CASES AND MATERIALS

Trademark and Unfair Competition Law

FOURTH EDITION

by

JANE C. GINSBURG
Morton L. Janklow Professor of
Literary and Artistic Property Law
Columbia University School of Law

JESSICA LITMAN
Professor of Law
University of Michigan

MARY L. KEVLIN
Cowan, Liebowitz and Latman, P.C.
Adjunct Professor, New York University School of Law

FOUNDATION PRESS

2007

THOMSON
───★───™
WEST

© 2001 FOUNDATION PRESS
© 2007 By FOUNDATION PRESS
        395 Hudson Street
        New York, NY 10014
        Phone Toll Free 1–877–888–1330
        Fax (212) 367–6799
        foundation–press.com

Printed in the United States of America

ISBN 978–1–59941–048–7

TEXT IS PRINTED ON 10% POST
CONSUMER RECYCLED PAPER

We dedicate the Fourth Edition to the Memory of David Goldberg, Esq.

*

PREFACE TO THE FOURTH EDITION

In the six years since we published the third edition of Trademark and Unfair Competition Law, the law of trademarks and unfair competition has become more international and more digital. That expansion, across borders and onto the Internet, has forced Congress and the courts to reexamine classic trademark doctrines and concepts. The increased permeability of national borders, the ubiquity of the Internet, and the emergence of new forms of product advertising have compelled reconsideration of the nature of "use in commerce" and caused some courts to question whether an effective trademark law can avoid extraterritorial impact. The Supreme Court decided three important cases: *Moseley v. V Secret Catalogue* (2003) sought to clarify the scope of the federal anti-dilution law. Congress at the end of 2006 responded to the Supreme Court's decision by enacting a significant amendment to the law's anti-dilution provisions. *Dastar Corp. v. Twentieth Century Fox Film Corp.* (2003) limited the use of the Lanham Act's false designation of origin provisions in cases seeking to vindicate interests in attribution. *KP Permanent Make-Up, Inc. v. Lasting Impression I, Inc.* (2004) clarified the scope of the statutory trademark fair use defense.

Internet-related trademark disputes have now arisen in every corner of trademark practice, and show up in nearly every chapter of the book. As we did in the 3d edition, however, we have taken up the special problems posed by trademarks and domain names in a chapter of their own. The issues in this chapter are largely the same as the issues raised in the 3d edition, but most of the cases and domain name dispute decisions are new.

We have integrated the international and comparative materials that once occupied their own chapter into the rest of the book. We have separated our treatment of "use in commerce;" we now take up the use in commerce issues surrounding establishing rights in a mark in Chapter 3, and the use in commerce issues arising in connection with infringement in chapter 6. We have reorganized the material in chapter 6 in response to its increasing complexity. We have completely revised our treatment of dilution to respond to the new anti-dilution law. We have, reluctantly, decided to eliminate the use of a single case as a "Prelude;" the law has grown sufficiently complex that no single case seemed to us to capture a large enough slice of it to qualify as a Prelude.

We have retained many of the successful features of earlier editions. The Casebook begins with introductory case law and secondary material on the concepts and policies underlying trademark law, and incorporates trademark policy concerns throughout the book. We have continued to include in-depth coverage of important advanced topics in the second half of the Casebook.

We wish to express appreciation to Professors Barton Beebe, Rob Denicola, Graeme Dinwoodie, Stacy Dogan, Rochelle Dreyfuss, Justin Hughes, Mark Janis, Mark Lemley, Sara Stadler, Rebecca Tushnet, and Jonathan Weinberg, and to Judge Alex Kozinski and William M. Borchard, Esq., for consenting to the use of excerpts of their work. We also thank Eric Schwartz, Esq., and Professor Coenraad Visser for their assistance with some of the international materials, and Richard Lehv, Esq. for signaling a variety of recent developments. Finally, we are especially grateful to Kevin Burdette, Columbia Law School class of 2007 (and New York City Opera 2005-06 and 2006-07 seasons), for extensive help with research and production.

June 2007

SUMMARY OF CONTENTS

TABLE OF CONTENTS

*

TABLE OF CASES

Principal cases are in bold type. Non-principal cases are in roman type. References are to Pages.

*

CASES AND MATERIALS

TRADEMARK AND UNFAIR COMPETITION LAW

*

CHAPTER 1

CONCEPTS OF TRADEMARKS AND UNFAIR COMPETITION

A. COMPETITION

Restatement of the Law (Third), Unfair Competition (Chapter 1. The Freedom to Compete)*

§ 1. GENERAL PRINCIPLES

One who causes harm to the commercial relations of another by engaging in a business or trade is not subject to liability to the other for such harm unless:

Endorses competition Generally

(a) the harm results from acts or practices of the actor actionable by the other under the rules of this Restatement relating to:

Actionable Unfair Competition

(1) deceptive marketing, as specified in Chapter Two;

(2) infringement of trademarks and other indicia of identification, as specified in Chapter Three;

(3) appropriation of intangible trade values including trade secrets and the right of publicity, as specified in Chapter Four; or from other acts or practices of the actor determined to be actionable as an unfair method of competition, taking into account the nature of the conduct and its likely effect on both the person seeking relief and the public; or

(b) the acts or practices of the actor are actionable by the other under federal or state statutes, international agreements, or general principles of common law apart from those considered in this Restatement.

Comment:

a. *The Freedom to Compete.* The freedom to engage in business and to compete for the patronage of prospective customers is a fundamental premise of the free enterprise system. Competition in the marketing of goods and services creates incentives to offer quality products at reasonable prices and fosters the general welfare by promoting the efficient allocation of economic resources. The freedom to compete necessarily contemplates the probability of harm to the commercial relations of other participants in the market. The fundamental rule stated in the introductory clause of this Section promotes competition by insuring that neither new entrants nor

---

existing competitors will be subject to liability for harm resulting solely from the fact of their participation in the market.

The freedom to compete implies a right to induce prospective customers to do business with the actor rather than with the actor's competitors. This Section permits a seller to seek to divert business not only from competitors generally, but also from a particular competitor. This Section is applicable to harm incurred by persons with whom the actor directly competes and to harm incurred by other persons affected by the actor's decision to enter or continue in business. Thus, the actor is not subject to liability to indirect competitors or to employees or suppliers of others who may be harmed by the actor's presence in the market. Liability is imposed under this Section, and under this Restatement generally, only in connection with harm resulting from particular methods of competition determined to be unfair.

The principle embodied in this Section is often loosely described as a "privilege" to compete. That characterization, however, is sometimes taken to imply that any intentional interference in the commercial relations of another is prima facie tortious, with the burden on the actor to establish an applicable privilege as an affirmative defense. There is as yet no consensus with respect to the allocation of the burdens of pleading and proof under the general tort of intentional interference with prospective economic relations. See Restatement, Second, Torts § 767, Comment k. However, in the case of harm resulting from competition in the marketplace, the privilege rationale appears inconsistent with the basic premise of our free enterprise system. Rather than adopting the view that such harm is prima facie tortious subject to a competitive privilege, this Restatement rejects the privilege rationale in favor of a general principle of non-liability. A person alleging injury through competition must therefore establish facts sufficient to subject the actor to liability under one or more of the rules enumerated in this Section.

———

International News Service v. Associated Press, 248 U.S. 215 (1918). In this landmark decision, the Supreme Court announced a "quasi-property" right in the dissemination of uncopyrightable information. At issue were news reports, published by AP on the East Coast, where they were copied by rival INS and relayed to INS' Midwest and West Coast papers, simultaneously or even ahead of their receipt by AP's local counterparts. The "quasi-" quality of the right derived from the scope of its enforceability: According to the Supreme Court majority, the right might be effective against competitors, but not against the public at large. In the course of the majority opinion, the Court invoked some agricultural metaphors which have remained firmly planted in the rhetoric of unfair competition:

Defendant admits that it is taking material that has been acquired by complainant as the result of organization and the expenditure of labor, skill and money, and which is salable by complainant for money, and that defendant in appropriating it and selling it as its own is endeavoring to reap where it has not sown, and by disposing of it to newspapers that are competitors of complainant's members is appropriating to itself the harvest of those who have sown. It is said that the elements of unfair competition are lacking because there is no attempt by defendant to palm off its goods as those of the complainant, characteristic of the most familiar, if not the most typical, cases of unfair competition. But we cannot concede that the right to equitable relief is confined to that class of cases.

The actual holding of INS was fairly narrow: it granted AP protection against its competitor during the period of initial dissemination of the information to AP's members. Nonetheless, because of the Court's willingness to find unfair competition beyond the traditional context of "passing off," as well as the opinion's fertile allusions, INS has come to stand for a general common law property right against "misappropriation" of commercial value. See generally Douglas G. Baird, The Story of INS v. AP: Property, Natural Monopoly, and the Uneasy Legacy of a Concocted Controversy, in Jane C. Ginsburg and Rochelle Cooper Dreyfuss, eds., INTELLECTUAL PROPERTY STORIES 9 (2006).

Cheney Bros. v. Doris Silk Corp.

35 F.2d 279 (2d Cir.1929), *cert. denied*, 281 U.S. 728, 50 S.Ct. 245, 74 L.Ed. 1145 (1930).

■ LEARNED HAND, J.:

The plaintiff, a corporation is a manufacturer of silks, which puts out each season many new patterns, designed to attract purchasers by their novelty and beauty. Most of these fail in that purpose, so that not much more than a fifth catch the public fancy. Moreover, they have only a short life, for the most part no more than a single season of eight or nine months. It is in practice impossible, and it would be very onerous if it were not, to secure design patents upon all of these; it would also be impossible to know in advance which would sell well, and patent only those. Besides, it is probable that for the most part they have no such originality as would support a design patent. Again, it is impossible to copyright them under the Copyright Act (17 USCA § 1 et seq.), or at least so the authorities of the Copyright Office hold. So it is easy for any one to copy such as prove successful, and the plaintiff, which is put to much ingenuity and expense in fabricating them, finds itself without protection of any sort for its pains.

Taking advantage of this situation, the defendant copied one of the popular designs in the season beginning in October, 1928, and undercut the plaintiff's price. This is the injury of which it complains. The defendant, though it duplicated the design in question, denies that it knew it to be the plaintiff's, and there thus arises an issue which might be an answer to the motion. However, the parties wish a decision upon the equity of the bill, and, since it is within our power to dismiss it, we shall accept its allegation, and charge the defendant with knowledge.

The plaintiff asks for protection only during the season, and needs no more, for the designs are all ephemeral. It seeks in this way to disguise the extent of the proposed innovation, and to persuade us that, if we interfere only a little, the solecism, if there be one, may be pardonable. But the reasoning which would justify any interposition at all demands that it cover the whole extent of the injury. A man whose designs come to harvest in two years, or in five, has prima facie as good right to protection as one who deals only in annuals. Nor could we consistently stop at designs; processes, machines, and secrets have an equal claim. The upshot must be that, whenever any one has contrived any of these, others may be forbidden to copy it. That is not the law. In the absence of some recognized right at common law, or under the statutes—and the plaintiff claims neither—a man's property is limited to the chattels which embody his invention. Others may imitate these at their pleasure.

This is confirmed by the doctrine of "nonfunctional" features, under which it is held that to imitate these is to impute to the copy the same authorship as the original. These decisions imply that, except as to these elements, any one may copy the original at will. Unless, therefore, there has been some controlling authority to the contrary, the bill at bar stands upon no legal right and must fail.

Of the cases on which the plaintiff relies, the chief is *International News Service v. Associated Press*, 248 U.S. 215. Although that concerned another subject-matter—printed news dispatches—we agree that, if it meant to lay down a general doctrine, it would cover this case; at least, the language of the majority opinion goes so far. We do not believe that it did. While it is of course true that law ordinarily speaks in general terms, there are cases where the occasion is at once the justification for, and the limit of, what is decided. This appears to us such an instance; we think that no more was covered than situations substantially similar to those then at bar. The difficulties of understanding it otherwise are insuperable. We are to suppose that the court meant to create a sort of common-law patent or copyright for reasons of justice. Either would flagrantly conflict with the scheme which Congress has for more than a century devised to cover the subject-matter.

Qua patent, we should at least have to decide, as *tabula rasa*, whether the design or machine was new and required invention; further, we must ignore the Patent Office whose action has always been a condition upon the creation of this kind of property. Qua copyright, although it would be simpler to decide upon the merits, we should equally be obliged to dispense with the conditions imposed upon the creation of the right. Nor, if we went so far, should we know whether the property so recognized should be limited to the periods prescribed in the statutes, or should extend as long as the author's grievance. It appears to us incredible that the Supreme Court should have had in mind any such consequences. To exclude others from the enjoyment of a chattel is one thing; to prevent any imitation of it, to set up a monopoly in the plan of its structure, gives the author a power which the Constitution allows only Congress to create.

QUESTIONS

1. Does not the protection sought in *Doris Silk* closely correspond to that granted in *INS* itself: exclusive reproduction rights for the very brief time of peak commercial value? Is there a principled distinction between the two? *See* Douglas G. Baird, *Common Law Intellectual Property and the Legacy of* International News Service v. Associated Press, 50 U. Chi. L. Rev. 411, 419 (1983), reporting that Judge Learned Hand "told other members of the panel in *Cheney* privately that *INS* 'is somewhat of a stumbling block,' and 'on principle it is hard to distinguish, and the language applies.'"

[handwritten margin note: L. Hand may have had diff Distinguishing]

2.   Precedent aside, did Judge Hand voice the better policy in his determination to favor the public domain of unpatented, uncopyrighted articles over plaintiff's claim to relief from parasitic competitors? Why, or why not?

Sears, Roebuck & Co. v. Stiffel Co.

376 U.S. 225, 84 S.Ct. 784, 11 L.Ed.2d 661 (1964).

[handwritten margin note: unpatentable Articles cannot be protected/monopolized under State law.]

■ MR. JUSTICE BLACK delivered the opinion of the Court:

The question in this case is whether a State's unfair competition law can, consistently with the federal patent laws, impose liability for or prohibit the copying of an article which is protected by neither a federal patent nor a copyright. The respondent, Stiffel Company, secured design and mechanical patents on a "pole lamp"—a vertical tube having lamp fixtures along the outside, the tube being made so that it will stand upright between the floor and ceiling of a room. Pole lamps proved a decided commercial success, and soon after Stiffel brought them on the market Sears, Roebuck & Company put on the market a substantially identical lamp, which it sold more cheaply, Sears' retail price being about the same as Stiffel's wholesale price. Stiffel then brought this action against Sears in the United States District Court for the Northern District of Illinois, claiming in its first count that by copying its design Sears had infringed Stiffel's patents and in its second count that by selling copies of Stiffel's lamp Sears had caused confusion in the trade as to the source of the lamps and had thereby engaged in unfair competition under Illinois law. There was evidence that identifying tags were not attached to the Sears lamps although labels appeared on the cartons in which they were delivered to customers, that customers had asked Stiffel whether its lamps differed from Sears', and that in two cases customers who had bought Stiffel lamps had complained to Stiffel on learning that Sears was selling substantially identical lamps at a much lower price.

[handwritten margin note: Pole Lamps]

[handwritten margin note: Evidence of confusion.]

The District Court, after holding the patents invalid for want of invention, went on to find as a fact that Sears' lamp was "a substantially exact copy" of Stiffel's and that the two lamps were so much alike, both in appearance and in functional details, "that confusion between them is likely, and some confusion has already occurred." On these findings the court held Sears guilty of unfair competition, enjoined Sears "from unfairly competing with [Stiffel] by selling or attempting to sell pole lamps identical to or confusingly similar to" Stiffel's lamp, and ordered an accounting to fix profits and damages resulting from Sears' "unfair competition."

The Court of Appeals affirmed, 313 F.2d 115. That court held that, to make out a case of unfair competition under Illinois law, there was no need to show that Sears had been "palming off" its lamps as Stiffel lamps; Stiffel had only to prove that there was a "likelihood of confusion as to the source of the products"—that the two articles were sufficiently identical that customers could not tell who had made a particular one. Impressed by the "remarkable sameness of appearance" of the lamps, the Court of Appeals upheld the trial court's findings of likelihood of confusion and some actual confusion, findings which the appellate court construed to mean confusion "as to the source of the lamps." The Court of Appeals thought this enough under Illinois law to sustain the trial court's holding of unfair competition, and thus held Sears liable under Illinois law for doing no more than copying and marketing an unpatented article. We granted certiorari to consider whether this use of a State's law of unfair competition is compatible with the federal patent law. 374 U.S. 826.

Before the Constitution was adopted, some States had granted patents either by special act or by general statute, but when the Constitution was adopted provision for a federal patent law was made one of the enumerated powers of Congress because, as Madison put it in The Federalist No. 43, the States "cannot separately make effectual provision" for either patents or copyrights. That constitutional provision is Art. I, § 8, cl. 8, which empowers Congress "To promote the Progress of Science and useful Arts, by securing for limited Times to Authors and Inventors the exclusive Right to their respective Writings and Discoveries." Pursuant to this constitutional authority, Congress in 1790 enacted the first federal patent and copyright law, 1 Stat. 109, and ever since that time has fixed the conditions upon which patents and copyrights shall be granted, see 17 U.S.C. §§ 1–216; 35 U.S.C. §§ 1–293. These laws, like other laws of the United States enacted pursuant to constitutional authority, are the supreme law of the land. *See Sperry v. Florida*, 373 U.S. 379 (1963). When state law touches upon the area of these federal statutes, it is "familiar doctrine" that the federal policy "may not be set at naught, or its benefits denied" by the state law. *Sola Elec. Co. v. Jefferson Elec. Co.*, 317 U.S. 173, 176 (1942). This is true, of course, even if the state law is enacted in the exercise of otherwise undoubted state power.

The grant of a patent is a statutory monopoly; indeed, the grant of patents in England was an explicit exception to the statute of James I prohibiting monopolies. Patents are not given as favors, as was the case of monopolies given by the Tudor monarchs, *see The Case of Monopolies (Darcy v. Allein)*, 11 Co. Rep. 84 b., 77 Eng. Rep. 1260 (K.B. 1602), but are meant to encourage invention by rewarding the inventor with the right, limited to a term of years fixed by the patent, to exclude others from the use of his invention. During that period of time no one may make, use, or sell the patented product without the patentee's authority. 35 U.S.C. § 271. But in rewarding useful invention, the "rights and welfare of the community must be fairly dealt with and effectually guarded." *Kendall v. Winsor*, 21 How. 322, 329 (1859). To that end the prerequisites to obtaining a patent are strictly observed, and when the patent has issued the limitations on its exercise are equally strictly enforced.... Finally, and especially relevant here, when the patent expires the monopoly created by it expires, too, and the right to make the article—including the right to make it in precisely the shape it carried when patented—passes to the public. *Kellogg Co. v. National Biscuit Co.*, 305 U.S. 111, 120–122 (1938); *Singer Mfg. Co. v. June Mfg. Co.*, 163 U.S. 169, 185 (1896).

Thus the patent system is one in which uniform federal standards are carefully used to promote invention while at the same time preserving free competition. Obviously a State could not, consistently with the Supremacy Clause of the Constitution, extend the life of a patent beyond its expiration date or give a patent on an article which lacked the level of invention required for federal patents. To do either would run counter to the policy of Congress of granting patents only to true inventions, and then only for a limited time. Just as a State cannot encroach upon the federal patent laws directly, it cannot, under some other law, such as that forbidding unfair competition, give protection of a kind that clashes with the objectives of the federal patent laws.

In the present case the "pole lamp" sold by Stiffel has been held not to be entitled to the protection of either a mechanical or a design patent. An unpatentable article, like an article on which the patent has expired, is in the public domain and may be made and sold by whoever chooses to do so. What Sears did was to copy Stiffel's design and to sell lamps almost identical to those sold by Stiffel. This it had every right to do under the federal patent laws. That Stiffel originated the pole lamp and made it popular is immaterial. "Sharing in the goodwill of an article unprotected by patent or trade-mark is the exercise of a right possessed by all—and in the free exercise of which the consuming public is deeply interested." *Kellogg Co. v. National Biscuit Co., supra*, 305 U.S., at 122. To allow a State by use of its law of unfair competition to prevent the copying of an article which represents too slight an advance to be patented would be to permit the State to block off from the public something which federal law has said belongs to the public. The result would be that while federal law grants only 14 or 17 years' protection to genuine inventions, *see* 35 U.S.C. §§ 154, 173, States could allow perpetual protection to articles too lacking in novelty to merit any patent at all under federal constitutional standards. This would be too great an encroachment on the federal patent system to be tolerated.

Sears has been held liable here for unfair competition because of a finding of likelihood of confusion based only on the fact that Sears' lamp was copied from Stiffel's unpatented lamp and that consequently the two looked exactly alike. Of course there could be "confusion" as to who had manufactured these nearly identical articles. But mere inability of the public to tell two identical articles apart is not enough to support an injunction against copying or an award of damages for copying that which the federal patent laws permit to be copied. Doubtless a State may, in appropriate circumstances, require that goods, whether patented or unpatented, be labeled or that other precautionary steps be taken to prevent customers from being misled as to the source, just as it may protect businesses in the use of their trademarks, labels, or distinctive dress in the packaging of goods so as to prevent others, by imitating such markings, from misleading purchasers as to the source of the goods. But because of the federal patent laws a State may not, when the article is unpatented and uncopyrighted, prohibit the copying of the article itself or award damages for such copying. *Cf. G. Ricordi & Co. v. Haendler*, 194 F.2d 914, 916 (C.A. 2d Cir. 1952). The judgment below did both and in so doing gave Stiffel the equivalent of a patent monopoly on its unpatented lamp. That was error, and Sears is entitled to a judgment in its favor.

Reversed.

Compco Corp. v. Day–Brite Lighting, Inc., 376 U.S. 234, 84 S.Ct. 779, 11 L.Ed.2d 669 (1964). In this companion case to *Sears, Roebuck v. Stiffel Lamp*, the work at issue, also a lighting fixture, had received a design patent, which a court subsequently invalidated. In holding the state unfair competition claim preempted, the Court stated:

Today we have held in *Sears, Roebuck & Co. v. Stiffel Co.*, *supra*, that when an article is unprotected by a patent or a copyright, state law may not forbid others to copy that article. To forbid copying would interfere with the federal policy, found in Art. I, § 8, cl. 8, of the Constitution and in the implementing federal statutes, of allowing free access to copy whatever the federal patent and copyright laws leave in the public domain. Here Day–Brite's fixture has been held not to be entitled to a design or mechanical patent. Under the federal patent laws it is, therefore, in the public domain and can be copied in every detail by whoever pleases. It is true that the trial court found that the configuration of Day–Brite's fixture identified Day–Brite to the trade because the arrangement of the ribbing had, like a trademark, acquired a "secondary meaning" by which that particular design was associated with Day–Brite. But if the design is not entitled to a design patent or other federal statutory protection, then it can be copied at will.

As we have said in *Sears*, while the federal patent laws prevent a State from prohibiting the copying and selling of unpatented articles, they do not stand in the way of state law, statutory or decisional, which requires those who make and sell copies to take precautions to identify their products as their own. A State of course has power to impose liability upon those who, knowing that the public is relying upon an original manufacturer's reputation for quality and integrity, deceive the public by palming off their copies as the original. That an article copied from an unpatented article could be made in some other way, that the design is "nonfunctional" and not essential to the use of either article, that the configuration of the article copied may have a "secondary meaning" which identifies the maker to the trade, or that there may be "confusion" among purchasers as to which article is which or as to who is the maker, may be relevant evidence in applying a State's law requiring such precautions as labeling; however, and regardless of the copier's motives, neither these facts nor any others can furnish a basis for imposing liability for or prohibiting the actual acts of copying and selling. *Cf. Kellogg Co. v. National Biscuit Co.*, 305 U.S. 111, 120 (1938). And of course a State cannot hold a copier accountable in damages for failure to label or otherwise to identify his goods unless his failure is in violation of valid state statutory or decisional law requiring the copier to label or take other precautions to prevent confusion of customers as to the source of the goods.

Since the judgment below forbids the sale of a copy of an unpatented article and orders an accounting for damages for such copying, it cannot stand.

QUESTION

Is the conflict articulated in *Sears–Compco* "constitutional" or "statutory," i.e., was state unfair competition law found to conflict with the patent and copyright clause of the federal constitution, or with the federal patent law? What is the consequence of the distinction?

Bonito Boats v. Thunder Craft Boats

489 U.S. 141, 109 S.Ct. 971, 103 L.Ed.2d 118 (1989).

[Plaintiff, a boat manufacturer, sought to enjoin defendant's use of a "direct molding process" to duplicate plaintiff's unpatented boat hulls. Plaintiff invoked a Florida statute that made "[i]t ... unlawful for any person to use the direct molding process to duplicate for the purpose of sale any manufactured vessel hull or component part of a vessel made by another without the written permission of that other person." Fla. Stat. § 559.94(2) (1987). The statute also made it unlawful for a person to "knowingly sell a vessel duplicated in violation of subsection (2)." The Florida Supreme Court held that the statute conflicted with the federal patent law and was therefore invalid under the Supremacy Clause of the federal Constitution. The Supreme Court affirmed.]

■ JUSTICE O'CONNOR delivered the opinion of the [unanimous] Court:

[The federal patent law requires a] backdrop of free competition in the exploitation of unpatented designs and innovations. The novelty and non-obviousness requirements of patentability embody a congressional understanding, implicit in the Patent Clause itself, that free exploitation of ideas will be the rule, to which the protection of a federal patent is the exception.... The ultimate goal of the patent system is to bring new designs and technology into the public domain through disclosure. State law protection for techniques and designs whose disclosure has already been induced by market rewards may conflict with the very purpose of the patent laws by decreasing the range of ideas available as the building blocks of further innovation. The offer of federal protection from competitive exploitation of intellectual property would be rendered meaningless in a world where substantially similar state law protections were readily available. To a limited extent the federal patent laws must determine not only what is protected but also what is free for all to use.

Thus ... state regulation of intellectual property must yield to the extent that it clashes with the balance struck by Congress in our patent laws. The tension between the desire to freely exploit the full potential of our inventive resources and the need to create an incentive to deploy those resources is constant. Where it is clear how the patent laws strike that balance in a particular circumstance, that is not a judgment the states may second guess....

We believe that the Florida statute at issue in this case so substantially impedes the public use of the otherwise unprotected design and utilitarian ideas embodied in unpatented boat hulls as to run afoul of the teaching of our decisions in *Sears* and *Compco*. It is readily apparent that the Florida statute does not operate to prohibit "unfair competition" in the usual sense that the term is understood. The law of unfair competition has its roots in the common-law tort of deceit: its general concern is with protecting consumers from confusion as to source. While that concern may result in the creation of "quasi-property rights" in communicative symbols, the focus is on the protection of consumers, not the protection of producers as an incentive to product innovation.

With some notable exceptions, including the interpretation of the Illinois law of unfair competition at issue in *Sears* and *Compco*, the common-law tort of unfair competition has been limited to protection against copying of nonfunctional aspects of consumer products which have acquired secondary meaning such that they operate as a designation of source. The "protection" granted a particular design under the law of unfair competition is thus limited to one context where consumer confusion is likely to result; the design "idea" itself may be freely exploited in all other contexts.

In contrast to the operation of unfair competition law, the Florida statute is aimed directly at preventing the exploitation of the design and utilitarian conceptions embodied in the product itself. Like the patentee, the beneficiary of the Florida statute may prevent a competitor from "making" the product in what is evidently the most efficient manner available and from "selling" the product when it is produced in that fashion. The Florida scheme offers this protection for an unlimited number of years to all boat hulls and their component parts, without regard to their ornamental or technological merit. Protection is available for subject matter for which patent protection has been denied or has expired, as well as for designs which have been freely revealed to the consuming public by their creators....

The Florida statute is aimed directly at the promotion of intellectual creation by substantially restricting the public's ability to exploit ideas that the patent system mandates shall be free for all to use. Like the interpretation of Illinois unfair competition law in *Sears* and *Compco*, the Florida statute represents a break with the tradition of peaceful coexistence between state market regulation and federal patent policy. The Florida law substantially restricts the public's ability to exploit an unpatented design in general circulation, raising the specter of state-created monopolies in a host of useful shapes and processes for which patent protection has been denied or is otherwise unobtainable. It thus enters a field of regulation which the patent laws have reserved to Congress. The patent statute's careful balance between public right and private monopoly to promote certain creative activity is a "scheme of federal regulation ... so pervasive as to make reasonable the inference that Congress left no room for the States to supplement it." *Rice v. Santa Fe Elevator Corp.*, 331 U.S. 218, 230 (1947).

Congress has considered extending various forms of limited protection to industrial design either through the copyright laws or by relaxing the restrictions on the availability of design patents. *See generally* Brown, *Design Protection: An Overview*, 34 UCLA L. Rev. 1341 (1987). Congress explicitly refused to take this step in the copyright laws, *see* 17 U.S.C. § 101; H. R. Rep. No. 94–1476, p. 55 (1976), and despite sustained criticism for a number of years, it has declined to alter the patent protections presently available for industrial design. It is for Congress to determine if the present system of design and utility patents is ineffectual in promoting the useful arts in the context of industrial design. By offering patent-like protection for ideas deemed unprotected under the present federal scheme, the Florida statute conflicts with the "strong federal policy favoring free competition in ideas which do not merit patent protection." *Lear, Inc. [v. Adkins*, 395 U.S. 653 (1969)], at 656. We therefore agree with the majority of the Florida Supreme Court that the Florida statute is preempted by the Supremacy Clause, and the judgment of that court is hereby affirmed.

It is so ordered.

QUESTIONS

1. Could a federal statute validly prohibit the copying of boat hulls and other unpatented utilitarian designs? *Cf.* 17 U.S.C. §§ 1301–1322 (Protection of Original Designs). Could such a law prohibit copying of designs that had been protected by a now-expired utility patent? *See TrafFix Devices v. Marketing Displays, infra*, Chapter 7.B.

2. Is it "unfair competition" to list as a work's author a person who did not in fact write the book? For example, for an unknown writer of thrillers to present her work as Stephen King's? Or to publish Stephen King's work under the unknown writer's name? Does it matter whether or not Stephen King's work is still protected by copyright? See *Dastar v. Twentieth Century Fox* (U.S. 2003), *infra* Chapter 10.

3. You are a federal judge called to decide a case presenting facts remarkably similar to those in *Cheney Bros. v. Doris Silk*. In light of *Bonito Boats*, what would you hold, and why?

Basketball Stats

National Basketball Association v. Motorola, 105 F.3d 841 (2d Cir.1997). Plaintiff NBA attempted to prevent Motorola and Sports Team Analysis and Tracking Systems (STATS) from divulging the scores of ongoing basketball games to users of Motorola's SportsTrax paging device. Defendants did not divert broadcast or computer feeds from the NBA or its licensees; instead, STATS' own reporters watched the games on television or listened to them on the radio, and keyed the relevant information into personal computers relayed by modem to STATS' host computer, which retransmitted the information. The court held that the information at issue did not qualify as "hot news," and that any protection of the information beyond the limited "hot news" context would be preempted by the federal copyright act. The court detailed its understanding of "hot news":

> We hold that the surviving "hot-news" INS-like claim is limited to cases where:
>
> "Hot News"
>
> (i) a plaintiff generates or gathers information at a cost; (ii) the information is time-sensitive; (iii) a defendant's use of the information constitutes free-riding on the plaintiff's efforts; (iv) the defendant is in direct competition with a product or service offered by the plaintiffs; and (v) the ability of other parties to free-ride on the efforts of the plaintiff or others would so reduce the incentive to produce the product or service that its existence or quality would be substantially threatened.

The NBA met the first two elements of this five-part test, the Second Circuit held, and made a credible showing under the fourth that Sports-Trax would compete with a new NBA-licensed service, "Gamestats," that in the future would offer pager access. But the NBA's failure under the third and fifth elements proved dispositive. Defendants did not free-ride, the court determined, because defendants do their own fact gathering, and "have their own network and assemble and transmit data themselves." There might have been free-riding and NBA might have had a stronger "hot news" claim, the court suggested, had defendants collected the information from Gamestats and simply retransmitted it to SportsTrax, rather than engaging in their own information collection and dissemination. In the absence of free riding, the fifth element could not be met, either. Here, again, the court suggested how, were free-riding shown, the fifth element could be made out. If defendants were simply diverting information feeds from Gamestats, then Gamestats would be incurring information-gathering costs that its competitors were not: "If the appropriation of facts from one pager to another pager service were allowed, transmission of current information on NBA games to pagers or similar devices would be substantially deterred because any potential transmitter would know that the first entrant would quickly encounter a lower cost competitor free-riding on the originator's transmissions."

B. TRADEMARKS

Until the enactment of the Lanham Act in 1946, United States trade-mark law was primarily a common law creature. The common law mark was acquired by use. If you used "ACME" as a mark for cheese in Pittsburgh, you acquired common law rights in the mark ACME for cheese sold in Pittsburgh. If you expanded your sale of ACME cheese to Akron and then Cleveland, your trademark rights expanded along with your use. In the Nineteenth Century, as businesses expanded their geographic reach, they increasingly collided with other businesses that had common law rights in the same or similar trademarks. In 1870, as part of a wholesale overhaul of copyright and patent laws, Congress enacted a statute purporting to give federal trademark rights to individuals or corporations who registered their marks in the Patent Office. In 1889, the Supreme Court held that law unconstitutional.

Trade–Mark Cases

100 U.S. 82, 25 L.Ed. 550, 10 Otto 82 (1879).

■ MR. JUSTICE MILLER delivered the opinion of the court.

. . . .

The entire legislation of Congress in regard to trade-marks is of very recent origin. It is first seen in sects. 77 to 84, inclusive, of the act of July 8, 1870, entitled "An Act to revise, consolidate, and amend the statutes relating to patents and copyrights." 16 Stat. 198. The part of this act relating to trade-marks is embodied in chap. 2, tit. 60, sects. 4937 to 4947, of the Revised Statutes.

It is sufficient at present to say that they provide for the registration in the Patent Office of any device in the nature of a trade-mark to which any person has by usage established an exclusive right, or which the person so registering intends to appropriate by that act to his exclusive use; and they make the wrongful use of a trade-mark, so registered, by any other person, without the owner's permission, a cause of action in a civil suit for damages. Six years later we have the act of Aug. 14, 1876 (19 Stat. 141), punishing by fine and imprisonment the fraudulent use, sale, and counterfeiting of Trademarks registered in pursuance of the statutes of the United States, on which the informations and indictments are founded in the cases before us.

The right to adopt and use a symbol or a device to distinguish the goods or property made or sold by the person whose mark it is, to the exclusion of use by all other persons, has been long recognized by the common law and the chancery courts of England and of this country, and by the statutes of some of the States. It is a property right for the violation of which damages may be recovered in an action at law, and the continued violation of it will be enjoined by a court of equity, with compensation for past infringement. This exclusive right was not created by the act of Congress, and does not now depend upon it for its enforcement. The whole system of trade-mark property and the civil remedies for its protection existed long anterior to that act, and have remained in full force since its passage.

These propositions are so well understood as to require neither the citation of authorities nor an elaborate argument to prove them.

As the property in trade-marks and the right to their exclusive use rest on the laws of the States, and, like the great body of the rights of person and of property, depend on them for security and protection, the power of Congress to legislate on the subject, to establish the conditions on which these rights shall be enjoyed and exercised, the period of their duration, and the legal remedies for their enforcement, if such power exist at all, must be found in the Constitution of the United States, which is the source of all the powers that Congress can lawfully exercise.

In the argument of these cases this seems to be conceded, and the advocates for the validity of the acts of Congress on this subject point to two clauses of the Constitution, in one or in both of which, as they assert, sufficient warrant may be found for this legislation.

The first of these is the eighth clause of sect. 8 of the first article. That section, manifestly intended to be an enumeration of the powers expressly granted to Congress, and closing with the declaration of a rule for the ascertainment of such powers as are necessary by way of implication to carry into efficient operation those expressly given, authorizes Congress, by the clause referred to, "to promote the progress of science and useful arts, by securing for limited times, to authors and inventors, the exclusive right to their respective writings and discoveries." . . . .

Any attempt, however, to identify the essential characteristics of a trade-mark with inventions and discoveries in the arts and sciences, or with the writings of authors, will show that the effort is surrounded with insurmountable difficulties.

The ordinary trade-mark has no necessary relation to invention or discovery. The trade-mark recognized by the common law is generally the growth of a considerable period of use, rather than a sudden invention. It is often the result of accident rather than design, and when under the act of Congress it is sought to establish it by registration, neither originality, invention, discovery, science, nor art is in any way essential to the right conferred by that act. If we should endeavor to classify it under the head of writings of authors, the objections are equally strong. In this, as in regard to inventions, originality is required. And while the word writings may be liberally construed, as it has been, to include original designs for engravings, prints, & c., it is only such as are original, and are founded in the creative powers of the mind. The writings which are to be protected are the fruits of intellectual labor, embodied in the form of books, prints, engravings and the like. The trade-mark may be, and generally is, the adoption of something already in existence as the distinctive symbol of the party using it. At common law the exclusive right to it grows out of its use, and not its mere adoption. By the act of Congress this exclusive right attaches upon registration. But in neither case does it depend upon novelty, invention, discovery, or any work of the brain. It requires no fancy or imagination, no genius, no laborious thought. It is simply founded on priority of appropriation. We look in vain in the statute for any other qualification or condition. If the symbol, however plain, simple, old, or well-known, has been first appropriated by the claimant as his distinctive trade-mark, he may by registration secure the right to its exclusive use. While such legislation may be a judicious aid to the common law on the subject of trade-marks, and may be within the competency of legislatures whose general powers embrace that class of subjects, we are unable to see any such power in the constitutional provision concerning authors and inventors, and their writings and discoveries.

The other clause of the Constitution supposed to confer the requisite authority on Congress is the third of the same section, which, read in connection with the granting clause, is as follows: "The Congress shall have power to regulate commerce with foreign nations, and among the several States, and with the Indian tribes."

The argument is that the use of a trade-mark—that which alone gives it any value—is to identify a particular class or quality of goods as the manufacture, produce, or property of the person who puts them in the general market for sale; that the sale of the article so distinguished is commerce; that the trade-mark is, therefore, a useful and valuable aid or instrument of commerce, and its regulation by virtue of the clause belongs to Congress, and that the act in question is a lawful exercise of this power.

Every species of property which is the subject of commerce, or which is used or even essential in commerce, is not brought by this clause within the control of Congress . . . . .

When, therefore, Congress undertakes to enact a law, which can only be valid as a regulation of commerce, it is reasonable to expect to find on the face of the law, or from its essential nature, that it is a regulation of commerce with foreign nations, or among the several States, or with the Indian tribes. If not so limited, it is in excess of the power of Congress. If its main purpose be to establish a regulation applicable to all trade, to commerce at all points, especially if it be apparent that it is designed to govern the commerce wholly between citizens of the same State, it is obviously the exercise of a power not confided to Congress.

We find no recognition of this principle in the chapter on trade-marks in the Revised Statutes. . . . If, for instance, the statute described persons engaged in a commerce between the different States, and related to the use of trade-marks in such commerce, it would be evident that Congress believed it was acting under the clause of the Constitution which authorizes it to regulate commerce among the States. . . . But no such idea is found or suggested in this statute . . . . .

It is therefore manifest that no such distinction is found in the act, but that its broad purpose was to establish a universal system of trade-mark registration, for the benefit of all who had already used a trade-mark, or who wished to adopt one in the future, without regard to the character of the trade to which it was to be applied or the residence of the owner, with the solitary exception that those who resided in foreign countries which extended no such privileges to us were excluded from them here.

. . . .

The questions in each of these cases being an inquiry whether these statutes can be upheld in whole or in part as valid and constitutional, must be answered in the negative. . . .

QUESTIONS

1. Does Justice Miller's analysis merely require Congress to identify the appropriate constitutional source for its authority to regulate trademarks, or does it place substantive limitations on the provisions of any trademark law Congress may enact? If it imposes substantive limitations, what are they?

2. Current views of the scope of Congress's commerce clause power are significantly more expansive than the views articulated in Justice Miller's decision. If Congress sought today to reenact the trademark laws it adopted in 1870 and 1876, as described in the opinion, would the constitution as it is currently understood pose any obstacle?

———

After the *Trade–Mark Cases*, Congress enacted a series of trademark registration statutes based on its commerce clause authority. Following the First World War, the trademark bar began efforts to draft a comprehensive federal trademark statute that would pass constitutional muster. See Edward S. Rogers, *The Lanham Act and the Social Function of Trademarks*, 14 L. & Contemp. Probs. 173, 177–84 (Spring 1949). It was not until 1946 that Congress finally enacted the Lanham Trademark Protection Act, which drew many of its substantive rules from years of common law trademark decisions. Twenty-first century trademark law in the United States still bears many signs of its common law origins.

WILLIAM M. BORCHARD, A TRADEMARK IS NOT A COPYRIGHT OR A PATENT (2007) (EXCERPTS)

Although trademarks, copyrights, patents, and trade secrets all concern intangible property rights and overlap to some extent, they differ from each other significantly. It may help to distinguish them by remembering that:

● Trademarks protect source identifications (marks of trade);

● Copyrights protect original literary and artistic expressions;

- Patents protect new and useful inventions; and
- Trade Secrets protect valuable secret information.

For example, think of a TV set in an ornamental cabinet. Trademark protection would apply to the brand name for the TV; copyright to the programs viewed on it and perhaps to the artistry of the cabinet; utility patent to new and non-obvious functional features of the electric circuitry; design patent to new, original and ornamental features of the cabinet; and trade secret to the know-how to manufacture the wiring efficiently.

What is a Trademark?

A **trademark** is a word, logo or package design, or a combination of them, used by a manufacturer or merchant to identify its goods and distinguish them from others. Trademarks include brand names identifying goods (Dole for canned pineapple) and trade dress consisting of the graphics, color or shape of packaging or, after sufficient use, of goods (Coca–Cola Bottle for a soft drink); service marks identifying services (McDonald's for a restaurant service); certification marks identifying goods or services meeting specified qualifications (Woolmark for apparel made of 100% wool); and collective marks identifying goods, services or members of a collective organization (The International Game Fish Association for a game fishing organization). The same legal principles generally apply to all of these terms, often simply called "marks."

. . . .

What is a Copyright?

A copyright seeks to promote literary and artistic creativity by protecting, for a limited time, what the U.S. Constitution broadly calls the "writing" of "authors." Copyrightable works include:

- literary, musical and dramatic works;
- pantomimes and choreographic works;
- pictorial, graphic and sculptural works (including the nonutilitarian design features of useful articles);
- motion pictures and other audiovisual works;
- sound recordings;
- computer programs;

- certain architectural works, and

- compilations of works and derivative works.

Copyright only protects particular expressions of ideas, not the ideas themselves. And a protectible work must be "original," i.e., not copied from another source (although two separately protectible works theoretically could be identical by coincidence). The work also must not be so elementary that it lacks sufficient creativity to be copyrightable.

Copyright owner's rights.

The creator basically has the exclusive rights to reproduce the work, to distribute the reproductions, to display and perform the work publicly, to make derivative works, and to authorize others to do any of these things. The creator of certain works of fine art also may have rights to control their attribution or modification. The performance right in a sound recording is limited to digital transmissions, such as webcasting, with lower royalty rates for small webcasters. However, you cannot lease or rent a phonograph record or computer program for commercial advantage without the consent of the copyright owner. . . .

What is a Patent?

A patent is granted only by the federal government. It lets the patentee exclude others from making, offering for sale or selling an invention within the U.S. or importing it into the U.S. It does not carry the affirmative right to make, use, sell or offer an item covered by the patent because one or more other patents may cover aspects of the same item.

You can obtain a utility patent (also called a functional or mechanical patent) for the following statutory classes of new and useful inventions:

- processes (chemical, mechanical or electrical procedures, such as a method for refining petroleum; or a business method of processing data or making calculations, and any technique used in athletics, instruction or personal skills, if it uses computer assisted implementation or it physically transforms an article or otherwise produces a useful, concrete and tangible result and is not directed to a law of nature, physical phenomena or an abstract idea);

- machines (mechanisms with moving parts, such as a motor);

- articles of manufacture (man-made products, such as a hand tool); and

- compositions of matter (chemical compounds, combinations or mixtures, such as a plastic).

In addition, you can obtain a **design patent** for a new original and ornamental design for an article of manufacture, and a **plant patent** for a new variety of seed or plant or any of its parts.

Whether an invention is made by a flash of genius or painstaking research, to be patentable it also must meet all of the following hard-to-satisfy criteria:

- "novelty" in that it was neither previously known to others (except for confidential information known to co-researchers under a joint research agreement), nor in public use in the U.S., nor patented or described in a printed publication anywhere, in each case more than 1 year before the U.S. application's filing date;

- "unobviousness" to a person having ordinary skill in the relevant art; and

- "utility" in that it has a useful purpose, actually works, and is not frivolous or immoral (although working models generally are no longer required to provide this attribute, except for inventions claimed to be perpetual motion devices). . . .

Overlap.

Various aspects of a single article may qualify for all four types of protection—trademark, copyright, patent and trade secret. For example, the distinctive trade dress on top of a candy box might be copyrighted and also might function as a trademark identifying the manufacturer. A computer program might be copyrighted and patented at the same time. A chemical product might be patented, but the manufacturing know-how may be a trade secret. Sometimes, you can get only one type of protection or else you must choose between inconsistent types of available protection. For instance, it might be inconsistent to place an unexplained statutory copyright notice (applicable only to published works) on a copy of an unpublished secret computer program.

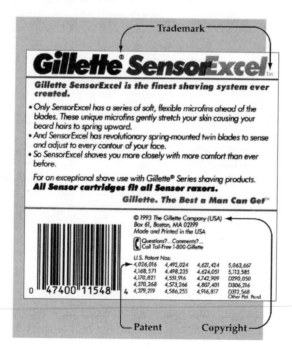

Step 9/4

Summary Table

	Trademarks	Copyrights	Patents
Nature	Commercial identifications of source such as words, designs, slogans, symbols, trade dress.	Original literary and artistic expressions such as books, paintings, music, records, plays, movies, software.	New and useful inventions and configurations of useful articles.
Scope	Protects against creating a likelihood of confusion; or diluting a famous mark.	Protects against unauthorized use or copying.	Excludes others from making, using, offering for sale or selling the invention in the U.S. or by importation into the U.S.
Purpose	Protects owners and public from unfair competition.	Encourages and rewards creative expression.	Encourages and rewards innovation.
How to Obtain Rights	Use mark in commerce or apply for federal registration.	Create work and fix it in tangible form. Registration confirms rights.	Apply for federal grant.
Principal Advantages of Registration	Nationwide priority rights; possibly conclusive evidence of validity and ownership; U.S. Customs recordation; increased anticounterfeiting remedies.	Statutory damages and attorney's fees; prima facie evidence of validity; U.S. Customs recordation.	Protection for non-secret inventions. May complement know-how that is a trade secret.
Basis for Registration	(1) Bona fide intention to use in commerce followed by actual use; (2) Non-U.S. owner's country of origin registration or application filed within 6 months prior to U.S. application, or extension to the U.S. of international registration, plus bona fide intention to use in commerce; or (3) Actual use in commerce.	Originality.	Novelty, unobviousness, utility.
Notice Requirements	Optional. "TM" or "SM" if unregistered; "®" or "Reg. U.S. Pat. & Tm. Off." if registered.	Optional after March 1, 1989. © or "Copyright" with year of first publication and name of owner.	Optional. "Patent applied for" or "Pat. Pending" after application; "Patent" or "Pat." plus registration number after grant.
Term of Rights	As long as used; registrations must be maintained by filing use declaration before each 6th and 10th anniversary; renewal required every 10 years.	Creations after January 1, 1978: author's lifetime plus 70 years, or if anonymous or work made for hire, earlier of 95 years from publication or 120 years from creation.	20 years from filing date (or sometimes 17 years from grant) for utility or plant patents, subject to periodic maintenance fees; 14 years from registration for design patents.
Infringement Prerequisites	Registration optional.	Registration required for U.S. nationals; optional for foreign nationals.	Issued patent required.
Infringement Standard	Likelihood of confusion, mistake or deception as to source or sponsorship; or dilution by blurring or tarnishment.	Unauthorized use or copying (access plus substantial similarity).	Unauthorized manufacture, use, sale, or offer for sale of devices or processes embodying the invention.
International Protection	(1) Individual countries or regions; (2) Community Trade Mark registration; or (3) Madrid Protocol centralized filing.	Usually protected without registration through international treaties.	Usually granted on a country-by-country basis with centralized filing available under the Patent Cooperation Treaty or European Patent Convention.

This summary is highly simplified and should only be used for a general comparison. • © 2007 Cowan, Liebowitz & Latman, P.C.

Hanover Star Milling Co. v. Metcalf

240 U.S. 403, 412–14, 36 S.Ct. 357, 60 L.Ed. 713 (1916).

■ MR. JUSTICE PITNEY delivered the opinion of the Court:

The redress that is accorded in trademark cases is based upon the party's right to be protected in the goodwill of a trade or business. The primary and proper function of a trademark is to identify the origin or ownership of the article to which it is affixed. Where a party has been in the habit of labeling his goods with a distinctive mark, so that purchasers recognize goods thus marked as being of his production, others are debarred from applying the same mark to goods of the same description, because to do so would in effect represent their goods to be of his production and would tend to deprive him of the profit he might make through the sale of the goods which the purchaser intended to buy. Courts afford redress or relief upon the ground that a party has a valuable interest in the goodwill of his trade or business, and in the trademarks adopted to maintain and extend it. The essence of the wrong consists in the sale of the goods of one manufacturer or vendor for those of another. *Canal Co. v. Clark*, 13 Wall. 311, 322; *McLean v. Fleming*, 96 U.S. 245, 251; *Manufacturing Co. v. Trainer*, 101 U.S. 51, 53; *Menendez v. Holt*, 128 U.S. 514, 520; *Lawrence Mfg. Co. v. Tennessee Mfg. Co.*, 138 U.S. 537, 546.

This essential element is the same in trademark cases as in cases of unfair competition unaccompanied with trademark infringement. In fact, the common law of trademarks is but a part of the broader law of unfair competition. *Elgin Watch Co. v. Illinois Watch Co.*, 179 U.S. 665, 674; *G. & C. Merriam Co. v. Saalfield*, 198 Fed. Rep. 369, 372; *Cohen v. Nagle*, 190 Massachusetts, 4, 8, 15; 5 A. & E. Ann. Cas. 553, 555, 558.

Common-law trademarks, and the right to their exclusive use, are of course to be classed among property rights, *Trademark Cases*, 100 U.S. 82, 92, 93; but only in the sense that a man's right to the continued enjoyment of his trade reputation and the goodwill that flows from it, free from unwarranted interference by others, is a property right, for the protection of which a trademark is an instrumentality. As was said in the same case (p. 94), the right grows out of use, not mere adoption. In the English courts it often has been said that there is no property whatever in a trademark, as such. Per Ld. Langdale, M.R., in *Perry v. Truefitt*, 6 Beav. 73; per Vice Chancellor Sir Wm. Page Wood (afterwards Ld. Hatherly), in *Collins Co. v. Brown*, 3 Kay & J. 423, 426; 3 Jur. N.S. 930; per Ld. Herschell in *Reddaway v. Banham*, A.C. 1896, 199, 209. But since in the same cases the courts recognized the right of the party to the exclusive use of marks adopted to indicate goods of his manufacture, upon the ground that "[a] man is not to sell his own goods under the pretense that they are the goods of another man; he cannot be permitted to practise such a deception, nor to use the means which contribute to that end. He cannot therefore be allowed to use names, marks, letters, or other indicia, by which he may induce purchasers to believe, that the goods which he is selling are the manufacture of another person" (6 Beav. 73); it is plain that in denying the right of property in a trademark it was intended only to deny such property right except as appurtenant to an established business or trade in connection with which the mark is used. This is evident from the expressions used in these and other English cases. Thus, in *Ainsworth v. Walmsley*, L.R. 1 Eq. Cas. 518, 524, Vice Chancellor Sir Wm. Page Wood said: "This court has taken upon itself to protect a man in the use of a certain trademark as applied to a particular description of article. He has no property in that mark per se, any more than in any other fanciful denomination he may assume for his own private use, otherwise than with reference to his trade. If he does not carry on a trade in iron, but carries on a trade in linen, and stamps a lion on his linen, another person may stamp a lion on iron; but when he has appropriated a mark to a particular species of goods, and caused his goods to circulate with this mark upon them, the court has said that no one shall be at liberty to defraud that man by using that mark, and passing off goods of his manufacture as being the goods of the owner of that mark."

In short, the trademark is treated as merely a protection for the goodwill, and not the subject of property except in connection with an existing business. The same rule prevails generally in this country, and is recognized in the decisions of this court already cited.

Stork Restaurant, Inc. v. Sahati et al.

166 F.2d 348 (9th Cir.1948).

■ GARRECHT, CIRCUIT JUDGE.

The appellant seeks to enjoin the appellees from using its trade name, "The Stork Club," and its insigne, consisting of a stork standing on one leg and wearing a high hat and a monocle. The complaint likewise asked for damages in the sum of $5,000, but that prayer was waived.

The court below entered judgment denying injunctive relief. From that judgment the present appeal has been taken.

1. The Facts

The appellant owns and operates a cafe and night club at No. 3 East 53d Street, New York, N.Y., known as "The Stork Club," described in a newsreel as "the best and most publicized night club in the entire world." The name had been used in New York by the appellant's two predecessor corporations since 1929.

As found by the court below, the appellant has been operating that establishment since on or about August 15, 1934. The cafe supplies "expensive food, beverages, music and dancing facilities," employs approximately 240 persons, and yields an average annual gross income of more than $1,000,000.

The appellant has spent more than $700,000 during the past eleven years in advertising on a nation-wide scale. This advertising was conducted through various media, including radio, newspapers, magazines, books, motion pictures, and established mailing lists. Another form of the publicity technique used by the appellant has been "cash advertising"—gifts to customers which included automobiles, 400 radios, one of which is an exhibit in this case; thousand dollar bills, none of which are exhibits here; five hundred dollar bottles of perfume, and "thousands" of thirty-five dollar bottles of perfume. Still another form of promotion has been "house advertising"—food and liquor given away to newspaper people, to radio, stage, and screen celebrities, and to "men in prominent and public life in the industrial world."

Newspapers throughout the country publish articles and photographs relating to the Stork Club. Many of America's leading syndicate writers mention it in their columns. Articles and advertisements relating to it appear in magazines of national circulation, and books have been written about it.

The club has been mentioned in many national hook-up radio programs, such as those of Bing Crosby, Frank Sinatra, Eddie Cantor, Walter Winchell, Jack Benny, Jimmy Durante, and Fred Allen.

A motion picture entitled "The Stork Club," produced by Paramount Pictures at a cost of nearly $1,700,000 and starring Betty Hutton and Barry Fitzgerald, was given 14,457 exhibitions throughout the United States, during a run of fifty-nine weeks, at a rental of $3,018,676.26. In northern California and adjacent territory, that picture was given 532 showings, during a run of sixty weeks, at a rental of $126,588.89. And in San Francisco alone, during a ten-day run at the Fox Theater, it was viewed by 83,729 persons. According to the deposition of George A. Smith, western sales manager for Paramount, one of the reasons for popularity of the picture was that "it had a very salable title, the popularity of the Stork Club was spread all over the United States." The Stork Club was paid $27,500 for the use of its name. Pathe News and "March of Time" have shown scenes from the Stork Club.

. . . .

[The court below found that] on or about April 6, 1945, the appellees "began the operation of, and continuously since that date have been operating and conducting a small bar, tavern and cocktail lounge at No. 200 Hyde Street, in * * * San Francisco * * * under the name of 'Stork Club' * * *." In another finding, the court indicated that a predecessor of the appellees had used the name at that location since March 1, 1943. The establishment has about ten stools at the bar, and will accommodate about fifty persons. It has about four steady employees, and serves only such food as is necessary to "conform with the law regulating the operation of bars." There are a few tables. There is no dancing, although the match pads distributed by the appellee for advertising purposes depict a dancing couple.

The appellees had a pianist "at one time," and when they "took over from the previous ownership there was a three-piece orchestra that they had on their payroll for probably two years." This orchestra continued with the appellees for about a month after the latter took over. The appellees have displayed a panel, suspended from the marquee and extending all around its three sides, with the word "Entertainment" emblazoned on each of the three sides. Napkins used in the appellee's establishment carried the picture of a stork standing on one leg and wearing a high hat, with the legend, "Stork Club * * * Finest Liquors. Expertly Blended Entertainment (sic)." Nicholas M. Sahati, one of the appellees, testified in this connection: "There might have been a few leftover napkins that the former owners had in the place when we took over, with the picture of a stork, which we used up, but never did order any napkins of that type. * * * I couldn't say exactly, maybe a few dozen. * * * There might have been a larger quantity; I have no method of knowing."

. . . .

3. *Trade Names and Trademarks Stand on a Similar Footing*

In California and elsewhere, a firmly established trade name receives the same protection from the law as a trade mark . . . . .

Accordingly, in the present inquiry it will be helpful to consider decisions dealing with trademarks as well as those concerned simply with trade names.

. . . .

10. *"Confusion of Source."*

We reach now what is perhaps the controlling principle in the instant case-that of "confusion of source," with its corollary, "dilution of good-will". . . .

In a situation where there is no direct competition between the parties, confusion of source may be defined as a misleading of the public by the imitation of "An attractive, reputable trade-mark or trade-name * * * not for the purpose of diverting trade from the person having the trade-mark or trade name to the imitator, but rather for the purpose of securing for the imitator's goods some of the good-will, advertising and sales stimulation of the trade-mark or trade name." Restatement, Id., at page 597.

> "One's interest in a trade-mark or trade name came to be protected, therefore, not only on competing goods, but on goods so related in the market to those on which the trade-mark or trade name is used that the good or ill repute of the one type of goods is likely to be visited upon the other. Thus one's interest in a trade-mark or trade name is protected against being subjected to the hazards of another's business." Restatement, Id., at pages 597–598.

The doctrine is well recognized in California. In [*Academy of Motion Picture Arts and Sciences v. Benson*, 15 Cal.2d 685, 689, 104 P.2d 650, 652], the Supreme Court of the State said: "The decisions of the courts for the most part are concerned with the principles application in respect to businesses which are directly competitive. But we perceive no distinction which, as a matter of law, should be made because of the fact that the plaintiff and the defendant are engaged in non-competing businesses. . . ."

Again, in *Winfield v. Charles*, 77 Cal.App.2d 64, 70, 175 P.2d 69, 74, the court reached the very heart of the problem when it observed: "Plaintiff has established a reputation for reliability and meritorious products. If articles which are not produced by him are attributed to him or associated with his name, the injury is obvious."

The rule has been repeatedly expounded by this and other Federal courts.

(a) "Reaping Where One Has Not Sown."

The decisions frequently refer to this sort of imitation as "reaping where one has not sown" or as "riding the coat-tails" of a senior appropriator of a trade name.

By whatever name it is called, equity frowns upon such business methods, and in proper cases will grant an injunction to the rightful user of the trade name.

. . . .

(b) A Disparity in the Size of the Respective Businesses Will Not Bar Injunctive Relief

[T]he appellees stress the fact that, "in comparison to appellant, (they) are in a most humble field of operation."

"Being humble," they continue, "in comparison to appellant this Court can very well deny any relief for unfair competition with appellant."

Humility is no doubt a virtue in many instances, but in a case of this type it affords no defense to a suit for an injunction against infringement of a trade name.

. . . .

(c) Mere Geographical Distance Does Not Obviate Danger of Confusion

The court found that, because of its business methods and its extensive publicity, the appellant's establishment, "conducted and operated under the name 'The Stork Club' and with the aforesaid insignia used in conjunction therewith, because and now is known to many persons in and about * * * San Francisco, * * * as a club in New York;" and that it "is patronized by visitors to New York * * * from * * * the metropolitan area of San Francisco * * *."

In these days of chain restaurants, one would not have to be uncommonly naive to assume that even a "humble" cafe at Turk and Hyde Streets, San Francisco, might be an unpretentious branch of a glittering New York night spot. A branch unit is usually less elaborate and impressive than the "mother house." As we shall see in a moment, however, equity will protect even the uncommonly naive against deception from unfair competition.

In any event, mere geographical distance is not of itself sufficient to preclude the possibility that a given establishment is a branch of an enterprise having its principal place of business elsewhere.

. . . .

(d) As to False Statements Obviously False

During the oral argument, it was suggested that any one driving by an unpretentious night club displaying the sign "Stork Club" in or near San Francisco, would hardly assume that the place was in any way affiliated with the celebrated New York establishment. It may well be true that a prudent and worldly-wise passerby would not be so deceived. The law, however, protects not only the intelligent, the experienced, and the astute. It safeguards from deception also the ignorant, the inexperienced, and the gullible.

That is the teaching of the Supreme Court of the United States, and it has been followed in this and in other circuits.

. . . .

11. Actual Loss of Trade Need Not be Shown to Warrant an Injunction.

The appellees stress the fact that the appellant has failed to show "that appellees' operation in any way has injured appellant," etc.

Neither under the California jurisprudence nor under the general law is such showing necessary. The California decisions, indeed, are overwhelmingly in accord on this point.

. . . .

[I]n the recent case of *Winfield v. Charles, supra,* 77 Cal.App.2d at page 70, 175 P.2d at page 73, we find the following succinct statement: "It is unnecessary, in such an action, to show that any person has been confused or deceived. It is the likelihood of deception which the remedy may be invoked to prevent."

This is undoubtedly the Federal rule. In *Adolph Kastor & Bros. v. Federal Trade Commission,* 2 Cir., 138 F.2d 824, 826, the court thus summarized the doctrine: "No one need expose his reputation to the trade practices of another, even though he can show no pecuniary loss."

. . . .

16. Conclusion

. . . .

The appellant is not here seeking to have the appellees mulcted in damages, nor is it striving to drive them out of business. It asks merely that its adversaries be compelled to desist from an unfair trade practice that threatens to "nibble away," "whittle away," or "dilute" the value of its dearly-bought prestige.

The appellant begs that the appellees, with an "infinity" of other names to choose from, divest themselves of plumage borrowed from the Stork.

In a word, the appellant is making a plea peculiarly calculated to move the conscience of a chancellor. It prays not for a sword, but for a shield.

The judgment is reversed, and the case is remanded to the lower court, with directions to grant to the appellant an injunction as prayed for in the complaint.

QUESTIONS

1. In what sense are consumers likely to be confused about the "source" of defendant's Stork Club?

2. If a company named its diaper service "The Stork Club," would plaintiff be entitled to force it to choose a different name? If not, why not?

Champion Spark Plug Co. v. Sanders

331 U.S. 125, 67 S.Ct. 1136, 91 L.Ed. 1386 (1947).

■ Opinion of the Court by MR. JUSTICE DOUGLAS, announced by MR. JUSTICE BLACK:

Petitioner is a manufacturer of spark plugs which it sells under the trade mark "Champion." Respondents collect the used plugs, repair and recondition them, and resell them. Respondents retain the word "Champion" on the repaired or reconditioned plugs. The outside box or carton in which the plugs are packed has stamped on it the word "Champion," together with the letter and figure denoting the particular style or type. They also have printed on them "Perfect Process Spark Plugs Guaranteed Dependable" and "Perfect Process Renewed Spark Plugs." Each carton contains smaller boxes in which the plugs are individually packed. These inside boxes also carry legends indicating that the plug has been renewed. But respondent company's business name or address is not printed on the cartons. It supplies customers with petitioner's charts containing recommendations for the use of Champion plugs. On each individual plug is stamped in small letters, blue on black, the word "Renewed," which at times is almost illegible.

Petitioner brought this suit in the District Court, charging infringement of its trade mark and unfair competition. The District Court found that respondents had infringed the trade mark. It enjoined them from offering or selling any of petitioner's plugs which had been repaired or reconditioned unless (a) the trade mark and type and style marks were removed, (b) the plugs were repainted with a durable grey, brown, orange, or green paint, (c) the word "REPAIRED" was stamped into the plug in letters of such size and depth as to retain enough white paint to display distinctly each letter of the word, (d) the cartons in which the plugs were packed carried a legend indicating that they contained used spark plugs originally made by petitioner and repaired and made fit for use up to 10,000 miles by respondent company.

The District Court denied an accounting.

The Circuit Court of Appeals held that respondents not only had infringed petitioner's trade mark but also were guilty of unfair competition. It likewise denied an accounting but modified the decree in the following respects: (a) it eliminated the provision requiring the trade mark and type and style marks to be removed from the repaired or reconditioned plugs; (b) it substituted for the requirement that the word "REPAIRED" be stamped into the plug, etc., a provision that the word "REPAIRED" or "USED" be stamped and baked on the plug by an electrical hot press in a contrasting color so as to be clearly and distinctly visible, the plug having been completely covered by permanent aluminum paint or other paint or lacquer; and (c) it eliminated the provision specifying the precise legend to be printed on the cartons and substituted therefor a more general one. 156 F.2d 488. The case is here on a petition for certiorari which we granted because of the apparent conflict between the decision below and *Champion Spark Plug Co. v. Reich*, 121 F.2d 769, decided by the Circuit Court of Appeals for the Eighth Circuit.

There is no challenge here to the findings as to the misleading character of the merchandising methods employed by respondents, nor to the conclusion that they have not only infringed petitioner's trade mark but have also engaged in unfair competition. The controversy here relates to the adequacy of the relief granted, particularly the refusal of the Circuit Court of Appeals to require respondents to remove the word "Champion" from the repaired or reconditioned plugs which they resell.

We put to one side the case of a manufacturer or distributor who markets new or used spark plugs of one make under the trade mark of another. *See Bourjois & Co. v. Katzel*, 260 U.S. 689. Equity then steps in to prohibit defendant's use of the mark which symbolizes plaintiff's good will and "stakes the reputation of the plaintiff upon the character of the goods." *Bourjois & Co. v. Katzel*, supra, p. 692.

We are dealing here with second-hand goods. The spark plugs, though used, are nevertheless Champion plugs and not those of another make. There is evidence to support what one would suspect, that a used spark plug which has been repaired or reconditioned does not measure up to the specifications of a new one. But the same would be true of a second-hand Ford or Chevrolet car. And we would not suppose that one could be enjoined from selling a car whose valves had been reground and whose piston rings had been replaced unless he removed the name Ford or Chevrolet. *Prestonettes, Inc. v. Coty*, 264 U.S. 359, was a case where toilet powders had as one of their ingredients a powder covered by a trade mark and where perfumes which were trade marked were rebottled and sold in smaller bottles. The Court sustained a decree denying an injunction where the prescribed labels told the truth. Mr. Justice Holmes stated, "A trade mark only gives the right to prohibit the use of it so far as to protect the owner's good will against the sale of another's product as his. When the mark is used in a way that does not deceive the public we see no such sanctity in the word as to prevent its being used to tell the truth. It is not taboo."

Cases may be imagined where the reconditioning or repair would be so extensive or so basic that it would be a misnomer to call the article by its original name, even though the words "used" or "repaired" were added.

[Citations omitted]. But no such practice is involved here. The repair or reconditioning of the plugs does not give them a new design. It is no more than a restoration, so far as possible, of their original condition. The type marks attached by the manufacturer are determined by the use to which the plug is to be put. But the thread size and size of the cylinder hole into which the plug is fitted are not affected by the reconditioning. The heat range also has relevance to the type marks. And there is evidence that the reconditioned plugs are inferior so far as heat range and other qualities are concerned. But inferiority is expected in most second-hand articles. Indeed, they generally cost the customer less. That is the case here. Inferiority is immaterial so long as the article is clearly and distinctly sold as repaired or reconditioned rather than as new. The result is, of course, that the second-hand dealer gets some advantage from the trade mark. But under the rule of *Prestonettes, Inc. v. Coty, supra*, that is wholly permissible so long as the manufacturer is not identified with the inferior qualities of the product resulting from wear and tear or the reconditioning by the dealer. Full disclosure gives the manufacturer all the protection to which he is entitled.

QUESTIONS

1.   Which disclaimer, the District Court's or the Court of Appeals', would be more likely to forestall consumer confusion?

2.   If "full disclosure gives the manufacturer all the protection to which he is entitled," should relief in all trademark infringement and unfair competition cases be limited to disclaimers and accurate labeling? If not, why not?

3.   Is the court's analogy to the sale of used cars persuasive?

4.   Imagine that you represent a client who wants to publish a how-to book on using Microsoft Windows Vista® software and Microsoft MSN®. She would like to call the book "Microsoft Windows Vista® and MSN®: An Unauthorized Guide." She plans to include a floppy disk with the book that contains some helpful add-on macros and shortcuts that she wrote herself, and that she maintains will help the novice user make the most of Windows Vista® and MSN®. Microsoft has an aggressive licensing program for its products, and your client neither meets Microsoft's specifications nor is willing to pay its licensing fee. What do you advise?

Ralph S. Brown, Jr., Advertising and the Public Interest: Legal Protection of Trade Symbols, 57 Yale L.J. 1165 (1948) [excerpts]*

The law of trade symbols is of modern development, largely judge-made and only partly codified. Its impetus comes from the demands of modern advertising, a black art whose practitioners are part of the larger army which employs threats, cajolery, emotions, personality, persistence and facts in what is termed aggressive selling. Much aggressive selling

* [footnotes omitted—Eds.]

involves direct personal relationships; advertising depends on the remote manipulation of symbols, most importantly of symbols directed at a mass audience through mass media, or imprinted on mass-produced goods. The essence of these symbols is distilled in the devices variously called trademarks, trade names, brand names, or trade symbols. To the courts come frequent claims for protection, made by those who say they have fashioned a valuable symbol, and that no one else should use it. Very recently, for example, the vendors of Sun–Kist oranges lost a court battle to prevent an Illinois baker from selling Sun–Kist bread. The highest court, in its most recent encounter with a like case, upheld the power of a manufacturer of rubber footwear to prevent the use of a red circle mark by a seller of rubber heels, which the plaintiff did not manufacture.

In these cases, a choice of premises and techniques is still open. One set of premises, which seems to subsume Justice Frankfurter's felicitous dictum, recognizes a primary public interest in protecting the seller who asks the court to enjoin "another [who] poaches upon the commercial magnetism of a symbol he has created." This expansive conception merits critical attention. Are all forms of poaching forbidden? Should they be, consistent with another premise? This one asserts, in the words of Judge Frank, "the basic common law policy of encouraging competition, and the fact that the protection of monopolies in names is but a secondary and limiting policy." The legal ties which bind together some apparently inconsistent decisions may be found, but not simply in an indiscriminate prohibition of poaching, nor yet in a presumption in favor of competition, no matter how compelling. Rather, courts move from these and other premises to refinements of doctrine.

It is proposed here to seek, in the milieu in which trade symbols are created and used, for data underlying both premises and dogma. This will require an independent evaluation of the institution of advertising. What do we get for the three billions of current annual outlay? Do we want it? Unfortunately, there is little consensus as to what values advertising serves. Its votaries have poured their most skillful symbols back in the soil from which they sprang. Its detractors, maddened by the success of this propaganda, would purge Radio City with fire and sword. One thing the examination will reveal is that what appear to be private disputes among hucksters almost invariably touch the public welfare. We shall therefore be concerned to ask, when courts protect trade symbols, whether their decisions further public as well as private goals.

The principal reason for advertising is an economic one—to sell goods and services. We can describe this process, and its economic effects, with relative confidence, compared to the obscurity which surrounds the psychological, cultural, or other social consequences of modern advertising. These may turn out to be more portentous than the affairs of the market-place. But the materials are uncollected or unrefined. In this survey we can only drop a handful of problems into a footnote. The reader must make his own judgments from his own observations, remembering, as we turn almost exclusively to economic discussion, that man does not live by bread alone.

Informative and Persuasive Advertising

The buying public submits to a vast outpouring of words and pictures from the advertisers, in which, mingled with exhortations to buy, is a modicum of information about the goods offered. From the point of view of the economic purist, imparting information is the only useful function of advertising. A perfect market demands a perfect enlightenment of those who buy and sell. One of the many imperfections of the real world is that, absent advertising, most buyers would have to go to a great deal of trouble to discover what is offered for sale. To the extent that the blandishments of sellers inform buyers what is to be bought, and at what price, advertising undoubtedly helps to quicken the stream of commerce.

Most advertising, however, is designed not to inform, but to persuade and influence. What is the occasion for such tremendous outlays on persuasion and influence in a well-ordered economic system? If we consider first the total stream of production and consumption, persuasive advertising seems only to consume resources that might be put to better use producing more goods and services. It does not increase total demand, it only increases wants. Effective demand arises, not from what we would like to have, but from the purchasing power of the community created by its productive power. We consume what we produce, and no more. Considering the economic welfare of the community as a whole, to use up part of the national product persuading people to buy product A rather than product B appears to be a waste of resources.

. . . .

The Sovereign Consumer

Defenders of the institution have two additional lines of defense. The first is that persuasive advertising creates a cluster of values, no less real because they are intangible. The second, related to the first, argues that the sovereign consumer has made a free election between those values and the austerities of price competition.

These considerations bring us to the consumer as an individual. As an individual, instead of a faceless component of mass purchasing power, he is a creature of infinite diversity, with, moreover, a soul. To make a complete analysis of what he gets from advertising, the relations of material rewards and spiritual values, as affected by advertising, would have to be considered. That task we must leave to the philosophers and the psychologists. As was indicated earlier, they have not yet performed it. The only arena which is at all adequately staked out is that of the economic conflict between seller and buyer. The agreed goal is the maximum satisfaction of each consumer, as determined by his free choice in disposing of his income. In a roundabout way, problems of aggregate output and investment, already discussed, bear on the same goal. Now we have to consider how persuasive advertising adds to or subtracts from the sum of the individual's satisfied wants.

What are the intangible values? One is said to be the assurance of reliability, because the advertiser wants to build up repeat sales, and cannot afford to sell patently unsatisfactory goods. Admitting, for the sake of getting on, that unadvertised brands offer a greater opportunity for "hit-and-run" frauds, the difficulty with this contention is that the hope of continued custom is quite unrelated to the magnitude of persuasive advertising. Nothing more than information as to source is necessary for the consumer to be able to repeat a satisfactory purchase.

Other values derive from the proposition in that cheapness is not enough. The buyer of an advertised good buys more than a parcel of food or fabric; he buys the pause that refreshes, the hand that has never lost its skill, the priceless ingredient that is the reputation of its maker. All these may be illusions, but they cost money to create, and if the creators can recoup their outlay, who is the poorer? Among the many illusions which advertising can fashion are those of lavishness, refinement, security, and romance. Suppose the monetary cost of compounding a perfume is trivial; of what moment is this if the ads promise, and the buyer believes, that romance, even seduction, will follow its use? The economist, whose dour lexicon defines as irrational any market behavior not dictated by a logical pecuniary calculus, may think it irrational to buy illusions; but there is a degree of that kind of irrationality even in economic man; and consuming man is full of it.

The taint of irrationality may be dispelled by asserting flatly that the utility of a good, that is, its capacity to satisfy wants, is measured exactly by what people will pay for it. If, as is undeniably the case, consumers will pay more for an advertised brand than for its unheralded duplicate, then consumers must get more satisfaction out of the advertised brand. The nature of the satisfaction is of concern only to the moralist. Though this argument can easily be pushed to absurdity—suppose it was to the interest of the advertisers to consume half the national product in persuasion?—it seems plausible if it is based on the dogma of consumer autonomy. Then anyone who questions the untrammeled use of influence by the seller and its uncoerced acceptance by the buyer is at best a Puritan, at worst a Fascist. The debate seems to end in a defense of freedom, for the advertiser as well as for the consumer.

But does the sovereign consumer have real freedom of choice? The first requisite of choice is an adequate presentation of alternatives. The classical economists who enthroned the consumer never dreamed that he would make his decisions under a bombardment of stupefying symbols. He should be informed, and willing to pay the necessary price for information. But the most charitable tabulations reveal relatively little information in advertising directed to consumers outside the classified columns and local announcements. National advertising is dominated by appeals to sex, fear, emulation, and patriotism, regardless of the relevance of those drives to the transaction at hand. The purchase of many advertised articles, then, has a raw emotional origin. Many others are compelled by the endless reiteration of the advertisers' imperative: eat lemons, drink milk, wear hats. Pseudo-information fills any gaps. It takes many forms. There is the bewildering manipulation of comparatives and superlatives: "No other soap washes cleaner"; "The world's most wanted pen." In the atomic age, precise scientific data are helpful. Bayer's Aspirin tells us that the tablet dissolves in two seconds. Whether the analgesic effect is then felt in one hour or two hours will no doubt be explained in time. Buick lists among its features such well-understood engineering terms as "Dynaflow Drive, taper-thru Styling, Vibra–Shielded Ride, Hi–Poised Fire-ball Power." The reader, after ten minutes with a magazine or the radio, can select his own examples of the types of influence that are thought to move the sovereign consumer.

The foundation of free choice, to repeat, is an adequate presentation of alternatives. Admittedly, many choices, for example in politics or religion, are presented under a smoke screen of exaggeration and emotion. But there are usually at least two sides to the argument. The choice between one highly advertised dentifrice and another is, in important respects, no choice at all. It cannot register a decision to support or reject institutional arrangements which, as had been shown, contribute to monopolistic waste of resources; it cannot reflect a preference to get more or less for one's money, to take an illusion or leave it. It is only a choice of between one illusion and another. That advertisers, despite their intramural rivalry, are aware that they stand on common ground, is shown by their united opposition to institutions which enlarge the consumer's alternatives. An instance is the forays and reprisals against the consumers' movement.

The forces which counter advertising propaganda may be listed as follows. First, as an individual protest, is the sentiment described as "sales resistance," a compound of realism, skepticism, and apathy. Second is organized sales resistance, the pressure for reform by the slow-moving consumers' organizations. Third, most important economically, is the still small voice of the lower price tag on an unadvertised substitute. Fourth, the nub of the present discussion, comes the shaping of legal institutions, either to curb the excesses of advertising or to foster the second and third forces just listed. It is intended to discuss in a later article the enforcement of truth in advertising, as an indication that freedom to persuade and influence has its boundaries, and the possible use of antitrust, taxation, or other devices to set new boundaries. The law also has to take a stand when the use or misuse of advertising has created measurable values for the advertiser, and "another poaches upon the commercial magnetism of the symbol." How much protection will be given the advertiser against the poacher? The answer is sought in the law of trade-marks and trade names.

Summary

Before assessing the relevance of that body of doctrine to the good and bad in advertising, it may be desirable to summarize the conclusions reached thus far. Advertising has two main functions, to inform and to persuade. With qualifications that need not be repeated, persuasive advertising is, for the community as a whole, just a luxurious exercise in talking ourselves into spending our incomes. For the individual firm, however, it is a potent device to distinguish a product from its competitors, and to create a partial immunity from the chills and fevers of competition. The result of successful differentiation is higher prices than would otherwise prevail. The aim, not always achieved, is higher profits. Whether persuasive advertising enhances the total flow of goods by promoting cost reductions is disputable. Whether it swells the flow of investment by the lure of monopoly profits is doubtful.

For the consumer who desires to get the most for his money, persuasive advertising displays a solid front of irrelevancy. The alternatives to what the advertisers offer are not adequately presented, and the choice among advertised products is loaded with a panoply of propaganda for which the buyer pays, whether he wants it or not. However, both buyer and seller profit from informative advertising. In a complex society, it is an indispensable adjunct to a free traffic in goods and services. The task before the courts in trade symbol cases, it may therefore be asserted, should be to pick out from the tangle of claims, facts, and doctrines they are set to unravel, the threads of informative advertising, and to ignore the persuasive. The two functions are very much intertwined in trade symbols, how confusingly will appear when we try to separate them.

. . . .

WILLIAM M. LANDES & RICHARD A. POSNER, TRADEMARK LAW: AN ECONOMIC PERSPECTIVE, XXX J. L. & Econ. 265, 268–70, 273–75 (1987) (excerpts)*

II.   The Economics of Trademarks

A.   Introduction

To oversimplify somewhat, a trademark is a word, symbol, or other signifier used to distinguish a good or service produced by one firm from the goods or services of other firms. Thus "Sanka" designates a decaffeinated coffee made by General Foods and "Xerox" the dry copiers made by Xerox Corporation. "Bib"—the "Michelin Man"—is the symbol of tires made by the Michelin Company. A stylized penguin is the symbol of a line of paperback books published by Penguin Books; a distinctively shaped green bottle is a trademark of the producer of Perrier bottled water; the color pink is a trademark for residential insulation manufactured by Owens–Corning.

1.   Benefits of Trademarks

Suppose you like decaffeinated coffee made by General Foods. If General Foods' brand had no name, then to order it in a restaurant or grocery store you would have to ask for "the decaffeinated coffee made by General Foods." This takes longer to say, requires you to remember more, and requires the waiter or clerk to read and remember more than if you can just ask for "Sanka." The problem would be even more serious if

---

* [footnotes omitted—Eds.]

General Foods made more than one brand of decaffeinated coffee, as in fact it does. The benefit of the brand name is analogous to that of designating individuals by last as well as first names, so that, instead of having to say "the Geoffrey who teaches constitutional law at the University of Chicago Law School—not the one who teaches corporations," you can say "Geoffrey Stone—not Geoffrey Miller."

To perform its economizing function a trademark or brand name (these are rough synonyms) must not be duplicated. To allow another maker of decaffeinated coffee to sell its coffee under the name "Sanka" would destroy the benefit of the name in identifying a brand of decaffeinated coffee made by General Foods (whether there might be offsetting benefits is considered later). It would be like allowing a second rancher to graze his cattle on a pasture the optimal use of which required that only one herd be allowed to graze. The failure to enforce trademarks would impose two distinct costs—one in the market for trademarked goods and the other in the distinct (and unconventional) market in language.

(a) The Market for Trademarked Goods. The benefits of trademarks in reducing consumer search costs require that the producer of a trademarked good maintain a consistent quality over time and across consumers. Hence trademark protection encourages expenditures on quality. To see this, suppose a consumer has a favorable experience with brand X and wants to buy it again. Or suppose he wants to buy brand X because it has been recommended by a reliable source or because he has had a favorable experience with brand Y, another brand produced by the same producer. Rather than investigating the attributes of all goods to determine which one is brand X or is equivalent to X, the consumer may find it less costly to search by identifying the relevant trademark and purchasing the corresponding brand. For this strategy to be efficient, however, not only must it be cheaper to search for the right trademark than for the desired attributes of the good, but also past experience must be a good predictor of the likely outcome of current consumption choices—that is, the brand must exhibit consistent quality. In short, a trademark conveys information that allows the consumer to say to himself, "I need not investigate the attributes of the brand I am about to purchase because the trademark is a shorthand way of telling me that the attributes are the same as that of the brand I enjoyed earlier."

Less obviously, a firm's incentive to invest resources in developing and maintaining (as through advertising) a strong mark depends on its ability to maintain consistent product quality. In other words, trademarks have a self-enforcing feature. They are valuable because they denote consistent quality, and a firm has an incentive to develop a trademark only if it is able to maintain consistent quality. To see this, consider what happens when a brand's quality is inconsistent. Because consumers will learn that the trademark does not enable them to relate their past to future consumption experiences, the branded product will be like a good without a trademark. The trademark will not lower search costs, so consumers will be unwilling to pay more for the branded than for the unbranded good. As a result, the firm will not earn a sufficient return on its trademark promotional expenditures to justify making them. A similar argument shows that a firm with a valuable trademark would be reluctant to lower the quality of its brand because it would suffer a capital loss on its investment in the trademark.

It should be apparent that the benefits of trademarks in lowering consumer search costs presuppose legal protection of trademarks. The value of a trademark is the saving in search costs made possible by the information or reputation that the trademark conveys or embodies about the brand (or the firm that produces the brand). Creating such a reputation requires expenditures on product quality, service, advertising, and so on. Once the reputation is created, the firm will obtain greater profits because repeat purchases and word-of-mouth references will generate higher sales and because consumers will be willing to pay higher prices for lower search costs and greater assurance of consistent quality. However, the cost of duplicating someone else's trademark is small—the cost of duplicating a label, design, or package where the required inputs are widely available. The incentive to incur this cost (in the absence of legal regulation) will be greater the stronger the trademark. The free-riding competitor will, at little cost, capture some of the profits associated with a strong trademark because some consumers will assume (at least in the short run) that the free rider's and the original trademark holder's brands are identical. If the law does not prevent it, free riding will eventually destroy the information capital embodied in a trademark, and the prospect of free riding may therefore eliminate the incentive to develop a valuable trademark in the first place.

. . . .

2. *The Costs of Legally Enforceable Trademarks*

These costs are modest, at least in the simple case of the "fanciful" mark, such as "Exxon" and "Kodak," which has no information content except to denote a specific producer or brand. Since the mark "goes with" the brand (in a sense explained later), the transfer of the mark is automatically effected by a transfer of the rights to make the branded product, as by a sale, or licensing, of production rights or assets. Rent seeking to stake out a trademark is not much of a problem either. Prior to establishing a trademark, the distinctive yet pronounceable combinations of letters to form words that will serve as a suitable trademark are as a practical matter infinite, implying a high degree of substitutability and hence a slight value in exchange. Finally, the costs of enforcement, though not trivial (especially where there is a danger of a brand name's becoming a generic name), are modest and (again putting aside the generic problem) do not include the cost in inefficient resource allocation from driving a wedge between price and marginal cost. A proper trademark is not a public good; it has social value only when used to designate a single brand.

We may seem to be ignoring the possibility that, by fostering product differentiation, trademarks may create deadweight costs, whether of monopoly or (excessive) competition. We have assumed that a trademark induces its owner to invest in maintaining uniform product quality, but another interpretation is that it induces the owner to spend money on creating, through advertising and promotion, a spurious image of high quality that enables monopoly rents to be obtained by deflecting consumers from lower-price substitutes of equal or even higher quality. In the case of products that are produced according to an identical formula, such as aspirin or household liquid bleach, the ability of name-brand goods (Bayer aspirin, Clorox bleach) to command higher prices than generic (nonbranded) goods has seemed to some economists and more lawyers an example of the power of brand advertising to bamboozle the public and thereby promote monopoly; and brand advertising presupposes trademarks—they are what enable a producer readily to identify his brand to the consumer. Besides the possibility of creating monopoly rents, trademarks may transform rents into costs, as one firm's expenditure on promoting its mark cancels out that of another firm. Although no monopoly profits are created, consumers may pay higher prices, and resources may be wasted in a sterile competition.

The short answer to these arguments is that they have gained no foothold at all in trademark law, as distinct from antitrust law. The implicit economic model of trademarks that is used in that law is our model, in which trademarks lower search costs and foster quality control rather than create social waste and consumer deception. A longer answer, which we shall merely sketch, is that the hostile view of brand advertising has been largely and we think correctly rejected by economists. The fact that two goods have the same chemical formula does not make them of equal quality to even the most coolly rational consumer. That consumer will be interested not in the formula but in the manufactured product and may therefore be willing to pay a premium for greater assurance that the good will actually be manufactured to the specifications of the formula. Trademarks enable the consumer to economize on a real cost because he spends less time searching to get the quality he wants. If this analysis is correct, the rejection by trademark law of a monopoly theory of trademarks is actually a mark in favor of the economic rationality of that law.

QUESTIONS

1. Have Landes and Posner adequately responded to the policy questions raised by Brown? How would you respond?

2. How different is the universe of protectable trademarks under the Landes & Posner discussion from the scope of "trade symbols" whose protection Brown discusses? Does that difference account for their different views?

3. Economist Jonathan Aldred suggests that that the argument that trademarks actually reduce consumer search costs is circular:

> What precisely is guaranteed to the consumer by a guarantee of origin? There is no guarantee regarding the product's function or fitness for purpose, nor that it has been made in a particular way or at a

particular location. . . . To a cynical economist, it seems that the only thing *guaranteed* to the consumer is that the trade mark owner will take a share of the profits on the sale of the product.

While Landes and Posner suggest that a trademark will give the owner of the mark an incentive to maintain a reputation for high quality products, Aldred responds that a mark owner has an interest in building its reputation but also has an interest in reducing its costs.

> Often the best way of achieving this combination is through sophisticated marketing, rather than making high quality products. Consumers come to *believe* the trade mark signals high quality, and may continue to do so even after purchase if the quality defects are hidden or debatable. As the central device in a marketing strategy, the trade-marked sign may be used by firms to mislead consumers rather than convey useful information, reputation arguments notwithstanding.

Aldred goes on to argue that Landes and Posner are too ready to accept that if consumers are willing to pay higher prices for products with well-known trademarks, that fact, without more, demonstrates that the trademarked products are better than their lower priced competitors. *See* Jonathan Aldred, *The Economic Rationale of Trademarks: An Economist's Critique, in* Lionel Bently, Jennifer Davis and Jane C. Ginsburg, eds., TRADE MARKS AND BRANDS: AN INTERDISIPLINARY CRITIQUE (Cambridge U. Press, forthcoming 2008). Do Landes & Posner have a persuasive response?

JESSICA LITMAN, BREAKFAST WITH BATMAN: THE PUBLIC INTEREST IN THE ADVERTISING AGE, 108 Yale L.J. 1717, 1725–1731 (1999) (excerpts)*

The expansion of the law of trade symbol protection has tracked two distinct but related trends. First has been an evolution in widely held views of the public interest. Ralph Brown argued in *Advertising and the Public Interest* that just because people paid more for products did not mean there had been any actual increase in productivity and welfare—rather, we had let ourselves be talked into paying more money for the same stuff. That, he insisted, was obviously in the interest of the producers whose advertising had persuaded the public to pay a higher price, but was wasteful for the public at large. Today, that once self-evident point is controversial. Productivity seems to be measured less by what people make than by what people are inclined to buy. What consumers are willing to pay has become synonymous with value. Commodification is the preeminent engine of progress. Transforming ephemeral figments into saleable property is a patriotic act, and the fact, without more, that an offer to sell something will find customers is reason enough to sanction its appropriation from the commons. There has been inexorable pressure to recognize as an axiom the

---

* [footnotes omitted—Eds.]

principle that if something appears to have substantial value to someone, the law must and should protect it as property. Recent years have seen an explosion of cases in which courts have relied on trademark-like rubrics to uphold claims to exclusive rights in names, faces, voices, gestures, phrases, artistic style, marketing concepts, locations, and references.

Second, the descriptive proposition that trade symbols have no intrinsic value has come to seem demonstrably inaccurate. The use of trademarks on promotional products has evolved from an advertising device for the underlying product line to an independent justification for bringing a so-called underlying product to market. Elvis Presley's estate has earned more annually in license fees than it did in the late singer's most profitable year. Warner Brothers has brought out a seemingly endless series of lackluster Batman sequels. Critics disliked the sequels, and their box office performances were mediocre, but the sales of Batman toys have more than made up for it. It is hard to maintain a straight face when asserting that the "Batman" mark has value only as an indicator that Batman-branded products are licensed by Warner Brothers. The worth of such valuable trade symbols lies less in their designation of product source than in their power to imbue a product line with desirable atmospherics.

Indeed, in the new orthodoxy, marketing *is* value. American industry seems to proceed on the assumption that we can make the consumer richer simply by revising a product's packaging, without having to make any changes in the product itself.

Consider the effort and expense that goes into distinguishing a Ford Taurus from a Mercury Sable and persuading customers to buy one rather than the other, when, after all, they're essentially the same car. Buying a truck? Agonize over whether you'd rather drive a Mazda B–Series (*Get in. Be moved.*), "the official truck of the AMA Motorcross Nationals," or haul your friends to the river, kayaks in tow, in a Ford Ranger (*Built Tough. Built To Last.*). The only major difference between them is the marketing. Auto companies can pitch their vehicles to specialized, niche markets without needing to redesign anything but the ad campaigns for their cars.

But why not? If the illusion of a vehicle custom-built for a particular sort of buyer is worth a couple of thousand dollars to a couple of million consumers, the customers will be happier, the auto companies will be wealthier, and the American economy will keep chugging along, picking up speed without burning additional coal. Anecdotal evidence suggests that many consumers don't feel duped, or, in any event, don't mind being duped. It isn't as if anyone has tried to conceal that the Sable and the Taurus are twins, that Advil and Motrin and generic ibuprofen are the exact same stuff, or that the reason that Tylenol and not some other brand of acetaminophen is "the pain reliever hospitals use most" is that McNeil sets the hospital price of Tylenol low enough to enable it to make that claim. At some level, most consumers know that; most of them have nonetheless settled on their own favorite advertised brands.

Moreover, there is something more going on than producers and consumers agreeing with each other to pretend that the atmospherics of product advertising are somehow reflected in the advertised products. Ask a child, and he'll persuade you that the difference between a box of Kellogg's Corn Flakes with a picture of Batman on it and some other box without one is real. There is nothing imaginary about it. It has nothing to do with the way the cereal tastes. What kids want isn't a nutritious part of a complete breakfast; they want Batman to have breakfast with them. One box supplies that; the other doesn't.

An important premise underlying Ralph Brown's analysis was that trade symbols themselves had no legitimate intrinsic value except insofar as they symbolized information about the products they accompanied. As a normative proposition, that would strike many consumers today as questionable; as a descriptive one, it is demonstrably untrue. Consumers have come to attach enormous value to trade symbols, and it is no longer uncommon to see the symbols valued far in excess of the worth of the underlying products they identify. In a very real sense, trade symbols are themselves often products: Toys are designed, perfumes are compounded, and breakfast cereals are devised for no better reason than to serve as a vehicle for the trade symbol du jour. If we have come to value the atmospherics embodied in advertising, shouldn't our law be reformed to protect them from unauthorized imitation?

At first glance, the syllogism seems to pack powerful intuitive appeal. Ralph Brown's argument relied on the axiom that what he called the persuasive function of trade symbols was of no value to the public at large; indeed, from the viewpoint of the public interest, the persuasive value of advertising was at best irrelevant and at worst pernicious. Affording it strong legal protection, therefore, seemed perverse. Whether or not that axiom described the U.S. economy in 1948, it seems naive in 1999. In today's world, the public has invested considerable spending dollars and a significant chunk of intangible goodwill in the atmospherics purveyed by advertisers. If society values the persuasive function of trade symbols more than it used to, then perhaps it ought to protect that persuasive function more powerfully than it used to.

To say that many consumers seem to attach real value to atmospherics, however, doesn't itself demonstrate that those atmospherics should be afforded legal protection. Many things have value. As Ralph Brown reminded us often, the essence of any intellectual property regime is to divide the valuable stuff subject to private appropriation from the valuable stuff that, precisely because of its importance, is reserved for public use. In the law of trade symbols, for instance, it has long been the rule that functional product features may not be protected, because they have too much value, not too little. Value, without more, does not tell us whether a particular item for which protection is sought belongs in the proprietary pile or the public one.

To agree to treat a class of stuff as intellectual property, we normally require a showing that, if protection is not extended, bad things will happen that will outweigh the resulting good things. But it would be difficult to argue that the persuasive values embodied in trade symbols are likely to suffer from underprotection. Indeed, the Mattels, Disneys, and Warner Brothers of the world seem to protect their atmospherics just fine without legal assistance. Not only can their target audiences tell the difference between, say, a Barbie doll and some other thirteen-inch fashion doll, but, regardless of features, they seem well-trained in the art of insisting on the Mattel product. Nor is the phenomenon limited to the junior set. The popularity of Ralph Lauren's Polo brand shirts or Gucci handbags is an obvious example.

To the extent that consumers want to purchase the higher-priced spread, they ought to be able to be sure that they are paying the higher price for the genuine branded article. If the concept of branding is itself legitimate, then we want to ensure consumers' protection against confusion or deception. Conventional trademark law does that. But, to stick with Lauren's Polo for a minute, what about consumers who want to pick up a polo shirt with some design on the chest at a good price? What if, instead, they want to buy this month's issue of *Polo* magazine (which follows the sport, not the fashion)? It seems obvious why Lauren might want to hinder the first and collect a license fee from the second, so it would hardly be perplexing if his company threatened to sue. There seems, nonetheless, to be no good reason why we should help him.

If competition is still the American way of doing business, then before we give out exclusive control of some coin of competition, we need, or should need, a justification. Protecting consumers from deception is the justification most familiar to trademark law, but it does not support assigning broad rights to prevent competitive or diluting use when no confusion seems likely. Supplying incentives to invest in the item that's getting the protection is another classic justification for intellectual property, and it is equally unavailing here. An argument that we would have an undersupply of good commercials if advertisers were not given plenary control over the elements in their ads cannot be made with a straight face. Finally, there is the perennially popular justification of desert. Producers have invested in their trade symbols, the argument goes; they have earned them, so they're entitled to them.

But so have we. The argument that trade symbols acquire intrinsic value—apart from their usefulness in designating the source—derives from consumers' investing those symbols with value for which they are willing to pay real money. We may want our children to breakfast with Batman. It may well increase the total utils in our society if every time a guy drinks a Budweiser or smokes a Camel, he believes he's a stud. We may all be better off if, each time a woman colors her hair with a L'Oreal product, she murmurs to herself *"and I'm worth it."* If that's so, however, Warner Brothers, Anheuser–Busch, R.J. Reynolds, and L'Oreal can hardly take all the credit. They built up all that mystique with their customers' money and active collaboration. If the customers want to move on, to get in bed with other products that have similar atmospherics, why shouldn't they? It's not very sporting to try to lock up the atmospherics.

To the extent, moreover, that the impulse to protect something beyond any prevention of consumer confusion derives from the perception that this thing has value, that it is something people want to buy, then giving its purveyor intellectual property protection is the wrong response. If the thing itself is valuable, if it is in some sense itself a product, then we want other purveyors to compete in offering it to consumers in their own forms and on their own terms. Competition is, after all, the premise of the system. Without competition, none of the rest of the rules make any practical sense.

QUESTIONS

1. On balance, do you see either benefit or harm from encouraging the public to perceive equivalent products as materially different from each other?

2. Articulate the justifications for protecting trademarks and other trade symbols from non-confusing use by others. Should it make a difference whether the use is commercial or non-commercial?

3. If kids want to eat breakfast with Batman, should any cereal manufacturer be entitled to put pictures of Batman on its cereal boxes without Warner Brothers' permission?

CHAPTER 2

WHAT IS A TRADEMARK?

A. SUBJECT MATTER OF TRADEMARK PROTECTION

Restatement (Third) of Unfair Competition*

§ 9. DEFINITIONS OF TRADEMARK AND SERVICE MARK

A trademark is a word, name, symbol, device, or other designation, or a combination of such designations, that is distinctive of a person's goods or services and that is used in a manner that identifies those goods or services and distinguishes them from the goods or services of others. A service mark is a trademark that is used in connection with services.

Comment:

. . . .

b. Historical origins of trademarks. The use of identifying marks on goods dates to antiquity. The original purpose of such marks was to indicate ownership. With the development of commercial trade the marks came to serve a different function—identification of the source of goods offered for sale in the marketplace.

The use of trademarks was well-known in Roman times, although it was apparently left to the defrauded purchaser to bring an action against a trademark infringer. The guild system of medieval England produced the first widespread use of trademarks. Distinctive production marks were required on goods manufactured by the local guilds. The purpose of such compulsory marking was primarily regulatory since the marks fixed responsibility for defective merchandise and facilitated enforcement of the territorial monopolies enjoyed by the guilds. The geographic expansion of markets and the development of more complex distribution systems eventually resulted in a new function for production marks. The marks served to identify the source of the goods to prospective purchasers who could then make their selections based upon the reputation, not merely of the immediate vendor, but also of the manufacturer. Manufacturers began to adopt marks expressly for the purpose of identifying their goods to prospective customers. The medieval production mark thus evolved into the modern trademark used by manufacturers, distributors, and other sellers to identify their goods and services in the marketplace.

. . . .

g. *Subject matter.* The subject matter of trademark law was initially limited to fanciful or arbitrary words and symbols. This limitation excluded not only descriptive words and symbols, but also other devices that could identify the source of goods, such as the physical appearance of the goods or the appearance of labels, wrappers, containers, or advertising materials that accompany the goods in the marketplace. When such features in fact served to distinguish the goods of a particular producer, they were protected, together with descriptive marks, in an action for unfair competition. As the distinctions between the actions for trademark infringement and unfair competition diminished, the law of trademarks eventually subsumed descriptive designations that had acquired significance as indications of source. Although the protection of product and packaging designs that are indicative of source remains subject to special limitations not applicable to other marks, they too have now been subsumed under the law of trademarks....

The definition of "trademark" adopted in this Section does not incorporate any technical limitations on the nature of the subject matter that may qualify for protection. Words remain the most common type of trademark, such as the word FORD used in connection with the sale of automobiles or KODAK used in connection with cameras. Numbers, letters, and slogans are also eligible for protection as trademarks, as are pictures, symbols, characters, sounds, graphic designs, product and packaging features, and other matter capable of identifying and distinguishing the goods or services of the user....

Kellogg Co. v. National Biscuit Co.

305 U.S. 111, 59 S.Ct. 109, 83 L.Ed. 73 (1938).

■ MR. JUSTICE BRANDEIS delivered the opinion of the Court:

This suit was brought in the federal court for Delaware by National Biscuit Company against Kellogg Company to enjoin alleged unfair competition by the manufacture and sale of the breakfast food commonly known as shredded wheat. The competition was alleged to be unfair mainly because Kellogg Company uses, like the plaintiff, the name shredded wheat and, like the plaintiff, produces its biscuit in pillow-shaped form.

Shredded wheat is a product composed of whole wheat which has been boiled, partially dried, then drawn or pressed out into thin shreds and baked. The shredded wheat biscuit generally known is pillow-shaped in form. It was introduced in 1893 by Henry D. Perky, of Colorado; and he was connected until his death in 1908 with companies formed to make and market the article. Commercial success was not attained until the Natural Food Company built, in 1901, a large factory at Niagara Falls, New York. In 1908, its corporate name was changed to "The Shredded Wheat Company;" and in 1930 its business and goodwill were acquired by National Biscuit Company.

Kellogg Company has been in the business of manufacturing breakfast food cereals since its organization in 1905. For a period commencing in

1912 and ending in 1919 it made a product whose form was somewhat like the product in question, but whose manufacture was different, the wheat being reduced to a dough before being pressed into shreds. For a short period in 1922 it manufactured the article in question. In 1927, it resumed manufacturing the product. . . .

In 1935, the District Court dismissed the bill. It found that the name "Shredded Wheat" is a term describing alike the product of the plaintiff and of the defendant; and that no passing off or deception had been shown. It held that upon the expiration of the Perky patent No. 548,086 issued October 15, 1895, the name of the patented article passed into the public domain. In 1936, the Circuit Court of Appeals affirmed that decree. Upon rehearing, it vacated, in 1937, its own decree and reversed that of the District Court, with direction "to enter a decree enjoining the defendant from the use of the name 'Shredded Wheat' as its trade-name and from advertising or offering for sale its product in the form and shape of plaintiff's biscuit in violation of its trade-mark; and with further directions to order an accounting for damages and profits." . . .

The plaintiff concedes that it does not possess the exclusive right to make shredded wheat. But it claims the exclusive right to the trade name "Shredded Wheat" and the exclusive right to make shredded wheat biscuits pillow-shaped. It charges that the defendant, by using the name and shape, and otherwise, is passing off, or enabling others to pass off, Kellogg goods for those of the plaintiff. Kellogg Company denies that the plaintiff is entitled to the exclusive use of the name or of the pillow-shape; denies any passing off; asserts that it has used every reasonable effort to distinguish its product from that of the plaintiff; and contends that in honestly competing for a part of the market for shredded wheat it is exercising the common right freely to manufacture and sell an article of commerce unprotected by patent.

First. The plaintiff has no exclusive right to the use of the term "Shredded Wheat" as a trade name. For that is the generic term of the article, which describes it with a fair degree of accuracy; and is the term by which the biscuit in pillow-shaped form is generally known by the public. Since the term is generic, the original maker of the product acquired no exclusive right to use it. As Kellogg Company had the right to make the article, it had, also, the right to use the term by which the public knows it. Ever since 1894 the article has been known to the public as shredded wheat. For many years, there was no attempt to use the term "Shredded Wheat" as a trade-mark. When in 1905 plaintiff's predecessor, Natural Food Company, applied for registration of the words "Shredded Whole Wheat" as a trade-mark under the so-called "ten year clause" of the Act of February 20, 1905, c. 592, § 5, 33 Stat. 725, William E. Williams gave notice of opposition. Upon the hearing it appeared that Williams had, as early as 1894, built a machine for making shredded wheat, and that he made and sold its product as "Shredded Whole Wheat." The Commissioner of Patents refused registration. The Court of Appeals of the District of Columbia affirmed his decision, holding that "these words accurately and aptly describe an article of food which ... has been produced ... for more than ten years...." *Natural Food Co. v. Williams,* 30 App. D.C. 348.

Moreover, the name "Shredded Wheat," as well as the product, the process and the machinery employed in making it, has been dedicated to the public. The basic patent for the product and for the process of making it, and many other patents for special machinery to be used in making the article, issued to Perky. In those patents the term "shredded" is repeatedly used as descriptive of the product. The basic patent expired October 15, 1912; the others soon after. Since during the life of the patents "Shredded Wheat" was the general designation of the patented product, there passed to the public upon the expiration of the patent, not only the right to make the article as it was made during the patent period, but also the right to apply thereto the name by which it had become known. As was said in *Singer Mfg. Co. v. June Mfg. Co.,* 163 U.S. 169, 185:

> "It equally follows from the cessation of the monopoly and the falling of the patented device into the domain of things public, that along with the public ownership of the device there must also necessarily pass to the public the generic designation of the thing which has arisen during the monopoly.... To say otherwise would be to hold that, although the public had acquired the device covered by the patent, yet the owner of the patent or the manufacturer of the patented thing had retained the designated name which was essentially necessary to vest the public with the full enjoyment of that which had become theirs by the disappearance of the monopoly."

It is contended that the plaintiff has the exclusive right to the name "Shredded Wheat," because those words acquired the "secondary meaning" of shredded wheat made at Niagara Falls by the plaintiff's predecessor. There is no basis here for applying the doctrine of secondary meaning. The evidence shows only that due to the long period in which the plaintiff or its predecessor was the only manufacturer of the product, many people have come to associate the product, and as a consequence the name by which the product is generally known, with the plaintiff's factory at Niagara Falls. But to establish a trade name in the term "shredded wheat" the plaintiff must show more than a subordinate meaning which applies to it. It must show that the primary significance of the term in the minds of the consuming public is not the product but the producer. This it has not done. The showing which it has made does not entitle it to the exclusive use of the term shredded wheat but merely entitles it to require that the defendant use reasonable care to inform the public of the source of its product.

The plaintiff seems to contend that even if Kellogg Company acquired upon the expiration of the patents the right to use the name shredded wheat, the right was lost by delay. The argument is that Kellogg Company, although the largest producer of breakfast cereals in the country, did not seriously attempt to make shredded wheat, or to challenge plaintiff's right to that name until 1927, and that meanwhile plaintiff's predecessor had expended more than $17,000,000 in making the name a household word and identifying the product with its manufacture. Those facts are without legal significance. Kellogg Company's right was not one dependent upon diligent exercise. Like every other member of the public, it was, and remained, free to make shredded wheat when it chose to do so; and to call the product by its generic name. The only obligation resting upon Kellogg Company was to identify its own product lest it be mistaken for that of the plaintiff.

Second. The plaintiff has not the exclusive right to sell shredded wheat in the form of a pillow-shaped biscuit—the form in which the article became known to the public. That is the form in which shredded wheat was made under the basic patent. The patented machines used were designed to produce only the pillow-shaped biscuits. And a design patent was taken out to cover the pillow-shaped form. Hence, upon expiration of the patents the form, as well as the name, was dedicated to the public. As was said in *Singer Mfg. Co. v. June Mfg. Co., supra,* p. 185:

> "It is self evident that on the expiration of a patent the monopoly granted by it ceases to exist, and the right to make the thing formerly covered by the patent becomes public property. It is upon this condition that the patent is granted. It follows, as a matter of course, that on the termination of the patent there passes to the public the right to make the machine in the form in which it was constructed during the patent. We may, therefore, dismiss without further comment the complaint, as to the form in which the defendant made his machines."

Where an article may be manufactured by all, a particular manufacturer can no more assert exclusive rights in a form in which the public has become accustomed to see the article and which, in the minds of the public, is primarily associated with the article rather than a particular producer, than it can in the case of a name with similar connections in the public mind. Kellogg Company was free to use the pillow-shaped form, subject only to the obligation to identify its product lest it be mistaken for that of the plaintiff.

Third. The question remains whether Kellogg Company in exercising its right to use the name "Shredded Wheat" and the pillow-shaped biscuit, is doing so fairly. Fairness requires that it be done in a manner which reasonably distinguishes its product from that of plaintiff.

Each company sells its biscuits only in cartons. The standard Kellogg carton contains fifteen biscuits; the plaintiff's twelve. The Kellogg cartons are distinctive. They do not resemble those used by the plaintiff either in size, form, or color. And the difference in the labels is striking. The Kellogg cartons bear in bold script the names "Kellogg's Whole Wheat Biscuit" or "Kellogg's Shredded Whole Wheat Biscuit" so sized and spaced as to strike the eye as being a Kellogg product. It is true that on some of its cartons it had a picture of two shredded wheat biscuits in a bowl of milk which was quite similar to one of the plaintiff's registered trademarks. But the name

Kellogg was so prominent on all of the defendant's cartons as to minimize the possibility of confusion.

Some hotels, restaurants, and lunchrooms serve biscuits not in cartons and guests so served may conceivably suppose that a Kellogg biscuit served is one of the plaintiff's make. But no person familiar with plaintiff's product would be misled. The Kellogg biscuit is about two-thirds the size of plaintiff's; and differs from it in appearance. Moreover, the field in which deception could be practiced is negligibly small. Only 2½ per cent of the Kellogg biscuits are sold to hotels, restaurants and lunchrooms. Of those so sold 98 per cent are sold in individual cartons containing two biscuits. These cartons are distinctive and bear prominently the Kellogg name. To put upon the individual biscuit some mark which would identify it as the Kellogg product is not commercially possible. Relatively few biscuits will be removed from the individual cartons before they reach the consumer. The obligation resting upon Kellogg Company is not to insure that every purchaser will know it to be the maker but to use every reasonable means to prevent confusion.

It is urged that all possibility of deception or confusion would be removed if Kellogg Company should refrain from using the name "Shredded Wheat" and adopt some form other than the pillow-shape. But the name and form are integral parts of the goodwill of the article. To share fully in the goodwill, it must use the name and the pillow-shape. And in the goodwill Kellogg Company is as free to share as the plaintiff. *Compare William R. Warner & Co. v. Eli Lilly & Co.,* 265 U.S. 526, 528, 530. Moreover, the pillow-shape must be used for another reason. The evidence is persuasive that this form is functional—that the cost of the biscuit would be increased and its high quality lessened if some other form were substituted for the pillow-shape.

Kellogg Company is undoubtedly sharing in the goodwill of the article known as "Shredded Wheat"; and thus is sharing in a market which was created by the skill and judgment of plaintiff's predecessor and has been widely extended by vast expenditures in advertising persistently made. But that is not unfair. Sharing in the goodwill of an article unprotected by patent or trade-mark is the exercise of a right possessed by all—and in the free exercise of which the consuming public is deeply interested. There is no evidence of passing off or deception on the part of the Kellogg Company; and it has taken every reasonable precaution to prevent confusion or the practice of deception in the sale of its product.

. . . .

QUESTIONS

1. The "Shredded Wheat" decision concerned the trademark protection available to the design of a product, and to its name, following expiration of patents covering the product and the processes and special machinery needed to manufacture it. Is the court holding that once such a patent expires, neither the product's shape nor its name can *ever* be the subject of a trademark? If not, under what circumstances is the assertion of trademark rights permissible?

2. Is trademark protection available for a word that accurately describes an article? For one that partially describes an article?

3. Is trademark protection available for a design for which a patent still subsists? For an unpatented design?

4. Justice Brandeis acknowledges that by adopting its predecessor's name and design the second-comer "is undoubtedly sharing in the goodwill of an article known as 'Shredded Wheat'; and thus is sharing in a market which was created by the skill and judgment of plaintiff's predecessor and has been widely extended by vast expenditures of advertising persistently made. But that is not unfair. Sharing in the goodwill of an article unprotected by patent or trademark is the exercise of a right possessed by all—and in the free exercise of which the consuming public is deeply interested."

In other words, one may share in the goodwill of the product, but not in that of the producer. What is the difference between these two kinds of "sharing"? How would you demonstrate the difference?

5. For a full exploration of the history and implications of the "Shredded Wheat" decision, see Graeme Dinwoodie, The Story of *Kellogg v. National Biscuit*: Breakfast with Brandeis, in Jane C. Ginsburg and Rochelle Cooper Dreyfuss, eds., Intellectual Property Stories 222 (2005).

1. Word Marks

Coca–Cola Co. v. Koke Co. of America

254 U.S. 143, 41 S.Ct. 113, 65 L.Ed. 189 (1920).

■ Mr. Justice Holmes delivered the opinion of the Court:

This is a bill in equity brought by the Coca–Cola Company to prevent the infringement of its trade-mark Coca–Cola and unfair competition with it in its business of making and selling the beverage for which the trademark is used. The District Court gave the plaintiff a decree. 235 Fed.408. This was reversed by the Circuit Court of Appeals. *Koke Co. v. Coca–Cola Co.*, 255 Fed. 894, 167 C. C. A. 214. Subsequently a writ of certiorari was granted by this Court. It appears that after the plaintiff's predecessors in title had used the mark for some years it was registered under the Act of Congress of March 3, 1881, and again under the Act of February 20, 1905. Both the Courts below agree that subject to the one question to be considered the plaintiff has a right to equitable relief. Whatever may have been its original weakness, the mark for years has acquired a secondary significance and has indicated the plaintiff's product alone. It is found that defendant's mixture is made and sold in imitation of the plaintiff's and that the word "Koke" was chosen for the purpose of reaping the benefit of the advertising done by the plaintiff and of selling the imitation as and for the plaintiff's goods. The only obstacle found by the Circuit Court of Appeals in the way of continuing the injunction granted below was its opinion that the trade-mark in itself and the advertisements accompanying it made such fraudulent representations to the public that the plaintiff had lost its claim to any help from the Court. That is the question upon which the writ of certiorari was granted and the main one that we shall discuss.

Of course a man is not to be protected in the use of a device the very purpose and effect of which is to swindle the public. But the defects of a plaintiff do not offer a very broad ground for allowing another to swindle him. The defense relied on here should be scrutinized with a critical eye. The main point is this: Before 1900 the beginning of the good will was more or less helped by the presence of cocaine, a drug that, like alcohol or caffeine or opium, may be described as a deadly poison or as a valuable item of the pharmacopoeia according to the rhetorical purposes in view. The amount seems to have been very small, but it may have been enough to begin a bad habit and after the Food and Drug Act of June 30, 1906, if not earlier, long before this suit was brought, it was eliminated from the plaintiff's compound. Coca leaves still are used, to be sure, but after they have been subjected to a drastic process that removes from them every characteristic substance except a little tannin and still less chlorophyll. The cola nut, at best, on its side furnishes but a small portion of the caffeine, which now is the only element that has appreciable effect. That comes mainly from other sources. It is argued that the continued use of the name imports a representation that has ceased to be true ... and that thus the very thing sought to be protected is used as a fraud.

The argument does not satisfy us. We are dealing here with a popular drink not with a medicine, and although what has been said might suggest that its attraction lay in producing the expectation of a toxic effect the facts point to a different conclusion. Since 1900 the sales have increased at a very great rate corresponding to a like increase in advertising. The name now characterizes a beverage to be had at almost any soda fountain. It means a single thing coming from a single source, and well known to the community. It hardly would be too much to say that the drink characterizes the name as much as the name the drink. In other words "Coca–Cola" probably means to most persons the plaintiff's familiar product to be had everywhere rather than a compound of particular substances.... [I]t has acquired a secondary meaning in which perhaps the product is more emphasized than the producer but to which the producer is entitled. The coca leaves and whatever of cola nut is employed may be used to justify the continuance of the name or they may affect the flavor as the plaintiff contends, but before this suit was brought the plaintiff had advertised to the public that it must not expect and would not find cocaine, and had eliminated everything tending to suggest cocaine effects except the name and the picture of the leaves and nuts, which probably conveyed little or nothing to most who saw it. It appears to us that it would be going too far to deny the plaintiff relief against a palpable fraud because possibly here and there an ignorant person might call for the drink with the hope for incipient cocaine intoxication. The plaintiff's position must be judged by the facts as they were when the suit was begun, not by the facts of a different condition and an earlier time.

SLOGANS

The Lanham Act's predecessor, the Trademark Act of 1905, made no provision for registration of slogans. Decisions construing this statute routinely refused registration on the premise that slogans were merely descriptive advertising features. *See generally* Beran, *Protection of Slogans in the Patent Office and the Courts*, 57 Trademark Rep. 219 (1967). The turning point came after adoption of the Lanham Act, in *American Enka Corp. v. Marzall*, 92 U.S.P.Q. 111 (D.D.C.1952). The court there recognized that the prior cases disfavoring registration defied the traditional trademark logic that a combination of words capable of distinguishing goods or services possesses trademark significance, and is therefore registrable. The *Marzall* court, holding registrable on the Principal Register the phrase "THE FATE OF A FABRIC HANGS BY A THREAD," noted that "certain combinations of words, albeit that they are also slogans, may properly function as trademarks."

The Commissioner of Patents adopted the *Marzall* approach in *Ex parte Robbins & Myers, Inc.,* 104 U.S.P.Q. 403 (1955), and held the slogan "MOVING AIR IS OUR BUSINESS" registrable on the Principal Register. Rejecting the Trademark Examiner's position that the phrase was merely descriptive for electric fans for circulating air, Assistant Commissioner Leeds stated that the phrase had "a certain double entendre which removes it from [the merely descriptive] category." The Commissioner also stressed that section 2 of the Lanham Act made clear that so long as a term is distinctive, it shall not be refused registration "on account of its nature." Thus, assigning slogans to second-class status violated the Lanham Act's nondiscrimination principle. Moreover, section 23 of the Lanham Act explicitly provides that slogans are registrable on the Supplemental Register. A slogan's descriptive feature, therefore, does not automatically disqualify it from registration.

What if the slogan is straightforwardly descriptive? Like other descriptive terms, a descriptive slogan can acquire secondary meaning through extensive, continuous and substantially exclusive use, and thus may achieve the secondary meaning requisite to protectable status. One such slogan was at issue in *Roux Labs. v. Clairol, Inc.,* 427 F.2d 823 (C.C.P.A.1970), where the court dismissed an opposition to registration on the Principal Register of the slogan "HAIR COLOR SO NATURAL ONLY HER HAIR DRESSER KNOWS FOR SURE" for "hair tinting, dyeing and coloring preparation." (The student may recall that in the advertisements for applicant's "Miss Clairol" product, the inquiry "Does she . . . or doesn't she?" preceded the disputed slogan. Another memorable slogan from this period for a similar product plaintively declared, "IF I HAVE ONLY ONE LIFE TO LEAD, LET ME LIVE IT AS A BLONDE!") In rejecting opposer's mere descriptiveness challenge, the court emphasized the pervasiveness of applicant's advertising and sales: from 1956–66, applicant sold over 50 million dollars worth of the product, and expended 22 million dollars in advertising containing the disputed slogan. "Conservatively estimated, there have been more than a billion audio impressions of this slogan on network television in the United States (one impression being one household having a TV set tuned to a given program at a given time)." The court thus held "we do not think the board erred in concluding that Clairol's slogan has made an impact upon the purchasing public separate from and in addition to the impact of its 'Miss Clairol' mark."

PERSONAL NAMES

Peaceable Planet v. Ty, Inc.

362 F.3d 986 (7th Cir.2004).

■ POSNER, J.

. . .

Like the defendant, the much larger and better known Ty Inc. . . ., Peaceable Planet makes plush toys in the shape of animals, filled with bean-like materials to give the toys a soft and floppy feel. Ty's plush toys are, of course, the famous "Beanie Babies."

In the spring of 1999, Peaceable Planet began selling a camel that it named "Niles." The name was chosen to evoke Egypt, which is largely desert except for the ribbon of land bracketing the Nile. The camel is a desert animal, and photos juxtaposing a camel with an Egyptian pyramid are common. The price tag fastened to Niles's ear contains information both about camels and about Egypt, and the Egyptian flag is stamped on the animal.

A small company, Peaceable Planet sold only a few thousand of its camels in 1999. In March of the following year, Ty began selling a camel also named "Niles." It sold a huge number of its "Niles" camels—almost two million in one year—precipitating this suit. The district court ruled that "Niles," being a personal name, is a descriptive mark that the law does not protect unless and until it has acquired secondary meaning, that is, until there is proof that consumers associate the name with the plaintiff's brand. Peaceable Planet did not prove that consumers associate the name "Niles" with its camel. . . .

The reluctance to allow personal names to be used as trademarks reflects valid concerns. . . . One of the concerns is a reluctance to forbid a person to use his own name in his own business. [Citations omitted.] Supposing a man named Brooks opened a clothing store under his name, should this prevent a second Brooks from opening a clothing store under his own (identical) name even though consumers did not yet associate the name with the first Brooks's store? It should not. [Citations omitted.]

Another and closely related concern behind the personal-name rule is that some names are so common—such as "Smith," "Jones," "Schwartz," "Wood," and "Jackson"—that consumers will not assume that two products having the same name therefore have the same source, and so they will not be confused by their bearing the same name. [Citations omitted.] If there are two bars in a city that are named "Steve's," people will not infer that they are owned by the same Steve.

The third concern, which is again related but brings us closest to the rule regarding descriptive marks, is that preventing a person from using his name to denote his business may deprive consumers of useful information. Maybe "Steve" is a well-known neighborhood figure. If he can't call his bar "Steve's" because there is an existing bar of that name, he is prevented from communicating useful information to the consuming public. [Citations omitted.] . . .

The personal-name "rule," it is worth noting, is a common law rather than statutory doctrine. All that the Lanham Act says about personal names is that a mark that is "primarily merely a surname" is not registrable in the absence of secondary meaning. 15 U.S.C. §§ 1052(e)(4), (f). There is no reference to first names. The reason for the surname provision is illustrated by the Brooks example. The extension of the rule to first names is a judicial innovation and so needn't be pressed further than its rationale, as might have to be done if the rule were codified in inflexible statutory language. Notice too the limitation implicit in the statutory term "primarily."

In thinking about the applicability of the rationale of the personal-name rule to the present case, we should notice first of all that camels, whether real or toy, do not go into business. Peaceable Planet's appropriation of the name "Niles" for its camel is not preventing some hapless camel in the Sahara Desert who happens to be named "Niles" from going into the water-carrier business under its own name. The second thing to notice is that "Niles" is not a very common name; in fact it is downright rare. And the third thing to notice is that if it were a common name, still there would be no danger that precluding our hypothetical Saharan water carrier from using its birth name "Niles" would deprive that camel's customers of valuable information. In short, the rationale of the personal-name rule is wholly inapplicable to this case.

What is more, if one wants to tie the rule in some fashion to the principle that descriptive marks are not protectable without proof of second meaning, then one must note that "Niles," at least when affixed to a toy camel, is a suggestive mark, like "Microsoft" or *Business Week,* or—coming closer to this case—like "Eor" used as the name of a donkey, or the proper names in *Circuit City Stores, Inc. v. CarMax, Inc., supra,* 165 F.3d at 1054, rather than being a descriptive mark. Suggestive marks are protected by trademark law without proof of secondary meaning. [Citations omitted.] Secondary meaning is not required because there are plenty of alternatives to any given suggestive mark. There are many more ways of suggesting than of describing. Suggestive names for camels include "Lawrence [of Arabia]" (one of Ty's other Beanie Babies *is* a camel named "Lawrence"); "Desert Taxi," "Sopwith" (the Sopwith Camel was Snoopy's World War I fighter plane), "Camelia," "Traveling Oasis," "Kamelsutra," "Cameleon," and "Humpy–Dumpy."

If "Niles" cannot be a protected trademark, it must be because to give it legal protection would run afoul of one of the purposes of the common law rule that we have identified rather than because it is a descriptive term, which it is not. But we have seen that it does not run afoul of any of those purposes. "Niles" is not the name of the defendant—it's not as if Peaceable Planet had named its camel "Ty Inc." or "H. Ty Warner." It also is not a common name, like "Smith" or "Jackson." And making Ty use a different name for its camel would not deprive the consumer of valuable information about Ty or its camel....

. . . .

2.   SERVICE MARKS

15 U.S.C. § 1053 [LANHAM ACT § 3]

Subject to the provisions relating to the registration of trademarks, so far as they are applicable, service marks shall be registrable, in the same manner and with the same effect as are trademarks, and when registered they shall be entitled to the protection provided in this chapter in the case of trademarks. Applications and procedure under this section shall conform as nearly as practicable to those prescribed for the registration of trademarks.

15 U.S.C. § 1127 [LANHAM ACT § 45]

The term "service mark" means any word, name, symbol, or device, or any combination thereof—

(1) used by a person, or

(2) which a person has a bona fide intention to use in commerce and applies to register on the principal register established by this Act,

to identify and distinguish the services of one person, including a unique service, from the services of others and to indicate the source of the services, even if that source is unknown. Titles, character names, and other distinctive features of radio or television programs may be registered as service marks notwithstanding that they, or the programs, may advertise the goods of the sponsor.

What is a "Service"?

Examples of service marks that we have already encountered in this casebook include Sears Roebuck & Co. (retail services) and Stork Restaurant (restaurant services). Neither the Lanham Act nor its legislative history defines "services." The Federal Circuit has noted that the term was "intended to have a broad scope" and was not defined because of "the plethora of services that the human mind is capable of conceiving." *In re*

Advertising & Marketing Development Inc., 821 F.2d 614 (Fed.Cir.1987). The Federal Circuit has broadly defined a "service" as "the performance of labor for the benefit of another." *Id.* at 2014. In order to constitute a service, therefore, it is necessary that it be for another. Services performed only for the benefit of the owner of the mark, such as advertising the owner's own goods, are not considered a service. *See, e.g., In re Dr. Pepper Co.*, 836 F.2d 508 (Fed.Cir.1987). What if instead of advertising one's own goods, the mark owner offers advertising space to others? *See In re Forbes*, 31 U.S.P.Q.2d 1315 (T.T.A.B.1994) (offering advertising space under mark NO GUTS, NO STORY found to be a service even though the advertising was placed in applicant's own publications such as *Forbes* magazine). What if a family-owned investment company engages in financial activities intended to benefit the family, but incidentally solicits co-investors, arranges joint ventures and advises U.S. individuals about investments in Asia; do these activities constitute a service? *See Morningside Group Ltd. v. Morningside Capital Group, L.L.C.*, 182 F.3d 133 (2d Cir.1999).

Unlike a trademark, a service mark is "used" when it is displayed in the advertising of services, as well as in their sale or offering. Nonetheless, courts have determined that the *first* use of a service mark for purposes of securing registration must be in connection with the offering, rather than the announcement, of the services. Hence, an advertising announcement that a service will shortly be available (for example, that a restaurant will be opening) will not constitute "use" for registration. The services must have been rendered in commerce. *See, e.g., In re Port Authority of New York*, 3 U.S.P.Q.2d 1453 (T.T.A.B.1987); TMEP § 1301.03(a).

3. Collective and Certification Marks

15 U.S.C. § 1054 [LANHAM ACT § 4]

Subject to the provisions relating to the registration of trademarks, so far as they are applicable, collective and certification marks, including indications of regional origin, shall be registrable under this Chapter, in the same manner and with the same effect as are trademarks, by persons, and nations, States, municipalities, and the like, exercising legitimate control over the use of the marks sought to be registered, even though not possessing an industrial or commercial establishment, and when registered they shall be entitled to the protection provided herein in the case of trademarks, except in the case of certification marks when used so as to represent falsely that the owner or a user thereof makes or sells the goods or performs the services on or in connection with which such mark is used. Applications and procedure under this section shall conform as nearly as practicable to those prescribed for the registration of trademarks.

15 U.S.C. § 1127 [LANHAM ACT § 45]

Collective Mark

The term "collective mark" means a trademark or service mark—

(1) used by the members of a cooperative, an association, or other collective group or organization, or

(2) which such cooperative, association, or other collective group or organization has a bona fide intention to use in commerce and files an application to register on the principal register established by this Act, and includes marks indicating membership in a union, an association, or other organization.

Certification Mark

The term "certification mark" means any word, name, symbol, or device, or any combination thereof—

(1) used by a person other than its owner, or

(2) which its owner has a bona fide intention to permit a person other than the owner to use in commerce and files an application to register on the principal register established by this Act,

to certify regional or other origin, material, mode of manufacture, quality, accuracy, or other characteristics of such person's goods or services or that the work or labor on the goods or services was performed by members of a union or other organization.

15 U.S.C. § 1064(5) [LANHAM ACT § 14(5)] provides for cancellation of certification mark:

> At any time in the case of a certification mark on the ground that the registrant (A) does not control, or is not able legitimately to exercise control over, the use of such mark, or (B) engages in the production or marketing of any goods or services to which the certification mark is applied, or (C) permits the use of the certification mark for purposes other than to certify, or (D) discriminately refuses to certify or to continue to certify the goods or services of any person who maintains the standards or conditions which such mark certifies. . . .

> Nothing in paragraph (5) shall be deemed to prohibit the registrant from using the certification mark in advertising or promoting recognition of the certification program or of the goods or services meeting the certification standards of the registrant. . . .

————

Collective and Certification Marks

There are two different types of collective marks: collective trademarks and service marks, and collective membership marks. Examples of collectives which may own either kind of collective marks include agricultural coops, unions and trade associations. Collective service marks are used by members of an organization to identify and distinguish their services. For example, REALTOR is the collective service mark of the National Association of Realtors. Collective membership marks, by contrast, are designations used by individual members to indicate that they are members of a group. Collective membership marks may be owned by collective organizations that never use the symbols of their organizations in connection with the commercialization of goods or services, such as fraternal benefit societies. See Ex Parte The Supreme Shrine of the Order of the White Shrine of Jerusalem, 109 U.S.P.Q. 248 (Comm'r. Pat. 1956). See also PRINCETON UNIVERSITY TRIANGLE CLUB, collective membership mark Reg. No. 737,669, issued Sept. 11, 1962, cited in, In re Triangle Club of Princeton University, 138 U.S.P.Q. 332 (TTAB 1963).

A certification mark, unlike a trademark or service mark, does not indicate the producer of the goods or services. Indeed, the owner of a certification mark is prohibited from using it as a mark to identify the source of its own goods or services. Rather, a certification mark functions as a symbol of guarantee or certification that the goods or services bearing the mark meet certain criteria or conditions. Examples include designations of regional origin such as ROQUEFORT for cheese produced in Roquefort, France, from blue-mold sheep's milk; designations that products meet certain standards, such as UL of Underwriter's Laboratory indicating compliance with safety standards; or designations that certify that labor on goods was performed by members of a union or organization, such as the UNITE HERE! label. Further, the owner of a certification mark cannot arbitrarily choose whom it will permit to use the mark, unlike the trademark or service mark owner who can choose its licensees. Indeed, the certification mark is subject to cancellation if the certifying organization excludes a potential user who meets the certifier's criteria. The Lanham Act's "certification mark cancellation provisions illustrate the legislative intent to protect a further public interest in free and open competition among producers and distributors of the certified product. By requiring certification mark holders to license all individuals who meet the certification criteria, the Lanham Act ensures that the market will include as many participants as can produce conforming goods. By preventing mark holders from becoming market participants, it removes incentives for mark holders to engage in anti-competitive conduct. The Lanham Act's cancellation provisions thus appear designed to promote free competition in the market for certified products." Idaho Potato Comm'n v. G & T Terminal Packaging, Inc., 425 F.3d 708 (9th Cir.2005) (citation omitted).

Like trademarks and service marks, collective and certification marks are protectable whether or not they are registered. Section 45 of the Lanham Act defines the term "mark" as "any trademark, service mark, collective mark, or certification mark entitled to registration under this Act *whether registered or not*" (emphasis added). Common law certification marks have been recognized by the Trademark Trial and Appeal Board, *see, e.g. Institut National Des Appellations d'Origine v. Brown–Forman Corp.*, 47 U.S.P.Q.2d 1875 (T.T.A.B.1998) (finding that COGNAC is a common law certification mark indicating brandy produced in the Cognac region of France and declining to dismiss opposition filed by French government agency charged with protecting national indications of origin, against registration of CANADIAN MIST AND COGNAC), and by the courts, *see, e.g., Florida v. Real Juices, Inc.*, 330 F.Supp. 428 (M.D.Fla.1971) (use by defendant of plaintiff's unregistered SUNSHINE TREE certification mark for citrus fruits a violation of Section 43(a) of Lanham Act).

Regional certification marks are sometimes challenged as being generic terms rather than as certifying the regional origin of goods. For example, ROQUEFORT for cheese and COGNAC for brandy have survived generic challenges. *See Community of Roquefort v. Faehndrich*, 303 F.2d 494 (2d Cir.1962); *Institut National Des Appellations d'Origine v. Brown–Forman Corp.*, 47 U.S.P.Q.2d 1875 (T.T.A.B.1998). Other terms such as "Swiss cheese" have been considered generic terms in the U.S. The difference between a valid regional certification mark and a generic term has been described by the Board as follows:

> In determining whether a designation, the use of which in fact is controlled by the certifier and is limited to products meeting the standards of regional origin established by the certifier, is a protectible regional certification mark, as opposed to an unprotectible generic name for the product, the issue is not whether the public is expressly aware of the certification function of the mark or the certification process underlying use of the mark, but rather is whether the public understands that goods bearing the mark come only from the region named in the mark. If use of the designation in fact is controlled by the certifier and limited to products meeting the certifier's standards of regional origin, and if purchasers understand the designation to refer only to products which are produced in the particular region, and not to products produced elsewhere, then the designation functions as a regional certification mark. Neither the statute nor the case law requires that purchasers also be expressly aware of the term's certification function, *per se*.
>
> In short, a regional certification mark will not be deemed to have become a generic term as applied to particular goods unless it appears that it has lost its significance as an indication of regional origin for those goods, e.g., by virtue of its having been used on goods which originate somewhere other than the place named in the mark.

Institut National Des Appellations d'Origine, 47 U.S.P.Q.2d at 1885 (citations omitted). For an analysis of whether the collective mark REALTOR has become generic, see Zimmerman v. National Association of Realtors, 70 U.S.P.Q.2d 1425 (T.T.A.B.2004).

QUESTIONS

1. Section 4 of the Lanham Act extends the general provisions relating to trademarks to collective and certification marks "in so far as the[se provisions] are applicable." Which provisions would not be applicable, and why?

2. Section 14(5) of the Lanham Act makes discriminatory refusal to certify the "goods or services of any person who maintains the standards or conditions which such mark certifies" a ground for cancellation of the registration of a certification mark. There is no equivalent provision for cancellation of a collective mark. Should there be?

Geographic Indications

The 1994 World Trade Organization Agreement on Trade Related Aspects of Intellectual Property (TRIPs), which the United States ratified in 1994 obliges Member States to protect "geographical indications." Article 22(1) defines these as:

> indications which identify a good as originating in the territory of a Member, or a region or locality in that territory, where a given quality, reputation, or other characteristic of the good is essentially attributable to its geographical origin.

Thus, not only must the goods originate in a particular place, but the goods would be (or would be perceived to be) qualitatively different if they came from some other place. For example, "Cuba" plays such a role in relation to tobacco, but not with respect to other goods grown or produced there, such as corn.

Article 22(2) obliges member states to prevent

> the use of any means in the designation or presentation of a good that indicates or suggests that the good in question originates in a geographical area other than the true place of origin in a manner that misleads the public as to the geographical origin of the good

As a result, not all use of a geographic term violates international norms. In particular, if to the national public, the term is generic–for example, Swiss cheese—its use cannot mislead as to the goods' geographical origin. Even terms, such as Feta, which some countries recognize as geographic indications (in this case, the EU) may not enjoy that status in others. TRIPs does not generally oblige one member State to adopt another's geographic indications TRIPs does, however, set out a more imperialistic standard for wines and spirits, see Note, infra.

Member States may implement TRIPs norms in a variety of ways, including application, and where necessary adaptation, of extant domestic trademark laws. Unites States' doctrine regarding certification marks may accomplish the task, but perhaps only part way. The following excerpt sets out the differences between the certification marks regime, and the much more specific French system of *Appellations d'origine contrôlées*.

JUSTIN HUGHES, CHAMPAGNE, FETA AND BOURBON: THE SPIRITED DEBATE ABOUT GEOGRAPHICAL INDICATIONS, 58 Hastings L.J. 299 (2006)

A "geographic identifier" could be any word, phrase, or symbol that designates the place where a product was produced regardless of reputation. So, "made in Patagonia" on ROM chips would be a geographical identifier even though Patagonia has no particular reputation for semiconductors. In contrast, a geographical indication (GI) designates the place where a product was produced and that the place is known to produce that item with particular desirable qualities. In the case of GI's there is a known land/qualities nexus. It follows that every geographical indication is a geographical identifier, but not vice versa.

Geographical indications are often geographic words coupled with the generic term for the product (e.g., Irish whiskey). Sometimes the geographic word stands alone (e.g., Scotch). Typically, the places are either towns (Roquefort, Chablis), or sub-national regions such as states (Idaho potatoes), departments (Cognac), or counties (Bourbon). The larger the region, the less likely it is that production factors will be both (a) consistent across the region and (b) unique to that region. Nonetheless, and despite resistance to the idea historically, names of countries can be protected as geographic indications one way or another in most legal systems, e.g., Canadian whiskey, Colombian coffee, or Swiss chocolate.

Finally, geographic indications are occasionally not names of places. For example, in Britain, "claret" has come to refer to red Bordeaux wines. Similarly, the European Union has spent years arguing over whether "feta" is a geographical indication belonging to Greece. A bottle style that has been historically used for, and identified with, a wine or spirit from one particular region might also be claimed as a geographical indication. . . .

With these basics in mind, it is useful to sketch out the two most divergent approaches to protecting geographical indications.

A.   The French System of Appellations D'Origine Contrôlées

Although there were some laws in France, Portugal, and Tuscany controlling wine labeling as early as the 14th and 15th century, appellations law is a modern phenomenon. In 1855, the Medoc vineyards of Bordeaux were classified. This move coincided, not incidentally, with the opening of the railroad between Bordeaux and Paris. The first modern French law to combat fraudulently labeled wines was passed in 1905, but France's first government committee on appellations of origin for wines and eaux de vie was not established until 1935. In 1947, that committee became the Institut National des Appellations d'Origine (INAO), now part of the Ministry of Agriculture.

The French system of appellations d'origine contrôlées (AOC) is founded on the idea of terroir. "Terroir" has no direct English translation, but the notion behind the Latinate word is simple: the product's qualities come with the territory. As one Australian wine critic describes it:

> terroir . . . translates roughly as "the vine's environment," but has connotations that extend right into the glass: in other words, if a wine tastes of somewhere, if the flavours distinctly make you think of a particular place on the surface of this globe, then that wine is expressing its terroir.

To put it less poetically, "terroir" is the idea of an "essential land/qualities nexus": French law defines an AOC as a region or locality name "that serves to designate a product of that origin whose qualities or characteristics are due to the geographic milieu, which includes natural and human elements."

Beliefs about terroir run deep in France, but not too deep, for if they did there might not be a justification for the elaborate regulatory structure governing production of AOC foodstuffs. The INAO regulates not just the geographic boundaries for each AOC, but all "conditions of production," including, for wine, the grape varietals, hectare production quotas, natural alcohol content during vinification, permitted irrigation, etc. The INAO regulations for AOC cheese place varying legal requirements on rennet used in coagulation, curd drainage, milk temperature at different points in curing, salting, and the use of lactic proteins. The INAO works with "interprofessional" committees organized around specific products. Based on committee recommendations, the INAO also establishes new appellations controlées.

French statutory law protects an AOC not just against unauthorized uses on products in the same category, but also against any commercial use of the indication "likely to divert or weaken the renown of the appellation d'origine." This standard seems roughly similar to the protection accorded famous trademarks under U.S. federal dilution law. In perhaps the best known application of this broad protection, the producers of sparkling wine from the Champagne region were able to stop Yves St. Laurent from marketing a perfume called "Champagne."

B. The American System of Certification and Collective Marks

In contrast to a separate system for protecting appellations, some countries, like the United States, subsume protection of geographical indications under trademark law. This is achieved through the categories of "certification marks" and "collective marks." Under U.S. law, a collective mark is a trademark "used by the members of a cooperative, an association, or other collective group or organization," a definition that could easily include a foodstuff producers' cooperative or trade association which imposes its own standards. Certification marks are used to "certify regional or other origin, material, mode of manufacture, quality, accuracy, or other characteristics of ... [the] good or service." Examples include the "Good Housekeeping" seal of approval, the "UL" mark (Underwriters' Laboratory), and various trademarks used to designate kosher foods.

A certification mark protects a geographical indication when it is used to "certify regional ... origin." For example, the state government of Idaho has three registered certification marks at the United States Patent and Trademark Office (USPTO) protecting different versions of "IDAHO POTATOES". Other examples of registered certification marks in the United States include PARMIGIANO–REGGIANO, ROQUEFORT, STILTON, CALIFORNIA for cheese, PARMA for ham, DARJEELING for tea, WASHINGTON for apples, and the FLORIDA SUNSHINE TREE for citrus.

To maintain USPTO registration of a certification mark, the mark holder must meet several standards.... But, unlike the INAO, as long as the certification standards are applied in a non-discriminatory fashion, the USPTO does not care what the certification standards are. Even less government oversight is involved in a "collective mark" which is owned by an association to which all the relevant producers belong. Collective marks are treated like regular trademarks,.... In short, government involvement with this kind of geographical indication is no different than it is with the trademarks HILTON HOTELS or PEPSI.

Like other trademarks, certification marks can develop as a matter of common law without USPTO registration.... The ability of certification mark rights to arise without any ex ante government role further distinguishes the American approach from a real AOC system.

Special protection for wines and spirits:

The TRIPS Agreement obliges Member States to accord additional protection to geographical indications for wines and spirits. While the general provision on geographic indications, art. 22(2) addresses uses that *mislead* the public as to geographical origin, art. 23(1) condemns a much broader scope of use of the designation:

> Each member shall provide the legal means for interested parties to prevent use of a geographical indication identifying wines for wines not originating in the place indicated by the geographical indication in question or identifying spirits for spirits not originating in the place indicated by the geographical indication in question, even where the true origin of the goods is indicated or the geographical indication is used in translation or accompanied by expressions such as 'kind,' 'type,' style,' 'imitation,' or the like.

The United States has implemented art. 23(1) through the following amendment to Lanham Act § 2(a):

> [A trademark shall be denied registration if it consists of] a geographical indication which, when used on or in connection with wines or spirits, identifies a place other than the origin of the goods and is first used on or in connection with wines or spirits by the applicant on or after [1996].

QUESTIONS:

1. Does § 2(a) fully satisfy the Unites States' international obligations under TRIPs?

2. May any of the following be registered? May any of the following be used? The mark for which registration is sought is set out in quotation marks. The goods are marketed using the entire phrase.

a. "Fabulous Fizz New York State Champagne." First use: 1990.

b. "Fabulous Fizz New York State Champagne." First use: 2000.

c. "Fabulous Fizz" New York State Champagne. First use: 2000.

d. "Fabulous Fizz Champagne Method" New York State Sparkling Wine. First use: 2000.

4. Trade Dress

Qualitex Co. v. Jacobson Products Co., Inc.

514 U.S. 159, 115 S.Ct. 1300, 131 L.Ed.2d 248 (1995).

■ Justice Breyer delivered the opinion of the Court:

The question in this case is whether the Lanham Trademark Act of 1946 (Lanham Act), 15 U.S.C. §§ 1051–1127 (1988 ed. and Supp. V), permits the registration of a trademark that consists, purely and simply, of a color. We conclude that, sometimes, a color will meet ordinary legal trademark requirements. And, when it does so, no special legal rule prevents color alone from serving as a trademark.

I

The case before us grows out of petitioner Qualitex Company's use (since the 1950's) of a special shade of green-gold color on the pads that it makes and sells to dry cleaning firms for use on dry cleaning presses. In 1989 respondent Jacobson Products (a Qualitex rival) began to sell its own press pads to dry cleaning firms; and it colored those pads a similar green-gold. In 1991 Qualitex registered the special green-gold color on press pads with the Patent and Trademark Office as a trademark. Registration No. 1,633,711 (Feb. 5, 1991). Qualitex subsequently added a trademark infringement count, 15 U.S.C. § 1114(1), to an unfair competition claim, § 1125(a), in a lawsuit it had already filed challenging Jacobson's use of the green-gold color.

Qualitex won the lawsuit in the District Court. 21 U.S.P.Q.2D (BNA) 1457 (C.D.Cal.1991). But, the Court of Appeals for the Ninth Circuit set aside the judgment in Qualitex's favor on the trademark infringement claim because, in that Circuit's view, the Lanham Act does not permit Qualitex, or anyone else, to register "color alone" as a trademark. 13 F.3d 1297, 1300, 1302 (1994).

The courts of appeals have differed as to whether or not the law recognizes the use of color alone as a trademark. Compare *NutraSweet Co. v. Stadt Corp.*, 917 F.2d 1024, 1028 (C.A.7 1990) (absolute prohibition against protection of color alone), with *In re Owens–Corning Fiberglas Corp.*, 774 F.2d 1116, 1128 (C.A.Fed.1985) (allowing registration of color pink for fiberglass insulation), and *Master Distributors, Inc. v. Pako Corp.*, 986 F.2d 219, 224 (C.A.8 1993) (declining to establish *per se* prohibition against protecting color alone as a trademark). Therefore, this Court granted certiorari. 512 U.S. (1994). We now hold that there is no rule absolutely barring the use of color alone, and we reverse the judgment of the Ninth Circuit.

II

The Lanham Act gives a seller or producer the exclusive right to "register" a trademark, 15 U.S.C. § 1052 (1988 ed. and Supp. V), and to prevent his or her competitors from using that trademark, § 1114(1). Both the language of the Act and the basic underlying principles of trademark law would seem to include color within the universe of things that can qualify as a trademark. The language of the Lanham Act describes that universe in the broadest of terms. It says that trademarks "include any word, name, symbol, or device, or any combination thereof." § 1127. Since human beings might use as a "symbol" or "device" almost anything at all that is capable of carrying meaning, this language, read literally, is not restrictive....

A color is also capable of satisfying the more important part of the statutory definition of a trademark, which requires that a person "use" or "intend to use" the mark

> "to identify and distinguish his or her goods, including a unique product, from those manufactured or sold by others and to indicate the source of the goods, even if that source is unknown." 15 U.S.C. § 1127.

True, a product's color is unlike "fanciful," "arbitrary," or "suggestive" words or designs, which almost *automatically* tell a customer that they refer to a brand. *Abercrombie & Fitch Co. v. Hunting World, Inc.*, 537 F.2d 4, 9–10 (C.A.2 1976) (Friendly, J.); see *Two Pesos, Inc. v. Taco Cabana, Inc.*, 505 U.S. ___, (1992) (slip op., at 6–7). The imaginary word "Suntost," or the words "Suntost Marmalade," on a jar of orange jam immediately would signal a brand or a product "source"; the jam's orange color does not do so. But, over time, customers may come to treat a particular color on a product or its packaging (say, a color that in context seems unusual, such as pink on a firm's insulating material or red on the head of a large industrial bolt) as signifying a brand. And, if so, that color would have come to identify and distinguish the goods—*i.e.* to "indicate" their "source"—much in the way that descriptive words on a product (say, "Trim" on nail clippers or "Car-Freshner" on deodorizer) can come to indicate a product's origin. See, *e.g., J. Wiss & Sons Co. v. W. E. Bassett Co.*, 59 C.C.P.A. 1269, 1271, 462 F.2d 567 (Pat.), 462 F.2d 567, 569 (1972); *Car-Freshner Corp. v. Turtle Wax, Inc.*, 268 F. Supp. 162, 164 (S.D.N.Y.1967). In this circumstance, trademark law says that the word (*e.g.*, "Trim"), although not inherently distinctive, has developed "secondary meaning." See *Inwood Laboratories, Inc. v. Ives Laboratories, Inc.*, 456 U.S. 844, 851, n. 11, 72 L. Ed. 2d 606, 102 S. Ct. 2182 (1982) ("secondary meaning" is acquired when "in the minds of the public, the primary significance of a product feature ... is to identify the source of the product rather than the product itself"). Again, one might ask, if trademark law permits a descriptive word with secondary meaning to act as a mark, why would it not permit a color, under similar circumstances, to do the same?

We cannot find in the basic objectives of trademark law any obvious theoretical objection to the use of color alone as a trademark, where that color has attained "secondary meaning" and therefore identifies and distinguishes a particular brand (and thus indicates its "source"). In principle, trademark law, by preventing others from copying a source-identifying mark, "reduces the customer's costs of shopping and making purchasing decisions," 1 J. McCarthy, McCarthy on Trademarks and Unfair Competition § 2.01[2], p. 2–3 (3d ed. 1994) (hereinafter McCarthy), for it quickly and easily assures a potential customer that *this* item—the item with this mark—is made by the same producer as other similarly marked items that he or she liked (or disliked) in the past. At the same time, the law helps assure a producer that it (and not an imitating competitor) will reap the financial, reputation-related rewards associated with a desirable product. The law thereby "encourages the production of quality products," *ibid.*, and simultaneously discourages those who hope to sell inferior products by capitalizing on a consumer's inability quickly to evaluate the quality of an item offered for sale. See, *e.g.*, 3 L. Altman, Callmann on Unfair Competition, Trademarks and Monopolies § 17.03 (4th ed. 1983); Landes & Posner, The Economics of Trademark Law, 78 T. M. Rep. 267, 271–272 (1988); *Park 'N Fly, Inc. v. Dollar Park and Fly, Inc.*, 469 U.S. 189, 198, 83 L. Ed. 2d 582, 105 S. Ct. 658 (1985); S. Rep. No. 100–515, p. 4 (1988). It is the source—distinguishing ability of a mark—not its ontological status as color, shape, fragrance, word, or sign—that permits it to serve these basic purposes. See Landes & Posner, Trademark Law: An Economic Perspective, 30 J. Law & Econ. 265, 290 (1987). And, for that reason, it is difficult to find, in basic trademark objectives, a reason to disqualify absolutely the use of a color as a mark.

Neither can we find a principled objection to the use of color as a mark in the important "functionality" doctrine of trademark law. The functionality doctrine prevents trademark law, which seeks to promote competition by protecting a firm's reputation, from instead inhibiting legitimate competition by allowing a producer to control a useful product feature. It is the province of patent law, not trademark law, to encourage invention by granting inventors a monopoly over new product designs or functions for a limited time, 35 U.S.C. §§ 154, 173, after which competitors are free to use the innovation. If a product's functional features could be used as trademarks, however, a monopoly over such features could be obtained without regard to whether they qualify as patents and could be extended forever (because trademarks may be renewed in perpetuity). See *Kellogg Co. v. National Biscuit Co.*, 305 U.S. 111, 119–120, 83 L. Ed. 73, 59 S. Ct. 109 (1938) (Brandeis, J.); *Inwood Laboratories, Inc., supra*, at 863 (White, J., concurring in result) ("A functional characteristic is 'an important ingredient in the commercial success of the product,' and, after expiration of a patent, it is no more the property of the originator than the product itself'") (citation omitted). Functionality doctrine therefore would require, to take an imaginary example, that even if customers have come to identify the special illumination-enhancing shape of a new patented light bulb with a particular manufacturer, the manufacturer may not use that shape as a trademark, for doing so, after the patent had expired, would impede competition—not by protecting the reputation of the original bulb maker, but by frustrating competitors' legitimate efforts to produce an equivalent illumination-enhancing bulb. See, *e.g., Kellogg Co., supra,* at 119–120 (trademark law cannot be used to extend monopoly over "pillow" shape of shredded wheat biscuit after the patent for that shape had expired). This Court consequently has explained that, "in general terms, a product feature is functional," and cannot serve as a trademark, "if it is essential to the use or purpose of the article or if it affects the cost or quality of the article," that is, if exclusive use of the feature would put competitors at a significant non-reputation-related disadvantage. *Inwood Laboratories, Inc.,* 456 U.S. at 850, n. 10. Although sometimes color plays an important role (unrelated to source identification) in making a product more desirable, sometimes it does not. And, this latter fact—the fact that sometimes color is not essential to a product's use or purpose and does not affect cost or quality—indicates that the doctrine of "functionality" does not create an absolute bar to the use of color alone as a mark. See *Owens–Corning,* 774 F.2d at 1123 (pink color of insulation in wall "performs no nontrademark function").

It would seem, then, that color alone, at least sometimes, can meet the basic legal requirements for use as a trademark. It can act as a symbol that distinguishes a firm's goods and identifies their source, without serving any other significant function. See U.S. Dept. of Commerce, Patent and Trademark Office, Trademark Manual of Examining Procedure § 1202.04(e), p. 1202–13 (2d ed. May, 1993) (hereinafter PTO Manual) (approving trademark registration of color alone where it "has become distinctive of the applicant's goods in commerce," provided that "there is [no] competitive need for colors to remain available in the industry" and the color is not "functional"); see also 1 McCarthy §§ 3.01[1], 7.26 ("requirements for qualification of a word or symbol as a trademark" are that it be (1) a "symbol," (2) "used ... as a mark," (3) "to identify and distinguish the seller's goods from goods made or sold by others," but that it not be "functional"). Indeed, the District Court, in this case, entered findings (accepted by the Ninth Circuit) that show Qualitex's green-gold press pad color has met these requirements. The green-gold color acts as a symbol. Having developed secondary meaning (for customers identified the green-gold color as Qualitex's), it identifies the press pads' source. And, the green-gold color serves no other function. (Although it is important to use *some* color on press pads to avoid noticeable stains, the court found "no competitive need in the press pad industry for the green-gold color, since other colors are equally usable." 21 U.S.P.Q.2D (BNA) at 1460.) Accordingly, unless there is some special reason that convincingly militates against the use of color alone as a trademark, trademark law would protect Qualitex's use of the green-gold color on its press pads.

III

Respondent Jacobson Products says that there are four special reasons why the law should forbid the use of color alone as a trademark. We shall explain, in turn, why we, ultimately, find them unpersuasive.

First, Jacobson says that, if the law permits the use of color as a trademark, it will produce uncertainty and unresolvable court disputes about what shades of a color a competitor may lawfully use. Because lighting (morning sun, twilight mist) will affect perceptions of protected color, competitors and courts will suffer from "shade confusion" as they try to decide whether use of a similar color on a similar product does, or does not, confuse customers and thereby infringe a trademark. Jacobson adds that the "shade confusion" problem is "more difficult" and "far different from" the "determination of the similarity of words or symbols." Brief for Respondent 22.

We do not believe, however, that color, in this respect, is special. Courts traditionally decide quite difficult questions about whether two words or phrases or symbols are sufficiently similar, in context, to confuse buyers. They have had to compare, for example, such words as "Bonamine" and "Dramamine" (motion-sickness remedies); "Huggies" and "Dougies" (diapers); "Cheracol" and "Syrocol" (cough syrup); "Cyclone" and "Tornado" (wire fences); and "Mattres" and "1–800–Mattres" (mattress franchisor telephone numbers). See, *e.g.*, *G. D. Searle & Co. v. Chas. Pfizer & Co.*, 265 F.2d 385, 389 (C.A.7 1959); *Kimberly–Clark Corp. v. H. Douglas Enterprises, Ltd.*, 774 F.2d 1144, 1146–1147 (C.A.Fed.1985); *Upjohn Co. v. Schwartz*, 246 F.2d 254, 262 (C.A.2 1957); *Hancock v. American Steel & Wire Co.*, 40 C. C. P. A. of New Jersey, 931, 935 (Pat.), 203 F.2d 737, 740–741 (1953); *Dial–A–Mattress Franchise Corp. v. Page*, 880 F.2d 675, 678 (C.A.2 1989). Legal standards exist to guide courts in making such comparisons. See, e.g., 2 McCarthy § 15.08; 1 McCarthy §§ 11.24–11.25 ("Strong" marks, with greater secondary meaning, receive broader protection than "weak" marks). We do not see why courts could not apply those standards to a color, replicating, if necessary, lighting conditions under which a colored product is normally sold. See Ebert, Trademark Protection in Color: Do It By the Numbers!, 84 T. M. Rep. 379, 405 (1994). Indeed, courts already have done so in cases where a trademark consists of a color plus a design, *i.e.*, a colored symbol such as a gold stripe (around a sewer pipe), a yellow strand of wire rope, or a "brilliant yellow" band (on ampules). See, *e.g., Youngstown Sheet & Tube Co. v. Tallman Conduit Co.*, 149 U.S.P.Q. (BNA) 656, 657 (TTAB 1966); *Amsted Industries, Inc. v. West Coast Wire Rope & Rigging Inc.*, 2 U.S.P.Q.2D (BNA) 1755, 1760 (TTAB 1987); *In re Hodes–Lange Corp.*, 167 U.S.P.Q. (BNA) 255, 256 (TTAB 1970).

Second, Jacobson argues, as have others, that colors are in limited supply. See, *e.g., NutraSweet Co.*, 917 F.2d at 1028; *Campbell Soup Co. v. Armour & Co.*, 175 F.2d 795, 798 (C.A.3 1949). Jacobson claims that, if one of many competitors can appropriate a particular color for use as a trademark, and each competitor then tries to do the same, the supply of colors will soon be depleted. Put in its strongest form, this argument would concede that "hundreds of color pigments are manufactured and thousands of colors can be obtained by mixing." L. Cheskin, Colors: What They Can Do For You 47 (1947). But, it would add that, in the context of a particular product, only some colors are usable. By the time one discards colors that, say, for reasons of customer appeal, are not usable, and adds the shades that competitors cannot use lest they risk infringing a similar, registered shade, then one is left with only a handful of possible colors. And, under these circumstances, to permit one, or a few, producers to use colors as trademarks will "deplete" the supply of usable colors to the point where a competitor's inability to find a suitable color will put that competitor at a significant disadvantage.

This argument is unpersuasive, however, largely because it relies on an occasional problem to justify a blanket prohibition. When a color serves as a mark, normally alternative colors will likely be available for similar use by others. See, *e.g., Owens–Corning*, 774 F.2d at 1121 (pink insulation). Moreover, if that is not so—if a "color depletion" or "color scarcity" problem does arise—the trademark doctrine of "functionality" normally would seem available to prevent the anticompetitive consequences that Jacobson's argument posits, thereby minimizing that argument's practical force.

The functionality doctrine, as we have said, forbids the use of a product's feature as a trademark where doing so will put a competitor at a significant disadvantage because the feature is "essential to the use or purpose of the article" or "affects [its] cost or quality." *Inwood Laboratories, Inc.*, 456 U.S. at 850, n. 10. The functionality doctrine thus protects competitors against a disadvantage (unrelated to recognition or reputation) that trademark protection might otherwise impose, namely their inability reasonably to replicate important non-reputation-related product features. For example, this Court has written that competitors might be free to copy the color of a medical pill where that color serves to identify the kind of medication (e.g., a type of blood medicine) in addition to its source. See *id.*, at 853, 858, n. 20 ("Some patients commingle medications in a container and rely on color to differentiate one from another"); see also J. Ginsburg, D. Goldberg, & A. Greenbaum, Trademark and Unfair Competition Law 194–195 (1991) (noting that drug color cases "have more to do with public health policy" regarding generic drug substitution "than with trademark law"). And, the federal courts have demonstrated that they can apply this doctrine in a careful and reasoned manner, with sensitivity to the effect on competition. Although we need not comment on the merits of specific cases, we note that lower courts have permitted competitors to copy the green color of farm machinery (because customers wanted their farm equipment to match) and have barred the use of black as a trademark on outboard boat motors (because black has the special functional attributes of decreasing the apparent size of the motor and ensuring compatibility with many different boat colors). See *Deere & Co. v. Farmhand, Inc.*, 560 F. Supp. 85, 98 (S.D.Iowa 1982), aff'd, 721 F.2d 253 (C.A.8 1983); *Brunswick Corp. v. British Seagull Ltd.*, 35 F.3d 1527, 1532 (C.A.Fed.1994), cert. pending, No. 94–1075; see also *Nor–Am Chemical v. O. M. Scott & Sons Co.*, 4

U.S.P.Q.2D (BNA) 1316, 1320 (E.D.Pa.1987) (blue color of fertilizer held functional because it indicated the presence of nitrogen). The Restatement (Third) of Unfair Competition adds that, if a design's "aesthetic value" lies in its ability to "confer a significant benefit that cannot practically be duplicated by the use of alternative designs," then the design is "functional." Restatement (Third) of Unfair Competition § 17, Comment *c*, pp. 175–176 (1995). The "ultimate test of aesthetic functionality," it explains, "is whether the recognition of trademark rights would significantly hinder competition." *Id.*, at 176.

The upshot is that, where a color serves a significant nontrademark function—whether to distinguish a heart pill from a digestive medicine or to satisfy the "noble instinct for giving the right touch of beauty to common and necessary things," G. K. Chesterton, Simplicity and Tolstoy 61 (1912)—courts will examine whether its use as a mark would permit one competitor (or a group) to interfere with legitimate (nontrademark-related) competition through actual or potential exclusive use of an important product ingredient. That examination should not discourage firms from creating aesthetically pleasing mark designs, for it is open to their competitors to do the same. See, *e.g., W. T. Rogers Co. v. Keene*, 778 F.2d 334, 343 (C.A.7 1985) (Posner, J.). But, ordinarily, it should prevent the anticompetitive consequences of Jacobson's hypothetical "color depletion" argument, when, and if, the circumstances of a particular case threaten "color depletion."

Third, Jacobson points to many older cases—including Supreme Court cases—in support of its position. In 1878, this Court described the common-law definition of trademark rather broadly to "consist of a name, symbol, figure, letter, form, or device, if adopted and used by a manufacturer or merchant in order to designate the goods he manufactures or sells to distinguish the same from those manufactured or sold by another." *McLean v. Fleming*, 96 U.S. 245, 254, 24 L. Ed. 828. Yet, in interpreting the Trademark Acts of 1881 and 1905, 21 Stat. 502, 33 Stat. 724, which retained that common-law definition, the Court questioned "whether mere color can constitute a valid trade-mark," *A. Leschen & Sons Rope Co. v. Broderick & Bascom Rope Co.*, 201 U.S. 166, 171, 50 L. Ed. 710, 26 S. Ct. 425 (1906), and suggested that the "product including the coloring matter is free to all who make it." *Coca–Cola Co. v. Koke Co. of America*, 254 U.S. 143, 147, 65 L. Ed. 189, 41 S. Ct. 113 (1920). Even though these statements amounted to dicta, lower courts interpreted them as forbidding protection for color alone. See, *e.g., Campbell Soup Co.*, 175 F.2d at 798, and n. 9; *Life Savers Corp. v. Curtiss Candy Co.*, 182 F.2d 4, 9 (C.A.7 1950) (quoting Campbell Soup).

These Supreme Court cases, however, interpreted trademark law as it existed before 1946, when Congress enacted the Lanham Act. The Lanham Act significantly changed and liberalized the common law to "dispense with mere technical prohibitions," S. Rep. No. 1333, 79th Cong., 2d Sess., 3 (1946), most notably, by permitting trademark registration of descriptive words (say, "U–Build–It" model airplanes) where they had acquired "secondary meaning." See *Abercrombie & Fitch Co.*, 537 F.2d at 9 (Friendly, J.). The Lanham Act extended protection to descriptive marks by making clear that (with certain explicit exceptions not relevant here),

> "nothing . . . shall prevent the registration of a mark used by the applicant which has become distinctive of the applicant's goods in commerce." 15 U.S.C. § 1052(f) (1988 ed., Supp. V).

This language permits an ordinary word, normally used for a nontrademark purpose (*e.g.*, description), to act as a trademark where it has gained "secondary meaning." Its logic would appear to apply to color as well. Indeed, in 1985, the Federal Circuit considered the significance of the Lanham Act's changes as they related to color and held that trademark protection for color was consistent with the

> "jurisprudence under the Lanham Act developed in accordance with the statutory principle that if a mark is capable of being or becoming distinctive of [the] applicant's goods in commerce, then it is capable of serving as a trademark." *Owens–Corning*, 774 F.2d at 1120.

In 1988 Congress amended the Lanham Act, revising portions of the definitional language, but left unchanged the language here relevant. § 134, 102 Stat. 3946, 15 U.S.C. § 1127. It enacted these amendments against the following background: (1) the Federal Circuit had decided *Owens–Corning*; (2) the Patent and Trademark Office had adopted a clear policy (which it still maintains) permitting registration of color as a trademark, see PTO Manual § 1202.04(e) (at p. 1200–12 of the January 1986 edition and p. 1202–13 of the May 1993 edition); and (3) the Trademark Commission had written a report, which recommended that "the terms 'symbol, or device' . . . not be deleted or narrowed to preclude registration of such things as a color, shape, smell, sound, or configuration which functions as a mark," The United States Trademark Association Trademark Review Commission Report and Recommendations to USTA President and Board of Directors, 77 T. M. Rep. 375, 421 (1987) (hereinafter Trademark Commission); see also 133 Cong. Rec. 32812 (1987) (statement of Sen. DeConcini) ("The bill I am introducing today is based on the Commission's report and recommendations"). This background strongly suggests that the language "any word, name, symbol, or device," 15 U.S.C. § 1127, had come to include color. And, when it amended the statute, Congress retained these terms. Indeed, the Senate Report accompanying the Lanham Act revision explicitly referred to this background understanding, in saying that the "revised definition intentionally retains . . . the words 'symbol or device' so as not to preclude the registration of colors, shapes, sounds or configurations where they function as trademarks." S. Rep. No. 100–515, at 44. In addition, the statute retained language providing that "no trademark by which the goods of the applicant may be distinguished from the goods of others shall be refused registration . . . on account of its nature" (except for certain specified reasons not relevant here). (15 U.S.C. § 1052 (1988 ed., Supp. V)).

This history undercuts the authority of the precedent on which Jacobson relies. Much of the pre–1985 case law rested on statements in Supreme Court opinions that interpreted pre-Lanham Act trademark law and were not directly related to the holdings in those cases. Moreover, we believe the Federal Circuit was right in 1985 when it found that the 1946 Lanham Act embodied crucial legal changes that liberalized the law to permit the use of color alone as a trademark (under appropriate circumstances). At a minimum, the Lanham Act's changes left the courts free to reevaluate the pre-existing legal precedent which had absolutely forbidden the use of color alone as a trademark. Finally, when Congress re-enacted the terms "word, name, symbol, or device" in 1988, it did so against a legal background in which those terms had come to include color, and its statutory revision embraced that understanding.

Fourth, Jacobson argues that there is no need to permit color alone to function as a trademark because a firm already may use color as part of a trademark, say, as a colored circle or colored letter or colored word, and may rely upon "trade dress" protection, under § 43(a) of the Lanham Act, if a competitor copies its color and thereby causes consumer confusion regarding the overall appearance of the competing products or their packaging, see 15 U.S.C. § 1125(a) (1988 ed., Supp. V). The first part of this argument begs the question. One can understand why a firm might find it difficult to place a usable symbol or word on a product (say, a large industrial bolt that customers normally see from a distance); and, in such instances, a firm might want to use color, pure and simple, instead of color as part of a design. Neither is the second portion of the argument convincing. Trademark law helps the holder of a mark in many ways that "trade dress" protection does not. See 15 U.S.C. § 1124 (ability to prevent importation of confusingly similar goods); § 1072 (constructive notice of ownership); § 1065 (incontestable status); § 1057(b) (prima facie evidence of validity and ownership). Thus, one can easily find reasons why the law might provide trademark protection in addition to trade dress protection.

IV

Having determined that a color may sometimes meet the basic legal requirements for use as a trademark and that respondent Jacobson's arguments do not justify a special legal rule preventing color alone from serving as a trademark (and, in light of the District Court's here undisputed findings that Qualitex's use of the green-gold color on its press pads meets the basic trademark requirements), we conclude that the Ninth Circuit erred in barring Qualitex's use of color as a trademark. For these reasons, the judgment of the Ninth Circuit is

REVERSED.

QUESTIONS

1. Color can be a highly distinctive feature of a product or its packaging. Hawaiian Punch® fruit juice drink, Pepto Bismol® medicine and Windex® glass cleaner are examples of products with distinctive coloration; Philadelphia® Cream Cheese and Coca Cola® are examples of products with widely recognized package colors. Color may also, however, function as a highly efficient symbol for conveying important information about the product. Sprite® soda is only one example of a citrus-flavored soft drink that has long been sold in a green can; over-the-counter drugs promoted as especially effective for night-time use, like Vick's NyQuil® and Tylenol® PM, are sold in boxes adorned with soothing blue tones, and unscented dishwashing liquids, like Dawn® Free and Palmolive® Sensitive Skin are commonly sold as colorless liquids in clear, colorless bottles. The Court in *Qualitex* determined that "color may sometimes meet the basic legal requirements for use as a trademark...." How would you articulate the test to determine whether a particular use of color in fact meets those legal requirements?

2. In Justice Breyer's view, can color alone ever qualify as a trademark without first acquiring secondary meaning?

———

Qualitex may have encouraged attempts to register single-color marks, but the Trademark Trial and Appeal Board has not always been receptive. In *In re Orange Communications Inc.*, 41 U.S.P.Q.2d 1036 (T.T.A.B.1996), the Board upheld the refusal to register a bright orange color for pay telephones, on the ground that the color was designed to be highly visible by passing motorists even in poor weather, and therefore was functional. In support of this determination, the Board cited its decision in *In re Howard S. Leight*, 39 U.S.P.Q.2d 1058 (T.T.A.B.1996), in which the Board had held that the bright and highly visible coral color of safety ear plugs was functional.

The color blue has spawned a relatively extensive and somewhat inconsistent caselaw. In *In re Hudson News Co.*, 39 U.S.P.Q.2d 1915 (T.T.A.B.1996), the Board sustained the refusal to register the color blue for newsstand and store decor. The Examiner had held the blue trade dress "*de jure* functional because it creates a soothing, calming environment which competitors should be free to create in their stores as well." The Board rejected this ground for refusal: "we do not see why a blue interior necessarily is beneficial to a retail newsstand. In this connection, there is no evidence to even suggest that a newsstand (or any other store) with a blue interior would attract more customers, and/or increase sales." Nonetheless, the Board upheld the Examiner's finding that the color was not inherently distinctive: the color "is quite pedestrian," and there was no evidence that the applicant had promoted the color as a service mark. By contrast, in 3M v. Intertape Polymer Group, 423 F.Supp.2d 958 (D.Minn. 2006), the PTO had registered the color blue for painter's tape, and the district court declined to grant the defendant summary judgment, holding that there remained disputed fact issues concerning the distinctiveness and functionality of the color. *See also Unique Sports Prods., Inc. v. Babolat VS*, 403 F.Supp.2d 1229 (N.D.Ga.2005)(light blue tennis racquet overgrip; denying summary judgment because material fact issues to resolve regarding secondary meaning and functionality); *Sazerac Company, Inc. v. Skyy Spirits Inc.*, 37 U.S.P.Q.2d 1731 (E.D.La.1995) (cobalt blue Skyy vodka bottle neither inherently distinctive nor entitled to protection by virtue of having acquired secondary meaning).

Claims involving the color yellow have produced similarly divergent outcomes, see, e.g., *Sportvision, Inc. v. Sportsmedia Tech. Corp.*, 2005 WL 1869350 (N.D.Cal.2005) ("virtual yellow first-down line used in football game broadcasts" held functional); *McNeil–PPC, Inc. v. Merisant Co.*, 2004 WL 3316380 (D.P.R.2004)(preliminary injunction granted producer of "Splenda" sugar substitute in yellow packs against "Same" artificial sweetener in yellow packets); *3M v. Beautone Specialties Co.*, 82 F.Supp.2d 997 (D.Minn.2000) (validity of "canary yellow" trademark for 3M's Post–It brand sticky notes cannot be resolved on summary judgment).

For commentary on colors as trademarks, *see, e.g.,* Paul Morico, *Protecting Color Per se in the Wake of Qualitex v. Jacobson*, 77 J. Pat. & TM Off. Soc. 571 (1995); Hillel Parness, Note, *The Curse of the Pink Panther: The Legacy of the Owens–Corning Fiberglas Dissent and Its Role in the Qualitex Supreme Court Appeal*, 18 Colum.–VLA J. L. & the Arts 327 (1994).

5. Other Identifying Indicia

If the protection of visual marks is well established, what about marks that appeal to the other senses? Can a musical chime serve as a trademark? What about a scent? A flavor? A touch? As Justice Breyer observed in *Qualitex*, the statutory definition of trademarks is not limited to words, logos or pictures, but extends to "any word, name, symbol, or device" used to indicate the source of goods. So long as a symbol or device in fact functions as a trademark in the marketplace, in the sense that it distinguishes a product from products of other producers and is perceived by consumers as an indicia of product source, is there any reason why it should not be protected as a trademark under the Lanham Act? The preamble of Section 2 of the Lanham provides that:

> No trademark by which the goods of the applicant may be distinguished from the goods of others shall be refused registration on the principal register *on account of its nature* ... (Emphasis added).

The Trademark Review Commission of the United States Trademark Association, in its review of the Trademark Act of 1946, "determined that the terms 'symbol, or device' should not be deleted or narrowed to preclude registration of such things as a color, shape, smell, sound, or configuration which functions as a mark." The United States Trademark Association Trademark Review Commission Report and Recommendations to USTA President and Board of Directors, 77 TMR 375, 421 (Sept.–Oct. 1987).

Courts interpret this flexible definition of a trademark as protecting non-graphic marks that have come to identify and distinguish the source of a service or a product. The registrability of an arbitrary, nonfunctional scent was addressed in *In re Clarke*, 17 U.S.P.Q.2d 1238 (T.T.A.B.1990). The Trademark Examining Attorney refused to register a mark for "sewing thread and embroidery yarn" that comprised "a high impact, fresh floral fragrance reminiscent of Plumeria blossoms." The examining attorney claimed that the "fragrance mark is analogous to other forms of product ornamentation in that it is not the type of matter which consumers would tend to perceive as an indication of origin." Analogies were made to other products that contain scents, such as cosmetics and cleaning products, where there is no showing that consumers regard the scent as an indication of source as opposed to a mere "pleasant feature of the goods." The Trademark Trial and Appeal Board held that the scented fragrance did function as a trademark for thread and embroidery yarn and found that:

> It is clear from the record that applicant is the only person who has marketed yarns and threads with a fragrance. That is to say, fragrance is not an inherent attribute or natural characteristic of applicant's goods but is rather a feature supplied by applicant. Moreover, applicant has emphasized this characteristic of her goods in advertising, promoting the scented feature of her goods. Applicant has demonstrated that customers, dealers and distributors of her scented yarns and threads have come to recognize applicant as the source of these goods.

The T.T.A.B. limited this holding to exclude "scents or fragrances of products which are noted for those features, such as perfumes, colognes or scented household products." *Compare In re Star Pharmaceuticals, Inc.*, 225 U.S.P.Q. 209 (T.T.A.B.1985) (where applicant failed to demonstrate that the features (colors) sought to be registered had been promoted as a source indicator).

Marks directed to the sense of taste have fared less well. *See, e.g., Perk Scientific, Inc. v. Ever Scientific, Inc.*, 77 U.S.P.Q.2d 1412 (E.D.Pa.2005) (lack of carbonation and flavor selection held functional for glucose tolerant beverage products); *In re N.V. Organon*, 79 U.S.P.Q.2d 1639 (T.T.A.B.2006) (orange flavor for antidepressants in quick-dissolving tablets and pills held functional for masking the unpleasant tastes of certain medicines). In *Organon*, the Board also held that consumers would not perceive the flavor as feature of the product rather than as an indicator of source. The Board expressed considerable doubt that flavor would ever be capable of serving as a trademark:

> [W]e are not blind to the practical considerations involved in the registration of flavor marks. Flavor perception is very subjective; what applicant considers to be a unique and distinctive orange flavor may be considered by patients as simply an orange flavor. Moreover, the Office's examination of flavor marks, not to mention litigation at the Board, would be very problematic.[10]

---

10. In the abstract, we see some difficulty in how a taste could function as a   trademark. As stated by Ms. Clarke in her law review article:

Further, it is not clear how taste would as a practical matter function as a trademark. A consumer generally has no access to the product's flavor prior to purchase. A trademark is defined as a word, name, symbol, or device that is used by a person "to identify and distinguish his or her goods, including a unique product, from those manufactured or sold by others and to indicate the source of the goods." Section 45 of the Trademark Act, 15 U.S.C. § 1127. Unlike color, sound and smell, there generally is no way for consumers routinely to distinguish products by sampling them before they decide which one to purchase. Generally, it would not be expected that prescribed antidepressants would be tasted prior to purchase so that a consumer, in conjunction with a physician, could distinguish one antidepressant from another on the basis of taste. Thus, the consumer, in making a purchasing decision involving either a prescribed medication or an over-the-counter medication, is unable to distinguish one pharmaceutical from another based on flavor. Consequently, it is difficult to fathom exactly how a flavor could function as a source indicator in the classic sense, unlike the situation with other nontraditional trademarks such as color, sound and smell, to which consumers may be exposed prior to purchase.

By contrast, the Trademark Office has registered a "sensory, touch mark," consisting of a "velvet textured covering on the surface of a bottle of wine." See Registration Number 3155702 (October 17, 2006).

Finally, with respect to sound marks, in an early decision, the T.T.A.B. refused a radio station's service mark application for "the sound made by a Ship's Bell Clock" consisting of "a series of bells tolled during the four, hour sequences, beginning with one ring at approximately a first half hour and increasing in number by one ring at approximately each half hour thereafter." *In re General Electric Broadcasting Co.*, 199 U.S.P.Q. 560 (T.T.A.B.1978). The Examining Attorney claimed that the radio station "is doing no more than telling its listeners the time by broadcasting the traditional maritime bells ringing in the traditional maritime sequence," and as such, the sequence is not a service mark. General Electric Broadcasting asserted that the sequence of maritime bells ringing served as a mark and not merely as a time-telling mechanism. There were instances where the sound would be made two minutes before or after the actual hour or half hour, showing the use of the tones as identification rather than solely time-telling devices. The T.T.A.B. agreed that the Lanham Act takes a "flexible approach toward the concept of what constitutes a service mark or a trademark, a flexibility that is required in order to keep up with

A flavor's subjectivity derives principally from its complexity. Flavors consist of three elements: aroma, taste (sweet, acid, bitter, or saline), and feeling. Numerous factors influence taste acuity, among them age, disease, and, for certain tastes, temperature. In addition, one's taste perception varies with practice, increasing the subjectivity of this sense. Thus, because of the subjectivity of flavor perception, the risk of inconsistent results would be substantial if the PTO examined flavors for trademark protection, or if a flavor trademark owner sought to enforce his rights in court. (footnotes omitted).

Nancy L. Clarke, Issues in the Federal Registration of Flavors as Trademarks for Pharmaceutical Products, [1993 U. Ill. L. Rev. 105] at 131.

the ever-changing ramifications brought about by . . . changing technologies.'' Generally, sounds may act as trademarks "where they assume a definitive shape or arrangement and are used in such a manner so as to create in the bearer's mind association of the sound with a service.'' However, the T.T.A.B. found that different standards apply for registration of sound marks because:

> . . . [U]nlike, the case of a trademark which is applied to the goods in such a manner as to create a visual and lasting impression upon a purchaser or prospective purchaser encountering the mark in the marketplace, a sound mark depends upon aural perception of the listener which may be as fleeting as the sound itself unless, of course, the sound is so inherently different or distinctive that it attaches to the subliminal mind of the listener to be awakened when heard and to be associated with the source or event with which it is struck.

The T.T.A.B. held that "arbitrary, unique or distinctive marks are registrable as such on the Principal Register without supportive evidence,'' but commonplace sounds can only be registered after a showing "that purchasers, prospective purchasers and listeners do recognize and associate the sound with services offered and/or rendered exclusively with a single, albeit anonymous, source.'' General Electric Broadcasting Co. had provided insufficient evidence to find that the sound mark had become distinctive of the radio station's services. By contrast, later efforts to register sound marks have proved more fruitful. AT&T has registered a sound mark consisting of the spoken letters "AT&T.'' The Harlem Globetrotters have registered the melody to the song "Sweet Georgia Brown'' as a service mark. Intel recently registered the five note sequence "D flat, D flat, G, D flat, A flat'' as a trademark for computer hardware.

A number of companies have registered cartoon characters as trademarks. *See, e.g., Viacom International v. Komm*, 46 U.S.P.Q.2d 1233 (T.T.A.B.1998) (Mighty Mouse). Courts have also given trademark or trademark-like protection to a broad array of non-traditional source designators ranging from the design of golf courses to performers' voices and likenesses under the rubric of false designation of origin. *See infra*, Chapters 7, 10, 12.

TRADEMARK ACTIONS BEFORE THE TRADEMARK TRIBUNALS AND BEFORE THE FEDERAL JUDICIAL COURTS

The previous note referred several times to the Trademark Trial and Appeal Board (T.T.A.B. or "Board''). This is a specialized body within the Patent and Trademark Office, an administrative agency. Claims arising out of trademark registration proceedings must first be brought before the T.T.A.B. If a Trademark Examiner has refused to register a mark, the applicant may appeal the refusal to the Board, 15 U.S.C. § 1070 (Lanham Act § 20). If this tribunal sustains the examiner's decision, the applicant may further appeal to the United States Court of Appeals for the Federal

Circuit (Fed. Cir.) or may have the Board's decision reviewed by a federal district court, 15 U.S.C. § 1071(a) (federal circuit), (b) (district court) (Lanham Act § 21(a), (b)). Before creation of the Federal Circuit in 1982, a substantially equivalent appellate tribunal was known as the Court of Customs and Patent Appeals (C.C.P.A.).

If the Examiner accepts the mark, it is published in the "Official Gazette" of the Patent and Trademark Office. At this point, owners of trademarks who believe the mark proposed for registration is likely to be confused with their marks may initiate opposition proceedings before the T.T.A.B. 15 U.S.C. § 1067 (Lanham Act § 17). The Board's decision may be appealed either to the Federal Circuit, or to any United States District Court that has jurisdiction over the parties. In addition, petitions to cancel a trademark registration, for example on the ground that the mark has become generic (see Chapter 5.A) or been abandoned (see Chapter 5.B), are brought to the T.T.A.B., whose decision may be appealed either to the Federal Circuit or to the appropriate U.S. District Court.

Trademark infringement actions may be initiated before federal district courts, if a federally registered mark is at issue or if the claim alleges a violation of Section 43 of the Lanham Act, a broad liability provision covering, inter alia, unregistered marks. In addition, federal courts hear state based trademark and unfair competition claims, either as claims joined to the federal trademark claim, see 28 U.S.C. § 1338(b), or, in the absence of a federal claim, pursuant to their diversity jurisdiction, if the amount in controversy exceeds $75,000, see 28 U.S.C. § 1332. Federal courts do not have exclusive jurisdiction over federal trademark infringement claims, unlike patent and copyright claims. *See* 28 U.S.C. § 1338(a). State courts therefore may also hear federal trademark infringement claims, as well as state based trademark and unfair competition claims.

As this summary indicates, the role of the Federal Circuit in trademark adjudication is far more limited than its role in patent adjudication. Not only does the Federal Circuit have exclusive jurisdiction over all appeals from patent tribunals, its exclusive jurisdiction also extends to all appeals of patent infringement decisions emanating from United States District Courts of general jurisdiction. Congress provided for the concentration of patent appeals in the Federal Circuit, and the elimination of appellate review by federal courts of general jurisdiction in the 1982 law creating the Court of Appeals for the Federal Circuit. Congress expressed concern that patent appeals to general federal appellate courts produced docket overload, discrepancy in legal doctrine, and conflict among the circuits. See S. Rep. No. 275, 97th Cong., 2d sess. 1–5 (1982). The Federal Circuit will also adjudicate a trademark appeal from a federal district court of general jurisdiction when the trademark claim was joined with a patent claim. Indeed, the Federal Circuit hears the trademark appeal even if the trademark claim is the only subject of the appeal. However, when the Federal Circuit hears a trademark appeal from a federal district court, the Federal Circuit does not rule on the basis of its own trademarks precedents, but applies the trademark law as developed in the circuit comprising the district court. *See, e.g., Cicena Ltd. v. Columbia Telecommunications Group*, 900 F.2d 1546 (Fed.Cir.1990).

Should appeals of trademark infringement decisions also be restricted to the Federal Circuit? If not, why are general federal (or state) courts more competent to adjudicate trademark claims than patent claims?

B.   DISTINCTIVENESS

1.   ARBITRARY, FANCIFUL, SUGGESTIVE AND DESCRIPTIVE TERMS

Abercrombie & Fitch Co. v. Hunting World, Inc.

537 F.2d 4 (2d Cir.1976).

■ FRIENDLY, CIRCUIT JUDGE.

[Abercrombie & Fitch claimed trademark rights in SAFARI for a variety of clothing items and accessories. The trial court found the term failed to distinguish Abercrombie's goods from other retailers' similar apparel. The Second Circuit upheld the lower court with respect to certain items, notably hats, but reversed as to others, for example, shoes and boots.]

It will be useful at the outset to restate some basic principles of trademark law, which, although they should be familiar, tend to become lost in a welter of adjectives.

The cases, and in some instances the Lanham Act, identify four different categories of terms with respect to trademark protection. Arrayed in an ascending order which roughly reflects their eligibility to trademark status and the degree of protection accorded, these classes are (1) generic, (2) descriptive, (3) suggestive, and (4) arbitrary or fanciful. The lines of demarcation, however, are not always bright. Moreover, the difficulties are compounded because a term that is in one category for a particular product may be in quite a different one for another,[6] because a term may shift from one category to another in light of differences in usage through time,[7] because a term may have one meaning to one group of users and a different one to others,[8] and because the same term may be put to different uses with respect to a single product.[9] In various ways, all of these complications are involved in the instant case.

A generic term is one that refers, or has come to be understood as referring, to the genus of which the particular product is a species. At

---

6. To take a familiar example, "Ivory" would be generic when used to describe a product made from the tusks of elephants but arbitrary as applied to soap.

7. *See, e.g., Haughton Elevator Co. v. Seeberger*, 85 U.S.P.Q. 80 (1950), in which the coined word "Escalator," originally fanci-

ful, or at the very least suggestive, was held to have become generic.

8. *See, e.g., Bayer Co. v. United Drug Co.*, 272 F. 505 (S.D.N.Y.1921).

9. *See* 15 U.S.C. § 1115(b)(4).

common law neither those terms which were generic nor those which were merely descriptive could become valid trademarks, *see Delaware & Hudson Canal Co. v. Clark,* 80 U.S. (13 Wall.) 311, 323 (1872) ("Nor can a generic name, or a name merely descriptive of an article or its qualities, ingredients, or characteristics, be employed as a trademark and the exclusive use of it be entitled to legal protection"). The same was true under the Trademark Act of 1905, *Standard Paint Co. v. Trinidad Asphalt Mfg. Co.,* 220 U.S. 446 (1911), except for marks which had been the subject of exclusive use for ten years prior to its enactment, 33 Stat. 726. While, as we shall see, . . . the Lanham Act makes an important exception with respect to those merely descriptive terms which have acquired secondary meaning, *see* § 2(f), 15 U.S.C. § 1052(f), it offers no such exception for generic marks. The Act provides for the cancellation of a registered mark if at any time it "becomes the common descriptive name of an article or substance," § 14(c).* This means that even proof of secondary meaning, by virtue of which some "merely descriptive" marks may be registered, cannot transform a generic term into a subject for trademark. As explained in *J. Kohnstam, Ltd. v. Louis Marx and Company,* 280 F.2d 437, 440 (C.C.P.A. 1960), no matter how much money and effort the user of a generic term has poured into promoting the sale of its merchandise and what success it has achieved in securing public identification, it cannot deprive competing manufacturers of the product of the right to call an article by its name. *See, accord, Application of Preformed Line Products Co.,* 323 F.2d 1007 (C.C.P.A. 1963); *Weiss Noodle Co. v. Golden Cracknel and Specialty Co.,* 290 F.2d 845 (C.C.P.A. 1961); *Application of Searle & Co.,* 360 F.2d 650 (C.C.P.A. 1966). We have recently had occasion to apply this doctrine of the impossibility of achieving trademark protection for a generic term, *CES Publishing Corp. v. St. Regis Publications, Inc.,* 531 F.2d 11 (1975). The pervasiveness of the principle is illustrated by a series of well-known cases holding that when a suggestive or fanciful term has become generic as a result of a manufacturer's own advertising efforts, trademark protection will be denied save for those markets where the term still has not become generic and a secondary meaning has been shown to continue. *Bayer Co. v. United Drug Co.,* 272 F. 505 (S.D.N.Y.1921) (L. Hand, D.J.); *DuPont Cellophane Co. v. Waxed Products Co.,* 85 F.2d 75 (2 Cir.) (A. N. Hand, C.J.), *cert. denied,* 299 U.S. 601 (1936); *King–Seeley Thermos Co. v. Aladdin Industries, Inc.,* 321 F.2d 577 (2 Cir.1963). A term may thus be generic in one market and descriptive or suggestive or fanciful in another.

The term which is descriptive but not generic[11] stands on a better basis. Although § 2(e) of the Lanham Act, 15 U.S.C. § 1052, forbids the

---

* Eds. note: After the 1988 amendments to the Lanham Act, § 14(3) provides for cancellation "at anytime if the registered mark becomes the generic name for the goods or services. . . ."

11. *See, e.g., W. E. Bassett Co. v. Revlon, Inc.,* 435 F.2d 656 (2 Cir.1970). A com-

mentator has illuminated the distinction with an example of the "Deep Bowl Spoon":

"Deep Bowl" identifies a significant characteristic of the article. It is "merely descriptive" of the goods, because it informs one that they are deep in the bowl portion. . . . It is not, however, "the com-

registration of a mark which, when applied to the goods of the applicant, is "merely descriptive," § 2(f) removes a considerable part of the sting by providing that "except as expressly excluded in paragraphs (a)–(d) of this section, nothing in this chapter shall prevent the registration of a mark used by the applicant which has become distinctive of the applicant's goods in commerce" and that the Commissioner may accept, as prima facie evidence that the mark has become distinctive, proof of substantially exclusive and continuous use of the mark applied to the applicant's goods for five years preceding the application. As indicated in the cases cited in the discussion of the unregistrability of generic terms, "common descriptive name," as used in §§ 14(c) and 15(4), refers to generic terms applied to products and not to terms that are "merely descriptive." In the former case any claim to an exclusive right must be denied since this in effect would confer a monopoly not only of the mark but of the product by rendering a competitor unable effectively to name what it was endeavoring to sell. In the latter case the law strikes the balance, with respect to registration, between the hardships to a competitor in hampering the use of an appropriate word and those to the owner who, having invested money and energy to endow a word with the good will adhering to his enterprise, would be deprived of the fruits of his efforts.

The category of "suggestive" marks was spawned by the felt need to accord protection to marks that were neither exactly descriptive on the one hand nor truly fanciful on the other—a need that was particularly acute because of the bar in the Trademark Act of 1905, 33 Stat. 724, 726, (with an exceedingly limited exception noted above) on the registration of merely descriptive marks regardless of proof of secondary meaning. *See Orange Crush Co. v. California Crushed Fruit Co.*, 297 F. 892 (D.C.Cir.1924). Having created the category the courts have had great difficulty in defining it. Judge Learned Hand made the not very helpful statement:

> It is quite impossible to get any rule out of the cases beyond this: That the validity of the mark ends when suggestion ends and description begins.

Franklin Knitting Mills, Inc. v. Fashionit Sweater Mills, Inc., 297 F. 247, 248 (2 Cir. 1923), *aff'd per curiam*, 4 F.2d 1018 (2 Cir.1925)—a statement amply confirmed by comparing the list of terms held suggestive with those held merely descriptive in 3 Callmann, Unfair Competition, Trademarks and Monopolies § 71.2 (3d ed.). Another court has observed, somewhat more usefully, that:

> A term is suggestive if it requires imagination, thought and perception to reach a conclusion as to the nature of the goods. A

mon descriptive name" of the article [since] the implement is not a deep bowl, it is a spoon.... "Spoon" is not merely descriptive of the article—it identifies the article—[and therefore] the term is generic.

Fletcher, *Actual Confusion as to Incontestability of Descriptive Marks*, 64 Trademark Rep. 252, 260 (1974). On the other hand, "Deep Bowl" would be generic as to a deep bowl.

term is descriptive if it forthwith conveys an immediate idea of the ingredients, qualities or characteristics of the goods.

Stix Products, Inc. v. United Merchants & Manufacturers, Inc., 295 F. Supp. 479, 488 (S.D.N.Y.1968)—a formulation deriving from *General Shoe Corp. v. Rosen,* 111 F.2d 95, 98 (4 Cir.1940). Also useful is the approach taken by this court in *Aluminum Fabricating Co. of Pittsburgh v. Season–All Window Corp.,* 259 F.2d 314 (2 Cir.1958), that the reason for restricting the protection accorded descriptive terms, namely the undesirability of preventing an entrant from using a descriptive term for his product, is much less forceful when the trademark is a suggestive word since, as Judge Lumbard wrote, 259 F.2d at 317:

> The English language has a wealth of synonyms and related words with which to describe the qualities which manufacturers may wish to claim for their products and the ingenuity of the public relations profession supplies new words and slogans as they are needed.

If a term is suggestive, it is entitled to registration without proof of secondary meaning. Moreover, as held in the *Season–All* case, the decision of the Patent Office to register a mark without requiring proof of secondary meaning affords a rebuttable presumption that the mark is suggestive or arbitrary or fanciful rather than merely descriptive.

It need hardly be added that fanciful or arbitrary terms[12] enjoy all the rights accorded to suggestive terms as marks—without the need of debating whether the term is "merely descriptive" and with ease of establishing infringement.

In the light of these principles we must proceed to a decision of this case.

"TECHNICAL TRADEMARKS"

Arbitrary, fanciful and suggestive marks are sometimes called "technical trademarks." As discussed in *Abercrombie, supra,* these marks may be registered without proof of "secondary meaning," that is, without demonstration that the public in fact recognizes these terms or symbols as indications of the source of the goods or services. On secondary meaning, see *infra,* section B.2.

One might inquire why technical trademarks are endowed with trademark significance *ab initio.* Why should the proprietor of a term used in the marketplace, once she has shown the term to be arbitrary, fanciful, or suggestive, not be required to make a further showing that the term, as

---

12. As terms of art, the distinctions between suggestive terms and fanciful or arbitrary terms may seem needlessly artificial. Of course, a common word may be used in a fanciful sense; indeed one might say that only a common word can be so used, since a coined word cannot first be put to a bizarre use. Nevertheless, the term "fanciful", as a classifying concept, is usually applied to words invented solely for their use as trademarks. When the same legal consequences attach to a common word, *i.e.,* when it is applied in an unfamiliar way, the use is called "arbitrary."

used, has developed a public following? Several considerations favor the rule conferring immediate trademark status on arbitrary, fanciful or suggestive terms. First, the nature of the term indicates that the public will inevitably perceive it as a trademark. We expect the public to conclude that a nondescriptive term associated with goods or services (*e.g.,* CREST toothpaste; CENTURY 21 real estate services) is intended to designate source. Second, one provider's appropriation of a nondescriptive term for use as a trademark does not disable competitors from describing their goods or services. The first user has not depleted the language of terms useful or necessary to the provision of information about the goods or services.

Third, and for many most importantly, first users, and potential competitors, require certainty regarding the trademark status of the term. If the term is inherently distinctive, and therefore not necessary for competition, the value of certainty outweighs whatever additional safeguard proof of actual source association might provide. As Judge Learned Hand observed in *Waldes v. International Mfrs.' Agency, Inc.,* 237 F. 502, 505 (S.D.N.Y.1916), given a technical trademark, "it is the priority of use alone that controls, even though, when the defendant comes into the field, [the mark] may not be fully established, or may not even be enough established to have associated largely in the public mind with the plaintiff's make. Were it not so, it would be of extreme difficulty to show at just what point in time the mark became associated with the maker in enough of his customers' minds to justify the inference that the defendant's use might have become confusing. Therefore, once his use begins, the rest of the public must avoid his fanciful mark."

Are Judge Hand's observations persuasive? Does it make a difference that, at the time of the *Waldes* decision, technical trademarks included arbitrary and fanciful terms, but not suggestive terms?

In The Matter of the Application of Quik–Print Copy Shops, Inc.

616 F.2d 523 (C.C.P.A.1980).

■ MILLER, J:

. . . .

The only issue before the board was the correctness of the examiner's refusal to register under section 2(e)(1) of the Lanham Act on the ground that the mark as applied to the stated services is merely descriptive thereof. The board, in affirming the examiner, said (203 U.S.P.Q. at 627):

> In the instant case, applicant is claiming use of the mark "QUIK–PRINT" for printing and duplication, which falls within the general category of "printing" [See: "The Random House College Dictionary"]. Thus, the question is what meaning, if any, does the term "QUIK–PRINT" invoke as to these services. There is no doubt but that "QUIK–PRINT" is the equivalent of "QUICK–

PRINT" and would be readily recognized as such, the word "QUICK" obviously would be equated with fast and promptly and when used with the word "PRINT" would immediately convey to customers that applicant's printing or duplication services will be rendered or completed in a short time or quickly. And since the "SAMEDAY SERVICE" offered by applicant through its advertising material emphasizes this quick service and attempts thereby to capitalize on it, it is obvious this is a desirable service and a desirable aspect of applicant's services that is conveyed to applicant's customers and potential customers by the term "QUIK–PRINT". Thus, "QUIK–PRINT" is equated with "FAST–PRINT" and therefore constitutes a term that others in the trade should be free to utilize in describing the speed in which they render their services. The aptness or desirability of the use of this term is demonstrated by the some twenty users of the same or a similar mark in connection with similar services noted by applicant in its application. Applicant has attempted to denigrate such use by urging that such use, as in its case, merely reflects a suggestive use of the term. However, it is believed that the widespread use of the term "QUIK–PRINT" throughout the United States by others including a number in the same state tends to establish that the term has lost whatever suggestiveness it may have possessed and has taken on and projects a descriptive significance of quick or fast printing services to the general public. . . .

The board further said that a registration on the supplemental register of QUIK PRINT, along with the other registrations of record, indicates that the practice of the PTO is to treat QUIK–PRINT as merely descriptive and to allow registration on the principal register only after a showing of secondary meaning under section 2(f) of the Lanham Act. It found "nothing in this record to establish that applicant has achieved a recognition or a secondary meaning in the mark 'QUIK–PRINT' in its marketing area." 203 U.S.P.Q. at 627.

OPINION

A mark is merely descriptive if it immediately conveys to one seeing or hearing it knowledge of the ingredients, qualities, or characteristics of the goods or services with which it is used; whereas, a mark is suggestive if imagination, thought, or perception is required to reach a conclusion on the nature of the goods or services. *In re Abcor Development Corp.*, 588 F.2d 811, 813–14, 200 U.S.P.Q. 215, 217–18 (CCPA 1978). Registration will be denied if a mark is merely descriptive of any of the goods or services for which registration is sought. *In re American Society of Clinical Pathologists*, 58 CCPA 1240, 442 F.2d 1404, 169 U.S.P.Q. 800 (1971). Therefore, the dispositive question is whether the mark QUIK–PRINT is merely descriptive of any of appellant's services.

Appellant argues that although the words "quick" and "print" used individually are well-known, mundane words useful to the trade, the term QUIK–PRINT is a fanciful and distinctive term not ordinarily usable in the trade to describe any quality, characteristic, or ingredient of the service; that, at most, the mark suggests to the consumer, after perception and analysis, that appellant can perform printing services within a short period of time; and that the board's use of perception, logical analysis, and mental gymnastics to prove that QUIK–PRINT is merely descriptive actually demonstrates that the mark is suggestive.

We do not agree. One of the services provided by appellant is printing. Clearly the term "QUIK" describes one of the qualities or characteristics of this service, namely: the speed with which it is done. Such speed is emphasized in appellant's advertising brochure, which offers a "SAME–DAY SERVICE." Because this quality or characteristic of appellant's service comes immediately to mind, we are satisfied that the mark QUIK–PRINT is merely descriptive. The board, contrary to appellant's argument, did not make use of perception, logical analysis, and mental gymnastics to prove that QUIK–PRINT is merely descriptive. Rather, it set forth a reasonable explanation in support of its finding that QUIK–PRINT would immediately convey knowledge of the essential character of appellant's service.

The decision of the board is *affirmed.*

In re Oppedahl & Larson, 373 F.3d 1171 (Fed.Cir.2004). In affirming the refusal to register "patents.com" for software that tracks patent records, the court nonetheless rejected the contention that the addition of the ".com" suffix made the composite term inherently distinctive.

The PTO ... argue[s] that ".com" possesses no source-identifying characteristics just as "Co." and "Corp." did not affect registrability in *Goodyear['s Rubber Manufacturing Co. v. Goodyear Rubber Co.*, 128 U.S. 598, 602, 32 L. Ed. 535, 9 S. Ct. 166, 1889 Dec. Comm'r Pat. 257 (1888)] ... which held that adding terms such as "Corp.," "Inc.," and "Co." to a generic term does not add any trademark significance to an otherwise unregistrable mark.... Although not a perfect analogy, the comparison of TLDs (i.e., ".com," ".org," etc.) to entity designations such as "Corp." and "Inc." has merit. The commercial impression created by ".com" is similar to the impression created by "Corp." and "Co.," that is, the association of a commercial entity with the mark. TLDs, however, can convey more than simply the organizational structure of the entity that uses the mark. For example, TLDs immediately suggest a relationship to the Internet. Thus, the per se rule in *Goodyear* that "Corp.," etc. never possess source-indicating significance does not operate as a per se rule, but more as a general rule, with respect to TLDs. ...

Appellant offers [a] hypothetical, Amazon.com, to argue that the addition of ".com" will generally, if not always, add source-identifying significance. According to appellant, saying the word "Amazon" to a person on the street may conjure images of a river or a fierce female warrior. In the hypothetical, however, the entire mark Amazon.com changes the impression to invoke an online retailer. This hypothetical, however, has a serious flaw in the context of this case. The Board must, of course, determine the commercial impression of a mark in the proper context of the goods or services associated with that mark. In its proper context, appellant's proposed hypothetical yields a different result. In context, appellant's hypothetical would state, "I bought this book from Amazon," and "I bought this book from Amazon.com." In that setting, the addition of ".com" adds no source-identifying significance, which is likely to be the case in all but the most exceptional case.

The "Amazon" hypothetical also illustrates another principle that the Board properly recognized, namely that TLD marks may obtain registration upon a showing of distinctiveness. Thus Amazon.com may well denote the source of services of an on-line retailer (rather than a used car dealer or some other association) because the mark has acquired that secondary meaning. The Board properly left that door open for this patents.com mark as well. . . .

. . . . [T]his court declines to adopt a per se rule that would extend trademark protection to all Internet domain names regardless of their use. Trademark law requires evaluation of a proposed mark to ascertain the commercial impression conveyed in light of the goods or services associated with the mark, not a simple check for ownership of an Internet address.

Appellant's goods include patent tracking software by means of the Internet. The term patents.com merely describes patent-related goods in connection with the Internet. The two terms combined do not create a different impression. Rather, the addition of ".com" to the term "patents" only strengthens the descriptiveness of the mark in light of the designation of goods in the application. . . .

———

As the *Abercrombie* court indicated, a term's distinctiveness depends on its context. Consider the following example. Labrador Software claimed trademark rights in the term "Labrador" for search engines, contending that the term was inherently distinctive. The product had not been marketed long enough to have acquired secondary meaning at the time that Labrador Software brought its infringement action against Lycos, who was using the image of a black Labrador dog for its rival search engine service. In *Labrador Software, Inc. v. Lycos, Inc.*, 32 F.Supp.2d 31 (D.Mass.1999), the court observed:

Under an abstract comparison of marks to product, a few of Plaintiff's marks appear, at first blush, to be suggestive. For example, without additional information, a consumer would likely have to use some imagination to conclude that the mark "LABRADOR" refers to a computer intranet service company.

The events giving rise to this lawsuit did not occur in a vacuum, however. Defendant proffers evidence showing that several other internet-related companies use (1) the word "retrieve," or some derivative thereof; and (2) images of Labrador dogs (or other dogs), in connection with their product/service.[2] The proliferation of marks identical or similar to Plaintiff's marks in the internet industry indicates that Plaintiff's marks are descriptive, rather than suggestive.[3] *See, e.g., Calamari [Fisheries Inc. v. The Village Catch, Inc.]*, 698 F.Supp. 994 [(D.Mass.1988)] at 1008 ("In determining whether a particular word has a descriptive or suggestive significance as applied to a field of merchandise or service, it is proper to take notice of the extent to which it has been used in trademarks by others in the same field."); 2 J. THOMAS MCCARTHY, MCCARTHY ON TRADEMARKS AND UNFAIR COMPETITION § 11:69 (4th ed. 1996) ("[I]f others are in fact using the term to describe their products, an inference of descriptiveness can be drawn.").

Accord, Radio Channel Networks, Inc. v. Broadcast.Com, Inc., 1999 WL 124455 (S.D.N.Y.1999) ("Radio Channel" for Internet website held descriptive for audio streaming website); *In re International Data Group*, 1998 WL 574343 (1998) ("Web Business" held merely descriptive for a variety of media "dealing with products and strategies on the Internet").

QUESTIONS

1. The *Abercrombie* decision supplies an often quoted enumeration and description of the four categories of terms in trademark law. Are you satisfied with the court's elaboration? What does the court mean when it denominates a generic term as "referring to the genus of which the

2. Defendant provided exhibits of the following products/services: (1) "Bess, Internet retriever for kids, families, and schools," (words quoted from web page), whose web page includes a large picture of what appears to be a chocolate Labrador dog; (2) "Retrieve It!," an internet search product from Macintosh whose web page includes a small picture of what appears to be a golden Labrador dog next to the words "Retrieve It!;" (3) "Black Lab Micro," a computer equipment seller/lessor whose web page includes a small picture of an indeterminate breed of dog, and two larger pictures of dog paws; (4) "SuperDog," a product designed to commerce-enable web sites, whose web page includes a large picture of what appears to be the head of a chocolate Labrador dog next to the name "SuperDog;" (5) "Nethound," a catalog of internet resources for a limited geographic area whose web page includes three pictures of a dog of indeterminate breed, plus pictures of a dog paw and a bone; (6) "Retriever!," an internet sales tool whose web site includes a picture of a black dog of indeterminate breed next to

the word "Retriever!;" (7) "Retriever," a computer file searcher whose web page includes a picture of a yellow dog next to the product name; (8) "Retriever" and "Retriever Reader," two products designed to facilitate internet downloading, whose web site includes the product names; (9) "Retriever for Windows 95/98/NT," a product designed to download files from the internet, whose web page includes two pictures of dogs of indeterminate breed; (10) "Retriever communications," an Australian mobile applications service provider whose web site includes pictures of what appear to be black dogs.

3. Evidence that numerous other internet-related companies use similar or identical marks is highly useful, given that "[t]he line between descriptive and suggestive terms is often blurred, and [that] the categorization of a name as 'descriptive' or 'suggestive' is frequently 'made on an intuitive basis' rather than as a result of a logical analysis susceptible of articulation." *Calamari*, 698 F.Supp. at 1008.

particular product is a species"? How do you know whether you are confronting a "genus" or a "species"? Does trademark law include a Linnean classification of goods and services?

2. Which of the following terms are "arbitrary or fanciful"? Which are "suggestive"? Which are "merely descriptive"?

a. "Big Star" for internet retailer of movie products. *See BigStar Entertainment, Inc. v. Next Big Star, Inc.*, 105 F.Supp.2d 185 (S.D.N.Y. 2000) (*suggestive*).

b. "Pet Pals" for pet safety program. *See P.A.W. Safety Charities v. Petco Animal Supplies, Inc.*, 2000 WL 284193 (N.D.Tex.2000) (*descriptive*).

c. "www.firstjewelry.com" for internet jewelry store. *See First Jewellery, Inc. v. Internet Shopping Network*, 53 U.S.P.Q.2d 1838 (S.D.N.Y.2000) (*suggestive*).

d. "Changing for the Better Every Day" for retail store slogan. *See K's Merchandise Mart v. Kmart Corporation*, 81 F.Supp.2d 923 (C.D.Ill. 2000) (*descriptive*).

e. "Battery Tender" for battery recharger. *See Deltona Transformer Corp. v. Wal–Mart Stores, Inc.*, 115 F.Supp.2d 1361 (M.D.Fla.2000) (*descriptive*).

f. "Soft–Chews" for soft, chewable, fast-dissolving pain relief tablets. *See Novartis Consumer Health, Inc. v. McNeil–PPC, Inc.*, 53 U.S.P.Q.2d 1406 (D.N.J.1999) (*descriptive*).

g. "Boston Dental" for dental services in Boston. *See Boustany v. Boston Dental Group*, 42 F.Supp.2d 100 (D.Mass.1999) (*descriptive*).

h. "Lawoffices" for a database of attorneys. *See DeGidio v. West Group Corp.*, 355 F.3d 506 (6th Cir.2004) (descriptive).

i. "Better–N–Butter" for oil-based butter substitute. *See Blendco v. Conagra*, 132 Fed.Appx. 520 (5th Cir.2005) (suggestive).

j. "Tumblebus" for a "mobile gym on wheels" (school buses retrofitted with gymnastics equipment). *See Tumblebus v. Cranmer*, 399 F.3d 754 (6th Cir.2005) (suggestive).

k. "Instant messenger" for computer services providing multiple user access to networks. *See In re America Online*, 77 U.S.P.Q.2d 1618 (T.T.A.B. 2006) (descriptive).

l. "Steelbuilding.com" for computerized on-line retail sales of pre-engineered metal buildings. *See In re Steelbuilding.com*, 415 F.3d 1293 (Fed.Cir.2005) (descriptive).

2.   Secondary Meaning

American Waltham Watch Co. v. United States Watch Co.

173 Mass. 85 (Mass.1899).

■ Holmes, J:

This is a bill brought to enjoin the defendant from advertising its watches as the "Waltham Watch" or "Waltham Watches," and from marking its watches in such a way that the word "Waltham" is conspicuous. The plaintiff was the first manufacturer of watches in Waltham, and had acquired a great reputation before the defendant began to do business. It was found at the hearing that the word "Waltham," which originally was used by the plaintiff in a merely geographical sense, now, by long use in connection with plaintiff's watches, has come to have a secondary meaning as a designation of the watches which the public has become accustomed to associate with the name. This is recognized by the defendant so far that it agrees that the preliminary injunction, granted in 1890, against using the combined words "Waltham Watch" or "Waltham Watches" in advertising its watches, shall stand and shall be embodied in the final decree.

The question raised at the hearing, and now before us, is whether the defendant shall be enjoined further against using the word "Waltham," or "Waltham, Mass.," upon the plates of its watches without some accompanying statement which shall distinguish clearly its watches from those made by the plaintiff. The judge who heard the case found that it is of considerable commercial importance to indicate where the defendant's business of manufacturing is carried on, as it is the custom of watch manufacturers so to mark their watches, but nevertheless found that such an injunction ought to issue. He also found that the use of the word "Waltham," in its geographical sense, upon the dial, is not important, and should be enjoined.

The defendant's position is that, whatever its intent and whatever the effect in diverting a part of the plaintiff's business, it has a right to put its name and address upon its watches; that to require it to add words which will distinguish its watches from the plaintiff's in the mind of the general public is to require it to discredit them in advance; and that, if the plaintiff by its method of advertisement has associated the fame of its merits with the city where it makes its wares instead of with its own name, that is the plaintiff's folly, and cannot give it a monopoly of a geographical name, or entitle it to increase the defendant's burdens in advertising the place of its works.

In cases of this sort, as in so many others, what ultimately is to be worked out is a point or line between conflicting claims, each of which has meritorious grounds and would be extended further were it not for the other. It is desirable that the plaintiff should not lose custom by reason of the public mistaking another manufacturer for it. It is desirable that the defendant should be free to manufacture watches at Waltham, and to tell the world that it does so. The two desiderata cannot both be had to their full extent, and we have to fix the boundaries as best we can. On the one hand, the defendant must be allowed to accomplish its desideratum in some way, whatever the loss to the plaintiff. On the other, we think the cases show that the defendant fairly may be required to avoid deceiving the public to the plaintiff's harm, so far as is practicable in a commercial sense.

It is true that a man cannot appropriate a geographical name, but neither can he a color, or any part of the English language, or even a proper name to the exclusion of others whose names are like his. Yet a color in connection with a sufficiently complex combination of other things may be recognized as saying so circumstantially that the defendant's goods are the plaintiff's as to pass the injunction line. So, although the plaintiff has no copyright on the dictionary or any part of it, he can exclude a defendant from a part of the free field of the English language, even from the mere use of generic words when the customers to another shop. So the name of a person may become so associated with his goods that one of the same name coming into the business later will not be allowed to use even his own name without distinguishing his wares. And so, we doubt not, may a geographical name acquire a similar association with a similar effect.

Whatever might have been the doubts some years ago, we think that now it is pretty well settled that the plaintiff, merely on the strength of having been first in the field, may put later comers to the trouble of taking such reasonable precautions as are commercially practicable to prevent their lawful names and advertisements from deceitfully diverting the plaintiff's custom.

We cannot go behind the finding that such a deceitful diversion is the effect and intended effect of the marks in question. We cannot go behind the finding that it is practicable to distinguish the defendant's watches from those of the plaintiff, and that it ought to be done. The elements of the precise issue before us are the importance of indicating the place of manufacture and the discrediting effect of distinguishing words on the one side, and the importance of preventing the inferences which the public will draw from the defendant's plates as they now are, on the other. It is not possible to weigh them against each other by abstractions or general propositions. The question is specific and concrete. The judge who heard the evidence has answered it, and we cannot say that he was wrong.

International Kennel Club of Chicago, Inc. v. Mighty Star, Inc.

846 F.2d 1079 (7th Cir.1988).

■ COFFEY, CIRCUIT JUDGE:

Plaintiff-appellee International Kennel Club of Chicago, Inc. ("IKC"), brought this action against the defendants-appellants Mighty Star, Inc. ("Mighty Star") and DCN Industries, Inc. ("DCN"), alleging that the defendants' use of the plaintiff's "International Kennel Club" name violates section 43(a) of the Lanham Act, 15 U.S.C. § 1125(a), as well as state statutory and common law. The district court granted the plaintiff's motion for a preliminary injunction against the defendants' use of the name. The defendants appeal. We affirm in part, reverse in part, and remand.

I.

A. *Plaintiff's use of the "International Kennel Club" name*

The IKC is an Illinois business corporation that sponsors dog shows in Chicago, and is a "show giving member club" of the American Kennel Club

("AKC"), a nationwide organization devoted to furthering the "sport" of showing purebred dogs. In addition to giving dog shows, the IKC serves as an information source for AKC activities in Chicago and provides assistance in the pedigree registration of purebred dogs with the AKC....

The IKC sponsors two major dog shows each year, with the annual spring show having an attendance of between 20,000 to 30,000 people. An average of 1,500 to 2,000 dogs are entered in plaintiff's shows, and for the spring 1986 show, entries came from 36 different states and various Canadian provinces. Persons who attend the plaintiff's shows are often interested in canine-related paraphernalia. While the IKC does not sell such items, private vendors rent booth space at plaintiff's shows at prices ranging from $600 to $800 per booth and sell dog-related items, including stuffed dogs. In 1985 and 1986, the annual revenue from the rental of booth space averaged $60,000.

In an effort to promote its activities, the IKC spent approximately $60,000 of its total revenue of $231,226 for fiscal year 1986 to hire a full-time staff person to handle the advertising of the dog shows and public relations. The paid advertising of the IKC, consisting of advertisements in magazines with a nationwide circulation such as the *American Kennel Club Gazette* and *Dog World Magazine*, as well as advertisements in the Chicago-area media, is primarily designed to reach canine enthusiasts (the dog "fancy" in trade parlance). The activities of the IKC have also been covered in a variety of national and local publications.[2]

B.   *Defendant's decision to market toy dogs under the name "International Kennel Club"*

For almost three decades, defendants DCN and its wholly-owned subsidiary Mighty Star have sold stuffed toys in the United States, Canada, England, Australia and Asia.... In the later part of 1985, the defendants decided to add to their product line of stuffed animals a line of stuffed "pedigree" dogs representing different breeds. The defendants state that at the time they had never heard of the plaintiff, and that they chose the name "International Kennel Club" in part because of the international scope of their business, and also because the products were toy dogs. The defendants utilized a marketing strategy whereby purchasers could "register" their dogs with the "International Kennel Club" and receive an "official International Kennel Club membership and pedigree certificate." Part of the defendants' registration strategy was to emphasize that the stuffed canines represent breeds "sanctioned by the International Kennel Club."…. Defendants' in-store advertising included plaques, buttons and

---

2. For instance, the IKC points to a poll conducted by *Kennel Review Magazine*, listing the International Kennel Club's show as one of the best in the country. A review of the plaintiff's activities between 1938 and 1984 in *Kennel Review Magazine* concluded that: "The International Kennel Club, after forty-five years, still remains a show of pres-

tige and education and still follows the original premise-that is to provide a showcase for the best of purebred dogs." The editor of *Kennel Review* also commented that "the International Kennel Club has long been a prestigious event, but in the last few years it has really put forth effort to become one of the most important events of the year."

counter displays, all of which referred to the "International Kennel Club Center," the "International Kennel Club," or the "IKC". . . .

After choosing the IKC name for its line of toy dogs, Mighty Star's counsel conducted a search of trade directories in major cities as well as a search of federally registered trademarks. The search disclosed two telephone directory listings in Chicago-one for "International Kennel" and one for the "International Kennel Club of Chicago." Nevertheless, counsel advised the defendants that the use of the International Kennel Club name would not infringe upon the plaintiff's name given the local scope of the plaintiff's operations and the fact that the plaintiff did not directly compete with Mighty Star or DCN. Thus, the defendants proceeded to market their line of stuffed dogs under that name without contacting the plaintiff to determine if the use of the International Kennel Club name would present a problem of infringement.

C. *Evidence of confusion allegedly caused by the marketing of the defendants' toy dogs under the "International Kennel Club" name*

In late March 1986—six months after learning of the plaintiff's existence—the defendants placed a full-page advertisement for their line of stuffed dogs in the April edition of the *Good Housekeeping* magazine. This advertisement was followed by ads in the June issues of *Better Homes and Gardens*, *Vogue*, and *Cosmopolitan* magazines that reached the public in mid-May. Following the publication of these ads, IKC officials began receiving telephone calls (at a rate of about one per day), letters, and personal inquiries from people expressing confusion as to the plaintiff's relationship to the International Kennel Club stuffed dogs. . . .

The IKC learned of the defendants' line of International Kennel Club toys at the plaintiff's spring dog show on March 29 through 30, 1986. Mr. Auslander, the Secretary and Treasurer of the IKC, testified that a vendor at the show brought one of the defendants' ads to his attention, and asked "why I was involved or why our club was involved in a venture of that type." Thereafter, in early April, the IKC began to receive letters of inquiry concerning the defendants' toy canines ... [one of which was from a vendor who expressed concern that the plaintiff's apparent selling of toy dogs] "conflicts with the stated aims of your involvement as a purebred dog club." The defendants' Executive Vice–President Sheldon Bernstein testified that neither Mighty Star nor DCN received any letters indicating confusion as to their relationship with the plaintiff.

After the plaintiff's spring 1986 dog show, Mr. Auslander attended between 15 and 20 other dog shows throughout the country during 1986. Auslander testified that at about half of these shows-including the shows in Florida, Wisconsin, Nebraska, Colorado, Massachusetts, California and Illinois-he was questioned about the relationship between the IKC and Mighty Star's toy dogs. Auslander further recounted that members of the board of directors of the American Kennel Club consulted him, expressing concern that the International Kennel Club might be involved in their sale. . . . Thereafter, at the request of the American Kennel Club, the plaintiff placed an ad disclaiming any relationship to the defendants' toys in the July issue of the American Kennel Club Gazette.

D.   *Plaintiff files suit and moves for a preliminary injunction*

Confronted with the complaints and inquiries noted above, the IKC filed the instant trademark infringement action on May 23, 1986, and simultaneously filed a motion to preliminarily enjoin Mighty Star and DCN's use of the International Kennel Club name. In response to the lawsuit, the defendants cancelled almost all of their advertising of the products bearing the plaintiff's name. One of the defendants' advertisements—placed in the September issue of *Good Housekeeping*—used the International Kennel Club name but contained a disclaimer of any relationship to the plaintiff's dog shows. This was the last advertisement that DCN and Mighty Star placed for their line of toy canines.

On July 14–16, 1986, the trial court held a hearing on the plaintiff's motion for injunctive relief and on July 21, 1986, ruled from the bench that the plaintiff was entitled to a preliminary injunction. . . .

II.

. . . .

A.   *Likelihood of success on the merits*

In order to prevail in its action under section 43(a) of the Lanham Act, the IKC must establish: (1) that it has a protectable trademark, and (2) a "likelihood of confusion" as to the origin of the defendant's product. [Citations omitted].

The first step in determining whether an unregistered mark or name is entitled to the protection of the trademark laws is to categorize the name according to the nature of the term itself. Trademarks that are fanciful, arbitrary [i.e. made-up terms like "Kodak"] or suggestive are fully protected, while "descriptive words (e.g. 'bubbly' champagne) may be trademarked only if they have acquired *secondary meaning*, that is, only if most consumers have come to think of the word not as descriptive at all but as the name of the product." *Blau Plumbing, Inc. v. SOS Fix–It, Inc.*, 781 F.2d 604, 609 (7th Cir.1986). . . . Hence, although a term's "primary" meaning is merely descriptive, if through use the public has come to identify the term with a plaintiff's product or service, the words have acquired a "secondary meaning" and would become a protectable trademark. *Gimix, Inc. v. J S & A Group, Inc.*, 699 F.2d 901, 907 (7th Cir.1983); *Miller Brewing Co. v. G. Heileman Brewing Co.*, 561 F.2d 75, 79 (7th Cir.1977), *cert. denied*, 434 U.S. 1025, 54 L. Ed. 2d 772, 98 S. Ct. 751 (1978). In other words, " 'secondary meaning' denotes an association in the mind of the consumer between the trade dress [or name] of a product and a particular producer." *Vaughan Manufacturing Co. v. Brikam Intern., Inc.*, 814 F.2d 346, 348 (7th Cir.1987). We agree with the district court that the phrase "International Kennel Club" fits within the category of descriptive words in that it "specifically describes a characteristic or ingredient of an article [or service]." *Miller Brewing Co.*, 561 F.2d at 79. Thus, the "International Kennel Club" name is entitled to trademark protection only if the name has acquired "secondary meaning," i.e. has become distinctive of the plaintiff's goods and/or services.

The defendants claim that the plaintiff's evidence introduced at the preliminary injunction hearing is insufficient to demonstrate that the plaintiff has better than a negligible chance of establishing that the "International Kennel Club" name acquired secondary meaning among the consuming public. "The factors which this court has indicated it will consider on the issue of secondary meaning include 'the amount and manner of advertising, volume of sales, the length and manner of use, direct consumer testimony, and consumer surveys.' " *Gimix, Inc.*, 699 F.2d at 907 (quoting *Union Carbide Corp. v. Ever–ready, Inc.*, 531 F.2d 366, 380 (7th Cir.), *cert. denied*, 429 U.S. 830, 50 L. Ed. 2d 94, 97 S. Ct. 91 (1976)). "Consumer testimony and consumer surveys are the only direct evidence on this question . . . the other factors are relevant in a more circumstantial fashion." *Id*. Not surprisingly, the defendants attack the absence of a consumer survey in the evidence produced by the plaintiff at the preliminary injunction hearing.

Despite this attack, we are not persuaded that the absence of a consumer survey is *per se* fatal to the plaintiff's request for a preliminary injunction. As noted previously, the trial court merely granted a *preliminary* injunction; it did not decide the case on the merits after allowing for full discovery. The IKC may be in a better position to produce a survey at a full trial on the merits. Thus, while the lack of survey evidence fails to support the plaintiff's request for preliminary relief, we are convinced that it does not necessarily destroy the plaintiff's entitlement to that relief. . . .

The remaining factors articulated in *Gimix* as material to the issue of secondary meaning weigh in favor of the trial court's conclusion that the International Kennel Club of Chicago "has acquired a secondary meaning like that among a small but very well-defined group of people in Chicago and elsewhere." In particular, the "amount and manner of advertising" and the "length and manner of use" of the International Kennel Club name yields a better than negligible chance of establishing secondary meaning. With respect to advertising, the plaintiff introduced evidence supporting the inference that the International Kennel Club has developed and maintained its reputation among canine enthusiasts through advertising carefully targeted to reach persons interested in the sport of showing purebred dogs. It has advertised in publications with a continent-wide circulation that are of interest to dog fanciers, including the *American Kennel Club Gazette, Kennel Review*, and *Dog World*. And because its shows are held in Chicago, the plaintiff advertises in regional publications of a more general appeal, including the major Chicago newspapers and magazines, as well as various local periodicals. Moreover, the plaintiff mails out as many as 15,000 "premium lists" prior to each show to persons on its mailing lists, and also employs a full-time public relations professional. In its most recent fiscal year, these advertising and public relations expenses have amounted to almost $60,000, or more than 42 percent of the club's total administrative and operating expenses. Viewed another way, these expenses come to more than 25 percent of the club's total revenues; further, the club's activities are often given extensive free publicity. As an example, both major Chicago newspapers have highlighted the plaintiff's dog shows and have designed and promoted special advertising supplements around those columns.

As evidence of secondary meaning, the International Kennel Club also introduced evidence that the club received a number and a variety of letters and phone calls asking about the defendants' toy dogs.... [T]he correspondence directed to the plaintiff provides support for the inference that when dog fanciers see the "International Kennel Club" name, they think of the plaintiff. Finally, the plaintiff has operated under and advertised the "International Kennel Club" name continuously for over 50 years. In our view, the club's half-century use of the name, combined with their advertising, substantial free publicity, and wide-ranging activities in support of dog groups, clearly renders the plaintiff's chances of establishing that the International Kennel Club name has acquired secondary meaning better than negligible.

. . . .

■ CUDAHY, CIRCUIT JUDGE, *dissenting*:

This seems to me a strange case of trademark infringement where likelihood of success on the merits and irreparable harm to the plaintiff are both exceedingly unclear. And the majority's rather selective statement of the facts does little to clarify the picture.

There is a loss to society in permitting one user to appropriate a descriptive term to the exclusion of others through the establishment of "secondary meaning." *See* R. Callmann, 3 *The Law of Unfair Competition Trademarks and Monopolies* § 19.29, at 109 (1983). Courts should therefore be adequately demanding in setting secondary meaning standards before issuing injunctions in aid of such appropriations.

In the present case, the majority finds that the plaintiff, "International Kennel Club of Chicago," had "better than a negligible chance" of showing that its name has acquired a secondary meaning by virtue of its use for many years, its advertising of semi-annual dog shows directed to a limited group of dog enthusiasts and its maintenance of a 15,000–person mailing list. The plaintiff spent less than $60,000 on advertising and public relations last year. Here the demands on the plaintiff have been so minimal that in the future almost anything will be susceptible to being claimed under the secondary meaning rubric.

The likelihood of confusion is equally uncertain. The plaintiff, a sponsor of live dog shows in Chicago, seeks to enjoin a national manufacturer of stuffed toy dogs. The plaintiff does not manufacture or distribute toy dogs, or goods of any kind. The closest the plaintiff comes to stuffed dogs is to rent booth space at its shows to merchants who may sell them along with a variety of other dog-related items. Thus, although the defendant's mark bears a high degree of similarity to the plaintiff's name, their respective products and services do not compete and are related only by their connection to the broad theme of "dogs." Further, evidence of actual consumer confusion about the origin of the toy dogs is, in the words of the district court, "hardly overwhelming."

The plaintiff has not suggested any economic harm it may be suffering as a result of confusion with the defendant's operation. There is no complaint, for example, of diminishing participation, by either dog breeders or vendors, in its dog shows. And evidence of potential harm to its reputation seems to center on a few letters and conversations inquiring into its connection with defendant's sales campaigns. The plaintiff alleges in effect that the inquiries are mildly embarrassing (or perhaps gently demeaning) because they taint it with commercialism. It is surely not clear to me, however, how any real harm is being done. In contrast, the defendant has expended hundreds of thousands of dollars advertising its line of stuffed dogs and thus will suffer considerable economic harm from this injunction.

To establish secondary meaning (and the right to appropriate descriptive terms from the public domain) it should be requisite either to show substantial expenditures for advertising—a real investment in the claimed secondary meaning—or actual evidence that consumers associate the descriptive term with the product or service, or both. In lieu of consumer surveys, letters or conversations might be acceptable if genuinely relevant and produced in sufficient volume. Here none of these paths has been followed in any kind of persuasive way. We are thus blazing an uncertain trail, which may allow prior users of the most descriptive of terms to win wide-ranging injunctions with only nominal showings of either harm or confusion. If this case can be a winner, it is difficult to imagine one that could lose.

Restatement (Third) of Unfair Competition*

§ 13. DISTINCTIVENESS; SECONDARY MEANING

A word, name, symbol, device, or other designation, or a combination of such designations, is "distinctive" under the rules stated in §§ 9–12 if:

(a) the designation is "inherently distinctive," in that, because of the nature of the designation and the context in which it is used, prospective purchasers are likely to perceive it as a designation that, in the case of a trademark, identifies goods or services produced or sponsored by a particular person, whether known or anonymous, or in the case of a trade name, identifies the business or other enterprise of a particular person, whether known or anonymous, or in the case of a collective mark, identifies members of the collective group or goods or services produced or sponsored by members, or in the case of a certification mark, identifies the certified goods or services; or

(b) the designation, although not "inherently distinctive," has become distinctive, in that, as a result of its use, prospective purchasers have come to perceive it as a designation that identifies goods, services, businesses, or members in the manner described in Subsection (a). Such acquired distinctiveness is commonly referred to as "secondary meaning."

Comment:

e. Secondary meaning. A designation that is not inherently distinctive, such as a word that describes the nature of the product on which it appears, nevertheless may become, as a result of its use by a specific person, uniquely associated with that person's goods, services, or business. Such acquired distinctiveness is called "secondary meaning." Secondary meaning does not connote a subordinate or rare meaning. It refers instead to a subsequent significance added to the original meaning of the term. Secondary meaning exists only if a significant number of prospective purchasers understand the term, when used in connection with a particular kind of good, service, or business, not merely in its lexicographic sense, but also as an indication of association with a particular, even if anonymous, entity. The concept of secondary meaning is also applicable to designations such as graphic designs, symbols, packaging features, and product designs. In these contexts secondary meaning denotes that the feature, although not inherently distinctive, has come through use to be uniquely associated with a particular source. A designation that has acquired secondary meaning thus distinguishes the goods, services, or business of one person from those of others.

When a designation has become distinctive through the acquisition of secondary meaning, it is protected under the same principles applicable to inherently distinctive designations. Protection extends, however, only to the secondary meaning that has attached to the designation. The trademark owner acquires no exclusive right to the use of the term in its original, lexicographic sense.

Rock & Roll Hall of Fame and Museum v. Gentile Productions

134 F.3d 749 (6th Cir.1998).

■ RYAN, CIRCUIT JUDGE:

I.

In 1988, The Rock and Roll Hall of Fame Foundation registered the words, "THE ROCK AND ROLL HALL OF FAME," as its service mark, on the principal register at the United States Patent and Trademark Office. In 1991, the Foundation commissioned I.M. Pei, a world famous architect, to design a facility for The Rock and Roll Hall of Fame and Museum in Cleveland, Ohio. Pei's design was brought to life on the edge of Lake Erie, in the form of The Rock and Roll Hall of Fame and Museum which opened in September 1995.

. . . .

The Museum states that its building design is "a unique and inherently distinctive symbol of the freedom, youthful energy, rebellion and movement of rock and roll music." Whatever its symbolism, there can be no doubt that the Museum's design is unique and distinctive. The front of the Museum is dominated by a large, reclining, triangular facade of steel and glass, while the rear of the building, which extends out over Lake Erie, is a striking combination of interconnected and unusually shaped, white buildings. On May 3, 1996, the State of Ohio approved the registration of the Museum's building design for trademark and service-mark purposes. The Museum has similar applications pending with the United States Patent and Trademark Office.

Charles Gentile is a professional photographer whose work is marketed and distributed through Gentile Productions. In the spring of 1996, Gentile began to sell, for $40 to $50, a poster featuring a photograph of the Museum against a colorful sunset. The photograph is framed by a black border. In gold lettering in the border underneath the photograph, the words, "ROCK N' ROLL HALL OF FAME," appear above the smaller, but elongated word, "CLEVELAND." Gentile's signature appears in small blue print beneath the picture of the building. Along the right-hand side of the photograph, in very fine print, is the following explanation: "(C)1996 Gentile Productions ... Photographed by: Charles M. Gentile[;] Design:

Division Street Design[;] Paper: Mead Signature Gloss Cover 80#[;] Printing: Custom Graphics Inc.[;] Finishing: Northern Ohio Finishing, Inc."

In reaction to Gentile's poster, the Museum filed a five-count complaint against Gentile in the district court. The Museum's complaint contends that the Museum has used both its registered service mark, "THE ROCK AND ROLL HALL OF FAME," and its building design as trademarks, and that Gentile's poster infringes upon, dilutes, and unfairly competes with these marks. The Museum's somewhat unusual claims regarding its building design, then, are quite unlike a claim to a service-mark right in a building design that might be asserted to prevent the construction of a confusingly similar building.

. . . .

The Museum submitted several exhibits in support of its motion. Of particular concern in the present dispute is a poster the Museum sells for $20. Although the Museum's poster, like Gentile's, features a photograph of the Museum at sunset, the photographs of the building in the two posters are very different. Gentile's photograph is a ground-level, close-up view of the Museum taken at a time when the building appears to be closed. It is an artistically appealing photograph of the Museum and virtually nothing else. In contrast, the Museum's poster features a photograph of the Museum, taken from an elevated and considerably more distant vantage point, on the Museum's opening night, when red carpet stretched from the Museum's front doors, and interior lights highlighted its dramatic glass facade. There is a great deal of detail in the foreground of the Museum's photograph including the full esplanade in front of the building, and even a portion of the highway adjacent to the property. It, too, is an artistically pleasing photograph of the Museum and its surrounding environment, but it is a very different picture than Gentile's.

The Museum's poster is framed by a white border, in which the words, "The Rock and Roll Hall of Fame and Museum—Cleveland," appear beneath the photograph. To the left of these words is a small circular designation, which appears to be a trademark (the "composite mark"). In the center of this composite mark is a triangle formed by six lines fanning out from a single point. The triangle is intersected by three horizontal lines, contains two dots running vertically, and may be intended to be evocative of the Museum's building design. In a circle around this triangular design are the words, "ROCK AND ROLL HALL OF FAME & MUSEUM."

In addition to the parties' posters, the record on appeal contains color copies of photographs of several items produced by the Museum; specifically, an advertisement for the Museum's opening, a paper weight, several postcards, and two T-shirts. One postcard features the same photograph which appears in the Museum's poster, one features a photograph of the rear of the Museum, and the third features six different close-up photographs of various parts of the Museum. One of the T-shirts bears a detailed drawing of the front of the Museum, a small drawing of the back of the

Museum, the composite mark, and the words, "The house that rock built." The other T-shirt features a similar drawing of the front of the Museum, set in front of several other buildings, and the words "Cleveland: Home of the Rock and Roll Hall of Fame + Museum." The paperweight is a "snow dome" that contains a three-dimensional rendition of the Museum, and bears the words, "Rock and Roll Hall of Fame," on its base. The advertisement for the opening night concert features a man reaching skyward with one of the Museum's paperweights. The composite mark appears on the bottom of the advertisement, and the triangular design from that mark appears on the left breast of the man holding the paperweight.

. . . .

On May 30, 1996, the district court concluded that the Museum had "shown a likelihood of success in proving its federal and state claims," and it granted the Museum's motion for a preliminary injunction. *Rock and Roll Hall of Fame and Museum, Inc. v. Gentile Prods.*, 934 F. Supp. 868, 872–73 (N.D.Ohio 1996). The district court explained, *inter alia*, that

> [a]s a result of the extensive advertising and promotional activities
> involving the [Museum's] "ROCK AND ROLL HALL OF FAME"
> and building design trademarks, the public has come to recognize
> these trademarks as being connected with or sold by the Museum,
> its official licensees and/or official sponsors.

Id. at 871. The district court found that the Museum's building design was a fanciful mark, and that Gentile's use of the Museum's building design and the words, "ROCK N' ROLL HALL OF FAME," was likely to cause confusion. *Id.* at 871–72. It then determined that the balance of equities favored granting the injunction, and it ordered Gentile to refrain from further infringements of the Museum's trademarks and to "deliver . . . for destruction all copies of defendants' poster in their possession." *Id.* at 872–73.

II.

. . . .

A trademark is a *designation*, "any word, name, symbol, or device, or any combination thereof," which serves "to identify and distinguish [the] goods [of the mark's owner] . . . from those manufactured or sold by others and to indicate the source of the goods, even if that source is unknown." 15 U.S.C. § 1127. Although some marks are classified as inherently distinctive and therefore capable of protection, *see generally Two Pesos, Inc. v. Taco Cabana, Inc.*, 505 U.S. 763, 768–69 (1992), it is not the case that all inherently distinctive symbols or words on a product function as trademarks. [Citations omitted]. Rather, in order to be protected as a valid trademark, a designation must create "a separate and distinct commercial impression, which . . . performs the trademark function of identifying the source of the merchandise to the customers." *In re Chemical Dynamics, Inc.*, 839 F.2d 1569, 1571 (Fed.Cir.1988); *see also* 1 J. McCarthy § 3:3.

. . . .

At the hearing on the Museum's motion, Gentile showed the district court a poster of an illustration of the Cleveland skyline, produced by another artist, that included the Museum as one building among many. Gentile also referred to a quilt or blanket which apparently depicts "all kinds of landmarks of Cleveland," again including the Museum among several others. In response to these exhibits, the Museum stated that "they illustrate something [that the Museum does not] think . . . [is] a problem because they show a whole collage of downtown buildings and scenes around Cleveland. That's not what [the Museum is] trying to stop." However, the Museum argued that Gentile's poster features nothing but the Museum and a sunset. According to the Museum, Gentile's production of his poster was like "going into a store, getting a bottle of [C]oke, taking a picture, [of it and] putting . . . [C]oke underneath."

Although we are mindful that we are called upon to settle only the present dispute, we have found the foregoing exchange from the hearing on the Museum's motion a helpful guidepost for our discussion.

On the one hand, although Gentile's exhibits, which depict the Museum as one landmark among others or as one of several buildings in the Cleveland lakefront skyline, present easier cases, their significance is consonant with our initial impression of Gentile's poster. That is to say that, when we view the photograph in Gentile's poster, we do not readily recognize the design of the Museum's building as an indicator of source or sponsorship. What we see, rather, is a photograph of an accessible, well-known, public landmark. Stated somewhat differently, in Gentile's poster, the Museum's building strikes us not as a separate and distinct mark *on the good*, but, rather, as the good itself.

On the other hand, the import of the Museum's Coke bottle example is not lost upon us. Indeed, the Museum's example is not entirely concocted, *see Coca-Cola Co. v. Gemini Rising, Inc.*, 346 F. Supp. 1183 (E.D.N.Y. 1972), and we accept that a photograph which prominently depicts another person's trademark might very well, wittingly or unwittingly, use its object as a trademark. However, after reviewing the record before us with this possibility in mind, we are not persuaded that the Museum uses its building design as a trademark. Thus, we are not dissuaded from our initial impression that the photograph in Gentile's poster does not function as a trademark.

The district court found that the Museum's building design is fanciful, that the Museum has used its building design as a trademark, and that "the public has come to recognize [the Museum's building design] trademark[] as being connected with or sold by the Museum." *Rock and Roll Hall of Fame*, 934 F. Supp. at 871. There are several problems with these critical findings. First, we find absolutely no evidence in the record which documents or demonstrates public recognition of the Museum's building design as a trademark. Such evidence might be pivotal in this case, but it is lacking. Indeed, we are at a loss to understand the district court's basis for this significant finding of fact.

Second, although no one could doubt that the Museum's building design is fanciful, it is less clear that a picture or a drawing of the Museum is fanciful in a trademark sense. Fanciful marks are usually understood as "totally new and unique combination[s] of letters or symbols" that are "invented or selected for the sole purpose of functioning as a trademark." 1 J. McCarthy § 11:5. Although the plaintiffs "invented" the Museum, the Museum's existence as a landmark in downtown Cleveland undermines its "fancifulness" *as a trademark*. A picture or a drawing of the Museum is not fanciful in the same way that a word like Exxon is when it is coined as a service mark. Such a word is distinctive as a mark because it readily appears to a consumer to have no other purpose. In contrast, a picture of the Museum on a product might be more readily perceived as ornamentation than as an identifier of source.

We recognize, of course, that a designation may serve both ornamental and source-identifying purposes, *see, e.g., WSM, Inc. v. Tennessee Sales Co.,* 709 F.2d 1084, 1087 (6th Cir.1983), and this brings us to our principal difficulty with the Museum's argument and the district court's judgment. As we described *supra*, although the Museum has used drawings or pictures of its building design on various goods, it has not done so with any consistency.... Several items marketed by the Museum display only the rear of the Museum's building, which looks dramatically different from the front. Drawings of the front of the Museum on the two T-shirts in the record are similar, but they are quite different from the photograph featured in the Museum's poster. And, although the photograph from the poster is also used on a postcard, another postcard displays various close-up photographs of the Museum which, individually and perhaps even collectively, are not even immediately recognizable as photographs of the Museum.

.   .   .   .

In reviewing the Museum's disparate uses of several different perspectives of its building design, we cannot conclude that they create a consistent and distinct commercial impression as an indicator of a *single* source of origin or sponsorship. To be more specific, we cannot conclude on this record that it is likely that the Museum has established a valid trademark in every photograph which, like Gentile's, prominently displays the front of the Museum's building, "no matter how dissimilar." Even if we accept that consumers recognize the various drawings and pictures of the Museum's building design as being drawings and pictures of the Museum, the Museum's argument would still fall short. Such recognition is not the equivalent of the recognition that these various drawings or photographs indicate a single source of the goods on which they appear. Consistent and repetitive use of a designation as an indicator of source is the hallmark of a trademark. Although the record before us supports the conclusion that the Museum has used its composite mark in this manner, it will not support the conclusion that the Museum has made such use of its building design.

In the end, then, we believe that the district court abused its discretion by treating the "Museum's building design" as a single entity, and by concomitantly failing to consider whether and to what extent the Museum's use of its building design served the source-identifying function that is the essence of a trademark. As we have noted, we find no support for the factual finding that the public recognizes the Museum's building design, in any form, let alone in all forms, as a trademark. In light of the Museum's irregular use of its building design, then, we believe that it is quite unlikely, on the record before us, that the Museum will prevail on its claims that Gentile's photograph of the Museum is an infringing trademark use of the Museum's building design.

. . . .

III.

For all of the foregoing reasons, we VACATE the judgment of the district court, and REMAND for further consideration.

■ BOYCE F. MARTIN, JR., CHIEF JUDGE, *dissenting*.

I cannot imagine a more cogent explanation of the meaning of a trademark than that offered by Justice Holmes in *Beech–Nut Co. v. Lorillard Co.*, 273 U.S. 629, 633 (1926).

> A trademark is not only a symbol of an existing good will, although it is commonly thought of only as that. Primarily it is a distinguishable token devised or picked out with the intent to appropriate it to a particular class of goods and with the hope that it will come to symbolize good will.

Id. Because I believe that the Museum has devised a distinguishable token, appropriated that token to a particular class of goods and plainly demonstrated quantifiable good will, I respectfully dissent.

The majority could have scarcely chosen a better analogy to adopt than that of the Coca–Cola bottle. Doubtless no symbol in the world is so readily recognized. This famous form serves two purposes: it allows the consumer to identify immediately what's inside the bottle; it also serves a utilitarian function by containing the Coca–Cola Company's primary product—Coca–Cola. Just as with a Coca–Cola bottle, more than one mark can serve to identify a single item. For example, the words "Coca–Cola", the signature script and the distinctive bottle shape are all trademarked. *See, e.g., Coca–Cola Co. v. Alma–Leo U.S.A., Inc.,* 719 F. Supp. 725, 726 (N.D.Ill.1989) (noting trademark of bottle shape); *Coca–Cola Co. v. Gemini Rising, Inc.,* 346 F. Supp. 1183, 1186–87 (E.D.N.Y.1972) (noting trademarks in product name and stylized script). All can be found on one product.

The Coke bottle analogy is significant for another reason. The trademarked shape of the bottle has three dimensions. Regardless of the angle from which it is viewed, it is still recognizable as a Coke bottle. When a Coke bottle is photographed it loses a dimension, but the subject of the picture remains recognizable as one of a trademarked, three dimensional figure. If a photograph of a trademark—for example, one of a Coke bottle— can be sold by the owner of the trademark in a poster form, that poster naturally must be recognized as one of the owner's "goods", albeit a derivative good.

In this case, the physical structure of the Museum, the I.M. Pei–designed building, is "the Coke bottle." *Webster's* defines *token* as "an outward sign or expression; symbol, emblem." Webster's New Collegiate Dictionary 1227 (1977). The Museum claims, as I am persuaded, that its building symbolizes something unique and protectable under the trademark laws of the United States. What that something is will arouse different feelings in whomever views the Museum, whether in person or through artists' renderings or photographs. Beyond embodying "the freedom, youthful energy, rebellion and movement of rock and roll music," the Museum building serves a utilitarian function. Like the Coke bottle, the building is also a container. Instead of containing a soft drink, the Museum envelops an array of tangible and intangible elements. It embraces nostalgia; it shelters memorabilia from one of this century's cardinal art forms; it also harbors a bazaar selling snow domes and postcards, T-shirts, baseball caps, and posters—souvenirs for the pilgrims of popular culture. It is this amalgam, of which posters are but a part, that is "the good itself." In short, it is the Coca–Cola in the bottle.

. . . .

There is no meaningful legal distinction between a three-dimensional and a two-dimensional trademark. I believe the Museum has a valid trademark in its building, and that a photographic image of the museum building could qualify as a trademark on merchandise. I do not read the Lanham Act to mean that simply because a trademark is also the subject of a poster it should enjoy any less protection.

I therefore respectfully dissent.

QUESTIONS

1. Is the showing required for secondary meaning different when the mark is a trade dress mark rather than a word mark? Should it be different? Why or why not? Should it matter whether the trade dress is the packaging of the product, or the shape ("configuration") of the product itself? *See Wal–Mart Stores v. Samara Brothers, infra,* Chapter 7.B.

2. Comedy III Productions is the assignee of all rights in the names, likenesses and trademarks of the Three Stooges. Comedy III seeks trademark protection for images of the Three Stooges as clothing appliques and for a famous film clip from *Disorder in the Court*, a Three Stooges movie no longer covered by copyright. What result? *See Comedy III Productions v. New Line Cinema*, 200 F.3d 593 (9th Cir.2000); *Comedy III Productions v. Class Publications*, 1996 WL 219636 (S.D.N.Y.1996).

3. Georgi brand vodka has introduced a new orange-flavored product; the label features a large "O" rendered as a vertical oval, with the outline of the "O" slightly wider along the sides (about one quarter inch thick) and narrowing at the top and bottom (about one eighth inch thick); the outline of the "O" is colored orange and decorated with two thin gold lines, one bordering the inside and one bordering the outside of the outline. Bacardi, a second-comer in the orange-flavored spirit market, also sports an outsize "O" on the "Bacardi O" label. Georgi's sales have not been sufficiently numerous to build secondary meaning in its "O" design, but Georgi's suit against Bacardi claims the design is inherently distinctive. Is Georgi's "O" design inherently distinctive, or rather merely descriptive? *See Star Indus. v. Bacardi*, 412 F.3d 373 (2d Cir.2005).

CHAPTER 3

OWNERSHIP AND USE

A. OWNERSHIP

Bell v. Streetwise Records, Ltd.

640 F.Supp. 575 (D.Mass.1986).

[This controversy concerned conflicting claims to trademark ownership of the term NEW EDITION for a singing group. The claimants were the performers; the defendant was the record producer who initially recorded and distributed their performances. The district court at first denied plaintiffs a preliminary injunction on the ground that plaintiffs' cancellation of their recording contract disentitled them to injunctive relief. Because it "did not view the 'unclean hands' doctrine as sufficient to justify continuation of public confusion," the First Circuit remanded, instructing the district judge "to take a fresh look at the ownership issue in light of all the evidence."]

■ ZOBEL, DISTRICT JUDGE:

Plaintiffs Bell, Bivins, Brown, DeVoe and Tresvant, members of a singing group, are known to teenagers across the nation and around the world by the name "New Edition." Together with their present recording company, MCA Records, Inc. ("MCA"), they seek to establish their exclusive right to appear, perform and record under that mark. Defendants and counterclaimants (hereinafter "defendants"), Boston International Music, Inc. ("BIM"), and Streetwise Records, Ltd. ("Streetwise") produced, recorded and marketed the first New Edition long-playing album, "Candy Girl," as well as the singles from that album. Defendants claim that they employed the five individual plaintiffs to serve as a public front for a "concept" which they developed, and to promote musical recordings embodying that "concept." Because the mark "New Edition" allegedly identifies those recordings, and not the group members, defendants assert that they are its rightful owners. Each side has asked that this court enjoin the other from using the mark.

The amended complaint charges defendants with violations of § 43(a) of the Lanham Act, 15 U.S.C.A. § 1125(a) (West 1982), of the Massachusetts antidilution statute, Mass. Gen. Laws ch. 110B, § 112 (West Supp. 1986), of the Massachusetts nonstatutory law of unfair competition, and of Mass. Gen. Laws ch. 93A, § 11 (West 1984), which prohibits unfair or deceptive acts or practices. Defendants' counterclaims mirror the claims of plaintiffs.

. . . .

The five plaintiffs, calling themselves New Edition, form one of the hottest song-and-dance acts on the entertainment scene today. They have released four albums, numerous singles and several videos. They have performed throughout this country, filling major concert halls. They have toured Britain and Germany, and have plans for an upcoming trip to Japan. They have appeared on television shows, at charity events, and—the crowning sign of success—they have even been featured in a COKE commercial.

The group got its start in 1981 when four of the five current members performed in a talent show at Roscoe's Lounge in Boston. They were each about thirteen years old at the time and they called themselves New Edition. Travis Gresham, who knew Bell and Tresvant from the marching band he directed, saw the show and thought they had potential. Within a week or two he became their manager and Brook Payne, who had collaborated with Bell, Bivins and Brown on an earlier endeavor, became their choreographer.

Gresham booked a series of performances for the group. Their sixth engagement, on November 15, 1981, was the "Hollywood Talent Night" at the Strand Theatre, where the group performed a medley of songs made famous by the Jackson Five. First prize and plaintiffs' goal for the night was a recording contract with Maurice Starr, president of defendant BIM [Boston International Music], who originated and organized the event. New Edition came in second but Starr, who had an agenda of his own, decided to work with them anyway.

. . . .

It was around this time that Starr began developing the "concept," which, in its final form, he dubbed "black bubble gum music of the eighties." The concept is essentially the Jackson Five updated by the addition of modern elements like synthesizers (electronic instrumentation) and rap (speaking parts). As early as 1972 Starr began to search for the right kids to act out his concept. In November 1981, when he first encountered Bell, Bivins, Brown and Tresvant, he was still looking.

Although he decided to work with them, Starr believed plaintiffs were short on talent. They had no training to speak of; none could read or write music. Nevertheless, he used the four boys to create a demonstration tape of a song he had composed earlier, entitled "Candy Girl." Starr played all the instruments, sang background vocals and did the arranging and mixing. He had to teach the thirteen-year-old group members everything, and while it is disputed whether lead singer Ralph Tresvant had to record his part bar-by-bar or note-by-note, it is clear Starr ran the show in the sound studio.

The tape was completed in the winter of 1982, and Starr expended considerable effort attempting to sell it to a recording company. He finally connected with Streetwise in the following fall. In the meantime, under the supervision of Gresham and Payne, plaintiffs continued to rehearse their dance routines and to perform locally. Starr played little if any role in these activities.

During this period Starr and the group members had three disagreements, all stemming from Starr's desire to make the group more like the Jackson Five. First, Starr insisted they acquire a fifth member. The boys resisted, but Starr prevailed. Plaintiffs selected Ronnie DeVoe, a nephew of Brook Payne, whom Starr approved. Second, he wanted the group to grow "afros." They refused. Third, and perhaps most significant, he wanted the newly expanded group to change its name to the MaJic Five [sic]; the upper case "J," not surprisingly, to evoke "Jackson." Plaintiffs were adamantly opposed and remained New Edition.

In November and December of 1982, Streetwise entered into separate recording contracts with each of the five plaintiffs, who were at the time approximately age fourteen. Each contract granted to Streetwise the exclusive right to use the name. Each, except Tresvant's, confirmed that the name "New Edition" was wholly owned by BIM.

Streetwise released the "Candy Girl" single in February 1983. The long-playing album—containing ten songs selected, produced, and for the most part written by Starr—came out the following June. Streetwise launched an unusually extensive and elaborate promotional campaign, placing advertisements in print and on radio, and producing three videos. After the single was released, plaintiffs—high school students at the time—performed every weekend night, in Massachusetts and beyond. At first they "lip-synched" to a recorded track; later they sang to a live band. For a period of time Starr accompanied them on these tours, announcing the group, playing instruments (four simultaneously, he testified), and performing background vocals. The records and the group were smash hits.

Sometime in the summer of 1983 plaintiffs began to perform without Starr. In August, they fired Gresham and Payne. That same month they performed in Britain and Germany. In September they acquired new management and in November they disaffirmed their contracts with Streetwise. After defendants revealed plans to issue New Edition records featuring five different young singers, and after they sought federal registration of the New Edition mark, plaintiffs commenced this lawsuit.

. . . .

Both sides concede that New Edition is a distinctive mark, protectable under state and federal law; it is accordingly unnecessary to pass on that issue. They also concede, and the opinion of the Court of Appeals assumes, that use of the mark by both plaintiffs and defendants will lead to public confusion. Thus this court must decide the sole remaining issue: who owns the mark.

I.

It is settled law that ownership of a mark is established by priority of appropriation. Priority is established not by conception but by bona fide usage. The claimant "must demonstrate that his use of the mark has been deliberate and continuous, not sporadic, casual or transitory." While it is not required that a product be an instant success the moment it hits the market, its usage must be consistent with a "present plan of commercial exploitation." Finally, while the Lanham Act is invoked only through use in interstate commerce, common law rights can be acquired through interstate or intrastate usage.

With these principles in mind, I make the following findings of fact. First, on the basis of testimony by Mr. Busby and by defendants' expert, Thomas Silverman, I find that there is only one relevant market at issue here: the entertainment market. Second, I find that as of the release of "Candy Girl" in February 1983—the first use in commerce—plaintiffs, calling themselves New Edition, had publicly performed in the local entertainment market on at least twenty occasions. Those performances (for which they frequently received compensation; albeit in nominal amounts), the promotional efforts by Travis Gresham on their behalf, their regular rehearsals with Gresham and Payne, their attempt to win a recording contract, and their hard work with Maurice Starr to further their career, all evidence a "present plan of commercial exploitation."

I accordingly conclude that plaintiffs have acquired legal rights to the mark New Edition through their prior use in intrastate commerce. Even if defendants' use had been the first in interstate commerce, they used the name simultaneously in Massachusetts, where plaintiffs had already appropriated it. And while it is well recognized that a junior user may occasionally acquire superior rights to a mark it used in good faith and in a different market, that was obviously not the case here. On this basis alone, plaintiffs own the mark.

II.

Even assuming there was no prior appropriation by the plaintiffs, however, they nonetheless own the mark under the controlling standard of law. Defendants correctly state that in the case of joint endeavors, where prior ownership by one of several claimants cannot be established, the legal task is to determine which party "controls or determines the nature and quality of the goods which have been marketed under the mark in question." The difficulty in performing that task in this case, however, is in deciding what the "goods" are. The parties have given the court little guidance in how to go about making that determination. Rather, each side baldly asserts the result that leads most logically to a decision in its favor. Defendants claim the goods are the recordings; plaintiffs claim they are the entertainment services of Bell, Bivins, Brown, DeVoe and Tresvant.

The role of "public association" in determining ownership has been much disputed in this case. Defendants have argued, and the Court of Appeals has confirmed, that the "finding that the public associate[s] the name NEW EDITION with the plaintiffs [does not compel] the conclusion that the name belong[s] to the plaintiffs." *Bell, supra,* 751 F.2d at 76. But defendants are wrong when they say that public association plays no part in determining ownership. It is crucial in establishing just what the mark has come to identify, *i.e.,* what the "goods" are.

In order to determine ownership in a case of this kind, a court must first identify that quality or characteristic for which the group is known by the public. It then may proceed to the second step of the ownership inquiry, namely, who controls that quality or characteristic.

As a preliminary matter, I find that the norm in the music industry is that an artist or group generally owns its own name. This case does not fit into one of the clearer exceptions to this rule. The name New Edition has not been assigned, transferred, or sold. Nor is New Edition a "concept group," whose name belongs to the person or entity that conceived both concept and name.

With respect to defendants, although Maurice Starr's contribution to the "Candy Girl" records was substantial, I find that all the functions he performed were consistent with the duties of a producer. He was credited and compensated separately for each role. Similarly, while Streetwise's promotional work was unusually extensive, and though it proceeded at considerable risk, marketing—or "educating your label," as one witness put it—is a normal function of a recording company.

With respect to the plaintiffs themselves, as noted elsewhere in this opinion, they existed and performed as New Edition long before defendants released "Candy Girl." They had already used songs of the Jackson Five. Their membership has been essentially constant; they were not, as defendants contend, replaceable actors in a play written by Maurice Starr. (*Compare Rick v. Buchansky,* [609 F. Supp. 1522, 226 U.S.P.Q. 449 (S.D.N.Y.), *appeal dismissed,* 770 F.2d 157 (2d Cir.1985)], where the four-person "Vito and the Salutations" had had twenty-two different members, including ten different "Vitos," to its one manager, Rick—who was found to own the name.) They were individual persons that the public came to know as such. While defendants would have us believe this is only the result of their successful promoting, I find that it was personality, not marketing, that led to the public's intimacy with plaintiffs. The "magic" that sold New Edition, and which "New Edition" has come to signify, is these five young men.

Based on the totality of the evidence, I conclude that the quality which the mark New Edition identified was first and foremost the five plaintiffs with their distinctive personalities and style as performers. The "goods" therefore are the entertainment services they provide. They and no one else controlled the quality of those services. They own the mark.

———

Robi v. Reed, 173 F.3d 736 (9th Cir.1999). This dispute concerned ownership of trademark rights to the name of the singing group "The Platters." Plaintiff was the widow of a former member of "The Platters," claimed to have received an assignment of the "Platters" name from her husband, and asserted exclusive rights in the group's name against the group's founder.

Paul Robi's rights derive from his membership in the singing group The Platters, of which he was a member when the group achieved fame. Paul Robi remained a member until 1965. Herb Reed, on the other hand, has been continuously associated with The Platters since 1953, a year before Paul Robi joined the group. As the district court noted, Herb Reed is the only member of the group who remained as the others left and were replaced.

In 1974 ... the California Superior Court ... recognized that "until January 1956, the name the 'Platters' was owned by five individuals comprising a group as a partnership." Thus, prior to 1956, the group, which included Reed and Robi, owned the mark collectively. Because the 1956 purported transfer of the rights to the mark to FPI was held invalid, *see Robi v. Five Platters, Inc.*, 838 F.2d 318 (9th Cir.1988); *Robi v. Five Platters, Inc.*, 918 F.2d 1439 (9th Cir.1990), the group maintained collective rights to the mark even after the purported transfer. As the district court documents indicate, Herb Reed was asserting his right to use the name in the early 1980s, and he continued to do so thereafter. Martha Robi, on the other hand, first used "The Platters" name in 1988, well after Herb Reed's use began in the 1950s; his claim to the name was asserted at least in the early 1980s.

Neither the Supreme Court nor the Ninth Circuit has directly discussed the status of a trademark for the name of a musical group when one of its members departs and continues to perform under the group's name. Courts that have confronted this problem have determined that members of a group do not retain rights to use the group's name when they leave the group. *See, e.g., HEC Enters., Ltd. v. Deep Purple, Inc.*, 213 U.S.P.Q. 991 (C.D.Cal.1980) (former members of a group prohibited from performing under the band's name when members of the original group, with certain replacement members, continued to use the name); *Kingsmen v. K–Tel Int'l, Ltd.*, 557 F.Supp. 178 (S.D.N.Y.1983) (holding, *inter alia*, that the former lead singer of The Kingsmen, who was with the group when it recorded the hit song "Louie Louie," did not have the right to use the name after his departure). It has been held also that there is no inalienable interest at stake that would attach to the departing member. *See Giammarese v. Delfino*, 197 U.S.P.Q. 162, 163 (N.D.Ill.1977) (former member of The Bucking-hams enjoined from performing under the name because he was "clearly not possessed of a sufficient proprietary interest in the name to justify his conveyance of the entire trade name for use by a new and entirely distinct musical group.") (quoting the unpublished Seventh Circuit opinion affirming the preliminary injunction); *cf. Boogie Kings v. Guillory*, 188 So.2d 445, 448 (La.App. 1966) (holding that individual members of The Boogie Kings had no right to transfer exclusive rights to use the name because it belonged to the band as a whole).

On the other hand, it has also been held that a person who remains continuously involved with the group and is in a position to control the quality of its services retains the right to use of the mark, even when that person is a manager rather than a performer. See *Rick v. Buchansky*, 609 F.Supp. 1522 (S.D.N.Y.1985). In the present case, as between Reed and Paul and Martha Robi, Reed is the person who has maintained continuity with the group and has been in a position to control the quality of its services. Reed is the only surviving member of the five singers who originally began with the group in 1953. He founded the group, gave the group its name, managed the group, and is the only member who has continuously performed with the group.

In contrast, Paul Robi left the group and never returned to it; moreover, he ceased to perform at all for a period of years, and is now deceased. Martha Robi, who claims the right to use "The Platters" name by assignment from Paul Robi, has never performed with that group and does not currently perform in any capacity. She asserts the right to use the name for performances by musicians who have also never had a connection with the original group or its evolving successor.

Under these circumstances, we hold that the district court was correct in ruling that Reed had a right to use of the name to the exclusion of Robi. We adopt the holdings of *HEC Enters., Ltd.* and *Kingsmen* and hold that when Paul Robi left the group, he took no rights to the service mark with him. Rather, the mark remained with the original group. Paul Robi therefore had nothing to assign to Martha Robi. Reed, who founded the group and is the only person who has remained and performed with it from its inception, retains the right to use of the service mark to the exclusion of Robi.

This holding is consistent with the basic purposes of trademark law and the Lanham Act. Allowing Martha Robi to organize a rival group called "The Platters" and allowing it to perform music as that group would lead to confusion among reasonable consumers. *See HEC Enters., Ltd.*, 213 U.S.P.Q. at 993 (holding, *inter alia*, that two bands performing under the name "Deep Purple" created a likelihood of confusion).

QUESTION

Suppose that after a three-year long association, the boy band 'N Tune breaks up because of creative differences. The members then split up to form two separate groups: one consists of three original band members and two replacements to fill the drummer and backup vocalist roles; the other consists of the original group's manager, two original band members, and three replacements including a new lead singer. What arguments would the two subgroups have to retain the band's original name? *See, e.g., Brother Records, Inc. v. Jardine*, 318 F.3d 900 (9th Cir.2003) (use of "Beach Boys" name in band formed by former member of the Beach Boys).

B. USE

Procter & Gamble Company v. Johnson & Johnson, Inc.

485 F.Supp. 1185 (S.D.N.Y.), *aff'd*, 636 F.2d 1203 (2d Cir.1980).

■ LEVAL, DISTRICT JUDGE:

Tampon Brand name protection

I.   *Introduction*

This is an action for trademark infringement, false designation of origin, unfair competition and trademark dilution. The plaintiff, Procter & Gamble Co. ("P&G"), an Ohio corporation, is one of the country's largest manufacturers of household and personal use products. The defendants are Johnson & Johnson Incorporated ("J&J") and its wholly-owned subsidiary Personal Products Company ("PPC"), both New Jersey corporations. PPC is the leading manufacturer of women's external menstrual protection products. The case raises interesting questions.

The defendants' trademarks which are alleged to infringe rights of the plaintiff are "Assure!" as used on a woman's menstrual tampon ...

The plaintiff's marks alleged to be infringed are "Sure" for an underarm anti-perspirant deodorant and for a woman's tampon, and "Assure" for a mouthwash and a shampoo.

Plaintiff seeks damages and injunctive relief. Defendants deny plaintiff's allegations and seek an order directing the cancellation of P&G's registration of the Sure tampon and Assure mouthwash and shampoo trademarks.

. . . . .

II.   *Facts*

The history of the development of the controversy is as follows:

a.   *P&G'S Establishment of its Marks*

In 1964 P&G acquired the trademark "Sure" for a personal deodorant from a prior owner. At the time P&G considered using the mark on two different products which it had in development. One was an anti-perspirant underarm deodorant which eventually entered test market in 1972 bearing the name "Sure" and which has since established itself as one of the best selling anti-perspirants in the country. The other was a woman's tampon which was to be P&G's first entry into the woman's sanitary protection field. Accordingly, P&G applied in 1964 for a federal trademark registration for "Sure" for tampons. As a deodorant mark, "Sure" was already registered by the predecessor.

P&G encountered clouds and potential obstacles to its use of the mark. Litigation with one adverse claimant was settled in 1968, following which the registration of "Sure" for tampons was granted by the patent office. In 1970, P&G succeeded in removing another potential cloud by buying from its owner the mark "Assure" which was registered for use on a mouthwash and a shampoo.

Also in 1970, P&G won a favorable resolution of a lawsuit brought by the manufacturer of a competing deodorant Arrid which sought to prevent P&G's use of "Sure" on the deodorant by reason of trademark rights in Arrid's advertising slogan "Use Arrid, to be sure". *Carter–Wallace, Inc. v. Procter & Gamble Co.*, 434 F.2d 794 (9 Cir.1970).

The anti-perspirant was ready for test marketing far in advance of the tampon. It was given the name Sure Anti-perspirant Deodorant and entered test market in 1972; it went national in 1973. Since it was introduced, over 300 million units have been sold bringing revenues to P&G of approximately $300,000,000. P&G has spent approximately $100,000,000 on the promotion of the product.

In 1974, P&G's tampon was ready to enter test market. The name Sure was not adopted. The name chosen was Rely. The marketing of Rely has expanded from year to year to the point that it is now sold in approximately two-thirds of the United States, including substantially all but the northeast.

Sure for tampons, since 1964, and Assure for mouthwash and shampoo, since 1970, have been carried by P&G in its "minor brands program". The minor brands program is designed by P&G to establish and maintain ownership rights over trademarks which have not been assigned by P&G to any commercially marketed product. One of the most hotly contested issues in this lawsuit is the legal effectiveness of this program to maintain ownership rights in the Assure and Sure-for-tampon marks for ten and sixteen years respectively.

b. J&J's Establishment of its Marks

Assure! Natural Fit Tampon.

For many years J&J's subsidiary PPC has been the country's leading manufacturer of women's external sanitary protection devices which have included the brand names Modess, Carefree and Stayfree. Although there was at one time a Modess tampon, it was not commercially successful; PPC has never successfully marketed a tampon. The tampon market has for many years been dominated by Tampax.

Since the early 1970's PPC has had under development a tampon, the subject of this lawsuit, which claims important technological improvements over prior products. The product development project was named Apex. The tampon eventually acquired the name Assure! Natural Fit Tampon. The principal technological improvements claimed have to do with high absorbency fibres and radial expansion. (The Tampax tampon expands in length, rather than radius, as it absorbs fluid). The Assure tampon also carries a deodorancy feature consisting of a masking fragrance, which was added to the product in 1976. . . . Assure, Rely and Playtex are expected to compete with one another to seek to take away from Tampax a share of its market dominance.

During the mid–1970's PPC searched extensively for an appropriate name for its product. Hundreds of names were considered and nearly twenty were tested for consumer reaction by market research specialists. PPC was interested in a name which would evoke confidence in the additional protection against leakage offered by the radial expansion technology. It was impressed with the name Rely which P&G had chosen for similar reasons.

The name Assure was first considered in 1974. A Miss Aikman, who was then in charge of the product's development at PPC, requested the office of legal counsel to ascertain the availability of the name. In response Michael J. Ryan, trademark counsel of J&J, commissioned a search of the trademark register. The trademark search revealed the existence of P&G's registration of the Sure mark for tampons as well as Sure for deodorant. On this basis Ryan furnished a standard-form provisional opinion stating that Assure "appears to be not available and registerable at this date." This was one of hundreds of routine requests of this nature handled annually by Ryan's office. It was one of many such requests emanating from the Apex project. Ryan's opinion was provisional and qualified by the word "appears". It was based solely on the face of the trademark register. Aikman apparently was aware of the existence of P&G's minor brand Sure tampon, as a packet of Sure tampons was found in her credenza by her successor.

In 1974 Mary McGuire took over responsibility for the development of the Apex Project at PPC. Consumer testing of the product at that time convinced McGuire that it was not ready for market. PPC had no prior experience with the use of super-absorbent fibres. The product did not work satisfactorily. Accordingly she directed her attention for nearly two years to the improvement of the technology. The process was expensive, laborious and time-consuming. . . . During McGuire's first two years on the project, little attention was given to the problem of naming as her primary attention was focussed on product improvement.

In the second half of 1976 attention returned to the naming problem. A large number of names was under consideration and many were submitted to Ryan for a routine check of the trademark register. Among them once again was the name Assure, no one remembering that it had been checked in 1974. Ryan again commissioned a trademark search. He delivered a second tentative opinion again stating the conclusion that the name appeared to be unavailable based on P&G registrations for Sure tampons and Assure shampoo.

In the fall of 1976 PPC conducted extensive name testing among consumers. The name "Assurance Plus" tested extremely well. Furthermore, it carried connotations which McGuire and her superiors considered desirable for the product. McGuire did not like the name because it was too long. Attention returned to the name Assure.

P&G was not known to be marketing either a Sure tampon or any product under the Assure label. Accordingly, Ryan was instructed to investigate further the legal availability of the name to determine whether the P&G registrations represented marks which were actively used in commerce, or whether the marks might be available in spite of the registrations. Ryan conducted an investigation. First he instructed the PPC sales force to canvas retail stores throughout the country to determine whether a P&G Sure tampon or Assure shampoo was being marketed. No such products were found in existence. Ryan also commissioned an outside investigator to explore the question ... [who] reported back that P&G's marketing personnel were unaware of the existence of such products. On the basis of the information available to him Ryan advised PPC's executives that the P&G registrations were no legal obstacle to PPC since P&G had not used the marks in commerce. He also concluded that P&G's use of Sure on an underarm anti-perspirant deodorant would not bar PPC's use of Assure on a tampon because of differences in the name and in the product categories. Ryan furnished his opinion to PPC's executives that the name Assure was legally available.

In January, 1977 PPC made initial token sales under an Assure label in order to qualify for registration. Subsequently, PPC filed an application to the Patent and Trademark Office of the U.S. Department of Commerce seeking to register the mark Assure for tampons. Not surprisingly, registration was refused on December 29, 1977 by reason of the P&G registration of Sure for tampons.

1977 and the early part of 1978 were devoted primarily to the development of an advertising strategy and copy.... [The initial ad campaign] told the consumer of three significant benefits to be derived from the product— protection, comfort and deodorancy. An obstacle to the use of this strategy lay in the rules of the National Association of Broadcasters Code. The Code authorities prohibit any reference to the deodorant qualities of the tampon except insofar as such reference is part of the product's name. Thus, in order to permit television advertising of the three benefits approach, the name was modified to Assure! Deodorant Tampons.

The [initial] advertising strategy was too diffuse and was not successful in testing. PPC continued to search for an advertising strategy....

Eventually McGuire and her [ad] team decided to focus on the most significant and unique benefit of the product, the radial expansion throughout its length, which permits it to adapt its shape to the shape of the vagina. This was thought to provide greater comfort and protection.... From these discussions emerged the "It fits" strategy incorporating a ... photographic display of the radial expansion. Print ads based on this concept tested extremely favorably. The development of television advertising faced another obstacle. The ever-vigilant NAB Code also forbids any reference to the fit of a tampon except as part of the product's name. Accordingly, the word deodorant was dropped from the name and instead the name became Assure! Natural Fit tampons. The television copy prepared on this theme also tested very well.... The "It fits" strategy was adopted. Final advertising was prepared and the product was finally named Assure! Natural Fit tampons.

The Assure tampon entered test market in Rochester in October, 1978 and in Portland in January, 1979. The test marketing was supported by the "It fits" print and television advertising. The print ads, which carry extensive copy, contain a mention of deodorancy, but it is given minimal importance in the overall impact of the ads. The television commercials, under the strictures of the NAB Code, contain no reference whatever to deodorancy, except that the package is visible on the screen with the word "deodorant" written on a corner of it. These advertising campaigns and the product sales have been successful. Second generation advertising has been developed to be used as follow-up in those markets. In the second generation advertising the deodorancy feature has been further diminished in importance.

Throughout the history of the Assure name selection and advertising strategy development there is no indication of any intention to trade on any association with P&G's Sure anti-perspirant trademark.

. . . .

III.   *The Contentions*

Plaintiff asserts that the Assure and the Sure & Natural marks infringe, compete unfairly with and dilute plaintiff's marks and that defendants' use of the marks would involve a false designation of origin.

Defendants contend insofar as plaintiff's claims are made on behalf of its Sure deodorant mark, that there is (1) no substantial likelihood of consumer confusion as to a common source of the products at issue; (2) no likelihood that P&G will use the Sure mark on a menstrual protection product; and (3) no threat to P&G's business reputation or to the strength of the Sure deodorant mark. Thus, defendants contend that no infringement, unfair competition, false designation of origin or unfair competition has been shown.

Insofar as plaintiff's claims are made on behalf of the minor brands, defendants contend that P&G has not established the right to trademark protection because it has not used the marks in commerce. Defendants seek an order directing the cancellation of these registrations.

. . . .

(b) P&G's Minor Brands

P&G's action is premised in part upon its registered ownership of the brands Sure for tampons and Assure for mouthwash and deodorant. PPC rebuts this part of plaintiff's claim by contending that P&G owns no rights in these marks, having failed to utilize them in commerce. In language of the Supreme Court dating from 1916:

"There is no such thing as property in a trade-mark except as a right appurtenant to an established business or trade in connection with which the mark is employed. The law of trade-marks is but a part of the broader law of unfair competition; the right to a particular mark grows out of its use, not its mere adoption; its function is simply to designate the goods as the product of a particular trader and to protect his good will against the sale of another's product as his; and it is not the subject of property except in connection with an existing business."

United Drug Co. v. Theodore Rectanus Co., 248 U.S. 90, 97, 39 S. Ct. 48, 51, 63 L. Ed. 141 (1918); *Hanover Star Milling Co. v. Metcalf*, 240 U.S. 403, 36 S. Ct. 357, 60 L. Ed. 713 (1916).

The defendant relies on Judge Friendly's landmark opinion in *La Societe Anonyme des Parfums Le Galion v. Jean Patou, Inc.*, 495 F.2d 1265 (2 Cir.1974) (the "Snob" case) to the effect that usage which is sporadic, nominal and intended solely for trademark maintenance is insufficient to establish and maintain trademark rights.

Broad statements of principle, however, will not answer for a particular case since "determining what constitutes sufficient use ... (is) a case-by-case task ... (and) the balance of the equities plays an important role in deciding whether defendant's use is sufficient...." *Snob*, 495 F.2d at 1274 n. 11; *Pab Produits v. Satinine Societa*, 570 F.2d 328, 334 (C.C.P.A.1978). Upon detailed review of all the pertinent facts, I have concluded that P&G does not own a protectable interest in the marks in question.

Most of the facts here are not in dispute, although there is some dispute concerning P&G's intentions and motives.

For many years P&G has maintained a formal program for the purpose of protecting its ownership rights in brand names which were not being actively used in commerce on its products. This program was entitled the "Minor Brands Program". In 1974 P&G's office of legal counsel circulated a memorandum institutionalizing the procedures to be followed for this brand maintenance program. The memorandum was revised in 1976 and was received in evidence at the trial. The memorandum begins by stating that the failure to use a trademark for two consecutive years may result in its loss. "The Minor Brands Sales Program is intended", it states, "to rebut any such inference of abandonment and thus maintain the company's ability to subsequently use the marks on goods in question as major brands." The memorandum directs that the trademark section of the legal division will annually prepare a list of every mark owned by the company. The list will be divided into three categories, to be designated as Major Brand, Minor Brand and No Value. A major brand is one which is currently marketed on a day to day basis. "A 'No Value' mark is one in which there is no current commercial interest ... All others automatically fall into the Minor Brand category." The memorandum goes on to state that each year the list will be reviewed with each division. "A diligent assessment will be made each year to place any marks which are in the Minor Brand category but which are unlikely to be selected for Major Brand usage within a reasonable period of time into the No Value category so as to keep Minor Brands to a minimum." The memorandum further instructs that when the list of minor brands has been reviewed each year, the trademark coordinator will pack 50 units of each product in the Minor Brand category and ship the 50 units to at least 10 states with a recommendation of alternation of states in succeeding years so as to achieve wide distribution. The shipments are made to normal customers for each type of product.

The evidence showed that the system functioned as follows. The distribution of goods in the Minor Brands Program is not handled by persons normally involved in P&G's merchandising operation. Indeed few employees at any level of P&G are even aware of the minor brands' existence. In each division of the company, one employee is charged with the distribution of minor brands. This "Minor Brands Coordinator" causes labels to be made and simple packages to be prepared for each minor brand. He then ships in accordance with the standing written instructions from trademark counsel. For all items in the Minor Brands Program regardless of size, cost or any other feature, the price billed is $2 per case.

As there are no products of P&G covered by these minor brands, the coordinator takes some other P&G product in the brand category to be shipped under the minor brand's label. P&G's Prell Shampoo is bottled under 13 different minor brand labels for annual shipment at $2 a case. P&G's Scope Mouthwash is bottled under 7 different minor brand labels for annual shipment. The situation as to tampons is particularly curious. Prior to 1974 when Rely was introduced, P&G had no such product. Accordingly, it was the practice to buy the tampons of other manufacturers and to repackage them under P&G's various minor brand tampon labels. PPC learned through documents produced at the trial that in the 1960's, its own Modess tampons had been purchased by P & G and repackaged and shipped under a "Sure" Tampon label. In recent years for its minor brand tampons, P&G has been purchasing and shipping Tampax. Although since 1974 P&G has had a tampon product of its own, the Minor Brands Coordinator for the paper goods division has continued to ship Tampax rather than P&G's own product, apparently through oversight.

None of P&G's catalogues, price lists or other published materials make any reference to the minor brands. Indeed it appears that virtually none of P & G's personnel is aware of their existence. No steps are taken to see whether these goods are actually sold by the recipients of the shipments. The only evidence received in the trial concerning any such resale was to the effect that once in 1977 the president of PPC had seen some P&G minor brands including Sure Tampons on the shelves of a store in Milwaukee and had bought a box.

The Minor Brands Program includes 127 different brand names. These names are applicable to approximately 180 product categories. In comparison with these numbers P&G currently has 60 major products. During the last ten years the number of new brands introduced into test markets was between 25 and 30. Thus if new brand introduction in test market were to continue at the same rate, P&G would have enough names in the Minor

Brands Program to service the next 50 years of product introductions (on the assumption that every new product utilized a minor brand name).

. . . .

Although the directive of legal counsel requires annual review for deletion from the minor brands program of brands which are of no commercial interest, the evidence suggests that this kind of policing does not command a high priority. Indeed the addition of names to the program seems to outpace deletions. The testimony of the P&G employee who controls minor brands for the toilet goods division established that this division, which introduced 5 new products into test in the last 10 years, has 25 to 30 minor brands reserved. He has been in his position for two years. During that time he added 10 names and dropped 4. One of his first acts was to drop the name SOAR for a deodorant because of its obvious inappropriateness. This testimony rather suggested that before his arrival in the position, little attention had been given to deletions. In the categories of mouthwash and shampoo which have 20 minor brand names between them, only 2 names had been dropped in 10 years.

P&G defends the validity of the Minor Brands Program on the grounds that it is commercially necessary. It argues that the development of new brands is an enormously lengthy process; numerous products are under development at any one time; and it is very hard to tell how soon a product under development will be ready for market. The process of name selection and registration is also time-consuming. If a product should become ready for market without prior provision having been made for a name, the product could be held up for quite some time while the name was being secured.

P&G points out further that names enter the Minor Brands Program in numerous different ways and under different circumstances. In some instances a name goes into the Minor Brands Program upon its retirement as a major brand, with the expectation of reviving it on a future product. In other instances a name is selected and entered in the program specially for a product which is under development and expected to enter the market in the reasonably near future. In other instances the names are chosen because of the expectation that several new products will be emerging in that category in the foreseeable future. P&G's witnesses testified that as to each of the 180 minor brands the company has a present intention to use that brand name on a commercially marketed product in the future.

I recognize that these contentions could well justify some portion of the Minor Brands Program. I pass judgment here only on the establishment and maintenance of the three brands in contention. I consider the overall program only for the light it sheds on intent and other issues that arise as to the brands in question.

P&G has claimed rights to the Sure Tampon brand since 1964. P&G contends that since it was in litigation over the right to use the name Sure from 1964 to 1968, it is not reasonably chargeable with failure to use the name during that period. Taking the facts in the light most favorable to

P&G, the Sure Tampon brand has resided in the Minor Brands Program for nearly 12 years, with approximately 50 cases being shipped once a year. The total revenues which P&G has realized from the sale of Sure Tampons are $874.70. During those years P&G has introduced one tampon product into the commercial market. It did not receive the name Sure. P&G personnel testified that the company now has four or five catamenial products under development and five tampon names in the Minor Brands Program. P&G's personnel testified that they intend to use each of the minor brand names on a product to be introduced. But Sure has not been assigned to any of the products. While there may well be persons at P&G who would like to use the Sure name on a tampon to be marketed in the future, for the reasons indicated in my discussion of the likelihood of P&G's bridging the gap I find it most unlikely that the Sure name will be assigned to a tampon while P&G's uses that name on an anti-perspirant.

P&G has owned the Assure mark for shampoo and mouthwash since 1970. The shampoo mark has been maintained as a minor brand since 1970 bringing in total revenues of $491.30. The mouthwash brand has been in the program for only three years bringing in total revenues of $161.50; apparently for the first six years the Assure mouth wash brand was not utilized at all. P&G has introduced a new mouthwash and a shampoo into test markets without selecting the name Assure.

Applying to these facts the reasoning of the Court of Appeals in the *Snob* case, I find that P&G "has never put (these brands) on the market in any meaningful way; indeed, it has given no indication (which I would regard as convincing) that it has any current plans to do so." "Trademark rights are not created by sporadic, casual, and nominal shipments of goods bearing a mark. There must a trade in the goods sold under the mark or at least an active and public attempt to establish such a trade" 495 F.2d at 1272–74, citing *Clairol, Inc. v. Holland Hall Products, Inc.*, 165 U.S.P.Q. 214 (Trademark Trial & App. Bd. 1970).

While P&G's annual shipment of 50 cases for periods of nine to twelve years may not be sporadic or casual, it is certainly nominal and does not represent a bona fide attempt to establish a trade in any meaningful way. As the *Snob* opinion further points out "(a) trademark maintenance program obviously cannot in itself justify a minimal sales effort, or the requirement of good faith commercial use would be read out of trademark law altogether." 495 F.2d at 1273 n. 10; *See Blue Bell, Inc. v. Jaymar-Ruby, Inc.*, 497 F.2d 433, 437 (2d Cir.1974).

I recognize that P&G's minor brands program might well be legally effective in other circumstances, as where a brand is reserved in connection with reasonably well-formulated plans to use it on a particular product under development, especially if the artificial maintenance does not continue for an unreasonably long time. See *PAB Produits*, 570 F.2d at 334 n. 10. But there must be a "present intent ... to market the trademarked product," *Snob*, 495 F.2d at 1272. P&G's vague, remote and almost abstract intentions for the Sure and Assure marks are not satisfactory....

A final consideration in assessing the validity of these three minor brands is the issue of bad faith and anti-competitive motive. The *Snob* court found as a factor supporting its decision that the principal and perhaps sole motive for the U.S. mark holder's maintenance program was to deprive a leading European competitor of the right to use that competitor's well-established European mark in the U.S. market. Defendant contends that the same kind of factor exists here. It maintains that P&G has no bona fide concern for the protection of the minor brands or of Sure antiperspirant, but rather that P&G's sole motive in bringing the lawsuit is to wound, confound and delay the Assure tampon which will be a formidable competitor to P&G's Rely.

To the extent that P&G's suit is brought on behalf of Sure antiperspirant, I believe it is brought in good faith. Although I have not found any likelihood of confusion or injury to the Sure anti-perspirant, P&G cannot be faulted for zealously protecting that trademark interest. Indeed, the trademark law not only encourages but requires one to be vigilant on pain of losing exclusive rights. *See* 3 Callmann ¶ 79.1. To the extent that the action was brought on behalf of these three minor brands, I believe that P&G had only negligible concern for their preservation. Regardless, the invocation of the minor brands rights is justifiable on the grounds that in going to war for Sure anti-perspirant, P&G was entitled to use all the ammunition it had.

. . . .

While P&G unavoidably has an anti-competitive interest in this lawsuit [keeping off the market the strongest competitor of its Rely tampon], its other justifiable interest overcomes the suggestion of bad faith. If the bringing of the lawsuit was justifiable on behalf of the Sure anti-perspirant mark, plaintiff was entitled to bring it even though it stood to benefit in other interests as well.

I conclude nonetheless that P&G owns no enforceable rights in Sure tampon brand or in the Assure mark and that its action on behalf of those interests must fail. P&G has failed to show that it established trademark rights through bona fide commercial use.

. . . .

QUESTIONS

1. What, exactly, did Proctor & Gamble fail to do in order to acquire enforceable rights in SURE brand tampons or ASSURE brand shampoo? Would it have sufficed to have made periodic sales of tampons and shampoo marked with the minor brand trademarks to regular customers at conventional prices? Would Judge Leval have been satisfied if Proctor & Gamble had designed distinctive packages for SURE tampons and ASSURE shampoo, and consistently packaged the products in those containers? Or, would it have been necessary for Proctor and Gamble to develop actual tampon and shampoo products and sell those products under the SURE and ASSURE marks?

2. Why does Proctor & Gamble have a minor brands program? Can you devise an alternative plan that would satisfy those commercial needs without the legal defects identified by Judge Leval?

"USE IN COMMERCE"
15 U.S.C. § 1227 [§ 45 OF THE LANHAM ACT]

In the construction of this Act, unless the contrary is plainly apparent from the context—

. . . .

Commerce. The word "commerce" means all commerce which may lawfully be regulated by Congress.

. . . .

Trademark. The term "trademark" includes any word, name, symbol, or device, or any combination thereof—

(1) used by a person, or

(2) which a person has a bona fide intention to use in commerce and applies to register on the principal register established by this Act,

to identify and distinguish his or her goods, including a unique product, from those manufactured or sold by others and to indicate the source of the goods, even if that source is unknown.

. . . .

Use in Commerce. The term "use in commerce" means the bona fide use of a mark in the ordinary course of trade, and not made merely to reserve a right in a mark. For purposes of this Act, a mark shall be deemed to be in use in commerce—

(1) on goods when—

(A) it is placed in any manner on the goods or their containers or the displays associated therewith or on the tags or labels affixed thereto, or if the nature of the goods makes such placement impracticable, then on documents associated with the goods or their sale, and

(B) the goods are sold or transported in commerce, and

(2) on services when it is used or displayed in the sale or advertising of services and the services are rendered in commerce, or the services are rendered in more than one State or the United States and a foreign country and the person rendering the services is engaged in commerce in connection with the services.

If a person in central Nebraska owned and operated a single grocery store named "Nebraska Bill's" that sold food exclusively to local residents, would his activities constitute "use in commerce" under the Lanham Act? What more do you need to know to address this question? Consider the following decision:

Larry Harmon Pictures Corp. v. Williams Restaurant Corp., 929 F.2d 662 (Fed.Cir.1991), *cert. denied,* 502 U.S. 823 (1991). Plaintiff, a corporation owned by Larry Harmon, a.k.a. Bozo the Clown, opposed registration of the mark "BOZO'S" for restaurant services. Applicant owned a single restaurant in Mason, Tennessee. Harmon asserted, inter alia, that registration should be denied because operation of a single restaurant did not constitute use in "commerce" within the meaning of the Lanham Act. The Court affirmed the Board's dismissal of the opposition.

Williams has operated BOZO'S pit barbecue restaurant in Mason, Tennessee, since 1932. Mason is about a 50 or 60 minute drive from Memphis, Tennessee, which is a large city and a major commercial center for the Mid–South region. The Memphis metropolitan statistical area comprises not only a portion of Tennessee, but also portions of Mississippi and Arkansas. As conceded by Harmon before the board, BOZO'S "restaurant is obviously popular with Memphis residents. . . . It is close enough (50–60 minutes) to make a pleasant outing from the city. Articles . . . from Memphis newspapers and magazines also refer to the restaurant's popularity with Memphis residents." In addition, BOZO'S restaurant has been at least mentioned in publications originating in New York, New York; Washington, D.C.; Dallas, Texas; Gila Bend, Arizona; and Palm Beach, Florida. Further, according to the board's opinion, "there is no dispute that BOZO'S restaurant services are rendered to interstate travelers" and Harmon "acknowledges that applicant's restaurant . . . serves some interstate travelers."

. . .

The only issue in this appeal is whether the board correctly concluded that the "use in commerce" requirement set forth in Section 3 of the Lanham Act is satisfied by the service in a single-location restaurant of interstate customers. Harmon argues that the use in commerce requirement of Section 3 cannot be satisfied by a single-location restaurant, such as BOZO'S, that serves only a minimal number of interstate travelers. In support of its argument, Harmon relies on *In re Bookbinder's Restaurant, Inc.*, 240 F.2d 365 (1957), in which a single-location restaurant in Philadelphia was not permitted to register its service mark. Harmon further contends that if the *Bookbinder's* rule—which it interprets to be that single-location restaurants, not located on an interstate highway, cannot be considered as rendering services in commerce—seems too restrictive, this court should adopt the test that a single-location restaurant is not entitled to register its service mark unless (1) it is located on an interstate highway, (2) at least 50% of its meals are served to interstate travelers, or (3) it regularly advertises in out-of-state media. We decline to circumscribe the statute in the manner suggested.

. . .

Congress has broad powers under the commerce clause of the United States Constitution, Art. 1, sec. 8, to regulate interstate commerce. In *In re Silenus Wines, Inc.*, this court's predecessor observed that the Lanham Act represented a change in the scope of federal trademark jurisdiction and that in making the change "Rep. Lanham and his subcommittee," and presumably the Congress, were "mindful of the broad scope of Congressional regulatory powers which the Supreme Court has sanctioned."

Harmon's position is based primarily on *In re Bookbinder's*, but in that case the court's decision reflects clearly the failure to prove any use in commerce. The court observed that "the record indicates that appellant operates a single restaurant in Philadelphia, Pennsylvania, and the services relied on are rendered in that city," and that "there are no affidavits or testimony of record and the application states merely that the mark is used 'for restaurant, catering and banquet services.'" The court also discounted as not probative the "unverified statement [by the applicant's attorney] that the services were offered to customers and prospective customers in states adjoining Pennsylvania."

In *In re Gastown, Inc.*, decided seven years after *Bookbinder's*, the CCPA again discussed the "use in commerce" requirement set forth in Section 3 of the Lanham Act. In *Gastown*, the appellant operated a chain of automobile and truck service stations, some of which were located on federal highways. Although the services rendered by the appellant were confined to the State of Ohio, some of appellant's customers had their legal situs in other states, were engaged in interstate commerce when served by appellant in Ohio, and were extended credit and billed in their respective domiciliary states. The court held that those circumstances established that the services had a direct effect on interstate commerce and were sufficient to show that applicant's mark was used in commerce within the meaning of Sections 3 and 45 of the Lanham Act.

. . .

While the facts supporting Williams' contention that its service mark is used in commerce are not as extensive, or as persuasive, as those in *Gastown*, we are convinced they are sufficient to satisfy the statutory requirement for registration. In *Gastown*, the court approved the Fifth Circuit's observation that in enacting the Lanham Act "it would seem that . . . Congress intended to regulate interstate and foreign commerce to the full extent of its constitutional powers." [Citations]

Again, in *Silenus Wines*, the CCPA pointed to the "broadened commerce provisions of the Lanham Act" and stated that the changed language regarding use in commerce in the Lanham Act "clearly involves a broadening of jurisdiction." ... Moreover, the *Silenus Wines* court found support for the broadened trademark jurisdiction in other federal courts' decisions which applied the infringement provisions of the Lanham Act:

> Our *Gastown* decision and this opinion are further fortified by the manner in which other federal courts have treated these terms, "use in commerce" and "commerce," when used in the infringement portion of the Lanham Act. Courts have uniformly held, in the infringement context, that "commerce" includes intrastate transactions that affect interstate or foreign commerce. We see no basis for the meaning of commerce in the registration context to be different from the meaning in the infringement context, particularly since the meanings both derive from the *same* definition in 15 USC 1127 (1976).

In *Silenus Wines*, the CCPA expressly rejected the position of the Patent and Trademark Office that the statute is ambiguous and that the various statements in legislative history "contradict and overshadow [the] statutory definition of commerce." The CCPA found instead that the Lanham Act contains "a clear and unambiguous definition of federal trademark jurisdiction" and that "with unambiguous language in a statute, it is improper to consider extrinsic sources like legislative history to raise ambiguities." It also noted that "while some of the other hearing participants appear to have taken a position contrary to the language of the statute, their opinions as to what the statute should have said will not be used to reverse clear, contrary language in the statute."

Thus, our predecessor court has unequivocally held that the definition of commerce in the Lanham Act means exactly what the statute says, i.e., "all commerce which may lawfully be regulated by Congress." In view of our precedent as to the scope of the use in commerce provision of the Lanham Act, we must reject Harmon's contention that its suggested non-statutory limitations, i.e., location on an interstate highway, or 50% of the meals furnished to interstate travelers, or regular advertising in out-of-state media, should be imposed on the registration of a mark used by a single-location restaurant.

The record here established that the BOZO'S mark has been used in connection with services rendered to customers traveling across state boundaries. It is not required that such services be rendered in more than one state to satisfy the use in commerce requirement. Harmon does not dispute that there has been some use in commerce of Williams' mark. It contends only that the volume of such activity was less than Williams' affidavit would indicate. Harmon, however, has produced no evidence to counter the proof of interstate activity by Williams. [Citations]

We therefore reject Harmon's argument that a certain increased threshold level of interstate activity is required before registration of the mark used by a single-location restaurant may be granted. The Lanham Act by its terms extends to all commerce which Congress may regulate. This court does not have the power to narrow or restrict the unambiguous language of the statute. Accordingly, we affirm the decision of the board.

QUESTIONS

1. Does the above decision afford sufficient guidance in determining whether the use is in "commerce" for Lanham Act purposes? If the goods are sold or the services are rendered in anything plausibly affecting interstate commerce, and the user wants to register the mark, is there a good policy reason *not* to register the mark? Once federally registered, the mark's existence is easily ascertained. Registration thus diminishes the likelihood of a national second-comer's unpleasant surprise at finding a local user of the same mark; registration affords notice to all potential adopters of the mark. Federal registration also confers nation-wide rights against subsequent adopters and users; would these be inappropriate if the registrant is truly local?

2. In January, a new company is formed to manufacture sports gear and apparel and to sell and distribute it online. The company, formed under the name Sports Galore, immediately registers a domain name for its Internet site under the name Sports–Galore.com. By February, Sports Galore has manufactured an initial line of t-shirts, bearing a plain-type Sports Galore label. Before bringing the inventory online, the company holds a contest to promote its launch by inviting website visitors to design a new logo for the company. The logo will emblazon the website and future clothing labels. In March, a winner is selected and promotional efforts are undertaken with the company name, web address, and logo to advertise the impending launch. The marketing encourages website visitors to register for prizes and gift certificates. In April, the website officially opens and makes its first sale. When did Sports Galore establish use in commerce for its name? For its logo?

C. ANALOGOUS USE

Maryland Stadium Authority v. Becker

806 F.Supp. 1236 (D.Md.1992), *aff'd*, 36 F.3d 1093 (4th Cir.1994).

■ MOTZ, DISTRICT COURT JUDGE:

The Maryland Stadium Authority (MSA) is a public corporation created in 1986 by the Maryland General Assembly to plan, build and operate a sports complex, including a baseball park. . . . In 1987 the General Assembly approved MSA's recommendation that the sports complex be constructed at Camden Yards, an area which for over a century had been a center of operations for the Baltimore & Ohio Railroad in downtown Baltimore.

In 1989 demolition of old buildings at the site commenced, and in early 1991 the superstructure of the new park began to rise from the ground. The park was scheduled to be completed for the start of the 1992 season, and throughout the summer of 1991, as public excitement grew, there was extensive public debate as to what it should be called. The two names most prominently mentioned were "Camden Yards" and "Oriole Park." In October 1991 the debate ended in compromise with the announcement that the name "Oriole Park at Camden Yards" had been chosen.

Construction proceeded apace during the long winter months, and on a cold but glorious afternoon in early April, 1992, the park was first opened for an exhibition game between the Baltimore Orioles and the New York Mets (a team last seen, unhappily, in Baltimore in the 1969 World Series). The following day the Orioles' official season began with a game against the Cleveland Indians (who, even more unhappily, had beaten the Orioles 19 out of 21 times in 1954 when Memorial Stadium, the Birds' former park, had been opened).

In the meantime, in July 1991, Becker had begun selling tee shirts outside Memorial Stadium. These tee shirts bore the lettering "Camden Yards means baseball," "Baltimore, Maryland," and "1992," and displayed a design including an oriole, crossed baseball bats and a baseball diamond. Becker continued his street vendoring until the last day of the 1991 baseball season. He also sold his shirts by direct mail, through sports bars and stores, and by advertising in a local publication known as the "Penny Saver."

On August 22, 1991, MSA wrote to Becker demanding that he cease use of the name Camden Yards. Becker did not respond to the letter, and MSA filed this suit on September 23, 1991.[3] Becker also argues that jurisdiction is lacking because MSA has not sold goods in interstate commerce. This argument too misses the plate. Promotion and advertising in interstate commerce is sufficient to confer jurisdiction under Section 43(a), see, e.g., New West Corp. v. NYM Co. of California, Inc., 595 F.2d 1194, 1199 (9th Cir.1979); Jellibeans, Inc., 716 F.2d at 838, and the record fully establishes that MSA promoted and advertised the Camden Yards

---

3. Becker contends that this Court lacks subject matter jurisdiction because MSA has not alleged that his infringement occurred in interstate commerce. There are two fallacies in this argument. First, this action is brought under Section 43(a) of the Lanham Act and that section (unlike Section 32(1) of the Act) does not require a defendant to have engaged in interstate commerce. See Jellibeans, Inc. v. Skating Clubs of Georgia, Inc., 716 F.2d 833, 839 (11th Cir.1983). Second, Becker admitted on deposition that he sold tee shirts in Virginia, Pennsylvania and Maryland and directly to consumers in California, Florida and Canada.

sports complex in several states. Moreover, baseball fans have come to the field at Camden Yards from afar, across state and national borders, in pursuit of their dreams. Occasionally, courtly bird watchers from the Carolinas and Virginias can be spotted in the stands.

. . . .

III.

As a threshold matter, Becker argues that MSA's use of the name Camden Yards as the name of the sports complex was insufficient to create trademark rights prior to July 1991 because MCA had not sold goods or services with the Camden Yards mark by that time. The argument is without merit. Although the sale or shipment of goods in commerce is necessary as part of a valid trademark application, the sale of goods or services using an unregistered mark is not necessary to establish use of the mark. Advertising and promotion is sufficient to obtain rights in a mark as long as they occur "within a commercially reasonable time prior to the actual rendition of service ..." and as long as the totality of acts "create[s] association of the goods or services and the mark with the user thereof." *New West Corp. v. NYM Co. of California, Inc.*, 595 F.2d 1194, 1200 (9th Cir.1979) (citing *Hotel Corp. of America v. Inn America, Inc.*, 153 U.S.P.Q. (BNA) 574, 576 (1967))....

A.   *Adoption and Use of the Mark*

The name Camden Yards first became associated with the proposed sports complex in 1987 when the Maryland General Assembly approved MSA's recommendation that the complex be constructed at the location of B & O's former railroad yard in Baltimore City. The General Assembly specifically defined the site as "85 acres in Baltimore City in the area bounded by Camden Street on the north, Russell Street on the west, Osten Street on the south, and Howard Street and Interstate 395 on the east." Md. Fin. Inst. Code Ann. § 13–709(f) (1992 Supp.).

MSA, itself, has referred to the project as the Camden Yards sports complex for many years. In November 1988 it formulated a "Camden Yards Sports Complex Development Plan" for "a major professional sports complex accommodating both a baseball park and a football stadium in the area of Camden Yards." This plan was disseminated to both the public and the press. Beginning in July 1989, MSA published a bi-monthly baseball newsletter that contained such phrases as "ball park at Camden Yards," "Camden Yards site," and "Camden Yards industrial area." The newsletter (as well as other brochures and pamphlets making reference to Camden Yards) was distributed to the press, to 2,500 readers and to members of the public who made inquiries about the new sports complex. Beginning in September 1989, MSA distributed to the press and sold to the public photographic renditions of the sports complex and baseball park, entitling them "Camden Yards Sports Complex" or "Camden Yards Ball Park." It also published drawings entitled "Camden Yards stadium properties" depicting the area where the sports complex was to be built. Likewise, its

1990 annual report, distributed to the Governor's office, members of the Maryland General Assembly, the news media and the Pratt Library, specifically referred to the Camden Yards sports complex.

MSA held a number of promotional events at Camden Yards which included media briefings and photo opportunities. At the "Wrecking Ball" and "Grand Slam" in June and November 1989, over 4,000 members of the public watched the demolition of various buildings which had been standing in the Camden Yards area. In February 1990, Pete Harnisch, Elrod Hendricks and Randy Milligan came to pitch, catch and hit the first balls thrown over the actual location of home plate at the new stadium. In April 1990, MSA began conducting regular tours of the Camden Yards sports complex. The name Camden Yards was used in publicizing all of these events.

MSA also generated public interest in the historical qualities of Camden Yards. In January 1990, it sponsored an "Archeological Open House" during which 1,000 people toured the location of the saloon once managed by George Herman Ruth, Sr., father of Babe Ruth. On March 27 and 28, 1990, it sponsored "Student Press Days" in which 200 middle and high school students studied the archeology of the area. It prepared a pamphlet detailing Camden Yards' archeological significance and distributed it to the Governor's Office, to the General Assembly, at locations visited by a mobile publicity van, to the Babe Ruth Museum and to members of the public who asked about the complex. MSA even designed a continuing education course, given at the University of Maryland, Baltimore County, entitled "The Camden Yards Ballpark—Baltimore's New Stadium," which covered various aspects of the sports complex, including the area's history and archeology.

Baltimore's 1991 baseball season was a remarkable one. While the team's performance on the field was rather dismal, attendance figures soared. Nostalgic and sentimental by nature, Oriole fans flocked to old Memorial Stadium to see a baseball game there just one more time. On the final day of the season, poignant closing ceremonies were held during which waves of Orioles from different eras streamed onto the field to say goodbye to the old ballpark on 33rd Street. But just as those ceremonies dramatically culminated in digging up home plate, transporting it by limousine and placing it at its new downtown home, so too throughout Memorial Stadium's last baseball season talk about the new ballpark had constantly been in the air. It represented the hope of the future and was on the mind and in the heart of every true Oriole fan. What would it be called? Oriole Park or Camden Yards? Controversy raged, from bar room to living room, from State House to penthouse. When it appeared that perhaps an impasse had been reached, such bland alternatives as "Harbor Stadium" crept into discussion. But one thing was certain: by the summer of 1991, whatever the official name of the ballpark might end up to be, Camden Yards had, as Becker's own tee shirts proclaimed, come to "mean baseball."

In short, at the time that Becker started his business, MSA's promotional efforts had already borne fruit. For any reasonable person to have made any association other than baseball with the Camden Yards name would have been as unlikely as Boog Powell hitting an inside-the-park home run, Paul Blair playing too deep, Brooks Robinson dropping a pop-up, Frank Robinson not running out a ground ball, Jim Palmer giving up a grand slam home run, Don Stanhouse pitching an easy 1–2–3 inning, or Cal Ripken, Jr., missing a game because of a cold. It is of such stuff that summary judgment is made. . . .

QUESTIONS

1. The Camden Yards ballpark had clearly generated much local goodwill before it opened, and even before the ballpark's construction was completed. Is this a case about protecting goodwill independently of actual use? And whose goodwill was at issue?

2. Could Becker legally sell T-shirts depicting the B & O Railroad at Camden Yards? Why, or why not? Could the nearby B & O Railroad Museum?

D. EXTRATERRITORIAL USE

The Lanham Act, § 45, defines "commerce" as "all commerce which may lawfully be regulated by Congress." What does this suggest about trademark uses occurring outside the U.S.? Congress' power extends to "commerce between the United States and a foreign country," but the Trademark Manual of Examining Procedures (4th edition) § 903 cautions against asserting that the mark was used in "foreign commerce" because "the term 'foreign' is not acceptable to specify the type of commerce in which a mark is used, because it does not clearly indicate that the mark is in use in a type of commerce that Congress can lawfully regulate. Unless the 'foreign commerce' involves the United States, Congress would not have the power to regulate it." What if the foreign user has promoted the mark and foreign enterprise to some extent in the U.S.? In *Buti v. Impressa Perosa, S.A.*, the parties disputed U.S. rights to the mark "Fashion Café" for fashion-theme restaurants and bars. Impressa, the alleged senior user, had opened a Fashion Cafe in Milan, and had plans to franchise the theme restaurant in other countries. To that end, Impressa's principal, Giorgio Santambrogio, traveled to the U.S. to promote the Fashion Cafe, distributing "literally thousands of T-shirts, cards and key chains with the [Milan] Fashion Cafe name and logo to persons associated with the modeling and fashion industry which entitled them to free meals at the Fashion Cafe." In rejecting Impressa's claims of rights arising from its use in Italy, the Second Circuit stressed the territorial nature of trademark rights; moreover, the court discounted the promotional activities in which Impressa had engaged in the U.S. Excerpts from the decision follow.

Buti v. Impressa Perosa, S.A., 139 F.3d 98 (2d Cir.), *cert. denied*, 525 U.S. 826 (1998). [W]e are concerned here not with the extraterritorial force of our trademark laws to regulate or redress the conduct of a foreign citizen in a foreign land, but with the ability of that foreign citizen to gain the protection of our trademark laws, and the degree of interaction with our nation's commerce that is required of him to receive that protection. Impressa nevertheless has implicitly acknowledged, through several pivotal concessions, that the question whether it may derive the benefits of the Lanham Act is dictated by . . . whether Impressa has conducted the affairs of its Milan Fashion Cafe in such a way as to "substantially affect" United States interstate or foreign commerce, and thereby fall within Congress's authority under the Commerce Clause. Thus Impressa conceded at oral argument that: (1) the food and drink services of the Milan Fashion Cafe form no part of the trade between Italy and the United States; and (2) Congress has no constitutional authority to regulate the operation of the Fashion Cafe in Milan. These admissions, even if only a recognition of the fact that Impressa's registration and use of the Fashion Cafe name in Italy has not, given the territorial nature of trademark rights, secured it any rights in the name under the Lanham Act . . . have dramatically narrowed the issue to be decided in this appeal.

"Services Rendered in Commerce"

[O]ne who registers and owns a trademark thereby "acquires the right to prevent his goods from being confused with those of others and to prevent his own trade from being diverted to competitors through their use of misleading marks." (Citation omitted). The right so acquired, however, exists only "as a right appurtenant to an established business or trade in connection with which the mark is employed." (Citation omitted). Under this rule, therefore, Santambrogio's mere advertising of the Fashion Cafe mark, standing alone, did not constitute "use" of the mark within the meaning of the Lanham Act. (Citations omitted).

The question thus remaining—apparently one of first impression in the federal courts—is whether Santambrogio's promotional activities in the United States merited Lanham Act protection for Impressa's mark based on the ongoing business of Impressa's Fashion Cafe in Milan. We agree with Magistrate Judge Peck's conclusion, adopted by Judge Schwartz, that Santambrogio's activities in the United States were insufficient to establish "use in commerce" of the Fashion Cafe name absent proof that Impressa offered any restaurant services in United States commerce. *See Buti*, 935 F.Supp. at 470–71. As the Magistrate Judge correctly noted, although courts may not have "addressed the issue of whether U.S. advertising of a foreign business establishes United States trademark rights, the [T.T.A.B.] has, adversely to Impressa."

The leading T.T.A.B. case in this area is *Mother's Restaurants Inc. v. Mother's Other Kitchen, Inc.*, 218 U.S.P.Q. 1046 (T.T.A.B.1983), in which an American restaurant applied to register the mark "Mother's Other Kitchen," and was opposed on the ground of likelihood of confusion by a chain of Canadian restaurants operating under the name "Mother's Pizza Parlor." The opposer claimed that it had made prior use of its mark in commerce through advertisements broadcast on Canadian radio stations with signals reaching the United States and promotional materials and coupons distributed at information booths along U.S. tourist routes in southern Ontario. *Id.* at 1047–48. The T.T.A.B. rejected the opposition to the extent that it was based on a claim of prior use of the mark in the United States, concluding that prior use and advertising of a mark in connection with goods or services marketed in a foreign country (whether said advertising occurs inside or outside the United States) creates no priority rights in said mark in the United States as against one who, in good faith, has adopted the same or similar mark for the same or similar goods or services in the United States prior to the foreigner's first use of the mark on goods or services sold and/or offered in the United States. . . . *Id.* at 1048. *See also Techex, Ltd. v. Dvorkovitz,* 220 U.S.P.Q. 81, 83 (T.T.A.B.1983) (holding same where it was "clear that opposer did not use its name in connection with the sale of goods or the performance of any service in the United States").[2]

The principle articulated in *Mother's Restaurants* was not new, the T.T.A.B. having said as much several times previously. *See, e.g.,* . . . *Greyhound Corp. v. Armour Life Ins. Co.,* 214 U.S.P.Q. 473, 474 (T.T.A.B. 1982) ("Advertising of a service, without performance of a service, will not support registration."). Moreover, the T.T.A.B. continues to adhere to the Mother's Restaurant position today. *See, e.g., Linville v. Rivard,* 41 U.S.P.Q.2d 1731, 1735–37 (T.T.A.B.1996) (Canadian company's promotion of its "Ultracuts" hair salons, including advertising by radio, television, newspaper that reached the United States, as well as handing out coupons and other materials at the North Dakota state fair, failed to "constitute[] use of the ULTRACUTS mark in commerce" because the company "rendered no hair dressing and beauty salon services in the United States during the relevant time period").

. . . [T]he T.T.A.B.'s ruling in *Mother's Restaurants* and other cases properly reserves United States trademark protection to those foreign companies whose actual "trade goes, attended by the use of [its] mark," into United States interstate or foreign commerce. So that the issue is no longer in doubt, we hold, in keeping with the T.T.A.B.'s longstanding view and the District Court's decision in this case, that the mere advertising or promotion of a mark in the United States is insufficient to constitute "use" of the mark "in commerce," within the meaning of the Lanham Act, where that advertising or promotion is unaccompanied by any actual rendering in the United States or in "commerce which may lawfully be regulated by

---

2. The T.T.A.B. indicated that the only exception to the rule in *Mother's Restaurants,* other than—implicitly—where the prior United States user failed to act in good faith, would be when "it can be shown that the foreign party's mark was . . . a 'famous' mark within the meaning of *Vaudable v. Montmartre, Inc.,* 193 N.Y.S.2d 332 (N.Y.Sup.Ct. 1959)." *Mother's Restaurants,* 218 U.S.P.Q. at 1048. In *Vaudable,* the owner of the well-known Paris restaurant Maxim's, which had received considerable publicity and recognition in the United States over many years, was granted a permanent injunction against the use of that name by a newly opened New York restaurant. *See* 193 N.Y.S.2d at 334–36; 4 McCARTHY § 29:4. The "famous mark" exception has no application here given that Impressa has made no claim under that doctrine and that the record would not support such an argument in any event.

Congress," 15 U.S.C. § 1127, of the services "in connection with which the mark is employed," *United Drug*, 248 U.S. at 97.

None of Impressa's arguments on appeal alter our conclusion. First, Impressa suggests that the relevant question in this case is more properly "whether Santambrogio's conduct could lawfully have been regulated by Congress," and Impressa endeavors at length to demonstrate that the advertising and promotional activities described above were "clearly within Congress' power to regulate under . . . the Commerce Clause." We have no quarrel, of course, with Impressa's contention that, "for example, Congress's consumer protection laws regulated the vouchers [that Santambrogio] distributed," and likely many other of his advertising activities in this country as well. But where the issue concerns what conduct is regulated by the Lanham Act, Impressa has got it precisely wrong by focusing on "Santambrogio's [advertising] conduct," as opposed to the business services in connection with which that advertising was performed. As Impressa has explicitly conceded in its briefs on appeal, it is "the restaurant services"—and not the advertising—that "must have been 'rendered in commerce'" in order for Impressa's activities to fall within the "advertising of services" branch of Lanham Act Section 45. *See* 15 U.S.C. § 1127 (service mark is deemed used in commerce when, *inter alia*, "it is used or displayed in the sale or advertising of services and the services are rendered in commerce").

Impressa also [contended that its promotional activities constituted "test marketing" sufficient to establish "use" in the U.S.] This argument is meritless. . . . [T]he record indicates that Santambrogio was attempting primarily to promote the Milan Fashion Cafe by distributing T-shirts and other items, including meal vouchers. . . . Impressa has failed to demonstrate "test market use" of the Fashion Cafe name such that its naked advertising in the United States—absent any rendering of restaurant services here—constituted "use in commerce" of the name within the meaning of the Act.[4]

QUESTION

If Santambrogio's Milan Fashion Cafe sponsored a series of fashion shows in the United States, would the result have been different in this case? Would it have been different had Santambrogio's Milan Fashion Cafe catered a few parties following fashion shows in the United States? What if the Milan establishment had an English-language website promoting the Fashion Cafe to American tourists?

International Bancorp, LLC v. Société des Bains de Mer et du Cercle des Etrangers à Monaco

329 F.3d 359 (4th Cir.2003).

■ Luttig, Circuit Judge:

Plaintiff companies appeal from the district court's summary judgment that their registration and use of forty-three domain addresses infringe a

---

4. In light of these shortcomings, we need not reach—and specifically express no opinion regarding—the validity of this puta- tive "test market" exception to the statutory definition of "use in commerce," 15 U.S.C. § 1127.

foreign corporation's rights under the Lanham Act and violate the [Lanham] Act, where the foreign corporation advertised its trademark domestically, but only rendered services under it abroad. . . .

I.

Appellee, Societe des Bains de Mer et du Cercle des Etrangers à Monaco ("SBM"), owns and operates historic properties in Monte Carlo, Monaco, including resort and casino facilities. One of its properties, a casino, has operated under the "Casino de Monte Carlo" trademark since 1863. The mark is registered in Monaco, but not in the United States. SBM promotes this casino, along with its other properties, around the world. For 18 years, SBM has promoted its properties from a New York office staffed with four employees. SBM's promotions within the United States, funded with $1 million annually, include trade show participation, advertising campaigns, charity partnerships, direct mail solicitation, telephone marketing, and solicitation of media coverage.

Appellants, the plaintiff companies, are five companies formed and controlled by a French national, which operate more than 150 web sites devoted to online gambling. Included in this roster are 53 web sites whose domain addresses incorporate some portion of the term "Casino de Monte Carlo."[1] These web sites, along with the gambling software they employ, also exhibit pictures of *the* Casino de Monte Carlo's exterior and interior, contain renderings that are strikingly similar to the Casino de Monte Carlo's interior, and make allusion to the geographic location of Monte Carlo, implying that they offer online gambling as an alternative to *their* Monaco-based casino, though they operate no such facility.

* * *

III.

The plaintiff companies first challenge the district court's determination that their use of 43 domain addresses violated 15 U.S.C. § 1125(a) of the Lanham Act, infringing on SBM's trademark. Central to their challenge is the claim that SBM did not have a protectible interest in the "Casino de Monte Carlo" mark, a prerequisite to SBM's ability to claim against the plaintiff companies under the Act. . . .

A.

. . . In their briefs and before the court below, the parties debate principally whether the activities of SBM's New York office conducted under the "Casino de Monte Carlo" mark constitute services rendered in interstate commerce. SBM, for its part, contends that the office's booking of reservations is a rendered service, and that its maintenance of the office,

---

1. *E.g.*, casinodemontecarlo.com, casinodemontecarlo.net, casinomontecarlo.com, casinomontecarlo.net, casinomontecarlo.org, and casino-montecarlo.net.

its advertising in this country, and its promotional web page attach the "Casino de Monte Carlo" mark for sales and advertising purposes to this interstate service, thereby satisfying the "use in commerce" requirement. The plaintiff companies argue, to the contrary, that there is no evidence in the record that the New York office books reservations to the casino, and that, as a result, the office engages in no activity beyond "mere advertising." They argue further that the casino gambling services are the only established business to which the trademark applies, and that *that* service, being rendered in Monaco, is not rendered in commerce that Congress may regulate....

Because SBM presented no record evidence that the New York office did anything other than advertise the "Casino de Monte Carlo" mark, if its case rested on this alone, the plaintiff companies would have the better of the argument. When they appeared before the court, however, we asked the parties to address themselves to the question of whether the casino services at issue were rendered in foreign trade, and the plaintiff companies conceded that the record contained evidence that United States citizens went to and gambled at the casino. This concession, when taken together with the undisputed fact that the Casino de Monte Carlo is a subject of a foreign nation, makes unavoidable the legal conclusion that foreign trade was present here, and that as such, so also was "commerce" under the Lanham Act.

Since the nineteenth century, it has been well established that the Commerce Clause reaches to foreign trade. And, for the same length of time, the Supreme Court has defined foreign trade as trade between subjects of the United States and subjects of a foreign nation. *See In re: Trade–Mark Cases*, 100 U.S. 82, 96, 25 L. Ed. 550, 1879 Dec. Comm'r Pat. 619 (1879) ("commerce with foreign nations means commerce between citizens of the United States and citizens and subjects of foreign nations"); ... And, of course, commerce does not solely apply "to traffic, to buying and selling, or the interchange of commodities ... Commerce, undoubtedly, is traffic, but it is something more: it is [commercial] intercourse." *Gibbons* v. *Ogden*, 22 U.S. 1, 189, 6 L. Ed. 23 (1824) (C.J. Marshall). Service transactions are clearly commercial intercourse, and by extension can clearly constitute foreign trade.... Thus, while SBM's promotions within the United States do not on their own constitute a use in commerce of the "Casino de Monte Carlo" mark, the mark is nonetheless used in commerce because United States citizens purchase casino services sold by a subject of a foreign nation, which purchases constitute trade with a foreign nation that Congress may regulate under the Commerce Clause. And SBM's promotions "use[ ] or display[ ] [the mark] in the sale or advertising of [these] services ... rendered in commerce." ...

The plaintiff companies' first argument fails because the *locality* in which foreign commercial intercourse occurs is of no concern to Congress' power under the Constitution to regulate such commerce.... The subject of foreign trade, as the Supreme Court noted in *In re: Trademark Cases*, *Henderson*, and *Holliday*, is defined not by where the trade occurs, but by the characteristics of the parties who engage in the trade, just as the [*U.S. v.*] *Holliday* Court [70 U.S. 407] concluded that the subject of Indian commerce is defined not by whether the commerce occurs on Indian territory, but rather by whether the trade brings United States citizens and tribal Indians together as transacting partners. *See also United States* v. *Mazurie,* 419 U.S. 544, 554, 42 L. Ed. 2d 706, 95 S. Ct. 710 (1975) ("This Court has repeatedly held that [the Indian commerce clause] affords Congress the power to prohibit or regulate the sale of alcoholic beverages to tribal Indians, *wherever situated . . .*" (emphasis added)). . . .

Nor, in modern times, has the Supreme Court ever suggested that Congress' authority over foreign trade is limited in the manner that the plaintiff companies suggest. To the contrary, when it has considered the scope of Congress' authority over foreign trade, the Court has emphasized the expansive nature of that authority. *See, e.g., Pfizer, Inc.* v. *India,* 434 U.S. 308, 313 n.11, 54 L. Ed. 2d 563, 98 S. Ct. 584 (1978) ("The Chief Justice's dissent seems to contend that the Sherman Act's reference to commerce with foreign nations was intended only to reach conspiracies affecting goods imported into this county. But the scope of congressional power over foreign commerce has never been so limited . . ." (citations omitted)). . . .

The plaintiff companies' second argument, that the purchase of gambling services by United States citizens at the Casino de Monte Carlo is not commerce because it does not have a substantial effect on the foreign commerce of the United States, also fails. The substantial effects test is not implicated here at all.

The Supreme Court has articulated the substantial effects test to ensure that Congress does not exceed its constitutional authority to regulate interstate commerce by enacting legislation that, rather than regulating interstate commerce, trammels on the rights of states to regulate purely intra-state activity for themselves pursuant to their police power. But while "Congress' power to regulate interstate commerce may be restricted by considerations of federalism and state sovereignty[,] it has never been suggested that Congress' power to regulate foreign commerce could be so limited." *Japan Line Ltd.* v. *Los Angeles County,* 441 U.S. 434, 448 n.13, 60 L. Ed. 2d 336, 99 S. Ct. 1813 (1979). . . . The rationale that underlies application of the substantial effects test in the analysis of congressional legislation purporting to regulate interstate commerce is therefore absent from analysis of congressional legislation purporting to regulate foreign commerce. . . .

The plaintiff companies, seeking to avoid the full import of this foreign trade analysis, ask us to be wary in addressing whether United States trademark protection can extend to services rendered abroad and suggest that other courts have decided this question in the negative with reasoning that should persuade us not to extend trademark protection in this instance. In particular, the plaintiff companies point to the Second Circuit's opinion in *Buti* v. *Perosa, S.R.L.,* 139 F.3d 98 (2nd Cir. 1998). . . .

Buti is not persuasive authority to us for several reasons, however. First, the *Buti* court did not analyze the application of the Lanham Act to foreign trade because, as it noted, the plaintiff, in a "pivotal concession[], . . . conceded at oral argument that . . . the food and drink services [it sells] form no part of the trade between Italy and the United States." *Id*. at 103. And in fact, even though the *Buti* court did not analyze trademark rights created via foreign trade, it did acknowledge the basis for such. *See id*. (noting that a key inquiry is "whether [the plaintiff] has conducted the affairs of its Milan Fashion Cafe in such a way as to 'substantially affect' United States interstate or *foreign commerce*, and thereby fall within Congress' authority under the Commerce Clause"). Secondly, even had the *Buti* plaintiff not explicitly conceded that his business was not foreign trade, it is not clear that the facts before the *Buti* court would have established that the plaintiff used the mark in that putative foreign trade. As the Second Circuit carefully noted, the restaurant undertook no "formal advertising or public relations campaign [aimed at United States citizens]." *Id*. at 100.

Here, SBM does *not* concede that its services do not constitute foreign trade when United States citizens purchase them. Instead, the plaintiff companies concede the very elements we conclude constitute foreign trade. And quite clearly SBM has used the mark in its foreign trade, formally, and at great cost, advertising its services intentionally to United States citizens under the "Casino de Monte Carlo" mark. Because SBM used its mark in the sale and advertising of its gambling services to United States citizens; because its rendering of gambling services to United States citizens constitutes foreign trade; because foreign trade is commerce Congress may lawfully regulate; and because commerce under the Lanham Act comprises all commerce that Congress may lawfully regulate, the services SBM renders under the "Casino de Monte Carlo" mark to citizens of the United States are services rendered in commerce, and the "use in commerce" requirement that the Lanham Act sets forth for the mark's protectibility is satisfied.

* * *

CONCLUSION

For the reasons provided herein, the judgment of the district court is affirmed.

AFFIRMED

◾ Diana Gribbon Motz, Circuit Judge, dissenting:

The majority reaches the unprecedented conclusion that an entity's use of its foreign trademark solely to sell services in a foreign country entitles it to trademark protection under United States law, even though the foreign mark holder has never used or registered its mark in the United States. In my view, the majority errs in holding that the protection of United States trademark law extends to a mark used exclusively in Monaco by a company incorporated there. For this reason and others set forth within, I respectfully dissent.

I.

. . .

Prior to today's holding, all existing authority ... concluded that use in the United States is necessary to meet the Lanham Act's use in commerce requirement. None of this authority has ever suggested that if one element of the use in commerce requirement—advertising—takes place in the United States while the other—the rendering of services—occurs outside the United States, there has been use in the United States. Both elements must occur in the United States in order to satisfy the use in commerce requirement.

Indisputably, SBM has satisfied the first element of the use in commerce requirement, for no one questions that SBM employed the Casino de Monte Carlo mark in the United States to advertise and promote the gambling services that it provides exclusively at its casino in Monaco. This is not and has never been a case about advertising. Rather, the question here is whether the second element of the use in commerce requirement has been satisfied, *i.e.* have the services that give rise to the Casino de Monte Carlo mark been rendered in commerce of the United States. . . .

A.

In this case, some United States citizens purchased "casino services" in Monaco from the Société des Bains de Mer et du Cercle des Etrangers à Monaco (SBM), a "subject of a foreign nation." The majority determines that those services "constitute trade with a foreign nation that Congress may regulate under the Commerce Clause." Based on this determination, the majority accords SBM, the holder of the foreign mark, "Casino de Monte Carlo," eligibility for trademark protection under the Lanham Act for that mark even though SBM has *never* used the mark in the United States.

SBM has not argued, and the district court did not hold, that the mark was entitled to protection under the Lanham Act simply because SBM used it to sell gambling services in Monaco to United States citizens. Nor did SBM argue, or the trial court hold, that these sales of gambling services in Monaco to United States citizens constitute foreign trade that has been regulated by Congress under the Lanham Act. Indeed, prior to today, no court, administrative agency, or treatise has ever espoused or adopted this theory.

Rather, it has long been recognized that use of a foreign mark in a foreign country creates no trademark rights under United States law. As the foremost trademark authority has explained, "for purposes of trademark rights in the United States, 'use' means use in the United States, not use in other nations." 2 J. Thomas McCarthy, McCarthy on Trademarks and Unfair Competition § 17.9 (4th ed. 2000) ("McCarthy") [other citation omitted].[3]

Until today, every court to address this issue has held that use of a *foreign trademark* in connection with goods and services sold *only* in a foreign country by a foreign entity does not constitute "use of the mark" in United States commerce sufficient to merit protection under the Lanham Act....

Nor is the rule any different when, as here, the mark is used in a foreign country in connection with services or goods *sold to United States citizens. See, e.g., Person's*, 900 F.2d at 1567–69 (rejecting argument that use of trademark on goods sold in Japan by Japanese company to a U.S. citizen could establish priority rights against person using mark first in the United States)....

Before concluding, I must note the potential consequences of adoption of the majority's rule. The rule announced by the majority today would mean that any entity that uses a foreign mark to advertise and sell its goods or services to United States citizens in a foreign country would be eligible for trademark protection under United States law. Such a rule threatens to wreak havoc over this country's trademark law and would have a stifling effect on United States commercial interests generally. Before investing in a mark, firms and individuals would be forced to scour the globe to determine when and where American citizens had purchased goods or services from foreign subjects to determine whether there were trademarks involved that might be used against them in ... an infringement action in the United States. On the other hand, SBM and companies like it would, under the majority's rule, suddenly acquire a windfall of potential United States trademark rights for all of the goods and services advertised to and purchased by United States citizens while traveling in their countries. Like some sort of foreign influenza, these new entitlements would accompany American travelers on their return home, creating a vast array of new duties for individuals in the United States seeking to use the same or similar marks on goods or services sold in the United States.

Of course, if the law required us to permit this sort of reverse imperialism, whereby foreign subjects would be allowed to colonize American markets with their foreign trademarks based on sales conducted exclusively abroad, we would have no choice but to allow it. But the law does not compel this. Rather, the majority's new theory is contrary to all extant authority. Applying this authority here leads to only one conclusion: SBM's use in Monaco of its "Casino de Monte Carlo" mark does not constitute "use in commerce" of the United States sufficient to gain protection under the Lanham Act. Therefore, the grant of summary judg-

---

3. This principle, that use in the United States provides the foundation for U.S. trademark rights, is a corollary of the well-established principle that trademark rights exist in each country solely as determined by that country's law. *See Ingenohl v. Olsen & Co.,* *Inc.*, 273 U.S. 541, 544, 71 L. Ed. 762, 47 S. Ct. 451 (1927) ("A trade-mark started elsewhere would depend for its protection in Honkong upon the law prevailing in Honkong and would confer no rights except by the consent of that law.")....

ment to SBM should be reversed. On this ground, the plaintiff companies were entitled to judgment as a matter of law.

QUESTIONS

1. Look at the sec. 27 definition of "use in commerce" in connection with *goods*. Suppose a brand of French clothing and accessories is sold only in France (often to American tourists), but the brand is advertised in U.S. travel magazines. Is that trademark "used in commerce?" If not, is there a reason the outcome should be so different for service marks?

2. What is the difference between SBM's U.S.-related exploitation of the mark and the Milan Fashion Café's?

3. If SBM had a website, accessible in the U.S., that allowed U.S. residents to book tables at the Monaco casino's restaurant, would this be a "use in commerce?" If the website allowed U.S. residents to gamble online, would this be a "use" in commerce?

4. The dissent emphasizes the territoriality of trademarks: rights arise where the mark is used. The same logic applies to infringement: rights are infringed where the goods or services bearing the alleged infringing mark are purveyed. If SBM has no use-based rights in the U.S., then offering casino services to U.S. websurfers is lawful (as a matter of U.S. trademark law; other laws may make this service problematic). But were SBM to allege a violation of the trademark law of Monte Carlo (where it does have rights), its claim would also fall short, because the public to whom the services are purveyed is located in the U.S., and U.S. law should therefore apply. As a result, no trademark law would prohibit Int'l. Bancorp from allegedly luring U.S. customers based on the fame of the SBM establishment. Does this outcome help explain the majority's expansive approach to use "in commerce"? Is there another approach to the problem of foreign marks that are well-known to U.S. consumers but that have not been physically exploited on U.S. shores? See Priority and Extraterritorial Use, *infra* next subsection.

E.   PRIORITY

Blue Bell, Inc. v. Farah Manufacturing Co.

508 F.2d 1260 (5th Cir.1975).

■ GEWIN, CIRCUIT JUDGE:

In the spring and summer of 1973 two prominent manufacturers of men's clothing created identical trademarks for goods substantially identical in appearance. Though the record offers no indication of bad faith in the design and adoption of the labels, both Farah Manufacturing Company (Farah) and Blue Bell, Inc. (Blue Bell) devised the mark "Time Out" for new lines of men's slacks and shirts. Both parties market their goods on a national scale, so they agree that joint utilization of the same trademark would confuse the buying public. Thus, the only question presented for our review is which party established prior use of the mark in trade. A response to that seemingly innocuous inquiry, however, requires us to define the chameleonic term "use" as it has developed in trademark law.[1]

After a full development of the facts in the district court both parties moved for summary judgment. The motion of Farah was granted and that of Blue Bell denied. It is not claimed that summary judgment procedure was inappropriate; the controversy presented relates to the application of the proper legal principles to undisputed facts. A permanent injunction was granted in favor of Farah but no damages were awarded, and Blue Bell was allowed to fill all orders for garments bearing the Time Out label received by it as of the close of business on December 5, 1973. For the reasons hereinafter stated we affirm.

Farah conceived of the Time Out mark on May 16, after screening several possible titles for its new stretch menswear. Two days later the firm adopted an hourglass logo and authorized an extensive advertising campaign bearing the new insignia. Farah presented its fall line of clothing, including Time Out slacks, to sales personnel on June 5. In the meantime, patent counsel had given clearance for use of the mark after scrutiny of current federal registrations then on file. One of Farah's top executives demonstrated samples of the Time Out garments to large customers in Washington, D.C. and New York, though labels were not attached to the slacks at that time. Tags containing the new design were completed June 27. With favorable evaluations of marketing potential from all sides, Farah sent one pair of slacks bearing the Time Out mark to each of its twelve regional sales managers on July 3. Sales personnel paid for the pants, and the garments became their property in case of loss.

Following the July 3 shipment, regional managers showed the goods to customers the following week. Farah received several orders and production began. Further shipments of sample garments were mailed to the rest of the sales force on July 11 and 14. Merchandising efforts were fully operative by the end of the month. The first shipments to customers, however, occurred in September.

Blue Bell, on the other hand, was concerned with creating an entire new division of men's clothing, as an avenue to reaching the "upstairs" market.... On June 18 Blue Bell management arrived at the name Time Out to identify both its new division and its new line of men's sportswear. Like Farah, it received clearance for use of the mark from counsel. Like Farah, it inaugurated an advertising campaign. Unlike Farah, however, Blue Bell did not ship a dozen marked articles of the new line to its sales

---

1. *Compare Western Stove Co. v. George D. Roper Corp.,* 82 F. Supp. 206 (S.D.Cal. 1949) (first commercial sale controls, despite opposing party's prior conception and advertisement of the mark) *with Charles Pfizer & Co. v. R. J. Moran Co.,* 125 U.S.P.Q. 201 (1960) (prior commercial sale is not determinative; drug manufacturer who first conceived of the mark and appended it to drugs for experimental purposes has rights superior to drug producer who initially placed goods on the market).

personnel. Instead, Blue Bell authorized the manufacture of several hundred labels bearing the words Time Out and its logo shaped like a referee's hands forming a T. When the labels were completed on June 29, the head of the embryonic division ... instructed shipping personnel to affix the new Time Out labels to slacks that already bore the "Mr. Hicks" trademark. The new tags, of varying sizes and colors, were randomly attached to the left hip pocket button of slacks and the left hip pocket of jeans. Thus, although no change occurred in the design or manufacture of the pants, on July 5 several hundred pair left [the division] with two tags.

Blue Bell made intermittent shipments of the doubly-labeled slacks thereafter, though the out-of-state customers who received the goods had ordered clothing of the Mr. Hicks variety. Production of the new Time Out merchandise began in the latter part of August, and Blue Bell held a sales meeting to present its fall designs from September 4–6. Sales personnel solicited numerous orders, though shipments of the garments were not scheduled until October.

By the end of October Farah had received orders for 204,403 items of Time Out sportswear, representing a retail sales value of over $2,750,000. Blue Bell had received orders for 154,200 garments valued at over $900,000. Both parties had commenced extensive advertising campaigns for their respective Time Out sportswear.

Soon after discovering the similarity of their marks, Blue Bell sued Farah for common law trademark infringement and unfair competition, seeking to enjoin use of the Time Out trademark on men's clothing. Farah counter-claimed for similar injunctive relief. The district court found that Farah's July 3 shipment and sale constituted a valid use in trade, while Blue Bell's July 5 shipment was a mere "token" use insufficient at law to create trademark rights.[2] While we affirm the result reached by the trial court as to Farah's priority of use, the legal grounds upon which we base our decision are somewhat different from those undergirding the district court's judgment.

2. The trial court reached the following conclusions of law:

4. Defendant Farah's shipment of TIME OUT labeled garments in interstate commerce on July 3, 1973, was a good faith step in a continuous and uninterrupted program of placing labeled goods on the market and soliciting orders therefor, and constituted a valid first use of the trademark. Such actions on the part of the Defendant Farah constituted use of the mark within the meaning of Art. 16.02, Business and Commerce Code of the State of Texas, in that TIME OUT labels were placed on tags or labels affixed to the goods and the goods were sold, displayed for sale, and otherwise publicly distributed in the state. Such use preceded any use of the trademark by Plaintiff Blue Bell.

5. Plaintiff Blue Bell's shipment of "MR. HICKS" garments carrying a supplemental "TIME OUT" label on July 5, 1973, was an attempt to reserve the trademark for a line of garments or line of business not yet established or existing. Such shipment was a token use insufficient in law to give Plaintiff prior rights to the trademark. Moreover, Plaintiff's claimed first use on such date came after Defendant's first use of the trademark.

Federal jurisdiction is predicated upon diversity of citizenship, since neither party has registered the mark pursuant to the Lanham Act. Given the operative facts surrounding manufacture and shipment from El Paso, the parties agree the Texas law of trademarks controls. In 1967 the state legislature enacted a Trademark Statute. Section 16.02 of the Act explains that a mark is "used" when it is affixed to the goods and "the goods are sold, displayed for sale, or otherwise publicly distributed." Thus the question whether Blue Bell or Farah established priority of trademark use depends upon interpretation of the cited provision. Unfortunately, there are no Texas cases construing § 16.02. This court must therefore determine what principles the highest state court would utilize in deciding such a question. In view of the statute's stated purpose to preserve common law rights, we conclude the Texas Supreme Court would apply the statutory provision in light of general principles of trademark law.

A trademark is a symbol (word, name, device or combination thereof) adopted and used by a merchant to identify his goods and distinguish them from articles produced by others. (Citations omitted). Ownership of a mark requires a combination of both appropriation and use in trade, *United Drug Co. v. Theodore Rectanus Co.,* 248 U.S. 90, 39 S. Ct. 48, 63 L.Ed. 141 (1918). Thus, neither conception of the mark, nor advertising alone establishes trademark rights at common law. Rather, ownership of a trademark accrues when goods bearing the mark are placed on the market.

The exclusive right to a trademark belongs to one who first uses it in connection with specified goods. *McClean v. Fleming,* 96 U.S. 245, 24 L.Ed. 828 (1877); 3 R. Callman, Unfair Competition, Trademarks and Monopolies § 76.2(c) (3d ed. 1969). Such use need not have gained wide public recognition, and even a single use in trade may sustain trademark rights if followed by continuous commercial utilization.

The initial question presented for review is whether Farah's sale and shipment of slacks to twelve regional managers constitutes a valid first use of the Time Out mark. Blue Bell claims the July 3 sale was merely an internal transaction insufficiently public to secure trademark ownership. After consideration of pertinent authorities, we agree.

Secret, undisclosed internal shipments are generally inadequate to support the denomination "use." Trademark claims based upon shipments from a producer's plant to its sales office, and vice versa, have often been disallowed. Though none of the cited cases dealt with sales to intracorporate personnel, we perceive that fact to be a distinction without a difference. The sales were not made to customers, but served as an accounting device to charge the salesmen with their cost in case of loss. The fact that some sales managers actively solicited accounts bolsters the good faith of Farah's intended use, but does not meet our essential objection: that the "sales" were not made to the public.

The primary, perhaps singular purpose of a trademark is to provide a means for the consumer to separate or distinguish one manufacturer's goods from those of another. Personnel within a corporation can identify an item by style number or other unique code. A trademark aids the public in selecting particular goods. As stated by the First Circuit:

> But to hold that a sale or sales are the *sine qua non* of a use sufficient to amount to an appropriation would be to read an unwarranted limitation into the statute, for so construed registration would have to be denied to any manufacturer who adopted a mark to distinguish or identify his product, and perhaps applied it thereon for years, if he should in practice lease his goods rather than sell them, as many manufacturers of machinery do. It seems to us that although evidence of sales is highly persuasive, the question of use adequate to establish appropriation remains one to be decided on the facts of each case, and that evidence showing, first, adoption, and, second, *use in a way sufficiently public to identify or distinguish the marked goods in an appropriate segment of the public mind as those of the adopter of the mark,* is competent to establish ownership. . . .

New England Duplicating Co. v. Mendes, 190 F.2d 415, 418 (1st Cir.1951) (Emphasis added). Similarly, the Trademark Trial and Appeal Board has reasoned:

> To acquire trademark rights there has to be an "open" use, that is to say, a use has to be made to the relevant class of purchasers or prospective purchasers since a trademark is intended to identify goods and distinguish those goods from those manufactured or sold by others. There was no such "open" use rather the use can be said to be an "internal" use, which cannot give rise to trademark rights.

Sterling Drug, Inc. v. Knoll A. G. Chemische Fabriken, supra, at 631.

Farah nonetheless contends that a recent decision of the Board so undermines all prior cases relating to internal use that they should be ignored. In *Standard Pressed Steel Co. v. Midwest Chrome Process Co.,* 183 U.S.P.Q. 758 (T.T.A.B. 1974), the agency held that internal shipment of marked goods from a producer's manufacturing plant to its sales office constitutes a valid "use in commerce" for registration purposes.

An axiom of trademark law has been that the right to register a mark is conditioned upon its actual use in trade. (Citations omitted). Theoretically, then, common law use in trade should precede the use in commerce upon which Lanham Act registration is predicated. Arguably, since only a trademark owner can apply for registration, any activity adequate to create registrable rights must perforce also create trademark rights. A close examination of the Board's decision, however, dispels so mechanical a view. The tribunal took meticulous care to point out that its conclusion related solely to registration use rather than ownership use.

> It has been recognized and especially so in the last few years that, in view of the expenditures involved in introducing a new product on the market generally and the attendant risk involved therein prior to the screening process involved in resorting to the

federal registration system and in the absence of an "intent to use" statute, a token sale or a single shipment in commerce *may be sufficient to support an application to register a trademark* in the Patent Office notwithstanding that the evidence may not show what disposition was made of the product so shipped. That is, the fact that a sale or a shipment of goods bearing a trademark was *designed primarily to lay a foundation for the filing of an application for registration* does not, per se, invalidate any such application or subsequent registration issued thereon.

. . . .

Inasmuch as it is our belief that a most liberal policy should be followed in a situation of this kind *[in which dispute as to priority of use and ownership of a mark is not involved]*, applicant's initial shipment of fasteners, although an intracompany transaction in that it was to a company sales representative, was a bona fide shipment. . . .

Standard Pressed Steel Co. v. Midwest Chrome Process Co., supra, at 764–65 (Emphasis added).

Priority of use and ownership of the Time Out mark are the only issues before this court. The language fashioned by the Board clearly indicates a desire to leave the common law of trademark ownership intact. The decision may demonstrate a reversal of the presumption that ownership rights precede registration rights, but it does not affect our analysis of common law use in trade. Farah had undertaken substantial preliminary steps toward marketing the Time Out garments, but it did not establish ownership of the mark by means of the July 3 shipment to its sales managers. The gist of trademark rights is actual use in trade. *Modular Cinemas of America, Inc. v. Mini Cinemas Corp.*, 348 F. Supp. 578 (S.D.N.Y.1972). Though technically a "sale", the July 3 shipment was not "publicly distributed" within the purview of the Texas statute.

Blue Bell's July 5 shipment similarly failed to satisfy the prerequisites of a bona fide use in trade. Elementary tenets of trademark law require that labels or designs be affixed to the merchandise actually intended to bear the mark in commercial transactions. *Persha v. Armour & Co.*, 239 F.2d 628 (5th Cir.1957). Furthermore, courts have recognized that the usefulness of a mark derives not only from its capacity to identify a certain manufacturer, but also from its ability to differentiate between different classes of goods produced by a single manufacturer. *Western Stove Co. v. George D. Roper Corp.*, 82 F. Supp. 206 (S.D.Cal.1949). Here customers had ordered slacks of the Mr. Hicks species, and Mr. Hicks was the fanciful mark distinguishing these slacks from all others. Blue Bell intended to use the Time Out mark on an entirely new line of men's sportswear, unique in style and cut, though none of the garments had yet been produced.

While goods may be identified by more than one trademark, the use of each mark must be bona fide. (Citation omitted). Mere adoption of a mark without bona fide use, in an attempt to reserve it for the future, will not create trademark rights. (Citation omitted). In the instant case Blue Bell's attachment of a secondary label to an older line of goods manifests a bad faith attempt to reserve a mark. We cannot countenance such activities as a valid use in trade. Blue Bell therefore did not acquire trademark rights by virtue of its July 5 shipment.

We thus hold that neither Farah's July 3 shipment nor Blue Bell's July 5 shipment sufficed to create rights in the Time Out mark. Based on a desire to secure ownership of the mark and superiority over a competitor, both claims of alleged use were chronologically premature. Essentially, they took a time out to litigate their differences too early in the game. The question thus becomes whether we should continue to stop the clock for a remand or make a final call from the appellate bench. While a remand to the district court for further factual development would not be improper in these circumstances, we believe the interests of judicial economy and the parties' desire to terminate the litigation demand that we decide, if possible, which manufacturer first used the mark in trade.

Careful examination of the record discloses that Farah shipped its first order of Time Out clothing to customers in September of 1973. Blue Bell, approximately one month behind its competitor at other relevant stages of development, did not mail its Time Out garments until at least October. Though sales to customers are not the *sine qua non* of trademark use, *see New England Duplicating Co. v. Mendes, supra,* they are determinative in the instant case. These sales constituted the first point at which the public had a chance to associate Time Out with a particular line of sportswear. Therefore, Farah established priority of trademark use; it is entitled to a decree permanently enjoining Blue Bell from utilization of the Time Out trademark on men's garments.

The judgment of the trial court is *affirmed.*

PROBLEMS

1. Your client, Ruprecht Murky, a media mogul, plans to launch a new periodical, *New Greed.* In January 2000, Murky, Inc. announced the impending publication to potential advertisers and sought their purchase of advertising space in the new venture. In February 2000 Murky, Inc. sent mailings to subscribers of its other periodicals, describing the kind of magazine *New Greed* would be, and offering special charter subscription rates. In March 2000 Murky, Inc. published a prototype issue of *New Greed* as a special center insert in one of Murky's nationally distributed magazines, *New Wealth.* The inaugural full issue of *New Greed* hit the newsstands in April 2000.

At the same time Murky, Inc. began elaborating its plans, Market Magazines (a smaller publisher) also determined to release a new publication, coincidentally called *New Greed.* Although Market Magazines was initially unaware of Murky's intended publication, Market learned of it by February. Market accordingly rushed its own production schedule. Later in February, it placed an advertisement in the national financial newspaper, the *Easy Street Journal,* announcing Market's forthcoming *New Greed.* In

March, it sent to newsstands a hastily put-together photocopied issue of *New Greed,* and released conventional four-color professionally printed issues beginning in May 2000.

Who owns the *New Greed* trademark? (Assume no one has filed for federal registration.) Would it make a difference if the periodical Market Magazines released in March were a fully professionally produced issue? *See The New West Corp. v. NYM Company of California, Inc.,* 595 F.2d 1194 (9th Cir.1979). For a more recent treatment of a similar problem, see *Marvel Comics Ltd. v. Defiant,* 837 F.Supp. 546 (S.D.N.Y.1993).

2. In October 1988, Pac–Tel began field testing a radio frequency based system for tracking fleet vehicles and recovering lost or stolen vehicles. In June 1989, Pac–Tel adopted the name Teletrac. In July 1989, Pac–Tel began a comprehensive public relations campaign to market its new service, including distributing press releases and giving interviews to print and electronic media. It also made presentations to prospective customers. In April 1990, Pac–Tel began making its service available on a commercial basis. Pac–Tel's first customer signed on in April 1990, although it did not begin paying for the service until December. From mid–1990 onward, Pac–Tel was developing customers among various vehicle fleet operating enterprises and had agreements with at least twenty four of them.

Meanwhile, in mid–1989, Allen Chance came up with the idea for a lost and found service using attachable tags with unique serial numbers. Finders of lost tagged items would use a toll free telephone number to report their discovery. In June 1989, Chance coined the name "TeleTrak" for the service.

In late summer 1989, Chance obtained a toll free number under the name "TeleTrak Lost and Found Hotline." He also obtained a mail drop and drew up a business plan. In October 1989, an unrelated company, Locksmith Ledger, included Chance's postcard in its own bulk mailing to 35,000 locksmiths. This post card announced the TeleTrak World Wide Toll Free Lost and Found Hotline. Chance received 128 responses from the mailing, but made no sales as a result.

In January 1991, Chance saw advertisements for Pac–Tel's Teletrac service. He conducted a trademark search and discovered no pending application on file with the United States Patent and Trademark Office (PTO). He filed a service mark application for "Teletrak Lost and Found Hotline" and a trademark application for "TeleTrak" claiming first use of the mark on December 28, 1990. Chance later claimed first use in October 1989, the time of the postcard mailer.

In February 1990, Chance sold a TeleTrak tag to a long time friend. Chance produced a one page typewritten registration form he prepared for the tag, number 11229, dated February 23, 1990. Chance could not state, however, how much the friend paid for the tag, how he paid for the tag, nor is there any record reflecting payment.

Pac–Tel has challenged the registration applications filed by Chance. Who first used the mark, as of when? Has either party established use analogous to trademark use sufficient to claim priority? See *Chance v. Pac–Tel Teletrac Inc.*, 242 F.3d 1151 (9th Cir.2001).

PRIORITY AND EXTRATERRITORIAL USE

What difference does it make to the analysis of priority if the senior user has been using the mark in another country? Normally, the principle of territoriality would make non U.S. use irrelevant (but see *Société des Bains de Mer, supra*). An exception for foreign "famous marks" might confer rights in the U.S. when the mark is well-known and the U.S. junior user has adopted the mark after it became famous in this country. Tourism, crossborder advertising and immigration may make a foreign mark, particularly one widely used in a neighboring country, well-known in this one. Such an exception, however, is highly contested, as the following decision illustrates.

ITC Limited v. Punchgini

482 F.3d 135 (2d Cir. 2007).

■ REENA RAGGI, CIRCUIT JUDGE:

This case requires us to decide, among other things, the applicability of the "famous marks" doctrine to a claim for unfair competition under federal and state law. Plaintiffs ITC Limited and ITC Hotels Limited (collectively "ITC") held a registered United States trademark for restaurant services: "Bukhara." They sued defendants, Punchgini, Inc., Bukhara Grill II, Inc., and certain named individuals associated with these businesses, in the United States District Court for the Southern District of New York (Gerard E. Lynch, Judge) claiming that defendants' use of a similar mark and related trade dress constituted trademark infringement, unfair competition, and false advertising in violation of federal and state law. ITC now appeals from the district court's award of summary judgment in favor of defendants on all claims. See ITC Ltd. v. Punchgini, Inc., 373 F. Supp. 2d 275 (S.D.N.Y. 2005).

Having reviewed the record de novo, we affirm the award of summary judgment on ITC's infringement claim, concluding, as did the district court, that ITC abandoned its Bukhara mark for restaurant services in the United States. To the extent ITC insists that the "famous marks" doctrine nevertheless permits it to sue defendants for unfair competition because its continued international use of the mark led to a federally protected right, we conclude that Congress has not yet incorporated that doctrine into federal trademark law.[2] Therefore, we affirm the award of summary

---

2. Although the term "famous marks" is often used to describe marks that qualify for protection under the federal anti-dilution statute, see 15 U.S.C. § 1125(c), the "famous marks" doctrine is, in fact, a different and distinct "legal concept under which a trademark or service mark is protected within a nation if it is well known in that nation even though the mark is not actually used or registered in that nation," 4 J. Thomas McCarthy, McCarthy on Trademarks and Unfair Competition, § 29.2, at 29–164 (4th ed. 2002). Thus, the famous marks doctrine might more aptly be described as the famous foreign marks

judgment on ITC's federal unfair competition claim. Whether the famous marks doctrine applies to a New York common law claim for unfair competition and, if so, how famous a mark must be to trigger that application, are issues not easily re-solved by reference to existing state law. Accordingly, we certify questions relating to these issues to the New York Court of Appeals, reserving our decision on this part of ITC's appeal pending the state court's response.

[The "Bukhrara" restaurant chain is named after a city in Uzbekistan on the legendary Silk Road between China and the West. Bukhara offers cuisine and decor inspired by the northwest frontier region of India. Since the original restaurant's beginnings in New Delhi in 1977, authorized Bukhara restaurants have opened in Hong Kong, Bangkok, Bahrain, Montreal, Bangladesh, Singapore, Kathmandu, Ajman, New York, and Chicago. ITC obtained US trademark registrations. "The Restaurant Magazine" (UK) declared Bukhara the Best Indian Restaurant in the world for 2004. The flagship New Delhi restaurant has also been voted the Best Restaurant in Asia and is the only Indian restaurant listed among the 50 Best Restaurants in the World. World famous celebrities, including Americans Bill Gates and President Clinton, have dined there and the restaurant is listed in leading American guidebooks, such as Frommer's. In 1991 and 1997, however, the New York and then the Chicago restaurants had closed. In 1999 former employees of the New York restaurant opened an unauthorized Bukhara Grill in New York; ITS brought a trademark infringement action alleging prior rights in the mark. The Second Circuit affirmed the district court's holding the ITC had abandoned its US trademark registrations when it closed all of its U.S. restaurants with no concrete plans to continue to offer restaurant services under the Bukhara mark. The court then addressed ITC's invocation of the "famous marks" doctrine.]

[ITC] submits that, because (1) since 1977, it has continuously used its Bukhara mark and trade dress outside the United States; and (2) that mark was renowned in the United States before defendants opened their first Bukhara Grill restaurant in New York in 1999, it has a priority right to the mark sufficient to claim section 43(a)(1)(A) protection in this country.

To explain why we disagree, we begin by discussing the principle of trademark territoriality. We then discuss the famous marks exception to this principle and the international treaties, implementing legislation, and policy concerns relied on by ITC in urging the application of this exception to this case.

a.   The Territoriality Principle

The principle of territoriality is basic to American trademark law. *See American Circuit Breaker Corp. v. Or. Breakers, Inc.*, 406 F.3d 577, 581 (9th Cir. 2005); *Kos Pharms., Inc. v. Andrx Corp.*, 369 F.3d 700, 714 (3d

---

doctrine. It is in this latter sense that we reference the famous marks doctrine on this appeal.

Cir. 2004); *Buti v. Impressa Perosa, S.R.L.*, 139 F.3d 98, 103 (2d Cir. 1998); *Person's Co. v. Christman*, 900 F.2d 1565, 1568–69 (Fed. Cir. 1990). As our colleague, Judge Leval, has explained, this principle recognizes that

> a trademark has a separate legal existence under each country's laws, and that its proper lawful function is not necessarily to specify the origin or manufacture of a good (although it may incidentally do that), but rather to symbolize the domestic goodwill of the domestic mark-holder so that the consuming public may rely with an expectation of consistency on the domestic reputation earned for the mark by its owner, and the owner of the mark may be confident that his goodwill and reputation (the value of the mark) will not be injured through use of the mark by others in domestic commerce.

Osawa & Co. v. B & H Photo, 589 F. Supp. 1163, 1171–72 (S.D.N.Y. 1984).[14]

Precisely because a trademark has a separate legal existence under each country's laws, ownership of a mark in one country does not automatically confer upon the owner the exclusive right to use that mark in another country. Rather, a mark owner must take the proper steps to ensure that its rights to that mark are recognized in any country in which it seeks to assert them. . . .

As we have already noted, United States trademark rights are acquired by, and dependent upon priority of use. The territoriality principle requires the use to be in the United States for the owner to assert priority rights to the mark under the Lanham Act. . . .

b. The Famous Marks Doctrine as an Exception to the Territoriality Principle

ITC urges us to recognize an exception to the territoriality principle for those foreign marks that, even if not used in the United States by their owners, have achieved a certain measure of fame within this country.

(1) Origin of the Famous Marks Doctrine

The famous marks doctrine is no new concept. It originated in the 1925 addition of Article 6bis to the Paris Convention for the Protection of Industrial Property, Mar. 20, 1883, as rev. at Stockholm, July 14, 1967, 21 U.S.T. 1583, 828 U.N.T.S. 305 ("Paris Convention"). Article 6bis, which by its terms applies only to trademarks, requires member states

---

14. The "territoriality principle" stands in contrast to the so-called "universality principle," which posits that "if a trademark [is] lawfully affixed to merchandise in one country, the merchandise would carry that mark lawfully wherever it went and could not be deemed an infringer although transported to another country where the exclusive right to the mark was held by some- one other than the owner of the merchandise." Osawa & Co. v. B & H Photo, 589 F. Supp. at 1171. The universality principle has been rejected in American trademark law. See American Circuit Breaker Corp. v. Or. Breakers, Inc., 406 F.3d at 581 (citing A. Bourjois & Co. v. Katzel, 260 U.S. 689, 43 S. Ct. 244, 67 L. Ed. 464, 1923 Dec. Comm'r Pat. 649 (1923)).

ex officio if their legislation so permits, or at the request of an interested party, to refuse or to cancel the registration, and to prohibit the use, of a trademark which constitutes a reproduction, an imitation, or a translation, liable to create confusion, of a mark considered by the competent authority of the country of registration or use to be well known in that country as being already the mark of a person entitled to the benefits of this Convention and used for identical or similar goods. These provisions shall also apply when the essential part of the mark constitutes a reproduction of any such well-known mark or an imitation liable to create confusion therewith.

Paris Convention, art. 6bis.[15] One commentator has observed that the "purpose" of Article 6bis "is to avoid the registration and use of a trademark, liable to create confusion with another mark already well known in the country of such registration or use, although the latter well-known mark is not, or not yet, protected in that country by a registration which would normally prevent the registration or use of the conflicting mark." G.H.C. Bodenhausen, Guide to the Application of the Paris Convention for the Protection of Industrial Property 90 (1968).

(2) The Famous Marks Doctrine in the United States

(a) State Common Law

The famous marks doctrine appears first to have been recognized in the United States by a New York trial court in a common law action for unfair competition in the use of a trademark. *See Maison Prunier v. Prunier's Rest. & Cafe*, 159 Misc. 551, 557–58, 288 N.Y.S. 529, 535–36 (N.Y. Sup. Ct. 1936). The owner of "Maison Prunier," a Paris restaurant with a branch in London, sought to enjoin defendants' operation of a New York City restaurant named "Prunier's Restaurant and Cafe." The New York restaurant had apparently adopted both the Paris restaurant's name and slogan ("Tout ce qui vient de la mer")[16] and boldly advertised itself as "The Famous French Sea Food Restaurant." While the French plaintiff conceded that it had never operated a restaurant in the United States, it nevertheless sought relief for the unauthorized use of its name and mark under the common law of unfair competition.

In ruling in favor of the plaintiff, the trial court first observed that "the right of a French corporation to sue here for protection against unfair competition was expressly granted in [Article 10bis of] the [Paris] convention between the United States and various other powers for the protection of industrial property." *Id.* at 554, 288 N.Y.S. at 532.[17] It then ruled that

---

15. The reach of Article 6bis was extended to service marks by Article 16(2) of the Agreement on Trade-Related Aspects of Intellectual Property Rights ("TRIPs"), see generally Uruguay Round Agreements Act, Pub. L. No. 103–465, 108 Stat. 4809 (1994) (codified as amended at scattered sections of the United States Code), which states that "Article 6bis of the Paris Convention shall apply, mutatis mutandis, to services."

16. "Everything that comes from the sea."

17. Article 10bis of the Paris Convention requires member states to "assure to nationals [of other member states] effective protection against unfair competition." Paris Convention, art. 10bis.

"actual competition in a product is not essential to relief under the doctrine of unfair competition." *Id.* at 555, 288 N.Y.S. at 533. The plaintiff was entitled to protection from "any injury which might result to it from the deception of the public through the unauthorized use of its trade name, or a trade name which would lead the public to believe that it was in some way connected with the plaintiff." *Id.* at 556, 288 N.Y.S. at 534 ... The Prunier court concluded that the French plaintiff was entitled to protection against unfair competition because its trademark enjoyed "wide repute" and the facts of the case indicated a total lack of good faith on the part of the defendants. *Id.* at 559, 288 N.Y.S. at 537. The basis of this holding, it should be noted, was not Article 6bis of the Paris Convention. Instead, the holding was based entirely on New York common law principles of unfair competition.

More than twenty years later, in *Vaudable v. Montmartre, Inc.*, 20 Misc. 2d 757, 193 N.Y.S.2d 332 (N.Y. Sup. Ct. 1959), another New York trial court granted a different Paris restaurant, "Maxim's," injunctive relief against a New York City restaurant that had appropriated its name, decor, and distinctive script style, all without permission. The court concluded that the lack of direct competition between the two restaurants was "immaterial" to a common law claim for unfair competition. *Id.* at 759, 193 N.Y.S.2d at 335. The only relevant question was whether "there had been a misappropriation, for the advantage of one person, of a property right belonging to another." *Id.* at 759, 193 N.Y.S.2d at 335. Noting that the Paris Maxim's had been in continuous operation since 1946, when it reopened after World War II, the court concluded that its owners had priority rights as against the junior American user by virtue of (1) their uninterrupted use of the mark abroad, and (2) the fame of the "Maxim's" mark among "the class of people residing in the cosmopolitan city of New York who dine out." *Id.* 758, 193 N.Y.S.2d at 334.

(b) Federal Actions

(i) Trademark Board Rulings

A quarter century later, the federal Trademark Trial and Appeal Board ("Trademark Board") invoked Vaudable's recognition of the famous marks doctrine in several inter partes proceedings. In *Mother's Rests., Inc. v. Mother's Other Kitchen, Inc.*, the Trademark Board stated in dictum that:

> [I]t is our view that prior use and advertising of a mark in connection with goods or services marketed in a foreign country (whether said advertising occurs inside or outside the United States) creates no priority rights in said mark in the United States as against one who, in good faith, has adopted the same or similar mark for the same or similar goods or services in the United States prior to the foreigner's first use of the mark on goods or services sold and/or offered in the United States at least unless it can be shown that the foreign party's mark was, at the time of the adoption and first use of a similar mark

by the first user in the United States, a "famous" mark within the meaning of *Vaudable v. Montmartre, Inc.*

218 U.S.P.Q. 1046 (T.T.A.B. 1983) (concluding that customers would be likely to confuse the "Mother's Pizza Parlour" trademark with the "Mother's Other Kitchen" trademark) (internal citation omitted).

That same year, the Trademark Board applied the same reasoning in *All England Lawn Tennis Club, Ltd. v. Creative Aromatiques*, 220 U.S.P.Q. 1069 (T.T.A.B. 1983), granting plaintiff's request to block registration of a trademark for "Wimbledon Cologne" even though plaintiff was not itself using the Wimbledon mark on any product sold in the United States. The Trademark Board observed that the Wimbledon mark had "acquired fame and notoriety as used in association with the annual championships within the meaning of Vaudable" and that "purchasers of applicant's cologne would incorrectly believe that said product was approved by or otherwise associated with the Wimbledon tennis championships and that allowance of the application would damage opposer's rights to the mark." *Id.* 218 U.S.P.Q. 1046.

Recently, the Trademark Board has reiterated in dicta that owners of well known foreign marks need not use those marks in the United States to challenge the registration of marks likely to promote confusion on the part of consumers. *See, e.g., First Niagara Ins. Brokers, Inc. v. First Niagara Fin. Group, Inc.*, 77 U.S.P.Q.2d 1334 (2005), overruled on other grounds by *First Niagara Ins. Brokers, Inc. v. First Niagara Fin. Group, Inc.*, No. 06–1202, 2007 U.S. App. LEXIS 367 (Fed. Cir. Jan. 9, 2007).

As this court has frequently observed, Trademark Board decisions, "while not binding on courts within this Circuit, are nevertheless 'to be accorded great weight'" under general principles of administrative law requiring deference to an agency's interpretation of the statutes it is charged with administering. *Buti v. Impressa Perosa S.R.L.*, 139 F.3d at 105 (quoting *Murphy Door Bed Co. v. Interior Sleep Sys., Inc.*, 874 F.2d 95, 101 (2d Cir. 1989)); *see also In re Dr Pepper Co.*, 836 F.2d 508, 510 (Fed. Cir. 1987). In applying this principle to this case, however, we identify a significant concern: nowhere in the three cited rulings does the Trademark Board state that its recognition of the famous marks doctrine derives from any provision of the Lanham Act or other federal law. Indeed, the federal basis for the Trademark Board's recognition of the famous marks doctrine is never expressly stated. Its reliance on *Vaudable* suggests that recognition derives from state common law. At least one Trademark Board member, however, has questioned whether state common law can support recognition of the famous marks doctrine as a matter of federal law:

> [I]t seems to me that the *Vaudable* decision according protection to the famous Maxim's restaurant in the United States ... is inapplicable in this case since that decision was based on a theory of unfair competition, namely misappropriation, under the law of the State of New York. Under Federal law, it seems to me that application of the well-known marks doctrine depends on whether the applicable text of the Paris

Convention ... and, in particular, Article 6bis of that Convention, is self-executing [so as to become part of federal law].

Mother's Rests., Inc. v. Mother's Other Kitchen, Inc., 1983 TTAB LEXIS 117, 218 U.S.P.Q. 1046, at *21 (Allen, concurring in part, dissenting in part) (internal citations omitted). Because we conclude that the Trademark Board's reliance on state law to recognize the famous marks doctrine falls outside the sphere to which we owe deference, we consider de novo the question of that doctrine's existence within federal trademark law.

(ii) Federal Case Law

To date, the Ninth Circuit Court of Appeals is the only federal appeals court to have recognized the famous marks doctrine as a matter of federal law. *See Grupo Gigante S.A. de C.V. v. Dallo & Co.*, 391 F.3d at 1088; cf. *International Bancorp, LLC v. Societe des Bains de Mer et du Cercle des Etrangers à Monaco*, 329 F.3d at 389 n.9 (Motz, J., dissenting) (noting that the famous marks doctrine has been applied so infrequently that its viability is uncertain). In *Grupo Gigante*, 391 F.3d at 1088, the Ninth Circuit considered whether the "Gigante" mark—registered and used by a large chain of grocery stores in Mexico since 1963—was sufficiently well known among Mexican–Americans in Southern California to afford it priority over a competing "Gigante" mark used by a separate chain of Los Angeles grocery stores. In resolving this question, the court ruled:

> [T]here is a famous mark exception to the territoriality principle. While the territoriality principle is a long-standing and important doctrine within trademark law, it cannot be absolute. An absolute territoriality rule without a famous-mark exception would promote consumer confusion and fraud. Commerce crosses borders. In this nation of immigrants, so do people. Trademark is, at its core, about protecting against consumer confusion and "palming off." There can be no justification for using trademark law to fool immigrants into thinking that they are buying from the store they liked back home.

Id. at 1094 (footnotes omitted).

In *Grupo Gigante*, the Ninth Circuit did not reference either the language of the Lanham Act nor Article 6bis of the Paris Convention to support recognition of the famous marks doctrine. Indeed, elsewhere in its opinion, the court specifically stated that the Paris Convention creates no "additional substantive rights" to those provided by the Lanham Act. *Id.* at 1100. The court also acknowledged that the famous marks doctrine is not recognized by California state law. *See id.* at 1101 (observing that cases cited by plaintiff "provide no support for the conclusion that use anywhere in the world suffices to establish priority in California"). Thus, it appears that the Ninth Circuit recognized the famous marks doctrine as a matter of sound policy: "An absolute territoriality rule without a famous marks exception would promote customer confusion and fraud." *Id.* at 1094.

This court has twice referenced the famous marks doctrine, but on neither occasion were we required to decide whether it does, in fact, provide a legal basis for acquiring priority rights in the United States for a foreign mark not used in this country. *See Buti v. Impressa Perosa, S.R.L.,* 139 F.3d at 104 n.2 (referencing Mother's Restaurant and Vaudable but, in the end, concluding that famous marks doctrine "has no application here given that Impressa has made no claim under that doctrine"); *see also Empresa Cubana del Tabaco v. Culbro Corp.,* 399 F.3d at 481 (declining to decide whether famous marks doctrine should be recognized because "even assuming that the famous marks doctrine is otherwise viable and applicable, the [Cuban] embargo bars [plaintiff] from acquiring property rights in the . . . mark through the doctrine").[19]

(c) Treaties Protecting Famous Marks and United States Implementing Legislation

ITC insists that Article 6bis of the Paris Convention, together with Article 16(2) of the Agreement on Trade–Related Aspects of Intellectual Property Rights ("TRIPs"), see Uruguay Round Agreements Act, Pub. L. No. 103–465, 108 Stat. 4809 (1994) (codified as amended at scattered sections of United States Code), provides legal support for its claim to famous marks protection. As previously noted, Article 6bis provides for member states to the Paris Convention, upon the request of an interested party,

> to prohibit the use of a trademark which constitutes a reproduction, an imitation, or a translation, liable to create confusion, of a mark considered by the competent authority of the country of registration or use to be well known in that country as being already the mark of a person entitled to the benefits of this Convention and used for identical or similar goods.

Paris Convention, art. 6bis. Further, TRIPs Article 16(2) extends Article 6 bis to service marks. . . .

[The court held that neither Paris Conv. art 6bis and TRIPs art. 16(2), nor Paris Conv. art. 10bis (addressing unfair competition) were self-executing and had not been implemented through § 44 of the Lanham Act.] . . . .

We further note that, in section 44(d) of the Lanham Act, Congress detailed circumstances under which the holders of foreign registered marks can claim priority rights in the United States, notably including among those circumstances actual or intended use in the United States within a specified time. See 15 U.S.C. § 1126(d) (affording United States priority rights from date of foreign registration if, *inter alia,* application for United States registration is filed within six months along with a statement of bona fide intent to use marks in commerce, but denying mark holder right to sue for acts committed prior to United States registration unless

---

19. In Empresa Cubana, however, we did observe, in dictum, that "[t]o the extent that a foreign entity attempts to utilize the famous marks doctrine as [a] basis for its right to a U.S. trade-mark and seeks to prevent another entity from using the mark in the United States, the claim should be brought under Section 43(a)." Id. at 480 n.10.

registration based on actual use in commerce).[26] Congress's specificity in dealing with registered marks cautions against reading a famous marks exception into sections 44(b) and (h), which nowhere reference the doctrine, much less the circumstances under which it would appropriately apply despite the fact that the foreign mark was not used in this country. We are mindful that Congress has not hesitated to amend the Lanham Act to effect its intent with respect to trademark protection, having done so almost thirty times since the statute took effect in 1947. See 1 McCarthy, supra, §§ 5–5–11, at 5–13–22. In light of these legislative efforts, the absence of any statutory provision expressly incorporating the famous marks doctrine or Articles 6bis and 16(2) is all the more significant. Before we construe the Lanham Act to include such a significant departure from the principle of territoriality, we will wait for Congress to express its intent more clearly.

(d) Policy Rationales Cannot, by Themselves, Support Judicial Recognition of the Famous Marks Doctrine Under Federal Law

Even if the Lanham Act does not specifically incorporate Article 6bis and Article 16(2) protections for famous foreign marks, ITC urges this court to follow the Ninth Circuit's lead and to recognize the famous marks doctrine as a matter of sound policy. *See Grupo Gigante S.A. de C.V. v. Dallo & Co.*, 391 F.3d at 1094 (recognizing famous marks doctrine because "[t]here can be no justification for using trademark law to fool immigrants into thinking that they are buying from the store they liked back home"). ITC argues that the United States cannot expect other nations to protect famous American trademarks if United States courts decline to afford reciprocal protection to famous foreign marks.

We acknowledge that a persuasive policy argument can be advanced in support of the famous marks doctrine. *See, e.g., De Beers LV Trademark Ltd. v. DeBeers Diamond Syndicate, Inc.*, 2005 U.S. Dist. LEXIS 9307, at *25 (noting that "[r]ecognition of the famous marks doctrine is particularly desirable in a world where international travel is commonplace and where the Internet and other media facilitate the rapid creation of business goodwill that transcends borders"); Frederick W. Mostert, Well–Known and Famous Marks: Is Harmony Possible in the Global Village?, 86 Trademark Rep. 103, 106 (1996) (arguing that "protection of the global trading system through the prevention of piracy and unfair exploitation of well-known marks has become essential"). The fact that a doctrine may promote sound policy, however, is not a sufficient ground for its judicial recognition, particularly in an area regulated by statute.... In light of the comprehensive and frequently modified federal statutory scheme for trademark protection set forth in the Lanham Act, we conclude that any policy arguments in favor of the famous marks doctrine must be submitted to Congress for it to determine whether and under what circumstances to accord federal

---

26. Because territoriality is the bedrock principle of trademark law, we understand the reference to "use in commerce" in the Lanham Act to contemplate use that, at some point in the transaction, implicates the United States.

recognition to such an exception to the basic principle of territoriality. *See Almacenes Exito S.A. v. El Gallo Meat Mkt., Inc.*, 381 F. Supp. 2d at 326–28. Absent such Congressional recognition, we must decline ITC's invitation to grant judicial recognition to the famous marks doctrine simply as a matter of sound policy. . . .

QUESTIONS

1. Having ruled that the "famous marks" doctrine exists only as a matter of state law, the Second Circuit certified the following questions to the New York Court of Appeals: Does New York recognize the famous marks doctrine? How famous must a mark be to come within the famous marks doctrine? With respect to the latter inquiry, the court suggested the New York court might clarify whether, assuming New York protects foreign famous marks, the standard was "secondary meaning plus," or a higher level, such as the fame required for antidilution protection. The court also referred to criteria set out in the World Intellectual Property Organization, Joint Recommendation Concerning Provisions on the Protection of Well–Known Marks (Sept. 1999), available at http://www.wipo.int/aboutip/en/development_iplaw/pub833.htm. Does it make sense to remit the questions of the existence and scope of the foreign famous marks doctrine to the 50 separate States? Do the potential consequences of this approach underlie the Second Circuit's suggestion that the New York Court of Appeals apply the WIPO criteria?

2. The court appears to recognize the shortcomings of the doctrine of territoriality in a world of cross-border consumer mobility, advertising, and Internet sales, see also Graeme Austin, The Story of Steele v. Bulova: Trademarks on the Line, in Jane C. Ginsburg and Rochelle Cooper Dreyfuss, INTELLECTUAL PROPERTY STORIES 395 (2006) (discussing "the tension between territoriality as a legal theory and the reality of the way goodwill in a brand gets to be created and expanded"). Nonetheless the Second Circuit concludes that the Lanham Act forecloses judicial adoption of the famous marks exception. Are you persuaded that the statute resists policy-informed interpretation in this context? Can you think of examples where courts have added policy glosses? Are they distinguishable?

Exceptions to Use–Based Priority

As we will see in the next chapter, on registration of trademarks, the first user's priority of rights yields to prior applicants for registration in two circumstances. First, an application filed under the § 1(b) intent to use procedure will trump a first user if the application's filing date predates the third party's actual use. Second, an application to register a foreign mark based on an application filed in the foreign country of origin up to six months before the U.S. filing will be given priority over a trademark first used in the U.S. before the U.S. filing, but after the date of the original foreign filing.

F.   CONCURRENT USE

United Drug Co. v. Theodore Rectanus Co.

248 U.S. 90 (1918).

■ MR. JUSTICE PITNEY delivered the opinion of the Court:

This was a suit in equity brought September 24, 1912, in the United States District Court for the Western District of Kentucky, by the present petitioner, a Massachusetts corporation, against the respondent, a Kentucky corporation, together with certain individual citizens of the latter State, to restrain infringement of trade-mark and unfair competition.

The essential facts are as follows: About the year 1877 Ellen M. Regis, a resident of Haverhill, Massachusetts, began to compound and distribute in a small way a preparation for medicinal use in cases of dyspepsia and some other ailments, to which she applied as a distinguishing name the word "Rex"—derived from her surname. The word was put upon the boxes and packages in which the medicine was placed upon the market, after the usual manner of a trade-mark. At first alone, and afterwards in partnership with her son under the firm name of "E. M. Regis & Company," she continued the business on a modest scale; in 1898 she recorded the word "Rex" as a trademark under the laws of Massachusetts; in 1900 the firm procured its registration in the United States Patent Office; in 1904 the Supreme Court of Massachusetts sustained their trade-mark right under the state law as against a concern that was selling medicinal preparations of the present petitioner under the designation of "Rexall remedies"; afterwards the firm established priority in the mark as against petitioner in a contested proceeding in the Patent Office; and subsequently, in the year 1911, petitioner purchased the business with the trade-mark right, and has carried it on in connection with its other business, which consists in the manufacture of medicinal preparations, and their distribution and sale through retail drug stores, known as "Rexall stores," situate in the different States of the Union, four of them being in Louisville, Kentucky.

Meanwhile, about the year 1883, Theodore Rectanus, a druggist in Louisville, familiarly known as "Rex," employed this word as a trade-mark for a medicinal preparation known as a "blood purifier." He continued this use to a considerable extent in Louisville and vicinity, spending money in advertising and building up a trade, so that—except for whatever effect might flow from Mrs. Regis' prior adoption of the word in Massachusetts, of which he was entirely ignorant—he was entitled to use the word as his trade-mark. In the year 1906 he sold his business, including the right to the use of the word, to respondent; and the use of the mark by him and afterwards by respondent was continuous from about the year 1883 until the filing of the bill in the year 1912.

Petitioner's first use of the word "Rex" in connection with the sale of drugs in Louisville or vicinity was in April, 1912, when two shipments of

"Rex Dyspepsia Tablets," aggregating 150 boxes and valued at $22.50, were sent to one of the "Rexall" stores in that city. Shortly after this the remedy was mentioned by name in local newspaper advertisements published by those stores. In the previous September, petitioner shipped a trifling amount—five boxes—to a drug store in Franklin, Kentucky, approximately 120 miles distant from Louisville. There is nothing to show that before this any customer in or near Kentucky had heard of the Regis remedy, with or without the description "Rex," or that this word ever possessed any meaning to the purchasing public in that State except as pointing to Rectanus and the Rectanus Company and their "blood purifier." That it did and does convey the latter meaning in Louisville and vicinity is proved without dispute. Months before petitioner's first shipment of its remedy to Kentucky, petitioner was distinctly notified (in June, 1911,) by one of its Louisville distributors that respondent was using the word "Rex" to designate its medicinal preparations, and that such use had been commenced by Mr. Rectanus as much as 16 or 17 years before that time.

There was nothing to sustain the allegation of unfair competition, aside from the question of trade-mark infringement. As to this, both courts found, in substance, that the use of the same mark upon different but somewhat related preparations was carried on by the parties and their respective predecessors contemporaneously, but in widely separated localities, during the period in question—between 25 and 30 years—in perfect good faith, neither side having any knowledge or notice of what was being done by the other. The District Court held that because the adoption of the mark by Mrs. Regis antedated its adoption by Rectanus, petitioner's right to the exclusive use of the word in connection with medicinal preparations intended for dyspepsia and kindred diseases of the stomach and digestive organs must be sustained, but without accounting for profits or assessment of damages for unfair trade. (Citations omitted). The Circuit Court of Appeals held that in view of the fact that Rectanus had used the mark for a long period of years in entire ignorance of Mrs. Regis' remedy or of her trade-mark, had expended money in making his mark well known, and had established a considerable though local business under it in Louisville and vicinity, while on the other hand during the same long period Mrs. Regis had done nothing, either by sales agencies or by advertising, to make her medicine or its mark known outside of the New England States, saving sporadic sales in territory adjacent to those States, and had made no effort whatever to extend the trade to Kentucky, she and her successors were bound to know that, misled by their silence and inaction, others might act, as Rectanus and his successors did act, upon the assumption that the field was open, and therefore were estopped to ask for an injunction against the continued use of the mark in Louisville and vicinity by the Rectanus Company.

The entire argument for the petitioner is summed up in the contention that whenever the first user of a trade-mark has been reasonably diligent in extending the territory of his trade, and as a result of such extension has in good faith come into competition with a later user of the same mark who in equal good faith has extended his trade locally before invasion of his field by the first user, so that finally it comes to pass that the rival traders are offering competitive merchandise in a common market under the same trade-mark, the later user should be enjoined at the suit of the prior adopter, even though the latter be the last to enter the competitive field and the former have already established a trade there. Its application to the case is based upon the hypothesis that the record shows that Mrs. Regis and her firm, during the entire period of limited and local trade in her medicine under the Rex mark, were making efforts to extend their trade so far as they were able to do with the means at their disposal. There is little in the record to support this hypothesis; but, waiving this, we will pass upon the principal contention.

The asserted doctrine is based upon the fundamental error of supposing that a trade-mark right is a right in gross or at large, like a statutory copyright or a patent for an invention, to either of which, in truth, it has little or no analogy. (Citations omitted). There is no such thing as property in a trade-mark except as a right appurtenant to an established business or trade in connection with which the mark is employed. The law of trade-marks is but a part of the broader law of unfair competition; the right to a particular mark grows out of its use, not its mere adoption; its function is simply to designate the goods as the product of a particular trader and to protect his good will against the sale of another's product as his; and it is not the subject of property except in connection with an existing business. *Hanover Milling Co. v. Metcalf*, 240 U.S. 403, 412–414.

The owner of a trade-mark may not, like the proprietor of a patented invention, make a negative and merely prohibitive use of it as a monopoly. [Citations omitted].

In truth, a trade-mark confers no monopoly whatever in a proper sense, but is merely a convenient means for facilitating the protection of one's goodwill in trade by placing a distinguishing mark or symbol—a commercial signature—upon the merchandise or the package in which it is sold.

It results that the adoption of a trade-mark does not, at least in the absence of some valid legislation enacted for the purpose, project the right of protection in advance of the extension of the trade, or operate as a claim of territorial rights over areas into which it thereafter may be deemed desirable to extend the trade. And the expression, sometimes met with, that a trade-mark right is not limited in its enjoyment by territorial bounds, is true only in the sense that wherever the trade goes, attended by the use of the mark, the right of the trader to be protected against the sale by others of their wares in the place of his wares will be sustained.

Property in trade-marks and the right to their exclusive use rest upon the laws of the several States, and depend upon them for security and protection; the power of Congress to legislate on the subject being only such as arises from the authority to regulate commerce with foreign nations and among the several States and with the Indian tribes. *Trade-Mark Cases*, 100 U.S. 82, 93.

Conceding everything that is claimed in behalf of the petitioner, the entire business conducted by Mrs. Regis and her firm prior to April, 1911, when petitioner acquired it, was confined to the New England States with inconsiderable sales in New York, New Jersey, Canada, and Nova Scotia. There was nothing in all of this to give her any rights in Kentucky, where the principles of the common law obtain. (Citations omitted). We are referred to no decision by the courts of that State, and have found none, that lays down any peculiar doctrine upon the subject of trade-mark law. There is some meager legislation, but none that affects this case....

It is not contended, nor is there ground for the contention, that registration of the Regis trade-mark under either the Massachusetts statute or the act of Congress, or both, had the effect of enlarging the rights of Mrs. Regis or of petitioner beyond what they would be under common-law principles. Manifestly, the Massachusetts statute could have no extraterritorial effect.... Nor is there any provision making registration equivalent to notice of rights claimed thereunder....

Undoubtedly, the general rule is that, as between conflicting claimants to the right to use the same mark, priority of appropriation determines the question. (Citations omitted). But the reason is that purchasers have come to understand the mark as indicating the origin of the wares, so that its use by a second producer amounts to an attempt to sell his goods as those of his competitor. The reason for the rule does not extend to a case where the same trade-mark happens to be employed simultaneously by two manufacturers in different markets separate and remote from each other, so that the mark means one thing in one market, an entirely different thing in another. It would be a perversion of the rule of priority to give it such an application in our broadly extended country that an innocent party who had in good faith employed a trade-mark in one State, and by the use of it had built up a trade there, being the first appropriator in that jurisdiction, might afterwards be prevented from using it, with consequent injury to his trade and good-will, at the instance of one who theretofore had employed the same mark but only in other and remote jurisdictions, upon the ground that its first employment happened to antedate that of the first-mentioned trader.

In several cases federal courts have held that a prior use of a trade-mark in a foreign country did not entitle its owner to claim exclusive trade-mark rights in the United States as against one who in good faith had adopted a like trade-mark here prior to the entry of the foreigner into this market. [Citations omitted].

The same point was involved in *Hanover Milling Co. v. Metcalf*, 240 U.S. 403, 415, where we said: "In the ordinary case of parties competing under the same mark in the same market, it is correct to say that prior appropriation settles the question. But where two parties independently are employing the same mark upon goods of the same class, but in separate markets wholly remote the one from the other, the question of prior appropriation is legally insignificant, unless at least it appear that the second adopter has selected the mark with some design inimical to the interests of the first user, such as to take the benefit of the reputation of his goods, to forestall the extension of his trade, or the like.''

In this case, as already remarked, there is no suggestion of a sinister purpose on the part of Rectanus or the Rectanus Company; hence the passage quoted correctly defines the status of the parties prior to the time when they came into competition in the Kentucky market. And it results, as a necessary inference from what we have said, that petitioner, being the newcomer in that market, must enter it subject to whatever rights had previously been acquired there in good faith by the Rectanus Company and its predecessor. To hold otherwise—to require Rectanus to retire from the field upon the entry of Mrs. Regis' successor—would be to establish the right of the latter as a right in gross, and to extend it to territory wholly remote from the furthest reach of the trade to which it was annexed, with the effect not merely of depriving Rectanus of the benefit of the good-will resulting from his long-continued use of the mark in Louisville and vicinity, and his substantial expenditures in building up his trade, but of enabling petitioner to reap substantial benefit from the publicity that Rectanus has thus given to the mark in that locality, and of confusing if not misleading the public as to the origin of goods thereafter sold in Louisville under the Rex mark, for, in that market, until petitioner entered it, ''Rex'' meant the Rectanus product, not that of Regis.

. . . .

Here the essential facts are so closely parallel to those that furnished the basis of decision in the *Allen & Wheeler Case,* reported *sub nom. Hanover Milling Co. v. Metcalf,* 240 U.S. 403, 419–420, as to render further discussion unnecessary. Mrs. Regis and her firm, having during a long period of years confined their use of the ''Rex'' mark to a limited territory wholly remote from that in controversy, must be held to have taken the risk that some innocent party might in the meantime hit upon the same mark, apply it to goods of similar character, and expend money and effort in building up a trade under it; and since it appears that Rectanus in good faith, and without notice of any prior use by others, selected and used the ''Rex'' mark, and by the expenditure of money and effort succeeded in building up a local but valuable trade under it in Louisville and vicinity before petitioner entered that field, so that ''Rex'' had come to be recognized there as the ''trade signature'' of Rectanus and of respondent as his successor, petitioner is estopped to set up their continued use of the mark in that territory as an infringement of the Regis trade-mark. Whatever confusion may have arisen from conflicting use of the mark is attributable to petitioner's entry into the field with notice of the situation; and petitioner cannot complain of this. . . .

Decree *affirmed.*

QUESTION

The *Rectanus* opinion concerns concurrent terrestrial use. What, if any, difference would it make if the senior user of the mark offered its goods via a website accessible throughout the US, and the junior user purveyed its goods from bricks-and-mortar stores located in a small number of states? What if the junior user also had a website? See also Chapter 4.B. *infra*.

Thrifty Rent–A–Car System v. Thrift Cars, Inc.

831 F.2d 1177 (1st Cir.1987).

■ DAVIS, CIRCUIT JUDGE:

In this trademark infringement suit brought by Thrifty Rent-a-Car System, Inc. (Thrifty), that firm and defendant Thrift Cars, Inc. (Thrift Cars) both appeal the decision of the district court for the District of Massachusetts (Young, J.), 639 F. Supp. 750. After a bench trial, the court enjoined Thrift Cars from conducting a car or truck rental or leasing business outside of Taunton, Massachusetts under the "Thrift Cars" name, and limited Thrift Cars' advertising to those media it had used prior to July 26, 1964, the date that Thrifty obtained federal registration of its own mark. Concomitantly, the court prohibited Thrifty from operating any of its business establishments in East Taunton, Massachusetts or from advertising in any media principally intended to target the East Taunton community. We affirm.

I. *Background*

A. *Thrifty Rent-a-Car System, Inc.*

Thrifty Rent-a-Car System traces its beginnings to March 3, 1958 when L.C. Crow, an individual, began renting cars in Tulsa, Oklahoma, under the tradename "Thrifty." In 1962, Stemmons, Inc., an Oklahoma corporation, purchased Crow's business and expanded the business to Houston, Texas, renting automobiles to customers under the "Thrifty" tradename. Stemmons subsequently changed its name to The Thrifty Rent-a-Car System, Inc. and expanded the business to Wichita, Kansas, Dallas, Texas and St. Louis, Missouri. On July 30, 1962, Thrifty Rent-a-Car made an application to the United States Patent Office to register the service mark "Thrifty Rent-a-Car System" and was granted that mark in July 1964. Thrifty expanded the business through both franchises and directly-owned rental agencies. In December 1967, a Thrifty Rent-a-Car outlet opened in Massachusetts. By the time of trial, Thrifty had become the fifth largest car rental agency worldwide, and operated car rental outlets in 23 locations in Massachusetts.

B. *Thrift Cars, Inc.*

Thrift Cars' rental business began in October 1962 and was incorporated in Massachusetts as Thrift Cars, Inc. Thrift Cars' owner and proprietor, Peter A. Conlon, at first began a modest car-rental service out of his home in East Taunton, Massachusetts. The East Taunton business was largely limited to what the car-rental industry considers a "tertiary market," that is, the market that serves individuals needing replacement cars to bridge the short term car rental and the longer term automobile lease. Thrift Cars provided customized service, arranging delivery of the rental car to the customer as well as pick-up at the termination of the rental period. In the years immediately following 1962, Thrift Cars delivered automobiles to Boston's Logan Airport and to various cities on Cape Cod and to Nantucket. Prior to Thrifty's federal registration in July 1964, Thrift Cars advertised in the Taunton area yellow pages telephone directory, in The Taunton Daily Gazette, The Cape Cod Times (a newspaper of general circulation servicing Cape Cod, Martha's Vineyard, and Nantucket) and in The Anchor (the newspaper of the Roman Catholic Diocese of Fall River). In 1963 Thrift Cars also advertised in The Inquirer and Mirror, a Nantucket newspaper. In 1970, some six years after Thrifty had obtained federal registration of its mark, Thrift Cars received a license to operate a car rental facility at the Nantucket airport, and Conlon, Thrift Cars' Chief Executive Officer, moved the major portion of the business to Nantucket.

The Nantucket facility, unlike the operation at East Taunton, was operated largely as a traditional car rental service, servicing the resort market. Customers came directly to the airport to arrange for rental and pick-up of the automobile. Thrift Cars' post–1970 Nantucket operation thus came into a direct clash with Thrifty, which was also operating a car rental facility directed to the resort market in the Cape Cod area.

C.   Litigation Below

Thrifty brought this action against Thrift Cars in federal district court, alleging trademark infringement and false designation of title under the Lanham Act. 15 U.S.C. § 1125(a) and §§ 1051–1127. The parties stipulated that the Thrift and Thrifty names are confusingly similar—as, of course, they are. The trial court found that Thrift Cars' business activities as of the critical date of July 26, 1964 (the date of Thrifty's registration) did not extend to areas beyond East Taunton, Massachusetts. The district court then enjoined Thrift Cars from using "Thrift" in conducting a car rental business outside of Taunton. The court also enjoined Thrift Cars from advertising in media directed outside of East Taunton, except in publications in which Thrift Cars had advertised prior to July 26, 1964.

Conversely, the court enjoined Thrifty from operating any business establishment in East Taunton and prohibited it from advertising in any media principally intended to target the East Taunton area.

Both parties appealed. Thrift Cars claims that the court erred by limiting its car rental activities under the "Thrift" name to Taunton, urging that this court expand its permissible business activities to southeastern Massachusetts, including Nantucket. Thrifty's cross-appeal argues that the district court erred in allowing Thrift Cars to conduct business in any locality under the Thrift Cars name because the business had not been continuous until trial, as required under the Lanham Act. In the alternative, Thrifty urges that the scope of Thrift Cars' business activities should be limited to East Taunton, not Taunton, because the record indicates that Thrift Cars' business had been limited to East Taunton, not to Taunton, prior to Thrifty's 1964 federal registration. Thrifty also says that the district court allowed Thrift Cars too broad an advertising base since it permitted Thrift Cars to advertise in publications directed outside of East Taunton.

II. *Discussion*

. . . .

Section 15 of the Lanham Act, 15 U.S.C. § 1065, provides that a party like Thrifty, which has successfully registered and continued using a federal service mark, has an incontestable right to use the mark throughout the United States in connection with the goods or services with which it has been used. *See Giant Food, Inc. v. Nation's Foodservice, Inc.,* 710 F.2d 1565, 1568 (Fed.Cir.1983). Lanham Act registration also puts all would-be users of the mark (or a confusingly similar mark) on constructive notice of the mark. 15 U.S.C. § 1072.

A. *"Limited area exception"*

However, Lanham Act § 33(b), 15 U.S.C. § 1115(b)(5), declares a "limited area" exception to that general premise of incontestability, an exception which the district court concluded was applicable in this case. The essence of the exception embodied in § 1115(b)(5) is based on common law trademark protection for remote users established by the Supreme Court in *Hanover Star Milling Co. v. Metcalf,* 240 U.S. 403 (1916), and *United Drug Co. v. Theodore Rectanus Co.,* 248 U.S. 90 (1918). Subsection (5) confers upon a junior user, such as Thrift Cars, the right to continued use of an otherwise infringing mark in a remote geographical area if that use was established prior to the other party's federal registration. The junior user is permitted to maintain a proprietary interest in the mark even though it has no general federal protection through registration. To be able to invoke the § 1115(b)(5) exception, however, the junior user must have used the mark continuously in that location and initially in good faith without notice of an infringing mark.

To sustain its "limited area" defense of 15 U.S.C. § 1115(b)(5), Thrift Cars was required to demonstrate (1) that it adopted its mark before Thrifty's 1964 registration under the Lanham Act, and without knowledge of Thrifty's prior use; (2) the extent of the trade area in which Thrift Cars used the mark prior to Thrifty's registration; and (3) that Thrift Cars has continuously used the mark in the pre-registration trade area. There is no issue that Thrift Cars had adopted its mark in good faith and without notice prior to Thrifty's registration. Rather, the questions are whether Thrift Cars had established a market presence in any locality, the extent of that market presence, and whether that market presence had been continuous within the meaning of § 1115(b)(5). The district court found that Thrift Cars' use of the service mark had been continuous in East Taunton within the meaning of § 1115(b)(5), but also found that it had not established a sufficient market presence outside of East Taunton (*i.e.,* in Nantucket or other areas of southeastern Massachusetts) to establish there a continuous market presence sufficient to confer on Thrift Cars trademark protection under the statute.

As the district court held, the scope of protection afforded by § 1115(b)(5) is limited. A pre-existing good faith user's rights are frozen to the geographical location where the user has established a market penetration as of the date of registration. Such users are unable thereafter to acquire additional protection superior to that obtained by the federal registrant. The district court therefore held that Thrift Cars' expansion into new market areas after the 1964 date of Thrifty's federal registration is not protected under § 1115(b)(5).

. . . .

B. *Thrift Cars did not demonstrate a continuous presence outside of East Taunton within the meaning of § 1115(b)(5)*

The district court found that Thrift Cars had not established a continuous presence in any area outside of East Taunton—prior to July 1964—adequate to satisfy the requirements of § 1115(b)(5). That finding was necessarily based on the hard facts and the inferences drawn from the trial evidence. The limited advertising Thrift Cars had done was not deemed sufficient to establish a presence outside East Taunton, nor were Thrift Cars' sporadic rentals in Nantucket and elsewhere in southeastern Massachusetts enough to sustain Thrift Cars' claim that it had already expanded out of East Taunton prior to Thrifty's federal registration. These findings are not clearly erroneous and we do not overturn the district court's findings on this matter.

We also note that the fact that Thrift Cars had desired to expand into the Nantucket market prior to July 1964 by unsuccessfully applying for a license to operate at the airport is not sufficient to meet the requirements of § 1115(b)(5). A mere desire, without more, will not confer upon Thrift Cars the ability to exclude Thrifty from Nantucket. The policy behind the Lanham Act is very strong and the party challenging the federal registrant has the burden of showing a continued and actual market presence in order to qualify for the "limited area" exception under the statute. The trial court permissibly found that Thrift Cars did not meet its burden in this respect.

C. *Thrift Cars' activities in East Taunton fall into the "limited area" defense of § 1115(b)(5)*

The more difficult question is whether Thrift Cars has established and maintained a continuous market presence in East Taunton so as to sustain an injunction against Thrifty in that region. Under § 1115(b)(5), the junior user must show that it has made continuous use of the mark prior to the issuance of the senior user's registration and must further prove continued use up until trial. Otherwise, the defense "dries up" and the junior user cannot assert rights in the limited trade area.

Here, the district court properly found that Thrift Cars established a significant enough market share in East Taunton prior to Thrifty's 1964 federal registration to constitute continuous use there at least until May 1970, when Conlon opened business operations in Nantucket. The pivotal issue is, however, whether Thrift Cars continued enough of a market presence in East Taunton after May 1970 (to the time of trial) to qualify for the § 1115(b)(5) defense. The district court made no specific findings on this precise matter (though its opinion reveals an implicit affirmative finding), and we think it is a close call whether Thrift Cars conducted a significant amount of business in East Taunton up until trial. Nevertheless, we believe that on this record Thrift Cars should be entitled to continue doing business in East Taunton and Thrifty should be enjoined from establishing a franchise there. First, the record shows that Thrift Cars continually advertised in media directed specifically to the East Taunton area such as the Taunton area telephone yellow pages, even after opening the Nantucket facility. The record also reveals that Thrift Cars made a showing of general reputation in the East Taunton area throughout the period involved by maintaining an East Taunton address and an East Taunton telephone number. We cannot say that the district court's inherent finding of continuous use should be upset.

Although Thrift Cars' business was solely in East Taunton, the district court prohibited its future conduct of any car or truck rental leasing business outside Taunton, Massachusetts. This was not error or an abuse of discretion. East Taunton is not a separate entity but simply an integral part of Taunton itself. In these circumstances, it is appropriate to direct the injunction to the overall entity. (East Taunton appears to be a popular name for or a colloquial designation for one part of Taunton.)

D. *The district court's injunction did not freeze Thrift Cars' business activities*

Thrift Cars argues that the district court's injunction is tantamount to freezing Thrift Cars' business activities rather than limiting the area in which those activities are conducted. We disagree. While we recognize that the automobile rental business, by its very nature, is mobile, and that we cannot, for example, prevent Nantucket residents from seeking out Thrift Cars in its protected East Taunton geographical area, the courts can prevent Thrift Cars from maintaining a rental agency in Nantucket using the Thrift Cars name. The district court considered East Taunton and Nantucket as two separate market areas, not parts of a single southeastern Massachusetts market, as Thrift Cars would have us believe. It is settled that a junior user can conduct its activities within the market it had carved out for itself before the senior user obtained federal registration. But there was no showing in this case that Nantucket is within the same market area as East Taunton. On the contrary, it seems clear that the major reason that Thrift Cars began to do significant business in Nantucket was because Conlon deliberately moved the major portion of the business there and opened up a rental counter at the Nantucket airport after Thrifty's registration. This action constituted an expansion out of the East Taunton area after the critical date of Thrifty's registration, not a continuation of business activities within the same market area. The result is that the district court's injunction did not freeze Thrift Cars' business activities, but merely confined them, correctly, to the market area it had established prior to Thrifty's federal registration.

E.   *The district court did not abuse its discretion by allowing Thrift Cars to advertise in those publications it had used prior to Thrifty's registration*

The district court allowed Thrift Cars to continue advertising in those media it had used prior to the critical date of July 26, 1964. Thrifty now urges that the court allowed Thrift Cars too broad an advertising distribution base, because it extended outside East Taunton to Cape Cod and Nantucket. Thrifty says that by permitting both parties to advertise in the major resort area publications, the court abused its discretion because substantial consumer confusion is likely to result.

We reject Thrifty's arguments and agree with the district court that to contract Thrift Cars' advertising base would be a punitive move. The district court did not allow Thrift Cars to advertise in any publications that it had not used prior to Thrifty's registration. On the contrary, the court simply authorized Thrift Cars to use only the same newspapers it had used prior to that critical date. While we recognize that some consumer confusion may result because there will be some overlap in advertising, the Lanham Act does not require the complete elimination of all confusion. We think, moreover, that the confusion spawned as a result of Thrift Cars' advertising will be minimal and should not significantly interfere with Thrifty's proprietary rights in its mark. Each party shall bear its own costs.

Affirmed.

Eds. Note: For a more recent decision addressing the geographic scope of a good faith junior user's operations, *see, e.g., All Video, Inc. v. Hollywood Entertainment Corp.*, 929 F.Supp. 262 (E.D.Mich.1996).

Dawn Donut Co. v. Hart's Food Stores, Inc., 267 F.2d 358 (2d Cir.1959). Dawn Donut has continuously used the trademark "Dawn" on bags of doughnut mix which it sells and ships to bakers in various states from its Michigan warehouse. Plaintiff also furnishes advertising and packaging material bearing the trademark "Dawn" and permits these bakers to sell goods made from the mixes to the consuming public under that trademark. The licensing of plaintiff's mark in connection with retail sales of doughnuts in New York has been confined to areas not less than 60 miles from defendant's trading area of Rochester, NY. While sales of Dawn Donut mix have been made to bakers in defendant's trading area, these bakers have not employed plaintiff's mark in connection with retail sales.

Defendant, Hart Food Stores, owns and operates a retail grocery chain in New York. The defendant's bakery distributes doughnuts with the imprint "Dawn" through these stores within the 45 mile radius of Rochester, NY. Defendant adopted the mark "Dawn" because of a slogan "Baked at midnight, delivered at Dawn." Defendant's adoption was subsequent to plaintiff's registration but without actual knowledge of plaintiff's use.

Plaintiff's marks were registered federally in 1927, and their registration was renewed in 1947. Therefore by virtue of the Lanham Act, 15 U.S.C.A. § 1072, the defendant had constructive notice of plaintiff's marks as of July 5, 1947, the effective date of the Act.

The Second Circuit nonetheless affirmed the district court's dismissal of plaintiff's complaint.

> As long as plaintiff and defendant confine their use of the mark "Dawn" in connection with the retail sale of baked goods to their present separate trading areas it is clear that no public confusion is likely.

> The decisive question then is whether plaintiff's use of the mark "Dawn" at the retail level is likely to be confined to its current area of use or whether in the normal course of its business, it is likely to expand the retail use of the mark into defendant's trading area. If such expansion were probable, then the concurrent use of the marks would give rise to the conclusion that there was a likelihood of confusion.

> Accordingly, because plaintiff and defendant use the mark in connection with retail sales in distinct and separate markets and because there is no present prospect that plaintiff will expand its use of the mark at the retail level into defendant's trading area, we conclude that there is no likelihood of public confusion arising from the concurrent use of the marks and therefore the issuance of an injunction is not warranted.... However, because of the effect we have attributed to the constructive notice provision of the Lanham Act, the plaintiff may later, upon a proper showing of an intent to use the mark at the retail level in defendant's market area, be entitled to enjoin defendant's use of the mark.

For a more recent expression of this principle, see **Emergency One v. American Fire Eagle Engine**, 332 F.3d 264 (4th Cir.2003):

> Although federal registration of a mark does not itself confer ownership rights, registration constitutes "prima facie evidence of the validity of the registered mark ..., of the registrant's ownership of the mark, and of the registrant's exclusive right to use the registered mark...." 15 U.S.C.A. § 1057(b) (West 1997). Moreover, the presumption of priority enjoyed by the registrant of a mark is "nationwide in effect." 15 U.S.C.A. § 1057(c). Thus, registration of a trademark under the Lanham Act "creates a presumption that the registrant is entitled to use the registered mark throughout the nation." *Draeger Oil Co. v. Uno–Ven Co.*, 314 F.3d 299, 302 (7th Cir.2002). By contrast, a user claiming ownership of a mark under common-law principles does not enjoy the benefit of the presumptions conferred by registration and must "establish his right to exclusive use"; in effect, registration

"shifts the burden of proof from the plaintiff ... to the defendant, who must introduce sufficient evidence to rebut the presumption of plaintiff's right to such [exclusive] use." *Pizzeria Uno Corp. v. Temple*, 747 F.2d 1522, 1529 (4th Cir. 1984) (internal quotation marks omitted). Accordingly, a plaintiff asserting a claim of infringement against common-law trademark ownership rights bears the burden of establishing its exclusive right to use the mark by actual use in a given territory.

The nature of common-law trademark rights in large measure determines the appropriate scope of any injunctive relief. Thus, the owner of common-law trademark rights in an unregistered mark is not entitled to injunctive relief in those localities where it has failed to establish actual use of the mark. By limiting injunctive relief to the territory where the mark is being used, courts ensure that a trademark does not precede its owner into "markets that [the owner's] trade has never reached." *Hanover Milling*, 240 U.S. at 416. For this reason, even the owner of a federally registered mark—who enjoys the presumption of nationwide priority—is not "entitled to injunctive relief except in the area actually penetrated" through use of the mark.[3] Accordingly, even though the senior user of an unregistered mark has established priority over a junior user through prior appropriation, injunctive relief is appropriate only in those areas where the senior user can show sufficient actual use. *See Spartan Food*, 813 F.2d at 1283–84 (reversing the award of injunctive relief to the extent that it covered territory beyond the area in which the senior user established actual use); *cf. Armand's Subway*, 604 F.2d at 849–50 (explaining that even though the owner of a registered trademark has an exclusive right of use that enjoys nationwide protection, "the protection is only potential in areas where the registrant in fact does not do business" and "[a] competing user could use the mark there until the registrant extended its business to the area").

QUESTIONS

1. How would the court have ruled in *United Drug* had § 33(b) of the Lanham Act [15 U.S.C. § 1115(b)] been in effect at the time of the Court's decision?

2. Was the court in *Dawn Donut* correct in concluding that there will be no confusion of the mark "Dawn" in the Rochester area? Had there been a likelihood of confusion in the *Dawn Donut* case, would the court have enjoined the defendant from using the mark? Does § 33(b)(5) of the Lanham Act help the defendant here?

3. The owner of a registered mark "has a nationwide *right*, but the injunctive *remedy* does not ripen until the registrant shows a likelihood of entry into the disputed territory.... [The junior user's] use of the mark can continue only so long as the federal registrant remains outside the market area." *Lone Star [Steakhouse & Saloon, Inc. v. Alpha of Virginia, Inc.*, 43 F.3d 922, 932 (4th Cir. 1995)] (internal quotation marks omitted).

3. Is *Dawn Donut* distinguishable from *Stork Club*, *supra*, Chapter 1? Suppose a Michigan resident drives through Western New York State? Is that traveler's potential confusion less cognizable than the New Yorker's who visits San Francisco?

4. Pegasus Pizza has a federally registered trademark for its retail pizza chain stores. It franchises hundreds of pizzerias in the southwest United States, and the company maintains a website on which it advertises its company. The website contains information on its pizzas, special Internet deals, and a store locator pointing website visitors to the pizzeria nearest them. Aside from the website, the company engages in no national advertising.

Pizza di Pegasus is an Italian restaurant that serves pizza and pasta. Its sole location is in Ithaca, New York. It advertises exclusively within its local college community through fliers and ads in newspapers.

Pegasus Pizza plans to expand its operations in the southeast United States, but it has no current plans to open pizzerias in New York.

Does the *Dawn Donut* rule protect the junior user Pizza di Pegasus under these facts? Would the result be different if Pegasus Pizza also sold frozen pizzas available in its pizzerias throughout the United States over its website? (For a discussion of the *Dawn Donut* rule and the Internet, *see* Thomas L. Casagrande, *The "Dawn Donut Rule": Still Standing (Article III, That Is) Even with the Rise of the Internet*, 90 Trademark Reptr. 723 (2000).)

5. Was the court in *Thrifty Rent–A–Car* correct in allowing the defendant to continue to advertise in the same media in which it had advertised prior to the plaintiff's federal registration? Does § 33(b)(5) of the Lanham Act dictate this result? Is this ruling consistent with *Dawn Donut*?

CHAPTER 4

REGISTRATION OF TRADEMARKS

A. THE PROCESS

WILLIAM M. BORCHARD, HOW TO GET AND KEEP A TRADEMARK, TRADEMARKS AND THE ARTS (2d Ed. 2000) (excerpt)

A. How to Clear a Proposed Mark

The best way to learn whether a conflicting mark is being used is to order a search report through one of the independent searching companies. The search report will purport to disclose all federal trademark registrations currently in effect, or which have been cancelled or have expired, for identical or similar marks applied to identical or closely related goods. It also will list state trademark registrations of interest, pertinent references in various relevant trade directories and on-line databases, and similar business names found in telephone directories or trade lists.

You should have the search report evaluated by an attorney experienced in the trademark field who can use expert judgment as to whether any potential problems exist, and if so, whether they can be cleared up....

B. How to Establish Rights in a Mark

Once you have cleared the trademark for adoption, the next step is either to start using the mark in the ordinary course of trade on or in connection with the goods or services or to file an intent-to-use application for federal registration (which will not be issued until the mark has been put into bona fide use). To use the trademark, it could be applied to labels or affixed to the goods or to containers for the goods. In the alternative, it could be applied directly to the goods themselves, or it could be shown on point-of-sale displays associated with the goods. Use of a trademark solely in invoices, bills of lading, packing slips or advertisements for the goods would not meet the technical requirements for obtaining trademark ownership rights.

The types of use for securing rights in a service mark are slightly different from those described above. The service mark may be used in advertisements, brochures, letterheads, signs or any other item used in either advertising or rendering the service.

In addition, the service must actually be rendered in federal commerce to be federally registrable. Generally, this means that the service must be rendered in more than one state. But if the service is in a location where its patrons are traveling from state to state such as on an interstate highway, the use in commerce requirement will be satisfied. For example, a vocal group would have to perform in at least two states in order to establish interstate use of its name, which might be exhibited to the general public on posters, print ads, fliers, tickets or theatre marquees. This procedure would make the group's name a federally registrable service mark for the entertainment services it has provided.

C. How to Obtain a Federal Registration of a Mark*

1. *Preparing the Application*

Once you have used the mark in commerce as described above, or once you have a bona fide intention to use the mark in commerce,[8] you can file an application to register it in the United States Patent and Trademark Office (hereinafter "PTO")....

The *minimum requirements* to receive a filing date for the application are as follows:

(a) Applicant's Name....

(b) A Name and Address for Correspondence....

(c) Drawing. Clear drawing of the mark suitable for printing on the certificate of registration must be part of the application or must accompany it. If the mark is not used in a stylized form of display, it may be registered in block-letter form and the drawing may be typed. However, if the mark has a particular style of lettering or incorporates a design, a pen and ink drawing may have to be prepared by a draftsman.

A sound mark—such as a musical signature—must be presented in an appropriate written description. A three-dimensional mark—such as a sculpture outside of a restaurant—must be presented in a line-drawing, not a photograph....

(d) Identification of Goods or Services. Identify in fairly specific ordinary terms the goods or services for which the mark has been or will be used, for example, t-shirts; prerecorded musical CD's and tapes; prerecorded video cassettes featuring motion pictures; entertainment services rendered by a vocal and instrumental group; motion picture distributorship services; restaurant services, etc. (At some point, you also must specify the official class in which the goods or services fall. The PTO follows the International Classification System which has 34 classes of trademarks and

---

* *Editors' Note.* This discussion does not apply to Requests for extensions of an International Registration to the United States under the Madrid Protocol, which have different procedures and requirements. *See* Note U.S. Adherence to Madrid Protocol, *infra* this chapter.

8. This intention must be more than a "wish list." It must be somewhat concrete, although it can be subject to one or more contingencies, and it is helpful if there is written evidence of this intent. *Commodore Electronics Ltd. v. Cbm KK*, 26 U.S.P.Q.2d 1503, 1507 (T.T.A.B.1993) (lack of documentary evidence is sufficient to prove that the applicant lacks a bona fide intention to use the mark in commerce).

11 classes of service marks ... A single application can cover the same mark in more than one class.)

(e) Filing Fee. The fee [is] $375 per class if the application is filed on paper. [I]f the application is filed electronically, there is a reduced fee of $325 per class and a further reduced fee of $275 per class if the goods/services description complies with the Trademark Office's Acceptable Identification of Goods and Services and if the application meets certain other conditions.

Other requirements that can be satisfied later, are as follows:

(f) Dates of Use. If the application is based on use of the mark, state the date the mark was first used anywhere, even in intrastate commerce, for each PTO class being covered. In addition, state the date the mark was first used in federal commerce in each PTO class. These two dates may or may not be the same.

If the application is based on intent-to-use, the use information will be included when the amendment or statement of use is filed during the prosecution of the application.

If the application is based on a Paris Convention country of origin application (filed during the previous 6 months) or a country of origin registration, no use information will be required. A true copy of the country of origin registration (with English translation) eventually will be needed, however.

(g) Specimens of Use. When the dates of use are required and are submitted, you also must submit one specimen showing the mark as actually used in each PTO class being covered. . . .

(h) Color Features of the Mark. If the mark always appears in a particular color which is to be regarded as a feature of the mark, explain where the colors appear and the nature of the colors.

(i) Declaration. The application at some point must be dated and signed immediately below a specified statement to the effect that the statements made in the application are true under penalties of perjury. . . .

. . . .

3. *Examination by the PTO*

Normally about six months after filing, the application is examined by a Trademark Attorney on the PTO's staff who reviews the application for form, completeness and registrability.

A mark may be considered unregistrable if it consists of or comprises: (1) immoral, deceptive or scandalous matter; or matter which may disparage or falsely suggest a connection with persons, living or dead, institutions, beliefs, or national symbols, or bring them into contempt or disrepute; (2) a name, portrait, or signature identifying a particular living individual except by his written consent; or (3) a mark which so resembles a mark registered in the PTO or a mark previously used in the United

States by another and not abandoned, as to be likely to cause confusion when applied to your goods or services.

If the mark is merely descriptive of the goods or services, such as the term "Non–Stop Music" for "radio broadcasting services," it is not registrable on the Principal Register without proof that it has had sufficient use and advertising to have become recognized as designating a source in addition to its descriptive connotation. This is sometimes known as acquiring a "secondary meaning." The same is true if the mark is deceptively misdescriptive, such as the term "The Jones Sisters" for a musical group having members with no family relationship; or geographically descriptive, such as the term "New York's Own" for handicrafts that come from New York State; or a surname such as "Smith's" for a dance company.[21]

The PTO's Trademark Attorney will also examine the PTO records to see if the mark is likely to cause confusion with any other trademark already on the Register or which is the subject of a pending application.

Often, the application encounters ... objections which can be dealt with through correspondence [or a telephone conversation with the Trademark Attorney]. The PTO issues ... an Office Action. The Office Action is dated and the applicant has six months from that date within which to respond....

A technical objection might be, for example, to identify the goods or services more precisely; to change the class; to add a disclaimer of a descriptive term incorporated in the mark; to prove that the mark has become distinctive through use, if that is appropriate; or to provide additional literature which will help the examination of the application. If the mark is refused registration because of a previously registered mark, an extended argument often is made, usually citing similar previously decided cases involving analogous facts or legal points.

4. *Publication for Opposition*

If the application is approved, it is then published in a weekly publication entitled the "Official Gazette of the U.S. Patent and Trademark Office." Publication ... means that it has satisfied all of the requirements of the PTO's Trademark Attorney. However, it also enables anyone who believes he or she will be damaged by application of the mark to oppose its registration.

An opposition, or request for extension of time to oppose, must be filed within thirty days from the date of publication. If an opposition is filed, a

---

21. [Lanham Act] §§ 2(e) and (f). Without proof of "secondary meaning," such a mark still can be registered on the Supplemental Register if it is in lawful use in commerce. *Id.* § 23. A Supplemental Register registration provides no substantive rights, but it ensures that the mark will appear on search reports, prevents anyone else from getting a Principal Register registration of the same mark for the same goods or services, and carries with it the right to use the same statutory notice of registration as applies to a Principal Register registration. A deceptive or geographically deceptively misdescriptive mark, such as "Viennese" for an orchestra from New Jersey, cannot be registered.

proceeding will be conducted before the Trademark Trial and Appeal Board of the PTO. The proceeding comes close to being a full trial with pre-trial discovery, testimony of witnesses, documentary evidence, legal briefs and possibly oral argument, and legal fees that can run very high.

If no opposition is filed and if the application is an intent-to-use application (that was not previously amended to a use application), the PTO will issue a Notice of Allowance. The applicant has six months in which to file a Statement of Use (with dates of first use and three specimens of use) accompanied by a filing fee of $150 per class. The deadline for filing the Statement of Use can be extended for six month intervals for up to 36 months after the Notice of Allowance was issued provided there is a reason for each extension after the first, there still is a bona fide intention to use the mark, and each extension request is accompanied by a filing fee of $150 per class covered. . . .

The application will mature to registration and a certificate will be issued within approximately three months from the date of publication (if no opposition is filed) or from acceptance of the Statement of Use. The entire registration process can take as long as one to two years from the date of filing, and substantially longer if there is an opposition proceeding or there are extensions for filing the Statement of Use.

D. How to Obtain State Registrations of a Mark

It sometimes is desirable to file an application with the Department of State in each state in which the mark has been used because it takes so long to obtain a federal registration, or because the mark may not have been used on goods or services in federally regulated commerce.[24]

State registrations are not given much weight in infringement actions because the applications are not examined for prior conflicts. But you generally can obtain a state registration in a matter of weeks and it will turn up on search reports so that subsequent users of the same or a similar mark will be alerted to the mark's existence. Moreover, a state registration constitutes evidence of a claim to exclusive trademark rights within all or at least part of the state, although that evidence is subject to rebuttal.

. . . .

E. Considering the Filing of Foreign Applications

If a mark will be used internationally, you should determine in which countries the goods will be marketed or the services rendered under the mark and then file applications to register the mark in those countries.

Most foreign countries will allow an application to be filed without prior use of the mark. In fact, many countries regard the first applicant to be the owner of the mark. If you wait for a mark to be successful in the United States before protecting it abroad, it may be too late in some countries since a local user may already have applied to register it there.

---

24. For an outline of the registration requirements of each state, *see* International Trademark Association, State Trademark and Unfair Competition Law (2006).

Marks often are registered on a country-by-country basis.... U.S. applicants may file a Community Trademark ("CTM") application, which if granted, covers all of the countries in the European Union. In addition, U.S. applicants, based on a U.S. application or registration, may file for an International Registration administered by the World Intellectual Property Organization ("WIPO") in Geneva and request extensions of the International Registration to countries that are members of the Madrid Protocol.

ADVANTAGES OF TRADEMARK REGISTRATION ON THE PRINCIPAL REGISTER

1. *Nationwide protection from the date of the application.* Once a mark is federally registered, the registrant's trademark rights relate back to the date of the trademark application, and give the registrant nationwide priority against a party adopting the same or similar mark after the date of the registrant's application. If a mark is left unregistered, common law protection may be limited to those areas in which the mark had actually been in use or become known. If a registrant does not apply for registration immediately upon use in commerce (or does not file an intent-to-use application), and another user innocently adopts a similar mark following the registrant's use, but prior to registrant's application, the registrant's entitlement to use the mark in the entire United States may be limited by the area of use in which the other user in good faith exploited the mark prior to the registrant's application.

2. *Incontestability.* If the registered mark is used continuously for five years, it may become incontestable. This means that the statute limits the challenges alleged infringers may bring to a registrant's right to use the mark to certain defenses specified in the statute. The other defenses are no longer available.

3. *Warning to others.* The registered mark will easily be found in trademark searches. Therefore, third parties should not blunder into using a similar mark for similar goods or services. Such blunders can result in expensive litigation if the second-comer refuses to relinquish its use of the mark. Moreover, if the mark is registered, its constructive date of first use will be the date the application for registration was filed. Because priority of use can be important in determining the rights of conflicting claimants to a mark, the registrant's constructive use date can make the difference in a priority conflict. This is particularly true for registrations made on the basis of intent to use applications. Finally, if the mark is registered, the Patent and Trademark Office will protect the mark by refusing to register any other mark that the Trademark Examiner considers likely to cause consumer confusion.

4. *Barring imports.* Goods produced abroad bearing infringing marks may be blocked at Customs, provided that the registrant is a U.S. citizen, and is not related in certain ways to the producer of the imported goods.

5. *Protection against counterfeiting.* Enhanced remedies are available against counterfeiters of trademarks registered on the Principal Register.

6. *Evidentiary advantages.* A registered mark is prima facie valid and enjoys other evidentiary presumptions.

7. *Use of the R symbol, or of the phrases "Registered in U.S. Patent Office" or "U.S. Pat. Off." to denote federal registration.* This notice informs the public that proprietary rights are recognized in the mark. The notice can be of importance with respect to marks which some might consider descriptive, generic, or merely ornamental.

8. *Confirms ownership and validity.* Trademarks can be important factors in the sale of a product line or of a company itself. Trademark registration greatly simplifies auditing and clearing title.

9. *Basis of Foreign Filings.* A U.S. application or registration can form the basis of an International Registration. *See* Note on Madrid Protocol, *infra* this section. Additionally, a U.S. application can be used as a basis for Paris Convention filing priority in Paris Convertion countries.

10. *Preemption of State Regulation.* 15 U.S.C. § 1121(b) [Lanham Act § 39(b)]

> No state or other jurisdiction of the United States or any political subdivision or any agency thereof may require alteration of a registered mark, or require that additional trademarks, service marks, trade names, or corporate names that may be associated with or incorporated into the registered mark be displayed in the mark in a manner differing from the display of such additional trademarks, service marks, trade names or corporate names con-templated by the registered mark as exhibited in the certificate of registration issued by the United States Patent and Trademark Office.

This rarely-invoked provision preserves the integrity of federal trade-marks from state law interference. In effect, the Lanham Act preempts state truth-in-labeling laws, when these would compel the registrant to change the trademark's presentation. The provision has been applied against state labeling measures that would have required alteration of trademarks, *see, e.g. Beatrice Foods Co. v. State of Wisconsin*, 223 U.S.P.Q. 75 (W.D.Wis.1983) (challenge by producer of BUTTERMATCH margarine against state dairy protection regulation that barred use of word "butter" in label of product not containing butter).

State and local zoning laws have presented a new source for § 39(b) challenges to state regulation. In this instance, a locality's "aesthetic zoning" regulations may, for example, require all merchants to display their store logos in a uniform style and color scheme. If the merchant is a franchisee, and the aesthetic ordinance commands changes to the appear-ance of the source-identifying symbols (think of pink arches for a Mc-Donalds outlet in a shopping center regulated under the ordinance) does the ordinance violate § 39(b)? A divided Ninth Circuit addressed this issue, one of first impression in the appellate courts, in *Blockbuster Videos, Inc. v. City of Tempe*, 141 F.3d 1295 (9th Cir.1998), and held that Tempe's local zoning ordinances, which required Video Updates to use a different color scheme on an exterior sign in a Tempe shopping mall from its federally registered mark, violated § 1121(b). The dissenting opinion interpreted § 1121(b) more narrowly as prohibiting across-the-board restrictions on displays of registered marks, rather than restriction only of exterior signage in a particular location to conform to aesthetic zoning regulations. *See also Lisa's Party City, Inc. v. Town of Henrietta*, 185 F.3d 12 (2d Cir.1999) (Second Circuit adopted interpretation in the *Blockbuster Videos* dissent).

THE SUPPLEMENTAL REGISTER

In addition to the Principal Register, Section 23 of the Lanham Act, 15 U.S.C. § 1091, directs the Director to maintain a Supplemental Register. Marks "not registrable on the Principal Register" may be registered on the Supplemental Register if they are "capable of distinguishing the applicant's goods or services." So long as the mark is "capable" of distinctiveness, it need not in fact distinguish applicant's goods or services from those of others. Thus, terms that are descriptive or geographic, or are surnames, may find a home on the Supplemental Register.

Although there was some doubt prior to the Trademark Law Revision Act of 1988 concerning whether a registration on the Supplemental Register constituted an admission that the mark was not distinctive, in 1988, Congress amended Section 27 of the Lanham Act, 15 U.S.C. § 1095, which now states:

> Registration of a mark on the supplemental register shall not constitute an admission that the mark has not acquired distinctiveness.

This amendment forecloses arguments that the supplemental registrant concedes that the mark has not built up secondary meaning. Nonetheless, does the amendment permit the argument that a supplemental registration constitutes an admission that the mark is not *inherently* distinctive? *See, e.g., Perma Ceram Enterprises, Inc. v. Preco Industries Ltd.*, 23 U.S.P.Q.2d 1134, 1137 n. 11 (T.T.A.B.1992).

Under Section 23, as amended, a domestic applicant's mark is now eligible for supplemental registration upon lawful use in commerce. May an application based on intent-to-use be filed on the Supplemental Register? The intent-to-use regime applies only to the Principal Register. However, an intent-to-use application can be amended to the Supplemental Register upon the filing of an amendment to the application alleging use. Trademark Rule 2.75(b), 37 C.F.R. § 2.75(b). In addition, applications based on a foreign registration in the country of origin need not allege use in order to be eligible for supplemental registration. Section 44 of the Lanham Act, 15 U.S.C. § 1126, permits registration by foreign applicants upon a claim of bona fide intention to use the mark.

Section 26 of the Lanham Act, 15 U.S.C. § 1094 explicitly provides that registrations on the Supplemental Register do not receive the same powerful statutory advantages as registrations on the Principal Register do, such as constituting prima facie evidence of validity of the mark, providing constructive notice and nationwide priority or providing a basis to stop infringing goods via Customs. Why then would applicants wish to register on the Supplemental Register? One reason is that the registration appears on search reports and may accordingly deter others from choosing a confusingly similar mark. Additionally, the PTO may cite a prior registration on the Supplemental Register against a mark considered confusingly similar. Finally, the registrant is permitted to use the registration notice and to sue in federal court.

THE NOTICE OF REGISTRATION

Although use of a notice of registration is permissive, important benefits attach to use of a notice "by displaying with the mark the words 'Registered in U.S. Patent and Trademark Office' or 'Reg. U.S. Pat. & Tm. Off.' or the letter R enclosed within a circle, thus ®." 15 U.S.C. § 1111. Failure to use such notice results in a bar to an award of profits or damages in an infringement suit involving a registered trademark absent a finding that a defendant had actual notice of the registration. *Id.* What effect does lack of a registration notice have in a section 43(a) claim for infringement of an unregistered mark? Section 35(a) of the Lanham Act, 15 U.S.C. § 1117(a), was amended to clarify that profits and damages are also available in section 43(a) claims, as well as in claims for infringement of a registered mark. Section 35(a) in turn is explicitly limited by the Section 29 (15 U.S.C. § 1111) bar against an award of damages or profits absent use of the registration notice or actual knowledge of registration. It appears, therefore, that in the case of a section 43(a) claim involving a registered mark that absence of registration notice would have the same preclusive effect. A section 43(a) claim involving an unregistered mark, however, would not require use of a registration notice, and thus arguably a plaintiff could claim profits and damages. Does it make sense to treat the unregistered mark more favorably in this circumstance?

The language "displaying with the mark" was interpreted in *Kransco Mfg. Inc. v. Hayes Specialties Corp.*, 33 U.S.P.Q.2d 1999 (E.D.Mich.1994), *aff'd in relevant part and vacated in part*, 77 F.3d 503 (Fed.Cir.1996), which involved a registered trademark in the sinuous seam of a two-panel footbag. The ® notice followed the registered word mark HACKY SACK, which was also near the sinuous seam. The back side of the packaging stated: "HACKY SACK is a brand name and registered trademark of [plaintiff]."

Judge Churchill in *Kransco* noted:

In the opinion of the Court, the plaintiff's footbag and package does a poor job of communicating to anyone that the encircled "R" refers to the sinuous seam as well as to the name "HACKY SACK," particularly in light of the statement on the package.

The defendant, however, has provided the Court with no authority whatsoever for its position that a statutory notice should be used in connection with each of several federally registered marks on one product. The defendant cannot claim estoppel based upon the limited words on the back of the package because its managing officers deny knowledge of the existence of the plaintiff's product and package.

As a matter of law, the encircled ''R'' on the plaintiff's footbag is displayed ''with the mark'' within the meaning of 15 U.S.C. § 1111 and the plaintiff would be entitled to recover profits even without proof that the defendant had actual notice of the registration.

MAINTENANCE AND RENEWAL OF REGISTRATION: SECTIONS 8 AND 9 OF THE LANHAM ACT

Section 8 of the Lanham Act, 15 U.S.C. § 1058, requires a registrant to file an affidavit that the mark is in use for at least some of the goods or services covered in the registration between the fifth and sixth year after the registration date (or within a six-month grace period thereafter for an additional fee). Goods or services not included in the use affidavit will be deleted from the registration. Absent any filing, the registration will be automatically cancelled by the PTO. The kind of ''use'' necessary is actual use in commerce, not mere token use designed nominally to preserve the mark. ''Special circumstances'' may excuse non-use of a mark where the registrant did not intend to abandon the mark. Examples of the ''special circumstances'' excusing non-use include governmental regulation or prohibition, and illness, fire or other catastrophe. *See* TMEP § 1604.11.

Section 9 of the Lanham Act, 15 U.S.C. § 1059, as amended in 1988, provides that ''each registration may be renewed for periods of ten years from the end of the expiring period upon payment of the prescribed fee and the filing of a verified application therefor.'' The registrant is now also required to file an affidavit under Section 8 in each 10th year (or within a 6 month grace period) that the mark is still in use in commerce for at least some of the goods or services covered in the registration, and attach a specimen or facsimile showing current use of the mark every ten years after a registration issues. Any goods or services not included in the use affidavit will be deleted from the registration. Failure to file the renewal and use affidavit will result in the registration's being automatically cancelled by the PTO.

U.S. REGISTRATION OF MARKS OWNED BY NON–U.S. APPLICANTS

The United States is a member of the Paris Convention for the Protection of Industrial Property. This is the leading multilateral treaty covering patents and trademarks. First promulgated in 1883 and originally ratified by eleven nations in 1884, it numbers 171 members as of January 2007, including all the industrialized nations. The current text of the

Convention is that of the 1967 Stockholm revision, and has been incorporated into the 1994 Agreement on Trade Related aspects of Intellectual Property (TRIPs), see art. 1.3. Like the Berne Convention for the Protection of Literary and Artistic works (the leading multilateral copyright treaty), the Paris Convention rests primarily upon the principle of national treatment. This is a nondiscrimination principle: member nations must treat the nationals or domiciliaries of other members as they would their own citizens (*see* art. 2). Unlike the Berne Convention, however, the Paris Convention does not automatically protect the trademark in all Paris Union countries once it is protected in one country. Rather, in most cases, protection depends upon securing a trademark (or patent) registration in each of the other member countries. The national treatment principle operates primarily to oblige member countries to grant trademark (or patent) owners from other member countries equal access to local trademark (or patent) registration procedures. *See, e.g., In re Rath,* 402 F.3d 1207 (Fed.Cir.2005)(Paris Convention is not self-executing; accordingly, applications for RATH and DR. RATH based on German registrations under section 44(e) are subject to scrutiny under Lanham Act's primarily merely a surname bar to registration).

A foreign applicant from a Paris Convention or WTO country may register a trademark in the United States in various ways. First, under the principle of national treatment, any foreign applicant who can allege use or intent to use in interstate or foreign commerce with the United States can file an application on the same basis as a U.S. applicant under section 1(a) [use] or section 1(b) [intent to use] of the Lanham Act.

In addition, the foreign applicant can obtain a registration in the United States on the basis of a prior registration in the applicant's country of origin. The country of origin is either the country in which the applicant "has a bona fide and effective industrial or commercial establishment," or, in the absence of a business establishment, the country of which the applicant is a domiciliary or a national. Lanham Act § 44(c), 15 U.S.C. § 1126(c). A mark duly registered in the foreign applicant's country of origin may be registered on the Principal Register if eligible, otherwise, on the Supplemental Register. As of the 1988 Lanham Act Amendments, the application must state the foreign applicant's bona fide intention to use the mark in commerce, but actual use is not required prior to registration. Together with the application, the foreign applicant must submit a true copy of the registration in the country of origin. Lanham Act § 44(e), 15 U.S.C. § 1126(e).

Moreover, a foreign applicant may apply to register the mark in the United States based on an application to register the mark in the country of origin. The U.S. application must be filed within six months of the date on which the application was first filed abroad. In addition, this application, as well as one based on a foreign registration, must comply in other ways with the requirements of the Lanham Act, including a statement that the applicant has a bona fide intention to use the mark in commerce. The U.S. application will receive the same force and effect as if it had been filed in the U.S. on the date on which it was first filed abroad. *See* Lanham Act § 44(d), 15 U.S.C. § 1126(d). However, the registration in the U.S. will not issue on this basis until the foreign registration has issued and a true copy has been sent to the USPTO.

The special benefits of section 44 of the Lanham Act are available to persons whose country of origin is a party to a treaty relating to trademarks to which the U.S. is also a party, such as the Paris Convention. A foreign applicant also qualifies for treatment under section 44 if the laws of the country of origin grant trademark rights to U.S. nationals on a reciprocal basis. Lanham Act § 44(b), 15 U.S.C. § 1126(b).

Once obtained, the foreign applicant's U.S. registration will be independent of the registration in the country of origin. The Lanham Act will govern the duration, validity, and transfer of rights under the U.S. registration. Lanham Act § 44(f), 15 U.S.C. § 1126(f). As a result, while a foreign national may obtain a U.S. registration without prior use in U.S. commerce, he must commence use in the United States within three years of issuance of the registration, or the statutory presumption of abandonment may be triggered.

A non-U.S. applicant may also avail itself of the Madrid Protocol's centralized filing mechanism discussed immediately below.

U.S. ADHERENCE TO THE MADRID PROTOCOL

The Madrid Protocol is an international trademark filing treaty among over 70 countries. The treaty allows non-U.S. applicants in member countries to extend their international registrations to the United States and allows domestic mark owners to obtain international registrations extending to member countries based upon the owner's U.S. applications or registrations. On November 2, 2002, President Bush signed the implementing legislation that added sections 60 through 74 to the Lanham Act (see sections 60 through 74 of the Lanham Act in the Statutory Appendix A). The international registration system is administered by the World Intellectual Property Organization ("WIPO") located in Geneva, the same organization that administers a number of international agreements pertaining to intellectual property. The mark owner can select the member countries to which the international registration will extend, and those countries then have the ability to accept or refuse the extension. The international registration offers several benefits, such as the ability to renew registrations and to record assignments in one place for a single registration that covers many countries.

A non-U.S. mark owner can extend the international registration it obtains from WIPO to the United States based on the international registration holder's "basic application" or "basic registration" in a Protocol country (other than the U.S.) in which it is a national, is domiciled or has a real and effective industrial or commercial establishment. The extension of the registration to the United States is submitted to the USPTO by WIPO and must be accompanied by a verified declaration that the international registration holder has a bona fide intent to use the mark in commerce. The date of the international registration (if the request for extension is filed in the international application) or the date the request for extension is recorded by WIPO (if the request is made after the international registration issued) is treated as the constructive first use date under section 7(c) of the Lanham Act. The USPTO examines the application as it normally does, and if it is approved, the application is published for opposition. In the event that no oppositions are filed or are overcome, the USPTO will issue a certificate of extension of protection that will have the same effect as a registration on the Principal Register. If the application is not approved by the USPTO or an opposition is filed, the USPTO will issue a notice of refusal within 18 months from the date on which WIPO transmits the request for extension to the USPTO, stating the grounds. In addition, the USPTO will issue a notice of the possibility of refusal within 18 months if an opposition is possible.

A unique feature of an international registration under the Protocol is that if the basic application or registration upon which the international registration is based is restricted, abandoned or cancelled with respect to some of all of the covered goods or services within 5 years of the international registration or more than 5 years if the change resulted from an action within the 5 years, then the extensions, including to the United States, will be similarly restricted, abandoned or cancelled. If the international registration is cancelled in whole or in part, the international registration holder has the option to transform its extension to the U.S. to a U.S. application under section 70(c) by filing an application in the U.S. for the same mark and goods or services covered by the cancelled registration within 3 months of the cancellation of the international registration. This application can be made under either section 1 or section 44 of the Lanham Act and will be accorded the same filing date as that of the international registration or recordal of the extension.

Once an extension of protection has issued, the international registration holder is not required to renew it at the USPTO under section 9 of the Lanham Act since renewal of the international registration takes place centrally through WIPO. However, the international registration holder is nevertheless required to submit to the USPTO declarations of use (or of excusable nonuse) under section 71 of the Lanham Act within 5 to 6 years after the certificate of extension to the U.S. has been issued and within the 6 month period prior to (or a 3–month grace period after) successive 10 year intervals after the certificate of extension issued. Compare the time periods specified in section 8 of the Lanham Act for registrations issued under section 1 or 44 of the Lanham Act. Are they the same as under the Section 71 time periods?

BASES OF REGISTRATION IN THE U.S.

Domestic applicants can generally apply in the U.S. either based on having made use of the mark in commerce in connection with the goods/services prior to filing under section 1(a) of the Lanham Act, *see* Borchard, How To Get and Keep a Trademark, *supra* (for discussion of the requirements), or based on a bona intent to use [ITU]the mark in commerce for such goods/services under section 1(b) of the Lanham Act. The Intent to Use basis will be examined in more detail *infra*, Chapter 4.B. In addition to these two bases, foreign applicants can also apply under section 44(d) or (e) of the Lanham Act, *see* U.S. Registration of Marks Owned by Non–U.S. Applicants, *supra*, or can extend an International Registration to the U.S. under the Madrid Protocol, *see* U.S. Adherence to the Madrid Protocol, *supra*. The chart on the following page summarizes the five bases on which applications may be filed to receive a federal registration or certificate of extension of protection.

	1(a) Use	1(b) ITU	44(e) Foreign Registration	44(d) Foreign Application	66 Protocol Extension
Application	application includes 1st use dates & specimens	application states bona fide ITU mark in commerce	application states bona fide ITU & includes a copy of foreign registration	application states bona fide ITU & includes copy of foreign application	WIPO sends request for extension of Int'l. Reg.[1] to U.S. which states bona fide ITU.
Examination	Office Action or approved for Publication	Office Action or approved for Publication	Office Action or approved for Publication	Office Action or approved for Publication then suspended pending foreign reg.	Office Action or approved for Publ.–18 mos. deadline to notify WIPO of refusal
Publication	Official Gazette	Official Gazette	Official Gazette	Official Gazette	Official Gazette
Opposition	either opposed successfully or reg. issues	either opposed successfully or Notice of Allowance issues	either opposed successfully or reg. issues	either opposed successfully or reg. issues if foreign reg. issues and is filed	either opposed successfully or Certificate of Extension of Protection issues[2]
Post Publication		S/U & specimens w/in 3 yrs. after N/A[3]—then Office Action or reg. issues			
Post Registration	§ 8 Use Aff. 5–6 yrs. after reg. (or w/in 6 mos. grace period)	§ 8 Use Aff. 5–6 yrs. after reg. (or w/in 6 mos. grace period)	§ 8 Use Aff. 5–6 yrs. after reg. (or w/in 6 mos. grace period)	§ 8 Use Aff. 5–6 yrs. after reg. (or w/in 6 mos. grace period)	§ 71 Use Aff. 5–6 yrs. after Cert. of Ext. of Protection
Renewal	§ 8 Use Aff. & renewal 9–10 yrs. after reg. (or 6 mos. grace period) & then every 10 yrs.	§ 8 Use Aff. & renewal 9–10 yrs. after reg. (or 6 mos. grace period) & then every 10 yrs.	§ 8 Use Aff. & renewal 9–10 yrs. after reg. (or 6 mos. grace period) & then every 10 yrs.	§ 8 Use Aff. & renewal 9–10 yrs. after reg. (or 6 mos. grace period) & then every 10 yrs.	§ 71 Use Aff. w/in 9½–10 yrs. after Cert. of Ext. (or 3 mos. grace period) & then every 10 yrs.[4]

[1.] If the underlying Basic Registration or Application in the home country on which the International Registration is based is cancelled in whole or in part within 5 years, the extension to the U.S. is similarly void or cancelled, but within 3 months, the applicant has the right of transformation under § 70(c) to file an application under § 1 or § 44 with the same priority filing date.

[2.] Extensions to oppose and oppositions against the Madrid extensions must be filed electronically–no amendments to oppositions are allowed.

[3.] An Applicant can seek extensions of time to file a Statement of Use in 6 month intervals after the Notice of Allowance. After the first extension, good cause must be stated in addition to a bona fide intent to use the mark.

[4.] The International Registration must be renewed through WIPO every 10 years. The section 71 use affidavit requirements are additional to maintain the U.S. extension and date from the Certificate of Extension of Protection rather than from the International Registration date.

10/2

B.   Priority: Intent to Use and Foreign Marks

1.   Intent to Use

15 U.S.C. § 1051(b) [LANHAM ACT § 1(b)]

(b) Application for bona fide intention to use trademark

(1) A person who has a bona fide intention, under circumstances showing the good faith of such person, to use a trademark in commerce may request registration of its trademark on the principal register hereby established by paying the prescribed fee and filing in the Patent and Trademark Office an application and a verified statement, in such form as may be prescribed by the Director.

(2) The application shall include specification of the applicant's domicile and citizenship, the goods in connection with which the applicant has a bona fide intention to use the mark, and a drawing of the mark.

(3) The statement shall be verified by the applicant and specify–

(A) that the person making the verification believes that he or she, or the juristic person in whose behalf he or she makes the verification, to be entitled to use the mark in commerce;

(B) the applicant's bona fide intention to use the mark in commerce;

(C) that, to the best of the verifier's knowledge and belief, no other person has the right to use the mark in commerce either in the identical form thereof or in such near resemblance thereto as to be likely, when used on or in connection with the goods of such person, to cause confusion, or cause mistake, or to deceive

THE POLICIES UNDERLYING "INTENT TO USE"

S. Rep. No. 100–515, 100th Cong., 2d Sess. 4–6, 22–26, 29–32, 38 (1988).

III.   DISCUSSION

INTENT TO USE

S. 1883 will improve the federal trademark registration system by eliminating the requirement that U.S. citizens and businesses, unlike their foreign counterparts, must use a mark in commerce before they can file an application to register it. The Lanham Act currently requires that a U.S. business or individual seeking to register a trademark in the United States first make use of the mark in interstate commerce before it can apply for registration.

Under current law, a trademark is considered to have been used when it is affixed to the product, its packaging, labels or hang tags and the product is sold or shipped in commerce. Similarly, a service mark is considered to have been used when the services are performed or advertised in commerce, such as by opening a hotel or a restaurant.

This requirement unfairly discriminates against U.S. citizens, as compared to foreign citizens, puts significant legal risks on the introduction of new products and services, and gives preference to certain industries over others, frequently disadvantaging small companies and individuals.

Today, the United States is the only developed country that requires use of a mark before an application for registration may be filed. Other countries, whose trademark laws are based on the common-law concept that rights in a mark are acquired by use, decided long ago that it is not in the interests of the business community to force business people to use a mark before its protection could be assured. In 1938, the United Kingdom converted to an intent-to-use system, and Canada converted in 1954.

This disparity between U.S. law and that of most other countries results in foreign applicants having an advantage over U.S. applicants in obtaining trademark registration rights. U.S. treaty obligations, reflected in Section 44 of the Lanham Act, require that foreign applicants, relying upon a home country registration, may register in the United States, notwithstanding their lack of use of the mark anywhere in the world. Moreover, foreign applicants can obtain a filing priority in the United States corresponding to the date they file their home application. Under current interpretations, this means that while a U.S. applicant is required to use its mark before applying, foreign nationals can apply for and obtain a U.S. registration without first using a mark in the United States or anywhere else. . . .

The Lanham Act's preapplication use requirement also creates unnecessary legal uncertainty for a U.S. business planning to introduce products or services into the marketplace. It simply has no assurance that after selecting and adopting a mark, and possibly making a sizable investment in packaging, advertising and marketing, it will not learn that its use of the mark infringes the rights another acquired through earlier use. In an age of national, if not global, marketing, this has a chilling effect on business investment. This effect is not merely theoretical, but is real. And it can be costly: Marketing a new product domestically often exceeds $30 million for a large company and can consume the life-savings of an individual or small entrepreneur.

Partially in recognition of the difficulties companies face in launching new products and services, and the sizable investments that may be at stake, regardless of a company's or individual's resources, the courts have sanctioned the practice of "token use." Token use is a contrived and commercially transparent practice—nothing more than a legal fiction. At the same time, token use is essential under current law because it recognizes present day marketing costs and realities; it reduces some of the legal and economic risks associated with entering the marketplace; and it nominally achieves the threshold "use" required to apply for federal registration and the creation of trademark rights in advance of commercial use.

Unfortunately, token use is not available to all businesses and industries. For example, it is virtually impossible to make the token use of a trademark on a large or expensive product such as an airplane. The same is true for service industries (that is, hotels, restaurants, and banks) prior to opening for business. Similarly, it is difficult for small business and individuals to avail themselves of token use because they frequently lack the resources or the knowledge to engage in the practice.

Token use is also troublesome for another reason. It allows companies to obtain registration based on minimal use. Often these companies change their marketing plans and subsequently do not make commercial use. The result is that the trademark register is clogged with unused marks, making the clearance of new marks more difficult and discouraging others from adopting and using marks which should otherwise be available.

Despite its numerous virtues, a registration system based on intent also carries some potential for abuse. A single business or individual might, for instance, attempt to monopolize a vast number of potential marks on the basis of a mere statement of intent to use the marks in the future. To minimize such risks, S. 1883 requires the specified intent to be bona fide. This bona fide requirement focuses on an objective good-faith test to establish that the intent is genuine.

S. 1883 addresses these problems and increases the integrity of the federal trademark registration system through the creation of a dual application system. It gives all applicants the choice of applying to register marks on the principal register on the basis of preapplication use in commerce, as they do now, or on the basis of a bona fide intention to use the mark in commerce. Since token use becomes unnecessary and inappropriate under the intent-to-use application system proposed by S. 1883, the definition of "use in commerce" in Section 45 of the Act is strengthened to reflect this significant change in the law. . . .

QUESTIONS

1. In *The Trouble with Trademarks*, 99 Yale L.J. 759 (1990), Professor Stephen Carter suggests that the 1988 Amendments make it far less costly to remove potentially useful trademarks from the public domain, at least temporarily, and thus threaten to impoverish the available market language, and raise entry barriers for later market entrants. Carter suggests that the PTO "should establish monetary or other penalties . . . to deter the filing of applications stating a bona fide intention to use the mark, when, in fact, the applicant has only an intention to keep others from using it." Would you favor the imposition of such penalties?

2.   An intent-to-use application may not be assigned "except to the successor to the business of the applicant, or portion thereof, to which the mark pertains." 15 U.S.C. § 1060. If an ITU application is assigned (together with other trademarks and applications) as collateral to a loan, does the assignment invalidate the ITU application? *See Clorox Co. v. Chemical Bank*, 40 U.S.P.Q.2d 1098 (T.T.A.B.1996).

Zirco Corp. v. American Telephone & Telegraph Co.

21 U.S.P.Q.2d 1542 (T.T.A.B.1991).

BY THE BOARD:

Opposer, on April 23, 1991, filed a notice of opposition to the registration of applicant's mark DATACEL for a portable cellular data transmission and reception system comprising a cellular transceiver integrated with a cellular protocol modem, which is the subject of an intent-to-use application filed on January 11, 1990. In its notice of opposition, opposer alleges, inter alia, that opposer has been the user of the mark DATACELL for a cellular adapter allowing linkage of substantially any and all telephone equipment to any cellular telephone since about April 15, 1990; that opposer has perfected its common law rights in its mark throughout the United States; that applicant's use of its mark in commerce, if any, is well after the first use date of opposer's mark; that opposer had no actual knowledge of applicant's intent-to-use application prior to its adoption and use of its mark; and that because of the similarities between opposer's and applicant's marks and because of the related nature of the goods provided by opposer under its mark and the goods proposed to be sold by applicant under its mark, there is a likelihood of confusion on the part of the trade and purchasing public.

Applicant, on July 1, 1991, has filed a motion to dismiss the opposition pursuant to Fed. R. Civ. P.12(b)(6) for failure to state a claim upon which relief may be granted. Applicant asserts that under Section 7(c) of the Trademark Act (15 USC § 1057(c)), as amended,[4] the filing of its intent-to-use application constitutes constructive use of its mark since the filing date of January 11, 1990 and thus opposer's allegations of first use of its mark on or about April 15, 1990, even if true, do not afford it a basis for relief, in that opposer, as a subsequent user, cannot be damaged.

Opposer has filed its opposition to the motion, arguing that it is clear from Section 7(c) that constructive use does not come into play until the mark has been registered and issued; that, accordingly, applicant does not have conferred upon it a nationwide right of priority of January 11, 1990

---

4. Section 7(c) reads:

Contingent upon the registration of a mark on the principal register provided by this Act, the filing of the application to register such mark shall constitute constructive use of the mark, conferring a right of priority, nationwide in effect, on or in connection with the goods or services specified in the registration against any other person except for a person whose mark has not been abandoned and who, prior to such filing:

(1) has used the mark;

(2) has filed an application to register the mark which is pending or has resulted in registration of the mark; or

(3) has filed a foreign application to register the mark on the basis of which he or she has acquired a right of priority, and timely files an application under Section 44(d) to register the mark which is pending or has resulted in registration of the mark.

until it uses the mark and registration is completed; that since applicant has not perfected constructive use of its mark, it cannot prevent opposer from acquiring common law rights in its mark; that opposer can exert these common law rights against parties which are junior to it, until the issuance of a dominating registration; and that since under Section 18 (15 USC § 1068), as amended, no judgment shall be entered in favor of an intent-to-use applicant before the mark is registered, if that applicant cannot prevail without establishing constructive use pursuant to Section 7(c),[5] no judgment can be made final herein in favor of applicant and thus the motion to dismiss must be denied. Opposer further contends that Section 7(c) is in violation of the commerce clause of the Constitution and as such can confer no rights on applicant.

Applicant has filed a reply, contending that opposer's position would require that an intent-to-use applicant make use of its mark before it could assert constructive use priority to prevail in an opposition and accordingly would defeat the purpose of the intent-to-use provisions of the Trademark Revision Act. Applicant argues that opposer cannot rely upon the acquisition of common law rights after the filing date of applicant's application; that the conditional language of Section 7(c) and Section 18 does not affect applicant's right to assert constructive use priority in this opposition, only the entry of final judgment in applicant's favor would be suspended pending issuance of a registration; and that the legislative history of the Trademark Law Revision Act reveals that the constitutionality of the intent-to-use provisions was thoroughly scrutinized and determined to be satisfactory.

Section 7(c) was added to the Lanham Act by the Trademark Law Revision Act of 1988 in order to provide constructive use, dating from the filing date of an application for registration on the principal register, for a mark registered on that register. As a review of the legislative history shows, the provision is intended to fix a registrant's nationwide priority rights in its mark from the filing date of its application whether the application is based on use or intent-to-use. This right of priority is to have legal effect comparable to the earliest use of a mark at common law. SENATE JUDICIARY COMMITTEE REPORT ON S. 1883, SENATE REPORT NO. 100–515 (September 15, 1988).

While constructive use is applicable to applications based on use as well as intent-to-use, the provision is considered to be essential to the intent-to-use system. Without this provision, an intent-to-use applicant would be vulnerable to theft of its mark or to innocent use of the mark by anyone after the filing of its application. Moreover, by according conditional rights to those who publicly disclose their marks, constructive use encourages the early filing of applications and the searching of trademark records prior to

---

5. Section 18, in pertinent part, reads:

... no final judgment shall be entered in favor of an applicant under section 1(b) before the mark is registered if such applicant cannot prevail without establishing constructive use pursuant to section 7(c).

the adoption and investment in new marks. SENATE JUDICIARY COMMITTEE REPORT ON S. 1883, *supra*.

Opposer's major contention is that under Section 7(c), constructive use is conditional upon registration of the mark and thus applicant, having neither used its mark nor having been issued a registration, is not entitled to assert any priority rights as of the filing date of its application in this opposition.

It is true that a reading of Section 7(c) alone, specifically of that portion which reads "[c]ontingent on the registration of a mark ..., the filing of the application to register such mark shall constitute constructive use of the mark ...," might be construed to limit an applicant's right to rely upon the constructive use date as the first use date of its mark to post-registration actions. But the Board does not believe that such a literal interpretation of Section 7(c) can be adopted. Instead this section must be read in conjunction with Sections 13 and 18 of the Trademark Act. Under Section 13, an opposition may be filed against any application for registration of a mark on the principal register, regardless of whether the application is based on use or intent-to-use. Under Section 18 the Board may render a decision on the opposition; it is only the entry of final judgment in favor of an intent-to-use applicant which must be deferred until the mark is registered, if that applicant cannot prevail without establishing constructive use pursuant to Section 7(c). If an intent-to-use applicant were not allowed to rely upon the constructive use date prior to actual use and registration of its mark, it would be rendered defenseless in any opposition against the registration of its mark based on likelihood of confusion. Constructive use would only function as a sword in affirmative actions by an intent-to-use applicant and only after the registration of its mark, never as a shield in actions against that applicant prior to the registration of its mark.

Accordingly, the Board finds that on its face the Lanham Act, as amended by the Trademark Law Revision Act, cannot be interpreted to limit an intent-to-use applicant's entitlement to rely upon the constructive use provision of Section 7(c) to the time after which it has used its mark and has been issued a registration. If the legislative history and the commentaries on the revised statute are taken into consideration, it is readily apparent that the constructive use provision was intended to foster the filing of intent-to use applications, to give an intent-to-use applicant a superior right over anyone adopting a mark after applicant's filing date (providing the applicant's mark is ultimately used and registered) and to prevent a third party from acquiring common law rights in a mark after the filing date of the intent-to-use application. With these being the aims of the constructive use provision, there can be no doubt but that the right to rely upon the constructive use date comes into existence with the filing of the intent-to-use application and that an intent-to-use applicant can rely upon this date in an opposition brought by a third party asserting common law rights. Whether this provision violates the commerce clause of the Constitution is not a matter falling within the jurisdiction of the Board.

In view thereof, applicant's motion to dismiss the opposition under Fed. R. Civ. P.12(b)(6) is well taken. Opposer's allegations of common law rights in its mark as of April 15, 1990, a date subsequent to applicant's constructive use date, are inadequate to support the ground of priority of use and likelihood of confusion and accordingly opposer has failed to set forth a claim upon which it can prevail.

Judgment in favor of applicant dismissing the opposition is hereby entered, subject to applicant's establishment of constructive use. The time for filing an appeal or for commencing a civil action will run from the date of the present decision. *See* Trademark Rules 2.129(d) and 2.145. When applicant's mark has been registered or the application becomes abandoned, applicant should inform the Board, so that appropriate action may be taken to terminate this proceeding.

QUESTION

1. After AT&T's DATACEL application was allowed, it was abandoned 6 months later for failure to file a Statement of Use. Many allowed intent-to-use applications are never perfected to registration. Does that fact place an undue burden on third parties like Zirco who would need to wait up to 3 years (if an applicant uses all allowed extensions to file its Statement of Use) to determine if a mark is clear?

WarnerVision Entertainment Inc. v. Empire of Carolina, Inc.

101 F.3d 259 (2d Cir.1996).

■ Van Graafeiland, Circuit Judge:

Empire of Carolina, Inc., Empire Industries, Inc. and Empire Manufacturing, Inc. (hereafter "Empire") and Thomas Lowe Ventures, Inc. d/b/a Playing Mantis (hereafter "TLV") appeal from orders of the United States District Court for the Southern District of New York (Baer, J.) preliminarily enjoining appellants from violating WarnerVision Entertainment Inc.'s trademark "REAL WHEELS," and denying Empire's cross-motion for injunctive relief. *See* 915 F. Supp. 639 and 919 F. Supp. 717. The appeal was argued on an emergency basis on May 31, 1996, and on June 12, 1996, we issued an order vacating the preliminary injunction with an opinion to follow. This is the opinion.

Appellants contend that the grant of preliminary relief in WarnerVision's favor should be reversed on any of several grounds. We limit our holding to one—the district court's misapplication of 15 U.S.C. § 1057(c), part of the intent-to-use ("ITU") provisions of the Lanham Act, to the facts of the instant case. This error constitutes an abuse of discretion. See *Reuters Ltd. v. United Press Int'l, Inc.*, 903 F.2d 904, 907 (2d Cir.1990).

Prior to 1988, an applicant for trademark registration had to have used the mark in commerce before making the application. Following the enactment of the ITU provisions in that year, a person could seek registration of a mark not already in commercial use by alleging a bona fide intent to use it. *See* 15 U.S.C. § 1051(b). Registration may be granted only if, absent a grant of extension, the applicant files a statement of commercial use within six months of the date on which the Commissioner's notice of allowance pursuant to 15 U.S.C. § 1063(b) is issued. *See* 15 U.S.C. § 1051(d); *see also Eastman Kodak Co. v. Bell & Howell Document Management Prods. Co.,* 994 F.2d 1569, 1570 (Fed.Cir.1993). The ITU applicant is entitled to an extension of another six months, and may receive further extensions from the Commissioner for an additional twenty four months. 15 U.S.C. § 1051(d)(2). If, but only if, the mark completes the registration process and is registered, the ITU applicant is granted a constructive use date retroactive to the ITU filing date. 15 U.S.C. § 1057(c). This retroactive dating of constructive use permits a more orderly development of the mark without the risk that priority will be lost. The issue we now address is whether the creator of a mark who files an ITU application pursuant to 15 U.S.C. § 1051(b) can be preliminarily enjoined from engaging in the commercial use required for full registration by 15 U.S.C. § 1051(d) on motion of the holder of a similar mark who commenced commercial use of its mark subsequent to the creator's ITU application but prior to the ITU applicant's commercial use. A brief statement of the pertinent facts follows.

On September 9, 1994, TLV sent the Patent and Trademark Office ("PTO") an ITU application for the mark "REAL WHEELS," stating an intent-to-use the mark in commerce on or in connection with "the following goods/services: wheels affiliated with 1/64th and 1/43rd scale toy vehicles." The application was filed on September 23, 1994. Around the same time, two other companies, apparently acting in innocence and good faith, decided that the "REAL WHEELS" mark would fit the products they were preparing to market. One of them, Buddy L, a North Carolina manufacturer that had been marketing toy replicas of vehicles for many years, selected the name for its 1995 line of vehicle replicas. The other, WarnerVision Entertainment Inc., found the name suitable for certain of its home videos which featured motorized vehicles. The videos and vehicles were shrink-wrapped together in a single package. Both companies ordered trademark searches for conflicts in the name, but, because TLV's application had not yet reached the PTO database, no conflict was found.

Both companies then filed for registration of their mark. However, because WarnerVision's application was filed on January 3, 1995, three days before Buddy L's, it was approved, and Buddy L's was rejected. Buddy L nonetheless continued with its marketing efforts and entered into negotiations with TLV for a possible license based on TLV's ITU application.

Unfortunately, Buddy L encountered financial problems, and on March 3, 1995, it filed for relief under Chapter 11 of the Bankruptcy Law as a debtor in possession. Thereafter, in an auction sale approved by the Bankruptcy Court, Buddy L sold substantially all of its assets to Empire. On October 20, 1995, Empire purchased from TLV all of TLV's title and interest in and to the REAL WHEELS product line, trademarks and good will associated therewith, including the September 23, 1994 ITU application. At the same time, Empire licensed TLV to use the REAL WHEELS mark for toy automobiles. On November 13, 1995, WarnerVision brought the instant action.

In granting the preliminary injunction at issue, the district court quoted the Supreme Court's admonition in *Connecticut Nat'l Bank v. Germain*, 503 U.S. 249, 253–54 (1992), to the effect that when the words of a statute are unambiguous, judicial inquiry as to its meaning is complete. 919 F. Supp. at 719. We do not quarrel with this statement as a general proposition; however, we question its application in the instant case. Section 1057(c) of Title 15, the statute at issue, provides that, "contingent on the registration of a mark ... the filing of the application to register such mark shall constitute constructive use of the mark, conferring a right of priority, nationwide in effect...." Empire is not claiming constructive use based on registration. Registration will not take place until after the section 1051(d) statement of use is filed and further examination is had of the application for registration. *See Eastman Kodak, supra*, 994 F.2d at 1570. Empire contends that the district court erred in granting the preliminary injunction which bars it from completing the ITU process by filing a factually supported statement of use.

We agree. Empire does not contend that the filing of its ITU application empowered it to seek affirmative or offensive relief precluding WarnerVision's use of the REAL WHEELS mark. It seeks instead to assert the ITU filing as a defense to WarnerVision's efforts to prevent it from completing the ITU registration process. In substance, Empire requests that the normal principles of preliminary injunction law be applied in the instant case. This accords with the stated intent of Congress that the Lanham Act would be governed by equitable principles, which Congress described as "the core of U.S. trademark jurisprudence." *See* S. Rep. No. 515, 100th Cong., 2d Sess. 30 (1988), reprinted in 1988 U.S.C.C.A.N. 5577, 5592.

. . . .

As the International Trademark Association ("ITA") correctly notes at page 9 of its amicus brief, if Empire's ITU application cannot be used to defend against WarnerVision's application for a preliminary injunction, Empire will effectively be prevented from undertaking the use required to obtain registration. In short, granting a preliminary injunction to Warner-Vision would prevent Empire from ever achieving use, registration and priority and would thus effectively and permanently terminate its rights as the holder of the ITU application. Quoting 2 MCCARTHY ON TRADEMARKS AND UNFAIR COMPETITION § 19.08[1][d] at 19–59 (3d ed. 1992), the ITA said "this result 'would encourage unscrupulous entrepreneurs to look in the record for new [intent-to-use] applications by large companies, rush in to make a few sales under the same mark and sue the large company, asking for a large settlement to permit the [intent-to-use] applicant to proceed on its plans for use of the mark.' " This vulnerability to pirates is precisely what the ITU enactments were designed to eliminate. See S. Rep. No. 515, *supra*, at 5592.

The Trademark Trial and Appeal Board believes that an ITU applicant should be able to defend against such piratical acts despite the fact that full registration has not yet been given. *See Larami Corp. v. Talk to Me Programs Inc.*, 36 U.S.P.Q.2d (BNA) 1840 (T.T.A.B. 1995); *Zirco Corp. v. American Tel. & Tel. Co.*, 21 U.S.P.Q.2d (BNA) 1542 (T.T.A.B. 1992). When the foregoing authorities were cited to the district court, the court correctly stated that it was not bound by them. 919 F. Supp. at 721. However, the district court was bound not to construe and apply the ITU provisions in such a manner as to effectively convert a preliminary injunction based largely on disputed affidavits into a final adjudication on the merits.

The ITU provisions permit the holder of an ITU application to use the mark in commerce, obtain registration, and thereby secure priority retroactive to the date of filing of the ITU application. Of course, this right or privilege is not indefinite; it endures only for the time allotted by the statute. But as long as an ITU applicant's privilege has not expired, a court may not enjoin it from making the use necessary for registration on the grounds that another party has used the mark subsequent to the filing of the ITU application. To permit such an injunction would eviscerate the ITU provisions and defeat their very purpose.

This is not to say that a holder of a "live" ITU application may never be enjoined from using its mark. If another party can demonstrate that it used the mark before the holder filed its ITU application or that the filing was for some reason invalid, then it may be entitled to an injunction. WarnerVision says that it made analogous use of the REAL WHEELS mark before TLV filed its ITU application and also that the assignment to Empire of TLV's ITU application was invalid. But the district court did not pass on these contentions, and we will not consider them in the first instance.

The district court based its grant of preliminary relief on the proposition that "the first party to adopt and use a mark in commerce obtains ownership rights," and held that "WarnerVision made prior use of the mark in commerce and is the senior user." 915 F. Supp. at 645. On the basis of the present record, that decision cannot stand. WarnerVision also contends that TLV's ITU application was not properly assigned to Empire because Empire did not succeed to a portion of TLV's business. *See* 15 U.S.C. § 1060. Like the claims of analogous use, this contention raises fact issues which should not be addressed in the first instance by this Court. We vacate that portion of the district court's orders that grants WarnerVision preliminary injunctive relief and remand to the district court for further proceedings not inconsistent with this opinion.

We affirm the district court's denial of Empire's application for a preliminary injunction enjoining WarnerVision from using the REAL WHEELS mark for toys outside the video cassette market. Empire does not claim that it may use TLV's ITU application offensively to obtain this injunction, and we express no opinion on this subject. Empire says only that Buddy L, a company it acquired in a bankruptcy sale, made analogous use of the mark prior to WarnerVision's first use of the mark. On the record before us, we cannot say that the district court abused its discretion in denying a preliminary injunction on this ground.

QUESTIONS

1. Early Bird Corp. filed an intent to use application for EARLY BIRD Brand shampoo on January 2000. Early Bird had been testing the product and expected to release it within the next year. In May of 2001, the Patent and Trademark Office sent Early Bird a notice of allowance. Sparrow Corp. began using the mark EARLY BIRD for shampoo on June 1, 2001. On October 15, 2001, Early Bird Corp. began selling large quantities of EARLY BIRD shampoo in interstate commerce and filed a statement of actual use with the PTO. What are the respective rights of Early Bird and Sparrow?

2. Same as above, except that Early Bird Corp., did not begin selling large quantities of EARLY BIRD shampoo in interstate commerce until January 2006. Beginning in April of 2004, however, having filed for all available extensions, Early Bird Corp. test markets the shampoo in interstate commerce.

3. Same as #2, except that, instead of test marketing, Early Bird shipped two cases of a different brand shampoo, overlaid with EARLY BIRD labels, in interstate commerce.

4. On January 1, 2005, Wriggle Foods Co. filed an intent to use application for FRUIT JUICY fruit-flavored chewing gum. On January 2, 2005, Chomp Chewing Gum Co. began using FRUIT JUICY for fruit-flavored chewing gum in interstate commerce. On December 31, 2005, Wriggle began using FRUIT JUICY in interstate commerce, and commenced an infringement action against Chomp. Chomp responded that the term FRUIT JUICY is descriptive of fruit-flavored chewing gum, and that Wriggle's intent to use application therefore is invalid. Chomp then asserts that it has prior rights to FRUIT JUICY because it had been using the term for three years and had established secondary meaning in the term. How should the court rule?

5. Ginger Spirits, Inc. filed an intent-to-use application on June 28, 1993 for the mark SOUTH BEACH BEER for "alcoholic beverages, namely beer." Ginger Spirits alleges that it first used the mark in commerce on October 4, 1994. The registration was issued on March 7, 1995.

Frank Salacuse filed an intent-to-use application on March 22, 1993 for the mark SOUTH BEACH for "brewed drinks, namely, beer and ale." Between March and August of 1993, Salacuse filed a total of 8 intent-to-use applications for the mark SOUTH BEACH. These applications were for products including wine and wine drinks; frozen drinks; pencil cases and other desk accessories; luggage; lingerie; furniture; motor vehicles; plastic sports bottles, portable insulated coolers, and insulated lunch boxes; school notebooks, calendars, diaries, and address books. Salacuse has also filed intent-to-use applications for SOBE and SO–BE–IT!, which are variations of SOUTH BEACH. With respect to these expanded applications, Salacuse did not have any documents bearing upon or supporting his intention to use the SOUTH BEACH mark in commerce.

In 1997, Salacuse filed a petition to cancel respondent's registration, alleging priority of use and likelihood of confusion under Trademark Act Section 2(d).

What affirmative defenses can Ginger Spirits assert? Does it matter that at the time he filed suit, Salacuse had not used the mark in commerce? Do the other seven intent-to-use applications have any bearing on this case? What effect does his lack of documentary evidence have on his claim of bona fide intent? *See Salacuse v. Ginger Spirits*, 44 U.S.P.Q.2d 1415 (T.T.A.B.1997); *Commodore Electronics Ltd. v. CBM Kabushiki Kaisha*, 26 U.S.P.Q.2d 1503 (T.T.A.B.1993); and *Dunn Computer Corp. v. Loudcloud, Inc.*, 133 F.Supp.2d 823 (E.D.Va.2001) (350 ITU applications of words incorporating the term "cloud.")

6. SureStream Inc. operates websites offering website design services under the domain names surestream.com and surestream.net. The domain names were registered on July 14, 1998; the websites were up and running by July 24, 1998. On August 3, 1998, RealNetworks filed an ITU application for SURE STREAM for streaming music services, and began use in September 1998. SureStream's websites and domain name registration had not appeared on the trademark search report commissioned by RealNetworks, but RealNetworks learned of SureStream's sites shortly after filing its ITU applications. RealNetworks requested that SureStream include on its websites a disclaimer of affiliation with RealNetworks, but SureStream refused, and, after converting the Surestream.com site to offer music streaming services, ultimately initiated a trademark infringement action against RealNetworks. SureStream's websites have generated no income, and received no visitors when they first went up. SureStream has been unable to attract traffic to the websites through well-placed links on the major search engines because RealNetworks had already obtained those placements for its websites. Who has prior use of the SureStream mark? *See Burns v. Realnetworks*, 359 F.Supp.2d 1187 (W.D.Okla.2004).

Eastman Kodak Co. v. Bell & Howell Document Management Products Co.

994 F.2d 1569 (Fed.Cir.1993).

■ MICHEL, CIRCUIT JUDGE:

Background

On October 12, 1990, B&H filed intent-to-use applications, under 15 U.S.C. § 1051(b), to register the numbers "6200," "6800" and "8100" on the Principal Register as trademarks for microfilm reader/printers. After initial examination of the applications, the trademark examining attorney approved the applications for publication in the PTO's *Official Gazette*.

. . . .

Kodak, a competitor of B&H in the manufacture and marketing of business equipment products, including microfilm reader/printers, timely filed a notice of opposition to registration of each of the three marks. Kodak alleged that the marks would be used solely as model designators for the reader/printers and therefore would be merely descriptive. Kodak argued that B&H had not shown that the marks had acquired secondary meaning and that, therefore, registration of the marks would be improper.

. . . .

B&H moved for summary judgment on the grounds that there were no genuine issues of material fact regarding the alleged mere descriptiveness of its applied-for number marks.... Kodak filed a cross-motion for summary judgment.

. . . .

On the issue of mere descriptiveness, the Board stated that it "believe[s] that it is possible for a numerical designation, which functions only in part to designate a model or grade, to be inherently distinctive and registrable without a showing of secondary meaning." *Eastman Kodak,* slip op. at 5 (citing *Neapco Inc. v. Dana Corp.,* 12 U.S.P.Q.2d 1746, 1748 (TTAB 1989)). Due to the nature of intent-to-use applications, the number marks at issue had not been used at the time of the opposition proceeding. Accordingly, the Board held that it could not determine whether the numerical designations "are merely descriptive or if they are registrable without a showing of secondary meaning." *Id.* The Board concluded that in such situations, where the descriptiveness issue could not be resolved until use had begun, the opposition should be dismissed without prejudice to the initiation of a cancellation proceeding against the mark if the mark is registered after the statement of use is filed. Consequently, the Board denied Kodak's motion for summary judgment, granted B&H summary judgment on the descriptiveness issue, and dismissed the oppositions without prejudice. As a result, B&H received a notice of allowance.

Discussion

The principal issue in this case is whether the Board's implied creation of a presumption in favor of the applicant for a numerical mark intended for use as more than a model designator is a reasonable interpretation of the Board's authority under the Lanham Act. We hold that it is.

. . . .

In the instant case, the Board's decision to grant B&H summary judgment and dismiss Kodak's opposition without prejudice, necessarily involved the Board's concluding that numerical designators are presumptively not merely descriptive under Lanham Act section 2(e), 15 U.S.C. § 1052(e), when applied for an intent-to-use application under section 1(b), 15 U.S.C. § 1051(b).... The statute on its face neither requires nor precludes the Board's interpretation.

Nor does the legislative history of the Trademark Law Revision Act of 1988 speak directly to this issue. The legislative history does demonstrate that Congress intended most marks applied for in an intent-to-use application ... to be reviewed for descriptiveness in the initial examination/pre-use stage of the intent-to-use application process. For example, Senate Report 515 states that "the absence of specimens at the time the application is filed will not affect examination on numerous fundamental issues of registrability (that is, descriptiveness, geographic or surname significance, or confusing similarity)." S. Rep. No. 515, 100th Cong., 2d Sess. 32 (1988), *reprinted in* 1988 U.S.C.C.A.N. 5577, 5595. With respect to the examination of the statement of use, which is filed after a notice of allowance has been issued, the Report states:

> The Patent and Trademark Office's examination of the statement of use will be only for the purpose of determining issues that could not have been fully considered during the initial examination of the application, that is, whether the person filing the statement of use is the applicant, whether the mark as used corresponds to the drawing submitted with the application, whether the goods or services were identified in the application and not subsequently deleted, and *whether the mark, as displayed in the specimens or facsimiles, functions as a mark.*

Id. at 34, 1988 U.S.C.C.A.N. at 5596 (emphasis added). As the highlighted phrase shows, Congress did intend the PTO to confirm, after the filing of the statement of use, that the intent-to-use mark, as displayed and used, actually "functions as a mark." ... And the legislative history itself emphasized that "[t]his provision [of the statute] permits the [PTO] to raise issues of registrability that might not be evident until the applicant makes available specimens showing the mark as used and/or clarifying the nature of the goods or services involved." H.R.Rep. No. 1028, 100th Cong., 2d Sess. 9 (1988). Thus, the statute and legislative history provide for the situation where, as here, the question of mere descriptiveness cannot be answered until after use has begun.

Furthermore, it is clear from the legislative history that Congress, for policy reasons, chose to sequence the opposition process before the use of an intent-to-use mark had commenced. *See* S. Rep. No. 515 at 32, 1988 U.S.C.C.A.N. at 5595 ("Subjecting an intent-to-use application to the opposition process before the applicant makes use of its mark is essential if the system is to achieve its goal of reducing uncertainty before the applicant invests in commercial use of the mark."). Accordingly, Congress knew that some issues of registrability could not be decided in opposition proceedings and would therefore have to be addressed in the post-use PTO examination or challenged in a cancellation proceeding after the mark was registered.

. . . .

Kodak argues, however, that the Board's interpretation is unreasonable because it would preclude asserting mere descriptiveness as a basis for denying registration of both word and number marks in intent-to-use applications. This argument is unavailing for several reasons. First, there are words and phrases that, as applied to certain goods, the examining attorney in the initial examination could certainly find to be prima facie merely descriptive. For example, an examining attorney could easily find that the term "reader/printer" applied to the microfilm reader/printers at issue here would be merely descriptive. ...Furthermore, the examining attorney may also find numbers that are intended for use *solely* as model designators to be prima facie merely descriptive.

. . . .

Second, Kodak's argument must assume that under circumstances such as these, after a notice of allowance is issued, intent-to-use marks will automatically be passed to registration. However, the statute provides for another examination of the mark after the statement of use is filed. 15 U.S.C. § 1051(d)(1). ...Moreover, the statute contemplates the need, in certain circumstances, for a complete reexamination: "Such examination may include an examination of the factors set forth in subsections (a) through (e) of section 1052." *Id.* In addition, the trademark regulations, promulgated by the PTO pursuant to authority granted by statute, *see id.* § 1123, provide that "[a] timely filed statement of use which meets the minimum requirements specified in paragraph (e) of this section *will be* examined in accordance with §§ 2.61 through 2.69." 37 C.F.R. § 2.88(f) (emphasis added). Thus, once the examining attorney establishes that the statement of use has met the minimum requirements set forth in 37 C.F.R. § 2.88(e), ... the regulation requires that the examining attorney reexamine the mark under the standards of the initial examination (37 C.F.R. §§ 2.61–2.69).

. . . .

Kodak further asserts that the Board's interpretation is unreasonable because it allegedly creates a different standard for registrability for intent-to-use applications from use-based applications with regard to descriptiveness, contrary to statutory design. Kodak is correct that the statute provides for the same substantive requirements to be met for intent-to-use and use-based applications. ...However, Kodak's argument misunderstands the character of the Board's action. The Board merely adopted a presumption that a numerical mark, which may be used at least in part as a model designator, is not merely descriptive in the absence of evidence of how it is actually used. Once B&H files its statement of use with specimens of actual use, the PTO will refuse registration if the marks are, indeed, used in a merely descriptive fashion, just as the PTO would deny such a mark registration in a use-based application. ...Thus, the standard that the PTO applies in either case is the same—only the timing of such review is different. Accordingly, the Board's interpretation is not unreasonable under this analysis.

Kodak contends that the difference in timing is sufficiently prejudicial to render the Board's interpretation unreasonable. Kodak argues particularly that the Board's decision relegates such questions of mere descriptiveness to a post-registration cancellation proceeding. Kodak maintains that the delay is prejudicial to it because in a cancellation proceeding, the registration at issue enjoys a presumption of validity. Kodak's argument is misplaced because, although the registration is considered prima facie valid, the challenger's burden of proof in both opposition and cancellation proceedings is a preponderance of the evidence. 2 J. Thomas McCarthy, McCarthy on Trademarks and Unfair Competition § 20.16 (3d ed. 1992).

. . . .

Because the Board's interpretation is consistent with the language and purposes of the statute, we hold that it is reasonable.

. . . .

Based on the foregoing, the Board's decision is *Affirmed.*

2.   FOREIGN MARKS

Recall the six-month priority allowed to foreign applications based on an application filed in the foreign country of origin up to six months prior to the U.S. filing, *supra* pp. 181–83. Under the ITU system, as we have seen, an ITU filing will give the applicant priority over a third party whose use postdates the filing, but precedes the applicant's use, so long as the applicant makes bona fide use of the mark within the allotted time. If the priority date recedes a further six months because the U.S. filing was based on a previous foreign filing, the foreign applicant may prevail not only over those who first use the mark after the filing, but also over U.S. applicants whose filings predated the non resident's U.S. filing, but postdate the filing in the country of origin. Consider the following problems: who has priority and why?

1.   On January 10, 2005, Koala Corp., an Australian company, filed an application in Australia for OUTDOORS for beer. On January 15, 2005, Armadillo Corp, a U.S. company, filed an intent-to-use application in the U.S. Patent and Trademark Office for OUTDOORS for beer. On March 1, 2005, Armadillo began to promote the impending arrival on the U.S. market of its OUTDOORS beer. On April 15, 2005, Koala began selling OUTDOORS beer in the U.S. On May 1, 2005, Armadillo began selling its OUTDOORS beer, and filed its Statement of Use in the PTO. On May 10, 2005, Koala filed a trademark application in the PTO citing its January 10 Australian filing. If Armadillo opposes issuance of Koala's registration:

  a.   Armadillo will prevail because it filed first in the U.S.

  b.   Armadillo will prevail because it has prior analogous use in the U.S.

  c.   Koala will prevail because it used first in the U.S.

  d.   Koala will prevail because it filed first.

2. Same facts as #1 above, except that Armadillo began promoting the arrival of its OUTDOORS beer on January 1, 2005.

    a. Armadillo will prevail because it filed first in the U.S.

    b. Armadillo will prevail because it has prior analogous use in the U.S.

    c. Koala will prevail because it used first in the U.S.

    d. Koala will prevail because it filed first.

3. Same facts as #1 above, except that Armadillo first sold its OUTDOORS beer on April 1, 2005.

    a. Armadillo will prevail because it filed first in the U.S.

    b. Armadillo will prevail because it has prior analogous use in the U.S.

    c. Armadillo will prevail because it used first in the U.S.

    d. Koala will prevail because it filed first.

4. Same facts as #1 above, except that Koala does not file in the PTO until July 15, 2005.

    a. Armadillo will prevail because it filed first in the U.S.

    b. Armadillo will prevail because it has prior analogous use in the U.S.

    c. Koala will prevail because it used first in the U.S.

    d. Koala will prevail because it filed first.

5. Same Facts as #4 above, except that Koala began selling its OUTDOORS beer in the U.S. on January 1, 2005.

    a. Armadillo will prevail because it filed first in the U.S.

    b. Armadillo will prevail because it has prior analogous use in the U.S.

    c. Koala will prevail because it used first in the U.S.

    d. Koala will prevail because it filed first.

C. Bars to Registration

1. Section 2(a) of the Lanham Act: Immoral, Scandalous, Disparaging or Deceptive Matter

Section 2(a) of the Lanham Act prohibits registration of a mark that

(a) consists of or comprises immoral, deceptive, or scandalous matter, or matter which may disparage or falsely suggest a connection with persons, living or dead, institutions, beliefs, or national symbols, or bring them into contempt, or disrepute.

Proof of distinctiveness cannot avail an applicant who is refused registration under Section 2(a); the bar is absolute. The four distinctive prongs of Section 2(a)–immoral or scandalous, disparaging, deceptive and false association–are discussed below.

a.   IMMORAL, SCANDALOUS OR DISPARAGING MARKS

In re Bad Frog Brewery, Inc., 1999 WL 149819 (T.T.A.B.). Applicant appealed from the Examining Attorney's denial of registration for BAD FROG BEER and design (depicted below) on the ground that the frog would be "immediately recognizable by the average consumer as 'flipping the bird' or 'giving the finger,' " and that this gesture "is widely recognized to be obscene." A majority of the Board reversed. First, the Board majority determined that Bad Frog's frog looked more amphibian than human, and would not be "perceived as giving the finger." Second, the majority concluded that the Examining Attorney had not established that "such a gesture, by a realistic looking animal, as opposed to a human, would be perceived as scandalous or immoral," especially since the frog was not "giving the finger to any individual or group." Citing "The Illustrated History of Flipping the Bird," an article from a 1997 issue of Gentleman's Quarterly, the majority indicated that far from being obscene, giving the finger had become "that most democratic of gestures," practiced by American soldiers, statesman, and celebrities.

Administrative Trademark Judge Simms disputed both of the majority's grounds. Applicant's labels left no doubt, he contended, as to the meaning of the Frog's gesture: "AN AMPHIBIAN WITH AN ATTITUDE," "HE JUST DON'T CARE," "DO IT FROGGY STYLE," "HE'S MEAN, GREEN AND OBSCENE," "HE'S NAKED, NASTY AND INSENSITIVE," and "FLIP THE BIRD, GET A FROG." As to the majority's second ground, Judge Simms retorted:

> Surely, the majority cannot be laying down a rule that registration should be allowed when any mark depicts an animal making this obscene gesture. A per se rule should not be estab-

lished that an animal making this gesture is somehow a registrable mark. Is a monkey, for example, depicted as making this gesture somehow less offensive than a depiction of a human being making this gesture? There is probably no more patently offensive gesture than this one, which is the non-verbal equivalent of an obscene expression. Moreover, I simply do not fathom why, in order to be considered scandalous, as the majority apparently contends, the obscene gesture must be directed at a particular person or group (presumably in the mark). The majority appears to be saying that, if applicant's mark showed the frog giving this gesture to a particular person or group, it would be more likely to be found unregistrable. I simply do not understand the logic of such a statement. It appears to me that the mere fact that the obscene expression is uttered in a mark or that the non-verbal gesture is made in a mark is sufficient to present a patently offensive mark for registration.

If you were an applicant for trademark registration, or for that matter, an Examining Attorney, how much guidance would this case afford toward future determinations of whether a proposed mark is immoral or scandalous? (Does the T.T.A.B.'s disclaimer at the head of its opinion, "This disposition is not citable as precedent of the T.T.A.B.," offer any hints?)

STANDING TO BRING A SECTION 2(a) CHALLENGE TO THE "IMMORAL" CHARACTER OF THE PROPOSED MARK

A mark is considered immoral or scandalous if a "substantial composite of the general public" would regard it as offensive. *See In re Mavety Media Group Ltd.*, 33 F.3d 1367 (Fed.Cir.1994). A divided panel of the Federal Circuit elaborated on the circumstances under which members of the public may oppose or seek to cancel the registration of a mark that the opponent/petitioner finds deeply offensive. In *Ritchie v. Simpson*, 170 F.3d 1092 (Fed.Cir.1999), a majority upheld a member of the general public's standing to oppose the registration of O.J. SIMPSON, O.J., and THE JUICE for a variety of goods:

> This court has made it clear that the officials of the PTO may not readily assume, without more, that they know the views of a substantial composite of the public. In this light, we have commended the practice of resolving the issue of whether a mark comprises scandalous matter by first permitting the mark to pass for publication, and then allowing interested members of a composite of the general public who consider the mark to be scandalous to bring opposition proceedings. By so doing, the PTO avoids the risk of pre-judging public attitudes toward a proposed registration based on ad hoc responses by government officials, while at the same time affording the affected public an opportunity to effectively participate in the question of whether the registration is proper. Thus, the policy behind the procedure for determining whether a mark is scandalous encourages, if not requires, partic-

ipation by members of the general public who seek to participate through opposition proceedings.

The starting point for a standing determination for a litigant before an administrative agency is . . . § 13 of the Lanham Act, . . . which provides:

> Any person who believes that he would be damaged by the registration of a mark upon the principal register may, upon payment of the prescribed fee, file an opposition in the Patent and Trademark Office, stating the grounds therefor. . . .

Section 13 of the Lanham Act establishes a broad class of persons who are proper opposers; by its terms the statute only requires that a person have a belief that he would suffer some kind of damage if the mark is registered. However, in addition to meeting the broad requirements of § 13, an opposer must meet two judicially-created requirements in order to have standing—the opposer must have a "real interest" in the proceedings and must have a "reasonable" basis for his belief of damage.

1.   The "Real Interest" Test

The opposer must have a direct and personal stake in the outcome of the opposition. . . . In no case has this court ever held that one must have a specific commercial interest, not shared by the general public, in order to have standing as an opposer . . . The crux of the matter is not how many others share one's belief that one will be damaged by the registration, but whether that belief is reasonable and reflects a real interest in the issue.

. . . .

In his notice of opposition against the marks at issue, Mr. Ritchie alleged, *inter alia,* that he would be damaged by the registration of the marks because the marks disparage his values, especially those values relating to his family. In addition, in his notice of opposition, Mr. Ritchie described himself as a "family man" who believes that the "sanctity of marriage requires a husband and wife who love and nurture one another," and as a member of a group that could be potentially damaged by marks that allegedly are synonymous with wife-beater and wife-murderer. Furthermore, Mr. Ritchie alleged that the marks are scandalous because they would "attempt to justify physical violence against women."

It would be inconsistent to deny standing . . . on the grounds that [his] concerns are widely shared. The Board erred by requiring the opposer in this case to somehow show that his interest is not shared by any substantial part of the general population. On the contrary, the purpose of the opposition proceeding is to establish what a substantial composite of the general public believes. The limitation placed upon standing in this case by the Board undermines this very purpose. . . .

directly imj
words, mark
group may k
example tha
ly possess a

A secon
of damage i
proposed tr;
damage. Th(
forms, inclu
groups repr(
mark." *Id.* .

Applyin;
finds that w
proceedings,
standing, th;
has a "reaso

Opposer
that is inher
he is a "lesb
his notice of
fourth-gener
mark is ther
the plaintiff
second meth
age.

In this 1
[O]pposer ha
belief of dam
personally of
committed by
to the USPT
ing applicant
allegations re
alleging that
conducted su
his belief in
throughout tl
cations (i.e. a
of the excerpt
opposer's gro
ing or offensi

. . . .

In sum, \
more than a r

2. *"Reasonable" Belief of Damage*

. . . . Mr. Ritchie alleges that he has obtained petitions signed by people from all over the United States who agree with him that the marks at issue are scandalous, denigrate their values, encourage spousal abuse and minimize the problem of domestic violence. Again, for purposes of the motion to dismiss on the pleadings for lack of standing, we accept as true all well-pled allegations. . . . Therefore, Mr. Ritchie's belief of damage, for purposes of the motion, has a reasonable basis in fact.

Judge Newman, *dissenting*, contested opposer's interest in the marks sought to be registered:

A person with no interest in the trademarks for which registration is sought—a "mere intermeddler," a "self-appointed guardian of the register"—does not meet even the minimal statutory requirements of 15 U.S.C. § 1063. The Lanham Act was not designed to convert federal trademark proceedings into a forum for attack on the morality of the registrant. Disapproval, by a member of the general public, of the applicant for registration, however notorious that applicant, does not provide standing to oppose registration of the applicant's commercial trademarks.

The panel majority, expressing concern lest a trademark examiner exercise moral judgment, instead opens federal agency procedures to satellite litigation initiated by any person who disapproves on moral grounds of the applicant for registration and alleges that others may share his disapproval. The panel majority has created a dangerous and facile opportunity for the intermeddling public to burden commercial rights in which it has no interest. . . .

QUESTION

Review the language of § 2(a): what does the unsavoriness of the *applicant* have to do with whether the *mark* "consists of or comprises" immoral or scandalous matter or matter "which may falsely suggest a connection with persons, living or dead, institutions, beliefs or national symbols, or bring them into contempt or disrepute"? Any time the PTO registers a mark that symbolizes an entity whose characteristics someone finds reprehensible, does that mean that the mark brings the objector's beliefs into contempt?

Michael J. McDermott v. San Francisco Women's Motorcycle

81 U.S.P.Q.2d 1212 (T.T.A.B.2006).

By The Board:

San Francisco Women's Motorcycle Contingent ("applicant") has applied to register the mark DYKES ON BIKES for "[e]ducation and [e]ntertainment [s]ervices in the nature of organizing, conducting, and promoting

2. A woman or wife.

1. *often offensive:* an American Indian woman

2. *usually disparaging:* WOMAN, WIFE.

Encyclopedia of North American Indians, Houghton Mifflin (College Division) (online version) The literal meaning of the word *squaw* is obscure, and its connotations have changed over time. Its origins are found among the northeastern tribes. In Massachusetts, *squd* referred to a younger woman. In Narragansett, *sunksquaw* meant "queen" or "lady." Despite these Algonquian-language origins, however, nonnatives applied the term to native women throughout North America. Over time it took on derogatory connotations as travelers referred to native women as *squaw drudges* and often used the term in opposition to Indian princess. Nonnatives often referred to women leaders as *squaw sachems* and nonnative men who married native women as *squaw men.* By the twentieth century the word *squaw* had developed multiple derogatory associations that had no connection with the word's original meaning.

. . . .

We find that the evidence made of record ... is sufficient to establish prima facie that applicant's marks disparage a substantial composite of Native Americans when used in the context of applicant's [Class 25] goods and [Class 35] services. The record includes statements from Native Americans that the term is "damaging and offensive," "the worst of the worst," an "insult" and "obscene." The record also demonstrates that the opinions of Native Americans regarding the term are not limited to particular contexts. Certainly, as a term considered "damaging and offensive," "the worst of the worst," an "insult" and "obscene," the term "squaw" is encompassed within the definition of "disparage." (Citation omitted) Additionally, the record includes a statement from Senator Ben Campbell, a Native American United States Senator, that the term is "one of four terms most offensive to Native Americans." *The Washington Post*, September 1993.... [E]ven if, as applicant maintains, the statements in the record attributed to Native Americans are those of Native American activists and of legislators who share the views of such activists, we do not discount such statements. Applicant would have us assume that the views of Native American activists and sympathetic legislators do not represent the views of a substantial composite of Native Americans. Applicant provides no basis for concluding that their views would not be shared by a substantial composite of Native Americans. Further, in light of the ex parte nature of this case and the Federal Circuit's recognition of the limited resources of examining attorneys, we do not discount the probative value of such evidence.

The record also shows that various states have taken the drastic and symbolic step of renaming geographic places containing the term "squaw" or banning the term "squaw" from geographic place names within the state. Of note is Maine Revised Statutes 1 M.R.S. § 1101 (2003), which characterizes "squaw" as "offensive," and includes the term "nigger" in the same statutory section, deeming each as an "offensive name." Also, Concurrent Resolution No. 94 of the Oklahoma Legislature (May 2000) describes the term "squaw" as "offensive to Native Americans," without limitation to a particular context.

Applicant's challenges to the legislative evidence on the basis that there are only a limited number of statutes that address "squaw" and that such statutes only address geographical place names and not the names of towns or villages, or the names of businesses, are not well taken. Even if "there are more than 1,000 geographical features in the United States" which have "squaw" in their names, and only seven out of thirty-six states have enacted legislation that applies to "geographical feature names" with "squaw," the fact that seven states have addressed the issue of names with "squaw" in them is significant. We cannot conclude from the absence of similar legislation to date in other states that those states consider the term to be inoffensive. Also, the statutory sections submitted by the examining attorney indicate that these seven states have enacted such statutes on the basis that the term is "offensive." As noted above, the Maine legislature has addressed the names of places containing "squaw" in the same statutory section as "nigger." *See* Maine Revised Statutes 1 M.R.S. § 1101 (2003)....

The record also contains evidence of Native American opposition to the term "squaw" as used in "Squaw Valley," which is the geographic location of applicant, part of applicant's trade name, and part of the trademark of applicant's claimed Registration Nos. 670261 (SQUAW VALLEY) and 1628589 (SQUAW VALLEY USA). *See* excerpted story from the April 6, 1997 edition of *The Saint Paul Pioneer Press*, stating that "the word 'squaw,' ... is offensive to some American Indians, and a national activist group is launching a campaign to remove it from more than 100 places throughout California—including the most famous of all: Squaw Valley."

... [T]he evidence offered by the examining attorney reflects that a substantial composite of Native Americans would consider the term SQUAW, when its meaning is a Native American woman or wife, to be disparaging regardless of context, including in connection with applicant's identified goods and services in International Classes 25 and 35. The evidence shows that this term, when it means a Native American woman or wife, is generally offensive to Native Americans, no matter what the goods or services with which the mark is used. Given the lesser evidentiary standard that is required of the USPTO in the ex parte context, it would be ludicrous to require an examining attorney to find statements from individuals in the relevant group stating that the term is offensive with respect to the specific goods and services in the application. Members of the affected group are not likely to make public statements regarding their feelings about the use of SQUAW with respect to specific goods or services. Rather, we can infer from the evidence about the generally offensive nature of the term when meaning a Native American woman or wife that the term is offensive no matter with what goods or services it is used.

. . . .

. . . We find that the examining attorney has made out a prima facie case of disparagement under Section 2(a).

b. *Did applicant rebut the examining attorney's evidence that, under the second prong of the Harjo I test, the mark is disparaging as used in connection with the goods and services in International Classes 25 and 35?*

. . . .

We note applicant's argument that its "mark is not used in connection with any other term or design element that would create an association with American Indians or any other identifiable person(s)," which was advanced by applicant to distinguish the present situation from those in other cases which had previously been cited by the examining attorney, namely, *Harjo I.* (Citations omitted).

It appears to us that this argument . . . goes to the first prong of the *Harjo I* test, namely, the "likely meaning" of the term in the mark. We agree that applicant's marks do not contain any design or logo elements, but are for word marks in standard character form. However, we are aware of no requirement in Section 2(a) or the case law interpreting Section 2(a) that to be found disparaging a mark must include design or logo elements which reinforce the connection with the referenced persons or symbol. In fact, in *In re Reemtsma Cigarettenfabriken G.m.b.H.,* 122 USPQ 339 (TTAB 1959), involving the mark SENUSSI for "cigarettes," the Board's decision does not refer to a design component in the applied-for mark, yet the Board found the mark to be disparaging to a Moslem sect whose tenets forbid the use of cigarettes.

. . . .

Thus, applicant's arguments directed against the examining attorney's evidence are not well taken. Applicant has not submitted any evidence which suggests that Native Americans do not view "squaw" as a non-disparaging term for its Class 25 and 35 goods and services.

Accordingly, we conclude that applicant has not rebutted either prong of the *Harjo I* test, and therefore we find that applicant has not rebutted the examining attorney's prima facie case of disparagement under Section 2(a).

. . . .

In our September 26, 2005 decision, the Board found that the meaning of SQUAW in applicant's marks, as used in connection with its identified skis and ski equipment in International Class 28, is applicant's Squaw Valley ski resort in California. The Board therefore held that the marks were not disparaging under the first part of the *Harjo I* test, i.e., the "likely meaning" of the matter in question was not a Native American woman or wife.

   . . . .

   . . . [T]he record shows that SQUAW VALLEY is well known in connection with the sport of skiing. Squaw Valley was the site of the 1960 Winter Olympics; *Encyclopedia Britannica* has an entry for "Squaw Valley" and identifies Squaw Valley as "world-famous"; Squaw Valley is mentioned in numerous newspaper articles in newspapers from all over the United States; and, according to the November 7, 1999 *Washington Post* article noted above, Squaw Valley is known for its challenging ski slopes. Further, the articles from the Nexis database submitted by applicant indicate that "Squaw" is used as a shortened form of "Squaw Valley." In view thereof, the examining attorney's contention that applicant is not "legally limited to using the mark in close approximation with the wording 'Squaw Valley USA,' " as appears on one of the specimens of use for applicant's International Class 28 goods, while true, is of no consequence— the wording "Squaw Valley USA" on skiing related goods is not necessary to create an association of SQUAW with applicant; rather, the term SQUAW, when used with skiing related goods, would be perceived as a reference to the Squaw Valley ski resort.

   The examining attorney also points out that there are no trade channel limitations in the identifications of goods and that "consumer[s] seeing those goods being sold in a ski shop not associated with Applicant would not necessarily perceive the meaning as the resort." Request for reconsideration at unnumbered p. 13. However, in view of the evidence of record, and particularly because many of the articles referring to "Squaw" are from locations in the United States distant from applicant's resort, we cannot accept the implication . . . that an association with applicant would only be created if the skis and skiing-related goods were sold in stores associated with applicant.

   The Board has, in analyzing refusals under Section 2(a), considered the meaning of a term as reflected by the goods on which the mark is used. In *In re In Over Our Heads, Inc.*, 16 USQP2d 1653 (TTAB 1990), the Board reversed a refusal to register the mark MOONIES (and design) for a doll which dropped its pants when a collapsible bulb was squeezed, thus exposing its buttocks. The examining attorney took the position that "the mark comprised scandalous matter which disparaged The Unification Church founded by the Reverend Sun Myung Moon." *id.* at 1653. However, the Board found that the term MOONIES had more than one meaning, and that the meaning of MOONIES, when used on the subject goods—dolls— would most likely be perceived as indicating that the doll "moons," and would not be perceived as referencing members of The Unification Church.

   Accordingly, we reiterate our finding that, when SQUAW is considered in connection with. . . items . . . directly connected with skiing, it is the Squaw Valley ski resort meaning of SQUAW, rather than the meaning of a

Native American woman or wife, that will come to the minds of consumers.
. . .

Because applicant has rebutted the examining attorney's showing regarding the "likely meaning" of the marks for the International Class 28 goods, it is not necessary for us to consider whether applicant has rebutted the second part of the *Harjo I* test, and the refusal to register the marks in Class 28 must be reversed. . . .

[T]he examining attorney's request for reconsideration is granted to the extent that the Section 2(a) refusal is affirmed for the application in International Classes 25 and 35.

QUESTIONS

1. Is the Board's conclusion that "squaw" is disparaging "regardless of context" with respect to applicant's Class 25 goods and Class 35 services consistent with its conclusion that the term is not disparaging for the Class 28 skiing-related goods?

2. What kind of evidence could applicant have submitted to rebut the Examiner's prima facie case of disparagement with respect to the Class 25 goods and Class 35 services? Would it help if applicant amended the descriptions of the apparel goods and the Class 35 retail store services with the limiting language "relating to a ski resort"? Why or why not?

3. Was the Board in *Squaw Valley* in essence saying that the Examiner can make a prima facie showing that a term is disparaging without reference to an applicant's goods/services under the second prong of the test? Consider the district court's criticism in *Harjo II* of the Board's failure to sufficiently analyze the disparaging nature of REDSKINS as viewed by Native Americans specifically in relation to the football team's services. Is the difference in *Squaw Valley* explained by the fact that it was an ex parte proceeding? What evidence would a plaintiff in an opposition or cancellation proceeding need to present in order to make a prima facie case?

4. In *Harjo II*, Pro–Football appealed the decision of the Trademark Trial and Appeal Board to a district court rather than to the Federal Circuit. Unlike the Federal Circuit, a district court can consider the matter *de novo* and can hear new evidence. Why do you think that Pro–Football chose the district court? Do you think the fact that the Board dismissed Pro–Football's First Amendment defense on the ground that it lacked jurisdiction to decide constitutional issues influenced the choice of appeal venues? Would there ever be good reasons for a losing party to appeal to the Federal Circuit rather than to seek a *de novo* review by a district court?

5. *Harjo I* involved a cancellation proceeding against REDSKINS registrations dating as far back as the 1960's. The Board held that the meaning of the mark should be determined at the time of the registrations in determining the issues of scandalousness and disparagement. In a cancellation proceeding, does it make sense to focus on the period when a registration issued, rather than the present? What if the meaning and/or perception of a term changes over time?

6. The measure of scandalous and immoral marks is the perception of a substantial composite of the general public; whereas, marks disparaging to a particular group are viewed through the lens of a substantial composite of that group. What if the disparaged group consists of a religion with 1,000 adherents, will the negative perceptions of 400 of them be sufficient to block a registration? Compare the standard for marks disparaging to a commercial entity or individual, which looks to the reaction of a "reasonable person of ordinary sensibilities." *See Greyhound Corp. v. Both Worlds, Inc.*, 6 U.S.P.Q.2d 1635 (T.T.A.B.1988) (design of defecating dog held disparaging to Opposer Greyhound Corp.).

b. SECTION 2(a): DECEPTIVE TERMS

In re ALP of South Beach Inc.

79 U.S.P.Q.2d 1009 (T.T.A.B.2006).

■ BUCHER, ADMINISTRATIVE TRADEMARK JUDGE:

ALP of South Beach Inc. seeks registration on the Supplemental Register of the term shown below:

for ... "restaurants providing full service to sit-down patrons, excluding cafeteria-style restaurants," in International Class 42.

This case is now before the Board on appeal from the final refusal of the Trademark Examining Attorney to register this designation based upon the ground that this term is deceptive under Section 2(a) of the Act.

We affirm the refusal to register.

The test for determining whether a mark is deceptive under Section 2(a) has been stated by the Court of Appeals for the Federal Circuit as:

(1) Is the term misdescriptive of the character, quality, function, composition or use of the goods (or services)?

(2) If so, are prospective purchasers likely to believe that the misdescription actually describes the goods (or services)?

(3) If so, is the misdescription likely to affect the decision to purchase?

In re Budge Manufacturing Co., Inc., 857 F.2d 773, 8 USPQ2d 1259, 1260 (Fed. Cir. 1988) [LOVEE LAMB held deceptive for seat covers not made of lambskin]. See also, *In re Woolrich Woolen Mills, Inc.*, 13 USPQ 2d 1235 (TTAB 1989) [WOOLRICH for clothing not made of wool found not to be deceptive under § 2(a)].

We find that the word CAFETERIA used in connection with restaurant services that explicitly exclude cafeteria-style restaurants does *misdescribe* the services. In fact, applicant appears to admit the same:

> Indeed, "cafeteria" is defined in Webster's New World Dictionary as "a self-service restaurant or lunchroom." ALP's restaurant is neither self-service nor a cafeteria....

Applicant's appeal brief, p. 5.

The next part of the *Budge* test is whether any prospective purchaser is likely to believe the misdescription. (Citations omitted)

The Trademark Examining Attorney argues from the evidence of record in this case that there are clearly restaurants that are categorized in restaurant guides, for example, as "cafeterias" ... The Trademark Examining Attorney argues from the record that some restaurant patrons prefer cafeteria-style restaurants for their variety of foods, convenience and overall value. Hence, at least some potential patrons are quite likely to believe that a restaurant calling itself CAFETERIA meets the common dictionary definition of a "cafeteria."

. . . .

We are not convinced, ... by applicant's arguments that everyone who comes into its CAFETERIA establishments knows in advance the nature of the restaurant.... [W]e cannot rely on applicant's allegations about its current marketing strategies. Any registration that issues from this application will be national in scope, and applicant clearly would not be limited to the two establishments it currently operates. Certainly, we cannot assume that word-of-mouth publicity and detailed restaurant reviews are the only ways prospective consumers would ever encounter the mark. We must presume that magazine advertisements, classified ad listings, and highway billboards could some day be part of applicant's marketing mix, or alternatively, that a prospective patron might well chance upon the restaurant when driving or walking by, and come in for a meal after seeing the signage on the exterior of the building.

It appears from a photograph of the Chelsea location that applicant's CAFETERIA mark is depicted on a canopy directly above floor-to-ceiling, glass garage-door panels. Applicant argues that any passerby could easily see that applicant's establishment is set up as a table-service restaurant. Accordingly, applicant contends that it would be impossible for the potential patron—even one having no familiarity with the nature of applicant's services—to be able to view the mark on the front of applicant's restaurant without simultaneously realizing applicant offers table service.

. . . .

We agree with applicant that what separates cases such as *Northwestern Golf [v. Acushnet Co.,* (226 USPQ 1985) (POWER STEP for golf clubs)] and *Econoheat* [218 USPQ 381 (TTAB 1983) (SOLAR QUARTZ for electric space heaters)](where marks were found not to be deceptively misdescriptive or deceptive) from the SILK and HYDE/HIDE cases cited by the Trademark Examining Attorney (where marks were found to be deceptively misdescriptive or deceptive), is that the Board found that merely contemplating the involved consumer items in the *Northwestern Golf* and *Econoheat* cases would be sufficient to enable a reasonable consumer to draw a correct conclusion about the nature of the respective products. (Citation omitted).

Applicant has pointed to cases where the casual observer of consumer products is presumed to be able to discover that the mark is obviously misdescriptive by looking at the involved goods. We do not find these cases involving a close-up visual examination of consumer items, such as golf clubs, [and] space heaters, . . . to be analogous to the allegedly misdescriptive service mark involved herein. Applicant has cited no cases saying that the owner of a service mark can advertise or display false information prominently about its services to prospective consumers, and then escape a finding of deceptiveness because the sale may ultimately not be consummated when the customer discovers the misrepresentation just in time to avoid the transaction.

We really cannot be sure what portion of prospective customers, at some point, actually believed the deceptive misdescription. In his affidavit, . . . one of applicant's principals states that only a very few prospective customers appeared to have any misimpressions about the nature of applicant's services. We view this acknowledgement as significant. That some prospective customers did have a misimpression about the nature of applicant's services indicates to us that others may also have been misled. . . .

We turn then to the third and final prong for deceptiveness under the *Budge* test. Having found that prospective patrons of applicant's restaurant are likely to believe that the misdescription actually describes the services, we must still determine whether the misdescription is likely to affect the decision to purchase.

This final prong of the *Budge* test has been restated as inquiring whether or not the misrepresentation would materially affect the decision to purchase the goods. . . .

Applicant dismisses the SILK and HIDE/HYDE cases, arguing in this case that a table service restaurant is preferable to a cafeteria. The SILK cases do discuss how silk is more desirable as a fabric than synthetic materials frequently used in its stead, or in a similar fashion, in the HIDE/HYDE cases, leather is found is more desirable to most consumers than are often-cheaper leather substitutes. By contrast, applicant's position . . . is that, for the majority of prospective diners, pushing a tray through a lunchroom line is not preferable to being seated at a table or booth with full table service provided by capable wait staff. In other words, applicant contends that if the instant case involves any "bait-and-switch" for some prospective patrons, the "switch" here is to a higher class of services.

. . . .

. . . [W]e conclude that there are features of a cafeteria that some prospective patrons will prefer to those of a table-service restaurant. Thus, whether or not restaurant services have significant attributes of a cafeteria may be material to the decision to patronize a particular establishment.

We turn then to applicant's argument that the prospective patrons who realize their mistake are able to walk away from the reservation desk before purchasing meals requiring full table service. . . .

. . . [W]hile descriptiveness or misdescriptiveness must be considered in relation to the services, this does not mean that prospective purchasers cannot be misled prior to arriving at the restaurant itself. Upon encountering applicant's mark for restaurant services in a promotional context, some share of prospective patrons will initially conclude, quite erroneously, that the referenced restaurant is, indeed, a cafeteria. Accordingly, we . . . find that the critical point for gauging whether or not potential patrons believe the misdescription inherent in applicant's service mark is earlier than applicant has argued.

Assume, as we must, that reasonable prospective patrons of these services see informational signage preceding an Interstate highway exchange notifying them of the availability of CAFETERIA restaurant services . . . and they pull off at the designated exit . . . Or perhaps another group of prospective patrons seeks out the restaurant based on a classified advertisement for "Cafeteria" under the heading "restaurant services," believing that it offers cafeteria services. Or maybe it is a hungry family merely driving or walking by that decides to come in for a cafeteria meal after seeing the signage on the canopy on the exterior of the building.

[A]pplicant takes the position that even consumers who may have been misled at some earlier timeframe, will discover their mistake once in the vicinity of the restaurant.

We . . . cannot say that reasonably prudent members of the public . . . would be able to ascertain from across the street or on the sidewalk that applicant's restaurant is not a cafeteria. . . .

True, the state of being misled may well be dispelled before the customer completes the purchase. Nonetheless, customers will have been misled by the name in the first place—causing them to decide to patronize the restaurant. The critical point is not when the customers walk into the restaurant or when they are handed a menu, but when they encounter the mark in an advertisement, informational road sign, or the signage on the exterior of the restaurant, and then . . . making a decision to purchase the services. . . . Irrespective of exactly where the patrons may be at the point they recognize the deception (e.g., parking across the street, walking down the sidewalk, standing at the reservation desk, or sitting at a table), we find that by the time the prospective patrons are faced with the choice of either completing the purchase of a meal different from the one sought or finding another restaurant, deception has already taken place.

... The mere fact that one may have decided to go to applicant's restaurant in order to patronize a true cafeteria, based solely upon applicant's choice of a deceptively misdescriptive name for a restaurant, is sufficient to meet the test of the final prong of the *Budge* test for deceptiveness.

Accordingly, we conclude that respondent's mark is deceptive under Section 2(a) of the Act.

■ ROGERS, ADMINISTRATIVE TRADEMARK JUDGE, dissenting:

... Does CAFETERIA misdescribe "the character, quality, function, composition or use" of applicant's recited services? The answer to this question is not as clear as it might appear at first glance.

The record suggests that consumers have various ideas of what makes a cafeteria a cafeteria, including value, familiar food, and a casual atmosphere.

. . . .

In sum, the term cafeteria is in part descriptive and in part misdescriptive of applicant's restaurant. Many consider it a restaurant that offers good value, although some do not, and the record is more supportive than not of a conclusion that the menu is much like that of a traditional cafeteria, albeit with some twists. In these respects, CAFETERIA may be viewed as more descriptive than misdescriptive of applicant's restaurant. On the other hand, what passes for a casual restaurant in New York City may not pass for a casual restaurant in many other areas of the country; and the absence of trays and self-service is clearly not at all like a traditional cafeteria. In this sense, CAFETERIA may be more misdescriptive than descriptive when used in conjunction with applicant's restaurant....

The first factor of the *Budge* test seeks a yes or no answer to the question whether a term is misdescriptive of identified goods or services. The mark in this case presents an issue of first impression, because the mixed record makes it impossible to answer the question in a simple yes or no fashion. For the sake of argument, however, I shall presume that the answer to the question is "Yes, CAFETERIA is misdescriptive of applicant's recited services." I turn then, to the second and third factors of *Budge*.

The second question of *Budge* is "are the prospective purchasers likely to believe that the misdescription actually describes the goods [or in this case services]?" ...

... There is nothing in the *Budge* majority opinion that suggests belief in a misdescription by unreasonable consumers would support a permanent refusal of registration under Section 2(a).

. . . Prohibitions against the registration of marks that would deceive consumers are contained in Sections 2(a), 2(d) and 2(e) of the Act. . . . [T]he proscriptions against registration of marks that would deceive ought to be read in a consistent manner.

Under Section 2(d), we do not bar registration of a mark that is likely to "deceive" only a gullible or unreasonable consumer as to source. Rather, we bar registration of a mark that is likely to confuse or deceive a reasonably prudent consumer. (Citations omitted)

Similarly, the Board has applied the reasonably prudent consumer test in assessing whether a mark is deceptively misdescriptive under Section 2(e)(1). (Citation omitted). And the same reasonableness requirement is applied when assessing whether a mark is primarily geographically deceptively misdescriptive under Section 2(e)(3). (Citation omitted).

Given that . . . the reasonably prudent purchaser standard is applied in evaluating whether a refusal of registration is warranted under Sections 2(d) and 2(e), the same standard should be applied in evaluating whether a refusal of registration is warranted under Section 2(a). . . . As Judge Nichols observed in the *Budge* concurring opinion, "unreasonable persons are likely to believe anything." *Budge,* 8 USPQ2d at 1262. Unreasonable beliefs should not permanently bar registration of a functioning, successful mark that an applicant seeks to register on the Supplemental Register.

. . . .

There may in this case be some concern about "initial interest deception," or whether prospective patrons of applicant's restaurant are subjected to a "bait and switch." There can be no deception, however, of those whose initial interest in applicant's restaurant is prompted by any of the restaurant reviews or entries from restaurant guides contained in this record. Applicant's restaurant plainly has not been reviewed as a cafeteria and, instead, has been reviewed as a sit-down restaurant. Any prospective patron whose interest was piqued by a review or guidebook entry would know what to expect.

On the other hand, . . . [e]ven reasonable consumers, passing by a restaurant with an awning emblazoned with the word CAFETERIA, might stop to see if it were a cafeteria. Yet these prospective patrons would have but to look at the restaurant or its menu to discover their misapprehension. This is scarcely the stuff of a "bait and switch" operation, for the prospective patron can easily turn away without having been hooked. Further, I am not aware of any extension of the doctrine of "initial interest confusion," so often discussed in the Internet context, to bar registration of marks that assertedly may deceive for a moment. I do not think it wise to rashly extend the doctrine to the case at hand. . . .

In this case, I have doubt about the extent of the misdescription assertedly created by applicant's mark; I do not think reasonable consumers would be deceived; and I do not think any misunderstanding that may be created in the minds of a very few consumers would be more than fleeting. Further, I do not find the record to support a conclusion that the absence of self-service trays from applicant's restaurants would be material to purchasing decisions of prospective diners. Accordingly, I would reverse the refusal of registration and register the mark on the Supplemental Register. . . .

QUESTIONS

1. Is the majority or dissenting opinion more persuasive in its deceptiveness determination? Do you agree with the dissent that the majority does not apply a reasonableness standard on the part of prospective customers?

2. Does the majority adequately explain the differences between consumers' ability to inspect golf clubs or space heaters on the one hand and their ability on the other hand to view a restaurant to determine that only table service is available? Should the initial interest confusion rationale apply equally to golf clubs as to restaurant services?

3. The dissenting opinion suggests that the first *Budge* question might be answered in the negative. What do you think?

4. Does the dissent conclude that the mark is deceptively misdecriptive under Section 2(e)(1)? If not, why would the mark only qualify for the Supplemental Register and not the Principal Register? See discussion *infra* about the difference between deceptive and deceptively misdescriptive terms.

THE DIFFERENCE BETWEEN DECEPTIVE TERMS AND "DECEPTIVELY MISDESCRIPTIVE" TERMS

Section 2(a) of the Lanham Act bars registration of any mark which "comprises . . . deceptive . . . matter . . ." This is an absolute bar and cannot be rescued under section 2(f) of the Lanham Act by showing that a mark "has become distinctive" through a showing of secondary meaning. Marks which are considered "merely . . . deceptively misdescriptive" of the goods or services of an applicant are also barred from registration under section 2(e)(1) of the Lanham Act. Such marks are registrable, however, if secondary meaning under section 2(f) can be demonstrated. The distinction between deceptive marks and merely deceptively descriptive marks thus can be significant.

If the answers to the first two questions in the *In re Budge* test (discussed in *In re Alp, supra*) are affirmative, (that is that the mark is misdescriptive of the goods/services and prospective purchases are likely to believe the misdescription), but the answer to the third question is negative, (that the misdescription is not material to the purchasing decision), then the mark is deceptively misdescriptive. *See, e.g., In re Woodward & Lothrop Inc.*, 4 U.S.P.Q.2d 1412 (T.T.A.B.1987). If only the first question is answered in the affirmative, then the mark may be arbitrary or suggestive since belief in the misdescription is key to a finding of deceptiveness.

QUESTIONS

Which of the following marks are deceptive? Which are deceptively misdescriptive? Arbitrary? Suggestive? Why?

1. ORGANIK for garments made of untreated, 100% natural cotton from plants that were not necessarily grown without chemicals or pesticides. *See In re Organik Technologies*, 41 U.S.P.Q.2d 1690 (T.T.A.B.1997).

2. BLANC DE CHINE for "porcelain, namely lamp bases, pots and figurines." Blanc de Chine is a term used to identify a valuable type of porcelain, made between the 15th and 19th centuries, in China. Antique Blanc de Chine figurines sell for over $10,000, although dishes may sell for $100 to $200. Applicant's porcelain goods contain no Blanc de Chine; its small bowls will be priced at $125, and a footed bowl will sell for $245. The Examining Attorney has rejected the mark as deceptive. Applicant contends that consumers cannot be deceived, either because they have never heard of Blanc de Chine, or because those who are familiar with the term know that it cannot apply to applicant's goods. How should the Board rule? *See In re Volk Art*, 1998 WL 377661 (T.T.A.B.1998).

3. TITANIUM for recreational vehicles. *See Glendale Int'l Corp. v. U.S.P.T.O.*, 374 F.Supp.2d 479 (E.D.Va.2005)

c.   SECTION 2(a): FALSE ASSOCIATION MARKS

In re White

80 U.S.P.Q.2d 1654 (T.T.A.B.2006).

■ HAIRSTON, ADMINISTRATIVE TRADEMARK JUDGE:

Julie White, a United States citizen and a member of the St. Regis Band of Mohawk Indians of New York, has applied to register MOHAWK (in standard character form) on the Principal Register as a trademark for "cigarettes."

The trademark examining attorney has refused registration under Section 2(a) of the Trademark Act, 15 U.S.C. § 1052(a), on the ground that when MOHAWK is used on cigarettes, it "may falsely suggest a connection with the federally recognized tribe the St. Regis Band of Mohawk Indians of New York."

. . .

The Section 2(a) refusal

Section 2(a) prohibits, inter alia, the registration of a mark if it "consists of or comprises . . . matter which may . . . falsely suggest a connection with persons, living or dead, institutions, beliefs, or national symbols." As the Court explained in *The University of Notre Dame du Lac v. J.C. Gourmet Food Imports Co., Inc.*, 703 F.2d 1372, 217 USPQ 505, 508 (Fed. Cir. 1983), Section 2(a) was designed to protect "the name of an individual or institution which was not a 'technical' trademark or 'trade name' upon which an objection could be made under Section 2(d).'' Further, the Court stated that Section 2(a) embraces the concepts of the right of privacy and the related right of publicity. To support a refusal under the "falsely suggests a connection" clause of Section 2(a), it is the examining attorney's burden to show: (1) that the mark is the same as, or a close approximation of, the name or identity previously used by another person or institution; (2) the mark would be recognized as such, in that it points uniquely and unmistakably to that person or institution; (3) the person or institution named by the mark is not connected with the activities performed by applicant under the mark; and (4) the fame or reputation of the person or institution is such that, when the mark is used with the applicant's goods or services, a connection with the person or institution would be presumed. *See Buffett v. Chi–Chi's, Inc.*, 226 USPQ 428 (TTAB 1985). *See also, In re Sloppy Joe's International Inc.*, 43 USPQ2d 1350 (TTAB 1997); and *In re Kayser–Roth Corp.*, 29 USPQ2d 1379 (TTAB 1993).

The examining attorney argues . . . that MOHAWK is the same as or a close approximation of the name for the federally recognized tribe the St. Regis Band of Mohawk Indians of New York, and . . . that the public would recognize MOHAWK as identifying this tribe, that is, the term MOHAWK points uniquely and unmistakably to the Mohawk tribe. . . . [T]he examining attorney relies on five dictionary excerpts, of which the following two are representative. One excerpt is from The American Heritage Dictionary of the English Language (Third Edition 1992 online edition) wherein "Mohawk" is defined as:

> a. A Native American people formerly inhabiting northeast New York along the Mohawk and upper Hudson valleys north to the St. Lawrence River with present-day populations chiefly in southern Ontario and extreme northern New York. The Mohawk were the easternmost member of the Iroquois confederacy.
>
> b. A member of the people.

Another excerpt is from the Merriam–Webster Online Dictionary wherein "Mohawk" is defined as:

> 1. a member of an American people of the Mohawk valley of New York;
>
> 2. the Iroquois language of the Mohawk people;
>
> 3. a hairstyle with a narrow center strip of upright hair and the sides shaved.

. . . .

We consider first whether MOHAWK is the same as or a close approximation of the designation for the federally recognized tribe St. Regis Band of Mohawk Indians of New York. . . . In this case, we are not persuaded by applicant's argument that MOHAWK is not the same as or a close approximation of the designation for the federally recognized St. Regis Band of Mohawk Indians of New York because the terms St. Regis and New York are not included in applicant's mark. We find that the dictionary definitions submitted by the examining attorney are sufficient to establish that MOHAWK is the same as or a close approximation of the federally recognized tribe St. Regis Band of Mohawk Indians of New York.

As to whether MOHAWK points uniquely and unmistakably to the Mohawk tribe, applicant argues that "the [Merriam–Webster Online Dictionary] excerpt defines the term 'Mohawk' to mean either (1) a member of an American Indian people of a specified place, (2) a language or (3) a type of haircut, but not as a tribe or certainly not the 'Mohawk Tribe,' with which the Examining Attorney has alleged a connection." (emphasis in original) (Applicant's brief at p. 7). Because the term "Mohawk" has "other" meanings, applicant argues that it cannot point uniquely and unmistakably to the Mohawk tribe. However, each of these other meanings is associated with the Mohawk tribe. The first is the name for a member of the Mohawk tribe. The second is the language spoken by the tribe, and the third is the name of a hairstyle associated with members of the tribe ... These other meanings, then, suggest that the term "Mohawk" is historically associated with the Mohawk tribe.

Applicant also argues that there are so many other uses of "Mohawk" and that the term appears in so many registrations and applications that "Mohawk" cannot be unmistakably associated with the Mohawk tribe. Applicant has made of record evidence to establish that "Mohawk" is the name of a ski resort, a college, two state forests, and a hiking trail. Further, applicant has submitted evidence which shows that "Mohawk" has been used by the U.S. Army as the name of an aircraft.

While at first blush this evidence of other uses of "Mohawk" would appear to suggest that the term is not unmistakably associated with the tribe, closer scrutiny reveals otherwise. The Mohawk Mountain ski resort and one of the Mohawk state forests are both located in northwest Connecticut, an area not far-removed from that part of "present-day" upstate New York which is inhabited by the Mohawk tribe. Mohawk college is located in Ontario, Canada, an area inhabited by the Mohawk tribe. Mohawk Trail State Forest in Massachusetts and the Mohawk (hiking) Trail are both located in the northern part of western Massachusetts, also an area near that part of "present-day" upstate New York which is inhabited by the Mohawk tribe. Insofar as the Mohawk (hiking) Trail is concerned, we note that the printout submitted by applicant for the trail shows a picture of a statue of a Native American. Thus, it is likely that the ski resort, college, both state forests, and hiking trail were named after the Mohawk tribe because of their close proximity to the lands inhabited by the Mohawk tribe. In regard to the use of "Mohawk" by the U.S. Army, we note that the printout submitted by applicant includes a depiction of a Native American which suggests that the aircraft also was named after the Mohawk tribe. Because these places and the aircraft appear to be named after the Mohawk tribe, these uses of "Mohawk" do not detract from the association of the name "Mohawk" with the Mohawk tribe. Thus, we are unable to conclude there from that the term "Mohawk" does not point uniquely to the Mohawk tribe.

. . . .

We now turn to the third factor in the Section 2(a) false suggestion analysis, that is, whether there is a connection of the type contemplated by Section 2(a) between applicant and the Mohawk tribe. The examining attorney argues that applicant does not have the type of connection contemplated by Section 2(a). It is the examining attorney's position that applicant's mere membership in the tribe is not enough and that there must be a commercial endorsement of her activities by the tribe.

. . . .

In the case of *In re Sloppy Joe's International Inc.*, 43 USPQ2d 1350 (TTAB 1997), the applicant sought to register the mark SLOPPY JOE'S and a representation of Ernest Hemingway for restaurant and bar services. In affirming the refusal of registration under Section 2(a) on the ground of a false suggestion of a connection with Ernest Hemingway, the Board held that Ernest "Hemingway's friendship with the original bar owner of Sloppy Joe's bar, his frequenting the bar and use of the back room as an office was not the kind of 'connection' contemplated by Section 2(a). Rather, a commercial connection, such as an ownership interest or commercial endorsement or sponsorship of applicant's services, would be necessary to entitle applicant to register the involved mark." *Id.* at 1354.

In the more recent case of *In re Los Angeles Police Revolver and Athletic Club, Inc.*, 69 USPQ2d 1630 (TTAB 2003), the applicant, a police athletic club, sought to register the mark TO PROTECT AND TO SERVE for clothing and beverage glasses. The identical phrase "To Protect and To Serve" is the official slogan of the Los Angeles Police Department (LAPD). In reversing the refusal to register under Section 2(a) on the ground of a false suggestion of a connection between the police athletic club and the LAPD, the Board found that the evidence demonstrated that the police athletic club and the LAPD had an extensive mutual relationship for decades. Although there was no formal or written agreement between the police athletic club and the LAPD concerning the club's activities, the evidence showed that the LAPD had "openly advanced the commercial activities of Applicant" and the Board found "a substantial commercial connection between applicant and the LAPD." *Id.* at 1633. The LAPD's endorsement or sponsorship of the club's specific goods, namely clothing and beverage glasses, was unnecessary; rather a general commercial connection between the club and the LAPD was sufficient.

The question, then, is whether a commercial connection has been established between applicant and the Mohawk tribe in light of the facts that applicant is a member of the tribe, the tribe has issued a license and d/b/a certificate to applicant's employer, Native American Trading Associates in connection with manufacturing tobacco products, and applicant has licensed use of her rights in the MOHAWK mark to Native American Trading Associates.

We recognize that, unlike the above cases, applicant is connected to the institution in this case, in the sense that she is a member of the Mohawk tribe. Yet, applicant is but one member of the tribe, and more than one individual can correctly claim a connection to the Mohawk tribe.

To overcome a Section 2(a) refusal in such a situation, a general commercial connection between the applicant and the institution is insufficient. Rather, the commercial connection must be specific and relate to the particular goods and services. In other words, there must be a specific endorsement, sponsorship or the like of the particular goods and services, whether written or implied.

On the facts of this case, we find that a specific commercial connection between applicant and the Mohawk tribe has not been proven. The license and d/b/a certificate issued by the Mohawk tribe to Native American Trading Associates is not evidence that the tribe endorses or is a sponsor of the cigarettes applicant intends to sell. We note that the license is general in nature and simply states that Native American Trading Associates has agreed to the rules and regulations regarding the manufacturing of tobacco products on the Mohawk tribe's reservation. The d/b/a certificate also is general in nature and states that Native American Trading Associates has requested and been approved to operate a tobacco manufacturing business on the reservation. Neither of these documents, however, is a specific endorsement or sponsorship of Native American Trading Associates' activities, and in turn, the cigarettes applicant intends to sell. Thus, we find that these documents do not evidence a specific commercial connection between applicant and the Mohawk tribe.

Further, this is not a situation where we can imply a specific commercial connection between applicant and the Mohawk tribe. While the tribe is undoubtedly aware of Native American Trading Associates' tobacco manufacturing activities, there is no evidence of a long-standing mutual relationship between Native American Trading Associates and the tribe. On the contrary, both the license and d/b/a certificate were issued in 2004 and both are for relatively short periods of time. Moreover, there is no evidence that the Mohawk tribe has openly advanced Native American Trading Associates' tobacco manufacturing activities. In short, this is not a situation where we can imply that the Mohawk tribe has specifically endorsed Native American Trading Associates' tobacco manufacturing activities, and in turn, the cigarettes applicant intends to sell.

The awarding of a federal registration to applicant individually for the mark MOHAWK for cigarettes would amount to the awarding of the tribe's "imprimatur" to the mark. In the absence of a specific commercial connection between the Mohawk tribe and applicant with respect to the goods involved herein, namely, cigarettes, we are unable to find the kind of commercial connection contemplated by Section 2(a).

As to the fourth factor of the Section 2(a) test, we must consider whether the name "Mohawk" is of sufficient fame or reputation that a connection with the federally recognized Mohawk tribe would be presumed by consumers of cigarettes. Here, the test is whether the name "Mohawk" per se is unmistakably associated with the Mohawk tribe, and as used, would point uniquely to the tribe.

The record shows that the Mohawk tribe inhabits New York and Canada. Further, the term "Mohawk" is readily found in dictionaries and in such listings it is defined as Native Americans who inhabit these areas. The Tiller publication discusses several commercial enterprises of the Mohawk tribe that would contribute to the fame and reputation of the tribe. The tribe began operating slot machines for gaming in the 1970's. It also operates a bingo hall which includes a full-service restaurant and a gift shop that sells souvenirs and discount cigarettes. There are two tribal-affiliated steel erector contractors doing business, and the reservation boasts the largest manufacturer of lacrosse sticks in the United States. Other tribal-affiliated businesses include cell phone systems, computers, smokeshops, construction contractors, and stores and galleries which feature handmade Indian arts and crafts. . . . This evidence is more than sufficient to establish that the Mohawk tribe is well known among residents in the region and visitors to the area.

Our final inquiry then is whether consumers of cigarettes would think only of the well-known Mohawk tribe when the name is used on or in connection with cigarettes. In this regard, the record is quite clear that many Native American tribes, the Mohawk and others, run smokeshops, many including Internet sales among their operations. In addition, the record is clear that Native Americans not only are engaged in large-scale marketing of cigarettes, but in manufacturing of Native American brands. As indicated, applicant has stated that she is a member of the Mohawk tribe which is in the business of manufacturing cigarettes through its licensee Native American Trading Associates.

The examining attorney submitted numerous web pages that reveal marketing of Native American brands of cigarettes. . . .

We find that purchasers of cigarettes would be aware of Native American manufacturing and marketing of Native American brand cigarettes, and, given the fame of the name of the Mohawk tribe, would think uniquely of the Mohawk tribe when they see MOHAWK as a mark used on or in connection with cigarettes.

In sum, we conclude that the record supports a refusal of registration of MOHAWK as a mark for cigarettes because use of the name of the federally recognized St. Regis Band of Mohawk Indians of New York would falsely suggest a connection between applicant and the Mohawk tribe.

QUESTION

Since the applicant is a member of the MOHAWK tribe, what is false about the association of the mark with the tribe?

2. Sections 2(b) and 2(c) of the Lanham Act

15 U.S.C. § 1052 [LANHAM ACT § 2]:

No trademark by which the goods of the applicant may be distinguished from the goods of others shall be refused registration on the principal register on account of its nature unless it—

. . . .

(b) Consists of or comprises the flag or coat of arms or other insignia of the United States, or of any State or municipality, or of any foreign nation, or any simulation thereof.

(c) Consists of or comprises a name, portrait, or signature identifying a particular living individual except by his written consent, or the name, signature, or portrait of a deceased President of the United States during the life of his widow, if any, except by the written consent of the widow.

REFUSALS UNDER 2(b)

Refusals to register a mark because a mark "consists of or comprises the flag or coat of arms, or other insignia of the United States, of any state or municipality, or of any foreign nation, or any simulation thereof" constitute an absolute bar. Moreover, unlike refusals based on Section 2(a), there is no requirement to show any additional element, such as disparagement or false association. T.M.E.P. § 1204. It is also not necessary that the mark consist exclusively of a governmental flag, coat of arms or other insignia if the mark includes such an element. *Id.* Do you believe that the following mark for condoms should be refused under Section 2(b)?

Is the design element a "simulation" of the American flag under Section 2(b)? Is the mark immoral or scandalous under Section 2(a)? *See In re Old Glory Condom Corp.*, 26 U.S.P.Q.2d 1216 (T.T.A.B.1993). A perusal of registered marks shows many with a flag design, suggesting that "simulation" has been interpreted to require fairly exact copying.

. . . .

Trademark Manual of Examining Procedure

§ 1206 Refusal on Basis of Name, Portrait or Signature of Particular Living Individual or Deceased U.S. President Without Consent

. . . .

Section 2(c) of the Trademark Act, 15 U.S.C. § 1052(c), bars the registration of a mark that consists of or comprises (whether consisting solely of, or having incorporated in the mark) a name, portrait or signature which identifies a particular living individual, or a deceased United States president during the life of his widow, except by the written consent of such individual or such president's widow.

Section 2(c) absolutely bars the registration of these marks on either Principal Register or the Supplemental Register

The purpose of requiring the consent of a living individual to the registration of his or her name, signature or portrait is to protect rights of privacy and publicity which living persons have in the designations which identify them....

§ 1206.01 Name, Portrait Or Signature

Section 2(c) explicitly pertains to any name, portrait or signature which identifies a particular living individual, or a deceased president of the United States during the life of the president's widow.

To identify a particular living individual, a name does not have to be the person's full name. *See Ross v. Analytical Technology Inc.*, 51 U.S.P.Q.2d 1269 (T.T.A.B.1999) (registration of opposer's surname without consent prohibited by § 2(c), where the record showed that because of opposer's reputation as an inventor in the field of electrochemical analysis, the relevant public would associate the goods so marked with opposer); *In re Steak and Ale Restaurants of America, Inc.*, 185 U.S.P.Q. 447 (T.T.A.B. 1975) (PRINCE CHARLES found to identify a particular living individual whose consent was not of record); *Laub v. Industrial Development Laboratories, Inc.*, 121 U.S.P.Q. 595 (T.T.A.B.1959) (LAUB, for flowmeters, found to identify the holder of a patent for flowmeters, whose written consent was not of record); *Reed v. Bakers Engineering & Equipment Co.*, 100 U.S.P.Q. 196, 199 (P.O.Ex.Ch.1954) (registration of REED REEL OVEN, for ovens, held to be barred by 2(c) without written consent of the designer and builder of the ovens, Paul N. Reed. " 'Name' in section 2(c) is not restricted to the full name of an individual but refers to any name regardless of whether it is a full name, or a surname or given name, or even a nickname, which identifies a particular living individual....") ...

§ 1206.02 Particular Living Individual or Deceased U.S. President

Section 2(c) applies to marks that comprise matter that identifies living individuals; it does not apply to marks that comprise matter that identifies deceased persons, except for a deceased president of the United States during the life of the president's widow. *See McGraw–Edison Co. v. Thomas Edison Life Insurance Co.*, 160 U.S.P.Q. 685 (T.T.A.B.1969), *vacated on other grounds*, 162 U.S.P.Q. 372 (N.D.Ill.1969) (opposition to the registration of THOMAS EDISON dismissed, the Board finding 2(c) inapplicable, as the particular individual whom the name identifies is deceased); *In re Masucci*, 179 U.S.P.Q. 829 (T.T.A.B.1973) (affirming refusal to register mark consisting of the name EISENHOWER, a portrait of President Dwight D. Eisenhower and the words PRESIDENT EISENHOWER REGISTERED PLATINUM MEDALLION #13, for greeting cards, on the ground that the mark comprises the name, signature or portrait of a deceased United States president without the written consent of his widow, under 2(c)).

The fact that a name appearing in a mark may actually be the name of more than one person does not negate the requirement for a written consent to registration, if the mark identifies, to the relevant public, a particular living individual or deceased United States president whose spouse is living. *In re Steak and Ale Restaurants of America, Inc.*, 185 U.S.P.Q. 447, 447 (T.T.A.B.1975) (affirming refusal to register PRINCE CHARLES, for meat, in the absence of consent to register by Prince Charles, a member of the English royal family. "Even accepting the existence of more than one living 'Prince Charles,' it does not follow that each is not a particular living individual.").

If it appears that a name, portrait or signature in a mark may identify a particular living individual but in fact the applicant devised the matter as fanciful, or believes it to be fanciful, a statement to that effect should be placed in the record. If appropriate, the statement that a name, portrait or signature does not identify a particular living individual will be printed in the Official Gazette and on the registration certificate....

QUESTION

1. May a third party register MARILYN MONROE for hosiery, or JAMES DEAN for motorcycle jackets under Section 2(c)? Would Section 2(a) of the Lanham Act bar registration?

2. Could an applicant register JIMMY CARTER for neckties?

3. SECTION 2(d) OF THE LANHAM ACT: CONFUSION

Section 2(d) of the Lanham Act provides, in relevant part, that a mark shall be refused registration if it

(d) consists of or comprises a mark which so resembles a mark registered in the Patent and Trademark Office, or a mark or trade name previously used in the United States by another and not abandoned, as to be likely, when used on or in connection with the goods of the applicant, to cause confusion, or to cause mistake, or to deceive....

Nutrasweet Co. v. K&S Foods, Inc.

4 U.S.P.Q.2d 1964 (T.T.A.B.1987).

■ KRUGMAN, MEMBER:

K&S Foods, Inc. has applied to register NUTRA SALT (SALT disclaimed) as a trademark for salt with trace minerals.

Registration has been opposed by The NutraSweet Company, formerly G.D. Searle & Co. As grounds for opposition, opposer asserts that it is the owner of the registered mark NUTRA–SWEET for a chemical compound used as a sweetening ingredient in the manufacture of food products and beverages; that it has continuously used its mark in various forms such as NUTRASWEET, NUTRA–SWEET and NUTRA SWEET in connection with sweeteners used as ingredients for food products since prior to the date of first use alleged by applicant and that applicant's mark so resembles opposer's previously used and registered mark as to be likely, when applied to applicant's goods, to cause confusion, mistake or to deceive. . . .

Opposer's priority in the NUTRASWEET mark has been established by competent testimony as well as by the introduction into evidence of status and title copies of a number of NUTRASWEET registrations. With respect to the marks and goods involved herein, the record shows that opposer manufactures and sells an artificial sweetener used in connection with a wide variety of foods, including, carbonated soft drinks, cereal, chewing gum, milk additives, cocoa mix, desserts, powdered soft drinks, tea, chewable vitamins, topping mix and shake mixes. In addition, opposer manufactures and sells a tabletop artificial sweetener under the EQUAL trademark which contains the NUTRASWEET ingredient. The NUTRA-SWEET mark appears on the packaging of most of the products containing the sweetening ingredient and most of the companies using the NUTRA-SWEET ingredient in their products mention the NUTRASWEET mark by name in their advertisements. The mark always appears on the packets of applicant's EQUAL sweetener.

Opposer has enjoyed considerable success in the marketing of the NUTRASWEET product. The record shows that sales of the NUTRA-SWEET product for use in various other products and for use in the EQUAL tabletop sweetener average $558 million annually with the EQUAL sweetener containing the NUTRASWEET ingredient accounting for approximately $125 million per year. The EQUAL product is sold through retail grocery stores as well as to the food service industry and appears in restaurants as well as in other institutional settings. Opposer's vice president of marketing and grocery products operations, Mr. Timothy Healy, testified that during the twelve months preceding the taking of his deposition (July 1, 1985), opposer spent approximately $25 million in advertising the NUTRASWEET mark on television, radio, in magazines and the like. Mr. Healy further testified that, during the same period, companies using the NUTRASWEET ingredient in their products have spent approximately $243 million advertising their products and that the majority of these advertisements mention the NUTRASWEET ingredient by name.

Applicant, in its brief on the case, concedes that NUTRASWEET is a famous mark. It is applicant's contention, however, that no confusion is likely from the use of the respective marks on the goods for the reasons that the marks as a whole are distinguishable; that applicant's NUTRA SALT mark is always used as two separate terms with NUTRA appearing above the term SALT while opposer's NUTRASWEET mark is a single term; that the goods are different, opposer applying its mark to a food sweetening ingredient incorporated into other food products sold under different primary trademarks with the NUTRASWEET mark used as a secondary mark; that applicant's trade channels comprise the ultimate consumer while opposer markets its NUTRASWEET product to manufacturers; that many third parties utilize NUTRA as part of their trademarks for foods and additives for foods and that no instances of actual confusion have occurred.

We are satisfied from the record that NUTRASWEET is a well recognized trademark for an artificial sweetening ingredient. Opposer has testified to the results of studies showing that the NUTRASWEET mark enjoys a high degree of customer recognition and awareness. The record further shows that in addition to being incorporated in many varieties of products, the NUTRASWEET ingredient is used in opposer's own EQUAL artificial sweetener product and that both the marks EQUAL and NUTRASWEET are used on the package for the product and both marks are used in promoting and advertising the product. While artificial sweeteners and salt with trace minerals are obviously different products, we think it likely that they would be sold in the same sections of grocery stores and supermarkets and would appear side by side in restaurants and on kitchen tabletops of ordinary consumers. We further note that the respective products are low-cost impulse type items where the purchasing decision is not likely to be as careful as it would be with a higher-priced product. In short, we conclude that the artificial sweetener and salt products are closely related, complementary products and that the use of the same or of a similar mark in connection with these products would likely result in confusion as to source or sponsorship.

Turning to the marks, it is clear that both marks share the identical prefix NUTRA. While the respective suffixes SWEET and SALT are obviously different in appearance and sound, these suffixes comprise generic designations as applied to the respective goods and are devoid of any source indicating capacity. We think it quite likely that purchasers familiar with the NUTRASWEET product, either as an ingredient in EQUAL artificial sweetener or as an ingredient in various other food products, would, upon viewing NUTRA SALT salt with trace minerals, be likely to believe that this was a new product line put out by the same producer as the NUTRASWEET producer or that the salt product was somehow associated with or sponsored by the people producing the NUTRASWEET product.

Applicant's argument that its mark always is used in special form with NUTRA appearing above SALT is not persuasive if only for the reason that the mark sought to be registered, as shown in the drawing in the application, is not in special form but, rather, is simply a typed drawing showing the term NUTRA SALT.

Applicant's argument regarding third-party uses of marks containing the formative NUTRA is unsupported by any evidence. While applicant has made of record a few third-party registrations which include the term NUTRA, this is not evidence of use of these marks or evidence of the extent to which any of these marks have been in use. *See generally* Sams, *Third Party Registrations in T.T.A.B. Proceedings,* 72 T.M.R. 297 (1982). We note, moreover, that applicant itself indicated that the formative NUTRA has no significance or meaning in applicant's relevant trade or industry.

Accordingly, we find the common formative NUTRA in the respective marks to be a strong element and nothing in the record is to the contrary.

Finally, while applicant has argued that there have been no instances of actual confusion, this fact is of no significance where, as here, applicant's sales have been *de minimis* and it is clear that there have been no opportunities for such confusion to arise.

In view of the foregoing, we find the respective marks to be sufficiently similar that their use on or in connection with the respective goods is likely to cause confusion for purposes of Section 2(d) of the Act.

Decision: The opposition is sustained and registration to applicant refused on the ground that the application is void *ab initio* in view of applicant's failure to use the mark in commerce at the time the application was filed and on the Section 2(d) ground of likelihood of confusion.

QUESTIONS

1. Would any mark for a food product prefixed "NUTRA–" encounter a section 2(d) refusal? Should it? What about a mark for a food product not produced by McDonald's Corp. prefixed "Mc"?

2. Suppose that, despite the Board's refusal to register NUTRA SALT, K&S Foods nonetheless marketed the goods, and that Nutrasweet Co. then sued K&S for trademark infringement. What, if any, preclusive effect should the Board's section 2(d) denial have on a subsequent civil action for trademark infringement? *Compare Levy v. Kosher Overseers Ass'n of America*, 104 F.3d 38 (2d Cir.1997), *with Jean Alexander Cosmetics, Inc. v. L'Oreal USA Inc.*, 458 F.3d 244 (3d Cir.2006) Should it matter if the judgment is granted by default? *See Santos v. Hecht*, 82 U.S.P.Q.2d 1542 (E.D.N.Y.2006).

3. In determining likelihood of confusion, the Board gives a broader scope of protection to famous marks. Should the test of fame in this context be the same as the test of fame for dilution under section 43(c)(1)? *See Palm Bay Imports, Inc. v. Veuve Clicquot Ponsardin Maison Fondee En 1772*, 396 F.3d 1369 (Fed.Cir.2005) ("While dilution fame is an either/or proposition—fame either does or does not exist—likelihood of confusion fame 'varies along a spectrum from very strong to very weak' ").

Marshall Field & Co. v. Mrs. Fields Cookies

25 U.S.P.Q.2d 1321 (T.T.A.B.1992).

■ Rooney, Member:

An application was filed by Mrs. Fields Cookies to register the mark MRS. FIELDS (as shown below) on the principal register under Section 2(f) for bakery goods, namely, cookies and brownies. Use since November 15, 1981 was alleged.

Registration has been opposed by Marshall Field & Company on the ground that applicant's mark so resembles the mark FIELD'S previously used and registered by opposer for retail department store services and the mark MARSHALL FIELD'S (as shown below) previously used and registered by opposer for baked goods and other foods and for retail department store services, as to be likely to cause confusion, mistake or deception.

Marshall Field's

. . . .

Subsequently, Marshall Field & Company . . . filed a petition to cancel the registrations of the marks MRS. FIELD'S COOKIES in the design shown below (the word, "cookies" disclaimed) for retail bakery store services;

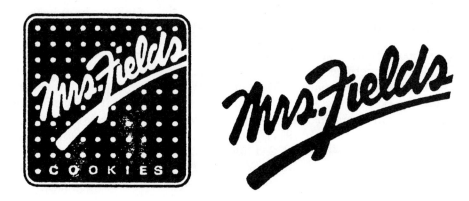

MRS. FIELD'S COOKIES in the same design with the same disclaimer for bakery goods, namely, cookies and brownies; and MRS. FIELDS, as shown below for retail bakery store services.

The grounds for cancellation are that petitioner has, for many years prior to respondent's date of first use, been engaged in the production and sale of baked goods and other foods and in rendering retail food and department store services . . . and that respondent's marks, as applied to its bakery goods and retail bakery store services, so resemble petitioner's marks as to be likely to cause confusion, mistake or deception.

. . . .

These two proceedings were consolidated upon motion made by respondent and approved by the Board.

. . . .

... [T]he facts revealed by the record show that petitioner has 26 department stores in the United States. [T]he company [also] issues catalogs and sells through mail and telephone orders. The main products in MARSHALL FIELD'S stores are apparel, housewares and furniture. In addition, MARSHALL FIELD'S stores contain restaurants and sell candy and bakery products. The first in-store restaurant was opened in 1890. There are 41 restaurants in 21 stores. There is a group of restaurants called Greener Fields and another group all having names of trees, such as, the Walnut Room and the Linden Room. Certain dishes on the menus of petitioner's restaurants are referred to by the name FIELD'S, such as, FIELD'S Special Sandwich and FIELD'S Covered Apple Pie. When this practice started is not quite clear, although there is testimony that it occurred at least as early as 1970. The bakeries use the name MARSHALL FIELD'S or MARSHALL FIELD'S GOURMET on their packaging, and those bakery goods which are considered MARSHALL FIELD'S specialties are sometimes, at the discretion of the department manager, labeled as FIELD'S, such as, Field's Pecan Pie. When this practice was initiated has not been established.

There has been a full-line bakery operating on the 13th floor of the Chicago store since 1920 producing breads, pies, cakes, tortes, cookies, muffins and wedding cakes which are baked fresh daily and are sold in the in-store bakeries or in the restaurants. There are five stores which have free-standing bakery counters and there are five bakeries that are outside of, but adjacent to, restaurants in MARSHALL FIELD'S stores. In 1988, petitioner had sales of just over a billion dollars. In the same year, petitioner's sales of baked goods amounted to $3 million.

... Since the 1940's petitioner has issued a catalog for packaged food items and includes packaged food items in its Christmas catalog. Petitioner makes candy which is sold in its retail stores and is also available through mail and telephone order catalogs. Petitioner's goods are packaged in bags, boxes and other packaging bearing its marks either in block print or in a distinctive script.

Petitioner employs various media for its advertising, i.e., radio, television, print and in-store distributed brochures. The evidence illustrates that petitioner's stores are often referred to as FIELD'S in newspaper and magazine articles as well as in books. Certain of the departments in the retail operations use the term FIELD'S, i.e., FIELD'S AFAR is a gift department, FIELD'S CHOICE, FIELD GEAR and FIELD MANOR are apparel departments, and there is also a FIELD'S FASHION SERVICE which is a shopping service for customers.

Petitioner owns registrations for the marks, MARSHALL FIELD'S for baked goods and other foods; MARSHALL FIELD'S for retail department store services; MARSHALL FIELD'S GOURMET and design for baked goods and other foods; FIELD'S for retail department store services; MARSHALL FIELD'S GOURMET for retail grocery store, mail and telephone order food services and restaurant services, FIELD GEAR for men's, women's and children's clothing; FIELD SPORT for men's and women's clothing; FIELD'S CHOICE for women's clothing; FIELD'S AFAR for clothing and retail department store services; and MARSHALL FIELD'S EXPRESSED for mail and telephone order services.

Respondent's business came into being in 1977 when Mrs. Debra Fields opened a cookie shop called MRS. FIELDS CHOCOLATE CHIP-PERY in Palo Alto, California. By 1981, there were 23 MRS. FIELDS CHOCOLATE CHIPPERY stores. The mark was used in the stores and on the packaging for the cookies. During this period, some of the stores carried only the name MRS. FIELDS because of size constraints or because of landlord specifications. In 1981, respondent began use of the marks MRS. FIELDS in script form and MRS. FIELDS COOKIES in script form on a polka dot background and began use of a red and white motif which was, and is, used in the stores on signs and uniforms and on the packaging. There are currently more than 400 MRS. FIELDS stores in the country. Respondent does not use FIELDS alone, although there were one or two instances, noted in publications, of references to respondent as FIELDS by third parties. However, in these instances this was the author's shorthand method of referring back to MRS. FIELDS, which had been previously mentioned.

The marks are also used by respondent's related company, La Petite Boulangerie, of which there are more than 100 and by Mrs. Fields Bakery stores, which number 8. The MRS. FIELDS mark has been licensed to Ambrosia Chocolate Company, a subsidiary of W. R. Grace Inc., for use on chocolate chips sold in supermarkets and grocery stores. Marriott Corporation has also sought a license from respondent to use the mark in connection with bakery and food service units in airports and toll road plazas. Figures for 1989 show that sales were $116 million dollars that year, having grown from $10 million in 1982.

The persona of Debra Fields is central to all of respondent's advertising and she has made and continues to make frequent public appearances at lectures, meetings, on television, etc. In addition, the company uses other methods of advertising such as television, radio, print and in-store point of purchase materials. Debra Fields estimated that about 5% of annual sales are spent on advertising. A great many articles have been written about the company and about Debra Fields in newspapers and magazines.

. . . .

Turning to the question of likelihood of confusion, petitioner's evidence of its ownership of valid and subsisting registrations of its pleaded marks make it unnecessary for us to examine the question of priority with respect to . . . the goods and services listed in the registrations. (Citation omitted). Apart therefrom, there is ample evidence of use of the marks MARSHALL FIELD'S for retail department store services for a very long period of time before the date of first use by respondent. There is also evidence that petitioner has used the mark FIELD'S as well for department store services, and that the public has come to recognize the mark FIELD'S in connection with the famous department store since before respondent's first use of its marks. There is further evidence that FIELD'S has been used to designate certain foods, including baked goods, on menus in petitioner's restaurants since at least 1970 and that at some time FIELD'S came to be used to designate certain specialty items in petitioner's bakeries.

. . . .

.... With respect to the services of these parties, it is noted that respondent's application and one of its registrations are for "bakery goods, namely, cookies and brownies" while the other two registrations are for retail bakery store services. Petitioner uses its marks FIELD'S and MARSHALL FIELD'S in relation to retail department store services. Petitioner has a number of bakeries and restaurants within its department stores and respondent has sold its bakery products in major department stores, i.e., Bloomingdale's and Macy's. We would have to conclude that there is a relationship between the parties' goods and services such that the use of the same or confusingly similar marks is likely to cause confusion, mistake or deception. The question to be resolved is whether the marks of these parties are so similar as to be likely to cause this confusion.

... [P]etitioner's Chairman Miller has testified that it was only because of the evolution of respondent's marks from MRS. FIELDS CHOCOLATE CHIPPERY to MRS. FIELDS COOKIES to MRS. FIELDS and the change from block letters to script that petitioner has come to believe that respondent's marks have become progressively closer to its own marks, thereby increasing the likelihood of confusion. It is Mr. Miller's testimony that:

> We would not have a problem with Mrs. Fields using her name in conjunction with cookies and baked goods products if it were not conflicting in design and color with Marshall Field's traditional signature and our use of color.

. . . .

With that in mind, we turn to the question of likelihood of confusion of the parties' marks. As to the mark MARSHALL FIELD'S, it is used in connection with all of the department store services performed by petitioner. There is no doubt that, for petitioner's department store services, the mark MARSHALL FIELD'S is extremely well known. There is also evidence that this mark is used in connection with petitioner's in-store bakeries and restaurants. For the most part, petitioner uses the mark MARSHALL FIELD'S GOURMET and design and MARSHALL FIELD'S on the packaging used in the bakeries and for those carry-out items sold in its restaurants.

Petitioner has argued that FIELD'S is the dominant part of the mark MARSHALL FIELD'S and that the purchasing public will assume upon seeing MRS. FIELDS on baked goods that there is a connection between the MRS. FIELDS bakeries and MARSHALL FIELD'S department stores.

With respect to that argument, we note that Field(s) is a common surname as shown by a number of telephone directories and in two dictionaries of surnames, *American Surnames*, 1969, Chilton Book Company and *A Dictionary of Surnames*, 1989, Oxford University Press, submitted by respondent. In addition, respondent has also introduced a number of third-party registrations of marks having as a component thereof the name FIELD(S) and its variations as well as deposition testimony of nine individuals involved in retail sales who use the name FIELD(S) in connection therewith.

It is duly noted that, except in the case of the deposition evidence, the remaining third-party evidence is subject to the objection that this material does not prove use of FIELD(S) by third parties. However, we do not have to find proof of use of FIELD(S) as a trade or service mark in order to conclude that this is a common surname easily recognized as such and that purchasers are accustomed to distinguishing between such common surnames by whatever slight differences may exist in the marks as a whole. In this case, the question is whether the addition of FIELD(S) of, on the one hand, the given name MARSHALL and, on the other, the title MRS., is enough of a difference to enable purchasers to make that distinction. We believe that, given the fame of MARSHALL FIELD'S for department store services and the fame shown to have been afforded to MRS. FIELDS for its bakery services and goods, the public will readily recognize the differences in the marks as used on the respective goods and services and are not likely to be confused as to the sources of the goods and services offered thereunder.

We recognize that MARSHALL FIELD'S is a famous mark and that famous marks are normally afforded a wide scope of protection. *See Kenner Parker Toys Inc. v. Rose Art Industries Inc.*, 22 U.S.P.Q.2d 1453 (Fed.Cir. 1992). However, in this case we are faced with a situation in which the respondent's mark has also achieved a significant degree of fame in the marketplace. It is because both marks are famous that we believe the public will easily recognize the differences in the marks and distinguish between them. It might have been a closer question had there been some evidence that MARSHALL FIELD'S used other familial terms with FIELD'S such as MISS FIELD'S, MR. FIELD'S or even GRANDMA FIELD'S. But the combining forms used by petitioner have altogether different connotations, such as, FIELD'S AFAR, FIELD'S CHOICE, FIELD GEAR, FIELD'S MANOR and FIELD'S FASHION SERVICE. Rather than causing an association to be assumed between MRS. FIELDS and MARSHALL FIELD'S, these combined terms are more likely to have the opposite effect.

... It appears to the Board that the script used in each mark is different enough that, combined with the differences in the words, purchasers are not likely to confuse the source of the goods or services offered thereunder because of the script forms in which they are presented. As for petitioner's arguments relative to trade dress, it is recognized that trade dress may have some effect as well in the public's perception of a mark. *See Kenner Parker Toys, Inc., supra*. However, we do not believe the trade dress used by these parties would foster a likelihood of confusion between these marks. Respondent uses the colors red and white on its packaging and signs while petitioner has frequently referred to its own color scheme as MARSHALL FIELD'S green. The only time respondent uses any green in its packaging is during the Christmas and St. Patrick's Day holidays, at which time the colors will be perceived as holiday decorations. We do not think that the parties' color schemes are likely to foster any confusion in the minds of purchasers.

There are a number of additional reasons which lead us to this conclusion. While there is abundant evidence of the fame of the mark MARSHALL FIELD'S, as used in connection with department store services, we are not convinced that MARSHALL FIELD'S is equally famous for bakery goods and services, except to the extent that they are sold within its department stores. That is to say, the evidence is clear that the restaurant and bakery store services of petitioner have always been confined to its own premises so that customers of petitioner would not expect to find a bakery belonging to petitioner standing alone in a shopping mall or on a city street. When they purchase baked goods in either the in-store bakeries or restaurants, customers know they are dealing with MARSHALL FIELD'S department store. As to those MRS. FIELDS bakeries located in Bloomingdale's and Macy's, it is unlikely that a bakery found in a competing department store would be attributed to petitioner.

Turning to petitioner's mark FIELD'S, the record shows that in addition to use as a service mark for department store services, FIELD'S is sometimes used to identify bakery products, such as, FIELD'S cheese cake, in bakery counter displays and is used to identify specialty items on menus in petitioner's restaurants, as in FIELD'S Famous Specialties, The FIELD'S Special or FIELD'S Fruit Cake. Although petitioner has achieved secondary meaning for the mark FIELD'S alone, as illustrated by petitioner's catalogs and the numerous publications referring to petitioner by that name, we agree with respondent that the secondary meaning of that mark is limited to department store services and does not extend to restaurant and bakery store services. The evidence strongly suggests that use of the mark FIELD'S in catalogs and in the stores is intended to be and is recognized as a shorthand reference to MARSHALL FIELD'S. As petitioner itself has suggested, companies are frequently called by shortened names, such as, Penney's for J.C. Penney's, Sears for Sears and Roebuck (even before it officially changed its name to Sears alone), Ward's for Montgomery Ward's, and Bloomies for Bloomingdale's. Moreover, we believe that FIELD'S for petitioner's services may be readily distinguished from MRS. FIELD'S for respondent's goods and services in the same way that KING'S for candy was held to be distinguishable from MISS KING'S for cakes. *See King Candy Company v. Eunice King's Kitchen, Inc.,* 182 U.S.P.Q. 108 (CCPA 1974).

. . . .

Finally, we are convinced that respondent's mark was not selected with any motive of trading on petitioner's good will. Nor do we believe that the selection of the sites for MRS. FIELDS cookie stores were made with any such intent. Rather, the evidence supports the contention that the site selections were made in accordance with the requirements discussed by Mr. Murphy during his deposition and that these requirements involved questions of traffic patterns, visibility, accessibility and opportunity. As to those stores in locations close to petitioner's stores, there appears to be no reason to believe that respondent located any of its stores near a MARSHALL FIELD'S store in order to trade on petitioner's good will.

. . . .

In view of the foregoing, the petitions for cancellation are denied, the opposition is dismissed and the counterclaim for cancellation is dismissed.

QUESTIONS

1. How much did it influence the Board that the Chicago department store used the MARSHALL FIELD'S mark on a variety of products? Should the Board give weight to the use of a prominent house mark to distinguish an applicant's or registrant's goods or services? In some cases the Board has considered the conjunction or proximity of a house mark irrelevant "since the marks may be used at any time without the respective house marks" *Sealy, Inc. v. Simmons Co.,* 265 F.2d 934, 937 (C.C.P.A.1959) (opposition proceeding, applicant's mark "BABY POSTURE" for mattresses held confusingly similar to opposer's mark "BABY POSTUREPEDIC" for mattresses, even though both parties used their marks together with their respective, well-known house marks "SIMMONS" and "SEALY"); *Blue Cross and Blue Shield Assoc. v. Harvard Community Health Plan Inc.,* 17 U.S.P.Q.2d 1075, 1077 (T.T.A.B.1990) (applicant's slogan THE CURE FOR THE BLUES held likely to cause confusion with opposer's BLUE CROSS/BLUE SHIELD marks and trade names, despite applicant's use of slogan in conjunction with house mark because applicant sought registration of slogan alone). In cases in the P.T.O. involving composite marks, the Board looks to all the circumstances to determine if an addition to a mark makes confusion unlikely. *Compare Mason Engineering and Design Corp. v. Mateson Chemical Corp.,* 225 U.S.P.Q. 956, 960 (T.T.A.B.1985) (opposer's use of house mark CLOUD 9 in conjunction with STERILAIRE mark did not dispel likelihood of confusion with applicant's STERILAIRE mark) *with In re Champion Oil Co.,* 1 U.S.P.Q.2d 1920, 1921 (T.T.A.B.1986) (mark TOP FORMULA–1, in which TOP was housemark, held not likely to cause confusion with prior registered mark FORMULA–1).

Should the weight accorded house marks be the same in the context of trademark infringement actions? *See* "Does Joining a House Mark to the Disputed Mark Reduce Likelihood of Confusion?" *infra,* Chapter 6.A.1.

2. Applying the analysis of *Marshall Field,* should BEN'S BREAD for bread mixes be found confusingly similar to the well-known UNCLE BEN'S mark for rice products? *See Uncle Ben's Inc. v. Stubenberg Int'l Inc.,* 47 U.S.P.Q.2d 1310 (T.T.A.B.1998).

3. An entrepreneur sells caps modeled after the *képi* of the French Foreign Legion, under the name LEGIONNAIRE. When the entrepreneur seeks to register the term as a trademark for the caps, both the French Foreign Legion and the American Legion oppose the registration on § 2(d) grounds. Who should prevail? *See American Legion v. Matthew*, 144 F.3d 498 (7th Cir.1998).

Person's Co., Ltd. v. Christman

900 F.2d 1565 (Fed.Cir.1990).

■ Smith, J:

Person's Co., Ltd. appeals from the decision of the Patent and Trademark Office Trademark Trial and Appeal Board (Board), which granted summary judgment in favor of Larry Christman and ordered the cancellation of appellant's registration for the mark "PERSON'S" for various apparel items. Appellant Person's Co. seeks cancellation of Christman's registration for the mark "PERSON'S" for wearing apparel on the following grounds: likelihood of confusion based on its prior foreign use, abandonment, and unfair competition within the meaning of the Paris Convention. We affirm the Board's decision.

Background

The facts pertinent to this appeal are as follows: In 1977, Takaya Iwasaki first applied a stylized logo bearing the name "PERSON'S" to clothing in his native Japan. Two years later Iwasaki formed Person's Co., Ltd., a Japanese corporation, to market and distribute the clothing items in retail stores located in Japan.

In 1981, Larry Christman, a U.S. citizen and employee of a sportswear wholesaler, visited a Person's Co. retail store while on a business trip to Japan. Christman purchased several clothing items bearing the "PERSON'S" logo and returned with them to the United States. After consulting with legal counsel and being advised that no one had yet established a claim to the logo in the United States, Christman developed designs for his own "PERSON'S" brand sportswear line based on appellant's products he had purchased in Japan. In February 1982, Christman contracted with a clothing manufacturer to produce clothing articles with the "PERSON'S" logo attached. These clothing items were sold, beginning in April 1982, to sportswear retailers in the northwestern United States. Christman formed Team Concepts, Ltd., a Washington corporation, in May 1983 to continue merchandising his sportswear line, which had expanded to include additional articles such as shoulder bags. All the sportswear marketed by Team Concepts bore either the mark "PERSON'S" or a copy of appellant's globe logo; many of the clothing styles were apparently copied directly from appellant's designs.

In April 1983, Christman filed an application for U.S. trademark registration in an effort to protect the "PERSON'S" mark. Christman believed himself to be the exclusive owner of the right to use and register the mark in the United States and apparently had no knowledge that appellant soon intended to introduce its similar sportswear line under the identical mark in the U.S. market. Christman's registration issued in September 1984 for use on wearing apparel.

In the interim between Christman's first sale and the issuance of his registration, Person's Co., Ltd. became a well-known and highly respected force in the Japanese fashion industry. The company, which had previously sold garments under the "PERSON'S" mark only in Japan, began implementing its plan to sell goods under this mark in the United States. According to Mr. Iwasaki, purchases by buyers for resale in the United States occurred as early as November 1982. This was some seven months subsequent to Christman's first sales in the United States. Person's Co. filed an application for U.S. trademark registration in the following year, and, in 1985, engaged an export trading company to introduce its goods into the U.S. market. The registration for the mark "PERSON'S" issued in August 1985 for use on luggage, clothing and accessories. After recording U.S. sales near 4 million dollars in 1985, Person's Co. granted California distributor Zip Zone International a license to manufacture and sell goods under the "PERSON'S" mark in the United States.

In early 1986, appellant's advertising in the U.S. became known to Christman and both parties became aware of confusion in the marketplace. Person's Co. initiated an action to cancel Christman's registration on the following grounds: (1) likelihood of confusion; ... Christman counterclaimed and asserted prior use and likelihood of confusion as grounds for cancellation of the Person's Co. registration.

After some discovery, Christman filed a motion with the Board for summary judgment on all counts. In a well-reasoned decision, the Board held for Christman on the grounds that Person's use of the mark in Japan could not be used to establish priority against a "good faith" senior user in U.S. commerce. The Board found no evidence to suggest that the "PERSON'S" mark had acquired any notoriety in this country at the time of its adoption by Christman. Therefore, appellant had no reputation or goodwill upon which Christman could have intended to trade, ... The Board granted summary judgment to Christman and ordered appellant's registration cancelled.

. . . .

Priority

The first ground asserted for cancellation in the present action is § 2(d) of the Lanham Act; each party claims prior use of registered marks which unquestionably are confusingly similar and affixed to similar goods.

Section 1 of the Lanham Act[10] states that "[t]he owner of a trademark used in commerce may register his trademark...." The term "commerce"

---

10. The case at bar is decided under the provisions of the Act in force prior to the enactment of the Trademark Law Revision Act of 1988.

is defined in Section 45 of the Act as "... all commerce which may be lawfully regulated by Congress." ...

In the present case, appellant Person's Co. relies on its use of the mark in Japan in an attempt to support its claim for priority in the United States. Such foreign use has no effect on U.S. commerce and cannot form the basis for a holding that appellant has priority here. The concept of territoriality is basic to trademark law; trademark rights exist in each country solely according to that country's statutory scheme. Christman was the first to use the mark in United States commerce and the first to obtain a federal registration thereon. Appellant has no basis upon which to claim priority and is the junior user under these facts.

Bad Faith

Appellant vigorously asserts that Christman's adoption and use of the mark in the United States subsequent to Person's Co.'s adoption in Japan is tainted with "bad faith" and that the priority in the United States obtained thereby is insufficient to establish rights superior to those arising from Person's Co.'s prior adoption in a foreign country. Relying on *Woman's World Shops, Inc. v. Lane Bryant, Inc.*, Person's Co. argues that a "remote junior user" of a mark obtains no right superior to the "senior user" if the "junior user" has adopted the mark with knowledge of the "senior user's" prior use.[18]

In *Woman's World*, the senior user utilized the mark within a limited geographical area. A junior user from a different geographical area of the United States sought unrestricted federal registration for a nearly identical mark, with the exception to its virtually exclusive rights being those of the known senior user. The Board held that such an appropriation with knowledge failed to satisfy the good faith requirements of the Lanham Act and denied the concurrent use rights sought by the junior user. Person's Co. cites *Woman's World* for the proposition that a junior user's adoption and use of a mark with knowledge of another's prior use constitutes bad faith. It is urged that this principle is equitable in nature and should not be limited to knowledge of use within the territory of the United States.

While the facts of the present case are analogous to those in *Woman's World*, the case is distinguishable in one significant respect. In *Woman's World*, the first use of the mark by both the junior and senior users was in United States commerce. In the case at bar, appellant Person's Co., while first to adopt the mark, was not the first user in the United States. Christman is the senior user, and we are aware of no case where a senior user has been charged with bad faith. The concept of bad faith adoption applies to remote junior users seeking concurrent use registrations; in such cases, the likelihood of customer confusion in the remote area may be

---

18. Appellant repeatedly makes reference to a "world economy" and considers Christman to be the remote junior user of the mark. Although Person's did adopt the mark in Japan prior to Christman's use in United States commerce, the use in Japan cannot be relied upon the acquire U.S. trademark rights. Christman is the senior user as that term is defined under U.S. trademark law.

presumed from proof of the junior user's knowledge. In the present case, when Christman initiated use of the mark, Person's Co. had not yet entered U.S. commerce. The Person's Co. had no goodwill in the United States and the "PERSON'S" mark had no reputation here. Appellant's argument ignores the territorial nature of trademark rights.

Appellant next asserts that Christman's knowledge of its prior use of the mark in Japan should preclude his acquisition of superior trademark rights in the United States. The Board found that, at the time of registration, Christman was not aware of appellant's intention to enter the U.S. clothing and accessories market in the future. Christman obtained a trademark search on the "PERSON'S" mark and an opinion of competent counsel that the mark was "available" in the United States. Since Appellant had taken no steps to secure registration of the mark in the United States, Christman was aware of no basis for Person's Co. to assert superior rights to use and registration here. Appellant would have us infer bad faith adoption because of Christman's awareness of its use of the mark in Japan, but an inference of bad faith requires something more than mere knowledge of prior use of a similar mark in a foreign country.

．　．　．　．

First Niagara Ins. v. First Niagara Financial, 476 F.3d 867 (Fed.Cir.2007). First Niagara Insurance, a Canadian corporation whose use of the mark in Canada dated to 1984, invoked § 2(d) to oppose a US company's ITU registration of First Niagara for financial services, including insurance brokerage. The Board dismissed the opposition on the ground that Opposer did not use its marks "in a type of commerce regulable by Congress." The Federal Circuit reversed.

> FN–Canada operates entirely out of Niagara Falls and Niagara-on-the-Lake, in Ontario, Canada, and has no physical presence (e.g., offices, employees, assets, etc.) in the United States. Moreover, FN–Canada is not licensed to act as an insurance broker in any country other than Canada. Nevertheless, FN–Canada's business does have connections to the United States. For example, FN–Canada sells insurance policies issued by United States-based underwriting companies. FN–Canada also sells, through insurance brokers in this country, policies to United States citizens having Canadian property. In other words, if an American owns property in Canada and needs insurance for that property, a domestic broker will contact FN–Canada, who will then provide an appropriate policy issued by one of FN–Canada's underwriters. The domestic broker and FN–Canada share the commission generated by the transaction.... FN–Canada does not own any registered United States marks; however, in its advertising (including advertising that "spills over" into the United States) and correspondence (including correspondence to customers and other business contacts in the United States) FN–Canada regularly uses several unregistered marks: "First Niagara," "First Niagara Insurance Brokers." ...

In the proceedings below, the Board based its analysis on the assumption that an "opposer's claim of prior use can succeed only if it has proved use of its marks in connection with services rendered in commerce lawfully regulated by Congress, as required under Section 45 of the Trademark Act, 15 U.S.C. § 1127." Such an assumption was unwarranted, however, in light of the plain language of the statute, which merely requires the prior mark to have been "used in the United States by another." 15 U.S.C. § 1052(d).... Indeed, as the Board observed in a footnote in its opinion, "[a]n opposer claiming priority under Section 2(d) may rely on use that is strictly intrastate and not regulable by Congress." That privilege attaches to all opposers, regardless of whether they are foreign or domestic. Thus, a foreign opposer can present its opposition on the merits by showing only use of its mark in the United States....

Under the correct test, it is clear that the Board erred in dismissing FN–Canada's oppositions. The record unquestionably reveals more than ample use of FN–Canada's marks in the United States to satisfy the use requirements of Section 2(d). Therefore, we are compelled to reverse the decision below. [The court declined to determine whether FN–Canada's US use was also "use in commerce."]

QUESTIONS

1. Is *Persons* still good law after *First Niagara*? If the PERSONS mark were known to U.S. tourists and Persons had first sold to buyers in Japan for resale in the U.S. before Christman had sold goods in the U.S. under the PERSONS mark, would the Japanese company have been entitled to register PERSONS in the U.S.? Would it have been able to oppose Christman's US registration of the same mark for the same goods?

2. Do you agree with *Person's* distinction between knowingly adopting a mark already in use in a limited geographic area within the U.S. (bad faith), and knowingly adopting a mark already in use outside the U.S. (good faith)? Is such a distinction good policy? For a general examination of the concept of trademark territoriality that underlies the distinction, *see, e.g.,* Graeme B. Dinwoodie, Trademarks and Territoriality: Detaching Trademark Law from the Nation–State, 41 Hous. L. Rev. 885 (2004).

––––––

Editors' Note: Sections 13 and 14 of the Lanham Act, 15 U.S.C. §§ 1063 and 1064, were amended in 1999 to permit oppositions and cancellations to be brought on the ground of dilution as set forth in Section 43(c), 15 U.S.C. § 1125(c). Dilution is not a bar to registration under section 2, and an Examiner cannot rely on dilution as a ground to refuse registration. Interested third parties, however, can institute an opposition or cancellation action on this basis. Examine the language in Section 13, 15 U.S.C. §§ 1063, which states that "any person who believes that he would be damaged by the registration of a mark ..., including as a result of dilution under Section 43(c)" may file an opposition. Could an opposer rely upon dilution under state law as a ground to oppose an application? *See Enterprise Rent–A–Car Co. v. Advantage Rent–A–Car, Inc.*, 330 F.3d 1333 (Fed.Cir.), *cert. denied*, 540 U.S. 1089 (2003) (state dilution not a ground for opposition). *See* Chapter 9, *infra*, for a discussion of dilution cases.

4. SECTION 2(e) OF THE LANHAM ACT: GEOGRAPHIC TERMS

Section 2(e) of the Lanham Act offers a variety of grounds for refusal to register. We have already encountered refusals on the basis that the mark is "merely descriptive," *see In re Quik–Print Copy Shops, Inc.* Chapter 2.B.1, *supra*, and that it is "deceptively misdescriptive," *see* Chapter 4.C.1.b. *supra*. Section 2(e) also bars from registration a mark which, *inter alia*

> (e) consists of a mark which . . . (2) when used on or in connection with the goods of the applicant is primarily geographically descriptive of them, except as indications of regional origin may be registrable under section 1054 of this title, (3) when used on or in connection with the goods of the applicant is primarily geographically deceptively misdescriptive of them, ...

Note that section 2(e)(2) refusals may be overcome by a showing pursuant to section 2(f) that the mark as used "has become distinctive of the applicant's goods in commerce." However, since the 1993 amendments to the Lanham Act, a showing of distinctiveness will no longer overcome a rejection on the ground that the mark is "primarily geographically deceptively misdescriptive" under section 2(e)(3):

> (f) Except as expressly excluded in paragraphs (a), (b), (c), (d), (e)(3) and (e)(5) of this section, nothing in this chapter shall prevent the registration of a mark used by the applicant which has become distinctive of the applicant's goods in commerce. The Commissioner may accept as prima facie evidence that the mark has become distinctive, as used on or in connection with the applicant's goods in commerce, proof of substantially exclusive and continuous use thereof as a mark by the applicant in commerce for the five years before the date on which the claim of distinctiveness is made. Nothing in this section shall prevent the registration of a mark which, when used on or in connection with the goods of the applicant, is primarily geographically deceptively misdescriptive of them, and which became distinctive of the applicant's goods in commerce before December 8, 1993. . . .

In re Joint–Stock Company "Baik"

80 U.S.P.Q.2d 1305 (T.T.A.B.2006).

■ KUHLKE, ADMINISTRATIVE TRADEMARK JUDGE:

Joint–Stock Company "Baik," a Russian company located in Irkutsk, Russia, has filed an application to register BAIKALSKAYA (in standard character form) on the Principal Register for "vodka" in International Class 33, alleging a bona fide intent to use the mark in commerce.

The examining attorney refused registration under Section 2(e)(2) of the Trademark Act, 15 U.S.C. § 1052(e)(2), on the ground that applicant's mark is primarily geographically descriptive of its goods: . . .

When the refusals were made final, applicant appealed. . . .We affirm the refusal to register under Section 2(e)(2).

Primarily Geographically Descriptive

In maintaining the refusal, the examining attorney argues that the "primary significance of the term BAIKALSKAYA is geographic" because translated from Russian this term means "from Baikal" (Br. p. 4) and BAIKAL is the name of a lake in Russia (Br. p. 5). Further, the examining attorney argues that a goods/place association is presumed because applicant is located in Irkutsk, a city near Lake Baikal, and its vodka "is manufactured and bottled with water piped directly from Lake Baikal." Br. p. 5. She argues that Lake Baikal is not an obscure location but rather a well-known lake and popular tourist destination and BAIKALSKAYA would be perceived by the relevant purchasers, consumers of Russian vodka, as such. She further notes that the translation "from Baikal" will not be lost on the approximately 706,000 Russian speakers in the United States.

In support of her position the examining attorney submitted an excerpt from a Russian/English language dictionary and a memorandum from the translations office of the Patent and Trademark Office showing the English translation of BAIKALSKAYA as "from Baikal" or "Baikal's." She also submitted the following entries from *The American Heritage Dictionary of the English Language* (3d ed. 1992):

> Baikal, Lake: A lake of south-central Russia. It is the largest freshwater lake in Eurasia and the world's deepest lake, with a maximum depth of 1,742.2m (5,712 ft).

> Irkutsk: A city of south-central Russia near the southern end of Lake Baikal. It is an industrial center and a major stop on the Trans–Siberian Railroad. Population, 598,000.

In addition, she submitted printouts of excerpts from a variety of publications retrieved from the Lexis/Nexis database that refer to Lake Baikal. . . .

The examining attorney also made of record content from three web-sites on the Internet featuring travel tours to Lake Baikal. . . . *See*, excerpts from www.tripadvisor.com, baikal.in-russia.com and www.waytorussia.net attached to Final Office Action (December 22, 2004).

Finally, regarding the number of people familiar with the Russian language in the United States, the examining attorney submitted printouts from several publications retrieved from the Lexis/Nexis database, as well as an excerpt from the CNN website, showing that there are approximately 706,000 Russian speakers in the United States. *See* www.cnn.com/2003.

In traversing the refusal, applicant first notes that it is the owner of a prior registration for BAIKALSKAYA vodka which was cancelled under Section 8 due to its failure to file a statement of continued use in view of its cessation of sales in the United States. Applicant argues that "The previous registration indicates that this mark is capable of functioning as an effective indicator of source for the Applicant." Br. p. 2. Continuing, applicant argues that Lake Baikal is remote and that the "vast majority of Americans are unlikely to be familiar with Russian geography in general and Lake Baikal in particular." Br. p. 4. Further, that only a very small portion of Americans visit Russia each year and that it "is common knowledge that the American public as a whole lacks even general geographic knowledge, ranking near the bottom of nearly all surveys of geographic knowledge among industrialized nations. Many Americans could not find the Atlantic Ocean on a globe and very few could name the five Great Lakes located in the United States." Br. p. 5. Applicant does not dispute the number of Russian speakers in the United States but argues that it is a very small percentage of the general population and that very few Americans visit "the remote location of Lake Baikal in Siberia." Br. p. 4. Applicant further argues that "the average American consumer does not speak or understand Russian, and thus would be highly unlikely to understand the meaning of the expression 'BAIKALSKAYA'." Br. p. 4.

The test for determining whether a term is primarily geographically descriptive is whether (1) the term in the mark sought to be registered is the name of a place known generally to the public, and (2) the public would make a goods/place association, that is, believe that the goods or services for which the mark is sought to be registered originate in that place. *See In re Societe Generale des Eaux Minerals de Vittel S.A.*, 824 F.2d 957, 3 USPQ2d 1450 (Fed. Cir. 1987) (hereinafter *Vittel*) (citations omitted). If the goods do in fact emanate from the place named in the mark, the goods/place association can be presumed. *In re Carolina Apparel*, 48 USPQ2d 1542 (TTAB 1998). One exception to that presumption is "if there exists a genuine issue raised that the place named in the mark is so obscure or remote that purchasers would fail to recognize the term as indicating the geographical source of the goods." *Vittel, supra* at 1451. In that situation, the examining attorney must submit evidence sufficient to establish a public association with that place. *Id.* The determination of the goods/place association is made not in the abstract, but rather in connection with the goods or services with which the mark is used and from the perspective of the relevant public for those goods or services. *See In re MCO Properties Inc.*, 38 USPQ2d 1154 (TTAB 1995) (FOUNTAIN HILLS geographically descriptive where relevant public for applicant's service of developing real estate includes people considering purchasing real property in Fountain Hills, Arizona). Finally, adjectival forms of geographic terms are also considered primarily geographically descriptive. *In re Jack's Hi–Grade Foods, Inc.*, 226 USPQ 1028, 1029 (TTAB 1985) (NEAPOLITAN for sausage emanating from United States primarily geographically deceptively misdescriptive); *Ex Parte La Union Agricola Sociedad Anonima*, 73 USPQ 233 (ComrPats 1947) (La Tarragonesa adjectival form of Tarragona indicating something from Tarragona geographically descriptive of brandy from Tarragona).

We first look at the significance of the term to the relevant public, who are consumers of vodka, including Russian vodka. As shown by the evidence, Lake Baikal is located in south-central Russia and is noted for its size, depth, volume of water and unique indigenous species. As indicated in the 1992 dictionary entry submitted by the examining attorney, Baikal is the world's deepest lake, and is located in Russia. The lake is the subject of numerous articles in U.S. publications on subjects ranging from tourism to ecology to oil production.

Baikal has been the subject of scientific and environmental/cultural exchanges between American and Russian citizens. (Citations omitted). Baikal and the surrounding region receive frequent mention in the United States press due to its attraction as a tourist destination and an energy pipeline project that is reported to be a threat to its natural beauty.(Citations omitted). We particularly note that the examples submitted by the examining attorney span the United States and include publications in Sacramento, California; Atlanta, Georgia; Bergen County, New Jersey and Bellingham, Washington. In addition, the examples include national publications with wide distribution such as *The Washington Post* and *The New York Times*.

The fact that BAIKALSKAYA is the adjectival form of a geographic term does not diminish its geographic significance. (Citation omitted). There is no question that Russian speakers living in the United States, according to the record approximately 706,000 in number, would immediately know that BAIKALSKAYA means "from Baikal." Thus, the evidence of record supports a finding that a significant portion of consumers would, upon seeing the word BAIKALSKAYA on a bottle of vodka, conclude that it is a place name and that the vodka came from there. Nor is there any evidence in the record to show an alternative primary meaning in the public mind. Applicant has not contended and the record does not reflect that the words BAIKAL and BAIKALSKAYA have any other meaning. On this record, we find that BAIKAL is not a remote or obscure place and its adjectival form retains its geographic significance.

We are not persuaded by applicant's argument that Americans have limited knowledge of world geography and that they "could not find the Atlantic Ocean on a globe." Aside from the fact that applicant submitted no evidence to support this statement, we are not concerned with "the American public as a whole." Rather, as noted above, we must determine the perception of a subset of Americans, purchasers of vodka, including Russian vodka. Moreover, the record shows that the public at large is exposed to references to Lake Baikal and certainly the Russian-speaking public is even more likely to be aware of the geographic significance of the mark because they are most likely either from Russia, have Russian relatives, or became familiar with Russia, including major geographic sites, when learning the language.

The facts of this case are distinguished from the cases relied on by applicant in support of its contention that its mark is not geographically descriptive. The cases of *Vittel, supra, In re Bavaria St. Pauli Brauerei AG*, 222 USPQ 926 (TTAB 1984), and *In re Brauerei Aying Franz Inselkammer KG*, 217 USPQ 73 (TTAB 1983), all involved the names of small villages which were not widely known, in contrast to the name of a significant lake, the deepest lake in the world. Moreover, the evidentiary record here, as opposed to the prior cases, is replete with numerous references to BAIKAL in various publications from various cities throughout the United States in addition to dictionary entries. We recognize that for an American consumer BAIKAL is not in the same category as MINNESOTA. *Compare In re JT Tobacconists, supra* (no question that Minnesota is not obscure or remote). However, to the extent applicant has raised an issue as to the possible remoteness or obscurity of the place, the examining attorney has submitted sufficient evidence from which we can infer that a significant portion of American vodka purchasers would conclude that BAIKALSKAYA refers to a place name. *Compare Vittel, supra.*

Turning to the second prong in the test, we presume a goods/place association because applicant is located near Lake Baikal, in the city of Irkutsk. *See In re Carolina Apparel, supra.* In addition, applicant has acknowledged that its vodka is made in Irkutsk. Moreover, applicant does not dispute the examining attorney's contention that its vodka is made from the water of Lake Baikal, or that it produces various vodkas from a location near Lake Baikal. . . .

In view of the above, we conclude that the proposed mark BAIKAL-SKAYA for use in connection with applicant's vodka is primarily geographically descriptive.

Finally, applicant's prior cancelled registration does not obviate the refusal. A cancelled registration is not entitled to any of the statutory presumptions of Section 7(b) of the Trademark Act. *See, e.g., In re Hunter Publishing Company*, 204 USPQ 957, 963 (TTAB 1979) (cancellation "destroys the Section [(b)] presumptions and makes the question of registrability 'a new ball game' which must be predicated on current thought."). *Cf. Action Temporary Services Inc. v. Labor Force Inc.*, 870 F.2d 1563, 10 USPQ2d 1307, 1309 (Fed. Cir. 1989) ("[A] canceled registration does not provide constructive notice of anything"). Moreover, prior decisions by examining attorneys are not binding on the Board. *In re Nett Designs Inc.*, 236 F.3d 1339, 57 USPQ2d 1564, 1566 (Fed. Cir. 2001).

QUESTION

Should the Board infer a goods/place association in the minds of potential purchasers when the goods come from the particular place named in the mark?

In re California Innovations, Inc.

329 F.3d 1334 (Fed.Cir.2003).

■ RADER, CIRCUIT JUDGE.

California Innovations, Inc. (CA Innovations), a Canadian-based corporation, appeals the Trademark Trial and Appeal Board's refusal to register its mark—CALIFORNIA INNOVATIONS. Citing section 2(e)(3) of the Lanham Act, 15 U.S.C. § 1052(e)(3) (2000), the Board concluded that the mark was primarily geographically deceptively misdescriptive. Because the Board applied an outdated standard in its analysis under § 1052(e)(3), this court vacates the Board's decision and remands.

I.

CA Innovations filed an intent-to-use trademark application, Serial No. 74/650,703, on March 23, 1995, for the composite mark CALIFORNIA INNOVATIONS and Design. The application sought registration for the following goods:

> automobile visor organizers, namely, holders for personal effects, and automobile trunk organizers for automotive accessories in International Class 12; backpacks in International Class 18; thermal insulated bags for food and beverages, thermal insulated tote bags for food or beverages, and thermal insulated wraps for cans to keep the containers cold or hot in International Class 21; and nylon, vinyl, polyester and/or leather bags for storage and storage pouches in International Class 22.

. . . .

The PTO ... refused registration under § 1052(e)(3), concluding that the mark was primarily geographically deceptively misdescriptive.

II.

The Lanham Act addresses geographical marks in three categories. The first category, § 1052(a), identifies geographically deceptive marks:

> No trademark by which the goods of the applicant may be distinguished from the goods of others shall be refused registration on the principal register on account of its nature unless it—(a) Consists of or comprises ... deceptive ... matter; ...

15 U.S.C. § 1052(a) (2000) (emphasis added). Although not expressly addressing geographical marks, § 1052(a) has traditionally been used to reject geographic marks that materially deceive the public. A mark found to be deceptive under § 1052(a) cannot receive protection under the Lanham Act. To deny a geographic mark protection under § 1052(a), the PTO must establish that (1) the mark misrepresents or misdescribes the goods, (2) the public would likely believe the misrepresentation, and (3) the misrepresentation would materially affect the public's decision to purchase the goods. *See In re Budge Mfg. Co.*, 857 F.2d 773, 775, 8 U.S.P.Q.2d 1259, 1260 (Fed. Cir. 1988). This test's central point of analysis is materiality because that finding shows that the misdescription deceived the consumer. *See In re House of Windsor*, 221 U.S.P.Q. 53, 56–57 (TTAB 1983).

The other two categories of geographic marks are (1) "primarily geographically descriptive" marks and (2) "primarily geographically deceptively misdescriptive" marks under § 1052(e). The North American Free Trade Agreement, *see* North American Free Trade Agreement, Dec. 17, 1992, art. 1712, 32 I.L.M. 605, 698 [hereinafter NAFTA], as implemented by the NAFTA Implementation Act in 1993, *see* NAFTA Implementation Act, Pub. L. No. 103–182, 107 Stat. 2057 (1993), has recently changed these two categories. Before the NAFTA changes, . . . [t]he law treated these two categories of geographic marks identically. . . .

. . . .

NAFTA and its implementing legislation obliterated the distinction between geographically deceptive marks and primarily geographically deceptively misdescriptive marks. Article 1712 of NAFTA provides:

1. Each party [United States, Mexico, Canada] shall provide, in respect of geographical indications, the legal means for interested persons to prevent:

(a) the use of any means in the designation or presentation of a good that indicates or suggests that the good in question originates in a territory, region or locality other than the true place of origin, in a manner that misleads the public as to the geographical origin of the good. . . .

See NAFTA, Dec. 17, 1992, art. 1712, 32 I.L.M. 605, 698. This treaty shifts the emphasis for geographically descriptive marks to prevention of any public deception. Accordingly, the NAFTA Act amended § 1052(e) to read:

No trademark by which the goods of the applicant may be distinguished from the goods of others shall be refused registration on the principal register on account of its nature unless it—

(e) Consists of a mark which . . . (1) when used on or in connection with the goods of the applicant is primarily geographically descriptive of them, except as indications of regional origin may be registrable under section 4 [15 U.S.C.S. § 1054], (2) when used on or in connection with the goods of the applicant is primarily geographically deceptively misdescriptive of them, . . .

(f) Except as expressly excluded in subsections (a), (b), (c), (d), (e)(3), and (e)(5) of this section, nothing herein shall prevent the registration of a mark used by the applicant which has become distinctive of the applicant's goods in commerce.

15 U.S.C. § 1052(e)–(f) (2000).

Recognizing the new emphasis on prevention of public deception, the NAFTA amendments split the categories of geographically descriptive and geographically deceptively misdescriptive into two subsections (subsections (e)(2) and (e)(3) respectively). Under the amended Lanham Act, subsection (e)(3)—geographically deceptive misdescription—could no longer acquire distinctiveness under subsection (f). Accordingly, marks determined to be primarily geographically deceptively misdescriptive are permanently denied registration, as are deceptive marks under § 1052(a).

Thus, § 1052 no longer treats geographically deceptively misdescriptive marks differently from geographically deceptive marks. Like geographically deceptive marks, the analysis for primarily geographically deceptively mis-descriptive marks under § 1052(e)(3) focuses on deception of, or fraud on, the consumer. The classifications under the new § 1052 clarify that these two deceptive categories both receive permanent rejection. Accordingly, the test for rejecting a deceptively misdescriptive mark is no longer simple lack of distinctiveness, but the higher showing of deceptiveness.

. . . .

Before NAFTA, the PTO identified and denied registration to a pri-marily geographically deceptively misdescriptive mark with a showing that (1) the primary significance of the mark was a generally known geographic location, and (2) "the public was likely to believe the mark identified the place from which the goods originate and that the goods did not come from there." *In re Loew's [Theatres, Inc.]*, 769 F.2d [764,] at 768 [Fed. Cir. 1985]. The second prong of the test represents the "goods-place association" between the mark and the goods at issue. This test raised an inference of deception based on the likelihood of a goods-place association that did not reflect the actual origin of the goods. A mere inference, however, is not enough to establish the deceptiveness that brings the harsh consequence of non-registrability under the amended Lanham Act. As noted, NAFTA and the amended Lanham Act place an emphasis on actual misleading of the public.

Therefore, the relatively easy burden of showing a naked goods-place association without proof that the association is material to the consumer's decision is no longer justified, because marks rejected under § 1052(e)(3) can no longer obtain registration through acquired distinctiveness under § 1052(f). To ensure a showing of deceptiveness and misleading before imposing the penalty of non-registrability, the PTO may not deny registra-tion without a showing that the goods-place association made by the consumer is material to the consumer's decision to purchase those goods. This addition of a materiality inquiry equates this test with the elevated standard applied under § 1052(a). [Citation omitted] This also properly reflects the presence of the deceptiveness criterion often overlooked in the "primarily geographically deceptively misdescriptive" provision of the statute. . . .

Since the NAFTA amendments, this court has dealt with two cases involving § 1052(e)(3). *Wada*, 194 F.3d 1297; *In re Save Venice New York, Inc.*, 259 F.3d 1346, 59 U.S.P.Q.2d 1778 (Fed. Cir. 2001). Although neither of those cases explores the effect of the NAFTA Act on the test for determining geographically deceptive misdescription, both cases satisfy the new NAFTA standard. "If there is evidence that goods like applicant's or goods related to applicant's are a principal product of the geographical area named by the mark, then the deception will most likely be found material and the mark, therefore, deceptive." *House of Windsor*, 221 U.S.P.Q. at 57. "If the place is noted for the particular goods, a mark for such goods which do not originate there is likely to be deceptive under § 2(a) and not registrable under any circumstances." *Loew's Theatres*, 769 F.2d at 768, n.6.

In *Save Venice*, this court affirmed the Board's refusal to register applicant's marks "THE VENICE COLLECTION" and "SAVE VENICE, INC." because of the "substantial evidence available showing that Venice, Italy is known for glass, lace, art objects, jewelry, cotton and silk textiles, printing and publishing." 259 F.3d at 1354 (emphasis added). Although the court in *Save Venice* did not expressly address the materiality issue, because it was not officially recognized in this context, the court emphasized that "all of the applicant's goods are associated with traditional Venetian products." *Id.* at 1350 (emphasis added). The court in *Save Venice* concluded that the public would mistakenly believe they were purchasing "traditional Venetian products" because the applicant's products were "indistinguishable" from the products traditionally originating in Venice. *Id.* at 1350–54. Thus, the record in *Save Venice* satisfies the test for deception.

Similarly, in *Wada*, this court affirmed the Board's refusal to register applicant's mark "NEW YORK WAYS GALLERY" because there was "evidence that showed . . . New York is well-known as a place where leather goods and handbags are designed and manufactured." *Wada*, 194 F.3d at 1299–1300 (emphasis added). Again, the court in *Wada* did not expressly make a finding that the goods-place association would materially influence the consumer. However, this court noted that the public, "upon encountering goods bearing the mark NEW YORK WAYS GALLERY, would believe that the goods" originate in New York, "a world-renown fashion center . . . well-known as a place where goods of this kind are designed, manufactured, or sold." *Id.* This showing that the place was not only well-known, but renowned for the products at issue supports a finding of materiality. *See House of Windsor*, 221 U.S.P.Q. at 57.

Thus, due to the NAFTA changes in the Lanham Act, the PTO must deny registration under § 1052(e)(3) if (1) the primary significance of the mark is a generally known geographic location, (2) the consuming public is likely to believe the place identified by the mark indicates the origin of the goods bearing the mark, when in fact the goods do not come from that place, and (3) the misrepresentation was a material factor in the consumer's decision.

As a result of the NAFTA changes to the Lanham Act, geographic deception is specifically dealt with in subsection (e)(3), while deception in general continues to be addressed under subsection (a). Consequently, this court anticipates that the PTO will usually address geographically deceptive marks under subsection (e)(3) of the amended Lanham Act rather than subsection (a). While there are identical legal standards for deception in each section, subsection (e)(3) specifically involves deception involving geographic marks.

III.

CA Innovations unequivocally states in its opening brief that its "petition seeks review only of that portion of the [Board's] decision that pertains to 'thermal insulated bags for food and beverages and thermal insulated wraps for cans' " as identified in International Class 21 in the application. Therefore, because of applicant's decision not to challenge the Board's judgment with respect to all goods other than those identified in class 21, that part of the Board's decision is not affected by this opinion.

The parties agree that CA Innovations' goods do not originate in California.

Under the first prong of the test—whether the mark's primary significance is a generally known geographic location—a composite mark such as the applicant's proposed mark must be evaluated as a whole.... It is not erroneous, however, for the examiner to consider the significance of each element within the composite mark in the course of evaluating the mark as a whole. *Save Venice*, 259 F.3d at 1352 (citations omitted).

The Board found that "the word CALIFORNIA is a prominent part of applicant's mark and is not overshadowed by either the word INNOVA-TIONS or the design element." Although the mark may also convey the idea of a creative, laid-back lifestyle or mindset, the Board properly recognized that such an association does not contradict the primary geographic significance of the mark. Even if the public may associate California with a particular life-style, the record supports the Board's finding that the primary meaning remains focused on the state of California. Nonetheless, this court declines to review at this stage the Board's finding that CA Innovations' composite mark CALIFORNIA INNOVATIONS and Design is primarily geographic in nature. Rather the PTO may apply the entire new test on remand.

The second prong of the test requires proof that the public is likely to believe the applicant's goods originate in California. The Board stated that the examining attorney submitted excerpts from the Internet and the NEXIS database showing "some manufacturers and distributors of backpacks, tote bags, luggage, computer cases, and sport bags ... headquartered in California." The Board also acknowledged articles "which make reference to companies headquartered in California which manufacture automobile accessories such as auto organizers," as well as the "very serious apparel and sewn products industry" in California.

A great deal of the evidence cited in this case relates to the fashion industry, which is highly prevalent in California due to Hollywood's influence on this industry. However, clothing and fashion have nothing to do with the products in question. At best, the record in this case shows some general connection between the state of California and backpacks and automobile organizers. However, because CA Innovations has limited its appeal to insulated bags and wraps, the above referenced evidence is immaterial. Therefore, this opinion has no bearing on whether the evidence of record supports a rejection of the application with regard to any goods other than those identified in CA Innovations' application under International Class 21, namely insulated bags and wraps.

CA Innovations argues that the examining attorney provided no evidence at all concerning insulated bags for food and wraps for cans in California. The Government contends that the evidence shows some examples of a lunch bag, presumed to be insulated, and insulated backpacks. According to the government, the evidence supports a finding of a goods-place association between California and insulated bags and wraps. This court has reviewed the publications and listings supplied by the examining attorney. At best, the evidence of a connection between California and insulated bags and wraps is tenuous. Even if the evidence supported a finding of a goods-place association, the PTO has yet to apply the materiality test in this case. This court declines to address that issue and apply the new standard in the first instance. Accordingly, this court vacates the finding of the Board that CA Innovations' mark is primarily geographically deceptively misdescriptive, and remands the case for further proceedings. On remand, the Board shall apply the new three-prong standard.

VACATED and REMANDED.

QUESTIONS

1. Applying the new test articulated in *In re California Innovations*, how should the Board rule on remand? Is the Board free to determine that the primary significance of CALIFORNIA INNOVATIONS is not a known place name but rather a phrase suggestive of a laid-back life style? What evidence would be required to determine that a mistaken belief that applicant's goods come from California would be material to purchasers?

2. Is "Japan Telecom" as a trade name for a California company in the business of selling and installing telephone and computer networking equipment primarily geographically deceptively misdescriptive? Does it influence the outcome if the company services mainly the Japanese–American community in California? *See Japan Telecom, Inc. v. Japan Telecom America Inc.*, 287 F.3d 866 (9th Cir.2002).

3. Does a mark's identification of services, rather than goods make any difference in applying the three-prong test for finding a mark primarily geographically deceptively misdescriptive? For example, how should the Trademark Office analyze the mark LE MARAIS, the name of a trendy neighborhood in Paris, for a restaurant located in New York City? Would it be sufficient for the Examiner to show that the Parisian neighborhood was well-known for restaurants to find that the term is primarily geographically deceptively misdescriptive? *See In re Les Halles De Paris J.V.*, 334 F.3d 1371 (Fed.Cir.2003).

"GEOGRAPHICALLY SUGGESTIVE" MARKS

Some place names convey general qualities in whose aura a trademark proprietor might wish her goods or services to bask. For example, "Paris" evokes high fashion and style, "Park Avenue" evokes wealth and luxury, "Wall Street" evokes wealth and power, "Dodge City" evokes the Wild West. "Hollywood" evokes the razzle dazzle of the entertainment industry. These kinds of marks might be dubbed "geographically suggestive," because they do not describe the place of the goods' origin, but they do (or are intended to) conjure up a variety of desirable associations with the place whose name the goods or services bear. Were you a Trademark Examiner, how would you rule on the following marks (assume in all cases that the goods are not in fact produced at the named locations):

  a. "Paris" for perfume;

  b. "Paris" for disposable diapers;

  c. "Park Avenue" for cigarettes, *cf. Philip Morris Inc. v. Reemtsma Cigarettenfabriken Gmbh*, 14 U.S.P.Q.2d 1487 (T.T.A.B.1990);

  d. "Wall Street" for desk organizers;

  e. "Dodge City" for chewing tobacco, *cf. In re Loew's Theatres, Inc.*, 769 F.2d 764 (Fed.Cir.1985);

  f. "Dodge City" for leather goods;

  g. "Swiss Army" for multiple-implement pocket knives, *cf. Forschner Group v. Arrow Trading*, 30 F.3d 348 (2d Cir.1994);

  h. "Hollywood Fries" for fast food restaurants, *cf. In re International Taste Inc.*, 53 U.S.P.Q.2d 1604 (T.T.A.B.2000).

  i. "Vegas" for playing cards, *cf. In re South Park Cigar, Inc.*, 82 U.S.P.Q.2d 1507 (T.T.A.B.2007).

Some courts have addressed the commercial advantage a trademark claimant may reap by linking itself to the desirable qualities associated with particular locales, even where there is no precise "goods-place association." In *Haagen–Dazs, Inc. v. Frusen Gladje*, 493 F.Supp. 73 (S.D.N.Y. 1980), the court rejected a trademark infringement claim brought by the originator of an ersatz–Scandinavian ice cream brand against a competitor who also adopted a name with "Scandinavian flair." The court declined to protect "plaintiff's unique Scandinavian marketing theme." By contrast, in another frozen confection controversy, despite the strong attraction of the suggestive power of ALASKA for ice cream, the court held that geographic designation susceptible to private appropriation. *See Alaska Incorporated v. Alaska Ice Cream Co.*, 34 U.S.P.Q.2d 1145 (E.D.Pa.1995).

5. SECTION 2(e) OF THE LANHAM ACT: SURNAMES AND OTHER ISSUES

15 U.S.C. § 1502 [LANHAM ACT § 2(e)(4)]

No trademark by which the goods of the applicant may be distinguished from the goods of others shall be refused registration on the principal register on account of its nature unless it—

(e) Consists of a mark which ... (4) is primarily merely a surname.

Trademark Manual of Examining Procedure

§ 1211   Refusal on Basis of Surname

. . . .

The Trademark Act, in § 2(e)(4), reflects the common law that exclusive rights in a surname *per se* cannot be established without evidence of long and exclusive use which changes its significance to the public from that of a surname of an individual to that of a mark for particular goods or services. The common law also recognizes that surnames are shared by more than one individual, each of whom may have an interest in using his surname in business and, by the requirement for evidence of distinctiveness, in effect, delays appropriation of exclusive rights in the name. *In re Etablissements Darty et fils*, 759 F.2d 15, 16 (Fed.Cir.1985), *aff'g* 222 U.S.P.Q. 260 (T.T.A.B.1984).

It is settled that the test to be applied in determining whether or not a mark is primarily merely a surname is its primary significance to the purchasing public. *See, e.g., Ex Parte Rivera Watch Corp.*, 106 U.S.P.Q. 145, 149 (Comm'r Pats.1955).

In re Quadrillion Publishing Ltd.

2000 WL 1195470 (Aug. 9, 2000).

■ BUCHER, ADMINISTRATIVE TRADEMARK JUDGE:

An intent-to-use application has been filed by Quadrillion Publishing Limited to register the mark "BRAMLEY" for a wide variety of books, magazines and stationery items in International Class 16.

The Trademark Examining Attorney has refused registration under Section 2(e)(4) of the Trademark Act, 15 U.S.C. § 1052(e)(4), on the ground that applicant's mark is primarily merely a surname. . . .

We *affirm* the refusal to register.

In support of her surname refusal, the Trademark Examining Attorney has made of record the results of her search of a database containing eighty million names, finding 433 "BRAMLEY" surname listings from PHONE-DISC POWERFINDER USA ONE 1997 (3rd ed.), as well as an excerpt from *Webster's Unabridged Third New International Dictionary*, 1986, showing that there is no listing of the term "Bramley" in that dictionary.

Applicant argues that the Trademark Examining Attorney has failed to establish a *prima facie* surname case. Applicant challenges the Trademark Examining Attorney's PHONEDISC evidence on the ground that the quantum of evidence submitted by the Examining Attorney is indeterminate of the primary significance of the term to purchasers. Applicant asserts that "Bramley" is also the name of a small village in England. In support of its position, applicant has submitted a map showing the village of Bramley in the county of Surrey, as well as a picture post card seeming to represent images of several buildings in the village of Bramley. Finally, applicant has also provided a copy of the *Oxford English Dictionary* where the term "Bramley" is defined as "a large green variety of cooking apple."

The test for determining whether a mark is primarily merely a surname is the primary significance of the mark to the purchasing public. (Citations omitted). The initial burden is on the Trademark Examining Attorney to establish a *prima facie* case that a mark is primarily merely a surname. *See In re Etablissements Darty et Fils*, 759 F.2d 15, 16, 225 U.S.P.Q. 652, 653 (Fed.Cir.1985). After the Trademark Examining Attorney establishes a *prima facie* case, the burden shifts to the applicant to rebut this finding.

The Board, in the past, has considered several different factors in making a surname determination under Section 2(e) (4): (i) the degree of surname rareness; (ii) whether anyone connected with applicant has the surname; (iii) whether the term has any recognized meaning other than that of a surname; and (iv) the structure and pronunciation or "look and sound" of the surname. *In re Benthin Management GmbH*, 37 U.S.P.Q.2d 1332 (T.T.A.B. 1995).

There is no doubt that the Trademark Examining Attorney has met her initial burden of establishing that "BRAMLEY" would be perceived by consumers as primarily merely a surname. In particular, the Trademark Examining Attorney has presented over four hundred "BRAMLEY" surname references from the PHONEDISC database, along with proof that the word "Bramley" does not appear in an unabridged, English-language dictionary. The Court of Appeals for the Federal Circuit has held that this type of evidence is sufficient to establish a *prima facie* surname case. *See Hutchinson Technology*, 852 F.2d at 554, 7 U.S.P.Q.2d at 1492; *Darty*, 759 F.2d at 16, 225 U.S.P.Q. at 653; *see also* 2 J. Thomas McCarthy, *McCARTHY ON TRADEMARKS AND UNFAIR COMPETITION*, § 13.30, p. 13–50 (4th ed. 1999).

The Trademark Examining Attorney's PHONEDISC evidence is collected from telephone directories and address books across the country. There is no magic number of directory listings required to establish a *prima facie* surname case. *In re Cazes*, 21 U.S.P.Q.2d 1796, 1797 (T.T.A.B. 1991); *In re Industrie Pirelli Societa per Azioni*, 9 U.S.P.Q.2d 1564, 1566

(T.T.A.B. 1988), *aff'd unpublished decision*, No. 89–1231 (Fed. Cir. 1989). It is reasonable to conclude from these submissions that "BRAMLEY," while obviously not as common as some other surnames, has had measurable public exposure.[2] Even if "BRAMLEY" is an uncommon surname, it is by no means a decidedly rare surname.[3] From more than four hundred "BRAMLEY" surname references in the PHONEDISC database, we conclude that "BRAMLEY" is a surname even if there are relatively few people in the United States having this name.

Applicant dismisses the hundreds of listings from the PHONEDISC database as representing "1/10,000 of 1%," or an "imperceptible sliver of the American population." However, we find this "percentage-of-the-entire-population" argument to be a hollow reed. The rich diversity of surnames in this country is amply reflected in the PHONEDISC computer database evidence. If one were to take a statistical measurement of this database for common names like "Smith" or "Jones," each would constitute a relatively small fraction of the total database content.

As to the second *Benthin* factor, we recognize that no one connected to applicant's organization has been shown to have the "Bramley" surname. If a Bramley were associated in some way with applicant, it could well indicate the public's recognition of the term as a surname. However, logic tells us that the converse is not necessarily true, i.e., the mere fact that this query comes up negative herein cannot compel the conclusion that consumers will perceive the term as a non-surname.

In weighing the third *Benthin* factor, we have considered applicant's contention that "Bramley" has recognized meanings other than that of a surname. However, both the *Benthin* decision and our primary reviewing court clearly require that the other meanings be "recognized" by a significant number of people. We do not believe that a significant number of people would recognize the other meanings proffered in this case because they are remote or obscure. Thus, they do not rebut the Examining Attorney's *prima facie* surname case. The mere fact that the word "Bramley" has two obscure or remote meanings is insufficient to show that it will not be perceived as "primarily merely a surname." Even applicant concedes that "Bramley" is ". . . the name of a very small village outside Guildford,

---

2. To the extent applicant contends that BRAMLEY is an uncommon surname, we would point out that even uncommon surnames may not be registrable on the Principal Register. *See Industrie Pirelli*, 9 U.S.P.Q.2d at 1566.

3. This evidence is far more significant than the number of listings presented in other cases where the surname has been categorized as "rare." *See e.g. Kahan & Weisz*, 508 F.2d at 832, 184 U.S.P.Q. at 422 (six DUC-HARME surname telephone directory listings); *In re Sava Research Corp.*, 32 U.S.P.Q. 2d 1380 (T.T.A.B. 1994) (one hundred SAVA surname telephone directory listings); *Benthin Management*, 37 U.S.P.Q.2d at 1333 (one hundred BENTHIN surname telephone directory listings); *In re Garan, Inc.*, 3 U.S.P.Q.2d 1537 (T.T.A.B. 1987) (six GARAN telephone directory listings and one NEXIS listing). This is one of four factors. Hence, the quantum of PHONEDISC evidence which may be persuasive for finding surname significance in one case may be insufficient in another because of differences in the surnames themselves and/or consideration of the other relevant surname factors. *Darty, supra*.

Surrey in England, which consists of a few houses, a post office and a general store." *See Harris–Intertype*, 518 F.2d at 631 n.4, 186 U.S.P.Q. at 239 n.4 (Harris, Missouri, population 174, and Harris, Minnesota, population 559 held obscure). Applicant certainly has not demonstrated that consumers in the United States would recognize that "Bramley" is the name of a tiny, rural village in England.[4]

Similarly, as to its other alleged non-surname meaning (i.e., a variety of apple), we note that according to applicant's own dictionary entry, the designation "Bramley's seedlings" comes from "M. Bramley, English butcher in whose garden it [the apple variety] may have first grown." Moreover, an entry from the *Oxford English Dictionary* combined with the absence of entries in several unabridged English language dictionaries commonly used in the United States suggests to us that this alleged non-surname significance is remote in the United Kingdom, that this alternate meaning is directly derived from an English surname, and that this particular non-surname meaning is nonexistent in the United States.

Finally, as to the fourth *Benthin* factor, contrary to applicant's contention, it is the view of the Board that "BRAMLEY" has the structure and pronunciation of a surname, not of an arbitrary designation. In fact, judging this matter simply by its look and feel, "BRAMLEY" seems to fit the archetype of British surnames having an "-ley" suffix, such as Bailey, Bradley, Buckley, Brantley or Barkley, and differs only in a single vowel from American surnames, Bromley, Brumley and Brimley.

Decision: The refusal to register the mark "BRAMLEY" under Section 2(e)(4) is affirmed.

QUESTIONS

1. If the user of a surname demonstrates that it has become distinctive within the meaning of Section 2(f), the name is entitled to registration. To what extent is the registrant entitled to exclusive use of the name? *See, infra*, Chapter 7.A

2. Fiore, which has over 5,000 telephone listings as a surname, means "flower" in Italian. Should Isabella Fiore be able to register FIORE for bags, luggage and other goods or should the application be refused as being primarily merely a surname? *See In re Isabella Fiore, LLC,* 75 U.S.P.Q.2d 1564 (T.T.A.B.2005).

NUMERALS, LETTERS AND INITIALS

Various products may carry model, grade or style designations that are helpful in identifying the goods to their producers and sellers, as well as to consumers. For example, most household appliances will carry a model

---

4. Surnames are routinely used as key parts of the names of streets, neighborhoods, towns, mountains and so forth, indicating the surnames of the people for whom they are named. Given that it is a common practice to name places after individuals, it would be surprising if the village of "Bramley" in Surrey could not also trace the historical origins of the village name to the surname of an English family that once lived there.

number in addition to the brand name. As a general rule, "A word, phrase, symbol, numeral or letter which merely differentiates between various grades, styles, colors or types of products, and does not designate their source, is not a protectable trademark. . . .Grade designations are analogous to descriptive terms, in that they serve the primary function of describing or supplying information about the product to the consumer." J. Gilson *et al.*, *Trademark Protection and Practice,* sec. 2.03[4][a] (2006).

A grade or style designation may nevertheless warrant protection as a trademark if, in addition to specifying the quality, style, or type of product, it also, and "primarily," designates the source of the goods. This is a fact question requiring analysis of the manner of use, the intent of the user, and the meaning understood by the consumer. *See, e.g., Ex Parte International Nickel Co., Inc.,* 115 U.S.P.Q. 365 (Com.Pat.1957) (registration allowed for "135" because it "identifies and distinguishes applicant's welding electrodes for welding particular alloys"); *Ex Parte Esterbrook Pen Co.,* 109 U.S.P.Q. 368 (Com.Pat.1956) (registration denied "2668" for penpoints for failure to demonstrate recognition "either in the trade or by consumers as a pen point made only by applicant"). Well-known model or style designations that consumers are likely to recognize as source designations include "747" and "DC10" for airplanes, and "501" for a model of LEVI'S jeans.

Combinations of letters or initials may also function as trademarks. *See, e.g., Eci Division of E–Systems, Inc. v. Environmental Communications Inc.,* 207 U.S.P.Q. 443 (T.T.A.B.1980) ("In fact, the marketing area is replete with well-known trademarks consisting of letters and, in particular, acronyms or nicknames derived from initial letters of the words forming their corporate names, such a 'GM,' 'GE,' 'RCA,' and 'NBC,' to name a few of which judicial notice may be taken.").

6.   SECTION 2(e)(5) OF THE LANHAM ACT: FUNCTIONALITY

15 U.S.C. § 1052(e)(5) [LANHAM ACT § 2(e)(5)]

No trademark by which the goods of the applicant may be distinguished from the goods of others shall be refused registration on the principal register on account of its nature unless it. . . .

(e) consists of a mark which . . . (5) comprises any matter that, as a whole, is functional.

Congress added Section 2(e)(5), 15 U.S.C. § 1052(e)(5), to the Lanham Act, barring the registration of functional features, in 1998. The amendment codified the longstanding practice of the PTO and the courts of holding functional features ineligible for trademark protection even if such features developed secondary meaning.

In re Howard Leight Industries, LLC

80 U.S.P.Q.2d 1507 (T.T.A.B.2006).

■ Grendel, Administrative Trademark Judge:

Applicant seeks registration on the Principal Register of the matter depicted below

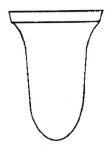

for goods identified in the application, as amended, as "earplugs for noise protection formed of slow recovery resilient foam material."

The Trademark Examining Attorney has issued a final refusal of registration on the ground that the matter sought to be registered is functional and thus unregistrable under Trademark Act Section 2(e)(5), 15 U.S.C. § 1052(e)(5), and on the alternative ground that if the matter is not functional, it is a configuration of the goods which has not acquired distinctiveness and which thus is not registrable pursuant to Trademark Act Section 2(f), 15 U.S.C. § 1052 (f).

. . . [W]e affirm the refusal to register. . . .

Functionality

Trademark Act Section 2(e)(5) precludes registration of "any matter that, as a whole, is functional." The Supreme Court has stated: "In general terms, a product feature is functional if it is essential to the use or purpose of the article or if it affects the cost or quality of the article." *Inwood Laboratories, Inc. v. Ives Laboratories, Inc.,* 456 U.S. 844, 214 USPQ 1, 4 n.10 (1982). The Supreme Court has called this *"Inwood* formulation" the "traditional rule" of functionality. *TrafFix Devices Inc. v. Marketing Displays Inc.,* 532 U.S. 23, 58 USPQ2d 1001, 1006 (2001).

The functionality doctrine is intended to encourage legitimate competition by maintaining the proper balance between trademark law and patent law. As the Supreme Court observed in *Qualitex Co. v. Jacobson Products Co.,* 514 U.S. 159, 34 USPQ2d 1161, 1163–64 (1995):

> The functionality doctrine prevents trademark law, which seeks to promote competition by protecting a firm's reputation, from instead inhibiting legitimate competition by allowing a producer to control a useful product feature. It is the province of patent law, not trademark law, to encourage invention by granting inventors a monopoly over new product designs or functions for a limited time, after which competitors are free to use the innovation. If a product's functional features could be used as trademarks, however, a monopoly over such features could be obtained without regard to whether they qualify as patents and could be extended forever (because trademarks may be renewed in perpetuity). That

is to say, the Lanham Act does not exist to reward manufacturers for their innovation in creating a particular device; that is the purpose of the patent law and its period of exclusivity. The Lanham Act, furthermore, does not protect trade dress in a functional design simply because an investment has been made to encourage the public to associate a particular functional feature with a single manufacturer or seller.

The Federal Circuit, our primary reviewing court, looks at four factors when it considers the issue of functionality: (1) the existence of a utility patent disclosing the utilitarian advantages of the design; (2) advertising materials in which the originator of the design touts the design's utilitarian advantages; (3) the availability to competitors of functionally equivalent designs; and (4) facts indicating that the design results in a comparatively simple or cheap method of manufacturing the product. *Valu Engineering Inc. v. Rexnord Corp.,* 278 F.3d 1268, 61 USPQ2d 1422, 1426 (Fed. Cir. 2002), citing *In re Morton–Norwich Products, Inc.,* 671 F.2d 1332, 213 USPQ 9, 15–16 (CCPA 1982). These are known as the *Morton-Norwich* factors.

The first *Morton-Norwich* factor is the existence of a utility patent disclosing the utilitarian advantages of the design. For purposes of this factor, we consider not only utility patents which are currently extant, but also expired utility patents. *See TrafFix Devices Inc., supra,* 58 USPQ2d at 1005–1007.

Regarding the evidentiary value of utility patents in the functionality determination, the Supreme Court has instructed as follows:

> A prior patent, we conclude, has vital significance in resolving the trade dress claim. A utility patent is strong evidence that the features therein claimed are functional. If trade dress protection is sought for those features the strong evidence of functionality based on the previous patent adds great weight to the statutory presumption that features are deemed functional until proved otherwise by the party seeking trade dress protection. Where the expired patent claimed the features in question, one who seeks to establish trade dress protection must carry the heavy burden of showing that the feature is not functional, for instance by showing that it is merely an ornamental, incidental or arbitrary aspect of the device.

TrafFix Devices Inc., supra, 58 USPQ2d at 1005. The Court further explained (in reference to the patented road sign design at issue in *TrafFix):*

> In a case where a manufacturer seeks to protect arbitrary, incidental, or ornamental aspects of features of a product found in the patent claims, such as arbitrary curves in the legs or an ornamental pattern painted on the springs, a different result might obtain. There the manufacturer could perhaps prove that those aspects do not serve a purpose within the terms of the utility patent. [The

patent and its prosecution history must be examined] to see if the feature in question is shown as a useful part of the invention. *TrafFix, supra*, 58 USPQ2d at 1007. . . .

Thus, in this case, we have reviewed applicant's utility patent as a whole, including its claims, in determining functionality under the first *Morton-Norwich* factor.

. . . .

It appears that a primary focus of the patented invention is the composition of the foam material out of which the earplug is formed (i.e., the foam consists of gas-filled cells which are larger in the center of the earplug than at the outside surface of the earplug, in order to better resist soiling and the pickup of water). However, it is clear that the patent also specifically discloses and claims the functional advantages of the shape of the earplug. . . . Claim 5 of the patent . . . claims "an earplug comprising: an earplug body having a largely bullet-shaped main body portion . . . and having a flared rearward portion of greater diameter than said main body portion." The patent's Description of the Preferred Embodiment likewise specifically identifies an earplug which includes "a largely bullet-shaped main body portion 12 and a flared rear end 14". . . .

The elements of the shape of the earplug, as disclosed and claimed in the patent, are not arbitrary or ornamental flourishes, nor are they merely incidental to the design and function of the earplug. Claim 1 specifies that the main body portion of the earplug has "a largely cylindrical outer surface" which is "constructed to enable its reception in the ear and having outer walls adapted to directly contact the surface of the ear canal." The cylindrical shape thus is not arbitrary or ornamental but instead serves an essential function, i.e., it allows the body of the earplug to directly contact the surface of the human ear canal, which likewise is cylindrical in shape. The patent repeatedly refers to the cylindrical shape of the main body portion of the earplug.

Likewise, the flanged or flared rear end of the earplug is not an arbitrary or incidental design flourish, but rather is essential to the proper functioning of the earplug. "Because of the flange, users tend to roll only the bullet-shaped or largely cylindrical body 12, while leaving the flanged end 14 at its full size. This reduces the possibility of deep insertion into the ear, and it reduces the difficulty of removing the earplug." See also Claim 4, which specifies that the earplug "has a flared rear end of greater diameter than said main body portion, . . . whereby to encourage rolling of only the main body portion but not the rear end."

. . . . .

. . . [W]e find that applicant's expired utility patent is strong evidence of the functionality of the earplug configuration applicant seeks to register. The bullet-shaped main body portion is one of only a few possible reasonable variations of the "cylindrical" shape repeatedly claimed and disclosed in the patent. The bullet-shaped main body (which allows for direct contact with the cylindrical surface of the ear canal) and the flared rear end (which helps prevent too-deep insertion and assists in removal of the earplug) are specifically claimed in Claim 5 of the patent, and are specifically disclosed in the first sentence of the patent's Description of the Preferred Embodiment. These features are more than merely *de facto* functional; rather, the patent shows that the earplug is in this shape because it works better in this shape. Both the disclosures and the claims of the patent reveal that the shape of the earplug is not a mere arbitrary, ornamental or incidental flourish, but rather serves an essential function in the use of the earplug, and affects the quality of the earplug.

In short, applicant's expired utility patent demonstrates the utilitarian advantages of the earplug design at issue, and we find that the first *Morton–Norwich* factor accordingly weighs heavily in favor of a finding of functionality.

There is no evidence of record showing that applicant touts the utilitarian advantages of its earplug design in its advertisements, nor that the design results in a comparatively simple or cheap method of manufacturing the product. The second and fourth *Morton-Norwich* factors accordingly do not support a finding of functionality in this case, and these factors are neutral in our analysis.

The third *Morton–Norwich* factor contemplates consideration of evidence of the availability to competitors of functionally equivalent designs. Regarding the applicability of this factor after the Supreme Court's decision in *TrafFix*, the Federal Circuit has noted, first, that the Court in *TrafFix*

> reaffirmed the "traditional rule" of *Inwood* that "a product feature is functional if it is essential to the use or purpose of the article or if it affects the cost or quality of the article." The Court further held that once a product feature is found to be functional under this "traditional rule," "there is no need to proceed further to consider if there is competitive necessity for the feature," and consequently "[t]here is no need.... to engage.... in speculation about other design possibilities.... Other designs need not be attempted."

Valu Engineering Inc. v. Rexnord Corp., supra, 61 USPQ2d at 1427. (Citations omitted.) The Federal Circuit then continued:

> Nothing in *TrafFix* suggests that consideration of alternative designs is not properly part of the overall mix, and we do not read the Court's observations in *TrafFix* as rendering the availability of alternative designs irrelevant. Rather, we conclude that the Court merely noted that once a product feature is found functional based on other considerations there is no need to consider the availability of alternative designs, because the feature cannot be given trade dress protection merely because there are alternative designs available. But that does not mean that the availability of alternative designs cannot be a legitimate source of evidence to determine whether a feature is functional in the first place.

Id.

In this case, as discussed above, we find that applicant's expired utility patent, which specifically discloses and claims the utilitarian advantages of applicant's earplug configuration and which clearly shows that the shape at issue "affects the . . . quality of the device," is a sufficient basis in itself for finding that the configuration is functional, given the strong weight to be accorded such patent evidence under *TrafFix.* Thus, under the Supreme Court's *TrafFix* test as interpreted by the Federal Circuit in *Valu Engineering,* because these "other considerations" (i.e., the disclosures and claims of the patent) establish the functionality of the design, "there is no need to consider the availability of alternative designs, because the feature cannot be given trade dress protection merely because there are alternative designs available." *Valu Engineering, supra,* 61 USPQ at 1427.

However, even if we consider the evidence of alternative designs that appears in the record, we conclude that such evidence is insufficient to overcome the contrary evidence of the functionality of applicant's design as specifically disclosed and claimed in applicant's expired utility patent, giving due weight to the patent as required by *TrafFix.*

Applicant has submitted a photograph of eight earplugs of various shapes, along with the drawings from twenty design patents for earplugs. Many of these alternative earplug designs do not appear to be functional equivalents to applicant's design because they lack either (or both) of the design features claimed and disclosed in applicant's expired utility patent, i.e., the cylindrical main body portion which allows the earplug to conform to the shape of the human ear canal, and the flared rear end which helps prevent too-deep insertion of the earplug and which aids in removing the earplug. Applicant's earplug shape clearly is one of but few possible alternative designs which provide these features and serve these functions.

However, even if some of these alternative designs are deemed to be functionally equivalent designs and thus are evidence in support of a finding of non-functionality, we find that this evidence is simply outweighed, in our functionality analysis, by the clear and strong evidence of functionality contained in applicant's expired utility patent.

For the reasons discussed above, we find that the earplug design depicted in applicant's trademark application drawing is functional. . . .

. . . .

Acquired Distinctiveness

Because applicant's design is functional, any evidence of distinctiveness is of no avail to applicant in support of registration. *See TrafFix, supra,* 58 USPQ2d at 1007 ("Functionality having been established, whether MDI's dual-spring design has acquired secondary meaning need not be considered"). (Citation omitted). However, . . . should applicant appeal and ultimately prevail on the issue of functionality, we also shall consider applicant's contention that its design has acquired distinctiveness. . . .

A product configuration is not inherently distinctive, and (if non-functional) may be registered on the Principal Register only upon a showing of acquired distinctiveness under Section 2(f). *See Wal–Mart Stores, Inc. v. Samara Brothers, Inc.,* 529 U.S. 205, 54 USPQ2d 1065 (2000). The burden of establishing acquired distinctiveness is on the applicant, who must establish acquired distinctiveness by a preponderance of the evidence. *Yamaha International Corporation v. Hoshino Gakki Co., Ltd.,* 840 F.2d 1572, 6 USPQ2d 1001 (Fed. Cir. 1988).

. . . .

We find that the evidence of record fails to establish, *prima facie,* that applicant's earplug configuration has acquired distinctiveness as a trademark. Applicant's claim of substantially exclusive and continuous use for over fifteen years does not suffice, in this case, to demonstrate acquired distinctiveness. *See In re Gibson Guitar Corp.,* 61 USPQ2d 1948 (TTAB 2001)(sixty-six years of use insufficient to establish acquired distinctiveness). Applicant's asserted U.S. sales of over one billion units in the years 2000–2002 is not particularly probative evidence of acquired distinctiveness, because although this seems like a large number, we cannot determine on this record what percentage of the market this number makes up. *See id.* ("As for the sales of 10,000 in a two-year period, again there is no evidence to show whether this is a large number of sales of guitars vis-à-vis the sales of other companies"). Moreover, although the sales figures might demonstrate that applicant has been successful in marketing its earplugs and that customers find applicant's earplugs to be quality merchandise worth purchasing, we cannot determine, from the sales figures, that purchasers view the shape of the earplug as a mark.

Applicant's asserted advertising expenditure of over $1.5 million in the past three years likewise does not persuade us that applicant's earplug configuration has acquired distinctiveness as a trademark. Indeed, there is nothing in applicant's advertisements or packaging from which we could determine that purchasers have been conditioned or educated to look to the shape of the earplugs, per se, as a source indicator. The advertisements include no "look for" instructions which might encourage purchasers to view the shape of the earplug as a trademark. Secondary meaning occurs when "in the minds of the public, the primary significance of [the configuration] is to identify the source of the product rather than the product itself". *Wal–Mart Stores, Inc., supra,* 54 USPQ2d at 1068. The photographs or drawings of the earplugs contained in applicant's advertisements and packaging would be used by purchasers to identify the product itself, and not the source of the product. Although applicant is correct in contending that goods may be sold under more than one mark, in this case applicant's advertisements and packaging encourage purchasers to view only the designation MAX(R) as the trademark for the goods; the shape of the goods would not be perceived as a mark.

In short, assuming that applicant's earplug design is not functional, we find that applicant has failed to establish, *prima facie,* that the design has acquired distinctiveness as a trademark. The design therefore is not registrable on the Principal Register pursuant to Section 2(f).

In re Gibson Guitar Corp.

61 U.S.P.Q.2d 1948 (T.T.A.B.2001).

■ SEEHERMAN, ADMINISTRATIVE TRADEMARK JUDGE:

Gibson Guitar Corp. has appealed from the final refusal of the Trademark Examining Attorney to register the design of a guitar body, shown below, for "stringed musical instruments, namely guitars." Applicant has described the mark as comprising "a fanciful design of the body of a guitar" and has stated that "the matter shown by the dotted lines is not a part of the mark and serves only to show the position of the mark on the goods."

Registration has been refused pursuant to Section 2(e)(5) of the Trademark Act, 15 U.S.C. 1052(e)(5), on the ground that the applied-for mark is de jure functional, and pursuant to Sections 1, 2 and 45 of the Trademark Act, 15 U.S.C. 1051, 1052 and 1127, on the ground that, if the product design is not de jure functional, it does not function as a mark, but is merely a configuration which has not acquired distinctiveness.

We turn first to the issue of whether the guitar configuration is de jure functional. A product feature is functional and cannot serve as a trademark if it is essential to the use or purpose of the article or it affects the cost or quality of the article. A functional feature is one the exclusive use of which would put competitors at a significant non-reputation-related disadvantage. *Qualitex Co. v. Jacobson Products Co.*, 514 U.S. 159, 34 USPQ2d 1161 (1995), quoted in *TrafFix Devices Inc. v. Marketing Displays Inc.*, 532 U.S. 23, 58 USPQ2d 1001, 1006 (2001).

In *In re Morton–Norwich Products, Inc.*, 671 F.2d 1332, 213 USPQ 9 (CCPA 1982), the Court set forth four factors to be considered in determining whether a product design is de jure functional: 1) the existence of a utility patent that discloses the utilitarian advantages of the design; 2) advertising materials in which the originator of the design touts the design's utilitarian advantages; 3) the availability to competitors of alternative designs; and 4) facts indicating that the design results from a comparatively simple or cheap method of manufacturing the product.

In this case, applicant has stated that there is no utility patent, nor is there any evidence that its guitar configuration results from a simpler or cheaper method of manufacture. Accordingly, these factors do not weigh in our decision.

With respect to the second factor, applicant's advertising materials tout the functional advantages of its guitar shape. Specifically, the advertisement for applicant's Epiphone guitar, submitted as Exhibits B and E to applicant's response filed on September 27, 1999, includes the following copy:

> The new Epiphone Advanced Jumbo TM (AJ) acoustics are different from any other ordinary dreadnought guitar. Our AJ body shape not only looks more like a bell, but also rings like a bell. The more rounded upper bout produces sweeter highs while the broader waist and wider lower bout creates more powerful lows. Combined with a solid Sitka spruce top, mahogany back and sides, reverse-belly TM rosewood bridge and AJ scalloped top bracing, this unique body shape creates a sound which is much more balanced and less "muddy" than other ordinary dreadnought acoustics.

This copy clearly indicates that the particular features of the applicant's configuration—the rounded upper bout, the broader waist, and the wider lower bout, provide certain acoustical advantages in terms of the sounds the guitar makes. "This unique body shape creates a sound which is much more balanced and less 'muddy' than other ordinary dreadnought acoustics."

We are not persuaded by applicant's argument that this advertisement does not tout the functional features of the guitar shape, but is merely puffery. Even if one cannot ascertain with specificity the sound of "sweeter highs", "more powerful lows", and a balanced and less muddy sound, the clear import of the advertisement is that the shape of the guitar is what produces a better musical sound.

With respect to the third factor, the availability of alternative designs, it is not clear, after *TrafFix Devices Inc. v. Marketing Displays Inc.*, *supra*, whether the availability of alternatives weighs as a factor in applicant's favor. In *TrafFix* the Court said that there is no need to engage in speculation about other design possibilities because the functionality of, in that case, the spring design,

> means that competitors need not explore whether other spring juxtapositions might be used. The dual-spring design is not an arbitrary flourish in the configuration of MDI's product; it is the reason the device works. Other designs need not be attempted.

Even assuming the availability of alternative designs remains a factor in determining whether a configuration is de jure functional, applicant has not shown that there are alternative guitar shapes which can produce the same sound as applicant's configuration. On the contrary, the evidence indicates that the specific shape of applicant's guitar is necessary for such sound. In particular, the literature for the Santa Cruz Guitar Company's "Vintage Jumbo Model," which appears identical in shape to the configuration sought to be registered, states that:

> "Round shouldered dreadnoughts have a unique sound," enthused Santa Cruz president Richard Hoover. "Their deep, rich, bass and sweet, strong treble really shine in chord-oriented styles like country, folk and blues." www.santacruzguitar.com

In view of the foregoing, we find that applicant's configuration is de jure functional.

QUESTION

When there is a pertinent patent, as was the case in *Howard Leight Industries*, do the other three *Morton-Norwich* factors play a significant role in determining functionality in the registration context? Should they?

CHAPTER 5

LOSS OF TRADEMARK RIGHTS

A. GENERICISM

1. DEVELOPMENT OF THE STANDARD

Recall the "Shredded Wheat" case, *Kellogg Co. v. National Biscuit Co.*, 305 U.S. 111 (1938), *supra*, Chapter 2.A. The court held Nabisco had no trademark rights in "Shredded Wheat," because that was "the term by which the biscuit in pillow shaped form is generally known by the public.... As Kellogg Company had the right to make the article, it had, also, the right to use the term by which the public knows it." If the name claimed as the brand is (or becomes) the "generic" name of the goods or services, principles of competition require that the name remain (or become) free for all purveyors to use. The cases that follow address both terms that initially served as trademarks but came to lose their source-denoting significance, and terms that aptly described the goods from the start, and may (or should) never have been trademarks.

Bayer Co. v. United Drug Co.
272 F. 505 (S.D.N.Y.1921).

■ LEARNED HAND, J:

[Plaintiff Bayer Co. was the holder of a recently-expired patent for acetylsalicylic acid, a pharmaceutical product that Bayer marketed under the name "Aspirin." Defendant, a competitor, was not only selling acetylsalicylic acid, but was doing so under the Aspirin designation. In response to Bayer's common-law trademark infringement suit, defendant asserted, *inter alia,* that Aspirin had become a commonly recognized name for the drug, and that once the patent expired, any person could not only manufacture and sell the drug, but could call it the name by which the public had come to know the goods.]

. . . .

The single question, as I view it, in all these cases, is merely one of fact: What do the buyers understand by the word for whose use the parties are contending? If they understand by it only the kind of goods sold them, I take it, it makes no difference whatever what efforts the plaintiff has made to get them to understand more. He has failed, and he cannot say that, when the defendant uses the word, he is taking away customers who wanted to deal with him, however closely disguised he may be allowed to keep his identity. So here the question is whether the buyers merely understood that the word "Aspirin" meant this kind of drug, or whether it meant that and more than that; i.e., that it came from the same single, though, if one please anonymous, source from which they had got it before. Prima facie I should say, since the word is coined and means nothing by itself, that the defendant must show that it means only the kind of drug to which it applies. The fact that it was patented until 1917 is material circumstances, but it is not necessarily controlling.

. . . .

In the case at bar the evidence shows that there is a class of buyers to whom the word "Aspirin" has always signified the plaintiff, more specifically indeed than was necessary for its protection. I refer to manufacturing chemists, to physicians, and probably to retail druggists. From 1899 it flooded the mails with assertions that "Aspirin" meant its own manufacture. This was done in pamphlets, advertisements in trade papers, on the packages and cartons, and by the gratuitous distribution of samples. True, after 1904 it abandoned the phrase "acetyl salicylic acid" for "monoaceticacidester of salicylicacid," but even that extraordinary collocation of letters was intelligible to these classes of buyers who, except possibly the more ignorant of the retail druggists, were measurably versed in the general jargon of pharmaceutical chemistry. Moreover, the drug continued to be generally known by the more tolerable phrase "acetyl salicylic acid," which also adequately described its chemical organization. As to these buyers the plaintiff has therefore, I think, made out a case at least to compel the addition of some distinguishing suffix, even though its monopoly had been more perfect than in fact it was.

The crux of this controversy, however, lies not in the use of the word to these buyers, but to the general consuming public, composed of all sorts of buyers from those somewhat acquainted with pharmaceutical terms to those who knew nothing of them. The only reasonable inference from the evidence is that these did not understand by the word anything more than a kind of drug to which for one reason or another they had become habituated. It is quite clear that while the drug was sold as powder this must have been so. It was dispensed substantially altogether on prescription during this period, and, although physicians appear to have used the terms, "Aspirin" or "acetyl salicylic acid" indifferently, it cannot be that such patients as read their prescriptions attributed to "Aspirin" any other meaning than as an ingredient in a general compound, to which faith and science might impart therapeutic virtue. Nor is there any evidence that such as may have seen both terms identified them as the same drug. I cannot speculate as to how many in fact did so. No packages could possibly have reached the consumer, nor was any advertising addressed to them; their only acquaintance with the word was as the name for a drug in whose curative properties they had got confidence.

In 1904, however, they began to get acquainted with it in a different way, for then all the larger manufacturing chemists began to make tablets, and the trade grew to extraordinary proportions. The consumer, as both sides agree, had long before the autumn of 1915 very largely abandoned consultation with physicians and assumed the right to drug himself as his own prudence and moderation might prescribe. In all cases—omitting for the moment the infringing product—the drug was sold in bottles labeled "Aspirin" with some indication of the name of the tablet maker, but none of the plaintiff. It is probable that by far the greater part of the tablets sold were in dozens or less, and that the bottles so labeled did not generally reach the hands of the consumer, but, even so, a not inconsiderable number of bottles of 100 were sold, and as to the rest they were sold only under the name "Aspirin." The consumer did not know and could not possibly know the manufacturer of the drug which he got, or whether one or more chemists made it in the United States. He never heard the name "acetyl salicylic acid" as applied to it, and without some education could not possibly have kept it in his mind, if he had. So far as any means of information at all were open to him, they indicated that it was made by most large chemists indiscriminately.

This being the situation up to the autumn of 1915, the defendant seems to me to have effectually rebutted any presumption which the coined word might carry.

. . . .

After the autumn of 1915 the plaintiff totally changed its methods, and thereafter no tablets reached the consumer without its own name. But it is significant that even then it used the word "Aspirin" as though it was a general term, although it is true that there was ample notice upon the bottles and boxes that "Aspirin" meant its manufacture. The most striking part of the label read, "Bayer—Tablets of Aspirin." While this did not show any abandonment of the name, which there has never been, it did show how the plaintiff itself recognized the meaning which the word had acquired, because the phrase most properly means that these tablets were Bayer's make of the drug known as "Aspirin." It presupposes that the persons reached were using the word to denote a kind of product. Were it not so, why the addition of "Bayer," and especially why the significant word "of"?

Disregarding this, however, it was too late in the autumn of 1915 to reclaim the word which had already passed into the public domain. If the consuming public had once learned to know "Aspirin" as the accepted name for the drug, perhaps it is true that an extended course of education might have added to it some proprietary meaning, but it would be very difficult to prove that it had been done in 17 months, and in any case the plaintiff does not try to prove it. The issue in this aspect, indeed, becomes whether during that period the word had obtained a secondary meaning, and I do not understand that any such thing is claimed. If it is, I own I cannot find any basis for it in the record. Probably what really happened was that the plaintiff awoke to the fact that on the expiration of the patent its trade-mark would be questioned, and strove to do what it could to relieve it of any doubts. Yet, had it not been indifferent to the results of selling to the consumer, it could have protected itself just as well as the time when consumers began to buy directly as in 1915. Nothing would have been easier than to insist that the tablet makers should market the drug in small tin boxes bearing the plaintiff's name, or to take over the sale just as it did later. Instead of this, they allowed the manufacturing chemists to build up this part of the demand without regard to the trade-mark. Having made that bed, they must be content to lie in it. Hence it appears to me that nothing happening between October, 1915, and March, 1917, will serve to turn the word into a trade-mark.

.   .   .   .

The case, therefore, presents a situation in which, ignoring sporadic exceptions, the trade is divided into two classes, separated by vital differences. One, the manufacturing chemists, retail druggists, and physicians, has been educated to understand that "Aspirin" means the plaintiff's manufacture, and has recourse to another and an intelligible name for it, actually in use among them. The other, the consumers, the plaintiff has, consciously I must assume, allowed to acquaint themselves with the drug only by the name "Aspirin," and has not succeeded in advising that the word means the plaintiff at all. If the defendant is allowed to continue the use of the word of the first class, certainly without any condition, there is a chance that it may get customers away from the plaintiff by deception. On the other hand, if the plaintiff is allowed a monopoly of the word as against consumers, it will deprive the defendant, and the trade in general, of the right effectually to dispose of the drug by the only description which will be understood. It appears to me that the relief granted cannot in justice to either party disregard this division; each party has won, and each has lost.

———

A factor that may have influenced the court in the Aspirin case was the trademark proprietor's improper, merely denominative use of the terms. Plaintiff's failure to use the terms in trademark fashion, or adequately to police others' use of the terms, resulted in the terms' loss of trademark significance. A similar result transpired regarding the term "cellophane," see *DuPont Cellophane Co. v. Waxed Products Co.,* 85 F.2d 75 (2d Cir.1936).

In *Stix Products, Inc. v. United Merchants & Mfrs., Inc.,* 295 F.Supp. 479 (S.D.N.Y.1968), Judge Weinfeld rejected a declaratory judgment plaintiff's assertion that CON–TACT had become generic for self-adhesive paper. The case indeed involved improper use of the trademark, but not by the trademark proprietor or its licensees. Rather, the court found that the proprietor's competitor (plaintiff in the action) had been using the term "contact paper" in connection with its self-adhesive paper product in order to render its competitor's trademark generic. Judge Weinfeld stated:

> Based upon the record, my trial notes and a study of the entire transcript, I find Shulman's [plaintiff's president] testimony unacceptable. His testimony, at times glib and facile, was marked by palpably evasive and irrelevant replies to critical inquiry. Its substance reveals a deliberate effort to conceal, behind a maze of

conflicting and equivocal explanations, Stix's true purpose in its use of "contact" in its advertising and promotional material. Shulman's purposeful conduct emerges from the entire record and is emphasized by demeanor evidence. His claim that by 1959 the word "contact" and related phrases had become generic for the goods was the product of his own creation. The conclusion is compelled that it was part of a planned and aggressive campaign to devitalize or destroy the value of United's mark in an effort to force it into the public domain.

The record, however, demonstrates that Stix failed of its purpose with the ultimate consumer. The majority of the purchasing public did not and does not now use the word "contact" or the phrases "contact paper" or "contact plastic" to describe self-adhesive decorative plastic products; they do not recognize or use such expressions as an indication of the nature or class of such products. The majority of those who do use the expression are aware that CON–TACT is a brand name, even apart from its hyphenated and stylized form, and use the terms interchangeably with United's CON–TACT mark to identify the product as coming from a single source; no matter how spelled, CON–TACT is recognized as a brand name for self-adhesive decorative plastics.

The Court concludes that Stix's use of "contact" in its captions, whether in lower case, with a capital "C," in block letters or without a hyphen, is a trademark use; it is not a primary or descriptive or generic use, but is an infringement of United's registered mark CON–TACT.

295 F.Supp. at 492. The *Stix* decision suggests that competitors may not "genericise" each other's marks. But the purpose of the genericism doctrine is to permit competitors to call their competing goods or services by their commonly-known names. Why, then, would a competitor's generic use of another's mark be wrongful?

PROTECTING TRADEMARKS AGAINST GENERICISM

As *Bayer* and other cases show, a trademark holder may lose trademark rights if the term ceases to indicate the source of the goods or services, and instead becomes synonymous with the goods or services. Companies employ various strategies to maintain trademark awareness, including placing advertisements directed toward the relevant public, and stressing the trademark significance of the term. Consider the following examples. Do you think they are an effective means of maintaining brand awareness?

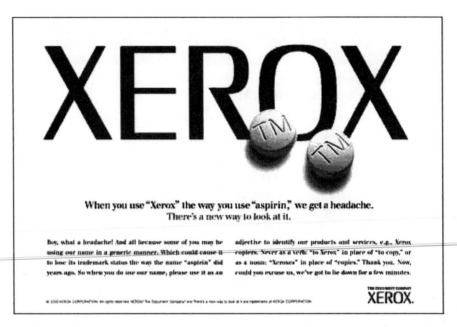

The following notice, posted on the trademark owner's website, illustrates another attempt to instill trademark awareness among consumers.

These trademark awareness advertisements exemplify a catchy attempt to prevent loss of trademark rights through popular misuse of the term. Trademark education endeavors, however, are not a recent phenomenon, as the following advertisement, which first appeared in 1920, attests.

(Advertisement)

The History of a Word

THE trademark "KODAK" was first applied, in 1888, to a camera manufactured by us and intended for amateur use. It had no "derivation." It was simply invented—made up from letters of the alphabet to meet our trademark requirements.

It was short and euphonious and likely to stick in the public mind, and therefore seemed to us to be admirably adapted to use in exploiting our new product.

It was, of course, immediately registered, and so is ours, both by such registration and by common law. Its first application was to the Kodak camera. Since then, we have applied it to other goods of our manufacture, as, for instance Kodak tripods, Kodak portrait attachments, Kodak film, Kodak film tanks and Kodak amateur printer.

The name "Kodak" does not mean that these goods must be used in connection with a Kodak camera, for, as a matter of fact, any of them may be used with other apparatus or goods. It simply means that they originated with, and are manufactured by, Eastman Kodak Company.

"Kodak," being our registered and common law trademark, cannot be rightly applied except to goods of our manufacture.

If you ask at the store for a Kodak camera, or Kodak film, or other Kodak goods and are handed something not of our manufacture, you are not getting what you specified, which is obviously unfair both to you and to us.

If it isn't an Eastman, it isn't a Kodak.

EASTMAN KODAK COMPANY, ROCHESTER, N.Y.

(First Appearance 1920)

Keeping company personnel and other business people attuned to proper trademark use is as important as maintaining public awareness, and can require its own education measures. The following brochure represents one such attempt.

In "How to Use a Trademark Properly," from TRADEMARK PROBLEMS AND HOW TO AVOID THEM (rev. ed. 1981), Sidney Diamond offered some rules of thumb to help prevent a trademark from degenerating into a generic term. He stressed that the product's generic name should accompany the trademark. The trademark is an adjective; it should never be used as a noun or as a verb. Thus, proper promotion of a GREMLIN brand washing machine would proclaim that "clothes come cleaner with a GREMLIN washing machine," rather than "clothes come cleaner with a Gremlin."

Similarly, the trademark owner should not exhort the consumer to "gremlinize" his clothing. Diamond counselled: "A simple test to apply to advertising copy is this: Would a complete thought be expressed if the trademark were omitted from the sentence?" Do the advertising materials you have just perused meet this test?

2.   IMPLEMENTING THE STANDARD: SURVEY EVIDENCE

King–Seeley Thermos Co. v. Aladdin Industries, Inc., 321 F.2d 577 (2d Cir.1963). King–Seeley owned eight trademark registrations for the word "Thermos." Aladdin Industries tried to sell its own vacuum-insulated containers as "thermos bottles," a term that it regarded as generic. Plaintiff King–Seeley sought to enjoin Aladdin Industries from using the term, and defendant countered seeking to cancel the registration of the word "thermos" for having become "a generic descriptive word in the English language ... as a synonym for 'vacuum insulated' container."

According to the District Court, King–Seeley's promotional campaign directed at the public for the "Thermos bottle" had the effect of making "thermos" a generic term descriptive of the product rather than its origin. Subsequent efforts by King–Seeley to police its trademark succeeded within the trade but failed to change public perception:

> The results of the survey [conducted at the behest of the defendant] were that about 75% of adults in the United States who were familiar with containers that keep the contents hot or cold, call such a container a "thermos"; about 12% of the adult American public know that "thermos" has a trade-mark significance, and about 11% use the term "vacuum bottle." This is generally corroborative of the court's conclusions drawn from the other evidence, except that such other evidence indicated that a somewhat larger minority than 12% was aware of the trade-mark meaning of "thermos"; and a somewhat larger minority than 11% used the descriptive term "vacuum" bottle or other container.

However, as there was an appreciable, though minority, segment of the consumer public which recognized plaintiff's trademarks, the District Court imposed certain restrictions and limitations on the use of the word "thermos" by defendant which were upheld by the 2d Circuit:

> Since in this case, the primary significance to the public of the word "thermos" is its indication of the nature and class of an

article rather than as an indication of its source, whatever duality of meaning the word still holds for a minority of the public is of little consequence except as a consideration in the framing of a decree. Since the great majority of those members of the public who use the word "thermos" are not aware of any trademark significance, there is not enough dual use to support King–Seeley's claims to monopoly of the word as a trademark.

No doubt, the *Aspirin* and *Cellophane* doctrine can be a harsh one for it places a penalty on the manufacturer who has made skillful use of advertising and has popularized his product. However, King–Seeley has enjoyed a commercial monopoly of the word "thermos" for over fifty years. During that period, despite its efforts to protect the trademark, the public has virtually expropriated it as its own. The word having become part of the public domain, it would be unfair to unduly restrict the right of a competitor of King–Seeley to use the word.

The court below, mindful of the fact that some members of the public and a substantial portion of the trade still recognize and use the word "thermos" as a trademark, framed an eminently fair decree designed to afford King–Seeley as much future protection as was possible. The decree provides that defendant must invariably precede the use of the word "thermos" by the possessive of the name "Aladdin"; that the defendant must confine its use of "thermos" to the lower-case "t"; and that it may never use the words "original" or "genuine" in describing its product. *See Bayer Co. v. United Drug Co.*, 272 F. 505 (S.D.N.Y.1921); *DuPont Cellophane Co. v. Waxed Products Co.*, 85 F.2d 75 (2 Cir.1936). In addition, plaintiff is entitled to retain the exclusive right to all of its present forms of the trademark "Thermos" without change. These conditions provide a sound and proper balancing of the competitive disadvantage to defendants arising out of plaintiff's exclusive use of the word "thermos" and the risk that those who recognize "Thermos" as a trademark will be deceived.

E.I. DuPont de Nemours & Co. v. Yoshida International, Inc.

393 F.Supp. 502 (E.D.N.Y.1975).

■ Neaher, District Judge:

[DuPont, trademark proprietors of the TEFLON mark for non-stick cookware coating, brought a trademark infringement action against YKK, the manufacturers of the EFLON easy-glide zipper. Among other defenses, YKK asserted that TEFLON was a generic term. Both parties introduced surveys purporting to show that the public did or did not perceive TEFLON to be the common noun for non-stick cookware coatings.]

YKK's principal proof of generic usage by the public comes from a second survey introduced into evidence. That survey, actually two nationwide studies conducted by a reputable professional survey research organization, The Sorenson Group, Inc., in September 1972, is entitled "Awareness and Name Identification of Non–Stick Coating Concept."

The first study ("Survey I") was conducted among adult women, 90.6% of whom expressed awareness of "kitchen pots and pans that have their inside surfaces coated by chemical substances to keep grease or food from sticking to them." Of the aware[51] respondents, 86.1% apparently mentioned only "TEFLON" or "TEFLON II" as their sole answer when asked, "What is the name ... or names of these pots and pans....?" Further, 71.7% of the aware women gave only "TEFLON" or "TEFLON II" as the name they would use to describe the pots and pans to a store clerk or friend. The figure was 79.3%, counting those who gave responses in addition to TEFLON or TEFLON II. Only 7.3% of the aware women identified DuPont as the manufacturer of the pots and pans.

The second study ("Survey II") was conducted among adult women, 89.4% of whom expressed some sort of awareness of "substances that manufacturers sometimes apply to the surfaces of certain products in order to prevent things from sticking to them." Of the aware respondents, 81.4% apparently mentioned only "TEFLON" or "TEFLON II" as their sole answer when asked, "What name or names are these substances called.... ?" Further, 60% of the aware women gave only "TEFLON" or "TEFLON II" as the name they would use to describe the pots and pans to a store clerk or friend. The figure was 70% counting those who gave other responses in addition to TEFLON or TEFLON II. Only 9.1% of the aware women identified DuPont as the manufacturer of the substances. Understandably enough, no one in either survey apparently ever mentioned polytetrafluoroethylene.

In response to these two surveys, DuPont introduced a second Burke survey, conducted telephonically by Burke Marketing Research, Inc., virtually on the eve of trial. It also contained two separate studies. In the first of these ("Survey A"), respondents of either sex who represented over the telephone to be over 18 years of age were told: "Protective coatings are sometimes applied by manufacturers to the inside of household utensils in order to prevent food and grease from sticking." They were then asked, "Do you know a brand name or trademark for one of these coatings?" Pursuing affirmative answers only, respondents were then asked, "What is that brand name or trademark?"

The results of the survey were that of the 60% of the respondents who reached the latter question, 80% of them—or 48% of the entire sample—answered "TEFLON." All respondents were then asked, "Can you think of any other words or terms to describe these coatings?" Among the TEFLON respondents to the prior question, 32% were able to supply an additional

---

51. "Aware" respondents were only those who indicated an awareness of the subject matter of the survey by responding in some affirmative fashion to an initial question, "Have you ever heard about these kitchen pots and pans....?"

term, the most frequently expressed of which was "Non–Stick." Sixty-eight percent knew no other words.

The second study ("Survey B") was conducted among adults in a similar fashion. By using the example of "Chevrolet—automobile" the interviewer first explained the difference between a brand name and a common name, and then asked whether each of eight names, including TEFLON, was a brand name or a common name. The results, as shown in more detail in the margin,[54] were that 68% of the respondents identified TEFLON as a brand name and 31% as a common name.

Naturally enough, the parties are in some conflict as to the import for this case of this wealth of statistics. Briefly stated, YKK contends that DuPont's Survey A confirms its own findings, because 68% of those who identified "TEFLON" as a brand name or trademark had no other word or term to describe the coatings. Accordingly, say defendants, this 68% regards "TEFLON" as the descriptive name of the non-stick substances, a figure that compares closely with their own. In response, DuPont argues that YKK's own studies are invalid because the way Survey I and Survey II questions were worded, it was not possible to determine "what percentage of the women who gave a TEFLON response did so in the belief or on the assumption that they were being asked for a brand name." DuPont also argues that the coding of "TEFLON only" responses in both of defendants' surveys were such that they included responses which clearly reflected proper, non-generic use of the TEFLON mark, *e.g.,* "TEFLON non-stick finish."

On a review of the exhibits, and especially the cross-examination of the author of YKK's surveys, Dr. Robert C. Sorensen, the court is satisfied that those surveys are ambiguous on the question of whether the responses truly reflect generic use of the TEFLON mark to the extent indicated.[56]

The fact is that the surveys do not really focus on the issue of the absence of *trademark* significance in public use of the word TEFLON. This is made clear by DuPont's own Survey A, which asked essentially the same question as did Survey II—name for non-stick coatings—but used the expression "brand name or trademark" rather than "name or names." It seems clear from the results that in all three surveys (I, II and A), respondents were, by the design of the questions, more often than not focusing on supplying the inquirer a "name," without regard to whether

54.

NAME	BRAND	COMMON	DON'T KNOW
	%	%	%
STP	90	5	5
THERMOS	51	46	3
MARGARINE	9	91	1
TEFLON	68	31	2
JELLO	75	25	1
REFRIGERATOR	6	94	—
ASPIRIN	13	86	—
COKE	76	24	—

Pl. Exh. 61, Table 2.

56. This is not wholly to reject defendants' contention that the surveys reveal some evidence and examples of generic use of TEFLON by the public. DuPont admits that they do. But as the discussion makes clear, "some evidence" of generic usage is not sufficient. Moreover, references, for example, to "Teflon pots and pans" are at best only ambiguous illustrations of generic use and hardly furnish the convincing proof required to overcome trademark or brand name usage for a non-stick coated pot or pan.

the principal significance of the name supplied was "its indication of the nature or class of an article, rather than an indication of its origin." *King–Seeley Thermos Co., supra,* 321 F.2d at 580.

The only survey which really gets down to this critical element of the case is Survey B. It stands unrebutted as evidence that, to the extent it accurately reflects public opinion, a substantial majority of the public continues to believe that TEFLON is a brand name. YKK criticizes the survey not for being unrepresentative, but for its failure to be tied to a particular product, and argues it is thus no evidence that TEFLON has trademark significance. That contention is without merit. In fact, the responses of the survey reveal that the public is quite good at sorting out brand names from common names, and, for TEFLON, answers the critical question left unanswered by the ambiguities inherent in Surveys I, II and A—that of the *principal significance* of the TEFLON mark to the public.[57] Not only have defendants failed to show that TEFLON's principal significance is as a common noun, plaintiff has succeeded in showing it to be a "brand name"—an indicator, in the words of DuPont's questionnaire, of a product "made by one company."

. . . .

Another, somewhat overlapping, factor is a considerable period of acquiescence by the trademark owner in generic use, possibly coupled with a failure to take adequate affirmative action to correct generic use thereafter. *See, e.g., King–Seeley Thermos Co., supra,* 321 F.2d at 578–79; *DuPont Cellophane Co., supra,* 85 F.2d at 78–80. In this case, there is *no* evidence that DuPont has been anything less than diligent in its efforts to protect the trademark significance of TEFLON from the outset, and continuously thereafter.

The foregoing makes clear that, on the facts of this case, YKK was required to make a rather clear and convincing showing that the principal significance of the word TEFLON to the public is as a term for non-stick coatings and finishes rather than its trademark significance. But no matter how defendants' burden is described, it simply has not been met on this record and the defense must fail.

. . . .

QUESTIONS

1. The "thermos" court placed great weight on the survey results. The survey requested respondents to supply a name for a container which keeps liquids hot or cold. Do you see any problems with this survey?

57. Also, . . . the court finds no significance in the evidence in Surveys I and II of the large proportion of the public unaware of the identify of DuPont as the manufacturer of TEFLON. As has been noted, such evidence has no bearing on the likelihood of confusion issue. It would be pertinent on the genericization issue only if the mark itself were an important component of the name of the manufacturing company, *e.g.,* Coca–Cola Bottling Co. But where, as here, the mark is entirely distinct from the identity of the manufacturer, such evidence is of no value.

2. In "thermos," although (according to the survey) 75% of the public perceived no trademark significance in the term, 25% did view the term as a trademark. What measures did the court prescribe to prevent confusing this segment of the public? Are there other measures you would recommend? (See materials *infra*, sub-part 3, "Genericism and Confusion.")

LEGISLATIVE "CLARIFICATION" OF STANDARDS TO ASSESS GENERICISM

In *Anti–Monopoly, Inc. v. General Mills Fun Group*, 684 F.2d 1316 (9th Cir.1982), the creator of the "Anti–Monopoly" board game (formerly known as the "Bust the Trust" board game), responding to notices of trademark infringement, brought an antitrust declaratory judgment claim against the producers of the well-known "Monopoly" real estate trading game. In the course of adjudicating the trademark infringement counter-claim, the Ninth Circuit reviewed several surveys, ultimately crediting a "motivation survey" that inquired into whether consumers purchased "Monopoly" because they liked Parker Brothers' products, or because they were "interested in playing 'Monopoly,' [they] don't much care who makes it." This ruling provoked a great outcry from trademark owners, as well as criticism from the academy, for disregarding the "single, if anonymous, source" rule, and for failing to recognize that trademarks serve a "dual purpose" of identifying both the producer of the goods, and the goods themselves. This is particularly true for "unique" goods, where the mark inevitably conveys product information as well as source information. That does not necessarily mean, however, that consumers do not perceive the trademark as a brand name. (Indeed, brand advertising endeavors to convince consumers that the trademark stands for goods whose qualities consumers should believe are unique and should find more appealing than the qualities symbolized by a rival brand.)

Congress responded remarkably rapidly, with the "Trademark Clarification Act of 1984." This legislation supplemented section 14 of the Lanham Act's provision on cancellation of trademark registrations of marks had become the "common descriptive name" of the goods or services, with the following specifications (in italics):

> *A registered mark shall not be deemed to be the common descriptive name of goods or services solely because such mark is also used as a name of or to identify a unique product or service. The primary significance of the registered mark to the relevant public rather than purchaser motivation shall be the test for determining whether the registered mark has become the common descriptive name of goods or services in connection with which it has been used.*

The legislation also modified the section 45 definitions of "trademark," "service mark" and "abandoned" as indicated in italics:

> The term "trademark" includes any word, name, symbol, or device or any combination thereof adopted and used by a manufacturer or merchant to identify and distinguish his goods, *including a unique*

product, from those manufactured or sold by others and to indicate the source of the goods, *even if that source is unknown.*

The term "service mark" means a mark used in the sale or advertising of services to identify and distinguish the services of one person, *including a unique service,* from the services of others and to indicate the source of the services, *even if that source is unknown.* ...

. . . .

A mark shall be deemed to be "abandoned"—

. . . .

(b) When any course of conduct of the registrant, including acts of omission as well as commission, causes the mark to lose its significance as an indication of origin. *Purchaser motivation shall not be a test for determining abandonment under this subparagraph.*

QUESTION

Public perception is key to trademark status. As the *Thermos* and *Anti–Monopoly* decisions indicate, however, the choice of method of assessing that perception can be hotly debated and sometimes dispositive. But, aren't all surveys inherently biased? Can you think of a survey that is not?

———

For further debate over survey evidence, *see e.g.,* Liefeld, *How Surveys Overestimate the Likelihood of Consumer Confusion,* 93 Trademark Rep. 939 (2003); Morrow and Corbin, *Pulling Confusion Surveys Back from an Illusory Brink: Reply to an Article of Dr. John Liefeld,* 94 Trademark Rep. 1372 (2004); Itamar Simonson, *An Empirical Investigation of the Meaning and Measure of "Genericness,"* 84 TMR 199 (1994); Folsom and Teply, *Surveying "Genericness" in Trademark Litigation,* 78 Trademark Rep. 1 (1988); Swann and Palladino, *Surveying "Genericness": A Critique of Folsom and Teply,* 78 Trademark Rep. 179 (1988); Folsom and Teply, *A Reply to Swann and Palladino's Critique of Folsom and Teply's Model Survey,* 78 Trademark Rep. 197 (1988); Greenbaum, Ginsburg & Weinberg, *A Proposal for Evaluating Genericism after "Anti–Monopoly",* 73 Trademark Rep. 101 (1983).

3. GENERICISM AND CONFUSION

"DE FACTO SECONDARY MEANING"

A trademark designates source. When the consuming public comes to recognize the term as identifying goods or services coming from a single, if anonymous, source, the term has acquired "secondary meaning," and is entitled to trademark status. Sometimes, however, as the "Shredded Wheat" decision exemplifies, the public may identify a term with a single source of origin, but the term is nonetheless not accorded trademark status. This phenomenon is, perhaps unhelpfully, known as "de facto secondary meaning."

There are two types of de facto secondary meaning. The first type arises in those situations in which the public does not recognize the term at issue as a brand name, but nonetheless may know that there is a single source for the goods. This occurs when the producer is the single source of the goods because it enjoys a patent monopoly, or because others are otherwise unable or unwilling to compete, and the producer has not been using the term applied to the goods in a proper trademark fashion. The other type of de facto secondary meaning occurs in those instances, such as the LITE beer case, *Miller Brewing Co. v. G. Heileman Brewing Co.*, 561 F.2d 75 (7th Cir.1977), where a producer selects as a trademark a term that is deemed to have been already the commonly recognized, *i.e.*, generic, name of the goods, but through substantial advertising, proper trademark use, and market dominance, succeeds in establishing public trademark recognition for this otherwise common name. In this case, there is real secondary meaning, because the public has come to understand the term as the producer's brand name. Nonetheless, the judicial result is the same—no trademark protection. *Anheuser-Busch v. Labatt*, 89 F.3d 1339 (8th Cir. 1996), *cert. denied*, 519 U.S. 1109 (1997) affords a more recent, but still beer-related example of selection of a mark deemed generic *ab initio*, in that case, "ice" beer.

Courts have held that a generic term cannot be converted into a trademark by means of de facto secondary meaning. The rationale for the statement is plain: if the term initially was, or has become, the common name of the goods, persons endeavoring to compete once the patent has expired—or once the market allows for competition—must be able to call the goods by their commonly recognized names. To permit a producer the exclusive use of a term that either was initially generic, or that has become generic, but that enjoys either type of de facto secondary meaning, would in effect afford that producer an improper monopoly in the goods. Thus, at bottom, the de facto secondary meaning doctrine reflects the legal conclusion that even if the public is aware that there has been only one source for the goods whose term is at issue, or even if the public further perceives the term as a brand name, that term must be held free for competitive use if it is in fact the commonly recognized name of the goods.

For examples of judicial treatment of trademark claims in terms perhaps born generic, but arguably associated with a single producer, consider the following decisions.

America Online Inc. v. AT&T Corp.

243 F.3d 812 (4th Cir.2001).

■ NIEMEYER, CIRCUIT JUDGE:

America Online, Inc. ("AOL") commenced this action against AT&T Corporation ("AT&T") for AT&T's alleged infringements of three trademarks that AOL claims in connection with its Internet services—"Buddy

List," "You Have Mail," and "IM." The district court entered summary judgment in favor of AT&T with respect to each mark, concluding that, as a matter of law, the alleged marks are generic and cannot be enforced as the exclusive property of AOL. For the reasons that follow, we conclude that the question whether "Buddy List" is a valid mark raises disputed issues of material fact and therefore cannot be resolved on summary judgment. With respect to the two other claimed marks, we affirm for the reasons given herein.

I.

Founded in 1985, AOL is now the world's largest Internet service provider, claiming more than 18 million members who pay a monthly fee for its services. These services include the facility to transmit and receive electronic mail ("e-mail") and a means to establish real-time communication ("chat") through "instant messaging."

In connection with its chat service, AOL uses "Buddy List" and "IM" to describe features of the service. The "Buddy List" enables the subscriber to create a list of identified screen names employed by other users with whom the subscriber wishes to communicate and displays which of those pre-selected users is currently using the AOL service. If a "Buddy" is identified by the "Buddy List" as online, the subscriber may then click a button labeled "IM," which are the initials of "instant messaging," and initiate a real-time chat session with the subscriber so identified on the "Buddy List." AOL has used "Buddy List" and "IM" since at least 1997. It has promoted these terms extensively, and it asserts now that it has a proprietary interest in them. In addition, with respect to "Buddy List," AOL obtained a certificate of registration on June 23, 1998, from the Patent and Trademark Office, indicating that the mark has been registered on the Principal Register and that AOL has used the mark as a service mark since August 31, 1995.

Also, in connection with its e-mail service, AOL advises its subscribers that they have received e-mail by displaying the words "You Have Mail," by playing a recording that announces, "You've got mail," and by depicting an icon of a traditional mailbox with the red flag raised. AOL contends that it has used these marks to describe its e-mail service since 1992, that it has promoted them extensively, and that it now has a proprietary interest in them.

AT&T, a competing Internet service provider, uses marks or phrases similar to those claimed by AOL in connection with its service to subscribers. It uses the terms "Buddy List," "You have Mail!," and "I M Here."

In December 1998, AOL commenced this action, seeking preliminary and permanent injunctive relief against AT&T to prohibit it from using marks similar to those asserted by AOL.... [In response] AT&T contended, among other things, that AOL's asserted marks were "common, generic terms for the e-mail, instant messaging, communication, and related services." It filed a counterclaim seeking a declaratory judgment that AOL's marks are not valid trademarks and requesting an order directing the Patent and Trademark Office to cancel the registration for "Buddy List."

The district court denied preliminary injunctive relief and, following discovery, granted AT&T summary judgment on the ground that all three of the claimed marks were generic and therefore incapable of functioning as trademarks. The court also directed that a copy of its order be sent to the Commissioner of Patents and Trademarks "in order to effect the cancellation of the BUDDY LIST mark." The district court rested its decision on evidence in the record obtained from third-party sources, including Internet dictionaries, published users' guides to both the Internet and to AOL services, use of the alleged marks by competitors, and use by AOL of the alleged marks in a manner suggesting their generic character. Although AOL proffered survey evidence in support of its contention that the marks "You Have Mail" and "Buddy List" were protected trademarks, the court considered the survey evidence irrelevant because it had concluded that the marks were generic and that words used generically cannot become trademarks by association. . . .

II. "Buddy List"

AOL's principal argument for the validity of "Buddy List" as a "suggestive" mark rests on the significance of its having obtained a certificate of registration from the Patent and Trademark Office ("PTO"). It argues that the district court erred in failing to give deference to the expert decision of the PTO to register the mark without requiring evidence of secondary meaning.

To address this argument, we must first recognize the statutory background against which a certificate of registration issues. When the Commissioner of Patents and Trademarks, in furtherance of an application of a registrant, lists a mark on the Principal Register, he issues a certificate of registration which provides the registrant with prima facie evidence of (1) the validity of the mark and its registration; (2) the registrant's ownership; and (3) the registrant's "exclusive right" to use the mark on or in connection with the goods and services specified in the certificate of registration. See 15 U.S.C. § 1057(b). And the Commissioner does not register a mark unless it meets the requirements established by statute. See, e.g., 15 U.S.C. §§ 1051, 1057, 1064. With a certificate of registration, therefore, the registrant obtains prima facie evidence that its mark is not generic in the eyes of the relevant public, see 15 U.S.C. § 1064(3), and that its mark is not "merely" descriptive, but at a minimum is descriptive and has obtained secondary meaning, see 15 U.S.C.§ 1052(e). . . .

AOL argues that the district court erred in failing to accord deference to this administrative proceeding before the PTO by which the Commissioner issued a certificate of registration, thus indicating that it owns a valid suggestive mark in "Buddy List."

.   .   .   .

The district court acknowledged that "Buddy List" "has been treated in a suggestive manner" according to some evidence. But it found that "the only reasonable conclusion which could be drawn from the evidence points to generic usage." Of particular importance to the Court was the fact that "virtually every third party which has used the phrase, including so many of AOL's competitors, use it as a generic phrase." AT&T ... maintains that the benefit accorded by AOL's registration of "Buddy List" was not "sufficient in light of the overwhelming evidence presented by AT&T. AT & T's 'compelling' and 'overwhelming' evidence of genericism amply supports the district court's ruling that no reasonable jury could find 'buddy list' anything other than generic." ...

Although we have observed that a district court should not freely substitute its opinion for that of the PTO, this observation was not made because the PTO was entitled to deference, but rather because its decision to register a mark, without requiring evidence of secondary meaning, was "powerful *evidence* that the registered mark is suggestive and not merely descriptive," id. (emphasis added); see also Petro Stopping Ctrs. L.P. v. James River Petroleum Inc., 130 F.3d 88, 93 (4th Cir.1997) (holding that the PTO's determination is "only prima facie evidence that the mark is suggestive," and, for that reason, "may be rebutted").

Accordingly, we conclude that in deciding whether "Buddy List" was generic, the district court ... was required to receive the certification of registration for "Buddy List" into evidence and treat that certificate as prima facie evidence of the validity of the mark—and, in this case, as prima facie evidence that it was suggestive. [The court held that the validity of "Buddy List" could not be determined on summary judgment.] ...

III.   "You Have Mail"

The district court concluded that the alleged mark "You Have Mail" functions primarily to inform AOL subscribers that they have e-mail, which the court found "is also known as mail." The court concluded that "when the common word or phrase is used as a mark for its ordinary meaning, the mark is generic." Accordingly, it ruled that AOL could not enforce "You Have Mail" as a trademark.

AOL argues that there is no evidence in the record that "You Have Mail" is "primarily perceived by consumers as 'the common name' of a service," as would meet the test of genericness stated in [our precedents]. It also contends that the district court erred in disregarding survey evidence that indicates that "You Have Mail" is associated with AOL. Finally, AOL argues that the Lanham Act does not exclude common phrases from the scope of protection—a principle that it contends the district court misunderstood.

AOL has not registered "You Have Mail" with the PTO, and therefore it must carry the burden of establishing the validity and its ownership of the mark as part of its larger burden in a trademark infringement action. That burden is to prove that it has a valid, protectable trademark and that the defendant is infringing its mark by creating confusion, or a likelihood thereof, by causing mistake, or by deceiving as to the attributes of its mark. See 15 U.S.C. §§ 1114, 1125. We agree with the district court that AOL did not meet this burden.

First, the record establishes, without contradiction, that "You Have Mail" has been used to inform computer users since the 1970s, a decade before AOL came into existence, that they have electronic mail in their electronic "mailboxes." . . . In the context of computer-based electronic communications across networked computers, the phrase "You Have Mail" has been used for the common, ordinary purpose of informing users of the arrival of electronic mail in their electronic mailboxes. In addition, books describing how a computer user is informed that he has e-mail on [the] UNIX [operating system] similarly reveal the functional nature of the phrase. For example, the following explanations for the presence of mail are described with "You Have Mail." . . .

—"Accessing your mail: Immediately upon logging in, should you have mail, you will see a message indicating: You Have Mail." Peter M. Birns et al., *UNIX for People* 242 (1985).

—"When you login your system, you are told whether you have electronic mail waiting for you. If there is mail waiting, you'll see a line like the following: You Have Mail." Kevin Reichard, *UNIX: The Basics* 160 (2d ed. 1998).

Furthermore, other companies that provide e-mail services have used "You Have Mail," or derivations thereof, to notify their subscribers of the arrival of e-mail messages. Prodigy Communications has used the spoken phrase, "You Have New Mail," since 1993 in connection with its online service. . . . Netcom, an Internet service provider, uses "You Have Mail" to inform users that they have e-mail. [Qualcomm, Banyan's "Beyond Mail Program," Care–Mail (a web-based e-mail provider), and "Internet Relay Chat" (a software program) all use "You Have New Mail" to notify users when they have e-mail.]

It is significant in the context of this usage that AOL has never registered "You Have Mail," nor has it attempted to enforce it as a mark prior to this action.

Second, in addition to the long and uninterrupted use by others of "You Have Mail," AOL's own use of "You Have Mail" has been inconsistent with its claim that the phrase is a trademark. Rather than describing a service that AOL offers—and indicating that it is describing such a service—AOL simply uses "You Have Mail" when the subscriber in fact has mail in the electronic mailbox. Once the user opens the new message, the phrase "You Have Mail" disappears from the user's screen. Moreover, if the subscriber does not have mail when he logs on, the screen does not display "You Have Mail." AOL's use of the phrase, conditioned on whether mail is present, does not describe AOL's e-mail service, but rather simply informs subscribers, employing common words to express their commonly used meaning, of the ordinary fact that they have new electronic mail in their mailboxes.

This functional manner in which AOL uses "You Have Mail" is consistent with a public perception of the phrase as describing whether or not mail is in an electronic mailbox, rather than as describing a service associated with AOL. For example, *America Online for Dummies*TM states, "You have two ways to see your new mail. One is pretty obvious. . . . The obvious one is the big picture button of a hand holding up some letters, emblazoned with a subtle notation You Have Mail. (I have seen *obvious* before and it looked a lot like this.)" John Kaufeld, *America Online for Dummies*TM 99 (1995). . . .

Indeed, AOL itself has made no claim that "You Have Mail" has been used to indicate anything but the information that the subscriber has mail. Even in its complaint, it asserts little more, alleging that it has used "You Have Mail . . . in connection with its automatic e-mail notification services for AOL Service members." The scope of this asserted use—to give notice of mail to subscribers—is no broader than the words' common meaning.

We agree with the district court that when words are used in a context that suggests only their common meaning, they are generic and may not be appropriated as exclusive property. But a debate over whether a word or phrase is being used in a context that communicates merely its common meaning can quickly become as metaphysical as the study of language itself. . . .

The task of distinguishing words or phrases functioning as trademarks from words or phrases in the "linguistic commons" begins with the development of an understanding of the common meaning of words and their common usage and then proceeds to a determination of whether the would-be trademark falls within this heartland of meaning and usage. The farther a would-be mark falls from the heartland of common meaning and usage, the more "distinctive" the would-be mark can become. At one level, this determination of word meaning and usage can be a question of law, but at another, it becomes a factual question as to what the relevant public perceives. The dichotomy between the legal question and the factual question is similar to that which exists in construing contracts—when meaning and usage are unambiguous, the court construes the contract, but when they are ambiguous, the factual question must be resolved by the factfinder. . . .

In the case before us, the record context of "You Have Mail" permits us to conclude as a matter of law that AOL's usage of the would be mark falls within the heartland of common meaning and usage and therefore that AOL may not exclude others from using the same words in connection with their e-mail service. This is indicated by two significant facts that remain undisputed. First, AOL uses "You Have Mail" functionally—consistently with that phrase's common meaning—to tell its subscribers they have mail. Second, others in the relevant industry have used and continue to use "you have mail," or a similar phrase, to announce the presence of an e-mail message in an electronic mailbox . . . . . We therefore agree with the district court that AOL may not enforce "You Have Mail" as a trademark in connection with its e-mail notification service.

AOL argues that its survey evidence indicates an association in the public's eye between "You Have Mail" and AOL and that this association is sufficient to permit a reasonable factfinder to conclude that "You Have Mail" is a trademark descriptive of its e-mail service that has acquired secondary meaning. AOL contends, therefore, that only a jury can decide whether "You Have Mail" is a trademark. Its evidence for secondary meaning consisted of a random survey of 507 Internet users whose households were "very likely paying to be receiving an Internet access service or an online service during the three months following the survey." The 507 respondents were divided into four groups: Group A, 250 respondents; Group B, 85; Group C, 86; and, Group D, 86. The respondents in Group A were first asked whether they had heard or seen the expression "You Have Mail." Those who answered affirmatively were then asked whether they associated that expression with one specific Internet or online service provider, or more than one provider. Those who associated the expression with one specific provider were then asked to identify the particular provider with whom they associated the phrase. Respondents in Groups B, C, and D were asked similar questions about different phrases. Instead of being queried for their reaction to "You Have Mail," respondents in Group B were asked about "New Mail Has Arrived"; respondents in Group C were asked about "Mail Is Here"; and, respondents in Group D were asked about "Mail Call." The results obtained from the answers given by the respondents in Groups B, C, and D were termed the "Control Condition," which, according to the design of the survey, was to provide "an important baseline against which to judge the strength of people's associations with the expression 'You Have Mail.' "

Out of the group that heard "You Have Mail," 41% of the respondents associated the phrase with a single Internet or online service provider, and 37% of the respondents associated the phrase with AOL. In Groups B, C, and D, only 9% of the respondents were able to associate the phrase they heard with a single Internet or online service provider, and only 5% were able to name a specific Internet or online service provider with which to associate the phrase they heard. . . .

At this summary-judgment stage of the proceedings, we must accept AOL's assertion that a portion of the public associates "You Have Mail" with AOL, the most widespread user of the phrase. But this fact does not reveal that the primary significance of the term "You Have Mail" to announce the arrival of new e-mail is not the functional, heartland usage of the phrase. . . . AOL's evidence of association may establish what is called "de facto secondary meaning," but such secondary meaning does not entitle AOL to exclude others from a functional use of the words. Stated otherwise, the repeated use of ordinary words functioning within the heartland of their ordinary meaning, and not distinctively, cannot give AOL a proprietary right over those words, even if an association develops between the words and AOL. . . .

We therefore conclude that "You Have Mail" has been and continues to be used by AOL and by others to alert online subscribers that there is electronic e-mail in their electronic mailboxes, and no more. This functional use of words within the heartland of their ordinary meaning cannot give rise to a trademark for the e-mail service when it is no more than the announcement of the arrival of a message. Because AOL has failed to establish its exclusive right to "You Have Mail," we affirm the district court's conclusion that AOL may not exclude others from use of those words in connection with its e-mail service.

IV. "IM"

Finally, AOL contends that the district court erred in refusing, based on a finding of genericness, to enforce "IM" as its trademark for its instant messaging service. The district court, reciting undisputed facts, concluded that "IM" is "an initialism" for "instant message," and that, despite their management's admonitions against using "IM" as a noun or a verb, AOL employees used "IM" as a noun or a verb in lieu of "instant message," such as in "They had an IM pending" or "Stop IM'ing me." The court also pointed to books, dictionaries, and glossaries defining "instant message" with the "IM" designation such as: "instant message, IM for short," or "instant message (IM)." It noted that Yahoo!, in promoting its pager service, claimed that it was providing "IMs." Based on these and similar facts, as well as the fact that AOL does not claim any proprietary interest in the phrase "instant messaging," the district court held that "IM stands for 'instant message' (as AOL admits), and because the primary significance of 'instant message' is to stand for an 'instant message,' the term . . . is generic."

AOL bases its claim to "IM" on its assertions that "IM" has frequently been associated by the media with AOL and that no other online or Internet service provider calls its real-time communications feature "IM." It argues that because it was one of the first companies to provide "IM," a jury could conclude that "IM" denotes the source, not the feature. But AOL has offered no evidence to support that contention. It can only contend in a conclusory manner that "IM" is a trademark rather than simply the product at issue. Accordingly, while we do not determine that "IM" is generic, we nevertheless agree with the district court's decision, based on this record, to deny AOL enforcement of "IM" as its trademark.

V.

In sum, we conclude that the validity of "Buddy List" cannot be resolved on summary judgment in view of genuine issues of material fact. Accordingly, we vacate the district court's order finding "Buddy List" generic, as well as its order directing cancellation of the certificate of registration for that mark, and remand for further proceedings. With respect to the district court's rulings denying enforcement of "You Have Mail" and "IM" as the trademarks of AOL, we affirm.

AFFIRMED IN PART, VACATED IN PART, AND REMANDED.

■ Luttig, Circuit Judge, concurring in part and dissenting in part:

[Judge Luttig dissented in part on the ground that whether or not the phrase "YOU HAVE MAIL" was generic, AOL has in fact been using the phrase "YOU'VE GOT MAIL." This phrase, Judge Luttig urged, was "sufficiently different from the phrase 'YOU HAVE MAIL' in both its grammatical dysfunctionality and likely secondary meaning, and possibly its genericness as well, as to render a decision on its protection a separate matter altogether from a decision as to protection for the feature that includes the phrase 'YOU HAVE MAIL.' "]

QUESTIONS

1. In what circumstances is it appropriate to hold the acronym for a generic phrase to itself be generic? Must the court find that the phrase itself is used generically, or is it enough that the initials stand for a generic phrase? In *Blinded Veterans Association v. Blinded American Veterans Foundation*, 872 F.2d 1035 (D.C.Cir.1989), the court determined that the term "Blinded Veterans" was generic for "formerly sighted former servicemen." The court then stated: "We need not deal separately with the question whether the initials 'BVA' are generic; if the full name is generic, an abbreviation is treated similarly." How, if at all, does the approach applied in *AOL* differ?

2. Was the phrase "you have mail" held generic because it fulfilled the function of notifying subscribers that they had mail? Because AOL had used it generically? Because others had? Is a phrase born generic if it is coined?

3. On remand, were you representing AT&T, how would you rebut the presumption that "Buddy List" is a valid trademark? If you were representing AOL what would you show in support of the presumption?

Harley Davidson v. Grottanelli, 164 F.3d 806 (2d Cir.1999). Harley Davidson, the well-known producer of motorcycles, brought a trademark infringement action against a garage and motorcycle repair service doing business as the "Hog Farm." Harley–Davidson claimed that the term HOG was a common law trademark for their motorcycles. The court determined that the term Hog was generic for large motorcycles:

    1. The Word "Hog" Applied to Motorcycles

    Public use of the word "hog". In the late 1960s and early 1970s, the word "hog" was used by motorcycle enthusiasts to refer to motorcycles generally and to large motorcycles in particular. The word was used that way in the press at least as early as 1965,[2]

2. *See* California: The Wild Ones, Newsweek, March 29, 1965, at 25 ("The state wide clan [of Hells' Angels] has its own beat argot (sample: a 'hog' is a big motorcycle)...."); Hell's Angels, Saturday Evening Post, Nov. 20, 1965, at 37 ("Some angels can dismantle a motorcycle in two hours. When they get through tinkering with it, the hog is a lean, dangerous beast."); see also Hunter S. Thompson, Hell's Angels 97 (1967) ("A columnist for the Los Angeles Times once described hogs as 'the kind of cycle the German couriers used to run down dogs and chickens—and people—in World War II: low brut-

and frequently thereafter,[3] prior to the 1980s when Harley first attempted to make trademark use of the term. Several dictionaries include a definition of "hog" as a motorcycle, especially a large one.[4] The October 1975 issue of Street Chopper contained an article entitled "Honda Hog," indicating that the word "hog" was generic as to motorcycles and needed a tradename adjective....

Harley–Davidson's use of the word "hog". In 1981, Harley–Davidson's new owners recognized that the term "hog" had financial value and began using the term in connection with its merchandise, accessories, advertising, and promotions. In 1983, it formed the Harley Owners' Group, pointedly using the acronym "H.O.G." In 1987, it registered the acronym in conjunction with various logos. It subsequently registered the mark "HOG" for motorcycles. That registration lists Harley–Davidson's first use as occurring in 1990.

Grottanelli's use of the word "hog". Grottanelli opened a motorcycle repair shop under the name "The Hog Farm" in 1969. Since that time his shop has been located at various sites in western New York. At some point after 1981, Grottanelli also began using the word "hog" in connection with events and merchandise. He has sponsored an event alternatively known as "Hog Holidays" and "Hog Farm Holidays," and sold products such as "Hog Wash" engine degreaser and a "Hog Trivia" board game.

. . . .

Discussion

I.   Use of the Word "Hog"

... Harley–Davidson acknowledged at oral argument that its state law claim fails if "hog" is generic as applied to large motorcycles. No manufacturer can take out of the language a word, even a slang term, that has generic meaning as to a category of products and appropriate it for its own trademark use....

ish machines, with drivers to match.'"). The earliest reference in the record to "hog" as referring to large motorcycles is the caption "Hog Heaven" in the June 1935 issue of Popular Mechanics. See Time Machine, Popular Mechanics, June 1995, at 16 (reprinting cover and caption of June 1935 issue).

3. *See, e.g.,* Outlaw Biker, May 1989, cover ("4,000 Find Hog Heaven at.... California Love Run"); Street Chopper, March 1975, at 10 ("HOG + $= CHOPPER"); see also Easyriders, May 1982, advertisement for Denver motorcycle shop ("HAWG STUFF"). The Magistrate Judge noted seven exhibits

showing the word "hog" or "hawg" referring generally to motorcycles.

4. *See* The Oxford Dictionary of Modern Slang (1992) ("hog noun U.S. A large, often old, car or motorcycle. 1967–."); American Heritage Dictionary (3d ed.1992) ("hog ... 4. Slang. A big, heavy motorcycle"); Eric Partridge, A Dictionary of Slang and Unconventional English (8th ed.1984) ("hog n.... 8. a homebuilt motorcycle...."); *see also* Glossary of Sportscycle Terms, Bike and Rider, Aug. 1992, at 84 ("HOG Old fashioned, heavyweight sportscycle.").

Though the Magistrate Judge made no ultimate finding as to whether "hog" was generic as applied to large motorcycles prior to Harley–Davidson's trademark use of the word, his subsidiary findings point irresistibly toward that conclusion. He found that there was "substantial evidence which would indicate that in those years the term referred to motorcycles (or motorcyclists) generally." He cited the various press and dictionary usages of the word that we have set forth above. Though not conclusive, dictionary definitions of a word to denote a category of products are significant evidence of genericness because they usually reflect the public's perception of a word's meaning and its contemporary usage. In this case, one dictionary cites a generic use of "hog" to mean a large motorcycle as early as 1967, long before Harley's first trademark use of the word,[8] and the recent dictionary editions continuing to define the word to mean a large motorcycle indicate that the word has not lost its generic meaning. We have observed that newspaper and magazine use of a word in a generic sense is "a strong indication of the general public's perception" that the word is generic. In this case, media use of "hog" to mean a large motorcycle began as early as 1935 and continued thereafter.

. . . .

Harley–Davidson suggests, albeit in a footnote, *see* Brief for Appellee at 18 n. 2, that it is entitled to trademark use of "HOG" as applied to motorcycles because a substantial segment of the relevant consumers began to use the term specifically to refer to Harley–Davidson motorcycles before the company made trademark use of the term. Some decisions have invoked this principle to accord a company priority as to its subsequent trademark use of a term. *See National Cable Television Ass'n, Inc. v. American Cinema Editors, Inc.*, 937 F.2d 1572 (Fed.Cir.1991) (mark "ACE"); *Volkswagenwerk AG v. Hoffman*, 489 F.Supp. 678 (D.S.C.1980) (mark "BUG"). Whether or not we would agree with these decisions, they present a significantly different situation. Neither "ACE" nor "BUG" was a generic term in the language as applied, respectively, to a category of film editors or a category of automobiles prior to the public's use of the terms to refer to the American Cinema Editors and Volkswagen cars. By contrast, "hog" was a generic term in the language as applied to large motorcycles before the public (or at least some segments of it) began using the word to refer to Harley–Davidson motorcycles. The public has no more right than a manufacturer to withdraw from the language a generic term, already applicable to the relevant category of products, and accord it trademark significance, at least as long as the term retains some generic meaning.

---

8. *See* The Oxford Dictionary of Modern Slang (1992) ("**hog**. noun U.S. A large, often old, car or motorcycle. 1967–.").

For all of these reasons, Harley–Davidson may not prohibit Grottanelli from using "hog" to identify his motorcycle products and services. Like any other manufacturer with a product identified by a word that is generic, Harley–Davidson will have to rely on all or a portion of its tradename (or other protectable marks) to identify its brand of motorcycles, e.g., "Harley Hogs."

———

Should it make a difference if the term is generic in a foreign language? In *Otokoyama Co. v. Wine of Japan Import*, 175 F.3d 266 (2d Cir.1999), the court reversed the district court's refusal to consider evidence of the generic meaning of "Otokoyama" in Japanese because:

> If *Otokoyama* in Japanese signifies a type of sake, and one United States merchant were given the exclusive right to use that word to designate its brand of sake, competing merchants would be prevented from calling their product by the word which designates that product in Japanese. Any Japanese-speaking customers and others who are familiar with the Japanese terminology would be misled to believe that there is only one brand of otokoyama available in the United States.…

> The meaning of otokoyama in Japanese, and particularly whether it designates sake, or a type or category of sake, was therefore highly relevant to whether plaintiff may assert the exclusive right to use that word as a mark applied to sake. Defendant should have been allowed to introduce evidence of otokoyama's meaning and usage in Japan to support its claim that the mark is generic and therefore ineligible for protection as a trademark.

See also Orto Conserviera v. Bioconserve, 49 U.S.P.Q.2d 2013 (S.D.N.Y. 1999) (court rejected plaintiff's assertion of trademark rights in "Bella di Cerignola," a type of olive known in Italy, but not then widely known in the U.S.).

———

TE–TA–MA Truth Foundation v. World Church of the Creator, 297 F.3d 662 (7th Cir.2002), *cert. denied*, 537 U.S. 1111 (2003).

The "Church of the Creator" and the "World Church of the Creator" have irreconcilable creeds. The Church of the Creator (the operating name of TE–TA–MA Truth Foundation—Family of URI, Inc.) [hereinafter Foundation] believes in universal love and respect. World Church of the Creator [hereinafter World Church], by contrast, does not worship God but instead depicts the "white race" as the "Creator" and calls for the elimination of Jews, blacks, and what it labels "mud races." Its slogan is: "Dedicated to the Survival, Expansion, and Advancement of the White Race".… Foundation charged World Church with trademark infringement, and World Church asserted the genericism of "Church of the Creator" in defense.

Reversing the district court, the Seventh Circuit, per Judge Easterbrook, found "Church of the Creator" to be descriptive rather than generic.

> Both sides moved for summary judgment, so each was required to introduce evidence to show that a material issue of disputed fact remained for decision. Confronted with the Foundation's motion, the World Church produced—nothing but a dictionary. It did not offer any evidence about how religious adherents use or understand the phrase as a unit. It offered only lexicographers' definitions of the individual words. That won't cut the mustard, because dictionaries reveal a range of historical meanings rather than how people use a particular phrase in contemporary culture. (Similarly, looking up the words "cut" and "mustard" would not reveal the meaning of the phrase we just used.)

> Contemporary usage does not treat "Church of the Creator" as the name for monotheistic religion—or any other genus of religion. If it were, then the World Church itself would be misusing the phrase, for it is not theistic in any traditional sense and has nothing in common with Judaism, Christianity, or Islam. The World Church's web site, and much of its literature, feature one international negation symbol (a circle with a diagonal bar) superimposed over a Star of David and another superimposed over a cross. It condemns the Bible as a hoax.

> A mark is "generic" when it has become the name of a product (e.g., "sandwich") for meat between slices of bread or class of products (thus "church" is generic). But "Church of the Creator" is descriptive, like "lite beer." It does not name the class of monotheistic religions. In the contemporary United States, variations on "Church of [Deity]" are used to differentiate individual denominations, not to denote the class of all religions. The list is considerable: Church of God; Church of God (Anderson, Indiana); First Church of God; Worldwide Church of God (see *Worldwide Church of God v. Philadelphia Church of God, Inc.*, 227 F.3d 1110 (9th Cir. 2000)); Church of God in Christ; Assembly of God; Korean Assembly of God; Church of the Nazarene; Church of Christ; United Church of Christ; Disciples of Christ; Church of Christ, Scientist; Church of Jesus Christ of Latter Day Saints. There is room for extension with Church of Our Savior, Church of the Holy Spirit, Church of the Holy Trinity, Church of Jehovah, and so on. Yet all of these are recognizable as denominational names, not as the designation of the religion to which the denominations belong. No Jewish, Islamic, Baha'i, or Unitarian group would say that it belongs to a "Church of the Creator"; and a Christian congregation would classify itself first into its denomination (e.g., Baptist, Lutheran, Russian Orthodox, Society of Friends), then into one of the major groupings (Roman Catholic, Orthodox, and Protestant), and finally into Christianity, but never into a "Church of the Creator." No one called or emailed a *Baptist* church to complain about its complicity in the hate-mongering of the World Church of the Creator; people recognized the name as denominational, and that's why protests ended up in the Church of the Creator's in box.

What is more, as these lists show, using "Church of the Creator" as a denominational name leaves ample options for other sects to distinguish themselves and achieve separate identities. It is not remotely like one firm appropriating the word "sandwich" and thus disabling its rivals from explaining to consumers what's to eat. When the line between generic and descriptive terms is indistinct—as it is, for example, with a phrase such as "liquid controls," see *Liquid Controls Corp. v. Liquid Control Corp.*, 802 F.2d 934 (7th Cir. 1986)—it is helpful to ask whether one firm's exclusive use of the phrase will prevent a rival from naming itself and describing its product. (As far as the Lanham Act is concerned, a denomination is a producer and religious services and publications are products. Neither side has questioned the application of trademark laws to religion.) Because there are so many ways to describe religious denominations, there is no risk that exclusive use of "Church of the Creator" will appropriate a theology or exclude essential means of differentiating one set of beliefs from another.

"DIAL 1–800–[G–E–N–E–R–I–C]"

A widespread marketing device exhorts consumers to contact a purveyor of goods or services by calling a seven-digit number whose corresponding letters spell out the name (or as close as possible) of the product or service proffered. Examples include "Dial-a-Mattress: M–A–T–T–R–E–S, and drop the last S for Savings," for home shopping and delivery of mattresses; "Dial L–A–W–Y–E–R–S" for legal counselling and litigation; "1–800–F–L–O–W–E–R–S" for flowers by wire; and "1–800–M–A–R–I–N–E–S" for recruiting to the ranks of "a few good men" [and women]. The first of these telephone numbers spawned controversy in the courts, for one provider had secured a local telephone designation in the pertinent digits, while the other obtained the equivalent 1–800 listing.

In *Dial-A-Mattress Franchise Corp. v. Page,* 880 F.2d 675 (2d Cir. 1989), the court determined that M–A–T–T–R–E–S was generic for mattresses, and therefore could not be subject to appropriation as a trademark. However, evidence indicated consumer confusion in the New York area arising out of a competitor's adoption of "1–800–M–A–T–T–R–E–S" when a New York business had previously adopted a local "M–A–T–T–R–E–S" telephone listing. Judge Newman stated:

> [T]his case cannot be decided solely upon the principles applicable to generic terms. Dial-a-Mattress is not seeking protection against a competitor's use of the word "mattress" solely to identify the competitor's name or product. What the plaintiff seeks is protection against a competitor's use of a confusingly similar telephone number and a confusingly similar means of identifying that number.... Plaintiff does not lose the right to protection against defendant's use of a confusingly similar number and a confusingly similar set of letters that correlate with that number on the telephone dial just because the letters spell a generic term. The principles limiting protection for the use of generic terms serve to

prevent a marketer from appropriating for its exclusive use words that must remain available to competitors to inform their customers as to the nature of the competitor's business or product. These principles do not require that a competitor remain free to confuse the public with a telephone number of the letters identifying that number that are deceptively similar to those of a first user.

The court therefore enjoined the proprietor of the 800 number from further exploitation of the same digits in the New York area. *See also Murrin v. Midco Comms., Inc.,* 726 F.Supp. 1195 (D.Minn.1989) (upholding plaintiff's service mark registration for "DIAL LAWYERS," but permitting defendant to continue to use the phrase in the New York metropolitan area, where defendant was the prior user).

QUESTIONS

1.   What if an entrepreneur obtained a vanity number identical to its competitor's, but varied one digit, anticipating that some consumers would misdial the competitor's number and accordingly call the entrepreneur's service? See Holiday Inns Inc. v. 800 Reservation, Inc., 86 F.3d 619 (6th Cir.1996) (1–800–HOLIDAY v 1–800–H0[zero]LIDAY), discussed in Chapter 11, Internet Domain Names.

2.   Suppose an entrepreneur registers mattress.com as a domain name, and then seeks to register mattress.com as a service mark, claiming substantial sales, advertising, and other indicia of secondary meaning. Should the Trademark Office register the mark as a service mark for bedding? See *In re Oppedahl & Larson, supra,* Chapter 2.B.1

B.   ABANDONMENT

1.   NON USE

15 U.S.C. § 1125 [LANHAM ACT § 45]

. . . .

Abandonment. A mark shall be deemed to be "abandoned" when either of the following occurs:

(1) When its use has been discontinued with intent not to resume such use. Intent not to resume may be inferred from circumstances. Nonuse for three consecutive years shall be prima facie evidence of abandonment. "Use" of a mark means the bona fide use of that mark made in the ordinary course of trade, and not made merely to reserve a right in a mark.

(2) When any course of conduct of the owner, including acts of omission as well as commission, causes the mark to become the generic name for the goods or services on or in connection with

which it is used or otherwise to lose its significance as a mark. Purchaser motivation shall not be a test for determining abandonment under this paragraph.

Silverman v. CBS, Inc.

870 F.2d 40 (2d Cir.), *cert. denied*, 492 U.S. 907 (1989).

■ NEWMAN, CIRCUIT JUDGE:

This appeal presents somewhat novel issues of both copyright and trademark law arising from the efforts of appellant Stephen M. Silverman to develop a musical based on the "Amos 'n' Andy" characters.... Silverman appeals from a judgment of the District Court for the Southern District of New York (Gerald L. Goettel, Judge) awarding [appellee] CBS damages, [attorney's fees,] declaratory relief, and an injunction. Because some "Amos 'n' Andy" materials are in the public domain while others remain subject to CBS copyrights, and because CBS has elected not to make commercial use of its "Amos 'n' Andy" radio and television programs, nor create new ones, since 1966, the issues primarily raised on this appeal are ... whether CBS has abandoned through non-use whatever trademarks it might have. We conclude that ... CBS's trademarks, if valid, have been abandoned.

Facts

The "Amos 'n' Andy" characters were created in 1928 by Freeman F. Gosden and Charles J. Correll, who wrote and produced for radio broadcasting "The Amos 'n' Andy Show." The show became one of the country's most popular radio programs. The characters in the Amos 'n' Andy programs were Black. Gosden and Correll, who were White, portrayed Amos and Andy on radio. The authors appeared in blackface in publicity photos. Black actors played the parts in the subsequent television programs.

Gosden and Correll assigned all of their rights in the "Amos 'n' Andy Show" scripts and radio programs to CBS Inc. in 1948. Gosden and Correll continued to create new "Amos 'n' Andy" scripts, which formed the basis for CBS radio programs. The radio programs continued until 1955. Beginning in 1951 CBS also broadcast an "Amos 'n' Andy" television series. The television series was aired on CBS affiliate stations until 1953 and continued in reruns and non-network syndication until 1966. CBS has not aired or licensed for airing any of the radio or television programs since 1966.

In 1981, Silverman began writing a script for a Broadway musical based on the "Amos 'n' Andy" characters.... Silverman sought a license to use the "Amos 'n' Andy" characters, but CBS refused.

Silverman filed this lawsuit seeking a declaration that the "Amos 'n' Andy" radio programs broadcast from March 1928 through March 1948 (the "pre–1948 radio programs") are in the public domain and that he is therefore free to make use of the content of the programs, including the characters, character names, and plots. He also sought a declaration that CBS has no rights in these programs under any body of law, including statutory and common law copyright law and trademark law. CBS asserted five counterclaims: (1) that Silverman's scripts infringed CBS's copyrights in the scripts for three post–1948 radio programs; (2) that the Silverman scripts violated section 43(a) of the Lanham Act, 15 U.S.C. § 1125(a) (1982), by infringing various CBS trademarks, including "AMOS 'N' ANDY," the names of various characters such as "George ('Kingfish') Stevens," "Madame Queen," and "Lightnin'," and various phrases such as "Scuse me for protruding," "splain dat," and "Holy mackral" (perhaps Amos's best-known contribution to the language); . . .

On the trademark side of the case, Judge Goettel ruled that the name "Amos 'n' Andy," as well as the names and appearances of "Amos 'n' Andy" characters and "other distinctive features of the . . . radio and television shows" are protectable marks. *Id.* at 1356. He then set down for trial the issue of whether CBS's non-use of the marks constituted abandonment. Finally, he ruled that the issue of trademark infringement, as well as the related issues of unfair competition and dilution, were premature in the absence of a staging of Silverman's musical. *Id.* at 1357–58.

After a bench trial on the issue of abandonment, Judge Goettel concluded that CBS had not abandoned its trademarks. *Silverman v. CBS,* 666 F. Supp. 575 (S.D.N.Y.1987) (*Silverman II*). . . .

The final judgment entered in the District Court included several provisions. Silverman was enjoined from "creating . . . distributing . . . or offering for sale any script, or permitting the display or performance publicly of any musical play based thereon, bearing or containing any substantial copy or derivative work based upon any episode of an Amos 'n' Andy radio or television program created by or for CBS in or after August 1948. . . ."

. . . .

Discussion

. . . .

1.   *Trademark Issues*

Silverman challenges the District Court's rulings that CBS has protectable trademarks in the "Amos 'n' Andy" names, characters, and other features of the radio and television programs, including phrases of dialogue, and that CBS has not abandoned these marks. We find it unnecessary to decide which features of the programs might give rise to protectable marks because we agree with Silverman that CBS has abandoned the marks.

Section 45 of the Lanham Act provides:

A mark shall be deemed to be "abandoned"—

(a) When its use has been discontinued with intent not to resume. Intent not to resume may be inferred from circumstances. Nonuse for two consecutive years shall be prima facie abandonment.

15 U.S.C. § 1127 (1982). There are thus two elements for abandonment: (1) non-use and (2) intent not to resume use. *See Saratoga Vichy Spring Co. v. Lehman,* 625 F.2d 1037, 1043 (2d Cir.1980). Two years of non-use creates a rebuttable presumption of abandonment. *Id.* at 1044.

On the undisputed facts of this case, CBS made a considered decision to take the "Amos 'n' Andy" television programs off the air. It took this action in response to complaints by civil rights organizations, including the NAACP, that the programs were demeaning to Blacks. By the time the abandonment issue came before the District Court, non-use of the AMOS 'N' ANDY marks had continued for 21 years. Although CBS has no current plans to use the marks within the foreseeable future, CBS asserts that it has always intended to resume using them at some point in the future, should the social climate become more hospitable.

Ordinarily, 21 years of non-use would easily surpass the non-use requirement for finding abandonment. *See, e.g., I.H.T. Corp. v. Saffir Publishing Corp.,* 444 F. Supp. 185 (S.D.N.Y.1978) (denying preliminary injunction to protect trademark after 12 years of non-use). The District Court concluded, however, that CBS had successfully rebutted the presumption of abandonment arising from its prolonged non-use by offering a reasonable explanation for its decision to keep the programs off the air and by asserting its intention to resume use at some indefinite point in the future. This conclusion raises a question as to the proper interpretation of the statutory phrase "intent not to resume": Does the phrase mean intent never to resume use or does it merely mean intent not to resume use within the reasonably foreseeable future?

We conclude that the latter must be the case. The statute provides that intent not to resume may be inferred from circumstances, and two consecutive years of non-use is prima facie abandonment. Time is thereby made relevant. Indeed, if the relevant intent were intent never to resume use, it would be virtually impossible to establish such intent circumstantially. Even after prolonged non-use, and without any concrete plans to resume use, a company could almost always assert truthfully that at some point, should conditions change, it would resume use of its mark.

We do not think Congress contemplated such an unworkable standard. More likely, Congress wanted a mark to be deemed abandoned once use has been discontinued with an intent not to resume within the reasonably foreseeable future. This standard is sufficient to protect against the forfeiture of marks by proprietors who are temporarily unable to continue using them, while it also prevents warehousing of marks, which impedes commerce and competition.

We are buttressed in this conclusion by the fact that the statute requires proof of "intent not to resume," rather than "intent to abandon." The statute thus creates no state of mind element concerning the ultimate issue of abandonment. On the contrary, it avoids a subjective inquiry on this ultimate question by setting forth the circumstances under which a mark shall be "deemed" to be abandoned. Of course, one of those circumstances is intent not to resume use, which is a matter of subjective inquiry.

But we think the provision, by introducing the two concepts of "deemed" abandonment and intent not to resume use, contemplates a distinction, and it is a distinction that turns at least in part on duration of the contemplated non-use.

Congress's choice of wording appears to have been deliberate. One early version of what became section 45 of the Lanham Act had provided that "[i]ntent to *abandon* may be inferred from the circumstances." H.R. Rep. 4744, 76th Cong., 1st Sess. (1939) (emphasis added). However, shortly thereafter a new bill modified this phrase by substituting "[i]ntent not to resume" for "[i]ntent to abandon." H.R. Rep. 6618, 76th Cong., 1st Sess. (1939).... We think that Congress, by speaking of "intent not to resume" rather than "intent to abandon" in this section of the Act meant to avoid the implication that intent never to resume use must be shown.[4]

This approach is consistent with our recent decisions concerning trademark abandonment.... [I]n *Defiance Button Machine Co. v. C & C Metal Products Corp.*, 759 F.2d 1053 (2d Cir.), *cert. denied*, 474 U.S. 844 (1985), we rejected an abandonment claim where, during a brief period of non-use, the proprietor tried to sell the mark, its associated goodwill, and some other assets and, upon failing to find a buyer, became a subsidiary of a company in its original line of trade and prepared to resume its business. In [that] case[], the proprietor of the mark had an intention to exploit the mark in the reasonably foreseeable future by resuming its use or permitting its use by others.

The undisputed facts of the pending case are entirely different. Unlike the proprietor[] in ... *Defiance Button*, CBS has not been endeavoring to exploit the value of its marks, failing to do so only because of lack of business opportunities. Instead, it has decided, albeit for socially commendable motives, to forgo whatever business opportunities may currently exist in the hope that greater opportunities, unaccompanied by adverse public reaction, will exist at some undefined time in the future.

... [A] proprietor may not protect a mark if he discontinues using it for more than 20 years and has no plans to use or permit its use in the reasonably foreseeable future. A bare assertion of possible future use is not enough.

We recognize the point, forcefully made by Judge Goettel, when he wrote:

It would be offensive to basic precepts of fairness and justice to penalize CBS, by stripping it of its trademark rights, merely

---

4. An early Supreme Court case involving abandonment under pre-Lanham Act, common law trademark said that proof of abandonment must include proof of an "intent to abandon." *Saxlehner v. Eisner & Mendelson Co.*, 179 U.S. 19, 31 (1900). In cases applying the Act, we have also on occasion used the phrase "intent to abandon," *see Saratoga Vichy Spring Co. v. Lehman, supra,* 625 F.2d at 1044, but decisions using the phrase have not faced the issue whether the requisite intent is never to resume use or not to resume in the reasonably foreseeable future. Where that choice matters, as in this case, the statutory phrase "intent not to resume" better describes the requisite mental element.

because it succumbed to societal pressures and pursued a course of conduct that it reasonably believes to be in the best interests of the community.

Silverman II, 666 F. Supp. at 581. Nonetheless, we believe that however laudable one might think CBS's motives to be, such motives cannot overcome the undisputed facts that CBS has not used its marks for more than 20 years and that, even now, it has no plans to resume their use in the reasonably foreseeable future. Though we agree with Judge Goettel that CBS should not be penalized for its worthy motive, we cannot adjust the statutory test of abandonment to reward CBS for such motive by according it protection where its own voluntary actions demonstrate that statutory protection has ceased. Moreover, we see nothing in the statute that makes the consequence of an intent not to resume use turn on the worthiness of the motive for holding such intent.

We are also mindful of the facts, relied on by the District Court, that show some minor activities by CBS regarding its properties, allegedly sufficient to rebut abandonment of the marks. These are CBS's actions in licensing the programs for limited use in connection with documentary and educational programs, challenging infringing uses brought to its attention, renewing its copyrights, and periodically reconsidering whether to resume use of the programs. But challenging infringing uses is not use, and sporadic licensing for essentially non-commercial uses of a mark is not sufficient use to forestall abandonment. *Cf. Exxon Corp. v. Humble Exploration Co., supra,* 695 F.2d at 102 (use must be "commercial use" to avoid abandonment). Such uses do not sufficiently rekindle the public's identification of the mark with the proprietor, which is the essential condition for trademark protection, nor do they establish an intent to resume commercial use. . . .

An adjudication of trademark rights often involves a balancing of competing interests. *See La Société Anonyme des Parfums Le Galion v. Jean Patou, Inc.,* 495 F.2d 1265, 1274 n. 11 (2d Cir.1974). In weighing the competing interests and reaching our conclusion concerning abandonment, we are influenced in part by the context in which this dispute arises—one in which the allegedly infringing use is in connection with a work of artistic expression. Just as First Amendment values inform application of the idea/expression dichotomy in copyright law, *see Harper & Row, Publishers, Inc. v. Nation Enterprises,* 471 U.S. 539, 556 (1985), in similar fashion such values have some bearing upon the extent of protection accorded a trademark proprietor against use of the mark in works of artistic expression.

Ordinarily, the use of a trademark to identify a commodity or a business "is a form of commercial speech and nothing more." *Friedman v. Rogers,* 440 U.S. 1, 11 (1979). Requiring a commercial speaker to choose words and labels that do not confuse or deceive protects the public and does not impair expression. (Citations omitted).

In the area of artistic speech, however, enforcement of trademark rights carries a risk of inhibiting free expression, *cf. L.L. Bean, Inc. v. Drake Publishers, Inc.,* 811 F.2d 26, 28–29 (1st Cir.), *cert. denied,* 107 S. Ct.

3254 (1987), not only in the case at hand but in other situations where authors might contemplate use of trademarks in connection with works of artistic expression. These risks add some weight to Silverman's claims.

From the standpoint of the proprietor of a mark in a work of artistic expression, there is also an interest in expression, along with the traditional trademark interest in avoiding public confusion as to source. Trademark law can contribute to a favorable climate for expression by complementing the economic incentive that copyright law provides to create and disseminate artistic works, *see Harper & Row Publishers, Inc. v. Nation Publishers, supra,* 471 U.S. at 558. In this case, however, the expression interest on CBS's side is markedly diminished by its decision to withhold dissemination of the works with which its marks are associated.

The interest of CBS, and the public, in avoiding public confusion, an interest obviously entitled to weight in every trademark case, is also somewhat diminished in the context of this case. This interest is not as weighty as in a case involving a non-artistic product whose trademark is associated with high quality or other consumer benefits. Though Silverman undoubtedly hopes that some of his audience will be drawn from those who favorably recall the "Amos 'n' Andy" programs, we doubt if many who attend Broadway musicals are motivated to purchase tickets because of a belief that the musical is produced by the same entity responsible for the movie, book, or radio or television series on which it is based. That is not to say that the musical is in a sufficiently distinct line of commerce to preclude all protection; the holder of a mark associated with a television series would normally be entitled to "bridge the gap" and secure some protection against an infringing use of the mark in connection with a Broadway musical. It is to say, however, that most theater-goers have sufficient awareness that the quality of a musical depends so heavily on a combination of circumstances, including script, score, lyrics, cast, and direction, that they are not likely to be significantly influenced in their ticket-purchasing decision by an erroneous belief that the musical emanated from the same production source as the underlying work.

The point must not be overstated. Trademark protection is not lost simply because the allegedly infringing use is in connection with a work of artistic expression. But in determining the outer limits of trademark protection—here, concerning the concept of abandonment—the balance of risks just noted is relevant and in some cases may tip the scales against trademark protection. These considerations are especially pertinent in the pending case where some aspects of the material claimed to be protected by trademark are in the public domain as far as copyright law is concerned.

For all of these reasons, we conclude that the undisputed facts establish abandonment of the AMOS 'N' ANDY marks.

. . . .

ITC Limited v. Punchgini, 482 F.3d 135 (2d Cir. 2007). The plaintiff ITC Hotels and Restaurants owns a chain of world-renowned Indian restaurants under the name Bukhara. (See supra, chapter 3.E.) "The restaurant's look is pure Flintstones: walls of boulders, solid-wood tables and menus printed on laminated sections of tree." ITC licensed the Bukhara trademark, for which it had obtained a U.S. registration, and trade dress to several franchisees, including one in New York City. The New York branch opened in 1986 and closed in 1991. In 1999, the defendants, former employees of the New York restaurant, opened a Bukhara Grill in New York. In addition to the name, defendants also allegedly emulated aspects of the prior restaurant's trade dress, including the rustic decor, heavy wooden menus, use of checkered bibs in lieu of napkins, and logo font. In 2000, ITC sent a cease and desist letter; the New York restaurant replied that the mark had been abandoned, and thus was legitimately taken up by the New York entrepreneurs. ITC ultimately sued in 2003. In response to defendants' motion for summary judgment, ITC conceded that it had not used the mark in the United States for over three years before defendants' appropriation, but it claimed a genuine issue of material fact as to its intent to resume use, sufficient to rebut the statutory presumption at trial and precluding summary judgment.

The Second Circuit affirmed the district court's findings that ITC had not rebutted the presumption of abandonment that arises from three years of non use. The court found that neither ITC's internal memoranda, nor its dealings with potential business partners, nor its plans to market packaged foods under the "Bukhara" brand evidenced a concrete intent to resume use of the mark *in the U.S.* It also found that while ITC had pursued franchise agreements around the world, none of the potential franchisees were located in the U.S.

(4) Bukhara Restaurants Outside the United States

Finally, ITC cites La Société Anonyme des Parfums le Galion v. Jean Patou, Inc. to support its argument that the continued operation of its Bukhara restaurants outside the United States demonstrates "an ongoing program to exploit the mark commercially," giving rise to an inference of an intent to resume the mark's use in this country, 495 F.2d 1265, 1272 (2d Cir. 1974). In fact, ITC's reliance on *Société Anonyme* is misplaced. In that case, this court ruled that a "meager trickle" of perfume sales within the United States—89 bottles sold over a period of 20 years—was insufficient to establish trade-mark rights in the United States. Id. Nothing in that case suggests that ongoing foreign use of a mark, by itself, supports an inference that the owner intends to re-employ a presumptively abandoned mark in the United States. Cf. id. at 1271 n.4 (noting "well-settled" view "that foreign use is ineffectual to create trademark rights in the United States"). Indeed, we identify no authority supporting that conclusion.

QUESTIONS

1. Were ITC's US contacts less extensive than those deemed to constitute "use in commerce" in *Société des Bains de Mer, supra,* Chapter 3.D, or "use" in the United States in *First Niagara Ins. v. First Niagara Financial,* 476 F.3d 867 (Fed.Cir.2007), *supra,* Chapter 4.B. Is there a reason to require a stronger showing of use in order to avoid abandonment of U.S. trademark rights than to establish U.S. trademark rights, or to have standing to oppose another's U.S. trademark registration?

2.   Nicole Bédé authors a successful French comic book series, *Les triplés*. In 1998, Nicole obtained a U.S. trademark registration on the basis of her French registration and her declaration of an intent to use the triplés mark in the U.S. (regarding U.S. registrations of foreign trademarks, see *infra*, Chapter 4.A). Although Nicole has sought and continues to seek U.S. licensees for an English-language version of her comic books, or for other merchandizing properties, she has so far been unsuccessful. Color Comics seeks to register the mark Triplets for a series of its own. Denied registration on the ground that Color's mark is likely to cause confusion with Nicole's, Color brings a cancellation action. How should the Board rule? *See Cromosoma S.A. v. Nicole Lambert*, 2005 WL 548068 (T.T.A.B.2005).

3.   Vincent George sold his eponymous family widget manufacturing business to Barton Robert, and returned home to Albania, his health shattered by long years of work. Fully recovered, George later returned to the U.S. and resumed manufacturing widgets under the same name. George's Widgets, Inc. brings a trademark infringement action, and George defends on the ground that he cannot "abandon" his own name. How should the court rule? *See Vais Arms, Inc. v. Vais*, 383 F.3d 287 (5th Cir.2004).

"THE SONG IS ENDED (BUT THE MELODY LINGERS ON)"*

Even long after a producer has ceased exploiting a mark, the term may continue to carry considerable residual goodwill. Most often, the mark's goodwill continues to redound to the benefit of the producer; even though the mark is no longer being used, the public continues to associate it with its former user. A new entrant's adoption of the mark for the same or related goods may thus prompt suspicion that it is seeking to reap the benefits of the goodwill remaining in the mark. In such a situation, a court may strain to avoid finding that an abandonment has occurred. For example, in *Exxon Corp. v. Humble Exploration Co.*, 695 F.2d 96 (5th Cir.1983), discussed in *Silverman*, the Fifth Circuit, having rejected an intent-not-to-abandon standard, remanded to the district court to determine if Exxon had an intent to resume use of the HUMBLE mark. The district court, 592 F.Supp. 1226 (N.D.Tex.1984), after surveying several abandonment decisions and observing that "each case is founded on its own facts," found certain special considerations underlying Exxon's three-year non-use of the HUMBLE mark. In particular, the court cited Exxon's efforts to replace its three regional marks, HUMBLE, ESSO, and ENCO, in the public mind with a single national mark, EXXON. Establishing the national brand required non-use of the regional brands, because "the very

---

* Editors' Note: Irving Berlin wrote his famous song, "The Song is Ended . . ." in the late 1920s.

strength of the HUMBLE mark made it difficult to find a use for HUMBLE which would not contaminate the EXXON mark." Nonetheless, the court found that Exxon had an "intent to make more than token use of HUMBLE," principally through its inclusion of the HUMBLE mark, along with the EXXON mark, on drums of petroleum products. The court held that "during the period of non-use, Exxon did not have an intent not to resume use of the HUMBLE mark and, further, that Exxon intended to resume commercial use of HUMBLE."

Even when the mark has been abandoned, courts may require the new adopter to take reasonable precautions to prevent confusion during the period of "residual significance" during which the "mark that has been abandoned ... is still associated by the public with its former holder," *Cumulus Media, Inc. v. Clear Channel*, 304 F.3d 1167 (11th Cir.2002) (upholding a preliminary injunction against a radio station which had adopted the name abandoned by a rival station thirteen months earlier). Cf. Note on "genericism and confusion," *supra*, Chapter 5.A.3.

Not all lingering goodwill evokes the reputation of the prior trademark owner. Sometimes the good will takes on a life of its own, no longer signaling the producer. This situation has arisen in the context of sports teams that relocate to a different city. *Indianapolis Colts Inc. v. Metropolitan Baltimore Football Club Limited Partnership*, 34 F.3d 410 (7th Cir. 1994), and *Major League Baseball Props. v. Sed Non Olet Denarius*, 817 F.Supp. 1103 (S.D.N.Y.1993), *vacated pursuant to settlement*, 859 F.Supp. 80 (S.D.N.Y.1994) represent different approaches to this problem. The latter case involved the unauthorized adoption of the term "Brooklyn Dodger" by a restaurant located in Brooklyn, New York. Decorated with Brooklyn Dodgers memorabilia, the restaurant sought to evoke the happy days of the baseball team's residence in the borough of Brooklyn—before the team's still-resented 1958 departure for Los Angeles. In response to the Los Angeles Dodgers' and Major League Baseball's suit for an injunction, the restaurant claimed that the "Brooklyn Dodgers" mark had been abandoned. The restaurant also disparaged any suggestion that it was seeking to capitalize on the Los Angeles' organization's goodwill: as the court described the testimony of one witness, "a life-long Brooklyn resident," "given the acrimonious abandonment of Brooklyn by Los Angeles, the idea of trading on Los Angeles' 'goodwill' in Brooklyn is almost 'laughable.' "

Although plaintiffs had not used the mark "Brooklyn Dodgers" between 1958 and 1981 (when plaintiffs began a limited licensing program for the mark), plaintiffs contended that the protected mark was simply "Dodgers," and that this mark had been in continuous use. The court rejected plaintiff's characterization of the mark:

> [I]n this context, "Brooklyn" is more than a geographic designation or appendage to the word "Dodgers." The *"Brooklyn* Dodgers" was a non-transportable cultural institution separate from the "Los Angeles Dodgers" or the "Dodgers" who play in Los Angeles. It is not simply the "Dodgers" (and certainly not the

"Los Angeles Dodgers") that defendants seek to invoke in their restaurant; rather, defendants specifically seek to recall the nostalgia of the cultural institution that was the "Brooklyn Dodgers." It was the "*Brooklyn* Dodgers" name that had acquired secondary meaning in New York in the early part of the century, prior to 1958. It was that cultural institution that Los Angeles abandoned.

The court held that plaintiffs' non-use of "*Brooklyn* Dodgers" for thirty-two years constituted an abandonment. Moreover, plaintiffs' partial resumption of use through the sporadic granting of licenses beginning in 1981 created only common-law rights in the term. Thus, plaintiffs could claim rights only in those locations and in those kinds of uses for which it had granted licenses. Because plaintiffs had not previously granted a license for restaurant use in Brooklyn (and because the court had already found that defendants' use was not likely to be confused with plaintiffs'), defendants were entitled to continue using the "Brooklyn Dodger" mark.

By contrast, in *Indianapolis Colts*, Judge Posner viewed the mark as "COLTS," independently of urban affiliation. Hence, the equally resented abandonment of Baltimore in 1984 by its former football team did not entitle the Canadian Football League (CFL) to adopt the name "Colts" in connection with its new team in Baltimore. Judge Posner declined to pair the good will of the team with its former home town:

> [Defendants] make a tremendous to-do over the fact that the district judge found that the Indianapolis Colts abandoned the trademark "Baltimore Colts" when they moved to Indianapolis. Well, of course; they were no longer playing football under the name "Baltimore Colts," so could not have used the name as the team's trademark.... The Colts' abandonment of a mark confusingly similar to their new mark neither broke the continuity of the team in its different locations—it was the same team, merely having a different home base and therefore a different geographical component in its name—nor entitled a third party to pick it up and use it to confuse [consumers] ... with regard to the identity, sponsorship, or league affiliation of the third party, that is, the new Baltimore team.

> A professional sports team is like Heraclitus's river: always changing, yet always the same.... [A]s far as the record discloses there is as much institutional continuity between the Baltimore Colts of 1984 and the Indianapolis Colts of 1994 as there was between the Baltimore Colts of 1974 and the Baltimore Colts of 1984.... There is, in contrast, no continuity, no links contractual or otherwise, nothing but a geographical site in common, between the Baltimore Colts and the Canadian Football League team that would like to use its name. Any suggestion that there is such continuity is false and potentially misleading.

QUESTIONS

1. Abandonment casts a mark into the public domain. It becomes free for another's adoption. However, if a mark held to have been abandoned nonetheless in fact continues to symbolize the producer's good will, how would you protect the interests of the public, and of the producer, in avoiding confusion?

2. Examine the current Lanham Act definition of "abandonment." The statute now provides that a mark shall be deemed abandoned "[w]hen its use has been discontinued with intent not to resume *such use.*" How does the addition of the italicized words affect analysis of abandonment claims? For example, how would you decide the *Humble* case given the current definition? Does this definition preclude protection on the basis of residual goodwill?

3. Recall the Second Circuit's *Silverman* statement: "Though Silverman undoubtedly hopes that some of his audience will be drawn from those who favorably recall the 'Amos 'n Andy' programs, we doubt if many who attend Broadway musicals are motivated to purchase tickets because of a belief that the musical is produced by the same entity responsible for the movie, book, or radio or television series on which it is based." What is the relevance of the "motivation" test to abandonment? To infringement?

4. Ferrari, the automobile manufacturer, ceased producing its well-known DAYTONA SPYDER model sports car in 1974. At that time and thereafter, Ferrari has had no plans to resume producing the sports car. However, Ferrari has continued to manufacture mechanical and body parts for the repair and servicing of existing DAYTONA SPYDER automobiles. Ferrari sells these parts through exclusive licensees who continue to service the DAYTONA cars. Moreover, these cars are still widely driven.

McBurnie specializes in manufacturing car assembly kits and completed cars, including a model it calls the "California Daytona Spyder." If Ferrari brings a trade dress infringement claim against McBurnie, how should the court rule on the issue of abandonment? How much weight would you place on the continuing service activities? How much on the strong residual goodwill in the DAYTONA SPYDER? *See Ferrari S.p.A. Esercizio Fabbriche Automobili e Corse v. McBurnie,* 11 U.S.P.Q.2d 1843 (S.D.Cal.1989).

2. ASSIGNMENT IN GROSS, NAKED LICENSING AND FAILURE TO POLICE

Clark & Freeman Corp. v. Heartland Co. Ltd.

811 F.Supp. 137 (S.D.N.Y.1993).

■ MARTIN, J:

This case involves the competing claims of two companies to the exclusive right to use the name "Heartland" in connection with their business operations. Defendants have been using the name since July of 1985 in connection with their sales of shirts, sweaters, trousers and jackets.

Plaintiffs first commenced using the name "Heartland" on April 26, 1986 in connection with the sale of men's shoes and boots.

Had each of the parties continued with their original operations, plaintiffs selling men's shoes and boots and defendants selling shirts, trousers and jackets, there would have been little need for either to seek the intervention of the Court. While some evidence of confusion was introduced at trial, such confusion was limited and not sufficient to justify interfering with the parties' continued operating in their separate lines of merchandise. Recently, however, plaintiffs have decided that they wish to launch a clothing line under the "Heartland" name and, thus, this lawsuit.

Although plaintiffs began using the name "Heartland" after defendants, plaintiffs claim priority because in 1987 they obtained an assignment of the "Heartland" name from Sears, Roebuck & Co. which had used the name since 1983 in connection with the sale of women's boots. Plaintiffs filed an application to register the "Heartland" mark with the U.S. Patent and Trademark Office on July 3, 1986. On November 25, 1986, the application was allowed and published in the Official Gazette. Nine days later on December 4, 1986, Sears notified plaintiffs of their prior use of the "Heartland" name and threatened to bring opposition proceedings. Ultimately, Sears agreed to settle the matter by assigning the "Heartland" name to plaintiffs in exchange for $15,000. The settlement was effected on April 6, 1987, and, on July 28, 1987, plaintiffs' mark was registered by the U.S. Patent and Trademark Office.

Since plaintiffs' own use of the name "Heartland" did not commence until after defendants' use of that trademark, plaintiffs can prevail in this action only if they have succeeded to the priority rights in the trademark "Heartland" which were enjoyed by Sears. Defendants contend, however, that the assignment of the trademark from Sears to plaintiffs was an assignment in gross and, therefore, plaintiffs may not tack on the period of *Sears'* prior use to defeat defendants' claim of priority.

Generally, an assignment of a trademark and its accompanying goodwill will entitle the assignee to "step into the shoes" of the assignor, gaining whatever priority the assignor might have had in the mark. [citations omitted] accord 15 U.S.C. § 1060.[2] However, where a trademark has been assigned "in gross," i.e. without the accompanying goodwill, then the assignment is invalid, and the "assignee" must instead rely upon his or her own use to establish priority.

Marshak v. Green, 746 F.2d 927 (2d Cir.1984), discusses the rationale behind the assignment in gross rule: "Use of the mark by the assignee in connection with a different goodwill and different product would result in a fraud on the purchasing public who reasonably assume that the mark

---

2. Although § 1060 applies only to registered trademarks, it parallels the common law rules of trademark assignment. [citations omitted] Thus, no distinction is made herein between cases discussing assignability of registered trademarks and those involving unregistered trademarks.

signifies the same thing, whether used by one person or another." *Id.* at 929.

Plaintiffs claim that the assignment is valid for two reasons: (1) Because Sears immediately ceased manufacture and marketing of its "Heartland" boots, there was an ipso facto transfer of goodwill to plaintiffs; (2) Because plaintiffs were applying the trademark to "substantially similar" goods, they had acquired the goodwill as well as the mark.

Plaintiffs' first argument can be easily dismissed. Plaintiffs cite no case establishing the proposition that forbearance by the assignor operates to transfer goodwill ipso facto. *Hy–Cross Hatchery, Inc. v. Osborne,* 303 F.2d 947, 950 (C.C.P.A. 1962) (using forbearance only as one element in transfer of goodwill determination). Indeed, if forbearance alone were sufficient, then discussion of "consumer deception" would be irrelevant, since an assignee could use the mark for any product desired as long as the assignor halted operations. Goodwill is not such a mechanistic concept.

Plaintiffs' second contention presents a closer question. It is well established that "courts have upheld such assignments if they find that the assignee is producing a product or performing a service substantially similar to that of the assignor and that the customers would not be deceived or harmed." *Marshak,* 746 F.2d at 930.[3] This is the case even if no physical or tangible assets have been transferred. The key question is whether plaintiffs produced a product "substantially similar" to that of *Sears* such that "the customers would not be deceived or harmed."

For these purposes, it is not dispositive that plaintiffs' footwear is of high quality. It is not merely the quality of the product, but its similarity to that produced by the assignor that determines whether goodwill has been transferred. "[A] trademark may be validly transferred without the simultaneous transfer of any tangible assets, as long as the recipient continues to produce goods of the same quality and nature previously associated with the mark." *Defiance Button,* 759 F.2d at 1059 (emphasis added). Plaintiffs' argument that customers cannot be harmed or deceived either because their shoes are of such high quality or because they are available for inspection prior to purchase misses the mark; by that rationale, plaintiffs could have produced the finest quality jet engines under the mark "Heartland" and claimed to have acquired Sears' goodwill in ladies boots. Substantial similarity demands more than quality.

Case law on "substantial similarity" is only moderately instructive, since the facts of each case are distinct and dispositive. ... Some courts have found "substantial similarity" even though the products differed in some respects. In *Main Street Outfitters v. Federated Dep't Stores,* 730 F. Supp. 289 (D.Minn.1989), "substantial similarity" was found to establish a goodwill transfer where the assignor had sold "all-weather coats and

---

3. Goodwill may also be transferred if "the purchaser is able to 'go on in real continuity with the past,'" *Bambu Sales, Inc. v. Sultana Crackers, Inc.,* 683 F. Supp. 899 (E.D.N.Y.1988), or if "there is a continuity of management," *Marshak,* 746 F.2d at 930. Neither of these occurrences has been alleged by plaintiffs....

women's coats" and the assignee was using the mark on "various items of clothing including jackets, rain wear and various items of apparel." *Id.* at 290. The court found dispositive that "[assignee] conducted a business of selling apparel, especially women's apparel, as had its assignor. The goods sold by [assignee] had substantially the same characteristics, that is: apparel, as those of the assignor." *Id.* at 292.

In *Mulhens & Kropff v. Ferd Muelhens, Inc.*, 38 F.2d 287, 293 (D.N.Y. 1929), the district court found assignor's and assignee's colognes to be "substantially similar" even though the assignor retained the secret formula to its cologne. But the court of appeals reversed, stating that "a majority of the court believe that assignment of the recipe is essential to give the assignee the exclusive right to a mark which denotes a product manufactured thereunder." 43 F.2d 937, 939 (2d Cir.), *cert. denied*, 282 U.S. 881, 51 S. Ct. 84 (1930).

In *Warner–Lambert Pharm. Co. v. General Foods Corp.*, 164 U.S.P.Q. 532 (T.T.A.B. 1970), the court found that assignor's mineral-vitamin pharmaceutical was not similar enough to assignee's anti-caries (tooth decay preventative) preparation in chewable tablet and capsule form to establish a transfer of goodwill.

Even minor differences can be enough to threaten customer deception. In the oft-cited *Pepsico, Inc. v. Grapette Co.*, 416 F.2d 285 (8th Cir.1969), the court found that assignor's cola-flavored syrup and assignee's pepper-flavored syrup were sufficiently different to prevent a transfer of goodwill, and thus invalidate the assignment: "[The assignee]'s intended use of the mark is one simply to describe its new pepper beverage. The evidence is clear that [the assignee] did not intend to adopt or exploit any 'goodwill' from the [trademark] and [the assignor]'s long association and use of it with a cola syrup." *Id.* at 289–90.

The facts of record in this case support a finding of assignment in gross here. Sears sold only women's pixie boots under the mark "Heartland," while plaintiffs immediately applied it only to men's shoes, then later to men's hiking boots. The markets for the two goods are substantially distinct; it is unlikely that men buying plaintiffs' "Heartland" shoes would be considering a reputation for footwear generally that Sears built by selling women's boots. That plaintiffs was using the "Heartland" mark before the assignment is also relevant, in that it tends to show that plaintiffs sought only to gain the ability to use the name "Heartland" rather than the goodwill associated with it. *Cf. Pepsico.* This is further supported by the fact that plaintiffs did not attempt to obtain the assignment from Sears until after Sears threatened to bring opposition proceedings to prevent plaintiffs from registering the "Heartland" trademark.

Since the assignment from Sears was an assignment in gross, defendants have shown priority in the use of the name "Heartland" and, therefore, plaintiffs may not enjoin defendants from using the "Heartland" name for the sale of its current line of products. . . .

CHAPTER 6

INFRINGEMENT

Start 10/23

332-3C

363-90

403-05

408-14

15 U.S.C. § 1114 [LANHAM ACT § 32(1)]

Any person who shall, without the consent of the registrant—

(a) use in commerce any reproduction, counterfeit, copy, or colorable imitation of a registered mark in connection with the sale, offering for sale, distribution, or advertising of any goods or services on or in connection with which such use is likely to cause confusion, or to cause mistake, or to deceive . . . shall be liable in a civil action by the registrant for the remedies hereinafter provided. . . .

A. LIKELIHOOD OF CONFUSION

1. FACTORS FOR ASSESSING LIKELIHOOD OF CONFUSION

Polaroid Corp. v. Polarad Elects. Corp., 287 F.2d 492 (2d Cir.), *cert. denied*, 368 U.S. 820 (1961). In this landmark decision, the Second Circuit enunciated eight factors for evaluating likelihood of confusion between non-identical goods or services:

1. The strength of plaintiff's mark;
2. the degree of similarity between plaintiff's and defendant's marks;
3. the proximity of the products or services;
4. the likelihood that plaintiff will bridge the gap;
5. evidence of actual confusion;
6. defendant's good faith in adopting the mark;
7. the quality of defendant's product or service;
8. the sophistication of the buyers.

Today Thinks... *** ***

The Second Circuit added, "even this extensive catalogue does not exhaust the possibilities—the court may have to take still other variables into account."

For example, unlike some circuits, the Second Circuit does not explicitly list a "channels of trade" factor, but the court has often considered the commercial environment(s) in which the public is likely to encounter the marks. The court has accordingly cautioned that side-by-side comparison of the marks is not probative if the public would not encounter the goods bearing the marks in the same place: "Whether simultaneous viewing by consumers is likely to result in confusion is not relevant when it is serial viewing that is at issue given the market context or the type of confusion claimed. In such a case, a district court must ask not whether differences are easily discernable on simultaneous viewing, but whether they are likely to be memorable enough to dispel confusion on serial viewing.... In the case before us, the district court's finding that no likelihood of confusion existed appears to have been the result, at least in part, of an inappropriate focus on the effect on consumers of simultaneous viewing of the handbags. The parties concede that, in the actual market-place, these products are not sold side-by-side, and are instead sold in different stores and on different websites." Louis Vuitton Malletier v. Burlington Coat Factory, 426 F.3d 532 (2d Cir.2005).

[handwritten margin note: Serial viewing, Not simultaneous]

The factors set forth above have come to be known in the Second Circuit as "the *Polaroid* factors." The *Polaroid* factors at first evolved as a measure of confusion between non-competing goods. Where marks used by the contending parties are the same and the products are directly competitive, there is obvious harm to the original trademark owner, for a second-comer is using the same mark on substitute goods. But what is the harm if the marks are the same, but the products are sufficiently different that no one would buy one product seeking or expecting to get the other? For example, if the same mark was used by plaintiff for milk, and by defendant for ice cream, would there be infringement? When a court confronted that question in *Borden Ice Cream v. Borden's Condensed Milk Co.*, 201 F. 510 (7th Cir.1912), it held that although both parties used the BORDEN mark, there was no infringement because the goods did not directly compete.

[handwritten margin note: Direct competition of goods]

This conclusion seems unduly cramped. Ice cream may not substitute for milk, but both are dairy products, and the public might well anticipate that a well-known milk producer had expanded into a closely related field. Indeed, the second-comer may well have adopted the mark with the intention of benefiting by any connection the public would draw between the milk producer (and its goodwill) and the eponymous ice cream product. Perhaps not surprisingly, *Borden* represents the end of the era in which only use of the same or very similar marks on directly competing goods could give rise to a finding of likelihood of confusion. Not long after the *Borden* decision, courts began to recognize the commercial realities underlying and resulting from a second-comer's selection of the same mark for closely related goods. Thus, five years later, the Second Circuit held that where AUNT JEMIMA was established as a mark for pancake batter, it was infringement to use the same mark for pancake syrup. *Aunt Jemima Mills Co. v. Rigney & Co.*, 247 F. 407 (2d Cir.1917), *cert. denied*, 245 U.S. 672 (1918).

[handwritten margin note: No longer valid.]

A decade later, the Second Circuit, per Judge Learned Hand, held the use of YALE for flashlights and batteries to infringe the well-known YALE mark used for locks and keys. *Yale Electric Corp. v. Robertson*, 26 F.2d 972 (2d Cir.1928). Courts have continued to recognize that the public may be

~~confused as to the source of goods or services in varying degrees~~ of ~~relatedness.~~

Other circuits have elaborated similar criteria. Although the factors weighed in making this determination vary to some degree from circuit to circuit, certain considerations seem to appear uniformly: the degree of similarity between the marks, the proximity of the products, the defendant's intent in selecting the allegedly infringing mark, evidence of actual confusion, and the strength of plaintiff's mark.

The factors enunciated by the Second Circuit in *Polaroid* have close analogues in other Circuits. The names various Circuits give the factors figure below:

Third Circuit: "Lapp" Factors, see *Century 21 Real Estate Corp. v. Lendingtree, Inc.*, 425 F.3d 211, 214 (3d Cir.2005);

Fourth Circuit: ~~"Pizzeria Uno"~~ factors, see *Anheuser–Busch, Inc. v. L. & L. Wings, Inc.*, 962 F.2d 316, 320 (4th Cir.1992), *cert. denied*, 506 U.S. 872 (1992);

Fifth Circuit: "Roto–Rooter" factors, see *Sno–Wizard Mfg., Inc. v. Eisemann Prods. Co.*, 791 F.2d 423, 428 (5th Cir.1986);

Sixth Circuit: "Frisch's" factors, see *Homeowners Group, Inc. v. Home Marketing Specialists, Inc.*, 931 F.2d 1100, 1106 (6th Cir.1991);

Seventh Circuit: "Helene Curtis" factors, see *Smith Fiberglass Prods., Inc. v. Ameron, Inc.*, 7 F.3d 1327, 1329 (7th Cir.1993);

Eighth Circuit: "Squirtco" factors, see *SquirtCo. v. Seven–Up Co.*, 628 F.2d 1086, 1091 (8th Cir.1980);

Ninth Circuit: "Sleekcraft" factors, see *E. & J. Gallo Winery v. Gallo Cattle Co.*, 967 F.2d 1280, 1290 (9th Cir.1992);

Tenth Circuit: "Beer Nuts" factors, see *Coherent, Inc. v. Coherent Technologies, Inc.*, 935 F.2d 1122, 1125 (10th Cir.1991)

See also *Keds Corp. v. Renee Int'l Trading Corp.*, 888 F.2d 215, 222 (1st Cir.1989); *Dieter v. B & H Industries of Southwest Florida, Inc.*, 880 F.2d 322, 326 (11th Cir.1989), *cert. denied*, 498 U.S. 950 (1990).*

Several courts and the Restatement suggest that "the list [of factors] is not exhaustive. Other variables may come into play depending on the particular facts presented." *AMF Inc. v. Sleekcraft Boats*, 599 F.2d 341, 348 n. 11 (9th Cir.1979); *Triumph Hosiery Mills, Inc. v. Triumph Int'l Corp.*, 308 F.2d 196, 198 (2d Cir.1962); Restatement (Third) of Unfair Competi-

---

* The appellate jurisdiction of the Court of Appeals for the Federal Circuit encompasses cases from any district court in the country which involves a patent question. 28 U.S.C. § 1295. Because trademark claims are sometimes combined with patent claims, the CAFC on occasion deals with the issue of likelihood of confusion on appeal from district courts in various circuits. In such cases, the CAFC applies the law of the regional circuit. *E.g., KeyStone Retaining Wall Systems, Inc. v. Westrock, Inc.*, 997 F.2d 1444, 1447 (Fed.Cir.1993).

tion § 21, Comment a (1993). For example, in *E. Remy Martin & Co. v. Shaw–Ross Int'l Imports, Inc.*, 756 F.2d 1525 (11th Cir.1985) (where a preliminary injunction was granted to plaintiff who alleged that F. REMY and REMY for sparkling wine infringed its marks, REMY, REMY MARTIN, and ST. REMY for cognac and brandy), the court, in considering the defendant's intent in adopting its mark, also addressed the "closely related issue" of defendant's abandonment of the mark. 756 F.2d at 1530, n.15.

While courts first articulated the *Polaroid* factors (and other Circuits' equivalents) to assess likelihood of confusion between dissimilar goods or services, the factors have come to be applied in all likelihood of confusion inquiries, including those involving the same or similar goods.

SIMILARITY OF SIGHT, SOUND AND MEANING

Both in the courts and before the Trademark Trial and Appeal Board, the degree of similarity between marks is one of the factors weighed in a likelihood of confusion analysis. Similarity is examined on three levels: sight, sound, and meaning. "Each must be considered as [it] is encountered in the marketplace. Although similarity is measured by the marks as a whole, similarities weigh more heavily than differences." *AMF Inc. v. Sleekcraft Boats*, 599 F.2d 341, 351 (9th Cir.1979).

[handwritten: Factor #2]

The court in *Borinquen Biscuit Corp. v. M.V. Trading Corp.*, 443 F.3d 112 (1st Cir.2006) upheld an injunction based on the similarity of the appearance and sound of the mark at issue ("Rica") used for round cookies (plaintiff's goods) and round crackers (defendant's goods). Likewise, ER-TEC (an acronym for Earth Technology Corporation) was held confusingly similar in sound and appearance to ERT (an acronym for Environmental Research and Technology, Inc.), notwithstanding that ERT appeared in block lettering and ERTEC in a modified block or script-like format. The court noted that "initials require less degree of similarity because by their nature they are abbreviations to be comprehended at a glance." *Earth Technology Inc. v. Environmental Research and Technology, Inc.*, 222 U.S.P.Q. 585, 588 (C.D.Cal.1983).

Similarity of meaning (*i.e.,* "the use of a designation which causes confusion because it conveys the same idea, or stimulates the same mental reaction," *Standard Oil Co. v. Standard Oil Co.*, 252 F.2d 65 (10th Cir.1958)) was found in *American Technical Industries, Inc. v. General Foam Plastics Corp.*, 200 U.S.P.Q. 244 (S.D.N.Y.1978) ("MOUNTAIN KING" for artificial Christmas trees held infringed by "ALPINE EMPEROR" for same goods); *In re Duofold*, 184 U.S.P.Q. 638 (T.T.A.B.1974) (design mark consisting of a representation of a golden eagle for shirts, jackets and shorts held confusingly similar to word mark "GOLDEN EAGLE" for coats and suits); *Rosenblum v. George Willsher & Co.*, 161 U.S.P.Q. 492 (T.T.A.B.1969) ("RED BULL" for scotch held confusingly similar to "TORO ROJO" for rum since "TORO ROJO" means "RED BULL" in Spanish); *Mitek Corp. v. Pyramid Sound Corp.*, 20 U.S.P.Q.2d

[handwritten: Similar Found]

1389 (N.D.Ill.1991) ("BLUE LIGHTENING" for audio speakers and "BLUE THUNDER" for audio speakers found confusingly similar); and *Aktiebolaget Electrolux v. Armatron Int'l, Inc.*, 999 F.2d 1 (1st Cir.1993) ("LEAF EATER" for a leaf shredder found to infringe "WEED EATER" for a grass trimmer); *Sanofi-Aventis v. Advancis Pharmaceutical Corp.*, 453 F.Supp.2d 834 (D.Del.2006)("AVENTIS" and "ADVANCIS" for pharmaceuticals found confusingly similar because both have meanings associated with movement, innovation, and advancing). However, the following cases held that the marks were not confusingly similar in meaning: *Burns Philp Food Inc. v. Modern Products Inc.*, 24 U.S.P.Q.2d 1157 (T.T.A.B.1992), *aff'd*, 1 F.3d 1252 (Fed.Cir.1993) (no likelihood of confusion between "SPICE ISLANDS" for spices and "SPICE GARDEN" for spices and seasonings); *ConAgra, Inc. v. George A. Hormel & Co.*, 990 F.2d 368 (8th Cir.1993) (no likelihood of confusion existed between "HEALTHY SELECTIONS" for food products and "HEALTHY CHOICE" for same goods); *Morrison Entertainment Group Inc. v. Nintendo of America, Inc.*, 56 Fed. Appx. 782 (9th Cir.2003)(no likelihood of confusion between "POKEMON" and "MONSTER IN MY POCKET" for similar goods because, even though the words mean the same thing–"Pokémon" is short for "Pocket Monster"–consumers assume "Pokémon" is fanciful).

Since similarity of sight, sound, or meaning is but one consideration in the likelihood of confusion calculus, such similarity may be established, yet confusion held not likely to exist. Hence, in *In re Unilever Limited*, 222 U.S.P.Q. 981 (T.T.A.B.1984), CLAX for industrial laundry detergents and powders was considered visually and phonetically similar to CLAK as applied to alkaline cleaner for food processing plants, where CLAX appeared in a stylized form with the "X" resembling a "K" and sounded like a pluralized version of CLAK. No likelihood of confusion was found, however, since the Board determined that the respective goods were "not competitive with each other, nor are they purchased by the same people under circumstances that would give use to the mistaken belief that one source was responsible for both products." 222 U.S.P.Q. at 983. *See also Shen Mfg. Co., Inc. v. Ritz Hotel, Ltd.*, 393 F.3d 1238 (Fed.Cir. 2004)("Although the marks are identical, the differences in the products as well as the weakness of Shen's mark lead us to dismiss [the] Opposition.").

E. & J. Gallo Winery v. Consorzio del Gallo Nero

782 F.Supp. 457 (N.D.Cal.1991).

■ JENSEN, DISTRICT JUDGE:

Background

This is an action for trademark infringement and dilution brought by plaintiff E. & J. Gallo Winery ("Gallo") against defendant Consorzio del Gallo Nero ("Gallo Nero"). Gallo, the largest winery in the United States, produces and sells a variety of wines featuring the "Gallo" trademark and is the owner of several federal registrations of the "Gallo" mark. Since 1933, Gallo has consistently used the "Gallo" name in relation to its wines and has sold some 2 billion bottles of wine bearing the "Gallo" mark to consumers through retail establishments of all types, including restaurants, grocery stores, wine shops, and liquor stores. Finally, over the past 50 years, Gallo has spent some $500 million in promoting the "Gallo" brand of wines, and Gallo's advertising is presently calculated to reach every consumer in the United States approximately 50–70 times a year.

Defendant Gallo Nero is an Italian trade association based in Florence, Italy, that promotes Chianti Classico wine produced by its individual members in the Chianti region of Italy. Prior to the formation of Gallo Nero in 1987, Chianti Classico producers were represented by the Consorzio Vino Chianti Classico ("CVCC"), which was formed in 1924. CVCC had consistently utilized the symbol of a black rooster, or "gallo nero," to represent its wines, a symbol with history of strong association with the Chianti region of Italy. In particular, the symbol appeared on the neck seal of its bottles, surrounded by the designation "Consorzio Vino Chianti Classico." The name of the successor organization, Consorzio del Gallo Nero, was selected on the basis of this association between the symbol and the wines of the Chianti region, and defendant has continued the tradition of using the black rooster symbol on its neck seals, substituting the designation "Consorzio del Gallo Nero" for the previous one. However, although Gallo Nero has produced such neck seals, they have not yet been used on any Gallo Nero wine distributed in the United States.

. . . .

Discussion

. . . .

1. *Strength of plaintiff's mark*

A registered mark is "presumed to be distinctive and should be afforded the utmost protection." Indeed, proper and current registration of a trademark is "conclusive evidence of the validity of the registered mark and of the registration of the mark, of the registrant's ownership of the mark, and of the registrant's exclusive right to use the registered mark in commerce." 15 U.S.C. § 1115(b). Therefore, in light of Gallo's current federal registration of several versions of the "Gallo" mark, plaintiff has established as an initial matter the validity and distinctiveness of the mark and Gallo's exclusive right to use the mark in promoting and selling its wines in the United States.

In addition to these statutory presumptions, the Gallo mark itself has been held by a sister court of this Circuit to have achieved "virtually universal recognition as a trademark for wine," and that it is "universally known both nationally and in California, and has become an extraordinarily strong and distinctive mark." *E. & J. Gallo Winery Cattle Co.,* 12 U.S.P.Q.2d 1657, 1661, 1667 (E.D.Cal.1989). This conclusion is further supported by Gallo's undisputed showing that it has used the Gallo mark in relation to its wines for over 50 years; it has spent some $500 million in advertising its wines distributed under the mark; and it has sold to consumers some 2 billion bottles of wine bearing the Gallo mark.

Gallo Nero contests the strength of the Gallo mark by noting that there are numerous third-party uses of the "Gallo" name, and that "Gallo" itself is merely a common surname and basic element of Italian vocabulary. However, "evidence of other unrelated potential infringers is irrelevant to claims of trademark infringement," and Gallo Nero has not shown that these third-party uses are in any way connected to the production, promotion, and sale of wine, much less that any of these uses has achieved significant consumer recognition. Therefore Gallo Nero's evidence of third-party uses is neither persuasive nor relevant to the issue of the strength of the "Gallo" mark.

Secondly, a family name is entitled to protection as a mark so long as it has acquired a recognized "secondary meaning" through use, advertising, and public recognition. "Gallo" has clearly become associated with wine in the United States such that its evolution to "secondary meaning" status may not be seriously questioned.

In conclusion, the Court finds that Gallo has established both its exclusive right to use the "Gallo" trademark under federal law and that the trademark itself is exceptionally strong when used in relation to the promotion and sale of wine in the United States. While the strength of plaintiff's mark is but one of several issues to be considered in determining whether there is likelihood of confusion between the parties' products, the Court notes that "a strong mark is 'afforded the widest ambit of protection from infringing uses.'"

2. *Similarity of marks used*

Similarity of marks is judged by their sound, appearance, and meaning. Gallo contends that the two marks share the total identity of the substantive term "Gallo" and are therefore substantially similar for purposes of trademark infringement.

Gallo Nero in opposition argues that its use of surrounding terms, *i.e.*, Consorzio del Gallo Nero, sufficiently distinguishes the latter from the "Gallo" mark to render the two uses dissimilar. However, it is undisputed that Gallo has valid, current federal registrations of the "Gallo" mark used in conjunction with other words, *e.g.*, "Ernest & Julio Gallo," and that Gallo has consistently combined the word "Gallo" with other descriptive terms, *e.g.*, "Gallo Premium Blush" and "Gallo Classic Burgundy." Therefore, as Gallo argues, there is a logical conclusion that consumers are accustomed to seeing the "Gallo" mark used in conjunction with other terms or surrounded by other words. The distinctive term in each instance is "Gallo," which, as discussed above, has clearly obtained a unique status when coupled with wine. Finally, this characteristic would seem to be particularly maintained with regard to non-Italian-speaking consumers when the "Gallo" mark is surrounded by the foreign terms "Consorzio" and "Nero." Again, for English speakers, the "stand out" or significant term in the phrase "Consorzio del Gallo Nero" is the word "Gallo" when the phrase is encountered on or in connection with a bottle of wine.

Gallo Nero also argues that the presentation of the terms on the bottle sufficiently distinguish the two uses such that defendant's use is dissimilar to plaintiff's. Thus, even if the subject marks are identical, "their similarity must be considered in light of the way the marks are encountered in the marketplace and the circumstances surrounding their purchase." Gallo Nero notes that the use of the term "Gallo" is always in conjunction with the term "Nero," and its proposed limitation to small script on the neck seal strengthens the immediate dissimilarity arising from the otherwise clearly different labels attached to the parties' bottles of wine.

Gallo does not respond to this particular argument, but the Court finds that Gallo Nero's argument, while having some merit, is neither dispositive nor persuasive on the issue of similarity between marks. As an initial matter, Gallo Nero is arguably well aware of the similarity of the "Gallo Nero" name to that of "Gallo" in light of defendant's interactions with foreign trademark offices. Specifically, in August 1984, defendant's predecessor, CVCC, sought to register the words "Gallo Nero" as a trademark in Canada. The application, however, was rejected because the Canadian trademark office concluded that "Gallo Nero" was likely to be confused with Gallo's registered marks. Moreover, just prior to commencing its U.S. marketing campaign, Gallo Nero opposed plaintiff's application to register "Ernest and Julio Gallo" in the United Kingdom on the ground that this mark would be "deceptive or confusing" with "Gallo Nero."

In conclusion, the Court finds that the continued use of the term "Gallo" as a manifestation of a federally registered mark or in conjunction with other terms establishes not only that the mark itself is strong, but that the consuming public will find the single term "Gallo" to be wholly and uniquely distinctive whenever it is used in conjunction with the promotion or sale of wine in the United States. Therefore, because "Gallo" is the single "dominant" or "substantive" term used by plaintiff on all its products—including the 2 billion bottles of wine already sold—defendant's use of the term "Gallo" even on a facially distinctive label or in conjunction with other terms does not divert this Court from its conclusion that, as a matter of law, the two terms are significantly similar for purposes of a finding of a likelihood of confusion between the two uses.

3. *Similarity of goods sold*

"When the goods produced by the alleged infringer compete for sales with those of the trademark owner, infringement usually will be found if the marks are sufficiently similar that confusion can be expected." Both parties are involved in the sale of wine, although of arguably different varieties. Gallo notes, however, that the Patent and Trademark Office has repeatedly found that wines of all types constitute a single class of goods. In fact, if Gallo Nero sought to register its name as a trademark, it would fall into the same class of goods as Gallo's trademarks. *See* 37 C.F.R. §§ 6.1, 6.2 (1990).

Gallo Nero in opposition contends that the wines themselves are distinct, one produced in Italy while the other in the United States.

Moreover, Gallo Nero's members produce only chianti wines, whereas Gallo effectively produces everything but Italian chianti. However, Gallo Nero cites no authority for finding a distinction between the wines produced by the parties, and representatives of Gallo Nero have themselves stated that Gallo Nero wines distributed in the United States are "in competition with every red wine that is being produced."

Therefore, the Court finds that the goods produced by Gallo and Gallo Nero are substantially similar for purposes of establishing a likelihood of confusion.

4.   *Similarity of marketing channels used*

Both parties market their products through retail establishments like wine shops and liquor stores, and utilize magazines for advertizing purposes. Gallo Nero effectively does not dispute Gallo's showing on this issue; indeed, Gallo Nero notes use of the same retail establishment in Washington, D.C., the Mayflower Wine & Spirits Shop, by both parties in selling their respective wines. Moreover, the above deposition testimony that Gallo Nero wines are in direct competition with those of other producers also supports a finding that the wines are marketed by similar means. Therefore the Court finds as a matter of law that both parties use similar marketing channels to distribute their wines.

5.   *Degree of care exercised by purchasers*

Confusion between marks is generally more likely where the goods at issue involve relatively inexpensive, "impulse" products to which the average, "unsophisticated" consumer does not devote a great deal of care and consideration in purchasing. Wine has been deemed an "impulse" product, and certainly so with respect to the average consumer, effectively compelling the consumer's reliance "on faith in the maker." *Taylor Wine Co. v. Bully Hill Vineyards, Inc.*, 569 F.2d 731, 733–34 (2d Cir.1978); see also *id.* ("The average American who drinks wine on occasion can hardly pass for a connoisseur of wines"). Indeed, Gallo Nero employees themselves have testified that the average American consumer is unlearned in the selection of wine.

The only opposition Gallo Nero offers to Gallo's characterization of the wine-buying public is a single 1959 case from the Middle District of Alabama, stating that "the wine-buying public—insofar as their selection and purchase of wine is concerned—is a highly discriminating group." *E. & J. Gallo Winery v. Ben R. Goltsman & Co.*, 172 F. Supp. 826, 830 (M.D.Ala.1959). That case, however, involved plaintiff's "THUNDERBIRD" fortified wine—with the "Gallo" name above—versus the defendant's "THUNDERBOLT"—with the words "Private Stock" immediately below—both products arguably failing any classification as "fine wines." Moreover, with all due respect to Alabama, it would seem common knowledge that wine was not a widely appreciated beverage in the South in 1959.

On balance then, the Court finds that Gallo Nero has failed to contest either through evidence or legal support the characterization of the wine-buying public as generally unsophisticated "impulse" buyers who are an "easy mark for a [trademark] infringer." Therefore the Court finds that the lack of consumer sophistication significantly enhances the likelihood of confusion between the two products.

6. *Evidence of actual confusion*

While evidence of actual consumer confusion provides strong support for a finding of a likelihood of confusion, "the failure to prove instances of actual confusion is not dispositive" of an infringement claim. Thus evidence of actual confusion "is merely one factor to be considered . . . and it is not determinative" if it is not shown. Therefore, at a minimum, the absence of actual confusion will not defeat an otherwise successful claim of infringement by Gallo as this Court must find only a *likelihood* of confusion.

Gallo Nero relies in significant part on the survey conducted by Dr. Jacob Jacoby, Merchants Council Professor of Consumer Behavior and Retail Management at the Stern School of Business, New York University, entitled "Consumer Perceptions of Wine Bottles Bearing the Consorzio del Gallo Nero Neck Seal" (the "Jacoby Survey"), to show that there is no likelihood of confusion between the parties' respective uses of the "Gallo" name. In the survey, individual participants were shown an array of eight bottles of red wine, including two bottles of Gallo wines and two bottles of Gallo Nero wines. Participants were then asked a series of questions designed to assess the likelihood of "point-of-sale" confusion as to the source of the respective wines. Dr. Jacoby found "only a trivial level of likely confusion as to source among these consumers," as "only three of the 216 respondents (1.4%) identified one or more E & J Gallo bottles and one or more Consorzio del Gallo Nero bottles as coming from the same source." Jacoby Survey at 3.

Gallo in response contends that the survey itself is irrelevant, and that even if it were, only 10 of the 216 respondents even referred to the neck seal. Thus Gallo argues that it is unclear whether each of the respondents even saw the critical mark being tested. Moreover, Gallo emphasizes that failure to show "actual" confusion under survey conditions is not dispositive of an infringement claim. Indeed, Gallo notes that it would be impossible at this stage to show actual confusion other than in the artificial setting of a survey as Gallo Nero has not sold a single bottle of wine in the U.S. bearing the words "Gallo Nero." Finally, Gallo proffers its own survey evidence conducted by Robert Lavidge of Elrick & Lavidge, a custom marketing research firm (the "Lavidge Survey"). In that survey, 512 respondents were shown the neck seal with the "Consorzio del Gallo Nero" designation, and another 512 were shown the advertisement which appeared in the *Wine Spectator* in 1986. Gallo reports that 43% of the respondents unequivocally associated the neck seal with the Ernest & Julio Gallo Winery, and 38% did so with regard to the advertisement. Lavidge Survey at 9–10.

Numerous courts hold a side-by-side comparison like the one conducted by Dr. Jacoby to be legally irrelevant in determining whether defendant's use of a similar mark leads to a finding of a likelihood of confusion. "The proper test for likelihood of confusion is not whether consumers would be confused in a side-by-side comparison of the products, but whether confusion is likely when a consumer, familiar with the one party's mark, is presented with the other party's goods alone." Based on the foregoing, it would seem that Gallo Nero's survey evidence is irrelevant to the issue of infringement and that Gallo's own evidence is both relevant and dispositive.

On the other hand, other authorities maintain that the proper survey evidence is that which attempts to most closely replicate the marketplace setting in which consumers will typically encounter the competing marks. Under such a view, then clearly the Gallo Nero survey has relevance in gauging a likelihood of consumer confusion when confronted with bottles of wine sporting the "Consorzio del Gallo Nero" name.

On summary judgment, drawing all inferences in the non-movant's favor, the Court finds nonetheless that there is *some* evidence of a likelihood of confusion under both surveys, even if the Jacoby Survey results in only a "trivial" showing. Moreover, even accepting that Gallo has overstated the results of its own survey, the "adjusted" statistics nonetheless establish that, again, there is *some* evidence of a likelihood of confusion as to source when a consumer is presented with allegedly infringing "Gallo Nero" name. While such showings are not overwhelming, given that no bottle of defendant's wine bearing the "Gallo Nero" name has ever been sold in the United States, and that failure to show actual confusion is not a prerequisite to finding a likelihood of confusion, the Court finds that Gallo Nero has sustained its burden on summary judgment with respect to this factor as well.

7. *Defendant's intent in adopting the "Gallo Nero" name*

Just as with actual confusion, a showing of intent is not necessary to support a finding of a likelihood of confusion. However, where an infringer adopts a particular name with knowledge of plaintiff's mark, courts presume that there was an intent to copy the mark.

The record here establishes that Gallo Nero was aware of the "Gallo" mark prior to beginning its U.S. marketing campaign in 1989, as demonstrated both by its predecessor's direct knowledge of the potentially infringing use of "Gallo" in its advertisements of "Gallo Nero" as well as the communications with the trademark offices of Canada and the United Kingdom.

Gallo Nero in opposition contends that there was no intent to infringe Gallo's marks because the adoption of the "Gallo Nero" name was made in good faith and for sound business reasons. The Court readily acknowledges the extensive and colorful tradition surrounding the relation between the "gallo nero" symbol and the Chianti region of Italy. Moreover, neither the Court nor Gallo has any qualms with Gallo Nero's continued use of the black rooster symbol to identify and distinguish its products in the U.S. marketplace. However, the present issue is not whether Gallo Nero had admirable motivations when it initially adopted its name in 1987, but whether Gallo Nero had knowledge of the potentially infringing effect its use of the "Gallo Nero" and "Consorzio del Gallo Nero" marks would have when it entered the U.S. wine market. The record establishes that Gallo Nero was so aware, and while there may be a question whether such knowledge rises to the level of willful infringement or bad faith, it shows nonetheless that Gallo Nero was at least cognizant of the potentially infringing nature of its use of the "Gallo" name.

8. *Conclusion*

Balancing the foregoing factors, the Court concludes that Gallo has established as a matter of law that it is entitled to summary judgment on its trademark infringement claim. Clearly the "Gallo" mark is a mighty fortress in the U.S. wine market, and use of that name on a bottle of competing wine marketed through similar channels leads to an initial finding of infringement. Compounded with defendant's knowledge that its use of the term "Gallo" in any combination would be deemed an infringement by Gallo–if not, in fact, by a federal district court–and some evidence showing a likelihood of confusion, the foregoing is sufficient to find that defendant's use of the term "Gallo" in conjunction with the promotion and sale of its wines in the United States would lead to a likelihood of consumer confusion with Gallo's products. Therefore Gallo is entitled to summary judgment on its infringement claim.

Banfi Products Corp. v. Kendall–Jackson Winery Ltd.

74 F.Supp.2d 188 (E.D.N.Y.1999).

■ PLATT, J:

Plaintiff Banfi Products Corporation commenced this action against defendant Kendall–Jackson Winery, Ltd. on March 14, 1996, seeking a declaratory judgment of non-infringement. In the alternative, plaintiff has asserted claims for: (1) trademark infringement in violation of the Lanham Act Section 32(1), 15 U.S.C. Section 1114; (2) unfair competition/ false designation of origin and false advertising, in violation of section 43(a) of the Lanham Act, 15 U.S.C. Section 1125(a); and (3) common law trademark infringement.

In response, defendant Kendall–Jackson Winery, Ltd. has asserted counterclaims for: (1) false designation of origin in violation of section 43(a) of the Lanham Act, 15 U.S.C. Section 1125(a); (2) unfair competition in violation of N.Y. Gen. Bus. Law Section 368–e; and (3) unfair business practices in violation of N.Y. Gen. Bus. Law Section 349. Additionally, Kendall–Jackson Winery, Ltd. seeks an order canceling Banfi's federal trademark registration No. 1,743,450 for COL–DI–SASSO.

. . . . For the following reasons, this Court finds that there is no likelihood of confusion.

Findings of Fact

A. Parties

Plaintiff Banfi Products Corporation ("Banfi") is a New York corporation whose principal place of business is in the Village of Old Brookville, Nassau County, New York. At present, Banfi is the largest importer of Italian wines in the United States, importing as much as sixty to seventy percent of all Italian wines coming into this country. Banfi also imports wines produced by its affiliated companies in Montalcino and Strevi, Italy. Domestically, Banfi produces a chardonnay wine in Old Brookville, New York, distributed primarily on Long Island and in Manhattan.

Defendant Kendall–Jackson Winery, Ltd. ("Kendall–Jackson") is a California corporation with its principal place of business in Santa Rosa, California. In 1994, Kendall–Jackson purchased the Robert Pepi Winery, located in Napa Valley, California.

B. COL–DI–SASSO

Banfi imports and sells COL–DI–SASSO, which is produced by an affiliate of Banfi in the Tuscan region of Italy. Dr. Ezio Rivella, Banfi's general manager of Italian operations, conceived of the name COL–DI–SASSO in Montalcino, Italy in 1989 or 1990. COL–DI–SASSO is an Italian term meaning "hill of stone." It was named for a particular rock known as "sasso," prevalent in the region of Tuscany.

Originally, COL–DI–SASSO was introduced as a Cabernet Sauvignon wine. Soon thereafter, however, Banfi changed COL–DI–SASSO to a 50–50 blend of Sangiovese and Cabernet. Banfi began selling this new blend in early 1993.

COL–DI–SASSO's trade dress is very distinctive. Its front label includes an orange-yellow depiction of a landscape, surrounded by a green-black marbleized background. The name COL–DI–SASSO is featured prominently on the front label, as are the words "Sangiovese" and "Cabernet." The back label includes the following legends: (1) "Red Table Wine of Tuscany;" (2) "Banfi S.R.L.;" (3) "50% Sangiovese–50% Cabernet Sauvignon;" (4)"Banfi Vinters;" and (5) "Produce of Italy." Additionally, the word "Banfi" appears in black script on the cork used in bottles of COL–DI–SASSO.

In 1991, Banfi introduced COL–DI–SASSO to the Italian market, and sold substantial quantities from that point forward throughout Europe. Banfi sent its first shipment of COL–DI–SASSO, consisting of two bottles, to the United States in late 1991. Yet commercial distribution and sales of COL–DI–SASSO in the U.S. did not commence until the Spring of 1992. On or about December 29, 1992, the United States Patent and Trademark Office ("PTO") issued Banfi federal trademark registration No. 1,743,450 for COL–DI–SASSO.

By late 1993, Banfi began to experience a sharp increase in U.S. sales of COL–DI–SASSO. To date, over 27,000 cases of COL–DI–SASSO have been sold in the United States. In 1998, Banfi's total U.S. sales in dollars of COL–DI–SASSO exceeded $1.3 million.

COL–DI–SASSO's success is attributable, in part, to the fact that Banfi expends vast sums of money each year on advertising and promotions for COL–DI–SASSO, to wit, $190,000 in 1998, $160,000 in 1997, $140,000 in 1996, and $113,000 in 1995. In promoting COL–DI–SASSO, Banfi uses point-of-sale materials such as displays, brochures, table tents, which are pieces of cardboard placed on restaurant tabletops featuring images of a designated wine bottle, and bottle collars placed over the necks of COL–DI–SASSO bottles.

Banfi sells COL–DI–SASSO to wine and spirit distributors throughout the United States, who in turn distribute the wine to restaurants and retail establishments. Banfi markets COL–DI–SASSO as an affordable, everyday Italian red wine. Accordingly, Banfi encourages its distributors to place the wine in discount liquor stores, supermarkets, and mid-range Italian restaurants such as the Olive Garden and Macaroni Grill. COL–DI–SASSO sells for between $8 and $10 per bottle in stores, and for anywhere from $16 to $23 per bottle in restaurants. Restaurants also feature COL–DI–SASSO by the glass as a promotional tool.

Since its introduction, COL–DI–SASSO has received generally favorable reviews from the media[, including the Houston Chronicle, the Providence Journal–Bulletin, the Washington Post, and the Port St. Lucie News.]

C.   ROBERT PEPI COLLINE DI SASSI

The other wine at issue in this case is ROBERT PEPI COLLINE DI SASSI, produced by the Robert Pepi Winery in Napa Valley, California. In July 1994, defendant Kendall–Jackson Winery ("Kendall–Jackson") purchased the Pepi winery and has continued to produce COLLINE DI SASSI ever since. In late 1989 or early 1990, Robert A. Pepi and his son Robert L. Pepi, founders of the Pepi winery, arrived at the name ROBERT PEPI COLLINE DI SASSI while eating dinner together.

Directly translated, ROBERT PEPI COLLINE DI SASSI means "Robert Pepi little hills of stone." The "Colline" element of ROBERT PEPI COLLINE DI SASSI is a three-syllable word pronounced "Col-ee-ne." Although ROBERT PEPI COLLINE DI SASSI is labeled solely as a Sangiovese varietal, it contains a small amount (typically 15%) of cabernet.

Since the introduction of ROBERT PEPI COLLINE DI SASSI, its trade dress has gone though several changes. Up through the 1993 vintage, the front label on bottles of ROBERT PEPI COLLINE DI SASSI was long and narrow with a jagged top edge. The words "Robert Pepi,""Colline Di Sassi," and "Napa Valley" all appeared on the front label in gold block lettering superimposed on a mauve background. Beginning with the 1994 vintage, the front label again was long and narrow, but was brown-black in hue with a jagged edge along the right side. The front label still contained the legends "Robert Pepi," "Colline Di Sassi," and "Napa Valley" in gold block lettering.

The current trade dress of ROBERT PEPI COLLINE DI SASSI consists of a rectangular wrap-around front label. The label is orange and cream, bearing the legend "Robert Pepi" in black script in the top left corner. The words "Colline Di Sassi" and "Napa Valley Sangiovese" are centered on the front label in black print. The back label reiterates that the wine is produced and bottled in Napa Valley California.

In September 1990, ROBERT PEPI COLLINE DI SASSI labels were approved by the Bureau of Alcohol, Tobacco and Firearms ("BATF"). Of considerable significance, the label approval application listed "ROBERT PEPI" as the "brand name" and "COLLINI (sic) DI SASSI" as the socalled "fanciful name." Thereafter, in October 1990, Pepi began to distribute the 1988 vintage of ROBERT PEPI COLLINE DI SASSI throughout the United States.

Since then, distribution of ROBERT PEPI COLLINE DI SASSI has been relatively limited. Annual case sales of defendant's wine have ranged from 133 cases in 1990, to 462 in 1991, 689 in 1992, 301 in 1993, 170 in 1994, 996 in 1995, 903 in 1996, 37 in 1997, and 1345 in 1998. Pepi did not produce a 1994 vintage of ROBERT PEPI COLLINE DI SASSI due to concerns over quality. Moreover, from 1990 through 1998, advertising expenditures for ROBERT PEPI COLLINE DI SASSI, both by Pepi and Kendall–Jackson, have been minimal.

Kendall–Jackson distributes ROBERT PEPI COLLINE DI SASSI to independent distributors, who in turn sell the wine to restaurants and retail stores. ROBERT PEPI COLLINE DI SASSI has been marketed as an high-end, limited production wine. In fact, after its purchase of the Pepi winery in 1994, Kendall–Jackson included ROBERT PEPI COLLINE DI SASSI as part of its "Artisans & Estates" stable of high-end, specialty wines. Accordingly, both Pepi and Kendall–Jackson have tried to place ROBERT PEPI COLLINE DI SASSI in better or high-priced restaurants and wine shops, as opposed to chain restaurants and discount stores. ROBERT PEPI COLLINE DI SASSI sells for $20 to $25 per bottle in stores, and from $35 to $45 or more in restaurants. Due to its high cost, ROBERT PEPI COLLINE DI SASSI generally is not sold by the glass in restaurants. . . .

D.   Nature of Dispute

This dispute arose in 1994 when John Mariani, Banfi's Chairman Emeritus, saw a reference to the Pepi wine in an article published in USA Today. The article, entitled "California vineyards take on an Italian accent," listed "ROBERT PEPI COLLINO (sic) DI SASSI" as one of several California wines using such Italian grape varietals as Sangiovese. It should be noted that up until the date of the USA Today article, John Mariani had never heard of the mark ROBERT PEPI COLLINE DI SASSI. John Mariani faxed the article to several officers of Banfi with the following handwritten direction: "[s]top Robert Pepi from using 'COLLINO (sic) DI

SASSI.' Ask JM. It is a region not in USA. Recall 'Walnut Creek' "
(emphasis added). Mr. Mariani objected to Pepi's use of the name "COL-
LINE DI SASSI" because, in his view, it was inappropriate for a California
wine to be using a name that implied a connection with the Grande Sasso,
a rock located in Italy's Appenine Mountains.[1]

A copy of Mariani's facsimile was presented to Philip Calderone,
Banfi's Vice President and General Counsel who, like Mariani, had not
heard of ROBERT PEPI COLLINE DI SASSI until that point. In response,
Calderone, without further discussing the matter with Banfi's owners,
wrote a letter to Pepi on March 9, 1994, demanding that Pepi cease
marketing ROBERT PEPI COLLINE DI SASSI because of the risk of
consumer confusion. The letter read as follows:

> Dear Mr. Pepi:
>
> It has come to the attention of Banfi Vinters that your winery is
> marketing a California red wine named Colline di Sassi. Being the U.S.
> trademark holder of the brand name Col di Sasso (sic) used for a
> tuscan red wine, Banfi feels there is a confusing similarity between the
> two brand names.
>
> I respectfully request that you choose another name for the
> referenced product, achieving a phase-out and cease and desist status
> on the "Colline di Sassi" name which conflicts with our trademark. A
> copy of our U.S. trademark is enclosed for your information, and I look
> forward to a written reply.
>
> Very truly yours,
>
>
> BANFI VINTERS
>
> /s/ Philip D. Calderone
>
> Vice President, Associate General Counsel

Pepi's reply letter, dated March 17, 1994, informed Banfi that its rights
in the mark were superior to Banfi's because Pepi obtained BATF approval
for the mark in 1990, whereas Banfi did not obtain federal trademark
registration of its mark until 1992. Pepi further agreed that there is, in
fact, "a confusing similarity in the two brand names" and therefore
requested that Banfi cease using the COL–DI–SASSO mark and withdraw
its trademark registration. Pepi attached various documents to its March
17th letter, including sales figures for ROBERT PEPI COLLINE DI SASSI
as well as the wine's BATF label approval.

---

1. John Mariani's mention of the name
"Walnut Creek" refers to Banfi's attempt [ ]
to use the mark "Walnut Creek" in connec-
tion with a wine it produced near Walnut
Creek, Chile. The BATF denied Banfi's appli-
cation for trademark protection, reasoning
that any use of the name Walnut Creek
might cause consumers to believe that the
wine is produced in Walnut Creek, California.
Thus, Banfi was forced to re-name the wine
WALNUT CREST. Compare Pepi's use of
"Robert Pepi" as its brand name on its
BATF application, as opposed to "Colline di
Sassi."

After conducting an investigation during which it reviewed sales figures, bills of lading, and trade articles relating to the two wines, Banfi concluded that there was no likelihood of confusion between COL–DI–SASSO and ROBERT PEPI COLLINE–DI–SASSI, and accordingly declined to cease using the COL–DI–SASSO mark. To further ensure that there would be no confusion, however, Banfi added the word "Banfi" in gold script along the side of COL–DI–SASSO's front label. In July 1994, defendant Kendall–Jackson purchased Pepi and continued to demand that Banfi cease using the COL–DI–SASSO mark.

In order to resolve this dispute once and for all, Banfi commenced the instant action pursuant to the Lanham Act, 15 U.S.C. Section 1051, et seq., seeking a judgment declaring that its use of the COL–DI–SASSO mark does not infringe Kendall–Jackson's use of ROBERT PEPI COLLINE DI SASSI, i.e., that there is no likelihood of confusion. In response, Kendall–Jackson asserted several counterclaims, arguing that it has priority, the marks are confusing, and therefore Banfi should be enjoined from using the COL–DI–SASSO mark.

E. Facts Relevant to Polaroid Analysis to Determine Likelihood of Confusion

Before this dispute developed, COL–DI–SASSO and ROBERT PEPI COLLINE DI SASSI co-existed for approximately four years without any evidence of actual confusion. No one associated with Banfi had ever heard of ROBERT PEPI COLLINE DI SASSI, nor had Pepi or Kendall–Jackson heard of COL–DI–SASSO. Similarly, there is no evidence that any consumer, distributor, retailer, or critic confused the two wines at issue in this case, as neither Banfi nor Kendall–Jackson ever received misdirected mail or telephone calls. Furthermore, to date, neither party has conducted a market study to determine whether there is, in fact, a likelihood of confusion. Accordingly, during oral argument on Banfi's Motion for Partial Summary Judgment on September 4, 1998, parties stipulated that there is no actual confusion between the two wines.

Moreover, it should be noted that there is widespread third-party use of names similar to COL–DI–SASSO and ROBERT PEPI COLLINE DI SASSI in the wine industry, including, inter alia, CA'DEL SOLO, COLLI-SENESI, COL D'ORCIA, COLLEMANORA, COLLE SOLATO, COLLI FIORENTINI, COLLINA RIONDA DI SERRALUNGA, COLLINE DI AMA, and COLLINE NOVARESI BIANCO.

In terms of the wine industry as a whole, it is well settled that retail wine stores typically segregate wine according to geographic origin, i.e., California, Italy, and Chile. Similarly, restaurant wine lists either separate wines from different countries, or at a minimum include some indication of each wine's geographic origin, along with the vinter's name and the year and price of the wine. In addition, while serving bottles of wine, waiters almost uniformly present the bottle so that the customer can examine the label and smell the cork, which, in the case of COL–DI–SASSO is imprinted with the word "Banfi."

Lastly, with respect to the sophistication of wine consumers, studies, like the one published by The U.S. Wine Market Impact Databank Review and Forecast, have indicated that wine drinkers tend to be older, wealthier, and better educated than the average population. Specifically, wine consumers "60 and over account for some 28% of all wine volume, while those between 50 and 59 consumer another 22 percent." In addition, "[t]he wine consumer is generally an affluent one—more than forty-one percent have incomes of at least $60,000." Finally, survey results indicate that "[a]t least half of the drinkers for all of the wine types (with the exception of Sangria) have some college education...."

Conclusions of Law

. . . .

1. Strength of Kendall–Jackson's Mark

. . . .

In the instant case, as Kendall–Jackson argues and Banfi more or less concedes, ROBERT PEPI COLLINE DI SASSI is an arbitrary mark because it has no meaning to the average consumer, nor does it suggest the qualities and features of the wine. However, a finding that a particular mark is arbitrary does not guarantee a determination that the mark is strong. Instead, this Court still must evaluate the mark's distinctiveness in the marketplace. Courts may consider several factors in determining a particular mark's distinctiveness in the marketplace. For example, the "strength of a mark is [ ] often ascertained by looking at the extent of advertising invested in it, and by the volume of sales of the product." In addition, "extensive third-party use can dilute the strength of a mark."

Here, ROBERT PEPI COLLINE DI SASSI is not particularly distinctive in the marketplace. In the first instance, Kendall–Jackson's advertising expenditures for ROBERT PEPI COLLINE DI SASSI over the last several years have been minimal. Kendall–Jackson's distribution of its wine also has been limited in scale. Furthermore, numerous vinters [sic] have used variations of the words "Colline" and "Sassi" in their respective marks. Accordingly, this first Polaroid factor weighs in favor of Banfi.

2. The Degree of Similarity Between the Two Marks

In determining whether the two marks are similar, and therefore likely to cause consumer confusion, courts should evaluate " 'the overall impression created by the logos and the context in which they are found and consider the totality of factors that could cause confusion among prospective purchasers.' " In doing so, courts may consider "the products' sizes, logos, typefaces and package designs, among other factors."

In the case at bar, the two marks are quite dissimilar. Banfi's mark, COL–DI–SASSO, is composed of three words, separated by hyphens, whereas Kendall–Jackson's ROBERT PEPI COLLINE DI SASSI is composed of five words with no hyphens. There are also phonetic differences between the two marks, to wit, the "Col" element of Banfi's COL–DI–SASSO has one syllable, while the "Colline" element of Kendall–Jackson's mark has three syllables and is pronounced "Col-ee-ne."[2] *See Buitoni Foods Corp. v. Gio. Buton*, 680 F.2d 290, 292 [216 U.S.P.Q. 558] (2d Cir.1982) (noting that differences in the pronunciation between the marks at issue rendered the degree of similarity insubstantial). In addition, the English translations of the two marks differ in that COL–DI–SASSO means "hill of stone," and ROBERT PEPI COLLINE DI SASSI translates into "Robert Pepi little hills of stone."

There are also several key distinctions between the products themselves and the overall impression created by the marks that would prevent consumer confusion. For instance, Banfi's front label includes an orange-yellow depiction of a landscape with a black marbleized background. The Banfi wine's front label features the COL–DI–SASSO name, along with the words "Sangiovese" and "Cabernet." Additionally, the word "Banfi" appears on the side of the front label in gold script and on the cork in black script. Banfi's back label features the legends "Produce of Italy," "Red Table Wine of Italy" and "Banfi Vinters."

By contrast, the front label of ROBERT PEPI COLLINE DI SASSI contains neither a depiction nor a marbleized background. Rather, the cream and orange label features the words "Robert Pepi" in the top left corner, with "Colline Di Sassi" and "Napa Valley Sangiovese" in the center. The back label plainly states that the wine is both produced and bottled in Napa Valley, California. Based on the foregoing, this factor also weighs in Banfi's favor.

3. The Proximity of the Products

Under this Polaroid factor, courts must assess whether the two products at issue compete with each other in the same market.... In doing so, courts should evaluate "the nature of the products themselves, as well as the structure of the relevant market." Differences in price between the two products also should be considered in measuring product proximity.

Taking these criteria in turn, this Court concludes that the products in this case differ in ways that may be deemed material to consumers. First, Banfi's COL–DI–SASSO is a 50–50 blend of Sangiovese and Cabernet. On the other hand, ROBERT PEPI COLLINE DI SASSI is both labeled and marketed solely as a Sangiovese, even though it contains a small percentage of Cabernet. Accordingly, COL–DI–SASSO is marketed as an affordable, everyday red wine, and as such is sold to distributors, who in turn market the wine to discount drug stores, supermarkets, and mid-range Italian restaurant chains. ROBERT PEPI COLLINE DI SASSI, marketed as a high-end, special occasion wine, is sold exclusively in fine restaurants and retail wine stores. In fact, Kendall–Jackson submitted no evidence to

---

2. Even if a prospective purchaser were to mispronounce Colline as a two-syllable word, its pronunciation still would differ from that of plaintiffs COL–DI–SASSO mark.

suggest that the two wines at issue were ever sold in the same location, be it restaurant or retail store.

Additionally, Banfi's COL–DI–SASSO is sold for $8 to $10 per bottle in stores, and $16 to $23 per bottle in restaurants. Conversely, ROBERT PEPI COLLINE DI SASSI is sold for double this price, i.e., $20 to $25 in stores, and $35 to $45 in restaurants. Banfi's wine is often sold by the glass in restaurants as a promotional tool, whereas Kendall–Jackson's is rarely, if ever, sold by the glass. Accordingly, this factor is of little help to Kendall–Jackson's claim that there is a likelihood of confusion.

4. The Likelihood That the Party Alleging Infringement Will "Bridge the Gap"

This factor considers whether Kendall–Jackson will enter Banfi's market.... Here, Kendall–Jackson has presented no evidence to suggest that it intends to produce a 50–50 blend of Sangiovese and Cabernet, produce and bottle a wine in Italy, or reduce the price of ROBERT PEPI COLLINE DI SASSI to match that of Banfi's COL–DI–SASSO. This factor, then, favors Banfi.

5. Actual Confusion

In the instant matter, Kendall–Jackson stipulated to the absence of actual confusion between the two products. Of equal significance, however, is the fact that Kendall–Jackson was ignorant of Banfi's use of the COL–DI–SASSO mark until 1994 when this dispute arose. This co-existence further buttresses this Court's finding that not only is there no actual confusion, but no likelihood of confusion as well.

6. The Alleged Infringer's Good Faith in Adopting the Mark

This factor considers "whether the [alleged infringer] adopted its mark with the intention of capitalizing on [the opposing party's] reputation and goodwill and any confusion between his and the senior user's product." ... One indication of a party's good faith is "the selection of a mark that reflects the product's characteristics."

Here, Banfi demonstrated that it conceived its mark at approximately the same time that Kendall–Jackson adopted its own mark, albeit in Italy as opposed to Napa Valley, California. Moreover, Banfi selected the COL–DI–SASSO name because the wine was produced in Tuscany, a region in which sasso rock is prevalent. Conversely, Pepi adopted its ROBERT PEPI COLLINE DI SASSI mark at a family meal, without any relation to "little hills of stone." Banfi also adopted the COL–DI–SASSO mark without ever having heard of ROBERT PEPI COLLINE DI SASSI. Furthermore, Banfi showed its continuing good faith by initiating this instant action, seeking resolution of both party's rights to the marks at issue. Accordingly, this factor weighs against a finding of likelihood of confusion.

7. The Quality of the Alleged Infringer's Product

Courts consistently have concluded that this factor primarily is concerned with "whether the senior user's reputation could be jeopardized by

virtue of the fact that the junior user's product is of inferior quality." ...
In the case at bar, the evidence establishes that Banfi's COL–DI–SASSO is
not of lesser quality than ROBERT PEPI COLLINE DI SASSI. On the
contrary, since it was first introduced in the United States, COL–DI–
SASSO has received favorable reviews from many critics. Thus, this factor
favors Banfi.

8.   The Sophistication of the Buyers

This final Polaroid factor considers "the general impression of the
ordinary consumer, buying under normal market conditions and giving the
attention such purchasers usually give in purchasing the product at issue."
... In this case, the only evidence relevant to this factor suggests that wine
purchasers are likely to be older, wealthier, and better educated than the
general population. Because Kendall–Jackson submitted no evidence to
contradict these findings, this factor weighs in Banfi's favor.

9.   Balancing the Polaroid Factors

In sum, all eight Polaroid factors favor Banfi, albeit in varying degrees.
Consequently, there is no likelihood that consumers will confuse Banfi's
COL–DI–SASSO, with Kendall–Jackson's ROBERT PEPI COLLINE DI
SASSI.

.   .   .   .

Conclusion

This Court has examined Kendall–Jackson's remaining claims and
finds that they are without merit. Accordingly, for the reasons stated
herein, this Court concludes that there is no likelihood of confusion
between the two marks at issue, and directs the Clerk of the Court to enter
judgment of non-infringement. In view of this conclusion, this Court
dismisses as meritless both parties [sic] remaining claims.

So ordered.

Sutter Home v. Madrona Vinyards, 2005 WL 701599 (N.D. Cal.
2005). Plaintiff Sutter Home is a large California winery, whose wines
include the "Ménage à Trois" series of wines, sold under the "Folie à
Deux" label. The wines sell at about $12 per bottle, and over 80,000 cases
have been sold since 1997. Defendant Madrona Vinyards is a small California winery, whose Rhone-style "Mélange de Trois" wines sell for $16 a
bottle; since 2001, Madrona has produced 1711 cases of "Mélange de
Trois," of which it has sold 1388. The court considered how the use by both
wines of a foreign language affected the analysis of the similarity of the
marks:

> Here, the court's attempt to evaluate the similarity of the relevant
> marks from the perspective of the average American wine purchaser is
> complicated by the fact that both marks are comprised of French
> words. Literally translated, plaintiff's "Ménage à Trois" mark refers to
> a household ("ménage") of three ("trois"), although it commonly

connotes a sexual relationship involving three persons. By way of comparison, defendant's "Mélange de Trois" means a "blend of three," a name that is intended both to reflect the fact that the wine is a blend of three grape varietals and to evoke the French origin of the Rhone varietals from which the wine is made. These definitions are distinctly different and would be perceived as such by anyone with even a passing familiarity with the French language.

The inquiry into the similarity of the two marks does not end there, however. As plaintiff points out, the sound and appearance of the two marks differ only in the substitution of two consonants in "Mélange" vis-a-vis "Ménage" and in the replacement of the preposition "de" with the word "a" as the second word of the marks. Plaintiff argues that these phonetic and orthographic parallels are sufficient to induce confusion in the average American consumer, who, being stubbornly monolingual, is unlikely to perceive the marks as anything more than "French-sounding" words.

In addressing the merits of plaintiff's argument, the court is guided by the so-called "doctrine of foreign equivalents." Under the doctrine, foreign words from common languages are translated into English before undertaking the confusing similarity analysis. However, the doctrine does not apply to every foreign word that appears in a trade-or service mark. Indeed, the Federal Circuit has characterized the doctrine as a "guideline" rather than an "absolute rule," observing that "it should be applied only when it is likely that the ordinary American purchaser would stop and translate the [foreign] word-into its English equivalent."

. . . . [While the doctrine is well-established in trademark registration proceedings,] there is no authoritative guidance on the question of whether the doctrine of foreign equivalents applies where, as here, both of the relevant marks are of foreign origin. The typical doctrine of foreign equivalents case involves the comparison of one foreign-word mark to a mark written in English, and there is some authority to suggest that the doctrine is operative only under those circumstances. However, another view would hold the doctrine to apply with equal force to the instant action despite the fact that the likelihood of confusion inquiry here entails the comparison of two foreign-word marks. As the Trademark Trial and Appeal Board observed in *In re Lar Mor International, Inc.*, 221 U.S.P.Q. 180 (T.T.A.B. 1983), "the fact that both marks may be comprised of foreign words should not mean that [a court] can disregard their meanings." *Id.* at 181. . . . [T]he question is whether the consumer is likely to translate the foreign words. "When it is unlikely that an American buyer will translate the foreign mark and will take it as is, then the doctrine of foreign equivalents will not be applied."

. . . . *Lar Mor*'s reliance on the doctrine of foreign equivalents to compare two foreign-word marks is merely an application of the general rule that two marks are confusingly similar only when their use "would cause confusion of any appreciable number of ordinary prudent purchasers as to source of the goods." This inquiry in turn depends on whether an "appreciable number of purchasers in the United States," who courts presume to speak English as well as the pertinent foreign language, will understand the meaning of the foreign-word mark at issue and translate that mark into its English equivalent. The court finds this standard applicable to the instant action and thus must consider whether an appreciable number of United States consumers of the parties' products would understand the meaning of the phrases "Ménage à trois" and "Mélange de trois."

... [P]laintiff's "Ménage à Trois" mark is so commonly used and understood that it could just as aptly be characterized as part of the lexicon of American English as it could be considered a foreign-language expression. The French words that comprise defendant's mark are almost as widely understood, particularly if one focuses on likely purchasers of the parties' wines. As defendant points out, the word "Mélange" is commonly used to describe wines such as defendant's "Mélange de Trois" that are comprised of a blend of more than one grape varietal. And of course, anyone with even a passing familiarity with the French language would understand the meaning of "de trois." Thus, the English-language definitions of the parties' marks are both familiar to an appreciable number of likely purchasers of the parties' products. The court therefore concludes that the dissimilar meaning of the parties' marks reduces the likelihood that consumers will be confused by defendant's use of the phrase "Mélange de Trois" in connection with the sale of wine.

Against these clearly different meanings, the court must weigh considerations of sound and appearance. *See Horn's, Inc. v. Sanofi Beaute Inc.*, 963 F.Supp. 318, 323 (S.D.N.Y. 1997) (*quoting* 3 J. Thomas McCarthy, Trademarks and Unfair Competition § 23:37, at 23–84 (4th ed. 1996)) (observing that even where the English translation of a foreign mark is used to determine similarity of meaning, "the foreign mark is used when examining similarity in sight and sound"). Plaintiff notes that the marks are each four syllables long and are consonant in significant respects. It is true that the confusion caused by these similarities in sound and appearance might in certain circumstance be mitigated by the information provided by the parties' trade dress and the use of other trademarks in association with the marks at issue here (e.g., "Madrona Vineyards"or "Folie à Deux"). However, while the "[u]se of differing names or distinctive logos in connection with similar marks can reduce the likelihood of confusion," it does not always do so. Plaintiff correctly points out that differences in trade dress and, to a lesser extent, differences in brand, cannot be relied on to distinguish the parties' products in an "on premises" setting, where consumers may order a glass of wine at a bar or make their purchasing decisions based on a restaurant wine list. Thus, it is certainly possible that some consumers, upon viewing or hearing the two marks, would be confused by their phonetic and orthographic similarity, although it is worth noting that wine lists, even by the glass, usually include the source of the wine.

In short, the court finds that a comparison of the definitions of the parties' marks weighs against a conclusion that consumer confusion is likely, whereas considerations of orthography and phonetics favor plaintiff's claim that the marks are confusingly similar. Balancing these disparate findings, the court concludes that the similarity of the parties' marks does not strongly favor either party. However, in the absence of any evidence in the record as it now stands that would quantify these conflicting inferences, the court finds that on balance this factor tips slightly in defendant's favor.

The court next found that the strength of the mark factor favored plaintiff, and that the products, as premium wines sold at similar prices, were closely proximate. By contrast, the "marketing channels used" differed markedly: plaintiff sells to wholesalers and retailers; defendant sells from its on-site tasting room and through wine clubs. The court did not find the parties' common use of websites to market their wines probative of similarity of marketing channels, given "the broad use of the Internet today." The court also found no intent to confuse consumers in defendant's selection of its "Mélange de trois" mark, pointing out that defendant's wine is indeed a blend of three grape varietals. The court held that Sutter Home had not established a likelihood of success on the merits of its infringement claim.

QUESTIONS

1. What are the salient differences that explain the different outcomes in the *E. & J. Gallo* and *Banfi* cases?

2. In evaluating the similarity of the marks, the *E. & J. Gallo Winery* court notes that "gallo" is a common Italian word, and that, in context, plaintiff's and defendant's marks have very different visual impacts, but concludes that "because 'Gallo' is the single 'dominant' or 'substantive' term used by plaintiff on all its products—including the 2 billion bottles of wine already sold—defendant's use of the term 'Gallo' even on a facially distinctive label or in conjunction with other terms" would be confusingly similar. Can you think of any use of the word "gallo" in connection with wine or wine-related products that would be sufficiently dissimilar to make confusion unlikely?

3. Review the court's treatment of the *E. & J. Gallo Winery* defendant's intent. Does the court conclude that Gallo Nero's initial adoption of of its mark was made in good faith, but that its later decision to use that mark on wine exported to the the U.S. was not? Does that make any sense?

4. Does "size matter"? Where defendant is a small producer, and particularly if its goods are high quality or addressed to an elite audience, is a court less likely to find confusion? *See Starbucks Corp. v. Black Bear Micro Roastery*, 2004 WL 2158120 (S.D.N.Y. 2004) (summary judgment for Starbucks denied in action against boutique producer of "Charbucks" dark-roasted coffee beans).

5. How effective are the Polaroid factors at guiding judicial discretion? Does the multi factor test supply meaningful boundaries, or is it a thinly disguised invitation to courts to do whatever they please? Are individual factors more probative of likelihood of confusion than others? Do some factors seem more easily manipulated than others?

Professor Barton Beebe, in a recent study of multifactor likelihood of confusion tests, finds an imbalance in the significance accorded each factor and a willingness by courts to "stampede" the less-significant factors. "Judges employ fast and frugal heuristics to short-circuit the multifactor test ... [and] rely upon a few factors or combinations of factors to make their decisions. The rest of the factors are at best redundant and at worst irrelevant." *An Empirical Study of the Multifactor Tests for Trademark Infringement*, 94 Cal. L. Rev. 1581, 1586 (2006).

6. Professors Beebe's study highlights an underlying judicial tension with regard to the *Polaroid* (or equivalent) factors. Compare the remarks of Judge Cardamone, and Judge Sprizzo's response, in *Centaur Communications, Ltd. v. A/S/M Communications, Inc.*, 830 F.2d 1217 (2d Cir.1987). In a suit by Marketing Week against AD WEEK's Marketing Week, Judge Cardamone, writing for the majority observed:

> This appeal, from a finding of trademark infringement, necessarily implicates the legal concepts of secondary meaning and likelihood of confusion, for which our precedents establish a long list of factors that must be considered, before a determination may be reached. Unfortunately, there is no shortcut. To reach a principled conclusion in a trademark case, it is just as essential to recite the right formulas as it was for Ali Baba to say "Open Sesame" in order to open the door to the treasure cave of the Forty Thieves.

830 F.2d at 1219.

Judge Sprizzo (of the Southern District of New York, sitting by designation) chafed in a concurring opinion:

> I do not share the view that a proper analysis of th[e] factors can or should be properly characterized as a recital of "the right formulas" akin to Ali Baba's magical incantation "Open Sesame," nor do I believe that a proper resolution of future cases raising these issues will be aided or enhanced by encouraging district court judges to perceive their function in the mechanistic fashion which that language suggests.

Id. at 1230.

Can you design a better test? What would it look like? How would it be applied?

INTENT

The court's treatment of intent in the *Gallo Nero* case invokes a line of authority recognizing that a defendant's intent to cause confusion is strong evidence that confusion is likely. What constitutes proof that defendant intended confusion is a more difficult question. Should such intent be inferred solely from defendant's adoption of a mark similar to that of the plaintiff, when other marks are available? Analytically, the inquiry into intent might in any event seem irrelevant. After all, the question is not whether the defendant sought to deceive consumers, but whether he is likely to have succeeded. To presume the bad intender succeeded may be to bootstrap the legal conclusion. Nonetheless, bad intent appears to weigh powerfully in courts' assessments. Professor Beebe, in his aforementioned study, *An Empirical Study of the Multifactor Tests for Trademark Infringement*, finds:

> Courts have long expressed conflicting views on what role the intent factor should and does play in the multifactor test. Some circuits have held, as the Second has, that a finding of bad faith intent creates a "rebuttable legal presumption that the actor's intent to confuse will be successful." Others have held that a finding of bad faith intent may "justify the inference" of confusing similarity or is entitled to "great weight," but have declined to establish a presumption.

> At the same time, certain circuits have declared that "intent is largely irrelevant in determining if consumers likely will be confused as to source." As one district court put it, "the presence or absence of intent does not impact the perception of consumers whose potential confusion is at issue." Notwithstanding the presumptive force it appears to accord to the intent factor, the Second Circuit has been particularly critical of it. . . .

> Other circuits, such as the Fifth, have declared the intent factor to be "critical" or "important" in the limited sense that while the "presence of intent constitutes strong evidence of confusion, the absence of intent is irrelevant in determining likelihood of consumer confusion." Fifth Circuit courts frequently state that "if the mark was adopted with the intent of deriving benefit from the reputation of [the plaintiff,] that fact alone may be sufficient to justify the inference that there is confusing similarity." However, they add, "the lack of guilt is immaterial to the evaluation." Courts that follow this approach typically reason that "one who intends to confuse is more likely to succeed in doing so" or that the defendant's intent "is relevant because it demonstrates the junior user's true opinion as to the dispositive issue, namely, whether confusion is likely." Some hold more precisely that "defendant's intent will indicate a likelihood of confusion only if an intent to confuse consumers is demonstrated via purposeful manipulation of the junior mark to resemble the senior's."

> The data strongly reject the hypothesis that the intent factor is irrelevant to the outcome of the multifactor test. In fact, they suggest that a finding of bad faith intent creates, if not in doctrine, then at least in practice, a nearly un-rebuttable presumption of a likelihood of confusion. All but one of the fifty preliminary injunction opinions in which the court found bad faith intent resulted in a finding of a

likelihood of confusion, and all but one of the seventeen bench trials in which the court found bad faith intent produced the same result....

It is black-letter doctrine across the circuits ... that bad faith intent may be inferred solely from the fact that the parties' marks are similar and the fact that the defendant had knowledge of the plaintiff's mark when it adopted its own, similar mark. The data suggest that this circumstantial inference is the leading basis for a finding of bad faith intent. District courts found bad faith in 102 of the 331 opinions sampled. In fifty-eight of these 102 opinions, the court based its finding of bad faith at least in part on the combination of similarity and defendant's knowledge. In thirty of these fifty-eight opinions, the court also based its finding on direct evidence of bad faith, such as documents produced by the defendant or actions of the defendant after receiving a cease and desist demand from the plaintiff....

Finally, what light do the data shed on the conflict among the courts concerning the proper role of intent in the multifactor analysis? ... [T]he intent factor data suggest that a finding of bad faith intent exerts excessive influence on the outcome of the multifactor test. The facile assumption, evidently quite pervasive among the courts, that if the defendant intended to confuse, then it succeeded in doing so does not do justice to the great diversity of trademark infringement fact patterns before the courts. Further, it loosens the focus of the multifactor analysis on what should be the overriding empirical question of whether consumers are likely to be confused. To be sure, in light of the defendant's bad faith, courts employ the multifactor test to reach what they deem to be the right result. But if trademark law seeks to prevent commercial immorality, then it should do so explicitly. An injunction should issue and damages be granted on that basis alone, and not on the basis of possibly distorted findings of fact as to the likelihood of consumer confusion.

DOES JOINING A HOUSE MARK TO THE DISPUTED MARK REDUCE LIKELIHOOD OF CONFUSION?

The *Gallo Nero* court rejected Gallo Nero's argument that its use of the term "Gallo" only in connection with well-known marks that wine consumers associate with its trade association–*i.e.*, only as part of the phrase "Consorzio del Gallo Nero," in conjunction with its black rooster mark, and on the neck seals of its wine bottles–obviated any likelihood of confusion. In *Vitarroz Corp. v. Borden, Inc.*, 644 F.2d 960 (2d Cir.1981), however, the court believed that the parties' use of their respective, well-known house marks on their packaging would help avoid confusion between "BRAVOS" for tortilla chips and "BRAVO'S" for salted crackers.

As the above cases illustrate, courts' treatment of this issue has not been consistent. In many infringement cases, the use of a house mark, or the defendant's addition of an allegedly distinguishing term to the mark at issue, has been held not to avoid confusion. *E.g., Americana Trading Inc. v. Russ Berrie & Co.*, 966 F.2d 1284 (9th Cir.1992) (defendant's display of housemark along with plaintiff's trademark WEDDING BEARS does not negate likelihood of confusion and, in fact, may create reverse confusion); *General Foods Corp. v. Borden, Inc.*, 191 U.S.P.Q. 674, 682 (N.D.Ill.1976) ("COUNTRY TIME" for a lemonade mix, which also bore house mark "GENERAL FOODS," held infringed by "COUNTY PRIZE" for a lemonade mix, which also bore house mark "BORDEN'S").

A number of cases involving trade dress infringement, however, have given great weight to the use of a prominent, recognized mark. *See, e.g., Conopco, Inc. v. May Dep't Stores Co.*, 46 F.3d 1556 (Fed.Cir.1994), *cert. denied*, 514 U.S. 1078 (1995), *infra*, Chapter 7.B.3 (defendant's private label look-a-like container and label did not infringe plaintiff's VASELINE INTENSIVE CARE trade dress where defendant's recognized mark and logo were prominently used); *L.A. Gear, Inc. v. Thom McAn Shoe Co.*, 988 F.2d 1117, 1134 (Fed.Cir.), *cert. denied*, 510 U.S. 908 (1993) (defendant's look-a-like fashion sneakers not confusingly similar to L.A. Gear's where parties' marks prominently appeared on sneakers); *Merriam–Webster Inc. v. Random House Inc.*, 35 F.3d 65 (2d Cir.1994), *cert. denied*, 513 U.S. 1190 (1995) (use of different logos and publisher names on two competing similar dictionaries "significantly" distinguished the two); *Bristol–Myers Squibb Co. v. McNeil–P.P.C., Inc.*, 973 F.2d 1033, 1046 (2d Cir.1992) (use of parties' EXCEDRIN and TYLENOL marks distinguished two otherwise highly similar trade dresses for competing analgesic products).; *Turtle Wax, Inc. v. First Brands Corp.*, 781 F.Supp. 1314, 1326 (N.D.Ill.1991) (prominent use of defendant's SIMONIZ mark on car wax product with similar trade dress to plaintiff's product noted as factor against finding likelihood of confusion).

For an example of a decision relying upon the use of house marks by both parties as a factor in diminishing any likelihood of confusion, *see Estee Lauder Inc. v. The Gap, Inc.*, 108 F.3d 1503 (2d Cir.1997) ("100%" for Old Navy's body lotion product not confusingly similar to "100%" for Estee Lauder's skin care product where house marks appeared on the parties' respective products which were sold in different channels of trade).

In **Bumble Bee Seafoods, L.L.C. v. UFS Industries, Inc.**, 2004 WL 1637017 (S.D.N.Y. 2004), Sally Sherman Foods highlighted its use of Bumble Bee brand tuna to make tuna salads, which Sally Sherman sold in five-pound tubs. A label on the lid of the tub truthfully stated that the salad was "made with Bumble Bee tuna." Bumble Bee claimed that the label would confuse consumers into believing that Bumble Bee had authorized or sponsored the Sally Sherman salads, and therefore sued to enjoin mention of its tuna brand on the lids of the salad containers.

> Should the makers of tuna salad be preliminarily enjoined from stating on its label that it is "Made with Bumble Bee Tuna" when the trademark to "Bumble Bee Tuna" is owned by another entity? The answer, in the context of the facts of this action, is "no." ...

> Bumble Bee is a leading provider of tuna in the United States and owns several well-established and widely recognized trademarks under

which it has marketed its products since 1910. Bumble Bee has created a Quality Assurance Program by which it authorizes tuna salad processing companies to manufacture and market tuna salad using its products and bearing its marks.

At the end of 2002, Bumble Bee and Sally Sherman discussed the possibility that Sally Sherman would become a participant in the Quality Assurance Program, thereby allowing Sally Sherman to use the Bumble Bee mark on its tuna salad. As part of that application process, Sally Sherman completed and passed a Quality Assurance Survey designed to screen potential participants in the Quality Assurance Program. As the next step in the application process, Bumble Bee then scheduled an onsite inspection at Sally Sherman's facilities, but Sally Sherman withdrew its application one week later.

Sally Sherman purchased a "substantial" amount of Bumble Bee tuna in 2003 "for use in making its tuna salad." In February 2004, Bumble Bee discovered that Sally Sherman distributed to delicatessens and supermarkets its five pound tubs of tuna salad, the lid of which stated: Sally Sherman Tuna Salad (with the Sally Sherman logo); Made with 100% Hellmann's Real Mayonnaise (with Hellmann's logo); Made with Bumble Bee Tuna (without the Bumble Bee logo). Bumble Bee had never authorized Sally Sherman to state "Made with Bumble Bee Tuna" on its lids. ...Extensive correspondence between Bumble Bee and Sally Sherman ensued; defendant insisted it was making fair use of Bumble Bee's name, triggering this litigation....

There is No Trademark Violation Because There Is No Deception

On the one hand, Bumble Bee concedes that Sally Sherman is entitled to list in small type within the ingredients on its tuna salad lids the words "made with Bumble Bee tuna a registered trademark of Bumble Bee Seafoods, LLC not affiliated." On the other hand, Sally Sherman concedes that it cannot simply label its tuna salad with "Bumble Bee" as the brand identifier. The lid at issue presents a use of Bumble Bee's trademark that lies somewhere between those examples. "Made with Bumble Bee Tuna" is not written along with the other ingredients; nor does the label falsely state that it is Bumble Bee Tuna Salad. This Court's analysis focuses upon whether the lids are deceptive—in other words, do they lead the consumer to believe that Bumble Bee is the source of Sally Sherman's tuna *salad* or endorses this tuna salad?

To understand whether these lids are deceptive, this Court's analysis begins with the specific audience that will read the label's contentious phrase: "Sally Sherman Tuna Salad: Made with Bumble Bee Tuna." These labels are affixed solely on five pound tubs of tuna salad and are sold exclusively to delicatessens and supermarkets for further sale out of the deli counter. The counterman will use the Sally Sherman product to sell to the retail customer a certain weight of tuna salad or it can be used to make sandwiches for the retail customer. The lidded tubs themselves do not find their way to the ultimate consumer of the tuna salad; the tubs are sold to commercial entities whose employees remove the tuna salad from the tubs to sell it in smaller quantities to the ultimate consumer.

There is nothing in the record of this action to support the proposition that a buyer for delicatessens and supermarkets lacks the commercial familiarity and sophistication to understand that Sally Sherman makes the tuna salad, and one component of that salad is Bumble Bee Tuna. Moreover, a deli buyer must affirmatively place an order with Sally Sherman—not Bumble Bee—for this tuna salad. The law permits the use of a component owner's trademark for descriptive use provided that use is not deceptive. . . . No reasonable deli buyer would be deceived after ordering tuna salad from Sally Sherman to think that instead he received Bumble Bee tuna salad. . . .

IS LIKELIHOOD OF CONFUSION A QUESTION OF FACT OR A QUESTION OF LAW?

Judicial attempts at characterizing the likelihood of confusion as an issue of law or fact, or both, have produced serious conflict among the circuits, and indeed, even within the circuits themselves. Clearly, the determination bears significantly on many aspects of a trademark case, including appeals, preliminary injunctions, and motions for summary judgment. Determining whether likelihood of confusion is an issue of law or fact greatly affects the standard of review applicable to federal appellate courts. Under F.R.C.P. 52(a), if the issue is one of fact, an appellate court must adopt the conclusion of the trial court unless it determines the underlying facts to be "clearly erroneous"—a "definite and firm conviction [of an appellate court] that a mistake has been committed." *See Inwood Laboratories, Inc. v. Ives Laboratories, Inc.,* 456 U.S. 844 (1982). The appellate court's authority is restricted in this manner because the trier of fact is deemed to be best situated to evaluate the evidence before it. However, if the likelihood of confusion issue is considered one of law, an appellate court may make an independent review of the facts and will not be bound by the lower court's conclusion.

Historically, likelihood of confusion has been labeled an issue of fact. The RESTATEMENT (THIRD) OF UNFAIR COMPETITION (1993) explains in a comment to § 21 "Proof of Likelihood of Confusion—Market Factors"

> m. *Question of law or fact.* Although the cases are not unanimous, whether the defendant's use of a trademark creates a likelihood of confusion is properly regarded as a question of fact. In jury trials the issue is submitted to the jury with appropriate instructions and the jury's determination is entitled to the usual deference accorded jury verdicts. In non-jury cases the findings of the trial judge concerning the likelihood of confusion should be subject to reversal only if clearly erroneous. Some courts have held that while findings relating to the relevant factors described in

this Section present questions of fact subject to a clearly erroneous standard of review, the balancing of those factors to determine the ultimate issue of likelihood of confusion is a question of law subject to de novo review. However, the likelihood of confusion is determined by the totality of the circumstances rather than the summation of discrete factors, and the better view, adopted by the majority of courts, regards likelihood of confusion as a question of fact subject to the clearly erroneous rule. The interpretation of the factors listed in this Section, such as the meaning of "strength: and its substantive relevance to the likelihood of confusion, remain issues of law."

Circuits have, more often than not, also classified it as such, and have thus applied the "clearly erroneous" standard of review. *Keds Corp. v. Renee Int'l Trading Corp.*, 888 F.2d 215 (1st Cir.1989); *American Home Products Corp. v. Barr Laboratories, Inc.*, 834 F.2d 368 (3d Cir.1987); *Pizzeria Uno Corp. v. Temple*, 747 F.2d 1522 (4th Cir.1984); *Marathon Mfg. Co. v. Enerlite Products Corp.*, 767 F.2d 214 (5th Cir.1985); *Smith Fiberglass Products, Inc. v. Ameron, Inc.*, 7 F.3d 1327 (7th Cir.1993); *Everest Capital Ltd. v. Everest Funds Management, Ltd.*, 393 F.3d 755 (8th Cir.2005); *Quiksilver, Inc. v. Kymsta Corp.*, 466 F.3d 749 (9th Cir.2006); *Sally Beauty Co., Inc. v. Beautyco, Inc.*, 304 F.3d 964 (10th Cir.2002); *Dieter v. B & H Industries of Southwest Florida, Inc.*, 880 F.2d 322 (11th Cir.1989), *cert. denied*, 498 U.S. 950 (1990); *see generally* 3 McCarthy, *supra*, § 23:73 (4th ed.2001).

By contrast, in viewing likelihood of confusion as a question of law, rather than fact, the Court of Appeals for the Federal Circuit provides itself with greater flexibility in reversing TTAB decisions since it may review the facts *de novo* and not pursuant to the "clearly erroneous" standard. *Giant Food, Inc. v. Nation's Foodservice, Inc.*, 710 F.2d 1565 (Fed.Cir.1983); *Shen Mfg. Co., Inc. v. Ritz Hotel, Ltd.*, 393 F.3d 1238 (Fed.Cir.2004).

In yet another approach, the Second and Sixth Circuits have characterized the issue as a mixed question of law and fact and have thereby established a two-level test to determine likelihood of confusion: the initial analysis of factors in the likelihood of confusion calculus (similarity of marks, identity of products, relationship between channels of trade, etc.) is deemed an exercise in fact finding, reviewable pursuant to the "clearly erroneous" standard. The ultimate determination of likelihood of confusion based on those factors, however, is viewed as a legal conclusion. *Bristol–Myers Squibb Co. v. McNeil–P.P.C., Inc.*, 973 F.2d 1033 (2d Cir.1992); *General Motors Corp. v. Lanard Toys, Inc.*, 468 F.3d 405 (6th Cir.2006). This double-layered approach has been questioned by the Supreme Court, which noted:

> Rule 52(a) broadly requires that findings of fact not be set aside unless clearly erroneous. It does not make exceptions or purport to exclude certain categories of fact findings from the obligation of a court of appeals to accept a district court's findings unless clearly erroneous. It does not divide facts into categories; in

particular, *it does not divide findings of fact into those that deal with "ultimate" and those that deal with "subsidiary" facts.*

Pullman–Standard, Div. of Pullman, Inc. v. Swint, 456 U.S. 273, *on remand,* 692 F.2d 1031 (5th Cir.1982) (emphasis added).

Predictably, the diverging viewpoints in this area have produced a muddled body of case law, characterized by such inconsistency among and within the circuits that it has become difficult to predict how a court will deal with a particular case.

2.   Initial Interest Confusion

Mobil Oil Corp. v. Pegasus Petroleum Corp.

818 F.2d 254 (2d Cir.1987).

■ Lumbard, Circuit Judge:

Mobil Oil Corporation brought this action in the Southern District charging Pegasus Petroleum Corporation with trademark infringement and unfair competition, 15 U.S.C. § 1114(1); false designation of origin, 15 U.S.C. § 1125(a); and trademark dilution, N.Y. Gen. Bus. Law § 368–d. On July 8, 1986, after a three-day bench trial, Judge MacMahon entered judgment for Mobil on each of its claims, dismissed Pegasus Petroleum's counterclaims seeking to cancel Mobil's trademark registration, and enjoined Pegasus Petroleum from using the mark "Pegasus" in connection with the petroleum industry or related businesses. We affirm.

Mobil, one of the world's largest corporations, manufactures and sells a vast array of petroleum products to industrial consumers and to the general public. Since 1931, Mobil has made extensive use of its well-known "flying horse" symbol—representing Pegasus, the winged horse of Greek mythology—in connection with its petroleum business. Mobil displays this registered trademark, usually in red, but occasionally in blue, black, white, or outline form, at virtually all its gasoline service stations (usually on an illuminated disk four feet in diameter); in connection with all petroleum products sold at its service stations; in connection with the sale of a variety of its other petroleum products; on its oil tankers, barges, and other vehicles; and on its letterhead. As the district court explained, it is "undisputed that Mobil's extensive use of the flying horse symbol for such a long period of time in connection with all of Mobil's commercial activity has rendered it a very strong mark. Indeed, counsel for [Pegasus Petroleum] could think of few trademarks, if any, that were stronger trademarks in American commerce today."

As part of its petroleum business, Mobil buys and sells crude and refined petroleum products in bulk, an activity known as oil trading, to insure a continuous flow of oil to its refineries, and ultimately to its customers. The oil trading market is tight-knit and sophisticated: It encompasses a select group of professional buyers and brokers, representing approximately 200 oil companies, wholesalers, and oil traders; deals are in the hundred of thousands, or millions of dollars, and in tens of tons; and, oil traders do not consummate deals with strangers except after a thorough credit check. Mobil does not use its flying horse symbol in connection with its oil trading business.

Pegasus Petroleum, incorporated in 1981, confines its activities to oil trading, and does not sell directly to the general public. Its founder, Gregory Callimanopulos, testified that he selected the name "Pegasus Petroleum" because he wanted a name with both mythical connotations and alliterative qualities. Callimanopulos admitted that he knew of Mobil's flying horse symbol when he picked the name, but claimed that he did not know that the symbol represented Pegasus or that Mobil used the word "Pegasus" in connection with its petroleum business. Shortly after the genesis of Pegasus Petroleum, Ben Pollner, then president of the company, sent a letter to 400–500 people in the oil trading business informing them about Pegasus Petroleum's formation. The letter stated that Pegasus Petroleum was part of the "Callimanopulos group of companies," and used an interlocking double P as a letterhead. Pegasus Petroleum has never used a flying horse symbol and sells no products with the name "Pegasus" on them.

In 1982, Mobil approached Pegasus Petroleum after learning of its use of the mark "Pegasus." When attempts to reach an agreement failed, Mobil filed the instant suit. The case proceeded to trial before Judge MacMahon, without a jury. After examining the criteria set forth in *Polaroid Corp. v. Polarad Electronics Corp.*, 287 F.2d 492, 495 (2d Cir.), *cert. denied,* 368 U.S. 820 (1961), Judge MacMahon concluded that "there is a sufficient likelihood of confusion between [Mobil's flying horse symbol] and [Pegasus Petroleum's use of the 'Pegasus' mark] to grant [Mobil] relief under the Lanham Act." Judge MacMahon also held for Mobil on its unfair competition, false designation, and antidilution claims; and enjoined Pegasus Petroleum's further use of the mark "Pegasus" in connection with the oil industry. With Mobil's consent, the injunction has been stayed, pending resolution of this appeal.

The Lanham Act prohibits the use of "any reproduction, counterfeit, copy, or colorable imitation of a registered mark" where "such use is likely to cause confusion, or to cause mistake, or to deceive." 15 U.S.C. § 1114(1)(a). To state a claim under this section, a plaintiff must show a "likelihood that an appreciable number of ordinarily prudent purchasers are likely to be misled, or indeed simply confused, as to the source of the goods in question." … We agree with both the district court's determination of each of the Polaroid factors and its balancing of those factors to arrive at its conclusion that Pegasus Petroleum infringed upon Mobil's senior mark—the flying horse.

Pegasus Petroleum does not dispute the district court's conclusion that the strength of Mobil's flying horse mark is "without question, and perhaps without equal." As an arbitrary mark—there is nothing suggestive of the petroleum business in the flying horse symbol—Mobil's symbol deserves "the most protection the Lanham Act can provide." *Lois Sportswear,*

U.S.A., Inc. v. Levi Strauss & Co., 799 F.2d 867, 871 (2d Cir.1986). On the
other hand, Pegasus Petroleum vigorously attacks the district court's
finding of similarity between the two marks. Pegasus Petroleum argues
that the district court erred by blindly equating the word "Pegasus" with
its pictorial representation—Mobil's flying horse. While we agree that
words and their pictorial representations should not be equated as a matter
of law, a district court may make such a determination as a factual matter.
See, e.g., Beer Nuts, Inc. v. King Nut Co., 477 F.2d 326, 329 (6th Cir.) ("It
is well settled that words and their pictorial representation are treated the
same in determining the likelihood of confusion between two marks."), *cert.
denied,* 414 U.S. 858 (1973); *Izod, Ltd. v. Zip Hosiery Co.,* 405 F.2d 575, 577
(C.C.P.A. 1969) ("Members of the purchasing public viewing appellant's
pictorial representation of a feline animal as applied to men's and women's
outer shirts and appellee's literal designation TIGER HEAD for men's
work socks might well and reasonably conclude that the respective goods of
the parties emanated from the same source."); *Instrumentalist Co. v.
Marine Corps League,* 509 F. Supp. 323, 328 (N.D.Ill.1981) ("the fact that
defendants' certificate most prominently displays a picture of Sousa (rather
than a literal transcription of his name) does not preclude a finding of
infringement"). Judge MacMahon made such a determination here:

> We find that the similarity of the mark exists in the strong
> probability that prospective purchasers of defendant's product will
> equate or translate Mobil's symbol for "Pegasus" and vice versa.

> We find that the word "Pegasus" evokes the symbol of the
> flying red horse and that the flying horse is associated in the mind
> with Mobil. In other words, the symbol of the flying horse and its
> name "Pegasus" are synonymous.

That conclusion finds support in common sense as well as the record.

The third *Polaroid* factor addresses the competitive proximity between
the two marks. Pegasus Petroleum points out that while Judge MacMahon
correctly found that Mobil and Pegasus Petroleum both compete in the oil
trading business, Mobil does not use its flying horse trademark in that
field. However, "direct competition between the products is not a prerequisite to relief. . . . Confusion, or the likelihood of confusion, not competition,
is the real test of trademark infringement." Both Mobil and Pegasus
Petroleum use their marks in the petroleum industry. *See, e.g., AMF Inc. v.
Sleekcraft Boats,* 599 F.2d 341, 350 (9th Cir.1979) (competitive proximity
may be found where goods are similar in use and function); *Syntex
Laboratories, Inc. v. Norwich Pharmacal Co.,* 437 F.2d 566 (2d Cir.1971)
(same).

Moreover, competitive proximity must be measured with reference to
the first two *Polaroid* factors: The unparalleled strength of Mobil's mark
demands that it be given broad protection against infringers. *See, e.g.,
James Burrough Ltd. v. Sign of Beefeater, Inc.,* 540 F.2d 266, 276 (7th
Cir.1976) ("A mark that is strong because of its fame or its uniqueness, is
more likely to be remembered and more likely to be associated in the public
mind with a greater breadth of products or services than is a mark that is

weak. . . ."); *R.J. Reynolds, Tobacco Co. v. R. Seelig & Hille,* 201 U.S.P.Q. 856, 860 (T.M.T.A.B. 1978) ("the law today rewards a famous or well-known mark with a larger cloak of protection than in the case of a lesser known mark because of the tendency of the consuming public to associate a relatively unknown mark with one to which they have long been exposed if the [relatively unknown] mark bears any resemblance thereto"). Mobil's ubiquitous presence throughout the petroleum industry further increases the likelihood that a consumer will confuse Pegasus Petroleum with Mobil. *See Armco, Inc. v. Armco Burglar Alarm Co.,* 693 F.2d 1155, 1161 (5th Cir.1982) ("Diversification makes it more likely that a potential customer would associate the non-diversified company's services with the diversified company, even though the two companies do not actually compete."). Finally, the great similarity between the two marks—the district court concluded that they were "synonymous"—entitles Mobil's mark to protection over a broader range of related products. *Cf. SquirtCo v. Seven–Up Co.,* 628 F.2d 1086, 1091 (8th Cir.1980) (closely related products require less similarity to support a finding of trademark infringement). We agree with the district court's finding of competitive proximity.

Our evaluation of the first three *Polaroid* factors, perhaps the most significant in determining the likelihood of confusion, *see Vitarroz v. Borden, Inc.,* 644 F.2d 960, 966 (2d Cir.1981), strongly supports the district court's conclusion that such a likelihood exists. The district court's finding under the fourth *Polaroid* factor that Pegasus Petroleum did not innocently select its potentially confusing mark reinforces this conclusion: Intentional copying gives rise to a presumption of a likelihood of confusion. *Perfect Fit Industries v. Acme Quilting Co.,* 618 F.2d 950, 954 (2d Cir.1980) (citing cases). The district court discredited Gregory Callimanopulos's testimony that "he did not intentionally choose the tradename 'Pegasus' with either the symbol of Mobil's flying horse or Mobil's wordmark in mind." The court explained:

> Mr. Callimanopulos is obviously an educated, sophisticated man who, from his prior shipping business, was familiar with the flying horse and from his own background and education and awareness of Greek mythology could not have escaped the conclusion that the use of the word "Pegasus" would infringe the tradename and symbol of the plaintiff.

In response, Pegasus Petroleum first contends that this finding is clearly erroneous given the objective evidence before the court, specifically pointing to its letter to the trade of June, 1982, which stated that it was a member of the Callimanopulos group of companies. While this correspondence was one piece of evidence for the district court to consider, it falls far short of establishing, by itself, Pegasus Petroleum's good faith. Pegasus Petroleum also notes that "actual and constructive notice of another company's prior registration of the mark . . . [is] not *necessarily* indicative of bad faith, because the presumption of an exclusive right to use a registered mark extends only so far as the goods or services noted in the registration certificate." *McGregor–Doniger, Inc. v. Drizzle, Inc.,* 599 F.2d

1126, 1137 (2d Cir.1979) (emphasis added). However, actual or constructive knowledge *may* signal bad faith. Indeed, "[i]n this circuit and others, numerous decisions have recognized that the second comer has a duty to so name and dress his product as to avoid all likelihood of consumers confusing it with the product of the first comer." *Harold F. Ritchie Inc. v. Chesebrough–Pond's, Inc.*, 281 F.2d 755, 758 (2d Cir.1960) (footnote omitted); *see generally* 2 J. McCarthy, *supra,* § 23:33 at 148 ("Where we can perceive freedom of choice with full knowledge of a senior user's mark, we can readily read into defendant's choice of a confusingly similar mark the intent to get a free ride upon the reputation of a well-known mark."). We believe the record clearly substantiates Judge MacMahon's inference of bad faith.

The existence of some evidence of actual confusion, the fifth *Polaroid* factor, further buttresses the finding of a likelihood of confusion. *See, e.g., World Carpets, Inc. v. Dick Littrell's New World Carpets,* 438 F.2d 482, 489 (5th Cir.1971) ("While . . . it is not necessary to show actual confusion . . . [t]here can be no more positive or substantial proof of the likelihood of confusion than proof of actual confusion.") (footnotes omitted). Both Mobil and Pegasus Petroleum offered surveys of consumers and of members of the oil trading industry as evidence relating to the existence of actual confusion between the two marks. The district court properly admitted these surveys into evidence, despite claims of statistical imperfections by both sides, as those criticisms affected the weight accorded to the evidence rather than its admissibility. After reviewing these surveys, Judge Macmahon concluded that there was "evidence of actual confusion." His decision was not clearly erroneous. *Id.*

Pegasus Petroleum argues that the absence of misdirected mail and telephone calls between the parties, and the fact that Pegasus Petroleum must post a letter of credit as security during its oil trading deals while Mobil need not, prove that no actual confusion between the two firms existed. This argument misunderstands the district court's opinion. Judge MacMahon found a likelihood of confusion not in the fact that a third party would do business with Pegasus Petroleum believing it related to Mobil, but rather in the likelihood that Pegasus Petroleum would gain crucial credibility during the initial phases of a deal. For example, an oil trader might listen to a cold phone call from Pegasus Petroleum—an admittedly oft-used procedure in the oil trading business—when otherwise he might not, because of the possibility that Pegasus Petroleum is related to Mobil. The absence of misdirected phone calls and the difference in the letter of credit requirements are other matters.

Pegasus Petroleum never rebutted the inference of a likelihood of confusion. The district court did not examine the sixth *Polaroid* factor— whether Mobil would "bridge the gap" by expanding its use of the flying horse symbol into the oil trading market (Mobil presently competes, but does not use its flying horse trademark, in the oil trading field). Nevertheless, "sufficient likelihood of confusion may be established although likelihood of bridging the gap is not demonstrated." *McGregor–Doniger, supra,*

599 F.2d at 1136. The absence of an intent to bridge the gap does not negate a finding of a likelihood of confusion in the market as presently constituted. The Lanham Act extends trademark protection to related goods in order to guard against numerous evils in addition to restraints on the possible expansion of the senior user's market, including consumer confusion, tarnishment of the senior user's reputation, and unjust enrichment of the infringer.

The seventh *Polaroid* factor suggests that the court examine the quality of Pegasus Petroleum's product. The district court made no findings on this issue. Pegasus Petroleum argues that its product—oil—does not differ from that sold by Mobil. However, a senior user may sue to protect his reputation even where the infringer's goods are of top quality. *See, e.g., Wesley–Jessen Div. of Schering Corp. v. Bausch & Lomb Inc.,* 698 F.2d 862, 867 (7th Cir.1983) ("Even if the infringer's goods are of high quality, the victim has the right to insist that its reputation not be imperiled by another's actions."); *James Burrough, Ltd. v. Ferrara,* 6 Misc. 2d 692, 694, 165 N.Y.S.2d 825, 826 (Sup. Ct. 1957) ("plaintiff is not required to put its reputation in defendant's hands, no matter how capable those hands may be"); 2 J. McCarthy, *supra,* § 24:5 at 176–77 ("If the other user sometime in the future engaged in false advertising, or cheated customs, or employed a rude salesperson, or simply sold some shoddy merchandise, the first user of the mark would suffer because buyers would link them together through the medium of the similar marks.").

We finally turn to the eighth *Polaroid* factor, the sophistication of purchasers. The district court concluded that, "even though defendant's business is transacted in large quantities only with sophisticated oil traders, there is still and nevertheless a likelihood of confusion." We agree. As explained above, the district court's concerns focused upon the probability that potential purchasers would be misled into an initial interest in Pegasus Petroleum. Such initial confusion works a sufficient trademark injury. The district court's concern had a sufficient basis in fact despite the sophistication of the oil trading market: Pegasus Petroleum admits that it solicits business through telephone calls to potential customers. Pegasus Petroleum also acknowledges that "[t]rust, in the oil industry, is of paramount importance." Finally, Mobil's Oil Trading Department executive, Thomas Cory, testified that he did not undertake an investigation of a new company before initially dealing with it. Such an investigation was undertaken only prior to the culmination of a deal.

For the foregoing reasons, we agree with the district court's finding that Pegasus Petroleum infringed on Mobil's registered flying horse trademark and therefore affirm its judgment. . . .

Affirmed.

Blockbuster Entertainment Group v. Laylco, Inc., 869 F.Supp. 505 (E.D.Mich.1994). Blockbuster challenged defendant's use of the name Video Busters. Video Busters finally argue that their use of a name confusingly similar to "Blockbuster Video" was not actionable under the

Lanham Act if customers were not likely to be confused at the time they actually rent video tapes in Video Busters' stores. Video Busters further contended that while consumers were likely to be confused initially by the similarity of the two stores' names, they were not likely to be confused once they entered Video Busters' stores to rent video cassettes because of the different appearance and layout of Video Busters and Blockbuster Video's stores.

The court relied on Sixth Circuit precedent, holding that the Lanham Act's protection was not limited to confusion at the "point of sale," *i.e.*, the time when actual purchases take place.

Point of sale confusion Not the issue

Rather, the Act protects against confusion among potential customers and protects the reputation among the general public of trade mark holders. (citations omitted) [T]he issue in a trade mark action is not limited to whether a purchaser would buy an allegedly infringing product thinking it was actually a product of or had some connection to the owner of the original mark. Instead, the court held that the issue is the degree of likelihood that the allegedly infringing name would attract potential customers based on the reputation earned by the owner of the original mark.

Therefore, the issue in this case is the degree of likelihood that the name "Video Busters" would attract potential customers based on the reputation built by Blockbuster. That a customer would recognize that Video Busters is not connected to Blockbuster after entry into a Video Busters store and viewing the Video Busters membership application, brochure, video cassette jacket, and store layout is unimportant. The critical issue is the degree to which Video Busters might attract potential customers based on the similarity to the Blockbuster name. The court finds that Video Busters might attract some potential customers based on the similarity to the Blockbuster name. Because the names are so similar and the products sold are identical, some unwitting customers might enter a Video Busters store thinking it is somehow connected to Blockbuster. Those customers probably will realize shortly that Video Busters is not related to Blockbuster, but under *Esercizio [Ferrari S.P.A. v. Roberts*, 944 F.2d 1235 (6th Cir.1991)] and *Grotrian [Helfferich, Schulz, Th. Steinweg Nachf. v. Steinway & Sons*, 523 F.2d 1331 (2d Cir.1975)] that is irrelevant.

QUESTION

Note the Second Circuit's discussion of the "actual confusion" and "sophistication of purchasers" factors in *Pegasus*. The court upheld the finding of likely confusion by highly sophisticated oil traders because defendant's use of the Pegasus name might evoke Mobil Oil and thereby secure defendant initial access to purchasers. Should this kind of "confusion" be cognizable, if the initial misimpression is dispelled by the time a purchase decision is made? Why or why not? *See also Elvis Presley Enterprises, Inc. v. Capece*, 141 F.3d 188 (5th Cir.1998) (considered the relevance of initial interest in defendant's VELVET ELVIS nightclub as a result of impressions that club might be associated with Presley or Presley merchandise).

FACILITATING INITIAL INTEREST CONFUSION ON THE INTERNET

Playboy Enterprises, Inc. v. Netscape Communications Corporation

354 F.3d 1020 (9th Cir.2004).

■ T.G. NELSON, CIRCUIT JUDGE:

Playboy Enterprises International, Inc. (PEI) appeals from the district court's grant of summary judgment in favor of Netscape Communications Corporation and Excite, Inc. PEI sued defendants for trademark infringement and dilution. We have jurisdiction pursuant to 28 U.S.C. § 1291. Because we conclude that genuine issues of material fact preclude summary judgment on both the trademark infringement and dilution claims, we reverse and remand.

I.   FACTS

This case involves a practice called "keying" that defendants use on their Internet search engines. Keying allows advertisers to target individuals with certain interests by linking advertisements to pre-identified terms. To take an innocuous example, a person who searches for a term related to gardening may be a likely customer for a company selling seeds. Thus, a seed company might pay to have its advertisement displayed when searchers enter terms related to gardening. After paying a fee to defendants, that company could have its advertisements appear on the page listing the search results for gardening-related terms: the ad would be "keyed" to gardening-related terms. Advertisements appearing on search result pages are called "banner ads" because they run along the top or side of a page much like a banner.

Defendants have various lists of terms to which they key advertisers' banner ads. Those lists include the one at issue in this case, a list containing terms related to sex and adult-oriented entertainment. Among the over–400 terms in this list are two for which PEI holds trademarks: "playboy" and "playmate." Defendants *require* adult-oriented companies to link their ads to this set of words. Thus, when a user types in "playboy," "playmate," or one of the other listed terms, those companies' banner ads appear on the search results page.

PEI introduced evidence that the adult-oriented banner ads displayed on defendants' search results pages are often graphic in nature and are confusingly labeled or not labeled at all. In addition, the parties do not dispute that buttons on the banner ads say "click here." When a searcher complies, the search results page disappears, and the searcher finds him or herself at the advertiser's website. PEI presented uncontroverted evidence that defendants monitor "click rates," the ratio between the number of times searchers click on banner ads and the number of times the ads are shown. Defendants use click rate statistics to convince advertisers to renew their keyword contracts. The higher the click rate, the more successful they deem a banner ad.

* * *

III. DISCUSSION

* * *

2. PEI's case for trademark infringement.

The "core element of trademark infringement," the likelihood of confusion, lies at the center of this case. No dispute exists regarding the other requirements set forth by the statute: PEI clearly holds the marks in question and defendants used the marks in commerce without PEI's permission.

PEI's strongest argument for a likelihood of confusion is for a certain kind of confusion: initial interest confusion. Initial interest confusion is customer confusion that creates initial interest in a competitor's product. Although dispelled before an actual sale occurs, initial interest confusion impermissibly capitalizes on the goodwill associated with a mark and is therefore actionable trademark infringement.

PEI asserts that, by keying adult-oriented advertisements to PEI's trademarks, defendants actively create initial interest confusion in the following manner. Because banner advertisements appear immediately after users type in PEI's marks, PEI asserts that users are likely to be confused regarding the sponsorship of unlabeled banner advertisements. In addition, many of the advertisements instruct users to "click here." Because of their confusion, users may follow the instruction, believing they will be connected to a PEI cite. Even if they realize "immediately upon accessing" the competitor's site that they have reached a site "wholly unrelated to" PEI's, the damage has been done: Through initial consumer confusion, the competitor "will still have gained a customer by appropriating the goodwill that [PEI] has developed in its [ ] mark."

PEI's theory strongly resembles the theory adopted by this court in *Brookfield Communications, Inc. v. West Coast Entertainment Corporation.* In *Brookfield*, a video rental company, West Coast Entertainment Corporation, planned on using "moviebuff.com" as a domain name for its website and using a similar term in the metatags for the site. Brookfield had trademarked the term "MovieBuff," however, and sued West Coast for trademark infringement. The court ruled in favor of Brookfield. It reasoned that Internet users entering Brookfield's mark (plus ".com") or searching for Brookfield's mark on search engines using metatags, would find themselves at West Coast's website. Although they might "realize, immediately upon accessing 'moviebuff.com,' that they have reached a site operated by West Coast and wholly unrelated to Brookfield," some customers who were originally seeking Brookfield's website "may be perfectly content with West

Coast's database (especially as it is offered free of charge)." Because those customers would have found West Coast's site due to West Coast's "misappropriation of Brookfield's goodwill" in its mark, the court concluded that Brookfield withstood summary judgment.

In this case, PEI claims that defendants, in conjunction with advertisers, have misappropriated the goodwill of PEI's marks by leading Internet users to competitors' websites just as West Coast video misappropriated the goodwill of Brookfield's mark. Some consumers, initially seeking PEI's sites, may initially believe that unlabeled banner advertisements are links to PEI's sites or to sites affiliated with PEI. Once they follow the instructions to "click here," and they access the site, they may well realize that they are not at a PEI-sponsored site. However, they may be perfectly happy to remain on the competitor's site, just as the *Brookfield* court surmised that some searchers initially seeking Brookfield's site would happily remain on West Coast's site. The Internet user will have reached the site because of defendants' use of PEI's mark. Such use is actionable.

Although analogies to *Brookfield* suggest that PEI will be able to show a likelihood of confusion sufficient to defeat summary judgment, we must test PEI's theory using this circuit's well-established eight-factor test for the likelihood of confusion to be certain. Accordingly, we turn to that test now.

The Ninth Circuit employs an eight-factor test, originally set forth in *AMF Inc. v. Sleekcraft Boats*, to determine the likelihood of confusion....

In the Internet context, courts must be flexible in applying the factors, as some may not apply. Moreover, some factors are more important than others. For example, a showing of actual confusion among significant numbers of consumers provides strong support for the likelihood of confusion. For that reason, we turn first to an examination of factor four: evidence of actual confusion.

a. *Factor 4: Evidence of Actual Confusion.*

The expert study PEI introduced establishes a strong likelihood of initial interest confusion among consumers. Thus, factor four alone probably suffices to reverse the grant of summary judgment.

PEI's expert, Dr. Ford, concluded that a statistically significant number of Internet users searching for the terms "playboy" and "playmate" would think that PEI, or an affiliate, sponsored banner ads containing adult content that appear on the search results page. When study participants were shown search results for the term "playboy," 51% believed that PEI sponsored or was otherwise associated with the adult-content banner ad displayed. When shown results for the term "playmate," 31% held the same belief. Using control groups, Dr. Ford also concluded that for 29% of those participants viewing "playboy" searches and 22% of those viewing "playmate" searches, the confusion stemmed from the targeting of the banner advertisements. The individuals were not confused by random, untargeted advertisements.

Defendants criticize Dr. Ford's procedures and conclusions. They offer their own interpretations of his data, with significantly lower rates of confusion. Defendants cite cases identifying probabilities of confusion of 7.6% and less as *de minimis* and then argue that Dr. Ford's results showed *de minimis* confusion as well. Their critique of Dr. Ford's methods and interpretations formed the basis of a motion to exclude his expert testimony and report before the district court. The district court denied that motion, however, and allowed the introduction of the evidence.

Defendants may have valid criticism of Dr. Ford's methods and conclusions, and their critique may justify reducing the weight eventually afforded Dr. Ford's expert report. The district court's evidentiary ruling is not before us on appeal, however, and weighing admissible evidence at this stage is improper. Defendants' arguments prove the point that a genuine issue of material fact exists regarding actual confusion. The presence of Dr. Ford's criticized (but uncontradicted) report, with its strong conclusions that a high likelihood of initial interest confusion exists among consumers, thus generates a genuine issue of material fact on the actual confusion issue.

Because actual confusion is at the heart of the likelihood of confusion analysis, Dr. Ford's report alone probably precludes summary judgment. In the interest of being thorough, however, we will examine the other seven *Sleekcraft* factors. On balance, they also support PEI.

b. *Factor One: Strength of the Mark.*

PEI has established that strong secondary meanings for its descriptive marks exist, and that a genuine issue of material fact exists as to whether it created the secondary meanings. Thus, the first *Sleekcraft* factor favors PEI.

At this point, defendants concede that they use the marks for their secondary meanings.[32] Thus, they concede that the marks have secondary meanings. They offer only a weak argument regarding the strength of the meanings. Given that defendants themselves use the terms precisely because they believe that Internet searchers associate the terms with their secondary meanings, disputing the strength of the secondary meanings is somewhat farfetched. The only meaningful dispute is whether PEI created the strong secondary meanings associated with the mark.

PEI offered evidence, in the form of expert reports, tending to show that PEI did create the secondary meanings of "playboy" and "playmate." PEI's expert evidence countered the defendants' expert evidence to the contrary, and suffices to generate a genuine issue of material fact on this issue.

---

32. Indeed, to argue that they use the marks for their primary meaning, as defendants did below, is absurd. Defendants obviously do not use the term "playmate," for example, for its dictionary definition: "a companion, especially of a child, in games and play." WEBSTER'S NEW WORLD DICTIONARY, 3d coll. ed. (1988).

c. *Factor Two: Proximity of the Goods.*

From an Internet searcher's perspective, the relevant "goods" are the links to the websites being sought and the goods or services available at those sites. The proximity between PEI's and its competitor's goods provides the reason Netscape keys PEI's marks to competitor's banner advertisements in the first place. Accordingly, this factor favors PEI as well.

d. *Factor Three: Similarity of the Marks.*

No doubt exists regarding this factor. Aside from their lack of capitalization, their font, and the fact that defendants use the plural form of "playmate," the terms defendants use are identical to PEI's marks. Thus, they are certainly similar.

e. *Factor Five: Marketing Channels Used.*

This factor is equivocal. PEI and the advertisers use identical marketing channels: the Internet. More specifically, each of their sites appears on defendants' search results pages. Given the broad use of the Internet today, the same could be said for countless companies. Thus, this factor merits little weight.

f. *Factor Six: Type of Goods and Degree of Consumer Care Expected.*

This factor favors PEI. Consumer care for inexpensive products is expected to be quite low. Low consumer care, in turn, increases the likelihood of confusion.

In addition to price, the content in question may affect consumer care as well. We presume that the average searcher seeking adult-oriented materials on the Internet is easily diverted from a specific product he or she is seeking if other options, particularly graphic ones, appear more quickly. Thus, the adult-oriented and graphic nature of the materials weighs in PEI's favor as well.

g. *Factor Seven: Defendants' Intent in Selecting the Mark.*

This factor favors PEI somewhat. A defendant's intent to confuse constitutes probative evidence of likely confusion: Courts assume that the defendant's intentions were carried out successfully. In this case, the evidence does not definitively establish defendants' intent. At a minimum, however, it does suggest that defendants do nothing to prevent click-throughs that result from confusion. Moreover, they profit from such click-throughs.

Defendants monitor "click-through" rates on the advertisements they display. That is, they monitor the number of times consumers are diverted to their advertisers' sites. They use the click-through rates as a way to gauge the success of the advertisements and to keep advertisers coming back to their services. Although some click-throughs may be the result of legitimate consumer interest, not confusion, some may be expected to result from confusion. Defendants will profit from both kinds of click-throughs. And they do nothing to ensure that only click-throughs based on legitimate interest, as opposed to confusion, occur.

PEI introduced evidence suggesting that labeling the advertisements would reduce click-through rates. It would also reduce confusion. However, although defendants control the content of advertisements in other contexts, defendants do not require that advertisers identify themselves on their banner ads. Moreover, they do not label the advertisements themselves. Perhaps even more telling, defendants refuse to remove the highly-rated terms "playboy" and "playmate" from their lists of keywords, even when advertisers request that they do so.

The above evidence suggests, at a minimum, that defendants do nothing to alleviate confusion, even when asked to do so by their advertisers, and that they profit from confusion. Although not definitive, this factor provides some evidence of an intent to confuse on the part of defendants. This factor thus favors PEI.

h. Factor Eight: Likelihood of Expansion of Product Lines.

Because the advertisers' goods and PEI's are already related, as discussed within factor two, this factor is irrelevant.

Having examined all of the *Sleekcraft* factors, we conclude that the majority favor PEI. Accordingly, we conclude that a genuine issue of material fact exists as to the substantial likelihood of confusion.

* * *

■ BERZON, CIRCUIT JUDGE, concurring:

I concur in Judge Nelson's careful opinion in this case, as it is fully consistent with the applicable precedents. I write separately, however, to express concern that one of those precedents was wrongly decided and may one day, if not now, need to be reconsidered *en banc.*

I am struck by how analytically similar keyed advertisements are to the metatags found infringing in *Brookfield Communications v. West Coast Entertainment Corp.*, 174 F.3d 1036 (9th Cir. 1999). In *Brookfield*, the court held that the defendant could not use the trademarked term "moviebuff" as one of its metatags. Metatags are part of the HTML code of a web page, and therefore are invisible to internet users. Search engines use these metatags to pull out websites applicable to search terms. *See also Promatek Indus., Ltd. v. Equitrac Corp.*, 300 F.3d 808, 812–13 (7th Cir. 2002) (adopting the *Brookfield* holding).

Specifically, *Brookfield* held that the use of the trademarked terms in metatags violated the Lanham Act because it caused "initial interest confusion." *Brookfield*, 174 F.3d at 1062–66. The court explained that even though "there is no source confusion in the sense that consumers know [who] they are patronizing, . . . there is nevertheless initial interest confusion in the sense that, by using 'moviebuff.com' or 'MovieBuff' to divert people looking for 'MovieBuff' to its website, [the defendant] improperly benefits from the goodwill that [the plaintiff] developed in its mark." *Id.* at 1062.

As applied to this case, *Brookfield* might suggest that there could be a Lanham Act violation *even if* the banner advertisements were clearly labeled, either by the advertiser or by the search engine. I do not believe that to be so. So read, the metatag holding in *Brookfield* would expand the reach of initial interest confusion from situations in which a party is initially confused to situations in which a party is never confused. I do not think it is reasonable to find initial interest confusion when a consumer is never confused as to source or affiliation, but instead knows, or should know, from the outset that a product or web link is not related to that of the trademark holder because the list produced by the search engine so informs him.

There is a big difference between hijacking a customer to another website by making the customer think he or she is visiting the trademark holder's website (even if only briefly), which is what may be happening in this case when the banner advertisements are not labeled, and just distracting a potential customer with another *choice*, when it is clear that it is a choice. True, when the search engine list generated by the search for the trademark ensconced in a metatag comes up, an internet user might *choose* to visit westcoastvideo.com, the defendant's website in *Brookfield*, instead of the plaintiff's moviebuff.com website, but such choices do not constitute trademark infringement off the internet, and I cannot understand why they should on the internet.

For example, consider the following scenario: I walk into Macy's and ask for the Calvin Klein section and am directed upstairs to the second floor. Once I get to the second floor, on my way to the Calvin Klein section, I notice a more prominently displayed line of Charter Club clothes, Macy's own brand, designed to appeal to the same people attracted by the style of Calvin Klein's latest line of clothes. Let's say I get diverted from my goal of reaching the Calvin Klein section, the Charter Club stuff looks good enough to me, and I purchase some Charter Club shirts instead. Has Charter Club or Macy's infringed Calvin Klein's trademark, simply by having another product more prominently displayed before one reaches the Klein line? Certainly not. . . .

Similarly, suppose a customer walks into a bookstore and asks for Playboy magazine and is then directed to the adult magazine section, where he or she sees Penthouse or Hustler up front on the rack while Playboy is buried in back. One would not say that Penthouse or Hustler had violated Playboy's trademark. This conclusion holds true even if Hustler paid the store owner to put its magazines in front of Playboy's.

One can test these analogies with an on-line example: If I went to Macy's website and did a search for a Calvin Klein shirt, would Macy's violate Calvin Klein's trademark if it responded (as does Amazon.com, for example) with the requested shirt and pictures of other shirts I might like to consider as well? I very much doubt it.

Accordingly, I simply cannot understand the broad principle set forth in *Brookfield*. Even the main analogy given in *Brookfield* belies its conclusion. The Court gives an example of Blockbuster misdirecting customers from a competing video store, West Coast Video, by putting up a highway billboard sign giving directions to Blockbuster but telling customers that a West Coast Video store is located there. *Brookfield*, 174 F.3d at 1064. Even though customers who arrive at the Blockbuster realize that it is not West Coast Video, they were initially misled and confused. *Id.*

But there was no similar misdirection in *Brookfield*, nor would there be similar misdirection in this case were the banner ads labeled or otherwise identified. The *Brookfield* defendant's website was described by the court as being accurately listed as westcoastvideo.com in the applicable search results. Consumers were free to choose the official moviebuff.com website and were not hijacked or misdirected elsewhere. I note that the billboard analogy has been widely criticized as inapplicable to the internet situation, given both the fact that customers were not misdirected and the minimal inconvenience in directing one's web browser back to the original list of search results. . . .

QUESTIONS

1. As a policy matter, should courts focus more on protecting the consuming public from confusion or on protecting companies from losing potential customers? Are the courts consistent in embracing one of these policies?

2. Does the fact that only one company can own a particular domain name mitigate confusion by consumers using the Internet? Are Internet users more savvy and less prone to initial confusion than consumers using other forms of communication?

3. A small Illinois quartet goes by the name Tom, Kate, Tim, and Sue. The large New York Broadway theatrical ticketing agency, TKTS, has a federal registration for its trademark, TKTS. Tom, Kate, Tim, and Sue registered the domain name tkts.com before TKTS thought to do it. They use it to update fans on current events, to notify prospective audience members of their performance schedule, and to sell tickets to their performances. Would TKTS have a claim against Tom, Kate, Tim, and Sue based on initial interest confusion?

4. The German automaker Porsche has a federally registered trademark for the name Porsche in relation to automobiles. It operates a website at Porsche.com to promote its line. Realizing that many people misspell the name, Cool Cars, an antique and collector car dealer registers the domain names for Porche.com, Porshe.com, and Porsch.com. Whenever a user types in these misspelled versions of the name, they are directed to the Cool Cars website, and the location bar on their Internet browser reads "Cool-Cars.com." Does Porsche have a claim against Cool Cars based on initial interest confusion? Cf. *Holiday Inns Inc. v. 800 Reservation, Inc.*, 86 F.3d 619 (6th Cir.1996)(misspelled "vanity" phone number).

———

3. DEFENDANT'S USE IN COMMERCE

a. INTERNET USES

1–800 Contacts, Inc. v. WhenU.com

414 F.3d 400 (2d Cir.2005).

The primary issue to be resolved by this appeal is whether the placement of pop-up ads on a C[omputer]-user's screen contemporaneously with either the 1–800 website or a list of search results obtained by the C-user's input of the 1–800 website address constitutes "use" under the Lanham Act.

[The District Court described defendant WhenU's Save Now advertising placement program. "When a computer user who has installed the SaveNow software (a 'SaveNow user') browses the Internet, the SaveNow software [that resides on the user's computer] scans activity conducted within the SaveNow user's Internet browser, comparing URLs, website addresses, search terms and webpage content accessed by the SaveNow user with a proprietary directory, using algorithms contained in the software. Entering an URL into the browser can 'trigger' the SaveNow software to deliver a 'pop-up' advertisement. When a user types a search word or URL into the Internet browser, the SaveNow software looks to see what category of products or services the address belongs to. In general, if the SaveNow user's Internet usage 'matches' information contained in the SaveNow directory, the SaveNow software will determine that an ad should be shown, will retrieve a pop-up advertisement from a server over the Internet, and will display that pop-up ad in a new window appearing on the user's computer screen. [Thus], when a user types in '1800contacts.com,' the URL for Plaintiff's website, the SaveNow software recognizes that the user is interested in the eye-care category, and retrieves from an Internet server a pop-up advertisement from that category." *1–800 Contacts, Inc. v. WhenU.com*, 309 F. Supp. 2d 467, 476 (S.D.N.Y. 2003).]

The district court reasoned that WhenU, by "causing pop-up advertisements for Defendant Vision Direct to appear when SaveNow users have specifically attempted to access [1–800]'s website, . . . [is] displaying [1–800]'s mark in the . . . advertising of . . . Vision Direct's services." *1–800 Contacts*, 309 F.Supp.2d at 489.

The fatal flaw with this holding is that WhenU's pop-up ads do not display the 1–800 trademark. The district court's holding, however, appears to have been based on the court's acceptance of 1–800's claim that WhenU's pop-up ads appear "on" and affect 1–800's website. *See, e.g., id.* at 479 (stating that WhenU has "no relationship with the companies on whose websites the pop-up advertisements appear") (emphasis omitted) (emphasis added). [But] the WhenU pop-up ads appear in a separate window that is prominently branded with the WhenU mark; they have has absolutely no tangible effect on the appearance or functionality of the 1–800 website.

More important, the appearance of WhenU's pop-up ad is not contingent upon or related to 1–800's trademark, the trademark's appearance on 1–800's website, or the mark's similarity to 1–800's website address. Rather, the contemporaneous display of the ads and trademarks is the result of the happenstance that 1–800 chose to use a mark similar to its trademark as the address to its web page and to place its trademark on its website. The pop-up ad, which is triggered by the C-user's input of 1–800's website address, would appear even if 1–800's trademarks were not displayed on its website. A pop-up ad could also appear if the C-user typed the

1–800 website address, not as an address, but as a search term in the browser's search engine, and then accessed 1–800's website by using the hyperlink that appeared in the list of search results.

In addition, 1–800's website address is not the only term in the SaveNow directory that could trigger a Vision Direct ad to "pop up" on 1–800's website. For example, an ad could be triggered by a C-user's search for "contacts" or "eye care," both terms contained in the directory, and then clicked on the listed hyperlink to 1–800's website.

Exemplifying the conceptual difficulty that inheres in this issue, the district court's decision suggests that the crux of WhenU's wrongdoing—and the primary basis for the district court's finding of "use"—is WhenU's alleged effort to capitalize on a C-user's specific attempt to access the 1–800 website. As the court explained it,

> WhenU.com is doing far more than merely "displaying" Plaintiff's mark. WhenU's advertisements are delivered to a SaveNow user when the user directly accesses Plaintiff's website—thus allowing Defendant Vision Direct to profit from the goodwill and reputation in Plaintiff's website that led the user to access Plaintiff's website in the first place.

1–800 Contacts, 309 F.Supp.2d at 490. Absent improper use of 1–800's trademark, however, such conduct does not violate the Lanham Act. *See TrafFix Devices, Inc. v. Marketing Displays, Inc.*, 532 U.S. 23, 29, 149 L.Ed.2d 164 (2001); *Kellogg Co. v. National Biscuit Co.*, 305 U.S. 111, 122, 83 L.Ed. 73 (1938) (holding that Kellogg's sharing in the goodwill of the unprotected "Shredded Wheat" market was "not unfair"); *see also* William P. Kratzke, *Normative Economic Analysis of Trademark Law*, 21 Memphis St. U. L. Rev. 199, 223 (1991) (criticizing importation into trademark law of "unjust enrichment" and "free riding" theories based on a trademark holder's goodwill). Indeed, it is routine for vendors to seek specific "product placement" in retail stores precisely to capitalize on their competitors' name recognition. For example, a drug store typically places its own store-brand generic products next to the trademarked products they emulate in order to induce a customer who has specifically sought out the trademarked product to consider the store's less-expensive alternative. WhenU employs this same marketing strategy by informing C-users who have sought out a specific trademarked product about available coupons, discounts, or alternative products that may be of interest to them.

1–800 disputes this analogy by arguing that unlike a drugstore, only the 1–800 website is displayed when the pop-up ad appears. This response, however, ignores the fact that a C-user who has installed the SaveNow software receives WhenU pop-up ads in a myriad of contexts, the vast majority of which are unlikely to have anything to do with 1–800 or the C-user's input of the 1–800 website address.

The cases relied on by 1–800 do not alter our analysis. As explained in detail by the court in *U-Haul*, they are all readily distinguishable because WhenU's conduct does not involve any of the activities those courts found to constitute "use." *U-Haul*, 279 F.Supp. at 728–29 (collecting cases).

Significantly, WhenU's activities do not alter or affect 1–800's website in any way. Nor do they divert or misdirect C-users away from 1–800's website, or alter in any way the results a C-user will obtain when searching with the 1–800 trademark or website address. *Compare Playboy Enters., Inc. v. Netscape Communications Corp.*, 354 F.3d 1020, 1024 (9th Cir. 2004) (holding that infringement could be based on defendant's insertion of unidentified banner ads on C-user's search-results page); *Brookfield Communications v. West Coast Entm't Corp.*, 174 F.3d 1036 (9th Cir. 1999) (holding that defendant's use of trademarks in "metatags," invisible text within websites that search engines use for ranking results, constituted a "use in commerce" under the Lanham Act); *see generally Bihari v. Gross*, 119 F.Supp.2d 309 (S.D.N.Y. 2000) (discussing *Brookfield* and similar cases).

In addition, unlike several other internet advertising companies, WhenU does not "sell" keyword trademarks to its customers or otherwise manipulate which category-related advertisement will pop up in response to any particular terms on the internal directory. *See, e.g., GEICO*, 330 F.Supp.2d at 703–04 (finding that Google's sale to advertisers of right to use specific trademarks as "keywords" to trigger their ads constituted "use in commerce"). In other words, WhenU does not link trademarks to any particular competitor's ads, and a customer cannot pay to have its pop-up ad appear on any specific website or in connection with any particular trademark. *See id.* at 704 (distinguishing WhenU's conduct on this basis). Instead, the SaveNow directory terms trigger categorical associations (e.g., www. 1800Contacts.com might trigger the category of "eye care"), at which point, the software will randomly select one of the pop-up ads contained in the eye-care category to send to the C-user's desktop.

Perhaps because ultimately 1–800 is unable to explain precisely how WhenU "uses" its trademark, it resorts to bootstrapping a finding of "use" by alleging other elements of a trademark claim. For example, 1–800 invariably refers to WhenU's pop-up ads as "unauthorized" in an effort, it would seem, to establish by sheer force of repetition the element of unauthorized use of a trademark. Not surprisingly, 1–800 cites no legal authority for the proposition that advertisements, software applications, or any other visual image that can appear on a C-user's computer screen must be authorized by the owner of any website that will appear contemporaneously with that image. The fact is that WhenU does not need 1–800's authorization to display a separate window containing an ad any more than Corel would need authorization from Microsoft to display its WordPerfect word-processor in a window contemporaneously with a Word word-processing window. Moreover, contrary to 1–800's repeated admonitions, WhenU's pop-up ads are authorized—if unwittingly—by the C-user who has downloaded the SaveNow software.

1–800 also argues that WhenU's conduct is "use" because it is likely to confuse C-users as to the source of the ad. It buttresses this claim with a survey it submitted to the district court that purportedly demonstrates, inter alia, that (1) a majority of C-users believe that pop-up ads that appear on websites are sponsored by those websites, and (2) numerous C-users are unaware that they have downloaded the SaveNow software. 1–800 also relies on several cases in which the court seemingly based a finding of trademark "use" on the confusion such "use" was likely to cause. *See, e.g., Bihari*, 119 F.Supp.2d at 318 (holding that defendant's use of trademarks in metatags constituted a "use in commerce" under the Lanham Act in part because the hyperlinks "effectively act[ed] as a conduit, steering potential customers away from Bihari Interiors and toward its competitors"); *GEICO*, 330 F.Supp.2d at 703–04 (finding that Google's sale to advertisers of right to have specific trademarks trigger their ads was "use in commerce" because it created likelihood of confusion that Google had the trademark holder's authority to do so). Again, this rationale puts the cart before the horse. Not only are "use," "in commerce," and "likelihood of confusion" three distinct elements of a trademark infringement claim, but "use" must be decided as a threshold matter because, while any number of activities may be "in commerce" or create a likelihood of confusion, no such activity is actionable under the Lanham Act absent the "use" of a trademark. Because 1–800 has failed to establish such "use," its trademark infringement claims fail.

800–JR Cigar, Inc. v. GoTo.com, Inc. et al.

437 F.Supp.2d 273 (D.N.J.2006).

■ LIFLAND, DISTRICT JUDGE.

. . . .

BACKGROUND

JR Cigar is a prominent seller of cigars at discount prices. JR Cigar has marketed its products for more than thirty years under the service mark "JR Cigars," more recently under other marks featuring the formatives "JR" or "JR Cigar," and, even more recently, under the trade name "jrcigars.com," which is the address for JR's Internet website that was launched in April 1999. JR Cigar is the ultimate owner of six federal trademarks that utilize the formative "JR" or "JR Cigar."

GoTo is a pay-for-priority Internet search engine formed in 1997. Its service reaches approximately 75% of all Internet users. A search engine allows users to find information by entering a search term and receiving a list of results. Pay-for-priority search engines solicit bids from advertisers for key words or phrases to be used as search terms, giving priority results on searches for those terms to the highest-paying advertiser. Thus, each advertiser's rank in the search results is determined by the amount of its bid on the search term entered by the user. The list of paid results on GoTo's web site discloses the amount of each advertiser's bid. Advertisers pay GoTo only when a user clicks on their listings in the search results. After all paying advertisers' sites are listed as search results, GoTo lists unpaid or "natural" search listings, i.e., those whose sites are most logically relevant to the search criteria. GoTo receives no revenue when a user clicks on unpaid listings.

Search terms are displayed on GoTo result pages only if a user enters those particular search terms. And if the search terms are displayed in web site descriptions in the search result listings, it is only because the owner of the listed web site included the term in its description for the listing.

It is arguable that GoTo does not use "jr cigar" or any other JR Cigar trademark to promote or advertise its own services. However, in addition to accepting bids for search terms and earning revenue therefrom, GoTo assists prospective and current advertisers in selecting search terms by providing an automated "Search Term Suggestion Tool." This tool enables an advertiser to assess the usefulness of a search term. When an advertiser enters a search term for which it is considering a bid, the Search Term Suggestion Tool applies various algorithms and automatically generates a list showing how many times that term and related terms were searched during the prior month. GoTo applies its standard editorial review process to search terms identified through the use of the Search Term Suggestion Tool.

Between April 1999 and June 2001, GoTo earned revenue of about $345 from paid listings for "jr cigar" and related search terms. Portions of that revenue stemmed from the term "jr" and clicks to web sites entirely unrelated to cigars, such as J & R Music. Another portion of this revenue resulted from clicks to a web site maintained by JR Cigar's attorneys.

JR Cigar itself did not pay GoTo for a priority listing, but some of its competitors (the non-search engine defendants) did. According to GoTo, some of the bids for "jr cigar" search terms were accepted because the advertisers' web sites contained content that was relevant to JR Cigar or its products under GoTo's relevancy guidelines. In other cases, GoTo accepted bids because its editors believed that the term "jr cigar" was a reference to a "junior" or small cigar.

In June 2000, JR became aware that GoTo was selling to the non-search engine defendants the right to use the term "JR Cigar" and slight variations of that term, including "J R Cigar," "J&R Cigar," "J–R Cigar," "JRCigars.com," and "800 JR Cigar" (collectively the "JR search terms"), as Internet keywords or other devices to generate advertising revenues for GoTo. According to JR Cigar, that enabled JR Cigar's competitors to "pass themselves off as JR" and "divert internet shoppers and purchasers from JR's website to their own competitive websites."

At no time did GoTo enter into any agreement with any advertiser encouraging the advertiser to bid on "jr cigar" or related search terms. According to GoTo, its advertisers represent to it that their web sites and search listings will not violate trademark rights of any third party. Moreover, GoTo claims that it exercises no control over the content of the web sites that appear among paid and unpaid listings.

At one time GoTo's "Editorial Manuals" and "Relevancy Guidelines" prohibited bidding on trademarks and on the names of advertisers' competitors, stating that:

- For line listings, GoTo does not permit the mention of specific competitors or bidding for search terms that are trademarked names;

- We do not accept search terms based on the products of our advertisers' competitors, unless our advertisers' websites present actual, significant information about their competitors' products by comparing them to their own.

These prohibitions were removed in 1999 and 2000, reportedly because it was impractical for editors to determine who owned trademarks and whether an advertiser's use was infringing.

On June 28, 2000, JR Cigar filed suit against GoTo ... GoTo responded to the receipt of the Complaint and demand letter by reviewing the paid listings for "jr cigar" and related search terms, and removed a number of listings that were not relevant. The two remaining paid listings include advertising by a JR Cigar attorney and by a site providing financial and other information about JR Cigar.

. . . .

DISCUSSION

. . . .

II. Parties' Arguments

JR Cigar seeks monetary and injunctive relief, arguing that GoTo (1) profited from the unauthorized sale of the JR marks as search terms to its customers; (2) used the JR marks to attract search customers to its site; and (3) created and implemented a scheme to divert Internet users seeking to find "jr cigar" to JR Cigar's competitors and rivals. JR Cigar argues that such conduct constitutes trademark infringement, unfair competition, and false designation of origin in violation of Sections 32(1) and 43(a) of the Lanham Act, 15 U.S.C. § 1114(1) and 1125(a), involving the unauthorized use of JR marks in interstate commerce in a manner that is likely to create confusion....

GoTo responds that JR Cigar seeks "broad veto power" well beyond the bounds afforded by trademark protection. The argument goes that the use of a trademark on GoTo's web site is consistent with applicable law allowing for comparative advertising, "gripe sites," and other cases of fair use. GoTo further argues that its paid listings service is much like other cases wherein courts have allowed use of another's trademark in domain names, as key words for banner advertisements, and in metatags (hidden codes that influence whether a web site appears in search engine results). In summary, GoTo maintains that it has not made trademark use of any JR Cigar search terms for its own services ...

. . . .

IV. Trademark Infringement and Unfair Competition Claims

. . . .

A. *Trademark Use*

First to be addressed is whether GoTo's "use" of JR marks—accepting bids that include "jr cigar" and like key search terms for purposes of priority listing—falls within the commercial use contemplated by statutory and common law trademark infringement prohibitions.

JR contends that GoTo's use of the "JR," "JR Cigar," and "800 JR Cigar" marks and variations of those marks are the sort of use contemplated by the Lanham Act, even though GoTo is not a distributor or direct competitor of JR Cigar. GoTo responds that the sale of JR marks is not "trademark use" attributable to GoTo, because it is the advertiser who selects the search term and uses it in conjunction with the content contained on the advertiser's website. GoTo perceives its involvement as merely limited to accepting the advertiser's bid on the search term after determining that the term is relevant to the advertiser's Web site.

The Court finds JR's position to be more persuasive. Instructive on this point is the *GEICO* case where GEICO brought suit against Google and Overture Services, Inc. (formerly GoTo, the defendant in the present action) based on their use of GEICO's trademarks in selling advertising on Google's and Overture's Internet search engines. GEICO alleged that Google and Overture operated Internet search engines that were used by Internet users to search the Internet for sites offering certain products or services. The search engines functioned by the Internet user entering search terms. *Id.* Those search terms were then compared with databases of websites maintained by the search engine, which resulted in a list of various websites matching the given search term.

Google and Overture also sold advertising linked to search terms. When an Internet user entered a search term, the results page displayed not only a list of websites generated by the search engine using neutral criteria, but also links to websites of paid advertisers, identified as "Sponsored Links." Id. GEICO alleged that the defendants' practice of selling advertising, by allowing GEICO's competitors to pay to have their ads appear next to the listings that resulted when GEICO's marks were entered as search terms, violated the Lanham Act, contributed to violations of the Act by third parties, and also constituted various state law torts.

Google and Overture moved to dismiss for failure to state a claim, arguing that the complaint failed to allege that defendants made trademark use of the marks. Specifically, defendants argued that their use of GEICO's marks was not "in commerce" and "in connection with the sale, offering for sale, distribution, or advertising of goods and services." Id. Defendants claimed that they only used GEICO's trademarks in their internal computer algorithms to determine which advertisements to show. The GEICO trademarks did not appear on the paid advertisements and therefore, Google and Overture argued, the Internet user could not be confused as to the origin of the advertised insurance products.

In its analysis, the *GEICO* court discussed recent cases holding that use of trademarks by software companies to generate pop-up Internet advertisements does not constitute "trademark use" of the marks under the Lanham Act. "Those cases are based on a finding that the mark were not used by the company making the pop-up software to identify the source of its goods and services.". See, e.g., *U-Haul Int'l, Inc. v. WhenU.com, Inc.*, 279 F. Supp. 2d 723, 727 (E.D.Va. 2003); see also *Wells Fargo & Co. v. WhenU.com, Inc.*, 293 F. Supp. 2d 734, 762 (E.D. Mich. 2003).

In the *U–Haul* and *Wells Fargo* cases, WhenU operated an Internet pop-up advertisement business. Its software program, called "SaveNow," was voluntarily downloaded by Internet users into their computers. To determine which pop-up ads to display, WhenU collected common search phrases, web addresses, and various keyword algorithms in an internal directory. The SaveNow program automatically scanned the user's Internet activity to discover whether that activity matched any information in the SaveNow directory. When the software identified a match, a pop-up advertisement was selected from among those provided by WhenU's clients and appeared on the Internet user's computer screen.

In finding that WhenU did not use plaintiffs' trademarks in commerce, the *U–Haul* and *Wells Fargo* courts both reasoned that WhenU did not sell the plaintiffs' trademarks to its customers or target specific websites, either in its software or in the selling of its services to advertisers. Rather, WhenU used the trademarks for a "pure machine-linking function" to internally associate terms with categories, and thus did not place the trademarks in commerce.

Similarly, in *1–800 Contacts, Inc. v. WhenU.com*, Inc., 414 F.3d 400 (2d Cir. 2005), the Second Circuit found that WhenU did not make "use" of the plaintiff's trademark. Although WhenU reproduced plaintiff's website address, www.1800Contacts.com, in its proprietary directory, the court found compelling the fact that WhenU "does not disclose the proprietary contents of the SaveNow directory to its advertising clients nor does it permit its advertising clients to request or purchase specified keywords to add to the directory." *Id.* at 409 (distinguishing *GEICO, supra*).

The *GEICO* court also noted other cases which held that the use of trademarks as advertising keywords by the Netscape and Excite search engines potentially created a likelihood of confusion and that there was no dispute that those defendants used the marks in commerce. See, e.g., *Playboy Enterprises, Inc. v. Netscape Commc'n Corp.*, 354 F.3d 1020, 1024 (9th Cir. 2004). Similarly, courts have found that the use of trademarks in metatags amount to "use in commerce" for purposes of the Lanham Act. See *Bihari v. Gross*, 119 F. Supp. 2d 309 (S.D.N.Y. 2000) (using plaintiff's trademarks as metatags in websites critical of plaintiff involved infringing use because those websites also contained hyperlinks to plaintiff's competitors); *Playboy Enter., Inc. v. Asiafocus Int'l*, Inc., 1998 U.S. Dist. LEXIS 10459, No. 97–734–A, 1998 WL 724000 (E.D. Va. April 10, 1998) (commercial use found where defendant embedded plaintiff's trademarks within defendant's website's computer source code (i.e., metatags) in order to attract consumers searching for plaintiff).

The *GEICO* court ultimately concluded that Overture made trademark use of GEICO's marks. The court found that the allegations of the complaint supported trademark use because "the complaint [was] addressed to more than the defendants' use of the trademarks in their internal computer coding." That is, the complaint addressed defendants' selling of and profiting from GEICO's marks.

The *GEICO* court distinguished the actions taken by defendant WhenU in the *U–Haul* case, stating:

> [W]hen defendants sell the rights to link advertising to plaintiff's trademarks, defendants are using the trademarks in commerce in a way that may imply that defendants have permission from the trademark holder to do so. This is a critical distinction from the U–Haul case, because in that case the only 'trademark use' alleged was the use of the trademark in the pop-up software—the internal computer coding. WhenU allowed advertisers to bid on broad categories of terms that included the trademarks, but did not market the protected marks themselves as keywords to which advertisers could directly purchase rights.

The distinction made by the *GEICO* court, italicized above, is applicable here. GoTo gives prominence in search results to the highest bidder by linking advertisers with certain trademarked terms. There is evidence in the record that, prior to the filing of JR's Complaint, GoTo accepted bids for the JR marks from no less than eleven of JR's competitors and ranked their priority on search results listings from highest to lowest based on who paid the most money. Such conduct is qualitatively different from the pop-up advertising context, where the use of trademarks in internal computer coding is neither communicated to the public nor for sale to the highest bidder.

Here, GoTo makes trademark use of the JR marks in three ways. First, by accepting bids from those competitors of JR desiring to pay for prominence in search results, GoTo trades on the value of the marks. Second, by ranking its paid advertisers before any "natural" listings in a search results list, GoTo has injected itself into the marketplace, acting as a conduit to steer potential customers away from JR to JR's competitors. Finally, through the Search Term Suggestion Tool, GoTo identifies those of JR's marks which are effective search terms and markets them to JR's competitors.[8] Presumably, the more money advertisers bid and the more frequently advertisers include JR's trademarks among their selected search terms, the more advertising income GoTo is likely to gain.

---

8. GoTo contends that its Search Term Suggestion Tool is an entirely automated utility that takes a term entered by the user and applies various algorithms to generate a list showing how many times that term was searched during the preceding month. Perhaps, but it is nonetheless clear to the Court that the Search Term Suggestion Tool permits GoTo to channel advertisers directly to JR's trademarks by demonstrating quantitatively the potential for successful advertising, thereby implicitly recommending those terms to advertisers.

For these reasons, the Court concludes that there are no disputed material issues of fact which would prevent the Court from concluding, as a matter of law, that GoTo is making trademark use of JR Cigar's trademarks. It must next be determined whether summary judgment is appropriate on the issue of whether GoTo's use of JR's trademarks creates a likelihood of confusion.

. . .

C. *Initial Interest Confusion*

A trademark violation based on initial interest confusion arises when a senior user's customers are diverted to a junior user's website offering similar products. The idea is that, upon arriving at the competitor's website, customers may be fully aware that the website is not JR's, but may buy from the competitor out of convenience or in the belief that JR's products are available from the competitor. See *Brookfield Commc'n. Inc. v. West Coast Entm't Corp.*, 174 F.3d 1036, 1064 (9th Cir. 1999).

The Third Circuit has held that initial interest confusion supports a violation of the Lanham Act. *Checkpoint*, 269 F.3d at 292. Initial interest confusion "occurs when a consumer is lured to a product by its similarity to a known mark, even though the consumer realizes the true identity and origin of the product before consummating a purchase." Id. at 294 (citing Eli Lilly & Co. v. Natural Answers, Inc., 233 F.3d 456 at 464 (7th Cir. 2000)). Without protection against initial interest confusion, an infringer receives a "free ride on the good will of the established mark." Id. at 295 (internal citations omitted). Indeed, "[c]onfining actionable confusion under the Lanham Act to confusion present at the time of purchase would undervalue the importance of a company's goodwill with its customers." *Id.*

Thus, courts have found that damage to a trademark holder results even where a consumer eventually becomes aware of the source's actual identity or where no actual sale occurs. See *Australian Gold, Inc. v. Hatfield*, 436 F.3d 1228, 1239 (10th Cir. 2006); *BigStar Entm't Inc. v. Next Big Star, Inc.*, 105 F. Supp. 2d 185 (S.D.N.Y. 2000).

> This damage can manifest itself in three ways: (1) the original diversion of the prospective customer's interest to a source that he or she erroneously believes is authorized; (2) the potential consequent effect of that diversion on the customer's ultimate decision whether to purchase caused by an erroneous impression that the two sources of a product may be associated; and (3) the initial credibility that the would—be buyer may accord to the infringer's products—customer consideration that otherwise may be unwarranted and that may be built on the strength of the protected mark, reputation and goodwill.

Australian Gold, 436 F.3d at 1239.

The probative value of initial interest confusion and its significance varies from case to case. Checkpoint, 269 F.3d at 297. Relevant factors include (1) product relatedness (i.e., whether the goods or services are similar; whether the products at issue directly compete), (2) the level of care exercised by consumers in making purchasing decisions, (3) the sophistication of the purchaser/consumer; and (4) the intent of the alleged infringer in adopting the mark. *Id.* at 296. "Initial interest confusion in the internet context derives from the unauthorized use of trademarks to divert internet traffic, thereby capitalizing on a trademark holder's good will." Australian Gold, 436 F.3d at 1239; see also Brookfield, 174 F.3d at 1064. Thus, in this factual context, evidence of the diversion of traffic away from JR's website to those of its competitors is also a significant factor.

Product Relatedness

This factor examines whether the goods and services are similar and whether the products at issue directly compete. GoTo again argues that it does not compete with JR, and that when the goods or services of the parties are dissimilar, there can be no initial interest confusion. The correct inquiry here is not whether the present parties are themselves competitors in the same business, but rather a comparison of the similarity of the goods and services being offered under the trademark being used by both.

GoTo and JR both used JR's marks—GoTo used JR's marks to promote its search engine services to cigar suppliers other than JR, and JR uses its marks to promote its own cigars. As discussed above in connection with the "Similarity of the Marks" and "Relationship of the Goods" *Lapp* factors, GoTo's use of the marks suggests an affiliation or connection between JR and GoTo based on GoTo's alleged infringing use of the marks.

Level of Care Exercised by Consumers in Making Purchasing Decisions and Sophistication of the Consumer

"When consumers do not exercise a high level of care in making their decisions, it is more likely that their initial confusion will result in a benefit to the alleged infringer from the use of the goodwill of the other firm." *Checkpoint*, 269 F.3d at 296–97. Cost of the product, the sophistication of the consumer, and the length of the purchasing process are relevant here. Unsophisticated buyers are more likely to be confused as to source or affiliation when confronted with similar trademarks, and there is an inverse relationship between the cost of a product and the amount of care the reasonably prudent buyer will use in acquiring it.

JR argues that "[t]he relatively modest price levels of [JR's] products—even for the more costly premium hand rolled cigars—suggest that ... consumers are unlikely to exercise undue care in purchasing many cigars. The moderate price levels further suggest that consumers may not be attentive to being redirected to the websites operated by JR's competitors from an internet search result that superficially appears to be directing the consumer to JR's website." (Pl. Br. at 14). GoTo does not respond to JR's arguments.

Without evidence in the record as to the price of JR's products, the sophistication of cigar buyers generally and JR's customers specifically, and the length of the purchasing process, all of which bear on whether an Internet user interested in cigars could be lured away from JR Cigar, the Court cannot address this issue. Upon hearing such evidence, the trier of the facts may find that consumers are unlikely to exercise care in their purchasing decisions and may not be attentive about being redirected away from JR's website, but JR's unsupported allegations on this issue are insufficient to meet its burden of proof on summary judgment.

Intent of Alleged Infringer in Adopting the Mark

The proper inquiry here is whether GoTo intentionally adopted JR's marks to create confusion among consumers making purchasing decisions. GoTo claims that it made fair use of JR's marks. JR claims that GoTo purposefully lured consumers away from its website to those of its competitors for financial gain. The factual issue of GoTo's intent is in dispute.

Evidence of Diversion Supporting the Likelihood of Confusion

JR points to evidence that Internet users who input JR Search Terms on GoTo's search engine were directed to a list including websites other than JR's website, the first eleven of which were paid listings. Between April 1999 and June 2001, while GoTo was selling the JR advertising rights to the highest bidders, JR Cigar maintains that approximately 20,000 of the 70,407 searches reflected in Rothman Conf. Ex. D were made on the GoTo search system, meaning Internet users were thwarted in their efforts to find JR's website on some 20,000 occasions. According to JR, such searches resulted in the Internet users who conducted these searches being shown 170,847 impressions or listings of sites other than the JR website and caused approximately 1,000 of those consumers to "click through" to the sites of JR's competitors. Indeed, during a two-month period between May and June 2000, GoTo averaged a 23.98% "diversion rate" in click-throughs to JR Cigar competitors. These statistics, JR contends, evidence a significant diversion of Internet traffic away from JR's website to those of its competitors, which, in turn, represents confusion created by GoTo's sale of advertising rights to JR's name.

GoTo responds that complaints of diversion of traffic from JR's website to those of its competitors, absent proof that any customers were actually confused, is insufficient to prove confusion. GoTo again contends that there has been no diversion of customers from plaintiff to defendant in that no one has bought a single cigar from GoTo. The Court finds that response unconvincing, because there is evidence that JR has suffered from the diversion occasioned by GoTo's bidding process and its use of JR's marks. See *Securacomm Consulting, Inc. v. Securacom Inc.*, 984 F. Supp. 286, 298 (D.N.J.1997) ("Infringement can be based upon confusion that creates initial customer interest, even though no actual sale is finally completed as a result of the confusion."), *rev'd on other grounds*, 166 F.3d 182, 186 (3d Cir. 1999) ("In this appeal, [appellant] does not challenge the district court's finding of infringement or order of injunctive relief.").

The statistical evidence of diversion of customers that JR has presented is arguably indicative of a likelihood of confusion. JR has come forward with evidence of diversion in support of actual confusion. GoTo does not contradict it. This state of the record favors JR, but the trier of fact must decide to credit this evidence of diversion of traffic away from JR's website to those of its competitors, in deciding whether there is a likelihood of confusion.

To summarize, the Court has concluded, as a matter of law, that GoTo made trademark use of JR's marks. As to the likelihood of confusion element, however, there are material issues in dispute; namely, ... the impact, if any, of initial interest confusion, and the fifth factor dealing with GoTo's intent in adopting the mark. These factors are highly relevant to the analysis of this action and preclude summary judgment for either party.

QUESTION

Do you understand the differences in how the *GoTo* and *WhenU* ad programs work? Are these sufficient to explain the different outcomes?

J.G. Wentworth S.S.C. v. Settlement Funding, LLC, 2007 WL 30115 (E.D. Pa. 2007). The court assessed Google's "Ad Words" program, which, like the GoTo program described in *JR Cigar* allows advertisers to bid on keywords as triggers for their ads.

> I find that defendant's participation in Google's AdWords program and defendant's incorporation of plaintiff's marks in its keyword meta tags constitute trademark use under the Lanham Act. Defendant focuses on the identification aspect of the use requirement, essentially arguing that use of plaintiff's marks in a method invisible to potential consumers precludes a finding of trademark use. But ... I recognize that defendant's use of plaintiff's marks to trigger internet advertisements for itself is the type of use consistent with the language in the Lanham Act which makes it a violation to use "in commerce" protected marks "in connection with the sale, offering for sale, distribution, or advertising of any goods or services," or "in connection with any goods or services."

The court nonetheless rejected plaintiff's initial interest theory of likelihood of confusion. The court held that the *Pegasus Petroleum* line of decisions were best understood as "bait and switch" cases: defendant's use of plaintiff's mark lured or trapped consumers into goods or services the consumers did not seek or desire. In the Ad Words context, by contrast,

> At no point are potential consumers "taken by a search engine" to defendant's website due to defendant's use of plaintiff's marks in meta tags. Rather, as in the present case, a link to defendant's website appears on the search results page as one of many choices for the potential consumer to investigate.... [T]he links to defendant's website always appear as independent and distinct links on the search result pages regardless of whether they are generated through Google's AdWords program or search of the keyword meta tags of defendant's website. Further, plaintiff does not allege that defendant's advertisements and links incorporate plaintiff's marks in any way discernable to internet users and potential customers.

J.G. Wentworth highlights a split in the caselaw and in the commentary regarding the nature of actionable "use." See also *Google, Inc. v. American Blind & Wallpaper Factory*, 2007 WL 1159950 (N.D.Cal.2007) (surveying cases, but following apparent Ninth Circuit precedent: "While the Second Circuit's decision in *1–800 Contacts* and the subsequent district court decisions may cause the Ninth Circuit to consider this [use in commerce] issue explicitly, the lengthy discussions of likelihood of confusion in *Brookfield* and *Playboy* would have been unnecessary in the absence of actionable trademark use."). In the typical trademark infringement controversy, the defendant has allegedly used plaintiff's mark as a trademark for its own goods or services. In the search engine cases, the defendant is using plaintiff's mark to trigger an advertisement or a link for defendant's goods or services, which defendant purveys under its own trademark. Must the "use" required for trademark infringement be as a trademark for defendant's goods or services? Consider the following:

GRAEME DINWOODIE & MARK JANIS, CONFUSION OVER USE: CONTEXTUALISM IN TRADEMARK LAW, 99 Iowa L. Rev. ___ (2007)(excerpt)

[A] number of scholars have argued that an unauthorized user of a mark is only liable, and should only be liable, when it uses the plaintiff's mark "as a mark." Under this approach, sometimes called the "trademark use" theory, the nature of the defendant's use serves as a threshold filter, requiring courts to engage in a preliminary inquiry regarding the nature of that use, thereby downgrading any analysis of its effects on consumer understanding. Indeed, courts following this new theory would not even reach the question of confusion absent the defendant's use being a "trademark use." The defendant would ipso facto be immune from liability. . . .

Proponents of the trademark use theory claim that trademark use has been an implicit (though largely unarticulated) principle of trademark law since before consumer confusion assumed its analytical dominance. They have been spurred to excavate the theory in the hopes of furthering a number of contemporary policy objectives, primarily with regard to contextual online advertising and affiliation merchandising. The trademark use theory threatens, however, to become even more pervasive–an all-purpose device by which to immunize a diverse set of practices from trademark claims. . . .

The range of contexts (such as product design, music counterfeiting, and brand merchandising) in which an argument of trademark use has been advanced of itself makes the theory one of the most important debates in contemporary trademark law. And its assertion in the worldwide litigation surrounding Google's advertising programs, from which the world's leading search engine generates 85% of its revenues, gives the theory an immediate and substantial commercial significance. With some over-simplification, advertisers pay Google to have their web pages appear on a list of sponsored links in response to a user query consisting of the trademark of a rival producer, prompting trademark infringement suits by the owners of the marks used in this fashion.

But the debate over trademark use implicates even more profound questions that permeate (and in some respects transcend) trademark law. For example, use-based doctrines are among the central elements in the narrative of trademark law as an efficiency mechanism, a narrative expounded by leading Chicago school scholars and embraced by the U.S. Supreme Court. Yet, technology is changing the ways that consumers search and shop. It is an open question whether the Chicago school analysis of search costs, persuasive in calibrating trademark law generally and invoked by trademark use proponents in support of the theory, adequately accounts for the dynamics of new information markets....

To be sure, persons claiming the existence of trademark rights must show that the mark in which rights are asserted is being used as a mark, but an allegation of infringement is not limited to equivalent uses by a defendant. Indeed, any interpretation to the contrary would render the statutory "fair use" defense superfluous. And, despite the best efforts of scholars to unearth supporting case law, the courts have never consistently articulated any such limitation on trademark suits. There are a number of appropriate limitations on trademark rights that may have the effect of permitting the types of third party uses that proponents of trademark use might wish to immunize from liability. But these are autonomous limits that do not, other than by happenstance, map on to the trademark use theory.

Stacey L. Dogan & Mark A. Lemley, Trademark and Consumer Search Costs on the Internet, 41 Hous. L. Rev. 777 (2004)(excerpt)

The Lanham Act prohibits only use of a trademark "in connection with" the offering of goods or services in commerce, and defines such a use as occurring in the context of services "when [the mark] is used or displayed in the sale or advertising of services and the services are rendered in commerce." It is the use of the mark to brand or advertise the defendant's services–so-called "trademark use"—that triggers trademark law.

The trademark use requirement serves a gatekeeper function, limiting the reach of trademark law without regard to a factual inquiry into consumer confusion. The rationale for the doctrine stems from the practical reality that it would be both unwise and impossible to permit trademark owners to control every use of their mark. People and businesses use trademarks every day, in conversation, in news reporting, in songs and in books. Trademark law has never given trademark owners exclusive control over any use of their marks. Rather, the law is designed to prevent consumer confusion by those who brand their own goods or services with a mark sufficiently similar to the plaintiff's mark that consumers may be deceived into believing there is some connection between the two. Individuals and companies may make reference to or use of a trademark without fear of liability unless they are making a trademark use.

The courts that have found Internet service companies liable for initial interest confusion err by holding that using a trademarked term as a "trigger" for supplying an advertisement is a trademark use of that term.... The courts appear to have been misled by the similarity in terminology of two very different elements of a trademark cause of action: the "use in commerce" requirement and the "trademark use" requirement. It is true that in both these cases the trademarks are used in interstate commerce in the minimal way necessary to invoke the jurisdiction of the federal courts. Unfortunately, an increasing number of courts apparently believe that satisfying this minimal requirement is the same as proving that the defendants had made trademark use of the plaintiff's brand. As a result, they do not analyze the requirement of trademark use directly. This is a crucial error....

Selling advertising space based on an Internet keyword that is also a trademark does not use that trademark as a brand. The Internet intermediary is not selling any product or service using those terms as an identifier. It is perhaps ... "allowing [the advertiser] to profit from the goodwill" of that mark. But it is not illegal simply to make money in a way that involves the use of a trademark. Indeed, courts considering analogous situations have rejected trademark claims on the ground that the defendant was not engaged in trademark use. For example, a number of plaintiffs have sued Internet domain name registrars such as Network Solutions for selling their trademark as a domain name to a cybersquatter who uses the name to infringe the trademark. There is no question that Network Solutions is trading on the goodwill of the trademark owner–it is making money by selling a domain name incorporating the mark itself. Nor is there any question that Network Solutions is engaged in interstate commerce. Nonetheless, courts uniformly hold that Network Solutions cannot be held liable as a direct infringer because it is not using the protected term as a trademark. The domain name registrants themselves may engage in trademark use by cybersquatting or confusing visitors to the site, but the company selling the domain names does not. [Editors' note: the *Network Solutions* decision appears *infra*, section B, page 429 of this Chapter.] ... By recognizing that advertisers may, in some cases, be engaged in trademark "use" in connection with their ads, we do not mean to suggest that purchasing a trademarked keyword constitutes such use. Trademark liability would arise, if at all, from the content and context of the ad itself, rather than the mere use of the mark as a classification tool. The speech-oriented objectives of the trademark use doctrine protect more than just intermediaries; they prevent trademark holders from asserting a generalized right to control language, an interest that applies equally–and sometimes especially–when the speaker competes directly with the trademark holder. The trademark use doctrine has broad application–because of it, newspapers are not liable for using a trademarked term in a headline, even if the use is confusing or misleading. Makers of telephone directories aren't liable for putting all the ads for taxi services together on the same page. Marketing surveyors aren't liable for asking people what they think of a competitor's brand-name product. Magazines aren't liable for selling advertising that relates to the content of their special issues, even when that content involves trademark owners.... [These users] may be making money from their "uses" of the trademark, and the uses may be ones the trademark owner objects to, but they are not trademark uses and are therefore not within the ambit of the statute.

b.   EXTRATERRITORIAL USE IN COMMERCE

Steele v. Bulova Watch Co.

344 U.S. 280, 73 S.Ct. 252, 97 L.Ed. 319 (1952).

■ MR. JUSTICE CLARK delivered the opinion of the Court:

The issue is whether a United States District Court has jurisdiction to award relief to an American corporation against acts of trademark infringement and unfair competition consummated in a foreign country by a citizen and resident of the United States. Bulova Watch Company, Inc., a New York corporation, sued Steele, petitioner here, in the United States District Court for the Western District of Texas. The gist of its complaint charged that "Bulova," a trade-mark properly registered under the laws of the United States, had long designated the watches produced and nationally advertised and sold by the Bulova Watch Company; and that petitioner, a United States citizen residing in San Antonio, Texas, conducted a watch business in Mexico City where, without Bulova's authorization and with the purpose of deceiving the buying public, he stamped the name "Bulova" on watches there assembled and sold. Basing its prayer on these asserted violations of the trademark laws of the United States, Bulova requested injunctive and monetary relief. Personally served with process in San Antonio, petitioner answered by challenging the court's jurisdiction over the subject matter of the suit and by interposing several defenses, including his due registration in Mexico of the mark "Bulova" and the pendency of Mexican legal proceedings thereon, to the merits of Bulova's claim. The trial judge, having initially reserved disposition of the jurisdictional issue until a hearing on the merits, interrupted the presentation of evidence and dismissed the complaint "with prejudice," on the ground that the court lacked jurisdiction over the cause. This decision rested on the court's findings that petitioner had committed no illegal acts within the United States. With one judge dissenting, the Court of Appeals reversed; it held that the pleadings and evidence disclosed a cause of action within the reach of the Lanham Trademark Act of 1946, 15 U.S.C. § 1051 *et seq.* The dissenting judge thought that "since the conduct complained of substantially related solely to acts done and trade carried on under full authority of Mexican law, and were confined to and affected only that nation's internal commerce, [the District Court] was without jurisdiction to enjoin such conduct." We granted certiorari, 343 U.S. 962.

Petitioner concedes, as he must, that Congress in prescribing standards of conduct for American citizens may project the impact of its laws beyond the territorial boundaries of the United States. Resolution of the jurisdictional issue in this case therefore depends on construction of exercised congressional power, not the limitations upon that power itself. And since we do not pass on the merits of Bulova's claim, we need not now explore every facet of this complex and controversial Act.

The Lanham Act, on which Bulova posited its claims to relief, confers broad jurisdictional powers upon the courts of the United States....

The record reveals the following significant facts which for purposes of a dismissal must be taken as true: Bulova Watch Company, one of the largest watch manufacturers in the world, advertised and distributed "Bulova" watches in the United States and foreign countries. Since 1929, its aural and visual advertising, in Spanish and English, has penetrated Mexico. Petitioner, long a resident of San Antonio, first entered the watch business there in 1922, and in 1926 learned of the trademark "Bulova." He subsequently transferred his business to Mexico City and, discovering that "Bulova" had not been registered in Mexico, in 1933 procured the Mexican registration of that mark. Assembling Swiss watch movements and dials and cases imported from that country and the United States, petitioner in Mexico City stamped his watches with "Bulova" and sold them as such. As a result of the distribution of spurious "Bulovas," Bulova Watch Company's Texas sales representative received numerous complaints from retail jewelers in the Mexican border area whose customers brought in for repair defective "Bulovas" which upon inspection often turned out not to be products of that company. Moreover, subsequent to our grant of certiorari in this case the prolonged litigation in the courts of Mexico has come to an end. On October 6, 1952, the Supreme Court of Mexico rendered a judgment upholding an administrative ruling which had nullified petitioner's Mexican registration of "Bulova."

On the facts in the record we agree with the Court of Appeals that petitioner's activities, when viewed as a whole, fall within the jurisdictional scope of the Lanham Act. This Court has often stated that the legislation of Congress will not extend beyond the boundaries of the United States unless a contrary legislative intent appears. The question thus is "whether Congress intended to make the law applicable" to the facts of this case. For "the United States is not debarred by any rule of international law from governing the conduct of its own citizens upon the high seas or even in foreign countries when the rights of other nations or their nationals are not infringed. With respect to such an exercise of authority there is no question of international law, but solely of the purport of the municipal law which establishes the duty of the citizen in relation to his own government." As Mr. Justice Minton, then sitting on the Court of Appeals, applied the principle in a case involving unfair methods of competition: "Congress has the power to prevent unfair trade practices in foreign commerce by citizens of the United States, although some of the acts are done outside the territorial limits of the United States." Nor has this Court in tracing the commerce scope of statutes differentiated between enforcement of legislative policy by the Government itself or by private litigants proceeding under a statutory right. The public policy subserved is the same in each case. In the light of the broad jurisdictional grant in the Lanham Act, we deem its scope to encompass petitioner's activities here. His operations and their effects were not confined within the territorial limits of a foreign nation. He bought component parts of his wares in the United States, and spurious "Bulovas" filtered through the Mexican border into this country; his competing goods could well reflect adversely on Bulova Watch Company's trade reputation in markets cultivated by advertising here as well as abroad. Under similar factual circumstances, courts of the United States have awarded relief to registered trademark owners, even prior to the advent of the broadened commerce provisions of the Lanham Act. Even when most jealously read, that Act's sweeping reach into "all commerce which may lawfully be regulated by Congress" does not constrict prior law or deprive courts of jurisdiction previously exercised. We do not deem material that petitioner affixed the mark "Bulova" in Mexico City rather than here, or that his purchases in the United States when viewed in isolation do not violate any of our laws. They were essential steps in the course of business consummated abroad; acts in themselves legal lose that character when they become part of an unlawful scheme. "[In] such a case it is not material that the source of the forbidden effects upon ... commerce arises in one phase or another of that program." In sum, we do not think that petitioner by so simple a device can evade the thrust of the laws of the United States in a privileged sanctuary beyond our borders.

. . . .

AFFIRMED.

■ Mr. Justice Black took no part in the decision of this case.

■ Mr. Justice Reed, with whom Mr. Justice Douglas joins, *dissenting*....

McBee v. Delica

417 F.3d 107 (1st Cir.2005).

■ Lynch, Circuit Judge.

It has long been settled that the Lanham Act can, in appropriate cases, be applied extraterritorially. *See Steele v. Bulova Watch Co.*, 344 U.S. 280, 73 S.Ct. 252, 97 L.Ed. 319 (1952). This case, dismissed for lack of subject matter jurisdiction, requires us, as a matter of first impression for this circuit, to lay out a framework for determining when such extraterritorial use of the Lanham Act is proper.

In doing so, we choose not to adopt the formulations used by various other circuits. *See, e.g., Reebok Int'l, Ltd. v. Marnatech Enters.*, 970 F.2d 552, 554–57 (9th Cir.1992); *Vanity Fair Mills v. T. Eaton Co.*, 234 F.2d 633, 642–43 (2d Cir.1956). The best-known test, the *Vanity Fair* test, asks (1) whether the defendant is an American citizen, (2) whether the defendant's actions have a substantial effect on United States commerce, and (3) whether relief would create a conflict with foreign law. 234 F.2d at 642–43. These three prongs are given an uncertain weight. Based on *Steele* and subsequent Supreme Court case law, we disaggregate the three prongs of the *Vanity Fair* test, identify the different types of "extraterritorial" application questions, and isolate the factors pertinent to subject matter jurisdiction.

Our framework asks first whether the defendant is an American citizen; that inquiry is different because a separate constitutional basis for jurisdiction exists for control of activities, even foreign activities, of an American citizen. Further, when the Lanham Act plaintiff seeks to enjoin sales in the United States, there is no question of extraterritorial application; the court has subject matter jurisdiction.

In order for a plaintiff to reach foreign activities of foreign defendants in American courts, however, we adopt a separate test. We hold that subject matter jurisdiction under the Lanham Act is proper only if the complained-of activities have a substantial effect on United States commerce, viewed in light of the purposes of the Lanham Act. If this "substantial effects" question is answered in the negative, then the court lacks jurisdiction over the defendant's extraterritorial acts; if it is answered in the affirmative, then the court possesses subject matter jurisdiction.

. . .

The plaintiff, Cecil McBee, an American citizen and resident, seeks to hold the defendant, Delica Co., Ltd. (Delica), responsible for its activities in Japan said to harm McBee's reputation in both Japan and the United States and for Delica's purported activities in the United States. McBee is a well-known American jazz musician; Delica is a Japanese corporation that adopted the name "Cecil McBee" for its adolescent female clothing line. McBee sued for false endorsement and dilution under the Lanham Act. . . . We conclude that the [district] court lacked jurisdiction over McBee's claims seeking (1) an injunction in the United States barring access to Delica's Internet website, which is written in Japanese, and (2) damages for harm to McBee due to Delica's sales in Japan. McBee has made no showing that Delica's activities had a substantial effect on United States commerce. . . .

I.

The relevant facts are basically undisputed. McBee, who lives in both Maine and New York, is a jazz bassist with a distinguished career spanning over forty-five years. He has performed in the United States and world-wide, has performed on over 200 albums, and has released six albums under his own name (including in Japan). He won a Grammy Award in 1989, was inducted into the Oklahoma Jazz Hall of Fame in 1991, and teaches at the New England Conservatory of Music in Boston. McBee has toured Japan several times, beginning in the early 1980s, and has performed in many major Japanese cities, including Tokyo. He continues to tour in Japan. McBee has never licensed or authorized the use of his name to anyone, except of course in direct connection with his musical performances, as for example on an album. In his own words, he has sought to "have [his] name associated only with musical excellence."

Delica is a Japanese clothing retailer. In 1984, Delica adopted the trade name "Cecil McBee" for a line of clothing and accessories primarily marketed to teen-aged girls. Delica holds a Japanese trademark for "Cecil McBee," in both Japanese and Roman or English characters, for a variety of product types. Delica owns and operates retail shops throughout Japan under the brand name "Cecil McBee"; these are the only stores where "Cecil McBee" products are sold. There are no "Cecil McBee" retail shops outside of Japan. Delica sold approximately $23 million worth of "Cecil McBee" goods in 1996 and experienced steady growth in sales in subsequent years; in 2002, Delica sold $112 million worth of "Cecil McBee" goods.... It is undisputed that [Delica] has never shipped any "Cecil McBee" goods outside of Japan. As described later, Delica's policy generally is to decline orders from the United States.

Delica operates a website, http://www.cecilmcbee.net, which contains pictures and descriptions of "Cecil McBee" products, as well as locations and telephone numbers of retail stores selling those products. The website is created and hosted in Japan, and is written almost entirely in Japanese, using Japanese characters (although, like the style book, it contains some English words). The website contains news about the "Cecil McBee" line, including promotions. Customers can log onto the site to access their balance of bonus "points" earned for making past "Cecil McBee" purchases, as well as information about how to redeem those points for additional merchandise. However, the site does not allow purchases of "Cecil McBee" products to be made online. The website can be viewed from anywhere in the Internet-accessible world.

McBee produced evidence that, when searches on Internet search engines (such as Google) are performed for the phrase "Cecil McBee," Delica's website (www.cecilmcbee.net) generally comes up as one of the first few results, and occasionally comes up first, ahead of any of the various websites that describe the musical accomplishments of the plaintiff. Certain other websites associated with Delica's "Cecil McBee" product line also come up when such searches are performed; like www.cecilmcbee.net, it is evident from the search results page that these websites are written primarily in Japanese characters.

In 1995, plaintiff McBee became aware that Delica was using his name, without his authorization, for a line of clothing in Japan. He contacted an American lawyer, who advised him that Delica was unlikely to be subject to personal jurisdiction in the United States. McBee retained a Japanese attorney, who sent a letter to Delica asking it to cease using the "Cecil McBee" name. When Delica declined, McBee petitioned the Japanese Patent Office to invalidate Delica's English-language trademark on "Cecil McBee."

On February 28, 2002, the Japanese Patent Office ruled Delica's trademark in Japan invalid. However, Delica appealed to the Tokyo High Court, which on December 26, 2002, vacated the decision of the Japanese

Patent Office. On remand, the Japanese Patent Office found for Delica and reinstated Delica's registration of the "Cecil McBee" trademark. McBee appealed that ruling to the Tokyo High Court and lost; the trademark reinstatement has become final.

In early 2002, Delica formulated a policy not to sell or ship "Cecil McBee" brand products to the United States and informed its managers throughout the company. Delica's admitted reason for this policy was to prevent McBee from being able to sue Delica in the United States.

. . .

[T]here is virtually no evidence of "Cecil McBee" brand goods entering the United States after being sold by Delica in Japan. McBee stated in affidavit that "[f]riends, fellow musicians, fans, students, and others . . . have reported seeing [his] name on clothing, shopping bags [and] merchandise (whether worn or carried by a young girl walking on the street in Boston or New York or elsewhere). . . ." But no further evidence or detail of these sightings in the United States was provided. McBee also provided evidence that Cecil McBee goods have occasionally been sold on eBay, an auction website that allows bids to be placed and items sold anywhere in the world. Most of the sellers were not located in the United States, and there is no evidence that any of the items were purchased by American buyers.

. . .

III.

A. Framework for Assessing Extraterritorial Use of the Lanham Act

. . .

The *Steele* Court did not define the outer limits of Congressional power because it was clear that the facts presented a case within those limits. The *Steele* Court explicitly and implicitly relied on two different aspects of Congressional power to reach this conclusion. First, it explicitly relied on the power of Congress to regulate "the conduct of its own citizens," even extraterritorial conduct. *Steele*, 344 U.S. at 285–86, 73 S.Ct. 252. This doctrine is based on an idea that Congressional power over American citizens is a matter of domestic law that raises no serious international concerns, even when the citizen is located abroad. . . .

Second, *Steele* also implicitly appears to rely on Congressional power over foreign commerce, although the Foreign Commerce clause is not cited- the Court noted that the defendant's actions had an impact on the plaintiff's reputation, and thus on commerce within the United States. . . .

When the purported infringer is not an American citizen, and the alleged illegal activities occur outside the United States, then the analysis is . . . appears to rest solely on the foreign commerce power. Yet it is beyond much doubt that the Lanham Act can be applied against foreign corporations or individuals in appropriate cases; no court has ever suggested that the foreign citizenship of a defendant is always fatal. . . .

The decisions of the Supreme Court in the antitrust context seem useful to us as a guide. The Court has written in this area, on the issue of extraterritorial application, far more recently than it has written on the Lanham Act, and thus the decisions reflect more recent evolutions in terms of legal analysis of extraterritorial activity. As the Court noted in *Steele*, Lanham Act violations abroad often radiate unlawful consequences into the United States, see 344 U.S. at 288, 73 S.Ct. 252. . . . One can easily imagine a variety of harms to American commerce arising from wholly foreign activities by foreign defendants. There could be harm caused by false endorsements, passing off, or product disparagement, or confusion over sponsorship affecting American commerce and causing loss of American sales. Further, global piracy of American goods is a major problem for American companies: annual losses from unauthorized use of United States trademarks, according to one commentator, now amount to $200 billion annually. In both the antitrust and the Lanham Act areas, there is a risk that absent a certain degree of extraterritorial enforcement, violators will either take advantage of international coordination problems or hide in countries without efficacious antitrust or trademark laws, thereby avoiding legal authority.

. . .

2.   Claim for Injunction Barring Access to Internet Website

McBee . . . argues that his claim for an injunction against Delica's posting of its Internet website in a way that is visible to United States consumers . . . does not call for an extraterritorial application of the Lanham Act. Here McBee is incorrect: granting this relief would constitute an extraterritorial application of the Act, and thus subject matter jurisdiction would only be appropriate if McBee could show a substantial effect on United States commerce. McBee has not shown such a substantial effect from Delica's website.

We begin with McBee's argument that his website claim, like his claim for Delica's sales into the United States, is not an extraterritorial application of the Lanham Act. McBee does not seek to reach the website because it is a method, by Delica, for selling "Cecil McBee" goods into the United States. In such a case, if a court had jurisdiction to enjoin sales of goods within the United States, it might have jurisdiction to enjoin the website as well, or at least those parts of the website that are necessary to allow the sales to occur. Rather, the injury McBee complains about from the website is that its mere existence has caused him harm, because United States citizens can view the website and become confused about McBee's relationship with the Japanese clothing company. In particular, McBee argues that he has suffered harm from the fact that Delica's website often comes up on search engines ahead of fan sites about McBee's jazz career.

Delica's website, although hosted from Japan and written in Japanese, happens to be reachable from the United States just as it is reachable from other countries. That is the nature of the Internet. The website is hosted and managed overseas; its visibility within the United States is more in the nature of an effect, which occurs only when someone in the United States decides to visit the website. To hold that any website in a foreign language, wherever hosted, is automatically reachable under the Lanham Act so long as it is visible in the United States would be senseless. The United States often will have no real interest in hearing trademark lawsuits about websites that are written in a foreign language and hosted in other countries.

McBee attempts to analogize the existence of Delica's website, which happens to be visible in any country, to the direct mail advertising that the *Vanity Fair* court considered to be domestic conduct and so held outside the scope of the extraterritoriality analysis. *See Vanity Fair*, 234 F.2d at 638–39. The analogy is poor for three reasons: first, the advertising in Vanity Fair was closely connected with mail-order sales; second, direct mail advertising is a far more targeted act than is the hosting of a website; and third, Delica's website, unlike the advertising in *Vanity Fair*, is in a foreign language.

Our conclusion that McBee's website claim calls for extraterritorial application of the Lanham Act is bolstered by a consideration of the now extensive case law relating to treatment of Internet websites with respect to personal jurisdiction. We recognize that the contexts are distinct, but the extraterritorial application of jurisdiction under the Lanham Act evokes concerns about territorial restraints on sovereigns that are similar to concerns driving personal jurisdiction. To put the principle broadly, the mere existence of a website that is visible in a forum and that gives information about a company and its products is not enough, by itself, to subject a defendant to personal jurisdiction in that forum. *See, e.g., Jennings v. AC Hydraulic A/S*, 383 F.3d 546, 549–50 (7th Cir.2004); *ALS Scan, Inc. v. Digital Serv. Consultants, Inc.*, 293 F.3d 707, 713–15 (4th Cir.2002).

Something more is necessary, such as interactive features which allow the successful online ordering of the defendant's products. The mere existence of a website does not show that a defendant is directing its business activities towards every forum where the website is visible; as well, given the omnipresence of Internet websites today, allowing personal jurisdiction to be premised on such a contact alone would "eviscerate" the limits on a state's jurisdiction over out-of-state or foreign defendants.

Similarly, allowing subject matter jurisdiction under the Lanham Act to automatically attach whenever a website is visible in the United States would eviscerate the territorial curbs on judicial authority that Congress is, quite sensibly, presumed to have imposed in this area.

Our conclusion does not make it impossible for McBee to use the Lanham Act to attack a Japan-based website; it merely requires that McBee first establish that the website has a substantial effect on commerce in the United States before there is subject matter jurisdiction under the Lanham Act. We can imagine many situations in which the presence of a website would ensure (or, at least, help to ensure) that the United States has a sufficient interest. The substantial effects test, however, is not met here.

Delica's website is written almost entirely in Japanese characters; this makes it very unlikely that any real confusion of American consumers, or diminishing of McBee's reputation, would result from the website's existence. In fact, most American consumers are unlikely to be able to understand Delica's website at all. Further, McBee's claim that Americans looking for information about him will be unable to find it is unpersuasive: the Internet searches reproduced in the record all turned up both sites about McBee and sites about Delica's clothing line on their first page of results. The two sets of results are easily distinguishable to any consumer, given that the Delica sites are clearly shown, by the search engines, as being written in Japanese characters. Finally, we stress that McBee has produced no evidence of any American consumers going to the website and then becoming confused about whether McBee had a relationship with Delica. . . .

QUESTIONS

1. In *Steele v. Bulova*, the defendant had targeted U.S. purchasers when it sold the spurious watches from a tourist town right across the Mexican border. In *Scotch Whisky Assoc. v. Barton Distilling Co.*, 489 F.2d 809 (7th Cir.1973), the defendants sold American whiskey in Panama under the name "Scotch." The purchasers of the spurious spirits were not U.S. nationals or residents (putting aside the question of U.S. soldiers in the then-Canal Zone), but some of the acts creating and assembling the deceptive packaging were accomplished in the U.S. *American Rice v. Arkansas Rice Growers Co-op. Assn.*, 701 F.2d 408 (5th Cir.1983), presented a more attenuated case for assertion of Lanham Act jurisdiction, for the purchasers resided and the packaging was created beyond U.S. borders. All parties, however, were U.S. entities. Is that all that is required to permit an assertion of Lanham Act jurisdiction with extraterritorial effect? *Cf. Reebok Int'l. v. American Sales Corp.*, 11 U.S.P.Q.2d 1229 (C.D.Cal.1989) (counterfeit designer sneakers manufactured in Taiwan and sold in Singapore and Japan; plaintiff alleged that defendants, California residents, had financed and directed the operations in Asia from the U.S., and particularly that the "purchase of the shoes was substantially financed by letters of credit and other financial documents issued by a number of California banks in this district upon instructions given by defendants here." Should the court retain jurisdiction?)

2. Suppose the Mexican Court had upheld the validity of the *Steele v. Bulova* defendant's Mexican registration of BULOVA. How should a U.S. court have analyzed the challenge to exercise of jurisdiction under the Lanham Act?

3. Recall the decisions addressing whether a foreign mark's "use" or "use in [US] commerce" suffices to vest the foreign entrepreneur with trademark rights in the US, or to confer standing to oppose a US registration, *supra*, Chapters 3.D, 3.E, and 4.C.3. Are those decisions consistent with *Steele v. Bulova*? With *McBee v. Delica*?

4. Relevant Public/Secondary Confusion

Mastercrafters Clock & Radio Co. v. Vacheron & Constantin–Le Coultre Watches, Inc.

221 F.2d 464 (2d Cir.), *cert. denied*, 350 U.S. 832 (1955).

■ Frank, Circuit Judge:

Mastercrafters Clock & Radio Co., the plaintiff below, is an American manufacturer of electric clocks. Vacheron & Constantin–Le Coultre Watches, Inc. (hereinafter referred to as "Vacheron"), defendant-counter-claimant, is an American importer and distributor of Swiss watches.

In 1952, when Mastercrafters launched the production and distribution of its Model 308 clock, Vacheron wired Mastercrafters and many of its customers-distributors that Model 308 was a counterfeit of the distinctive appearance and configuration of the Atmos clock, distributed by Vacheron, and that Vacheron would commence legal action if necessary. Following these telegrams, Vacheron started state-court suits against several of Mastercrafters' distributors for damages and an injunction. Mastercrafters, faced with a cancellation of orders for its Model 308 from distributors being sued in the state courts, countered by bringing the present action seeking a declaratory judgment that its Model 308 does not unfairly compete with Vacheron, and asking damages allegedly resulting from Vacheron's suits against Mastercrafters' distributors and an injunction to restrain further prosecution of those suits. Vacheron counterclaimed for damages from alleged unfair competition and for an injunction restraining the manufacture and distribution of Model 308. . . .

The [trial] judge found that, before plaintiff began production of its Model 308, the Atmos clock "was readily distinguishable from all other clocks then on the market by virtue of its appearance"; that plaintiff's Model 308 copied that appearance; that plaintiff "undoubtedly intended to, and did, avail itself of an eye-catching design and hoped to cater to the price-conscious purchaser who desires to own a copy of a luxury design clock regardless of mechanism or source"; that the Atmos clock sold for not less than $175 while plaintiff's sold for $30 or $40; that on "two or three occasions Model 308 has been described as 'a copy of Atmos,'" once by a representative of plaintiff at an exhibit in Chicago, on the other occasions by distributors of plaintiff's clock; that "since the introduction of the Model 308, Vacheron's salesmen have encountered considerable sales resistance" and its sales have "fallen off"; and that these facts undoubtedly prove "the uniqueness and even the aesthetic qualities of" the Atmos clock. He further found that three customers inquired as to "the lower priced Atmos" and that others "said they knew where they 'could get a clock for $30 or $40 just like the Atmos.'" But he held there was no unfair competition by plaintiff because (a) more than one person lawfully distributed the Atmos clock and therefore there was no single source, (b) there was no evidence to show that the public cared what was the ultimate source, and (c) plaintiff's clock was plainly marked and advertised as plaintiff's.

Absent a design patent or a secondary meaning, of course there would be no actionable harm by plaintiff. But the existence of a secondary meaning, attaching to the unique appearance of the Atmos clock, is not precluded by the mere fact that more than one person distributed that clock in the same area. The actionable harm, in a secondary-meaning case, may result either from the likelihood (a) of loss of customers or (b) of loss of reputation, or (c) of both. Such loss can result from the customer's belief that the competing article derives from the same source as that of the party complaining; and it matters not whether the customers know just who is the source. The ultimate source here was the Swiss manufacturer, while the intermediate sources, in this country, were the defendant and Cartier. All three had actionable claims against plaintiff, if its conduct did or was likely to injure the reputation of the ultimate source of the Atmos clock, for all three legitimately enjoyed the benefits of that reputation.

True, a customer examining plaintiff's clock would see from the electric cord, that it was not an "atmospheric" clock. But, as the judge found, plaintiff copied the design of the Atmos clock because plaintiff intended to, and did, attract purchasers who wanted a "luxury design" clock. This goes to show at least that some customers would buy plaintiff's cheaper clock for the purpose of acquiring the prestige gained by displaying what many visitors at the customers' homes would regard as a prestigious article. Plaintiff's wrong thus consisted of the fact that such a visitor would be likely to assume that the clock was an Atmos clock. Neither the electric cord attached to, nor the plaintiff's name on, its clock would be likely to come to the attention of such a visitor; the likelihood of such confusion suffices to render plaintiff's conduct actionable.

Plaintiff's intention thus to reap financial benefits from poaching on the reputation of the Atmos clock is of major importance. Of course, where there is no likelihood of confusion—as, *e.g.,* where the alleged infringing article is not in a sufficiently adjacent field—then an alleged infringer's intent becomes irrelevant, since an intent to do a wrong cannot transmute a lawful into an unlawful act. But where the copying is unlawful, if only there is a likelihood of confusion, then the intent of the copier becomes decidedly relevant: It gives rise to a powerful inference that confusion is likely, and puts on the alleged infringer the burden of going forward with proof that it is not. Here the plaintiff's intent is unmistakable; accordingly, plaintiff had the burden of going forward with proof showing an absence of such likelihood; and that burden plaintiff did not discharge. Consequently, we do not accept the judge's findings as to the absence of unfair competition by plaintiff.

Since plaintiff was guilty of unfair competition, the judgment against defendant must be reversed. We remand with directions to dismiss plaintiff's complaint and, on the counterclaim, to grant an injunction against plaintiff, and to ascertain the damages to defendant. . . .

The trial judge should determine whether defendant should also be awarded a sum equal to plaintiff's profits from sales of the infringing clock. We do not now decide that such an amount should be awarded but leave that matter to be decided, in the first instance at any rate, by the trial judge.

Reversed and remanded.

QUESTIONS

1. So long as the actual purchaser is not confused regarding the source of the goods, why should it matter under trademark and unfair competition law that the purchaser's friends may be misled (or even that the purchaser sought to mislead his friends)?

2. Is "copying for the purpose of acquiring prestige" trademark infringement?

3. Do you understand why "associating" goods or services with a trademark owner is "confusing"? Do you agree?

Munsingwear, Inc. v. Jockey International

31 U.S.P.Q.2d 1146 (D.Minn.), *aff'd*, 39 F.3d 1184 (8th Cir.1994).

■ DOTY, DISTRICT COURT JUDGE:

This matter is before the court on plaintiff Munsingwear's motion for a preliminary injunction and defendant Jockey's motion for summary judgment. Based on a review of the file, record, and proceedings herein, the court grants Jockey's motion and denies Munsingwear's motion.

BACKGROUND

This matter involves the marketing of a horizontal-fly version of mens' [sic] underwear by Jockey. Jockey first introduced its horizontal-fly[1] briefs under the "Jockey Pouch" ("Pouch") name in June 1992. The Pouch line consisted of briefs with the horizontal-fly and the "JOCKEY" trademark woven into the waistband. They were sold through Jockey's standard lines of commerce. The packaging consisted of standard cellophane wrapped around the brief with the "JOCKEY" trademark and Jockey Design trademark on both the front and back of the packaging.

Munsingwear instituted this action against Jockey claiming trademark infringement under § 43(a) of the Lanham Act, common law trademark infringement, and deceptive trade practices. Munsingwear based these claims on its alleged preexisting trademark rights in the horizontal-fly (or H–FLY) mark. While not having actual federal registration of the H–FLY, Munsingwear claims it is entitled to protection based upon its continuous use of the design since 1946, reinforced by millions of dollars of advertising.

Munsingwear now moves for a preliminary injunction to prevent Jockey from manufacturing, distributing and selling Pouch underwear.

---

1. A horizontal-fly is exactly as it is described. Rather than running vertical, or parallel with the leg, the horizontal-fly is perpendicular to the leg and looks generally like a pocket.

Jockey moves for summary judgment claiming that there is no likelihood of confusion between the two manufacturers' underwear as a matter of law.

DISCUSSION

. . . .

Before undertaking the six factor *Squirtco* analysis, the court must initially determine which products are to be compared. In this action two alternatives exist, either the pre-sale or post-sale product. The pre-sale product consists of the underwear as packaged and sold to the consuming public, seen in Figures 1 and 2 of Jockey's motion for summary judgment. The post-sale product consists of the actual individual briefs themselves. Determination of which products are to be compared is made by referring to how consumers will encounter the two products. *Lindy Pen Co., Inc. v. Bic Pen Corp.*, 725 F.2d 1240 (9th Cir.1984) (Similarity of marks considered in light of the way they are encountered in the marketplace and the circumstances surrounding their purchase.)

Jockey contends that the overall combination and arrangement of the package design elements, the pre-sale product, should serve as the basis of analysis. Evidence submitted in support of that contention shows that underwear is purchased in single or multi-unit cellophane wrapped packages that indicate source and style information.

Munsingwear claims that, while the products are purchased as packaged, consumers base their buying decision on other factors. Among those cited are the consumer's desire for certain styles and purchase place exposure to the product while it is on mannequins. Munsingwear contends that the combination of the two factors often leads to the subsequent purchasing decision and thus likelihood of customer confusion. Munsingwear equates this display technique to post-sale exposure which serves as the basis for its argument that consumers will be confused.

The courts that have decided the question have split as to whether pre-sale products or post-sale product provide the proper basis for analysis. The Eighth Circuit has not yet ruled on this issue. On the facts of this case, the argument for pre-sale exposure is stronger because any relevant consumer confusion will likely occur prior to sale, if at all. As customarily worn, underwear is concealed by other articles of clothing. The general public does not ordinarily see underwear in the same manner and to the extent that it views outerwear. Thus, the potential for customer confusion is not as great as it could be for other articles of clothing. *Lois Sportswear, U.S.A., Inc. v. Levi Strauss & Co.*, 631 F. Supp. 735, 228 U.S.P.Q. 648 (S.D.N.Y.1985), *aff'd*, 799 F.2d 867, 872–73 (2d Cir.1986). In *Levi* the Second Circuit held that potential confusion may exist in consumers seeing appellant's jeans worn outside the retail store absent any identifying labels that may be attached at the time of purchase. *Id.* The inherently concealed nature of worn underwear diminishes the concern for post-sale confusion noted by the *Levi* court. Thus Munsingwear's reliance on *Levi* is misplaced.

The lack of post-sale exposure of the product to the general public reduces the risk that any customers will be confused as to source.

a. Similarity

The first step in the *Squirtco* analysis is to compare the two products as they are encountered by the consuming public. Examination of the two product packages reveals that they are not similar. The Jockey package consists of a cardboard insert that has a picture of a man wearing the style of underwear the package contains. The "JOCKEY POUCH" label is written across the top with the "JOCKEY" and Jockey logo trademarks. Finally, the material makeup of the underwear is also listed as well as the size and manufacturer's barcodes. The Munsingwear package does not have a cardboard insert but rather consists of a "band and medallion" through the middle of the package. The medallion has the kangaroo design with "MUNSINGWEAR KANGAROO BRIEF" encircling the drawing. Under the band is the Munsingwear trade mark. The Munsingwear package also lists sizes. When viewed side by side, it is obvious which package is produced by which manufacturer. Thus, the court finds that there is no substantial similarity between the two products.

b. Proximity

While competitive proximity is not controlled by the two manufactures, both products are sold in the men's department of stores. Munsingwear cites an individual instance where the two products were sold side-by-side; Jockey contends that this is not the usual course of business and is unusual. However, whether Munsingwear and Jockey are sold side-by-side becomes irrelevant when the market is viewed. In a market controlled by only a few producers it is inevitable that one brand will be located near another. Efficiency and customer assistance dictate that many stores will display and sell all similar products in relatively close proximity. Thus, the court finds that due to the nature of the product, it is highly likely that the two products will be sold in relatively close proximity, but that this is a function of market decisions made by individual stores rather than by the litigants.

c. Intent to Pass–Off

Munsingwear next argues that Jockey formed a specific intent to pass-off its "Pouch" underwear as Munsingwear's "H–Fly" underwear. Jockey contends that the existing strength of its trademark and the amount spent in advertising indicate that this is not the case. Jockey claims that its marketing of Pouch underwear is a form of competition for market share rather than an attempt to pass-off its underwear as that of Munsingwear.

Viewing the two packages together, the court finds that it is evident that there is no intent to pass off. First, the two packages prominently indicate who the manufacturer is. Second, the individual pieces of underwear have the manufacturer's name permanently stitched into the waistband. Based upon these factors, the court finds that Jockey has no intent to pass off its underwear as that of Munsingwear.

d. Actual Confusion

[The court found no evidence probative of actual confusion]

e. Survey Evidence

[No surveys were submitted.]

f. Costs and Conditions of Purchase

Finally, the court must consider the costs and conditions surrounding the purchase of the two products. Generally, the more sophisticated the average consumer of a product is, the less likely it is that similarities in trade dress and trademarks will result in confusion concerning the source or sponsorship of the product. *Bristol–Myers Squibb Co. v. McNeil–P.P.C., Inc.*, 973 F.2d 1033 (2d Cir.1992). In this action, both parties suggest that its products are purchased in a retail setting and that the costs are similar and relatively inexpensive. The purchasers of relatively inexpensive goods are held to a lesser standard of purchasing care and do not give much thought to the purchase of such inexpensive goods. *Specialty Brands, Inc. v. Coffee Bean Distributors, Inc.*, 748 F.2d 669 (Fed.Cir.1984); c.f., *Beer Nuts, Inc. v. Clover Club Foods, Co.*, 805 F.2d 920 (10th Cir.1986); *Sun–Fun Products, Inc. v. Suntan Research & Development, Inc.*, 656 F.2d 186 (5th Cir.1981). Therefore, due to the inexpensive nature of the products, the court finds that the relevant consumer is not generally sophisticated and gives little thought to the purchasing decision.

Upon review of the facts in this case, and applying the *Squirtco* analysis, the court finds that the dissimilarity between the two products in their pre-sale condition, the lack of an intent to pass off by Jockey and the lack of actual customer confusion all weigh heavily in Jockey's favor. The relatively close proximity of the two products during retail sale, the unsophisticated decision making process of the average consumer and the lack of a survey to establish or disprove actual confusion weigh in favor of neither party. Therefore, the court finds that Jockey has established that no likelihood of confusion exists between the two products.

5. REVERSE CONFUSION

Harlem Wizards Entertainment Basketball, Inc. v. NBA Properties, Inc., 952 F.Supp. 1084 (D.N.J.1997). The Harlem Wizards is a "show basketball" team. Founded in 1962, the team plays exhibition games in which competitive basketball play is interspersed with comedic antics and tricks. The Wizards do not, typically, sell tickets to their "games"; rather, they market themselves to third party organizations, which hire them to appear at fairs, festivals and charity programs. The Harlem Wizards have performed throughout the United States and internationally. The team sells souvenir t-shirts, sweatshirts, caps, basketballs and posters bearing the Wizards logo at its games and appearances, but does not market them to retail stores. The Washington Bullets were an NBA professional basketball team. The team's owner had been concerned for some time that the Bullets name had unfortunately violent connotations. On February 22, 1996, the Bullets announced that beginning in the 1997–98 season, the Washington Bullets would formally change their name to the Washington Wizards. The Harlem Wizards filed a trademark infringement suit, alleging reverse confusion. The court began by distinguishing reverse confusion cases from conventional trademark infringement:

> In an ordinary trademark infringement case, the alleged trademark infringer takes advantage of the reputation and good will of a senior trademark owner by adopting a similar or identical mark. In contrast, reverse confusion arises when a larger, more powerful entity adopts the trademark of a smaller, less powerful trademark user and thereby causes confusion as to the origin of the senior trademark user's goods or services. Because the junior user is a larger company with greater financial ability and trademark recognition in the marketplace, it can easily overwhelm the senior user by flooding the market with promotion of its similar trademark. The strength of the junior user's promotional campaigns leads consumers to believe that the senior user's products derive from that of the junior user or that the senior user is actually the trademark infringer. As a result, the senior user "loses the value of the trademark—its product identity, corporate identity, control over its goodwill and reputation, and ability to move into new markets." The federal courts and legal commentators have observed that failure to recognize reverse confusion would essentially immunize from unfair competition liability companies that have well established trade names and the financial ability to advertise a senior mark taken from smaller, less powerful competitors.

The court analyzed the claim by applying the Third Circuit's version of the *Polaroid* factors. It concluded that the degree of similarity between the two teams' services was the most important indicator of likelihood of confusion.

> The Court first addresses whether the services offered by the parties are similar because in its view, this factor is the most dispositive regarding the existence of any likelihood of confusion. Courts have held that where the goods and services offered by the plaintiff and defendant are dissimilar or non-competitive, consumer confusion is less likely to occur. . . .

> . . . Plaintiff would have this Court simply lump the services of plaintiff and defendants under the heading of basketball or entertainment and, on that basis alone, find that the parties engage in confusingly similar services. Numerous cases, however, illustrate that even when two products or services fall within the same general field, it does not mean that the two products or services are sufficiently similar to create a likelihood of confusion.

Meaningful differences between the products and services are often cited as a factor tending to negate reverse confusion, even when the products are superficially within the same category. . . .

The show basketball performed by plaintiff is markedly distinct from NBA competitive basketball in myriad ways. As a show basketball team, plaintiff simply does not play NBA level competitive basketball. Even accepting plaintiff's contention that it has on many occasions played genuinely competitive basketball during the first and third quarters of its games, it is undisputed that the remaining quarters are reserved for comedy routines and fancy tricks. It is inconceivable that the NBA would adopt such a "show" format. Plaintiff also plays against any team put together by the organization that purchases its services. Consequently, its competition is ordinary citizens and not serious NBA level athletes. Furthermore, as a show basketball team, plaintiff does not play in a league, whereas in the NBA, league competition is an intrinsic element of the sport. Also in contrast to the NBA, a large proportion of plaintiff's performances are non-game appearances such as school assembly programs. And with respect to plaintiff there is no proof that the athletic quality of its average player is similar to that of an NBA team member. These are but a few examples of the dissimilarity between the parties' services. Therefore, the court finds that when every aspect of the two teams is compared, there is glaring dissimilarity. Any similarity between the two teams is superficial and the result of creating over-inclusive categories that are irrelevant to the likelihood of confusion.

The court's analysis of the remaining factors confirmed its conclusion that no confusion was likely:

The similarities between the channels of trade and target audiences of the two teams are closely related and therefore, the Court considers these two factors together. The channels of trade that plaintiff uses are not similar to those used by defendants. Plaintiff established that it targets event organizers at high schools, colleges, and charitable organizations and advertises through direct mail solicitation, participation at trade shows, and trade magazines. Plaintiff does not advertise on television, radio or in the popular print media. Plaintiff's merchandise is only available as souvenirs at its games and appearances. In contrast, the Washington Bullets, as a NBA member team, advertises its services directly to sports fans through television and print media and its merchandise is widely available in retail stores. Moreover, as a show basketball team, plaintiff competes with other show and comedy basketball teams for customers and not with the NBA. For example, plaintiff frequently refers to the Harlem Globetrotters in its advertisements and promotional material because it is seeking to reach that more famous team's audience. Therefore, the Court finds that plaintiff has failed to establish that it shares the same channels of trade and target audience as defendants.

. . . .

It is widely accepted as true that consumers are less likely to be confused about the origin of specific goods or services if such goods are expensive because the amount of care and attention expended by consumers increases proportionately as the price of the desired goods or services increases. Plaintiff's goods and services include games, appearances and merchandise. Harlem Wizards' tickets typically sell for between five and eight dollars while NBA tickets are significantly more expensive, requiring somewhat of an inheritance as a paying source. It is not surprising therefore, that the average NBA fan earns about $60,000 a year. Given the disparity between ticket prices of the plaintiff and the NBA alone, it is unlikely that likelihood of confusion exists between the parties' services. Moreover, NBA fans are generally sophisticated and knowledgeable of their sport; they read about their favorite teams in the sports pages or listen to sports reporting and commentary on television and radio. Therefore, the Court finds it unlikely that consumers will attend a Harlem Wizards' game expecting to see NBA basketball or purchase NBA tickets expecting to see the Harlem Wizards perform show basketball.

. . . .

Based on the evidence presented, the Court finds that there are no other factors that would lead consumers to believe that plaintiff offers services similar to the NBA. For nearly thirty-five years, plaintiff has limited its services to show basketball, a service that is separate and distinct from NBA basketball. Plaintiff has not shown that it plans to chart a new course by entering the world of professional competitive basketball. The evidence presented inevitably leads to the conclusion that under these circumstances, a wizard is not a wizard. Therefore, for the reasons stated, the Court finds that the Washington Bullets' adoption of the Washington Wizards as its new name poses no likelihood of injury to the Harlem Wizards in the marketplace and dismisses plaintiff's federal and state law claims.

Dreamwerks Production, Inc. v. SKG Studio, 142 F.3d 1127 (9th Cir.1998). In this suit brought by a convention organizer specializing in STAR TREK themes, Judge Kozinski adopted a reverse confusion analysis quite different from the *Washington Wizards* court's.

In the usual infringement case, these factors are applied to determine whether the junior user is palming off its products as those of the senior user. Would a consumer who finds a running shoe marked Mike be bamboozled into thinking that it was manufactured by Nike? In a reverse infringement case, like ours, there is no question of palming off, since neither junior nor senior user wishes to siphon off the other's goodwill. The question in such cases is whether consumers doing business with the senior user might mistakenly believe that they are dealing with the junior user. More specifically, the question here is whether a reasonable consumer attending a Dreamwerks-sponsored convention might do so believing that it is a convention sponsored by DreamWorks.[3]

Before performing a Vulcan mind meld on the "reasonably prudent consumer," we note that if this were an ordinary trademark case rather than a reverse infringement case—in other words if DreamWorks had been there first and Dreamwerks later opened up a business running entertainment-related conventions—there would be little doubt that DreamWorks would have stated a case for infringement sufficient to survive summary judgment.[4] The reason for this, of course, is that a famous mark like DreamWorks SKG casts a long shadow. Does the result change in a reverse infringement case because the long shadow is cast by the junior mark? We think not.[5]

Three of the *Sleekcraft* factors are pivotal here: (1) arbitrariness of the mark; (2) similarity of sight, sound and meaning; and (3) relatedness of the goods. "Dreamwerks" is an arbitrary and fictitious mark deserving of strong protection. Had Dreamwerks chosen a descriptive mark like Sci–Fi Conventions Inc., or a suggestive mark like Sci–Fi World, some confusion with the marks of legitimate competitors might be expected. DreamWorks argues that the word "Dream" makes the Dreamwerks mark suggestive of a company which brings sci-fi dreams to life. But "Dream" is used in too many different ways to suggest any particular meaning to the reasonable consumer.[8] At best, "Dream-

---

3. Or more precisely for our purposes, the question is whether the district court erred in holding that Dreamwerks had failed to establish a triable issue of fact with respect to this. The distinction is important because it requires us to draw reasonable inferences—about the workings of the entertainment industry, the mind set of trekkies attending conventions and so on—in favor of Dreamwerks.

4. The unusual posture of the case has caused DreamWorks SKG, the holder of the famous mark, to make an argument that is quite uncharacteristic for someone in its position. Namely, it argues that the plaintiff's mark (and therefore its own) deserves relatively narrow protection. DreamWorks may someday find itself in a case where its position is reversed, and discover that the arguments it made in our case come back to haunt it. See, e.g., *Russell v. Rolfs*, 893 F.2d 1033, 1037 (9th Cir.1990) (applying judicial estoppel).

5. In an infringement case involving "forward" confusion, a more well-known senior mark suggests greater likelihood of confusion because a junior user's mark is more likely to be associated with a famous mark. In a reverse confusion case, however, we must focus on the strength of the junior user's mark. *See Sands, Taylor & Wood Co. v. Quaker Oats Co.*, 978 F.2d 947, 959 (7th Cir.1992). The concern here is that convention-goers will think DreamWorks SKG is sponsoring the Star Trek conventions. So the greater the power of DreamWorks' mark in the marketplace, the more likely it is to capture the minds of Dreamwerks customers.

8. Consider how "Dream" works itself into the commercial lexicon:

Dream Team (the 1992 Olympic basketball team)
Dream Lover (a movie)
Dream Land (an electric blanket manufacturer)

werks" conjures images related to fantasy, hope or reverie. It's too great a mental leap from hopes to Star Trek conventions for us to treat the mark as suggestive. The Dreamwerks mark deserves broad protection.

Sight, sound and meaning is easy. There is perfect similarity of sound, since "Dreamwerks" and "DreamWorks" are pronounced the same way. There is also similarity of meaning: Neither literally means anything, and to the extent the words suggest a fantasy world, they do so equally.[9] Similarity of sight presents a slightly closer question. The man-in-the-moon DreamWorks logo, when presented in the full regalia of a movie trailer, is quite distinctive. But "DreamWorks" often appears in the general press and in Industry magazines without the logo, leaving only the slight difference in spelling. Spelling is a lost art; many moviegoers might think that Miramax and Colombia Pictures are movie studios. Moreover, a perceptive consumer who does notice the "e" and lower-case "w" in Dreamwerks might shrug off the difference as an intentional modification identifying an ancillary division of the same company. While we recognize that spelling matters, we're not sure substituting one vowel for another and capitalizing a middle consonant dispels the similarity between the marks.

The clincher is the relatedness of the goods. Twenty years ago DreamWorks may have had an argument that making movies and promoting sci-fi merchandise are different businesses promoting different products. But movies and sci-fi merchandise are now as complementary as baseball and hot dogs. The main products sold at Dreamwerks conventions are movie and TV collectibles and memorabilia; the lectures, previews and appearances by actors which attract customers to Dreamwerks conventions are all dependent, in one way or another, on the output of entertainment giants like DreamWorks.

The district court emphasized that Dreamwerks has carved out a narrow niche in the entertainment marketplace, while DreamWorks controls a much broader segment. Dreamwerks targets trekkies; DreamWorks targets everyone. But the relatedness of each company's prime directive isn't relevant. Rather, we must focus on Dreamwerks'

Dream Weaver (a new Web page editor)
Dreamcoat (Joseph and the Amazing Technicolor . . .)
DreamWriter (a line of laptop computers)
Dreamgirls (a Broadway show)
Dreamwatch (a sci-fi magazine)
DreamPerks (a promotion by Northwest Airlines)

9. "Dreamwork" seems to have two more specific but lesser-known meanings. In psychiatry, "dream-work" is a term coined by Sigmund Freud to refer to the work a dream does by bringing out one's fears, anxieties and hopes, thereby helping balance one's personality. *See* Sigmund Freud, The Interpretation of Dreams 174–75 (A.A. Brill trans.,

Random House 1950). The term "dreamwork" has even spilled over into academic film analysis, where the viewing of a film (sitting in the dark, passive) is often analogized to a dream. *See, e.g.*, Paul Coates, The Sense of an Ending: Reflections on Kieslowski's Trilogy, Film Quarterly, Dec. 1, 1996 (discussing dreamwork in Blue). Since we can hardly expect the reasonable consumer to discover this film-specific meaning, we think it is appropriate to also treat the DreamWorks mark as simply calling to mind vague notions of fantasy, hope or reverie.

customers and ask whether they are likely to associate the conventions with DreamWorks the studio. Entertainment studios control all sorts of related industries: publishing, clothing, amusement parks, computer games and an endless list of toys and kids' products. In this environment it's easy for customers to suspect DreamWorks of sponsoring conventions at which movie merchandise is sold.[10] Other studios are rapidly expanding their merchandising outlets: Universal Studios has theme parks in California, Florida and Japan with dozens of stores selling movie-related products, and Disney is helping transform New York's Times Square into a G-rated shopping center. Dreamwerks convention-goers might well assume that DreamWorks decided to ride the coattails of Spielberg's unparalleled reputation for sci-fi/adventure films (Jaws, E.T., Close Encounters, Raiders, Jurassic Park) into the sci-fi merchandising business.[11]

Attrezzi v. Maytag, 436 F.3d 32 (1st Cir.2006). Plaintiff operates a single retail store of the same name in Portsmouth, New Hampshire, specializing in fine kitchen products and services (the store's name, in Italian, means "tools" or "equipment"). The shop opened in June 2002, and also sells over the internet. The store's proprietor obtained a New Hampshire trademark registration for "Attrezzi" in November 2003.

Maytag, the well-known appliance maker, selected the same word, "Attrezzi," in the spring of 2003 as the name for a new line of small electric kitchen appliances that Maytag was preparing to launch. Plaintiff also sells such appliances although it does not carry Maytag's products. Before launching its line, Maytag conducted a trademark search and learned of plaintiff's business. Maytag's in-house trademark counsel warned that this created "a problem," Maytag sought federal registration for the Attrezzi mark. Plaintiff opposed the registration and initiated suit in the federal District of New Hampshire. A jury found reverse confusion and the First Circuit affirmed. In applying that Circuit's confusion factors, the Court observed:

> Both use the word Attrezzi and to this extent the marks are identical rather than merely similar. On the other hand, Maytag uses the word only in conjunction with the term Jenn–Air (i.e., Jenn–Air Attrezzi), which could help diminish the chance of confusion. (citations

---

10. According to Jeffrey Katzenberg's deposition testimony, DreamWorks has no current plans to sponsor conventions. But DreamWorks does not dispute that it plans to hawk mass quantities of commercial goods in addition to the movies themselves. People attending Dreamwerks conventions may not know about Katzenberg's plans and could easily assume that DreamWorks has spun off a Star Trek marketing division.

11. Promoting sci-fi merchandise may or may not amount to the same thing as sponsoring conventions. But how would a Dreamwerks customer know the difference? If an entertainment studio can own the movie, the theatres which show the movie, the newspapers which list the movie, the television networks which advertise the movie, the magazines which review the movie, the stores which sell the toys, clothing and posters associated with the movie, the amusement parks with rides based on the movie and the rights to the movie-related merchandise itself, then why wouldn't a studio also sponsor a convention which celebrates movies and sells movie-related products?

omitted). Yet since the alleged harm is reverse confusion, to the extent Jenn–Air is itself the more recognized label the linkage could actually aggravate the threat to Attrezzi LLC.

Turning to the overlap of products, Maytag fairly points out that its Jenn–Air Attrezzi products are appliances while Attrezzi LLC uses the Attrezzi term to represent its entire retail business. But Attrezzi LLC itself sells small electric appliances alongside its gourmet foods and dinnerware. This is not a case in which two products are so dissimilar as to make confusion highly unlikely; and the more similar the marks are, the less necessary it is that the products themselves be very similar to create confusion.

Channels of trade, advertising modes, and prospective customers— a set of factors often considered together—also cut both ways. Maytag is a national manufacturer selling through stores and catalogues while Attrezzi LLC operates a single retail store engaged in local sales. But both use websites—Attrezzi LLC has customers in many states—and searches using the terms Attrezzi or Jenn–Air Attrezzi turn up both companies' websites. Both parties aim at basically the same high-end customers, a point in favor of Attrezzi LLC, but conceivably customer sophistication could also ameliorate confusion.

Attrezzi LLC's evidence of actual confusion, often deemed the best evidence of possible future confusion (citations omitted), is limited but real: [for example,] eight e-mails mistakenly sent to it rather than Maytag through Attrezzi LLC's website (complaining of problems with Jenn–Air Attrezzi products).....

Finally, the respective strengths of the junior and senior marks-in a nutshell, their respective renown-are regarded as relevant. Attrezzi LLC offered some evidence of regional success, showing that its retail business "has been mentioned or featured" in publications such as the Boston Globe and Accent Magazine, and that it received an award from Business NH magazine in 2003 for its Attrezzi branding campaign. Maytag showed large national expenditures to promote Jenn–Air At-trezzi; yet in a reverse confusion case, the relatively greater strength of a junior user like Maytag may hurt, rather than help, its defense.

QUESTIONS

1. The *Harlem Wizards* court found confusion unlikely chiefly because of the disparity between professional competitive basketball and show basketball. The difference between the two sorts of basketball, as the court noted, reduces the likelihood that fans seeking to view one Wizards' event would instead find to their chagrin that they had purchased tickets to the other Wizards' event. The more difficult question is whether that difference makes it less likely that consumers will come to believe that the Harlem Wizards show basketball team derives from the NBA team, or that it is the Harlem Wizards who are infringing the NBA team's trademark and seeking to appropriate the NBA team's goodwill. How did the court resolve that question? Do you agree?

2. In *Attrezzi*, both parties adopted a mark meaning "equipment" for kitchen equipment. The First Circuit addressed the "doctrine of foreign equivalents," but nonetheless held the mark suggestive, in part because Maytag, having responded to the PTO's initial denial of registration by urging the mark's suggestive qualities, was not now well-placed to call the mark descriptive. But when a mark straddles the suggestive/descriptive line, should the court's assessment of its strength be any more skeptical when the claim is for reverse confusion than for "forward" confusion?

3. Amazon Bookstore in Minneapolis, Minnesota advertises itself as the oldest women's bookstore in North America. Amazon began in 1970, when two women collected feminist books and sold them out of their home. In the mid–1970s, Amazon moved to the city's Lesbian Resource Center. In 1980, the bookstore moved again, to a commercial storefront. During the 1980s, Amazon expanded; it began to fill mail orders for feminist books from customers in other cities, other states, and Canada. Finally, in 1985, the bookstore moved to its current home in downtown Minneapolis. Amazon Bookstore never applied to register its name as a trade or service mark. Since the mid–1970s, the store has been run as a woman-owned workers' cooperative.

Amazon.com is a virtual bookstore, and the largest bookseller on the World Wide Web. The brainchild of Jeff Bezos, Amazon.com sells books by mail order over the World Wide Web. It keeps its overhead down by avoiding the need to stock any inventory whatsoever. Rather, it places orders directly with publishers for all books ordered by its customers. Bezos registered the Internet domain name **amazon.com** with Network Solutions, Inc., and then incorporated the company as Amazon.com, Inc. in Washington State in 1994. It first opened its virtual doors in April of 1995, at <http://www.amazon.com>. Amazon.com filed a use-based application to register AMAZON.COM as a service mark for "retail book distribution services" on October 23, 1995, citing a first use in commerce date of April 15, 1995. Registration was issued on July 15, 1997.

In 1996, Amazon Bookstore decided to open a home page on the World Wide Web. The domain name **amazon.com** was not available, so Amazon Bookstore registered the domain **amazonfembks.com** and set up a home page at <http://www.amazonfembks.com>. The website gives the history ("herstory", actually) of the bookstore, directions to the bookstore, news (updated monthly) about new releases, recommended books, special services, and bookstore-sponsored reading groups and activities. It also includes an online book order form. The Amazon Bookstore home page explains:

> *"We have no connection to amazon.com except that they took our name. They are a big cyberspace bookstore in Seattle. We are a small independent worker-cooperative women-owned business."*

Notwithstanding the disclaimer, however, Amazon Bookstore receives e-mail from customers trying to reach Amazon.com, and e-mail from customers under the impression that Amazon.com is the online version of Amazon Bookstore.

In the spring of 1999, Amazon Bookstores sued Amazon.com for trademark infringement, asserting both likelihood of confusion and reverse confusion claims.

Can the bookstore prevent the registration of AMAZON BOOKS? Does it matter that the bookstore began selling books from its own site on the Web after Amazon.com had launched its operations? Is Amazon Bookstore entitled to oust Amazon.com from use of the AMAZON.COM mark for the sale of books? What arguments would you make on the bookstore's behalf, and how would you expect Amazon.com to respond?

4. Surfvivor is a coined word, and a trademark registered for Hawaiian beach-themed products, and has been in use in Hawaii for some years before the inauguration of the reality-television show, *Survivor*. The show's producers have licensed "Survivor" for a variety of consumer merchandise, including beachwear. The producers were aware of the Surfvivor mark when they adopted Survivor for the television show. There has been no evidence of actual confusion of the marks. How should the court rule on Surfvivor's reverse confusion claim? *See Surfvivor Media v. Survivor Productions*, 406 F.3d 625 (9th Cir.2005).

B. Secondary Liability for Trademark Infringement

Under what circumstances may a person other than the direct infringer be held liable for that person's trademark infringing acts? In *AT&T v. Winback*, 42 F.3d 1421, 1433–34 (3d Cir.1994) The Third Circuit recognized that indirect liability could arise under the Lanham Act:

> There is a good reason for this: the Lanham Act is derived generally and purposefully from the common law tort of unfair competition, and its language parallels the protections afforded by state common law and statutory torts.... The Act federalizes a common law tort. In construing the Act, then, courts routinely have recognized the propriety of examining basic tort liability concepts to determine the scope of liability.... Applying the analysis to the facts of this case, it is clear that liability based on agency principles is often appropriate.

Courts generally recognize two different bases of derivative liability: Contributory infringement, for inducing infringement or knowingly supplying the means to infringe; and vicarious liability imposed under the principles of agency law. The Restatement (Third) of Unfair Competition would impose liability for contributory infringement when "... (a) the actor intentionally induces the third person to engage in the infringing conduct; or (b) the actor fails to take reasonable precautions against the occurrence of the third person's infringing conduct in circumstances in which the infringing conduct can be reasonably anticipated." RESTATEMENT (THIRD) OF UNFAIR COMPETITION § 26. Vicarious liability turns on the defendant's deriving a financial benefit from the infringement, and especially on its ability to control the conduct of the direct infringer. See, e.g., *Procter & Gamble Co. v. Haugen*, 317 F.3d 1121 (10th Cir. 2003)(rejecting vicarious liability of corporation for acts of independent distributors outside corporation's control who disparaged P&G products and insinuated that P&G was in league with Satan). As you review the following materials, consider the extent to which the two bases are in fact distinct.

Inwood Labs., Inc. v. Ives Labs., Inc.

456 U.S. 844, 102 S.Ct. 2182, 72 L.Ed.2d 606 (1982).

■ JUSTICE O'CONNOR delivered the opinion of the Court:

This action requires us to consider the circumstances under which a manufacturer of a generic drug, designed to duplicate the appearance of a similar drug marketed by a competitor under a registered trademark, can be held vicariously liable for infringement of that trademark by pharmacists who dispense the generic drug.

I

In 1955, respondent Ives Laboratories, Inc. (Ives), received a patent on the drug cyclandelate, a vasodilator used in long-term therapy for peripheral and cerebral vascular diseases. Until its patent expired in 1972, Ives retained the exclusive right to make and sell the drug, which it did under the registered trademark CYCLOSPASMOL. Ives marketed the drug, a white powder, to wholesalers, retail pharmacists, and hospitals in colored gelatin capsules. Ives arbitrarily selected a blue capsule, imprinted with "Ives 4124," for its 200 mg dosage and a combination blue-red capsule, imprinted with "Ives 4148," for its 400 mg dosage.

After Ives' patent expired, several generic drug manufacturers, including petitioners Premo Pharmaceutical Laboratories, Inc., Inwood Laboratories, Inc., and MD Pharmaceutical Co., Inc. (collectively the generic manufacturers), began marketing cyclandelate.[2] They intentionally copied the appearance of the CYCLOSPASMOL capsules, selling cyclandelate in 200 mg and 400 mg capsules in colors identical to those selected by Ives.

The marketing methods used by Ives reflect normal industry practice. Because cyclandelate can be obtained only by prescription, Ives does not direct its advertising to the ultimate consumer. Instead, Ives' representatives pay personal visits to physicians, to whom they distribute product literature and "starter samples." Ives initially directed these efforts toward convincing physicians that CYCLOSPASMOL is superior to other vasodilators. Now that its patent has expired and generic manufacturers have entered the market, Ives concentrates on convincing physicians to indicate

---

2. The generic manufacturers purchase cyclandelate and empty capsules and assemble the product for sale to wholesalers and hospitals. The petitioner wholesalers, Darby Drug Co., Inc., Rugby Laboratories, Inc., and Sherry Pharmaceutical Co., Inc., in turn, sell to other wholesalers, physicians, and pharmacies.

on prescriptions that a generic drug cannot be substituted for CYCLOS-PASMOL.

The generic manufacturers also follow a normal industry practice by promoting their products primarily by distribution of catalogs to wholesalers, hospitals, and retail pharmacies, rather than by contacting physicians directly. The catalogs truthfully describe generic cyclandelate as "equivalent" or "comparable" to CYCLOSPASMOL. In addition, some of the catalogs include price comparisons of the generic drug and CYCLOSPASMOL and some refer to the color of the generic capsules. The generic products reach wholesalers, hospitals, and pharmacists in bulk containers which correctly indicate the manufacturer of the product contained therein.

A pharmacist, regardless of whether he is dispensing CYCLOSPASMOL or a generic drug, removes the capsules from the container in which he receives them and dispenses them to the consumer in the pharmacist's own bottle with his own label attached. Hence, the final consumer sees no identifying marks other than those on the capsules themselves.

II

A

Ives instituted this action in the United States District Court for the Eastern District of New York under §§ 32 and 43(a) of the Trademark Act of 1946 (Lanham Act), 60 Stat. 427, as amended, 15 U.S.C. § 1051 et seq., and under New York's unfair competition law, N. Y. Gen. Bus. Law § 368–d (McKinney 1968).

Ives' claim under § 32, 60 Stat. 437, as amended, 15 U.S.C. § 1114, derived from its allegation that some pharmacists had dispensed generic drugs mislabeled as CYCLOSPASMOL.[8] Ives contended that the generic manufacturers' use of lookalike capsules and of catalog entries comparing prices and revealing the colors of the generic capsules induced pharmacists illegally to substitute a generic drug for CYCLOSPASMOL and to mislabel the substitute drug CYCLOSPASMOL. Although Ives did not allege that the petitioners themselves applied the Ives trademark to the drug products they produced and distributed, it did allege that the petitioners contributed to the infringing activities of pharmacists who mislabeled generic cyclandelate.

Ives' claim under § 43(a), 60 Stat. 441, 15 U.S.C. § 1125(a), alleged that the petitioners designated the origin of their products by copying the capsule colors used by Ives and by promoting the generic products as equivalent to CYCLOSPASMOL. In support of its claim, Ives argued that

---

8. The claim involved two types of infringements. The first was "direct" infringement, in which druggists allegedly filled CYCLOSPASMOL prescriptions marked "dispense as written" with a generic drug and mislabeled the product as CYCLOSPASMOL. The second, "intermediate" infringement, occurred when pharmacists, although authorized by the prescriptions to substitute, allegedly mislabeled a generic drug as CYCLOSPASMOL. The one retail pharmacy originally named as a defendant consented to entry of a decree enjoining it from repeating such actions. 455 F.Supp., at 942.

the colors of its capsules were not functional[10] and that they had developed a secondary meaning for the consumers.[11]

Contending that pharmacists would continue to mislabel generic drugs as CYCLOSPASMOL so long as imitative products were available, Ives asked that the court enjoin the petitioners from marketing cyclandelate capsules in the same colors and form as Ives uses for CYCLOSPASMOL. In addition, Ives sought damages pursuant to § 35 of the Lanham Act, 60 Stat. 439, as amended, 15 U.S.C. § 1117.

B

The District Court denied Ives' request for an order preliminarily enjoining the petitioners from selling generic drugs identical in appearance to those produced by Ives. 455 F. Supp. 939 (1978). Referring to the claim based upon § 32, the District Court stated that, while the "knowing and deliberate instigation" by the petitioners of mislabeling by pharmacists would justify holding the petitioners as well as the pharmacists liable for trademark infringement, Ives had made no showing sufficient to justify preliminary relief. Id., at 945. Ives had not established that the petitioners conspired with the pharmacists or suggested that they disregard physicians' prescriptions.

The Court of Appeals for the Second Circuit affirmed. 601 F.2d 631 (1979). To assist the District Court in the upcoming trial on the merits, the appellate court defined the elements of a claim based upon § 32 in some detail. Relying primarily upon *Coca–Cola Co. v. Snow Crest Beverages, Inc.*, 64 F.Supp. 980 (Mass. 1946), *aff'd*, 162 F.2d 280 (CA1), *cert. denied*, 332 U.S. 809 (1947), the court stated that the petitioners would be liable under § 32 either if they suggested, even by implication, that retailers fill bottles with generic cyclandelate and label the bottle with Ives' trademark or if the petitioners continued to sell cyclandelate to retailers whom they knew or had reason to know were engaging in infringing practices. 601 F.2d, at 636.

C

After a bench trial on remand, the District Court entered judgment for the petitioners. 488 F.Supp. 394 (1980). Applying the test approved by the Court of Appeals to the claim based upon § 32, the District Court found that the petitioners had not suggested, even by implication, that pharmacists should dispense generic drugs incorrectly identified as CYCLOSPASMOL.

In reaching that conclusion, the court first looked for direct evidence that the petitioners intentionally induced trademark infringement. Since

---

10. In general terms, a product feature is functional if it is essential to the use or purpose of the article or if it affects the cost or quality of the article. See *Sears, Roebuck & Co. v. Stiffel Co.*, 376 U.S. 225, 232 (1964); *Kellogg Co. v. National Biscuit Co.*, 305 U.S. 111, 122 (1938).

11. To establish secondary meaning, a manufacturer must show that, in the minds of the public, the primary significance of a product feature or term is to identify the source of the product rather than the product itself. See *Kellogg Co. v. National Biscuit Co.*, supra, at 118.

the petitioners' representatives do not make personal visits to physicians and pharmacists, the petitioners were not in a position directly to suggest improper drug substitutions. Cf. *William R. Warner & Co. v. Eli Lilly & Co.*, 265 U.S. 526, 530–531 (1924); *Smith, Kline & French Laboratories v. Clark & Clark*, 157 F.2d 725, 731 (CA3), *cert. denied*, 329 U.S. 796 (1946). Therefore, the court concluded, improper suggestions, if any, must have come from catalogs and promotional materials. The court determined, however, that those materials could not "fairly be read" to suggest trademark infringement. 488 F.Supp. at 397.

The trial court next considered evidence of actual instances of mislabeling by pharmacists, since frequent improper substitutions of a generic drug for CYCLOSPASMOL could provide circumstantial evidence that the petitioners, merely by making available imitative drugs in conjunction with comparative price advertising, implicitly had suggested that pharmacists substitute improperly. After reviewing the evidence of incidents of mislabeling, the District Court concluded that such incidents occurred too infrequently to justify the inference that the petitioners' catalogs and use of imitative colors had "impliedly invited" druggists to mislabel. *Ibid.* Moreover, to the extent mislabeling had occurred, the court found it resulted from pharmacists' misunderstanding of the requirements of the New York Drug Substitution Law, rather than from deliberate attempts to pass off generic cyclandelate as CYCLOSPASMOL. *Ibid.*

The District Court also found that Ives failed to establish its claim based upon § 43(a). In reaching its conclusion, the court found that the blue and blue-red colors were functional to patients as well as to doctors and hospitals: many elderly patients associate color with therapeutic effect; some patients commingle medications in a container and rely on color to differentiate one from another; colors are of some, if limited, help in identifying drugs in emergency situations; and use of the same color for brand name drugs and their generic equivalents helps avoid confusion on the part of those responsible for dispensing drugs. *Id.*, at 398–399. In addition, because Ives had failed to show that the colors indicated the drug's origin, the court found that the colors had not acquired a secondary meaning. *Id.*, at 399.

Without expressly stating that the District Court's findings were clearly erroneous, and for reasons which we discuss below, the Court of Appeals concluded that the petitioners violated § 32. 638 F.2d 538 (1981). The Court of Appeals did not reach Ives' other claims. We granted certiorari, 454 U.S. 891 (1981), and now reverse the judgment of the Court of Appeals.

III

A

As the lower courts correctly discerned, liability for trademark infringement can extend beyond those who actually mislabel goods with the mark of another. Even if a manufacturer does not directly control others in the chain of distribution, it can be held responsible for their infringing activities under certain circumstances. Thus, if a manufacturer or distributor intentionally induces another to infringe a trademark, or if it continues to supply its product to one whom it knows or has reason to know is engaging in trademark infringement, the manufacturer or distributor is contributorially responsible for any harm done as a result of the deceit. See *William R. Warner & Co. v. Eli Lilly & Co., supra*; *Coca–Cola Co. v. Snow Crest Beverages, Inc., supra*.

It is undisputed that those pharmacists who mislabeled generic drugs with Ives' registered trademark violated § 32. However, whether these petitioners were liable for the pharmacists' infringing acts depended upon whether, in fact, the petitioners intentionally induced the pharmacists to mislabel generic drugs or, in fact, continued to supply cyclandelate to pharmacists whom the petitioners knew were mislabeling generic drugs. The District Court concluded that Ives made neither of those factual showings.

B

In reviewing the factual findings of the District Court, the Court of Appeals was bound by the "clearly erroneous" standard of Rule 52(a), Federal Rules of Civil Procedure. *Pullman–Standard v. Swint, ante*, p. 273. That Rule recognizes and rests upon the unique opportunity afforded the trial court judge to evaluate the credibility of witnesses and to weigh the evidence. *Zenith Radio Corp. v. Hazeltine Research, Inc.*, 395 U.S. 100, 123 (1969). Because of the deference due the trial judge, unless an appellate court is left with the "definite and firm conviction that a mistake has been committed," *United States v. United States Gypsum Co.*, 333 U.S. 364, 395 (1948), it must accept the trial court's findings.

IV

In reversing the District Court's judgment, the Court of Appeals initially held that the trial court failed to give sufficient weight to the evidence Ives offered to show a "pattern of illegal substitution and mislabeling in New York...." 638 F.2d, at 543. By rejecting the District Court's findings simply because it would have given more weight to evidence of mislabeling than did the trial court, the Court of Appeals clearly erred. Determining the weight and credibility of the evidence is the special province of the trier of fact. Because the trial court's findings concerning the significance of the instances of mislabeling were not clearly erroneous, they should not have been disturbed.

Next, after completing its own review of the evidence, the Court of Appeals concluded that the evidence was "clearly sufficient to establish a § 32 violation." *Ibid.* In reaching its conclusion, the Court of Appeals was influenced by several factors. First, it thought the petitioners reasonably could have anticipated misconduct by a substantial number of the pharmacists who were provided imitative, lower priced products which, if substituted for the higher priced brand name without passing on savings to consumers, could provide an economic advantage to the pharmacists. *Ibid.*

Second, it disagreed with the trial court's finding that the mislabeling which did occur reflected confusion about state law requirements. *Id.* at 544. Third, it concluded that illegal substitution and mislabeling in New York are neither *de minimis* nor inadvertent. *Ibid.* Finally, the Court of Appeals indicated it was further influenced by the fact that the petitioners did not offer "any persuasive evidence of a legitimate reason unrelated to CYCLOSPASMOL" for producing an imitative product. *Ibid.*

Each of those conclusions is contrary to the findings of the District Court. An appellate court cannot substitute its interpretation of the evidence for that of the trial court simply because the reviewing court "might give the facts another construction, resolve the ambiguities differently, and find a more sinister cast to actions which the District Court apparently deemed innocent." *United States v. Real Estate Boards*, 339 U.S. 485, 495 (1950).

V

The Court of Appeals erred in setting aside findings of fact that were not clearly erroneous. Accordingly, the judgment of the Court of Appeals that the petitioners violated § 32 of the Lanham Act is reversed.

Although the District Court also dismissed Ives' claims alleging that the petitioners violated § 43(a) of the Lanham Act and the state unfair competition law, the Court of Appeals did not address those claims. Because § 43(a) prohibits a broader range of practices than does § 32, as may the state unfair competition law, the District Court's decision dismissing Ives' claims based upon those statutes must be independently reviewed. Therefore, we remand to the Court of Appeals for further proceedings consistent with this opinion.

Reversed and remanded.

QUESTIONS

1. Under what circumstances is it appropriate to impose liability on a business that is not itself infringing any trademark rights, but that is facilitating or profiting from trademark infringement by others? Should the landlord of a store that deals in infringing merchandise be held liable as a contributory infringer? The ad agency that prepares ads for infringing products? The celebrity who endorses infringing goods?

2. Should it make a difference whether Inwood's generic cyclandelate differs in any material way from Ives' cyclospasmol? May Inwood use blue and red capsules for for generic cyclandelate in higher or lower doses than the 400 mg. capsule? If not, why not?

Hard Rock Café Licensing Corp. v. Concession Services, Inc.

955 F.2d 1143 (7th Cir.1992).

■ CUDAHY, CIRCUIT JUDGE:

The Hard Rock Café Licensing Corporation (Hard Rock) owns trademarks on several clothing items, including t-shirts and sweatshirts, and apparently attempts to exploit its trademark monopoly to the full. In the summer of 1989, Hard Rock sent out specially trained private investigators to look for counterfeit Hard Rock Café merchandise. The investigators found Iqbal Parvez selling counterfeit Hard Rock t-shirts from stands in the Tri–State Swap–O–Rama and the Melrose Park Swap–O–Rama, flea markets owned and operated by Concession Services Incorporated (CSI). The investigators also discovered that Harry's Sweat Shop (Harry's) was selling similar items. Hard Rock brought suit against Parvez, CSI, Harry's and others not relevant to this appeal under the Lanham Trademark Act, 15 U.S.C. §§ 1051 *et seq.* (1988). Most of the defendants settled, including Parvez, who paid Hard Rock some $30,000. CSI and Harry's went to trial.

After a bench trial, the district court found that both remaining defendants violated the Act and entered permanent injunctions forbidding Harry's to sell merchandise bearing Hard Rock's trademarks (whether counterfeit or genuine) and forbidding CSI to permit the sale of such merchandise at its flea markets. The court also awarded treble damages against Harry's. The court did not, however, award attorney's fees against either defendant.

All of the parties who participated in the trial appealed.... [Harry's appeal is dismissed for having been filed too late.] Finding errors of law and a fatal ambiguity in the findings of fact, we vacate the judgment against CSI, vacate the denial of attorney's fees and remand for further proceedings.

I

. . . .

A. *The Parties and Their Practices*

1. *Concession Services, Inc.*

In the summer of 1989, CSI owned and operated three "Swap–O–Rama" flea markets in the Chicago area: the Tri–State, in Alsip, Illinois; the Melrose Park, in Melrose Park, Illinois; and the Brighton Park, in Chicago itself. Although Parvez sold counterfeits at the Tri–State Swap–O–Rama and at Melrose Park, testimony at trial concentrated on the operations at the Tri–State....

CSI generates revenue from a flea market in four ways. First, it rents space to vendors for flat fees.... Second, CSI charges a reservation and storage fee to those vendors who want to reserve the same space on a month-to-month basis. Third, CSI charges shoppers a nominal 75 cents admission charge. Fourth, CSI runs concession stands inside the market. To promote its business, CSI advertises the markets, announcing "BARGAINS" to be had, but does not advertise the presence of any individual vendors or any particular goods.

Supervision of the flea markets is minimal. CSI posts a sign at the Tri–State prohibiting vendors from selling "illegal goods." It also has "Rules For Sellers" which prohibit the sale of food or beverages, alcohol, weapons, fireworks, live animals, drugs and drug paraphernalia and subversive or un-American literature. Other than these limitations, vendors can, and do, sell almost any conceivable item. Two off-duty police officers provide security and crowd control.... These officers also have some duty to ensure that the vendors obey the Sellers' Rules. The manager of the Tri–State, Albert Barelli, walks around the flea market about five times a day, looking for problems and violations of the rules. No one looks over the vendors' wares before they enter the market and set up their stalls, and any examination after that is cursory. Moreover, Barelli does not keep records of the names and addresses of the vendors. The only penalty for violating the Seller's Rules is expulsion from the market.

James Pierski, the vice president in charge of CSI's flea markets, testified that CSI has a policy of cooperating with any trademark owner that notifies CSI of possible infringing activity. But there is no evidence that this policy has ever been carried into effect. Before this case, there have been a few seizures of counterfeit goods at Swap–O–Rama flea markets. In no case was CSI informed of a pending seizure, involved in a seizure or notified as to the ultimate disposition of the seized goods. On the other hand, CSI did not investigate any of the seizures, though it knew they had occurred.

2.   *Harry's Sweat Shop*

Harry's is a small store in Darien, Illinois, owned and operated by Harry Spatero. The store sells athletic shoes, t-shirts, jackets with the names of professional sports teams and the like. Spatero testified that the store contains over 20,000 different items.... Harry's buys most of its t-shirts from Supply Brokers of Pennsylvania, a firm which specializes in buying up stocks from stores going out of business. Spatero testified that Supply Brokers sends him largely unidentified boxes of shirts which he may choose to return after looking them over. But Spatero testified that Harry's also bought shirts from people who came around in unmarked vans, offering shirts at a discount. The store kept no records of the sources of its inventory.

3.   *Hard Rock Licensing Corp.*

Hard Rock owns the rights to a variety of Hard Rock trademarks. The corporation grants licenses to use its trademarks to the limited partnerships that own and operate the various Hard Rock Café restaurants. These restaurants are the only authorized distributors of Hard Rock Café merchandise, but apparently this practice of exclusivity is neither publicized nor widely known. The shirts themselves are produced by Winterland Productions, which prints logos on blank, first quality t-shirts that it buys from Hanes, Fruit-of-the-Loom and Anvil. According to the manager of the Chicago Hard Rock Café, Scott Floersheimer, Winterland has an agreement with Hard Rock to retain all defective Hard Rock shirts. Thus, if Winterland performs as agreed, all legitimate Hard Rock shirts sold to the public are well-made and cleanly printed.

The Chicago Hard Rock Café has done very well from its business. Since 1986, it has sold over 500,000 t-shirts at an average gross profit of $10.12 per shirt.

B.   *The Investigation*

National Investigative Services Corporation (NISCOR) carried out the search for counterfeit merchandise on Hard Rock's behalf. Another firm, Trademark Facts, Inc., trained NISCOR's investigators to recognize counterfeit merchandise. Recognizing counterfeit Hard Rock goods was apparently easy. Any shirt not sold in a Hard Rock Café restaurant was, unless second-hand, counterfeit. Other than this, the investigators were instructed to check for the manufacturer of the t-shirt, a registration or trademark symbol, the quality of the printed design, the color of the design, the quality of the shirt stock and the price. But as to these latter factors (except for the price), Floersheimer testified that even he would have trouble distinguishing a good counterfeit from a legitimate t-shirt.

The investigators visited both the Melrose Park and the Tri–State Swap–O–Ramas and observed Iqbal Parvez (or his employees) offering more than a hundred Hard Rock t-shirts for sale. Cynthia Myers, the chief investigator on the project, testified that these shirts were obviously counterfeit. The shirts were poor quality stock, with cut labels and were being sold for $3 apiece (a legitimate Hard Rock shirt, we are told, goes for over $14). Harry's had four Hard Rock shirts for sale, sitting on a discount table for $3.99 each. The district court found that these too were of obviously low quality, with cut labels and cracked and worn designs. Nonetheless, both Parvez and Harry's were selling t-shirts made by approved manufacturers. Parvez was selling Hanes t-shirts, and Harry's was selling Fruit-of-the-Loom.

At no point before filing suit did Hard Rock warn Harry's or CSI (or Parvez, whose supplier Hard Rock was trying to track down) that the shirts were counterfeits.

C.   *The District Court Proceedings*

Hard Rock brought suit against the defendants in September 1989, alleging violations of sections 32 and 43 of the Lanham Act. 15 U.S.C. §§ 1114 & 1125 (1988). Pending trial, the court entered temporary restraining orders and then preliminary injunctions against both CSI and Harry's. Harry's got rid of its remaining Hard Rock t-shirts, and CSI told any vendors selling Hard Rock merchandise in its flea markets to get rid of their stock as well. There have been no more violations.

After a bench trial, the district court entered permanent injunctions against both defendants and ordered Harry's to pay treble damages based on Hard Rock's lost profits on four t-shirts (in sum, $120). The court denied Hard Rock's request for attorney's fees. The court's reasoning is crucial to the resolution of this appeal.... The court concluded that both defendants were "guilty of willful blindness that counterfeit goods were being sold on [their] premises." Another sentence follows, however, which somewhat dilutes the impact of the preceding finding: "Neither defendant took reasonable steps to detect or prevent the sale of Hard Rock Café counterfeit T-shirts on its premise [sic]." This suggests mere negligence.

Willful blindness, the court said, "is a sufficient basis for a finding of violation of the Lanham Act. *Louis Vuitton S.A. v. Lee,* 875 F.2d 584, 590 (7th Cir.1989)." As to CSI's argument that it did not actually sell the offending goods, the court observed that CSI is not "merely a landlord; it also advertises and promoted the activity on its premises, sells admission tickets to buyers and supervises the premises. Under these circumstances it must also take reasonable precautions against the sale of counterfeit products."

II

The Lanham Trademark Act protects consumers from deceptive claims about the nature and origin of products. (Citations omitted). But the Lanham Act also protects trademarks as a form of intellectual property. In this case, the Act protects Hard Rock's investment in a fashionable image and a reputation for selling high quality goods. *See Inwood Laboratories, Inc. v. Ives Laboratories, Inc.,* 456 U.S. 844, 854 (1982) (citations omitted).

A.   *Secondary Liability*

The most interesting issue in this case is CSI's liability for Parvez's sales. Hard Rock argues that CSI has incurred both contributory and vicarious liability for the counterfeits, and we take the theories of liability in that order.

It is well established that "if a manufacturer or distributor intentionally induces another to infringe a trademark, or if it continues to supply its product to one whom it knows or has reason to know is engaging in trademark infringement, the manufacturer or distributor is contributorially responsible for any harm done as a result of the deceit." *Id.* at 854 (footnote omitted). Despite this apparently definitive statement, it is not clear how the doctrine applies to people who do not actually manufacture or distribute the good that is ultimately palmed off as made by someone else. A temporary help service, for example, might not be liable if it furnished Parvez the workers he employed to erect his stand, even if the help service knew that Parvez would sell counterfeit goods. Thus we must ask whether the operator of a flea market is more like the manufacturer of a mislabeled good or more like a temporary help service supplying the purveyor of goods. To answer questions of this sort, we have treated trademark infringement as a species of tort and have turned to the common law to guide our inquiry into the appropriate boundaries of liability.

CSI characterizes its relationship with Parvez as that of landlord and tenant. Hard Rock calls CSI a licensor, not a landlord. Either way, the Restatement of Torts tells us that CSI is responsible for the torts of those it permits on its premises "knowing or having reason to know that the other is acting or will act tortiously. . . ." RESTATEMENT (SECOND) OF TORTS § 877(c) & cmt. D (1979). The common law, then, imposes the same duty on landlords and licensors that the Supreme Court has imposed on manufacturers and distributors. In the absence of any suggestion that a trademark violation should not be treated as a common law tort, we believe that the *Inwood Labs.* test for contributory liability applies. CSI may be liable for trademark violations by Parvez if it knew or had reason to know of them. But the factual findings must support that conclusion.

The district court found CSI to be willfully blind. Since we have held that willful blindness is equivalent to actual knowledge for purposes of the Lanham Act, *Lee,* 875 F.2d at 590, this finding should be enough to hold CSI liable (unless clearly erroneous). But we very much doubt that the district court defined willful blindness as it should have. To be willfully blind, a person must suspect wrongdoing and deliberately fail to investigate. *Id.* The district court, however, made little mention of CSI's state of mind and focused almost entirely on CSI's [duty to and] failure to take precautions against counterfeiting. . . . In short, it looks as if the district court found CSI to be negligent, not willfully blind.

This ambiguity in the court's findings would not matter if CSI could be liable for failing to take reasonable precautions. But CSI has no affirmative duty to take precautions against the sale of counterfeits. Although the "reason to know" part of the standard for contributory liability requires CSI (or its agents) to understand what a reasonably prudent person would understand, it does not impose any duty to seek out and prevent violations. Restatement (Second) of Torts § 12(1) & cmt. A (1965). . . . Thus the district court's findings do not support the conclusion that CSI bears contributory liability for Parvez's transgressions.

Before moving on, we should emphasize that we have found only that the district court applied an incorrect standard. We have not found that the evidence cannot support the conclusion that CSI was in fact willfully blind. . . . One might infer from the[] facts that Barelli suspected that the shirts were counterfeits but chose not to investigate.

On the other hand, we do not wish to prejudge the matter. . . . The circumstantial evidence that Barelli suspected the shirts to be counterfeit is, at best, thin. On remand, the district court may choose to develop this issue more fully.

Polo Ralph Lauren Corp. v. Chinatown Gift Shop, 855 F.Supp. 648 (S.D.N.Y.1994). Polo, Rolex Watch, and Louis Vuitton brought a trademark infringement suit against retailers of allegedly counterfeit merchandise and their landlords. Jolania, the owner of one of the buildings, argued that, since it had not itself infringed any trademark, but had merely leased premises on which allegedly infringing activity occurred, the suit against it should be dismissed. The court disagreed. Plaintiffs' complaint alleged that Jolania was aware that its tenant was selling counterfeit goods on the premises and did nothing to prevent the activity. The court held that that claim, if proved, would constitute contributory infringement under the *Inwood Laboratories* and *Hard Rock Café Licensing Corp.* standard.

Lockheed Martin Corporation v. Network Solutions, Inc.

194 F.3d 980 (9th Cir.1999).

■ TROTT, CIRCUIT JUDGE:

I

This appeal concerns the NSI registration scheme for domain-name combinations.... An interested reader may wish to review the district court's in-depth discussion of the Internet technology that forms the basis of this cause of action. 985 F. Supp. at 951–53.

When a third party seeks to maintain an Internet web site, that party must reserve a location, called an Internet Protocol ("IP") Address, and do the necessary programming. When an Internet user accesses the third party's web site, the user enters the domain-name combination that corresponds to the IP Address and is routed to the host computer. An industry of surrogate hosts has developed, where an Internet Service Provider licenses space on its computers to a third-party web-site operator.... [A separate organization] provide[s] the translation service from an entered domain-name combination to the appropriate IP Address.

A

At all relevant times, NSI was the sole National Science Foundation contractor in charge of registering domain-name combinations for the top-level domains <.gov>, <.edu>, <.com>, <.org>, and <.net>. (For clarity, we set off Internet-related character strings with the carat symbols ("< >").) After registration, NSI entered the combination and the corresponding IP Address in its database, permitting automatic translation when an Internet user entered a domain-name combination.

When registering with NSI to receive a domain-name combination, an applicant submits NSI's "template" electronically over the Internet. On approval, NSI puts the domain-name combination in its database in conjunction with the correct IP Address. NSI then routes Internet users who enter a certain domain-name combination to the registrant's computer. At the time of argument on this appeal, NSI was receiving approximately 130,000 registrations per month, although evidence indicates that the number of monthly registrations has been increasing steadily and is possibly much larger today. Ninety percent of templates are processed electronically, and the entire registration process for each application requires between a few minutes and a few hours. Ten percent of the time, an employee of NSI reviews the application. Human intervention might occur because of an error in filling out the form or because the applied-for domain name includes a "prohibited" character string—such as specific variations on the words Olympic, Red Cross, or NASA, and certain "obscene" words. NSI also performs a conflict check on all applications, which compares an application to other registered domain-name combinations. However, NSI does not consult third parties during the registration process, check for a registrant's right to use a particular word in a domain-name combination, or monitor the use of a combination once registered. NSI is also not an Internet Service Provider. It performs none of the "hosting" functions for a web site.

NSI does maintain a post-registration dispute-resolution procedure. Anyone who feels that his or her rights are violated by the domain-name combination maintained by a registrant can submit a certified copy of a trademark registration to NSI. NSI then requires the registrant to obtain a declaratory judgment of the right to maintain the domain-name combination. If the registrant fails to do so, its registration is terminated.

B

Lockheed owns and operates "The Skunk Works," an aircraft design and construction laboratory. Since 1943, The Skunk Works has developed prototypes of this country's first jet fighter, the U–2 and SR–71 spy planes, and the F–117 and F–22 fighter planes.... "Skunk Works" is a registered and incontestable service mark.

II

Third parties, not involved in this litigation, have registered domain-name combinations with NSI which are variations on the phrase "skunk works." These include:

<skunkworks.com>,

<skunkworks.net>,

<skunkwrks.com>,

<skunkwerks.com>,

<skunkworx.com>,

<theskunkworks.com>,

<skunkworks1.com>,

<skunkworks.org>,

<skunkwear.com>,

<the-skunkwerks.com>,

<skunkwurks.com>, and

<theencryptedskunkworks.com>.

Lockheed alleges that many of these registrations infringe and dilute its "Skunk Works" service mark.

Lockheed sent two letters, on May 7 and June 18, 1996, bringing the <skunkworks.com> and <skunkworks.net> registrations to NSI's attention. Lockheed's letters informed NSI of its belief that the third-party registrants were infringing or diluting Lockheed's service mark. Lockheed requested that NSI cancel the allegedly offending registrations. Lockheed also requested that NSI cease registering domain-name combinations that included "Skunk Works" or variations on the phrase and report to Lockheed all such domain-name combinations contained in its registry. NSI took no action on Lockheed's requests, informing Lockheed by letter that Lockheed had failed to comply with the terms of NSI's dispute resolution policy. . . .

Lockheed sued NSI on October 22, 1996, claiming contributory service mark infringement, infringement, unfair competition, and service mark dilution, all in violation of the Lanham Act, and also seeking declaratory relief. The complaint alleged that four specific domain-name registrations infringed or diluted Lockheed's "Skunk Works" service mark. . . . NSI moved for summary judgment. The district court . . . granted summary judgment to NSI.

. . . .

IV

Contributory infringement occurs when the defendant either intentionally induces a third party to infringe the plaintiff's mark or supplies a product to a third party with actual or constructive knowledge that the product is being used to infringe the service mark. *Inwood Lab., Inc. v. Ives Lab., Inc.*, 456 U.S. 844, 853–54 (1982). Lockheed alleges only the latter basis for contributory infringement liability and therefore must prove that NSI supplies a product to third parties with actual or constructive knowledge that its product is being used to infringe "Skunk Works." *Id.* at 854.

The district court assumed for purposes of summary judgment that third parties were infringing Lockheed's "Skunk Works" service mark, and NSI does not ask us to affirm an the alternate. . . . We are thus left to consider two issues on Lockheed's contributory infringement cause of action: (1) whether NSI supplied a product to third parties and (2) whether NSI had actual or constructive knowledge of any infringement. Because we accept the district court's excellent analysis on the first question, *see* 985 F. Supp. at 960–62, we affirm summary judgment without reaching the second.

A

Under the plain language of the *Inwood Lab.* formulation, to be liable for contributory infringement, NSI must supply a "product" to a third party with which the third party infringes Lockheed's service mark. 456 U.S. at 854. In *Inwood Lab.*, the Supreme Court considered an action against a manufacturer of generic pharmaceuticals. *Id.* at 847. Non-party pharmacists packaged the defendant's less-expensive generic pills, but labeled them with the plaintiff's brand name. *Id.* at 850. The plaintiff stated a cause of action for contributory infringement by alleging that the defendant "continued to supply [the product] to pharmacists whom the petitioners knew were mislabeling generic drugs." *Id.* at 855.

Inwood Lab. has been applied in the broader context of renting booth space at a flea market. *See Hard Rock Cafe Licensing Corp. v. Concession Servs., Inc.*, 955 F.2d 1143, 1148–49 (7th Cir.1992). In *Hard Rock*, the Seventh Circuit explicitly addressed the distinction between a product and a service. . . . The court [] held that space at a flea market was more comparable to pharmaceuticals than to manpower, in part because of the close comparison between the legal duty owed by a landlord to control illegal activities on his or her premises and by a manufacturer to control illegal use of his or her product. *Id.* at 1149. We adopted the *Hard Rock* analysis in *Fonovisa, Inc. v. Cherry Auction, Inc.*, 76 F.3d 259 (9th Cir. 1996), holding that a flea market could be liable for contributory infringement if it "supplied the necessary marketplace" for the sale of infringing products. *Id.* at 265 (citing *Hard Rock*, 955 F.2d at 1149).

Hard Rock and *Fonovisa* teach us that when measuring and weighing a fact pattern in the contributory infringement context without the convenient "product" mold dealt with in *Inwood Lab.*, we consider the extent of control exercised by the defendant over the third party's means of infringement. (Citations omitted). Direct control and monitoring of the instrumentality used by a third party to infringe the plaintiff's mark permits the expansion of *Inwood Lab.*'s "supplies a product" requirement for contributory infringement.

B

The case at bench involves a fact pattern squarely on the "service" side of the product/service distinction suggested by *Inwood Lab* and its offspring. All evidence in the record indicates that NSI's role differs little from that of the United States Postal Service: when an Internet user enters a domain-name combination, NSI translates the domain-name combination to the registrant's IP Address and routes the information or command to the corresponding computer. . . . NSI does not supply the domain-name combination any more than the Postal Service supplies a street address by performing the routine service of routing mail. As the district court correctly observed,

> Where domain names are used to infringe, the infringement does not result from NSI's publication of the domain name list, but from the registrant's use of the name on a web site or other Internet form of communication in connection with goods or services. . . . NSI's involvement with the use of domain names does not extend beyond registration.

985 F. Supp. at 958.

The "direct control and monitoring" rule established by *Hard Rock* and *Fonovisa* likewise fails to reach the instant situation. The district court correctly recognized that NSI's rote translation service does not entail the kind of direct control and monitoring required to justify an extension of the "supplies a product" requirement. *See* 985 F. Supp. at 962 ("While the landlord of a flea market might reasonably be expected to monitor the merchandise sold on his premises, NSI cannot reasonably be expected to monitor the Internet."). Such a stretch would reach well beyond the contemplation of *Inwood Lab.* and its progeny.

. . . .

NSI is not liable for contributory infringement as a matter of law.

QUESTIONS

1. Recall the *WhenU* and *JR Cigar* cases, *supra* this Chapter, section A.3.a. In *WhenU*, the court found that the defendant had not "used" plaintiff's marks when it allowed its customers to key their pop up ads to users' entry of the URL for plaintiff's website, as well as to users' entry of generic search terms, such as "contacts" and "eye care." Suppose, however, the pop up advertisements were found to infringe plaintiff's marks (for example, by confusing consumers as to plaintiff's sponsorship or approval of the advertised products). Would WhenU be held a contributory infringer or vicariously liable for the advertisers' infringements?

2. In *JR Cigar*, GoTo, the defendant search engine, keyed plaintiff's trademark as a search term to generate priority links to its customers' websites. The court held that GoTo had "used" plaintiff's trademark, but denied summary judgment on the question whether its use was likely to cause confusion. The court also observed:

> As summary judgment is inappropriate on JR's claims for trademark infringement and unfair competition, the Court need not consider GoTo's affirmative "fair use" defense, except to note that use of JR's marks by GoTo is probably fair in terms of its search engine business; that is, where GoTo permits bids on JR marks for purposes of comparative advertising, resale of JR's products, or the provision of information about JR or its products. However, fairness would dissipate, and protection under a fair use defense would be lost, if GoTo wrongfully participated in someone else's infringing use. Thus, the factual issue of whether GoTo's conduct supports a fair use defense is for the trier of fact.

Suppose that the court found that a sponsored link to a user search for JR products was an infringing use. How would it analyze the issue of whether "GoTo wrongfully participated in someone else's infringing use"?

C.   STATUTORY DEFENSES/INCONTESTABILITY

1.   INCONTESTABILITY

15 U.S.C. § 1065 [LANHAM ACT § 15]

Except on a ground for which application to cancel may be filed at any time under paragraphs (3) and (5) of section 14 of this Act, and except to the extent, if any, to which the use of a mark registered on the principal register infringes a valid right acquired under the law of any State or Territory by use of a mark or trade name continuing from a date prior to the date of registration under this Act of such registered mark, the right of the registrant to use such registered mark in commerce for the goods or services on or in connection with which such registered mark has been in continuous use for five consecutive years subsequent to the date of such registration and is still in use in commerce, shall be incontestable: Provided, that—

(1) there has been no final decision adverse to registrant's claim of ownership of such mark for such goods or services, or to registrant's right to register the same or to keep the same on the register; and

(2) there is no proceeding involving said rights pending in the Patent and Trademark Office or in a court and not finally disposed of; and

(3) an affidavit is filed with the Commissioner within one year after the expiration of any such five-year period setting forth those goods or services stated in the registration on or in connection with which such mark has been in continuous use for such five consecutive years and is still in use in commerce, and the other matters specified in paragraphs (1) and (2) of this section; and

(4) no incontestable right shall be acquired in a mark which is the generic name for the goods or services or a portion thereof, for which it is registered.

Park 'N Fly, Inc. v. Dollar Park and Fly, Inc.

469 U.S. 189, 105 S.Ct. 658, 83 L.Ed.2d 582 (1985).

■ JUSTICE O'CONNOR delivered the opinion of the Court.

In this case we consider whether an action to enjoin the infringement of an incontestable trade or service mark may be defended on the grounds that the mark is merely descriptive. We conclude that neither the language of the relevant statutes nor the legislative history supports such a defense.

I.

Petitioner operates long-term parking lots near airports. After starting business in St. Louis in 1967, petitioner subsequently opened facilities in Cleveland, Houston, Boston, Memphis, and San Francisco. Petitioner applied in 1969 to the United States Patent and Trademark Office (Patent Office) to register a service mark consisting of the logo of an airplane and the words "Park 'N Fly." The registration issued in August 1971. Nearly six years later, petitioner filed an affidavit with the Patent Office to establish the incontestable status of the mark. As required by § 15 of the Trademark Act of 1946 (Lanham Act), 60 Stat. 433, as amended, 15 U.S.C. § 1065, the affidavit stated that the mark had been registered and in continuous use for five consecutive years, that there had been no final adverse decision to petitioner's claim of ownership or right to registration, and that no proceedings involving such rights were pending. Incontestable status provides, subject to the provisions of § 15 and 33(b) of the Lanham

Act, "conclusive evidence of the registrant's exclusive right to use the registered mark...." § 33(b), 15 U.S.C. § 1115(b).

Respondent also provides long-term airport parking services, but only has operations in Portland, Oregon. Respondent calls its business "Dollar Park and Fly." Petitioner filed this infringement action in 1978 in the United States District Court for the District of Oregon and requested the court permanently to enjoin respondent from using the words "Park and Fly" in connection with its business. Respondent counterclaimed and sought cancellation of petitioner's mark on the grounds that it is a generic term. See § 14(c), 15 U.S.C. § 1064(c). Respondent also argued that petitioner's mark is unenforceable because it is merely descriptive....

After a bench trial, the District Court found that petitioner's mark is not generic and observed that an incontestable mark cannot be challenged on the grounds that it is merely descriptive.

The Court of Appeals for the Ninth Circuit reversed. 718 F.2d 327 (1983). The District Court did not err, the Court of Appeals held, in refusing to invalidate petitioner's mark. *Id.*, at 331. The Court of Appeals noted, however, that it previously had held that incontestability provides a defense against the cancellation of a mark, but it may not be used offensively to enjoin another's use. *Ibid.* Petitioner, under this analysis, could obtain an injunction only if its mark would be entitled to continued registration without regard to its incontestable status.... Based on its own examination of the record, the Court of Appeals then determined that petitioner's mark is in fact merely descriptive, and therefore respondent should not be enjoined from using the name "Park and Fly." *Ibid.*

The decision below is in direct conflict with the decision of the Court of Appeals for the Seventh Circuit in *Union Carbide Corp. v. Ever–Ready, Inc.*, 531 F.2d 366, *cert. denied*, 429 U.S. 830 (1976). We granted certiorari to resolve this conflict, 465 U.S. 1078 (1984), and we now *reverse*.

II.

. . . .

This case requires us to consider the effect of the incontestability provisions of the Lanham Act in the context of an infringement action defended on the grounds that the mark is merely descriptive. Statutory construction must begin with the language employed by Congress and the assumption that the ordinary meaning of that language accurately express-es the legislative purpose. [Citation omitted] With respect to incontestable trade or service marks, § 33(b) of the Lanham Act states that "registration shall be conclusive evidence of the registrant's exclusive right to use the registered mark" subject to the conditions of § 15 and certain enumerated defenses. Section 15 incorporates by reference subsections (c) and (e) of § 14, 15 U.S.C. § 1064. An incontestable mark that becomes generic may be canceled at any time pursuant to § 14(c). That section also allows cancellation of an incontestable mark at any time if it has been abandoned, if it is being used to misrepresent the source of the goods or services in connection with which it is used, or if it was obtained fraudulently or contrary to the provisions of § 4, 15 U.S.C. § 1054, or §§ 2(a)–(c), 15 U.S.C. §§ 1052(a)–(c).

One searches the language of the Lanham Act in vain to find any support for the offensive/defensive distinction applied by the Court of Appeals. The statute nowhere distinguishes between a registrant's offensive and defensive use of an incontestable mark. On the contrary, § 33(b)'s declaration that the registrant has an "exclusive right" to use the mark indicates that incontestable status may be used to enjoin infringement by others. A conclusion that such infringement cannot be enjoined renders meaningless the "exclusive right" recognized by the statute. Moreover, the language in three of the defenses enumerated in § 33(b) clearly contemplates the use of incontestability in infringement actions by plaintiffs. *See* §§ 33(b)(4)–(6), 15 U.S.C. §§ 1115(b)(4)–(6).

The language of the Lanham Act also refutes any conclusion that an incontestable mark may be challenged as merely descriptive. A mark that is merely descriptive of an applicant's goods or services is not registrable unless the mark has secondary meaning. Before a mark achieves incontestable status, registration provides prima facie evidence of the registrant's exclusive right to use the mark in commerce. § 33(a), 15 U.S.C. § 1115(a). The Lanham Act expressly provides that before a mark becomes incontestable an opposing party may prove any legal or equitable defense which might have been asserted if the mark had not been registered. *Ibid.* Thus, § 33(a) would have allowed respondent to challenge petitioner's mark as merely descriptive if the mark had not become incontestable. With respect to incontestable marks, however, § 33(b) provides that registration is conclusive evidence of the registrant's exclusive right to use the mark, subject to the conditions of § 15 and the seven defenses enumerated in § 33(b) itself. Mere descriptiveness is not recognized by either § 15 or § 33(b) as a basis for challenging an incontestable mark.

The statutory provisions that prohibit registration of a merely descriptive mark but do not allow an incontestable mark to be challenged on this ground cannot be attributed to inadvertence by Congress. The Conference Committee rejected an amendment that would have denied registration to any descriptive mark, and instead retained the provisions allowing registration of a merely descriptive mark that has acquired secondary meaning. *See* H.R. Conf. Rep. No. 2322, 79th Cong., 2d Sess., 4 (1946) (explanatory statement of House managers). The Conference Committee agreed to an amendment providing that no incontestable right can be acquired in a mark that is a common descriptive, *i.e.*, generic, term. *Id.*, at 5. Congress could easily have denied incontestability to merely descriptive marks as well as to generic marks had that been its intention.

The Court of Appeals in discussing the offensive/defensive distinction observed that incontestability protects a registrant against cancellation of his mark. 718 F.2d, at 331. This observation is incorrect with respect to marks that become generic or which otherwise may be canceled at any time pursuant to §§ 14(c) and (e). Moreover, as applied to marks that are merely descriptive, the approach of the Court of Appeals makes incontestable status superfluous. Without regard to its incontestable status, a mark that has been registered five years is protected from cancellation except on the grounds stated in §§ 14(c) and (e). Pursuant to § 14, a mark may be canceled on the grounds that it is merely descriptive only if the petition to cancel is filed within five years of the date of registration. § 14(a), 15 U.S.C. § 1064(a). The approach adopted by the Court of Appeals implies that incontestability adds nothing to the protections against cancellation already provided in § 14. The decision below not only lacks support in the words of the statute, it effectively emasculates § 33(b) under the circumstances of this case.

III.

Nothing in the legislative history of the Lanham Act supports a departure from the plain language of the statutory provisions concerning incontestability. Indeed, a conclusion that incontestable status can provide the basis for enforcement of the registrant's exclusive right to use a trade or service mark promotes the goals of the statute. The Lanham Act provides national protection of trademarks in order to secure to the owner of the mark the goodwill of his business and to protect the ability of consumers to distinguish among competing producers. The opportunity to obtain incontestable status by satisfying the requirements of § 15 thus encourages producers to cultivate the goodwill associated with a particular mark. This function of the incontestability provisions would be utterly frustrated if the holder of an incontestable mark could not enjoin infringement by others so long as they established that the mark would not be registrable but for its incontestable status.

Respondent argues, however, that enforcing petitioner's mark would conflict with the goals of the Lanham Act because the mark is merely descriptive and should never have been registered in the first place. Representative Lanham, respondent notes, explained that the defenses enumerated in § 33(b) were "not intended to enlarge, restrict, amend, or modify the substantive law of trademarks either as set out in other sections of the act or as heretofore applied by the courts under prior laws." 92 Cong. Rec. 7524 (1946). Respondent reasons that because the Lanham Act did not alter the substantive law of trademarks, the incontestability provisions cannot protect petitioner's use of the mark if it were not originally registrable. Moreover, inasmuch as petitioner's mark is merely descriptive, respondent contends that enjoining others from using the mark will not encourage competition by assisting consumers in their ability to distinguish among competing producers.

These arguments are unpersuasive. Representative Lanham's remarks, if read in context, clearly refer to the effect of the defenses enumerated in § 33(b).[6] There is no question that the Lanham Act altered existing law

---

6. Representative Lanham made his remarks to clarify that the seven defenses enumerated in § 33(b) are not substantive rules of law which go to the validity or enforceabili-

concerning trademark rights in several respects.... Most significantly, Representative Lanham himself observed that incontestability was one of "the valuable new rights created by the act." 92 Cong. Rec. 7524 (1946).

Respondent's argument that enforcing petitioner's mark will not promote the goals of the Lanham Act is misdirected. Arguments similar to those now urged by respondent were in fact considered by Congress in hearings on the Lanham Act. For example, the United States Department of Justice opposed the incontestability provisions and expressly noted that a merely descriptive mark might become incontestable. Hearings on H.R. 82, at 59–60 (statement of the U.S. Dept. of Justice). This result, the Department of Justice observed, would "go beyond existing law in conferring unprecedented rights on trade-mark owners," and would undesirably create an exclusive right to use language that is descriptive of a product. *Id.*, at 60; *see also* Hearings on H.R. 102, at 106–107, 109–110 (testimony of Prof. Milton Handler); *id.*, at 107, 175 (testimony of attorney Louis Robertson). These concerns were answered by proponents of the Lanham Act, who noted that a merely descriptive mark cannot be registered unless the Commissioner finds that it has secondary meaning. *Id.*, at 108, 113 (testimony of Karl Pohl, U.S. Trade Mark Assn.). Moreover, a mark can be challenged for five years prior to its attaining incontestable status. *Id.*, at 114 (remarks of Rep. Lanham)....

The alternative of refusing to provide incontestable status for descriptive marks with secondary meaning was expressly noted in the hearings on the Lanham Act. Also mentioned was the possibility of including as a defense to infringement of an incontestable mark the "fact that a mark is a descriptive, generic, or geographical term or device." *Id.*, at 45, 47. Congress, however, did not adopt either of these alternatives. Instead, Congress expressly provided in §§ 33(b) and 15 that an incontestable mark could be challenged on specified grounds, and the grounds identified by Congress do not include mere descriptiveness.

The dissent echoes arguments made by opponents of the Lanham Act that the incontestable status of a descriptive mark might take from the public domain language that is merely descriptive.... Congress has already addressed concerns to prevent the "commercial monopolization" of descriptive language. The Lanham Act allows a mark to be challenged at any time if it becomes generic, and, under certain circumstances, permits the non-trademark use of descriptive terms contained in an incontestable mark. Finally, if "monopolization" of an incontestable mark threatens economic competition, § 33(b)(7), 15 U.S.C. § 1115(b)(7), provides a defense on the grounds that the mark is being used to violate federal antitrust laws. At

ty of an incontestable mark. 92 Cong.Rec. 7524 (1946). Instead, the defenses affect the evidentiary status of registration where the owner claims the benefit of a mark's incontestable status. If one of the defenses is established, registration constitutes only prima facie and not conclusive evidence of the owner's right to exclusive use of the mark. *Ibid.* *See also* H.R. Conf. Rep. No. 2322, 79th Cong., 2d Sess., 6 (1946) (explanatory statement of House managers).

bottom, the dissent simply disagrees with the balance struck by Congress in determining the protection to be given to incontestable marks.

Respondent argues that the decision by the Court of Appeals should be upheld because trademark registrations are issued by the Patent Office after an *ex parte* proceeding and generally without inquiry into the merits of an application.... The facts of this case belie the suggestion that registration is virtually automatic. The Patent Office initially denied petitioner's application because the examiner considered the mark to be merely descriptive. Petitioner sought reconsideration and successfully persuaded the Patent Office that its mark was registrable.

... If the Patent Office examiner determines that an applicant appears to be entitled to registration, the mark is published in the Official Gazette. § 12(a), 15 U.S.C. § 1062(a). Within 30 days of publication, any person who believes that he would be damaged by registration of the mark may file an opposition. § 13, 15 U.S.C. § 1063. Registration of a mark provides constructive notice throughout the United States of the registrant's claim to ownership. § 22, 15 U.S.C. § 1072. Within five years of registration, any person who believes that he is or will be damaged by registration may seek to cancel a mark. § 14(a), 15 U.S.C. § 1064(a). A mark may be canceled at any time for certain specified grounds, including that it was obtained fraudulently or has become generic. § 149(c), 15 U.S.C. § 1064(c).

The Lanham Act, as the dissent notes, authorizes courts to grant injunctions "according to principles of equity." § 34, 15 U.S.C. § 1116.... Whatever the precise boundaries of the courts' equitable power, we do not believe that it encompasses a substantive challenge to the validity of an incontestable mark on the grounds that it lacks secondary meaning. To conclude otherwise would expand the meaning of "equity" to the point of vitiating the more specific provisions of the Lanham Act.... Our responsibility ... is not to evaluate the wisdom of the legislative determinations reflected in the statute, but instead to construe and apply the provisions that Congress enacted.

. . . .

We conclude that the holder of a registered mark may rely on incontestability to enjoin infringement and that such an action may not be defended on the grounds that the mark is merely descriptive.... Respondent urges that we nevertheless affirm the decision below based on the "prior use" defense recognized by 33(b)(5) of the Lanham Act. Alternatively, respondent argues that there is no likelihood of confusion and therefore no infringement justifying injunctive relief. The District Court rejected each of these arguments, but they were not addressed by the Court of Appeals. 718 F.2d, at 331–332, n.4. That court may consider them on remand. The judgment of the Court of Appeals is reversed, and the case is remanded for further proceedings consistent with this opinion.

It is so ordered.

[Dissenting opinion of Justice Stevens is omitted.]

INCONTESTABLE REGISTRATION AND STRENGTH OF THE MARK

The *Park 'N Fly* majority held that once incontestable, a mark's registration may not be challenged on the ground that the mark is merely descriptive. Does the *Park 'N Fly* decision also mean that the distinctiveness of a mark is irrelevant to the analysis of likelihood of confusion? At first, courts unanimously distinguished defenses asserting the mere descriptiveness of a mark in order to challenge the validity of a registration, from arguments that the mark, as descriptive, was weak and therefore less prone to be confused with other, similar marks. For example, the court in *Source Services Corp. v. Source Telecomputing Corp.*, 635 F.Supp. 600 (N.D.Ill.1986), observed:

> *Park 'N Fly* teach[es] the conclusive presumption of secondary meaning merely means an alleged infringer is not permitted to raise descriptiveness as a defense against the validity of plaintiff's mark. That says nothing about the expected reactions of actual marketplace consumers. [P]laintiffs must still provide a factual predicate showing consumers are likely to confuse defendants' products with their own. And the more descriptive a mark is in fact, the less likely that sort of confusion will be.

Accord, Lone Star Steakhouse & Saloon, Inc. v. Alpha of Virginia, Inc., 43 F.3d 922 (4th Cir.1995); *Munters Corp. v. Matsui America, Inc.*, 909 F.2d 250 (7th Cir.), *cert. denied*, 498 U.S. 1016 (1990). *See also Oreck Corp. v. U.S. Floor Systems, Inc.*, 803 F.2d 166 (5th Cir.1986), *cert. denied*, 481 U.S. 1069 (1987). ("*Park 'N Fly* says nothing to preclude this argument [of absence of likelihood of confusion]. Incontestable status does not make a weak mark strong."); *Entrepreneur Media, Inc. v. Smith*, 279 F.3d 1135 (9th Cir.2002).

Some courts, however, have expressed a contrary view. In *Dieter v. B & H Industries*, 880 F.2d 322 (11th Cir.1989), *cert. denied*, 498 U.S. 950 (1990), the Eleventh Circuit noted that the question "[w]hether 'incontestable' status affects the strength of the mark for purposes of 'likelihood of confusion' determinations . . . is an issue of first impression in this circuit." The court "decline[d] to follow" the *Source Services Corp.* decision (*supra*):

> We hold that incontestable status is a factor to be taken into consideration in likelihood of confusion analysis. Because [plaintiff's] mark is incontestable, then it is presumed to be at least descriptive with secondary meaning, and therefore a relatively strong mark.

See also Wynn Oil Co. v. American Way Service Corp., 943 F.2d 595 (6th Cir.1991) (incontestable marks are presumed strong).

Which position makes more sense to you? Does the text of Section 33(b) of the Lanham Act, 15 U.S.C. § 1115(b), assist your determination? This provision states that once incontestability has been achieved, "the registration shall be conclusive evidence of the validity of the registered mark. . . . and of the registrant's exclusive right to use the registered mark in commerce" (emphasis supplied). On its face, does the Lanham Act "make a weak mark strong"? Should it?

In *Gruner + Jahr v. Meredith Corp.*, 991 F.2d 1072 (2d Cir.1993), the publishers of PARENTS magazine claimed that PARENTS' DIGEST, a separately-distributed supplement to defendant's LADIES HOME JOURNAL, was a title likely to be confused with plaintiff's publication. The district court had denied injunctive relief, in part because it found plaintiff's mark to be descriptive and weak. On appeal, plaintiff urged "that its uncontestable [sic] trademark registration status precludes defendant's using the fact that plaintiff's mark was merely descriptive as a defense in this infringement suit."

After reviewing the text of Lanham Act § 33(b), the court stated:

> What this means is that a defendant in an infringement suit— where plaintiff has an incontestable mark because of five years' registration—may not succeed in a defense that declares the mark is entitled to no protection because it is descriptive. As the Supreme Court instructs, the holder of a registered mark may enjoin its infringement relying on the mark's incontestability against a defense that the mark is merely descriptive. *See Park 'N Fly, Inc.* . . . . Hence, it must be concluded that for purposes of establishing its protectability in an infringement suit Gruner + Jahr's PARENTS is a strong mark entitled to be protected.

However, the court emphasized that an incontestable mark may nonetheless lack the strength necessary to prevail in a likelihood of confusion analysis. Analyzing the "strength of the mark" factor in the confusion test, the court continued:

> Gruner + Jahr suggests the district court properly found that the registered trademark PARENTS had acquired strong secondary meaning as an incontestable mark and was therefore strong, but that it erred when it inconsistently concluded the mark was descriptive and therefore weak. To the contrary, the district court carefully and, in our view, properly distinguished between the strength of the trademark PARENTS and the weak, descriptive nature of what it called the "mere word 'parents'." Those findings are perfectly consistent.

> First, Judge Knapp found that the mark PARENTS was strong since it was an incontestable registered trademark, having necessarily acquired secondary meaning. Thus, Gruner + Jahr's descriptive registered trademark was correctly found to be strong for purposes of protectability. At the same time, the trademark registration of the title PARENTS in its distinctive typeface did not confer an exclusive right to plaintiff on variations of the word "parent," such term being more generic than descriptive.

> The district court therefore did not make inconsistent findings when it noted that the "mere word" parents could be considered weak. On other occasions, we have found that the strength of an

incontestable registered trademark could be overcome by the use of a descriptive or weak portion of the mark. *See, e.g., W.W.W. Pharmaceutical Co. v. The Gillette Co.*, 984 F.2d 567 (2d Cir.1993) (incontestable registered trademark for "Sportstick" lip balm not infringed by Gillette's "Sport Stick" deodorant); *Western Pub.*, 910 F.2d at 60 (noting that despite over 100 registered trademarks in "Little Golden Books" family, use of term "golden" alone might be descriptive); *cf. Pirone v. MacMillan, Inc.*, 894 F.2d 579 (2d Cir.1990) (observing in case of a proper noun that registration does not remove it from the general language or reduce it to exclusive possession of registrant for all purposes).

[W]e think it now established that the strength of a descriptive mark made incontestably distinctive for protectability purposes by registration for more than five years is a matter also properly considered by a trial court on the issue of likelihood of confusion. [citations omitted] In analyzing the strength of the mark for likelihood of confusion purposes, we observe again that the actual trademark registration in this case protects not the name or the word "parents," but rather the stylized logo of that name including the unusual form and shape of the letters comprising the word. Any presumption of distinctiveness for likelihood of confusion purposes is lessened by the dissimilarity of the two magazine logos before us. The fact that the term "parents" resides in the public domain, lessens the possibility that a purchaser would be confused and think the mark came from a particular single source.

Further, registering the proper noun "parents" as a trademark scarcely can be held to have removed it from being available for use by others, or grant exclusive possession of this property right to the trademark registrant. This view is given particular force by the Trademark Law Revision Act of 1988, Pub. L. No. 100–667 (1988), which amended 15 U.S.C. § 1115(a) and (b) and made clear that incontestability does not relieve the trademark owner from the requirement of proving likelihood of confusion. Consequently, the finding by the district court that the "parents" portion of the mark—divorced from the stylized typeface and its particular placement on the magazine cover—was extremely weak was not clearly erroneous.

2.   DEFENSES TO INCONTESTABLY REGISTERED MARKS

SECTION 33 of the LANHAM ACT

We have already encountered a variety of defenses. For example, a defendant may raise as a defense to an infringement claim objections such as those that furnish the basis for rejecting an application for trademark registration. The grounds that the Lanham Act sets forth in section 14 as bases for cancelling a mark, may also be invoked as defenses to infringement claims. These grounds include fraud, abandonment, genericism and functionality. Any mark, including one that has become incontestable, may be cancelled at any time if it is abandoned or functional, was obtained fraudulently or becomes generic.

Section 33(a) of the Lanham Act provides that a registration is prima facie evidence of the registrant's right to exclusive use of the registered mark in connection with the goods or services covered by the registration subject to legal and equitable defenses, including those set forth in section 33(b). An incontestable registration is "conclusive" of the owner's exclusive right to use of the marks, but incontestability only applies to the goods/services covered by the incontestable registration. *See Sears, Roebuck & Co. v. Sears Realty Co.*, 1990 WL 198712 (N.D.N.Y. 1990) (incontestability of plaintiffs' SEARS registrations unavailable where such registrations did not cover the gasoline, fuel and convenience store services of defendant). Section 33(b) of the Lanham Act delineates nine exceptions to a registered mark's incontestable status as acquired under section 15. Because they are affirmative defenses, an alleged infringer has the burden of pleading and proving them. These defenses apply to contestable as well as incontestable marks.

As noted by the Supreme Court in *Park 'N Fly, supra*, the effect of establishing a section 33(b) defense is evidentiary so that "registration constitutes only prima facie and not conclusive evidence of the owner's right to exclusive use of the mark." All legal and common law defenses are then applicable. *See* 15 U.S.C. § 1115. Courts nevertheless frequently treat an established defense as conclusive on the merits. This approach reaches the same result as long as the court does not interpret the statutory defense more narrowly than the common law defense which might otherwise be applied. *See generally*, J. T. McCarthy, McCarthy on Trademarks and Unfair Competition § 32:153 (4th ed.).

A brief review of the § 33(b) defenses follows:

(1) *Fraudulent acquisition of trademark registration or of incontestable right to use mark.*

This defense is explored in more detail *infra*, Chapter 6.C.2.a.

(2) *Abandonment of the mark.*

Abandonment is a ground for cancelling a mark at any time, and may also be raised as a defense in an infringement suit. Abandonment, which was explored in detail *supra*, Chapter 5, includes non-use with intent not to resume, allowing a mark to become generic and uncontrolled licensing.

(3) *Use of the mark to misrepresent source.*

Similar to an unclean hands defense, this exception to incontestability includes intentionally false and misleading designations of origin, nature, or ingredients of registrant's goods. Courts have read this defense narrowly. In *W.E. Bassett Co. v. Revlon, Inc.*, 354 F.2d 868 (2d Cir.1966), for example, the defendant argued that plaintiff's misleading advertisements amounted to section 33(b)(3) false designation. The court disagreed: "any advertising errors were unintentional and *de minimis* in effect and there was no public deception by Bassett."

(4) *Use of mark in a descriptive sense other than as a trademark (the so-called "fair use" defense).*

The trademark fair use defense privileges non-trademark descriptive uses under some conditions. It is explored in more detail *infra*, Chapter 6.C.2.b

(5) *Limited territory defense.*

The limited territory defense was discussed in connection with concurrent use in Chapter 3.C, *supra*. This exception to an incontestable registration applies to a junior user who adopts a mark innocently before the senior user registers it, and who has used the mark continuously ever since. However, the benefits of the defense are restricted to the area of continuous use by the junior user prior to the plaintiff's registration (or application filing date for registrations resulting from applications filed after November 16, 1989, the effective date of The Trademark Revision Act of 1988). The area where continuous use by the defendant is established will thereafter be off-limits to the plaintiff and, conversely, use of the mark by the defendant in all other areas is barred. While the defendant may not subsequently extend the territory in which he uses the mark, he may be able to expand his business within his defined boundaries. *See Safeway Stores, Inc. v. Safeway Quality Foods, Inc.*, 433 F.2d 99 (7th Cir.1970).

(6) *Prior registration by defendant.*

Where the alleged infringer registered and used the mark prior to the registration of plaintiff and did not abandon it, the senior registrant may continue to use its mark, but only within the area where it was used prior to registration by plaintiff. This defense would seem to be useful only in situations in which two marks that were not confusingly similar when they were registered (because the products, geographic regions, or marks themselves were sufficiently dissimilar at the time to obviate confusion) later become confusingly similar. Even with that limitation, however, it seems peculiar to limit the senior registrant to a restricted geographic area at the behest of the junior registrant, even where the junior registrant has obtained a certificate of incontestability. Perhaps unsurprisingly, then, there is little case law invoking section 33(b)(6).

(7) *Use of mark to violate anti-trust laws.*

The antitrust defense is rarely successful. *See, e.g., Helene Curtis Industries v. Church & Dwight Co.*, 560 F.2d 1325, 1336 (7th Cir.1977), *cert. denied*, 434 U.S. 1070 (1978).

(8) *Functionality.*

Although functionality was not initially enumerated as a separate defense to incontestability under section 33, courts and the Board treated it as one until the Fourth Circuit's decision in *Shakespeare Co. v. Silstar Corp.*, 9 F.3d 1091 (4th Cir.1993), *cert. denied*, 511 U.S. 1127 (1994). *Silstar* held that functionality could not be asserted as a defense to an incontestable registration because the defense was not explicitly included in the statute. Sections 14 and 33 were amended in 1998 by Congress to include functionality explicitly both as a basis of cancellation and as a defense to incontestable marks. The amendment has been held to codify existing law in order to correct the reasoning in *Silstar. See Pudenz v. Littlefuse, Inc.*, 177 F.3d 1204 (11th Cir.1999). For a discussion of the functionality defense, *see* Chapter 4.C, *supra*, and Chapter 7.B, *infra*.

(9) *Equitable principles.*

Added in 1988, § 33(b)(9) explicitly makes "equitable principles, including laches, estoppel, and acquiescence" applicable defenses to incontestably registered marks. Laches, for purposes of objecting to registration of a mark, dates from the publication of the mark for opposition. *See National Cable Television Ass'n v. American Cinema Editors, Inc.*, 937 F.3d 1572 (Fed.Cir.1991). Because of the public interest in avoiding confusion, however, where the marks and goods or services of the parties are substantially similar and confusion is inevitable, laches has been held unavailable even where established. *See, e.g., Turner v. Hops Grill & Bar, Inc.*, 52 U.S.P.Q.2d 1310 (T.T.A.B.1999). Laches is discussed in more detail *infra*, Chapter 6.C.2.d.

In addition to the nine defenses listed in section 33(b), that section refers to section 15 as a further limit on incontestable status. Section 33(b) begins: "To the extent that the right to use the registered mark has become incontestable under section 15." Section 15 in turn incorporates additional defenses through its reference to section 14(3) (which inter alia refers to genericism, required conditions for obtaining a collective or certification mark and the statutory bars to registration set forth in section 2(a) (b) and (c)) and to section 14(5) (which refers to misuses of a certification mark).

QUESTIONS

1. After eliminating the defenses which still can be asserted against an incontestable registration, are any useful defenses precluded apart from descriptiveness such as was involved in *Park 'N Fly?*

2. Plaintiff, your client, owns an incontestable Federal registration for LAWSTORE for providing general consumer legal services such as will-drafting, uncontested divorces, and title searches. Defendant has adopted LAWSTORE in connection with a similar business. The term at issue was invented by plaintiff and does not appear in any dictionary. Several legal practitioners had adopted LAWSTORE in connection with their legal services operations, but when advised of plaintiff's registration they agreed to stop using the term. What defense do you expect defendant to raise, and what arguments do you plan to make in response?

a. FRAUD ON THE TRADEMARK OFFICE

What Constitutes Fraud?

In order to establish fraud, a material and knowing misrepresentation must be shown. The registrant's failure to reveal that a mark was commonly used in a generic or descriptive sense in the industry was held to be fraud in *G. Levor & Co., Inc. v. Nash, Inc.*, 123 U.S.P.Q. 234 (T.T.A.B. 1959). In *Hank Thorp, Inc. v. Minilite, Inc.*, 474 F.Supp. 228 (D.Del.1979), the court found fraud by a registrant who knew he was not the owner of the mark. In *Orient Express Trading Co. v. Federated Department Stores*, 842 F.2d 650 (2d Cir.1988), the court noted that fraudulent statements made in a trademark registration application "may not be the product of mere error or inadvertence, but must indicate a deliberate attempt to mislead the PTO." Under that standard, the court found that the registrant had fraudulently misrepresented its dates of first use and the scope of its subsequent use of its marks. A registrant's failure to reveal the widespread use of a mark by others was held to be fraudulent in *Bart Schwartz International Textiles, Ltd. v. Federal Trade Commission*, 289 F.2d 665 (C.C.P.A.1961). Making intentionally false statements in the incontestability declaration was held to be fraud in *Robi v. Five Platters, Inc.*, 918 F.2d 1439 (9th Cir.1990). *See also Daesang Corp. v. Rhee Bros., Inc.*, 77 U.S.P.Q.2d 1753 (D.Md. 2005)(failure of registrant to inform PTO that transliteration of mark meant Soon Chang, a place in Korea well known for sauces of the type covered by the application, and that registrant's customers would be aware of this association constituted fraud on the PTO). Even if fraud is proven, however, a trademark owner retains its common law rights, which can be used as a basis to challenge third parties.

The question of what constitutes an "intentional" material misstatement has been expanded by the recent line of Trademark Trial and Appeal Board cases discussed below.

Medinol Ltd. v. Neuro Vasx, 67 U.S.P.Q.2d 1205 (T.T.A.B. 2003). Neuro Vasx filed an intent-to-use based application for "medical devices, namely, neurological stents and catheters." At the time it filed its statement of use (and at all times since,) it used the mark on catheters but not on stents. In its statement of use, however, Neuro Vasx stated that it was using the mark on both. Faced with Medinol's cancellation petition alleging fraud on the Trademark Office, Neuro Vasx admitted an error, and agreed that the registration should be cancelled as to stents, but should be maintained with respect to the medical equipment on which it had in fact been using the mark. The Board rejected Neuro Vasx's contention that fraud required a showing of specific intent to deceive and instead found: "the appropriate inquiry.... is not into the registrant's subjective intent, but rather into the objective manifestations of that intent" and concluded:

Respondent's explanation for the misstatement (which we accept as true)—that the inclusion of stents in the notice of allowance was "apparently overlooked"—does nothing to undercut the conclusion that respondent knew or should have known that its statement of use was materially incorrect. Respondent's knowledge that its mark was not in use on stents—or its reckless disregard for the truth—is all that is required to establish intent to commit fraud in the procurement of a registration. While it is clear that not all incorrect statements constitute fraud, the relevant facts in this record allow no other conclusion. We find that respondent's material misrepresentations made in connection with its statement of use were fraudulent.

Standard Knitting v. Toyota, 77 U.S.P.Q.2d 1917 (T.T.A.B. 2006). Standard Knitting opposed issuance of a registration for TUNDRA for automobiles, on the ground that opposer had used the TUNDRA and TUNDRA SPORT marks for clothing. Toyota rejoined by seeking cancellation of opposer's registrations on the ground that the marks had not been used on the claimed clothing, and that opposer's Chief Executive Officer knew this when he signed the use-based applications and the statement of use for one application based on an intent to use. Opposer's Chief Operating Officer:

> indicate[d] that he did not make any effort to confirm that the marks TUNDRA and TUNDRA SPORT were in fact then being used on each of the goods listed in the applications when the applications were filed, and that he made no effort to verify what goods were in fact then being sold, and sold in the United States, although he admitted that there were sources of documentary information that could have been consulted (possibly invoices, if not destroyed and if they could be located), or price lists and cost sheets, for at least some of the goods.

> As support for his claim of current use on all of the identified goods, Mr. Groumoutis [the COO] states that he "had personal knowledge or knowledge of looking at past brochures that they, in fact, had done those in the past" [the meaning of "done" in this context being unclear], and he indicates that some brochures would have been current, and some three or more years old. At various points in his deposition, he states that he may have discussed the goods to be included in the applications . . . , and would have asked "have we ever sold these goods" or have we made, or did we make these goods or that he "may have spoken" . . . to find out if the list was correct but "it may have been just general, are we using these, yes, we are, and that would have been the end of it." However, when asked by applicant's counsel, "did you make any . . ." [then proceeding to list items of children's clothing], Mr. Groumoutis answered "not sure" as to children's sweaters, and "no" as to hats, jackets, coats, t-shirts, vests, shorts and shirts for children.

The Company's CEO, who signed the registration application was no more assiduous:

Mr. Wang [the CEO] states that Mr. Groumoutis,

Told me that this was an application to register, I think it was to register our trademark. I asked him, if he has read it. And he said yes. I asked him if it was accurate. And he said yes. And I signed it.

Mr. Wang indicated that he did not look at any other documents in connection with the applications at that time and that the process took five minutes.

Finding it clear from the record that the marks were not in fact in use on most of the goods claimed, the Board addressed whether opposer's officers' statements were fraudulent:

Mr. Wang, who signed the underlying applications for these registrations, did not personally know, at the time of signing, whether or not certain of the identified goods, specifically, hats and coats, were being sold under the TUNDRA mark in the United States. He also stated that to his personal knowledge hats, jackets, coats and shorts were not being sold under the TUNDRA SPORT mark in the United States. Mr. Wang relied on Mr. Groumoutis's representation that the applications were accurate. However, that representation turned out to be false.

It is opposer's contention that the false statement was the result of an honest mistake, and not due to any fraudulent intent; that opposer was making and selling a variety of clothing items; that the evidence, including invoices and spec sheets, shows that all of the listed products were actually made and/or sold by Standard Knitting, and substantiates the first use dates for each of its challenged registrations; that opposer did not know or understand the legal meaning of "use in commerce" and that its understanding of use was that the item was made or was sold; and that opposer had a reasonable belief, after making inquiries, that the marks were being used with the listed goods. As to the statement of use, opposer argues that it was filed on the basis of a mistaken belief that use was being made . . . and that the mark was in use with at least some goods as of the statement of use date.

Mr. Groumoutis's asserted mistake, assuming it truly was a mistake, was not a reasonable one. The language in the application that the mark "is now in use in commerce" is clear, and its meaning is unambiguous. It was not reasonable for Mr. Groumoutis to believe that if the items of clothing were ever made or sold, even if the last sale took place 20 years ago, it would support a claim that the mark "is" in use on the goods. . . .

Mr. Groumoutis clearly understood, prior to filing the applications, that "use" of a mark meant use in the United States. Given that none of Standard Knitting's clothing was made in the United States, Mr. Groumoutis could not have honestly believed that "use" simply meant that the goods were "made." This is not a situation where opposer misunderstood the significance of the statements it signed. Rather, opposer disregarded the significance.

Considering that Mr. Groumoutis did not personally know whether the marks were in use on children's clothing in the United States, he was obligated to inquire and to the extent he did inquire, by looking at prior registrations, relying on his attorney's representations, and asking [company employees] whether the goods were ever made or sold, those inquiries were grossly insufficient. *See Medinol* ("Statements made with such degree of solemnity clearly are—or should be—investigated thoroughly prior to signature and submission to the USPTO.").... Opposer is charged with knowing what it is signing and by failing to make any appropriate inquiry, [opposer's officer] signed the statement of use with a "reckless disregard for the truth."

QUESTIONS

1. Were opposers' officers in *Medinol* and *Standard Knitting* uncommonly ignorant, or is the TTAB requiring that a company's top officers know more about daily operations than they normally would or should?

2. Australian musicians file a use-based application in the U.S. for entertainment services for which they own an Australian registration. In fact, the mark has only been used in Australia and not in the U.S. Would the foreign applicants' honest (but erroneous) belief that their use was sufficient to file a use-based application in the U.S. be enough to overcome a *Medinol*-based fraud claim in an opposition? After the opposition is brought, could the musicians amend the basis of their application to § 44(e) based on their Australian registration? *See Hurley Int'l LLC v. Volta*, 2007 WL 196407 (T.T.A.B.2007).

b. FAIR USE

As we have seen, most of the defenses, including those to incontestably registered marks, concern the nature of the mark, or of the trademark owner's use of the mark. By contrast, two of the § 33(b) defenses focus on the other party's use. We have already examined one of these two defenses, the good-faith junior user exception, set forth at § 33(b)(5), in the materials on acquisition of trademark rights and concurrent use, *supra*, Chapter 3.C.2. The other defense, trademark "fair use" (not to be confused with the eponymous, but quite different, exception to copyright infringement), applies when an alleged infringer has used a term in good faith primarily to describe a product, rather than to identify it with a particular source, the use will be held not to infringe the plaintiff's trademark which it resembles.

United States Shoe Corp. v. Brown Group Inc.

740 F.Supp. 196 (S.D.N.Y.), *aff'd*, 923 F.2d 844 (2d Cir.1990).

■ LEVAL, J:

Plaintiff United States Shoe Corp. ("U.S. Shoe"), asserts trademark violation and unfair competition against Brown Group, Inc., in connection with the advertising and sale of women's dress shoes. Plaintiff advertises its women's dress pumps under the slogan and musical jingle, "Looks Like a Pump, Feels Like a Sneaker." Defendant has launched an advertising campaign that compares its pump to a sneaker and asserts that it "feels like a sneaker." Plaintiff seeks a preliminary injunction barring defendant from using the phrase. An evidentiary hearing was held on submission.

Background

The facts are largely undisputed. In August 1987, the plaintiff began to sell walking shoes under the Easy Spirit trademark. In or around October 1988, the plaintiff introduced under the same trademark a line of "comfortable women's dress pumps" which were intended to incorporate design and comfort elements of the plaintiff's walking shoes. Since that time, Easy Spirit pumps have been promoted and advertised by associating them with sneakers, and in particular by using the slogan or tag line, "Looks Like a Pump, Feels Like a Sneaker." This slogan has been prominently featured in plaintiff's print ads, point of purchase displays, catalog sheets and promotional brochures. It has also been used in a widely distributed television commercial, in which the slogan is sung while women are pictured playing basketball in Easy Spirit dress shoes. The plaintiff spent more than nine million dollars on advertising including the slogan in 1988 and 1989. During this time, sales increased dramatically. Sales of Easy Spirit pumps increased between 56% and 133% in the relevant market in the several weeks following runs of plaintiff's television commercial.

The defendant is the manufacturer and distributor of the NaturalSport line of walking shoes, and also of the Townwalker, a comfortable women's dress pump considered to be one of the key competitors of the Easy Spirit dress pump. In mid–1988, defendant retained the advertising agency D'Arcy, Masius, Benton & Bowles ("D'Arcy") to develop an ad campaign for the Townwalker and other NaturalSport shoes. D'Arcy recommended a campaign to communicate the basic product concept of the Townwalker: "a sneaker in a pump." D'Arcy submitted several proposed print ads for the Townwalker to the defendant, including some which used the slogan, "The pump that feels like a sneaker." The defendant rejected these ads, in part because of their similarity to plaintiff's advertising slogan, "Looks Like a Pump, Feels Like a Sneaker," of which defendant was aware. . . .

The print advertisement ultimately selected by defendant features a photograph of a women's pump with the headline, "Think Of It As A Sneaker With No Strings Attached." The text of the ad includes the phrase, "And when we say it feels like a sneaker, we're not just stringing you along." The ad includes the NaturalSport logo, the slogan, "Walk Our Way" and the words "From Naturalizer," which defendant uses to advertise other styles of shoe in the NaturalSport line.

THINK OF IT AS A SNEAKER
WITH NO STRINGS ATTACHED.

Slip into the NaturalSport TownWalker. It has all the cushioning and support of our high performance walking shoes. And when we say it feels like a sneaker, we're not just stringing you along.

WALK OUR WAY

FROM NATURALIZER.

Plaintiff contends that the Townwalker ad's statement "And when we say it feels like a sneaker" is deliberately meant to mislead consumers into believing the Townwalker is the brand previously advertised by the slogan, "Looks Like a Pump, Feels Like a Sneaker," and thus cause consumers to purchase defendant's pump rather than plaintiff's. Plaintiff alleges that this constitutes a violation of the Lanham Act, as well as unfair competition and trademark violation under state common law.

.   .   .   .

Defendant's use of the words "feels like a sneaker" falls squarely within the "fair use" defense codified in Section 33(b)(4) of the Lanham Act. The fair use doctrine provides a statutory defense to a trademark infringement claim when "the use of the name, term or device charged to be an infringement is a use, otherwise than as a trade or service mark, . . . of a term or device which is *descriptive of and used fairly and in good faith only to describe* to users the goods or services of such party, or their geographic origin." 15 U.S.C. § 1115(b)(4) (emphasis added). The purpose of the defense is to prevent the trademark rights of one party from being extended to preclude another party from the description of his product to the public. [Citation omitted]. When the plaintiff chooses a mark with descriptive qualities, the fair use doctrine recognizes that "he cannot altogether exclude some kinds of competing uses," "particularly those which use words in their primary descriptive and non-trademark sense." *Abercrombie & Fitch Co. v. Hunting World, Inc.*, 537 F.2d 4, 12 (2d Cir.1976). (Citations omitted).

An understanding of statutory fair use doctrine depends on the purposes and justifications of the trademark law. In general, the law disfavors the grant of exclusive monopoly rights. Exceptions exist, however, where the grant of monopoly rights results in substantial benefits to society. Because of the benefits to society resulting from the ability easily to recognize the goods or services of a purveyor or manufacturer, the trademark law grants the exclusive right to employ an identifying mark. A reciprocal benefit results. The merchant is thereby permitted to profit from a well earned reputation; the public is thereby enabled to choose the products produced by those who have satisfied them in the past, avoid those that have disappointed and recognize an unknown quantity as exactly that. The benefits are great, and because potential identifying marks exist in virtually inexhaustible supply, the cost of the monopoly to society is minimal.

The cost-free aspect of the trademark depends, however, on the exclusivity being practiced only over identifiers that are not needed by others for trade communication. If only one manufacturer of candy were permitted to call the product "candy"; if only one were permitted to say that it is "lemon flavored," then society would not be enriched but impoverished. Society would be deprived of useful information about competing products, and one supplier would receive an unfair and unjustified advantage over competitors. Thus the trademark law presumptively forbids the establishment of rights over "generic" or "descriptive" marks—marks that define or describe the product. An exception was permitted, however, to a user of a descriptive mark who over time had built up a customer recognition (secondary meaning) in the mark. It would be unfair to permit competitors to piggyback on the reputation earned by such a merchant. Thus a showing of acquired secondary meaning would overcome the presumptive ineligibility of descriptive words to exclusive reservation.

A user of a descriptive word may acquire the exclusive right to use that descriptive word as *an identifier* of the product or source. This, however, does not justify barring others from using the words in good faith *for descriptive purposes* pertinent to their products. Returning to the example of the candy manufacturers, the fact that one might acquire trademark rights over a descriptive identifier like "chewy" or "lemon flavored" cannot deprive society of the opportunity to be advised by other manufacturers that their candy is chewy or lemon flavored. Therefore, notwithstanding the establishment of trademark rights over a descriptive term by a showing that it has acquired secondary meaning, the statute preserves in others the right to the use of such terms "fairly and in good faith only to describe [and not to designate] the goods or services." 15 U.S.C. § 1115(b)(4). The purpose of this provision is to ensure that the according of monopoly trademark rights over descriptive marks (upon a showing of acquired secondary meaning) will not overbroadly deprive society of the use of those terms in their descriptive sense in commercial communication.

In this case, the defendant uses the phrase "feels like a sneaker" in a descriptive sense, claiming a virtue of the product. It essentially restates the key selling claim of defendant's product—that the Townswalker shoe was designed specifically to incorporate the comfort of athletic shoes.

Moreover, defendant is not using the phrase as an identifier or trademark to indicate origin or source. That function is performed in defendant's ad by the NaturalSport logo, which is prominently displayed, and by the slogan, "Walk our Way . . . From Naturalizer." Defendant's use of the words "feels like a sneaker" is not even as a caption or slogan, but as a fragment of a sentence in small print. In short, defendant uses the words "otherwise than as a trade or service mark, . . . fairly and in good faith only to describe to users the goods" marketed by defendant. 15 U.S.C. § 1115(b)(4). Under the fair use doctrine, such a use is not an infringement. There is no justification for permitting plaintiff to monopolize an essentially descriptive phrase which claims virtues, simply because plaintiff may have been the first to employ it in widely distributed advertisements.

Plaintiff, furthermore, has not demonstrated a sufficient likelihood of confusion as to source to justify a finding of infringement. Descriptive advertising claiming a product's virtues is likely to be understood as such rather than as an identifier of source. No confusion should be presumed from the defendant's use of descriptive words similar to plaintiff's, because the consumer is likely to understand that it is the claimed features of both products that are being discussed, and not their origin. Notwithstanding that plaintiff may have built up consumer recognition in its slogan and musical jingle, there is no reason to suppose that consumers will assume that any manufacturer who claims his shoes feel like a sneaker is the plaintiff. This is a standard descriptive approach to a claim of comfort and is unlikely to be understood as an identifier. Plaintiff has not met its burden of demonstrating that defendant's ad is likely to confuse consumers as to the source of defendant's product.

Car–Freshner Corp. v. S.C. Johnson & Son Inc.

70 F.3d 267 (2d Cir.1995).

■ LEVAL, J.

This action for trademark infringement involves the principle that the public's right to use language and imagery for descriptive purposes is not defeated by the claims of a trademark owner to exclusivity.

Plaintiff Car–Freshner Corporation sells air fresheners for cars in the shape of a pine tree. Over a number of years, Car–Freshner has sold millions of such pine-tree-shaped fresheners. Its air fresheners are made of flat scented cardboard and come in a variety of colors and odors, including a green pine-scented version. They have a string attached to the top of the tree, so that they can be hung from the rear-view mirror of an automobile. We assume that plaintiff has established trademark rights in the pine-tree shape of its product and in the name "Little Tree," which it uses on some of its products.

Defendant S.C. Johnson & Son, Inc., sells air fresheners under the trademark name "Glade." Johnson's "Glade" products include a line of air fresheners called "Plug–Ins," designed to be plugged into electrical outlets. Glade Plug–Ins have a plastic casing that holds a replaceable fragrance cartridge of scented gel. When the unit is plugged in, the electrical current warms the gel, causing release of the fragrance into the air. During the Christmas holiday season, Johnson sells a pine-tree-shaped, plug-in air freshener called "Holiday Pine Potpourri" under its Glade Plug–Ins trademark.

Car–Freshner brought this action against Johnson, claiming that Johnson's sale of its pine-tree-shaped plug-in freshener violates Car–Freshner's trademark rights in the pine-tree shape of its air fresheners and in its mark "Little Tree." ... Johnson, in addition to denying that its use of a pine-tree shape creates a likelihood of confusion, asserted the affirmative defense known in trademark law as fair use.

Johnson moved for summary judgment, arguing that the dissimilarity between the two products and the fair use defense precluded a finding of infringement as a matter of law. The district court rejected Johnson's claim of fair use and granted summary judgment to Car–Freshner on that issue. The court ruled that the defense of fair use applies only when the plaintiff's mark is descriptive, and is not applicable here because the court found plaintiff's mark to be suggestive. The district court nonetheless granted summary judgment to Johnson on the ground that the plaintiff's and defendant's tree-shaped products were sufficiently dissimilar that there was no likelihood consumers would be confused as to the source of the two products. Accordingly, judgment was awarded to the defendant Johnson.

Car–Freshner appeals. Johnson cross-appeals, arguing that the district court erred in its fair use determination. We affirm the district court's grant of summary judgment in favor of Johnson, but on grounds of fair use.

. . . .

The district court rejected Johnson's claim of fair use because it believed such a defense could be mounted only against a mark classed as "descriptive" in the four-tiered hierarchy of trademark law—generic, descriptive, suggestive, and arbitrary or fanciful. *See Abercrombie*, 537 F.2d at

9–11. (Citation omitted). Although there is authority for that proposition, *see Institute for Scientific Info. v. Gordon and Breach, Science Publishers, Inc.*, 931 F.2d 1002, 1010 (3d Cir.), *cert. denied*, 502 U.S. 909, 116 L. Ed. 2d 245, 112 S. Ct. 302 (1991); *Cullman Ventures, Inc. v. Columbian Art Works, Inc.*, 717 F. Supp. 96, 133 (S.D.N.Y.1989); 3A Callmann § 21.24, at 212, we believe that notion is misguided.[1] It is true that the doctrine can apply only to marks consisting of terms or images with descriptive qualities. That is because only such terms or images are capable of being used by others in their primary descriptive sense. But it should make no difference whether the plaintiff's mark is to be classed on the descriptive tier of the trademark ladder (where protection is unavailable except on a showing of secondary meaning). What matters is whether the defendant is using the protected word or image descriptively, and not as a mark. (Citations omitted).

Whether the mark is classed as descriptive (and thus ineligible for protection without secondary meaning) depends on the relationship between the mark and the product described. Thus words like SWEET or CHEWY would be descriptive for a candy, but would be suggestive, or even arbitrary or fanciful, if used in connection with bed sheets, a computer, or an automobile. Regardless whether the protected mark is descriptive, suggestive, arbitrary, or fanciful as used in connection with the product or service covered by the mark, the public's right to use descriptive words or images in good faith in their ordinary descriptive sense must prevail over the exclusivity claims of the trademark owner. *See Dowbrands, L.P. v. Helene Curtis, Inc.*, 863 F. Supp. 963, 966–69 (D.Minn.1994) (fair use defense is not limited to descriptive marks); Restatement (Third) of Unfair Competition § 28 cmt. a ("Trademark rights ... extend only to the source significance that has been acquired by such terms, not to their original descriptive meanings."). An auto manufacturer's use of the mark SWEET for its cars could not deprive anyone of the right to use that word in good faith in its ordinary descriptive sense and not as a trademark. Thus a candy manufacturer would remain free to advertise the sweetness of its candies without worry about the trademark owner's bridging the gap and going into the candy business. If any confusion results to the detriment of the markholder, that was a risk entailed in the selection of a mark with descriptive attributes.

Section 1115(b)(4) includes no prerequisite that the mark sought to be protected be on the descriptive tier. . . .

---

1. We do not agree with the district court in *Cullman*, 717 F. Supp. at 133, that this limitation was imposed by the Fifth Circuit in *Zatarains, Inc. v. Oak Grove Smokehouse, Inc.*, 698 F.2d 786 (5th Cir.1983). It is true the *Zatarains* opinion asserts that "the holder of a protectable descriptive mark" is subject to the fair use defense, *id.* at 791, and that "the 'fair use' defense applies only to descriptive terms." *Id.* at 796. We read these passages to use the term "descriptive" in its primary sense and not as a reference to the second tier of the trademark ladder. If we are mistaken and the Fifth Circuit intended a rule that the fair use defense can be asserted only against marks on the second tier, we disagree. In our view, such a holding would be contrary to reason, the statutory language, and the bulk of persuasive authority.

In short, fair use permits others to use a protected mark to describe aspects of their own goods, provided the use is in good faith and not as a mark. *See* 15 U.S.C. § 1115(b)(4). That is precisely the case here. Johnson's use of the pine-tree shape describes two aspects of its product. The pine tree refers to the pine scent of its air freshening agent. Furthermore, as a Christmas tree is traditionally a pine tree, the use of the pine-tree shape refers to the Christmas season, during which Johnson sells this item. Johnson's use of the pine-tree shape is clearly descriptive. There is no indication that Johnson uses its tree shape as a mark. Its pine-tree-shaped air fresheners come in boxes prominently bearing the "Glade Plug–Ins" trademark as well as Johnson's corporate logo. Each unit has "Glade" imprinted across the front of the product itself.

Car–Freshner contends that Johnson adopted the mark in bad faith and therefore cannot claim fair use. Car–Freshner bases its argument primarily on the fact that Johnson adopted its tree shape with knowledge of Car–Freshner's use of the tree shape and without consulting counsel. There is no merit to this argument. As Johnson was fully entitled to use a pine-tree shape descriptively notwithstanding Car–Freshner's use of a tree shape as a mark, the fact that it did so without consulting counsel has no tendency to show bad faith. *See U.S. Shoe*, 740 F. Supp. at 199 (defendant's knowledge of plaintiff's success with mark is insufficient to show bad faith); Restatement (Third) of Unfair Competition § 28 cmt. d (1995) (describing examples of bad faith).

We therefore reverse the district court's grant of summary judgment to Car–Freshner on the defense of fair use and direct entry of summary judgment in favor of Johnson on that issue. We thus affirm the dismissal of Car–Freshner's complaint.

QUESTIONS

1. Since 1996, THE RADIO CHANNEL website at "www.radiochannel.com" has offered a directory of radio stations and radio advertising information. Recently, an Internet webcaster has organized its live and on-demand television programming, radio programming, music and other media content offered to its subscribers at <www.broadcast.com>, into sixteen channels by content, including a "Radio Channel" for radio programming. When the words "radio channel" are typed into one popular search engine, the webcaster's site is listed before THE RADIO CHANNEL website in the list of hits. How would you decide the webcaster's fair use defense? Would it make a difference if, instead of sixteen content channels, the webcaster provided only one called "Radio Channel"? *Cf. Radio Channel Networks, Inc. v. Broadcast.Com, Inc.*, 1999 WL 124455 (S.D.N.Y.1999), *aff'd w/out op.*, 201 F.3d 432 (2d Cir.1999).

2. Consider a t.v. commercial for golf clubs with swing music in the background which, during 5 seconds of a 30 second commercial, shows three golfers in succession swinging their clubs preceded by the phrase on the screen "Swing, Swing, Swing." In a suit by the owner of the rights in the well-known swing song "Sing, Sing, Sing (with a Swing)," how would you decide a fair use defense? Would it affect your analysis if the advertising agency had initially approached the owner of the song, but decided not to use the song for reasons of costs? *EMI Catalogue Partnership v. Hill, Holliday, Connors, Cosmopulos, Inc.*, 228 F.3d 56 (2d Cir.2000).

3. International Stamp Art, Inc. designs and produces note cards and greeting cards bearing reproductions of postage stamp art. For certain of these products, ISA used a perforation design to serve as a border for the card's design or illustration. ISA has obtained a trademark registration for the perforated border design. The U.S. Postal Service also issues greeting cards incorporating the designs of postage stamps, and which display a perforated border. In response to ISA's infringement action, the Postal Service contends that the perforated border is being used as an integral aspect of the image of a postage stamp. Is the Postal Service making a descriptive use "other than as a mark" that would qualify it for the § 33(b)(4) exception? *See International Stamp Art v. U.S. Postal Service*, 78 U.S.P.Q.2d 1116 (N.D. Ga. 2005).

KP Permanent Make–Up, Inc. v. Lasting Impression I, Inc.

543 U.S. 111, 125 S.Ct. 542, 160 L.Ed.2d 440 (2004).

■ JUSTICE SOUTER.

The question here is whether a party raising the statutory affirmative defense of fair use to a claim of trademark infringement, 15 U.S.C. § 1115(b)(4), has a burden to negate any likelihood that the practice complained of will confuse consumers about the origin of the goods or services affected. We hold it does not.

I

Each party to this case sells permanent makeup, a mixture of pigment and liquid for injection under the skin to camouflage injuries and modify nature's dispensations, and each has used some version of the term "micro color" (as one word or two, singular or plural) in marketing and selling its product. Petitioner KP Permanent Make–Up, Inc., claims to have used the single-word version since 1990 or 1991 on advertising flyers and since 1991 on pigment bottles. Respondents Lasting Impression I, Inc., and its licensee, MCN International, Inc. (Lasting, for simplicity), deny that KP began using the term that early, but we accept KP's allegation as true for present purposes.... In 1992, Lasting applied to the United States Patent and Trademark Office (PTO) under 15 U.S.C. § 1051 for registration of a trademark consisting of the words "Micro Colors" in white letters separated by a green bar within a black square. The PTO registered the mark to Lasting in 1993, and in 1999 the registration became incontestable. § 1065.

It was also in 1999 that KP produced a 10–page advertising brochure using "microcolor" in a large, stylized typeface, provoking Lasting to demand that KP stop using the term. Instead, KP sued Lasting in the Central District of California, seeking, on more than one ground, a declaratory judgment that its language infringed no such exclusive right as Lasting claimed. Lasting counterclaimed, alleging, among other things, that KP had infringed Lasting's "Micro Colors" trademark.

KP sought summary judgment on the infringement counterclaim, based on the statutory affirmative defense of fair use, 15 U.S.C. § 1115(b)(4). After finding that Lasting had conceded that KP used the term only to describe its goods and not as a mark, the District Court held that KP was acting fairly and in good faith because undisputed facts showed that KP had employed the term "microcolor" continuously from a time before Lasting adopted the two-word, plural variant as a mark. Without inquiring whether the practice was likely to cause confusion, the court concluded that KP had made out its affirmative defense under § 1115(b)(4) and entered summary judgment for KP on Lasting's infringement claim.

On appeal, 328 F.3d 1061 (2003), the Court of Appeals for the Ninth Circuit thought it was error for the District Court to have addressed the fair use defense without delving into the matter of possible confusion on the part of consumers about the origin of KP's goods. The reviewing court took the view that no use could be recognized as fair where any consumer confusion was probable, and although the court did not pointedly address the burden of proof, it appears to have placed it on KP to show absence of consumer confusion. (Citation omitted) Since it found there were disputed material facts relevant under the Circuit's eight-factor test for assessing the likelihood of confusion, it reversed the summary judgment and remanded the case.

We granted KP's petition for certiorari, 540 U.S. 1099, 540 U.S. 1099, 157 L. Ed. 2d 811, 124 S. Ct. 981 (2004), to address a disagreement among the Courts of Appeals on the significance of likely confusion for a fair use defense to a trademark infringement claim, and the obligation of a party defending on that ground to show that its use is unlikely to cause consumer confusion. (Citations omitted).

... We now vacate the judgment of the Court of Appeals.

II

A

The holder of a registered mark (incontestable or not) has a civil action against anyone employing an imitation of it in commerce when "such use is likely to cause confusion, or to cause mistake, or to deceive." § 1114(1). Although an incontestable registration is "conclusive evidence ... of the registrant's exclusive right to use the ... mark in commerce," § 1115(b), the plaintiff's success is still subject to "proof of infringement as defined in section 1114," § 1115(b). And that, as just noted, requires a showing that the defendant's actual practice is likely to produce confusion in the minds of consumers about the origin of the goods or services in question. (Citations omitted) This plaintiff's burden has to be kept in mind when reading the relevant portion of the further provision for an affirmative defense of fair use, available to a party whose

> "use of the name, term, or device charged to be an infringement is a use, otherwise than as a mark, ... of a term or device which is descriptive of and used fairly and in good faith only to describe the goods or services of such party, or their geographic origin...."
> § 1115(b)(4).

Two points are evident. Section 1115(b) places a burden of proving likelihood of confusion (that is, infringement) on the party charging infringement even when relying on an incontestable registration. And Congress said nothing about likelihood of confusion in setting out the elements of the fair use defense in § 1115(b)(4).

Starting from these textual fixed points, it takes a long stretch to claim that a defense of fair use entails any burden to negate confusion. It is just not plausible that Congress would have used the descriptive phrase "likely to cause confusion, or to cause mistake, or to deceive" in § 1114 to describe the requirement that a markholder show likelihood of consumer confusion, but would have relied on the phrase "used fairly" in § 1115(b)(4) in a fit of terse drafting meant to place a defendant under a burden to negate confusion. "[W]here Congress includes particular language in one section of a statute but omits it in another section of the same Act, it is generally presumed that Congress acts intentionally and purposely in the disparate inclusion or exclusion." *Russello v. United States,* 464 U.S. 16, 23, 78 L. Ed. 2d 17, 104 S. Ct. 296 (1983) (quoting *United States v. Wong Kim Bo,* 472 F.2d 720, 722 (CA5 1972)) (alteration in original).[4]

Nor do we find much force in Lasting's suggestion that "used fairly" in § 1115(b)(4) is an oblique incorporation of a likelihood-of-confusion test developed in the common law of unfair competition. Lasting is certainly correct that some unfair competition cases would stress that use of a term by another in conducting its trade went too far in sowing confusion, and would either enjoin the use or order the defendant to include a disclaimer. (Citations omitted). But the common law of unfair competition also tolerated some degree of confusion from a descriptive use of words contained in another person's trademark. (Citations omitted). While these cases are consistent with taking account of the likelihood of consumer confusion as one consideration in deciding whether a use is fair, *see* Part II–B, *infra,* they do not stand for the proposition that an assessment of confusion alone may be dispositive. Certainly one cannot get out of them any defense burden to negate it entirely.

---

4. Not only that, but the failure to say anything about a defendant's burden on this point was almost certainly not an oversight, not after the House Subcommittee on Trade-marks declined to forward a proposal to provide expressly as an element of the defense that a descriptive use be " '[un]likely to de-ceive the public.' " Hearings on H.R. 102 et al. before the Subcommittee on Trade–Marks of the House Committee on Patents, 77th Cong., 1st Sess., 167–168 (1941) (hereinafter Hearings) (testimony of Prof. Milton Handler).

Finally, a look at the typical course of litigation in an infringement action points up the incoherence of placing a burden to show nonconfusion on a defendant. If a plaintiff succeeds in making out a prima facie case of trademark infringement, including the element of likelihood of consumer confusion, the defendant may offer rebutting evidence to undercut the force of the plaintiff's evidence on this (or any) element, or raise an affirmative defense to bar relief even if the prima facie case is sound, or do both. But it would make no sense to give the defendant a defense of showing affirmatively that the plaintiff cannot succeed in proving some element (like confusion); all the defendant needs to do is to leave the factfinder unpersuaded that the plaintiff has carried its own burden on that point. A defendant has no need of a court's true belief when agnosticism will do. Put another way, it is only when a plaintiff has shown likely confusion by a preponderance of the evidence that a defendant could have any need of an affirmative defense, but under Lasting's theory the defense would be foreclosed in such a case. "[I]t defies logic to argue that a defense may not be asserted in the only situation where it even becomes relevant." *Shakespeare Co. v. Silstar Corp.,* 110 F.3d at 243. Nor would it make sense to provide an affirmative defense of no confusion plus good faith, when merely rebutting the plaintiff's case on confusion would entitle the defendant to judgment, good faith or not.

· · · ·

B

Since the burden of proving likelihood of confusion rests with the plaintiff, and the fair use defendant has no free-standing need to show confusion unlikely, it follows (contrary to the Court of Appeals's view) that some possibility of consumer confusion must be compatible with fair use, and so it is. The common law's tolerance of a certain degree of confusion on the part of consumers followed from the very fact that in cases like this one an originally descriptive term was selected to be used as a mark, not to mention the undesirability of allowing anyone to obtain a complete monopoly on use of a descriptive term simply by grabbing it first. (Citation omitted). The Lanham Act adopts a similar leniency, there being no indication that the statute was meant to deprive commercial speakers of the ordinary utility of descriptive words. "If any confusion results, that is a risk the plaintiff accepted when it decided to identify its product with a mark that uses a well known descriptive phrase." *Cosmetically Sealed Industries, Inc. v. Chesebrough–Pond's USA Co.,* 125 F.3d at 30. *See also Park 'N Fly, Inc. v. Dollar Park & Fly, Inc.,* 469 U.S. 189, 201, 83 L. Ed. 2d 582, 105 S. Ct. 658 (1985) (noting safeguards in Lanham Act to prevent commercial monopolization of language); *Car–Freshner Corp. v. S. C. Johnson & Son, Inc.,* 70 F.3d 267, 269 (CA2 1995) (noting importance of "protect[ing] the right of society at large to use words or images in their primary descriptive sense"). This right to describe is the reason that descriptive terms qualify for registration as trademarks only after taking on secondary meaning as "distinctive of the applicant's goods," *15 U.S.C. § 1052(f),* with the registrant getting an exclusive right not in the original, descriptive sense, but only in the secondary one associated with the markholder's goods, 2 McCarthy, *supra*, § 11:45 ("The only aspect of the mark which is given legal protection is that penumbra or fringe of secondary meaning which surrounds the old descriptive word").

While we thus recognize that mere risk of confusion will not rule out fair use, we think it would be improvident to go further in this case, for deciding anything more would take us beyond the Ninth Circuit's consideration of the subject. It suffices to realize that our holding that fair use can occur along with some degree of confusion does not foreclose the relevance of the extent of any likely consumer confusion in assessing whether a defendant's use is objectively fair. Two Courts of Appeals have found it relevant to consider such scope, and commentators and *amici* here have urged us to say that the degree of likely consumer confusion bears not only on the fairness of using a term, but even on the further question whether an originally descriptive term has become so identified as a mark that a defendant's use of it cannot realistically be called descriptive. *See Shakespeare Co. v. Silstar Corp.,* [110 F.3d] at 243 ("[T]o the degree that confusion is likely, a use is less likely to be found fair ..." (emphasis omitted)); *Sunmark, Inc. v. Ocean Spray Cranberries, Inc.,* 64 F.3d at 1059; Restatement (Third) of Unfair Competition.

Since we do not rule out the pertinence of the degree of consumer confusion under the fair use defense, we likewise do not pass upon the position of the United States, as *amicus*, that the "used fairly" requirement in § 1115(b)(4) demands only that the descriptive term describe the goods accurately. Tr. of Oral Arg. 17. Accuracy of course has to be a consideration in assessing fair use, but the proceedings in this case so far raise no occasion to evaluate some other concerns that courts might pick as relevant, quite apart from attention to confusion. The Restatement raises possibilities like commercial justification and the strength of the plaintiff's mark. Restatement § 28. As to them, it is enough to say here that the door is not closed.

III

In sum, a plaintiff claiming infringement of an incontestable mark must show likelihood of consumer confusion as part of the prima facie case, 15 U.S.C. § 1115(b), while the defendant has no independent burden to negate the likelihood of any confusion in raising the affirmative defense that a term is used descriptively, not as a mark, fairly, and in good faith, § 1115(b)(4).

Because we read the Court of Appeals as requiring KP to shoulder a burden on the issue of confusion, we vacate the judgment and remand the case for further proceedings consistent with this opinion.

KP Permanent Make–Up, Inc. v. Lasting Impression I, Inc., 408 F.3d 596 (9th Cir.2005). On remand, the Ninth Circuit interpreted the Supreme Court's statement that its holding did "not foreclose the relevance of the extent of any likely consumer confusion in assessing whether a defendant's use is objectively fair'' and reversed summary judgment for the declaratory judgment plaintiff because there were genuine issues of fact as to likelihood of confusion:

> The fair use defense only comes into play once the party alleging infringement has shown by a preponderance of the evidence that confusion is likely. *See KP II*, 125 S. Ct. at 549. We hold in accordance with *Shakespeare Co.*, 110 F.3d at 243, that the degree of customer confusion remains a factor in evaluating fair use.
>
> Summary judgment on the defense of fair use is also improper. There are genuine issues of fact that are appropriate for the fact finder to determine in order to find that the defense of fair use has been established. Among the relevant factors for consideration by the jury in determining the fairness of the use are the degree of likely confusion, the strength of the trademark, the descriptive nature of the term for the product or service being offered by KP and the availability of alternate descriptive terms, the extent of the use of the term prior to registration of the trademark, and any differences among the times and contexts in which KP has used the term.

QUESTION

Is the Ninth Circuit's multifactor test for determining fair use a good one? Is it consistent with *Park & Fly*?

c.   NOMINATIVE FAIR USE

Nominative fair use is not a statutory defense to an incontestable registration. Some courts have recognized this close cousin to fair use when a mark is used not to describe the defendant's product, but to refer fairly to a plaintiff or its goods or services. Congress has also recognized nominative fair use as an exception to dilution protection in § 1125(c)(3), as revised in 2006. *See infra,* Chapter 9.B.

New Kids on the Block v. News America Publishing

971 F.2d 302 (9th Cir.1992).

■ KOZINSKI, CIRCUIT JUDGE:

The individual plaintiffs perform professionally as The New Kids on the Block, reputedly one of today's hottest musical acts. This case requires us to weigh their rights in that name against the rights of others to use it in identifying the New Kids as the subjects of public opinion polls.

Background

No longer are entertainers limited to their craft in marketing themselves to the public. This is the age of the multi-media publicity blitzkrieg: Trading on their popularity, many entertainers hawk posters, T-shirts, badges, coffee mugs and the like—handsomely supplementing their incomes while boosting their public images. The New Kids are no exception; the record in this case indicates there are more than 500 products or services bearing the New Kids trademark. Among these are services taking advantage of a recent development in telecommunications: 900 area code numbers, where the caller is charged a fee, a portion of which is paid to the call recipient. Fans can call various New Kids 900 numbers to listen to the New Kids talk about themselves, to listen to other fans talk about the New Kids, or to leave messages for the New Kids and other fans. The defendants, two newspapers of national circulation, conducted separate polls of their readers seeking an answer to a pressing question: Which one of the New Kids is the most popular? USA Today's announcement contained a picture of the New Kids and asked, "Who's the best on the block?" The announcement listed a 900 number for voting, noted that "any USA Today profits from this phone line will go to charity," and closed with the following:

New Kids on the Block are pop's hottest group. Which of the five is your fave? Or are they a turn off? ... Each call costs 50 cents. Results in Friday's Life section.

The Star's announcement, under a picture of the New Kids, went to the heart of the matter: "Now which kid is the sexiest?" The announcement, which appeared in the middle of a page containing a story on a New Kids concert, also stated:

Which of the New Kids on the Block would you most like to move next door? STAR wants to know which cool New Kid is the hottest with our readers.

Readers were directed to a 900 number to register their votes; each call cost 95 cents per minute.

Fearing that the two newspapers were undermining their hegemony over their fans, the New Kids filed a shotgun complaint in federal court [alleging, *inter alia*, violations of the Lanham Act and of California unfair competition law]. The two papers raised the First Amendment as a defense, on the theory that the polls were part and parcel of their "news-gathering activities." The district court granted summary judgment for defendants.

Discussion

While the district court granted summary judgment on First Amendment grounds, we are free to affirm on any ground fairly presented by the record. Indeed, where we are able to resolve the case on nonconstitutional grounds, we ordinarily must avoid reaching the constitutional issue. Therefore, we consider first whether the New Kids have stated viable claims on their various causes of action.

... A trademark is a limited property right in a particular word, phrase or symbol. And although English is a language rich in imagery, we need not belabor the point that some words, phrases or symbols better convey their intended meanings than others. Indeed, the primary cost of recognizing property rights in trademarks is the removal of words from (or perhaps non-entrance into) our language. Thus, the holder of a trademark will be denied protection if it is (or becomes) generic, i.e., if it does not relate exclusively to the trademark owner's product. This requirement allays fears that producers will deplete the stock of useful words by asserting exclusive rights in them....

A related problem arises when a trademark also describes a person, a place or an attribute of a product. If the trademark holder were allowed exclusive rights in such use, the language would be depleted in much the same way as if generic words were protectable. Thus trademark law recognizes a defense where the mark is used only "to describe the goods or services of [a] party, or their geographic origin." 15 U.S.C. § 1115(b)(4). "The 'fair-use' defense, in essence, forbids a trademark registrant to appropriate a descriptive term for his exclusive use and so prevent others from accurately describing a characteristic of their goods." *Soweco, Inc. v. Shell Oil Co.*, 617 F.2d 1178, 1185 (5th Cir.1980). Once again, the courts will hold as a matter of law that the original producer does not sponsor or endorse another product that uses his mark in a descriptive manner.

With many well-known trademarks, such as Jell–O, Scotch tape and Kleenex, there are equally informative non-trademark words describing the products (gelatin, cellophane tape and facial tissue). But sometimes there is no descriptive substitute, and a problem closely related to genericity and descriptiveness is presented when many goods and services are effectively identifiable only by their trademarks. For example, one might refer to "the two-time world champions" or "the professional basketball team from Chicago," but it's far simpler (and more likely to be understood) to refer to the Chicago Bulls. In such cases, use of the trademark does not imply sponsorship or endorsement of the product because the mark is used only to describe the thing, rather than to identify its source.

Indeed, it is often virtually impossible to refer to a particular product for purposes of comparison, criticism, point of reference or any other such purpose without using the mark. For example, reference to a large automobile manufacturer based in Michigan would not differentiate among the Big Three; reference to a large Japanese manufacturer of home electronics would narrow the field to a dozen or more companies. Much useful social and commercial discourse would be all but impossible if speakers were under threat of an infringement lawsuit every time they made reference to a person, company or product by using its trademark....

A good example of this is *Volkswagenwerk Aktiengesellschaft v. Church*, 411 F.2d 350 (9th Cir.1969), where we held that Volkswagen could not prevent an automobile repair shop from using its mark. We recognized that in "advertising [the repair of Volkswagens, it] would be difficult, if not impossible, for [Church] to avoid altogether the use of the word 'Volkswagen' or its abbreviation 'VW,' which are the normal terms which, to the public at large, signify appellant's cars." *Id.* at 352. Church did not suggest to customers that he was part of the Volkswagen organization or that his repair shop was sponsored or authorized by VW; he merely used the words "Volkswagen" and "VW" to convey information about the types of cars he repaired. Therefore, his use of the Volkswagen trademark was not an infringing use.

The First Circuit confronted a similar problem when the holder of the trademark "Boston Marathon" tried to stop a television station from using the name.... Similarly, competitors may use a rival's trademark in advertising and other channels of communication if the use is not false or misleading. *See, e.g., Smith v. Chanel, Inc.*, 402 F.2d 562 (9th Cir.1968) (maker of imitation perfume may use original's trademark in promoting product).

Cases like these are best understood as involving a non-trademark use of a mark—a use to which the infringement laws simply do not apply.... Indeed, we may generalize a class of cases where the use of the trademark does not attempt to capitalize on consumer confusion or to appropriate the cachet of one product for a different one. Such nominative use of a mark— where the only word reasonably available to describe a particular thing is pressed into service—lies outside the strictures of trademark law: Because it does not implicate the source-identification function that is the purpose of trademark, it does not constitute unfair competition; such use is fair because it does not imply sponsorship or endorsement by the trademark holder. "When the mark is used in a way that does not deceive the public we see no such sanctity in the word as to prevent its being used to tell the truth." *Prestonettes, Inc. v. Coty*, 264 U.S. 359, 368, 68 L. Ed. 731, 44 S. Ct. 350 (1924) (Holmes, J.).

To be sure, this is not the classic fair use case where the defendant has used the plaintiff's mark to describe the defendant's own product. Here, the New Kids trademark is used to refer to the New Kids themselves. We therefore do not purport to alter the test applicable in the paradigmatic fair use case. If the defendant's use of the plaintiff's trademark refers to something other than the plaintiff's product, the traditional fair use inquiry will continue to govern. But, where the defendant uses a trademark to describe the plaintiff's product, rather than its own, we hold that a commercial user is entitled to a nominative fair use defense provided he meets the following three requirements: First, the product or service in question must be one not readily identifiable without use of the trademark; second, only so much of the mark or marks may be used as is reasonably necessary to identify the product or service; and third, the user must do nothing that would, in conjunction with the mark, suggest sponsorship or endorsement by the trademark holder. The New Kids do not claim there was anything false or misleading about the newspapers' use of their mark. Rather, the first seven causes of action, while purporting to state different claims, all hinge on one key factual allegation: that the newspapers' use of the New Kids name in conducting the unauthorized polls somehow implied that the New Kids were sponsoring the polls. It is no more reasonably possible, however, to refer to the New Kids as an entity than it is to refer to the Chicago Bulls, Volkswagens or the Boston Marathon without using the trademark. Indeed, how could someone not conversant with the proper names of the individual New Kids talk about the group at all? While plaintiffs' trademark certainly deserves protection against copycats and those who falsely claim that the New Kids have endorsed or sponsored them, such protection does not extend to rendering newspaper articles, conversations, polls and comparative advertising impossible. The first nominative use requirement is therefore met.

Also met are the second and third requirements. Both The Star and USA Today reference the New Kids only to the extent necessary to identify them as the subject of the polls; they do not use the New Kids' distinctive logo or anything else that isn't needed to make the announcements intelligible to readers. Finally, nothing in the announcements suggests joint sponsorship or endorsement by the New Kids. The USA Today announcement implies quite the contrary by asking whether the New Kids might be "a turn off." The Star's poll is more effusive but says nothing that expressly or by fair implication connotes endorsement or joint sponsorship on the part of the New Kids.

The New Kids argue that, even if the newspapers are entitled to a nominative fair use defense for the announcements, they are not entitled to it for the polls themselves, which were money-making enterprises separate and apart from the newspapers' reporting businesses. According to plaintiffs, defendants could have minimized the intrusion into their rights by using an 800 number or asking readers to call in on normal telephone lines which would not have resulted in a profit to the newspapers based on the conduct of the polls themselves.

The New Kids see this as a crucial difference, distinguishing this case from *Volkswagenwerk*, *WCBV–TV* and other nominative use cases. The New Kids' argument in support of this distinction is not entirely implausible: They point out that their fans, like everyone else, have limited resources. Thus a dollar spent calling the newspapers' 900 lines to express loyalty to the New Kids may well be a dollar not spent on New Kids products and services, including the New Kids' own 900 numbers. In short, plaintiffs argue that a nominative fair use defense is inapplicable where the use in question competes directly with that of the trademark holder.

We reject this argument. While the New Kids have a limited property right in their name, that right does not entitle them to control their fans' use of their own money. Where, as here, the use does not imply sponsorship or endorsement, the fact that it is carried on for profit and in competition with the trademark holder's business is beside the point. *See, e.g., Universal City Studios, Inc. v. Ideal Publishing Corp.*, 195 U.S.P.Q. 761 (S.D.N.Y. 1977) (magazine's use of TV program's trademark "Hardy Boys" in connection with photographs of show's stars not infringing). Voting for their favorite New Kid may be, as plaintiffs point out, a way for fans to articulate their loyalty to the group, and this may diminish the resources available for products and services they sponsor. But the trademark laws do not give the New Kids the right to channel their fans' enthusiasm (and dollars) only into items licensed or authorized by them. *See International Order of Job's Daughters v. Lindeburg & Co.*, 633 F.2d 912 (9th Cir.1990) (no infringement where unauthorized jewelry maker produced rings and pins bearing fraternal organization's trademark). The New Kids could not use the trademark laws to prevent the publication of an unauthorized group biography or to censor all parodies or satires which use their name. We fail to see a material difference between these examples and the use here.

QUESTION

Although the court declares that "the trademark laws do not give the New Kids the right to channel their fans' enthusiasm (and dollars) only into items licensed or authorized by them," is such channelling not in fact the goal of a trademark licensing program? Moreover, some courts have protected such programs against unauthorized third-party merchandise. *See, e.g., Warner Bros. Inc. v. Gay Toys, Inc.*, 724 F.2d 327 (2d Cir.1983); *Processed Plastic Co. v. Warner Communications, Inc.*, 675 F.2d 852 (7th Cir.1982) (both finding trademark infringement by unlicensed toy cars bearing the Dukes of Hazzard "General Lee" insignia). Are these cases distinguishable from *New Kids*? *See also Dow Jones & Company, Inc. v. International Securities, Exchange, Inc.*, 451 F.3d 295 (2d Cir.2006).

d. LACHES

Pro–Football, Inc. v. Harjo

415 F.3d 44 (D.C.Cir.2005).

■ PER CURIAM.

. . . . Because we find that the district court applied the wrong standard in evaluating laches as to at least one of the [petitioners], we remand the record to the district court to revisit this issue.

. . . . 15 U.S.C. § 1064(3) provides that if a mark is registered in violation of section 1052(a), "any person who believes that he is or will be damaged by the registration" may file a petition "at any time" with the PTO to cancel the registration. This triggers a proceeding before the TTAB, *see* 15 U.S.C. § 1067, which takes evidence and determines whether to cancel the mark. Yet another provision, 15 U.S.C. § 1069, states that "in all . . . proceedings equitable principles of laches, estoppel, and acquiescence, where applicable may be considered and applied."

This case concerns the registrations of six trademarks owned by Pro–Football, the corporate owner of the Washington Redskins football team, that include the word "Redskin." The first—"The Redskins" written in a stylized script—was registered in 1967, three more in 1974, another in 1978, and the sixth—the word "Redskinettes"—in 1990. Pro–Football uses all these marks in connection with goods and services related to its football team, including merchandise and entertainment services.

In 1992, seven Native Americans petitioned for cancellation of the registrations, claiming that the marks had disparaged Native Americans at the times of registration and had thus been registered in violation of section 1052(a). Pro–Football defended its marks, arguing among other things that laches barred the Native Americans' claim. Rejecting this argument, the TTAB found laches inapplicable due to the "broader interest—an interest beyond the personal interest being asserted by the present petitioners—in preventing a party from receiving the benefits of registration where a trial might show that respondent's marks hold a substantial segment of the population up to public ridicule." *Harjo v. Pro–Football Inc.*, 1994 TTAB LEXIS 9, 30 U.S.P.Q.2d 1828, 1831 (TTAB 1994).

. . . In a lengthy opinion, the TTAB concluded that a preponderance of the evidence showed the term "redskin" as used by Washington's football team had disparaged Native Americans from at least 1967 onward. The TTAB cancelled the registrations. Cancellation did not require Pro–Football to stop using the marks, but it did limit the team's ability to go after infringers under the Lanham Act.

Pursuant to 15 U.S.C. § 1071(b), Pro–Football filed suit in the U.S. District Court for the District of Columbia, seeking reinstatement of its registrations on the grounds that: (1) laches barred the Native Americans' petition; (2) the TTAB's finding of disparagement was unsupported by substantial evidence; and (3) section 1052(a) violates the First and Fifth Amendments to the U.S. Constitution both facially and as applied by the TTAB. Although in suits challenging TTAB decisions parties may introduce new evidence in the district court, (citation omitted), in this case the only such evidence of note related to laches. After discovery, the parties cross-moved for summary judgment. Without reaching the constitutional issues, the district court granted summary judgment to Pro–Football on the alternate grounds that laches barred the Native Americans' petition and that the TTAB's conclusion of disparagement was unsupported by substantial evidence. *Pro–Football, Inc. v. Harjo*, 284 F. Supp. 2d 96 (D.D.C. 2003). This appeal followed.

II.

An equitable doctrine, "laches is founded on the notion that equity aids the vigilant and not those who slumber on their rights." *NAACP v. NAACP Legal Def. & Educ. Fund, Inc.*, 243 U.S. App. D.C. 313, 753 F.2d 131, 137 (D.C. Cir. 1985). This defense, which Pro–Football has the burden of proving, (citation omitted) "requires proof of (1) lack of diligence by the party against whom the defense is asserted, and (2) prejudice to the party asserting the defense." *Nat'l R.R. Passenger Corp. v. Morgan*, 536 U.S. 101, 121–22, 153 L. Ed. 2d 106, 122 S. Ct. 2061 (2002) (internal quotation marks omitted). In this case, the Native Americans contend both that the statute bars the defense of laches and that even were laches an available defense, Pro–Football has failed to prove it.

The Native Americans' statutory argument runs as follows: because section 1064(3) permits petitions alleging wrongful registration under section 1052(a) to be filed "at any time," laches is not a valid defense in cancellation proceedings. We disagree. The words "at any time" demonstrate only that the act imposes no statute of limitations for bringing petitions. Those words have nothing to do with what equitable defenses may be available during cancellation proceedings. Indeed, under the Native Americans' logic, equitable defenses would never be available as long as cancellation petitions are brought within the specified statute of limitations—"at any time" for petitions alleging wrongful registration under section 1052(a) or certain other grounds, see 15 U.S.C. § 1064(3)-(5), and "within five years" of registration for petitions brought for all other reasons, *see id.* § 1064(1). This would make section 1069, which explicitly permits consideration of laches and other equitable doctrines, meaningless as to cancellation petitions. For this reason, we disagree with the Third Circuit's suggestion that laches is not an available defense to cancellation petitions brought pursuant to section 1064(3), *see Marshak v. Treadwell,* 240 F.3d 184, 193–94 & n.4 (3d Cir. 2001). Instead, we join the Federal Circuit, *see Bridgestone/Firestone Research, Inc. v. Auto. Club de L'Ouest de la France,* 245 F.3d 1359, 1360–61 (Fed. Cir. 2001) (permitting the defense of laches to a cancellation petition brought under section 1064(3)), and our own district court, *see Pro–Football, Inc. v. Harjo,* 57 U.S.P.Q.2d 1140, 1145 (D.D.C. 2000), in concluding that the statute does not bar the equitable defense of laches in response to section 1064(3) cancellation petitions.

The Native Americans also offer several reasons why, in their view, the district court erred in its assessment of laches in this case. At this point, we need only consider one: their claim that the district court mistakenly started the clock for assessing laches in 1967—the time of the first mark's registration—for *all* seven Native Americans, even though one, Mateo Romero, was at that time only one year old.

We agree with the Native Americans that this approach runs counter to the well-established principle of equity that laches runs only from the time a party has reached his majority....

Pro–Football asserts that were we to apply this principle here, it "would logically mean that trademark owners could never have certainty, since a disparagement claim could be brought by an as yet unborn claimant for an unlimited time after a mark is registered." Appellee's Br. at 48. At the least, this assertion is overstated—only owners of those trademarks that may disparage a population that gains new members (as opposed to one that disparages, say, a single corporate entity, *see, e.g., Greyhound Corp. v. Both Worlds Inc.,* 6 U.S.P.Q.2d 1635 (TTAB 1988)), would face such a prospect. But even if registrations of some marks would remain perpetually at risk, it is unclear why this fact authorizes—let alone requires—abandonment of equity's fundamental principle that laches attaches only to parties who have unjustifiably delayed in bringing suit.

. . . .

In assessing prejudice, the district court should address both trial and economic prejudice. As to trial prejudice, the court should consider the extent to which Romero's post-majority delay resulted in a "loss of evidence or witnesses supporting [Pro–Football's] position," *see Gull Airborne Instruments,* 694 F.2d at 844. As to economic prejudice, we express no view as to how such prejudice should be measured where, as here, what is at stake is not the trademark owner's right to use the marks but rather the owner's right to Lanham Act protections that turn on registration. We encourage the district court to take briefing on whether economic prejudice should be measured based on the owner's investment in the marks during the relevant years, on whether the owner would have taken a different course of action—e.g., abandoned the marks—had the petitioner acted more diligently in seeking cancellation, or on some other measure.

III.

While retaining jurisdiction over the case, we remand the record to the district court for the purpose of evaluating whether laches bars Mateo Romero's claim.

So ordered.

QUESTIONS

1. Does the Circuit Court's decision in *Harjo* mean that a mark can always be challenged on grounds of disparagement as long as the challenger is a member of the allegedly disparaged group who was not born at the time of the registration? Does this make sense?

2. What evidence of prejudice should Pro–Football submit on remand?

D.   SOVEREIGN IMMUNITY

College Savings Bank v. Florida Prepaid Postsecondary Education Expense Board

527 U.S. 666, 119 S.Ct. 2219, 144 L.Ed.2d 605 (1999).

■ JUSTICE SCALIA delivered the opinion of the Court:

The Trademark Remedy Clarification Act (TRCA), 106 Stat. 3567, subjects the States to suits brought under § 43(a) of the Trademark Act of 1946 (Lanham Act) for false and misleading advertising, 60 Stat. 441, 15 U.S.C. § 1125(a). The question presented in this case is whether that provision is effective to permit suit against a State for its alleged misrepresentation of its own product—either because the TRCA effects a constitutionally permissible abrogation of state sovereign immunity, or because the TRCA operates as an invitation to waiver of such immunity which is automatically accepted by a State's engaging in the activities regulated by the Lanham Act.

I.

. . . [T]he Eleventh Amendment, . . . provides:

"The Judicial power of the United States shall not be construed to extend to any suit in law or equity, commenced or prosecuted against one of the United States by Citizens of another State, or by Citizens or Subjects of any Foreign State."

Though its precise terms bar only federal jurisdiction over suits brought against one State by citizens of another State or foreign state, we have long recognized that the Eleventh Amendment accomplished much more: It repudiated ... that the jurisdictional heads of Article III superseded the sovereign immunity that the States possessed before entering the Union....

While this immunity from suit is not absolute, we have recognized only two circumstances in which an individual may sue a State. First, Congress may authorize such a suit in the exercise of its power to enforce the Fourteenth Amendment—an Amendment enacted after the Eleventh Amendment and specifically designed to alter the federal-state balance. *Fitzpatrick v. Bitzer*, 427 U.S. 445 (1976). Second, a State may waive its sovereign immunity by consenting to suit. *Clark v. Barnard*, 108 U.S. 436, 447–448 (1883). This case turns on whether either of these two circumstances is present.

II.

... The TRCA amends § 43(a) by defining "any person" to include "any State, instrumentality of a State or employee of a State or instrumentality of a State acting in his or her official capacity." § 3(c), 106 Stat. 3568. The TRCA further amends the Lanham Act to provide that such state entities "shall not be immune, under the eleventh amendment of the Constitution of the United States or under any other doctrine of sovereign immunity, from suit in Federal court by any person, including any governmental or nongovernmental entity for any violation under this Act," and that remedies shall be available against such state entities "to the same extent as such remedies are available ... in a suit against" a nonstate entity. § 3(b) (codified in 15 U.S.C. § 1122).

Petitioner College Savings Bank is a New Jersey chartered bank located in Princeton, New Jersey. Since 1987, it has marketed and sold CollegeSure certificates of deposit designed to finance the costs of college education. College Savings holds a patent upon the methodology of administering its CollegeSure certificates. Respondent Florida Prepaid Postsecondary Education Expense Board (Florida Prepaid) is an arm of the State of Florida. Since 1988, it has administered a tuition prepayment program designed to provide individuals with sufficient funds to cover future college expenses. College Savings brought a patent infringement action against Florida Prepaid in United States District Court in New Jersey. That action is the subject of today's decision in *Florida Prepaid Postsecondary Ed. Expense Bd. v. College Savings Bank*. In addition, and in the same court, College Savings filed the instant action alleging that Florida Prepaid violated § 43(a) of the Lanham Act by making misstatements about its own tuition savings plans in its brochures and annual reports.

... The District Court granted Florida Prepaid's motion to dismiss [on the ground of sovereign immunity]. The Court of Appeals affirmed. We granted *certiorari*.

III.

We turn first to the contention that Florida's sovereign immunity was validly abrogated. Our decision three Terms ago in *Seminole Tribe, supra,* held that the power "to regulate Commerce" conferred by Article I of the Constitution gives Congress no authority to abrogate state sovereign immunity. As authority for the abrogation in the present case, petitioner relies upon § 5 of the Fourteenth Amendment, which we held ... could be used for that purpose.

Section 1 of the Fourteenth Amendment provides that no State shall "deprive any person of ... property ... without due process of law." Section 5 provides that "the Congress shall have power to enforce, by appropriate legislation, the provisions of this article." We made clear in *City of Boerne v. Flores*, 521 U.S. 507 (1997), that the term "enforce" is to be taken seriously—that the object of valid § 5 legislation must be the carefully delimited remediation or prevention of constitutional violations. Petitioner claims that, with respect to § 43(a) of the Lanham Act, Congress enacted the TRCA to remedy and prevent state deprivations without due process of two species of "property" rights: (1) a right to be free from a business competitor's false advertising about its own product, and (2) a more generalized right to be secure in one's business interests. Neither of these qualifies as a property right protected by the Due Process Clause.

As to the first: The hallmark of a protected property interest is the right to exclude others. That is "one of the most essential sticks in the bundle of rights that are commonly characterized as property." *Kaiser Aetna v. United States*, 444 U.S. 164, 176, 62 L. Ed. 2d 332, 100 S. Ct. 383 (1979). That is why the right that we all possess to use the public lands is not the "property" right of anyone—hence the sardonic maxim, explaining what economists call the "tragedy of the commons," *res publica, res nullius*. The Lanham Act may well contain provisions that protect constitutionally cognizable property interests—notably, its provisions dealing with infringement of trademarks, which are the "property" of the owner because he can exclude others from using them. *See, e.g., K Mart Corp. v. Cartier, Inc.*, 485 U.S. 176, 185–186, 99 L. Ed. 2d 151, 108 S. Ct. 950 (1988) ("Trademark law, like contract law, confers private rights, which are themselves rights of exclusion. It grants the trademark owner a bundle of such rights"). The Lanham Act's false-advertising provisions, however, bear no relationship to any right to exclude; and Florida Prepaid's alleged misrepresentations concerning its own products intruded upon no interest over which petitioner had exclusive dominion.

. . . .

. . . We turn next to the question whether Florida's sovereign immunity, though not abrogated, was voluntarily waived.

IV.

. . . [O]ur "test for determining whether a State has waived its immunity from federal-court jurisdiction is a stringent one." [Citations omitted]. Generally, we will find a waiver either if the State voluntarily invokes our jurisdiction, [citations omitted] or else if the State makes a "clear declaration" that it intends to submit itself to our jurisdiction. . . .

There is no suggestion here that respondent Florida Prepaid expressly consented to being sued in federal court. Nor is this a case in which the State has affirmatively invoked our jurisdiction. Rather, petitioner College Savings and the United States both maintain that Florida Prepaid has "impliedly" or "constructively" waived its immunity from Lanham Act suit. They do so on the authority of *Parden v. Terminal R. Co. of Ala. Docks Dept.*, 377 U.S. 184 (1964)—an elliptical opinion that stands at the nadir of our waiver (and, for that matter, sovereign immunity) jurisprudence. In *Parden*, we permitted employees of a railroad owned and operated by Alabama to bring an action under the Federal Employers' Liability Act (FELA) against their employer....

... [I]n *Welch v. Texas Dept. of Highways and Public Transp.*, 483 U.S. 468 (1987), although we expressly avoided addressing the constitutionality of Congress's conditioning a State's engaging in Commerce–Clause activity upon the State's waiver of sovereign immunity, we said there was "no doubt that *Parden*'s discussion of congressional intent to negate Eleventh Amendment immunity is no longer good law," and overruled *Parden* "to the extent [it] is inconsistent with the requirement that an abrogation of Eleventh Amendment immunity by Congress must be expressed in unmistakably clear language," 483 U.S. at 478, and n.8.

. . . .

We think that the constructive-waiver experiment of *Parden* was ill conceived, and see no merit in attempting to salvage any remnant of it.... *Parden* broke sharply with prior cases, and is fundamentally incompatible with later ones. We have never applied the holding of *Parden* to another statute, and in fact have narrowed the case in every subsequent opinion in which it has been under consideration. In short, *Parden* stands as an anomaly in the jurisprudence of sovereign immunity, and indeed in the jurisprudence of constitutional law. Today, we drop the other shoe: Whatever may remain of our decision in *Parden* is expressly overruled.

To begin with, we cannot square *Parden* with our cases requiring that a State's express waiver of sovereign immunity be unequivocal. The whole point of requiring a "clear declaration" by the State of its waiver is to be certain that the State in fact consents to suit. But there is little reason to assume actual consent based upon the State's mere presence in a field subject to congressional regulation.

. . . .

Recognizing a congressional power to exact constructive waivers of sovereign immunity through the exercise of Article I powers would also, as a practical matter, permit Congress to circumvent the antiabrogation holding of *Seminole Tribe*. Forced waiver and abrogation are not even different sides of the same coin—they are the same side of the same coin....

Nor do we think that the constitutionally grounded principle of state sovereign immunity is any less robust where, as here, the asserted basis for constructive waiver is conduct that the State realistically could choose to abandon, that is undertaken for profit, that is traditionally performed by private citizens and corporations, and that otherwise resembles the behavior of "market participants." . . . [I]t is hard to say that that limitation has any more support in text or tradition than, say, limiting abrogation or constructive waiver to the last Friday of the month. Since sovereign immunity itself was not traditionally limited by these factors, and since they have no bearing upon the voluntariness of the waiver, there is no principled reason why they should enter into our waiver analysis.

. . . .

Concluding, for the foregoing reasons, that the sovereign immunity of the State of Florida was neither validly abrogated by the Trademark Remedy Clarification Act, nor voluntarily waived by the State's activities in interstate commerce, we hold that the federal courts are without jurisdiction to entertain this suit against an arm of the State of Florida. The judgment of the Third Circuit dismissing the action is *affirmed*.

■ JUSTICE STEVENS, dissenting:

. . . .

The procedural posture of this case requires the Court to assume that Florida Prepaid is an "arm of the State" of Florida because its activities relate to the State's educational programs. But the validity of that assumption is doubtful if the Court's jurisprudence in this area is to be based primarily on present-day assumptions about the status of the doctrine of sovereign immunity in the 18th century. Sovereigns did not then play the kind of role in the commercial marketplace that they do today. . . .

The majority . . . assumes that petitioner's complaint has alleged a violation of the Lanham Act, but not one that is sufficiently serious to amount to a "deprivation" of its property. I think neither of those assumptions is relevant to the principal issue raised in this case, namely, whether Congress had the constitutional power to authorize suits against States and state instrumentalities for such a violation. In my judgment the Constitution granted it ample power to do so. Section 5 of the Fourteenth Amendment authorizes Congress to enact appropriate legislation to prevent deprivations of property without due process. Unlike the majority, I am persuaded that the Trademark Remedy Clarification Act was a valid exercise of that power, even if Florida Prepaid's allegedly false advertising in this case did not violate the Constitution. My conclusion rests on two premises that the Court rejects.

. . . [I]n my opinion "the activity of doing business, or the activity of making a profit," *ante* at 8, is a form of property. The asset that often appears on a company's balance sheet as "good will" is the substantial equivalent of that "activity." . . . A State's deliberate destruction of a going business is surely a deprivation of property within the meaning of the Due Process Clause. . . .

[The dissenting opinion of JUSTICE BREYER is omitted.]

NOTE

Justice Scalia draws a distinction between the Lanham Act's trademark provisions, which he concedes involve property rights, and its false advertising provisions, which he holds do not. On that basis, might the Trademark Remedy Clarification Act effectively abrogate state sovereign immunity to suits for trademark infringement under section 32? It would appear not. On the same day the Court handed down its decision in *College Savings Bank v. Florida*, it issued a decision in the companion case, *Florida Prepaid Postsecondary Education Expense Board v. College Savings Bank*, 527 U.S. 627 (1999), involving the validity of the Patent Remedy Clarification Act, Pub. L. 102–560, 106 Stat. 4230 (1992). The Court of Appeals for the Federal Circuit held that Congress had properly exercised its power under the 14th Amendment to abrogate state sovereign immunity to patent infringement suits. The Supreme Court reversed. Justice Rehnquist's majority opinion agreed both that Congress had clearly intended to abrogate state sovereign immunity and that patents could be considered property. The court held however, that the legislative record contained scant support for the assertion that states' avoiding patent infringement by pleading sovereign immunity amounted to "widespread and persisting deprivation of constitutional rights," and that the Patent Remedy Clarification Act swept too broadly:

> The historical record and the scope of coverage therefore make it clear that the Patent Remedy Act cannot be sustained under § 5 of the Fourteenth Amendment. The examples of States avoiding liability for patent infringement by pleading sovereign immunity in a federal-court patent action are scarce enough, but any plausible argument that such action on the part of the State deprived patentees of property and left them without a remedy under state law is scarcer still. The statute's apparent and more basic aims were to provide a uniform remedy for patent infringement and to place States on the same footing as private parties under that regime. These are proper Article I concerns, but that Article does not give Congress the power to enact such legislation after *Seminole Tribe*.

Has the Court left any room for abrogating state sovereign immunity to trademark suits? May state governments safely ignore the Lanham Act's infringement provisions?

CHAPTER 7

FALSE DESIGNATION OF ORIGIN

15 U.S.C. § 1125(a)(1)(A) [LANHAM ACT § 43(a)(1)(A)]

(1) Any person who, on or in connection with any goods or services, or any container for goods, uses in commerce any word, term, name, symbol, or device, or any combination thereof, or any false designation of origin, false or misleading description of fact, or false or misleading representation of fact, which—

> (A) is likely to cause confusion, or to cause mistake, or to deceive as to the affiliation, connection, or association of such person with another person, or as to the origin, sponsorship, or approval of his or her goods, services, or commercial activities by another person,

> . . . .

shall be liable in a civil action by any person who believes that he or she is or is likely to be damaged by such act.

A.   SECTION 43(a) OF THE LANHAM ACT AND UNREGISTERED MARKS

DC Comics v. Powers

465 F.Supp. 843 (S.D.N.Y.1978).

■ DUFFY, J.

This is a trademark action involving use of the name Daily Planet both as the title of a news publication and in connection with a myriad of consumer products. Plaintiff, D C Comics, Inc., charges that the continued use of the name Daily Planet by defendants, the Daily Planet, Inc. and its President, Jerry Powers, is violative of § 43(a) of the Lanham Act, 15 U.S.C. § 1125(a), (hereinafter "the Act") and constitutes unfair competition resulting in dilution of plaintiff's common law trademark under the law of New York. Jurisdiction is founded upon 28 U.S.C. § 1338(a), (b) and upon the principles of pendent jurisdiction.

In June of 1938, plaintiff's predecessors created the fictional character called Superman the "man of steel who, with powers and abilities beyond those of mortal men, fights a never ending battle for truth, justice and the American way." The Daily Planet serves a dual function in relation to the

Superman character. Primarily, it is the name of the fictitious Metropolis newspaper which employs Superman's alter ego, together with the other central characters in the Superman story. The Daily Planet is also the title of a promotional news column appearing from time-to-time within Superman comic books.

Defendants are the moving forces behind an underground news publication called the Daily Planet. The Daily Planet appeared between the years 1969 through 1973. Since its demise in 1973, the Daily Planet lay dormant until recently when defendants demonstrated a great interest in its resuscitation.

Upon commencement of the instant action, defendants moved for a preliminary injunction to preclude plaintiff from any use of the name Daily Planet including the advertisement, promotion, distribution or sale of any products in connection with the multi-million dollar cinema production of "Superman", scheduled to be released in just a few weeks by plaintiff's parent, Warner Communications. Plaintiff has cross moved for injunctive relief seeking to preclude defendants from any use of the Daily Planet.

. . . .

Both plaintiff and defendants claim that as a result of a prior appropriation and use of the name Daily Planet, they each possess exclusive rights to its use. What is really at issue, however, is whether either party to this action is entitled to exclusive exploitation of the name Daily Planet based on the expected wave of public interest in the Superman character calculated to result from the release of the Superman movie.

. . . .

Merits of the Case

It is undisputed that neither plaintiff nor defendants presently hold a registered trademark in the Daily Planet and, therefore, any rights to the exclusive use thereof are to be determined solely under the common law of trademarks. *D. M. & Antique Import Corp. v. Royal Saxe Corp.*, 311 F. Supp. 1261, 1271 (S.D.N.Y.1970).

The Superman character has, since its creation in 1938, been featured in comic books, comic strips and on radio and television. The Daily Planet first appeared in the Superman story in 1940. Since then, the Daily Planet has played a key role, not only in the Superman story, but also in the development of the Superman character. In addition, plaintiff has gone to great effort and expense throughout the long history of Superman to utilize the Superman character in connection with a myriad of products born of the Superman story. Indeed, to this end plaintiff employed the Licensing Corporation of America to act as its agent in the licensing of the Superman character to persons wishing to use it in connection with a given product. These products have included school supplies, toys, costumes, games and clothes.

At the hearing before me, Joseph Grant, the President of the Licensing Corporation of America, explained the licensing procedures for the D C

Comics, Inc. and in particular the Superman characters. He testified that his corporation, at the behest of D C Comics, Inc., licenses the Superman story as a package. Thus, the typical licensing agreement would permit use not only of Superman, but of all the Superman characters. Mr. Grant concluded that while the Daily Planet was never singled out in any licensing agreement, he believed it to be part and parcel of the typical licensing agreement. Indeed, it was clearly established that the Daily Planet has been prominently featured on many products emanating from these licensing agreements.

In contrast, defendants' relationship with the term Daily Planet has been both brief and, at best, sporadic. Defendants' first published their newspaper in 1969 in Miami, Florida and called it "The Miami Free Press." Thereafter, the name went through a series of changes from "The Miami Free Press and The Daily Planet", to "The Daily Planet and The Miami Free Press" and finally to "The Daily Planet." In 1970, Powers registered the name Daily Planet as the trademark for the paper. It was also during this period that Powers caused the incorporation of the Daily Planet, Inc.

There was testimony from the defendant Powers that the Daily Planet was distributed at the Woodstock Music Festival in Woodstock, New York and at the Atlanta Pop Festival in Georgia. I am willing to believe that to be true. Much of Power's other testimony, however, strains credibility.

Despite defendants' dream of creating a paper with national appeal, the Daily Planet remained throughout its brief history essentially a local affair and, as such, was published between 1969 through 1973 on an irregular basis. Powers also testified that from its inception, the Daily Planet was plagued with financial problems. Finally, in 1973, its financial woes became overwhelming and the paper folded.

Thereafter, Powers left Florida and began work on a new underground publication called "Superstar." At least two issues of "Superstar" were published at this time. It appears that the majority of defendants' time and efforts were devoted to the promotion of this new publication. Consequently, defendants permitted their trademark registration of Daily Planet to lapse and it was subsequently cancelled by the Office of Patent and Trademark Registration in 1976.

In light of the foregoing, it is apparent that only plaintiff has demonstrated an association of such duration and consistency with the Daily Planet sufficient to establish a common law trademark therein. The totality of evidence demonstrates that the Daily Planet has over the years become inextricably woven into the fabric of the Superman story.

Defendants, on the other hand, have offered very little to evidence either a substantial or genuine interest in the Daily Planet. More importantly, however, upon the demise of the Daily Planet in 1973, I find that defendants engaged in a course of conduct evidencing an intent to abandon any interests they may have acquired therein. The fact that defendants permitted their registration of the Daily Planet to lapse and thereafter began to publish another paper of the same nature as the Daily Planet under the name "Superstar" is dispositive of this intent and supports a finding of abandonment.

Turning in particular to plaintiff's claim under section 43(a) of the Lanham Act, 15 U.S.C. § 1125(a), it is not a prerequisite for remedial action thereunder that the mark in issue be registered.[Citations] Consequently, under this section, a common law trademark is entitled to the same protection as its statutory counterpart. A plaintiff, therefore, is entitled to remedial action under this section if the defendant has affixed plaintiff's mark to his goods in such a fashion as to misrepresent to the public the source of the goods.

Although it is imperative in the instant action for plaintiff to demonstrate that defendants' use of the Daily Planet is likely to either confuse or deceive purchasers as to the source of items bearing the mark, [citation], liability will attach even though plaintiff is not in direct competition with the defendants.[5]

. . . .

Applying these principles to the case at bar, it is evident that plaintiff has demonstrated a probability of success on the merits sufficient to warrant the equitable relief requested.

. . . .

. . . . I find substantial evidence indicating that the adoption by defendants of the name Daily Planet in 1969 was merely an attempt to cash in on the Superman story and its notoriety. Powers admitted that he was aware of the relationship between the Daily Planet and the Superman story when he first decided to use the name. It was also established that there were, throughout the brief history of Powers' Daily Planet, numerous references in the paper not only to the Superman character, but also to the Superman story, for example:

(i) A lead article entitled "Superman smokes super dope";

(ii) A promotional campaign to encourage new subscriptions employing the phrase "Join the Planet Army in Metropolis";[7]

(iii) Use of the phrase "Watchdog of Metropolis" as its slogan;

(iv) Numerous drawings of the Superman character;

(v) Use of a masthead which was an exact replica of the Daily Planet insignia appearing in numerous Superman comic books.

Thus, it is quite apparent that defendants, both in adopting the Daily Planet as the title of their newspaper and in its publication, intended to at least confuse, if not to deceive the public as to the origin of the publication.

. . . .

---

5. Accordingly, the fact that plaintiff never published an actual paper entitled the Daily Planet is neither a barrier to the instant suit nor to preliminary equitable relief.

7. Metropolis is "the resident city of Superman and the scene of the vast majority of his adventures." See The Great Superman Book, The Complete Encyclopedia of the Folk Hero of America, at 223. (Plaintiff's Exhibit 14 herein).

Moreover, while plaintiff may have been somewhat less than diligent in policing its mark, in light of the local appeal and limited distribution (geographic and numeric) of defendants' publication, I am not convinced that their lack of diligence was so great as to warrant loss of their trademark.

In light of the foregoing, the defendants' continued use of the Daily Planet is likely to cause irreparable injury to plaintiff's business reputation, good will and to its common law trademark.

Accordingly, defendants' motion for preliminary relief is denied and plaintiff's motion for a preliminary injunction is granted.

So ordered.

THE MEANING OF "ORIGIN"

Both the "false designation of origin" provision in section 43(a), and its companion "false representation" provision were initially designed to provide a civil remedy for misbranding of products. "Origin" was intended to mean geographic origin, enabling a perfumery to recover if its competitor labeled a bottle of Canadian perfume "Parfum de France." *See* Trade–Marks: Hearings on H.R. 13486 Before the House Committee on patents, 69th Cong. 87 (1927). Courts, however, gave "false designation of origin" a broad construction, interpreting origin to encompass the source or sponsor of a product. Since infringing an unregistered, common-law trademark is likely to confuse purchasers about the source (or origin) of the marked product, courts entertained actions for infringement of unregistered trademarks as suits for false designation of origin of the marked products. Thus, section 43(a) quickly grew in importance. Several of the cases in earlier chapters, including [*Maryland Stadium Authority v. Becker* in Chapter 3 and *Munsingwear v. Jockey* in chapter 6] involved unregistered trademarks and were brought under section 43(a).

In the Night Kitchen is the title of an illustrated book by Maurice Sendak, which was first published by Harper Collins in 1970. The book tells the story of a young boy who wakes up in the middle of the night and falls out of his pajamas and into a bowl of batter in the night kitchen. The book has been continuously in print since it first appeared.

Your clients have opened a catering business under the name "Night Kitchen Catering." They have printed up business cards:

Your clients have also posted a website at www.inthenightkitchen.com, which describes their business and features sample menus. Do you see a likelihood of confusion?

B.   TRADE DRESS

Two Pesos, Inc. v. Taco Cabana, Inc.

505 U.S. 763, 112 S.Ct. 2753, 120 L.Ed.2d 615 (1992).

■ JUSTICE WHITE delivered the opinion of the Court:

[handwritten: Resolution of trade Dress Circuit split.]

The issue in this case is whether the trade dress[1] of a restaurant may be protected under § 43(a) of the Trademark Act of 1946 (Lanham Act), 60 Stat. 441, 15 U.S.C. § 1125(a) (1982 ed.), based on a finding of inherent distinctiveness, without proof that the trade dress has secondary meaning.

I

Respondent Taco Cabana, Inc., operates a chain of fast-food restaurants in Texas. The restaurants serve Mexican food. The first Taco Cabana restaurant was opened in San Antonio in September 1978, and five more restaurants had been opened in San Antonio by 1985. Taco Cabana describes its Mexican trade dress as

"a festive eating atmosphere having interior dining and patio areas decorated with artifacts, bright colors, paintings and murals. The patio includes interior and exterior areas with the interior patio capable of being sealed off from the outside patio by overhead garage doors. The stepped exterior of the building is a festive and vivid color scheme using top border paint and neon stripes. Bright awnings and umbrellas continue the theme." 932 F.2d 1113, 1117 (C.A.5 1991).

1. The District Court instructed the jury: " 'Trade dress' is the total image of the business. Taco Cabana's trade dress may include the shape and general appearance of the exterior of the restaurant, the identifying sign, the interior kitchen floor plan, the decor, the menu, the equipment used to serve food, the servers' uniforms and other features reflecting on the total image of the restaurant." The Court of Appeals accepted this definition and quoted from *Blue Bell* *Bio–Medical v. Cin–Bad, Inc.,* 864 F.2d 1253, 1256 (C.A.5 1989): "The 'trade dress' of a product is essentially its total image and overall appearance." *See* 932 F.2d 1113, 1118 (C.A.5 1991). It "involves the total image of a product and may include features such as size, shape, color or color combinations, texture, graphics, or even particular sales techniques." *John H. Harland Co. v. Clarke Checks, Inc.,* 711 F.2d 966, 980 (C.A.11 1983).

In December 1985, a Two Pesos, Inc., restaurant was opened in Houston. Two Pesos adopted a motif very similar to the foregoing description of Taco Cabana's trade dress. Two Pesos restaurants expanded rapidly in Houston and other markets, but did not enter San Antonio. In 1986, Taco Cabana entered the Houston and Austin markets and expanded into other Texas cities, including Dallas and El Paso where Two Pesos was also doing business.

In 1987, Taco Cabana sued Two Pesos in the United States District Court for the Southern District of Texas for trade dress infringement under § 43(a) of the Lanham Act, 15 U.S.C. § 1125(a) (1982 ed.),[2] and for theft of trade secrets under Texas common law. The case was tried to a jury, which was instructed to return its verdict in the form of answers to five questions propounded by the trial judge. The jury's answers were: Taco Cabana has a trade dress; taken as a whole, the trade dress is nonfunctional; the trade dress is inherently distinctive;[3] the trade dress has not acquired a secondary meaning[4] in the Texas market; and the alleged infringement creates a likelihood of confusion on the part of ordinary customers as to the source or association of the restaurant's goods or services. Because, as the jury was told, Taco Cabana's trade dress was protected if it either was inherently distinctive or had acquired a secondary meaning, judgment was entered awarding damages to Taco Cabana. In the course of calculating damages, the trial court held that Two Pesos had intentionally and deliberately infringed Taco Cabana's trade dress.[5]

The Court of Appeals ruled that the instructions adequately stated the applicable law and that the evidence supported the jury's findings. In particular, the Court of Appeals rejected petitioner's argument that a finding of no secondary meaning contradicted a finding of inherent distinctiveness.

2. Section 43(a) provides: "Any person who shall affix, apply, or annex, or use in connection with any goods or services, or any container or containers for goods, a false designation of origin, or any false description or representation, including words or other symbols tending falsely to describe or represent the same, and shall cause such goods or services to enter into commerce, and any person who shall with knowledge of the falsity of such designation of origin or description or representation cause or procure the same to be transported or used in commerce or deliver the same to any carrier to be transported or used, shall be liable to a civil action by any person doing business in the locality falsely indicated as that of origin or in the region in which said locality is situated, or by any person who believes that he is or is likely to be damaged by the use of any such false description or representation." 60 Stat. 441.

This provision has been superseded by § 132 of the Trademark Law Revision Act of 1988, 102 Stat. 3946, 15 U.S.C. § 1121.

3. The instructions were that to be found inherently distinctive, the trade dress must not be descriptive.

4. Secondary meaning is used generally to indicate that a mark or dress "has come through use to be uniquely associated with a specific source." Restatement (Third) of Unfair Competition § 13, Comment *e*. (Tent. Draft No. 2, Mar. 23, 1990). "To establish secondary meaning, a manufacturer must show that, in the minds of the public, the primary significance of a product feature or term is to identify the source of the product rather than the product itself." *Inwood Laboratories, Inc. v. Ives Laboratories, Inc.,* 456 U.S. 844, 851, n. 11 (1982).

5. The Court of Appeals agreed: "The weight of the evidence persuades us, as it did Judge Singleton, that Two Pesos brazenly copied Taco Cabana's successful trade dress, and proceeded to expand in a manner that foreclosed several important markets within Taco Cabana's natural zone of expansion." 932 F.2d, at 1127, n.20.

[handwritten margin note: Secondary Meaning needed only when TM is not inherently Distinctive]

In so holding, the court below followed precedent in the Fifth Circuit. In *Chevron Chemical Co. v. Voluntary Purchasing Groups, Inc.,* 659 F.2d 695, 702 (C.A.5 1981), the court noted that trademark law requires a demonstration of secondary meaning only when the claimed trademark is not sufficiently distinctive of itself to identify the producer; the court held that the same principles should apply to protection of trade dresses. The Court of Appeals noted that this approach conflicts with decisions of other courts, particularly the holding of the Court of Appeals for the Second Circuit in *Vibrant Sales, Inc. v. New Body Boutique, Inc.,* 652 F.2d 299 (1981), *cert. denied,* 455 U.S. 909 (1982), that § 43(a) protects unregistered trademarks or designs only where secondary meaning is shown. *Chevron, supra,* at 702. We granted certiorari to resolve the conflict among the Courts of Appeals on the question whether trade dress which is inherently distinctive is protectable under § 43(a) without a showing that it has acquired secondary meaning.[6] 112 S. Ct. 964 (1992). We find that it is, and we therefore affirm.

II

The Lanham Act was intended to make "actionable the deceptive and misleading use of marks" and "to protect persons engaged in . . . commerce against unfair competition." § 45, 15 U.S.C. § 1127. Section 43(a) "prohibits a broader range of practices than does § 32," which applies to registered marks, *Inwood Laboratories, Inc. v. Ives Laboratories, Inc.,* 456 U.S. 844, 858 (1982), but it is common ground that § 43(a) protects qualifying unregistered trademarks and that the general principles qualifying a mark for registration under § 2 of the Lanham Act are for the most part applicable in determining whether an unregistered mark is entitled to protection under § 43(a).

A trademark is defined in 15 U.S.C. § 1127 as including "any word, name, symbol, or device or any combination thereof" used by any person "to identify and distinguish his or her goods, including a unique product, from those manufactured or sold by others and to indicate the source of the goods, even if that source is unknown." In order to be registered, a mark must be capable of distinguishing the applicant's goods from those of others. § 1052. Marks are often classified in categories of generally increasing distinctiveness; following the classic formulation set out by Judge Friendly, they may be (1) generic; (2) descriptive; (3) suggestive; (4) arbitrary; or (5) fanciful. See *Abercrombie & Fitch Co. v. Hunting World, Inc.,* 537 F.2d 4, 9 (C.A.2 1976). The Court of Appeals followed this classification and petitioner accepts it. Brief for Petitioner 11–15. The latter three categories of marks, because their intrinsic nature serves to identify a particular source of a product, are deemed inherently distinctive and are entitled to protection. In contrast, generic marks—those that "refer to the genus of which the particular product is a species," *Park 'N Fly, Inc. v. Dollar Park and Fly, Inc.,* 469 U.S. 189, 194 (1985), citing *Abercrombie & Fitch, supra,* at 9—are not registrable as trademarks. *Park 'N Fly, supra,* at 194.

---

6. We limited our grant of certiorari to the above question on which there is a conflict. We did not grant certiorari on the second question presented by the petition, which challenged the Court of Appeals' acceptance of the jury's finding that Taco Cabana's trade dress was not functional.

Marks which are merely descriptive of a product are not inherently distinctive. When used to describe a product, they do not inherently identify a particular source, and hence cannot be protected. However, descriptive marks may acquire the distinctiveness which will allow them to be protected under the Act. Section 2 of the Lanham Act provides that a descriptive mark that otherwise could not be registered under the Act may be registered if it "has become distinctive of the applicant's goods in commerce." §§ 2(e), (f), 15 U.S.C. §§ 1052(e), (f). See *Park 'N Fly, supra,* at 194, 196. This acquired distinctiveness is generally called "secondary meaning." See *ibid.; Inwood Laboratories, supra,* at 851, n. 11; *Kellogg Co. v. National Biscuit Co.,* 305 U.S. 111, 118 (1938). The concept of secondary meaning has been applied to actions under § 43(a).

The general rule regarding distinctiveness is clear: an identifying mark is distinctive and capable of being protected if it *either* (1) is inherently distinctive *or* (2) has acquired distinctiveness through secondary meaning. RESTATEMENT (THIRD) OF UNFAIR COMPETITION, § 13, pp. 37–38, and Comment *a* (Tent. Draft No. 2, Mar. 23, 1990). *Cf. Park 'N Fly, supra,* at 194. It is also clear that eligibility for protection under § 43(a) depends on nonfunctionality. *See, e.g., Inwood Laboratories, supra,* at 863 (White, J., concurring in result). It is, of course, also undisputed that liability under § 43(a) requires proof of the likelihood of confusion.

The Court of Appeals determined that the District Court's instructions were consistent with the foregoing principles and that the evidence supported the jury's verdict. Both courts thus ruled that Taco Cabana's trade dress was not descriptive but rather inherently distinctive, and that it was not functional. None of these rulings is before us in this case, and for present purposes we assume, without deciding, that each of them is correct. In going on to affirm the judgment for respondent, the Court of Appeals, following its prior decision in *Chevron,* held that Taco Cabana's inherently distinctive trade dress was entitled to protection despite the lack of proof of secondary meaning. It is this issue that is before us for decision, and we agree with its resolution by the Court of Appeals. There is no persuasive reason to apply to trade dress a general requirement of secondary meaning which is at odds with the principles generally applicable to infringement suits under § 43(a). . . .

. . . .

This brings us to the line of decisions by the Court of Appeals for the Second Circuit that would find protection for trade dress unavailable absent proof of secondary meaning. . . . In *Vibrant Sales, Inc. v. New Body Boutique, Inc.,* 652 F.2d 299 (1981), the plaintiff claimed protection under § 43(a) for a product whose features the defendant had allegedly copied. The Court of Appeals held that unregistered marks did not enjoy the "presumptive source association" enjoyed by registered marks and hence could not qualify for protection under § 43(a) without proof of secondary meaning. *Id.* at 303, 304. The court's rationale seemingly denied protection for unregistered but inherently distinctive marks of all kinds, whether the claimed mark used distinctive words or symbols or distinctive product design. The court thus did not accept the arguments that an unregistered mark was capable of identifying a source and that copying such a mark could be making any kind of a false statement or representation under § 43(a). This holding is in considerable tension with the provisions of the Act. If a verbal or symbolic mark or the features of a product design may be registered under § 2, it necessarily is a mark "by which the goods of the applicant may be distinguished from the goods of others," 60 Stat. 428, and must be registered unless otherwise disqualified. Since § 2 requires secondary meaning only as a condition to registering descriptive marks, there are plainly marks that are registrable without showing secondary meaning. These same marks, even if not registered, remain inherently capable of distinguishing the goods of the users of these marks. Furthermore, the copier of such a mark may be seen as falsely claiming that his products may for some reason be thought of as originating from the plaintiff.

Some years after *Vibrant,* the Second Circuit announced in *Thompson Medical Co. v. Pfizer Inc.,* 753 F.2d 208 (C.A.2 1985), that in deciding whether an unregistered mark is eligible for protection under § 43(a), it would follow the classification of marks set out by Judge Friendly in *Abercrombie & Fitch,* 537 F.2d, at 9. Hence, if an unregistered mark is deemed merely descriptive, which the verbal mark before the court proved to be, proof of secondary meaning is required; however, "suggestive marks are eligible for protection without any proof of secondary meaning, since the connection between the mark and the source is presumed." 753 F.2d, at 216. The Second Circuit has nevertheless continued to deny protection for trade dress under § 43(a) absent proof of secondary meaning, despite the fact that § 43(a) provides no basis for distinguishing between trademark and trade dress.

The Fifth Circuit was quite right in *Chevron,* and in this case, to follow the *Abercrombie* classifications consistently and to inquire whether trade dress for which protection is claimed under § 43(a) is inherently distinctive. If it is, it is capable of identifying products or services as coming from a specific source and secondary meaning is not required. This is the rule generally applicable to trademark, and the protection of trademarks and trade dress under § 43(a) serves the same statutory purpose of preventing deception and unfair competition. There is no persuasive reason to apply different analysis to the two. The "proposition that secondary meaning must be shown even if the trade dress is a distinctive, identifying mark, [is] wrong, for the reasons explained by Judge Rubin for the Fifth Circuit in *Chevron.*" *Blau Plumbing, Inc. v. S.O.S. Fix-it, Inc.,* 781 F.2d 604, 608 (C.A.7 1986). The Court of Appeals for the Eleventh Circuit also follows *Chevron, Ambrit, Inc. v. Kraft, Inc.,* 805 F.2d 974, 979 (1986), and the Court of Appeals for the Ninth Circuit appears to think that proof of secondary meaning is superfluous if a trade dress is inherently distinctive. *Fuddruckers, Inc. v. Doc's B. R. Others, Inc.,* 826 F.2d 837, 843 (1987).

It would be a different matter if there were textual basis in § 43(a) for treating inherently distinctive verbal or symbolic trademarks differently from inherently distinctive trade dress. But there is none. The section does not mention trademarks or trade dress, whether they be called generic, descriptive, suggestive, arbitrary, fanciful, or functional. Nor does the concept of secondary meaning appear in the text of § 43(a). Where secondary meaning does appear in the statute, 15 U.S.C. § 1052 (1982 ed.), it is a requirement that applies only to merely descriptive marks and not to inherently distinctive ones. We see no basis for requiring secondary meaning for inherently distinctive trade dress protection under § 43(a) but not for other distinctive words, symbols, or devices capable of identifying a producer's product.

Engrafting onto § 43(a) a requirement of secondary meaning for inherently distinctive trade dress also would undermine the purposes of the Lanham Act. Protection of trade dress, no less than of trademarks, serves the Act's purpose to "secure to the owner of the mark the goodwill of his business and to protect the ability of consumers to distinguish among competing producers. National protection of trademarks is desirable, Congress concluded, because trademarks foster competition and the maintenance of quality by securing to the producer the benefits of good reputation." *Park 'N Fly*, 469 U.S., at 198, citing S. Rep. No. 1333, 79th Cong., 2d Sess., 3–5 (1946) (citations omitted). By making more difficult the identification of a producer with its product, a secondary meaning requirement for a nondescriptive trade dress would hinder improving or maintaining the producer's competitive position.

Suggestions that under the Fifth Circuit's law, the initial user of any shape or design would cut off competition from products of like design and shape are not persuasive. Only nonfunctional, distinctive trade dress is protected under § 43(a). The Fifth Circuit holds that a design is legally functional, and thus unprotectable, if it is one of a limited number of equally efficient options available to competitors and free competition would be unduly hindered by according the design trademark protection. This serves to assure that competition will not be stifled by the exhaustion of a limited number of trade dresses.

On the other hand, adding a secondary meaning requirement could have anticompetitive effects, creating particular burdens on the start-up of small companies. It would present special difficulties for a business, such as respondent, that seeks to start a new product in a limited area and then expand into new markets. Denying protection for inherently distinctive nonfunctional trade dress until after secondary meaning has been established would allow a competitor, which has not adopted a distinctive trade dress of its own, to appropriate the originator's dress in other markets and to deter the originator from expanding into and competing in these areas.

As noted above, petitioner concedes that protecting an inherently distinctive trade dress from its inception may be critical to new entrants to the market and that withholding protection until secondary meaning has been established would be contrary to the goals of the Lanham Act. Petitioner specifically suggests, however, that the solution is to dispense with the requirement of secondary meaning for a reasonable, but brief period at the outset of the use of a trade dress. Reply Brief for Petitioner

11–12. If § 43(a) does not require secondary meaning at the outset of a business' adoption of trade dress, there is no basis in the statute to support the suggestion that such a requirement comes into being after some unspecified time.

III

We agree with the Court of Appeals that proof of secondary meaning is not required to prevail on a claim under § 43(a) of the Lanham Act where the trade dress at issue is inherently distinctive, and accordingly the judgment of that court is affirmed.

It is so ordered.

■ JUSTICE STEVENS, *concurring* in the judgment:

As the Court notes in its opinion, the text of § 43(a) of the Lanham Act, 15 U.S.C. § 1125(a), "does not mention trademarks or trade dress." *Ante,* at 11. Nevertheless, the Court interprets this section as having created a federal cause of action for infringement of an unregistered trademark or trade dress and concludes that such a mark or dress should receive essentially the same protection as those that are registered. Although I agree with the Court's conclusion, I think it is important to recognize that the meaning of the text has been transformed by the federal courts over the past few decades. I agree with this transformation, even though it marks a departure from the original text, because it is consistent with the purposes of the statute and has recently been endorsed by Congress.

. . . .

In light of the general consensus among the Courts of Appeals that have actually addressed the question, and the steps on the part of Congress to codify that consensus, *stare decisis* concerns persuade me to join the Court's conclusion that secondary meaning is not required to establish a trade dress violation under § 43(a) once inherent distinctiveness has been established. Accordingly, I concur in the judgment, but not in the opinion of the Court.

QUESTIONS

1. In *Dirk Laureyssens v. Idea Group, Inc.,* 964 F.2d 131 (2d Cir.1992), the Court of Appeals for the Second Circuit concluded that protecting trade dress that had not acquired secondary meaning would be inconsistent with the language and purpose of trademark law because:

> Where there is no actual secondary meaning in a trade dress, the purchasing public simply does not associate the trade dress with a particular producer. Therefore, a subsequent producer who adopts an imitating trade dress will not cause confusion, mistake, or deception as to the "origin, sponsorship, or approval" of the goods. Second, a junior producer's use of imitating trade dress bears no "false designation of origin" because, in the absence of secondary

meaning in the senior producer's trade dress, the imitating trade dress suggests no particular origin to the consuming public. What is Justice White's response to this objection?

2.   Common law ownership of trademarks extended only to the geographic area of actual use. One of the advantages of registration on the principal register is that it permits the registrant to claim nationwide priority in the mark except as against actual senior users in the geographic areas of their actual use before registration. In *Two Pesos*, Justice White found "no persuasive reason" to analyze the infringement of unregistered marks under section 43(a) differently from the analysis applied to registered marks. One result of this analysis is that it permits Taco Cabana to claim priority over the actual senior user in the city of Houston, without having registered its trade dress. How might that affect the incentives Congress has put in place to encourage registration?

3.   Plaintiff seeks to register a design as a trademark, but the PTO rejects the application for lack of distinctiveness. What, if any, relevance should the PTO's action have on plaintiff's § 43(a) suit to protect the design from trade dress infringement? *See Dunn v. Gull*, 990 F.2d 348 (7th Cir.1993).

4.   You represent the owner of ROLLERECORDS, a trendy new music store and cafe doing a brisk business at the local shopping mall. ROLLERE-CORDS customers are greeted at the door with a complimentary pair of roller skates, and encouraged to zip through the aisles while selecting CDs or DVDs to purchase, or ordering refreshments at the store's stand-up bar. The music selection is geared to contemporary teens; the food is heavy on greasy snacks and sugary treats (no alcohol is served); and the decor is wall-to-wall concrete painted with bright enamel paint. Your client believes that her concept will be the next marketing breakthrough, and seeks to ensure that she will have the opportunity to exploit it, without competition, throughout the U.S. She seeks your advice on whether she should apply to register any aspects of her new business, and, if so, which ones. What do you advise?

1.   WHEN IS A DESIGN INHERENTLY DISTINCTIVE?

Wal–Mart Stores, Inc. v. Samara Brothers, Inc.

529 U.S. 205, 120 S.Ct. 1339, 146 L.Ed.2d 182 (2000).

■ JUSTICE SCALIA delivered the opinion of the Court:

In this case, we decide under what circumstances a product's design is distinctive, and therefore protectable, in an action for infringement of unregistered trade dress under § 43(a) of the Trademark Act of 1946 (Lanham Act), 60 Stat. 441, as amended, 15 U.S.C. § 1125(a).

I

Respondent Samara Brothers, Inc., designs and manufactures children's clothing. Its primary product is a line of spring/summer one-piece seersucker outfits decorated with appliques of hearts, flowers, fruits, and the like. A number of chain stores, including JCPenney, sell this line of clothing under contract with Samara.

Petitioner Wal–Mart Stores, Inc., is one of the nation's best known retailers, selling among other things children's clothing. In 1995, Wal–Mart contracted with one of its suppliers, Judy–Philippine, Inc., to manufacture a line of children's outfits for sale in the 1996 spring/summer season. Wal–Mart sent Judy–Philippine photographs of a number of garments from Samara's line, on which Judy–Philippine's garments were to be based; Judy–Philippine duly copied, with only minor modifications, 16 of Samara's garments, many of which contained copyrighted elements. In 1996, Wal–Mart briskly sold the so-called knockoffs, generating more than $1.15 million in gross profits.

In June 1996, a buyer for JCPenney called a representative at Samara to complain that she had seen Samara garments on sale at Wal–Mart for a lower price than JCPenney was allowed to charge under its contract with Samara. The Samara representative told the buyer that Samara did not supply its clothing to Wal–Mart. Their suspicions aroused, however, Samara officials launched an investigation, which disclosed that Wal–Mart and several other major retailers–Kmart, Caldor, Hills, and Goody's—were selling the knockoffs of Samara's outfits produced by Judy—Philippine.

After sending cease-and-desist letters, Samara brought this action in the United States District Court for the Southern District of New York against Wal–Mart, Judy—Philippine, Kmart, Caldor, Hills, and Goody's for copyright infringement under federal law, consumer fraud and unfair competition under New York law, and—most relevant for our purposes—infringement of unregistered trade dress under § 43(a) of the Lanham Act, 15 U.S.C. § 1125(a). All of the defendants except Wal–Mart settled before trial.

After a weeklong trial, the jury found in favor of Samara on all of its claims. Wal–Mart then renewed a motion for judgment as a matter of law, claiming, inter alia, that there was insufficient evidence to support a conclusion that Samara's clothing designs could be legally protected as distinctive trade dress for purposes of § 43(a). The District Court denied the motion, 969 F. Supp. 895 (S.D.N.Y.1997), and awarded Samara damages, interest, costs, and fees totaling almost $1.6 million, together with injunctive relief, *see* App. to Pet. for Cert. 56–58. The Second Circuit affirmed the denial of the motion for judgment as a matter of law, 165 F.3d 120 (1998), and we granted certiorari, 528 U.S. 808 (1999).

II

The Lanham Act provides for the registration of trademarks, which it defines in § 45 to include "any word, name, symbol, or device, or any combination thereof used or intended to be used to identify and distinguish a producer's goods ... from those manufactured or sold by others and to indicate the source of the goods...." 15 U.S.C. § 1127. Registration of a mark under § 2 of the Act, 15 U.S.C. § 1052, enables the owner to sue an infringer under § 32, 15 U.S.C. § 1114; it also entitles the owner to a presumption that its mark is valid, see § 7(b), 15 U.S.C. § 1057(b), and ordinarily renders the registered mark incontestable after five years of continuous use, see § 15, 15 U.S.C. § 1065. In addition to protecting registered marks, the Lanham Act, in § 43(a), gives a producer a cause of action for the use by any person of "any word, term, name, symbol, or device, or any combination thereof . . . which . . . is likely to cause confusion . . . as to the origin, sponsorship, or approval of his or her goods. . . ." 15 U.S.C. § 1125(a). It is the latter provision that is at issue in this case.

The breadth of the definition of marks registrable under § 2, and of the confusion-producing elements recited as actionable by § 43(a), has been held to embrace not just word marks, such as "Nike," and symbol marks, such as Nike's "swoosh" symbol, but also "trade dress"—a category that originally included only the packaging, or "dressing," of a product, but in recent years has been expanded by many courts of appeals to encompass the design of a product. *See, e.g., Ashley Furniture Industries, Inc. v. Sangiacomo N. A., Ltd.*, 187 F.3d 363 (C.A.4 1999) (bedroom furniture); *Knitwaves, Inc. v. Lollytogs, Ltd.*, 71 F.3d 996 (C.A.2 1995) (sweaters); *Stuart Hall Co., Inc. v. Ampad Corp.*, 51 F.3d 780 (C.A.8 1995) (notebooks). These courts have assumed, often without discussion, that trade dress constitutes a "symbol" or "device" for purposes of the relevant sections, and we conclude likewise. "Since human beings might use as a 'symbol' or 'device' almost anything at all that is capable of carrying meaning, this language, read literally, is not restrictive." *Qualitex Co. v. Jacobson Products Co.*, 514 U.S. 159 (1995). This reading of § 2 and § 43(a) is buttressed by a recently added subsection of § 43(a), § 43(a)(3), which refers specifically to "civil actions for trade dress infringement under this chapter for trade dress not registered on the principal register." 15 U.S.C.A. § 1125(a)(3) (Oct. 1999 Supp.).

The text of § 43(a) provides little guidance as to the circumstances under which unregistered trade dress may be protected. It does require that a producer show that the allegedly infringing feature is not "functional," see § 43(a)(3), and is likely to cause confusion with the product for which protection is sought, see § 43(a)(1)(A), 15 U.S.C. § 1125(a)(1)(A). Nothing in § 43(a) explicitly requires a producer to show that its trade dress is distinctive, but courts have universally imposed that requirement, since without distinctiveness the trade dress would not "cause confusion . . . as to the origin, sponsorship, or approval of the goods," as the section requires. Distinctiveness is, moreover, an explicit prerequisite for registration of trade dress under § 2, and "the general principles qualifying a mark for registration under § 2 of the Lanham Act are for the most part applicable in determining whether an unregistered mark is entitled to protection under § 43(a)." *Two Pesos, Inc. v. Taco Cabana, Inc.*, 505 U.S. 763 (1992) (citations omitted).

In evaluating the distinctiveness of a mark under § 2 (and therefore, by analogy, under § 43(a)), courts have held that a mark can be distinctive in one of two ways. First, a mark is inherently distinctive if "its intrinsic nature serves to identify a particular source." *Ibid.* In the context of word marks, courts have applied the now-classic test originally formulated by Judge Friendly, in which word marks that are "arbitrary" ("Camel" cigarettes), "fanciful" ("Kodak" film), or "suggestive" ("Tide" laundry detergent) are held to be inherently distinctive. *See Abercrombie & Fitch Co. v. Hunting World, Inc.*, 537 F.2d 4, 10–11 (C.A.2 1976). Second, a mark has acquired distinctiveness, even if it is not inherently distinctive, if it has developed secondary meaning, which occurs when, "in the minds of the public, the primary significance of a mark is to identify the source of the product rather than the product itself." *Inwood Laboratories, Inc. v. Ives Laboratories*, Inc., 456 U.S. 844, 851, n. 11, 72 L. Ed. 2d 606, 102 S. Ct. 2182 (1982).

The judicial differentiation between marks that are inherently distinctive and those that have developed secondary meaning has solid foundation in the statute itself. Section 2 requires that registration be granted to any trademark "by which the goods of the applicant may be distinguished from the goods of others"—subject to various limited exceptions. 15 U.S.C. § 1052. It also provides, again with limited exceptions, that "nothing in this chapter shall prevent the registration of a mark used by the applicant which has become distinctive of the applicant's goods in commerce"—that is, which is not inherently distinctive but has become so only through secondary meaning. § 2(f), 15 U.S.C. § 1052(f). Nothing in § 2, however, demands the conclusion that every category of mark necessarily includes some marks "by which the goods of the applicant may be distinguished from the goods of others" without secondary meaning—that in every category some marks are inherently distinctive.

Indeed, with respect to at least one category of mark—colors—we have held that no mark can ever be inherently distinctive. *See Qualitex*, 514 U.S. at 162–163. In *Qualitex*, petitioner manufactured and sold green-gold dry-cleaning press pads. After respondent began selling pads of a similar color, petitioner brought suit under § 43(a), then added a claim under § 32 after obtaining registration for the color of its pads. We held that a color could be protected as a trademark, but only upon a showing of secondary meaning. Reasoning by analogy to the *Abercrombie & Fitch* test developed for word marks, we noted that a product's color is unlike a "fanciful," "arbitrary," or "suggestive" mark, since it does not "almost automatically tell a customer that it refers to a brand," *ibid.*, and does not "immediately ... signal a brand or a product 'source,'" 514 U.S. at 163. However, we noted that, "over time, customers may come to treat a particular color on a product or its packaging ... as signifying a brand." 514 U.S. at 162–163. Because a color, like a "descriptive" word mark, could eventually "come to indicate a product's origin," we concluded that it could be protected upon a showing of secondary meaning. *Ibid.*

It seems to us that design, like color, is not inherently distinctive. The attribution of inherent distinctiveness to certain categories of word marks and product packaging derives from the fact that the very purpose of attaching a particular word to a product, or encasing it in a distinctive packaging, is most often to identify the source of the product. Although the words and packaging can serve subsidiary functions—a suggestive word mark (such as "Tide" for laundry detergent), for instance, may invoke positive connotations in the consumer's mind, and a garish form of packaging (such as Tide's squat, brightly decorated plastic bottles for its liquid laundry detergent) may attract an otherwise indifferent consumer's attention on a crowded store shelf—their predominant function remains source identification. Consumers are therefore predisposed to regard those symbols as indication of the producer, which is why such symbols "almost automatically tell a customer that they refer to a brand," 514 U.S. at 162–163, and "immediately . . . signal a brand or a product 'source,' " 514 U.S. at 163. And where it is not reasonable to assume consumer predisposition to take an affixed word or packaging as indication of source—where, for example, the affixed word is descriptive of the product ("Tasty" bread) or of a geographic origin ("Georgia" peaches)—inherent distinctiveness will not be found. That is why the statute generally excludes, from those word marks that can be registered as inherently distinctive, words that are "merely descriptive" of the goods, § 2(e)(1), 15 U.S.C. § 1052(e)(1), or "primarily geographically descriptive of them," see § 2(e)(2), 15 U.S.C. § 1052(e)(2). In the case of product design, as in the case of color, we think consumer predisposition to equate the feature with the source does not exist. Consumers are aware of the reality that, almost invariably, even the most unusual of product designs—such as a cocktail shaker shaped like a penguin—is intended not to identify the source, but to render the product itself more useful or more appealing.

The fact that product design almost invariably serves purposes other than source identification not only renders inherent distinctiveness problematic; it also renders application of an inherent-distinctiveness principle more harmful to other consumer interests. Consumers should not be deprived of the benefits of competition with regard to the utilitarian and esthetic purposes that product design ordinarily serves by a rule of law that facilitates plausible threats of suit against new entrants based upon alleged inherent distinctiveness. How easy it is to mount a plausible suit depends, of course, upon the clarity of the test for inherent distinctiveness, and where product design is concerned we have little confidence that a reasonably clear test can be devised. Respondent and the United States as amicus curiae urge us to adopt for product design relevant portions of the test formulated by the Court of Customs and Patent Appeals for product packaging in *Seabrook Foods, Inc. v. Bar–Well Foods, Ltd.*, 568 F.2d 1342 (1977). That opinion, in determining the inherent distinctiveness of a product's packaging, considered, among other things, "whether it was a 'common' basic shape or design, whether it was unique or unusual in a particular field, and whether it was a mere refinement of a commonly-adopted and well-known form of ornamentation for a particular class of goods viewed by the public as a dress or ornamentation for the goods." *Id.* at 1344 (footnotes omitted). Such a test would rarely provide the basis for summary disposition of an anticompetitive strike suit. Indeed, at oral argument, counsel for the United States quite understandably would not give a definitive answer as to whether the test was met in this very case, saying only that "this is a very difficult case for that purpose." Tr. of Oral Arg. 19.

It is true, of course, that the person seeking to exclude new entrants would have to establish the nonfunctionality of the design feature, *see* § 43(a)(3), 15 U.S.C. A. § 1125(a)(3) (Oct. 1999 Supp.)—a showing that may involve consideration of its esthetic appeal, *see Qualitex*, 514 U.S. at 170. Competition is deterred, however, not merely by successful suit but by the plausible threat of successful suit, and given the unlikelihood of inherently source-identifying design, the game of allowing suit based upon alleged inherent distinctiveness seems to us not worth the candle. That is especially so since the producer can ordinarily obtain protection for a design that is inherently source identifying (if any such exists), but that does not yet have secondary meaning, by securing a design patent or a copyright for the design—as, indeed, respondent did for certain elements of the designs in this case. The availability of these other protections greatly reduces any harm to the producer that might ensue from our conclusion that a product design cannot be protected under § 43(a) without a showing of secondary meaning.

Respondent contends that our decision in *Two Pesos* forecloses a conclusion that product-design trade dress can never be inherently distinctive. In that case, we held that the trade dress of a chain of Mexican restaurants, which the plaintiff described as "a festive eating atmosphere having interior dining and patio areas decorated with artifacts, bright colors, paintings and murals," 505 U.S. at 765 (internal quotation marks and citation omitted), could be protected under § 43(a) without a showing of secondary meaning, see 505 U.S. at 776. *Two Pesos* unquestionably establishes the legal principle that trade dress can be inherently distinctive, see, e.g., 505 U.S. at 773, but it does not establish that product-design trade dress can be. *Two Pesos* is inapposite to our holding here because the trade dress at issue, the decor of a restaurant, seems to us not to constitute product design. It was either product packaging—which, as we have discussed, normally is taken by the consumer to indicate origin—or else some tertium quid that is akin to product packaging and has no bearing on the present case.

Respondent replies that this manner of distinguishing *Two Pesos* will force courts to draw difficult lines between product-design and product-packaging trade dress. There will indeed be some hard cases at the margin: a classic glass Coca–Cola bottle, for instance, may constitute packaging for those consumers who drink the Coke and then discard the bottle, but may constitute the product itself for those consumers who are bottle collectors, or part of the product itself for those consumers who buy Coke in the classic glass bottle, rather than a can, because they think it more stylish to drink from the former. We believe, however, that the frequency and the difficulty of having to distinguish between product design and product packaging will be much less than the frequency and the difficulty of having to decide when a product design is inherently distinctive. To the extent there are close cases, we believe that courts should err on the side of caution and classify ambiguous trade dress as product design, thereby requiring secondary meaning. The very closeness will suggest the existence of relatively small utility in adopting an inherent-distinctiveness principle, and relatively great consumer benefit in requiring a demonstration of secondary meaning.

We hold that, in an action for infringement of unregistered trade dress under § 43(a) of the Lanham Act, a product's design is distinctive, and therefore protectible, only upon a showing of secondary meaning. The judgment of the Second Circuit is reversed, and the case is remanded for further proceedings consistent with this opinion.

It is so ordered.

QUESTIONS

1. Justice Scalia distinguishes between product design, product packaging, and "some tertium quid that is akin to product packaging." What is that "tertium quid"? Can you think of an example?

2. How should courts distinguish between trade dress and product design? In *In re Slokevage*, 441 F.3d 957 (Fed.Cir.2006), the manufacturer of Flash Dare brand sportswear sought to register a mark consisting of the phrase "Flash Dare" flanked by two peek-a-boo holes in the rear hip area. The applicant argued that the mark was trade dress; the court concluded that it was product design:

> Slokevage urges that her trade dress is not product design because it does not alter the entire product but is more akin to a label being placed on a garment. We do not agree. The holes and flaps portion are part of the design of the clothing—the cut-out area is not merely a design placed on top of a garment, but is a design incorporated into the garment itself. Moreover, while Slokevage urges that product design trade dress must implicate the entire product, we do not find support for that proposition. Just as the product design in Wal–Mart consisted of certain design features featured on clothing, Slokevage's trade dress similarly consists of design features, holes and flaps, featured in clothing, revealing the similarity between the two types of design.
>
> In addition, the reasoning behind the Supreme Court's determination that product design cannot be inherently distinctive is also instructive to our case. The Court reasoned that, unlike a trademark whose "predominant function" remains source identification, product design often serves other functions, such as rendering the "product itself more useful or more appealing." *Wal–Mart*, 529 U.S. at 212, 213. The design at issue here can serve such utilitarian and aesthetic functions. For example, consumers may purchase Slokevage's clothing for the utilitarian purpose of wearing a garment or because they find the appearance of the garment particularly desirable. Consistent with the Supreme Court's analysis in *Wal–Mart*, in such cases when the purchase implicates a utilitarian or aesthetic purpose, rather than a

(Court applying Sticky trade Dress v. Product Design Problem source-identifying function, it is appropriate to require proof of acquired distinctiveness.

Finally, the Court in *Wal–Mart* provided guidance on how to address trade dress cases that may be difficult to classify: "To the extent that there are close cases, we believe that courts should err on the side of caution and classify ambiguous trade dress as product design, thereby requiring secondary meaning." 529 U.S. at 215. Even if this were a close case, therefore, we must follow that precedent and classify the trade dress as product design. We thus agree with the Board that Slokevage's trade dress is product design and therefore that she must prove acquired distinctiveness in order for her trade dress mark to be registered.

Stop 11/20   Continue on p. 515

2.   FUNCTIONALITY REVISITED

15 U.S.C. § 1125(a)(3)[LANHAM ACT § 43(a)(3)]

(3) In a civil action for trade dress infringement under this chapter for trade dress not registered on the principal register, the person who asserts trade dress protection has the burden of proving that the matter sought to be protected is not functional.

Tie Tech, Inc. v. Kinedyne Corp., 296 F.3d 778 (9th Cir.2002). Tie Tech sued Kinedyne for marketing a device that was "virtually indistinguishable" from Tie Tech's Safecutt web cutter.

Safecut had succeeded in registering the overall design of the device as a trademark on the principal register in 1998. Kinedyne argued that the product configuration was functional and therefore unprotectable. The 9th Circuit agreed:

To begin, there is nothing inherently wrong with Kinedyne's interest in copying the SAFECUT's configuration: "The requirement of nonfunctionality is based 'on the judicial theory that *there exists a fundamental right 'o compete through imitation of a competitor's product*, which right can only be *temporarily* denied by the patent or copyright laws.'" *Clamp*[*Mfg. Co. v. Enco Mfg. Co.*,], 870 F.2d at 516 (quoting *Morton–Norwich*, 671 F.2d at 1336 (emphasis added)). Consequently, as early as *Vuitto.   ·t Fils S.A. v. J. Young Enters., Inc.*, 644 F.2d 769, 775 (9th Cir. 1981)], we characterized the distinction between "features which constitute the actual benefit that the consumer wishes to purchase," which do not engender trademark protection, "as distinguished from an assurance that a particular entity made, sponsored, or endorsed a product," which, if incorporated into the product's design by virtue of arbitrary embellishment, does have trademark significance. 644 F.2d at 774 (internal quotations and citations omitted); *see also Qualitex Co. v. Jacobson Prods. Co.*, 514 U.S. 159, 164, 115 S.Ct. 1300, 131 L.Ed.2d 248 (1995) ("The functionality doctrine prevents trademark law, which seeks to promote competition by protecting a firm's reputation, from instead inhibiting legitimate competition by allowing a producer to control a useful product feature.").

Unfortunately for Tie Tech, it has not pointed to any evidence of distinctiveness of the SAFECUT design other than those elements essential to its effective use. Instead, Tie Tech suggests something different when it claims that it "is not asking that Kinedyne be barred from having a webcutter with an enclosed blade, a slot and prong to guide the webbing into the blade, or even an opening through which the user can put their [sic] hand," but instead that Kinedyne should "be barred from arranging those elements into a shape that mimics that of the SAFECUT tm." In other words, Tie Tech argues that the overall appearance of its cutter, and not its separate functional parts, is what deserves protection as a non-functional aspect of its configuration. This cannot be the case. Where the plaintiff only offers evidence that "the whole is nothing other than the assemblage of functional parts," our court has already foreclosed this argument, holding that "it is semantic trickery to say that there is still some sort of separate 'overall appearance' which is non-functional." *Leatherman [Tool Group, Inc. v. Cooper Industries, Inc.*, 199 F.3d 1009 (9th Cir.1999)], at 1013.

Likewise, Tie Tech's evidence of alternative designs fails to raise a material factual issue under *Leatherman*. As was the case with the pocket tool at issue in *Leatherman*, Tie Tech has presented evidence that there are other webcutters with a variety of appearances and features that effectively cut webbing. In particular, Tie Tech cites to a trade journal which evaluated several webcutters including the SAFE-CUT and another, the Ortho, which is strikingly similar to Kinedyne's original cutter and is described in the article as "the simplest design— a rectangle with rounded corners [that] several testers found . . . cut the webbing faster than any of the other products." As for the SAFECUT, its shape was "lauded immediately"; one tester was quoted as saying "I like the grip. . . . It seems like a natural shape." Narrowing their preferences down to the Ortho and the SAFECUT, the article's testers

> split on their ultimate preference in web cutters. But all present agreed that either of the two finalists—Ortho's Web Cutter or Tie Tech's Safecut—admirably did the job. They both ripped through

the test webbing in a single motion. *It simply came down to personal preference.* (Emphasis added).

This evidence certainly supports Tie Tech's contention that adequate alternative designs exist which "admirably" do the job, but to Tie Tech's detriment, it goes further. Because the product review not only demonstrates that a design such as the Ortho may be "highly functional and useful," it also undisputedly shows that the Ortho does not "offer *exactly* the same features as [the SAFECUT]," in particular the secured-grip handle, and thus fails as matter of law to support Tie Tech's interest in precluding competition by means of trademark protection. *Id.* at 1013–14 (emphasis in original).

In *Leatherman* we held that a product's manufacturer "does not have rights under trade dress law to compel its competitors to resort to alternative designs which have a different set of advantages and disadvantages. Such is the realm of patent law." *Id.* at 1014 n.7. Here, Tie Tech does not dispute that some customers may prefer a specific functional aspect of the SAFECUT, namely its closed-grip handle, even though other functional designs may ultimately get the job done just as well. As *Leatherman* reminds us, though, a customer's preference for a particular functional aspect of a product is wholly distinct from a customer's desire to be assured "that a particular entity made, sponsored, or endorsed a product." *Id.* at 1012 (quoting *Vuitton*, 644 F.2d at 774). Whereas the latter concern encompasses the realm of trademark protection, the former does not. We therefore conclude on this record that the district court appropriately granted summary judgment in favor of Kinedyne.

TrafFix Devices, Inc. v. Marketing Displays, Inc.
532 U.S. 23, 121 S.Ct. 1255, 149 L.Ed.2d 164 (2001).

■ JUSTICE KENNEDY delivered the opinion of the Court:

Temporary road signs with warnings like "Road Work Ahead" or "Left Shoulder Closed" must withstand strong gusts of wind. An inventor named Robert Sarkisian obtained two utility patents for a mechanism built upon two springs (the dual-spring design) to keep these and other outdoor signs upright despite adverse wind conditions. The holder of the now-expired Sarkisian patents, respondent Marketing Displays, Inc. (MDI), established a successful business in the manufacture and sale of sign stands incorporating the patented feature. MDI's stands for road signs were recognizable to buyers and users (it says) because the dual-spring design was visible near the base of the sign.

This litigation followed after the patents expired and a competitor, TrafFix Devices, Inc., sold sign stands with a visible spring mechanism that looked like MDI's. MDI and TrafFix products looked alike because they were. When TrafFix started in business, it sent an MDI product abroad to have it reverse engineered, that is to say copied. Complicating matters, TrafFix marketed its sign stands under a name similar to MDI's. MDI used the name "WindMaster," while TrafFix, its new competitor, used "Wind-Buster."

MDI brought suit under the Trademark Act of 1964 (Lanham Act), 60 Stat. 427, as amended, 15 U.S.C. § 1051 *et seq.*, against TrafFix for trademark infringement (based on the similar names), trade dress infringement (based on the copied dual-spring design) and unfair competition. TrafFix counterclaimed on antitrust theories. After the United States District Court for the Eastern District of Michigan considered cross-motions for summary judgment, MDI prevailed on its trademark claim for the confusing similarity of names and was held not liable on the antitrust counterclaim; and those two rulings, affirmed by the Court of Appeals, are not before us.

I

We are concerned with the trade dress question. The District Court ruled against MDI on its trade dress claim. 971 F. Supp. 262 (E.D.Mich. 1997). After determining that the one element of MDI's trade dress at issue was the dual-spring design, *id.*, at 265, it held that "no reasonable trier of fact could determine that MDI has established secondary meaning" in its alleged trade dress, *id.*, at 269. In other words, consumers did not associate the look of the dual-spring design with MDI. As a second, independent reason to grant summary judgment in favor of TrafFix, the District Court determined the dual-spring design was functional. On this rationale secondary meaning is irrelevant because there can be no trade dress protection in any event. In ruling on the functional aspect of the design, the District Court noted that Sixth Circuit precedent indicated that the burden was on MDI to prove that its trade dress was nonfunctional, and not on TrafFix to show that it was functional (a rule since adopted by Congress, see 15 U.S.C. § 1125(a)(3) (1994 ed., Supp. V)), and then went on to consider MDI's arguments that the dual-spring design was subject to trade dress protection. Finding none of MDI's contentions persuasive, the District Court concluded MDI had not "proffered sufficient evidence which would enable a reasonable trier of fact to find that MDI's vertical dual-spring design is *non*-functional." *Id.*, at 276. Summary judgment was entered against MDI on its trade dress claims.

The Court of Appeals for the Sixth Circuit reversed the trade dress ruling. 200 F.3d 929 (1999). The Court of Appeals held the District Court had erred in ruling MDI failed to show a genuine issue of material fact regarding whether it had secondary meaning in its alleged trade dress, *id.*, at 938, and had erred further in determining that MDI could not prevail in any event because the alleged trade dress was in fact a functional product configuration, *id.*, at 940. The Court of Appeals suggested the District Court committed legal error by looking only to the dual-spring design when evaluating MDI's trade dress. Basic to its reasoning was the Court of Appeals' observation that it took "little imagination to conceive of a hidden dual-spring mechanism or a tri or quad-spring mechanism that might avoid infringing [MDI's] trade dress." *Ibid.* The Court of Appeals explained that "[i]f TrafFix or another competitor chooses to use [MDI's] dual-spring design, then it will have to find *some other way* to set its sign apart to avoid infringing [MDI's] trade dress." *Ibid.* It was not sufficient, according to the Court of Appeals, that allowing exclusive use of a particular feature such as the dual-spring design in the guise of trade dress would "hinde[r] competition somewhat." Rather, "[e]xclusive use of a feature must 'put competitors at a *significant* non-reputation-related disadvantage' before trade dress protection is denied on functionality grounds." *Ibid.* (quoting *Qualitex Co. v. Jacobson Products Co.*, 514 U.S. 159, 165 (1995)). In its criticism of the District Court's ruling on the trade dress question, the Court of Appeals took note of a split among Courts of Appeals in various other Circuits on the issue whether the existence of an expired utility patent forecloses the possibility of the patentee's claiming trade dress protection in the product's design. 200 F.3d, at 939. Compare *Sunbeam Products, Inc. v. West Bend Co.*, 123 F.3d 246 (C.A.5 1997) (holding that trade dress protection is not foreclosed), *Thomas & Betts Corp. v. Panduit Corp.*, 138 F.3d 277 (C.A.7 1998) (same), and *Midwest Industries, Inc. v. Karavan Trailers, Inc.*, 175 F.3d 1356 (C.A.Fed.1999) (same), with *Vornado Air Circulation Systems, Inc. v. Duracraft Corp.*, 58 F.3d 1498, 1500 (C.A.10 1995) ("Where a product configuration is a significant inventive component of an invention covered by a utility patent ... it cannot receive trade dress protection"). To resolve the conflict, we granted certiorari. 530 U.S. 1260 (2000).

II

It is well established that trade dress can be protected under federal law. The design or packaging of a product may acquire a distinctiveness which serves to identify the product with its manufacturer or source; and a design or package which acquires this secondary meaning, assuming other requisites are met, is a trade dress which may not be used in a manner likely to cause confusion as to the origin, sponsorship, or approval of the goods. In these respects protection for trade dress exists to promote competition. As we explained just last Term, see *Wal–Mart Stores, Inc. v. Samara Brothers, Inc.*, 529 U.S. 205 (2000), various Courts of Appeals have allowed claims of trade dress infringement relying on the general provision of the Lanham Act which provides a cause of action to one who is injured when a person uses "any word, term name, symbol, or device, or any combination thereof ... which is likely to cause confusion ... as to the origin, sponsorship, or approval of his or her goods." 15 U.S.C. § 1125(a)(1)(A). Congress confirmed this statutory protection for trade dress by amending the Lanham Act to recognize the concept. Title 15 U.S.C. § 1125(a)(3) (1994 ed., Supp. V) provides: "In a civil action for trade dress infringement under this chapter for trade dress not registered on the principal register, the person who asserts trade dress protection has the burden of proving that the matter sought to be protected is not functional." This burden of proof gives force to the well-established rule that trade dress protection may not be claimed for product features that are functional. *Qualitex, supra,* at 164–165; *Two Pesos, Inc. v. Taco Cabana, Inc.*, 505 U.S. 763, 775 (1992). And in *Wal–Mart, supra,* we were careful to caution against misuse or over-extension of trade dress. We noted that "product design almost invariably serves purposes other than source identification." *Id.*, at 213.

Trade dress protection must subsist with the recognition that in many instances there is no prohibition against copying goods and products. In general, unless an intellectual property right such as a patent or copyright protects an item, it will be subject to copying. As the Court has explained, copying is not always discouraged or disfavored by the laws which preserve our competitive economy. *Bonito Boats, Inc. v. Thunder Craft Boats, Inc.*, 489 U.S. 141, 160 (1989). Allowing competitors to copy will have salutary effects in many instances. "Reverse engineering of chemical and mechanical articles in the public domain often leads to significant advances in technology." *Ibid.*

The principal question in this case is the effect of an expired patent on a claim of trade dress infringement. A prior patent, we conclude, has vital significance in resolving the trade dress claim. A utility patent is strong evidence that the features therein claimed are functional. If trade dress protection is sought for those features the strong evidence of functionality based on the previous patent adds great weight to the statutory presumption that features are deemed functional until proved otherwise by the party seeking trade dress protection. Where the expired patent claimed the features in question, one who seeks to establish trade dress protection must carry the heavy burden of showing that the feature is not functional, for instance by showing that it is merely an ornamental, incidental, or arbitrary aspect of the device.

In the case before us, the central advance claimed in the expired utility patents (the Sarkisian patents) is the dual-spring design; and the dual-spring design is the essential feature of the trade dress MDI now seeks to establish and to protect. The rule we have explained bars the trade dress claim, for MDI did not, and cannot, carry the burden of overcoming the strong evidentiary inference of functionality based on the disclosure of the dual-spring design in the claims of the expired patents.

The dual springs shown in the Sarkisian patents were well apart (at either end of a frame for holding a rectangular sign when one full side is the base) while the dual springs at issue here are close together (in a frame designed to hold a sign by one of its corners). As the District Court recognized, this makes little difference. The point is that the springs are necessary to the operation of the device....

The rationale for the rule that the disclosure of a feature in the claims of a utility patent constitutes strong evidence of functionality is well illustrated in this case. The dual-spring design serves the important purpose of keeping the sign upright even in heavy wind conditions; and, as confirmed by the statements in the expired patents, it does so in a unique and useful manner. As the specification of one of the patents recites, prior art "devices, in practice, will topple under the force of a strong wind." U.S. Patent No. 3,662,482, col. 1. The dual-spring design allows sign stands to resist toppling in strong winds. Using a dual-spring design rather than a single spring achieves important operational advantages. For example, the specifications of the patents note that the "use of a pair of springs . . . as opposed to the use of a single spring to support the frame structure prevents canting or twisting of the sign around a vertical axis," and that, if not prevented, twisting "may cause damage to the spring structure and may result in tipping of the device." U.S. Patent No. 3,646,696, col. 3. In the course of patent prosecution, it was said that "[t]he use of a pair of spring connections as opposed to a single spring connection . . . forms an important part of this combination" because it "forc[es] the sign frame to tip along the longitudinal axis of the elongated ground-engaging members." App. 218. The dual-spring design affects the cost of the device as well; it was acknowledged that the device "could use three springs but this would unnecessarily increase the cost of the device." App. 217. These statements made in the patent applications and in the course of procuring the patents demonstrate the functionality of the design. MDI does not assert that any of these representations are mistaken or inaccurate, and this is further strong evidence of the functionality of the dual-spring design.

III

In finding for MDI on the trade dress issue the Court of Appeals gave insufficient recognition to the importance of the expired utility patents, and their evidentiary significance, in establishing the functionality of the device. The error likely was caused by its misinterpretation of trade dress principles in other respects. As we have noted, even if there has been no previous utility patent the party asserting trade dress has the burden to establish the nonfunctionality of alleged trade dress features. MDI could not meet this burden. Discussing trademarks, we have said " '[i]n general terms, a product feature is functional,' and cannot serve as a trademark, 'if it is essential to the use or purpose of the article or if it affects the cost or quality of the article.' " *Qualitex*, 514 U.S., at 165 (quoting *Inwood Laboratories, Inc. v. Ives Laboratories, Inc.*, 456 U.S. 844, 850, n. 10 (1982)). Expanding upon the meaning of this phrase, we have observed that a functional feature is one the "exclusive use of [which] would put competitors at a significant non-reputation-related disadvantage." 514 U.S., at 165. The Court of Appeals in the instant case seemed to interpret this language to mean that a necessary test for functionality is "whether the particular product configuration is a competitive necessity." 200 F.3d, at 940. See also *Vornado*, 58 F.3d, at 1507 ("Functionality, by contrast, has been defined both by our circuit, and more recently by the Supreme Court, in terms of competitive need"). This was incorrect as a comprehensive definition. As explained in *Qualitex*, *supra*, and *Inwood*, *supra*, a feature is also functional when it is essential to the use or purpose of the device or when it affects the cost or quality of the device. The *Qualitex* decision did not purport to displace this traditional rule. Instead, it quoted the rule as *Inwood* had set it forth. It is proper to inquire into a "significant non-reputation-related disadvantage" in cases of aesthetic functionality, the question involved in *Qualitex*. Where the design is functional under the *Inwood* formulation there is no need to proceed further to consider if there is a competitive necessity for the feature. In *Qualitex*, by contrast, aesthetic functionality was the central question, there having been no indication that the green-gold color of the laundry press pad had any bearing on the use or purpose of the product or its cost or quality.

The Court has allowed trade dress protection to certain product features that are inherently distinctive. *Two Pesos*, 505 U.S., at 774. In *Two Pesos*, however, the Court at the outset made the explicit analytic assumption that the trade dress features in question (decorations and other features to evoke a Mexican theme in a restaurant) were not functional. *Id.*, at 767, n. 6. The trade dress in those cases did not bar competitors from copying functional product design features. In the instant case, beyond serving the purpose of informing consumers that the sign stands are made by MDI (assuming it does so), the dual-spring design provides a unique and useful mechanism to resist the force of the wind. Functionality having been established, whether MDI's dual-spring design has acquired secondary meaning need not be considered.

There is no need, furthermore, to engage, as did the Court of Appeals, in speculation about other design possibilities, such as using three or four springs which might serve the same purpose. 200 F.3d, at 940. Here, the functionality of the spring design means that competitors need not explore whether other spring juxtapositions might be used. The dual-spring design is not an arbitrary flourish in the configuration of MDI's product; it is the reason the device works. Other designs need not be attempted.

Because the dual-spring design is functional, it is unnecessary for competitors to explore designs to hide the springs, say by using a box or framework to cover them, as suggested by the Court of Appeals. *Ibid*. The dual-spring design assures the user the device will work. If buyers are assured the product serves its purpose by seeing the operative mechanism that in itself serves an important market need. It would be at cross-purposes to those objectives, and something of a paradox, were we to require the manufacturer to conceal the very item the user seeks.

In a case where a manufacturer seeks to protect arbitrary, incidental, or ornamental aspects of features of a product found in the patent claims, such as arbitrary curves in the legs or an ornamental pattern painted on the springs, a different result might obtain. There the manufacturer could perhaps prove that those aspects do not serve a purpose within the terms of the utility patent. The inquiry into whether such features, asserted to be trade dress, are functional by reason of their inclusion in the claims of an expired utility patent could be aided by going beyond the claims and examining the patent and its prosecution history to see if the feature in question is shown as a useful part of the invention. No such claim is made here, however. MDI in essence seeks protection for the dual-spring design alone. The asserted trade dress consists simply of the dual-spring design, four legs, a base, an upright, and a sign. MDI has pointed to nothing arbitrary about the components of its device or the way they are assembled. The Lanham Act does not exist to reward manufacturers for their innovation in creating a particular device; that is the purpose of the patent law

[handwritten margin note: Dual springs are essential to function. Not ornamental Design.]

and its period of exclusivity. The Lanham Act, furthermore, does not protect trade dress in a functional design simply because an investment has been made to encourage the public to associate a particular functional feature with a single manufacturer or seller. The Court of Appeals erred in viewing MDI as possessing the right to exclude competitors from using a design identical to MDI's and to require those competitors to adopt a different design simply to avoid copying it. MDI cannot gain the exclusive right to produce sign stands using the dual-spring design by asserting that consumers associate it with the look of the invention itself. Whether a utility patent has expired or there has been no utility patent at all, a product design which has a particular appearance may be functional because it is "essential to the use or purpose of the article" or "affects the cost or quality of the article." *Inwood*, 456 U.S., at 850, n. 10.

TrafFix and some of its *amici* argue that the Patent Clause of the Constitution, Art. I, § 8, cl. 8, of its own force, prohibits the holder of an expired utility patent from claiming trade dress protection. . . . We need not resolve this question. If, despite the rule that functional features may not be the subject of trade dress protection, a case arises in which trade dress becomes the practical equivalent of an expired utility patent, that will be time enough to consider the matter. The judgment of the Court of Appeals is reversed, and the case is remanded for further proceedings consistent with this opinion.

It is so ordered.

QUESTION

Justice Kennedy's opinion describes the facts in *Qualitex* as raising the question of "aesthetic functionality," and suggests that, in such a case, "it is proper to inquire into a 'significant non-reputation-related disadvantage.'" If plaintiff claims a feature that affects neither the cost nor quality of its product as protectable trade dress, can defendant argue that the attractiveness of plaintiff's design is itself a product feature, and that prohibiting defendant from copying it would impose a significant non-reputation-related disadvantage on plaintiff's competitors? In particular, can ornamental product features be protected as trade dress?

Eco Manufacturing LLC v. Honeywell International Inc., 357 F.3d 649 (7th Cir.2003).

Eco Manufacturing proposes to make a thermostat similar in appearance to Honeywell's well-known circular, convex model with a round dial. . . .

... This appeal is from the district court's order declining to issue a preliminary injunction that would block Eco from bringing its product to market. ...[T]he district court concluded that the shape of Honeywell's thermostat is functional—or, to be precise, that the likelihood of such a finding after a trial on the merits is sufficiently high, and damages are sufficiently easy to calculate if Honeywell turns out to win in the end, that Eco should be allowed to sell its competing product while the litigation proceeds. ...

Honeywell's lead argument in this court is that it does not matter whether, or to what extent, the thermostat's shape is functional. That is so, Honeywell submits, because the trademark registration became incontestable in 1996, before Eco brought a competing product to market. Once a mark has been used for five years following registration, it becomes "incontestable". 15 U.S.C. § 1065. Incontestability is "conclusive evidence of the validity of the registered mark and ... the registrant's exclusive right" to use the mark in commerce. 15 U.S.C. § 1115(b). *See Park'N Fly, Inc. v. Dollar Park and Fly, Inc.*, 469 U.S. 189, 105 S.Ct. 658, 83 L.Ed.2d 582 (1985).

The words "incontestable" and "exclusive" sound more impressive than the legal rights that the Lanham Act actually conveys, however. Section 1065 says that even "incontestable" marks must yield to prior users, and that the protection dissipates if the mark becomes generic. Moreover, and more to the point, § 1065 says that a claim based on an incontestable mark may be defeated "on a ground for which application to cancel may be filed at any time under paragraphs (3) and (5) of section 1064 of this title". Section 1064(3) provides that a mark may be cancelled if it is, or becomes, functional. Thus incontestability does not avoid the question whether the thermostat's round shape is functional.

. . .

It is not hard to think of three ways in which a round thermostat could be functional, at least in principle. First, rectangular objects may clash with other architectural or decorative choices. Just as a building designed by Ludwig Mies van der Rohe demands controls made from regular or semi-regular polyhedra, so a building designed by Frank Gehry could not tolerate boxy controls. Second, round thermostats (and other controls) may reduce injuries, especially to children, caused by running into protruding sharp corners. Third, people with arthritis or other disabilities may find it easier to set the temperature by turning a large dial (or the entire outer casing of the device) than by moving a slider or pushing buttons on boxes. The record does not contain much along any of these lines, but they are sufficiently plausible to disable Honeywell from prevailing at this preliminary stage, given the burden it bears as a result of the expired patents. Although the three possibilities we have mentioned do not show that roundness is "essential" to a thermostat, that's not required. *TrafFix* rejected an equation of functionality with necessity; it is enough that the design be useful. The Justices told us that a feature is functional if it is essential to the design *or* it affects the article's price or quality. 532 U.S. at 33.

Thus the district court did not abuse its discretion in holding that Eco may go forward with a round thermostat—at its own risk, of course, should the decision come out otherwise on the merits. Although we have not endorsed all of the district court's legal analysis, it would be pointless to remand for another hearing on interlocutory relief. The case should proceed expeditiously to final decision; another "preliminary" round would waste everyone's time. It would be especially inappropriate to direct the district judge to issue a preliminary injunction when issues other than functionality remain to be addressed. Eco contends, for example, that Honeywell bamboozled the Patent and Trademark Office when seeking registration during the 1980s, and material deceit would scotch this enforcement action whether or not the trade dress is functional. We do not express any view on that issue, or any ultimate view about functionality; it is enough to say that the record compiled to date adequately supports the district judge's interlocutory decision.

"AESTHETIC FUNCTIONALITY"

Au–Tomotive Gold, Inc. v. Volkswagen of America, Inc.

457 F.3d 1062 (9th Cir.2006).

■ McKEOWN, CIRCUIT JUDGE:

This case centers on the trademarks of two well-known automobile manufacturers—Volkswagen and Audi. The question is whether the Lanham Act prevents a maker of automobile accessories from selling, without a license or other authorization, products bearing exact replicas of the trademarks of these famous car companies. Au–Tomotive Gold, Inc. ("Auto Gold") argues that, as used on its key chains and license plate covers, the logos and marks of Volkswagen and Audi are aesthetic functional elements of the product—that is, they are "the actual benefit that the consumer wishes to purchase"—and are thus unprotected by the trademark laws.

Accepting Auto Gold's position would be the death knell for trademark protection. It would mean that simply because a consumer likes a trademark, or finds it aesthetically pleasing, a competitor could adopt and use the mark on its own products. Thus, a competitor could adopt the distinctive Mercedes circle and tri-point star or the well-known golden arches of McDonald's, all under the rubric of aesthetic functionality.

The doctrine of aesthetic functionality has a somewhat checkered history. In broad strokes, purely aesthetic product features may be protected as a trademark where they are source identifying and are not functional. On the other hand, where an aesthetic product feature serves a "significant non-trademark function," the doctrine may preclude protection as a trademark where doing so would stifle legitimate competition. *Qualitex Co. v. Jacobson Products Co.*, 514 U.S. 159, 170, 115 S. Ct. 1300, 131 L. Ed. 2d 248 (1995). Taken to its limits, as Auto Gold advocates, this doctrine would permit a competitor to trade on any mark simply because there is some "aesthetic" value to the mark that consumers desire. This approach distorts both basic principles of trademark law and the doctrine of functionality in particular.

Auto Gold's incorporation of Volkswagen and Audi marks in its key chains and license plates appears to be nothing more than naked appropriation of the marks. The doctrine of aesthetic functionality does not provide a defense against actions to enforce the trademarks against such poaching. Consequently, we reverse the district court's grant of summary judgment in favor of Auto Gold on the basis of aesthetic functionality. We also reverse the denial of Volkswagen and Audi's motion for summary judgment with respect to infringement and dilution and remand for further proceedings.

BACKGROUND

Volkswagen and Audi are manufacturers of automobiles, parts and accessories that bear well-known trademarks, including the names Volkswagen and Audi, the encircled VW logo, the interlocking circles of the Audi logo, and the names of individual car models. The marks are registered in the United States and have been in use since the 1950s.

Auto Gold produces and sells automobile accessories to complement specific makes of cars, including Cadillac, Ford, Honda, Lexus, Jeep, Toyota, and others. In 1994, Auto Gold began selling license plates, license plate frames and key chains bearing Volkswagen's distinctive trademarks and, in 1997, began selling similar products bearing Audi's distinctive trademarks. The marks used are exact replicas of the registered trademarks or, in at least some cases, genuine trademark medallions purchased from Volkswagen dealers; Auto Gold states that it "applies authentic [Volkswagen and Audi] logos to its marquee license plates."

According to Auto Gold, its goods serve a unique market. Consumers want these accessories "to match the chrome on their cars; to put something on the empty space where the front license tag would otherwise go; or because the car is a [Volkswagen or Audi], they want a [Volkswagen or Audi]-logo plate." Both Auto Gold and Volkswagen and Audi serve this market. Auto Gold sells its license plates, license plate covers, and key rings with Volkswagen and Audi trademarks to the wholesale market, including car dealers, auto accessory dealers and other merchants. Volkswagen and Audi, for their operations in the United States, license an independent marketing firm to sell license plates, covers, and key chains directly to consumers.

Auto Gold has license and marketing agreements with several car manufacturers, authorizing sales of auto accessories bearing those companies' trademarks. Despite several attempts to secure similar arrangements with Volkswagen and Audi, Auto Gold is not authorized to sell products with their trademarks. Instead, Auto Gold products are accompanied by disclaimers that deny any connection to Volkswagen or Audi. The disclaimers are not visible once the product is removed from the packaging and in use, nor are the disclaimers always clear. For example, some labels state that the product "may or may not" be dealer approved, and Auto Gold's website identifies its goods as "Factory authorized licensed products."

. . . .

ANALYSIS

The central question before us, discussed in Part I, is the scope of the doctrine of the "aesthetic functionality" and its application to the Volkswagen and Audi trademarks as they appear on Auto Gold's products . . . . .

I.   AESTHETIC FUNCTIONALITY

   A.   TRADEMARK LAW AND AESTHETIC FUNCTIONALITY

The principal role of trademark law is to ensure that consumers are able to identify the source of goods. *Qualitex*, 514 U.S. at 164. Protecting the source-identifying role of trademarks serves two goals. First, it quickly and easily assures a potential customer that *this* item—the item with the mark—is made by the same producer as other similarly marked products. At the same time, the law helps "assure a producer that it (and not an imitating competitor) will reap the financial, reputation-related rewards associated with a desirable product." *Id.; see also Avery Dennison Corp. v. Sumpton*, 189 F.3d 868, 873 (9th Cir. 1999).

A functional product feature does not, however, enjoy protection under trademark law. *See Qualitex*, 514 U.S. at 164. The Supreme Court has instructed that a feature is functional if it is "essential to the use or purpose of the article [or] affects [its] cost or quality." *Inwood Labs., Inc. v. Ives Labs., Inc.*, 456 U.S. 844, 851 n. 10, 102 S. Ct. 2182, 72 L. Ed. 2d 606 (1982). The *Inwood Laboratories* definition is often referred to as "utilitarian" functionality, as it relates to the performance of the product in its intended purpose. Thus, "[t]he functionality doctrine prevents trademark law, which seeks to promote competition by protecting a firm's reputation, from instead inhibiting legitimate competition by allowing a producer to control a useful product feature." *Qualitex*, 514 U.S. at 164.

Extending the functionality doctrine, which aims to protect "useful" product features, to encompass unique logos and insignia is not an easy transition. Famous trademarks have assumed an exalted status of their own in today's consumer culture that cannot neatly be reduced to the historic function of trademark to designate source. Consumers sometimes buy products bearing marks such as the Nike Swoosh, the Playboy bunny ears, the Mercedes tri-point star, the Ferrari stallion, and countless sports franchise logos, for the appeal of the mark itself, without regard to whether it signifies the origin or sponsorship of the product. As demand for these marks has risen, so has litigation over the rights to their use as claimed "functional" aspects of products. [Citations]

The results reached in these various aesthetic functionality cases do not easily weave together to produce a coherent jurisprudence, although as a general matter courts have been loathe to declare unique, identifying logos and names as functional. To understand how the concept of functionality applies to the case before us, broad invocations of principle are not particularly helpful. Instead, we find it useful to follow the chronological development and refinement of the doctrine.

The doctrine of aesthetic functionality is often traced to a comment in the 1938 Restatement of Torts:

> When goods are bought largely for their aesthetic value, their features may be functional because they definitely contribute to that value and thus aid the performance of an object for which the goods are intended.

Restatement of Torts § 742, comment a (1938) (see Restatement 3d of Unfair Competition, § 17 (1995)). Two examples of products with aesthetic functional features were offered, with very little comment—a heart-shaped candy box and a distinctive printing typeface.

Nearly fifteen years later, the doctrine blossomed in *Pagliero v. Wallace China Co.*, an action by Wallace China, a manufacturer of vitrified china, to prohibit a competitor from using a series of decorative patterns and a corresponding list of names. *See* 198 F.2d 339 (9th Cir. 1952). Neither the patterns nor the names were covered by registered trademarks or patents; instead, Wallace claimed secondary meaning, primarily that customers associated the patterns with Wallace, due to extensive advertising and a reputation for quality. *Id*. at 342. In ruling on Wallace's claim, we loosely echoed the 1938 Restatement in articulating the line between aesthetic appeal and functionality:

> [W]here the features are "functional" there is normally no right to relief. "Functional" in this sense might be said to connote other than a trade-mark purpose. If the particular feature is an important ingredient in the commercial success of the product, the interest in free competition permits its imitation in the absence of a patent or copyright....

Applying that test, the china patterns were deemed "functional" because the "attractiveness and eye-appeal" of the design is the primary benefit that consumers seek in purchasing china. *Id.* at 343–44. Thus, Wallace's designs were not "mere arbitrary embellishment," but were at the heart of basic consumer demand for the product and could not be protected as trademarks.

Almost thirty years later, *Pagliero* was revived in a Ninth Circuit case involving an effort by the International Order of Job's Daughters to preclude a jewelry maker from selling jewelry bearing the Job's Daughters insignia. *See International Order of Job's Daughters v. Lindeburg & Co.,* 633 F.2d 912 (9th Cir. 1980). Because the defendant's products bearing the Job's Daughters mark were sold "on the basis of their intrinsic value, not as a designation of origin or sponsorship," the defendant argued that they were functional under *Pagliero. Id.* at 918.

The court acknowledged that a "name or emblem" could, in some cases, "serve simultaneously as a functional component of a product and a trademark," and accordingly called for a "close analysis of the way in which [the defendant] is using the Job's Daughters insignia." *Id.* at 917–19. The court observed that Job's Daughters had submitted no evidence that the defendant's use of the mark either caused confusion as to source or was likely to do so and suggested that the emblem did not designate a source at all. Accordingly, the Job's Daughters insignia, as used by the defendant, was unprotected. *Id.* at 920.

Job's Daughters, with its collective mark, was a somewhat unique case and its broad language was soon clarified and narrowed. In *Vuitton [et Fils S.A. v. J. Young Enters., Inc.,* 644 F.2d 769 (9th Cir. 1981)], we confronted bare counterfeiting of Louis Vuitton handbags with minor alterations to the familiar LV logo and fleur-de-lis insignia. 644 F.2d at 774. ...Significantly, in *Vuitton,* we emphatically rejected the notion that "any feature of a product which contributes to the consumer appeal and saleability of the product is, as a matter of law, a functional element of that product." *Id.* at 773. Indeed, "a trademark which identifies the source of goods and incidentally services another function may still be entitled to protection." *Id.* at 775. Under *Vuitton,* the mere fact that the mark is the "benefit that the consumer wishes to purchase" will not override trademark protection if the mark is source-identifying. *Id.* at 774. With *Vuitton,* aesthetic functionality was dealt a limiting but not fatal blow; the case was remanded for trial. *Id.* at 776.

. . . .

The Supreme Court has yet to address aesthetic functionality as it applies to logos and insignia, in contrast to product features. The Court has, however, outlined the general contours of functionality and aesthetic functionality. As noted earlier, in *Inwood Laboratories*, the Court offered a simple definition of functionality: "a product feature is functional if it is essential to the use or purpose of the article or if it affects the cost or quality of the article." 456 U.S. at 850 n. 10 (citing *Kellogg Co. v. National Biscuit Co.*, 305 U.S. 111, 122, 59 S. Ct. 109, 83 L. Ed. 73, 1939 Dec. Comm'r Pat. 850 (1938)).

More recently, in *Qualitex*, the Court considered whether a color (a distinctive green-gold used on dry cleaning press pads) could be protected as a trademark. Observing that color alone can meet the basic legal requirement for a trademark, namely that it acts "as a symbol that distinguishes a firm's goods and identifies their source," the Court concluded that the use of color as a trademark is not *per se* barred by the functionality doctrine. *Qualitex*, 514 U.S. at 165–66 ("And, this latter fact—the fact that sometimes color is not essential to a product's use or purpose and does not affect cost or quality—indicates that the doctrine of 'functionality' does not create an absolute bar to the use of color alone as a mark"). The green-gold color of the dry cleaner pads served a trade-mark (i.e., source-identifying) function. Additionally, the use of *some* color on the pads served a non-trademark function—namely, to "avoid noticeable stains." *Id.* at 166. The Court underscored, however, that functionality protects against a competitive disadvantage "unrelated to recognition or reputation." *Id.* at 169. Accordingly, because "the [district] court found 'no competitive need in the press pad industry for the green-gold color, since other colors are equally usable,'" functionality did not defeat protection. *Id.* at 166.

The Court's most recent explication of aesthetic functionality is found in a case surprisingly not cited by the parties—*TrafFix Devices, Inc. v. Marketing Displays, Inc.*, 532 U.S. 23, 121 S. Ct. 1255, 149 L. Ed. 2d 164 (2001). In *TrafFix*, a company that held an expired patent for a dual-spring road sign design argued that the visible appearance of the design constituted protectable trade dress. In considering whether the dual spring mechanism was a functional aspect of the product, the Court clarified *Qualitex's* emphasis on competitive necessity and the overall test for functionality. Rather than paraphrase the decision, and to be absolutely clear, we quote extensively from the passages that set out the appropriate inquiry for functionality.

The Supreme Court emphasized that *Qualitex* did not displace the traditional *Inwood Laboratories* utilitarian definition of functionality. " '[I]n general terms, a product feature is functional,' and cannot serve as a trademark, 'if it is essential to the use or purpose of the article or if it affects the cost or quality of the article.' " *TrafFix*, 532 U.S. at 32 (quoting *Qualitex*, 514 U.S. at 165); *see also Inwood Labs.*, 456 U.S. at 850 n. 10. The Court noted that *Qualitex* "expand[ed] upon" the *Inwood Laboratories* definition, by observing that "a functional feature is one the 'exclusive use of [which] would put competitors at a significant non-reputation-related disadvantage.' " *TrafFix*, 532 U.S. at 32 (quoting *Qualitex*, 514 U.S. at 165) (alteration in original).

The Court explained the interplay between these two statements of functionality. If a feature is functional under *Inwood Laboratories*, the inquiry ends and the feature cannot be protected under trademark law. *Id.* As the Court elaborated, "there is no need to proceed further to consider if there is a competitive necessity for the feature." *Id.* at 33. Thus, in *Traf-Fix*, once the dual-spring mechanism met the traditional functionality test by making the signs more wind resistant, "there [was] no need to proceed further to consider if there is competitive necessity for the feature" and likewise no need "to engage . . . in speculation about other design possibilities." *Id.* at 33.

By contrast, the Court went on to suggest that "[i]t is proper to inquire into a 'significant non-reputation-related disadvantage' in cases of aesthetic functionality, the question involved in *Qualitex*." *Id.* The Court described aesthetic functionality as "the central question [in *Qualitex*], there having been no indication that the green-gold color of the laundry press pad had any bearing on the use or purpose of the product or its cost or quality." *Id.*

As to functionality, we read the Court's decision to mean that consideration of competitive necessity may be an appropriate but not necessary element of the functionality analysis. If a design is determined to be functional under the traditional test of *Inwood Laboratories* there is no need to go further to consider indicia of competitive necessity, such as the availability of alternative designs. *Accord Valu Eng'g, Inc. v. Rexnord Corp.*, 278 F.3d 1268, 1275–76 (Fed. Cir. 2002). However, in the context of aesthetic functionality, such considerations may come into play because a "functional feature is one the 'exclusive use of [which] would put competitors at a significant non-reputation related disadvantage.' " *TrafFix*, 532 U.S. at 32 (quoting *Qualitex*, 514 U.S. at 165); *see also Dippin' Dots, Inc. v. Frosty Bites Distrib., L.L.C.*, 369 F.3d 1197, 1203 (11th Cir. 2004); *Eppendorf–Netheler–Hinz GMBH v. Ritter GMBH*, 289 F.3d 351, 356 (5th Cir. 2002).

B. AESTHETIC FUNCTIONALITY AND AUTO GOLD'S USE OF VOLKSWAGEN AND AUDI'S PRODUCTS

So where do we stand in the wake of forty years of trademark law scattered with references to aesthetic functionality? After *Qualitex* and *TrafFix*, the test for functionality proceeds in two steps. In the first step, courts inquire whether the alleged "significant non-trademark function" satisfies the *Inwood Laboratories* definition of functionality—"essential to the use or purpose of the article [or] affects [its] cost or quality." *TrafFix*, 532 U.S. at 32–33 (citing *Inwood Laboratories*, 456 U.S. at 850, n. 10). If this is the case, the inquiry is over—the feature is functional and not protected. *TrafFix*, 532 U.S. at 33. In the case of a claim of aesthetic functionality, an alternative test inquires whether protection of the feature as a trademark would impose a significant non-reputation-related competitive disadvantage. *Id.; and see also Qualitex*, 514 U.S. at 165.

We now address the marks at issue in this case. Volkswagen and Audi's trademarks are registered and incontestable, and are thus presumed to be valid, distinctive and non-functional. *Aromatique, Inc. v. Gold Seal, Inc.*, 28 F.3d 863, 868–69 (8th Cir. 1994). Auto Gold, thus, must show that the marks are functional under the test set forth above. To satisfy this requirement, Auto Gold argues that Volkswagen and Audi trademarks are functional features of its products because "the trademark is the feature of the product which constitutes the actual benefit the consumer wishes to purchase." While that may be so, the fact that a trademark is desirable does not, and should not, render it unprotectable. Auto Gold has not shown that Volkswagen and Audi's marks are functional features of Auto Gold's products. The marks are thus entitled to trademark protection.

At the first step, there is no evidence on the record, and Auto Gold does not argue, that Volkswagen and Audi's trademarks are functional under the utilitarian definition in *Inwood Laboratories* as applied in the Ninth Circuit in *Talking Rain. See* 349 F.3d at 603–04. That is to say, Auto Gold's products would still frame license plates and hold keys just as well without the famed marks. Similarly, use of the marks does not alter the cost structure or add to the quality of the products.

We next ask whether Volkswagen and Audi's marks, as they appear on Auto Gold's products, perform some function such that the " 'exclusive use of [the marks] would put competitors at a significant non-reputation-related disadvantage. ' "*TrafFix*, 532 U.S. at 32 (quoting *Qualitex*, 532 U.S. at 165). As an initial matter, Auto Gold's proffered rationale—that the trademarks "constitute[] the actual benefit the consumer wishes to purchase"—flies in the face of existing caselaw. We have squarely rejected the notion that "any feature of a product which contributes to the consumer appeal and saleability of the product is, as a matter of law, a functional element of that product." *Vuitton*, 644 F.2d at 773 . . . . .

Even viewing Auto Gold's position generously, the rule it advocates injects unwarranted breadth into our caselaw. *Pagliero*, *Job's Daughters*, and their progeny were careful to prevent "the use of a trademark to monopolize a design feature which, *in itself and apart from its identification of source*, improves the usefulness or appeal of the object it adorns." *Vuitton*, 644 F.2d at 774 (discussing *Pagliero*, 198 F.2d 339) (emphasis added). The concept of an "aesthetic" function that is non-trademark-related has enjoyed only limited application. In practice, aesthetic functionality has been limited to product features that serve an aesthetic purpose wholly independent of any source-identifying function. *See Qualitex*, 514 U.S. at 166 (coloring dry cleaning pads served nontrademark purpose by avoiding visible stains); *Publications Int'l, Ltd. v. Landoll, Inc.*, 164 F.3d 337, 342 (7th Cir. 1998) (coloring edges of cookbook pages served nontrademark purpose by avoiding color "bleeding" between pages); *Brunswick Corp. v. British Seagull Ltd.*, 35 F.3d 1527, 1532 (Fed. Cir. 1994) (color black served nontrademark purpose by reducing the apparent size of outboard boat engine); *Pagliero*, 198 F.2d at 343 (china patterns at issue were attractive and served nontrademark purpose because "one of the essential selling features of hotel china, if, indeed, not the primary, is the design").

It is difficult to extrapolate from cases involving a true aesthetically functional feature, like a box shape or certain uses of color, to cases involving well-known registered logos and company names, which generally have no function apart from their association with the trademark holder. The present case illustrates the point well, as the use of Volkswagen and Audi's marks is neither aesthetic nor independent of source identification. That is to say, there is no evidence that consumers buy Auto Gold's products solely because of their "intrinsic" aesthetic appeal. Instead, the alleged aesthetic function is indistinguishable from and tied to the mark's source-identifying nature.

By Auto Gold's strident admission, consumers want "Audi" and "Volkswagen" accessories, not beautiful accessories. This consumer demand is difficult to quarantine from the source identification and reputation-enhancing value of the trademarks themselves. [Citation] The demand for Auto Gold's products is inextricably tied to the trademarks themselves. *See Qualitex*, 514 U.S. at 170 (identifying "legitimate (nontrademark-*related*) competition" as the relevant focus in determining functionality) (emphasis added). Any disadvantage Auto Gold claims in not being able to sell Volkswagen or Audi marked goods is tied to the reputation and association with Volkswagen and Audi.

. . . .

We hold that Volkswagen and Audi's marks are not functional aspects of Auto Gold's products. These marks, which are registered and have achieved incontestable status, are properly protected under the Lanham Act against infringement, dilution, false designation of source and other misappropriations.

QUESTION

Cartier sells expensive luxury watches. It promotes its watches through extensive advertising campaigns. Globe Jewelry makes watches that resemble Cartier watches in outward appearance, but retail for significantly lower prices. Globe's watches are almost indistinguishable from Cartier watches in design and shape, but do not bear the Cartier mark. Cartier sues Globe for trade dress infringement, claiming that Globe has infringed the trade dress of these Cartier watches:

Globe contends that the designs of the watches are functional, and therefore cannot be protected as trade dress. How should the court rule? *See Cartier, Inc. v. Four Star Jewelry Creations, Inc.*, 348 F.Supp.2d 217 (S.D.N.Y.2004).

3.   TRADE DRESS INFRINGEMENT

Gibson Guitar Corp. v. Paul Reed Smith Guitars

423 F.3d 539 (6th Cir.2005).

[Gibson Guitar Corporation has manufactured the Les Paul solid body guitar since 1952. Gibson registered the shape of the Les Paul guitar on the principal register in 1987. The mark is incontestable. Paul Reed Smith Guitars(PRS) introduced the Singlecut, a similarly shaped solid-body guitar, in 2000. Gibson sued PRS for trademark infringement. The district court granted Gibson's summary judgment motion on its trademark claim, and PRS appealed. Gibson conceded before the district court and on appeal that there was no point-of-sale confusion between its Les Paul guitars and PRS's SingleCut guitars. It nonetheless argued that the similarity in guitar shapes was likely to cause actionable confusion before and after the point of sale.]

■ KAREN NELSON MOORE, CIRCUIT JUDGE.

   1.   Gibson's Theories of Purchaser Confusion

   Gibson argues that despite the lack of actual confusion at the point of sale, the district court's decision can be affirmed under a theory of either initial-interest confusion (the theory relied on by the district court), post-sale confusion, or some combination of the two. Initial-interest confusion takes place when a manufacturer improperly uses a trademark to create initial customer interest in a product, even if the customer realizes, prior to purchase, that the product was not actually manufactured by the trademark-holder. [Citations] Post-sale confusion occurs when use of a trademark leads individuals (other than the purchaser) mistakenly to believe that a product was manufactured by the trademark-holder [Citation]. We conclude that neither initial-interest confusion, nor post-sale confusion, nor any combination of two, is applicable in this case.

Gibson Les Paul Guitar   PRS Singlecut Guitar

a. Initial–Interest Confusion

. . . .

Gibson essentially argues that the shape of the PRS guitar leads consumers standing on the far side of the room in a guitar store to believe they see Gibson guitars and walk over to examine what they soon realize are PRS guitars. We decline to adopt such a broad reading of the initial-interest-confusion doctrine. Many, if not most, consumer products will tend to appear like their competitors at a sufficient distance. Where product shapes themselves are trademarked, such a theory would prevent competitors from producing even *dissimilar* products which might appear, from the far end of an aisle in a warehouse store, somewhat similar to a trademarked shape. Accordingly, we hold that initial-interest confusion cannot substitute for point-of-sale confusion on the facts of this case.

b. Post–Sale Confusion

The one published case where we have applied post-sale confusion is also clearly distinguishable from the present case. *Esercizio [v. Roberts*, 944 F.2d 1235 (6th Cir. 1991), *cert. denied*, 505 U.S. 1219 (1992)], a trade-dress case, involved Ferrari sports cars which were manufactured in deliberately limited quantities "in order to create an image of exclusivity." *Esercizio*,

944 F.2d at 1237. The alleged infringer built fiberglass kits intended to be "bolted onto the undercarriage of another automobile such as a Chevrolet Corvette or a Pontiac Fiero" in order to make the "donor car" look like a far-more-expensive Ferrari. *Id.* at 1238. Our concern in *Esercizio* was that "Ferrari's reputation in the field could be damaged by the marketing of Roberts' [clearly inferior] replicas." *Id.* at 1245. Such a concern is not present here, where Gibson concedes that PRS guitars are not clearly inferior to Gibson guitars. Accordingly, post-sale confusion cannot serve as a substitute for point-of-sale confusion in this case.

c. Gibson's Smoky–Bar Theory of Confusion

Finally, Gibson argues that, taken together, the initial-interest-confusion and post-sale-confusion doctrines should be extended to include something that we can only describe as a "smoky-bar theory of confusion." Initial-interest-confusion doctrine, which we have already rejected on the facts of this case, applies when allegedly improper use of a trademark attracts potential purchasers to consider products or services provided by the infringer. Post-sale-confusion doctrine, which we have also rejected on the facts of this case, applies when allegedly improper use of protected trade dress on a lower-quality product diminishes the reputation of the holder of the rights to that trade dress. In the smoky-bar context, however, Gibson does not suggest that consumer confusion as to the manufacturer of a PRS guitar would lead a potential purchaser to consider purchasing a PRS, rather than a Gibson, or that Gibson's reputation is harmed by poor-quality PRS guitars. Rather, Gibson argues that this confusion occurs when potential purchasers see a musician playing a PRS guitar and believe it to be a Gibson guitar:

> In the context of guitar sales, initial interest confusion is of real consequence. Guitar manufacturers know that they can make sales by placing their guitars in the hands of famous musicians. On a distant stage, a smoky bar, wannabe musicians see their heroes playing a guitar they then want.

Gibson Br. at 20–21. As Gibson concedes that PRS produces high-quality guitars, we do not believe such an occurrence could result in confusion harmful to Gibson. If a budding musician sees an individual he or she admires playing a PRS guitar, but believes it to be a Gibson guitar, the logical result would be that the budding musician would go out and purchase a Gibson guitar. Gibson is helped, rather than harmed, by any such confusion.

2. The Summary Judgment Motions

We have determined as a matter of law that initial-interest confusion, post-sale confusion, and Gibson's "smoky-bar theory of confusion" cannot be used to demonstrate infringement of the trademark at issue in this case. Gibson has conceded that point-of-sale confusion does not occur between these high-priced guitars, and our review of the record does not suggest otherwise. Accordingly, there is simply no basis on which Gibson can show confusion that would demonstrate trademark infringement in violation of the Lanham Act. *See KP Permanent Make–Up, Inc. v. Lasting Impression I, Inc.*, 543 U.S. 111 (2004) (noting that a claim of trademark infringement under the Lanham Act "requires a showing that the defendant's actual practice is likely to produce confusion in the minds of consumers about the origin of the goods or services in question"). Accordingly, PRS, rather than Gibson, must be granted summary judgment on Gibson's trademark-infringement claim.

. . . .

■ KENNEDY, CIRCUIT JUDGE, concurring in part and dissenting in part.

I agree that the district court erred in granting summary judgment in favor of Gibson and I also agree that Gibson cannot maintain its trademark infringement claim either on a theory of likelihood of confusion at the point-of-sale (for it has disclaimed that a consumer could be confused at the point-of-sale) or on a theory of post-sale confusion. However, because I believe that a product shape trademark holder should be able to present evidence to maintain a trademark infringement claim on the theory of initial-interest confusion, I dissent with respect to this issue.

. . . .

The majority's reason for rejecting the application of initial interest confusion to product shapes is based upon the concern that since many product shapes within the same category will appear similar when viewed from a sufficient distance, if the initial-interest confusion doctrine were applied to product shapes, a product shape trademark holder could prevent competitors from producing even dissimilar products that appeared from a sufficient distance to be somewhat similar to a trademarked shape. This concern, however, is misplaced. Evidence that a competitor's product shape is similar to a trademark holder's product shape when viewed from afar is irrelevant unless the product shape trademark holder maintains that its product shape identifies its source when viewed from afar. For if a product shape trademark holder does not assert that its product shape identifies its source when viewed from a certain distance, then any alleged confusion between the trademark holder's product shape and a competitor's product shape would not support the trademark holder's claim for infringement. If a product shape trademark holder does assert that its product shape serves to identify the product's source when viewed from a distance where many competitor products appear substantially the same, then this will be evidence that the trademark holder's product shape does not identify its source. If most product shapes in the same product category have similar shapes, a product shape trademark holder will have a difficult time establishing that its trademark identifies the source of its product when viewed from afar, for the further one is away from a product, the more similar products in the same category will look to each other and, thus, the less likely a product shape will identify the source of the product (i.e. serve as a trademark) from that vantage point. In other words, a product shape trademark holder will not be able to present probative evidence of initial interest confusion unless it first shows that its product shape identifies its source when viewed from the vantage point where the confusion is alleged to have occurred.

Best Cellars Inc. v. Grape Finds at Dupont, Inc.

90 F.Supp.2d 431 (S.D.N.Y.2000).

■ SWEET, DISTRICT COURT JUDGE:

. . . .

Findings of Fact

Best Cellars operates retail wine stores in New York, New York, Brookline, Massachusetts, and Seattle, Washington. The company was founded by Joshua Wesson ("Wesson"), Green, and Richard Marmet ("Marmet").

Wesson is an internationally recognized wine expert who has worked in the field since 1979. He has received national and international awards as a sommelier. For several years, he worked for top New York and Boston restaurants, helping to select their wine lists. In 1986, he started a wine consulting business, the clients of which included both top restaurants and other businesses. Throughout this period, he also wrote numerous articles on wine. In 1989, he co-authored, with David Rosengarten, an award-winning book entitled "Red Wine With Fish," which discussed the concept of "wine by style," i.e., categorizing wine by taste and weight, rather than by grape type or place of origin.

Wesson continued to promote the "wine by style" concept through additional writings and frequent speaking engagements. In the early 1990's, he began to think about developing a new kind of retail wine store where people who knew little or nothing about wine could feel as comfortable when shopping as wine connoisseurs, and in which the "wine by style" concept could be implemented. The name "Best Cellars" came to him in 1993.

In 1994 or 1995, Wesson began to include Green, who at the time was working at Acker Merrall & Condit, an upscale New York retail wine store, in the discussions for the new store. In 1995, Wesson met Marmet, a practicing lawyer who had written all of the wine sections for Food and Wine magazine's cookbooks. Wesson, Green, and Marmet then set out to make the Best Cellars concept a reality.

Wesson, with the input of Marmet and Green, spent considerable time before and during the design phase of the first Best Cellars store refining the "wine by style" concept. Wesson eventually reduced the "world of wine" to eight taste categories: sparkling wines, light-, medium-, and full-bodied white wines, light-, medium-, and full-bodied red wines, and dessert wines. For each category, he selected, after a long winnowing process, a single word to serve as a "primary descriptor." Words which were "runners-up" for each category became "secondary descriptors." The eight primary descriptors are: "fizzy" (for sparkling wine), "fresh" (light-bodied white), "soft" (medium-bodied white), "luscious" (full-bodied white), "juicy" (light-bodied red), "smooth" (medium-bodied red), "big" (full-bodied red), and "sweet" (dessert wine). This conceptual reduction is the heart of the Best Cellars "system."

A principal reason Wesson reduced the world of wine to eight taste categories was in order to demystify wine for casual, non-connoisseur purchasers who might be intimidated purchasing wine in a traditional wine store, where wines are customarily organized by grape type and place of origin. To the uninitiated, of course, grape type and place of origin provide no ready clues to a wine's flavor. In addition, the vast number of grape types and places of origin could easily overwhelm a novice. For these same reasons, Wesson also decided to limit the number of wines for sale at Best Cellars to approximately one hundred, and to price those wines at ten dollars or less. It was also decided to offer fifteen or twenty more expensive wines for "special occasions."

. . . .

The design for the first Best Cellars retail store—on the Upper East Side in Manhattan—evolved to contain the following elements:

For each of the eight taste categories in the Best Cellars system, [Seattle design firm] Hornall Anderson came up with a corresponding color and a graphic image (an "icon-identifier") both to evoke and to reinforce the sensory associations of each category. Thus, for example, the "fizzy" category (sparkling wines) is represented by an ice-blue color and an icon suggesting bubbles rising, while the "fresh" category (light-bodied white wines) is represented by a lime-green color and an icon suggesting a slice of citrus fruit. The icon-identifiers, which are computer-manipulated drawings, are also meant to suggest wine stains. Before settling on the iconographic drawings, Hornall Anderson discussed the use of computer-enhanced photographs with Best Cellars. It was decided to reserve the use of photographic images for holiday and other special promotions.

The Rockwell architectural design is simple, elegant, and striking. The wines are primarily displayed along the perimeter walls of the store. A display bottle for each wine stands upright on a stainless-steel wire pedestal slightly above eye-level, so that the label on the bottle may be viewed by the customer. Under each display bottle, at eye-level, is a "shelf-talker": a 4″ x 4″ info card, designed by Hornall Anderson, providing the name of the wine, its vintage, a five-or six-line description of its taste, the type of grape from which it is made, its place of origin, a "FYI" blurb (often mentioning foods which the wine would complement), and its price. The top third of the shelf-talker has a color strip corresponding to the Best Cellars taste category to which the wine belongs.

Below each display bottle and its shelf-talker, nine additional bottles of the same wine are stored in a vertically arrayed racking system. The bottles in the vertical array lie horizontally in translucent Plexiglas tubes. The tubes are masked by a wall of light wood (American Sycamore) through which the individual bottles protrude slightly. Each of the openings through which the bottles protrude is trimmed with a thin ring of stainless steel. Because the perimeter walls of the store are built out so that they are flush with the "walls" of the racking system, and because the perimeter walls are built of the same light wood, it creates the impression that the bottles are literally stored in cubbyholes in the walls of the store.

The racking system, which is patented by Marmet, Wesson, and Trimble, is lit from behind, which causes the bottles to glow but does not harm the wine. The bottles can be placed in the tubes so that either the cork end or the bottom of the bottle is visible. Both methods of display are utilized, although the bottom method is more prevalent. The overall effect, which is quite striking, is of rows and rows of glowing bottles in the walls of the store. The wine is thus a decorative element.

Beneath the wall racks are drawers for storing additional bottles of wine. The drawers also serve a visual aesthetic function, providing a border strip between the racks and the floor, similar to baseboard molding or wainscotting. In addition, if the racks were to extend all the way to the floor, customers would have to stoop excessively to retrieve the lowest bottles. Thus, there is also an ergonomic aspect to the design.

The "walls of wine" do not extend along the entire perimeter of the store. The wall facing the street is glass, as is typical for a retail store, in order to attract passing foot traffic. The back wall has a limited amount of traditional "open shelving," i.e., shelves on which the non-display bottles of wine stand upright underneath the display bottles. In addition, the cash wrap[3] is recessed into the back wall, and to the right of the cash wrap (from the perspective of a customer looking into the store from the street entrance), there is a large placard on the wall explaining the Best Cellars system through the use of the primary and secondary descriptors, the colors, and the icon identifiers for the eight categories.

Above the wall racks are large signs, designed by Hornall Anderson, with the name of each taste category, together with its assigned color and icon-identifier. The categories are arranged in the following order as one moves clockwise around the store from the doorway: fizzy, fresh, soft, luscious, juicy, smooth, big, and sweet (corresponding to sparkling, light-, medium-, and full-bodied white, light-, medium-, and full-bodied red, and dessert wine, respectively). The wines displayed beneath each individual sign belong to the category identified by the sign. Also, affixed to each bottle of wine is a label with the Best Cellars name and logo, and the color, icon-identifier, and name of the category into which the wine has been classified.

Of course, the fixtures perimeter—the wine racks, the signs, and the storage drawers—while dominant in the design, are not its only elements. There is a plaster ceiling with track lighting, and a poured concrete floor. The wall behind the cash wrap is a burgundy-colored plaster with copper powder mixed in. The store has no fixed aisles, but in the floor space is a wooden table with benches, used for displays and wine tastings, and a

---

3. A "cash wrap" is a term for the area in a retail store where the retail goods are paid for and, if applicable, packaged by employees.

mobile cart, designed by Rockwell, with a stove and cook top for food preparation to accompany the wine tastings.

The dominant architectural material in the store is light wood. Stainless steel is used as a highlight: in the wire pedestals holding the display bottles, in the rings circling the holes in the racking system, and as trim on the cash wrap.

. . . .

Many of the design elements described above are not found in any other retail wine store, with the exception of Grape Finds. On average, a retail wine store in the U.S. carries about 500 different kinds of wine, displayed not only along the perimeter but throughout the floor space by the use of freestanding or built-in shelves. . . . No other store has a uniform display of shelf-talkers at eye level. No store arranges wine by taste category, along the perimeter, backlit in vertical arrays of nine, with storage cabinets underneath.

Other stores do, however, merchandise wine by displaying a single upright bottle, with additional bottles of the same wine stored in racks or open shelving beneath the display bottle. Light wood is a common material in retail stores generally and has been used in retail wine stores.

The concept of categorizing wine by taste and style, while it had not previously been utilized in any retail wine store, has been utilized by various writers of books on wine. These writers use differing numbers of categories. For example, Serena Sutcliffe, author of "The Wine Handbook," uses 14 categories. Fiona Beckett uses 12 categories in one book and 13 in another.

The Manhattan Best Cellars store opened in November 1996. It has received local, national, and international press coverage from a wide variety of general interest and wine industry publications, including Harper's, BusinessWeek, the Wall Street Journal, Food and Wine, and Wine and Spirits. The store has also been highlighted on local and national television programs, during which Wesson or other Best Cellars employees have been interviewed. An article in Wine Business Monthly, a publication serving the wine industry, stated that "Best Cellars is unlike any wine store that ever existed on Main Street, in cyberspace, or anywhere else."

. . . .

At some point prior to October 14, 1998, Best Cellars terminated Hornall Anderson (before the opening of the Brookline store, in October 1998) due to disagreement over how to improve Best Cellars' trade dress.

The Grape Finds story begins with Mazur, who attended Columbia Business School in New York from 1996 through May 1998, when he received an M.B.A. Mazur wanted to run his own business, and he had an interest in wine. While at Columbia, he discovered the Best Cellars New York store, which he has visited at least ten times. Mazur has also visited the Best Cellars web site between 100 and 200 times, and has downloaded hundreds of articles about Best Cellars from the LEXIS–NEXIS database.

Mazur had studied and admired Starbucks' phenomenally successful remerchandising of coffee retailing and saw in the Best Cellars model a way to do a similar remerchandising of wine retailing. Seeking to capitalize on Best Cellars' innovations, Mazur began to draft a business plan, cutting and pasting descriptions of the Best Cellars concept and design from the articles downloaded from LEXIS–NEXIS and substituting "Grape Finds" for "Best Cellars."

After graduation, Mazur moved to the Washington, D.C. metropolitan area and began to implement a plan to open a Grape Finds retail wine store using the Best Cellars conceptual model. Mazur was assisted in his enterprise by his father, Jack Mazur, from whom at least some business advice and some funding came. Jack Mazur is a former attorney who surrendered his license to practice law in conjunction with a lawsuit initiated against him for fraud.

[In 1999, Mazur purchased a liquor store in the Dupont Circle are of Washington DC. He hired architect Theodore Adamstein to design the interior of the store and Hornall Anderson to do the graphic design.] The store opened on December 3, 1999.

The leased space is narrow and deep, with one large window looking out onto the street. The exterior of the store has a curved awning above the window, which echoes the vaulted ceiling inside the store. The echo is continued with a long, curved door handle. A purple blade sign "slices" through the awning. The Grape Finds logo bears no resemblance to the Best Cellars logo.

Inside, there are many marked similarities to the Best Cellars store. First, the display is organized according to eight taste categories: CRISP-finds, MELLOWfinds, RICHfinds, FRUITYfinds, SMOOTHfinds, BOLD-finds, BUBBLYfinds, and SWEETfinds, corresponding to light-, medium-, and full-bodied whites, light-, medium-, and full-bodied reds, sparkling, and dessert wines (i.e., the same eight categories in the Best Cellars classification system).[5]

Mazur admitted that he copied the Best Cellars category system. Moreover, many of the Grape Finds primary and secondary descriptors ... were copied from the primary and secondary descriptors used by Best Cellars, although the words were rearranged slightly. In many cases, words among the Best Cellars secondary descriptors appear as primary descriptors in the Grape Finds system, while Best Cellars' primary descriptors appear among Grape Finds' secondary descriptors.

As with Best Cellars, Grape Finds has assigned to each taste category a corresponding color and icon-identifier, likewise designed by Hornall Anderson. The categories are likewise arranged in the store in systematic order. There are approximately 100 value-priced wines displayed around the perimeter of the store. Most significantly, each display wine is placed

---

5. These categories, which form the heart of the Grape Finds "system," also appear throughout Grape Finds' promotional materials, on its web site, and in its business plan and private placement memorandum.

slightly above eye-level, on a stainless steel pedestal held in place by stainless steel wire. At eye-level, directly underneath the display bottle, is a square shelf-talker, formatted, once again, by Hornall Anderson, containing almost the identical set of information as the Best Cellars shelf talkers. Under each Grape Finds shelf-talker, nine bottles are horizontally stored in a stainless steel rack. The bottles are held in stainless-steel cradles lined with cork to protect the bottles. There is no "wall" concealing the bottles as there is in the Best Cellars stores, yet the effect of the nine-bottle vertical array wrapping around the perimeter of the store gives the same design feel of a "wall of wine." Moreover, lights above the racks are directed down; much of this light bounces against the wall behind the racks, thereby indirectly backlighting the bottles and causing them to glow. As in Best Cellars, beneath the racks are storage cabinets, creating the same visual look of an equivalent to baseboard molding or wainscotting.

On the walls above the bottle racks, around the perimeter of the store, as in Best Cellars' stores, are large signs denoting the categories. While the signs were created as a continuous thirty-foot-long computer-enhanced photographic mural, the presence of vertical stainless-steel blades (which divide the category sections), and the need to chop the mural into at least three sections (one continuous section along the left wall (from the perspective of a customer looking into the store from the doorway), and two sections along the right wall, broken up by the cash wrap, above which is a color-coded placard explaining the Grape Finds system) reduces the sense of a continuous mural and makes it more similar to the Best Cellars wall signs.

Each mural section corresponds to, and serves to identify, one of the eight categories in the Grape Finds system. Thus, each section has a unique, computer-enhanced photograph of wine swirling in a glass, the title of the category (e.g., "MELLOWfinds," "RICHfinds"), and a corresponding color palette.

The combination of these visual elements—color-coded, iconographic wall signs identifying taste categories, single display bottles on stainless-steel wire pedestals along the store perimeter, identical color-coded textually formatted square shelf talkers below the display bottles, vertical arrays of nine glowing bottles stacked horizontally, and a strip of cabinets or drawers between the wine racks and the floor—dominates the overall look of both the Best Cellars and the Grape Finds stores.

There are differences between the two stores. The Grape Finds store has a vaulted ceiling, meant to evoke a wine cellar. It is a prominent design feature. The floor of the store is cork. There are eleven mobile boxes in the store which can be used as seats, for display, and for storage of additional cases of wine. The boxes are arranged in varying ways on the store floor.

There is an alcove space at the back of the store where a wooden table and several chairs are located for wine tastings. In the alcove there is also traditional shelving with smoked glass panels. Grape Finds does not have a mobile cart for food preparation.

Stainless steel is more prominent in the Grape Finds design. As mentioned, there are stainless steel blades running from floor to ceiling, dividing the categories. On each blade is written the primary and the secondary descriptors for the Grape Finds category marked off by that blade.

The cash wrap is on wheels, has a linoleum top, has shelves along the front and top, is curved, and is finished with metal. It is located at the middle of one of the long walls.

There is no burgundy wall in the Grape Finds store.

The layout of the Grape Finds store resembles a wine bottle, though Adamstein testified that this was more happenstance based on the configuration of the lease space than deliberate design.

. . . .

Although Mazur testified that he did not intend to copy the Best Cellars trade dress or brochure, Mazur is not a credible witness. . . .

Conclusions of Law

. . . .

a. *Trade Dress Infringement*

. . . .

To establish a claim of trade dress infringement under § 43(a), a plaintiff must demonstrate (1) "that its trade dress is either inherently distinctive or that it has acquired distinctiveness through a secondary meaning," (2) "that there is a likelihood of confusion between defendant's trade dress and plaintiff's," *Fun–damental Too [v. Gemmy Industries*, 111 F.3d 993 (2d Cir. 1997),], *111 F.3d at 999* (citing *Two Pesos, 505 U.S. at 769–70); see also Jeffrey Milstein [v. Greger, Lawlor, Roth, Inc.*, 58 F.3d 27 (2d Cir.1995)], at 31, and (3) where, as here, the dress has not been registered, that the design is non-functional. See *15 U.S.C. § 1125*(a)(3).

i. *Best Cellars' Trade Dress Is Inherently Distinctive*

The inherent distinctiveness of a trademark or trade dress is evaluated under the test set forth by Judge Friendly in *Abercrombie & Fitch Co. v. Hunting World, Inc., 537 F.2d 4, 9 (2d Cir.1976)*. [Citations] Under the *Abercrombie* test,

> trade dress is classified on a spectrum of increasing distinctiveness as generic, descriptive, suggestive, or arbitrary/fanciful. Suggestive and arbitrary or fanciful trade dress are deemed inherently distinctive and thus always satisfy the first prong of the test for protection. A descriptive trade dress may be found inherently distinctive if the plaintiff establishes that its mark has acquired secondary meaning giving it distinctiveness to the consumer. A generic trade dress receives no Lanham Act protection.

Fun–damental Too, 111 F.3d at 1000 (citing *Two Pesos,* 505 U.S. at 768–69*).* "Although each element of a trade dress individually might not be inherently distinctive, it is the combination of elements that should be the focus of the distinctiveness inquiry. Thus, if the overall dress is arbitrary, fanciful, or suggestive, it is distinctive despite its incorporation of generic [or functional] elements." *Jeffrey Milstein,* 58 F.3d at 32. Because there is a "virtually unlimited" number of ways to combine elements to make up the total visual image that constitutes a trade dress, "a product's trade dress typically will be arbitrary or fanciful and meet the inherently distinctive requirement for § 43(a) protection." *Fun–damental Too,* 111 F.3d at 1000 (citing *Mana Prods., Inc. v. Columbia Cosmetics Mfg., Inc.,* 65 F.3d 1063, 1069 (2d Cir.1995); *Chevron Chem. Co. v. Voluntary Purchasing Groups, Inc.,* 659 F.2d 695, 703 (5th Cir.1981)).[11]

On the other hand, "an idea, a concept, or a generalized type of appearance" cannot be protected under trade dress law, although "the concrete expression of an idea in a trade dress has received protection." *Jeffrey Milstein,* 58 F.3d at 32–33 (citing cases). This can be a difficult distinction to draw, and in doing so "a helpful consideration will be the purpose of trade dress law: to protect an owner of a dress in informing the public of the source of its products, without permitting the owner to exclude competition from functionally similar products." *Id.* at 33.

Best Cellars has met its burden under the standard for a preliminary injunction, set forth above, of establishing the inherent distinctiveness of its trade dress. Under the *Abercrombie* analysis, the trade dress of Best Cellars is arbitrary. This arbitrary trade dress consists of the total visual image which a customer entering a Best Cellars store encounters—an image that was acknowledged as unique by both Mazur and Adamstein in their testimony. As described above in the "Facts" section of this opinion, a huge number of articles written about the Best Cellars stores have focused on the distinctiveness of their look. The unique design—both the architectural component and the graphical component—has been further acknowledged in numerous awards. The point does not need to be belabored; the Best Cellars stores look like no other wine stores. Best Cellars achieved its goal of designing an "anti-wine store." As such, the trade dress is not suggestive of the product being sold, let alone descriptive or generic.

Best Cellars sets forth fourteen specific elements which it believes constitute the uniqueness of its trade dress: (1) eight words differentiating taste categories; (2) eight colors differentiating taste categories; (3) eight computer-manipulated images differentiating taste categories; (4) taste categories set above display fixtures by order of weight; (5) single display bottles set on stainless-steel wire pedestals; (6) square 4x4 shelf talkers with text arranged by template; (7) shelf talkers positioned at eye level, below each display bottle; (8) bottles vertically aligned in rows of nine; (9)

---

11. Under this standard, many trade dresses are likely to be found to be inherently distinctive. Fears of a slippery slope, however, are alleviated because the ease of meeting the inherent distinctiveness prong is balanced in trade dress cases by the difficulty of meeting the likelihood of confusion prong.

storage closets located beneath vertically aligned bottles; (10) materials palette consisting of light wood and stainless steel; (11) mixture of vertical racks and open shelving display fixtures; (12) no fixed aisles; (13) bottles down and back-lit; and (14) limited selection (approximately 100) of value-priced wines.

The essence of the look, however, is the "wall of wine," i.e., the color-coded, iconographic wall signs identifying eight taste categories above single display bottles on stainless-steel wire pedestals which run along the store perimeter, above identical color-coded textually formatted square shelf-talkers, above vertical arrays of nine glowing bottles stacked horizontally, above a strip of cabinets or drawers which extend to the floor.

Defendants put forth several reasons why Best Cellars' trade dress is not inherently distinctive, but none is compelling. First, Defendants maintain that Best Cellars has failed to meet its burden of demonstrating that its trade dress is non-functional. . . . See 15 U.S.C. § 1125(a)(3). A feature of a trade dress is functional when it is " 'essential to the use or purpose of the article or if it affects the cost or quality of the article,' that is, if the exclusive use of the feature would put competitors at a significant non-reputation-related disadvantage." *Qualitex Co. v. Jacobson Prods. Co.,* 514 U.S. 159, 165(1995) (quoting *Inwood Lab., Inc. v. Ives Lab., Inc.,* 456 U.S. 844, 850 n. 10 (1982)). . . .

Under this legal standard, it is unnecessary to examine laboriously, and in detail, each element of Best Cellars' claimed trade dress in order to make a determination of non-functionality. . . . [T]here is nothing inherently functional about a vertical array of identical bottles of wine to begin with. There are countless examples of wine stores which do not use vertical arrays; indeed, many of the design ideas generated by Rockwell in the planning stages involved non-vertical arrays. In fact, many of the elements of Best Cellars' trade dress, while containing arguably functional components, contain equally non-functional components.

In any event, Best Cellars has made a sufficient showing that at least some of the elements of its trade dress are not commonly used or functional, which is all that is required under the law. See *Jeffrey Milstein,* 58 F.3d at 32.

. . . .

Defendants are correct that Best Cellars cannot protect under trade dress law its concept of selling wine by taste. However, protection is possible for the "concrete expression" of the concept in the trade dress that Best Cellars has developed. *Jeffrey Milstein,* 58 F.3d at 33.

Finally, Defendants maintain that Best Cellars cannot show that it has developed secondary meaning in its trade dress. However, as a matter of law, of course, such a showing is not required if inherent distinctiveness has been shown, as it has been in this case. See *Two Pesos,* 505 U.S. at 769.

ii.   There Is a Substantial Likelihood of Confusion Between the Trade Dresses of Best Cellars and Grape Finds

Courts in this Circuit apply an eight-factor test, drawn from *Polaroid Corp. v. Polarad Electronics Corp.*, 287 F.2d 492 (2d Cir.1961), to determine the likelihood of confusion between the trade dress of two competitors.... While the factors are meant to be a guide, the inquiry ultimately hinges on whether an ordinarily prudent person would be confused as to the source of the allegedly infringing product. Here, that inquiry can be put as follows: is there a substantial likelihood that an ordinarily prudent consumer would, when standing in the Grape Finds store, think he was standing in a Best Cellars store? As the eight-factor analysis below will demonstrate, the answer to that question, weighing the facts in the context of a preliminary injunction hearing, is yes.

1.   Strength of the Trade Dress

. . . .

Arbitrary dress is by its very nature distinctive and strong. [Citation] However, this strength may be diminished by the existence of similar dresses used in connection with similar products. [Citation] Dresses that lack distinctiveness and fall on the lower end of the scale are classified as weak and are entitled to limited scope of protection....

Under this standard, Best Cellars' trade dress is quite strong. As set forth above, the dress is best classified as ''arbitrary'' under the *Abercrombie* analysis. Moreover, there is no similar dress used in connection with the retail sale of wine. Finally, although it is not required here in order to find that the dress is strong, there is evidence that the dress has acquired secondary meaning. While there is no evidence of advertising expenditures or customer studies linking the dress to a source, there has been an abundance of unsolicited media coverage of Best Cellars, there is demonstrated sales success, and the dress has been exclusively used by Best Cellars since the fall of 1996. Also, as set forth below, the Grape Finds trade dress involves a deliberate attempt to copy the Best Cellars dress. These facts provide at least some evidence of secondary meaning. In sum, Best Cellars' trade dress is quite strong.

2.   Similarity Between the Trade Dresses

. . . .

As described above, the dominant visual element of both the Best Cellars and the Grape Finds store is the wall of wine. Neither the vaulted ceiling, nor the exterior, nor the cork floor, nor the multi-purpose cubes, nor the steel racking system, nor any other difference in the Grape Finds store, significantly modifies the overall visual effect achieved by merchandising the eight categories of wines almost exclusively along the perimeter walls of the store, with display bottles set at a uniform height, identical shelf talkers, nine bottles lying on their side in a vertical array, wall signs above and cabinets below. While the Grape Finds trade name is displayed both outside and inside the store, the name is not recognizable and thus carries less weight. In sum, the evidence demonstrates a significant probability that numerous ordinarily prudent customers in the Grape Finds store will be confused as to whether they are, in fact, in a Best Cellars store.

3. The Proximity of the Products

. . . .

The products here are indisputably similar: value-priced bottles of wine. As for the structure of the relevant market, there are also similarities. The class of customers is nearly identical. Both stores target consumers who are not necessarily wine connoisseurs. No evidence has been presented about advertising. The channels through which the goods are sold are the stores themselves, as well as mail-order sales through the respective web sites.

Moreover, while there is certainly a geographical distance between the Grape Finds store in Washington, D.C. and the nearest Best Cellars store in Manhattan, Best Cellars has already received nationwide recognition of its product and conducts mail-order sales in many states. More crucially, it is undisputed that both Grape Finds and Best Cellars envision a "national rollout" of stores. . . .

In sum, there is considerable proximity between the products.

4. Bridging the Gap

. . . . Here, there is no gap to bridge: Best Cellars and Grape Finds sell the same products in the same field. This factor, therefore, also favors Best Cellars.

5. Evidence of Actual Confusion

Best Cellars has presented some evidence of actual confusion. Several individuals who know Wesson and Marmet informed them that a "copycat" or "knock off" store was opening in Washington, and several customers were overheard outside the Grape Finds store remarking that it looked like a store in Brookline, while a customer inside the store asked whether Grape Finds had a sister store in New York and Boston. Because no survey or other type of systematic research was conducted, however, too much weight cannot be attached to this evidence. The comments are anecdotal, and it is possible that confusion arose because the concepts—selling wine by taste—are similar.

However, "it is black letter law that actual confusion need not be shown to prevail under the Lanham Act, since actual confusion is very difficult to prove and the Act requires only a likelihood of confusion as to source." *Lois Sportswear, U.S.A. v. Levi Strauss & Co.*, 799 F.2d 867, 875 (2d Cir.1986); *see Centaur Communications*, 830 F.2d at 1227. Given the very brief period of time Grape Finds was open prior to the hearing on this preliminary injunction, it is understandable that Best Cellars would not be able to gather more evidence of actual confusion. *See Time Inc. Magazine*

Co. v. Globe Communications Corp., 712 F.Supp. 1103, 1111 (S.D.N.Y. 1989). Since some evidence of actual confusion has been presented, this factor also weighs, however slightly, in favor of Best Cellars.

6. Grape Finds' Bad Faith

. . . .

Given the overwhelming evidence of copying by Mazur of so many aspects of the Best Cellars business, it strains credulity to think that the reproduction of the trade dress—in particular, the "wall of wine"—in the Grape Finds store was not meant to capitalize on the reputation, goodwill, and any confusion between Grape Finds and Best Cellars. . . .

7. The Quality of Grape Finds' Products

No evidence has been presented that Grape Finds' products are inferior to those of Best Cellars. This factor therefore favors Grape Finds.

8. Sophistication of Purchasers

. . . .

This factor also favors Best Cellars. Both stores are specifically targeting non-sophisticated wine purchasers, and the overwhelming majority of wines sold in each store are priced at the lower end of the spectrum.

. . . .

iii. Best Cellars Is Entitled to a Preliminary Injunction on its Lanham Act Claim

Because Best Cellars has demonstrated a substantial likelihood that (1) its trade dress is distinctive, and (2) that there is a likelihood of confusion between its trade dress and the trade dress of Grape Finds, it has demonstrated that it is likely to prevail on the merits of its trade dress claim. As set forth above, because it has demonstrated a substantial likelihood of confusion, irreparable harm is assumed. Therefore, it has met the requirements for a preliminary injunction.

Grape Finds will be enjoined from continuing to display its eight categories of wines in the precise configuration of its present "wall of wine," which is the essential visual element of Best Cellars' trade dress. It must find a way to display its wines other than by single display bottles at a uniform height around the perimeter of the store, with shelf-talkers underneath, with nine bottles lying horizontally in a vertical array. Altering its trade dress in this manner will suffice to eliminate confusion between the two stores.

The other aspects of the Grape Finds store which Best Cellars has claimed are infringing do not have to be changed. Thus, the use of eight words, colors, and images to describe eight categories, of light wood and stainless steel, of open flooring, of wall signs above the display bottles and wine racks, and of a limited selection of value-priced wines can be retained.

.   .   .   .

QUESTION

What are the elements of Best Cellars' protected trade dress? The colors, names and images designating its eight taste categories? The light wood and stainless steel décor? The color-coded wall signs? The layout and arrangement of wine bottles? On pages 526–27, Judge Sweet lists 14 elements that plaintiff claimed as elements of its protected trade dress. How many of these elements does Judge Sweet determine are entitled to protection? How many of these elements did Grape Finds copy?

Best Cellars v. Wine Made Simple, 320 F.Supp.2d 60 (S.D.N.Y. 2003). Best Cellars brought a trade dress infringement suit against a second purveyor of wines by taste categories. Like Grape Finds, defendant Wines Made Simple operated a wine store that sold moderately priced wines sorted into eight taste categories. Judge Gerard Lynch agreed with Best Cellars that the trade dress of its stores was inherently distinctive, but found it more difficult to determine whether Wines Made Simple infringed it:

> Plaintiff Best Cellars owns and operates four wine stores, including its flagship store on the Upper East Side of Manhattan, which pursue the novel marketing strategy of organizing wines by taste category rather than by grape type or country of origin. The flagship store has a clean, crisp, modern decor that demonstrates that the owners invested energy and capital in the design of the store as well as in the development of the marketing theme. Best Cellars opened its flagship store in November 1996. . . . The interior design included wine racks built into a wall, which consist of tubes to hold bottles of wine horizontally, creating the appearance of a grid of steel rimmed holes in a light wood-paneled wall. The graphic design elements include computer-generated icons and brightly colored signs associated with each taste category.
>
> . . .
>
> Like Best Cellars, Bacchus aims to sell wine to novice wine consumers by organizing the store's inventory by taste category, and by retailing modestly-priced wines in an imaginatively-decorated store. The Bacchus stores have a Mediterranean-themed decor consisting of white stucco and dark wood beams, and display wine bottles horizontally in racks which are constructed to resemble a grid of holes in a white stucco wall.
>
> . . .
>
> In this case, it is undisputed that there are a number of similarities between the interior designs of plaintiff's and defen-

dants' stores. Both stores have racks of wine arranged around the perimeter of the store. The wine racks store the wine bottles horizontally in what appears to be a grid of holes in a wall. Both stores have one display bottle of wine presented vertically above a column of that identical wine stored horizontally in holes. Both stores have a method of illuminating the wine racks from behind the wine bottles. Both stores separate wine into eight taste categories, in addition to one to two other non-taste-based categories. Each taste category is identified by single words describing a taste property. Both stores have a farm table for display. Both stores have signs above the wine racks indicating the category stored in that area. Both stores use index card identifiers posted at eye-level on the wine racks describing individual wines. Both stores use different individual colors on signs and index cards to identify the categories of wine. Both stores sell books about wine as well as wineglasses and other items related to wine drinking. Both stores stock approximately 100 different varieties of wine that retail for less than 20 dollars a bottle.

On the other hand, it is also undisputed that there are a number of dissimilar elements between the store designs. Plaintiff's dominant building materials are blonde wood paneling and stainless steel detail, while defendants use primarily white stucco and dark-brown stained wood beams. Plaintiff's store prominently features large color-coded signs containing unique computer-generated graphics that serve as iconic identifiers for the different categories of wine. In fact, plaintiff has won numerous awards for its computer-generated graphics and has sought and received trademark protection for those graphic designs. Defendants utilize no such icon-coding system, and rely instead on tarnished-looking metal signs with no pictorial image to identify the different categories of wine. The lettering of defendants' category signs appears to be roughly cut out of the sheet of metal that comprises each sign. While each sign is of the same colored metal, the lettering of each sign is in the unique color associated with the category of wine. Plaintiff's and defendants' stores use different colors and different names to delineate categories of wine. Plaintiff has sought and received trademark protection for the specific words used to identify six of its eight taste categories. Plaintiff does not allege that defendants infringed any trademarked element of plaintiff's trade dress such as the icon identifiers or the specific category names. The only graphic image associated with defendants' store is a classically-styled painted "fresco" of Bacchus, the Roman god of wine for whom the store is named. In contrast, plaintiff's trade dress does not associate its store with any personality, either human or divine, and plaintiff's store features modern computer graphic images, not faux-classical painted images. The names of the stores too are not similar. To state the obvious, the name "Best Cellars" is a play on words, punning between a "best seller" as a popular consumer item, and a "best cellar" in the sense of a superior wine collection. The name "Bacchus" straightforwardly references a mythological enjoyer of wine. It is undisputed that the store names figure prominently in both defendants' and plaintiff's respective trade dress.

Overall Visual Image

What *is* disputed is the overall effect of the interior decor of the wine stores on consumer perception of those stores. Courts are instructed to proceed very carefully with respect to the similarity of the overall impression of trade dress, because issues of consumer confusion are normally factual in nature and thus rarely appropriate for summary judgment. [Citation] A judge can look at photographs of the respective stores and form his or her own opinion of how similar they appear. Undoubtedly, there will be cases where the similarity is so patent, or the divergence so dramatic, that reasonable jurors necessarily must agree that the appearances are either closely similar or distinctly different. But in most cases, the subjectivity of perception counsels judges not to assume that their assessment of overall similarity will necessarily be shared by all reasonable jurors. In this case, as is apparent from the listing of similar and different features of the stores' trade dress, the question is really whether the similar features or the divergent ones dominate the viewer's response to the overall "look" of the stores. This is a matter about which reasonable people can easily differ.

In this case, moreover, the interaction of marketing theme with trade dress presents an additional complication. " 'An idea, a concept, or a generalized type of appearance' cannot be protected under trade dress law, although 'the concrete expression of an idea in a trade dress has received protection.' " *Grape Finds*, 90 F.Supp.2d at 451, quoting *Jeffrey Milstein*, 58 F.3d at 32–33 (internal citations omitted). The idea of marketing wine by taste, however innovative it may be, is not protected by trade dress law, and Best Cellars cannot invoke the Lanham Act to preserve a monopoly on operating retail stores that categorize wines by taste. "Uniqueness of an idea and not the trade dress itself is not a proper basis upon which a court can base a finding that a trade dress is capable of being a source identifier. The connection must be between the trade dress and the product, not the idea and the product." *Sports Traveler* [*Inc. v. Advance Magazine Publishers, Inc.*, 25 F.Supp.2d 154, 163 (S.D.N.Y. 1998)], 25 F.Supp.2d at 163.

In this case, plaintiff claims, in effect, that its (formerly) unique marketing style is part of its trade dress. Uniqueness of marketing style is not a factor in the *Polaroid* test, and this Court will discount marketing theme in its analysis of the similarity of the trade dresses because that alone is not the focus of the legal inquiry. When the analytic focus is trained on trade dress, that is, on the general appearance of the interior decor of the stores which includes a marketing concept, rather than on marketing ideas alone, then the stores appear similar in some key respects, and dissimilar on others. Plaintiff's store is characterized by light wood-paneled walls, stainless steel finishings and brightly colored computer-generated icons. Defendants' store, by contrast, presents an atmosphere distinguished by white stucco walls with dark wood beams, rusted metal signs, and a classically-styled painting of the Roman god of wine. Rather than slavishly imitating plaintiff's decor, defendants have deviated from it in very significant ways. The similarity of the wine rack system is apparent, but is merely one element in the general appearance of the stores. The similarity of the categories of wine is also apparent, but the stores use different names for the categories and different colors associated with the categories as well as very different signs. Reasonable viewers could well disagree about whether the similarities outweigh the differences, or vice versa, in determining the overall similarity or differences of the decor.

Conclusion

Because in this case the similarity of the marks element is at the heart of the consumer confusion prong of the trade dress infringement test, and because reasonable minds could disagree as to the degree of similarity, this question is not suited for summary judgment. For this reason, and because there are material issues of fact as to virtually all of the Polaroid factors in this case, plaintiff's and defendants' cross-motions for summary judgment on the Lanham Act 43(a) claim for injunctive relief are denied.

QUESTIONS

1. Philip Morris, makers of Marlboro cigarettes, sued Cowboy Cigarettes for trade dress infringement. Cowboy markets its Cowboys Cigarettes in a red package showing the silhouette of a cowboy on a horse. The Cowboys package design does not resemble the design of the Marlboros package, but Philip Morris argues that its long use of cowboy imagery to promote Marlboros is itself trade dress, and Cowboy's use of cowboy imagery and the Cowboys name constitutes trade dress infringement. How should the court rule? *See Philip Morris USA v. Cowboy Cigarette*, 70 U.S.P.Q.2d 1092 (S.D.N.Y.2003).

2. J.K. Rowling's Harry Potter books have been wildly successful. The books follow Harry, a talented young wizard, through his years as a student at Hogwarts School of Witchcraft and Wizardry. The U.S. book publishing, motion picture and merchandising rights are owned by Scholastic Books and Warner Brothers Pictures. Warner Brothers has made five Harry Potter movies, and has tentative plans for a sixth and seventh. Warner Brothers has registered the marks HARRY POTTER and HOGWARTS for motion pictures, toys, calendars, figurines, candy, clothing, and art.

The Fox Creek School is a non-profit private school. Although Fox Creek's tuition is substantial, it is not able to meet its budget on tuition alone. It relies on outside foundation support and a variety of fundraising activities for additional funds. The most important of its fundraising activities is a summer day camp program, which it views both as a chance to recruit new potential students and an opportunity to raise significant funds to offset the substantial deficit incurred during the school year. The summer camp program offers one-week sessions to children from age 5 to age 13, focusing on a variety of subjects. Recent summer sessions have featured Spanish, astronomy, Arabic, filmmaking, computer programming, gardening, Japanese, chemistry, and tournament chess.

By far the most popular and successful summer camp program at Fox Creek is one that it calls "A Week at Hogwarts." Fox Creek introduced the Hogwarts camp four years ago. The camp was full within a week of its announcement. The following year, Fox Creek offered two one-week sessions of Hogwarts camp, but was unable to fulfill demand. Last year, Fox Creek ran three one-week sessions; this coming year, it is planning on at least four. The camp is inspired by and based on J.K. Rowling's Harry Potter books and the Warner Brothers movies derived from those books.

Fox Creek advertises its camp on its website, in flyers it distributes to its students, and in ads placed in local newspapers. The ads, which do not mention either Scholastic Books or Warner Brothers, explain that

> *A Week at Hogwarts* is our overwhelmingly popular Harry Potter camp. Fox Creek is transformed into Hogwarts School, where the summer campers learn sorcery and spells, play Quidditch, and encounter many of the characters from the Harry Potter books. Summer fun at its best!

Fox Creek has not sought permission from Rowling, Warner Brothers, or Scholastic Books to operate its camp. Do you see a likelihood of confusion?

Conopco, Inc. v. May Dept. Stores Co.

46 F.3d 1556 (Fed.Cir.1994), *cert. denied*, 514 U.S. 1078, 115 S.Ct. 1724, 131 L.Ed.2d 582 (1995).

■ PLAGER, CIRCUIT JUDGE:

Defendants May Department Stores Co. (May), Venture Stores, Inc. (Venture), The Benjamin Ansehl Co. (Ansehl), and Kessler Containers Ltd. (Kessler) appeal the judgment of the District Court for the Eastern District of Missouri, entered January 2, 1992 after a bench trial. *Conopco, Inc. v. May Dep't Stores Co.*, 784 F. Supp. 648, 24 U.S.P.Q.2d 1721 (E.D.Mo.1992). The District Court ruled that defendants willfully infringed a package of proprietary rights owned by plaintiff Conopco, Inc. d/b/a Chesebrough–Pond's U.S.A. Co. (Conopco) relating to a relaunch of Conopco's Vaseline Intensive Care Lotion (VICL) product....

. . . . .

BACKGROUND

In 1986, Conopco decided to "relaunch" VICL, a product it had been marketing for over 20 years. Conopco wanted to enhance that product's therapeutic image and to further distance it from private label brands, which had been eroding its sales. Accordingly, it set about developing a new bottle shape and label for the product. It also set about developing a new formula for the lotion. Conopco's objective was to reduce the lotion's greasiness while maintaining its thickness and smooth skin feel.

In 1988, Conopco decided upon a revised bottle shape and label for the relaunched product. By 1989, it decided upon a lotion formula. Conopco discovered that the combination of two ingredients—isoparaffin and DEA-cetyl phosphate—resulted in a synergistic increase in the viscosity of the lotion. By adding these two ingredients to its lotion, Conopco found that it could decrease the amount of mineral oil used. Since mineral oil is heavy and greasy, Conopco was thus able to achieve a reduction in greasiness without a corresponding decrease in viscosity.

After filing a patent application on the new formula, Conopco initiated the relaunch. It began shipping the product to retailers and aggressively promoting it. By the fall of 1989, the product was on the shelves of virtually every major retailer and drug store in the United States. Between the fall of 1989 and March of 1990, Conopco spent over $37 million to advertise and promote the product.

Ansehl is a manufacturer of private label hand lotions, which it distributes through retailers such as Venture, who also handle national brands such as the revised VICL product. Kessler is a manufacturer of containers, and May is Venture's corporate parent.

In January 1989, Ansehl became aware of Conopco's plans to relaunch VICL. Accordingly, it developed a private label product to compete with the revised VICL product. Together with Kessler, it developed a container for the product. In conjunction with Venture, it developed the labelling that would be affixed to the container. Soon after Conopco initiated the VICL relaunch, Ansehl began marketing its product through several retailers, including Venture.

In March 1990, Conopco sent Venture a letter asserting that the Ansehl product infringed the proprietary rights Conopco had then accumulated in the revised VICL product (trademark and trade dress). In May 1990, May, Venture's parent, responded denying infringement of those rights.... In August 1990, Conopco filed suit against the defendants in the District Court for the Eastern District of Missouri....

. . . .

On January 2, 1992, the court, in the decision that gave rise to defendants' appeals, entered after a bench trial judgment in favor of plaintiff. *Conopco, Inc. v. May Dep't Stores Co.*, 784 F. Supp. 648, 24 U.S.P.Q.2d 1721 (E.D.Mo.1992). The court found that ... all defendants had willfully infringed plaintiff's trademark and trade dress rights. The court found the case to be exceptional, and that enhanced damages were warranted. The court awarded ... trebled damages of $281,622 for the trademark and trade dress infringement. The court also awarded costs, attorney fees, prejudgment interest, a recall order, and an injunction. It also imposed joint and several liability on the defendants. These appeals followed.

DISCUSSION

. . . .

B. Trade Dress and Trademark Infringement Issues

The trade dress and trademark infringement issues raise substantive legal issues over which this court does not have exclusive subject matter jurisdiction. Accordingly, it is our practice to defer to the law of the regional circuit in which the district court sits, in this case the Eighth Circuit, to resolve them. *See Payless Shoesource, Inc. v. Reebok Int'l Ltd.*, 998 F.2d 985, 987, 27 U.S.P.Q.2d 1516, 1518 (Fed.Cir.1993).

1. Trade Dress

Conopco's trade dress infringement claim was brought pursuant to section 43(a) of the Lanham Act (codified as amended at 15 U.S.C. § 1125(a) (1988)). Conopco seeks injunctive and monetary relief. In the Eighth Circuit, the elements to be proved in a claim for trade dress infringement differ depending on whether injunctive or monetary relief is being sought. *See Woodsmith Publishing Co. v. Meredith Corp.*, 904 F.2d 1244, 1247 n. 5, 15 U.S.P.Q.2d 1053, 1055 n. 5 (8th Cir.1990); *Co–Rect Products, Inc. v. Marvy! Advertising Photography*, Inc., 780 F.2d 1324, 1329–30, 228 U.S.P.Q. 429, 432 (8th Cir.1985). To establish entitlement to monetary relief, a plaintiff must show actual confusion, while to establish entitlement to injunctive relief, it is sufficient if the plaintiff establishes likelihood of confusion. *Woodsmith*, 904 F.2d at 1247 n.5, 15 U.S.P.Q.2d at 1055 n.5. The difficulty of proving actual confusion understandably is greater than that of proving likelihood of confusion. *See PPX Enters. v. Audio Fidelity Enterprises*, 818 F.2d 266, 271, 2 U.S.P.Q.2d 1672, 1675 (2d Cir.1987); *Schutt Mfg. Co. v. Riddell, Inc.*, 673 F.2d 202, 206, 216 U.S.P.Q. 191, 194 (7th Cir.1982). We consider first Conopco's claim for monetary relief, then its claim for injunctive relief.

a. Monetary Relief–Actual Confusion

In the Eighth Circuit, the question of actual confusion vel non is one of fact subject to the clearly erroneous standard of review. *Prufrock Ltd., Inc. v. Lasater*, 781 F.2d 129, 132–33, 228 U.S.P.Q. 435, 437 (8th Cir.1986) (discussing standard of review for trade dress infringement claim). The trial court based its finding of actual confusion on two factors. The first is the testimony of a consumer, Mrs. Sickles. The second is a presumption of actual confusion arising from the "overwhelming evidence that defendants intended to deceive and confuse the public in connection with the Venture skin care lotion product."

In her testimony, Mrs. Sickles stated that she purchased a private label brand of VICL—the Target brand—thinking it to have originated from Conopco. The problem with the testimony is that Mrs. Sickles's confusion arose at least in part from her assumption, erroneous as applied to this case, that national brand manufacturers secretly market private label brands. First, there is no evidence that this assumption is widely held by the relevant consumers, the vantage point from which the confusion issue must ultimately be addressed. Second, under the circumstances of this case, in which the national brand is being sold side-by-side with the private label brand, the assumption is at best counter-intuitive—it assumes that a national brand manufacturer would embark on a scheme to deliberately erode its sales of the national brand.[8]

Thus, Mrs. Sickles's experience appears to have been atypical and an isolated incident. Isolated instances of actual confusion do not justify an award of monetary relief when there is a reasonable explanation in the record which serves to discount their importance. (Citations omitted). Accordingly, that testimony is legally insufficient to sustain the court's award of monetary relief.

Actual confusion is normally proven "through the use of direct evidence, i.e., testimony from members of the buying public, as well as through circumstantial evidence, e.g., consumer surveys or consumer reaction tests." *PPX Enters. v. Audio Fidelity Enterprises*, 818 F.2d 266, 271, 2 U.S.P.Q.2d 1672, 1675 (2d Cir.1987). A presumption of actual confusion arising from an intent to deceive is neither. Thus, the question is whether such a judicially-created presumption constitutes a sufficient basis to sustain the trial court's award of monetary relief.

. . . .

This is a case in which a retailer markets a national brand product and at the same time markets its own private label product in direct competition. The retailer packages its product in a manner to make it clear to the consumer that the product is similar to the national brand, and is intended for the same purposes. At the same time, the retailer clearly marks its product with its private logo, and expressly invites the consumer to compare its product with that of the national brand, by name.

With the rise of regional and national discount retailers with established names and logos, retailers who market both national brands and their own private label brands in direct competition, this form of competition has become commonplace and well-known in the marketplace. When such packaging is clearly labeled and differentiated—as was the case here, see the discussion in the next section—we are unwilling to attribute to the Eighth Circuit, absent clear precedent so requiring, a rule that would make such competition presumptively unlawful.

---

8. The circumstance in which the private label brand is being sold through different commercial channels than the national brand might present a different case.

The District Court erred in concluding that under Eighth Circuit law actual confusion could be presumed from defendants' intent to copy the overall package design. Consequently, there is a complete absence of proof of actual confusion, the required element in plaintiff's claim for monetary relief. The court's award of monetary relief is thus not sustainable, and is reversed.

b.   *Injunctive Relief—Likelihood of Confusion*

.   .   .   .

The trial court concluded that likelihood of confusion had been established on the basis of the following findings: that plaintiff's marks are strong, the trade dress of the two products is "extremely similar", the two products are "directly competitive", the defendants "acted with deliberate intent to imitate and infringe the revised VICL trade dress", a presumption of likelihood of confusion arising from defendants' intent to deceive and copy, and the presence of actual confusion. As noted, supra, the court's finding of actual confusion was erroneous because of a complete failure of proof. Thus, our task is to determine whether the other findings are sufficient to support the court's finding of likelihood of confusion.

We conclude that they are not. Even accepting these other findings as true, they are at best merely inferentially or presumptively relevant to the likelihood of confusion issue. A factor more probative of that issue, which the court in its opinion failed to address, is the significance of the black and white diagonally-striped Venture logo prominently situated on the front of the original and relaunched Venture products. Photographs comparing the original and relaunched Conopco products with the corresponding Venture products, reproduced below, show the prominent placement of that logo on the front of the Venture products:

COMPARISON OF ORIGINAL VICL AND VENTURE BOTTLES

COMPARISON OF REVISED VICL AND VENTURE BOTTLES

The unique and extensive appearance of that logo in the store parking lot, on store signs, on employees' badges, in Venture's frequent and periodic print and television advertisements, and on other private label items sold by Venture, the large volume of Venture's annual sales ($1.3 billion in 1990), and the dearth of evidence that consumers ever purchased the Venture brand thinking it to have originated from Conopco despite the extended (over 10 year) period over which the original and relaunched products were sold alongside the Venture brand, give rise to the expectation that consumers identify the logo with Venture, rather than Conopco, and use that logo to successfully distinguish between the two brands.

The fact that Venture (and other retailers) compete in the manner described, which is all that the evidence establishes, is simply insufficient to amount to proof that there is in the minds of consumers a likelihood of confusion about whose product is whose . . . . .

[T]he marketing device employed by defendants in this case is neither new nor subtle. The cases have approved the general practice in a variety of settings, at least to the extent of not finding a violation of the Lanham Act absent a showing by the plaintiff that real consumers have real confusion or likelihood of it with regard to the origin of the products involved. We are thus left with a "definite and firm conviction" that the District Court erred in concluding that likelihood of confusion had been established. *United States v. United States Gypsum Co.*, 333 U.S. 364, 395, 92 L. Ed. 746, 68 S. Ct. 525 (1948); *see also Colorado v. New Mexico*, 467 U.S. 310, 316, 81 L. Ed. 2d 247, 104 S. Ct. 2433 (1984). The court thus clearly erred in awarding injunctive relief, and the judgment of the court in that regard is reversed. We reverse the court's judgment of trade dress infringement, and its award of costs, attorney fees, and prejudgment interest as they relate to this issue. We further reverse the court's finding of willfulness, the determination that the case is exceptional, and the determination that enhanced damages are warranted as they relate to trade dress infringement. The injunction and recall order are vacated as they relate to this issue.

. . . .

QUESTIONS

1. Was May using the copied elements of the Vaseline Intensive Care trade dress as a trademark for its private label lotion?

2. In any large chain supermarket or pharmacy you can find national brand products on shelves beside private brand equivalents. Some of the private brand imitations are identical in formulation to their national brand models; others are more distantly related. Some of the private brand packages merely note their comparability to a national brand product, while others have packages designed to duplicate the characteristic features of the national brand trade dress. What policy reasons support permitting this degree of imitation?

3. Recall the "fair use" defense in section 33(b)(4), discussed, *supra*, Chapter 6.C. If Conopco's VICL trade dress were registered on the Principal Register, would Venture's imitation of it qualify as fair use?

4. In footnote 8 of the court's opinion, it notes that "[t]he circumstance in which the private label brand is sold through different commercial channels than the national brand might present a different case." How should such a case be resolved?

McNeil–PPC, Inc. v. Guardian Drug Co., 984 F.Supp. 1066 (E.D.Mich.1997). In a case involving a look-alike private-label lactose intolerance remedy, the court enjoined defendant Arbor Drugs from using a trade dress for its ARBOR ULTRA LACTASE product virtually identical to plaintiff's LACTAID ULTRA trade dress. The court found unpersuasive the facts that defendant's product bore its ARBOR house mark as well as a "compare to" statement and a disclaimer. The court distinguished the *Conopco* case on the ground that the parties' products had been competing for 10 years. The court was also unimpressed with defendant's arguments that its house brand and "compare to" strategy would dispel any confusion. The court reasoned:

Defendant further argues that its "shelf talker" sign directing the customer to compare the price of Arbor's product to that of the national brand, together with its multi-million dollar price comparison advertising campaign in the Detroit Metropolitan area, combine to insure that the buying public will not be confused. The Court disagrees. Because Defendant is mimicking Plaintiff's packaging and placing the products side-by-side on the shelf, the price comparison signs and advertising do not dispel customer confusion as to the source or origin of the Arbor product. The signs and advertising can be read as actually telling customers "Our Arbor product is the same product as the national brand, only cheaper." Furthermore, if Arbor's goal were truly to "compare" its product to the national brand, it would have made its package as distinct as possible from that of Plaintiff's product. Thus, the Court does not deem Defendant's "shelf talkers" or advertising to dispel customer confusion as to the source or origin of the Arbor product.

Defendant also argues that its entire marketing/store identification scheme is actually a comparison campaign designed not to confuse the consumer but to get the consumer to compare and contrast the products. Defendant contends that this comparison approach can be seen in the fact that the lettering of the brand-name "Arbor" on the ULTRA LACTASE package is the same as the lettering on its store signs and on its store clerks' uniforms and badges. Thus, Defendant argues that no intent to confuse can be inferred. The Court is not persuaded by this argument, either. If it were truly Defendant's intent merely to invite customers to compare its product with the national brand with no intent to confuse consumers, Defendant would have packaged its product in its store colors—orange/red and yellow—instead of Plaintiff's blue and white combination. This would have clearly drawn comparison rather than confusion.

Defendant also argues that to prevail on its Lanham Act claim of trade dress infringement, it is not enough for Plaintiff to show that customers are likely to be confused at the initial stage where they are drawn in or when they reach for the product on the shelf, but rather that it must show likelihood of confusion at the actual point of sale. This argument is not supported by Sixth Circuit precedent. In *Esercizio v. Roberts*, the court explicitly rejected the "point of sale" argument. The Court reasoned, "Since Congress intended to protect the reputation of the manufacturer as well as to protect purchasers, the [Lanham] Act's protection is not limited to confusion at the point of sale." 944 F.2d at 1245.

. . . .

It is clear to the Court that, taken as a whole, it was defendant's intent in appropriating Plaintiff's trade dress, not only in its packaging but also in its advertising, to confuse or "hook" customers at the initial point of contact with the product, thus initially drawing the customers to its product through the similarity in trade dress. That the customer might realize that Defendant's product is not Plaintiff's before he gets to the check-out counter to pay for it is irrelevant. Even if the consumer realizes that the Arbor product is not the same as the national brand once he picks the product up off the shelf and reads the label, Defendant has already accomplished what it set out to do, which is to confuse the consumer at the point when he first reaches for the product on the shelf. It is at that point that the damage is done. Defendant has already succeeded in utilizing the Plaintiff's trade dress to get the customer to consider buying its product. In this Court's view, this is sufficient to constitute a trade dress violation.

QUESTION

Did the *McNeil* court reach a different outcome from the *Conopco* court because of factual differences between the cases? Did the fact that the *McNeil* case involved an over-the-counter remedy rather than hand lotion make a difference? Which decision is more persuasively reasoned? Should initial interest confusion be actionable?

C. FALSE DESIGNATION OF ORIGIN

America Online v. LCGM, 46 F.Supp.2d 444 (E.D.Va.1998).

AOL, an Internet service provider located in the Eastern District of Virginia, provides a proprietary, content-based online service that provides its members (AOL members) access to the Internet and the capability to receive as well as send e-mail messages. AOL registered "AOL" as a trademark and service mark in 1996 and has registered its domain name "aol.com" with the InterNIC. At the time this cause of action arose, defendant LCGM, Inc. was a Michigan corporation which operated and transacted business from Internet domains offering pornographic web sites. Plaintiff alleges that defendant ... operates Internet domains offering pornographic web sites. ...

AOL alleges that defendants, in concert, sent unauthorized and unsolicited bulk e-mail advertisements ("spam") to AOL customers. AOL's Unsolicited Bulk E-mail Policy and its Terms of Service bar both members and nonmembers from sending bulk e-mail through AOL's computer systems. Plaintiff estimates that defendants, in concert with their "site partners," transmitted more than 92 million unsolicited and bulk e-mail messages advertising their pornographic Web sites to AOL members from approximately June 17, 1997 to January 21, 1998. ...

Plaintiff alleges that defendants harvested, or collected, the e-mail addresses of AOL members in violation of AOL's Terms of Service. Defendants have admitted to maintaining AOL memberships to harvest or collect the e-mail addresses of other AOL members. . . .

Plaintiff alleges that defendants forged the domain information "aol.com" in the "from" line of e-mail messages sent to AOL members. Defendants have admitted to creating the domain information "aol.com" through an e-mail sending program, and to causing the AOL domain to appear in electronic header information of its commercial e-mails. . . . Plaintiffs assert that as a result, many AOL members expressed confusion about whether AOL endorsed defendants' pornographic Web sites or their bulk e-mailing practices. Plaintiff also asserts that defendants e-mail messages were sent through AOL's computer networks. Defendants have admitted to sending e-mail messages from their computers through defendants' network *via* e-mail software to AOL, which then relayed the messages to AOL members. . . .

. . . .

Plaintiff alleges that defendants' actions injured AOL by consuming capacity on AOL's computers, causing AOL to incur technical costs, impairing the functioning of AOL's e-mail system, forcing AOL to upgrade its computer networks to process authorized e-mails in a timely manner, damaging AOL's goodwill with its members, and causing AOL to lose customers and revenue. Plaintiff asserts that between the months of December 1997 and April 1998, defendants' unsolicited bulk e-mails generated more than 450,000 complaints by AOL members.

Count I: False Designation of Origin Under the Lanham Act

The undisputed facts establish that defendants violated 15 U.S.C. § 1125(a)(1) of the Lanham Act. . . .

. . . The elements necessary to establish a false designation violation under the Lanham Act are as follows: (1) a defendant uses a designation; (2) in interstate commerce; (3) in connection with goods and services; (4) which designation is likely to cause confusion, mistake or deception as to origin, sponsorship, or approval of defendant's goods or services; and (5) plaintiff has been or is likely to be damaged by these acts. . . .

Each of the false designation elements has been satisfied. First, defendants clearly use the "aol.com" designation, incorporating the registered trade and service mark AOL in their e-mail headers. Second, defendants' activities involved interstate commerce because all e-mail sent to AOL members were routed from defendants' computers in Virginia. Third, the use of AOL's designation was in connection with goods and services as defendants' e-mails advertised their commercial web sites. Fourth, the use of "aol.com" in defendants' e-mails was likely to cause confusion as to the origin and sponsorship of defendants' goods and services. Any e-mail recipient could logically conclude that a message containing the initials "aol.com" in the header would originate from AOL's registered Internet domain, which incorporates the registered mark "AOL." *AOL v IMS*, 24 F. Supp. 2d 548 [(E.D.Va. 1998)]. The recipient of such a message would be led to conclude the sender was an AOL member or AOL, the Internet Service Provider. Indeed, plaintiff alleges that this designation did cause such confusion among many AOL members, who believed that AOL sponsored and authorized defendants' bulk e-mailing practices and pornographic web sites. Finally, plaintiff asserts that these acts damaged AOL's technical capabilities and its goodwill. The defendants are precluded from opposing these claims due to their failure to comply with discovery orders. Therefore, there is no genuine issue of material fact in regards to this Count, and the Court holds the plaintiff is entitled to summary judgment on Count I.

QUESTIONS

1. What is the nature of the likely confusion experienced by recipients of LCGM's unsolicited electronic mail? Are they likely to believe that AOL sent the spam, or that one of AOL's subscribers sent the spam? In what sense is a forged email return address a false designation of origin?

2. *My Neighbor Totoro* is an animated Japanese film for children produced and distributed in Japan by Studio Ghibli. The film, set in the 1950s, tells the story of an encounter between two children and a "Totoro"–a giant magical furry forest creature. Disney has the exclusive U.S. distribution rights to the film and has released it on DVD. Studio Ghibli sells a line of Totoro-related merchandise in toy stores and free standing Studio Ghibli stores and in the Studio Ghibli Museum in Japan, and has registered TOTORO on the principal register in the United States as a mark for computer games, alarm clocks, ball point pens, toys, jewelry, briefcases, luggage, and clothing. Recently, a Japanese restaurant opened in a Midwestern college town under the name "Totoro." The proprietor of the restaurant has no relationship to Studio Ghibli or Disney; she just really enjoyed the movie. Do you see a likelihood of confusion?

Dastar Corporation v. Twentieth Century Fox Film Corporation

539 U.S. 23, 123 S.Ct. 2041, 156 L.Ed.2d 18 (2003).

■ JUSTICE SCALIA delivered the opinion of the Court.

In this case, we are asked to decide whether § 43(a) of the Lanham Act, 15 U.S.C. § 1125(a), prevents the unaccredited copying of a work....

I

In 1948, three and a half years after the German surrender at Reims, General Dwight D. Eisenhower completed *Crusade in Europe*, his written account of the allied campaign in Europe during World War II. Doubleday published the book, registered it with the Copyright Office in 1948, and granted exclusive television rights to an affiliate of respondent Twentieth Century Fox Film Corporation (Fox). Fox, in turn, arranged for Time, Inc., to produce a television series, also called *Crusade in Europe*, based on the book, and Time assigned its copyright in the series to Fox. The television series, consisting of 26 episodes, was first broadcast in 1949. It combined a soundtrack based on a narration of the book with film footage from the United States Army, Navy, and Coast Guard, the British Ministry of Information and War Office, the National Film Board of Canada, and unidentified "Newsreel Pool Cameramen." In 1975, Doubleday renewed the copyright on the book.... Fox, however, did not renew the copyright on the *Crusade* television series, which expired in 1977, leaving the television series in the public domain.

In 1988, Fox reacquired the television rights in General Eisenhower's book, including the exclusive right to distribute the *Crusade* television series on video and to sub-license others to do so. Respondents SFM Entertainment and New Line Home Video, Inc., in turn, acquired from Fox the exclusive rights to distribute *Crusade* on video. SFM obtained the negatives of the original television series, restored them, and repackaged the series on videotape; New Line distributed the videotapes.

Enter petitioner Dastar. In 1995, Dastar decided to expand its product line from music compact discs to videos. Anticipating renewed interest in World War II on the 50th anniversary of the war's end, Dastar released a video set entitled *World War II Campaigns in Europe*. To make *Campaigns*, Dastar purchased eight beta cam tapes of the *original* version of the *Crusade* television series, which is in the public domain, copied them, and then edited the series. Dastar's *Campaigns* series is slightly more than half as long as the original *Crusade* television series. Dastar substituted a new opening sequence, credit page, and final closing for those of the *Crusade* television series; inserted new chapter-title sequences and narrated chapter introductions; moved the "recap" in the *Crusade* television series to the beginning and retitled it as a "preview"; and removed references to and images of the book. Dastar created new packaging for its *Campaigns* series and (as already noted) a new title.

Dastar manufactured and sold the *Campaigns* video set as its own product. The advertising states: "Produced and Distributed by: *Entertainment Distributing*" (which is owned by Dastar), and makes no reference to the *Crusade* television series. Similarly, the screen credits state "DASTAR CORP presents" and "an ENTERTAINMENT DISTRIBUTING Production," and list as executive producer, producer, and associate producer, employees of Dastar. The *Campaigns* videos themselves also make no reference to the *Crusade* television series, New Line's *Crusade* videotapes, or the book. Dastar sells its *Campaigns* videos to Sam's Club, Costco, Best Buy, and other retailers and mail-order companies for $25 per set, substantially less than New Line's video set.

In 1998, respondents Fox, SFM, and New Line brought this action alleging that Dastar's sale of its *Campaigns* video set infringes Doubleday's copyright in General Eisenhower's book and, thus, their exclusive television rights in the book. Respondents later amended their complaint to add claims that Dastar's sale of *Campaigns* "without proper credit" to the *Crusade* television series constitutes "reverse passing off"[1] in violation of § 43(a) of the Lanham Act, 15 U.S.C. § 1125(a)....

The Court of Appeals for the Ninth Circuit affirmed the judgment for respondents on the Lanham Act claim, but reversed as to the copyright claim and remanded. With respect to the Lanham Act claim, the Court of Appeals reasoned that "Dastar copied substantially the entire *Crusade in Europe* series created by Twentieth Century Fox, labeled the resulting product with a different name and marketed it without attribution to Fox [,and] therefore committed a 'bodily appropriation' of Fox's series." *Id.*, at 314. It concluded that "Dastar's 'bodily appropriation' of Fox's original [television] series is sufficient to establish the reverse passing off."

II

The Lanham Act was intended to make "actionable the deceptive and misleading use of marks," and "to protect persons engaged in ... commerce against unfair competition." 15 U.S.C. § 1127. While much of the Lanham Act addresses the registration, use, and infringement of trademarks and related marks, § 43(a), 15 U.S.C. § 1125(a) is one of the few provisions that goes beyond trademark protection. As originally enacted, § 43(a) created a federal remedy against a person who used in commerce either "a false designation of origin, or any false description or representation" in connection with "any goods or services." 60 Stat. 441. As the Second Circuit accurately observed with regard to the original enactment, however—and as remains true after the 1988 revision—§ 43(a) "does not have boundless application as a remedy for unfair trade practices," *Alfred Dunhill, Ltd.* v. *Interstate Cigar Co.*, 499 F.2d 232, 237 (1974). "Because of its inherently limited wording, § 43(a) can never be a federal 'codification' of the overall law of 'unfair competition,' " 4 J. McCarthy Trademarks and Unfair Competition § 27:7, p. 27–14 (4th ed. 2002) (McCarthy), but can apply only to certain unfair trade practices prohibited by its text.

Although a case can be made that a proper reading of § 43(a), as originally enacted, would treat the word "origin" as referring only "to the geographic location in which the goods originated," *Two Pesos, Inc.* v. *Taco Cabana, Inc.*, 505 U.S. 763, 777, 120 L. Ed. 2d 615, 112 S. Ct. 2753 (1992) (Stevens, J., concurring in judgment), the Courts of Appeals considering the issue, beginning with the Sixth Circuit, unanimously concluded that it "does not merely refer to geographic origin, but also to origin of source or manufacture," *Federal–Mogul–Bower Bearings, Inc.* v. *Azoff*, 313 F.2d 405, 408 (1963), thereby creating a federal cause of action for traditional

---

1. Passing off (or palming off, as it is sometimes called) occurs when a producer misrepresents his own goods or services as someone else's. See, *e.g., O. & W. Thum Co.* v. *Dickinson*, 245 F. 609, 621 (CA6 1917). "Reverse passing off," as its name implies, is the opposite: The producer misrepresents someone else's goods or services as his own. See, *e.g., Williams* v. *Curtiss–Wright Corp.*, 691 F.2d 168, 172 (CA3 1982).

trademark infringement of unregistered marks. See 4 McCarthy § 27:14; *Two Pesos, supra*, at 768, 120 L. Ed. 2d 615, 112 S Ct 2753. Moreover, every Circuit to consider the issue found § 43(a) broad enough to encompass reverse passing off. [Citations] The Trademark Law Revision Act of 1988 made clear that § 43(a) covers origin of production as well as geographic origin. Its language is amply inclusive, moreover, of reverse passing off—if indeed it does not implicitly adopt the unanimous court-of-appeals jurisprudence on that subject. [Citations]

Thus, as it comes to us, the gravamen of respondents' claim is that, in marketing and selling *Campaigns* as its own product without acknowledging its nearly wholesale reliance on the *Crusade* television series, Dastar has made a "false designation of origin, false or misleading description of fact, or false or misleading representation of fact, which . . . is likely to cause confusion . . . as to the origin . . . of his or her goods." That claim would undoubtedly be sustained if Dastar had bought some of New Line's *Crusade* videotapes and merely repackaged them as its own. Dastar's alleged wrongdoing, however, is vastly different: it took a creative work in the public domain—the *Crusade* television series—copied it, made modifications (arguably minor), and produced its very own series of videotapes. If "origin" refers only to the manufacturer or producer of the physical "goods" that are made available to the public (in this case the videotapes), Dastar was the origin. If, however, "origin" includes the creator of the underlying work that Dastar copied, then someone else (perhaps Fox) was the origin of Dastar's product. At bottom, we must decide what § 43(a)(1)(A) of the Lanham Act means by the "origin" of "goods."

III

The dictionary definition of "origin" is "the fact or process of coming into being from a source," and "that from which anything primarily proceeds; source." Webster's New International Dictionary 1720–1721 (2d ed. 1949). And the dictionary definition of "goods" (as relevant here) is "[w]ares; merchandise." *Id.*, at 1079. We think the most natural understanding of the "origin" of "goods"—the source of wares—is the producer of the tangible product sold in the marketplace, in this case the physical *Campaigns* videotape sold by Dastar. The concept might be stretched (as it was under the original version of § 43(a)) to include not only the actual producer, but also the trademark owner who commissioned or assumed responsibility for ("stood behind") production of the physical product. But as used in the Lanham Act, the phrase "origin of goods" is in our view incapable of connoting the person or entity that originated the ideas or communications that "goods" embody or contain. Such an extension would not only stretch the text, but it would be out of accord with the history and purpose of the Lanham Act and inconsistent with precedent.

Section 43(a) of the Lanham Act prohibits actions like trademark infringement that deceive consumers and impair a producer's goodwill. It forbids, for example, the Coca–Cola Company's passing off its product as Pepsi–Cola or reverse passing off Pepsi–Cola as its product. But the brand-loyal consumer who prefers the drink that the Coca–Cola Company or PepsiCo sells, while he believes that that company produced (or at least stands behind the production of) that product, surely does not necessarily believe that that company was the "origin" of the drink in the sense that it was the very first to devise the formula. The consumer who buys a branded product does not automatically assume that the brand-name company is the same entity that came up with the idea for the product, or designed the product—and typically does not care whether it is. The words of the Lanham Act should not be stretched to cover matters that are typically of no consequence to purchasers.

It could be argued, perhaps, that the reality of purchaser concern is different for what might be called a communicative product—one that is valued not primarily for its physical qualities, such as a hammer, but for the intellectual content that it conveys, such as a book or, as here, a video. The purchaser of a novel is interested not merely, if at all, in the identity of the producer of the physical tome (the publisher), but also, and indeed primarily, in the identity of the creator of the story it conveys (the author). And the author, of course, has at least as much interest in avoiding passing-off (or reverse passing-off) of his creation as does the publisher. For such a communicative product (the argument goes) "origin of goods" in § 43(a) must be deemed to include not merely the producer of the physical item (the publishing house Farrar, Straus and Giroux, or the video producer Dastar) but also the creator of the content that the physical item conveys (the author Tom Wolfe, or—assertedly—respondents).

The problem with this argument according special treatment to communicative products is that it causes the Lanham Act to conflict with the law of copyright, which addresses that subject specifically. The right to copy, and to copy without attribution, once a copyright has expired, like "the right to make [an article whose patent has expired]—including the right to make it in precisely the shape it carried when patented—passes to the public." *Sears, Roebuck & Co.* v. *Stiffel Co.*, 376 U.S. 225, 230 (1964); see also *Kellogg Co.* v. *National Biscuit Co.*, 305 U.S. 111, 121–122 (1938). "In general, unless an intellectual property right such as a patent or copyright protects an item, it will be subject to copying." *TrafFix Devices, Inc.* v. *Marketing Displays, Inc.*, 532 U.S. 23, 29 (2001). The rights of a patentee or copyright holder are part of a "carefully crafted bargain," *Bonito Boats, Inc.* v. *Thunder Craft Boats, Inc.*, 489 U.S. 141, 150–151 (1989), under which, once the patent or copyright monopoly has expired, the public may use the invention or work at will and without attribution. Thus, in construing the Lanham Act, we have been "careful to caution against misuse or over-extension" of trademark and related protections into areas traditionally occupied by patent or copyright. *TrafFix*, 532 U.S., at 29. "The Lanham Act," we have said, "does not exist to reward manufacturers for their innovation in creating a particular device; that is the purpose of the patent law and its period of exclusivity." *Id.*, at 34. Federal trademark law "has no necessary relation to invention or discovery," *Trade–Mark Cases*, 100 U.S. 82, 94 (1879), but rather, by preventing competitors from copying "a source-identifying mark," "reduces the customer's costs of shopping and making purchasing decisions," and "helps assure a producer that it (and not an imitating competitor) will reap the financial, reputation-related rewards associated with a desirable product," *Qualitex Co.* v. *Jacobson Products Co.*, 514 U.S. 159, 163–164 (1995) (internal quotation marks and citation omitted). Assuming for the sake of argument that Dastar's representation of itself as the "Producer" of its videos amounted to a representation that it originated the creative work conveyed by the videos, allowing a cause of action under § 43(a) for that representation would create a species of mutant copyright law that limits the public's "federal right to 'copy and to use,' " expired copyrights, *Bonito Boats*, *supra*, at 165.

When Congress has wished to create such an addition to the law of copyright, it has done so with much more specificity than the Lanham Act's ambiguous use of "origin." The Visual Artists Rights Act of 1990, § 603(a), 104 Stat. 5128, provides that the author of an artistic work "shall have the right . . . to claim authorship of that work." 17 U.S.C. § 106A(a)(1)(A). That express right of attribution is carefully limited and focused: It attaches only to specified "work[s] of visual art," § 101, is personal to the artist, §§ 106A(b) and (e), and endures only for "the life of the author," at § 106A(d)(1). Recognizing in § 43(a) a cause of action for misrepresentation of authorship of noncopyrighted works (visual or otherwise) would render these limitations superfluous. A statutory interpretation that renders another statute superfluous is of course to be avoided. . . .

Reading "origin" in § 43(a) to require attribution of uncopyrighted materials would pose serious practical problems. Without a copyrighted work as the basepoint, the word "origin" has no discernable limits. A video of the MGM film *Carmen Jones*, after its copyright has expired, would presumably require attribution not just to MGM, but to Oscar Hammerstein II (who wrote the musical on which the film was based), to Georges Bizet (who wrote the opera on which the musical was based), and to Prosper Merimee (who wrote the novel on which the opera was based). In many cases, figuring out who is in the line of "origin" would be no simple task. Indeed, in the present case it is far from clear that respondents have that status. Neither SFM nor New Line had anything to do with the production of the *Crusade* television series—they merely were licensed to distribute the video version. While Fox might have a claim to being in the line of origin, its involvement with the creation of the television series was limited at best. Time, Inc., was the principal if not the exclusive creator, albeit under arrangement with Fox. And of course it was neither Fox nor Time, Inc., that shot the film used in the *Crusade* television series. Rather, that footage came from the United States Army, Navy, and Coast Guard, the British Ministry of Information and War Office, the National Film Board of Canada, and unidentified "Newsreel Pool Cameramen." If anyone has a claim to being the *original* creator of the material used in both the *Crusade* television series and the *Campaigns* videotapes, it would be those groups, rather than Fox. We do not think the Lanham Act requires this search for the source of the Nile and all its tributaries.

Another practical difficulty of adopting a special definition of "origin" for communicative products is that it places the manufacturers of those products in a difficult position. On the one hand, they would face Lanham Act liability for *failing* to credit the creator of a work on which their lawful copies are based; and on the other hand they could face Lanham Act liability for *crediting* the creator if that should be regarded as implying the creator's "sponsorship or approval" of the copy, 15 U.S.C. § 1125(a)(1)(A). In this case, for example, if Dastar had simply "copied [the television series] as *Crusade in Europe* and sold it as *Crusade in Europe*," without changing the title or packaging (including the original credits to Fox), it is hard to have confidence in respondents' assurance that they "would not be here on a Lanham Act cause of action," Tr. of Oral Arg. 35.

Finally, reading § 43(a) of the Lanham Act as creating a cause of action for, in effect, plagiarism—the use of otherwise unprotected works and inventions without attribution—would be hard to reconcile with our previous decisions. For example, in *Wal–Mart Stores, Inc.* v. *Samara Brothers, Inc.*, 529 U.S. 205 (2000), we considered whether product-design trade dress can ever be inherently distinctive. Wal–Mart produced "knock-offs" of children's clothes designed and manufactured by Samara Brothers, containing only "minor modifications" of the original designs. *Id.*, at 208. We concluded that the designs could not be protected under § 43(a) without a showing that they had acquired "secondary meaning," *id.*, at 214, so that they " 'identify the source of the product rather than the product itself,' " *id.*, at 211, (quoting *Inwood Laboratories, Inc.* v. *Ives Laboratories, Inc.*, 456 U.S. 844, 851, n. 11 (1982)). This carefully considered limitation would be entirely pointless if the "original" producer could turn around and pursue a reverse-passing-off claim under exactly the same provision of the Lanham Act. Samara would merely have had to argue that it was the "origin" of the designs that Wal–Mart was selling as its own line. It was not, because "origin of goods" in the Lanham Act referred to the producer of the clothes, and not the producer of the (potentially) copyrightable or patentable designs that the clothes embodied.

. . . .

In sum, reading the phrase "origin of goods" in the Lanham Act in accordance with the Act's common-law foundations (which were *not* designed to protect originality or creativity), and in light of the copyright and patent laws (which *were*), we conclude that the phrase refers to the producer of the tangible goods that are offered for sale, and not to the author of any idea, concept, or communication embodied in those goods. Cf. 17 U.S.C. § 202 [17 U.S.C.S. § 202] (distinguishing between a copyrighted work and "any material object in which the work is embodied"). To hold otherwise would be akin to finding that § 43(a) created a species of perpetual patent and copyright, which Congress may not do.

Bretford Manufacturing, Inc. v. Smith System Manufacturing Corporation

419 F.3d 576 (7th Cir.2005).

■ EASTERBROOK, CIRCUIT JUDGE.

Bretford makes a line of computer tables that it sells under the name Connectiont. Since 1990 many of these tables have featured one rather than two legs on each end. The leg supports a sleeve attached to a V-shaped brace, making it easy to change the table's height while keeping the work surface stable. Although the sleeve and brace together look like a Y, Bretford calls it the V–Design table, and we employ the same usage.

This illustration, from Bretford's web site, shows the idea:

Between 1990 and 1997 Bretford was the only seller of computer tables with a V-shaped height-adjustment system. It sold about 200,000 V–Design tables during that period. Smith System, one of Bretford's competitors, decided to copy the sleeve and brace for its own line of computer tables. Smith System made its initial sales of the knockoff product to the Dallas school system in 1997, and this trademark litigation quickly followed.

Invoking § 43(a) of the Lanham Act, 15 U.S.C. § 1125(a), Bretford contends that the V-shaped design is its product's trade dress, which Smith System has infringed. It also contends that Smith System engaged in "reverse passing off" when it incorporated some Bretford hardware into a sample table that it showed purchasing officials in Dallas. The parties waived their right to a jury trial, and the district court held evidentiary hearings and issued opinions over a number of years. Although at one point the judge found Smith System liable and awarded damages in Bretford's favor, he reversed course in light of *Wal–Mart Stores, Inc. v. Samara Brothers, Inc.*, 529 U.S. 205 (2000), and *Dastar Corp. v. Twentieth Century Fox Film Corp.*, 539 U.S. 23 (2003). The appeal presents two principal questions: whether Smith System is entitled to copy Bretford's design, and, if yes, whether it was nonetheless wrongful for Smith System to use Bretford components in a sample table shown to the Dallas buyers.

. . . .

The district court found that V-shaped legs do not signal Bretford as a source. The record supports this conclusion; indeed, Bretford has *no* evidence that the leg design prompts "Bretford" in buyers' minds. There are no surveys and no evidence of actual confusion. Both Bretford and Smith System sell through distributors and field representatives to sophisticated buyers who know exactly where their goods are coming from.

Many buyers ask for tables with V-shaped legs, and Bretford insists that this shows that they want its Connectionst furniture; quite the contrary, this form of specification does more to imply that the leg design is functional than to show that anyone cares who makes the table. In the end, all Bretford has to go on is the fact that it was the only maker of such tables for eight years and spent more than $4 million to promote sales. If that were enough to permit judgment in its favor, new entry would be curtailed unduly by the risk and expense of trademark litigation, for *every* introducer of a new design could make the same sort of claim. "Consumers should not be deprived of the benefits of competition with regard to the utilitarian and esthetic purposes that product design ordinarily serves by a rule of law that facilitates plausible threats of suit against new entrants based on alleged inherent distinctiveness." *Wal–Mart*, 529 U.S. at 213.

. . . .

When Smith System decided to copy Bretford's table, it subcontracted the leg assemblies to a specialized metal fabricator, whose initial efforts were unsatisfactory. This left Smith System in a bind when the Dallas school system asked to see a table. Smith System cobbled a sample together by attaching the leg assembly from a Bretford table (which Smith System had repainted) to a top that Smith System had manufactured itself. (Who supplied other components, such as the cable guides and grommets, is disputed but irrelevant.) Dallas was satisfied and placed an order. All of the tables delivered to Dallas included legs manufactured by Smith System's subcontractor. Nonetheless, Bretford contends, by using its leg assemblies on even the one sample, Smith System engaged in reverse passing off and must pay damages.

Passing off or palming off occurs when a firm puts someone else's trademark on its own (usually inferior) goods; reverse passing off or misappropriation is selling someone else's goods under your own mark. See *Roho, Inc. v. Marquis*, 902 F.2d 356, 359 (5th Cir. 1990). It is not clear what's wrong with reselling someone else's goods, if you first buy them at retail. If every automobile sold by DeLorean includes the chassis and engine of a Peugeot, with DeLorean supplying only the body shell, Peugeot has received its asking price for each car sold and does not suffer any harm. Still, the Supreme Court said in *Dastar* that "reverse passing off" can violate the Lanham Act if a misdescription of goods' origin causes commercial injury. . . .

Dastar added that the injury must be a *trademark* loss—which is to say, it must come from a misrepresentation of the goods' origin. Dastar thus had the right (so far as the Lanham Act is concerned) to incorporate into its videos footage taken and edited by others, provided that it manufactured the finished product and did not mislead anyone about who should be held responsible for shortcomings. No one makes a product from scratch, with trees and iron ore entering one end of the plant and a finished consumer product emerging at the other. Ford's cars include Fram oil filters, Goodyear tires, Owens–Corning glass, Bose radios, Pennzoil lubricants, and many other constituents; buyers can see some of the other producers' marks (those on the radio and tires for example) but not others, such as the oil and transmission fluid. Smith System builds tables using wood from one supplier, grommets (including Teflon from du Pont) from another, and vinyl molding and paint and bolts from any of a hundred more sources—the list is extensive even for a simple product such as a table. If Smith System does not tell du Pont how the Teflon is used, and does not inform its consumers which firm supplied the wood, has it violated the Lanham Act? Surely not; the statute does not condemn the way in which all products are made.

Legs are a larger fraction of a table's total value than grommets and screws, but nothing in the statute establishes one rule for "major" components and another for less costly inputs. The right question, *Dastar* holds, is whether the consumer knows who has produced the finished product. In the *Dastar* case that was Dastar itself, even though most of the product's economic value came from elsewhere; just so when Smith System includes components manufactured by others but stands behind the finished product. The portion of § 43(a) that addresses reverse passing off is the one that condemns false designations of origin. "Origin" means, *Dastar* holds, "the producer of the tangible product sold in the marketplace". 539 U.S. at 31. As far as Dallas was concerned, the table's "origin" was Smith System, no matter who made any component or subassembly.

Much of Bretford's argument takes the form that it is just "unfair" for Smith System to proceed as it did, making a sale before its subcontractor could turn out acceptable leg assemblies. Businesses often think competition unfair, but federal law encourages wholesale copying, the better to drive down prices. Consumers rather than producers are the objects of the law's solicitude. . . .

AFFIRMED.

QUESTIONS

1. What is the difference between "false designation of origin" and ordinary trademark infringement? One obvious answer is that section 43(a) permits suits even when no registered trademark is involved. Putting to one side the fact that false designation of origin claims vindicate trademark-like interests in trademark-like symbols, is there any difference between the sort of conduct that is actionable as trademark infringement under section 32 and the conduct reached by section 43(a)?

2.   In *Bretford*, Judge Easterbrook questions the policy justification for reading the Lanham Act to permit recovery for reverse passing off: "It's not clear what's wrong with reselling someone else's goods, if you first buy them at retail." If the trademark owner has already made a profit on a retail sale, why might it object to some other seller's reselling the product under a different trademark? Are those objections persuasive?

3.   If Smith wants to use Bretford's V-shaped leg assemblies as components of its tables, may it advertise that it does so? *Cf. Bumble Bee Seafoods v. UFS Industries, supra* Chapter 6.A.

CHAPTER 8

ADVERTISING

In the mid 1990s, Pillsbury introduced a convenience breakfast food product to compete with Kellogg's Pop Tarts® Pillsbury launched its new "Toaster Strudel®" with a television commercial that began with an exterior shot of a suburban home. A boy ran out of the house, and we heard his mother's voice calling "Don't forget your PopTart®" The boy grabbed his PopTart® and ran down to the sidewalk where he met another boy. He asked him, "Got the Toaster Strudel®?" He then traded his PopTart® for a small package.

The camera cut away to a picture of the delectable Toaster Strudel®, while a voice-over explained its delicious qualities.

The commercial returned to a shot of the two boys as they arrived in school and walked into the school locker room. The first boy asked his friend "What do you do with all those PopTarts®?" Just then, the friend pulled open his locker door, and a tower of dozens of stacked PopTarts® overbalanced and spilled out of the locker and onto the floor. Cut to a picture of the Toaster Strudel® box. "Toaster Strudel®," said the voice-over. "Something good just popped up."

Actionable? The use does not seem to come within the literal terms of section 33(b)(4)'s fair use defense, explored *supra* chapter 6.C.2. Indeed, at the beginning of the commercial, viewers may well have believed that they were watching an ad for PopTarts®. An analogous potential for initial confusion, later dispelled, led to liability in *Mobil Oil Corp v. Pegasus Petroleum*, and *Blockbuster Entertainment Group v. Laylco, Inc., supra,* Chapter 6. Should the same principle apply here? Does it matter whether Toaster Strudel® is in fact more delicious than PopTarts®?

During a particularly heated competition among the manufacturers of over-the-counter antacids, the makers of Tagamet® aired a television commercial claiming that physicians overwhelmingly prescribed Tagamet® in preference to Pepcid®. The makers of Pepcid®, meanwhile, were broadcasting a commercial claiming that 8 out of 10 doctors recommended Pepcid® over Tagamet®. Both claims could not be true; both, in fact, were false. *See SmithKline Beecham Consumer Healthcare v. Johnson & Johnson–Merck Consumer Pharmaceuticals Company*, 906 F.Supp. 178 (S.D.N.Y.1995). Under what circumstances should a complaint that an ad is false, misleading or deceptive state a claim under the Lanham Act?

Chapter 8 examines the Lanham Act's application to product advertising. Section A surveys the caselaw dealing with use of other entities' marks in connection with ostensibly truthful comparative advertising. Section B examines the Lanham Act's treatment of false and deceptive advertising.

A. Comparative Advertising

Smith v. Chanel, Inc.

402 F.2d 562 (9th Cir.1968).

■ Browning, J:

Appellant R. G. Smith, doing business as Ta'Ron, Inc., advertised a fragrance called "Second Chance" as a duplicate of appellees' "Chanel No. 5," at a fraction of the latter's price. Appellees were granted a preliminary injunction prohibiting any reference to Chanel No. 5 in the promotion or sale of appellants' product. This appeal followed.

The action rests upon a single advertisement published in "Specialty Salesman," a trade journal directed to wholesale purchasers. The advertisement offered "The Ta'Ron Line of Perfumes" for sale. It gave the seller's address as "Ta'Ron Inc., 26 Harbor Cove, Mill Valley, Calif." It stated that the Ta'Ron perfumes "duplicate 100% perfect the exact scent of the world's finest and most expensive perfumes and colognes at prices that will zoom sales to volumes you have never before experienced!" It repeated the claim of exact duplication in a variety of forms.

The advertisement suggested that a "Blindfold Test" be used "on skeptical prospects," challenging them to detect any difference between a well-known fragrance and the Ta'Ron "duplicate." One suggested challenge was, "We dare you to try to detect any difference between Chanel #5* (25.00) and Ta'Ron's 2nd Chance. $7.00."

In an order blank printed as part of the advertisement each Ta'Ron fragrance was listed with the name of the well-known fragrance which it purportedly duplicated immediately beneath. Below "Second Chance" appeared "(Chanel #5)." The asterisk referred to a statement at the bottom of the form reading "Registered Trade Name of Original Fragrance House."

Appellees conceded below and concede here that appellants "have the right to copy, if they can, the unpatented formula of appellees' products." Moreover, for the purposes of these proceedings, appellees assume that "the products manufactured and advertised by [appellants] are *in fact* equivalents of those products manufactured by appellees." (Emphasis in original.) Finally, appellees disclaim any contention that the packaging or labeling of appellants' "Second Chance" is misleading or confusing.

I

The principal question presented on this record is whether one who has copied an unpatented product sold under a trademark may use the trademark in his advertising to identify the product he has copied. We hold that he may, and that such advertising may not be enjoined under either the Lanham Act, 15 U.S.C. § 1125(a) (1964), or the common law of unfair competition, so long as it does not contain misrepresentations or create a reasonable likelihood that purchasers will be confused as to the source, identify, or sponsorship of the advertiser's product.

This conclusion is supported by direct holdings in *Saxlehner v. Wagner*, 216 U.S. 375, 30 S. Ct. 298, 54 L. Ed. 525 (1910); *Viavi Co. v. Vimedia Co.*, 245 F. 289 (8th Cir.1917), and *Societe Comptoir de L'Industrie Cotonniere Etablissements Boussac v. Alexander's Dept. Stores, Inc.*, 299 F.2d 33, 1 A.L.R.3d 752 (2d Cir. 1962).

In *Saxlehner* the copied product was a "bitter water" drawn from certain privately owned natural springs. The plaintiff sold the natural water under the name "Hunyadi Janos," a valid trademark. The defendant was enjoined from using plaintiff's trademark to designate defendant's "artificial" water, but was permitted to use it to identify plaintiff's natural water as the product which defendant was copying.

Justice Holmes wrote:

> We see no reason for disturbing the finding of the courts below that there was no unfair competition and no fraud. The real intent of the plaintiff's bill, it seems to us, is to extend the monopoly of such trademark or trade name as she may have to a monopoly of her type of bitter water, by preventing manufacturers from telling the public in a way that will be understood, what they are copying and trying to sell. But the plaintiff has no patent for the water, and the defendants have a right to reproduce it as nearly as they can. *They have a right to tell the public what they are doing, and to get whatever share they can in the popularity of the water by advertising that they are trying to make the same article, and think that they succeed. If they do not convey, but, on the contrary, exclude, the notion that they are selling the plaintiff's goods, it is a strong proposition that when the article has a well-known name they have got the right to explain by that name what they imitate.* By doing so, they are not trying to get the good will of the name, but the good will of the goods. 216 U.S. at 380–381, 30 S. Ct. at 298, 299 (citations omitted) (emphasis added).

In *Viavi Co. v. Vimedia Co.*, plaintiff sold unpatented proprietary medicinal preparations under the registered trademark "Viavi," and local sellers of defendant's medicinal preparations represented to prospective purchasers that Vimedia products "were the same or as good as Viavi" preparations. The court held, "[in] the absence of such a monopoly as a patent confers, any persons may reproduce the articles, if they can, and may sell them under the representation that they are the same article, if they exclude the notion that they are the plaintiff's goods." 245 F. at 292.

In *Societe Comptoir de L'Industrie Cotonnière Etablissements Boussac v. Alexander's Dept. Stores, Inc.*, the defendant used plaintiff's registered trademarks "Dior" and "Christian Dior" in defendant's advertising in identifying plaintiff's dresses as the original creations from which defendant's dresses were copied. The district court refused to grant a preliminary injunction.

The appellate court considered plaintiff's rights under both the Lanham Act and common law. Noting that the representation that defendant's dresses were copies of "Dior" originals was apparently truthful and that there was no evidence of deception or confusion as to the origin or sponsorship of defendant's garments (299 F.2d at 35), the court disposed of the claim of right under the Lanham Act as follows:

> In any proceeding under the Lanham Act the gist of the proceeding is a "false description or representation," 15 U.S.C.A. § 1125(a), or a use of the mark which "is likely to cause confusion or mistake or to deceive purchasers as to the source of origin of such goods or services," 15 U.S.C.A. § 1114(1).... Registration bestows upon the owner of the mark the limited right to protect his good will from possible harm by those uses of another as may engender a belief in the mind of the public that the product identified by the infringing mark is made or sponsored by the owner of the mark.... *The Lanham Act does not prohibit a commercial rival's truthfully denominating his goods a copy of a design in the public domain, though he uses the name of the designer to do so. Indeed it is difficult to see any other means that might be employed to inform the consuming public of the true origin of the design.* 299 F.2d at 36 (citations omitted) (emphasis added).

. . . .

The rule rests upon the traditionally accepted premise that the only legally relevant function of a trademark is to impart information as to the source or sponsorship of the product. Appellees argue that protection should also be extended to the trademark's commercially more important function of embodying consumer good will created through extensive, skillful, and costly advertising. The courts, however, have generally confined legal protection to the trademark's source identification function for reasons grounded in the public policy favoring a free, competitive economy.

Preservation of the trademark as a means of identifying the trademark owner's products, implemented both by the Lanham Act and the common law, serves an important public purpose.[13] It makes effective competition possible in a complex, impersonal marketplace by providing a means through which the consumer can identify products which please him and reward the producer with continued patronage. Without some such method

---

13. It also serves two substantial private interests of the owner: It protects him from diversion of sales through a competitor's use of his trademark or one confusingly similar to it; and it protects his reputation from the injury that could occur if the competitor's goods were inferior.

of product identification, informed consumer choice, and hence meaningful competition in quality, could not exist.

. . . .

A related consideration is also pertinent to the present case. Since appellees' perfume was unpatented, appellants had a right to copy it, as appellees concede. There was a strong public interest in their doing so, "[for] imitation is the life blood of competition. It is the unimpeded availability of substantially equivalent units that permits the normal operation of supply and demand to yield the fair price society must pay for a given commodity." *American Safety Table Co. v. Schreiber*, 269 F.2d 255, 272 (2d Cir.1959). But this public benefit might be lost if appellants could not tell potential purchasers that appellants' product was the equivalent of appellees' product. "A competitor's chief weapon is his ability to represent his product as being equivalent and cheaper . . . ." Alexander, *Honesty and Competition*, 39 So. Cal. L. Rev. 1, 4 (1966). The most effective way (and, where complex chemical compositions sold under trade names are involved, often the only practical way) in which this can be done is to identify the copied article by its trademark or trade name. To prohibit use of a competitor's trademark for the sole purpose of identifying the competitor's product would bar effective communication of claims of equivalence. Assuming the equivalence of "Second Chance" and "Chanel No. 5," the public interest would not be served by a rule of law which would preclude sellers of "Second Chance" from advising consumers of the equivalence and thus effectively deprive consumers of knowledge that an identical product was being offered at one third the price.

As Justice Holmes wrote in *Saxlehner v. Wagner*, the practical effect of such a rule would be to extend the monopoly of the trademark to a monopoly of the product. The monopoly conferred by judicial protection of complete trademark exclusivity would not be preceded by examination and approval by a governmental body, as is the case with most other government-granted monopolies. Moreover, it would not be limited in time, but would be perpetual.

Against these considerations, two principal arguments are made for protection of trademark values other than source identification.

The first of these, as stated in the findings of the district court, is that the creation of the other values inherent in the trademark require "the expenditure of great effort, skill and ability," and that the competitor should not be permitted "to take a free ride" on the trademark owner's "widespread goodwill and reputation."

. . . .

A large expenditure of money does not in itself create legally protectable rights. Appellees are not entitled to monopolize the public's desire for the unpatented product, even though they themselves created that desire at great effort and expense. As we have noted, the most effective way (and in some cases the only practical way) in which others may compete in satisfying the demand for the product is to produce it and tell the public they have done so, and if they could be barred from this effort appellees would have found a way to acquire a practical monopoly in the unpatented product to which they are not legally entitled.

Disapproval of the copyist's opportunism may be an understandable first reaction, "[but] this initial response to the problem has been curbed in deference to the greater public good." *American Safety Table Co. v. Schreiber,* 269 F.2d at 272. By taking his "free ride," the copyist, albeit unintentionally, serves an important public interest by offering comparable goods at lower prices. On the other hand, the trademark owner, perhaps equally without design, sacrifices public to personal interests by seeking immunity from the rigors of competition.

Moreover, appellees' reputation is not directly at stake. Appellants' advertisement makes it clear that the product they offer is their own. If it proves to be inferior, they, not appellees, will bear the burden of consumer disapproval.

The second major argument for extended trademark protection is that even in the absence of confusion as to source, use of the trademark of another "creates a serious threat to the uniqueness and distinctiveness" of the trademark, and "if continued would create a risk of making a generic or descriptive term of the words" of which the trademark is composed.

The contention has little weight in the context of this case. Appellants do not use appellees' trademark as a generic term. They employ it only to describe appellees' product, not to identify their own. They do not label their product "Ta'Ron's Chanel No. 5," as they might if appellees' trademark had come to be the common name for the product to which it is applied. Appellants' use does not challenge the distinctiveness of appellees' trademark, or appellees' exclusive right to employ that trademark to indicate source or sponsorship. For reasons already discussed, we think appellees are entitled to no more. . . .

We are satisfied, therefore, that both authority and reason require a holding that in the absence of misrepresentation or confusion as to source or sponsorship a seller in promoting his own goods may use the trademark of another to identify the latter's goods. The district court's contrary conclusion cannot support the injunction.

. . . . .

"If You Like Plaintiff, You'll Love Defendant"

Sequels to *Smith v. Chanel* have pitted well-known name brand producers against second comers proposing substitute goods in advertisements proclaiming, "if you like [x's expensive product], you'll love [our cheaper identical product]." Like/love advertisements involving "smell-alike" perfumes have spawned litigation in several courts, with disparate results. In *Calvin Klein Cosmetics v. Parfums de Coeur,* 824 F.2d 665 (8th Cir.1987), the appellate court rejected challenges by the producers of "Calvin Klein's OBSESSION" scent against the like/love advertisements of the producers of CONFESS. Plaintiffs had asserted that the frequent and emphatic reference to the OBSESSION mark in defendant's advertisements and point-of-sale displays created confusion regarding Calvin Klein's sponsorship or origination of the CONFESS perfume. The court found that the overall commercial context of the CONFESS promotion, including defendant's prominent use of the phrase "Designer Imposters by Parfums de Coeur" in connection with its like/love slogan, dispelled likelihood of consumer confusion.

By contrast, in *Charles of the Ritz Group Ltd. v. Quality King Distributors, Inc.*, 832 F.2d 1317 (2d Cir.1987), a different federal appellate court reached a different result regarding a like/love campaign setting Yves St. Laurent's OPIUM perfume against defendant's OMNI substitute. Applying the *Polaroid* factors, the trial court determined, and the Second Circuit affirmed, that a series of like/love slogans were inadequate to allay likely consumer confusion. Defendant's first rejected slogan stated: "If you like OPIUM, you'll love OMNI." The second rejected slogan stated: "If you like OPIUM, a fragrance by Yves St. Laurent, you'll love OMNI, a fragrance by Deborah International Beauty." The third rejected slogan, and the subject of the appeal, repeated the second slogan, but accompanied it with a disclaimer: "If you like OPIUM, a fragrance by Yves St. Laurent, you'll love OMNI, a fragrance by Deborah International Beauty. Yves St. Laurent and Opium are not related in any manner to Deborah International Beauty and Omni." Elements supporting the finding of likelihood of confusion included the visual similarity of the marks OPIUM and OMNI and of the products' trade dress, and evidence of actual consumer confusion. Significantly, the Second Circuit further held that the burden was on defendant "to introduce empirical evidence that the disclaimer actually lessens consumer confusion as required to overcome such a previous finding [of likelihood of confusion]."

More recently, in *Tommy Hilfiger Licensing, Inc. v. Nature Labs, L.L.C.*, 221 F. Supp. 2d 410 (S.D.N.Y. 2002), plaintiff, owner of the TOMMY HILFIGER mark for fragrances, sued defendant for marketing a "TIMMY HOLEDIGER" perfume for dogs using the slogan: *"If you like Tommy Hilfiger Your Pet Will Love Timmy Holedigger."* The court concluded that because defendant's product was an obvious parody, there was no likelihood of confusion.

QUESTIONS

1. It makes intuitive sense to permit defendant to label his goods truthfully to inform the consumer what the goods are, even if that label explicitly mentions a competing product. Defendant has a right to manufacture perfumes under the same unpatented formula as Chanel's; defendant therefore can inform the public of the identity of formulae and scents. But should truthful labeling necessarily extend to the use of a competitor's trademark? A second-comer may be entitled to make identical goods, but does it follow that he may sell them by reference to the mark, and goodwill, of another producer? Why not limit the second-comer to the truthful statement of the formula, or of other descriptive information, without identifying the rival producer's mark?

2. Your client is a producer of smell-alike perfumes. He presents you with the following advertisement. What problems do you see?

3. Does it help to view "like/love" slogans as an "invitation to compare" the original goods and the proposed substitute? What information does the consumer need to make the comparison? *Cf. Ross Cosmetics Distribution Ctrs. v. United States*, 34 U.S.P.Q.2d 1758 (Ct Int'l. Trade 1994), *infra*, Chapter 13.D (preventing importation of confusingly labelled "like/love" perfume substitute).

WHY ARE WE GIVING AWAY

OUR FULL-SIZED ¼ OZ. VERSIONS OF GIORGIO, OPIUM, CHANEL NO. 5, L'AIR DU TEMPS AND OSCAR DE LA RENTA

Only $2.00 Each?

FREE with every order over $12.00. A full ¼ oz. bottle of Hallbrook's version of Joy — the world's most expensive perfume.

TRADEMARKS AND BOTTLE DESIGNS ARE THE EXCLUSIVE PROPERTY OF ORIGINAL MANUFACTURERS.

As part of a nationwide marketing campaign to prove that our perfumes are the most authentic versions of these world famous originals, we are giving away full ¼ oz. bottles for the astonishing publicity price of only $2.00 each to every person who completes the order form shown here within the next 30 days.

Giorgio, Opium, Chanel No. 5, L'Air du Temps and Oscar de la Renta are all perfume classics. But many people cannot readily afford the luxury price tag of even a ¼ oz. bottle. Now Hallbrook has unlocked the secrets of the World's Greatest Perfumes and we're confident our versions are the best in the country today. Aged and blended from natural essences and sumptuous perfume oils, our perfumes are so expertly mixed, so close to the originals we challenge you to tell the difference.

To prove it, we're giving away our versions for just $2.00 each in the hope that you will purchase our full-sized perfumes from now on...at a fraction of the price of the originals. Over 600,000 satisfied customers tell us that our perfumes are among the most glorious and desirable in the world.

These nationally advertised perfumes will not be sold at this price by the company in any store. There is a limit of sixteen (16) bottles per address at this price, but if your request is made early enough (within the next 15 days) you may request up to thirty-two (32) or two complete sets. Orders mailed within the next 15 days which are over $12.00 will also receive a FREE bottle of our version of Joy — the world's most expensive fragrance.

Conn. residents add sales tax. Make checks payable to Value Fair.

The famous brand	Reg. retail price	Our Version	Our Price	Quantity	Total
Giorgio	$75.00	601	$2.00		
Opium	$72.50	602	$2.00		
Chanel No. 5	$65.00	603	$2.00		
Oscar de la Renta	$60.00	604	$2.00		
L'air du Temps	$110.00	605	$2.00		
Escape	$85.00	606	$2.00		
Gio	$75.00	607	$2.00		
Tresor	$75.00	608	$2.00		
Beautiful	$70.00	609	$2.00		
Obsession	$65.00	611	$2.00		
Poison	$75.00	612	$2.00		
Amarige	$75.00	613	$2.00		
Passion	$80.00	614	$2.00		
Giorgio Red	$75.00	615	$2.00		
Eternity	$94.00	616	$2.00		
White Diamonds	$82.00	617	$2.00		
Sung	$96.00	618	$2.00		

Please allow 4-6 weeks for delivery.

56-MKT

Shipping & Handling	$3.50	
Sub Total		
CT res. add sales tax		
Total Enclosed	$	

VALUE FAIR™
P.O. Box 3505
Wallingford, CT 06492

Please rush my FULL SIZE 1/4 oz. versions of the fragrances I have checked. I am including only $3.50 for postage and handling regardless of how many I order.

☐ My order value exceeds $12.00. Please send a FREE 1/4 oz. bottle of Hallbrook's version of Joy.

☐ Check/Money Order Enclosed

☐ Charge to my VISA

☐ Charge to my Master Card

SATISFACTION GUARANTEED

Name _____
Address _____
City _____
State _____ Zip _____
Account # _____

4. Suppose that Ta'Ron not only promoted "Second Chance" as identical to "Chanel No. 5," but offered customers, with each bottle of "Second Chance," an empty, recycled bottle of "Chanel No. 5," anticipating (but not expressly directing) that customers would fill the Chanel bottle with the Ta'Ron substitute, and discard the Ta'Ron bottle. Any liability under the Lanham Act? What if Ta'Ron did not supply the Chanel bottles, but its advertisements encouraged customers to transfer "Second Chance" to any leftover Chanel bottles the customers might have? What if Ta'Ron neither said nor supplied anything regarding refills of old Chanel bottles, but Ta'Ron were nonetheless aware (and expected) that many customers would do exactly that?

5. Davidoff manufactures premium cigars. JR Tobacco sells a "J*R Alternatives" line of copied cigars, which JR advertises as "duplicating as closely as possible the size, shape, taste, origin and wrapper cover" of the premium cigars from which they were copied, including several Davidoff cigars. Other ads for the entire J*R Alternatives line insist that "in many instances the cigars sold under the super premium label, the premium label, and our J*R label are the identical product!" Davidoff insists that the J*R cigars are far inferior, and that the only features of its premium cigars that JR actually copied were their size, shape and wrapper color. Are JR's ads actionable? Who should bear the burden of proof regarding the comparability of the cigars and the steps taken to achieve it? *See JR Tobacco of America v. Davidoff of Geneva*, 957 F.Supp. 426 (S.D.N.Y.1997).

August Storck K.G. v. Nabisco, Inc.

59 F.3d 616 (7th Cir.1995).

■ EASTERBROOK, CIRCUIT JUDGE:

It happened a long time ago in the little village of Werther. There, the candymaker, Gustav Nebel, created his very finest candy, taking real butter, fresh cream, white and brown sugars, a pinch of salt, and lots of time. And because these butter candies tasted especially delicious, he called the candy "Werther's Original", in honor of his little village of Werther. So reads the pitch on a bag of Werther's® Original candies. Nabisco surely developed its competing candy a different way—in a chemist's lab, followed by testing in focus groups. Nabisco concluded that Nebel used too much sugar for modern tastes and worries; it substituted isomalt, hydrogenated glucose syrup, and acesulfame potassium. Its packaging of Life Savers® Delites™ screams: *"25 percent LOWER IN CALORIES THAN WERTHER'S® ORIGINAL * CANDY"*. August Storck K.G., which makes and sells Werther's® Original, learned about Life Savers Delites™ from prototype trade samples; the candy is not scheduled for introduction until this coming August. Storck did not appreciate the comparison and filed this suit under the Lanham Act, 15 U.S.C. §§ 1114, 1125(a), arguing that Nabisco was about to infringe its trademark and trade dress. The district court issued a preliminary injunction, forbidding Nabisco to use the packaging it has devised. 1995 U.S. Dist. LEXIS 3486 (N.D. Ill.). Nabisco tells us that if it must come up with new packaging the new candy cannot be introduced until 1996.

The prototype packaging for Life Savers® Delites™ that Storck attached to the complaint used the words "Werther's Original" without either the ® symbol or the asterisk that Nabisco will include in the product offered for sale. The asterisk refers to a disclaimer: "WERTHER'S® ORIGINAL is a registered trademark of and is made by August Storck KG. Storck does not make or license Life Savers Delites™." Nabisco assures us that it does not (and never did) plan to market a product without the ® symbol or disclaimer, and that it told Storck so. Before the district judge issued the injunction, Nabisco gave him a copy of the consumer packaging. The judge remarked that if he had seen Nabisco's revised packaging earlier "the Court's ruling might have been different"—and then issued the injunction anyway. Yet Nabisco did not yield to the pressure of litigation, demonstrating in the process that an injunction is essential to prevent it from returning to its preferred practices; Nabisco's corporate policy calls for the use of an ® symbol and disclaimer when mentioning rivals' products. That an injunction could have been appropriate to prevent the use of Storck's registered trademark without the symbol and disclaimer does not mean that it is appropriate once the judge learns that all prospect of an improper use has vanished. Quite the contrary, the injunction hampers a form of competition highly beneficial to consumers.

We reproduce at the end of this opinion Storck's packaging and Nabisco's proposed packaging. (Nabisco plans to introduce four different Life Savers® Delites™ collections; we show only the two that refer to Storck's product.) It is hard to see how anyone could think that the Life Savers® Delites™ package contains Werther's® Original candies or has anything to do with Storck's product. Life Savers®, one of the most famous brand names in American life, is emblazoned on the package of Life Savers® Delites™; the candy-gulping public will quickly grasp that the point of the diagonal stripe containing the Werther's® Original name is to distinguish the two candies—to say that one is different from, and better than, the other. Trademarks designate the origin and quality of products. *Qualitex Co. v. Jacobson Products Co.*, 131 L. Ed. 2d 248, 115 S. Ct. 1300 (1995); *Green River Bottling Co. v. Green River Corp.*, 997 F.2d 359 (7th Cir.1993); William M. Landes & Richard A. Posner, *Trademark Law: An Economic Perspective*, 30 J.L. & ECON. 265 (1987). A use of a rival's mark that does not engender confusion about origin or quality is therefore permissible. *Prestonettes Inc. v. Coty*, 264 U.S. 359, 68 L. Ed. 731, 44 S. Ct. 350 (1924); *Saxlehner v. Wagner*, 216 U.S. 375, 54 L. Ed. 525, 30 S. Ct. 298 (1910); *Calvin Klein Cosmetics Corp. v. Lenox Laboratories, Inc.*, 815 F.2d 500 (8th Cir.1987); *G.D. Searle & Co. v. Hudson Pharmaceutical Corp.*, 715 F.2d 837 (3d Cir.1983). The use is not just permissible in the sense that one firm is entitled to do everything within legal bounds to undermine a rival;

it is beneficial to consumers. They learn at a glance what kind of product is for sale and how it differs from a known benchmark. Storck does not say that Nabisco's claim is false. That Life Savers® Delites™ are 25 percent lower in calories than Werther's® Original candies is something consumers may want to know before deciding which candy to buy.

Both the FTC and the FDA encourage product comparisons. The FTC believes that consumers gain from comparative advertising, and to make the comparison vivid the Commission "encourages the naming of, or reference to competitors". 16 C.F.R. § 14.15(b). A "comparison" to a mystery rival is just puffery; it is not falsifiable and therefore is not informative. Because comparisons must be concrete to be useful, the FDA's regulations implementing the Nutrition Labeling and Education Act of 1990, 21 U.S.C. § 301 note, prefer that the object of a nutritional comparison be the market leader (a "comparison" to a product consumers do not recognize is as useless as a comparison to an anonymous rival) or an average of the three leading brands. 21 C.F.R. § 101.13(j)(1)(ii)(A). Werther's® Original is the top selling butter cream hard candy, so Nabisco's claim follows the FDA's guideline.

Under the circumstances, the district judge's statement that the use of the Werther's® Original mark on the Life Savers® Delites™ package creates a "possibility" of confusion cannot support an injunction. Many consumers are ignorant or inattentive, so some are bound to misunderstand no matter how careful a producer is. *See Gammon v. GC Services Limited Partnership*, 27 F.3d 1254, 1258–60 (7th Cir.1994) (concurring opinion). If such a possibility created a trademark problem, then all comparative references would be forbidden, and consumers as a whole would be worse off.

Likelihood of confusion in a trademark case is a factual issue, and appellate review is deferential. *Scandia Down Corp. v. Euroquilt, Inc.*, 772 F.2d 1423, 1428 (7th Cir.1985). But the district court did not hold an evidentiary hearing. Nabisco and Storck informed us at oral argument that to this day no one has conducted the surveys customary in trademark cases, showing the packaging or product to consumers and asking: "Who makes this?" or "Are these two products made by the same firm?" Perhaps the packages are confusing after all; we make little of the disclaimer, which few consumers will read. *International Kennel Club v. Mighty Star, Inc.*, 846 F.2d 1079, 1093 (7th Cir.1988). But all the district court found—all that it could find on this record—is that Nabisco's packaging uses Storck's mark and that confusion is possible. That is not enough to postpone the introduction of a new product. When deciding whether to grant or withhold equitable relief a court must give high regard to the interest of the general public, which is a great beneficiary from competition. Although the benefits of competition do not justify the introduction of products that engender substantial confusion, *see Abbott Laboratories v. Mead Johnson & Co.*, 971 F.2d 6, 18–19 (7th Cir.1992), when the plaintiff's showing is as thin as Storck's the interests of the public carry the day. Damages in trademark cases are hard to measure, but the possibility of compensation offers sufficient protection to a trademark owner, when an injunction bids fair to stifle competition and injure consumers in order to ward off occasional confusion. Even substantial deference to the district court's balancing of the equities cannot save an injunction when the judge overstates the private injury and disregards the public interest in competition. *See Abbott Laboratories*, 971 F.2d at 11–13; *Lawson Products, Inc. v. Avnet, Inc.*, 782 F.2d 1429, 1433 (7th Cir.1986); *American Hospital Supply Corp. v. Hospital Products Ltd.*, 780 F.2d 589, 593–94 (7th Cir.1986); *Roland Machinery Co. v. Dresser Industries, Inc.*, 749 F.2d 380, 387–88 (7th Cir.1984).

Storck argues not only that Nabisco infringes its trademark but also that the Life Savers® Delites™ package infringes its trade dress. Quoting from *Storck USA, L.P. v. Farley Candy Co.*, 797 F. Supp. 1399, 1406 (N.D.Ill.1992), the judge concluded that "the overall appearance of the Werther's Original package, including the layout of the trade dress elements, creates a distinctive and arbitrary visual impression." The "trade dress elements" the judge had in mind apparently are those in the "Old World Recipe" inset, which shows a quaint village behind two pitchers pouring white fluids together. We say "apparently" because the judge did not describe the "trade dress elements"; but we cannot suppose that he meant the mound of unwrapped candies that occupy the bottom third of the package, because he crossed out of Storck's proposed injunction a prohibition on using a package depicting a mound of candies. Having held that Storck's "trade dress elements" are distinctive, and therefore protectable without proof of secondary meaning, *Two Pesos, Inc. v. Taco Cabana, Inc.*, 120 L. Ed. 2d 615, 112 S. Ct. 2753 (1992), the district court immediately concluded that Storck is entitled to relief; it did not explain how or to what extent Nabisco's packages use the protected elements. The court stated, without supporting reasoning, that "the likelihood of confusion is a possibility as Nabisco's package is currently designed." Once again, the district judge apparently believed that a "possibility" of confusion justifies a restriction on competition, which it does not. The lack of findings makes deference impossible and the injunction untenable.

The Life Savers® Delites™ butter toffee package shows a pitcher, an urn of milk, a stick of butter, and a mound of candies against a pastel yellow background; the vertical stripe is green. The "European Collection" package shows a butter churn, a coffee grinder, leaves of mint, and a mound of candies against a strawberry background; again the vertical stripe is green. Neither package shows two fluids being poured together in front of a picturesque town, the element that the district court in Farley Candy thought distinctive. Neither package uses Storck's color (a cream brown or tan). All of Nabisco's packages have a bold vertical stripe, in contrasting color, that Storck's lacks. Nabisco's packages are about half the size of Storck's and are taller than they are wide; Storck's is wider than it is tall. Both packages have banners, which are common graphic elements. Nabisco uses a convex yellow banner, with blue lettering, at the bottom center of the package; Storck uses a concave brown banner, with white lettering, in the upper left. The device of a banner is not independently protectable. *Storck USA, L.P. v. Farley Candy Co.*, 821 F. Supp. 524, 529 (N.D.Ill.1993), *affirmed*, 14 F.3d 311 (7th Cir.1994). And these banners are not similar.

Doubtless the overall appearance is what matters. *Kohler Co. v. Moen, Inc.*, 12 F.3d 632, 641 n. 11 (7th Cir.1993). Dissecting a product or package into components can cause a court to miss an overall similarity. *Two Pesos*, 112 S. Ct. at 2758; *Scandia Down*, 772 F.2d at 1431; *Roulo v. Russ Berrie & Co.*, 886 F.2d 931, 936 (7th Cir.1989). But neither survey evidence nor testimony in this record supports a conclusion that consumers would see these packages as similar in any respect beyond the mound of candies—which is such a common visual cue to the product inside, and so obviously functional, that it cannot be a protected trade dress. *Schwinn Bicycle Co. v. Ross Bicycles, Inc.*, 870 F.2d 1176, 1190 (7th Cir.1989). The differences between the packages are so great that it is impossible (on this record) to believe that Nabisco is taking advantage of Storck's goodwill, or even that its industrial designers have taken a free ride on the work of Storck's graphic arts department. It may be that after a full trial the record will support Storck's claims; the current record does not.

The preliminary injunction is reversed. So that Nabisco may proceed with the introduction of Life Savers® Delites™ on schedule, the mandate will issue today.

B. False Representations

Section 43(a)(1)(B); 15 U.S.C. § 1125(a)(1)(B)

Any person who, on or in connection with any goods or services, or any container for goods, uses in commerce any word, term, name, symbol, or device, or any combination thereof, or any false designation of origin, false or misleading description of fact, or false or misleading representation of fact, which—

. . . .

(2) in commercial advertising or promotion, misrepresents the nature, characteristics, qualities, or geographic origin of his or her or another person's goods, services, or commercial activities,

shall be liable in a civil action by any person who believes that he or she is or is likely to be damaged by such act.

Remarks of Rep. Kastenmeier, *Cong. Rec.,* Oct. 19, 1988, H 10420–21

Subsection (a) currently covers false designations of origin and false descriptions or representations with regard to a person's own products. It has been held, however, that Section 43(a) does not cover such statements with regard to the products of another. To rectify this situation, it was proposed to add the words "or another person's" to Section 43(a).

The proposal thus raised the issue of commercial defamation in the context of Section 43(a) and, as a result, a host of constitutional problems. The proposal was not limited to commercial speech, and appeared to apply to private citizens, the news media, and business competitors alike. No scienter was required. In addition, the subsection appeared to cover false statements of opinion as well as fact.

To avoid legitimate constitutional challenge, it was necessary to carefully limit the reach of the subsection. Because Section 43(a) will not provide a kind of commercial defamation action, the reach of the section specifically extends only to false and misleading speech that is encompassed within the "commercial speech" doctrine by the United States Supreme Court. In addition, subsection (a) will extend only to false and misleading statements of fact. As noted in the discussion of Section 32(2), critical constitutional protections modify the changes made in Section 43(a), and certain "innocent" disseminators of material that constitutes a violation of subsection (a) are protected from liability. Thus, through Section 32(2), innocent dissemination and communication of false and misleading advertising, including promotional material, by the media are excluded from the reach of Section 43(a). For a defendant who is a member of the media to be found liable under Section 43(a), the plaintiff must show that the defendant was not "innocent" under Section 32(2) and, as noted, that state of mind must encompass the *New York Times v. Sullivan* standard.

S. 1882 is limited in another important sense. It uses the word "commercial" to describe advertising or promotion for business purposes, whether conducted by for-profit or non-profit organizations or individuals. Political advertising and promotion is political speech, and therefore not encompassed by the term "commercial." This is true whether what is being promoted is an individual candidacy for public office, or a particular political issue or point of view. It is true regardless of whether the promoter is an individual or a for-profit entity. However, if a political or other similar organization engaged in business conduct incidental to its political functions, then the business conduct would be considered "commercial" and would fall within the confines of this section....

As Jerome Gilson, the noted trademark commentator, has written about USTA's proposal to limit the proposed change in Section 43(a) to commercial speech:

> Under this proposed change only false or misleading "advertising or promotion" would be actionable, whether it pertained to the advertiser itself or another party. The change would exclude all other misrepresentations from Section 43(a) coverage. These others are the type which raise free speech concerns, such as a Consumer Report which reviews and may disparage the quality of stereo speakers or other products, misrepresentations made by interested groups which may arguably disparage a company and its products because of the company's failure to divest its South African holdings, and disparaging statements made by commentators concerning corporate product liability and injuries to the public (e.g., A.H. Robins and the Dalkon shield cases, or the Manville Corporation asbestos cases). All of these would be judged by first amendment law (including New York Times v. Sullivan) and not Section 43(a) law ... Product disparagement based on false representations would be actionable only if they were made in the context of advertising or promotion, not in connection with Consumer Report publications.

As Mr. Gilson correctly notes, the proposed change in Section 43(a) should not be read in any way to limit political speech, consumer or editorial comment, parodies, satires, or other constitutionally protected material. Nor should it be read to change the standards in current law with respect to comparative advertising, which assists consumers in choosing among various competing products. The section is narrowly drafted to encompass only clearly false and misleading commercial speech.

The provision in Section 43(a) granting consumers standing to sue has been deleted from the bill. This provision would have clarified that consumers have standing to sue under Section 43(a). The plain meaning of the statute already includes consumers, since it grants any "person" the right to sue.

The committee's decision not to include proposed provisions relating to dilution, material omissions, and tarnishment and disparagement in Section 43 is carried forward. By this decision, current law remains in effect.

QUESTIONS

1. As discussed above, the 1988 amendments to § 43(a) expanded the realm of actionable deceptive advertisements. Is this a positive development, or should the trademark law revision have taken the opposite approach, and have eliminated private law federal false advertising claims altogether? After all, isn't more speech, in the form of replies or counter statements by the aggrieved producer, a better way than curtailing a competitor's claims to combat allegedly false speech in the market?

2. How should a court determine whether a contested representation is true or false?

1. COMMERCIAL ADVERTISING OR PROMOTION

The Procter & Gamble Company v. Amway Corporation

242 F.3d 539 (5th Cir.2001).

■ JERRY E. SMITH, CIRCUIT JUDGE:

. . . .

I.

P&G, a manufacturer and distributor of numerous household products, has been plagued by rumors of links to Satanism since the late 1970's or early 1980's. The most common variant of the rumor is that the president of P&G revealed on a television talk show that he worships Satan; that many of P&G's profits go to the church of Satan; and that there is no harm in such disclosure, because there are no longer enough Christians left in the United States for such devilish activities to make a difference. The rumor often was circulated in the form of a written flier that listed numerous P&G products and called for a boycott.

. . . .

The rumor re-surfaced on April 20, 1995, when an Amway distributor named Randy Haugen forwarded it to other Amway distributors via a telephone messaging system for Amway distributors known as "AmVox."[2]

2. AmVox is a communication system that Amway sells to its distributors to facilitate communication between and among them. Haugen received the rumor about P&G from another Amway distributor via AmVox and forwarded it to all his distributors saying, "This is a great message. Listen to it." The message was:

Hey, Jeff, this is Roger Patton. I wanted to run something by you real quick that I think you'll find pretty interesting. I was just talking to a guy the other night about this very subject and it just so happens that a guy brings information in, lays it on my desk this morning, so here it goes. It says the president of

Haugen is a highly successful Amway distributor with a network of tens of thousands to possibly 100,000 distributors underneath him throughout Utah, Nevada, Texas, Mexico, and Canada. . . .

There is no evidence that Haugen knew the rumor was false when he spread it; in fact, he testified that he believed it to be true. The rumor circulated in his and other distribution networks. Some Amway distributors printed fliers containing the rumor, circulating them to consumers, with a message saying, "We offer you an alternative." The fliers also gave contact information for Amway distributors . . . . .

Within days of the initial message containing the rumor, Haugen sent a short retraction via AmVox. Shortly thereafter, an Amway representative contacted Haugen and delivered a copy of a P&G "truth kit," which explains that the rumor is false. The Amway representative asked Haugen to issue another retraction via AmVox. Using the AmVox system, Haugen then sent out a second, more detailed, retraction. Despite Haugen's retractions, the rumor continued to circulate in Haugen's network and at least one other network for some time.

. . . .

IV.

P&G avers that the district court erred in ruling that P&G was required to prove "actual malice"[11] to prevail on its § 43(a) claim for disparagement of commercial activities. The actual-malice standard has developed in cases involving defamation of public figures. P&G argues that strict liability and not actual malice applies in a commercial speech[12] case under the Lanham Act.

Procter & Gamble appeared on the Phil Donahue Show on March 1st of '95. He announced that due to the openness of our society, he was coming out of the closet about his association with the Church of Satan. He stated that a large portion of the profits from the Procter & Gamble products go to support a satanic church. When asked by Donahue if stating this on television would hurt his business, his reply was there are not enough Christians in the United States to make a difference. And below it has a list of the Procter & Gamble products, which I'll read: [list of 44 P&G Brands] and says if you're not sure about a product, look for the symbol of the ram's horn that will appear on each product beginning in April. The ram's horn will form the 666 which is known as Satan's number. I tell ya, it really makes you count your blessings to have available to all of us a business that will allow us to buy all the products that we want from

our own shelf and I guess my real question is, if people aren't being loyal to themselves and buying from their own business, then whose business are they supporting and who are they buying from. Love ya. Talk to you later. Bye.

11. "Actual malice" is a term of art meaning that the speaker knew the statement was false when spoken or in fact entertained serious doubt about its truth. *Peter Scalamandre & Sons, Inc. v. Kaufman*, 113 F.3d 556, 560 (5th Cir. 1997). Actual malice must be proven by clear and convincing evidence. *Id.*

12. The First Amendment affords less protection to commercial speech and none to *false* commercial speech. *Va. State Bd. of Pharm. v. Va. Citizens Consumer Council, Inc.*, 425 U.S. 748, 771–72, 48 L. Ed. 2d 346, 96 S. Ct. 1817 (1976). No party questions that the speech linking P&G to Satanism is false.

Amway makes two arguments in response. First, acknowledging that the Lanham Act covers only commercial speech, Amway urges that the speech here is not commercial and that therefore a § 43(a) claim will not lie.[13] Second, and alternatively, Amway argues that even if the speech is commercial, the actual-malice standard should apply, because the Satanism rumor is an issue of public concern, and P&G is a "limited-purpose public figure" with respect to the rumor.

Thus, to determine what P&G is required to prove to prevail on its § 43(a) claim that Amway misrepresented its associations and commercial activities, we first must determine whether the spreading of the false Satanism rumor is "commercial" speech. . . .

A.

We begin by examining what is meant by, and what protections extend to, "commercial speech." First, we consider whether the commercial speech line of cases, which mainly deals with government regulation of speech, should apply in this case of a private action for false speech. Second, we examine the historical development of the commercial speech exception to the full protections granted by the First Amendment. In making this examination, we pay particular attention to the characteristics that the Supreme Court has said make certain speech "commercial" and therefore worthy of less protection. Third, we take the facts of the case *sub judice* and apply the test set out in *Bolger v. Youngs Drug Products Corp.*, 463 U.S. 60, 77 L. Ed. 2d 469, 103 S. Ct. 2875 (1983), for determining whether a specific instance of speech is commercial. Our application of the *Bolger* test is what ultimately determines whether the speech is commercial.

. . . .

2.

. . . .

Commercial speech has been defined, at its core, as speech that merely proposes a commercial transaction. *Virginia [State Pharmacy Board v. Virginia Citizens Consumer Council, Inc.*, 425 U.S. 748 (1976)] at 762.

---

13. In *Seven–Up Co. v. Coca–Cola Co.*, 86 F.3d 1379, 1383 n.6 (5th Cir. 1996), we held that the Lanham Act extends only to false or misleading speech that is encompassed within the Supreme Court's commercial speech doctrine:

> The "commercial" requirement was inserted to ensure that § 43(a) does not infringe on free speech protected by the First Amendment. See 135 Cong. Rec. H1216–17 (daily ed. Apr. 13, 1989) (statement of Rep. Kastenmeier) ("The proposed change in section 43(a) should not be read in any way to limit political speech, consumer or editorial comment, parodies, satires, or other constitutional-

ly protected material. . . . The section is narrowly drafted to encompass only clearly false and misleading commercial speech."); 134 Cong.Rec. 31,851 (Oct. 19, 1988) (statement of Rep. Kastenmeier) (commenting that the reach of § 43(a) "specifically extends only to false and misleading speech that is encompassed within the 'commercial speech' doctrine developed by the United States Supreme Court"). *See generally Gordon & Breach Science Publishers S.A., STBS v. Am. Inst. of Physics*, 859 F. Supp. 1521, 1533–34 (1994) (discussing the legislative history of the Lanham Act).

Because such speech traditionally has been thought less valuable than political speech, which is at the core of the First Amendment, commercial speech is not accorded the full protections given to political speech, speech on matters of public concern, and speech regarding public figures. In fact, for a time it was thought that commercial speech might not be worthy of any First Amendment protection.

In *Virginia State Board*, the Court finally decided that commercial speech should receive some protection, holding that a state may not prohibit pharmacists from truthfully advertising the prices at which they sell drugs. The Court suggested, however, that instead of the strict scrutiny with which courts review most restrictions on speech, a lower standard of scrutiny is appropriate for commercial speech. The Court noted that false or misleading commercial speech should receive no protection, because commercial speech merely gives information to consumers about a producer's goods, and any false information either has no value or is harmful.

> [I]n defining something as commercial speech, the Court says we are to rely on "the 'commonsense' distinction between speech proposing a commercial transaction, which occurs in an area traditionally subject to government regulation, and other varieties of speech." *Ohralik v. Ohio State Bar Ass'n*, 436 U.S. 447, 455–56, 56 L. Ed. 2d 444, 98 S. Ct. 1912 (1978).

Further, although Amway argues that the Satanism rumor is a matter of public concern, which should make the speech noncommercial, the Court "has made clear that advertising which 'links a product to a current public debate' is not thereby entitled to the constitutional protection afforded noncommercial speech." *Bolger*, 463 U.S. at 68 (quoting *Central Hudson*, 447 U.S. at 563, n.5). Thus, in *Bolger* the Court held that informational pamphlets mailed by a condom manufacturer directly to the public constituted commercial speech, even though the pamphlets spoke about matters of public concern.

. . . . .

3.

We now apply the test the Court has set out to determine whether a specific instance of speech is commercial. In *Bolger*, the Court recognized three factors that help determine whether speech is commercial: (i) whether the communication is an advertisement, (ii) whether the communication refers to a specific product or service, and (iii) whether the speaker has an economic motivation for the speech. If all three factors are present, there is "strong support" for the conclusion that the speech is commercial. *Bolger*, 463 U.S. at 67.

Here we consider the *Bolger* factors in reverse order[25] and conclude that the third—the motivation of the speaker—is determinative. This factor

---

25. The *Bolger* test easily disposes of any question as to whether the fliers that were printed by Amway distributors and giv-en to customers or potential customers were commercial speech—they plainly were. These fliers, associating P&G with Satanism and

has not yet been decided by the trier of fact, so we remand for that to be done.

The second factor is easily satisfied—the message did refer to specific products of P&G's. The first factor—whether the speech is an advertisement—seems to collapse into the third factor in this case. Certainly the repetition of the rumor via AmVox was not an advertisement in the classic sense, but whether it could be considered as a negative advertisement against P&G seems to depend on the determination of the third factor—whether the speaker had an economic motivation for the speech. If Haugen or others who repeated this rumor did have economic motivations, then the message resembles an advertisement seeking to encourage downline distributors to eschew P&G and buy Amway. If the motivation was not economic, then this looks more like a case of individuals' repeating false speech on a matter of public concern.

This question of the speaker's motivation will also help to clear up the difficulty in determining whether the characteristics of commercial speech summarized in *U.S. Healthcare* were present here. If the speakers were economically motivated, then issues of the quality of the speech, its durability, and the knowledge the speakers had of the relevant market and products become both more relevant and easier to determine.

Thus, on remand, if the trier of fact finds that the motivation behind the Amway distributors' repetition of the rumor to other distributors was not economic, the speech is not commercial, and there can be no Lanham Act claim. On the other hand, if an economic motivation is found, the speech is commercial, and a violation of the Lanham Act may be found.

The question whether an economic motive existed is more than a question whether there was an economic incentive for the speaker to make the speech; the *Bolger* test also requires that the speaker acted *substantially* out of economic motivation. Thus, for example, speech that is principally based on religious or political convictions, but which may also benefit the speaker economically, would fall short of the requirement that the speech was economically motivated. We stress that we are not shortening the *Bolger* test to a single factor—whether the speaker's motive was economic—but rather, we conclude that the other two *Bolger* factors are not conclusive, and therefore the motive factor is determinative.

This does not mean that whenever the primary motivation for speech is economic, the speech is commercial. As the Court said in *Bolger*, finding all three factors merely provides "strong support" for the proposition that the speech is commercial. The difference between commercial speech and noncommercial speech is, after all, "a matter of degree." *City of Cincinnati v. Discovery Network, Inc.*, 507 U.S. 410, 423, 123 L. Ed. 2d 99, 113 S. Ct.

suggesting Amway products as alternatives to P&G products, (i) were advertisements—i.e., they proposed a commercial transaction, (ii) they referred to specific products, and (iii) the distributors plainly had an economic motive in distributing them.

1505 (1993). We can well imagine cases in which a speaker's primary motivation is economic, but the speech nonetheless is protected.[30]

. . . .

P&G's Lanham Act claim for disparagement of its commercial activities is remanded for fact-finding to determine whether the primary motivation of the Amway disseminators of the Satanism rumor was economic. If it was, then the speech is commercial; if not, the speech was noncommercial, and no Lanham Act claim is available.

QUESTIONS

1. If a consumer publication's product evaluations contain false or misleading representations of fact, are the product reviews actionable under § 43(a)(1)(B)? *Cf. Bose Corp. v. Consumers Union,* 466 U.S. 485 (1984). What if an advertising-supported magazine publishes an allegedly misleading article that rates the products of its advertisers more highly than the products of non-advertisers?

2. If unionized airline mechanics take out misleading newspaper ads claiming that their airline's maintenance practices are unsafe, may the airline recover under the Lanham Act? Would your answer be different if the ad were placed by a competing airline?

2. LITERAL FALSEHOOD

Coca–Cola Co. v. Tropicana Prods., Inc.

690 F.2d 312 (2d Cir.1982).

■ CARDAMONE, J:

A proverb current even in the days of ancient Rome was "seeing is believing." Today, a great deal of what people see flashes before them on their TV sets. This case involves a 30–second television commercial with simultaneous audio and video components. We have no doubt that the byword of Rome is as valid now as it was then. And, if seeing something on TV has a tendency to persuade a viewer to believe, how much greater is the impact on a viewer's credulity when he both sees and hears a message at the same time?

In mid-February of 1982 defendant Tropicana Products, Inc. (Tropicana) began airing a new television commercial for its Premium Pack orange juice. The commercial shows the renowned American Olympic athlete Bruce Jenner squeezing an orange while saying "It's pure, pasteurized juice as it comes from the orange," and then shows Jenner pouring the fresh-squeezed juice into a Tropicana carton while the audio states "It's the only leading brand not made with concentrate and water."

---

30. Labor cases come to mind as an example.

Soon after the advertisement began running, plaintiff Coca–Cola Company (Coke, Coca–Cola), maker of Minute Maid orange juice, brought suit in the United States District Court for the Southern District of New York against Tropicana for false advertising in violation of section 43(a) of the Lanham Act.... Coke claimed the commercial is false because it incorrectly represents that Premium Pack contains unprocessed, fresh-squeezed juice when in fact the juice is pasteurized (heated to about 200 degrees Fahrenheit) and sometimes frozen prior to packaging. The court below denied plaintiff's motion for a preliminary injunction to enjoin further broadcast of the advertisement pending the outcome of this litigation. In our view preliminary injunctive relief is appropriate.

. . . .

II. *Irreparable Injury*

Perhaps the most difficult element to demonstrate when seeking an injunction against false advertising is the likelihood that one will suffer irreparable harm if the injunction does not issue. It is virtually impossible to prove that so much of one's sales will be lost or that one's goodwill will be damaged as a direct result of a competitor's advertisement. Too many market variables enter into the advertising-sales equation. Because of these impediments, a Lanham Act plaintiff who can prove actual lost sales may obtain an injunction even if most of his sales decline is attributable to factors other than a competitor's false advertising. In fact, he need not even point to an actual loss or diversion of sales.

The Lanham Act plaintiff must, however, offer something more than a mere subjective belief that he is likely to be injured as a result of the false advertising; he must submit proof which provides a reasonable basis for that belief. The likelihood of injury and causation will not be presumed, but must be demonstrated in some manner.

Two recent decisions of this Court have examined the type of proof necessary to satisfy this requirement. Relying on the fact that the products involved were in head-to-head competition, the Court in both cases directed the issuance of a preliminary injunction under the Lanham Act. *Vidal Sassoon,* 661 F.2d at 227; *Johnson & Johnson,* 631 F.2d at 189–91. In both decisions the Court reasoned that sales of the plaintiffs' products would probably be harmed if the competing products' advertising tended to mislead consumers in the manner alleged.[3] Market studies were used as evidence that some consumers were in fact misled by the advertising in issue. Thus, the market studies supplied the causative link between the advertising and the plaintiffs' potential lost sales; and thereby indicated a likelihood of injury.

---

3. In *Vidal Sasoon* consumers were allegedly misled to believe that "Body on Tap" shampoo was an all-around superior product. In *Johnson & Johnson* consumers were allegedly misled into thinking that using NAIR depilatory with baby oil would obviate the need for using baby oil alone to moisturize the skin after shaving.

Applying the same reasoning to the instant case, if consumers are misled by Tropicana's commercial, Coca–Cola probably would suffer irreparable injury. Tropicana and Coca–Cola are the leading national competitors for the chilled (ready-to-serve) orange juice market. If Tropicana's advertisement misleads consumers into believing that Premium Pack is a more desirable product because it contains only fresh-squeezed, unprocessed juice, then it is likely that Coke will lose a portion of the chilled juice market and thus suffer irreparable injury.

Evidence in the record supports the conclusion that consumers are likely to be misled in this manner. A consumer reaction survey conducted by ASI Market Research, Inc. and a Burke test, measuring recall of the commercial after it was aired on television, were admitted into evidence, though neither one was considered by the district court in reference to irreparable injury. The trial court examined the ASI survey regarding the issue of likelihood of success on the merits, and found that it contained various flaws which made it difficult to determine for certain whether a large number of consumers were misled. We do not disagree with those findings. We note, moreover, that despite these flaws the district court ruled that there were at least a small number of clearly deceived ASI interviewees. Our examination of the Burke test results leads to the same conclusion, *i.e.*, that a not insubstantial number of consumers were clearly misled by the defendant's ad. Together these tests provide sufficient evidence of a risk of irreparable harm because they demonstrate that a significant number of consumers would be likely to be misled. The trial court should have concluded, as did this Court in *Vidal Sassoon* and *Johnson & Johnson*, that the commercial will mislead consumers and, as a consequence, shift their purchases from plaintiff's product to defendant's. Coke, therefore, demonstrated that it is likely to suffer irreparable injury.

III. *Likelihood of Success on the Merits*

Once the initial requisite showing of irreparable harm has been made, the party seeking a preliminary injunction must satisfy either of the two alternatives regarding the merits of his case. We find that Coca–Cola satisfies the more stringent first alternative because it is likely to succeed on the merits of its false advertising action.

Coke is entitled to relief under the Lanham Act if Tropicana has used a false description or representation in its Jenner commercial. *See* 15 U.S.C. § 1125(a). When a merchandising statement or representation is literally or explicitly false, the court may grant relief without reference to the advertisement's impact on the buying public. When the challenged advertisement is implicitly rather than explicitly false, its tendency to violate the Lanham Act by misleading, confusing or deceiving should be tested by public reaction.

In viewing defendant's 30–second commercial at oral argument, we concluded that the trial court's finding that this ad was not facially false is an error of fact. Since the trial judge's finding on this issue was based solely on the inference it drew from reviewing documentary evidence, consisting of the commercial, we are in as good a position as it was to draw an appropriate inference. We find, therefore, that the squeezing-pouring sequence in the Jenner commercial is false on its face. The visual component of the ad makes an explicit representation that Premium Pack is produced by squeezing oranges and pouring the freshly-squeezed juice directly into the carton. This is not a true representation of how the product is prepared. Premium Pack juice is heated and sometimes frozen prior to packaging. Additionally, the simultaneous audio component of the ad states that Premium Pack is "pasteurized juice as it comes from the orange." This statement is blatantly false—pasteurized juice does not come from oranges. Pasteurization entails heating the juice to approximately 200 degrees Fahrenheit to kill certain natural enzymes and microorganisms which cause spoilage. Moreover, even if the addition of the word "pasteurized" somehow made sense and effectively qualified the visual image, Tropicana's commercial nevertheless represented that the juice is only squeezed, heated and packaged when in fact it may actually also be frozen.

Hence, Coke is likely to succeed in arguing that Tropicana's ad is false and that it is entitled to relief under the Lanham Act. The purpose of the Act is to insure truthfulness in advertising and to eliminate misrepresentations with reference to the inherent quality or characteristic of another's product. The claim that Tropicana's Premium Pack contains only fresh-squeezed, unprocessed juice is clearly a misrepresentation as to that product's inherent quality or characteristic. Since the plaintiff has satisfied the first preliminary injunction alternative, we need not decide whether the balance of hardships tips in its favor.

Because Tropicana has made a false representation in its advertising and Coke is likely to suffer irreparable harm as a result, we reverse the district court's denial of plaintiff's application and remand this case for issuance of a preliminary injunction preventing broadcast of the squeezing-pouring sequence in the Jenner commercial.

QUESTION

In *Coca–Cola v. Tropicana* the Second Circuit distinguishes between explicitly and implicitly false statements. In the latter instance, no injunction will issue without evaluation of the advertisement's impact on the buying public. Why should plaintiffs complaining of explicitly false statements not also be required to demonstrate that the advertisement in fact tends to deceive?

United Industries Corp. v. Clorox Co., 140 F.3d 1175 (8th Cir. 1998). In a case involving competing roach bait products, defendant's commercial was described by the court as follows:

> The commercial at issue, entitled "Side by Side" ... depicts a split-screen view of two roach bait products on two kitchen countertops. The lighting is dark. On the left, one sees the Maxattrax box; on the right, a generic "Roach Bait" box that is vaguely similar to the packaging of the Combat brand sold by Clorox. An

announcer asks the question: "Can you guess which bait kills roaches in 24 hours?" The lights then come up as the camera pans beyond the boxes to reveal a clean, calm, pristine kitchen, uninhabited by roaches, on the Maxattrax side. On the other side, the kitchen is in a chaotic state: cupboards and drawers are opening, items on the counter are turning over, paper towels are spinning off the dispenser, a spice rack is convulsing and losing its spices, all the apparent result of a major roach infestation. At the same time, the message "Based on lab tests" appear in small print at the bottom of the screen. The two roach bait boxes then reappear on the split-screen, and several computer-animated roaches on the "Roach Bait" side appear to kick over the generic box and dance gleefully upon it. The final visual is of the Maxattrax box only, over which the announcer concluded, "to kill roaches in 24 hours, it's hot-shot Maxattrax. Maxattrax, it's the no-wait roach bait."

The court rejected Clorox's arguments of both literal and implicit falsity. The evidence indicated that roaches died within 24 hours of contact with Maxattrax roach bait; however, the Maxattrax would not clear up a roach infestation problem within 24 hours. In rejecting Clorox's literal falsity argument (that Maxattrax would clear up an infestation problem within a day) based on the visual elements of the commercial, the court stated:

> [W]e conclude that the district court did not err in determining that the Maxattrax commercial did not convey explicit visual messages that were literally false. The depiction of a Maxattrax box in a pristine, roach-free kitchen, coupled with the depiction of a kitchen in disarray in which animated roaches happily dance about on a generic roach trap, is not sufficient, in our view, to constitute literal falsity in the manner in which it was presented. When the context is considered as a whole, moreover, the audio component of the advertisement, emphasizing only the 24–hour time frame and quick roach kill with no mention of complete infestation control, fosters ambiguity regarding the intended message and renders the commercial much more susceptible to differing, plausible interpretations.

The court further rejected Clorox's contentions that the ad was implicitly false because Clorox's failed to present consumer reaction evidence to demonstrate the ad's impact on viewers.

Schick Manufacturing, Inc. v. The Gillette Company, 372 F.Supp.2d 273 (D.Conn.2005). Schick sued Gillette, claiming that Gillette's advertising for its M3 Power Razor System violated section 43(a)(1)(B):

> Gillette's original advertising for the M3 Power centered on the claim that "micro-pulses raise hair up and away from skin," thus allowing a consumer to achieve a closer shave. This "hair-raising" or hair extension claim was advertised in various media, including the internet, television, print media, point of sale materials, and product

packaging. For example, Gillette's website asserted that, in order to combat the problem of "facial hair growing in different directions," the M3 Power's "micro-pulses raise hair up and away from skin ..." Of Gillette's expenditures on advertising, 85% is spent on television advertising. At the time of the launch, the television advertising stated, "turn on the first micro-power shaving system from Gillette and turn on the amazing new power-glide blades. Micro-pulses raise the hair, so you shave closer in one power stroke." The advertisement also included a 1.8 second-long animated dramatization of hairs growing. In the animated cartoon, the oscillation produced by the M3 Power is shown as green waves moving over hairs. In response, the hairs shown extended in length in the direction of growth and changed angle towards a more vertical position.

    . . .

Gillette conceded during the hearing that the M3 Power's oscillations do not cause hair to change angle on the face. Its original advertisements depicting such an angle change are both unsubstantiated and inaccurate. Gillette also concedes that the animated portion of its television advertisement is not physiologically exact insofar as the hairs and skin do not appear as they would at such a level of magnification and the hair extension effect is "somewhat exaggerated." The court finds that the hair "extension" in the commercial is greatly exaggerated. Gillette does contend, however, that the M3 Power's oscillations cause beard hairs to be raised out of the skin. Gillette contends that the animated product demonstration showing hair extension in its revised commercials is predicated on its testing showing that oscillations cause "trapped" facial hairs to lengthen from the follicle so that more of these hairs' length is exposed. Gillette propounds two alternative physiological bases for its "hair extension" theory. First, Gillette hypothesizes that a facial hair becomes "bound" within the follicle due to an accumulation of sebum and corneocytes (dead skin cells). Gillette contends that the oscillations could free such a "bound" hair. Second, Gillette hypothesizes that hairs may deviate from their normal paths in the follicle and become "trapped" outside the path until vibrations from the M3 Power restore them to their proper path.

    . . .

The challenged advertising consists of two basic components: an animated representation of the effect of the M3 Power razor on hair and skin and a voice-over that describes that effect. The animation, which lasts approximately 1.8 seconds, shows many hairs growing at a significant rate, many by as much as four times the original length. During the animation, the voice-over states the following: "Turn it on and micropulses raise the hair so the blades can shave closer." Schick asserts that this M3 Power advertising is false in three ways: first, it asserts the razor changes the angle of beard hairs; second, it portrays a false amount of extension; and third, it asserts that the razor raises or extends the beard hair.

With regard to the first claim of falsity, if the voiceover means that the razor changes the angle of hairs on the face, the claim is false. Although Gillette removed the "angle changing" claim from its television advertisements, it is unclear whether it has completely removed all material asserting this angle-change claim. The court concludes that the current advertising claim of "raising" hair does not unambiguously mean to changes angles.[8] See *Novartis Consumer Health, Inc. v. Johnson & Johnson–Merck Consumer Pharms. Co.*, 290 F.3d 578, 587 (3d Cir.2002) ("only an unambiguous message can be literally false"). Thus, the revised advertising is not literally false on this basis.

With regard to the second asserted basis of falsity, the animation, Gillette concedes that the animation exaggerates the effect that the razor's vibration has on hair. Its own tests show hairs extending approximately 10% on average, when the animation shows a significantly greater extension. The animation is not even a "reasonable approximation," which Gillette claims is the legal standard for nonfalsity. Here, Schick can point to Gillette's own studies to prove that the animation is false. *See McNeil–P.C.C., Inc.*, 938 F.2d at 1549.

Gillette argues that such exaggeration does not constitute falsity. However, case law in this circuit indicates that a defendant cannot argue that a television advertisement is "approximately" correct or, alternatively, simply a representation in order to excuse a television ad or segment thereof that is literally false. *S.C. Johnson & Son, Inc.*, 241 F.3d at 239–40 (finding that depiction of leaking plastic bag was false where rate at which bag leaked in advertisement was faster than rate tests indicated); *Coca-Cola Co.*, 690 F.2d at 318 (finding that advertisement that displaced fresh-squeezed orange juice being poured into a Tropicana carton was false). Indeed, "[the Court of Appeals has] explicitly looked to the visual images in a commercial to assess whether it is literally false." *S.C. Johnson*, 241 F.3d at 238.[9]

Gillette's argument that the animated portion of its advertisement need not be exact is wrong as a matter of law. Clearly, a cartoon will not exactly depict a real-life situation, here, e.g., the actual uneven surface of a hair or the details of a hair plug. However, a party may not distort an inherent quality of its product in either graphics or animation. Gillette acknowledges that the magnitude of beard hair extension in the animation is false. The court finds, therefore, that any claims with respect to changes in angle and the animated portion of Gillette's current advertisement are literally false.

8. It is the words "up and away" when combined with "raises" that suggest both extension and angle changes.

9. At least one other circuit has held that picture depictions can constitute false advertising. *Scotts Co. v. United Indus. Corp.*, 315 F.3d 264 (4th Cir.2002) (finding that while ambiguous graphic on packaging did not constitute literally false advertising, an unambiguous graphic could do so).

QUESTION

Johnson & Johnson, maker of Mylanta® antacid introduced Mylanta® Night Time Strength antacid, a formulation with more active ingredients per teaspoon than regular Mylanta. Ads for the new product described it as "made just for night-time heartburn," and "specially formulated for night time heartburn." The maker of Maalox® insists that the name of the product and the supporting ads are literally false, because they claim that Mylanta Night Time Strength is specially formulated, and therefore better than other antacids at reliving night-time heartburn, and that they claim that Mylanta Night Time Strength provides heartburn relief through the night. Maalox seeks to force Johnson and Johnson to stop running the ads and to rename its product. Johnson & Johnson concedes that the only difference between regular Mylanta and Mylanta Night Time Strength is that the latter is more concentrated, but it insists that neither the name of the product nor its ads contain any literal falsity. How should the court rule? *See Novartis Consumer Health v. Johnson & Johnson–Merck Consumer Pharmaceuticals*, 290 F.3d 578 (3d Cir.2002).

Clorox Co. Puerto Rico v. Proctor & Gamble Commercial Co.

228 F.3d 24 (1st Cir.2000).

■ LIPEZ, CIRCUIT JUDGE:

"Mas blanco no se puede" (Whiter is not possible) was the advertising tag line used by the defendant, the Proctor and Gamble Commercial Company, to sell its detergent, Ace con Blanqueador (Ace with whitener), in Puerto Rico. The Clorox Company Puerto Rico cried foul, complaining that no detergent brings out the white like its chlorine bleach when used with a detergent. Proctor & Gamble modified its pitch, inviting consumers to "Compare con su detergente ... Mas blanco no se puede" (Compare with your detergent ... Whiter is not possible). Unimpressed by this change, Clorox sued, alleging, inter alia, that the advertisements were false and misleading in violation of Section 43(a) of the Lanham Act, 15 U.S.C. § 1125(a). After Clorox moved for a preliminary injunction, the district court dismissed the false advertising claim sua sponte. Concluding that Clorox has stated a claim under § 43(a) of the Lanham Act, we vacate the dismissal and remand to the district court for further proceedings.

I.

We present the facts in the light most favorable to Clorox, the party opposing the dismissal of the complaint. *See Langadinos v. American Airlines, Inc.*, 199 F.3d 68, 69 (1st Cir.2000). In 1989, Proctor & Gamble introduced in Puerto Rico Ace con Blanqueador, a powdered laundry detergent that contains a non-chlorine whitening agent described as a "color-safe oxygen bleach" with a patented "activator," the same formula used in powdered Tide with Bleach marketed in the continental United States. In 1997, Proctor & Gamble introduced a liquid version of Ace containing a "compound of high levels of sulfactants and enzymes which function as a whitener and a color enhancer," the same formula used in liquid Tide with Bleach Alternative.

The Original Doorstep Challenge Campaign

Proctor & Gamble conducted some consumer studies in 1997 and determined that an obstacle to obtaining an enhanced market share for Ace con Blanqueador was the public's perception that chlorine bleach was necessary to get clothes white. Using this new information, Proctor & Gamble implemented an advertising campaign to counter the perception of consumers that chlorine bleach was necessary, and to convince them that Ace was a superior option to using a lower-priced detergent in conjunction with chlorine bleach. This "Doorstep Challenge" included a series of television advertisements in which Francisco Zamora, a television celebrity in Puerto Rico, visited women in their homes to ask them about their laundry practices and to elicit their praise for Ace. In the commercials depicting powdered Ace, the overriding theme was that chlorine bleach was not necessary to get clothes white if washed with Ace. The commercials pitching liquid Ace also emphasized its enhanced whitening capacity, but did not specifically mention chlorine bleach. Each commercial closed with the tag line, "Whiter is not possible," a slogan Proctor & Gamble had been using since powdered Ace arrived on the market in 1989.

For instance, the "Evelyn" commercial for powdered Ace went as follows:

> Francisco: Do you use Ace?
>
> She: No . . .
>
> Fco: What is your laundry routine?
>
> She: I put in the three detergents I use, I throw in a bit of chlorine and I let it soak until the next day. I waste a lot of time . . . but to accomplish what I want I have to do it that way.
>
> Fco: I dare you to wash your white garments with Ace and nothing else!
>
> She: Without chlorine?
>
> . . . .
>
> Fco: Without chlorine . . . we're going to wash all these.
>
> She: I don't think so . . .
>
> She: The truth is . . . that's whiteness, that's whiteness! So now I'm going to save money, time . . .
>
> . . . .
>
> [VISUAL: Whiter is not possible.]

The Promotional Mailing

As part of its campaign to sell Ace, Proctor & Gamble sent a promotional brochure and product sample to consumers in Puerto Rico. The first page of the brochure depicted a bowling ball imprinted with the word "Ace" standing in front of several bowling pins that resembled Clorox bottles. The caption read: "Da en el blanco con una sola tirada," (hit the [white] spot with just one shot). The second and third pages of the brochure contained additional pictures surrounded by punchy statements in Spanish like, "Dare to pass the test. Wash with Ace and nothing else," "Say goodbye to the complications of chlorine and other cleaners," and "Resist the 'bombs.'[1] Put your ACE con Blanqueador to the test." Like the television commercials, the brochure ended with the tag line, "Whiter is not possible!"

The Modified Campaign

In January 1998, the Clorox Company, which markets in Puerto Rico a brand of chlorine-based liquid bleach called Clorox, sent a letter to Proctor & Gamble complaining that the Doorstep Challenge campaign was false and misleading, and demanding that Proctor & Gamble stop running the television advertisements. Although Proctor & Gamble would not alter the theme of its advertising, it agreed to soften the tag line by adding the qualification, "compare with your detergent," before the phrase "whiter is not possible."

The qualification did not satisfy Clorox. In March 1998, Clorox filed this lawsuit, alleging in its complaint violations of Section 43(a) of the Lanham Act, 15 U.S.C. § 1125(a)....

Clorox sought to permanently enjoin Proctor & Gamble from "making any claims that Ace gets clothes 'the whitest possible,' *without* the use of Clorox." (Emphasis in original). Additionally, Clorox sought damages and attorneys' fees under § 43(a) of the Lanham Act. Finally, Clorox moved for a preliminary injunction on its Lanham Act claim. In connection with the motion for a preliminary injunction, the parties conducted document production and depositions and submitted to the court relevant evidentiary materials, including consumer surveys, statements of experts, and the testimony of various witnesses. The district court did not hear oral argument.

In March 1999, ... the district court dismissed the Lanham Act claim sua sponte. This appeal followed....

II.

. . . .

B. *The Lanham Act False Advertising Claims*

. . . .

A plaintiff can succeed on a false advertising claim by proving either that an advertisement is false on its face or that the advertisement is literally

---

1. The combination of detergent and chlorine bleach is called "la bomba" in Puerto Rico.

true or ambiguous but likely to mislead and confuse consumers. *See Southland Sod Farms v. Stover Seed Co.*, 108 F.3d 1134, 1139 (9th Cir.1997); *Castrol, Inc. v. Pennzoil Co.*, 987 F.2d 939, 943 (3d Cir.1993); *Abbott Labs. v. Mead Johnson & Co.*, 971 F.2d 6, 13 (7th Cir.1992). If the advertisement is literally false, the court may grant relief without considering evidence of consumer reaction. *See United Indus. Corp. v. Clorox Co.*, 140 F.3d 1175, 1180 (8th Cir.1998). In the absence of such literal falsity, an additional burden is placed upon the plaintiff to show that the advertisement, though explicitly true, nonetheless conveys a misleading message to the viewing public. *See Sandoz Pharms. Corp. v. Richardson–Vicks, Inc.*, 902 F.2d 222, 228–29 (3d Cir.1990). To satisfy its burden, the plaintiff must show how consumers have actually reacted to the challenged advertisement rather than merely demonstrating how they could have reacted. *See id.* at 229.

Clorox's amended complaint alleged that Proctor & Gamble's original and modified Doorstep Challenge television campaigns, as well as the promotional brochure, were false and misleading. Specifically, Clorox alleged that the Doorstep Challenge advertisements and promotions conveyed the false and misleading message to the Puerto Rican public that Ace con Blanqueador gets clothes as white or whiter than a detergent used with chlorine bleach. Clorox also alleged that the name "Ace con Blanqueador" is literally false with respect to Ace liquid detergent.

The district court's analysis of the Lanham Act claim consisted of two paragraphs in which it reasoned that Clorox "has failed to state a claim" under the Lanham Act because it could not establish that Proctor & Gamble's advertisements contained false or misleading statements. In particular, it found that the tag line appearing in the modified campaign commercials, "Compare with your detergent ... Whiter is not possible," was not false because it compared Ace only to other detergents, not to detergents used with chlorine bleach. The court also stated that, "Ace's comparison claim" was not actionable under the Lanham Act because it was "mere puffing."

. . . .

We analyze Clorox's various allegations de novo, ... focusing on (1) the allegations of literal falsity, (2) the allegations of misleading advertising, and (3) the concept of "puffery."

1. *Claims of Literal Falsity*

Clorox challenged two features of Proctor & Gamble's advertising campaign as literally false. First, Clorox alleged that the television commercials that aired in the original and modified campaign claimed that Ace gets clothes as white or whiter than chlorine bleach. According to Clorox, that claim is literally false because tests prove that chlorine bleach whitens better than detergent used alone. Second, Clorox alleged that the name, "Ace con Blanqueador," is literally false with respect to Ace liquid detergent because it falsely suggests that Ace liquid contains whitener or bleach.

a. *The Television Advertisements*

Whether an advertisement is literally false is typically an issue of fact. *See Mead Johnson & Co. v. Abbott Labs.*, 209 F.3d 1032, 1034 (7th Cir.2000) (denying petition for rehearing and amending prior panel opinion). At least two factual questions must be answered in evaluating the accuracy of any particular advertisement. First, a factfinder must determine the claim conveyed by the advertisement. *See United Indus. Corp.*, 140 F.3d at 1181 (applying clearly erroneous standard to review of district court's factual determination regarding the claim conveyed by an advertisement for roach bait); *Johnson & Johnson v. GAC Int'l, Inc.*, 862 F.2d 975, 979 (2d Cir.1988). Once the claim made by the advertisement has been determined, the factfinder must then evaluate whether that claim is false. *See Castrol*, 987 F.2d at 944.

In the case at hand, the parties focus their attention solely upon the first of these factual determinations. The complaint asserts that in head-to-head whitening tests, Clorox achieved "by far, superior results" to Ace. Clorox also emphasizes that "Ace's own boxes" state that in certain cases, for better results, the consumers must use chlorine bleach. In reviewing the motion to dismiss, we therefore assume as true that chlorine bleach whitens better than Ace and that a contrary claim would be literally false. The primary dispute between the parties is not which product whitens better,[8] but rather whether any of Proctor & Gamble's advertisements make a claim of whitening superiority over chlorine bleach.

Although factfinders usually base literal falsity determinations upon the explicit claims made by an advertisement, they may also consider any claims the advertisement conveys by "necessary implication." [Citations] A claim is conveyed by necessary implication when, considering the advertisement in its entirety, the audience would recognize the claim as readily as if it had been explicitly stated. . . .

. . . .

We conclude that Clorox has stated a claim that Proctor & Gamble's original Doorstep Challenge commercials are literally false. These commercials juxtapose a tag line, "Whiter is not possible," with images of consumers who normally used bleach to achieve white clothes and who are favorably impressed by the results obtained from using Ace alone. The overall theme of the commercials is that bleach is unnecessary if clothes are washed with Ace, and, in fact, many of the consumers visited by Zamora are congratulated at the end of the commercials for passing "the Ace whiteness challenge without chlorine." Some of the commercials also suggest that eliminating chlorine from the laundry process will save consumers time or money, or curtail the negative side effects of washing clothes with chlorine. A factfinder could reasonably conclude that, viewed

---

8. Indeed, Proctor & Gamble does not challenge on appeal Clorox's assertion that chlorine bleach in combination with a detergent gets clothes whiter than its Ace detergent.

in their entirety, these advertisements claim that Ace is equal or superior in whitening ability to a detergent and bleach combination.

The modified Doorstep Challenge campaign continued the same visual comparisons, as well as the congratulatory comments for passing the "Ace whiteness challenge without chlorine," but added the words "Compare your detergent" to the "Whiter is not possible" tag line shown at the bottom of the screen at the end of the commercials. Although this change may render the comparative claim of the advertisements more ambiguous, we nonetheless conclude that it remains reasonable to interpret these advertisements as making by necessary implication a superiority claim for Ace over chlorine bleach. Consequently, the court erred in dismissing Clorox's literal falsity claims with respect to both Doorstep Challenge campaigns.

> b.   *The Name "Ace con Blanqueador"*

Clorox also alleged that the name, "Ace con Blanqueador," as applied to liquid Ace, is literally false. According to Clorox, the word "blanqueador" implies that liquid Ace has whitening capabilities like bleach. Clorox alleged that this is literally false because in its liquid form Ace does not contain bleach or whitening agents. Instead, it contains only a "color enhancer." Clorox emphasizes that liquid Ace uses the same formula as "Tide with Bleach Alternative" whose name, unlike "blanqueador," clearly signifies the absence of bleach. Proctor & Gamble responds that "blanqueador" means "whitener," and that the name cannot be literally false because tests show that the agents added to liquid Ace produce greater whiteness than detergents without those agents.

Clorox's allegations about the use of the name "Ace con Blanqueador" for the liquid detergent state a claim for literal falsity. Although "blanqueador," meaning "whitener," is broad enough to encompass both bleach and non-bleach whitening agents, the question remains whether liquid Ace is properly described as containing "whitening agents" of any sort. Clorox has alleged that it is not, insisting that Ace's ingredients are properly termed "color enhancers." Although the distinction between a "whitening agent" and a "color enhancer" eludes us, we must credit that allegation in this appeal from a 12(b)(6) dismissal. If Clorox succeeds in proving that liquid Ace contains only an "enhancer," rather than a "whitener," and if it further establishes the other elements of a false advertising claim, see supra note 6, it will be entitled to relief under the Lanham Act because Proctor & Gamble's designation of Ace liquid detergent as "Ace con Blanqueador" would be literally false.

> 2.   *Claims of Misleading Advertising*

In addition to its claims of literal falsity, Clorox has alleged in its complaint that the Ace advertising campaign, even if true or ambiguous, makes an implied claim that is misleading to consumers. This second theory of recovery under the Lanham Act is independent of a literal falsity theory. *See, e.g., Coca–Cola, Co. v. Tropicana Prods., Inc.*, 690 F.2d 312, 317 (2d Cir.1982). Unlike the requirements of a claim of literal falsity, the plaintiff alleging a misleading advertisement has the burden of proving that a substantial portion of the audience for that advertisement was actually misled. *See Rhone–Poulenc Rorer*, 19 F.3d at 134 (citing *U.S. Healthcare v. Blue Cross*, 898 F.2d 914, 922 (3d Cir.1990)). An advertisement's propensity to deceive the viewing public is most often proven by consumer survey data. *See id.* 19 F.3d at 129–30. Clorox appended to the amended complaint a consumer survey prepared by David Whitehouse of Gaither International/Puerto Rico, Inc. The survey consisted of a series of open-ended questions followed by several follow-up probes. In reliance on the survey, the complaint alleges that:

> In open-ended questions, 35% of respondents of its scientifically valid survey responded that the main message of the Doorstep Challenge Campaign was that, with ACE, there is no need to use other products for maximum whitening performance. In addition, when the respondents were asked if "the Detergent in the Ad (ACE) Leaves Clothes as White or Whiter than If One Uses Bleach," 47% totally agreed and 20% somewhat agreed with that statement. Plainly, the Doorstep Challenge Campaign has been amply shown to be likely to cause consumer deception.

Clorox has also alleged in its complaint that "in its promotional activities and advertisements," Proctor & Gamble "deceived and confused the public, causing consumers to wrongly believe they are buying a detergent that possesses the same qualities and characteristics as a detergent used with CLOROX."

The court was required to credit Clorox's allegations. It could not conduct its own evaluation of the advertising copy because whether advertising is misleading depends on "what message was actually conveyed to the viewing audience." *Smithkline Beecham Corp.*, 960 F.2d at 298; *see also Rhone–Poulenc Rorer*, 19 F.3d at 129. In deciding whether a message is "misleading," the message conveyed is discerned by "public reaction," not by judicial evaluation. [Citations] That is, absent some other defect in its proof of the elements of a false advertising claim, ... if Clorox's consumer survey data (or Proctor & Gamble's own market research data) shows that the advertisements "deceived a substantial portion of the intended audience," *U.S. Healthcare*, 898 F.2d at 922, Clorox is entitled to relief under the Lanham Act. Hence, the claims asserting misleading advertising were improperly dismissed.

. . . .

3. *Puffery*

Finally, the statements, "Compare with your detergent.... Whiter is not possible," and "Whiter is not possible," are not non-actionable puffing. " 'Puffing' is exaggerated advertising, blustering, and boasting upon which no reasonable buyer would rely...." *McCarthy* § 27:38. "A specific and measurable advertisement claim of product superiority ... is not puffery." *Southland Sod Farms*, 108 F.3d at 1145 (claim that turfgrass seed requires "50% less mowing" was not puffery); *see also Castrol, Inc.*, 987 F.2d at 946 (claim that motor oil provides "longer engine life and better engine protection" was not puffery). Whether the "Doorstep Challenge" campaign conveys the message that Ace gets clothes whiter than chlorine bleach, or compares Ace with other detergents without implying that it whitens better than chlorine bleach, the claim is specific and measurable, not the kind of vague or subjective statement that characterizes puffery. Indeed, Proctor & Gamble concedes in its brief that its claim in its modified campaign, "Compare with your detergent ... Whiter is not possible," is not puffery. It contends that it is a true statement supported by its studies comparing Ace con Blanqueador with other detergents.

The original campaign tag line, "Whiter is not possible," is a closer call on the puffing issue. Standing alone, that statement might well constitute an unspecified boast, and hence puffing. In context, however, the statement invites consumers to compare Ace's whitening power against either other detergents acting alone or detergents used with chlorine bleach. Despite this ambiguity, it is a specific, measurable claim, and hence not puffing.

. . . .

III.

Pursuant to § 43(a) of the Lanham Act, Clorox has stated a claim for literal falsity relating to the name of the Ace liquid detergent, "Ace con Blanqueador." Clorox has also stated claims for literal falsity and for misleading advertising with respect to the commercials aired in both the original and modified Doorstep Challenge advertising campaigns, as well as the promotional brochure. The district court erred by dismissing these claims pursuant to Rule 12(b)(6). We must vacate its judgment and remand the Lanham Act claims to the district court for further proceedings consistent with this decision.

QUESTIONS

1. Mueller's is a regional brand of pasta available only in the North Eastern United States. The company labels packages of its pasta "America's favorite pasta." The best selling brand of pasta in the U.S. is not Mueller's, but Barilla, which is available throughout the United States. The manufacturer of Barilla claims that the "America's Favorite Pasta" label is a false and misleading representation of fact. Mueller insists that the phrase is mere puffing, and therefore not actionable. How should the court rule? *See American Italian Pasta Co. v. New World Pasta*, 371 F.3d 387 (8th Cir.2004).

2. In the 1860s, Piotr Arsenvitch Smirnov began a vodka trade house in Russia named "P.A. Smirnov in Moscow." During his lifetime, P.A. Smirnov built his trade house into a nationally and internationally renowned vodka distillery, winning numerous awards. In 1886, Smirnov was named the "Official Purveyor to the Russian Imperial Court." Smirnov died in 1898, leaving his distillery to his sons Piotr, Nikolai, Vladimir, Sergei, and Alexey. Piotr bought out his brothers' interest in the distillery, and he and his wife operated it until his death in 1910. Piotr's wife Eugenie continued to run the distillery until the Bolshevik government nationalized all distilleries in 1918. Meanwhile, Vladimir Smirnov emigrated to Europe, and opened a distillery under the name "Pierre Smirnoff & Sons." He later sold his rights in the name to Heublein, which introduced a Smirnoff brand vodka into the United States. That vodka was and continues to be distilled and bottled in the United States, and has become a best-selling brand. Bottles of Smirnoff vodka bear a label suggesting the vodka's Russian origin and imperial seal. Meanwhile, when the Soviet Union dissolved, Eugenie's daughter reopened a Smirnov distillery in Moscow. She sues Heublein under § 43(a), arguing that it falsely advertises its Smirnoff vodka as the prizewinning Russian vodka introduced in Moscow by P.A. Smirnov. What result? *See Joint Stock Society v. UDV North America*, 266 F.3d 164 (3d Cir.2001).

Johnson & Johnson Vision Care, Inc. v. Ciba Vision Corp., 348 F.Supp.2d 165 (S.D.N.Y.2004). Johnson & Johnson, the maker of ACUVUE contact lenses, sued Ciba Vision, alleging that ads promoting CIBA's O_2 OPTIX contact lenses were literally false. O_2OPTIX lenses have greater oxygen permeability than ACUVUE lenses, a feature that CIBA claimed made the lenses both more comfortable and better for the health of the wearer's cornea. CIBA's O_2OPTIX ads, directed at eye care professionals, asserted that in a clinical study, "75% of lens wearers preferred O_2OPTIX to ACUVUE ADVANCE. The #1 reason was comfort." Johnson & Johnson argued that CIBA's clinical trial supported neither claim. In the trial, 20 contact lens wearers wore a Johnson & Johnson ACUVUE ADVANCE lens in one eye and a CIBA O_2OPTIX lens in the other eye for four weeks. At several points during the study participants were asked which lens they preferred, and were asked to choose a reason for that preference. At the end of the study, five participants indicated a preference for ACUVUE ADVANCE, and 15 (or 75%) indicated a preference for O_2OPTIX. When asked the reason for their preference, however, two of the participants who chose ACUVUE and five of the participants who chose O_2OPTIX said that they had made a random choice between the two lenses. Eight of the participants who chose O_2OPTIX (and none of the participants who chose ACCUVUE) identified "Comfort" as the reason for their preference.

Evaluating the data, the court concluded that participants who claimed to have made a random choice did not prefer one lens to the other. Thus, of the 20 participants, 10 preferred O_2OPTIX, three preferred ACCUVUE, and 7 had no preference. The court agreed with Johnson & Johnson that CIBA's claim that "75% of lens wearers preferred O_2OPTIX to ACUVUE ADVANCE" was literally false. The court, however, held that the study supported CIBA's claim that comfort was the #1 reason: "comfort was clearly selected as the primary reason more often than any of the other reasons mentioned in the study, and all 8 of the persons who chose comfort as the primary reason made O_2OPTIX their overall preference choice."

Solvay Pharmaceuticals, Inc. v. Ethex Corporation, 2004 WL 742033 (D. Minn. 2004). Solvay, the producer of Creon brand enzyme supplement, brought a § 43(a) claim against its competitor, alleging that marketing representing that the competing product, Pangestyne, was equivalent or comparable to Creon was false and misleading. The defendant argued that the dispute required a determination whether Creon and Pangestyne were in fact comparable and that the matter was therefore exclusively within the jurisdiction of the FDA. The court disagreed:

> The Court is thus satisfied that Solvay could, based on the allegations in the complaint, prove that Pangestyme and Creon are not substitutable, alternatives, equivalent, or comparable, and that any advertisement to the contrary is literally false. Such a claim does not require the Court to determine anything within the particular jurisdiction of the FDA and is within the purview of the Lanham Act. Plaintiff's claims will therefore not be dismissed on this basis.

3.   MISLEADING REPRESENTATION

Polar Corp. v. Coca–Cola Co.

871 F.Supp. 1520 (D.Mass.1994).

■ GORTON, DISTRICT JUDGE:

Polar Corporation ("Polar"), a manufacturer of carbonated sodas distributed in the Northeast, has filed a complaint seeking a declaratory judgment against The Coca–Cola Co. ("Coca–Cola"). Polar requests a court order declaring that it is entitled to broadcast a certain television commercial which depicts an animated polar bear throwing a can of Coca–Cola classic ("Coke") into a trash barrel labeled "Keep the Arctic Pure" and then drinking, with satisfaction, a can of Polar Seltzer. The defendant, Coca–Cola, has filed a motion for a temporary restraining order (treated here as a motion for a preliminary injunction) to enjoin Polar from broadcasting the commercial and otherwise infringing or diluting Coca–Cola trademarks, including the so-called "Coca–Cola Polar Bears."

The thirty-second, television commercial at issue in this case features a computer-generated polar bear that examines a Coke can, makes an unhappy sound and flips the can over his shoulder into a trash bin. A sign over the bin reads "Keep the Arctic Pure." The polar bear then reaches down into the freezing, Arctic water and pulls out a can of Polar Seltzer. He (or she) then drinks the Polar soda and smiles contentedly.

To be entitled to a preliminary injunction, pursuant to Fed.R.Civ.P. 65, Coca–Cola, the moving party, must show: 1) a likelihood of success on the merits, 2) potential irreparable harm if the injunction is not granted, 3) that injury to Coca–Cola, if the injunction is denied, outweighs the harm the injunction would cause Polar, if imposed, and 4) that the public interest would not be adversely affected by granting the injunction. *United Steel-*

workers of America v. Textron, Inc., 836 F.2d 6, 7 (1st Cir. 1987). *See also Gately v. Commonwealth*, 2 F.3d 1221, 1224 (1st Cir.1993); *Camel Hair and Cashmere Inst. of Am. v. Associated Dry Goods Corp.*, 799 F.2d 6, 12 (1st Cir.1986).

Coca–Cola argues that Polar's commercial violates the Lanham Act by disparaging the purity and the quality of Coke.

This Court finds that, by causing the polar bear to throw the can of Coke into a trash bin labeled "Keep the Arctic Pure," Polar has implied that Coke is not pure. Because there is no evidence suggesting that Coke is not "pure," the Court concludes that Polar has misrepresented the nature and quality of Coke. Coca–Cola has, therefore, shown a likelihood of success under 15 U.S.C. § 1125(a)(1)(B). *See Johnson & Johnson–Merck Consumer Pharmaceuticals Co. v. Rhone–Poulenc Rorer Pharmaceuticals, Inc.*, 19 F.3d 125, 129 (3d Cir.1994). *See generally Note, To Tell the Truth: Comparative Advertising and the Lanham Act Section 43(a)*, 36 CATH. U. L. REV. 565 (1987) (describing how the Lanham Act evolved to create a cause of action against false advertising).

The Court further finds that Coca–Cola, engaged in an industry that relies heavily on the consumer's perception of quality and purity, has shown a potential for irreparable harm if the injunction is not granted. Moreover, that harm outweighs any injury that Polar would suffer as a result of the injunction, especially because Polar, in effect, would be enjoined only from misrepresenting the nature and quality of Coke. Finally, the public interest would not be adversely affected by the issuance of an injunction.

Accordingly, this Court concludes that Coca–Cola has met its burden under Fed.R.Civ.P. 65 and is entitled to a preliminary injunction. Therefore, Coca–Cola's motion for preliminary injunction sought pursuant to paragraph (a) of its proposed order is ALLOWED, and this Court ORDERS that:

> Polar, its officers, agents, servants, employees and attorneys, and those persons in active concert or participation with Polar during the pendency of this action are enjoined from broadcasting, causing to be broadcast, publishing, disseminating or distributing, in any way, directly or indirectly, the television commercial for Polar brand soft drinks that features a polar bear discarding a Coke can into a trash barrel.

So ordered.

Coors Brewing Co. v. Anheuser–Busch Co.

802 F.Supp. 965 (S.D.N.Y.1992).

■ MUKASKEY, DISTRICT JUDGE:

Plaintiff, Coors Brewing Company, sues Anheuser–Busch Companies, Inc. and D'Arcy Masius Benton & Bowles, Anheuser–Busch's advertising agency, claiming that Anheuser–Busch's recent promotional campaign violates § 43(a) of the Lanham Act, New York unfair competition law, and §§ 349 and 350 of New York General Business Law. Plaintiff has sought a preliminary injunction prohibiting defendants' continued use of the advertisements at issue. For the reasons set forth below, plaintiff's application for a preliminary injunction is denied.

I.

Since 1978, Coors has been expanding from the western United States into a nationwide market. Also since 1978, Coors has marketed a reduced-calorie beer called Coors Light. Coors manufactures its line of beers, including Coors Light, using a process that the beer industry calls "high gravity brewing." During the 30 to 60 days it takes to produce the "high gravity" brew, it is cooled to about 4 to 5 degrees centigrade. When the aging process is completed, the brew is filtered to remove yeast and other microbes. The temperature of the brew then is reduced further, to approximately minus 1 degree centigrade. Finally, the high gravity brew, whose alcohol content exceeds the statutory maximum for beer, is "blended" with water.

Most Coors Light is processed fully, *i.e.*, brewed, blended, and bottled, in Golden, Colorado. However, somewhere between 65% (plaintiff's figure) and 85% (defendants' figure) of the Coors Light supplied to the Northeast is "blended" and bottled in Virginia. Using "special insulated railcars," plaintiff transports the high gravity brew from Colorado to Virginia, where plaintiff adds Virginia water to the brew, further filters the mixture, and then bottles it.

Defendant Anheuser–Busch produces a reduced-calorie beer called Natural Light. Like Coors Light, Natural Light is produced by a process of "high gravity" brewing. Apparently, the only material difference between the processes used to produce Coors Light and Natural Light is that Natural Light is pasteurized, a process that involves heating, whereas Coors Light is brewed at low temperatures.[1] In addition, Natural Light apparently is processed entirely—*i.e.*, brewed, blended, and bottled—in regional Anheuser–Busch breweries.

Defendants recently began an advertising campaign comparing Natural Light with Coors Light. That campaign includes radio, television, and point-of-sale advertisements, which, not surprisingly, promote Natural Light at the expense of Coors Light.

Defendants' 30-second television commercial consists of a series of images accompanied by the following narrative:

1. The parties have disputed vigorously whether the taste of beer, unlike the taste of milk, is adversely affected by pasteurization. Coors says it is; Anheuser–Busch say it isn't. They have also disputed, in this forum and elsewhere, other features of their products and their advertising, defendants having gone so far as to accuse Coors of "*ad hominem* attacks on Natural Light." (Def. Mem. at 13) However, *de gustibus cerevesiae non scit lex*.

This is a railroad tanker. [flash the image of a railway tanker] This is the taste of the Rockies. [flash the image of a can of Coors Light] Tanker. [image of a railway tanker] Rockies. [image of a can of Coors Light]

Actually, a concentrated form of Coors Light leaves Colorado in a tanker and travels to Virginia, where local water dilutes the Rockies concentrate before it's sent to you.

So what's it gonna be, the Rockies concentrate or an ice cold Natural Light that leaves our local breweries fresh and ready to drink? Like this [picture of a Natural Light delivery truck], not like this [picture of railway tanker].

So drink fresh, cold Natural Light and don't be railroaded.

The phrase "don't be railroaded" is accompanied by the image of a can of Coors Light atop a railroad car, over which is superimposed a circle with a diagonal line through its center—the international safety warning symbol.

Similarly, defendants' radio advertisements portray a dialogue between two (male) beer-drinkers. One beer-drinker asks the other, "Did you know that Coors Light ships beer concentrate in railroad tanker cars?" The first beer-drinker then continues: "Yeah, all the way from Colorado—1,500 miles to Virginia. That's where they add local water."

In addition, defendants have been distributing printed materials to be displayed by retailers. These point-of-sale materials assert that Coors Light is made from concentrate while Natural Light is fresh. These materials also contain the logo "Don't be railroaded" above the image a Coors Light inside the international safety warning symbol.

Plaintiff argues that the Natural Light advertisements imply that "differences in production make Natural Light 'fresh' in a way in which Coors Light is not." In other words, those advertisements imply that Natural Light is "fresher" than Coors Light because Natural Light leaves the factory ready to drink while Coors Light leaves Colorado in a "concentrate" form, which is diluted when it reaches Coors' plant in Virginia.

Plaintiff also contends that by broadcasting nationally the Natural Light advertisements, defendants lead consumers outside the Northeast to believe erroneously that their Coors Light is shipped to Virginia to be diluted before being shipped to their regional retailers.

II. *Lanham Act Claims*

The Second Circuit has held that in order to obtain injunctive relief against a false or misleading advertising claim[2] pursuant to section 43(a) of the Lanham Act, a plaintiff must demonstrate either: (1) that an advertise-

---

2. Under § 43(a), a merchant's false or misleading claim may relate either to its own product or another's product.

ment is literally false; or (2) that the advertisement, though literally true, is likely to mislead and confuse customers.

1. *Literal Falsehoods*

In the case at hand, Coors contends that the challenged advertisements contain two literal falsehoods: (1) that "Coors Light is made from 'concentrate' that is 'diluted' with water"; and (2) that "Coors Light travels to Virginia 'before it's sent to you.'"

As to defendants' advertising claim that Coors Light is made from a concentrate, Coors has failed to prove literal falsehood. The challenged commercial states that Coors Light travels from Colorado to Virginia in "a concentrated form" and asks, "So what's it gonna be, the Rockies concentrate or an ice cold Natural Light ...?" Relying on 27 C.F.R. § 25.11, which provides that a "concentrate is produced from beer by the removal of water," plaintiff would define "concentrate" only as a substance from which water has been removed. However, defendants proffer another, equally plausible definition of "concentrate," namely, "a concentrated substance" or "concentrated form of something." In addition, when "concentrate" is used as an adjective, it means "concentrated." In turn, "concentrated" means "(1) rich in respect to a particular or essential element: strong, undiluted; (2) intense...." WEBSTER'S THIRD NEW INTERNATIONAL DICTIONARY 469 (1986). Because the term "concentrate" is equally open to either party's definition, defendants' advertising claim that Coors Light is made from a concentrate is ambiguous at most. Therefore, the commercial's reference to concentrate is not literally false.

In addition, plaintiff argues that the commercial's claim that Coors Light is diluted is literally false. However, dilute means, *inter alia*, "to make thinner or more liquid by admixture (as with water); to make less concentrated: diminish the strength, activity, or flavor of...." *Id.* 633. It is undisputed that water is added to the "high gravity" brew—or concentrate—to produce the final product. That process makes the concentrate less concentrated. Therefore, neither is defendants' use of the term dilute literally false.

Plaintiff also challenges as literally false, except as applied to the Northeast, defendants' claim that Coors Light travels to Virginia before it is distributed to consumers. However, Anheuser–Busch "represents that the commercials will not be broadcast on any 'superstations' or other media that can be received outside of the Northeast." Therefore, this portion of plaintiff's application for injunctive relief is moot.

2. *Implied Falsehoods*

Plaintiff contends that by repeatedly stating that Coors Light is made from concentrate and is diluted, and by showing Coors Light being shipped from Colorado in railway cars while stating that Natural Light leaves Anheuser–Busch factories fresh and ready to drink, defendants' commercial implies three falsehoods: (1) that Natural Light is not also made by a process of "high gravity" brewing; (2) that all of the Coors Light sold in the

Northeast has been "blended" with Virginia water; and (3) that there is a difference between Colorado Coors and Virginia Coors.

A claim for implied falsehood rises or falls on a plaintiff's evidence of consumer confusion, *i.e.*, market surveys. In the case at hand, plaintiff retained a market research and behavioral consulting firm called Leo J. Shapiro and Associates ("Shapiro") to conduct market surveys. Philip Johnson, Shapiro's president, has submitted an affidavit setting forth the results of those surveys; he also testified—sort of—at the preliminary injunction hearing.

Between August 7 and 10, 1992, Shapiro conducted consumer surveys in shopping malls located in Boston, Philadelphia, Washington, D.C., New York, Los Angeles, and Kansas City. In all, Shapiro interviewed 200 men and 100 women who were over 21 years old and who had consumed beer in the preceding four weeks; 50 people were interviewed at each location.

Survey respondents were shown the challenged Natural Light television advertisement. After respondents had been shown the advertisement once, they were asked the following two questions:

Question 2a: Now, tell me what you recall about the commercial I just showed you?

Probe: What else was it about?

Question 2b: And, what was the central theme or message in this commercial? What were they trying to tell you?

After respondents were asked, and answered, Questions 2a and 2b, the commercial was played a second time. Respondents then were asked six more questions:

Question 4: What, if anything, did this commercial tell you about Coors Light beer?

Probe: What else?

Question 5: Based on this commercial, do you believe that Coors Light and Natural Light are made the same way, or are they made differently?

If different: In what way is Coors Light made differently than Natural Light?

Question 6: And, based on the commercial, do you believe there is any difference between Coors Light and Natural Light in terms of the freshness of the products?

If yes: In what way is Coors Light different from Natural Light in terms of freshness?

Question 7: Based on the commercial, do you believe there is any difference between Coors Light and Natural Light in terms of the purity or naturalness of the products?

If yes: In what way is Coors Light different from Natural Light in terms of purity or naturalness?

Question 8: Do you feel that seeing this commercial would encourage You to drink Coors Light beer, discourage you from drinking Coors Light beer, or would it make no difference? Why do you say that?

Probe: Why else?

Question 9: By the way, do you believe that this commercial is talking about the Coors Light beer that is available where you buy beer? Why do you say that?

In answer to Question 5, whether based on the commercial respondents believed that Coors Light and Natural Light were made the same way or different ways, 67% of all respondents answered that they believed the two beers were made in different ways while 21% of all respondents answered that they believed the two beers were made the same way. Of those respondents who answered that the two beers were made in different ways, (i) 29% stated that they believed that "Coors is diluted/watered down/Natural Light is not," (ii) 25% stated that "Coors/Coors Light made from concentrate/Natural Light is not," and (iii) 13% stated that "Coors made in two places/Natural Light from one place." There were at least 20 other responses specifying differences between how the two beers are made, but those responses are not relevant to the case at hand.

Based on the answers to Question 5, plaintiff argues that 67% of all respondents falsely believed, based on the commercial in question, that Natural Light and Coors Light are made differently. Adding the category of respondents who said that they believed that "Coors is diluted/watered down/Natural Light is not" (29%), and the category of respondents who said that they believed that "Coors/Coors Light made from concentrate/Natural Light is not" (25%), the total percentage of the 67% of respondents who had been misled by the commercial into thinking that Natural Light is not made by a process of high gravity brewing is 54%. This means that, based on plaintiff's survey, 36.18% of *all* respondents were misled by defendants' commercial as to the differences between how the two beers are made.

In the case at hand, plaintiff's reliance on the answers elicited by Question 5 is misplaced because that question is leading and thus produced unreliable results. By asking whether, "based on the commercial," the respondent believes Coors Light and Natural Light are made the same way or different ways, Question 5 assumes that the commercial conveys some message comparing how the two beers are made. But, in response to the open-ended questions—Questions 2a and 2b—a statistically insignificant percentage of respondents remarked on differences between the processes by which the two beers are made. This jump in the percentage of respondents whose answers indicate a mistaken belief that Natural Light is not also made by a process of high gravity brewing from between 3% and 9% to 36.18% further suggests the leading nature of Question 5.

Question 5 is leading also in that it asks whether an obviously comparative advertisement, which disparages one product and promotes another, suggests or does not suggest a difference in the way the two products are made. This inquiry in itself implies, because the advertisement invidiously compares one product with another, that the advertisement does suggest a difference in the way the two products are made. Moreover, Question 5 failed to inform respondents that they also could respond that they did not know if the commercial implied that Coors Light and Natural Light are made by different processes. This omission further undermines the reliability of the answers elicited by Question 5. For the above reasons, I do not credit Question 5 with probative value.

By contrast, I find that the survey's open-ended questions, 2a and 2b, were generally reliable. Questions 2a and 2b elicited answers going principally to plaintiff's claims of literal falsehood, which I have rejected. In answer to Question 2a, the bulk of respondents remarked that Coors Light is made from concentrate (20%), is "diluted/watered down" (32%), is transported by railway tanker (26%), and travels a long distance before it reaches customers (20%).

Because Johnson lumped together the percentage of respondents who said that Coors Light is diluted and the percentage of respondents who said that Coors Light is watered down, the 32% figure is uninformative. While I have found that it is literally true that in one sense Coors Light is "diluted," Coors Light does not appear to be "watered down," in the sense of containing more water than beer should or than Natural Light does. However, because I have no way of knowing what percentage of respondents said that Coors Light is diluted and what percentage said that Coors Light is watered down, this category of responses has no probative value. *See* Darrell Huff, *How to Statisticulate,* in How to Lie with Statistics 110–20 (1954).

Plaintiff has invited me to enjoin the advertisement at issue despite any blemishes in Shapiro's survey technique based on the "general thrust of [the] survey rather than its quantitative results." Here, the "thrust" is to be found in the "quantitative results," or it is not to be found at all. I decline to imagine "thrust" in the absence of evidence. Nor is there significance in defendants' failure to conduct a survey of their own. The burden is plaintiff's, and defendants may rely on that if they choose. Accordingly, because I have found that the results of Question 5 are unreliable and that those results of Questions 2a and 2b that support plaintiff's claims are either ambiguous or are statistically insignificant, I find that plaintiff has failed to prove that the challenged commercial is likely to mislead consumers into believing that, unlike Coors Light, Natural Light is not made by a process of "high gravity" brewing.

As to plaintiff's two remaining implied falsehood claims, that (i) *all* of the Coors Light sold in the Northeast has been "blended" with Virginia water, and (ii) there is a difference between Colorado Coors and Virginia Coors, plaintiff has failed to support either of these claims with any extrinsic evidence; none of the survey questions even arguably addresses these claims. Moreover, I find that plaintiff is estopped to argue the third alleged falsehood, *i.e.*, that there is a difference between Colorado Coors and Virginia Coors. Plaintiff has promoted its beers, including Coors Light, as "the taste of the Rockies," based on use of water from the Rocky Mountains. After having advertised for years that Coors beers tasted better than other beers because Coors beers are made from Rocky Mountain water, Coors now cannot seek an equitable remedy that would prohibit defendants' hoisting Coors by its own petard.

For the above reasons, I find that plaintiff has failed to substantiate its implied falsehood claims with reliable extrinsic evidence.

It goes almost without saying that the balance of hardships between these major brewers seems evenly balanced. Certainly, plaintiff has made no showing that the balance tips decidedly in its favor.

For the above reasons, plaintiff's application for a preliminary injunction prohibiting defendants' continued use of the challenged Natural Light commercial is denied.

So ordered.

McNeil–PPC, Inc. v. Pfizer Inc.

351 F.Supp.2d 226 (S.D.N.Y.2005).

■ CHIN, D.J.

In June 2004, defendant Pfizer Inc. ("Pfizer") launched a consumer advertising campaign for its mouthwash, Listerine Antiseptic Mouthrinse. Print ads and hang tags featured an image of a Listerine bottle balanced on a scale against a white container of dental floss, as shown above.

The campaign also featured a television commercial called the "Big Bang." In its third version, which is still running, the commercial announces that "Listerine's as effective as floss at fighting plaque and gingivitis. Clinical studies prove it." Although the commercial cautions that "there's no replacement for flossing," the commercial repeats two more times the message that Listerine is "as effective as flossing against plaque and gingivitis." The commercial also shows a narrow stream of blue liquid flowing out of a Cool Mint Listerine bottle, then tracking a piece of dental floss being pulled from a white floss container, and then swirling around and between teeth—bringing to mind an image of liquid floss.

In this case, plaintiff McNeil–PPC, Inc. ("PPC"), the market leader in sales of string dental floss and other interdental cleaning products, alleges that Pfizer has engaged in false advertising in violation of § 43(a) of the Lanham Act, 15 U.S.C. § 1125(a), and unfair competition in violation of state law. PPC contends that Pfizer's advertisements are false and misleading in two respects. First, PPC contends that Pfizer's literal (or explicit) claim that "clinical studies prove" that Listerine is "as effective as floss against plaque and gingivitis" is false. Second, PPC contends that Pfizer's advertisements also implicitly are claiming that Listerine is a replacement for floss—that all the benefits of flossing may be obtained by rinsing with Listerine—and that this implied message is false and misleading as well.

Before the Court is PPC's motion for a preliminary injunction enjoining Pfizer from continuing to make these claims in its advertisements. For the reasons set forth below, I conclude that Pfizer's advertisements are false and misleading. PPC's motion is granted and a preliminary injunction will be issued. My findings of fact and conclusions of law follow.

STATEMENT OF THE CASE

A.   *The Facts*

1.   *The Parties and Their Products*

PPC, a wholly-owned subsidary of Johnson & Johnson ("J&J"), manufactures and markets consumer oral health products. PPC is the market leader in the sales of interdental cleaning products, including dental floss—waxed or unwaxed string used to mechanically remove food and debris from between the teeth and underneath the gumline. . . .

J&J invented floss nearly 100 years ago. PPC's products include the Reach Access Daily Flosser (the "RADF"), a toothbrush-like device with a snap-on head (to be replaced after each use) containing a piece of string floss. The RADF was launched in August 2003. PPC also sells a battery-powered version of the RADF, called the Reach Access Power Flosser.

Pfizer manufactures and markets consumer and pharmaceutical products, including Listerine, an essential oil-containing antimicrobial mouthrinse. According to its label, Listerine:

Kills germs that cause Bad Breath, Plaque & the gum disease Gingivitis.

Listerine has been "accepted" by the American Dental Association (the "ADA") and bears the ADA seal of acceptance on its label. The label instructs users to rinse with Listerine full strength for 30 seconds, each morning and night. Listerine also comes in several flavors, including Cool Mint, Fresh Burst, and Natural Citrus.

2.   *Oral Hygiene and Oral Diseases*

Plaque is a biofilm comprised of a thin layer of bacteria that forms on teeth and other surfaces of the mouth. Food debris caught between teeth provides a source of nutrition for this bacteria and will help the bacteria multiply, grow, and persist. Plaque build-up may cause gingivitis, an inflammation of the superficial gum tissues surrounding the tooth. Gingivitis is common, affecting some two-thirds of the U.S. population. Its symptoms include red, inflamed, swollen, puffy, or bleeding gums. Periodontitis is inflammation that develops in deeper tissues, and involves the bone and connection to the tooth (the periodontal ligament). Periodontitis is less common, affecting some 10–15% (more or less) of the population, although it becomes more prevalent with age. It is a major cause of tooth loss.

. . .

The removal of plaque and the prevention of plaque build-up are critical to addressing both gingivitis and periodontitis. In addition, although it is less clear, controlling plaque also helps prevent or reduce "caries"—cavities or dental decay. The ADA recognizes that "plaque is responsible for both tooth decay and gum disease."

The most common method of mechanically removing plaque is brushing, and today the use of toothbrushes and fluoridated toothpastes is "almost universal." Brushing, however, does not adequately remove plaque. In part, this is because many people do not brush properly or they brush less than the recommended two minutes twice a day. In part, it is also because for most people "toothbrushing alone cannot effectively control interproximal plaque," i.e., the plaque in the hard-to-reach places between the teeth. As a consequence, removal of plaque from the interproximal areas by additional methods is particularly important, for it is in these areas between the teeth that plaque deposits appear early and become more prevalent. The direct interproximal area is the area where there is "the most stagnation" and where "periodontal disease usually starts."

Traditionally, the "most widely recommended" mechanical device for removing interproximal plaque is dental floss. . . . Flossing provides a number of benefits. It removes food debris and plaque interdentally and it also removes plaque subgingivally. As part of a regular oral hygiene program, flossing helps reduce and prevent not only gingivitis but also periodontitis and caries.

Some 87% of consumers, however, floss either infrequently or not at all. Although dentists and dental hygienists regularly tell their patients to floss, many consumers do not floss or rarely floss because it is a difficult and time-consuming process.

As a consequence, a large consumer market exists to be tapped. If the 87% of consumers who never or rarely floss can be persuaded to floss more regularly, sales of floss would increase dramatically. PPC has endeavored, with products such as the RADF and the Power Flosser, to reach these consumers by trying to make flossing easier.

At the same time, Pfizer has recognized that there is enormous potential here for greater sales of Listerine as well. Pfizer has come to realize that if it could convince consumers who were reluctant flossers that they could obtain the benefits of flossing by rinsing with Listerine, it would be in a position to see its sales of Listerine increase dramatically.

In the context of this case, therefore, Pfizer and PPC are competitors.

3.   *The Listerine Studies*

Pfizer sponsored two clinical studies involving Listerine and floss: the "Sharma Study" and the "Bauroth Study." These studies purported to compare the efficacy of Listerine against dental floss in controlling plaque and gingivitis in subjects with mild to moderate gingivitis.

[Both studies divided subjects with mild to moderate gingivitis into three groups. One group received instruction in flossing and a supply of dental floss, and was directed to brush twice and floss once every day for six months. The second group was given a supply of Listerine and asked to brush twice and rinse twice every day for six months. The final group was given a supply of a placebo rinse and told to brush and rinse twice daily. The subjects returned to the clinic every month for a dental exam and new supplies. After three months, the Listerine and flossing groups had fewer symptoms of gingivitis than the control group. After six months, the Listerine results were better than the flossing results. The authors of both studies suggested that the most probable reason was that the subjects failed to floss consistently in the later months of the study.]

Neither the Bauroth Study nor the Sharma Study purported to examine whether Listerine could replace floss, and neither study examined the efficacy of Listerine with respect to severe gingivitis or periodontitis or tooth decay or the removal of food debris. In addition, neither study considered the adjunctive effects of Listerine when used in addition to brushing and flossing.

. . .

7. *The Consumer Advertising Campaign*

The consumer advertising campaign was launched in June 2004. . . .

In the third version of the Big Bang, which continues to run, the commercial announces that "Listerine's as effective as floss at fighting plaque and gingivitis. Clinical studies prove it." The commercial cautions that "there's no replacement for flossing," but states that "if you don't floss like you should, you can get its plaque-fighting benefits by rinsing." The commercial goes on to repeat two more times the message that Listerine is "as effective as flossing against plaque and gingivitis."

The commercial also shows a narrow stream of blue liquid flowing out of a Cool Mint Listerine bottle, then tracking a piece of dental floss being pulled from a white floss container, and then swirling around and between teeth—bringing to mind an image of liquid floss. In a superscript that appears briefly on-screen, the commercial also tells viewers to "ask your dental professional."

Pfizer also published print ads, including a freestanding circular with a manufacturer's discount coupon featuring a bottle of Cool Mint Listerine balanced equally on a scale opposite a floss container (similar to the image used in the professional campaign). The ad proclaims that Listerine "Is Clinically Proven To Be As Effective as Floss at Reducing Plaque & Gingivitis between the Teeth." In small print near the bottom of the page, the ad states: "Floss Daily." There is no instruction telling consumers to consult their dentists.

Pfizer also used a hang tag and shoulder labels on its bottles of Listerine. The hang tag features the scale image and is similar to the print ad just described. The shoulder label has gone through three versions. The first version (which was red) stated: "Now Clinically Proven As Effective As Floss," with the words in much smaller print "Against Plaque and Gingivitis Between the Teeth." (PXs 98, 162). The second version (which is blue) reads the same as the first, with the addition in small print of the words: "Ask Your Dentist. Floss Daily." A third version (which is gold and red) is being or is about to be distributed and reads: "As Effective As Floss Against Plaque & Gingivitis Between Teeth," with the following words in smaller print: "Ask Your Dentist. Not a Replacement for Floss."

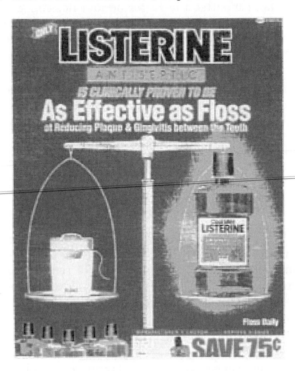

Pfizer has also featured the "as effective as flossing" claim on its website for Listerine. The first page of the website shows the Cool Mint Listerine bottle shaking, with the stream of blue liquid flowing out (as in the Big Bang commercial), and forming the words "Listerine Antiseptic is as effective as flossing," with a footnote to the words: "Against plaque and gingivitis between teeth. Use as directed. Ask your dentist. Not a replacement for floss." The first page also states:

It's clinically proven.

A quick easy rinse with Listerine Antiseptic, twice a day, is actually as effective as floss. Because Listerine Antiseptic gets between teeth to kill the germs that cause plaque and gingivitis. Ask your dentist. You'll find out that Listerine Antiseptic truly is the easy way to a healthy mouth.

The website has an entire section entitled "Effective As Floss," spanning many pages. In a question-and-answer section, the website addresses frequently asked questions, including the following:

Question 3 Most people don't like to floss/don't make the time to floss. Isn't this new data telling people that they don't have to floss?

Answer—No, flossing is essential in preventing gum disease because it helps remove food particles and plaque from between the teeth, areas where the toothbrush can't reach. However, optimal plaque control through brushing and flossing alone can sometimes be difficult to achieve. We believe that the results [of the two studies] suggest the importance of adding an antiseptic mouthwash to patients' daily oral healthcare. . . .

. . .

8. *The Surveys*

In September and October 2004, at PPC's request, a consumer research firm, Bruno and Ridgway Research Associates, conducted three consumer surveys in connection with this case, in malls and shopping centers in ten different locations throughout the United States. The first was intended to determine the message that consumers took away from the Big Bang commercial. The second sought to determine the message that consumers took away from the first of the three shoulder labels. The third sought to measure the pre-existing beliefs of consumers regarding the use of Listerine and floss.

In the first survey, consumers were shown the third version of Big Bang twice and then asked a series of questions about the ideas that were communicated to them by the commercial. The survey found that 50% of the respondents took away the message that "you can replace floss with Listerine." . . .

In the second survey, eligible consumers were shown a Listerine bottle with the first (or red) version of the shoulder label. They were asked essentially the same questions as were asked in the first survey. Some 45% of the consumers took away the message that Listerine could be used instead of floss. . . .

In the third survey, a control survey, consumers were asked their "pre-existing beliefs" regarding Listerine and floss; the intent was to determine the number of people who did not recall seeing the commercials but who still believed that Listerine could be used instead of floss. A minority of those surveyed did not recall seeing Big Bang, and of those 19% stated the opinion that Listerine could be used in place of floss. . . .

The surveyors then took the three surveys together, subtracted the 19% figure from the 50% and 45% figures, respectively, and concluded that 31% of those who saw the commercial and 26% of those who viewed the shoulder label took away a replacement message.

. . .

DISCUSSION

. . .

I conclude that PPC has demonstrated a likelihood of success on both its literal falsity claim and on its implied falsity claim. I address each claim in turn.

a. Literal Falsity

Pfizer's advertisements make the explicit claim that "clinical studies prove that Listerine is as effective as floss against plaque and gingivitis." As Pfizer purports to rely on "clinical studies," this is an "establishment claim" and PPC need only prove that "the [studies] referred to ... were not sufficiently reliable to permit one to conclude with reasonable certainty that they established the proposition for which they were cited." *Castrol [Inc. v. Quaker State Corp.*, 977 F.2d 57 (2d Cir. 1992)] at 62–63. Two questions are presented: first, whether the Sharma and Bauroth Studies stand for the proposition that "Listerine is as effective as floss against plaque and gingivitis"; and second, assuming they do, whether the studies are sufficiently reliable to permit one to draw that conclusion with "reasonable certainty."

First, even putting aside the issue of their reliability, the two studies do not stand for the proposition that "Listerine is as effective as floss against plaque and gingivitis." The two studies included in their samples only individuals with mild to moderate gingivitis. They excluded individuals with severe gingivitis or with any degree of periodontitis, and they did not purport to draw any conclusions with respect to these individuals. Hence, the literal claim in Pfizer's advertisements is overly broad, for the studies did not purport to prove that Listerine is as effective as floss "against plaque and gingivitis," but only against plaque and gingivitis in individuals with mild to moderate gingivitis. The advertisements do not specify that the "as effective as floss" claim is limited to individuals with mild to moderate gingivitis. Consequently, consumers who suffer from severe gingivitis or periodontitis (including mild periodontitis) may be misled by the ads into believing that Listerine is just as effective as floss in helping them fight plaque and gingivitis, when the studies simply do not stand for that proposition.

Second, the two studies were not sufficiently reliable to permit one to conclude with reasonable certainty that Listerine is as effective as floss in fighting plaque and gingivitis, even in individuals with mild to moderate gingivitis. What the two studies showed was that Listerine is as effective as floss when flossing is not done properly. The authors of both studies recognized that the plaque reductions in the flossing groups were lower than would be expected and hypothesized that "behavioral or technical causes" were the reason. . . .

Hence, the studies did not "prove" that Listerine is "as effective as floss." Rather, they proved only that Listerine is "as effective as improperly-used floss." The studies showed only that Listerine is as effective as floss when the flossing is not performed properly. . . .

Pfizer and its experts argue that the two studies are reliable, notwithstanding the indications that the participants in the flossing group did not floss properly, because these conditions reflect "real-world settings." But the ads do not say that "in the real world," where most people floss rarely or not at all and even those who do floss have difficulty flossing properly, Listerine is "as effective as floss." Rather, the ads make the blanket assertion that Listerine works just as well as floss, an assertion the two studies simply do not prove. Although it is important to determine how a product works in the real world, it is probably more important to first determine how a product will work when it is used properly.

. . .

Accordingly, I hold that PPC is likely to succeed on its claim of literal false advertisement.

b. Implied Falsity

In considering the claim of implied falsity, in accordance with Second Circuit law, I determine first the message that consumers take away from the advertisements and second whether that message is false.

(i) The Implicit Message

Pfizer argues that its advertisements do not implicitly send the message that Listerine is a replacement for floss. I disagree. Rather, I find that Pfizer's advertisements do send the message, implicitly, that Listerine is a replacement for floss—that the benefits of flossing may be obtained by rinsing with Listerine, and that, in particular, those consumers who do not have the time or desire to floss can switch to Listerine instead.

First, the words and images used in the advertisements confirm that this is the message being sent. The words ("as effective as floss") and images (a stream of blue liquid tracking floss as it is removed from a floss container and then swirling between and around teeth; a bottle of Listerine balanced equally on a scale against a container of floss) convey the impression that Listerine is the equal to floss.

Second, the Ridgway survey is convincing and was conducted in a generally objective and fair manner. . . . The Ridgway surveys show that 31% and 26% of the consumers who saw Big Bang and the shoulder label, respectively, took away the message that "you can replace floss with Listerine." Hence, a substantial percentage of the consumers who saw the advertisements took away a replacement message.

. . .

Accordingly, I conclude that the Pfizer ads send an implicit message that Listerine is a replacement for floss.

(ii) Falsity

The final inquiry, then, is whether the implicit message sent by the Pfizer ads is false. Pfizer argues that even assuming the advertisements do send a replacement message, the message is true: Listerine provides all the benefits of flossing.

Pfizer's position is based on two premises. First, Pfizer contends, the Sharma and Bauroth Studies prove that Listerine is as effective as floss in fighting plaque and gingivitis. Second, Pfizer contends, no clinical proof exists to show that flossing provides any benefit other than fighting plaque and gingivitis—there is no clinical proof that flossing reduces tooth decay or periodontitis. Indeed, Pfizer asserts, this notion is a "myth," and goes so far as to argue that there is no proof that reducing plaque will reduce caries or periodontitis. Hence, Pfizer continues, because Listerine does everything that floss can do, Listerine therefore provides all the benefits of floss—and consumers can "toss the floss" and replace it with Listerine.

These arguments are rejected. I conclude that the implicit message sent by Pfizer's advertisements is false, for Listerine is not a replacement for floss.

First, as discussed above, Pfizer's initial premise is wrong. The Sharma and Bauroth Studies do not prove that Listerine is just as effective as floss in fighting plaque and gingivitis. They prove only that Listerine is just as effective in fighting plaque and gingivitis as improperly-used floss. One simply cannot conclude from the two studies that Listerine is just as effective as flossing when the flossing is performed properly.

Second, Pfizer's second premise is wrong as well: there is substantial, convincing clinical, medical, and other proof to show that flossing does fight tooth decay and periodontitis and that Listerine is not a replacement for flossing.

Flossing provides certain benefits that Listerine does not. Floss penetrates subgingivally to remove plaque and biofilm below the gumline. Flossing, as part of a regular oral prevention program, also can reduce periodontitis. Flossing also reduces tooth decay and has an anti-caries effect. Finally, flossing removes food debris interdentally, including pieces of food trapped between the teeth that rinsing cannot dislodge. Numerous articles confirm that tooth decay and periodontitis can be reduced or prevented through interdental plaque control methods, including flossing.
. . .

Other substantial evidence also demonstrates, overwhelmingly, that flossing is important in reducing tooth decay and periodontitis and that it cannot be replaced by rinsing with a mouthwash. . . .

Finally, of course, dentists and hygienists have been telling their patients for decades to floss daily. They have been doing so for good reason. The benefits of flossing are real—they are not a "myth." Pfizer's implicit message that Listerine can replace floss is false and misleading.

CONCLUSION

In sum, I find that PPC has demonstrated that it will suffer irreparable harm if a preliminary injunction is not issued, and I find further that PPC has demonstrated a likelihood of success on both its literal falsity claim and on its implied falsity claim. . . . In addition, I find that Pfizer's false and misleading advertising also poses a public health risk, as the advertisements present a danger of undermining the efforts of dental professionals—and the ADA—to convince consumers to floss on a daily basis.

QUESTIONS

1. Lazar Khidekel was a Russian painter who died in 1986, leaving his unsold paintings to his son, Mark. Rene and Claude Boule are French art collectors who specialize in Russian art, and own paintings attributed to Lazar Khidekel. In the late 1980s, Rene and Claude met Mark. He examined their collection and, at their request (and in return for $8000), executed a certificate of authenticity attesting that sixteen of their paintings were authentic Lazar Khidekel works. In 1992, Rene and Claude loaned those paintings to the Musée d'art de Joliette in Canada for a special exhibit.

Several years later, Mark moved to New York City and sought to sell his late father's paintings. He arranged for the exhibition of his father's work at a gallery, and advertised the show as the "first ever North American exhibition" of Khidekel's work. He sent a letter to 25 important art galleries in which he claimed that the paintings shown in the 1992 exhibit at the Musee d'art de Jolliette were not authentic Khidekels. He later arranged to be interviewed by ARTnews magazine. In the interview as it appeared in the magazine, Mark complained that unscrupulous and dishonest art dealers had misrepresented thousands of fraudulent artworks as his father's paintings. He identified Rene and Claude's collection as a fraudulent one, and maintained that he had viewed their collection, and immediately advised them that none of the paintings they owned had been painted by his father.

The Boules are furious. They consult you to find out whether Mark's letter or the interview published in ARTnews might be actionable. Can they recover under § 43(a)? Why or why not? *See Boule v. Hutton*, 328 F.3d 84 (2d Cir.2003).

2. Digital Widgets has secured several patents but not yet exploited them. To get the capital to take its inventions to market, Digital Widgets borrowed substantial sums of money from a venture capital firm, and assigned its patents as collateral for the loan. Unfortunately, in today's sluggish economy, Digital Widgets was unable to find the right marketing partner. It failed to market its inventions and defaulted on its loan payments. The venture capital firm informed it that it would therefore foreclose on the loan and take sole control of the collateral. In a desperate maneuver to stave off bankruptcy, Digital Widgets issued a press release and bought a full-page advertisement in *Investors Weekly* seeking additional funding. Both the press release and the advertisement claimed that Digital Widgets presented a unique and worthwhile investment opportunity because of the unrealized value of the patents that it owned. The venture capital firm sues for false advertising, claiming that it is the true owner of the patents, and Digital Widget's representations to the contrary are therefore false representations under 43(a)(1)(b). Digital Widgets concedes that it misrepresented the ownership of the patents, but argues that its only false representation was in connection with patents, not products, and it was therefore not actionable under section 43(a). How should the court rule? *See Digigan v. Invalidate,* 52 UCC Rep.Serv.2d 1022 (S.D.N.Y.2004).

4.   STANDING TO ASSERT A § 43(A) CLAIM

Representative Kastenmeier's remarks, *supra* pages 569–71, refer to Congress' decision not to include an addition to Section 43(a) explicitly providing for consumer standing to sue. His remarks implied that the issue is clear: the "plain meaning" of the statute already conferred consumer standing. Despite the provision's extensive language authorizing suit by "any person who believes that he is likely to be damaged by the use of any such false description or representation," however courts have ruled that only competitors had standing to assert a Section 43(a) claim of false representation. *See, e.g., Barrus v. Sylvania,* 55 F.3d 468 (9th Cir.1995). *Serbin v. Ziebart* is representative.

Serbin v. Ziebart International Corp., 11 F.3d 1163 (3d Cir.1993). Sara Serbin brought suit under section 43(a) against the Ziebart Corporation, claiming that she had purchased Ziebart's "Super Rust Protection" policy relying on Ziebart's false representations comparing the scope of its policy to the scope of standard, new car rust-protection warranties, and on Ziebart's false descriptions of the expansiveness of its own coverage. After reviewing the legislative history of the 1946 Lanham Act and the 1988 amendments, scholarly commentary on standing decisions, and the case law of various circuits, the Court of Appeals for the Third Circuit concluded that consumers may not sue under section 43(a):

> The question of policy that underlies these appeals is not whether false advertising is a bad thing. It is, and consumers are victimized by it. The question of policy is what institution, or set of institutions, should be charged with identifying false advertising, ameliorating its malign consequences, and, in the long run, shrinking its dominion. State courts have substantial authority in this field by virtue of judge-made misrepresentation law, and some state legislatures have, through such legislation as the Uniform Deceptive Trade Practices Act, undertaken to widen that authority. Congress conferred a measure of public enforcement authority on the Federal Trade Commission and, through section 43(a) of the Lanham Act, has vested in the federal courts jurisdiction to entertain certain categories of private law suits predicated on claims of false advertising. Given this commitment of institutional resources to the cause of consumers injured by false advertising, if Congress had intended to make the additional commitment involved in recognizing a federal tort of misrepresentation and in bestowing access to federal fora without regard to the amount in issue, we are confident that the legislative history of the Lanham Act would

have borne clear witness to that commitment. Because we find no clear indication of such an unusual commitment and because we are satisfied that section 43(a) had an important, though narrower and quite distinct purpose, we join the Second Circuit in holding that Congress, when authorizing federal courts to deal with claims of false advertising, did not contemplate that federal courts should entertain claims brought by consumers.

Ortho Pharmaceutical Corp. v. Cosprophar, Inc., 32 F.3d 690 (2d Cir.1994). Ortho, which markets RETIN–A, a prescription acne medication shown to be effective at diminishing wrinkles on sun-damaged skin, and RENOVA, a treatment developed especially for sun-damaged skin with the same active ingredient, filed suit against Cosprophar, seeking to prevent it from claiming that its ANTI–AGE line of cosmetics contained the naturally-occurring form of the chemical in Retin–A, and that ANTI–AGE products diminished wrinkles. The court ruled that Ortho had failed to make the requisite showing of standing:

This circuit has adopted a flexible approach toward the showing a Lanham Act plaintiff must make on the injury and causation component of its claim. We have held that, while a plaintiff must show more than a "subjective belief" that it will be damaged, it need not demonstrate that it is in direct competition with the defendant or that it has definitely lost sales because of the defendant's advertisements. *Coca–Cola Co.*[*v. Tropicana Products*, 690 F.2d 312 (2d Cir.1982)] at 316; *see also Johnson & Johnson* [*v. Carter–Wallace, Inc.*, 631 F.2d 186 (2d Cir.1980)] at 190. However, we have also maintained that "the likelihood of injury and causation will not be presumed, but must be demonstrated in some manner." *Coca–Cola Co.*, 690 F.2d at 316; *see also Johnson & Johnson*, 631 F.2d at 190. The type and quantity of proof required to show injury and causation has varied from one case to another depending on the particular circumstances. On the whole, we have tended to require a more substantial showing where the plaintiff's products are not obviously in competition with defendant's products, or the defendant's advertisements do not draw direct comparisons between the two. *Compare McNeilab, Inc. v. American Home Prods. Corp.*, 848 F.2d 34, 38 (2d Cir.1988) (district court did not err by presuming harm after finding that advertisement for over-the-counter pain reliever made misleading comparison to specific competing product) *with Johnson & Johnson*, 631 F.2d at 190 (requiring manufacturer of baby oil to show indication of actual injury and causation when seeking to enjoin non-comparative commercial for depilatory); *see also Coca–Cola*, 690 F.2d at 316 n.2 (noting that plaintiff in *Johnson & Johnson* was required to prove the element of competition because its product was "not obviously competing . . . for the same consumer dollars").

Here, the district court found that "Ortho and Cosprophar are not in direct competition given the nature of their products: one is a drug requiring a doctor's prescription, the other is a cosmetic available in a pharmacy." Without disputing this finding, Ortho claims that it will be harmed by Cosprophar's advertising in three ways. First, it asserts that consumers who currently buy Cosprophar's cosmetics consequently will not buy RETIN–A. Second, it claims that consumers who are dissatisfied with Cosprophar's cosmetics will be discouraged from buying Ortho's products in the future. Third, it claims that consumers who like Cosprophar's cosmetics will continue to purchase them and will thus have no occasion to try either RETIN–A or RENOVA. As proof of this injury, Ortho relies solely on (a) Cosprophar's advertisements, and (b) statements made by a Cosprophar employee that its cosmetics were introduced to take advantage of the publicity surrounding transretinoic acid. The able district judge determined that this evidence was insufficient to establish that Ortho would likely be injured by Cosprophar's conduct. We agree.

. . . .

Under the standards of this Circuit, Ortho has failed to present sufficient evidence to establish that it will likely be damaged by Cosprophar's conduct. While Cosprophar's advertisements draw comparisons to the active ingredient in Ortho's drugs, their substance is not sufficient to establish that Ortho has standing to pursue a Lanham Act claim. Ortho has not shown that consumers see Cosprophar's cosmetics as a substitute for either RETIN–A or RENOVA. Without such proof, it would be just as reasonable to believe that consumers who buy Cosprophar's cosmetics will also buy Ortho's drugs or, alternatively, that the type of consumer who buys Cosprophar's over-the-counter products is not the type who would seek out a prescription drug. Because consumer behavior is unpredictable, and because of the general rule in our Circuit against making presumptions of injury and causation favorable to the plaintiff, we affirm the district court's decision dismissing Ortho's Lanham Act claims for lack of standing.

CHAPTER 9

DILUTION

A. THE CONCEPT OF DILUTION

SARA K. STADLER, THE WAGES OF UBIQUITY IN TRADEMARK LAW, 88 Iowa L. Rev. 731 (2003) (Excerpts)

Introduction

... [D]ilution was born in 1927, when the Harvard Law Review published an article in which its author, Frank Schechter, warned that the distinctiveness of truly unique trademarks was in danger of being "whittled away" (diluted) by the use of those trademarks on unrelated goods, and proposed that if nothing else, trademark law should be an instrument for the preservation of this uniqueness.[8] Courts initially were hostile to the radical theories that Schechter proposed, but in the end, scholars and practitioners convinced courts that Schechter had described a harm that deserved to be remedied—a harm that, in 1995, Congress defined as "the lessening of the capacity of a famous mark to identify and distinguish goods or services, regardless of the presence or absence of ... likelihood of confusion, mistake, or deception."[11]

Unfortunately, this harm was not the one that Schechter described. In promulgating and interpreting the trademark law, Congress and most courts have assumed that by "unique," Schechter meant "distinctive and famous"—in other words, that Schechter meant his dilution remedy to cover every famous word or phrase that happened to have acquired the ability to function as a trademark. A closer review of the Schechter text reveals, however, that Schechter intended his remedy to apply not to famous marks, but to a select class of highly distinctive (indeed, for the most part, inherently distinctive) trademarks that were, like most trademarks of his day, synonymous with a single product or product class. When viewed against the backdrop of modern marketing techniques, this definition of uniqueness reveals a growing state of what I term "ubiquity" in the trademark world—one in which trademark owners are deliberately destroying the uniqueness of their marks by using them to identify a diversity of products, or more generally, product myths and entire lifestyles. Worse,

---

8. Frank I. Schechter, The Rational Basis of Trademark Protection, 40 Harv. L. Rev. 813 (1927).

11. Federal Trademark Dilution Act of 1995, Pub. L. No. 104–98, 4, 109 Stat. 985, 986 (1995), amending 15 U.S.C. 1127 (2000). *Editors' Note*: The FTDA was subsequently amended in 2006. *See infra* Chapter 9.B for the amended text.

613

this ubiquity has gone unchecked, as courts often cite ubiquitous usage as evidence that a mark is famous and thus protectible under dilution law . . .

. . . .

I. *Frank Schechter, Trademark Dilution, and the State of Ubiquity*

. . . [T]he Trademark Act of 1905, even as amended in 1920, proscribed the use of an existing trademark only on "merchandise of substantially the same descriptive properties as those set forth in the registration," and as Schechter repeatedly (and unhappily) pointed out, courts tended to construe this language fairly narrowly . . .

Schechter . . . saw plenty of harm in tolerating such peculiarities as "Kodak bath tubs," and he began to argue for making that harm actionable. . . . To [Schechter's] way of thinking, if asking whether consumers were misled failed to result in an injunction against, inter alia, "Kodak bath tubs," then courts needed to find another touchstone. . . .

. . . Schechter['s] . . . theory would rest on a simple, if unspoken, premise: owners of qualifying trademarks suffered injury whenever others used those marks without permission. For Schechter, this premise not only solved the "non-competing goods" problem, but it also compensated companies for making the investments that transformed words, phrases, and symbols into agents of "selling power."[86] For Schechter, trademarks were not merely (or even primarily) the means by which producers identified themselves as the sources of their goods. Trademarks had become part of the "goods" themselves.

. . . In [Schechter's] view, the value of a "symbol depended in large part upon its uniqueness." What did he mean by this? Were distinctiveness and uniqueness the same thing?

A close reading of Rational Basis indicates that the uniqueness . . . consisted of classic trademark "distinctiveness" plus something more. Consider his examples: marks to which Schechter attributed "very little distinctiveness in the public mind" included the laudatory "Blue Ribbon" and "Gold Medal" and the descriptive "Simplex." None of these marks qualified as a technical trademark, but Schechter did not limit his reasoning to the question whether these marks were "coined" (i.e., fanciful), arbitrary, or suggestive on the one hand, or whether they were descriptive on the other. Blue Ribbon not only was laudatory, but it also had been "used, with or without registration, for all kinds of commodities or services, more than sixty times." Gold Medal, too, had been "as extensively and variously applied." Simplex had been registered, in whole or in part, "approximately sixty" times by numerous parties and had been "applied to so diversified a variety of products as windows, wires, concrete pilings, golf practice machines, letter openers, air brakes, inks and buttons." Contrast these marks with the ones Schechter meant to protect:

---

86. *See* Schechter, *supra* note 8, at 819.

"Rolls–Royce," "Aunt Jemima's," "Kodak," "Mazda," "Corona," "Nujol," and "Blue Goose," are coined, arbitrary or fanciful words or phrases that have been added to rather than withdrawn from the human vocabulary by their owners, and have, from the very beginning, been associated in the public mind with a particular product, not with a variety of products, and have created in the public consciousness an impression or symbol of the excellence of the particular product in question.[113]

Schechter had painted a picture of what, to him, was a unique trademark: "arbitrary or fanciful words or phrases ... associated ... with a particular product." These were the types of trademarks Schechter proposed to protect under his new theory.

There are several concepts packed into this definition, but trademark fame—the headliner in litigation arising under the Federal Trademark Dilution Act—is not one of them. Instead, Schechter required the mark to possess, in ascending order of uniqueness components: (1) a level of distinctiveness in the marketplace, also known as secondary meaning, or the ability to indicate source to the public (a mark must "have created in the public consciousness an impression or symbol of the excellence of the particular product in question"); (2) a level of distinctiveness in the mark itself (a mark must be a "coined, arbitrary or fanciful word[] or phrase[]"); and (3) a singularity of association between the mark and the underlying product (a mark must be "associated in the public mind with a particular product, not with a variety of products"). The "and" in this construction is important. Schechter thought a trademark had to possess each one of these qualities before it was capable of being whittled away by offending uses.

... To Schechter, only ... highly distinctive marks, with their "impress upon the public consciousness," were capable of being vitiated by third party uses on unrelated goods. Because his "coined, arbitrary, or fanciful" language tracks the definition of a technical trademark, Schechter probably meant to limit his dilution remedy to those marks that would have qualified for federal registration under the 1905 Act. We must content ourselves with "probably" because Schechter made a mistake in characterizing the "Rolls–Royce" mark as a "coined, arbitrary or fanciful word"; the compound phrase "Rolls–Royce" was formed by combining two surnames, and thus the mark would properly have been categorized as a trade name—albeit, according to courts at the time, a highly protectible one. On the whole, though, the marks Schechter believed to possess uniqueness were those that courts would term "inherently distinctive" today ...

... Schechter added one more layer to his definition of uniqueness. In order to qualify for protection against dilution, ... a mark must "have, from the very beginning, been associated in the public mind with a particular product, not with a variety of products."

Schechter understood that trademarks standing for one thing were both valuable and vulnerable to those who would make them stand for

---

113. Schechter, *supra* note 8, at 829 (emphasis added) (citations omitted).

more than one thing. They were the trademarks he deemed "most in need of protection." Indeed, he wrote that "the preservation of the uniqueness of a trademark should constitute the only rational basis for its protection." As for marks standing for many things, they had already been vitiated—for them. . . . it was too late to preserve uniqueness through the application of the dilution doctrine.

. . . .

Schechter believed it was high time for courts to remedy the "real injury in . . . such [unrelated goods] cases," which was the gradual whittling away or dispersion of the identity and hold upon the public mind of the mark or name by its use upon non-competing goods. The more distinctive or unique the mark, the deeper is its impress upon the public consciousness, and the greater its need for protection against vitiation or dissociation from the particular product in connection with which it has been used.

As Schechter warned, if " 'Kodak' may be used for bath tubs and cakes, 'Mazda' for cameras and shoes, or 'Ritz–Carlton' for coffee, these marks must inevitably be lost in the commonplace words of the language, despite the originality and ingenuity in their contrivance." Of equal concern, the "vast expenditures" each producer spent in advertising those marks would be lost as well. This set of harms would come to be known as trademark "dilution"—a remedy that Schechter termed "the very essence of any rational system of individual and exclusive trade symbols."[146]

. . . .

The years following the passage of the Lanham Act saw state legislatures in key states enact legislation prohibiting what they termed "injury to business reputation or of dilution of the distinctive quality" of a mark, notwithstanding the absence of consumer confusion "as to the source of goods or services." In enacting these dilution laws, state legislatures borrowed from Schechter, but (intentionally or not) failed to adopt the remedy he had prescribed. When Massachusetts passed such a law in 1947, it did so only after amending the original bill, in which the Massachusetts House of Representatives—like Schechter—had proposed to protect "only a 'coined or peculiar word' or 'unique symbol.' " [T]he Massachusetts Senate . . . passed the much broader "dilution of the distinctive quality" language . . . Illinois followed with a longer (but equally broad) version in 1953. In 1955, New York and Georgia followed . . . And when a similar dilution provision found its way into the Model State Trademark Act in 1963, the floodgates opened. By 1994, the year before Congress enacted its federal dilution statute, 25 states had adopted some form of legislation outlawing the dilution of the "distinctive quality" of marks.

Legislation, of course, is not always synonymous with acceptance. With a few exceptions, courts refused to enforce the plain language of the dilution statutes. To judges comfortable with traditional trademark in-

146. Schechter note 8 *supra* at 833.

fringement, dilution was a radical remedy. Its most vocal critics charged that the dilution doctrine gave trademark owners "rights in gross"—i.e., exclusive rights in a trade symbol regardless of how (or even whether) it was being used to identify goods.

... Congress returned to dilution in 1995.... [T]he bill proscribed dilution of the "distinctive quality" of a famous mark, which was defined as "the lessening of the capacity of a famous mark to identify and distinguish goods or services."[241] Schechter was invoked repeatedly throughout the proceedings. And if the language of the new section 43(c) indicated a preoccupation with fame, those involved in the legislative process clearly believed themselves to be enacting the remedy of which Schechter had conceived.

. . . .

II. *Will the Real Dilution Doctrine Please Stand Up?*

A. Ubiquity as a Form of Dilution

... Marketing experts tell us not to worry about encountering a Pepsi brand single malt whisky or Chanel brand galoshes because Pepsico, Inc. and Chanel, Inc. would never market these products; single malt whisky and galoshes would be inconsistent with the "myths" surrounding Pepsi and Chanel, respectively. Some trademark scholars, taking their cue from the marketers, have defined dilution in terms of this myth disturbance. Dilution is, to them, "the impairment of brand equity caused by a use of the mark that creates associations and images inconsistent with the equity." Thus (the argument goes), if Pepsi were to make single malt whiskey, it would risk diluting its myth (youth), but if it made spandex "midriff" tops in candy colors, it would not. Not only is this interpretation of dilution inconsistent with the writings of Schechter, but more importantly, this interpretation ignores—and thus devalues—the product associations that the Pepsis of the world possess. When dilution, as Schechter conceived it, "happens," it not only disturbs the source signal broadcast by every distinctive mark, but it also disturbs the product signal—the one that links the Pepsi mark to carbonated cola beverages.

To be sure, a unique (and therefore dilutible) trademark does not possess only a product association. Unique trademarks are highly distinctive as well, which makes them able to identify a single, if anonymous, source. These trademarks thus possess the ability to create two types of associations in the minds of consumers: a source association (e.g., Pepsico, Inc.) and a product association (carbonated cola beverages). "Pepsi" is dilutible because, like Coke, Pepsi "means a single thing coming from a single source.... It hardly would be too much to say that the drink characterizes the name as much as the name the drink." [*Coca-Cola v. Koke Co.*, 254 U.S. 143, 146 (1920)]. This ability to create source and product associations is what Schechter termed "selling power." When a mark is diluted, both associations are disturbed. If, for example, the Pepsi

241. See 15 U.S.C. 1127 (2000).

mark were used by Company X in connection with a single malt whisky, "Pepsi" not only would come to mean two sources (Pepsico, Inc. and Company X), but it also would come to mean two products (carbonated cola beverages and single malt whisky). Pepsico, Inc. would be able to safeguard the source identification function of its mark under infringement law, of course, but it also would have recourse to dilution law, which would enable the company to protect the link between mark and "particular product" as well.

Schechter was right when he wrote that without uniqueness, there can be no "selling power"; without selling power, there can be no "dissociation from the particular product in connection with which [the mark] has been used"; and without this whittling away, there can be no dilution. . . . To the extent the distinctiveness of a mark alone is impaired, infringement offers a remedy (assuming, of course, the trademark owner can prove that consumer confusion is likely). But when a mark possesses "mere" distinctiveness, when a mark has plenty to say about source but nothing to say about product, when a mark does not possess uniqueness, there simply is nothing to "dilute."

. . . What if the trademark owner is the one transforming a unique symbol into a ubiquitous one? Judges, lawyers, and even scholars appear to have assumed that . . . trademark owners are perfectly free to engage in acts that, if perpetrated by others, would be held to cause dilution under the doctrine as presently applied. Worse, courts have held that ubiquity only adds to the fame of the mark—an element of the modern dilution cause of action that, contrary to popular belief, never was part of the doctrine as Schechter conceived it. [I]f we believe what we have been saying about what dilution is, then we must acknowledge that the acts of trademark owners can have the same dilutive effects as can the acts of third parties. The source association that a mark possesses may be left intact, or even strengthened, when the owner of that mark engages in ubiquitous branding practices, but the product association is destroyed—and with it, uniqueness.

Ubiquity is dilution, for in each case, the "uniqueness" of the mark, as Schechter defined that term, is vitiated . . . Hundreds, perhaps thousands of trademarks are in danger of losing their "unique distinctiveness" every day, and not because of anything trademark pirates are doing. Trademark owners are doing the damage themselves.

QUESTIONS

1. What marks today would Schechter's conception of dilution protect? MCDONALD'S? WINDOWS? ETCH–A–SKETCH? LEXUS?

2. Consider the mark VIRGIN, which has been used or licensed for diverse goods and services from a record label to airline services, or the Ralph Lauren POLO brand that has been promoted as synonymous with a trendy lifestyle and applied to numerous products from apparel and fragrances to home furnishings. Is the author suggesting that these famous marks should not be entitled to dilution protection? Do you agree?

3.   What is the harm, if any, to consumers from dilution of a "unique" or "singular" mark of the type for which Schechter advocated? *See* Graeme Austin, "Trademarks and the Burdened Imagination," 69 Brooklyn L. Rev. 827 (2004).

Ty Inc. v. Perryman

306 F.3d 509 (7th Cir.2002), *cert. denied*, 538 U.S. 971, 123 S.Ct. 1750 (2003).

■ POSNER, CIRCUIT JUDGE.

Ty Inc., the manufacturer of Beanie Babies, the well-known beanbag stuffed animals, brought this suit for trademark infringement against Ruth Perryman. Perryman sells second-hand beanbag stuffed animals, primarily but not exclusively Ty's Beanie Babies, over the Internet. Her Internet address ("domain name"), a particular focus of Ty's concern, is bargainbeanies.com. She has a like-named Web site (http://www. bargainbeanies.com) where she advertises her wares. Ty's suit is based on the federal antidilution statute, 15 U.S.C. § 1125(c), which protects "famous" marks from commercial uses that cause "dilution of the distinctive quality of the mark." *See Nabisco, Inc. v. PF Brands, Inc.*, 191 F.3d 208, 214–16 (2d Cir. 1999). The district court granted summary judgment in favor of Ty and entered an injunction that forbids the defendant to use "BEANIE or BEANIES or any colorable imitation thereof (whether alone or in connection with other terms) within any business name, Internet domain name, or trademark, or in connection with any non-Ty products." Perryman's appeal argues primarily that "beanies" has become a generic term for beanbag stuffed animals and therefore cannot be appropriated as a trademark at all, and that in any event the injunction (which has remained in effect during the appeal) is overbroad.

The fundamental purpose of a trademark is to reduce consumer search costs by providing a concise and unequivocal identifier of the particular source of particular goods. The consumer who knows at a glance whose brand he is being asked to buy knows whom to hold responsible if the brand disappoints and whose product to buy in the future if the brand pleases. This in turn gives producers an incentive to maintain high and uniform quality, since otherwise the investment in their trademark may be lost as customers turn away in disappointment from the brand. A successful brand, however, creates an incentive in unsuccessful competitors to pass off their inferior brand as the successful brand by adopting a confusingly similar trademark, in effect appropriating the goodwill created by the producer of the successful brand. The traditional and still central concern of trademark law is to provide remedies against this practice.

Confusion is not a factor here, however, with a minor exception discussed at the end of the opinion. Perryman is not a competing producer of beanbag stuffed animals, and her Web site clearly disclaims any affiliation with Ty. But that does not get her off the hook. The reason is that state and now federal law also provides a remedy against the "dilution" of a trademark, though as noted at the outset of this opinion the federal statute is limited to the subset of "famous" trademarks and to dilutions of them caused by commercial uses that take place in interstate or foreign commerce. "Beanie Babies," and "Beanies" as the shortened form, are famous trademarks in the ordinary sense of the term: "everybody has heard of them" . . . Ty's trademarks are household words. And Perryman's use of these words was commercial in nature and took place in interstate commerce, and doubtless, given the reach of the aptly named World Wide Web, in foreign commerce as well.

But what is "dilution"? There are (at least) three possibilities relevant to this case, each defined by a different underlying concern. First, there is concern that consumer search costs will rise if a trademark becomes associated with a variety of unrelated products. Suppose an upscale restaurant calls itself "Tiffany." There is little danger that the consuming public will think it's dealing with a branch of the Tiffany jewelry store if it patronizes this restaurant. But when consumers next see the name "Tiffany" they may think about both the restaurant and the jewelry store, and if so the efficacy of the name as an identifier of the store will be diminished. Consumers will have to think harder—incur as it were a higher imagination cost—to recognize the name as the name of the store. [citations omitted] So "blurring" is one form of dilution.

Now suppose that the "restaurant" that adopts the name "Tiffany" is actually a striptease joint. Again, and indeed even more certainly than in the previous case, consumers will not think the striptease joint under common ownership with the jewelry store. But because of the inveterate tendency of the human mind to proceed by association, every time they think of the word "Tiffany" their image of the fancy jewelry store will be tarnished by the association of the word with the strip joint. [citations omitted] So "tarnishment" is a second form of dilution. Analytically it is a subset of blurring, since it reduces the distinctness of the trademark as a signifier of the trademarked product or service.

Third, and most far-reaching in its implications for the scope of the concept of dilution, there is a possible concern with situations in which, though there is neither blurring nor tarnishment, someone is still taking a free ride on the investment of the trademark owner in the trademark. Suppose the "Tiffany" restaurant in our first hypothetical example is located in Kuala Lumpur and though the people who patronize it (it is upscale) have heard of the Tiffany jewelry store, none of them is ever going to buy anything there, so that the efficacy of the trademark as an identifier will not be impaired. If appropriation of Tiffany's aura is nevertheless forbidden by an expansive concept of dilution, the benefits of the jewelry store's investment in creating a famous name will be, as economists say, "internalized"—that is, Tiffany will realize the full benefits of the investment rather than sharing those benefits with others—and as a result the amount of investing in creating a prestigious name will rise.

This rationale for antidilution law has not yet been articulated in or even implied by the case law, although a few cases suggest that the concept of dilution is not exhausted by blurring and tarnishment, *see Panavision Int'l,L.P. v. Toeppen*, 141 F.3d 1316, 1326 (9th Cir. 1998); *Intermatic, Inc. v. Toeppen*, 947 F. Supp. 1227, 1238–39 (N.D. Ill. 1996); *Rhee Bros., Inc. v. Han Ah Reum Corp.*, 178 F.Supp.2d 525, 530 (D. Md. 2001), and the common law doctrine of "misappropriation" might conceivably be invoked in support of the rationale that we have sketched. (Citation omitted). The validity of the rationale may be doubted, however. The number of prestigious names is so vast (and, as important, would be even if there were no antidilution laws) that it is unlikely that the owner of a prestigious trademark could obtain substantial license fees if commercial use of the mark without his consent were forbidden despite the absence of consumer confusion, blurring, or tarnishment. Competition would drive the fee to zero since, if the name is being used in an unrelated market, virtually every prestigious name will be a substitute for every other in that market.

None of the rationales we have canvassed supports Ty's position in this case. Perryman is not producing a product, or a service, such as dining at a restaurant, that is distinct from any specific product; rather, she is selling the very product to which the trademark sought to be defended against her "infringement" is attached. You can't sell a branded product without using its brand name, that is, its trademark. Supposing that Perryman sold only Beanie Babies (a potentially relevant qualification, as we'll see), we would find it impossible to understand how she could be thought to be blurring, tarnishing, or otherwise free riding to any significant extent on Ty's investment in its mark. To say she was would amount to saying that if a used car dealer truthfully advertised that it sold Toyotas, or if a muffler manufacturer truthfully advertised that it specialized in making mufflers for installation in Toyotas, Toyota would have a claim of trademark infringement. Of course there can be no aftermarket without an original market, and in that sense sellers in a trademarked good's aftermarket are free riding on the trademark. But in that attenuated sense of free riding, almost everyone in business is free riding.

Ty's argument is especially strained because of its marketing strategy.... *Ty, Inc. v. GMA Accessories, Inc.*, 132 F.3d 1167, 1173 (7th Cir. 1997), Ty deliberately produces a quantity of each Beanie Baby that fails to clear the market at the very low price that it charges for Beanie Babies. The main goal is to stampede children into nagging their parents to buy the new Baby lest they be the only kid on the block who doesn't have it. A byproduct (or perhaps additional goal) is the creation of a secondary market, like the secondary market in works of art, in which prices on scarce Beanie Babies are bid up to a market-clearing level. Perryman is a middleman in this secondary market, the market, as we said, that came into existence as the result, either intended or foreseen, of a deliberate marketing strategy. That market is unlikely to operate efficiently if sellers who specialize in serving it cannot use "Beanies" to identify their business. Perryman's principal merchandise is Beanie Babies, so that to forbid it to use "Beanies" in its business name and advertising (Web or otherwise) is like forbidding a used car dealer who specializes in selling Chevrolets to mention the name in his advertising.

It is true that Web search engines do not stop with the Web address; if Perryman's Web address were www.perryman.com but her Web page mentioned Beanies, a search for the word "Beanies" would lead to her Web page. Yet we know from the events that led up to the passage in 1999 of the Anticybersquatting Consumer Protection Act, 15 U.S.C. § 1125(d), that many firms value having a domain name or Web address that signals their product. (The "cybersquatters" were individuals or firms that would register domain names for the purpose of selling them to companies that wanted a domain name that would be the name of their company or of their principal product.) After all, many consumers search by typing the name of a company in the Web address space (browser) on their home page rather than by use of a search engine. We do not think that by virtue of trademark law producers own their aftermarkets and can impede sellers in the aftermarket from marketing the trademarked product.

We surmise that what Ty is seeking in this case is an extension of antidilution law to forbid commercial uses that accelerate the transition from trademarks (brand names) to generic names (product names). Words such as "thermos," "yo-yo," "escalator," "cellophane," and "brassiere" started life as trademarks, but eventually lost their significance as source identifiers and became the popular names of the product rather than the name of the trademark owner's brand, and when that happened continued enforcement of the trademark would simply have undermined competition with the brand by making it difficult for competitors to indicate that they were selling the same product—by rendering them in effect speechless. Ty is doubtless cognizant of a similar and quite real danger to "Beanie Babies" and "Beanies." Notice that the illustrations we gave of trademarks that became generic names are all descriptive or at least suggestive of the product, which makes them better candidates for genericness than a fanciful trademark such as "Kodak" or "Exxon." Ty's trademarks likewise are descriptive of the product they denote; its argument that "Beanies" is "inherently distinctive" (like Kodak and Exxon), and therefore protected by trademark law without proof of secondary meaning, is nonsense. A trademark that describes a basic element of the product, as "Beanies" does, is not protected unless the owner can establish that the consuming public accepts the word as the designation of a brand of the product (that it has acquired, as the cases say, secondary meaning). [citations omitted] As the public does with regard to "Beanies"—for now. But because the word is catchier than "beanbag stuffed animals," "beanbag toys," or "plush toys," it may someday "catch on" to the point where the mark becomes generic, and then Ty will have to cast about for a different trademark.

Although there is a social cost when a mark becomes generic—the trademark owner has to invest in a new trademark to identify his brand—there is also a social benefit, namely an addition to ordinary language. A nontrivial number of words in common use began life as trademarks. An interpretation of antidilution law as arming trademark owners to enjoin uses of their mark that, while not confusing, threaten to render the mark generic may therefore not be in the public interest. Moreover, the vistas of litigation that such a theory of dilution opens up are staggering. Ty's counsel at argument refused to disclaim a right to sue the publishers of dictionaries should they include an entry for "beanie," lowercased and defined as a beanbag stuffed animal, thus accelerating the transition from trademark to generic term. He should have disclaimed such a right. (Citations omitted).

We reject the extension of antidilution law that Ty beckons us to adopt, but having done so we must come back to the skipped issue of confusion. For although 80 percent of Perryman's sales are of Ty's products, this means that 20 percent are not, and on her Web page after listing the various Ty products under such names as "Beanie Babies" and "Teenie Beanies" she has the caption "Other Beanies" and under that is a list of products such as "Planet Plush" and "Rothschild Bears" that are not manufactured by Ty. This is plain misdescription, in fact false advertising, and supports the last prohibition in the injunction, the prohibition against using "Beanie" or "Beanies" "in connection with any non-Ty products." That much of the injunction should stand. But Ty has not demonstrated any basis for enjoining Perryman from using the terms in "any business name, Internet domain name, or trademark."

We can imagine an argument that merely deleting "Other Beanies" is not enough; that if the other beanbag stuffed animals look much like Ty's, consumers might assume they are "Beanies," or if not, that they still might associate "Beanies" with these other animals, causing the term to lose its distinctness as the name of Ty's products. But we do not understand Ty to be seeking a broadening of the injunction to require a disclaimer as to the source of the non-Ty products sold by Perryman. This however is a matter that can be pursued further on remand. . . .

QUESTIONS

1. Did Judge Posner consider defendant's use of BEANIES in connection with non-Ty products to be dilution? Should he have?

2. Is Judge Posner's characterization of tarnishment as a sub-species of blurring persuasive?

3. Do you agree that use of "Beanies" as part of Perryman's domain and business names does not dilute the distinctiveness of plaintiff's BEANIE BABIES mark? Do uses that tend to genericize a mark dilute its distinctiveness? Should every business in the aftermarket for a product be entitled to use the brand name in its own name or domain name?

Rebecca Tushnet, Gone in 60 Milliseconds: Trademark Law and Cognitive Science, 86 Texas L. Rev. ___ (forthcoming 2007) (Excerpts)

I. Introduction

. . . .

Trademark dilution has been subjected to two persistent criticisms: First, that its proponents haven't identified any real harm caused by dilution, and second, that dilution isn't really an "it"—we have no clear idea of what it means for there to be dilution. Cognitive models offer hope of answering these objections by conceiving of dilution as an increase in mental or internal search costs. Consumers allegedly have more difficulty recalling, recognizing and producing a diluted trademark, and correspondingly are less likely to purchase products or services branded with that mark.

. . . .

H.   The Appeal of the Internal Search Costs/Cognitive Model

. . . .

[C]ognitive processing models . . . offer an attractive definition of dilution, one that creates a pleasing symmetry between dilution and traditional–now "external"–search cost models of infringement. Dilution imposes mental–"internal"–search costs on consumers, which is why dilution is harmful. Judge Posner has ably set forth the fundamentals of the cognitive model, and Jacob Jacoby, a prominent ₋ ₋ trademark expert, has seized on Posner's explanations as confirmation of his framework for measuring dilution experimentally.

A.   Blurring

In *Ty, Inc. v. Perryman*, [306 F.3d 509 (7th Cir.2002)], Judge Posner . . . contrasted infringement to dilution, which he saw as dealing with internal search costs–difficulties not in figuring out whether two products or services are from the same source, but in retrieving the mark from memory in the first place.

In the cognitive model, blurring takes place when a single term activates multiple, non-confusing associations in a consumer's mind. Meanings or concepts . . . are linked by mental networks. Concepts are activated through links in the network, triggering related concepts. Activation happens very fast, and if it doesn't continue, an unreinforced word or concept can die away. . . .

Blurring involves relatively extended activation of two different meanings for a mark, until the consumer sorts out the proper referent. The basic theory is that an unrelated, nonconfusing mark similar to a famous mark adds new associations to a preexisting network, which slows processing time, especially if the junior mark has a very different meaning than the senior mark. . . .

In 2000, Maureen Morrin and Jacob Jacoby conducted an experiment that can be used to bolster the internal search costs model.[11] The study had participants view diluting ads for Dogiva dog biscuits, Heineken popcorn, and Hyatt legal services. The ads were "tombstone" ads–print-only and

---

11.   *See* Maureen Morrin & Jacob Jacoby, *Trademark Dilution: Empirical Measures*   *for an Elusive Concept*, 19 J. PUB. POL'Y & MARKETING 265 (2000).

highly informational ... Computers measured how long it took for participants to identify the senior marks after exposure to the junior marks. Morrin and Jacoby found that exposure to dilutive ads slowed participants' accuracy and response time in associating some brands with product categories and attributes, such as linking Godiva to chocolate and rich taste. Heineken beer was similarly affected by ads for Heineken popcorn, though Hyatt hotels were not affected by ads for Hyatt legal services.

... Other researchers conducted paper-and-pencil versions of the experiment using aided recall, so that respondents were required to retrieve distinctive aspects of a brand when presented with the brand name, and required to retrieve the brand name when presented with the brand's distinctive aspects. The results also showed measurable dilutive effects.[12] Dilution proponents maintain that delayed responses, like decreased accuracy in linking brands to categories and products, are likely to affect purchasing decisions, given that advertisers often only have a few seconds—or even milliseconds—to catch consumers' attention....

[A] considerable advantage of the search costs explanation of blurring is that it converts dilution into a protection for consumers as well as for producers. After all, we know that external search costs are inefficient and therefore welfare-diminishing for consumers. It seems natural that internal search costs would also decrease efficiency. Thus, a focus on the workings of the consumer's diluted mind produces a response to Judge Kozinski's more skeptical take on dilution, in which he found the FTDA less justified than infringement law because it served only trademark owners' interests and did not protect consumers. [See Mattel, Inc. v. MCA Records, Inc., 296 F.3d 894, 905 (9th Cir.2002).] The Supreme Court, for the moment, has sided with Judge Kozinski, [See Moseley v. V Secret Catalogue, Inc., 537 U.S. 418, 429 (2003) ("Unlike traditional infringement law, the prohibitions against trademark dilution are not motivated by an interest in protecting consumers.")], but it has not had the occasion to address the search costs argument directly.

B. Tarnishment

In Posner's model, dilution by tarnishment also involves interference with cognitive processing, but of a different kind. Judge Posner posited a strip joint named Tiffany's, and assumed that reasonable consumers do not think it has any connection with the jewelry store. Nevertheless, "because of the inveterate tendency of the human mind to proceed by association, every time [people who know about the strip joint think of the word 'Tiffany'] their image of the fancy jewelry store will be tarnished by the association of the word with the strip joint." [Ty, 306 F.3d at 511]. This "inveterate tendency" can be equated to the psychological concept of activation discussed above....

[D]ilution by tarnishment would mean that the idea of Tiffany's-the-strip-joint remains at least slightly activated after a reference to Tiffany's-

---

12. See Chris Pullig et al., *Brand Dilution: When Do New Brands Hurt Existing Brands?*, J. Marketing, Spring 2006, at 52, 52, 61–62.

the-jewelry-store, decreasing the overall positive value associated with Tiffany's-the-jewelry-store. . . .

Though it was decided on confusion grounds, *Balducci v. Anheuser–Busch*, a case against a humor magazine's parody ad for Michelob Oily, is one of Jacoby's prime examples of tarnishment. Participants in his study were shown either an ad for Michelob Dry or the mock ad for Michelob Oily. Thirty-seven percent of those shown the Michelob Oily ad "associat[ed] a negative meaning with Michelob or Anheuser–Busch," while no one who saw a Michelob Dry ad did so.[21] Such negative meanings attach to the senior mark directly, rather than being mediated through a second, unrelated product. . . .

C.   Free Riding

Finally, Posner offers a third possible meaning of dilution, which is simply free riding. The example is a Tiffany's restaurant in Kuala Lumpur, which grabs some of the luster of Tiffany's-the-jeweler because of the same tendency to make associations that explains tarnishment and blurring. People in Kuala Lumpur know about the jewelry store but would never patronize it, so no jewelry store customers have their mental models of Tiffany's distorted in any way. But non-customers now have multiple associations with Tiffany's, and their recognition of the famous mark is impaired. Posner is dubious about this rationale, and the new federal dilution law seems to have taken it off the table for federal claims, though it may still be viable under state law. This definition focuses on the mental processes of the junior user's customers, not the senior user's, but is otherwise quite similar to the definition of blurring. . . .

III.   Critiquing the Cognitive Model of Dilution

. . . .

A.   Context Effects

In the *Perryman* case, Judge Posner did not explain why it was a problem for consumers to have to think harder to figure out the entity to which "Tiffany's" refers. In fact, he did not define what it means to think harder. With blurring, the result of the existence of Tiffany's-the-restaurant is that we need more context to figure out which Tiffany's someone is talking about, but we generally have that context. When we're primed with a context, like "computers," Apple is on a par with Microsoft, even though it's a classically pre-diluted mark. Product categories, images in ads, and even distinctive fonts can provide immediate context for a mark. . . .

Product categories provide an important type of context. Robert Peterson and his confederates surveyed major product categories and trademarks, examining typicality (the extent to which naming a brand caused a

---

21. Jacoby [2001], *supra* note [], at 1060. Twenty-two percent said the Michelob Oily ad made them less likely to buy Michelob, and twenty percent said they were less likely to drink it, compared to seven and five percent, respectively, of those who saw the Michelob Dry ad. *See id.* at 1061.

respondent to produce its major product category, as McDonald's would produce "fast food") and dominance (the extent to which naming a product category caused a respondent to produce a brand as the first that came to mind). Leading brands' typicality was much greater than their dominance, on average three times greater.[25] In other words, marks are easy to recognize as category members without being at the top of a respondent's mind in the category. Moreover, the differences between recognition when prompted with a brand and recognition when prompted with a category may have significant real-world effects. Even if the Heineken name in the abstract produces less association with beer because of Heineken popcorn, consumers may still identify it as a beer if they're prompted with the category, and when they go to the store to buy beer, it will be right there on the shelf. Consumers just do not confront trademarks in the abstract very often....

Why, then, did laboratory studies reveal an apparent dilutive effect from a single exposure to Dogiva biscuits and Heineken popcorn? One possibility is that the test environment was itself decontextualizing, depriving subjects of the cues they'd ordinarily use to distinguish a dilutive use from a senior mark. Morrin and Jacoby told their test subjects, students who were taking marketing courses, that they'd be tested on the information provided in the ads, which themselves were not the image-and emotion-laden appeals to which consumers are generally subjected. This method made it likely that information would be primary, not the contextual, emotional associations that serve to distinguish brands in the real world.

B.   Association Sets and Uncommon Words

.   .   .   .

Jerre Swann ... has been a major proponent of using cognitive theories to justify and define dilution. He cites psychological studies to show that adding unrelated associations to a famous mark causes dilution and interferes with consumers' ability to retrieve the mark because " ' "[R]are words [like KODAK] are more distinctively encoded than (are) common words," ' and words that have a limited number of 'association set[s]' (e.g., 'Cheer' for an encouraging shout and an all-temperature detergent), can likewise be readily retrieved.... 'Some empirical research has shown that the greater the number of associations a word has the more difficult it is for the individual initially to encode the word in memory or later to recall the word.' "[29]

Swann's citation to the work of Joan Meyers–Levy supposedly shows that increasing the association set size of a brand decreases the consumer's

25. *See* Robert A. Peterson et al, *Trademark Dilution and the Practice of Marketing*, 27 J. ACAD. MARKETING SCI. 255, 261 (1999). Half of the brands with typicality over 90% showed low levels of dominance. *See id.* at 262.

29. Jerre B. Swann, Sr., *Dilution Redefined for the Year 2000*, 37 HOUS. L. REV. 729, 755 (2000) (citing Joan Meyers–Levy, *The Influence of a Brand Name's Association Set Size and Word Frequency on Brand Memory*, 16 J. CONSUMER RES. 197 (1989)) (alterations in original).

ability to retrieve any particular concept. There are at least three problems
with this extrapolation. First, the underlying research uses a definition of
"association set" ... as the number of words that are named by at least
two people when a large number are asked the first word that comes to
mind in response to a target word. Unless a dilutive use was the first thing
that came to mind, it would not affect this measure of association. Second
and relatedly, even if a dilutive use dominated some respondents' minds, it
would only increase the set size by one. The underlying research does not
come close to identifying any effect from a one-association increase. Third,
Meyers–Levy does not measure change, though Swann applies her work to
change over time; her research, like that of others in the field, compares
words with existing high and low measured frequency and association set
sizes.

Still, assuming those problems away, the Meyers–Levy research may
have implications for famous brands. High-frequency words are easy to
process, and thus we don't encode them distinctively, meaning that we
don't pay much attention to them. If they're used as brand names, we'll
have trouble remembering the brand. Low-frequency words are relatively
difficult to encode, and thus we process them more meaningfully. Given
that advertisers have trouble getting consumers to pay attention to advertising in general, ... low-frequency words seem more desirable as marks.
Meyers–Levy offers Ivory as an example of a low-frequency word that
therefore relates strongly to soap. When a word is low-frequency, a particular use will cause people to encode only relevant information presented in
context, because their attention will be drawn to specific attributes of the
word (for Ivory, color and not elephants). Thus, with a low-frequency word,
even a large association set size won't interfere with memory. "Indeed, it is
possible that memory might be somewhat enhanced as the size of the
association set increases [for low-frequency words] because more associations will be available to relate meaningfully to the brand in a distinctive
manner." By contrast, a use that takes a mark from low to high frequency
or increases the associations of a high-frequency mark creates a branding
problem by making the mark harder to recognize.

Meyers–Levy experimented with fictitious antiperspirants, blemish
medications, and disposable razors, choosing brand names from words with
known frequencies and association set sizes. Low-frequency words (fifteen
or fewer uses per million words) were Crisp, Moose, Bribe, Cork, Shove,
and Dusk. High-frequency words (one hundred or more per million) were
Yard, Lake, Room, Cloud, Day, and Round.

Experimental subjects heard ads for products, which they were told
were existing regional brands, and instructed to consider how clear, grammatical, and professionally written the ads were. Then they were asked to
recall and write down all statements they could remember from the ads.
Then, they were shown lists of brand names, instructed that some might be
"impostors," and asked to indicate whether they recognized the brands.
The results showed that, for high-frequency brand names, recall was poorer
(both immediately and at 24 hours) for words with a large association set

size. With low-frequency brand names, recall was similar regardless of set size.

That sounds like good reason for marketers to minimize the associations evoked by their famous brands. The flaw is the assumption that famous brand names are high-frequency, or can be made so by dilution. . . . In the 2003 release of the American National Corpus, . . . only one of the top forty brands–[MICROSOFT]–in BusinessWeek's Best Global Brands 2006 had frequencies approaching one hundred per million words. Kodak, Swann's example of a famous mark subject to dilution, had a frequency of approximately seven per million, Hyatt and Godiva were slightly above one, and Heineken was below one. Thus, even dilutive uses that doubled the frequency of exposure to these marks would still leave them low-frequency. There just aren't that many high-frequency words.

The one psychological study I have found that specifically addressed trademarks and frequency effects found that popular brands were recognized with a speed and accuracy similar to that of low-frequency words.[40] Meyers–Levy's work, then, can be read to suggest that dilution does not harm many famous trademarks, because adding associations to low-frequency words doesn't interfere with retrieval or recognition—and may even help.

C.   Reaffirmation Effects

. . . [T]here are reasons to think that at least some dilutive uses can reinforce, rather than chip away at, the strength of a mark. Any delay in recognizing which Tiffany's or which Apple a particular use refers to may be compensated for by easier recall of the marks.

In essence, exposure to near variants or uses in other contexts makes the trademark more familiar and thus more easily retrieved from memory. This process can add value in the same way that marketers think preexisting associations carried by descriptive or suggestive terms add value to a trademark. Words with multiple associations may be more easily activated, or reference to one word may "prime" us to recall a similar word. Tiffany's-the-restaurant may make us think of Tiffany's-the-jeweler's when we are at lunch thinking of gifts for Mother's Day. In one experiment that was supposed to provide evidence for the cognitive model of tarnishment, exposure to ads for a Hyatt tattoo parlor actually increased preference for Hyatt hotels. (An important caveat, however, is that priming effects, like dilution effects, are typically small and could be unimportant to famous marks.)

Beyond priming, dilutive uses may increase the richness of a term's associations. Multiplication of associations can aid recall of trademarks comprising uncommon words. The cognitive model of dilution posits that consumers don't like to think hard. . . . Recall that low-frequency words are

---

40. *See* Antonia Kronlund, *Remembering Words and Brand Names After the Perception of Discrepancies*, http://www.sfu.ca/āmantona/Kronlund.pdf (last visited Aug. 2, 2006) (brands tested included Camel and Marlboro for cigarettes, Levis and Wrangler for jeans, Coke and Pepsi for soda, and Tide and Sunlight for detergent).

remembered better because they require more processing to encode in memory–an instance of "thinking hard" that's useful to trademark owners. In essence, there may be a tradeoff between ease and richness of processing. Some difficulty in retrieval prompts more mental processing, which itself leads to better long-term memory for the relevant concepts. The delayed response times that Jacoby and Morrin saw as evidence of dilution when they tested subjects with a single recognition test could have improved the strength of the diluted marks in the long run.

. . . .

Priming makes it particularly unlikely that a glancing exposure to a dilutive mark will cause harm to the senior brand. If a consumer isn't paying attention and doesn't process the mark, it will just be a subliminal reminder, without generating new and inconsistent meanings. If a consumer's attention is caught, however, we simply don't know how that will play out in any particular case–whether it will ultimately reinforce the original, as the Hyatt tattoo parlor reinforces Hyatt hotels, or dilute it. When the effect can be either positive or negative, it is a mistake to adopt as the theory of dilution an explanation that always posits a negative effect.

D. What About Tarnishment?

. . . There is very little empirical work in this area. Marketing researchers have, however, been extremely interested in a related question: When a strong existing brand introduces a new product extension that is bad, or enters into a marketing alliance with a partner who turns out to have reputation problems, does that reflect poorly on the originally strong and popular core brand? The research suggests that dilution by tarnishment through the use of a similar mark on a shoddy product is unlikely in the absence of confusion, because consumers have relatively robust mental concepts of strong brands.[63] If they are given a reason to distinguish an authorized extension or co-branded product from the core brand–for example, a name like "Courtyard by Marriott" instead of "Marriott Courtyard" or "Coke BlaK" instead of "Coke"–they will do so, and negative opinions about the extension will not return to harm opinions of the core brand. If consumers make those distinctions for authorized line extensions, it seems implausible that, absent confusion, they will transfer negative opinions between unrelated products or services.

V. Normative Implications

Given the evidence discussed . . . the cognitive model of dilution lacks enough empirical support to justify its adoption as a general theory underlying dilution law. There is still too much we don't know about how

---

63. *See, e.g.*, Stephen J. Hoch, *Product Experience Is Seductive*, 29 J. CONSUMER RES. 448, 451 (2002) ("Using a simple associative learning procedure, [researchers] showed that, in a few trials, people learn brand associations that later block the learning of new predictive attribute associations.") (citation omitted); Deborah Roedder John et al., *The Negative Impact of Extensions: Can Flagship Products Be Diluted?*, J. MARKETING, Jan. 1998, at 19, 20 ("[B]eliefs about the flagship product [of a strong brand] are 'encapsulated' and extremely resistant to change") [citations omitted].

consumers process marks in the marketplace. At a minimum, the evidence suggests that we cannot predict that any particular dilutive use will produce the difficulties posited by the cognitive model.

. . . .

QUESTIONS

1. Is there anything left of Judge Posner's concept of dilution by blurring as protecting a consumer's mental search cost in light of the research examined by Professor Tushnet? How about dilution by tarnishment?

2. Could the concept of free riding support application of a dilution remedy? In what situations?

B. FEDERAL DILUTION

1. FEDERAL STATUTE

HISTORY OF THE FEDERAL DILUTION STATUTE

As noted in the Stadler excerpt *supra*, many state legislatures and courts adopted dilution remedies beginning in the 1940s. However, trademark owners continued to press for a federal statute in light of the lack of uniformity of the state laws. Although Congress considered including dilution within its revision to the Lanham Act in 1988 as recommended in the *Report and Recommendations* of the USTA Trademark Review Commission, 77 TMR 375 (1987), the federal anti-dilution proposal was not ultimately included in the Trademark Law Revision Act of 1988. Seven years later, however, the Federal Trademark Dilution Act of 1995 ("FTDA") was enacted and added a new § 43(c) to the Lanham Act as well as a definition of dilution in § 45 as "the lessening of the capacity of a famous mark to identify and distinguish goods or services, regardless of the presence or absence of—(1) competition between the owner of the famous mark and other parties, or (2) likelihood of confusion, mistake or deception." The FTDA provided that owners of famous marks were entitled to relief against a "commercial use in commerce of a mark or trade name" that "causes dilution of the distinctive quality of the mark." The statute listed a number of factors to determine whether a mark "is distinctive and famous."

Uniformity, however, was not the result. Courts offered differing interpretations of the FTDA with respect to whether a mark qualified as famous if it possessed just niche or regional fame, whether marks had to be inherently distinctive to qualify as "distinctive" and whether tarnishment was even covered by the statute. See generally Clarissa Long, *Dilution*, 106 Colum.L.Rev. 1029 (2006). The most important split among courts, however, involved the standard for proving liability. Was likelihood of dilution enough or did a plaintiff need to prove actual dilution of its mark? The Supreme Court in *Moseley v. V Secret Catalogue*, 537 U.S. 418 (2003) resolved the latter conflict among the circuits and held that the FTDA dictated the higher standard of proving actual dilution.

In response to the cries for reform by trademark owners, Congress passed the Trademark Dilution Revision Act of 2006 ("TDRA of 2006"), *infra,* which became effective on October 6, 2006.

Trademark Dilution Revision Act of 2006

15 U.S.C. § 1125(c) [SECTION 43(c) LANHAM ACT]

(c) dilution by Blurring; dilution by Tarnishment.

(1) *Injunctive relief.* Subject to the principles of equity, the owner of a famous mark that is distinctive, inherently or through acquired distinctiveness, shall be entitled to an injunction against another person who, at any time after the owner's mark has become famous, commences use of a mark or trade name in commerce that is likely to cause dilution by blurring or dilution by tarnishment of the famous mark, regardless of the presence or absence of actual or likely confusion, of competition, or of actual economic injury.

(2) *Definitions.* (A) For purposes of paragraph (1), a mark is famous if it is widely recognized by the general consuming public of the United States as a designation of source of the goods or services of the mark's owner. In determining whether a mark possesses the requisite degree of recognition, the court may consider all relevant factors, including the following:

(i) The duration, extent, and geographic reach of advertising and publicity of the mark, whether advertised or publicized by the owner or third parties.

(ii) The amount, volume, and geographic extent of sales of goods or services offered under the mark.

(iii) The extent of actual recognition of the mark.

(iv) Whether the mark was registered under the Act of March 3, 1881, or the Act of February 20, 1905, or on the principal register.

(B) For purposes of paragraph (1), "dilution by blurring" is association arising from the similarity between a mark or trade name and a famous mark that impairs the distinctiveness of the famous mark. In determining whether a mark or trade name is likely to cause dilution by blurring, the court may consider all relevant factors, including the following:

(i) The degree of similarity between the mark or trade name and the famous mark.

(ii) The degree of inherent or acquired distinctiveness of the famous mark.

(iii) The extent to which the owner of the famous mark is engaging in substantially exclusive use of the mark.

(iv) The degree of recognition of the famous mark.

(v) Whether the user of the mark or trade name intended to create an association with the famous mark.

(vi) Any actual association between the mark or trade name and the famous mark.

(C) For purposes of paragraph (1), "dilution by tarnishment" is association arising from the similarity between a mark or trade name and a famous mark that harms the reputation of the famous mark.

(3) *Exclusions.* The following shall not be actionable as dilution by blurring or dilution by tarnishment under this subsection:

(A) Any fair use, including a nominative or descriptive fair use, or facilitation of such fair use, of a famous mark by another person other than as a designation of source for the person's own goods or services, including use in connection with—

(i) advertising or promotion that permits consumers to compare goods or services; or

(ii) identifying and parodying, criticizing, or commenting upon the famous mark owner or the goods or services of the famous mark owner.

(B) All forms of news reporting and news commentary.

(C) Any noncommercial use of a mark.

(4) *Burden of proof.* In a civil action for trade dress dilution under this Act for trade dress not registered on the principal register, the person who asserts trade dress protection has the burden of proving that—

(A) the claimed trade dress, taken as a whole, is not functional and is famous; and

(B) if the claimed trade dress includes any mark or marks registered on the principal register, the unregistered matter, taken as a whole, is famous separate and apart from any fame of such registered marks.

(5) *Additional remedies.* In an action brought under this subsection, the owner of the famous mark shall be entitled to injunctive relief as set forth in section 34. The owner of the famous mark shall also be entitled to the remedies set forth in sections 35(a) and 36 [15 USCS § 1117(a) and 1118], subject to the discretion of the court and the principles of equity if—

(A) the mark or trade name that is likely to cause dilution by blurring or dilution by tarnishment was first used in commerce by the person against whom the injunction is sought after the date of enactment of the Trademark Dilution Revision Act of 2006 [enacted Oct. 6, 2006]; and

(B) in a claim arising under this subsection—

(i) by reason of dilution by blurring, the person against whom the injunction is sought willfully intended to trade on the recognition of the famous mark; or

(ii) by reason of dilution by tarnishment, the person against whom the injunction is sought willfully intended to harm the reputation of the famous mark.

(6) *Ownership of valid registration a complete bar to action.* The ownership by a person of a valid registration under the Act of March 3, 1881, or the Act of February 20, 1905, or on the principal register under this Act shall be a complete bar to an action against that person, with respect to that mark, that—

(A)

(i) is brought by another person under the common law or a statute of a State; and

(ii) seeks to prevent dilution by blurring or dilution by tarnishment; or

(B) asserts any claim of actual or likely damage or harm to the distinctiveness or reputation of a mark, label, or form of advertisement.

QUESTIONS

1. Will the revised statute create more uniformity? Does it require actual or likely dilution? Do regionally famous or niche fame marks qualify for protection? Must a mark be inherently distinctive to qualify? Is tarnishment actionable?

2. How helpful are the factors listed in the statute for determining "dilution by blurring"?

3. Does the statute define "tarnishment"?

4. Does the inclusion of protection against dilution in the federal statute cure the problem of checkerboard jurisprudence under state law? Are state statutes pre-empted under the federal provision? *See* § 43(c)(6). Does § 43(c)(6)(B) suggest that ownership of a federal registration is a complete bar to a federal dilution claim? If so, could this be a drafting error?

5. Are the ubiquitous marks discussed in Professor Stadler's excerpted article, *supra* this chapter, such as VIRGIN and POLO, likely to qualify for dilution protection under the federal statute?

6. Consider section 43(c)(3). How would the *New Kids on the Block v. News American Publishing, supra* Chapter 6.C., be decided under the statute? Would defendant's use of the famous CHANEL #5 mark in *Smith v. Chanel, Inc., supra* Chapter 8.A. constitute actionable dilution?

7. In Disney's video "George of the Jungle 2," the villains drive bulldozers with recognizable CATERPILLAR trademarks to destroy Ape Mountain, and the narrator refers to the bulldozers as "deleterious dozers" and "maniacal machines." In the comedy film "Dickie Roberts: Former Child Star," the protagonist comically misuses a SLIP 'N SLIDE yellow water slide which results in his injury. This scene appears in advertisements and trailers for the film. Do the owners of the CATERPILLAR or SLIP 'N SLIDE marks have a viable federal dilution claim? *See Caterpillar Inc. v. Walt Disney Co.*, 287 F.Supp.2d 913 (C.D.Ill.2003) and *Wham–O, Inc. v. Paramount Pictures Corp.*, 286 F.Supp.2d 1254 (N.D.Cal.2003). *See also* Chapter 12, *infra.*

2.   Word Marks

Chew Toy Case

Louis Vuitton Malletier S.A. v. Haute Diggity Dog, LLC

464 F.Supp.2d 495 (E.D.Va.2006).

■ Cacheris, District Court Judge.

This matter comes before the Court on Plaintiff's and Defendants' cross-motions for summary judgment. This "dog of a case" gave the Court a great amount of facts to chew upon and applicable law to sniff out. Nonetheless, having thoroughly gnawed through the record, this Court finds that no material dispute of fact remains, and summary judgment is appropriate on all counts. For the following reasons, the Court will deny Plaintiff's motion and grant Defendants' motion.

I. Background

Plaintiff, Louis Vuitton Malletier S.A., ("LVM") is a manufacturer of luxury consumer goods, including luggage and handbags. In 1896, LVM created a Monogram Canvas Pattern Design mark and trade dress, which includes, *inter alia,* an entwined L and V monogram with three motifs and a four pointed star, and is used to identify its products. In 2002, Vuitton introduced a new signature design in collaboration with Japanese designer Takashi Murakami. LVM manufactures a limited number of high-end pet products, such as leashes and collars that range in price from $250 to $1600.

Plaintiff filed this action on March 24, 2006 against Defendants Haute Diggity Dog, LLC ("HDD"), Victoria Dauernheim, and Woofies, LLC d/b/a Woofie's Pet Boutique. HDD is a company that markets plush stuffed toys and beds for dogs under names that parody the products of other companies. HDD sells products such as Chewnel #5, Dog Perignon, Chewy Vuiton, and Sniffany & Co. in pet stores, alongside other dog toys, bones, beds, and food, and most are priced around $10. Plaintiff's complaint specifically refers to HDD's use of the mark "Chewy Vuiton" and alleges that this mark, as well as other marks and designs that imitate Plaintiff's trademarks and copyrights, violate Plaintiff's trademark, trade dress, and copyright rights. Plaintiff and Defendants have filed cross-motions for summary judgment. These motions are currently before the Court.

. . . .

III.   Analysis
Count I: Trademark Infringement

. . . .

. . . . Defendants do not deny that the marks are similar, but argues that the name "Chewy Vuiton" and the associated marks and colorings are a parody of the Vuitton name and marks. Plaintiff's marks contain an interlocking L and V, with two distinct coloring patterns, printed on leather women's handbags.[1] The marks used by Defendants are an interlocking C and V with similar coloring schemes and patterns. There is no doubt that the two are similar. Nonetheless, this Court has considered the evidence, and finds that two simultaneous messages are conveyed by Defendants' marks and dress. The marks and dress are similar enough for the average consumer to recognize a humorous association with the Vuitton mark, without likely confusing that same customer that it *really is* a Vuitton product. The similarities do exist, but they are necessary as part of the parody, for without them, no parody exists.

. . . .

iii. Trade and Marketing Channels

While Vuitton makes some pet products such as collars and leashing, ranging in price from $215 to $1600, the items are high-end and mainly made of fine leather. To the contrary, the "Chewy Vuiton" line consists of plush chew toys and beds, mostly priced below $20, made for pets to destroy or sleep upon. Plaintiff points out that Chewy Vuiton beds sell for $120, which is somewhat comparable to a $215 collar made by Vuitton. However, this argument is unconvincing. The dog bed mentioned is the single most expensive item made by HDD, and many dog beds range from $50 to $100 in price. On the other hand Vuitton's limited number of pet products begin at $215, the most expensive being priced at $1600. Contrary to dog beds, these prices are clearly high-end for collars, leashes, and pet carriers.

. . . .

[The court concluded that there was no likelihood of confusion.]

Count II: Dilution

Plaintiff seeks an injunction under the Federal Trademark Dilution Act (FTDA), *15 U.S.C. § 1125(c)*. The Trademark Dilution Act provides

---

1. Plaintiff's trade dress includes one design with a white background and a pastel color pattern consisting of blue, pink, yellow, green, and brown marks (Vuitton Monogram Multicolor), including the interlocking L and V. An additional trade dress offered by the Plaintiff includes a brown background with red cherries and green stems (Vuitton Cerises). Both of Plaintiff's trade dresses are printed on leather handbags. Defendants offer products that look similar, but also different. Defendants' mark and dress are slightly different in color and contain an interlocking C and V. But most importantly, they are printed on a plush dog toy or a dog bed. Defendants do not make high-end leather products or actual purses.

that the owner of a famous mark can enjoin "another person's commercial use in commerce of a mark or trade name, if such use begins after the mark has become famous and causes dilution of the distinctive quality of the mark." *CareFirst of Maryland, Inc. v. First Care,* 434 F.3d 263, 274 (4th Cir. 2006) (citing 15 U.S.C. § 1127). The Fourth Circuit has defined dilution as "the lessening of the capacity of a famous mark to identify and distinguish goods or services." *Id.*

While a court may find dilution even where it does not find likelihood of confusion, *Id.,* the Supreme Court has held that the dilution statute "unambiguously requires a showing of actual dilution, rather than a likelihood of dilution." *Moseley v. Secret Catalogue, Inc.,* 537 U.S. 418, 433, 123 S. Ct. 1115, 155 L. Ed. 2d 1 (2003). Actual dilution occurs by either a blurring of the mark's identification or a tarnishment of the positive associations the mark has come to convey. *See id.* This action commenced on March 24, 2006. However, following the commencement of litigation, the dilution statute was amended by Congress to exclude the "actual dilution" requirement in place of a "likely dilution" one. *See* Trademark Dilution Revision Act of 2006, Pub. L. No. 109–312, 120 Stat. 1730 (amending *15 U.S.C. § 1125(c) (1946)*). This Court must therefore decide the retroactive effect of the amended statute.

In *Landgraf v. USI Film Products, Inc.,* 511 U.S. 244, 114 S. Ct. 1483, 128 L. Ed. 2d 229 (1994), the Supreme Court established a two-part test to determine the retroactive effect of a statute. First, a court should determine "whether Congress has expressly prescribed the statute's proper reach." *Id. at 280.* In an instance where Congress has proscribed an effective date, courts must respect the will of Congress. *Id.* Second, when Congress has not proscribed an effective date, a court must determine if the statute will "impair rights a party possessed when [it] acted, increase a party's liability for past conduct, or impose new duties with respect to transactions already completed." *Id.* If it does, then a court should not apply the new statute to the pending case. *Id.; see also Altizer v. Deeds,* 191 F.3d 540, 545 (4th Cir. 1999) (quoting *Landgraf,* 511 U.S. at 280). However, the Supreme Court also stated that "relief by injunction operates *in futuro* and the right to it must be determined as of the time of the hearing." *American Steel Foundries v. Tri–City Central Trades,* 257 U.S. 184, 201, 42 S. Ct. 72, 66 L. Ed. 189 (1921); *see also Landgraf,* 511 U.S. at 273–74. In this case, Plaintiff has pled for injunctive relief on the issue of dilution. *See* Compl. at P78. Therefore, the amended statute will apply in this case.

A. Dilution by Blurring

Dilution by blurring is association arising from the similarity between a mark or trade name and a famous mark that impairs the distinctiveness of the famous mark. *See* Trademark Dilution Revision Act of 2006, Pub. L. No. 109–312, 120 Stat. 1730. Dilution by blurring occurs when consumers mistakenly associate a famous mark with goods and services of a junior mark, thereby diluting the power of the senior mark to identify and distinguish associated goods and services. *Ringling Bros.–Barnum & Bailey*

Combined Shows, Inc. v. Utah Div. of Travel Dev., 955 F. Supp. 605, 616 (E.D. Va. 1997) (citing *Mead Data Cent., Inc. v. Toyota Motor Sales, U.S.A., Inc.*, 875 F.2d 1026, 1031 (2d Cir. 1989)). According to the amended statute, in determining whether a mark or trade name is likely to cause dilution by blurring, the court may consider all relevant factors, including the following:

(i) the degree of similarity between the mark or trade name and the famous mark;

(ii) the degree of inherent or acquired distinctiveness of the famous mark;

(iii) the extent to which the owner of the famous mark is engaging in substantially exclusive use of the mark;

(iv) the degree of recognition of the famous mark;

(v) whether the user of the mark or trade name intended to create an association with the famous mark; and

(vi) any actual association between the mark or trade name and the famous mark.

Trademark Dilution Revision Act of 2006, Pub. L. No. 109–312, 120 Stat. 1730. Since the Fourth Circuit has not offered opinion on the new "likelihood of dilution" standard, for guidance this Court looks to the Second Circuit's application of *New York General Business Law § 360–l*, which incorporates the likelihood of dilution standard now adopted by Congress. Using this standard, the Second Circuit and its district courts have held on numerous occasions that in the case of parody, "the use of famous marks in parodies causes no loss of distinctiveness, since the success of the use depends upon the continued association with the plaintiff." *See Yankee Publ'g, Inc. v. News Am. Publ'g, Inc.*, 809 F. Supp. 267, 282 (S.D.N.Y. 1992) (applying New York statute); *see also Tommy Hilfiger*, 221 F. Supp. 2d at 422–23 products may have little diluting effect, particularly where it is obvious that the defendant intends the public to associate the use with the true owner; *Hormel*, 73 F.3d at 506 (finding no likelihood that defendant's puppet "Spa'am" would dilute the association of the Hormel mark with "Spam" lunchmeat).

Defendants do not dispute that the Plaintiff's mark is strong and famous. Nonetheless, this Court finds no likelihood that the parody of Plaintiff's mark by Defendants will result in dilution of Plaintiff's mark. This Court finds, like the New York and Second Circuit courts, the mark continues to be associated with the true owner, Louis Vuitton. Its strength is not likely to be blurred by a parody dog toy product. Instead of blurring Plaintiff's mark, the success of the parodic use depends upon the continued association with Louis Vuitton. This Court finds that no reasonable trier of fact could conclude that Plaintiff's mark is diluted by blurring in this case, and summary judgment is appropriate. Accordingly, Defendants' motion for summary judgment will be granted for dilution by blurring.

B.   Dilution by Tarnishment

Tarnishment occurs when the plaintiff's trademark is likened to products of low quality, or is portrayed in a negative context. *Deere & Co. v. MTD Prods.*, 41 F.3d 39, 43 (2d Cir. 1994). When the association is made through harmless or clean puns and parodies, however, tarnishment is unlikely. *Jordache Enters. v. Hogg Wyld, Ltd.*, 625 F. Supp. 48, 57 (D.N.M. 1985), *aff'd*, 828 F.2d 1482 (10th Cir. 1987). Plaintiff's assertions that Chewy Vuiton products tarnish LVM's marks by associating "inferior products" with the Vuiton name are baseless, and without merit. Plaintiff provides neither examples of actual tarnishment, nor any evidence that shows likely tarnishment. At oral argument, Plaintiff provided only a flimsy theory that a pet may some day choke on a Chewy Vuiton squeak toy and incite the wrath of a confused consumer against Louis Vuitton. Therefore, even taking into account the amended statute, this Court concludes that no reasonable trier of fact could find for the Plaintiff on the issue of dilution by tarnishment. Accordingly, this Court will grant summary judgment in favor of the Defendants on this issue.

QUESTIONS

1. Why did the district court list the statutory factors for blurring and then fail to analyze any of them? Was the parodic nature of defendant's use a sufficient justification?

2. Does the federal dilution statute's exemption for "fair use" cover parody? Consider the CHEWY VUITON "parody" dog bed shown below:

Chewy Vuiton Bed

Does the exemption cover the CHEWY VUITON dog bed? Why or why not?

Ringling Bros.–Barnum & Bailey Combined Shows, Inc. v. Utah Division of Travel Development, 170 F.3d 449 (4th Cir.), *cert. denied,* 528 U.S. 923, 120 S.Ct. 286, 145 L.Ed.2d 239 (1999). Plaintiff circus owner of the mark THE GREATEST SHOW ON EARTH sued defendant for use of the slogan THE GREATEST SNOW ON EARTH to promote travel to Utah. The following survey conducted by plaintiff was interpreted by the district court to show a lack of dilution. Do you agree?

> ... [Ringling's] survey was conducted by interviewing individuals at seven shopping malls throughout the country, including one in Utah. At each location, randomly selected shoppers were presented with a card containing the fill-in-the-blank statement "THE GREATEST _____ ON EARTH" and were asked what word or words they would use to complete the phrase. If the shoppers completed the statement, they were asked with whom or what they associated the completed statement. And, they were asked further whether they could think of any other way to complete the statement, and with whom or what they associated the resulting statement.
>
> The survey results showed that in Utah (1) 25% of the respondents completed the statement THE GREATEST _____ ON EARTH with only the word "show" and associated the completed statement with the Circus; (2) 24% completed the statement with only the word "snow" and associated the completed statement with Utah; and (3) 21% of respondents completed the statement with "show" and associated the result with the Circus and also completed the statement with "snow" and associated the completed statement with Utah. The survey further showed that outside of Utah (1) 41% of respondents completed the statement THE GREATEST _____ ON EARTH with only the word "show" and associated the completed statement with the Circus; (2) 0% completed the statement with only the word "snow" and associated the completed statement with Utah; and (3) fewer than 0.5% of respondents completed the statement with "show" and associated the result with the Circus and also completed the statement with "snow" and associated the completed statement with Utah.

QUESTIONS

1.   Terri Welles, a model named Playboy's "Playmate of the Year 1981," refers to this fact in her website promoting her services. The references appear in headings and text in the visible portion of the website as well as in the meta-tag or invisible portion of the site. Meta-tags are key words which guide search engines to a particular site by subject matter. Ms. Welles has not used any Playboy marks as a domain name. Playboy Magazine sues for trademark infringement and for federal dilution. How should a court rule on Ms. Welles's fair use defense to trademark infringement under section 33(b)(4) and to Ms. Welles's fair comparative advertising defense to dilution under section 43(c)(3)(A)? *Cf. Playboy Enterprises, Inc. v. Welles,* 279 F.3d 796 (9th Cir.2002) and *infra* Chapter 12.

2.   Would use of the well-known "aol.com" or "hotmail.com" designations as a header in unsolicited bulk e-mails sent to thousands of subscribers of those Internet services constitute dilution under the federal statute? Would it matter if the subject of the e-mail were a solicitation for pornography? For software? *See America Online, Inc. v. IMS*, 24 F.Supp.2d 548 (E.D.Va. 1998); *Hotmail Corp. v. Van Money Pie, Inc.*, 47 U.S.P.Q.2d 1020 (N.D.Cal. 1998).

3.   If a company buys banner advertising from an internet search engine so that its advertising will appear on screen whenever certain search words are typed in by a computer user, can those key words include a famous trademark without offending the dilution statute? *Cf. Playboy Enterprises Inc. v. Netscape Communications Corp.*, 55 F.Supp.2d 1070 (C.D.Cal.), *aff'd*, 202 F.3d 278 (9th Cir.1999).

3.   TRADE DRESS

   Hershey Foods Corp. v. Mars, Inc., 998 F.Supp. 500 (M.D.Pa.1998). Hershey, maker of REESE's Peanut Butter Cup and REESE'S PIECES candies, sued Mars, maker of M & M's Peanut Butter candy, claiming that a portion of the REESE's orange, yellow and brown trade dress was famous and was being diluted by the M & M's similarly colored packaging. On a motion for preliminary injunction, the court considered the statutory factors for determining fame under the 1996 FDTA and concluded that Hershey had clearly established inherent or acquired distinctiveness, a high degree of recognition in the trading areas and channels used by the parties, long duration and extent of use, nationwide geographic extent, and sufficient duration and extent of advertising. Nevertheless, the court found that Hershey failed to establish that its trade dress was "famous" because the remaining two factors favored the defendant and outweighed the significance of the other factors which favored Hershey. The court stated:

   Factor G: the nature and extent of use of the same or similar marks by third parties.

   The defendant argues that this factor does not favor the plaintiff because numerous third-party food companies use marks that are similar to the Reese's abbreviated trade dress by employing a similar combination of the colors orange, brown and yellow.

   The plaintiff counters in two ways. First, Hershey argues that the trade dress the defendant relies on is not the same or similar to the Reese's trade dress at issue in this case. Second, it is not sufficient for the defendant merely to point out third-party uses of certain elements of the contested trade dress. Hershey contends that Mars must also establish that such third-party use confuses consumers as to source. . . .

   We reject the plaintiff's argument. First, the [cited cases] deal with infringement under section 1125(a), and while the framework for analyzing the distinctiveness of a mark can be borrowed from such cases for use in a section 1125(c) case, it is obvious that the relevant passages are dealing with confusion, the essential element of an infringement claim but irrelevant to a dilution claim. Second, and in a related point, because we deal here with section 1125 (c) and the statutory criteria for determining fame, we need only follow the statute, and if it simply requires us to determine the nature and extent of the use of the same or similar marks by third parties, we need not go further and determine confusion. Other courts have not imposed this additional requirement in connection with Factor G. We note also that they have looked outside the relevant market for similar marks. [Citations omitted.] ... We believe the defendant has pointed out at least several examples of similar dress in the food industry.

Factor H: whether the mark was registered ...

The Reese's abbreviated trade dress is not federally registered. Federal registration is not a requirement to protect a mark, but a failure to register counts against a finding of fame. A person would be expected to register a famous mark.

Weighing the Factors

... [W]e do not consider the fame analysis to be a mere arithmetical exercise. We would expect most businesses hoping to succeed under the federal dilution act to be able to satisfy factors A, B, C, D, E, and F. Many companies doing business nationwide should be able to.

The important factors for us are G and H. The trade dress Hershey seeks to protect here, a particular combination of orange, brown and yellow, is similar to enough third-party marks in the food industry that we hesitate to preliminarily enjoin Mars' use of the color scheme on its M & M's peanut butter dress. Despite the evidence from the consumer survey, since plaintiff is not relying on its trade name, logo, and sawtoothed bar, the dress does not seem worthy of protection as famous.

Factor H is also significant because Hershey has registered its complete trade dress and has attempted to register its background orange but has never attempted to register the trade dress at issue here.

We conclude that the abbreviated Reese's trade dress at issue in this case has not been shown to be famous and Hershey has failed to establish the first element of its dilution claim.

QUESTIONS

1. Do you agree with the emphasis given by the court in the *Hershey* case to the third-party use factor in determining fame? *See also Hasbro Inc. v. Clue Computing Inc.*, 66 F.Supp.2d 117 (D.Mass.1999), *aff'd per curiam*, 232 F.3d 1 (1st Cir.2000) (CLUE for board games insufficiently famous in view of third party uses shown). Should such third-party uses only be considered when they are nationwide? Is this a factor in determining fame under the revised federal statute?

2.   Should the registration of a plaintiff's mark be significant in determining fame of a mark? Do you agree with the emphasis placed on this factor by the *Hershey* court, especially in the context of trade dress? Is registration a factor in determining fame under the revised federal statute?

3.   If *Hershey* were decided under the revised federal dilution statute would the result be different? Does unregistered trade dress qualify for protection? Under what conditions? *See, e.g., I.P. Lund Trading ApS v. Kohler Co.*, 163 F.3d 27 (1st Cir.1998) (award winning, unregistered faucet design insufficiently famous to qualify for dilution protection).

4.   Defendant was a licensee of the popular children's cartoon show CatDog. The show stars a two-headed creature that is half dog and half cat, each with distinct personalities. Fish is the favorite food of and symbol for the cat half and a bone is the preferred food and symbol for the dog half. Defendant licensee manufacturers small orange crackers in three shapes— half are the CatDog character, one-quarter are bone shaped and one quarter are fish-shaped as shown below. Pepperidge Farm, the manufacturer of the highly popular GOLDFISH crackers (shown below) sues, alleging federal dilution of its goldfish-shaped crackers. How should the court rule under the revised federal dilution statute? *Cf. Nabisco, Inc. v. PF Brands, Inc.*, 191 F.3d 208 (2d Cir.1999).

C.   DILUTION UNDER STATE LAW

The following cases apply state anti-dilution law. The federal law limits claims to "famous" marks. As you examine the following cases, consider whether courts applying state anti-dilution law set forth equivalent limits on the class of marks eligible to invoke anti-dilution claims. Should they? *See generally* Caroline Chicoine and Jennifer Visintine, *The Role of State Trademark Dilution Statutes in Light of The Trademark Dilution Revision Act of 2006*, 96 TMR 1155 (2006).

Ringling Bros.–Barnum & Bailey Combined Shows, Inc. v. Celozzi–Ettelson Chevrolet, Inc.

855 F.2d 480 (7th Cir.1988).

■ CUMMINGS, CIRCUIT JUDGE:

Ringling Bros.–Barnum & Bailey Combined Shows, Inc., owners of the trademark "The Greatest Show on Earth," obtained a preliminary injunction prohibiting Celozzi–Ettelson Chevrolet, Inc., an Illinois car dealership, from using the slogan "The Greatest Used Car Show on Earth." On appeal, Celozzi–Ettelson challenges the injunction as improper under the Illinois Anti–Dilution Act, challenges the Anti–Dilution Act as preempted by federal trademark law, and challenges the district court's finding that Ringling Bros. would suffer irreparable harm if a preliminary injunction was not issued. We reject each of Celozzi–Ettelson's challenges and affirm.

I

Ringling Bros. circus owns the trademark "The Greatest Show on Earth." The district court found that although originally this mark was primarily descriptive and weak, through continued use it has become a celebrated and famous mark that the public associates with the circus. Annually, approximately 10 million people in 80 cities in 48 states attend performances of "The Greatest Show on Earth." To attract an audience of 10 million people, in 1987 Ringling Bros. spent in excess of 10 million dollars heavily promoting "The Greatest Show on Earth" through a variety of techniques including print, radio and television advertisements, outdoor billboards, direct mail and souvenirs. In addition, prior to circus perform-ances in major cities, Ringling Bros. often enters into joint promotions with local companies in which Ringling Bros. provides circus tickets to retailers who in turn pay for print advertisements that feature their service in association with "The Greatest Show on Earth" and offer the retailers' customers free tickets to the circus. In October 1985, Ringling Bros. entered into such a joint promotion with Hanley Dawson Automobile Dealership in Chicago.

. . . .

Celozzi–Ettelson, located in Elmhurst, Illinois, is a car dealership that sells both new and used cars, ranking first in Illinois in the number of used cars sold and second nationally in the number of new Chevrolet cars sold. In June 1985, it erected two signs on its showroom roof that in big, bold, red circus-style letters proclaimed Celozzi–Ettelson "The Greatest Used Car Show on Earth." Beginning in mid–1986, these signs were also visible in a television advertisement for Celozzi–Ettelson that included a view of the premises. . . .

When Ringling Bros. became aware of Celozzi–Ettelson's use of the phrase "The Greatest Used Car Show on Earth," Ringling Bros. wrote Celozzi–Ettelson demanding that it immediately cease all further use of the phrase. Celozzi–Ettelson refused to comply and Ringling Bros. filed a motion for a preliminary injunction. The district court granted the motion on the ground that Celozzi–Ettelson's use of the phrase violated the Illinois Anti–Dilution Act.

II

The Illinois Anti–Dilution Act permits the owner of a mark to obtain an injunction enjoining the use by another of a similar mark "if there exists a likelihood . . . of dilution of the distinctive quality of the mark, . . . notwithstanding the absence of competition between the parties or of confusion as to the source of goods or services." Ill. Rev. Stat. Ch. 140, § 22. The injunctive relief provided by the Act grants protection to trade-marks beyond that provided by the classic "likelihood of confusion" test under the Lanham Act. 15 U.S.C. § 1051 et seq. The additional protection prevents the gradual whittling away of trademarks' distinctiveness through use by third parties on non-confusing, non-competing products.

Under the Illinois Act, "an injunction must be granted if the prior user can show that the mark is distinctive and that the subsequent user's use dilutes that distinctiveness." *Hyatt Corp. v. Hyatt Legal Services*, 736 F.2d

1153, 1157 (7th Cir.1984), *cert. denied*, 469 U.S. 1019 (emphasis added)....

. . . .

. . . Celozzi–Ettelson's slogan is deceptively similar to Ringling Bros.' entire mark. As noted above, the car dealer did not merely use the words "The Greatest Used Cars" or "The Greatest Used Cars on Earth"; it used "The Greatest [Used Car] Show on Earth." Any dissimilarity caused by the insertion of the words "Used Car" is countered by the fact that Celozzi–Ettelson presented its slogan in a manner designed to evoke the circus, using big, bold, red circus-style lettering. Protecting Ringling Bros.' distinctive mark from the dilution that would result from Celozzi–Ettelson's similar slogan will not grant Ringling Bros. a monopoly over other common laudatory phrases.

Celozzi–Ettelson also argues that the mark is not distinctive because it is composed of a widely used phrase rather than a coined word such as "Polaroid." The fact that a mark is coined or invented may make distinctiveness easier to show, but it is neither necessary nor sufficient to establish distinctiveness. The length of time the mark has been used, the scope of advertising and promotions, the nature and extent of the business and the scope of the first user's reputation are also important factors that must be considered in determining the distinctiveness of a mark. *Hyatt*, 736 F.2d at 1158.

Looking at the relevant factors, we see that "The Greatest Show on Earth" has been used by Ringling Bros. for almost 100 years; that $10 million is spent annually advertising "The Greatest Show on Earth" throughout the country and approximately $50 million in revenue is derived from services rendered under the mark; and that the scope of Ringling Bros.' reputation as "The Greatest Show on Earth" is nationwide. Thus the district court clearly did not abuse its discretion when it determined that the mark "The Greatest Show on Earth," although not coined, is nevertheless distinctive.

Celozzi–Ettelson also makes the unique argument that "distinctive" means something different under the Anti–Dilution Act than it does under the Lanham Act. However, even if Celozzi–Ettelson had cited some authority in support of this argument, we would have no reason to evaluate its dubious merit because the district court applied the definition of "distinctive" used by this Court in *Hyatt* to evaluate a claim under the Anti–Dilution Act. *See* 736 F.2d at 1158. The district court's discussion followed the factors establishing distinctiveness outlined in *Hyatt* and noted the parallels between the two cases. Therefore, even if two different definitions did exist, no error occurred because the district court would have relied on the correct one.

. . . .

IV

Celozzi–Ettelson's final argument challenges the district court's finding that Ringling Bros. would suffer irreparable harm if the preliminary injunction did not issue. The thrust of Celozzi–Ettelson's argument is that because there is no finding of likelihood of confusion, Ringling Bros.' reputation cannot be tarnished and its mark cannot be blurred. While acknowledging that a likelihood of confusion is not a requisite for a finding of dilution, Celozzi–Ettelson nevertheless concludes that without a likelihood of confusion Ringling Bros. can suffer no legal damages from defendant's use of the phrase "The Greatest Used Car Show on Earth."

Celozzi–Ettelson's argument is based on a misconstruction of the Anti–Dilution Act. First, it is nonsensical to argue that although a likelihood of confusion is not necessary to establish the existence of dilution, it is necessary to obtain an injunction preventing further dilution. Second, the underlying premise of the anti-dilution doctrine is that unlike the immediate, and often measurable, injury caused by confusion, "dilution is an infection which, if allowed to spread, will inevitably destroy the advertising value of the mark." Thus the very nature of dilution, insidiously gnawing away at the value of a mark, makes the injury "remarkably difficult to convert into damages." *Hyatt*, 736 F.2d at 1158. The lack of confusion that Celozzi–Ettelson argues as a factor negating damages is actually a factor establishing the unquantifiable, and thus irreparable, nature of the injury. Without a likelihood of confusion there is no effective way to measure the loss of audience or potential growth—to identify the specific persons who do not attend the circus or to ascertain the businesses that do not enter into joint promotions—because of Celozzi–Ettelson's use of the slogan "The Greatest Used Car Show on Earth." *See Hyatt*, 736 F.2d at 1158.

Finally, by its nature, the injury caused by dilution will almost always be irreparable. The harm caused by dilution is, for example, that the distinctiveness of the name "Polaroid" and the favorable association that accrued to it by virtue of Polaroid's commercial success would be undermined by the use of similar names in connection with other non-competing and non-confusing products. With other uses, the word "Polaroid" would no longer immediately call to mind the highly regarded cameras made by the Polaroid Corporation. The mental image would be blurred, at least to anyone who had dealt with the other products or seen their advertising. "It is the same dissonance that would be produced by selling cat food under the name 'Romanoff,' or baby carriages under the name 'Aston Martin.' " This dissonance constitutes irreparable harm that cannot be measured and can only be prevented through an injunction. The district court correctly determined that Celozzi–Ettelson's use of the slogan "The Greatest Used Car Show on Earth" would blur the strong association the public now has between Ringling Bros.' mark and its circus and thus inflict irreparable harm.

. . . .

QUESTIONS

1. Should violation of a state anti-dilution statute support a nationwide injunction?

2. Would the outcome in *Ringling Bros.* have been different had the defendant not used circus-style lettering in its slogan and had it acted in good faith? To what extent should the defendant's intent to siphon off the goodwill of the plaintiff's mark be a factor in deciding dilution cases? Is bad faith a factor in the revised federal dilution statute?

Mead Data Central, Inc. v. Toyota Motor Sales, U.S.A., Inc.

875 F.2d 1026 (2d Cir.1989).

■ Van Graafeiland, Circuit Judge:

Toyota Motor Sales, U.S.A., Inc. and its parent, Toyota Motor Corporation, appeal from a judgment of the United States District Court for the Southern District of New York (Edelstein, J.) enjoining them from using LEXUS as the name of their new luxury automobile and the division that manufactures it. The district court held that, under New York's antidilution statute, N.Y. Gen. Bus. Law § 368–d,* Toyota's use of LEXUS is likely to dilute the distinctive quality of LEXIS, the mark used by Mead Data Central, Inc. for its computerized legal research service. On March 8, 1989, we entered an order of reversal, stating that an opinion would follow. This is the opinion.

. . . .

The Parties and Their Marks

Mead and Lexis

. . . Since 1972, Mead has provided a computerized legal research service under the trademark LEXIS. Mead introduced evidence that its president in 1972 "came up with the name LEXIS based on Lex which was Latin for law and I S for information systems." In fact, however, the word "lexis" is centuries old. . . .

It can be found today in at least sixty general dictionaries or other English word books. . . . Moreover, its meaning has not changed significantly from that of its Latin and Greek predecessors; e.g., "Vocabulary, the total set of words in a language" (American Heritage Illustrated Encyclopedic Dictionary); "A vocabulary of a language, a particular subject, occupation, or activity" (Funk & Wagnalls Standard Dictionary). . . .

Moreover, the record discloses that numerous other companies had adopted "Lexis" in identifying their business or its product. . . .

Nevertheless, through its extensive sales and advertising in the field of computerized legal research, Mead has made LEXIS a strong mark in that field, and the district court so found. In particular, the district court accepted studies proffered by both parties which revealed that 76 percent of attorneys associated LEXIS with specific attributes of the service provided by Mead. However, among the general adult population, LEXIS is recog-

---

* *Editor's Note:* The New York statute was renumbered and is now § 360–l.

nized by only one percent of those surveyed, half of this one percent being attorneys or accountants. The district court therefore concluded that LEXIS is strong only within its own market.

[T]he LEXIS mark is printed in block letters with no accompanying logo.

Toyota and Lexus

... On August 24, 1987 Toyota announced a new line of luxury automobiles to be called LEXUS. The cars will be manufactured by a separate LEXUS division of Toyota, and their marketing pitch will be directed to well-educated professional consumers with annual incomes in excess of $50,000. Toyota had planned to spend $18 million to $20 million for this purpose during the first nine months of 1989.

Before adopting the completely artificial name LEXUS for its new automobile, Toyota secured expert legal advice to the effect that "there is absolutely no conflict between 'LEXIS' and 'LEXUS.'" Accordingly, when Mead subsequently objected to Toyota's use of LEXUS, Toyota rejected Mead's complaints. The district court held correctly that Toyota acted without predatory intent in adopting the LEXUS mark.

. . . .

The LEXUS mark is in stylized, almost script-like lettering and is accompanied by a rakish L logo.

The Law

The brief legislative history accompanying section 368–d describes the purpose of the statute as preventing "the whittling away of an established trade-mark's selling power and value through its unauthorized use by others upon dissimilar products." 1954 N.Y. Legis. Ann. 49 (emphasis supplied). If we were to interpret literally the italicized word "its," we would limit statutory violations to the unauthorized use of the identical established mark.... However, since the use of obvious simulations or markedly similar marks might have the same diluting effect as would an appropriation of the original mark, the concept of exact identity has been broadened to that of substantial similarity. Nevertheless, in keeping with the original intent of the statute, the similarity must be substantial before the doctrine of dilution may be applied.

Indeed, some courts have gone so far as to hold that, although violation of an antidilution statute does not require confusion of product or source, the marks in question must be sufficiently similar that confusion may be created as between the marks themselves. We need not go that far. We hold only that the marks must be "very" or "substantially" similar and that, absent such similarity, there can be no viable claim of dilution.

The district court's opinion was divided into two sections. The first section dealt with Toyota's alleged violation of the Lanham Act, and the second dealt with the alleged dilution of Mead's mark under New York's antidilution statute. The district court made several findings on the issue of similarity in its Lanham Act discussion; it made none in its discussion of section 368–d. [I]f the district court's statement in its Lanham Act discussion that "in everyday spoken English, LEXUS and LEXIS are virtually identical in pronunciation" was intended to be a finding of fact rather than a statement of opinion, we question both its accuracy and its relevance. The word LEXUS is not yet widely enough known that any definitive statement can be made concerning its pronunciation by the American public. However, the two members of this Court who concur in this opinion use "everyday spoken English," and we would not pronounce LEXUS as if it were spelled LEXIS. Although our colleague takes issue with us on this point, he does not contend that if LEXUS and LEXIS are pronounced correctly, they will sound the same. We liken LEXUS to such words as "census," "focus" and "locus," and differentiate it from such words as "axis," "aegis" and "iris."[2] If we were to substitute the letter "i" for the letter "u" in "census," we would not pronounce it as we now do. Likewise, if we were to substitute the letter "u" for the letter "i" in "axis," we would not pronounce it as we now do.

. . . .

In addition, we do not believe that "everyday spoken English" is the proper test to use in deciding the issue of similarity in the instant case. Under the Constitution, there is a " 'commonsense' distinction between speech proposing a commercial transaction, which occurs in an area traditionally subject to government regulation, and other varieties of speech." "The legitimate aim of the anti-dilution statute is to prohibit the unauthorized use of another's trademark in order to market incompatible products or services," and this constitutes a "legitimate regulation of commercial speech." "Advertising is the primary means by which the connection between a name and a company is established . . .," . . . and oral advertising is done primarily on radio and television. When Mead's speech expert was asked whether there were instances in which LEXUS and LEXIS would be pronounced differently, he replied, "Yes, although a deliberate attempt must be made to do so. . . . They can be pronounced distinctly but they are not when they are used in common parlance, in everyday language or speech." We take it as a given that television and radio announcers usually are more careful and precise in their diction than is the man on the street. Moreover, it is the rare television commercial that does not contain a visual reference to the mark and product, which in the instant case would be the LEXUS automobile. We conclude that in the field of commercial advertising, which is the field subject to regulation, there is no substantial similarity between Mead's mark and Toyota's.

There are additional factors that militate against a finding of dilution in the instant case. Such a finding must be based on two elements. First,

---

2. Similarly, we liken LEXUS to NEXXUS, a nationally known shampoo, and LEXIS to NEXIS, Mead's trademark for its computerized news service. NEXXUS and NEXIS have co-existed in apparent tranquility for almost a decade.

plaintiff's mark must possess a distinctive quality capable of dilution. Second, plaintiff must show a likelihood of dilution. . . .

Distinctiveness for dilution purposes often has been equated with the strength of a mark for infringement purposes. It also has been defined as uniqueness or as having acquired a secondary meaning. A trademark has a secondary meaning if it "has become so associated in the mind of the public with that entity . . . or its product that it identifies the goods sold by that entity and distinguishes them from goods sold by others." In sum, the statute protects a trademark's "selling power." However, the fact that a mark has selling power in a limited geographical or commercial area does not endow it with a secondary meaning for the public generally.

The strength and distinctiveness of LEXIS is limited to the market for its services—attorneys and accountants. Outside the market, LEXIS has very little selling power. Because only one percent of the general population associates LEXIS with the attributes of Mead's service, it cannot be said that LEXIS identifies that service to the general public and distinguishes it from others. Moreover, the bulk of Mead's advertising budget is devoted to reaching attorneys through professional journals.

This Court has defined dilution as either the blurring of a mark's product identification or the tarnishment of the affirmative associations a mark has come to convey. Mead does not claim that Toyota's use of LEXUS would tarnish affirmative associations engendered by LEXIS. The question that remains, therefore, is whether LEXIS is likely to be blurred by LEXUS.

Very little attention has been given to date to the distinction between the confusion necessary for a claim of infringement and the blurring necessary for a claim of dilution. Although the antidilution statute dispenses with the requirements of competition and confusion, it does not follow that every junior use of a similar mark will dilute the senior mark in the manner contemplated by the New York Legislature.

As already stated, the brief legislative history accompanying section 368–d described the purpose of the statute as preventing "the whittling away of an established trade-mark's selling power and value through its unauthorized use by others upon dissimilar products." The history disclosed a need for legislation to prevent such "hypothetical anomalies" as "Dupont shoes, Buick aspirin tablets, Schlitz varnish, Kodak pianos, Bulova gowns, and so forth," and cited cases involving similarly famous marks.

It is apparent from these references that there must be some mental association between plaintiff's and defendant's marks.

> [I]f a reasonable buyer is not at all likely to link the two uses of the trademark in his or her own mind, even subtly or subliminally, then there can be no dilution. . . . [D]ilution theory presumes some kind of mental association in the reasonable buyer's mind between the two party's [sic] uses of the mark.

. . . .

This mental association may be created where the plaintiff's mark is very famous and therefore has a distinctive quality for a significant percentage of the defendant's market. However, if a mark circulates only in a limited market, it is unlikely to be associated generally with the mark for a dissimilar product circulating elsewhere. As discussed above, such distinctiveness as LEXIS possesses is limited to the narrow market of attorneys and accountants. Moreover, the process which LEXIS represents is widely disparate from the product represented by LEXUS. For the general public, LEXIS has no distinctive quality that LEXUS will dilute.

The possibility that someday LEXUS may become a famous mark in the mind of the general public has little relevance in the instant dilution analysis since it is quite apparent that the general public associates nothing with LEXIS. On the other hand, the recognized sophistication of attorneys, the principal users of the service, has substantial relevance. Because of this knowledgeable sophistication, it is unlikely that, even in the market where Mead principally operates, there will be any significant amount of blurring between the LEXIS and LEXUS marks.

. . . .

■ Sweet, Circuit Judge, *concurring*:

. . . .

This case raises an issue that is likely to arise rarely in dilution law—the prospect that a junior mark may become so famous that it will overwhelm the senior mark. Dilution under this theory might occur where the senior user's advertising and marketing have established certain associations for its product among a particular consumer group, but the junior mark's subsequent renown causes the senior user's consumers to draw the associations identified with the junior user's mark. Here, for example, Toyota seeks to associate LEXUS with luxury and the carriage trade, which Mead fears may overwhelm LEXIS's association with indispensability and economy.

The district court found dilution based upon the anticipated renown of the LEXUS mark. Survey evidence revealed that seventy-two percent of the general public associated LEXIS either with Mead's service or with nothing at all. The fact that only two percent of the population recognized LEXIS as being associated with Mead's service indicates that the vast majority of the general public associated LEXIS with nothing at all. The district court noted:

> The parties have stipulated that in the first nine months of 1989, Toyota expects to spend between $18 million and $23 million on media advertising. Awareness of the LEXUS mark is likely to spread far beyond its potential purchasers through television, radio, billboards and other print advertising. . . . In short, the LEXUS mark is itself likely to become the sort of "famous" or "celebrated" mark, which Toyota claims is entitled to protection under § 368–d. The effect will surpass "whittling away"—it will

dwarf the LEXIS mark.... A hypothetical will perhaps clarify this conclusion. Suppose the telephone surveys conducted in this case were conducted two or three years after the introduction of the LEXUS line of automobiles, with the concomitant blitz of advertising and media attention. The court doubts whether three-quarters of the general population would respond that the word LEXUS brought nothing to mind. Moreover, it is more than likely that, even among Mead customers, the word "lexis" might first bring to mind Toyota's car.

. . . .

The district court found a likelihood of dilution, reasoning that Toyota's promotional campaign for its LEXUS automobile "will dwarf the LEXIS mark," and that Toyota acted in bad faith—although without predatory intent—by launching its LEXUS line "without any regard for its effect on the LEXIS mark." . . .

. . . .

The only finding that supports a likelihood of dilution is the district court's conclusion that LEXUS eventually may become so famous that members of the general public who now associate LEXIS or LEXUS with nothing at all may associate the terms with Toyota's automobiles and that Mead's customers may think first of Toyota's car when they hear LEXIS. This analysis is problematic. First, section 368–d protects a mark's selling power among the consuming public. Because the LEXIS mark possesses selling power only among lawyers and accountants, it is irrelevant for dilution analysis that the general public may come to associate LEXIS or LEXUS with Toyota's automobile rather than nothing at all. Second, the district court offered no evidence for its speculation that LEXUS's fame may cause Mead customers to associate "lexis" with Toyota's cars. It seems equally plausible that no blurring will occur—because many lawyers and accountants use Mead's services regularly, their frequent association of LEXIS with those services will enable LEXIS's mark to withstand Toyota's advertising campaign.

Therefore, even if we accept the district court's finding regarding the renown of the LEXUS mark, however, reversal still is required. The differences in the marks and in the products covered by the marks, the sophistication of Mead's consumers, the absence of predatory intent, and the limited renown of the LEXIS mark all indicate that blurring is unlikely.

Conclusion

For the reasons set forth above, I concur.

QUESTION

The LEXIS/LEXUS case presents certain peculiarities. First, the plaintiff's mark was highly distinctive, but only to a limited segment of the public. Second, at least in the district court's view, as the larger, more widely-known company, Toyota's adoption of a mark very similar to Mead's could lead to a kind of reverse dilution: LEXUS will overwhelm LEXIS, and members of the public who subsequently become familiar with LEXIS might believe that Mead was seeking to profit by Toyota's goodwill. Do you think the court adequately addressed either the problem of "whittling away" Mead's goodwill among the public familiar with LEXIS, or the problem of reverse dilution?

Deere & Co. v. MTD Products, Inc.

41 F.3d 39 (2d Cir.1994).

■ NEWMAN, CIRCUIT JUDGE:

This appeal in a trademark case presents a rarely litigated issue likely to recur with increasing frequency in this era of head-to-head comparative advertising. The precise issue, arising under the New York anti-dilution statute, N.Y.Gen.Bus.Law § 368–d (McKinney 1984), is whether an advertiser may depict an altered form of a competitor's trademark to identify the competitor's product in a comparative ad. The issue arises on an appeal by defendant-appellant MTD Products, Inc. ("MTD") from the August 9, 1994, order of the United States District Court for the Southern District of New York (Lawrence M. McKenna, Judge) granting a preliminary injunction to plaintiff-appellee Deere & Company ("Deere") and Deere's cross-appeal to broaden the scope of the injunction beyond New York State, 860 F. Supp. 113. The injunction prevents MTD from airing a television commercial that shows an animated version of the leaping deer that has become appellee's well-known logo

. . . Though we find MTD's animated version of Deere's deer amusing, we agree with Judge McKenna that the television commercial is a likely violation of the anti-dilution statute. We therefore affirm the preliminary injunction.

Background

. . . For over one hundred years, Deere has used a deer design ("Deere Logo") as a trademark for identifying its products and services. Deere owns numerous trademark registrations for different versions of the Deere Logo. Although these versions vary slightly, all depict a static, two-dimensional silhouette of a leaping male deer in profile. The Deere Logo is widely recognizable and a valuable business asset.

MTD . . . manufactures and sells lawn tractors. In 1993, W.B. Doner & Company ("Doner"), MTD's advertising agency, decided to create and produce a commercial—the subject of this litigation—that would use the Deere Logo, without Deere's authorization, for the purpose of comparing Deere's line of lawn tractors to MTD's "Yard–Man" tractor. The intent was to identify Deere as the market leader and convey the message that Yard–Man was of comparable quality but less costly than a Deere lawn tractor.

Doner altered the Deere Logo in several respects. For example, as Judge McKenna found, the deer in the MTD version of the logo ("Commercial Logo") is "somewhat differently proportioned, particularly with respect to its width, than the deer in the Deere Logo." Doner also removed the name "John Deere" from the version of the logo used by Deere on the front of its lawn tractors, and made the logo frame more sharply rectangular.

More significantly, the deer in the Commercial Logo is animated and assumes various poses. Specifically, the MTD deer looks over its shoulder, jumps through the logo frame (which breaks into pieces and tumbles to the ground), hops to a pinging noise, and, as a two-dimensional cartoon, runs, in apparent fear, as it is pursued by the Yard–Man lawn tractor and a barking dog. Judge McKenna described the dog as "recognizable as a breed that is short in stature," and in the commercial the "fleeing deer appears to be even smaller than the dog. . . ."

[T]he District Court ... found that Deere had demonstrated a likelihood of prevailing on its dilution claim and granted preliminary injunctive relief limited to activities within New York State. . . . [T]he Court concluded that Deere had not shown a likelihood of success on the merits of its Lanham Act claim.

. . . .

Discussion

. . . .

In order to prevail on a section 368–d dilution claim, a plaintiff must prove, first, that its trademark either is of truly distinctive quality or has acquired secondary meaning, and, second, that there is a "likelihood of dilution." [Citation]. A third consideration, the predatory intent of the defendant, may not be precisely an element of the violation, but, as we discuss below, is of significance, especially in a case such as this, which involves poking fun at a competitor's trademark.

MTD does not dispute that the Deere Logo is a distinctive trademark that is capable of dilution and has acquired the requisite secondary meaning in the marketplace. *See Allied Maintenance Corp. v. Allied Mechanical Trades, Inc.*, 42 N.Y.2d 538, 545, 399 N.Y.S.2d 628, 632, 369 N.E.2d 1162, 1166 (1977). Therefore, the primary question on appeal is whether Deere can establish a likelihood of dilution of this distinctive mark under section 368–d.

Likelihood of Dilution.

Traditionally, this Court has defined dilution under section 368–d "as either the blurring of a mark's product identification or the tarnishment of the affirmative associations a mark has come to convey." [Citations omitted].

In previous cases, "blurring" has typically involved "the whittling away of an established trademark's selling power through its unauthorized use by others upon dissimilar products." *Mead Data*, 875 F.2d at 1031 (describing such " 'hypothetical anomalies' as 'DuPont shoes, Buick aspirin tablets, Schlitz varnish, Kodak pianos, Bulova gowns, and so forth' ") (quoting legislative history of section 368–d) (citation omitted). Thus, dilution by "blurring" may occur where the defendant uses or modifies the plaintiff's trademark to identify the defendant's goods and services, raising the possibility that the mark will lose its ability to serve as a unique identifier of the plaintiff's product.

"Tarnishment" generally arises when the plaintiff's trademark is linked to products of shoddy quality, or is portrayed in an unwholesome or unsavory context likely to evoke unflattering thoughts about the owner's product. In such situations, the trademark's reputation and commercial value might be diminished because the public will associate the lack of quality or lack of prestige in the defendant's goods with the plaintiff's unrelated goods, or because the defendant's use reduces the trademark's reputation and standing in the eyes of consumers as a wholesome identifier of the owner's products or services.

. . . .

The District Court noted that "the instant case [wa]s one of first impression" because it involved a defendant's use of a competitor's trademark to refer to the competitor's products rather than to identify the defendant's products. For this reason, the traditional six-factor test for determining whether there has been dilution through blurring of a trademark's product identification was not fully applicable.[8] Focusing only on the alteration of the static Deere Logo resulting from MTD's animation, the Court concluded that MTD's version constituted dilution because it was likely to diminish the strength of identification between the original Deere symbol and Deere products, and to blur the distinction between the Deere Logo and other deer logos in the marketplace, including those in the insurance and financial markets. Although we agree with the District Court's finding of a likelihood of dilution, we believe that MTD's commercial does not fit within the concept of "blurring," but, as we explain below, nonetheless constitutes dilution.

The District Court's analysis endeavored to fit the MTD commercial into one of the two categories we have recognized for a section 368–d claim. However, the MTD commercial is not really a typical instance of blurring, [citation], because it poses slight if any risk of impairing the identification of Deere's mark with its products. Nor is there tarnishment, which is usually found where a distinctive mark is depicted in a context of sexual activity, obscenity, or illegal activity. [Citations]. But the blurring/tarnishment dichotomy does not necessarily represent the full range of uses that can dilute a mark under New York law. [Citations].

In giving content to dilution beyond the categories of blurring or tarnishment, however, we must be careful not to broaden section 368–d to prohibit all uses of a distinctive mark that the owner prefers not be made.

---

8. *See Mead Data*, 875 F.2d at 1035 (Sweet, J., concurring) (suggesting that courts evaluating blurring claims look at (1) similarity of the marks, (2) similarity of the products covered by the marks, (3) sophistication of consumers, (4) predatory intent, (5) renown of the senior mark, and (6) renown of the junior mark).

Several different contexts may conveniently be identified. Sellers of commercial products may wish to use a competitor's mark to identify the competitor's product in comparative advertisements. *See, e.g., R.G. Smith v. Chanel, Inc.*, 402 F.2d 562, 567 (9th Cir.1968) (perfume manufacturer used competitor's mark in comparative advertisements; injunction denied). As long as the mark is not altered, such use serves the beneficial purpose of imparting factual information about the relative merits of competing products and poses no risk of diluting the selling power of the competitor's mark. Satirists, selling no product other than the publication that contains their expression, may wish to parody a mark to make a point of social commentary, *see, e.g., Stop the Olympic Prison v. United States Olympic Committee*, 489 F. Supp. 1112, 1123 (S.D.N.Y.1980) (poster used defendant's trademark to criticize trademark owner's involvement with proposed prison; injunction denied), to entertain, *see, e.g., L.L. Bean v. Drake Publishers, Inc.*, 811 F.2d 26 (1st Cir.) (satiric magazine parodying L.L. Bean catalogue; injunction denied), *cert. denied*, 483 U.S. 1013, 107 S.Ct. 3254, 97 L.Ed.2d 753 (1987), or perhaps both to comment and entertain, *see, e.g., Girl Scouts of USA v. Personality Posters Manufacturing Co.*, 304 F. Supp. 1228, 1233 (S.D.N.Y.1969) (poster depicting pregnant Girl Scout to suggest humorously that trademark owner's traditional image of chastity and wholesomeness was somewhat illusory; injunction denied). Such uses risk some dilution of the identifying or selling power of the mark, but that risk is generally tolerated in the interest of maintaining broad opportunities for expression. [Citation].

Sellers of commercial products who wish to attract attention to their commercials or products and thereby increase sales by poking fun at widely recognized marks of noncompeting products, *see, e.g., Eveready Battery Co., Inc. v. Adolph Coors Co.*, 765 F. Supp. 440 (N.D.Ill.1991) (beer manufacturer spoofed Energizer Bunny trademark; preliminary injunction under Lanham Act and state dilution statute denied), risk diluting the selling power of the mark that is made fun of. When this occurs, not for worthy purposes of expression, but simply to sell products, that purpose can easily be achieved in other ways. The potentially diluting effect is even less deserving of protection when the object of the joke is the mark of a directly competing product. *See, e.g., Wendy's International, Inc. v. Big Bite, Inc.*, 576 F. Supp. 816 (S.D.Ohio 1983) ("fast-food" chain made fun of "fast-food" competitors' trademarks; preliminary injunction granted under Lanham Act). The line-drawing in this area becomes especially difficult when a mark is parodied for the dual purposes of making a satiric comment and selling a somewhat competing product. *See, e.g., Yankee Publishing Inc. v. News America Publishing Inc.*, 809 F. Supp. 267 (S.D.N.Y.1992) (magazine satirized another magazine; injunction denied).

Whether the use of the mark is to identify a competing product in an informative comparative ad, to make a comment, or to spoof the mark to enliven the advertisement for a noncompeting or a competing product, the scope of protection under a dilution statute must take into account the degree to which the mark is altered and the nature of the alteration. Not every alteration will constitute dilution, and more leeway for alterations is appropriate in the context of satiric expression and humorous ads for noncompeting products. But some alterations have the potential to so lessen the selling power of a distinctive mark that they are appropriately proscribed by a dilution statute. Dilution of this sort is more likely to be found when the alterations are made by a competitor with both an incentive to diminish the favorable attributes of the mark and an ample opportunity to promote its products in ways that make no significant alteration.

We need not attempt to predict how New York will delineate the scope of its dilution statute in all of the various contexts in which an accurate depiction of a distinctive mark might be used, nor need we decide how variations of such a mark should be treated in different contexts. Some variations might well be de minimis, and the context in which even substantial variations occur may well have such meritorious purposes that any diminution in the identifying and selling power of the mark need not be condemned as dilution.

Wherever New York will ultimately draw the line, we can be reasonably confident that the MTD commercial challenged in this cases crosses it. The commercial takes a static image of a graceful, full-size deer—symbolizing Deere's substance and strength—and portrays, in an animated version, a deer that appears smaller than a small dog and scampers away from the dog and a lawn tractor, looking over its shoulder in apparent fear. Alterations of that sort, accomplished for the sole purpose of promoting a competing product, are properly found to be within New York's concept of dilution because they risk the possibility that consumers will come to attribute unfavorable characteristics to a mark and ultimately associate the mark with inferior goods and services. [Citations omitted].

Significantly, the District Court did not enjoin accurate reproduction of the Deere Logo to identify Deere products in comparative advertisements. MTD remains free to deliver its message of alleged product superiority without altering and thereby diluting Deere's trademarks. The court's order imposes no restriction on truthful advertising properly comparing specific products and their "objectively measurable attributes." FTC Policy Statement on Comparative Advertising, 16 C.F.R. § 14.15 n. 1 (1993). In view of this, the District Court's finding of a likelihood of dilution was entirely appropriate, notwithstanding the fact that MTD's humorous depiction of the deer occurred in the context of a comparative advertisement.

. . . .

Conclusion

The order of the District Court granting a preliminary injunction as to activities within New York State is affirmed.

Hormel Foods Corp. v. Jim Henson Productions, Inc., 73 F.3d 497 (2d Cir.1996). The Second Circuit affirmed a finding of no infringement and no dilution of plaintiff's well-known SPAM mark for canned luncheon meat. Defendant used a wild boar character named Spa'am in a Muppet movie and on related merchandising items. Spa'am is portrayed as a leader of a wild boar tribe that worships Muppet character Miss Piggy.

In discussing the tarnishment prong of dilution, the Court noted:

Tarnishment can occur through a variety of uses. Some cases have found that a mark is tarnished when its likeness is placed in the context of sexual activity, obscenity, or illegal activity. [Citations omitted.] However, tarnishment is not limited to seamy conduct. [Citations omitted.] Hormel argues that the image of Spa'am, as a "grotesque," "untidy" wild boar will "inspire negative and unsavory associations with SPAM luncheon meat." Both Hormel and Amicus Curiae rely heavily on our recent decision in *Deere, supra,* for the proposition that products that "poke fun at widely recognized marks of non-competing products, risk diluting the selling power of the mark that is made fun of." 41 F.3d at 44 [citation omitted]. Their reliance is misplaced.

In *Deere,* [w]e found that there was no blurring because there was little risk of impairing the identification of Deere's mark with its products. Noting that tarnishment "is usually found where a distinctive mark is depicted in a context of sexual activity, obscenity, or illegal activity," we held that the "blurring/tarnishment dichotomy does not necessarily represent the full range of uses that can dilute a mark under New York law." *Id.* at 44. We found a violation of the anti-dilution statute because "alterations of that sort, accomplished for the sole purpose of promoting a competing product ... risk the possibility that consumers will come to attribute unfavorable characteristics to a mark and ultimately associate the mark with inferior goods and services." *Id.* at 45. This holding mirrors the rationale of the tarnishment doctrine. Thus, although the court below understood *Deere* to create a new category of dilution, we find that our decision in *Deere* is better understood as a recognition of a broad view of tarnishment, where that doctrine had been sometimes narrowly confined.

The sine quo non of tarnishment is a finding that plaintiff's mark will suffer negative associations through defendant's use. Hormel claims that linking its luncheon meat with a wild boar will adversely color consumer's impressions of SPAM. However, the district court found that Spa'am, a likeable, positive character, will not generate any negative associations. Moreover, contrary to Hormel's contentions, the district court also found no evidence that Spa'am is unhygienic or that his character places Hormel's mark in an unsavory context. Indeed, many of Henson's own plans involve placing the Spa'am likeness on food products. In addition, the court noted that a simple humorous reference to the fact that SPAM is made from pork is unlikely to tarnish Hormel's mark. Absent any showing that Henson's use will create negative associations with the SPAM mark, there was little likelihood of dilution. [Citation omitted.]

Moreover, unlike *Deere*, Henson's merchandise will not be in direct competition with that of Hormel. This is an important, even if not determinative, factor. "Dilution of this sort is more likely to be found when the alterations are made by a competitor with both an incentive to diminish the products in ways that make no significant alteration." *Deere, supra,* 41 F.3d at 45. Here, Henson does not seek to ridicule SPAM in order to sell more of its competitive products; rather, the parody is part of the product itself. Without Spa'am, the joke is lost. Indeed, we were mindful of this problem in *Deere* when we noted that "the line-drawing in this area becomes especially difficult when a mark is parodied for the dual purposes of making a satiric comment and selling a somewhat competing product." *Id.* Thus, in *Deere* we did not proscribe any parody or humorous depiction of a mark. Overall, we took a cautious approach, stating that "we must be careful not to broaden section 368–d to prohibit all uses of a distinctive mark that the owner prefers not to be made." *Id.* at 44.

Therefore, in the instant case, where (1) there is no evidence that Henson's use will cause negative associations, (2) Henson is not a direct competitor, and (3) the parody inheres in the product, we find that there is no likelihood of dilution under a tarnishment theory.

QUESTIONS

1. Consider the view of The Restatement (Third) of the Law of Unfair Competition § 25(2) which provides:

> (2) One who uses a designation that resembles the trademark, trade name, collective mark, or certification mark of another, not in a manner that is likely to associate the other's mark with the goods, services, or business of the actor, but rather to comment on, criticize, ridicule, parody, or disparage the other or the other's goods, services, business, or mark, is subject to liability without proof of a likelihood of confusion only if the actor's conduct meets the requirements of a cause of action for defamation, invasion of privacy, or injurious falsehood.

Would the result in *Deere* be different under The Restatement view? If so, which is the better view? Is a *Deere*-type claim available under § 43(c)? *See* § 43(c)(3)(A).

2. The lesser requirements for distinctiveness under some state statutes as compared with the more stringent federal dilution requirements have led to different outcomes for federal and state dilution claims in the same case. *See, e.g., New York Stock Exchange, Inc. v. New York, New York Hotel LLC*, 293 F.3d 550 (2d Cir.2002). *Cf. Pfizer, Inc. v. Y2K Shipping & Trading, Inc.*, 70 U.S.P.Q.2d 1592 (E.D.N.Y.2004) (having withdrawn federal dilution claim after Supreme Court's decision in *Moseley*, owner of VIAGRA mark for a pharmaceutical for erectile dysfunction succeeded on its New York state dilution ground against the mark TRIAGRA for a treatment for the same condition). How do you think the TRIAGRA case would be decided under the revised federal statute?

3. Are there other situations where state dilution laws may provide a remedy not covered by the federal statute? How about marks that possess only local or niche fame? Are state-based remedies desirable?

CHAPTER 10

AUTHORS' AND PERFORMERS' RIGHTS

A. AUTHORS' AND PERFORMERS' RIGHTS OF ATTRIBUTION

Gilliam v. American Broadcasting Companies, Inc.

538 F.2d 14 (2d Cir.1976).

■ LUMBARD, CIRCUIT JUDGE:

Plaintiffs, a group of British writers and performers known as "Monty Python," appeal from a denial by Judge Lasker in the Southern District of a preliminary injunction to restrain the American Broadcasting Company (ABC) from broadcasting edited versions of three separate programs originally written and performed by Monty Python for broadcast by the British Broadcasting Corporation (BBC). We agree with Judge Lasker that the appellants have demonstrated that the excising done for ABC impairs the integrity of the original work. We further find that the countervailing injuries that Judge Lasker found might have accrued to ABC as a result of an injunction at a prior date no longer exist. We therefore direct the issuance of a preliminary injunction by the district court.

. . . .

[The Monty Python group wrote scripts for BBC's thirty-minute television program entitled "Monty Python's Flying Circus." Monty Python and BBC entered into a detailed scriptwriters' agreement under which BBC retained final authority to make changes, but only minor changes could be made to the scripts without prior consultation with the writers. Furthermore, once the program was recorded, nothing in the agreement entitled BBC to alter the program. This agreement also entitled BBC to license the programs for viewing overseas.

In 1973, BBC licensed to Time–Life Films the right to distribute in the United States the Monty Python series. Time–Life was permitted to edit the programs only "for insertion of commercials, applicable censorship or governmental . . . rules and regulations, and National Association of Broadcasters and time segment requirements." This clause was not included in the scriptwriters' agreement between Monty Python and BBC. In July 1975, ABC agreed with Time–Life to broadcast two ninety-minute specials each comprising three thirty-minute Monty Python programs. ABC broadcast the first of the specials on October 3, 1975. Monty Python was allegedly "appalled" at the discontinuity and "mutilation" that had resulted from the editing. Twenty-four minutes of the original 90 minutes of recording had been omitted, partially to make time for commercials, and partially because ABC found some of the material offensive or obscene.]

. . . .

In early December, Monty Python learned that ABC planned to broadcast the second special on December 26, 1975. . . . [Monty Python] filed this action to enjoin the broadcast and for damages. Following an evidentiary hearing, Judge Lasker found that "the plaintiffs have established an impairment of the integrity of their work" which "caused the film or program . . . to lose its iconoclastic verve." . . . Nevertheless, the judge denied the motion for the preliminary injunction on the grounds that it was unclear who owned the copyright in the programs produced by BBC from the scripts written by Monty Python; that there was a question of whether Time–Life and BBC were indispensable parties to the litigation; that ABC would suffer significant financial loss if it were enjoined a week before the scheduled broadcast; and that Monty Python had displayed a "somewhat disturbing casualness" in their pursuance of the matter.

Judge Lasker granted Monty Python's request for more limited relief by requiring ABC to broadcast a disclaimer during the December 26 special to the effect that the group dissociated itself from the program because of the editing. A panel of this court, however, granted a stay of that order until this appeal could be heard and permitted ABC to broadcast, at the beginning of the special, only the legend that the program had been edited by ABC. We heard argument on April 13 and, at that time, enjoined ABC from any further broadcast of edited Monty Python programs pending the decision of the court.

. . . .

[The court first held that the editing exceeded the scope of the contractual grant and violated plaintiffs' rights under copyright to prepare derivative works.]

. . . .

[T]he appellants claim that the editing done for ABC mutilated the original work and that consequently the broadcast of those programs as the creation of Monty Python violated the Lanham Act § 43(a), 15 U.S.C. § 1125(a). This statute, the federal counterpart to state unfair competition laws, has been invoked to prevent misrepresentations that may injure plaintiff's business or personal reputation, even where no registered trademark is concerned. It is sufficient to violate the Act that a representation of a product, although technically true, creates a false impression of the product's origin. *See Rich v. RCA Corp.*, 390 F. Supp. 530 (S.D.N.Y.1975) (recent picture of plaintiff on cover of album containing songs recorded in distant past held to be a false representation that the songs were new).

These cases cannot be distinguished from the situation in which a television network broadcasts a program properly designated as having been written and performed by a group, but which has been edited, without the writer's consent, into a form that departs substantially from the original work. "To deform his work is to present him to the public as the creator of a work not his own, and thus makes him subject to criticism for work he has not done." In such a case, it is the writer or performer, rather than the network, who suffers the consequences of the mutilation, for the public will have only the final product by which to evaluate the work. Thus, an allegation that a defendant has presented to the public a "garbled," distorted version of plaintiff's work seeks to redress the very rights sought to be protected by the Lanham Act, 15 U.S.C. § 1125(a), and should be recognized as stating a cause of action under that statute. *See Autry v. Republic Productions, Inc.,* 213 F.2d 667 (9th Cir.1954); *Jaeger v. American Intn'l Pictures, Inc.,* 330 F. Supp. 274 (S.D.N.Y.1971), which suggests the violation of such a right if mutilation could be proven.

. . . [After viewing and comparing the edited and the unedited versions of the program], [w]e find that the truncated version at times omitted the climax of the skits to which appellants' rare brand of humor was leading and at other times deleted essential elements in the schematic development of a story line.[12] We therefore agree with Judge Lasker's conclusion that the edited version broadcast by ABC impaired the integrity of appellants' work and represented to the public as the product of appellants what was actually a mere caricature of their talents. We believe that a valid cause of action for such distortion exists and that therefore a preliminary injunction may issue to prevent repetition of the broadcast prior to final determination of the issues.[13]

. . . .

■ GURFEIN, CIRCUIT JUDGE *concurring*:

I concur in my brother Lumbard's scholarly opinion, but I wish to comment on the application of Section 43(a) of the Lanham Act, 15 U.S.C. § 1125(a).

12. A single example will illustrate the extent of distortion engendered by the editing. In one skit, an upper-class English family is engaged in a discussion of the tonal quality of certain words as "woody" or "tinny." The father soon begins to suggest certain words with sexual connotations as either "woody" or "tinny," whereupon the mother fetches a bucket of water and pours it over his head. The skit continues from this point. The ABC edit eliminates this middle sequence so that the father is comfortably dressed at one moment and, in the next moment, is shown in a soaken condition without any explanation for the change in his appearance.

13. Judge Gurfein's concurring opinion suggests that since the gravamen of a complaint under the Lanham Act is that the original of goods had been falsely described, a legend disclaiming Monty Python's approval of the edited version would preclude violation of that Act. We are doubtful that a few words could erase the indelible impression that is made by a television broadcast, especially since the viewer has no means of comparing the truncated version with the complete work in order to determine for himself the talents of plaintiffs. Furthermore, a disclaimer such as the one originally suggested by Judge Lasker in the exigencies of an impending broadcast last December, would go unnoticed by viewers who tuned into the broadcast a few minutes after it began.

We therefore conclude that Judge Gurfein's proposal that the district court could find some form of disclaimer would be sufficient might not provide appropriate relief.

I believe that this is the first case in which a federal appellate court has held that there may be a violation of Section 43(a) of the Lanham Act with respect to a common-law copyright. The Lanham Act is a trademark statute, not a copyright statute. Nevertheless, we must recognize that the language of Section 43(a) is broad. It speaks of the affixation or use of false designations of origin or false descriptions or representations, but proscribes such use "in connection with any goods or services." It is easy enough to incorporate trade names as well as trademarks into Section 43(a) and the statute specifically applies to common-law trademarks, as well as registered trademarks. Lanham Act § 45, 15 U.S.C. § 1127.

. . . .

The Copyright Act provides no recognition of the so-called *droit moral,* or moral rights of authors. Nor are such rights recognized in the field of copyright law in the United States. If a distortion or truncation in connection with a use constitutes an infringement of copyright, there is no need for an additional cause of action beyond copyright infringement. An obligation to mention the name of the author carries the implied duty, however, as a matter of contract, not to make such changes in the work as would render the credit line a false attribution of authorship.

So far as the Lanham Act is concerned, it is not a substitute for *droit moral* which authors in Europe enjoy. If the licensee may, by contract, distort the recorded work, the Lanham Act does not come into play. If the licensee has no such right by contract, there will be a violation in breach of contract. The Lanham Act can hardly apply literally when the credit line correctly states the work to be that of the plaintiffs which, indeed it is, so far as it goes. The vice complained of is that the truncated version is not what the plaintiffs wrote. But the Lanham Act does not deal with artistic integrity. It only goes to misdescription of origin and the like.

The misdescription of origin can be dealt with, as Judge Lasker did below, by devising an appropriate legend to indicate that the plaintiffs had not approved the editing of the ABC version.[1] With such a legend, there is no conceivable violation of the Lanham Act. If plaintiffs complain that their artistic integrity is still compromised by the distorted version, their claim does not lie under the Lanham Act, which does not protect the copyrighted work itself but protects only against the misdescription or mislabelling.

So long as it is made clear that the ABC version is not approved by the Monty Python group, there is no misdescription of origin. So far as the content of the broadcast itself is concerned, that is not within the proscription of the Lanham Act when there is no misdescription of the authorship.

I add this brief explanation because I do not believe that the Lanham Act claim necessarily requires the drastic remedy of permanent injunction. That form of ultimate relief must be found in some other fountainhead of equity jurisprudence.

---

1. I do not imply that the appropriate legend be shown only at the beginning of the broadcast. That is a matter for the District Court.

Dastar Corporation v. Twentieth Century Fox Film Corporation

539 U.S. 23 (2003).

[See Chapter 7.C supra, page 545]

QUESTION

The text of § 43(a) construed in *Gilliam* is not identical to the version the Supreme Court interpreted in *Dastar*. Notably, the *Gilliam* version placed false designations of origin and false representations in the same section of the statute. Did *Gilliam* concern a false designation of origin, or a false representation? If the former, is it still good law after *Dastar*? If the latter?

Antidote Int'l Films v. Bloomsbury Publishing PLC, 467 F.Supp.2d 394 (S.D.N.Y.2006). The plaintiff, a film producer, had purchased an option to produce a motion picture based on the novel *Sarah*, by the enigmatic cult writer J.T. Leroy, whose personal history was as dramatic as his fictional characters. It turns out, however, that "J.T. Leroy" was also a fiction, one elaborately devised and maintained by the actual author, her family, and the publisher.

Plaintiff alleges that defendants' representations "that the novel Sarah was authored by a person known as 'J.T. Leroy'" and that "Sarah is a semi-autobiographical novel based on actual experiences and hardships suffered by the fictional persona known as 'J.T. Leroy,'" together with defendants' other representations "of and relating to the false personal history of the persona known as 'J.T. Leroy'" together "constitute a false designation of origin under § 43(a)(1)(A) of the Lanham Act."

This claim is foreclosed by the Supreme Court's decision in *Dastar Corp. v. Twentieth Century Fox Film Corp.*, 539 U.S. 23, 123 S.Ct. 2041, 156 L.Ed.2d 18 (2003). In *Dastar*, the Supreme Court addressed whether the word "origin" in the Lanham Act could be read to refer to the author of a work, such as a novel, rather than to the producer of the physical book. The Court recognized that "[t]he purchaser of a novel is interested not merely, if at all, in the identity of the producer of the physical tome (the publisher), but also, and indeed primarily, in the identity of the creator of the story it conveys (the author)." The Court refused, however, to accord "special treatment" to "communicative products"—that is, to read the word "origin" in the Lanham Act to cover the authors of communicative products—on the ground that such treatment would "cause[] the Lanham Act to conflict with the law of copyright, which addresses that subject specifically." *Id.* Accordingly, the Court held that the phrase "origin" of "goods" in the Lanham Act "refers to the producer of the tangible goods that are offered for sale, and not to the author of any idea, concept, or communication embodied in those goods."

Plaintiff argues that in spite of *Dastar*, this Court should accord "special treatment" to the communicative product at issue in this case, the novel Sarah, and treat the author of the work (the fictional "J.T. Leroy"), rather than the producer of the physical books (defendant Bloomsbury), as the "origin" of the book under the Lanham Act. Plaintiff argues that *Dastar* does not preclude such treatment because the plaintiff in *Dastar* was attempting to vindicate a copyright claim that was unavailable because the underlying work was in the public domain, whereas in this case Antidote is not trying to vindicate any copyright. But nothing in *Dastar* suggests that communicative products such as novels may be accorded "special treatment" under the Lanham Act where no copyright claim is available. Rather, *Dastar* holds that the fact that copyright law covers "communicative products" prevents these products from being accorded "special treatment" under the Lanham Act regardless of whether a viable copyright claim exists in a given case. Accordingly, plaintiff cannot prevail on its Lanham Act claim because, pursuant to *Dastar*, Bloomsbury is the "origin"—that is, the manufacturer—of the physical books in which the novel Sarah is printed, and plaintiff does not claim that Bloomsbury was not properly designated as such.

Plaintiff further attempts to distinguish *Dastar* by arguing that defendants' false representations here are likely to cause confusion not only with respect to the "origin" of Sarah, but also with respect to "the affiliation, connection, or association of [Bloomsbury] with another person," that is, "the imaginary 'J.T. LeRoy.'" § 43(a)(1)(A).... [S]uch allegations ... simply restate plaintiff's claim that Bloomsbury falsely designated the origin of Sarah—which fails for the reasons set out above—in different terms. *Dastar* holds that a claim for false designation origin is unavailable where the "origin" in question is the authorship of a communicative work. This holding necessarily applies with equal force to any claim for "false ... representation[s]" with respect to the "affiliation ... of [one] person with another person," where, as here, one person is the publisher of a novel and the other is the author of the novel, because the holding of *Dastar* would be meaningless if a false authorship claim could be recast in this manner....

Turning to Count II, defendants Bloomsbury, Underdogs, and Albert sought in their motions to dismiss this count, which alleges false advertising under § 43(a)(1)(B) of the Lanham Act, on the ground that it was also precluded by *Dastar*. Section 43(a)(1)(B) prohibits misrepresentations going to "the nature, characteristics, qualities, or geographic origin of ... goods." Plaintiff alleges that defendants' representations that "(a) 'J.T. Leroy' exists, (b) the novel Sarah was authored by 'J.T. Leroy' and (c) Sarah is based on the personal, real-life experiences of its author constitute false advertising under § 43(a)(1)(B) of the Lanham Act." In large part, these allegations mirror the false authorship claims that *Dastar* precludes under § 43(a)(1)(A). Plaintiff nonetheless argues that *Dastar* leaves open the possibility that some false authorship claims could be vindicated under the auspices of § 43(a)(1)(B)'s prohibition on false advertising. In particular, plaintiff relies on the suggestion in *Dastar* that if the defendant in that case had substantially copied the public-domain video at issue and, "in advertising or promotion," had attempted "to give purchasers the impression that the video was quite different" from the public-domain work, the original producers of the public domain work "might have a cause of action ... for misrepresentations under the 'misrepresents the nature, characteristics [or] qualities' provision of § 43(a)(1)(B)." *Dastar*, 539 U.S. at 38.

However, while this language might be read to suggest that the Supreme Court was leaving open the possibility of a claim arising from a misrepresentation going to the substance of a work, rather than the work's authorship, in the instant case, with respect to claims that sound in false authorship, the holding in *Dastar* that the word "origin" in § 43(a)(1)(A) refers to producers, rather than authors, necessarily implies that the words "nature, characteristics, [and] qualities" in § 43(a)(1)(B) cannot be read to refer to authorship. If authorship were a "characteristic[]" or "qualit[y]" of a work, then the very claim *Dastar* rejected under § 43(a)(1)(A) would have been available under § 43(a)(1)(B).

As *Antidote* illustrates, decisions subsequent to *Dastar* have read that ruling to limit sharply if not eliminate invocation of the Lanham Act to advance claims for authorship credit. *See e.g., Chivalry Film Prods. v. NBC Universal, Inc.,* 2006 WL 89944 (S.D.N.Y.2006) (screenwriter claimed producer of "Meet the Parents" copied his script and misattributed screenplay to third parties; court held *Dastar* required dismissal of misattribution claim)*; A Slice of Pie Prods. v. Wayans Bros. Entm't,* 392 F.Supp.2d 297 (D. Conn. 2005) (same re film "White Chicks"); *Keane v. Fox,* 297 F.Supp.2d 921 (S.D.Tex.2004), where the court dismissed plaintiff's claim that, as the originator of the idea of the "American Idol" television series, and developer of the "American Idol" mark, he should have been recognized and paid. The court held that Keane had not developed trademark rights in the term "American Idol." The court also ruled against any claim in the concept of the television series, citing *Dastar*: "the Lanham Act does not create a cause of action for 'plagiarism,' that is, 'the use of otherwise unprotected works and inventions without attribution;'" *Williams v. UMG,* 281 F.Supp.2d 1177 (C.D.Cal.2003)(rejecting "reverse passing off" claim when film writer and director's name was left off the credits of a documentary on which he collaborated; court acknowledged that Ninth Circuit precedent had recognized such claims in similar contexts, but that *Dastar* now "precludes plaintiff's Lanham Act claim" in still-copyrighted as well as public domain works); *Hustlers v. Thomasson,* 73 U.S.P.Q.2d 1923 (N.D.Ga. 2004) (holding that *Dastar*'s limitation of false designation of origin claims to the producer of physical copies bars not only claims by authors, but also by publishers; the court also follows *Williams v. UMG Recordings* in holding *Dastar* not limited to works in the public domain); *Mays & Assoc. v. Euler,* 370 F.Supp.2d 362 (D.Md.2005) (after *Dastar*, no Lanham Act claim for non-attribution of authorship of web design portfolio); *JB Oxford & Co. v. First Tenn. Bank Nat'l Ass'n.,* 427 F.Supp.2d 784 (M.D.Tenn.2006) (no § 43(a) claim against advertiser who allegedly copied plaintiff's advertisement and substituted its name for plaintiff's). *See also Wilchcombe v. Teevee Toons, Inc.,* 2007 WL 438296 (N.D.Ga.2007), (entertaining § 43(a)(1)(B) claim brought by a co-author allegedly improperly credited on a CD's liner notes, but rejecting the claim on the merits, on the grounds that plaintiff failed to prove he was a commercial creditor of the defendants; that the CD insert containing the inaccurate co-authorship information did not qualify as commercial advertising or promotion because "the public received the CD inserts only after buying the Album, and therefore they could not have had a material effect on purchasing decisions".)

For critiques of *Dastar* and its implications for authors and the public, see, e.g., F. Gregory Lastowka, *The Trademarks Function of Authorship*, 85 B.U. L. Rev. 1171 (2005); Jane C. Ginsburg, *The Right to Claim Authorship in United States Trademark and Copyright Law*, 41 U. HOUS. L. REV. 263 (2004).

QUESTIONS

1. Octavian, Antony, and Lepidus have co-authored several editions of a Roman Law casebook. The book is a best-seller in a limited market. For the most recent edition, however, the authors have had a falling-out, and Lepidus has not participated in the latest revision. If Lepidus' name nonetheless remains on the book cover and inside title pages, would he have any Lanham Act claim to compel its removal? If his name is omitted from the cover and title pages, would he have any Lanham Act claim to compel its reinstatement?

2. After *Dastar*, would it matter that ABC retained the title "*Monty Python's* Flying Circus" (emphasis added)? Would broadcasting an altered version thus be a "false designation of origin"? Would it be a "false or misleading description of fact . . . which is likely to cause . . . mistake or to deceive as to [Monty Python's] approval" of the ABC broadcast?

3. Would using Monty Python's name for ABC's truncated broadcast be a "misrepresent[ation of] the nature" of the program? In the latter case, would that misrepresentation have occurred "in commercial advertising or promotion," as required by § 43(a)(1)(B)? Is *Antidote* correct that a § 43(a)(1)(B) claim is simply an end-run around the unavailability of a § 43(a)(1)(A) claim, and ought accordingly to be dismissed? Are the interests underlying those claims identical?

4. *Dastar* declares that reading section 43(a) to create a claim against plagiarism would be inconsistent with the Supreme Court's opinions in *Wal–Mart v. Samara Brothers* and *TrafFix* (both *supra* Chapter 7), and *Bonito Boats* (*supra* Chapter 1). Can you distinguish those cases?

5. *Dastar* addressed a claim of "reverse passing off." Would it make a difference if the claim were for traditional passing off? Suppose the discovery of an obscure anonymous 16th-century English play, falsely published as a newly-unearthed work of Shakespeare. Has the publisher violated § 43(a)(1)(A)? Has it violated any other provision of the Lanham Act?

King v. Innovation Books

976 F.2d 824 (2d Cir.1992).

■ MINER, CIRCUIT JUDGE:

Defendants-appellants, Allied Vision, Ltd. and New Line Cinema Corporation, appeal from an order of the United States District Court for the

Southern District of New York (Motley, J.) granting a preliminary injunction in favor of plaintiff-appellee Stephen King in connection with King's claims under the Lanham Act and New York law. King, who is the author of such best-selling horror thrillers as *The Shining, Carrie* and *Salem's Lot*, contended that Allied and New Line falsely designated him as the originator of the motion picture "The Lawnmower Man," which was produced by Allied and distributed in North America by New Line. The injunction, which prohibits any use of King's name "on or in connection with" the movie, encompasses two forms of credit to which King objected: (i) a possessory credit, describing the movie as "Stephen King's The Lawnmower Man," and (ii) a "based upon" credit, representing that the movie is "based upon" a short story by King. For the reasons that follow, we affirm the district court's order to the extent that it prohibits use of the possessory credit, but reverse the order to the extent that it prohibits use of the "based upon" credit.

BACKGROUND

In 1970, King wrote a short story entitled "The Lawnmower Man" (the "Short Story"). The Short Story, published in 1975 and running about ten printed pages in length, involves Harold Parkette, a homeowner in the suburbs. Parkette begins to neglect his lawn after an incident in which the boy who usually mows his lawn mows over a cat. By the time Parkette focuses his attention again on his overgrown lawn, the boy has gone away to college. Parkette therefore hires a new man to mow his lawn. The lawnmower man turns out to be a cleft-footed, obese and vile agent of the pagan god Pan. The lawnmower man also is able to move the lawnmower psychokinetically (that is, by sheer force of mind).

After starting the lawnmower, the lawnmower man removes his clothing and crawls after the running mower on his hands and knees, eating both grass and a mole that the mower has run over. Parkette, who is watching in horror, phones the police. Using his psychokinetic powers, however, the lawnmower man directs the lawnmower after Parkette, who is chopped up by the lawnmower's blades after being chased through his house. The Short Story ends with the discovery by the police of Parkette's entrails in the birdbath behind the home.

In 1978, King assigned to Great Fantastic Picture Corporation the motion picture and television rights for the Short Story. The assignment agreement, which provided that it was to be governed by the laws of England, allowed the assignee the "exclusive right to deal with the [Short Story] as [it] may think fit," including the rights

> (i) to write film treatments [and] scripts and other dialogue versions of all descriptions of the [Short Story] and at all times to add to[,] take from[,] use[,] alter[,] adapt ... and change the [Short Story] and the title[,] characters[,] plot[,] theme[,] dialogue[,] sequences and situations thereof. ...

(ii) to make or produce films of all kinds ... incorporating or based upon the [Short Story] or any part or parts thereof or any adaptation thereof.

In return, King received an interest in the profits of "each" film "based upon" the Short Story.

In February 1990, Great Fantastic transferred its rights under the assignment agreement to Allied, a movie production company.... In May 1990, Allied commissioned a screenplay for a feature-length film entitled "The Lawnmower Man." The screenplay was completed by August 1990, and pre-production work on the movie began in January 1991. By February 1991, Allied began to market the forthcoming movie by placing advertisements in trade magazines and journals.

The picture generally was described as "Stephen King's The Lawnmower Man," and as "based upon" a short story by King. Actual filming of the movie began in May 1991. About one month later, Allied ... licensed New Line ... to distribute the movie in North America....

King learned of the forthcoming movie in early October 1991, from an article in a film magazine. He then contacted Rand Holston, an agent handling King's film rights, in an attempt to gather information about the film; asked Chuck Verrill, his literary agent, to obtain a "rough cut" of the movie; and instructed Jay Kramer, his lawyer, to inform Allied that King did not like the idea of a possessory credit (a form of credit apparently portended by the article).

By letter dated October 9, 1991, Kramer advised Allied that King "did not want" a possessory credit to appear on the film. Kramer also requested a copy of the movie and the tentative movie credits King was to receive. In another letter to Allied dated October 21, 1991 ... Kramer advised that "we emphatically object" to the possessory credit contained in the screenplay, and noted that he had yet to receive a copy of the tentative credits.

It appears that King learned of New Line's involvement with the film in November 1991. On King's direction, Verrill contacted New Line for a copy of the film. Verrill was informed that a copy would not be available until January 1992. Verrill contacted New Line again on February 6, 1992, but this produced no copy of the film either. Kramer and Holston shortly advised New Line, in a February 18, 1992 telephone call with New Line's President of Production Sara Risher, that King was "outraged" that the movie was being described as "Stephen King's The Lawnmower Man."

In a February 28, 1992 letter, Kramer again insisted to Risher that the possessory credit was a "complete misrepresentation," and attached copies of the October 1991 letters sent to Allied. As of this time, New Line had paid the balance of the price due to Allied for purchase of the distribution rights, had expended about $7.5 million in advertising and marketing costs, and had become committed to release the movie in theaters throughout North America.

On March 3, 1992, four days or so before release of the movie in theaters, King viewed a copy of the movie in a screening arranged by Allied and New Line. The protagonist of the two hour movie is Dr. Lawrence Angelo. Experimenting with chimpanzees, Dr. Angelo develops a technology, based on computer simulation, known as "Virtual Reality," which allows a chimp to enter a three-dimensional computer environment simulating various action scenarios. Dr. Angelo hopes to adapt the technology for human use, with the ultimate goal of accelerating and improving human intelligence.

Eventually, Dr. Angelo begins experimenting with his technology on Jobe, who mows lawns in Dr. Angelo's neighborhood and is referred to as "the lawnmower man." Jobe, a normal-looking young man, is simple and possesses a childlike mentality. Dr. Angelo is able greatly to increase Jobe's intellect with Virtual Reality technology. However, the experiment spins out of control, with Jobe becoming hostile and violent as his intelligence and mental abilities become super-human. In the build-up to the movie's climax, Jobe employs his newly acquired psychokinetic powers to chase Dr. Angelo's neighbor (a man named Harold Parkette) through his house with a running lawnmower, and to kill him. The police discover the dead man's remains in the birdbath behind his home, and, in the climax of the movie, Dr. Angelo destroys Jobe . . . .

DISCUSSION

.   .   .   .

I.   *Likelihood of Success on the Merits* . . .

A.   *The Possessory Credit*

We perceive no error in the district court's conclusion that King is likely to succeed on the merits of his objection to the possessory credit. The district court was entirely entitled to conclude, from the testimony at the preliminary injunction hearing, that a possessory credit ordinarily is given to the producer, director or writer of the film; and that the credit at a minimum refers to an individual who had some involvement in, and/or gave approval to, the screenplay or movie itself. In contrast to other films for which he has been given a possessory credit, King had no involvement in, and gave no approval of, "The Lawnmower Man" screenplay or movie.

Under the circumstances, therefore, the arguments advanced by Allied and New Line as to why the possessory credit is not false, that the other movie credits make clear that King was not the producer, director or writer of the film, and that King has in the past received a possessory credit where he merely approved in advance of the screenplay or movie, do not alter the conclusion that King is likely to succeed on his challenge to the possessory credit. Appellants also contend that King offered no evidence of public confusion in relation to the possessory credit. As will be detailed in our discussion of irreparable harm, however, there was some such evidence offered. In any event, as the district court recognized, no evidence of public confusion is required where, as is the case with the possessory credit, the attribution is false on its face.

B. *The "Based Upon" Credit*

As the district court recognized, a "based upon" credit by definition affords more "leeway" than a possessory credit. The district court nevertheless concluded that the "based upon" credit at issue here is misleading and likely to cause confusion to the public, reasoning in essence that the "climactic scene from the Short Story is inserted into the film in a manner wholly unrelated to the Plot of the film," and that the credit "grossly exaggerates" the relationship between the Short Story and the film. . . . We believe that in so heavily weighing the proportion of the film attributable to the Short Story in the course of finding the "based upon" credit to be misleading and confusing, the district court applied a standard without sufficient support in the testimony and applicable law.

John Breglio, an attorney of the law firm of Paul, Weiss, Rifkind, Wharton & Garrison specializing in entertainment law, testified as an expert witness for King. Breglio opined that the term "based upon," in the context of royalty obligations under King's assignment agreement, was not identical to the term "based upon" in a movie credit. After speaking of a test of "substantial similarity" between the literary work and movie, and opining that there was not substantial similarity between the Short Story and the film, Breglio went on to state that the industry standard for determining the meaning of a "based upon" movie credit is very similar to that used by copyright lawyers in examining issues of copyright infringement. Breglio further explained that this standard involved looking "at the work as a whole and how much protected material from the underlying work appears in the derivative work."

Indeed, in cases of alleged copyright infringement it has long been appropriate to examine the quantitative and qualitative degree to which the allegedly infringed work has been borrowed from, and not simply the proportion of the allegedly infringing work that is made up of the copyrighted material. [citations omitted] Accordingly, the propriety of the "based upon" credit should have been evaluated with less emphasis on the proportion of the film attributable to the Short Story, and with more emphasis on the proportion, in quantitative and qualitative terms, of the Short Story appearing in the film. Where a movie draws in material respects from a literary work, both quantitatively and qualitatively, a "based upon" credit should not be viewed as misleading absent persuasive countervailing facts and circumstances. Our concern is the possibility that under the district court's apparent approach, substantially all of a literary work could be taken for use in a film and, if unrelated ideas, themes and scenes are tacked on or around the extracted work, a "based upon" credit would be deemed misleading. In the case before us, the apparent "core" of the ten page Short Story, a scene in which a character called "the lawnmower man" uses psychokinetic powers to chase another character through his house with a running lawnmower and thereby kill him, is used in the movie. In both the movie and the Short Story, the remains of the murdered man (who is named Harold Parkette in both works) are found in the birdbath by the police; the two police officers in both works have the same names and engage in substantially similar dialogue. As King himself described it, "the core of my story, such as it is, is in the movie." The red lawnmower seen in the movie also appears to be as described in the Short Story. A brief reference to the Pan mythology of the Short Story appears in the movie as well; dialogue between Jobe and another character includes a reference to "Pan pipes of the little people in the grass."

We recognize that several important and entertaining aspects of the Short Story were not used in the film, and that conversely the film contains a number of elements not to be found in the Short Story. However, when the resemblances between the Short Story and the motion picture at issue here are considered together, they establish to our satisfaction that the movie draws in sufficiently material respects on the Short Story in both qualitative and quantitative aspects. Nor are there any persuasive countervailing facts or circumstances in the record to lead us away from the conclusion that the "based upon" credit is proper in this case. King himself apparently was not bothered much (if at all) by the "based upon" credit, in marked contrast to his sustained and strong objections to the possessory credit, until shortly before he initiated this suit. He has not pointed us to evidence in the record of industry or public perception of, or confusion over, the "based upon" credit beyond the thoughts offered by Breglio. Professor George Stade, Vice Chairman of the English Department at Columbia University and King's other expert witness, did opine that, despite similarities, the movie was not based upon the Short Story. However, even Professor Stade indicated at one point in his testimony that "substantial" portions of the Short Story appear in the film. . . .

It is undoubtedly the case that King's assignment agreement does not permit Allied to use King's name fraudulently, and we express no view as to the degree of overlap between the term "based upon" in the King assignment agreement and the term "based upon" in a theatrical credit. However, we do note that the agreement contemplates substantial alterations to the Short Story, and even obligates Allied to give King credit in the case of a film "based wholly or substantially upon" the Short Story. We think that King would have cause to complain if he were *not* afforded the "based upon" credit.

Miramax Films Corp. v. Columbia Pictures Ent., 996 F.Supp. 294 (S.D.N.Y.1998). The producers of the very successful horror film, Scream, directed by Wes Craven, brought a § 43(a) false advertising claim against the producers of another horror film, I Know What You Did Last Summer, which the defendants touted as "From the Creator of Scream," and "From the Creator of Scream Comes a New Chapter in Terror," and "Last Time He Made You Scream, This Time You Won't Have the Chance." In fact, Wes Craven did not direct Summer; the only link between the films was the screenwriter, who created an original screenplay for Scream, and adapted a novel for Summer. The screenwriter did not identify himself as the "creator" of either film, but affirmed that Craven "is the person most reasonably perceived to be the 'creator' of Scream." The court credited survey evidence that showed that many respondents thought Summer had been produced or directed by the producers or director of Scream, and that only 2% of the respondents believed that the common link between the films was the screenwriter. Reviewing prior related cases, including *King v. Innovation Books,* and *Allen v. National Video,* 610 F.Supp. 612 (S.D.N.Y. 1985) (excerpted *infra,* Chapter 10.B), the court concluded that:

> The harm which presumptively faced King and Allen is present here, namely the wrongful attribution of responsibility for a movie over which plaintiff has no control and the potential for loss of reputation with the public. The fact that the designation of origin in *King* was literally false, whereas the designation here is misleading, does not diminish the likelihood that plaintiff has been harmed; nor does the fact that in both *King* and *Allen* the designation was to a named person, whereas here it is to the more ambiguous "creator" of "Scream." The fact that the false designation in *King* was literally false and referred by name to Stephen King is relevant to the determination of whether the designation was "likely to cause confusion" within the meaning of 15 U.S.C. § 1125(a)(1)(A). . . . Although plaintiff cannot rely on the presumption of confusion which would be available in a case of literal falseness such as *King*, plaintiff has affirmatively demonstrated that defendants' advertisements have confused consumers in the relevant market about the source of "Summer." The type of harm which flows from this confusion does not depend on whether the confusion results from a literally false designation of origin as opposed to a "misleading" designation of origin. While a literally false designation might, depending on the circumstances of any given case, be presumed to cause a greater degree of harm, it is the type of harm—not its degree—that permits the reviewing court to presume irreparable injury.

QUESTION

Is the "type of harm" at issue in *King* and *Miramax* still cognizable after *Dastar*? Under what section of the Lanham Act?

B.   RIGHT OF PUBLICITY

An accoutrement of celebrity is the ability to exploit the commercial value of one's identity. For example, a rock band might sell posters, t-shirts, and buttons adorned with its logo and with the images and names of the performers. *See, e.g., Bi–Rite Enterprises v. Button Master*, 555 F.Supp. 1188 (S.D.N.Y.1983). Celebrity identity can extend beyond name and image to vocal style, and even to phrases long associated with the individual. *See, e.g., Midler v. Ford Motor Co.*, 849 F.2d 460 (9th Cir.1988) (vocal identity); *Carson v. Here's Johnny Portable Toilets, Inc.*, 698 F.2d 831 (6th Cir.1983) ("Heeeeeeere's Johnny").

The coverage that trademark law affords against unlicensed exploitations of identity, however, does not fully correspond to the interests the celebrity seeks to protect, because the underlying policies of trademark law seek to ensure accuracy of source identification, rather than to secure rights in identifying symbols *in gross*. Thus, if the use of a rock band's logo on a button suggests that the goods came from or were authorized by that group, the Lanham Act will provide relief. Where, however, the use of a rock band's logo on a button is deemed to perform the informational function of identifying the group, without misleading consumers as to the provenance or approval of the button, there is no violation of the Lanham Act. The *Bi–Rite* decision illustrates this distinction:

> Functionality in this context means that consumers desire the mark for its intrinsic value and not as a designation of origin. [Citations omitted]. When a mark ... is exploited [by third parties] for its intrinsic value, Congress has implicitly determined that society's interest in free competition overrides the owner's interest in reaping monopoly rewards.

555 F.Supp. 1188 (S.D.N.Y.1983). Put another way, "allegiance" uses of celebrity names arguably do not use those names *as a trademark* for the goods (t-shirts, etc.) brandishing the names, and therefore do not infringe the mark. For the debate over whether liability arises only from use as a mark, as opposed to capitalizing on goodwill, see *supra*, Chapter 6.A.3. See also *infra*, Chapter 12, *Trademarks as Speech*.

The "right of publicity", developed most extensively by California courts and adopted in some form in many other states (there is at present no federal right of publicity statute), affords more sweeping protection to the commercial interest that a celebrity has cultivated in his identity. It grants to that person an exclusive right to control the commercial value of his name and likeness and to prevent others from exploiting that value without permission. The right of publicity recognizes the investment that a person makes in developing a public image, and it prevents unjust enrichment by others who would exploit the resulting goodwill.

An individual claiming a violation of his right of publicity must show: (1) that the defendant used his name or likeness; (2) that the appropriation of his name or likeness was to the "defendant's advantage, commercially or otherwise"; (3) that he did not consent to this use; and (4) that he suffered an "injury" as a result. Laws v. Sony Music Entertainment, Inc., 448 F.3d 1134, 1138 (9th Cir. 2006).

A celebrity can normally establish publicity value for his identity. The notion of identity extends to groups just the same as it does to individuals, provided that the group in question has established a primary identity such as a rock band. Neither courts nor state statutes have extended this protection of identity to corporate entities, however. In the materials that follow, consider the differences in rationale and scope between trademark claims and right of publicity claims invoking protection of personally identifying indicia.

Allen v. National Video, Inc.

610 F.Supp. 612 (S.D.N.Y.1985).

■ MOTLEY, CHIEF DISTRICT JUDGE:

This case arises because plaintiff, to paraphrase Groucho Marx, wouldn't belong to any video club that would have him as a member. More precisely, plaintiff sues over an advertisement for defendant National Video (National) in which defendant Boroff, allegedly masquerading as plaintiff, portrays a satisfied holder of National's movie rental V.I.P. Card. Plaintiff asserts that the advertisement appropriates his face and implies his endorsement, and that it therefore violates his statutory right to privacy, his right to publicity, and the federal Lanham Act's prohibition of misleading advertising. Plaintiff, basing jurisdiction on diversity of citizenship, seeks an injunction against Boroff and defendant Smith, Boroff's agent, and damages against all defendants.

Defendants, while conceding that Boroff looks remarkably like plaintiff, deny that the advertisement appropriates plaintiff's likeness or that it poses a likelihood of consumer confusion. In addition, defendants Smith and Boroff seek indemnity under an alleged contract with defendant National, and charge that National violated Boroff's own privacy rights and breached the contract in using Boroff's picture without a required disclaimer and by placing it in media not authorized by the contract. National disputes that it ever entered into the alleged contract, and claims instead to have a general release from Boroff.

. . . .

Facts

The following facts are not in dispute. Plaintiff Woody Allen is a film director, writer, actor, and comedian. Among the films plaintiff has directed are "Annie Hall," which won several Academy Awards, "Manhattan," "Bananas," "Sleeper," "Broadway Danny Rose," and, most recently, "The Purple Rose of Cairo." In addition to being a critically successful artist, plaintiff has for more than 15 years been a major international celebrity. Although he has not often lent his name to commercial endeavors other than his own projects, plaintiff's many years in show business have made his name and his face familiar to millions of people. This familiarity, and plaintiff's reputation for artistic integrity, have significant, exploitable, commercial value.

The present action arises from an advertisement, placed by National to promote its nationally franchised video rental chain, containing a photograph of defendant Boroff taken on September 2, 1983. The photograph portrays a customer in a National Video store, an individual in his forties, with a high forehead, tousled hair, and heavy black glasses. The customer's elbow is on the counter, and his face, bearing an expression at once quizzical and somewhat smug, is leaning on his hand. It is not disputed that, in general, the physical features and pose are characteristic of plaintiff.

The staging of the photograph also evokes associations with plaintiff. Sitting on the counter are videotape cassettes of "Annie Hall" and "Bananas," two of plaintiff's best known films, as well as "Casablanca" and "The Maltese Falcon." The latter two are Humphrey Bogart films of the 1940's associated with plaintiff primarily because of his play and film "Play It Again, Sam," in which the spirit of Bogart appears to the character played by Allen and offers him romantic advice. In addition, the title "Play It Again, Sam" is a famous, although inaccurate, quotation from "Casablanca."

The individual in the advertisement is holding up a National Video V.I.P. Card, which apparently entitles the bearer to favorable terms on movie rentals. The woman behind the counter is smiling at the customer and appears to be gasping in exaggerated excitement at the presence of a celebrity.

The photograph was used in an advertisement which appeared in the March 1984 issue of "Video Review," a magazine published in New York and distributed in the Southern District, and in the April 1984 issue of "Take One," an in-house publication which National distributes of its franchisees across the country. The headline on the advertisement reads "Become a V.I.P. at National Video. We'll Make You Feel Like a Star." The copy goes on to explain that holders of the V.I.P. card receive "hassle-free movie renting" and "special savings" and concludes that "you don't need a famous face to be treated to some pretty famous service."

The same photograph and headline were also used on countercards distributed to National's franchisees. Although the advertisement that ran in "Video Review" contained a disclaimer in small print reading "Celebrity double provided by Ron Smith's Celebrity Look–Alike's, Los Angeles, Calif.," no such disclaimer appeared in the other versions of the advertisement.

. . . .

Plaintiff maintains that these undisputed facts require the court to enter summary judgment for him on his right to privacy, right of publicity, and Lanham Act claims. He urges the court to find, as a matter of law, that defendants used his picture or portrait for commercial purposes without his permission, and that the advertisements were materially misleading and likely to result in consumer confusion as to his endorsement of National's services.

Defendants insist that other disputed facts require denial of plaintiff's motion. Although defendants concede that they sought to evoke by reference plaintiff's general persona, they strenuously deny that they intended to imply that the person in the photograph was actually plaintiff or that plaintiff endorsed National.... According to defendants, the idea of the advertisement is that even people who are *not* stars are *treated* like stars at National Video. They insist that the advertisement depicts a "Woody Allen fan," so dedicated that he has adopted his idol's appearance and mannerisms, who is able to live out his fantasy by receiving star treatment at

National Video. The knowing viewer is supposed to be amused that the counter person actually believes that the customer is Woody Allen.

Defendants urge that this interpretation cannot be rejected as a matter of law, and that if defendant Boroff merely appeared as someone who looks like Woody Allen, but not as Woody Allen himself, then plaintiff's rights were not violated. Defendants further seek summary judgment against plaintiff on the basis that plaintiff has offered no actual evidence that anyone was actually deceived into thinking that the photograph was of him. . . . Smith and Boroff further urge that they never misrepresented Boroff as plaintiff, that they had insisted that National include a disclaimer in all advertisements using the photo, and they are therefore guilty of no wrongful conduct and cannot be held liable for the misdeeds of National.

.   .   .   .

[The court declined to award Allen summary judgment on his New York privacy and publicity claims, on the ground that the N.Y. Civil Rights statute protects rights in the plaintiff's "portrait or picture"; when a look-alike portrays a celebrity, a reasonable jury could find that the advertisement did not display Allen's likeness, but that of the look-alike.]

Lanham Act Claim

Plaintiff seeks summary judgment on his claim under section 43(a) of the federal Lanham Act, 15 U.S.C. section 1125(a) (West 1982) ("the Act"), which prohibits false descriptions of products or their origins. . . .

The Act has . . . been held to apply to situations that would not qualify formally as trademark infringement, but that involve unfair competitive practices resulting in actual or potential deception. To make out a cause of action under the Act, plaintiff must establish three elements: 1) involvement of goods or services, 2) effect on interstate commerce, and 3) a false designation of origin or false description of the goods or services.

Application of the act is limited, however, to potential deception which threatens economic interests analogous to those protected by trademark law. One such interest is that of the public to be free from harmful deception. Another interest, which provides plaintiff here with standing, is that of the "trademark" holder in the value of his distinctive mark. . . .

A celebrity has a . . . commercial investment in the "drawing power" of his or her name and face in endorsing products and in marketing a career. The celebrity's investment depends upon the good will of the public, and infringement of the celebrity's rights also implicates the public's interest in being free from deception when it relies on a public figure's endorsement in an advertisement. The underlying purposes of the Lanham Act therefore appear to be implicated in cases of misrepresentations regarding the endorsement of goods and services.

The Act's prohibitions, in fact, have been held to apply to misleading statements that a product or service has been endorsed by a public figure. In *Geisel v. Poynter Products, Inc.*, 283 F. Supp. 261 (S.D.N.Y.1968), plaintiff, the well-known children's book author and artist known as "Dr. Seuss," sought to enjoin the use of his distinctive pseudonym in connection with dolls based on his characters. The court held that "a 'false representation,' whether express or implied, that a product was authorized or approved by a particular person is actionable under [the Act]." The court further held that liability attached not just for descriptions that are literally false, but for those that create a "false impression." *Geisel,* 283 F. Supp. at 267. "The plaintiff is not required to prove actual palming off. A showing of the likelihood of consumer confusion as to the source of the goods is sufficient." *Id.* (citation omitted). Finally, the court held that a showing of actual consumer deception was not required in order to [justify] injunctive relief under the Act, so long as a "tendency to deceive" was demonstrated. *Id.* at 268.

In *Cher v. Forum International, Ltd.,* 213 U.S.P.Q. 96 (C.D.Cal.1982), plaintiff, a popular singer and actress, brought a similar Lanham Act claim. Plaintiff sued when an interview she had granted to "US" magazine was sold to "Forum" magazine, a publication of Penthouse International. "Forum" published the interview and advertised it widely, falsely implying that plaintiff read and endorsed "Forum" and had granted the magazine an exclusive interview. *Id.* at 99–100. The court held that the Act "extends to misrepresentations in advertising as well as labeling of products and services in commerce", *id.* at 102, and noted that no finding of an actual trademark is required under the Act. *Id.* "The Lanham Act proscribes any false designation or representation in connection with any goods or services in interstate commerce," a standard which plaintiff Cher had met. *Id.*

Geisel and *Cher* suggest that the unauthorized use of a person's name or photograph in a manner that creates the false impression that the party has endorsed a product or service in interstate commerce violates the Lanham Act. Application of this standard to the case at bar, however, is complicated by defendants' use of a look-alike for plaintiff, rather than plaintiff's actual photograph, as in *Cher,* or pseudonym, as in *Geisel.* Unlike the state law privacy claim . . ., the plaintiff's Lanham Act theory does not require the court to find that defendant Boroff's photograph is, as a matter of law, plaintiff's "portrait or picture." The court must nevertheless decide whether defendant's advertisement creates the likelihood of consumer confusion over whether plaintiff endorsed or was otherwise involved with National Video's goods and services. *See Geisel,* 283 F. Supp. at 267.[8]

This inquiry requires the court to consider whether the look-alike employed is sufficiently similar to plaintiff to create such a likelihood—an

---

8. The court rejects defendants' argument that the perception that plaintiff appeared in National's advertisement does not give rise to an inference that he endorses their product. It is disingenuous to suggest that consumers would assume no more than that plaintiff had been hired as an actor. When a public figure of Woody Allen's stature appears in an advertisement, his mere presence is inescapably to be interpreted as an endorsement. *Cf. Negri v. Schering Corp.,* 333 F. Supp. 102, 105 (1971); *Onassis v. Christian Dior N.Y., Inc.,* 122 Misc. 603, 472 N.Y.S.2d 254, 258–59 (S. Ct. N.Y. Co. 1983). Moreover, defendant's pose in National's advertisement—smiling at the camera while holding up the V.I.P. card—is the classic stance of the product spokesperson.

inquiry much like that made in cases involving similar, but not identical, trademarks. The court therefore finds it helpful, in applying the likelihood of confusion standard to the facts of this case, to refer to traditional trademark analysis. . . .

The first factor . . . , the strength of plaintiff's mark, concerns the extent to which plaintiff has developed a favorable association for his mark in the public's mind. There is no dispute that plaintiff's name and likeness are well-known to the public, and that he has built up a considerable investment in his unique, positive public image. Plaintiff's "mark", to analogize from trademark law, is a strong one.

The similarity of the "marks"—*i.e.*, the similarity of plaintiff to defendant Boroff . . . has already been addressed above. While the court was unable to hold that defendant Boroff's photograph was as a matter of law plaintiff's portrait or picture, the resemblance between the two is strong and not disputed.

Under the third factor, proximity of the products, the court notes that while plaintiff does not own a video rental chain, he is involved in producing and distributing his own motion pictures, and he is strongly identified with movies in the public mind. The audience at which National Video's advertisement was aimed—movie watchers—is therefore the same audience to which plaintiff's own commercial efforts are directed. There is no requirement under the Act that plaintiff and defendant actually be in competition.

The court has declined to rely on plaintiff's proffered consumer survey, and plaintiff has submitted no other evidence of actual confusion. . . . [S]uch evidence, although highly probative of likelihood of confusion, is not required.

The sophistication of the relevant consuming public is measured under the fifth factor. The average reader of "Video Review" or customer of National Video is likely to be comparatively sophisticated about movies, such that a good number of them arguably would realize that plaintiff did not actually appear in the photograph. This is relevant to the question of whether the advertisement contained plaintiff's "portrait or picture." However, given the close resemblance between defendant Boroff's photograph and plaintiff, there is no reason to believe that the audience's relative sophistication eliminates all likelihood of confusion; at a cursory glance, many consumers, even sophisticated ones, are likely to be confused.

The final factor is the good or bad faith of defendants. While plaintiff has not established that defendants acted intentionally to fool people into thinking that plaintiff actually appeared in the advertisement, defendants admit that they designed the advertisement intentionally to evoke an association with plaintiff. They must therefore at least have been aware of the risk of consumer confusion, which militates against a finding that their motives were completely innocent. . . . The failure of defendant National to include any disclaimer on all but one of the uses of the photograph also supports a finding of, at best, dubious motives.

A review of all these factors leads the court to the inescapable conclusion that defendants' use of Boroff's photograph in their advertisement creates a likelihood of consumer confusion over plaintiff's endorsement or involvement. In reaching this conclusion, the court notes several distinctions between plaintiff's Lanham Act and privacy claims which make this case more appropriate for resolution under the Lanham Act.

First and most important, the likelihood of confusion standard applied herein is broader than the strict "portrait or picture" standard under the Civil Rights Law. Evocation of plaintiff's general persona is not enough to make out a violation of section 51, but it may create a likelihood of confusion under the Lanham Act. As the Second Circuit held in the trademark context, "In order to be confused, a consumer need not believe that the owner of the mark actually produced the item and placed it on the market. The public's belief that the mark's owner sponsored or otherwise approved the use satisfies the confusion requirement." *Dallas Cowboys Cheerleaders, Inc. v. Pussycat Cinema, Ltd.*, 604 F.2d 200, 204–05 (2d Cir.1979) (citations omitted). *See also Estate of Elvis Presley v. Russen*, 513 F. Supp. 1339, 1371 (D.N.J.1981). Similarly, even if the public does not believe that plaintiff actually appeared in the photograph, it may be led to believe by the intentional reference to plaintiff that he is somehow involved in or approves of their product. This broader standard is justified since the Lanham Act seeks to protect not just plaintiff's property interest in his face, but the public's interest in avoiding deception.

Second, the likelihood of confusion standard is easier to satisfy on the facts of this case. Enough people may realize that the figure in the photograph is defendant Boroff to negate the conclusion that it amounts to a "portrait or picture" of plaintiff as a matter of law. All that is necessary to recover under the Act, however, is that a *likelihood* of confusion exists. While defendants, as noted above, have urged an interpretation of the advertisement which might defeat a finding of "portrait or picture," the court finds that no such explanation can remove the likelihood of confusion on the part of "any appreciable number of ordinarily prudent" consumers.

. . . .

In seeking to forestall summary judgment, defendants Smith and Boroff maintain that the disclaimer which they insisted be included in the advertisement would have avoided consumer confusion. The court disagrees. Even with regard to the one version of the advertisement in which the requisite disclaimer was included, there exists a likelihood of consumer confusion. The disclaimer, in tiny print at the bottom of the page, is unlikely to be noticed by most readers as they are leafing through the magazine. Moreover, the disclaimer says only that a celebrity double is being used, which does not in and of itself necessarily dispel the impression that plaintiff is somehow involved with National's products or services. To be effective, a disclaimer would have to be bolder and make clear that plaintiff in no way endorses National, its products, or its services. Having gone to great lengths to evoke plaintiff's image, defendants must do more than pay lip service to avoiding confusion. The disclaimer provided is insufficient as a matter of law.

. . . .

Defendants have argued that any injunction against them must be limited in geographical scope to New York State. While such a limitation might be required for an injunction under the New York Civil Rights Law, given the differences in privacy law among different jurisdictions, an injunction under the Lanham Act need not be so limited. Plaintiff enjoys a nationwide reputation, and defendants advertised a nationally franchised business through a national magazine. The harm sought to be prevented is clearly not limited to the New York area, and the injunction must therefore be national in scope.

Plaintiff seeks an injunction preventing defendants from presenting defendant Boroff as plaintiff in advertising. Defendant Boroff argues that any such injunction would interfere impermissibly with his ability to earn a living and his First Amendment rights. . . . .

What plaintiff legitimately seeks to prevent is not simply defendant Boroff dressing up as plaintiff, but defendant *passing himself off* as plaintiff or an authorized surrogate. Therefore, defendant must be enjoined from appearing in advertising that creates the likelihood that a reasonable person might believe that he was really plaintiff or that plaintiff had approved of his appearance. Defendant may satisfy the injunction by ceasing his work as a Woody Allen look-alike, but he may also satisfy it by simply refusing to collaborate with those advertisers, such as National Video in this case, who recklessly skirt the edges of misrepresentation. Defendant may sell his services as a look-alike in any setting where the overall context makes it completely clear that he is a look-alike and that plaintiff has nothing to do with the project—whether that is accomplished through a bold and unequivocal disclaimer, the staging of the photograph, or the accompanying advertising copy. . . . .

Editors' note: Woody Allen's lawsuits against look-alike Boroff and Ron Smith Celebrity Look–Alike agency did not end with this case. In *Allen v. Men's World*, 679 F.Supp. 360 (S.D.N.Y.1988), Allen prevailed against an advertising agency and its client regarding an advertisement for Men's World depicting an Allen-esque Boroff, this time with a clarinet. The court rejected defendants' contention that res judicata should bar the claim; an earlier contempt action against Smith and Boroff for the Men's World advertisement alleging violation of the *National Video* having failed on what the court deemed "technical" grounds, *Allen v. National Video, Inc.*, No. 84 Civ. 2764 (CBM) (S.D.N.Y. June 25, 1986).

QUESTIONS

1. Judge Motley found that Woody Allen was not entitled to summary judgment on his privacy claim because a reasonable jury could find that others would interpret the advertisement as portraying a Woody Allen look-alike rather than Woody Allen himself. She also found that Woody Allen *was* entitled to summary judgment on his Lanham Act claim because no reasonable jury could find that the ads do not falsely represent that Allen endorsed National Video. Are those two findings consistent?

2. *Allen v. National Video* illustrates successful invocation of the Lanham Act to control rights in likeness, where New York Civil Rights Law failed to secure relief. But how pertinent are the *"Polaroid* factors" to assessing confusion as to personal endorsements?

3. Apple Corps, the licensing agent and business affairs manager for the group The Beatles, has charged Buttonmaster with violation of The Beatles' right of publicity. Buttonmaster has been selling buttons with images of the group, their name, and logo, but claims that it executed agreements with each of the four Beatles before they transferred their rights to Apple Corps. Assuming Buttonmaster had valid agreements with the individual performers, what effect do those agreements have on the right of publicity of the group? *See Apple Corps. Ltd. v. Button Master, P.C.P.,* 47 U.S.P.Q.2d 1236 (E.D.Pa.1998).

Midler v. Ford Motor Co.

849 F.2d 460 (9th Cir.1988).

■ NOONAN, CIRCUIT JUDGE:

This case centers on the protectibility of the voice of a celebrated chanteuse from commercial exploitation without her consent. Ford Motor Company and its advertising agency, Young & Rubicam, Inc., in 1985 advertised the Ford Lincoln Mercury with a series of nineteen 30 or 60 second television commercials in what the agency called "The Yuppie Campaign." The aim was to make an emotional connection with Yuppies, bringing back memories of when they were in college. Different popular songs of the seventies were sung on each commercial. The agency tried to get "the original people," that is, the singers who had popularized the songs, to sing them. Failing in that endeavor in ten cases the agency had the songs sung by "sound-alikes." Bette Midler, the plaintiff and appellant here, was done by a sound-alike.

Midler is a nationally known actress and singer. She won a Grammy as early as 1973 as the Best New Artist of that year. Records made by her since then have gone Platinum and Gold. She was nominated in 1979 for an Academy award for Best Female Actress in *The Rose,* in which she portrayed a pop singer. Time hailed her in its March 2, 1987 issue as "a legend" and "the most dynamic and poignant singer-actress of her time."

When Young & Rubicam was preparing the Yuppie Campaign it presented the commercial to its client by playing an edited version of Midler singing "Do You Want To Dance," taken from the 1973 Midler album, "The Divine Miss M." After the client accepted the idea and form of the commercial, the agency contacted Midler's manager, Jerry Edelstein. The conversation went as follows: "Hello, I am Craig Hazen from Young and Rubicam. I am calling you to find out if Bette Midler would be interested in doing ...?'' Edelstein: "Is it a commercial?" "Yes." "We are not interested."

Undeterred, Young & Rubicam sought out Ula Hedwig whom it knew to have been as one of "the Harlettes" a backup singer for Midler for ten years.

At the direction of Young & Rubicam, Hedwig then made a record for the commercial. The Midler record of "Do You Want To Dance" was first played to her. She was told to "sound as much as possible like the Bette Midler record," leaving out only a few "aahs" unsuitable for the commercial. Hedwig imitated Midler to the best of her ability.

After the commercial was aired Midler was told by "a number of people" that it "sounded exactly" like her record of "Do You Want To Dance." Hedwig was told by "many personal friends" that they thought it was Midler singing the commercial. Ken Fritz, a personal manager in the entertainment business not associated with Midler, declares by affidavit that he heard the commercial on more than one occasion and thought Midler was doing the singing.

Neither the name nor the picture of Midler was used in the commercial; Young & Rubicam had a license from the copyright holder to use the song. At issue in this case is only the protection of Midler's voice. The district court described the defendants' conduct as that "of the average thief. They decided, 'If we can't buy it, we'll take it.' " The court nonetheless believed there was no legal principle preventing imitation of Midler's voice and so gave summary judgment for the defendants. Midler appeals.

The First Amendment protects much of what the media do in the reproduction of likenesses or sounds. A primary value is freedom of speech and press. *Time, Inc. v. Hill,* 385 U.S. 374, 388 (1967). The purpose of the media's use of a person's identity is central. If the purpose is "informative or cultural" the use is immune; "if it serves no such function but merely exploits the individual portrayed, immunity will not be granted." Felcher and Rubin, *Privacy, Publicity and the Portrayal of Real People by the Media,* 88 Yale L.J. 1577 1596 (1979). Moreover, federal copyright law preempts much of the area. "Mere imitation of a recorded performance would not constitute a copyright infringement even where one performer deliberately sets out to simulate another's performance as exactly as possible." Notes of Committee on the Judiciary, 17 U.S.C.A. § 114(b). It is in the context of these First Amendment and federal copyright distinctions that we address the present appeal.

Nancy Sinatra once sued Goodyear Tire and Rubber Company on the basis of an advertising campaign by Young & Rubicam featuring "These Boots Are Made For Walkin'," a song closely identified with her; the female singers of the commercial were alleged to have imitated her voice and style and to have dressed and looked like her. The basis of Nancy Sinatra's complaint was unfair competition; she claimed that the song and the arrangement had acquired "a secondary meaning" which, under California law, was protectible. This court noted that the defendants "had paid a very substantial sum to the copyright proprietor to obtain the license for the use of the song and all of its arrangements." To give Sinatra damages for their use of the song would clash with federal copyright law. Summary judgment for the defendants was affirmed. *Sinatra v. Goodyear Tire & Rubber Co.*, 435 F.2d 711, 717–718 (9th Cir.1970), *cert. denied*, 402 U.S. 906 (1971). If Midler were claiming a secondary meaning to "Do You Want To Dance" or seeking to prevent the defendants from using that song, she would fail like Sinatra. But that is not this case. Midler does not seek damages for Ford's use of "Do You Want To Dance," and thus her claim is not preempted by federal copyright law. A voice is not copyrightable. What is put forward as protectable here is more personal than any work of authorship.

Bert Lahr once sued Adell Chemical Co. for selling Lestoil [cleaning fluid] by means of a commercial in which an imitation of Lahr's voice accompanied a cartoon of a duck. Lahr alleged that his style of vocal delivery was distinctive in pitch, accent, inflection, and sounds. The First Circuit held that Lahr had stated a cause of action for unfair competition, that it could be found "that defendant's conduct saturated plaintiff's audience, curtailing his market." *Lahr v. Adell Chemical Co.*, 300 F.2d 256, 259 (1st Cir.1962). That case is more like this one. But we do not find unfair competition here. One-minute commercials of the sort the defendants put on would not have saturated Midler's audience and curtailed her market. Midler did not do television commercials. The defendants were not in competition with her. *See Halicki v. United Artists Communications, Inc.*, 812 F.2d 1213 (9th Cir.1987).

California Civil Code section 3344 is also of no aid to Midler. The statute affords damages to a person injured by another who uses the person's "name, voice, signature, photograph or likeness, in any manner." The defendants did not use Midler's name or anything else whose use is prohibited by the statute. The voice they used was Hedwig's, not hers. The term "likeness" refers to a visual image not a vocal imitation. The statute, however, does not preclude Midler from pursuing any cause of action she may have at common law; the statute itself implies that such common law causes of action do exist because it says its remedies are merely "cumulative." *Id.* § 3344(g).

The companion statute protecting the use of a deceased person's name, voice, signature, photograph or likeness states that the rights it recognizes are "property rights." *Id.* § 990(b). By analogy the common law rights are also property rights. Appropriation of such common law rights is a tort in California. *Motschenbacher v. R.J. Reynolds Tobacco Co.*, 498 F.2d 821 (9th Cir.1974). In that case what the defendants used in their television commercial for Winston cigarettes was a photograph of a famous professional racing driver's racing car. The number of the car was changed and a wing-like device known as a "spoiler" was attached to the car; the car's features of white pinpointing, an oval medallion, and solid red coloring were retained. The driver, Lothar Motschenbacher, was in the car but his features were not visible. Some persons, viewing the commercial, correctly inferred that the car was his and that he was in the car and was therefore endorsing the product. The defendants were held to have invaded a "proprietary interest" of Motschenbacher in his own identity. *Id.* at 825.

Midler's case is different from Motschenbacher's. He and his car were physically used by the tobacco company's ad; he made part of his living out of giving commercial endorsements. But as Judge Koelsch expressed it in *Motschenbacher,* California will recognize an injury from "an appropriation of the attributes of one's identity." *Id.* at 824. It was irrelevant that Motschenbacher could not be identified in the ad. The ad suggested that it was he. The ad did so by emphasizing signs or symbols associated with him. In the same way the defendants here used an imitation to convey the impression that Midler was singing for them.

Why did the defendants ask Midler to sing if her voice was not of value to them? Why did they studiously acquire the services of a sound-alike and instruct her to imitate Midler if Midler's voice was not of value to them? What they sought was an attribute of Midler's identity. Its value was what the market would have paid for Midler to have sung the commercial in person.

A voice is more distinctive and more personal than the automobile accouterments protected in *Motschenbacher*. A voice is as distinctive and personal as a face. The human voice is one of the most palpable ways identity is manifested. We are all aware that a friend is at once known by a few words on the phone. At a philosophical level it has been observed that with the sound of a voice, "the other stands before me." D. Ihde, *Listening and Voice* 77 (1976). A fortiori, these observations hold true of singing, especially singing by a singer of renown. The singer manifests herself in the song. To impersonate her voice is to pirate her identity.

We need not and do not go so far as to hold that every imitation of a voice to advertise merchandise is actionable. We hold only that when a distinctive voice of a professional singer is widely known and is deliberately imitated in order to sell a product, the sellers have appropriated what is not theirs and have committed a tort in California. Midler has made a showing, sufficient to defeat summary judgment, that the defendants here for their own profit in selling their product did appropriate part of her identity.

Reversed and remanded for trial.

QUESTIONS

1. *Allen* and *Midler* concern the protection of commercial identity against look-alikes and sound-alikes. Curiously, neither case was decided on right-of-publicity grounds. In both instances, the courts determined that the pertinent state right of publicity statutes protected individuals' actual image or voice against appropriation, but did not redress simulations of visual or vocal appearance. In *Allen* the court found a likelihood that readers of the advertisement would believe the look-alike was Allen, or at least appeared with Allen's consent or endorsement, and therefore determined that Lanham Act § 43(a) had been violated. In *Midler,* the court rejected an unfair competition claim on the ground that the producers of the advertisement were not in competition with a plaintiff who "did not do television commercials." (Query whether the court's concept of competition is well-founded.) Instead, the court found misappropriation of a common law "property right" in vocal identity.

As a result, in the two cases *supra* concerning unauthorized exploitation of commercial persona studied here, courts have applied different, arguably inconsistent, bodies of state and federal law. Does this make sense? Do these two cases present qualitatively different issues requiring a diversity of legal regimes?

2. Recall the *Allen* court's discussion of the geographic scope of the injunction. Because the court found a violation of federal law, issuance of a nation-wide injunction would not pose sister-state federalism problems. What if the court had found only a state law violation? For example, suppose that many state right of privacy/publicity statutes prohibit only appropriation of a celebrity's actual image, but some state statutes also reach look-alikes. What, if any, geographic limits should a court place on a state-law injunction against unauthorized commercial exploitation of a look-alike? Should Congress federalize the right of publicity?

3. What are examples of *permissible* unauthorized exploitations of celebrity look-alikes or sound-alikes?

4. Nova Wines has for many years sold California wines under a variety of brand names associated with Marilyn Monroe, including "Marilyn Merlot" and the "Velvet Collection," featuring photographs of Marilyn Monroe on the labels. Nova holds an exclusive license to use, on wine, the registered trademark "Marilyn Monroe," as well as common law trademarks for Monroe's name, image and likeness from the Monroe estate. It has been the sole winery using photographs of Marilyn Monroe on wine for nearly twenty years, and this trade dress has achieved secondary meaning. Rival winery Adler Fels has obtained a copyright license from the photographer who created the images used on the Nova labels, and has begun selling a "Red Velvet Collection" of wine whose labels feature one of the same photographs as used on the Nova "Velvet Collection" labels. In response to Nova's trademark and right of publicity claims, Adler Fels invokes its right under copyright law to reproduce and distribute copies of the image it licensed from the photographer. How should the court resolve the alleged conflict between copyright and trademark-publicity rights? See *Nova Wines, Inc. v. Adler Fels Winery LLC*, 467 F.Supp.2d 965 (N.D.Cal.2006), *infra* Chapter 13.A.

White v. Samsung Electronics America, Inc.

971 F.2d 1395 (9th Cir.1992), *petition for rehearing and rehearing en banc denied*, 989 F.2d 1512 (9th Cir.), *cert. denied*, 508 U.S. 951, 113 S.Ct. 2443, 124 L.Ed.2d 660 (1993).

■ GOODWIN, CIRCUIT JUDGE:

This case involves a promotional "fame and fortune" dispute. In running a particular advertisement without Vanna White's permission, defendants Samsung Electronics America, Inc. (Samsung) and David Deutsch Associates, Inc. (Deutsch) attempted to capitalize on White's fame to enhance their fortune. White sued, alleging infringement of various intellectual property rights, but the district court granted summary judgment in favor of the defendants. We affirm in part, reverse in part, and remand.

Plaintiff Vanna White is the hostess of *"Wheel of Fortune,"* one of the most popular game shows in television history. An estimated forty million people watch the program daily. Capitalizing on the fame which her participation in the show has bestowed on her, White markets her identity to various advertisers.

The dispute in this case arose out of a series of advertisements prepared for Samsung by Deutsch. The series ran in at least half a dozen publications with widespread, and in some cases national, circulation. Each of the advertisements in the series followed the same theme. Each depicted a current item from popular culture and a Samsung electronic product. Each was set in the twenty-first century and conveyed the message that the Samsung product would still be in use by that time. By hypothesizing outrageous future outcomes for the cultural items, the ads created humorous effects. For example, one lampooned current popular notions of an unhealthy diet by depicting a raw steak with the caption: "Revealed to be health food. 2010 A.D." Another depicted irreverent "news"-show host Morton Downey Jr. in front of an American flag with the caption: "Presidential candidate. 2008 A.D."

The advertisement which prompted the current dispute was for Samsung video-cassette recorders (VCRs). The ad depicted a robot, dressed in a wig, gown, and jewelry which Deutsch consciously selected to resemble White's hair and dress. The robot was posed next to a game board which is instantly recognizable as the *Wheel of Fortune* game show set, in a stance for which White is famous. The caption of the ad read: "Longest-running game show. 2012 A.D." Defendants referred to the ad as the "Vanna White" ad. Unlike the other celebrities used in the campaign, White neither consented to the ads nor was she paid.

Following the circulation of the robot ad, White sued Samsung and Deutsch in federal district court under: (1) California Civil Code § 3344; (2) the California common law right of publicity; and (3) § 43(a) of the Lanham Act, 15 U.S.C. § 1125(a). The district court granted summary judgment against White on each of her claims. White now appeals.

. . .

II.   *Right of Publicity*

White ... argues that the district court erred in granting summary judgment to defendants on White's common law right of publicity claim. The district court dismissed White's claim, reasoning that defendants had not appropriated White's "name or likeness" with their robot ad. We agree that the robot ad did not make use of White's name or likeness. However, the common law right of publicity is not so confined.

. . .

In *Midler*, this court held that, even though the defendants had not used Midler's name or likeness, Midler had stated a claim for violation of her California common law right of publicity because "the defendants . . . for their own profit in selling their product did appropriate part of her identity" by using a Midler sound-alike.

In *Carson v. Here's Johnny Portable Toilets, Inc.*, 698 F.2d 831 (6th Cir.1983), the defendant had marketed portable toilets under the brand name "Here's Johnny"—Johnny Carson's signature "Tonight Show" introduction—without Carson's permission. The district court had dismissed Carson's Michigan common law right of publicity claim because the defendants had not used Carson's "name or likeness." *Id.* at 835. In reversing the district court, the sixth circuit found "the district court's conception of the right of publicity ... too narrow" and held that the right was implicated because the defendant had appropriated Carson's identity by using, inter alia, the phrase "Here's Johnny." *Id.* at 835–37.

These cases teach not only that the common law right of publicity reaches means of appropriation other than name or likeness, but that the specific means of appropriation are relevant only for determining whether the defendant has in fact appropriated the plaintiff's identity. The right of publicity does not require that appropriations of identity be accomplished through particular means to be actionable. . . .

Although the defendants in these cases avoided the most obvious means of appropriating the plaintiffs' identities, each of their actions directly implicated the commercial interests which the right of publicity is designed to protect. As the *Carson* court explained:

> [t]he right of publicity has developed to protect the commercial interest of celebrities in their identities. The theory of the right is that a celebrity's identity can be valuable in the promotion of products, and the celebrity has an interest that may be protected from the unauthorized commercial exploitation of that identity. . . . If the celebrity's identity is commercially exploited, there has been an invasion of his right whether or not his "name or likeness" is used.

Carson, 698 F.2d at 835. It is not important how the defendant has appropriated the plaintiff's identity, but whether the defendant has done so. *Motschenbacher, Midler,* and *Carson* teach the impossibility of treating the right of publicity as guarding only against a laundry list of specific means of appropriating identity. . . .

Indeed, if we treated the means of appropriation as dispositive in our analysis of the right of publicity, we would not only weaken the right but effectively eviscerate it. . . . The identities of the most popular celebrities are not only the most attractive for advertisers, but also the easiest to evoke without resorting to obvious means such as name, likeness, or voice.

. . . .

Viewed separately, the individual aspects of the advertisement in the present case say little. Viewed together, they leave little doubt about the celebrity the ad is meant to depict. The female-shaped robot is wearing a long gown, blond wig, and large jewelry. Vanna White dresses exactly like this at times, but so do many other women. The robot is in the process of turning a block letter on a gameboard. Vanna White dresses like this while turning letters on a game-board but perhaps similarly attired Scrabble-playing women do this as well. The robot is standing on what looks to be the *Wheel of Fortune* game show set. Vanna White dresses like this, turns letters, and does this on the *Wheel of Fortune* game show. She is the only one. Indeed, defendants themselves referred to their ad as the "Vanna White" ad. We are not surprised.

Television and other media create marketable celebrity identity value. Considerable energy and ingenuity are expended by those who have achieved celebrity value to exploit it for profit. The law protects the celebrity's sole right to exploit this value whether the celebrity has achieved her fame out of rare ability, dumb luck, or a combination thereof. We decline Samsung and Deutch's invitation to permit the evisceration of the common law right of publicity through means as facile as those in this case. Because White has alleged facts showing that Samsung and Deutsch had appropriated her identity, the district court erred by rejecting, on summary judgment, White's common law right of publicity claim.

V.   *Conclusion*

In remanding this case, we hold only that White has pleaded claims which can go to the jury for its decision.

Affirmed in part, reversed in part, and remanded.

————

On petition for rehearing and rehearing en banc:

ORDER

The panel has voted unanimously to deny the petition for rehearing. Judge Pregerson has voted to reject the suggestion for rehearing en banc, and Judge Goodwin so recommends. Judge Alarcon has voted to accept the suggestion for rehearing en banc.

The full court has been advised of the suggestion for rehearing en banc. An active judge requested a vote on whether to rehear the matter en banc. The matter failed to receive a majority of the votes of the nonrecused active judges in favor of en banc consideration. Fed. R. App. P. 35.

The petition for rehearing is DENIED and the suggestion for rehearing en banc is REJECTED.

■ KOZINSKI, CIRCUIT JUDGE, with whom CIRCUIT JUDGES O'SCANNLAIN and KLEINFELD join, *dissenting* from the order rejecting the suggestion for rehearing *en banc*:

I

Saddam Hussein wants to keep advertisers from using his picture in unflattering contexts.[1] Clint Eastwood doesn't want tabloids to write about him.[2] Rudolf Valentino's heirs want to control his film biography.[3] The Girl

---

1.   *See* Eben Shapiro, *Rising Caution on Using Celebrity Images,* N.Y. TIMES, Nov. 4, 1992, at D20 (Iraqi diplomat objects on right of publicity grounds to ad containing Hussein's picture and caption "History has shown what happens when one source controls all the information").

2.   *Eastwood v. Superior Court,* 149 Cal. App.3d 409, 198 Cal.Rptr. 342 (1983).

Scouts don't want their image soiled by association with certain activities.[4] George Lucas wants to keep Strategic Defense Initiative fans from calling it "Star Wars."[5] Pepsico doesn't want singers to use the word "Pepsi" in their songs.[6] .... Guy Lombardo wants an exclusive property right to ads that show big bands playing on New Year's Eve.[7] Uri Geller thinks he should be paid for ads showing psychics bending metal through telekinesis.[8] Paul Prudhomme, that household name, thinks the same about ads featuring corpulent bearded chefs.[9] And scads of copyright holders see purple when their creations are made fun of.[10]

3. *Guglielmi v. Spelling–Goldberg Prods.*, 25 Cal.3d 860, 160 Cal.Rptr. 352, 603 P.2d 454 (1979) (Rudolph Valentino); *see also Maheu v. CBS, Inc.*, 201 Cal.App.3d 662, 668, 247 Cal.Rptr. 304 (1988) (aide to Howard Hughes). *Cf.* Frank Gannon, *Vanna Karenina*, in VANNA KARENINA AND OTHER REFLECTIONS (1988) (A humorous short story with a tragic ending. "She thought of the first day she had met VR—SKY. How foolish she had been. How could she love a man who wouldn't even tell her all the letters in his name?").

4. *Girl Scouts v. Personality Posters Mfg.*, 304 F.Supp. 1228 (S.D.N.Y.1969) (poster of a pregnant girl in a Girl Scout uniform with the caption "Be Prepared").

5. *Lucasfilm Ltd. v. High Frontier*, 622 F.Supp. 931 (D.D.C.1985).

6. Pepsico Inc. claimed the lyrics and packaging of grunge rocker Tad Doyle's "Jack Pepsi" song were "offensive to and [are] likely to offend [its] customers," in part because they "associate [Pepsico] and its Pepsi marks with intoxication and drunk driving." Russell, *Doyle Leaves Pepsi Thirsty for Compensation*, BILLBOARD, June 15, 1991, at 43. Conversely, the Hell's Angels recently sued Marvel Comics to keep it from publishing a comic book called "Hell's Angel," starring a character of the same name. Marvel settled by paying $35,000 to charity and promising never to use the name "Hell's Angel" again in connection with any of its publications. Marvel, *Hell's Angels Settle Trademark Suit*, L.A. Daily J., Feb. 2, 1993, § II, at 1.

Trademarks are often reflected in the mirror of our popular culture. *See* TRUMAN CAPOTE, BREAKFAST AT TIFFANY'S (1958); KURT VONNEGUT, JR., BREAKFAST OF CHAMPIONS (1973); TOM WOLFE, THE ELECTRIC KOOL–AID ACID TEST (1968) (which, incidentally, includes a chapter on the Hell's Angels); Larry Niven, *Man of Steel, Woman of Kleenex*, in ALL THE MYRIAD WAYS (1971); LOOKING FOR MR. GOODBAR (1977);

THE COCA-COLA KID (1985) (using Coca–Cola as a metaphor for American commercialism); THE KENTUCKY FRIED MOVIE (1977); HARLEY DAVIDSON AND THE MARLBORO MAN (1991); *The Wonder Years* (ABC 1988–present) ("Wonder Years" was a slogan of Wonder Bread); Tim Rice & Andrew Lloyd Webber, *Joseph and the Amazing Technicolor Dream Coat* (musical).

Hear Janis Joplin, *Mercedes Benz*, on PEARL (CBS 1971); Paul Simon, *Kodachrome*, on THERE GOES RHYMIN' SIMON (Warner 1973); Leonard Cohen, *Chelsea Hotel*, on THE BEST OF LEONARD COHEN (CBS 1975); Bruce Springsteen, *Cadillac Ranch*, on THE RIVER (CBS 1980); Prince, *Little Red Corvette*, on 1999 (Warner 1982); dada, *Dizz Knee Land*, on PUZZLE (IRS 1992) ("I just robbed a grocery store—I'm going to Disneyland/I just flipped off President George—I'm going to Disneyland"); Monty Python, *Spam*, on THE FINAL RIP OFF (Virgin 1988); Roy Clark, *Thank God and Greyhound [You're Gone]*, on ROY CLARK'S GREATEST HITS VOLUME I (MCA 1979); Mel Tillis, *Coca–Cola Cowboy*, on THE VERY BEST OF (MCA 1981) ("You're just a Coca–Cola cowboy/You've got an Eastwood smile and Robert Redford hair....").

Dance to Talking Heads, POPULAR FAVORITES 1976–92: SAND IN THE VASELINE (Sire 1992); Talking Heads, *Popsicle*, on *id.* *Admire* Andy Warhol, CAMPBELL'S SOUP CAN. *Cf.* REO Speedwagon, 38 Special, and Jello Biafra of the Dead Kennedys.

7. *Lombardo v. Doyle, Dane & Bernbach, Inc.*, 58 A.D.2d 620, 396 N.Y.S.2d 661 (1977).

8. *Geller v. Fallon McElligott*, 1991 WL 640574 (S.D.N.Y.1991) (involving a Timex ad).

9. *Prudhomme v. Procter & Gamble Co.*, 800 F.Supp. 390 (E.D.La.1992).

10. *E.g., Acuff–Rose Music, Inc. v. Campbell*, 972 F.2d 1429 (6th Cir.1992);

Something very dangerous is going on here. Private property, including intellectual property, is essential to our way of life. It provides an incentive for investment and innovation; it stimulates the flourishing of our culture; it protects the moral entitlements of people to the fruits of their labors. But reducing too much to private property can be bad medicine. Private land, for instance, is far more useful if separated from other private land by public streets, roads and highways. Public parks, utility rights-of-way and sewers reduce the amount of land in private hands, but vastly enhance the value of the property that remains. So too it is with intellectual property. Overprotecting intellectual property is as harmful as underprotecting it. Creativity is impossible without a rich public domain. Nothing today, likely nothing since we tamed fire, is genuinely new: Culture, like science and technology, grows by accretion, each new creator building on the works of those who came before. Overprotection stifles the very creative forces it's supposed to nurture.[11]

The panel's opinion is a classic case of overprotection. Concerned about what it sees as a wrong done to Vanna White, the panel majority erects a property right of remarkable and dangerous breadth: Under the majority's opinion, it's now a tort for advertisers to remind the public of a celebrity. Not to use a celebrity's name, voice, signature or likeness; not to imply the celebrity endorses a product; but simply to evoke the celebrity's image in the public's mind. This Orwellian notion withdraws far more from the public domain than prudence and common sense allow. It's bad law, and it deserves a long, hard second look.

II

Samsung ran an ad campaign promoting its consumer electronics. The ads were meant to convey—humorously—that Samsung products would still be in use twenty years from now.

The ad that spawned this litigation starred a robot dressed in a wig, gown and jewelry reminiscent of Vanna White's hair and dress; the robot was posed next to a Wheel-of-Fortune-like game board. The caption read "Longest-running game show. 2012 A.D." The gag here, I take it, was that Samsung would still be around when White had been replaced by a robot.

Perhaps failing to see the humor, White sued, alleging Samsung infringed her right of publicity by "appropriating" her "identity." Under California law, White has the exclusive right to use her name, likeness, signature and voice for commercial purposes. But Samsung didn't use her name, voice or signature, and it certainly didn't use her likeness. The ad

---

Cliffs Notes v. Bantam Doubleday Dell Publishing Group, Inc., 886 F.2d 490 (2d Cir. 1989); *Fisher v. Dees*, 794 F.2d 432 (9th Cir. 1986); *MCA, Inc. v. Wilson*, 677 F.2d 180 (2d Cir.1981); *Elsmere Music, Inc. v. NBC*, 623 F.2d 252 (2d Cir.1980); *Walt Disney Prods. v. The Air Pirates*, 581 F.2d 751 (9th Cir.1978); *Berlin v. E.C. Publications, Inc.*, 329 F.2d 541 (2d Cir.1964); *Lowenfels v. Nathan*, 2 F.Supp. 73 (S.D.N.Y.1932).

11. *See* Wendy J. Gordon, *A Property Right in Self Expression: Equality and Individualism in the Natural Law of Intellectual Property*, 102 YALE L.J. 1533, Part IV(A) (1993).

just wouldn't have been funny had it depicted White or someone who resembled her—the whole joke was that the game show host(ess) was a robot, not a real person. No one seeing the ad could have thought this was supposed to be White in 2012.

The district judge quite reasonably held that, because Samsung didn't use White's name, likeness, voice or signature, it didn't violate her right of publicity. 971 F.2d at 1396–97. Not so, says the panel majority: The California right of publicity can't possibly be limited to name and likeness. If it were, the majority reasons, a "clever advertising strategist" could avoid using White's name or likeness but nevertheless remind people of her with impunity, "effectively eviscerating" her rights. To prevent this "evisceration," the panel majority holds that the right of publicity must extend beyond name and likeness, to any "appropriation" of White's "identity"— anything that "evokes" her personality. *Id.* at 1398–99.

III

But what does "evisceration" mean in intellectual property law? Intellectual property rights aren't like some constitutional rights, absolute guarantees protected against all kinds of interference, subtle as well as blatant. They cast no penumbras, emit no emanations: The very point of intellectual property laws is that they protect only against certain specific kinds of appropriation. I can't publish unauthorized copies of, say, *Presumed Innocent*; I can't make a movie out of it. But I'm perfectly free to write a book about an idealistic young prosecutor on trial for a crime he didn't commit.[14] So what if I got the idea from *Presumed Innocent*? So what if it reminds readers of the original? Have I "eviscerated" Scott Turow's intellectual property rights? Certainly not. All creators draw in part on the work of those who came before, referring to it, building on it, poking fun at it; we call this creativity, not piracy.[15] Newton himself may have borrowed this phrase from Bernard of Chartres, who said something similar in the early twelfth century. Bernard in turn may have snatched it from Priscian, a sixth century grammarian. *See Lotus Dev. Corp. v. Paperback Software Int'l,* 740 F.Supp. 37, 77 n. 3 (D.Mass.1990).

The majority isn't, in fact, preventing the "evisceration" of Vanna White's existing rights; it's creating a new and much broader property right, a right unknown in California law.[16] Neither have we previously interpreted California law to cover pure "identity." *Midler v. Ford Motor Co.,* 849 F.2d 460 (9th Cir.1988), and *Waits v. Frito–Lay, Inc.,* 978 F.2d

---

14. It would be called "Burden of Going Forward with Evidence," and the hero would ultimately be saved by his lawyer's adept use of Fed. R. Evid. 301.

15. In the words of Sir Isaac Newton, "if I have seen further it is by standing on [the shoulders] of Giants." Letter to Robert Hooke, Feb. 5, 1675/1676.

16. In fact, in the one California case raising the issue, the three state Supreme

Court Justices who discussed this theory expressed serious doubts about it. *Guglielmi v. Spelling–Goldberg Prods.,* 25 Cal.3d 860, 864 n. 5, 160 Cal.Rptr. 352, 355, 603 P.2d 454 n. 5 (1979) (Bird, C.J., concurring) (expressing skepticism about finding a property right to a celebrity's "personality" because it is "difficult to discern any easily applied definition for this amorphous term").

1093 (9th Cir.1992), dealt with appropriation of a celebrity's voice. *See id.* at 1100–01 (imitation of singing style, rather than voice, doesn't violate the right of publicity). *Motschenbacher v. R.J. Reynolds Tobacco Co.*, 498 F.2d 821 (9th Cir.1974), found a violation of the right of publicity, but stressed that, though the plaintiff's likeness wasn't directly recognizable by itself, the surrounding circumstances would have made viewers think the likeness was the plaintiff's. *Id.* at 827; *see also Moore v. Regents of the Univ. of Cal.*, 51 Cal.3d 120, 138, 271 Cal.Rptr. 146, 157, 793 P.2d 479 (1990) (construing *Motschenbacher* as "holding that every person has a proprietary interest in his own likeness"). It's replacing the existing balance between the interests of the celebrity and those of the public by a different balance, one substantially more favorable to the celebrity. Instead of having an exclusive right in her name, likeness, signature or voice, every famous person now has an exclusive right to anything that reminds the viewer of her. After all, that's all Samsung did: It used an inanimate object to remind people of White, to "evoke [her identity]," 971 F.2d at 1399.[17] Note also that the majority's rule applies even to advertisements that unintentionally remind people of someone. California law is crystal clear that the common-law right of publicity may be violated even by unintentional appropriations. *Id.* at 417 n.6, 198 Cal.Rptr. at 346 n.6; *Fairfield v. American Photocopy Equipment Co.*, 138 Cal.App.2d 82, 87, 291 P.2d 194 (1955).

Consider how sweeping this new right is. What is it about the ad that makes people think of White? It's not the robot's wig, clothes or jewelry; there must be ten million blond women (many of them quasi-famous) who wear dresses and jewelry like White's. It's that the robot is posed near the *"Wheel of Fortune"* game board. Remove the game board from the ad, and no one would think of Vanna White. But once you include the game board, anybody standing beside it—a brunette woman, a man wearing women's clothes, a monkey in a wig and gown—would evoke White's image, precisely the way the robot did. It's the *"Wheel of Fortune"* set, not the robot's face or dress or jewelry that evokes White's image. The panel is giving White an exclusive right not in what she looks like or who she is, but in what she does for a living.[18]

17. Some viewers might have inferred White was endorsing the product, but that's a different story. The right of publicity isn't aimed at or limited to false endorsements, *Eastwood v. Superior Court*, 149 Cal.App.3d 409, 419–20, 198 Cal.Rptr. 342, 348 (1983); that's what the Lanham Act is for.

18. Once the right of publicity is extended beyond specific physical characteristics, this will become a recurring problem: Outside name, likeness and voice, the one thing that most reliably reminds the public of someone are the actions or roles they're famous for. A commercial with an astronaut setting foot on the moon would evoke the image of Neil Armstrong. Any masked man on horseback would remind people (over a certain age) of Clayton Moore. And any number of songs—"My Way," "Yellow Submarine," "Like a Virgin," "Beat It," "Michael, Row the Boat Ashore," to name only a few—instantly evoke an image of the person or group who made them famous, regardless of who is singing. *See also* Carlos V. Lozano, *West Loses Lawsuit over Batman TV Commercial*, L.A. Times, Jan. 18, 1990, at B3 (Adam West sues over Batman-like character in commercial); *Nurmi v. Peterson*, 10 U.S.P.Q.2d (BNA) 1775, 1989 U.S. Dist. LEXIS 9765 (C.D.Cal.1989) (1950s TV movie hostess "Vampira" sues 1980s TV hostess "Elvira"); text accompanying notes 7–8 (law-

This is entirely the wrong place to strike the balance. Intellectual property rights aren't free: They're imposed at the expense of future creators and of the public at large. Where would we be if Charles Lindbergh had an exclusive right in the concept of a heroic solo aviator? If Arthur Conan Doyle had gotten a copyright in the idea of the detective story, or Albert Einstein had patented the theory of relativity? If every author and celebrity had been given the right to keep people from mocking them or their work? Surely this would have made the world poorer, not richer, culturally as well as economically.

This is why intellectual property law is full of careful balances between what's set aside for the owner and what's left in the public domain for the rest of us: The relatively short life of patents; the longer, but finite, life of copyrights; copyright's idea-expression dichotomy; the fair use doctrine; the prohibition on copyrighting facts; the compulsory license of television broadcasts and musical compositions; federal preemption of overbroad state intellectual property laws; the nominative use doctrine in trademark law; the right to make soundalike recordings.[20] All of these diminish an intellectual property owner's rights. All let the public use something created by someone else. But all are necessary to maintain a free environment in which creative genius can flourish.

The intellectual property right created by the panel here has none of these essential limitations: No fair use exception; no right to parody; no idea-expression dichotomy. It impoverishes the public domain, to the detriment of future creators and the public at large. Instead of well-defined, limited characteristics such as name, likeness or voice, advertisers will now have to cope with vague claims of "appropriation of identity," claims often made by people with a wholly exaggerated sense of their own fame and significance. Future Vanna Whites might not get the chance to create their personae, because their employers may fear some celebrity will claim the persona is too similar to her own.[21] The public will be robbed of parodies of

---

suits brought by Guy Lombardo, claiming big bands playing at New Year's Eve parties remind people of him, and by Uri Geller, claiming psychics who can bend metal remind people of him). *Cf. Motschenbacher*, where the claim was that viewers would think plaintiff was actually in the commercial, and not merely that the commercial reminded people of him.

20. *See* 35 U.S.C. § 154 (duration of patent); 17 U.S.C. §§ 302–305 (duration of copyright); 17 U.S.C. § 102(b) (idea-expression dichotomy); 17 U.S.C. § 107 (fair use); *Feist Pubs., Inc. v. Rural Tel. Serv. Co.*, 111 S.Ct. 1282, 288, 113 L.Ed.2d 358 (1991) (no copyrighting facts); 17 U.S.C. §§ 115, 119(b) (compulsory licenses); *Bonito Boats, Inc. v. Thunder Craft Boats, Inc.*, 489 U.S. 141, 109 S.Ct. 971, 103 L.Ed.2d 118 (1989) (federal

preemption); *New Kids on the Block v. News America Publishing, Inc.*, 971 F.2d 302, 306–308 (9th Cir.1992) (nominative use); 17 U.S.C. § 114(b) (soundalikes); *accord G.S. Rasmussen & Assocs. v. Kalitta Flying Serv., Inc.*, 958 F.2d 896, 900 n. 7 (9th Cir.1992); Daniel A. Saunders, *Comment, Copyright Law's Broken Rear Window*, 80 CALIF. L. REV. 179, 204–05 (1992). *But see Midler v. Ford Motor Co.*, 849 F.2d 460 (9th Cir.1988).

21. If Christian Slater, star of "Heathers," "Pump up the Volume," "Kuffs," and "Untamed Heart"—an alleged Jack Nicholson clone—appears in a commercial, can Nicholson sue? Of 54 stories on LEXIS that talk about Christian Slater, 26 talk about Slater's alleged similarities to Nicholson. Apparently it's his nasal wisecracks and killer smiles, ST. PETERSBURG TIMES, Jan. 10, 1992, at 13, his

celebrities, and our culture will be deprived of the valuable safety valve that parody and mockery create. Moreover, consider the moral dimension, about which the panel majority seems to have gotten so exercised. Saying Samsung "appropriated" something of White's begs the question: Should White have the exclusive right to something as broad and amorphous as her "identity"? Samsung's ad didn't simply copy White's schtick—like all parody, it created something new. True, Samsung did it to make money, but White does whatever she does to make money, too; the majority talks of "the difference between fun and profit," 971 F.2d at 1401, but in the entertainment industry fun is profit. Why is Vanna White's right to exclusive for-profit use of her persona—a persona that might not even be her own creation, but that of a writer, director or producer—superior to Samsung's right to profit by creating its own inventions? Why should she have such absolute rights to control the conduct of others, unlimited by the idea-expression dichotomy or by the fair use doctrine?

To paraphrase only slightly *Feist Publications, Inc. v. Rural Telephone Service Co.*, 111 S.Ct. 1282, 1289–90, 113 L.Ed.2d 358 (1991), it may seem unfair that much of the fruit of a creator's labor may be used by others without compensation. But this is not some unforeseen byproduct of our intellectual property system; it is the system's very essence. Intellectual property law assures authors the right to their original expression, but encourages others to build freely on the ideas that underlie it. This result is neither unfair nor unfortunate: It is the means by which intellectual property law advances the progress of science and art. We give authors certain exclusive rights, but in exchange we get a richer public domain. The majority ignores this wise teaching, and all of us are the poorer for it.

VII

For better or worse, we are the Court of Appeals for the Hollywood Circuit. Millions of people toil in the shadow of the law we make, and much of their livelihood is made possible by the existence of intellectual property rights. But much of their livelihood—and much of the vibrancy of our culture—also depends on the existence of other intangible rights: The right to draw ideas from a rich and varied public domain, and the right to mock, for profit as well as fun, the cultural icons of our time.

In the name of avoiding the "evisceration" of a celebrity's rights in her image, the majority diminishes the rights of copyright holders and the public at large. In the name of fostering creativity, the majority suppresses it. Vanna White and those like her have been given something they never had before, and they've been given it at our expense. I cannot agree.

eyebrows, OTTAWA CITIZEN, Jan. 10, 1992, at E2, his sneers, BOSTON GLOBE, July 26, 1991, at 37, his menacing presence, USA TODAY, June 26, 1991, at 1D, and his sing-song voice, Gannett News Service, Aug. 27, 1990 (or, some say, his insinuating drawl, L.A. TIMES, Aug. 22, 1990, at F5). That's a whole lot more than White and the robot had in common.

QUESTIONS

1. Judge Kozinski's dissent from denial of rehearing in the *Vanna White* case is both witty and eloquent. The judge reveals broad familiarity with contemporary cultural icons, and makes his arguments in a thoroughly charming way. Is his characterization of the majority's opinion in the case fair? Is his underlying objection to this particular expansion of common law intellectual property rights (if expansion it be) sound?

2. Does it make sense to say that Vanna White owns her letter-turning "persona"? Did she create the persona? If, as Judge Kozinski suggests, there is no persona without juxtaposition to the wheel, shouldn't the *Wheel of Fortune* producers enjoy the good-will built-up in the persona, and a right against unauthorized commercial exploitation?

Rogers v. Grimaldi

875 F.2d 994 (2d Cir.1989).

■ NEWMAN, CIRCUIT JUDGE:

Appellant Ginger Rogers and the late Fred Astaire are among the most famous duos in show business history. Through their incomparable performances in Hollywood musicals, Ginger Rogers and Fred Astaire established themselves as paragons of style, elegance, and grace. A testament to their international recognition, and a key circumstance in this case, is the fact that Rogers and Astaire are among that small elite of the entertainment world whose identities are readily called to mind by just their first names, particularly the pairing "Ginger and Fred." This appeal presents a conflict between Rogers' right to protect her celebrated name and the right of others to express themselves freely in their own artistic work. Specifically, we must decide whether Rogers can prevent the use of the title "Ginger and Fred" for a fictional movie that only obliquely relates to Rogers and Astaire.

Rogers appeals from an order of the District Court for the Southern District of New York (Robert W. Sweet, Judge) dismissing on summary judgment her claims that defendants-appellees Alberto Grimaldi, MGM/UA Entertainment Co., and PEA Produzioni Europee Associate, S.R.L., producers and distributors of the motion picture "Ginger and Fred," violated the Lanham Act, 15 U.S.C. § 1125(a) (1982), and infringed her common law rights of publicity and privacy. *Rogers v. Grimaldi*, 695 F. Supp. 112 (S.D.N.Y.1988). Although we disagree with some of the reasoning of the District Court, we affirm.

I. *Background*

Appellant Rogers has been an international celebrity for more than fifty years. In 1940, she won an Academy Award for her performance in the motion picture "Kitty Foyle." Her principal fame was established in a series of motion pictures in which she co-starred with Fred Astaire in the 1930s and 1940s, including "Top Hat" and "The Barkleys of Broadway."

There can be no dispute that Rogers' name has enormous drawing power in the entertainment world. Rogers has also used her name once for a commercial enterprise other than her show business career. In the mid–1970s, she licensed J.C. Penney, Inc. to produce a line of GINGER ROGERS lingerie. Rogers is also writing her autobiography, which she hopes to publish and possibly sell for adaptation as a movie.

In March 1986, appellees produced and distributed in the United States and Europe a film entitled "Ginger and Fred," created and directed by famed Italian film-maker Federico Fellini. The film tells the story of two fictional Italian cabaret performers, Pippo and Amelia, who, in their heyday, imitated Rogers and Astaire and became known in Italy as "Ginger and Fred." The film focuses on a televised reunion of Pippo and Amelia, many years after their retirement. Appellees describe the film as the bittersweet story of these two fictional dancers and as a satire of contemporary television variety shows.

The film received mixed reviews and played only briefly in its first run in the United States. Shortly after distribution of the film began, Rogers brought this suit, seeking permanent injunctive relief and money damages. Her complaint alleged that the defendants (1) violated section 43(a) of the Lanham Act, 15 U.S.C. § 1125(a) (1982), by creating the false impression that the film was about her or that she sponsored, endorsed, or was otherwise involved in the film, [and] (2) violated her common law right of publicity, . . .

After two years of discovery, the defendants moved for summary judgment. In opposition to the motion, Rogers submitted a market research survey purporting to establish that the title "Ginger and Fred" misled potential movie viewers as to Rogers' connection with the film. Rogers also provided anecdotal evidence of confusion, including the fact that when MGM/UA publicists first heard the film's title (and before they saw the movie), they began gathering old photographs of Rogers and Astaire for possible use in an advertising campaign.

The District Court granted summary judgment to the defendants. Judge Sweet found that defendants' use of Rogers' first name in the title and screenplay of the film was an exercise of artistic expression rather than commercial speech. 695 F. Supp. at 120. He then held that "[b]ecause the speech at issue here is not primarily intended to serve a commercial purpose, the prohibitions of the Lanham Act do not apply, and the Film is entitled to the full scope of protection under the First Amendment." *Id.* at 120–21. The District Judge also held that First Amendment concerns barred Rogers' state law right of publicity claim. *Id.* at 124. . . .

II. *Discussion*

A. *Lanham Act*

. . . .

The District Court ruled that because of First Amendment concerns, the Lanham Act cannot apply to the title of a motion picture where the title is "within the realm of artistic expression," 695 F. Supp. at 120, and is not "primarily intended to serve a commercial purpose," *id.* at 121. Use of the title "Ginger and Fred" did not violate the Act, the Court concluded, because of the undisputed artistic relevance of the title to the content of the film. *Id.* at 120. In effect, the District Court's ruling would create a nearly absolute privilege for movie titles, insulating them from Lanham Act claims as long as the film itself is an artistic work, and the title is relevant to the film's content. We think that approach unduly narrows the scope of the Act.

Movies, plays, books, and songs are all indisputably works of artistic expression and deserve protection. Nonetheless, they are also sold in the commercial marketplace like other more utilitarian products, making the danger of consumer deception a legitimate concern that warrants some government regulation. Poetic license is not without limits. The purchaser of a book, like the purchaser of a can of peas, has a right not to be misled as to the source of the product. Thus, it is well established that where the title of a movie or a book has acquired secondary meaning—that is, where the title is sufficiently well known that consumers associate it with a particular author's work—the holder of the rights to that title may prevent the use of the same or confusingly similar titles by other authors. Indeed, it would be ironic if, in the name of the First Amendment, courts did not recognize the right of authors to protect titles of their creative work against infringement by other authors. *Cf. Harper & Row, Publishers, Inc. v. Nation Enterprises,* 471 U.S. 539, 556–60 (1985) (noting that copyright law fosters free expression by protecting the right of authors to receive compensation for their work).

Though First Amendment concerns do not insulate titles of artistic works from all Lanham Act claims, such concerns must nonetheless inform our consideration of the scope of the Act as applied to claims involving such titles. Titles, like the artistic works they identify, are of a hybrid nature, combining artistic expression and commercial promotion. The title of a movie may be both an integral element of the film-maker's expression as well as a significant means of marketing the film to the public. The artistic and commercial elements of titles are inextricably intertwined. Film-makers and authors frequently rely on word-play, ambiguity, irony, and allusion in titling their works. Furthermore, their interest in freedom of artistic expression is shared by their audience. The subtleties of a title can enrich a reader's or a viewer's understanding of a work. Consumers of artistic works thus have a dual interest: They have an interest in not being misled and they also have an interest in enjoying the results of the author's freedom of expression. For all these reasons, the expressive element of titles requires more protection than the labeling of ordinary commercial products.[3]

---

3. In other respects, trademark law has also accorded greater leeway for the use of titles than for names of ordinary commercial products, thus allowing breathing space for

Because overextension of Lanham Act restrictions in the area of titles might intrude on First Amendment values, we must construe the Act narrowly to avoid such a conflict. *See Silverman v. CBS,* 870 F.2d 40, 48 (2d Cir.1989).

Rogers contends that First Amendment concerns are implicated only where a title is so intimately related to the subject matter of a work that the author has no alternative means of expressing what the work is about. This "no alternative avenues of communication" standard derives from *Lloyd Corp. v. Tanner,* 407 U.S. 551, 566–67 (1972), and has been applied by several courts in the trademark context.

In the context of titles, this "no alternative" standard provides insufficient leeway for literary expression. In *Lloyd,* the issue was whether the First Amendment provided war protesters with the right to distribute leaflets on a shopping center owner's property. The Supreme Court held that it did not. But a restriction on the *location* of a speech is different from a restriction on the *words* the speaker may use. *See Denicola, supra,* at 197. As the Supreme Court has noted, albeit in a different context, "[W]e cannot indulge the facile assumption that one can forbid particular words without running a substantial risk of suppressing ideas in the process." *Cohen v. California,* 403 U.S. 15, 26 (1971).[4]

Thus, the "no alternative avenues" test does not sufficiently accommodate the public's interest in free expression, while the District Court's rule—that the Lanham Act is inapplicable to all titles that can be considered artistic expression—does not sufficiently protect the public against flagrant deception. We believe that in general the Act should be construed to apply to artistic works only where the public interest in avoiding consumer confusion outweighs the public interest in free expression. In the context of allegedly misleading titles using a celebrity's name, that balance will normally not support application of the Act unless the title has no artistic relevance to the underlying work whatsoever, or, if it has some artistic relevance, unless the title explicitly misleads as to the source or the content of the work.[5]

free expression. A confusingly similar title will not be deemed infringing unless the title alleged to be infringed, even if arbitrary or fanciful, has acquired secondary meaning. *See* 1 J. McCarthy, *Trademarks and Unfair Competition* § 10.2 (1984).

4. This Circuit employed the "no alternative avenues of communication" standard in *Dallas Cowboys Cheerleaders, Inc. v. Pussycat Cinema, Ltd.,* 604 F.2d 200, 206 (2d Cir.1979). As we stated in *Silverman,* however, that case involved a pornographic movie with blatantly false advertising. 870 F.2d at 48 n. 5. Advertisements for the movie were explicitly misleadingly, stating that the principal actress in the movie was a former Dallas Cowboys' cheerleader. We do not read *Dallas Cowboys Cheerleaders* as generally precluding all consideration of First Amendment concerns whenever an allegedly infringing author has "alternative avenues of communication."

5. This limiting construction would not apply to misleading titles that are confusingly similar to other titles. The public interest in sparing consumers this type of confusion outweighs the slight public interest in permitting authors to use such titles.

The reasons for striking the balance in this manner require some explanation. A misleading title with no artistic relevance cannot be sufficiently justified by a free expression interest. For example, if a film-maker placed the title "Ginger and Fred" on a film to which it had no artistic relevance at all, the arguably misleading suggestions as to source or content implicitly conveyed by the title could be found to violate the Lanham Act as to such a film.

.   .   .   .

Similarly, titles with at least minimal artistic relevance to the work may include explicit statements about the *content* of the work that are seriously misleading. For example, if the characters in the film in this case had published their memoirs under the title "The True Life Story of Ginger and Fred," and if the film-maker had then used that fictitious book title as the title of the film, the Lanham Act could be applicable to such an explicitly misleading description of content.[6]

But many titles with a celebrity's name make no explicit statement that the work is about that person in any direct sense; the relevance of the title may be oblique and may become clear only after viewing or reading the work. As to such titles, the consumer interest in avoiding deception is too slight to warrant application of the Lanham Act. Though consumers frequently look to the title of a work to determine what it is about, they do not regard titles of artistic works in the same way as the names of ordinary commercial products. Since consumers expect an ordinary product to be what the name says it is, we apply the Lanham Act with some rigor to prohibit names that misdescribe such goods. But most consumers are well aware that they cannot judge a book solely by its title any more than by its cover. We therefore need not interpret the Act to require that authors select titles that unambiguously describe what the work is about nor to preclude them from using titles that are only suggestive of some topics that the work is not about. Where a title with at least some artistic relevance to the work is not explicitly misleading as to the content of the work, it is not false advertising under the Lanham Act.

This construction of the Lanham Act accommodates consumer and artistic interests. It insulates from restriction titles with at least minimal artistic relevance that are ambiguous or only implicitly misleading but leaves vulnerable to claims of deception titles that are explicitly misleading as to source or content, or that have no artistic relevance at all.

With this approach in mind, we now consider Rogers' Lanham Act claim to determine whether appellees are entitled to summary judgment. . . .

Rogers essentially claims that the title "Ginger and Fred" is false advertising. Relying on her survey data, anecdotal evidence, and the title

---

6. In offering this example and others in this opinion, we intend only to indicate instances where Lanham Act coverage might be available; whether in such instances a violation is established would depend on the fact-finder's conclusions in light of all the relevant facts and circumstances.

itself, she claims there is a likelihood of confusion that (1) Rogers produced, endorsed, sponsored, or approved the film, and/or (2) the film is about Rogers and Astaire, and that these contentions present triable issues of fact. In assessing the sufficiency of these claims, we accept Judge Sweet's conclusion, which is not subject to dispute, that the title "Ginger and Fred" surpasses the minimum threshold of artistic relevance to the film's content. The central characters in the film are nicknamed "Ginger" and "Fred," and these names are not arbitrarily chosen just to exploit the publicity value of their real life counterparts but instead have genuine relevance to the film's story. We consider separately the claims of confusion as to sponsorship and content.

The title "Ginger and Fred" contains no explicit indication that Rogers endorsed the film or had a role in producing it. The survey evidence, even if its validity is assumed,[8] indicates at most that some members of the public would draw the incorrect inference that Rogers had some involvement with the film. But that risk of misunderstanding, not engendered by any overt claim in the title, is so outweighed by the interests in artistic expression as to preclude application of the Lanham Act. We therefore hold that the sponsorship and endorsement aspects of Rogers' Lanham Act claim raise no "genuine" issue that requires submission to a jury.

Rogers' claim that the title misleads consumers into thinking that the film is *about* her and Astaire also fails. Indeed, this case well illustrates the need for caution in applying the Lanham Act to titles alleged to mislead as to content. As both the survey and the evidence of the actual confusion among the movie's publicists show, there is no doubt a risk that some people looking at the title "Ginger and Fred" might think the film was about Rogers and Astaire in a direct, biographical sense. For those gaining that impression, the title is misleading. At the same time, the title is entirely truthful as to its content in referring to the film's fictional protagonists who are known to their Italian audience as "Ginger and Fred." Moreover, the title has an ironic meaning that is relevant to the film's content. As Fellini explains in an affidavit, Rogers and Astaire are to him "a glamorous and care-free symbol of what American cinema represented during the harsh times which Italy experienced in the 1930s and 1940s." In the film, he contrasts this elegance and class to the gaudiness and banality of contemporary television, which he satirizes. In this sense,

---

8. The survey sampled 201 people who said they were likely to go to a movie in the next six months. Half of those surveyed were shown a card with the title "Ginger and Fred" on it; the other half were shown an actual advertisement for the movie. Of these 201, 38 percent responded "yes" to the question: "Do you think that the actress, Ginger Rogers, had anything to do with this film, or not?" Of these respondents, a third answered yes to the question: "Do you think Ginger Rogers was involved in any way with making this film or not?" In other words, about 14 percent of the total 201 surveyed found that the title suggested that Rogers was involved in making the film.

Appellees contend that the survey used "leading" questions, making the survey results invalid. Without resolving this issue, we will assume for the purposes of this appeal that the survey was valid.

the title is not misleading; on the contrary, it is an integral element of the film and the film-maker's artistic expression.

This mixture of meanings, with the possibly misleading meaning not the result of explicit misstatement, precludes a Lanham Act claim for false description of content in this case. To the extent that there is a risk that the title will mislead some consumers as to what the work is about, that risk is outweighed by the danger that suppressing an artistically relevant though ambiguous title will unduly restrict expression.

For these reasons, we hold that appellees are entitled to summary judgment on Rogers' claim that the title gives the false impression that the film is about Rogers and Astaire.

B. *State Law Claims*

1. *Right of Publicity*

Because the District Judge decided Rogers' state law claims on the ground of broad First Amendment protection, he did not decide which state's law applies to those claims. 695 F. Supp. at 121 n. 5. Although we reach the same result as the District Court, we think the correct approach is to decide the choice of law issue first and then to determine if Rogers has a triable claim under the applicable substantive law, before reaching constitutional issues.

A federal court sitting in diversity or adjudicating state law claims that are pendent to a federal claim must apply the choice of law rules of the forum state. The New York Court of Appeals has clearly stated that "right of publicity" claims are governed by the substantive law of the plaintiff's domicile because rights of publicity constitute personalty. Rogers is an Oregon domiciliary, and thus Oregon law governs this claim.

Oregon courts, however, have not determined the scope of the common law right of publicity in that state. We are therefore obliged to engage in the uncertain task of predicting what the New York courts would predict the Oregon courts would rule as to the contours of a right of publicity under Oregon law.

. . . . .

. . . We believe that New York courts would, as a matter of substantive interpretation, presume that the unsettled common law of another state would resemble New York's but that they would examine the law of the other jurisdiction and that of other states, as well as their own, in making an ultimate determination as to the likely future content of the other jurisdiction's law. That is the task we now undertake.

The common law right of publicity, where it has been recognized, grants celebrities an exclusive right to control the commercial value of their names and to prevent others from exploiting them without permission. *See Bi–Rite Enterprises v. Button Master,* 555 F. Supp. 1188, 1198–99 (S.D.N.Y. 1983). Because the right of publicity, unlike the Lanham Act, has no likelihood of confusion requirement, it is potentially more expansive than the Lanham Act. Perhaps for that reason, courts delineating the right of publicity, more frequently than in applying the Lanham Act, have recognized the need to limit the right to accommodate First Amendment concerns.

In particular, three courts, citing their concern for free expression, have refused to extend the right of publicity to bar the use of a celebrity's name in the title and text of a fictional or semi-fictional book or movie. *See Hicks v. Casablanca Records,* 464 F. Supp. 426 (S.D.N.Y.1978); *Frosch v. Grosset & Dunlop, Inc.,* 75 A.D.2d 768, 427 N.Y.S.2d 828 (1st Dep't 1980); *Guglielmi v. Spelling–Goldberg Productions,* 603 P.2d 454, 455 (Cal.1979) (Bird, C.J., concurring).

Guglielmi involved a suit by a nephew of the late film star Rudolph Valentino to bar a television broadcast entitled "Legend of Valentino: A Romantic Fiction" as a violation of Valentino's right of publicity. The Court dismissed the action for failure to state a claim. In a concurrence joined by three members of the Court, Chief Justice Bird stated: "[P]rominence invites creative comment. Surely, the range of free expression would be meaningfully reduced if prominent persons in the present and recent past were forbidden topics for the imaginations of authors of fiction." 603 P.2d at 460.[12]

Chief Justice Bird noted that a cause of action might have existed had the defendant, for example, published "Rudolph Valentino's Cookbook," and neither the recipes nor the menus described were in any fashion related to Valentino. *Id.* at 457 n. 6. But she said that as long as the use of a celebrity's name was not "wholly unrelated" to the individual nor used to promote or endorse a collateral commercial product, the right of publicity did not apply. *Id.* Similarly, New York's Appellate Division said in *Frosch* that the right of publicity did not bar the use of a celebrity's name in a title so long as the item was a literary work and not "simply a disguised commercial advertisement for the sale of goods or services." 427 N.Y.S.2d at 829.

We think New York would recognize similar limits in Oregon law on the right of publicity. We note, for example, that the Oregon Supreme Court has on occasion interpreted the free speech clause of the Oregon Constitution as providing broader protection for free expression than that mandated by the federal Constitution. In light of the Oregon Court's concern for the protection of free expression, New York would not expect Oregon to permit the right of publicity to bar the use of a celebrity's name in a movie title unless the title was "wholly unrelated" to the movie or was "simply a disguised commercial advertisement for the sale of goods or services."

Here, as explained above, the title "Ginger and Fred" is clearly related to the content of the movie and is not a disguised advertisement for the

---

12. The majority of the in banc court did not discuss the First Amendment issues, rejecting the claim instead on the ground that the right of publicity expires on the death of the person protected. 603 P.2d at 455.

sale of goods or services or a collateral commercial product. We therefore hold that under Oregon law the right of publicity does not provide relief for Rogers' claim.[13]

. . . .

III. *Conclusion*

In sum, we hold that section 43(a) of the Lanham Act does not bar a minimally relevant use of a celebrity's name in the title of an artistic work where the title does not explicitly denote authorship, sponsorship, or endorsement by the celebrity or explicitly mislead as to content. Similarly, we conclude that Oregon law on the right of publicity, as interpreted by New York, would not bar the use of a celebrity's name in a movie title unless the title was "wholly unrelated" to the movie or was "simply a disguised commercial advertisement for the sale of goods or services." Under these standards, summary judgment was properly entered on the undisputed facts of this case, rejecting the Lanham Act and right of publicity claims. . . .

We therefore affirm the judgment of the District Court.

Editors' Note: The First Amendment issues raised in *Rogers v. Grimaldi* will be explored further in Chapter 12, Trademarks as Speech. See also *ETW Corp. v. Jireh Publishing, infra* this Chapter.

QUESTION

Does the *Rogers* decision suggest a form of "fair use" akin to copyright law's fair use (17 U.S.C. § 107), limiting both Lanham Act and state publicity claims regarding artistic uses of the names of celebrities whose fame has made them symbols of popular culture? Should a similar exception be created for artistic uses of trademarks whose fame has made them symbols of popular culture? *See infra*, Chapter 12.

O'Grady v. Twentieth Century Fox, 2003 WL 24174616 (E.D.Tex. 2003). The magistrate judge recommended denial of defendant Fox's motion for summary judgment regarding plaintiff's false advertising claim, but recommended granting summary judgment on the misappropriation claim. Plaintiff, Scott O'Grady, a pilot shot down over Bosnia, had written a best-selling book about his experiences, and also featured in a BBC docudrama. Fox subsequently, without O'Grady's participation, made a movie "loosely based" on the same events. When originally filmed, the docudrama was titled "Missing in Action." The U.S. distributor subsequently re-titled it

---

13. As in our ruling on the Lanham Act claim, we need not, and do not, reach the issue of whether the First Amendment would preclude a state from giving broader application to the right of publicity. The Supreme Court explored the First Amendment limits on the right of publicity in *Zacchini v. Scripps–Howard Broadcasting Co.*, 433 U.S. 562 (1977), holding that the First Amendment does not preclude an award of damages to a performer for violation of the right of publicity where a television news program broadcasts a performer's entire act. But the Court explicitly recognized each state's authority to define the right more narrowly. *Id.* at 578–79.

"Behind Enemy Lines: The Scott O'Grady Story." The Fox film was titled "Behind Enemy Lines." O'Grady alleged that Fox's publicity for its motion picture gave the false and misleading impression that O'Grady endorsed the movie or that it was his story.

The court rejected O'Grady's claim alleging misappropriation of his right of publicity: "the protection of name or likeness under Texas law does not include a person's life story." As to the false advertising claim, however, the magistrate judge ruled that facts necessary to its resolution remained in dispute:

> Plaintiff contends the title *Behind Enemy Lines: The Scott O'Grady Story* used in connection with the Rebroadcast [of the BBC docudrama] to promote the Movie *Behind Enemy Lines* is misleading and gives rise to an actionable claim. In addition, Plaintiff complains that even without the titles, the entire Rebroadcast is false and misleading because of the intermixing of advertisements, promotions, interviews, and other materials [promoting the Fox movie] into the true docudrama, giving viewers the false impression that Plaintiff endorsed the Movie or the Movie was Plaintiff's story.

> [Because the claim concerns advertisements for the movie, rather than the movie itself] there is a fact issue whether this is a case about commercial speech, in which case the *Rogers* test may not apply. Even if the Court were to apply the "hybrid speech" test utilized in *Rogers,* there is a genuine issue of material fact whether the title and Defendants' actions in creating the Rebroadcast are artistically related to the expressive elements of the Movie to qualify for First Amendment protection or whether the Rebroadcast is nothing more than a misleading advertisement for the Movie.

ETW Corp. v. Jireh Publishing, Inc.

332 F.3d 915 (6th Cir.2003).

■ GRAHAM, DISTRICT JUDGE.

Plaintiff–Appellant ETW Corporation ("ETW") is the licensing agent of Eldrick "Tiger" Woods ("Woods"), one of the world's most famous professional golfers. Woods, chairman of the board of ETW, has assigned to it the exclusive right to exploit his name, image, likeness, and signature, and all other publicity rights. ETW owns a United States trademark registration for the mark "TIGER WOODS" (Registration No. 2,194,381) for use in connection with "art prints, calendars, mounted photographs, notebooks, pencils, pens, posters, trading cards, and unmounted photographs."

Defendant–Appellee Jireh Publishing, Inc. ("Jireh") of Tuscaloosa, Alabama, is the publisher of artwork created by Rick Rush ("Rush"). Rush, who refers to himself as "America's sports artist," has created paintings of famous figures in sports and famous sports events. A few examples include Michael Jordan, Mark McGuire, Coach Paul "Bear" Bryant, the Pebble Beach Golf Tournament, and the America's Cup Yacht Race. Jireh has produced and successfully marketed limited edition art prints made from Rush's paintings.

In 1998, Rush created a painting entitled *The Masters of Augusta*, which commemorates Woods's victory at the Masters Tournament in Augusta, Georgia, in 1997. At that event, Woods became the youngest player ever to win the Masters Tournament, while setting a 72–hole record for the tournament and a record 12–stroke margin of victory. In the foreground of Rush's painting are three views of Woods in different poses. In the center, he is completing the swing of a golf club, and on each side he is crouching, lining up and/or observing the progress of a putt. To the left of Woods is his caddy, Mike "Fluff" Cowan, and to his right is his final round partner's caddy. Behind these figures is the Augusta National Clubhouse. In a blue background behind the clubhouse are likenesses of famous golfers of the past looking down on Woods. These include Arnold Palmer, Sam Snead, Ben Hogan, Walter Hagen, Bobby Jones, and Jack Nicklaus. Behind them is the Masters leader board.

The limited edition prints distributed by Jireh consist of an image of Rush's painting which includes Rush's signature at the bottom right hand corner. Beneath the image of the painting, in block letters, is its title, "The Masters Of Augusta." Beneath the title, in block letters of equal height, is the artist's name, "Rick Rush," and beneath the artist's name, in smaller upper and lower case letters, is the legend "Painting America Through Sports."

As sold by Jireh, the limited edition prints are enclosed in a white envelope, accompanied with literature which includes a large photograph of Rush, a description of his art, and a narrative description of the subject painting. On the front of the envelope, Rush's name appears in block letters inside a rectangle, which includes the legend "Painting America Through Sports." Along the bottom is a large reproduction of Rush's signature two inches high and ten inches long. On the back of the envelope, under the flap, are the words "Masters of Augusta" in letters that are three-eights of an inch high, and "Tiger Woods" in letters that are one-fourth of an inch high. Woods's name also appears in the narrative description of the painting where he is mentioned twice in twenty-eight lines of text. The text also includes references to the six other famous golfers depicted in the background of the painting as well as the two caddies. Jireh published and marketed two hundred and fifty 22 1/2″ x 30″ serigraphs and five thousand 9″ x 11″ lithographs of *The Masters of Augusta* at an issuing price of $700 for the serigraphs and $100 for the lithographs.

ETW filed suit against Jireh on June 26, 1998, in the United States District Court for the Northern District of Ohio, alleging trademark infringement in violation of the Lanham Act, 15 U.S.C. § 1114; ... and violation of Woods's right of publicity under Ohio common law. Jireh counterclaimed, seeking a declaratory judgment that Rush's art prints are protected by the First Amendment and do not violate the Lanham Act. Both parties moved for summary judgment. The district court granted Jireh's motion for summary judgment and dismissed the case. *See ETW*

Corp. v. Jireh Pub., Inc., 99 F.Supp.2d 829 (N.D. Ohio 2000). ETW timely perfected an appeal to this court.

II.   *Trademark Claims Based on the Unauthorized Use of the Registered Trademark "Tiger Woods"*

ETW claims that the prints of Rush's work constitute the unauthorized use of a registered trademark in violation of the Lanham Act, 15 U.S.C. § 1114, ...

ETW claims that Jireh infringed the registered mark "Tiger Woods" by including these words in marketing materials which accompanied the prints of Rush's painting. The words "Tiger Woods" do not appear on the face of the prints, nor are they included in the title of the painting. The words "Tiger Woods" do appear under the flap of the envelopes which contain the prints, and Woods is mentioned twice in the narrative which accompanies the prints.

The Lanham Act provides a defense to an infringement claim where the use of the mark "is a use, otherwise than as a mark, ... which is descriptive of and used fairly and in good faith only to describe the goods ... of such party[.]" 15 U.S.C. § 1115(b)(4); ... In evaluating a defendant's fair use defense, a court must consider whether defendant has used the mark: (1) in its descriptive sense; and (2) in good faith.

A celebrity's name may be used in the title of an artistic work so long as there is some artistic relevance. *See Rogers v. Grimaldi*, 875 F.2d 994, 997 (2nd Cir. 1989); *New York Racing Ass'n v. Perlmutter Publ'g, Inc.*, No. 95–CV–994, 1996 WL 465298 at *4 (N.D.N.Y. July 19, 1996) (finding the use of a registered mark on the title of a painting protected by the First Amendment). The use of Woods's name on the back of the envelope containing the print and in the narrative description of the print are purely descriptive and there is nothing to indicate that they were used other than in good faith. The prints, the envelopes which contain them, and the narrative materials which accompany them clearly identify Rush as the source of the print. Woods is mentioned only to describe the content of the print.

The district court properly granted summary judgment on ETW's claim for violation of its registered mark, "Tiger Woods," on the grounds that the claim was barred by the fair use defense as a matter of law.

III.   *Trademark Claims Under 15 U.S.C. § 1125(a) Based on the Unauthorized Use of the Likeness of Tiger Woods*

. . .

ETW has registered Woods's name as a trademark, but it has not registered any image or likeness of Woods. Nevertheless, ETW claims to have trademark rights in Woods's image and likeness. Section 43 (a) of the Lanham Act provides a federal cause of action for infringement of an unregistered trademark which affords such marks essentially the same protection as those that are registered....

Here, ETW claims protection under the Lanham Act for any and all images of Tiger Woods. This is an untenable claim. ETW asks us, in effect, to constitute Woods himself as a walking, talking trademark. Images and likenesses of Woods are not protectable as a trademark because they do not perform the trademark function of designation. They do not distinguish and identify the source of goods. They cannot function as a trademark because there are undoubtedly thousands of images and likenesses of Woods taken by countless photographers, and drawn, sketched, or painted by numerous artists, which have been published in many forms of media, and sold and distributed throughout the world. No reasonable person could believe that merely because these photographs or paintings contain Woods's likeness or image, they all originated with Woods.

We hold that, as a general rule, a person's image or likeness cannot function as a trademark. Our conclusion is supported by the decisions of other courts which have addressed this issue. In *Pirone v. MacMillan, Inc.,* 894 F.2d 579 (2nd Cir. 1990), the Second Circuit rejected a trademark claim asserted by the daughters of baseball legend Babe Ruth. The plaintiffs objected to the use of Ruth's likeness in three photographs which appeared in a calendar published by the defendant. The court rejected their claim, holding that "a photograph of a human being, unlike a portrait of a fanciful cartoon character, is not inherently 'distinctive' in the trademark sense of tending to indicate origin." *Id.* at 583. The court noted that Ruth "was one of the most photographed men of his generation, a larger than life hero to millions and an historical figure[.]" *Id.* The Second Circuit Court concluded that a consumer could not reasonably believe that Ruth sponsored the calendar:

> [A]n ordinarily prudent purchaser would have no difficulty discerning that these photos are merely the subject matter of the calendar and do not in any way indicate sponsorship. No reasonable jury could find a likelihood of confusion.

Id. at 585. The court observed that "under some circumstances, a photograph of a person may be a valid trademark—if, for example, a particular photograph was consistently used on specific goods." *Id.* at 583. The court rejected plaintiffs' assertion of trademark rights in every photograph of Ruth.

In *Estate of Presley v. Russen*, 513 F. Supp. 1339, 1363–1364 (D.N.J. 1981), the court rejected a claim by the estate of Elvis Presley that his image and likeness was a valid mark. The court did find, however, as suggested by the Second Circuit in *Pirone*, that one particular image of Presley had been consistently used in the advertising and sale of Elvis Presley entertainment services to identify those services and that the image could likely be found to function as a mark.

In *Rock and Roll Hall of Fame*, the plaintiff asserted trademark rights in the design of the building which houses the Rock and Roll Hall of Fame in Cleveland, Ohio, and claimed that defendant's poster featuring a photograph of the museum against a colorful sunset was a violation of its trademark rights. 134 F.3d at 751. This court, with one judge dissenting, reversed the judgment of the district court which granted plaintiff's request for a preliminary injunction. After reviewing the evidence, the majority concluded:

> In reviewing the Museum's disparate uses of several different perspectives of its building design, we cannot conclude that they create a consistent and distinct commercial impression as an indicator of a single source of origin or sponsorship. To be more specific, we cannot conclude on this record that it is likely that the Museum has established a valid trademark in every photograph which, like Gentile's, prominently displays the front of the Museum's building.

Id. at 755. In reaching this conclusion, this court approved and followed *Pirone* and *Estate of Presley.*

Here, ETW does not claim that a particular photograph of Woods has been consistently used on specific goods. Instead, ETW's claim is identical to that of the plaintiffs in *Pirone*, a sweeping claim to trademark rights in every photograph and image of Woods. Woods, like Ruth, is one of the most photographed sports figures of his generation, but this alone does not suffice to create a trademark claim.

The district court properly granted summary judgment on ETW's claim of trademark rights in all images and likenesses of Tiger Woods.

* * *

D.   *Right of Publicity Claim*

[The court discussed its own and other circuits' decisions in right of publicity cases.]

In *Comedy III Productions, Inc. v. Gary Saderup, Inc.,* 25 Cal. 4th 387, 106 Cal. Rptr. 2d 126, 21 P.3d 797 (2001), the California Supreme Court adopted a transformative use test in determining whether the artistic use of a celebrity's image is protected by the First Amendment. Saderup, an artist with over twenty-five years experience in making charcoal drawings of celebrities, created a drawing of the famous comedy team, The Three Stooges. The drawings were used to create lithographic and silk screen masters, which were then used to produce lithographic prints and silk screen images on T-shirts. Comedy III, the owner of all rights to the former comedy act, brought suit against Saderup under a California statute, which grants the right of publicity to successors in interest of deceased celebrities.

The California Supreme Court found that Saderup's portraits were entitled to First Amendment protection because they were "expressive works and not an advertisement or endorsement of a product." *Id.* at 396, 21 P.3d at 802....

The court rejected the proposition that Saderup's lithographs and T-shirts lost their First Amendment protection because they were not original single works of art, but were instead part of a commercial enterprise designed to generate profit solely from the sale of multiple reproductions of likenesses of The Three Stooges:

[T]his position has no basis in logic or authority. No one would claim that a published book, because it is one of many copies, receives less First Amendment protection than the original manuscript.... [A] reproduction of a celebrity image that, as explained above, contains significant creative elements is entitled to as much First Amendment protection as an original work of art.

Id. at 408, 21 P.3d at 810.

Borrowing part of the fair use defense from copyright law, the California court proposed the following test for distinguishing between protected and unprotected expression when the right of publicity conflicts with the First Amendment:

When artistic expression takes the form of a literal depiction or imitation of a celebrity for commercial gain, directly trespassing on the right of publicity without adding significant expression beyond that trespass, the state law interest in protecting the fruits of artistic labor outweighs the expressive interests of the imitative artist.

On the other hand, when a work contains significant transformative elements, it is not only especially worthy of First Amendment protection, but it is also less likely to interfere with the economic interest protected by the right of publicity....

Accordingly, First Amendment protection of such works outweighs whatever interest the state may have in enforcing the right of publicity.

Id. at 405, 21 P.3d at 808 (footnote and citations omitted). Later in its opinion, the California court restated the test as follows:

Another way of stating the inquiry is whether the celebrity likeness is one of the "raw materials" from which an original work is synthesized, or whether the depiction or imitation of the celebrity is the very sum and substance of the work in question.

Id. at 406, 21 P.3d at 809.

Finally, citing the art of Andy Warhol, the court noted that even literal reproductions of celebrity portraits may be protected by the First Amendment.

Through distortion and the careful manipulation of context, Warhol was able to convey a message that went beyond the commercial exploitation of celebrity images and became a form of ironic social comment on the dehumanization of celebrity itself.... Although the distinction between protected and unprotected expression will sometimes be subtle, it is no more so than other distinctions triers of fact are called on to make in First Amendment jurisprudence.

Id. at 408–409, 106 Cal.Rptr.2d 126, 21 P.3d 797, 21 P.3d at 811 (citations and footnote omitted).

. . .

E. *Application of the Law to the Evidence in this Case*

The evidence in the record reveals that Rush's work consists of much more than a mere literal likeness of Woods. It is a panorama of Woods's victory at the 1997 Masters Tournament, with all of the trappings of that tournament in full view, including the Augusta clubhouse, the leader board, images of Woods's caddy, and his final round partner's caddy. These elements in themselves are sufficient to bring Rush's work within the protection of the First Amendment. The Masters Tournament is probably the world's most famous golf tournament and Woods's victory in the 1997 tournament was a historic event in the world of sports. A piece of art that portrays a historic sporting event communicates and celebrates the value our culture attaches to such events. It would be ironic indeed if the presence of the image of the victorious athlete would deny the work First Amendment protection. Furthermore, Rush's work includes not only images of Woods and the two caddies, but also carefully crafted likenesses of six past winners of the Masters Tournament: Arnold Palmer, Sam Snead, Ben Hogan, Walter Hagen, Bobby Jones, and Jack Nicklaus, a veritable pantheon of golf's greats. Rush's work conveys the message that Woods himself will someday join that revered group.

Turning first to ETW's Lanham Act false endorsement claim, we agree with the courts that hold that the Lanham Act should be applied to artistic works only where the public interest in avoiding confusion outweighs the public interest in free expression. The *Rogers* test is helpful in striking that balance in the instant case. We find that the presence of Woods's image in Rush's painting *The Masters Of Augusta* does have artistic relevance to the underlying work and that it does not explicitly mislead as to the source of the work. We believe that the principles followed in *Cardtoons*, *Hoffman* and *Comedy III* are also relevant in determining whether the Lanham Act applies to Rush's work, and we find that it does not. . . .

In regard to the Ohio law right of publicity claim, we conclude that Ohio would construe its right of publicity as suggested in the Restatement (Third) of Unfair Competition, Chapter 4, Section 47, Comment d., which articulates a rule analogous to the rule of fair use in copyright law. Under this rule, the substantiality and market effect of the use of the celebrity's image is analyzed in light of the informational and creative content of the defendant's use. Applying this rule, we conclude that Rush's work has substantial informational and creative content which outweighs any adverse effect on ETW's market and that Rush's work does not violate Woods's right of publicity.

We further find that Rush's work is expression which is entitled to the full protection of the First Amendment and not the more limited protection afforded to commercial speech. When we balance the magnitude of the speech restriction against the interest in protecting Woods's intellectual property right, we encounter precisely the same considerations weighed by the Tenth Circuit in *Cardtoons*. These include consideration of the fact that through their pervasive presence in the media, sports and entertainment celebrities have come to symbolize certain ideas and values in our society

and have become a valuable means of expression in our culture. As the Tenth Circuit observed "celebrities . . . are an important element of the shared communicative resources of our cultural domain." *Cardtoons*, 95 F.3d at 972.

In balancing these interests against Woods's right of publicity, we note that Woods, like most sports and entertainment celebrities with commercially valuable identities, engages in an activity, professional golf, that in itself generates a significant amount of income which is unrelated to his right of publicity. Even in the absence of his right of publicity, he would still be able to reap substantial financial rewards from authorized appearances and endorsements. It is not at all clear that the appearance of Woods's likeness in artwork prints which display one of his major achievements will reduce the commercial value of his likeness.

While the right of publicity allows celebrities like Woods to enjoy the fruits of their labors, here Rush has added a significant creative component of his own to Woods's identity. Permitting Woods's right of publicity to trump Rush's right of freedom of expression would extinguish Rush's right to profit from his creative enterprise.

After balancing the societal and personal interests embodied in the First Amendment against Woods's property rights, we conclude that the effect of limiting Woods's right of publicity in this case is negligible and significantly outweighed by society's interest in freedom of artistic expression.

Finally, applying the transformative effects test adopted by the Supreme Court of California in *Comedy III*, we find that Rush's work does contain significant transformative elements which make it especially worthy of First Amendment protection and also less likely to interfere with the economic interest protected by Woods' right of publicity. Unlike the unadorned, nearly photographic reproduction of the faces of The Three Stooges in *Comedy III*, Rush's work does not capitalize solely on a literal depiction of Woods. Rather, Rush's work consists of a collage of images in addition to Woods's image which are combined to describe, in artistic form, a historic event in sports history and to convey a message about the significance of Woods's achievement in that event. Because Rush's work has substantial transformative elements, it is entitled to the full protection of the First Amendment. In this case, we find that Woods's right of publicity must yield to the First Amendment.

. . .

■ CLAY, CIRCUIT JUDGE, dissenting.

. . .

I. Trademark Claims Based on Defendant's Unauthorized Use of the Unregistered Mark—§ 43(a) of the Lanham Act, 15 U.S.C. § 1125(a)

. . .

Simply stated, contrary to the majority's contention, the jurisprudence clearly indicates that a person's image or likeness *can* function as a trademark as long as there is evidence demonstrating that the likeness or image was used as a trademark; which is to say, the image can function as a trademark as long as there is evidence of consumer confusion as to the source of the merchandise upon which the image appears. *See, e.g., Rock & Roll*, 134 F.3d at 753. . . .

Inasmuch as Plaintiff proffered evidence of consumer confusion as to Woods' affiliation with or sponsorship of the poster, Plaintiff proffered evidence that it has used this image of Tiger Woods "as a trademark." . . .

With that said, it is difficult to conceive how the majority arrives at its conclusion that Plaintiff "does not claim that a particular photograph of Woods has been consistently used on specific goods" but instead makes "a sweeping claim to trademark rights in every photograph and image of Woods." As indicated in the outset of this discussion, Plaintiff's complaint specifically takes issue with the image of Woods as depicted in Rush's *Masters of Augusta* print and, moreover, Plaintiff has come forward with strong evidence of consumer confusion to support its claim that this image of Woods has been used as a trademark for purposes of supporting its § 43(a) claim. The majority's failure to acknowledge the significance of this evidence constitutes a fatal flaw in its analysis . . .

Finally, as explained in the next section, even by adopting the Second Circuit's balancing approach when considering a Lanham Act claim involving an artistic expression, Plaintiff's likelihood of confusion evidence should, and indeed must, be considered in deciding Plaintiff's claim for infringement of the unregistered mark. As the Second Circuit has also proclaimed, "trademark protection is not lost simply because the alleging infringing use is in connection with an artistic expression." *Cliffs Notes, Inc. v. Bantam Doubleday Dell Publ'g Group, Inc.*, 886 F.2d 490, 493 (2d Cir. 1989) (alteration in *Cliffs Notes*) (quoting *Silverman v. CBS Inc.*, 870 F.2d 40, 49 (2d Cir. 1989)).

. . .

Even under the *Rogers* standard, it is necessary for this case to be remanded on the issue of Plaintiff's false endorsement claim since questions of fact remain as to the degree of consumer confusion associated with Rush's print and Woods' endorsement thereof. To hold otherwise not only runs counter to the approach espoused in *Rogers* and its progeny, but to the express word of Congress: that a plaintiff may prevail on a Lanham Act claim if he can prove that the use in commerce of the trademark "in connection with goods or services" is "*likely to cause confusion, to cause mistake, or to deceive* as to the affiliation, connection, or association of such person with another person, or as to the origin, sponsorship, or approval of his or her goods, services, or commercial activities by another person. . . ." 15 U.S.C. § 1125(a)(1)(A) (emphasis added). This is not to say that the ultimate outcome here would necessarily be a favorable one for Plaintiff; however, a jury should be able to make that decision after hearing all of the evidence presented by Plaintiff, as opposed to the majority's truncated and abbreviated approach which fails to engage in any meaningful consideration of pertinent and relevant evidence of consumer confusion, and fails to engage in any significant balancing of the interests.

. . .

V.   Ohio Common Law Right of Publicity Claim

. . .

Despite the various commentary and scholarship assessing the virtues and drawbacks to the right of publicity when compared to First Amendment principles, the fact remains that the right of publicity is an accepted right and striking the balance between an individual's right of publicity against the speaker's First Amendment right is not an easy one. Bearing in mind the principles justifying the two rights, it is clear why Woods' right of publicity does not bow to Defendant's First Amendment rights in this case.

B.   Woods' Right of Publicity Claim in this Case

. . .

In the instant case, where we are faced with an expressive work and the question of whether that work is protected under the First Amendment, the reasoning and transformative test set forth in *Comedy III* are in line with the Supreme Court's reasoning in *Zacchini* as well as in harmony with the goals of both the right to publicity and the First Amendment. Applying the test here, it is difficult to discern any appreciable transformative or creative contribution in Defendant's prints so as to entitle them to First Amendment protection. "A literal depiction of a celebrity, even if accomplished with great skill, may still be subject to a right of publicity challenge. The inquiry is in a sense more quantitative than qualitative, asking whether the literal and imitative or the creative elements predominate in the work." *Comedy III*, 21 P.3d at 809 (footnote omitted).

Indeed, the rendition done by Rush is nearly identical to that in the poster distributed by Nike. Although the faces and partial body images of other famous golfers appear in blue sketch blending in the background of Rush's print, the clear focus of the work is Woods in full body image wearing his red shirt and holding his famous swing in the pose which is nearly identical to that depicted in the Nike poster. Rush's print does not depict Woods in the same vein as the other golfers, such that the focus of the print is not the Masters Tournament or the other golfers who have won the prestigious green jacket award, but that of Woods holding his famous golf swing while at that tournament. Thus, although it is apparent that Rush is an adequately skilled artist, after viewing the prints in question it is also apparent that Rush's ability in this regard is "subordinated to the overall goal of creating literal, conventional depictions of [Tiger Woods] so as to exploit his ... fame [such that Rush's] right of free expression is outweighed by [Woods'] right of publicity." *See id.* at 811.

In fact, the narrative that accompanies the prints expressly discusses Woods and his fame:

> But the center of their [other golfers'] gaze is 1997 winner Tiger Woods, here flanked by his caddie, "Fluff", and final round player partner's (Constantino Rocca) caddie on right, displaying that awesome swing that sends a golf ball straighter and truer than should be humanly possible. Only his uncanny putting ability serves to complete his dominating performance that lifts him alongside the Masters of Augusta.

Accordingly, contrary to the majority's conclusion otherwise, it is clear that the prints gain their commercial value by exploiting the fame and celebrity status that Woods has worked to achieve. Under such facts, the right of publicity is not outweighed by the right of free expression. *See Comedy III*, 21 P.3d at 811 (noting that the marketability and economic value of the defendant's work was derived primarily from the fame of the three celebrities that it depicted and was therefore not protected by the First Amendment).

This conclusion regarding Plaintiff's right of publicity claim is in harmony with that regarding Plaintiff's claims brought under the Lanham Act. As the Restatement explains:

> Proof of deception or confusion is not required in order to establish an infringement of the right of publicity. However, if the defendant's unauthorized use creates a false suggestion of endorsement or a likelihood of confusion as to source or sponsorship, liability may also be imposed for deceptive marketing or trademark or trade name infringement.

Restatement, *supra* § 46 cmt. b, 537.

Because Plaintiff has come forward with evidence of consumer confusion as to Woods' sponsorship of the products in question, it is for the jury to decide whether liability should be imposed for Plaintiff's claims brought under the Lanham Act, and this is true whether employing the balancing approach set forth in *Rogers* or simply employing the eight-factor test in the traditional sense. The majority's failure to do so in this case is in complete contravention to the intent of Congress, the principles of trademark law, and the well-established body of jurisprudence in this area. . . .

———

Consider whether right of publicity claims require first amendment analyses like those undertaken in *ETW v. Jireh*. Where, for example, a state right of publicity statute provides a right of action for nonconsensual use of a person's name or likeness "for purposes of trade," is it clear that "trade" encompasses all for-profit expressive uses? **Tyne v. Time Warner Entertainment**, 901 So.2d 802 (Fla.2005), concerned a claim brought by the families of the fishermen who died in what became memorialized in a non fiction book and film as "The Perfect Storm." The Florida Supreme

Court, ruling on a question certified by the Eleventh Circuit, interpreted the Florida statute, which prohibited a person to "publicly use for purposes of trade or for any commercial or advertising purpose the name, portrait, photograph, or other likeness of any natural person without the express written or oral consent to such use ..." Section 540.08, Florida Statutes (2000). The Florida Supreme Court adopted the reasoning of a lower court in *Loft v. Fuller*, 408 So.2d 619 (Fla. 4th DCA 1981), which had declined to find that the statute covered a claim by the family of an airline pilot who died in a crash against a book and a motion picture containing non fiction accounts of the disaster.

In our view, section 540.08, by prohibiting the use of one's name or likeness for trade, commercial or advertising purposes, is designed to prevent the unauthorized use of a name to directly promote the product or service of the publisher. Thus, the publication is harmful not simply because it is included in a publication that is sold for a profit, but rather because of the way it associates the individual's name or his personality with something else. Such is not the case here.

While we agree that at least one of the purposes of the author and publisher in releasing the publication in question was to make money through sales of copies of the book and that such a publication is commercial in that sense, this in no way distinguishes this book from almost all other books, magazines or newspapers and simply does not amount to the kind of commercial exploitation prohibited by the statute. We simply do not believe that the term "commercial," as employed by Section 540.08, was meant to be construed to bar the use of people's names in such a sweeping fashion. We also believe that acceptance of appellants' view of the statute would result in substantial confrontation between this statute and the first amendment to the United States Constitution guaranteeing freedom of the press and of speech. Having concluded that the publication as alleged is not barred by Section 540.08, we need not decide if, under the allegations of the complaint, the book was of current and legitimate public interest, thus removing it entirely from the scope of the statute.

In **Nussensweig v. DiCorcia**, 11 Misc.3d 1051, 814 N.Y.S.2d 891 (Sup.Ct.2006), DiCorcia, a professional photographer, made a series of prints of candid, unstaged photos taken of passers-by in Times Square. DiCorcia did not seek or obtain consent to photograph any of the people whose likenesses were included in his series, in which the plaintiff Nussensweig's readily-identifiable image appeared. DiCorcia admitted to creating 10 edition prints of the photograph of plaintiff, plus 3 artist's proofs. The series, including the photograph of plaintiff, was exhibited at a well-known gallery, which also published a catalogue containing reproductions of all the photographs in the series, including the photograph of plaintiff. A substantial number of catalogues were distributed to the public during the period of the gallery exhibition. Plaintiff holds a deep religious conviction that the use of his image for commercial and public purposes violates his religion. In particular he believes that defendants' use of his image violates the second commandment prohibition against graven images, and has therefore demanded that DiCorcia cease selling and displaying his photograph. DiCorcia responded that the photographs were not being used for either "advertising" or "trade" because the photograph of plaintiff was "art" and thus fell outside the prohibition of the New York civil rights statute §§ 50 and 51. Plaintiff rejoined that DiCorcia's photographs were displayed in a commercial gallery and were for sale, as were the catalogs. Should the court consider "what is art"? Should the sale of the photographs (in originals or as reproduced in the catalogs) make them objects of "trade" under the statute?

QUESTIONS

1. Brutus Forte, a New York domiciliary, is a musician who, under the pseudonym Brute Force, is an extremely popular entertainer, performing in the "heavy metal" genre of rock music. Brute Force has a distinctive vocal style, consisting in part of grunts and squawks that evoke a variety of barnyard fauna, principally pigs and turkeys. Perhaps not surprisingly, the song with which Brute Force opens and closes his live performances is his own, rather violent and idiosyncratic, version of "Old MacDonald Had a Farm." Brute Force often appears on stage, in music videos, and on album covers dressed in a turkey suit.

Brute Force has become a pop culture icon, and advertisers have sought to take advantage of his popularity by soliciting his participation in a variety of commercials. However, seeking to maintain his artistic purity, Brute Force has refused to perform in or to authorize any commercials incorporating sounds or images from his live or recorded performances.

Tina's Turkeys is a successful poultry producer in Illinois. Tina's has just aired a commercial on a local television station that depicts a person in a turkey suit, striking an aggressive attitude. The turkey suit completely encloses its wearer. Next to the individual in the turkey suit is a roast turkey attractively arranged on a serving platter. The sound track plays "Old MacDonald Had a Farm" in a traditional arrangement, but accompanied by sounds of squawking turkeys and grunting pigs. These sounds were taken from a sound effects recording. A voice-over declares "As tough as this turkey is (close up of the person in the turkey suit), that's how tender our's is (close up of the roast turkey). You don't have to be a brute to enjoy a good turkey.... Tina's Turkeys."

Mr. Forte asks you, his lawyer, what claims he might have against Tina's Turkeys, what defenses he should anticipate, and your evaluation of the likely outcome.

2. Basketball star Kareem Abdul–Jabbar's birth name was Ferdinand Lewis Alcindor. During college and his early years in the National Basketball Association, he was known as Lew Alcindor. In college, he converted to Islam, and in 1971 recorded his name as Kareem Abdul–Jabbar. He has played basketball and endorsed products under the name Kareem Abdul–Jabbar ever since. At the time the controversy arose, he had not used "Lew Alcindor" commercially for over ten years. General Motors Corp. aired a television commercial recalling the college championship record of Lew Alcindor, and implying that their Oldsmobile car is an equivalent champion in its field. GMC did not obtain Abdul–Jabbar's consent to use his former name in its commercial. In response to Abdul–Jabbar's lawsuit alleging violation of his California law right of publicity, GMC has contended that Abdul–Jabbar has abandoned the Lew Alcindor name. How should the court rule? *See Abdul–Jabbar v. GM*, 85 F.3d 407 (9th Cir.1996).

3. Ernest Hemingway (1899–1961) lived in Key West, Florida from 1929 through 1940. After his death, the house where he lived was purchased by residents of Key West, who opened the "Hemingway Home Museum" in 1964. (The house was empty when the museum's owners bought it, but they furnished it with a combination of items once owned by Hemingway, and items similar to those he probably owned during the period of his residence.) The museum is a tourist attraction; visitors to Key West can take conducted tours through the author's former residence. The building became a national historic landmark in 1968. Beginning in July 1981, and continuing until this year, the Hemingway Home Museum has sponsored an annual "Hemingway Days" festival in Key West. The festival combines kitsch (Hemingway look-alike contests, sales of Hemingway souvenirs, arm wrestling contests) with more high-brow events (storytelling contests, fishing and golf events, short story competitions, readings from Hemingway's work).

Meanwhile, in 1988, Hemingway's three sons, Patrick, John and Gregory, hired an agent to help them gain control over their father's name and likeness. They formed the Hemingway Ltd. Corporation, and applied for federal trademark registration for their father's name and likeness. Registration issued in 1992 for HEMINGWAY as a service mark for the services of "licensing others the rights to use and/or exploit the name and likeness of Ernest Hemingway." The brothers have recently licensed a limited edition Hemingway Mont Blanc pen ($600.00) and a Hemingway line of glasses frames ($300.00 and up).

Recently, Hemingway Ltd. got in touch with the owners of the museum and insisted that it controlled the use of the Hemingway name and likeness. It proposed that the museum remit a royalty of 10% of the gross proceeds from all museum and the annual festival activities. The president of the museum declined, and the brothers filed suit for trademark infringement, unfair competition, and violation of their late father's right of publicity. They seek a preliminary injunction against this year's Hemingway Days festival. How should the court rule?

4. In the wake of the success of the television series *Cheers*, Host International Co, a franchisor of airport cocktail lounges, has obtained permission from Paramount, *Cheers'* producer, to recreate the television show bar's decor and to feature at the bar animatronic figures resembling two of the characters from the show. The actors who portray these characters have now alleged that Host has violated the California publicity right statute and California common law by appropriating their likenesses for the figures. Host responds that the Vanna White case forecloses the actors' claim with respect to the robots, and further urges that all it has appropriated is the characters (with Paramount's permission), not the identities of the actors. How should the court rule? *See Wendt v. Host International, Inc.*, 125 F.3d 806 (9th Cir.1997), *reh. den.* 197 F.3d 1284 (Kozinski, J. dissenting).

5. With respect to the following exhibits, what claims do you foresee? By whom against whom?

6. Major League Baseball publishes statistics of each player's performance. For batters, these include batting average, home runs and RBIs (runs batted in), for pitchers, the win-loss record and the ERA (earned run average). Organizers of baseball "fantasy leagues" assemble imaginary teams based on the players' statistics. The league organizers also use the statistics to calculate the "winning" team at season's end. Some fantasy leagues award cash prizes; the fantasy leagues have become a multi million dollar business. Major League Baseball, asserting the ballplayers' rights of publicity, has demanded that the leagues take a license to use the names and statistics of the ballplayers. The fantasy leagues reply that these are unprotectable facts not subject to ownership on any theory. What arguments can you make for the players and MLB? What arguments for the leagues? Who should prevail? See *C.B.C. Distrib. & Mktg., Inc. v. Major League Baseball Advanced Media, L.P.*, 443 F.Supp.2d 1077 (E.D.Mo.2006).

C. Merchandising

Hon. Alex Kozinski, Essay: Trademarks Unplugged, 68 N.Y.U. L. Rev. 960, 961–962 (1993).

There's a growing tendency to use trademarks not just to identify products but also to enhance or adorn them, even to create new commodities altogether. There was a time when the name of a shirt's manufacturer was discreetly sewn inside the collar. Izod and Pierre Cardin changed all that, making the manufacturer's logo an integral part of the product itself. Do you like a particular brand of beer? Chances are you can buy a T-shirt that telegraphs your brand loyalty. Some people put stickers on their cars announcing their allegiance to the Grateful Dead. Go figure.

It's a pretty good deal all around. The consumer gets a kick out of it, and the manufacturer gets free advertising, solidifying its name recognition and reinforcing brand loyalty. What's more, it's lucrative—not merely in enhancing sales of the product, but also as a separate profit center. Think, for example, how much money is made in products associated with sports teams and blockbuster movies.

When trademarks are used in this way, they acquire certain functional characteristics that are different from—and sometimes inconsistent with—their traditional role as identifiers of source. Where trademarks once served only to tell the consumer who made the product, they now often enhance it or become a functional part of it. This trend raises questions about whether—and to what extent—the law should protect trademarks when they are pressed into service as separate products.

QUESTIONS

1. Judge Kozinski suggests that, because trademarks are now "doing all kinds of work they weren't originally meant to do," the law of trademarks must be revised in order to keep up: "It seems to me that we should confront this new reality head on, probably by amending the Lanham Act." How would you frame such an amendment?

2. The Apple Computer Corporation advertises its iPod MP3 player with an ad campaign that features black silhouettes of happy iPod customers wearing white iPods against a brightly colored background. Apple has used this theme for print ads, web ads, billboards and television commercials. The ad campaign has been very well received.

Recently, three Apple iPod fans launched a small business in which they will take any digital photograph and turn it into a silhouette styled to resemble an iPod advertisement. They charge $20 for each photo, and offer their service from a website at www.ipodmyphoto.com. Customers can upload digital photos using the website, pay with a credit card, and download the "iPod-ized" versions a week later. Editing the image to add an iPod, complete with earbud wires, is optional, and carries no additional charge. Business has been brisk. The majority of the orders involve pictures of babies and children, pets, and recently married couples. The website includes several sample photographs:

The service has neither sought nor received permission from Apple for any of its activities. Small print at the bottom of the ipodmyphoto.com web page explains: *"iPod is the property of Apple Computer. iPod My Photo is not affiliated with Apple Computer in any way except that we love iPods."* Can Apple secure an injunction against the service? If not, why not?

Boston Athletic Ass'n v. Sullivan

867 F.2d 22 (1st Cir.1989).

■ BOWNES, J.:

In this service mark infringement case, Boston Athletic Association (BAA) and Image Impact, Inc. (Image) appeal the denial of their motion for summary judgment and the concurrent granting of the defendants', Mark Sullivan d/b/a Good Life (Sullivan) and Beau Tease, Inc. (Beau Tease), motion for summary judgment. This case arises out of the sale by the defendants of T-shirts (hereinafter called shirts) and other wearing apparel with designs alleged to infringe on BAA's service marks "Boston Marathon," "BAA Marathon" and its unicorn logo. We agree with the district court that there are no genuine issues of material fact, but disagree with the district court's determination of which side was entitled to summary judgment. We, therefore, reverse.

. . . .

II.   *The Start in State Court*

We have taken the facts mainly from the district court opinions. BAA is a charitable organization whose principal activity has been conducting the Boston Marathon since it was first run in 1897. The race is run annually from Hopkinton to Boston on Patriots' Day, the third Monday in April. In recent years, a day or two prior to the race an exposition has been put on by Conventures, Inc. under BAA's sponsorship. At the exposition, various businesses set up booths and sell shirts, running apparel, and sports items. The registered runners also pick up their numbers and official materials from the BAA booth.

Defendant Sullivan, a resident of Hopkinton, Massachusetts, retails wearing apparel under the name "Good Life" at a store in Hopkinton. Defendant Beau Tease, Inc. is a Massachusetts corporation doing business in Cambridge. It imprints and distributes merchandise, including shirts, to the trade.

In an effort to defray the costs of the race, BAA began an active campaign to market its name via licensing agreements. It registered the names "Boston Marathon" and "BAA Marathon" and its unicorn logo in Massachusetts in 1983 and "Boston Marathon" in the United States Patent and Trademark Office in 1985.

As early as 1978, the defendants were imprinting and selling shirts with the name "Boston Marathon" and various other terms including the year on them. In 1984, defendant Sullivan negotiated an agreement under which Beau Tease sold to BAA a large quantity of shirts which BAA gave away to the athletes and volunteers during the 1985 race. In 1986, Image, through its President, Mickey Lawrence, entered into an exclusive license with BAA for the use of BAA's service marks on wearing apparel including shirts. Starting in 1986, Image and BAA gave notice to imprinters, wholesalers, and retailers that Image was the exclusive licensee of the BAA and that any unauthorized use on merchandise of the name "Boston Marathon," or a similar name or a colorable imitation thereof, would violate the exclusive rights of BAA and its licensee.

By March of 1986, Beau Tease was imprinting and Sullivan was selling in the Boston area shirts imprinted as follows:

1986 Marathon

[picture of runners]

Hopkinton–Boston

.   .   .   .

In late 1986 and early 1987, Beau Tease began to imprint and Sullivan began to retail shirts and other apparel imprinted as follows:

1987 Marathon

[picture of runners]

Hopkinton–Boston

The 1987 shirts and the 1986 shirts were of poorer quality than plaintiffs' both as to manufacture and materials. The defendants were planning to sell their shirts and other items at the exposition.

III.   *The Contestants Reach Federal Court*

In 1987, the exposition was held on Saturday April 18 and the race on Monday April 20. On April 1, 1987, BAA and Image filed suit in the United States District Court for the District of Massachusetts alleging that defendants' 1986 and 1987 shirts, with the logos described above, infringed BAA's marks. The complaint alleged confusion in violation of the Lanham Act, 15 U.S.C. § 1114.... The complaint also included ... state law counts for dilution, sale of counterfeits and imitations, and unauthorized use of a name. Along with the complaint, plaintiffs filed a motion for a preliminary injunction, seeking to stop the manufacture and sale of any article bearing the name "Boston Marathon" or any similar name.

. . . .

The district court[] ... found that BAA's marks were its most valuable asset and were at all relevant times valid and enforceable. It found that an average person would infer sponsorship by someone of a product carrying the logo "Boston Marathon," and that defendants' logos referred to the marathon. The court stated that there was a dispute whether the public would associate BAA with the Boston Marathon but that this dispute was not material. It held that the public would not infer that the defendants' logos were sponsored by BAA.... The court also held that BAA's rights did not extend beyond the use of its exact service marks. The court ruled as a matter of law that there was no confusion between the defendants' and plaintiffs' shirts. The court concluded its opinion: "More precisely, this Court rules that the specific T-shirt logo challenged in this action does not, as a matter of law, give rise to any colorable confusion with products authorized by the BAA as part of its sponsorship of the particular road race in question." Judgment for the defendants was entered.... This appeal followed.

IV.   *BAA's Right to Run*

Defendants argue that they should prevail because BAA's marks are entitled to no protection for two reasons: 1. "Boston Marathon" has become a generic term inasmuch as it now refers to both the race and the services rendered by BAA; and 2. defendants' use of "Boston Marathon" on shirts from 1978 constitutes a prior usage.

. . . .

The burden of proof is on the party seeking to have a registered mark declared a generic to show that it has become so under the above test. Here, the defendants have introduced no evidence on the issue of "primary significance" and thus, have failed to meet the burden of proof.

With respect to prior usage, it is axiomatic that "registration does not create the underlying right in a trademark. That right, which accrues from the use of a particular name or symbol, is essentially a common law property right...." Therefore, BAA's failure to register its marks until the mid–1980s is not dispositive. Furthermore, a mark provides protection not only for the product or service to which it is originally applied but also to related items or services.

Here, the uncontradicted evidence, consisting mainly of media references to the race, especially newspaper and magazine articles, shows that: 1. the race was originally called the Boston Athletic Association or Boston A.A. Marathon; 2. since 1917, the race has also been called the Boston Marathon; and 3. since at least 1977, a year before defendants' "prior usage," BAA used the names "B.A.A. Marathon" and "Boston Marathon" interchangeably. This use by BAA undercuts defendants' prior use claim as to the words *per se*. As for the use of the words on shirts and other running apparel, such apparel is related to the service provided by BAA, the race, and BAA is entitled to enjoin use of its marks on such items. We agree with the district court that BAA has had valid and enforceable marks for the entire relevant time frame.

V.   *The Longest Stretch: Likelihood of Confusion*

Having held that BAA has enforceable rights in its marks, we turn to the central issue in this and most infringement cases: the likelihood of confusion. Claims for infringement of a registered trademark are governed by § 32(1) of the Lanham Act, 15 U.S.C. § 1114(1)....

In order to determine whether defendants' shirts are "likely to cause confusion ...," we must first ask, "confusion as to *what*?" In the "typical" trademark infringement case, the "likelihood of confusion" inquiry centers on whether members of the purchasing public are likely to mistake defendants' products or services for plaintiffs' protected products or services within the same category. One question before us is whether members of the purchasing public are likely to mistake defendants' T-shirts for those of plaintiffs. This was the main issue that was addressed and decided below.

There is, however, a distinct but inseparably related issue, not adverted to directly below, that is involved in this case. Defendants are using the Boston Marathon sponsored and operated by the BAA to promote the sale of goods which are adorned so as to capitalize on the race. This implicates what is called a "promotional goods" issue. Under this issue, the "likelihood of confusion" inquiry focuses upon whether the purchasing public is likely to believe that the sponsor of the Boston Marathon produces, licenses, or otherwise endorses defendants' shirts.

. . . .

A.   *Confusion of Goods*

[The court weighed eight factors in assessing likelihood of confusion: (1) the similarity of the marks; (2) the similarity of the goods; (3) the relationship between the parties' channels of trade; (4) the relationship between the parties' advertising; (5) the classes of prospective purchasers; (6) evidence of actual confusion; (7) the defendant's intent in adopting its mark; and (8) the strength of the plaintiff's mark.

In examining the evidence favorable to the defendants, the court found that the plaintiffs had proved that the purchasing public was likely to confuse defendant's shirts with those of plaintiffs.]

. . . .

5. *Classes of Prospective Purchasers*

[With respect to the fifth factor,] we . . . address the district court's initial division of the purchasing public into two classes. [T]he court split the purchasing public into a class of those interested enough in racing to attend the exposition and all others. It found that only the former were likely to connect BAA with the Boston Marathon, and thus, were the only ones likely to infer sponsorship of defendants' products by BAA. In its summary judgment decision, the court stated that there was a genuine issue as to the public's knowledge of BAA's sponsorship of the Marathon but that this issue was not material because resolution of the issue would not alter the outcome.

Distinctions based on expertise can be useful in analyzing likelihood of confusion, but we find no reason for such a distinction here. Unlike the sophisticated hospital personnel involved in *Astra* [*Astra Pharmaceutical Products, Inc. v. Beckman Instruments, Inc.,* 718 F.2d 1201 (1st Cir.1983)] or the expert camera buffs in *Pignons* [*Pignons S.A. de Mecanique de Precision v. Polaroid Corp.,* 657 F.2d 482 (1st Cir.1981)], it is the general public that is the market for shirts commemorating the Boston Marathon. In making its distinction, the court appears to have reasoned as follows: defendants' logos mean "Boston Marathon"; Boston Marathon shirts imply sponsorship by someone; the public (as opposed to those who attend the exposition) does not know that BAA sponsors the Marathon; therefore, the public cannot infer that BAA sponsors defendants' shirts. The key step in this reasoning—the public's lack of knowledge of BAA's sponsorship of the race—is not supported in the record. Indeed, the evidence is to the contrary. Plaintiffs submitted voluminous, uncontradicted evidence, in the form of numerous newspaper and magazine articles dating back to 1897, videotapes of television broadcasts, and encyclopedia entries, all showing that the public was continually exposed to the fact of BAA's sponsorship of the Boston Marathon. Defendants argue that the plaintiffs' evidence is not sufficient to show the public's knowledge because a public poll was not conducted. The lack of survey data, however, does not fatally undercut plaintiffs' claims. The defendants offered no evidence tending to contradict plaintiffs' assertions. Plaintiffs were not bound to a particular form of evidence. A poll might have been more accurate, but the lack of one does not nullify the evidence plaintiffs did introduce.

We find that no genuine issue of fact exists as to the public's general awareness of BAA's sponsorship of the Boston Marathon; there was, therefore, no reason to divide the purchasing public into two classes.

6. *Evidence of Actual Confusion*

Mickey Lawrence, president of Image Impact, reported in her affidavit that she had encountered a shopper at the Filene's department store who expressed surprise when Lawrence told her that defendants' shirt, which the shopper was wearing, was not an "official" Boston Marathon shirt. The district court refused to consider this account, holding that it was inadmissible hearsay. We think that the account was not hearsay, however, because it was not "offered in evidence to prove the truth of the matter asserted." Fed. R. Evid. 801(c). The statement was made not to prove that the defendants' shirts were in fact officially authorized, but rather to show that the declarant, a member of the public, *believed* that they were officially authorized.

Lawrence described two other instances where members of the public had bought defendants' shirts believing them to be officially sponsored shirts; one incident involved a 1986 shirt bought at the exposition, the other a 1987 shirt bought at the race. She also described events occurring at her booth during the 1986 exposition:

> People would come over after they had been shopping. They would get to our booth and they would say, oh, I think I like that T-shirt better. Can I exchange this one? And they would take out a [1986] . . . shirt [sold by defendants].

> . . . .

> And I would tell them or one of the salespeople would say, that isn't one of our shirts. You will have to return it where you bought it. And then there would be indignation of, well, it's a Boston Marathon shirt. Why can't I return it at the Boston Marathon booth? This happened many times to many of the people who were selling, all of the people that we had hired to do it. And it happened throughout the course of the race—of the expo.

While not as accurate as a survey might have been, this evidence shows that some people were actually confused as to who sponsored defendants' shirts. This factor, then, weighs in favor of a likelihood of confusion.

7. *Defendants' Intent in Adopting Their Marks*

The facts can only be interpreted to mean that defendants sought to profit from BAA's sponsorship of the Boston Marathon. The defendants chose designs that obviously referred to the Marathon, put those designs on the same types of clothing sold by the plaintiffs, sold those shirts at the same time and in the same manner as the plaintiffs to the same general purchasing public. Defendants' actions clearly show their intent to trade on BAA's sponsorship and management of the Boston Marathon.

 . . . .

B. *The Promotional Goods Issue*

The question here is whether the purchasing public is likely to believe that the sponsor of the Boston Marathon, produces, licenses or endorses defendants' shirts. Whether or not purchasers happen to know that the sponsor of the Boston Marathon is an organization called the "Boston Athletic Association" is irrelevant to this "likelihood of confusion" analysis. *See* 15 U.S.C. § 1127, as amended (defining "service mark" as a mark "indicat[ing] the source of the services, even if that source is unknown"). In order to establish infringement in a promotional goods case, it has traditionally been the plaintiff's burden to show that prospective purchasers are in fact likely to be confused or misled into thinking that the defendant's product was produced, licensed, or otherwise sponsored by the plaintiff.

The facts bearing on this type of confusion have been, to a great extent, already set forth in our "confusion of goods" analysis. We therefore only summarize them here. The applicable law is, however, discussed *in extenso*.

There can be no doubt that the language and design on defendant's shirts intentionally calls attention to an event that has long been sponsored and supported by the BAA—an event that is, in fact, the subject of its registered mark. Defendants' shirts are clearly designed to take advantage of the Boston Marathon and to benefit from the good will associated with its promotion by plaintiffs. Defendants thus obtain a "free ride" at plaintiffs' expense. In the oft quoted words of the Supreme Court in *International News Service v. Associated Press,* 248 U.S. 215 (1918), because the Boston Marathon has achieved its renown as a result of BAA's "expenditure of labor, skill, and money," such unlicensed use of BAA's mark would permit defendants to "reap where [they have] not sown." *Id.* at 239. Like Rosie Ruiz, a notorious imposter in the 1980 Boston Marathon, defendants would be given a medal without having run the course.

Under these facts, the plaintiffs have to prove, of course, that the defendants are trading on plaintiffs' mark and good will. We do not think, however, that plaintiffs also have to prove that members of the public will actually conclude that defendants' product was *officially* sponsored by the Marathon's sponsor (whoever that sponsor may be). One difficulty with presenting such proof is that few people, other than legal specialists, could venture an informed opinion on whether someone using the logo of the sponsor of a sporting event is required to have the permission of the event's sponsor. Lacking such knowledge, the question of approval is pure guesswork. To ask a factfinder to determine whether the public would think that defendants' shirts were "authorized" or "official" shirts is to ask it to resolve a confusing and, in many contexts, virtually meaningless question. Asking a factfinder to make such a determination also raises a problem of circularity:

> If consumers think that most uses of a trademark require authorization, then in fact they will require authorization because the owner can enjoin consumer confusion caused by unpermitted uses

or charge for licenses. And if owners can sue to stop unauthorized uses, then only authorized uses will be seen by consumers, creating or reinforcing the perception that authorization is necessary. This is a "chicken and the egg" conundrum. [Citations omitted].

The pertinent case law recognizes the difficulty of asking factfinders to decide whether particular uses are "authorized". The Fifth Circuit has held that a factual showing of confusion about source or sponsorship need not be made in order to enjoin a manufacturer of cloth emblems from the unlicensed sale of National Hockey League team emblems.... More recently, the Eleventh Circuit affirmed an injunction against the sale of "Battlin' Bulldog Beer," with cans emblazoned with the University of Georgia's canine mascot, in part on the ground that " 'confusion' may relate to the public's knowledge that the *trademark*, which is 'the triggering mechanism' for the sale of the products, originates with the plaintiff." *University of Georgia Athletic Ass'n v. Laite,* 756 F.2d 1535, 1546 (11th Cir.1985) (citing *Boston Professional Hockey Ass'n,* 510 F.2d at 1012) (emphasis in original).

Other examples of such increased concern with a mark holder's rights can be found in decisions by both the Second and Seventh Circuits to enjoin toy manufacturers from the unlicensed manufacture and sale of toy cars. *Warner Bros. v. Gay Toys, Inc.,* 658 F.2d 76 (2d Cir.1981), *decision on appeal after remand,* 724 F.2d 327 (2d Cir.1983); *Processed Plastic Co. v. Warner Communications, Inc.,* 675 F.2d 852 (7th Cir.1982). In each case plaintiff's evidence showed that children bought defendant's toy car (or prevailed on their parents to buy it for them) because they identified it with the "General Lee" car on plaintiff's "Dukes of Hazzard" television show. There was no probative evidence showing that the children or their parents were likely to believe that the television show's producers had authorized or licensed the toy. Nevertheless, the courts held that the evidence that purchasers recognized defendant's toy as plaintiff's "General Lee" car was sufficient to provide the required "likelihood of confusion."

In *Gay Toys,* the Second Circuit moved quickly from the evidence of the purchasers' recognition of the car as the "General Lee" car to the inference that "many of the consumers did confuse the 'Dixie Racer' [defendant's toy car] with the 'General Lee' and assumed that the car was sponsored by Warner Bros." 658 F.2d at 79. As the district court noted on remand, the Second Circuit's opinion seemed to "creat[e] a conclusive presumption that if children are reminded of the 'General Lee' by seeing a facsimile thereof, they will assume distribution of the facsimile to have been 'sponsored' by plaintiff." *Warner Bros. v. Gay Toys, Inc.,* 553 F. Supp. 1018, 1021 (S.D.N.Y.), *aff'd,* 724 F.2d 327 (2d Cir.1983). In *Processed Plastic,* the Seventh Circuit, in its opinion affirming an injunction against the toy manufacturer, emphasized the defendant's admission that it had "deliberately copied the 'General Lee' car to capitalize on the popularity of the TV show." *Processed Plastic Co.,* 675 F.2d at 857 (emphasis added). The court noted that in cases of intentional copying, the second comer is generally "presumed to have intended a confusing similarity of appearance and to have succeeded in doing so." *Id.* (citation omitted). Following this line of cases, the court held that the toymaker "did not introduce evidence to rebut the inference that its intentional copying of the 'General Lee' car effectively created confusion on the part of the consuming public." *Id.* at 858.

In the present case, we adopt a similar presumption. Given the undisputed facts that (1) defendants intentionally referred to the Boston Marathon on its shirts, and (2) purchasers were likely to buy the shirts precisely because of that reference, we think it fair to presume that purchasers are likely to be confused about the shirt's source or sponsorship. We presume that, at the least, a sufficient number of purchasers would be likely to assume—mistakenly—that defendants' shirts had some connection with the official sponsors of the Boston Marathon. In the absence of any evidence that effectively rebuts this presumption of a "likelihood of confusion," we hold that plaintiffs are entitled to enjoin the manufacture and sale of defendants' shirts.

Our holding that there is a rebuttable presumption in BAA's favor is consistent with the holdings of other courts in analogous cases of intentional copying. For example, the Second Circuit has held that when there is intentional copying of a product's trade dress, "the second comer will be presumed to have intended to create a confusing similarity of appearance and will be presumed to have succeeded." *Perfect Fit Indus., Inc. v. Acme Quilting Co.,* 618 F.2d 950, 954 (2d Cir.1980) (citations omitted).

In the present case, the facts clearly show that defendants intentionally referred to the Boston Marathon on their shirt in order to create an identification with the event and, thus, to sell their shirts. This evidence is itself sufficient to raise the inference of a likelihood of confusion. Given this presumption in favor of plaintiffs and the fact that defendants offered no evidence that would rebut the presumption, there is no genuine issue of material fact about the "likelihood of confusion."

We acknowledge that a trademark, unlike a copyright or patent, is not a "right in gross" that enables a holder to enjoin all reproductions. In Justice Holmes's words, "When the mark is used in such a way that does not deceive the public we see no such sanctity in the word as to prevent it being used to tell the truth. It is not taboo." *Prestonettes, Inc. v. Coty,* 264 U.S. 359 (1924). But when a manufacturer intentionally uses another's mark as a means of establishing a link in consumers' minds with the other's enterprise, and directly profits from that link, there is an unmistakable aura of deception. Such a use is, by its very nature, "likely to cause confusion, or to cause mistake, or to deceive." 15 U.S.C. § 1114(1). Unless the defendant can show that there is in fact no likelihood of such confusion or deception about the product's connection to the trademark holder, such a use can be enjoined.

QUESTIONS

1. Did Sullivan use "Boston Marathon" as a trademark for his t-shirts? Should the use have been considered a nominative fair use?

2. Consider the "rebuttable presumption" of likelihood of confusion arising from the combination of Sullivan's intentional copying and the commercial attraction of the Boston Marathon name. If the presumption were to apply in contexts other than merchandizing rights, would it alter the outcomes of other decisions encountered in this casebook?

WCVB–TV v. Boston Athletic Association

926 F.2d 42 (1st Cir.1991).

■ BREYER, J.:

The Boston Athletic Association ("BAA"), its licensing agent (Pro-Serv), and Channel 4 (WBZ–TV) appeal the district court's refusal to enjoin Channel 5 (WCVB–TV) from televising the Boston Marathon. They point out 1) that the BAA has spent a great deal of money over the years promoting the annual Patriot's Day marathon event, 2) that it has registered the words "Boston Marathon" as a trade, or service mark, in connection with the event, 3) that it has licensed (for a fee) Channel 4 to broadcast the event on television, 4) that it has not licensed Channel 5 to broadcast the event or to use its mark, 5) that Channel 5 broadcast the event last year anyway, and intends to do so in 1991, simply by placing television cameras in the streets along the marathon route, and 6) that Channel 5 used the words "Boston Marathon" on the screen in large letters before, during, and after the event. They argue that Channel 5, by broadcasting the words "Boston Marathon" in connection with the event, violated federal trademark law. They asked the district court to issue a preliminary injunction, it refused to do so, and they have appealed that refusal.

In our view, the district court's refusal to grant the preliminary injunction was lawful. The dispositive legal issue concerns "customer confusion." A trademark, or service mark, is an "attention getting symbol" used basically, and primarily, to make clear to the customer the origin of the goods or the service. Trademark law prohibits the unauthorized use of such a mark, but only where doing so creates a "likelihood of confusion" about who produces the goods or provides the service in question. *See* 15 U.S.C. § 1114(1); 15 U.S.C. § 1125(a); *Boston Athletic Ass'n v. Sullivan,* 867 F.2d 22, 28–35 & n. 11 (1st Cir.1989); *see also Quabaug Rubber Co. v. Fabiano Shoe Co.,* 567 F.2d 154, 160 (1st Cir.1977). Unless a plaintiff can convince a district court that it will likely show such a "likelihood of confusion" on the merits of its trademark claim (or can convince a court of appeals that the district court abused its discretion), it is not entitled to a preliminary injunction. Yet, we cannot find in the record before us sufficient evidence of relevant customer confusion, arising out of Channel 5's use of the words "Boston Marathon," to require the district court to issue the preliminary injunction that the appellants seek.

Obviously, we do not have before us the common, garden variety type of "confusion" that might arise with typical trademark infringement. This is not a heartland trademark case, where, for example, plaintiff uses the words "Big Tom" to mark his apple juice, defendant (perhaps a big man called Tom) uses the same words (or perhaps similar words, e.g., "Large Tommy") on his own apple juice label, and plaintiff says customers will confuse defendant's apple juice with his own. *See, e.g., Beer Nuts, Inc. v. Clover Club Foods Co.,* 805 F.2d 920 (10th Cir.1986) ("Beer Nuts" and "Brew Nuts" confusingly similar); 2 J. McCARTHY § 23.3 at 56 ("Cases where a defendant uses an identical mark on competitive goods hardly ever find their way into the appellate reports ... [and] are 'open and shut' ..."). No one here says that Channel 5 is running its own marathon on Patriot's Day, which a viewer might confuse with the BAA's famous Boston Marathon.

Rather, BAA argues that the confusion here involved is somewhat special. It points to cases where a defendant uses a plaintiff's trademark in connection with a different type of good or service and a plaintiff claims that the public will wrongly, and confusedly, think that the defendant's product somehow has the plaintiff's official "O.K." or imprimatur. The Eleventh Circuit, for example, found trademark law violated when the defendant, without authorization, used the plaintiff's football team mark, a bulldog, not in connection with a different football team, but, rather, on his beer mugs. *See University of Georgia Athletic Ass'n v. Laite,* 756 F.2d 1535 (11th Cir.1985). This circuit has found trademark law violated, when the defendant, without authorization, used this very appellant's foot race mark, "Boston Marathon," on his t-shirts, sold during the event, permitting the customer to wrongly or confusedly think that his t-shirts were somehow "official." *See Sullivan, supra.* BAA goes on to say that Channel 5's use of those words will lead viewers, wrongly, and confusedly, to believe that Channel 5 (like the t-shirt seller) has a BAA license or permission or authorization to use the words, i.e., that it broadcasts with the BAA's official imprimatur. It also notes that this court, in *Sullivan,* listed circumstances that create a "rebuttable presumption" of confusion. And, it quotes language from *Sullivan,* in which this court, citing *International News Service v. Associated Press,* 248 U.S. 215, 39 S. Ct. 68, 63 L. Ed. 211 (1918), said that the defendant's t-shirts were "clearly designed to take advantage of the Boston Marathon and to benefit from the good will associated with its promotion by plaintiffs," and that defendants obtained a "free ride" at the plaintiffs' expense; they "reap where [they have] not sown." *Sullivan,* 867 F.2d at 33. Appellants say that Channel 5 is doing the same here.

In our view, the cases BAA cites, and *Sullivan* in particular, do not govern the outcome of this case. Nor can we find a likelihood of any relevant confusion here. First, the *Sullivan* opinion, taken as a whole, makes clear that the court, in using the language appellants cite, referring to a "free ride," and taking "advantage" of another's good will, did not intend to depart from ordinary principles of federal trademark law that make a finding of a "likelihood of confusion" essential to a conclusion of "violation." As a general matter, the law sometimes protects investors from the "free riding" of others; and sometimes it does not. The law, for example, gives inventors a "property right" in certain inventions for a limited period of time; *see* 35 U.S.C. §§ 101 *et seq.*; it provides copyright protection for authors; *see* 17 U.S.C. §§ 101 *et seq.*; it offers certain protections to trade secrets. But, the man who clears a swamp, the developer of a neighborhood, the academic scientist, the school teacher, and millions of others, each day create "value" (over and above what they are paid) that the law permits others to receive without charge. Just how, when and where the law should protect investments in "intangible" benefits or goods is a matter that legislators typically debate, embodying the results in specific statutes, or that common law courts, carefully weighing relevant competing interests, gradually work out over time. The trademark statute does not give the appellants any "property right" in their mark except "the right to prevent confusion." *See Quabaug Rubber Co.,* 567 F.2d at 160. And, nothing in *Sullivan* suggests the contrary.

Second, the "rebuttable presumption" of confusion that this court set forth in Sullivan does not apply here. We concede that the *Sullivan* court said that "there is a rebuttable presumption" of confusion "about the shirts' source or sponsorship" arising from the fact that the defendants used the words "Boston Marathon" on the shirts, which use made customers more likely to buy the shirts. The court wrote that when a manufacturer intentionally uses another's mark as a means of establishing a link in consumers' minds with the other's enterprise, and directly profits from that link, there is an unmistakable aura of deception. *Sullivan,* 867 F.2d at 35. As we read these words, they mean that the *Sullivan* record indicated that the defendant wanted to give the impression that his t-shirt was an "official" t-shirt, a fact that, in the sports world, might give a shirt, in the eyes of sports fans, a special "cachet." It makes sense to presume confusion about a relevant matter (namely, official sponsorship) from such an intent, at least in the absence of contrary evidence.

Here, however, there is no persuasive evidence of any intent to use the words "Boston Marathon" to suggest official sponsorship of Channel 5's broadcasts. To the contrary, Channel 5 offered to "broadcast whatever disclaimers" the BAA might want ("every thirty seconds, every two minutes, every ten minutes") to make certain no one thought the channel had any special broadcasting status. Nor is there any evidence that Channel 5 might somehow profit from viewers' wrongly thinking that the BAA had authorized its broadcasts. Indeed, one would ordinarily believe that television viewers (unlike sports fans who might want to buy an official t-shirt with the name of a favorite event, team or player) wish to see the event and do not particularly care about the relation of station to event-promoter.

Third, and perhaps most importantly, the record provides us with an excellent reason for thinking that Channel 5's use of the words "Boston Marathon" would not confuse the typical Channel 5 viewer. That reason consists of the fact that those words do more than call attention to Channel 5's program; they also describe the event that Channel 5 will broadcast. Common sense suggests (consistent with the record here) that a viewer who sees those words flash upon the screen will believe simply that Channel 5 will show, or is showing, or has shown, the marathon, not that Channel 5 has some special approval from the BAA to do so. In technical trademark jargon, the use of words for descriptive purposes is called a "fair use," and the law usually permits it even if the words themselves also constitute a trademark. *See* 15 U.S.C. § 1115(b)(4) (statutory fair use defense); *Zatarains, Inc. v. Oak Grove Smokehouse, Inc.,* 698 F.2d 786, 796 (5th Cir.1983) (fair use established if mark descriptive, not used in trademark sense, and used in good faith). If, for example, a t-shirt maker placed the words "Pure Cotton" (instead of the words "Boston Marathon") on his t-shirts merely to describe the material from which the shirts were made, not even a shirt maker who had a registered trademark called "Pure Cotton" could likely enjoin their sale. As Justice Holmes pointed out many years ago, "when the mark is used in a way that does not deceive the public we see no such sanctity in the word as to prevent its being used to tell the truth." *Prestonettes, Inc. v. Coty,* 264 U.S. 359, 368, 44 S. Ct. 350, 351, 68 L. Ed. 731 (1924).

This is not a case where it is difficult to decide whether a defendant is using particular words primarily as a mark, i.e., as an "attention getting symbol," or primarily as a description. Here there is little in the record before us to suggest the former (only the large size of the words on the screen); while there is much to show the latter (timing, meaning, context, intent, and surrounding circumstances). Consequently, the appellants have shown no real likelihood of relevant confusion.

We also note that the only federal court which has decided a case nearly identical to the one before us, a case in which a station planning to televise a public parade was sued by the parade's promoter who had granted "exclusive" rights to another station, reached a conclusion similar to the one we draw here. *See Production Contractors, Inc. v. WGN Continental Broadcasting Co.,* 622 F. Supp. 1500, 1504 (N.D.Ill.1985). Reviewing the promoter's Lanham Act claim that the "unauthorized" broadcast would create a "false impression" of sponsorship, the court concluded that it fell "far short of establishing likelihood of confusion" among viewers that the defendant station was the "official" or "authorized" broadcaster of the parade. *See id.* at 1504–05. Similarly, we do not see how Channel 5's broadcast could likely confuse viewers that it bore the imprimatur of the BAA.

The district court's denial of the motion for preliminary injunction is AFFIRMED.

QUESTION

On June 15, 2004, the Detroit Pistons stunned basketball fans by winning the NBA Basketball championship against the heavily favored Los Angeles Lakers. The Detroit Free Press celebrated the victory with a story splashed across its front page, headlined "R–E–S–P–E–C–T." The story featured a large image of members of the team, in their uniforms, at the end the game. To commemorate the event, the Free Press created souvenir posters and tee-shirts bearing a reproduction of the front page of its June 16 paper. The Free Press offers the posters and tee shirts for sale at its website and, on the day of the Pistons victory parade, dispatched 20 teenagers to sell tee-shirts to fans in the crowd. The Pistons have objected to the sale of tee-shirts and posters bearing Pistons and NBA logos, insisting that the Free Press is not entitled to reproduce Pistons and NBA marks outside of the newspaper. The Free Press claims it has a right to sell images of its front page whether the images are presented on newsprint, on cotton, or in any other medium. What are the best arguments to be made on the Pistons' behalf? How should the Free Press respond to them?

C H A P T E R   11

INTERNET DOMAIN NAMES

A. THE DOMAIN NAME SYSTEM

JONATHAN WEINBERG, ICANN AND THE PROBLEM OF LEGITIMACY, 50 Duke L.J. 187 (2000)(excerpt)*

. . . .

I. How We Got Here

A. *Early History of the Internet*

For a long time after computers were developed, they were solitary objects; one computer could not talk with another. Researchers achieved a milestone in 1965 when they used an ordinary telephone line to connect a computer at the Massachusetts Institute of Technology with another in California, allowing them to share programs and data across a substantial distance. In order to allow computers to communicate effectively, though, computer scientists had to devise an entirely new way, known as packet switching, of transmitting information over phone lines.

A unit of the Department of Defense called the Defense Advanced Research Projects Agency, or DARPA, funded research into how to connect computers together into networks. With DARPA's support, scientists began to connect computers at various universities into a new network called the ARPANET. Data was transmitted over the ARPANET at a rate of 50,000 bits per second—blindingly fast at the time, but not too far off the speed any ordinary user with an off-the-shelf modem can achieve today. In 1972, researchers developed the first e-mail program. This, for the first time, enabled the use of computers for long-distance person-to-person communication.

Computer networks began springing up wherever researchers could find someone to pay for them. The Department of Energy set up two networks, NASA set up another, and the National Science Foundation (NSF) provided seed money for yet another. In each case, far-flung researchers were able to use the network to communicate and share their work via e-mail.

Scientists developed a technology called TCP/IP to connect all of these networks together. When the ARPANET adopted TCP/IP, people using ARPANET computers could communicate with people using computers on any other TCP/IP network. The technique of linking different networks

---

together was referred to as internetworking or internetting, and the resulting "network of networks" was the Internet. By the mid–1980s, though, the number of interconnected hosts was still small.

The National Science Foundation saw the chance to change that. NSF helped fund a high-speed backbone to link networks serving thousands of research and educational institutions around the United States. By 1992, there were more than one million host computers connected to the Internet. At the same time, scientists were developing new ways to use an Internet connection. At a research center in Switzerland, scientists developed a key new application: the World Wide Web, which permitted users to link documents, programs, or video clips residing on different machines almost anywhere in the world.

B.   Internet Addressing

In any system of networked computing, there has to be some mechanism enabling one computer to locate another. If I want to send e-mail to a buddy in Boise, the system needs to have some way to find his mail server so that it can direct the information there. Internet engineers came up with this solution: Each "host" computer connected to the Internet was assigned an Internet protocol (IP) address, which consisted of a unique 32–bit number, usually printed in dotted decimal form, such as 128.127.50.224. Dr. Jon Postel of the University of Southern California's Information Sciences Institute (ISI) assumed the task of assigning blocks of IP addresses to computer networks. Because no two computers had the same IP address, it was possible to locate any computer on the Internet simply by knowing its IP address. TCP/IP made possible a system of routing that permitted a user to dispatch a message onto the Internet, knowing only the IP address of the computer he wished to reach, with confidence that the message would eventually reach its intended destination.

In addition to an IP address, each host computer had a name, such as SRI–NIC. A Network Information Center maintained a hosts.txt table translating names to IP addresses for every host. A user could send e-mail specifying only the name of the relevant host; his computer would consult the hosts.txt table to determine the relevant IP address. There were two advantages to this dual system of names and addresses. First, IP addresses were opaque and hard to remember. Names were rather more user-friendly. It was inconvenient for a user to have to remember and type in a different IP address for every Internet resource he sought to access or e-mail message he wished to send. It was much easier to use a short name with semantic meaning. Second, the use of names made it possible for network operators to change the configuration of their networks, and therefore change the IP addresses associated with various machines, without disrupting communications with the outside world.

This system worked well so long as the number of computers attached to the Internet was small. As that number grew, however, it became clear that the Internet needed a more sophisticated addressing structure than the hosts.txt table could provide. By 1983, the size of that table and the frequency of its updates were "near the limit of manageability." Accordingly, scientists, including Postel and Paul Mockapetris, also of the Information Sciences Institute, developed the "domain name system" (DNS). The domain name system retains the user-friendliness of mapping each IP address to a domain name such as threecats.net or law.wayne.edu. The new system differs from the old approach, though, in key respects.

First, the DNS defines a hierarchical name space. That name space is divided into top-level domains, or TLDs. Each top-level domain is divided into second-level domains, and so on. Under the plan developed by Postel and Mockapetris, there were seven generic, three-letter top-level domains: .com, .net, .org, .edu, .gov, .mil, and .int. In addition, there were two-letter country code top-level domains such as .jp, .us, and .fr. At the outset, it was thought that .com would be used by commercial entities, .net by entities involved with the Internet networking infrastructure, .org by nonprofit organizations, and .edu by educational institutions. Today, the restrictions on the first three of these have long since fallen away. The largest top-level domain by far is .com, with more than sixteen million second-level domain names as of this writing; .net and .org come next.

Within the name space pyramid, the structure replicates itself. The owner of each second-level domain is at the apex of a pyramid consisting of the third-level domains (if any) within that second-level domain, and so on. This hierarchy makes possible (but does not mandate) functional, geographical, or other organization of any portion of the name space.

The hierarchy also makes it easier for name-to-number translation to be distributed. There is no single central server that must be queried every time an Internet-connected computer needs to map a domain name to an IP address. Rather, at the apex of the DNS pyramid is a set of thirteen root servers, each of which lists the IP addresses of the computers containing the zone files for each of the top-level domains. At the next level are the computers holding those top-level domain zone files, each of which lists the IP addresses of the name servers for each second-level domain it controls, and so on. When a user looking for a particular Internet resource types in a domain name, his computer begins at the bottom of the pyramid: it queries a set of local DNS servers, specified in its software, to find the IP address corresponding to that domain name. If those local servers do not know the answer, they move the request up the line.

By virtue of the structure of the DNS, the ability to modify (or to refuse to modify) the root zone files in the root servers carries with it considerable power. If a user types in a domain name incorporating a top-level domain that is unknown to the root servers, then the DNS will be unable to find the corresponding computer. The power to control the root servers is the power to decide (1) which top-level domains are visible in the name space and (2) which name servers are authoritative for those top-level domains—that is, which entities get to say who controls the various second-level domains in that top-level domain.

On the other hand, there is no requirement that any particular end user send his DNS queries to a name server that references the root zone described above. Users can point their computers at entirely different DNS servers that, in turn, point to different root servers, referencing a different set of top-level domains. Such alternative top-level domains and alternative root servers in fact exist, so that if one points one's computer at the right DNS server, one can send e-mail to addresses that the rest of the Internet does not recognize, such as <richard@vrx.zoo> or <richard@tangled. web>. Very few Internet users, though, look to alternative root servers. The vast majority rely on the single set of authoritative root servers, historically supervised by Jon Postel, that have achieved canonical status.

Once the DNS got underway in 1985, the day-to-day job of registering second-level domains in the generic top-level domains was handled by the Stanford Research Institute (SRI) under contract to the U.S. Department of Defense. The Defense Department, which had long funded ISI as part of its funding of almost all of the Internet's early development, also entered into contracts under which it funded the activities of Dr. Postel and other Information Sciences Institute staff in coordinating IP address allocation and oversight of the domain name system. These activities came to be referred to as the Internet Assigned Numbers Authority (IANA). Later on, the National Science Foundation took over the role of funding the civilian part of the Internet infrastructure. The National Science Foundation entered into a cooperative agreement with a company named Network Solutions, Inc. (NSI) to perform the registration services that had been handled earlier by SRI. NSI agreed to register second-level domains in .com, .net, .org, and .edu and to maintain those top-level domains' master databases. Those services were underwritten by the National Science Foundation and were free to users.

Jessica Litman, The DNS Wars, 4 J. Small & Emerging Bus. L. 149 (2000)(excerpt).*

Until 1993, the National Science Foundation prohibited anyone from making commercial use of the Internet. When the NSF decommissioned the Internet backbone ..., and stopped prohibiting commercial use, it foresaw a gradual increase in commercial Internet activity, and a growing, if still modest demand for commercial domain names in the .com top level domain, so it subcontracted the job of registering .com domain names to a small company named Network Solutions, which immediately put 2 1/2 employees on the job. Network Solutions registered .com domain names on a first-come first-served basis, just as all the Internet domain names had always been allocated.

Back in 1993 and 1994, nobody had any idea that the Internet was going to become the engine of electronic commerce within the next few years. People registered domain names in .com for a variety of reasons. There were some companies, like Clue Computing or Amazon.com, who registered their names as domain names because they planned to do business over the Internet. There were fans. A guy named Jef Poskanzer, for instance, registered acme.com because he'd always been a big fan of

---

* [most footnotes omitted].

Wile E Coyote. Then, there were domain name speculators: folks who believed that the Internet would be an important business tool some day, and domain names would be valuable commodities, and so they registered a whole slew of domain names they believed someone would someday pay money to own.

It's hard to know how to think about domain name speculators. These folks saw some unclaimed property that they believed would be valuable someday, and so they invested in it. Turns out they were right. Our society thinks about that sort of activity in different ways depending on the circumstances. Sometimes we encourage it: If the potentially valuable resource is land, or gold or pork bellies, or stock in some start-up company, we tend to think of the successful speculator as an admirable entrepreneur. Sometimes, we disapprove. If someone is stockpiling huge reserves of medicine or water or food in case the Y2K bug plunges society back into the dark ages, we tend to call it either greedy or silly. Sometimes, we simply won't permit it: If the potential valuable resource is a trademark, and someone tries to register it and put it in her trademark warehouse, in case she gets the chance to sell it to someone else some day, she can't.

In any event, there were domain name speculators, who were either business investors or cybersquatters, depending on your religion, and they registered potentially useful names like drugs.com, and also names they figured that businesses out there would want, like panavision.com. Some of them were planning on simply grabbing up unclaimed but commercially valuable domain names and selling them to the companies likely to want them at a substantial markup. A variation involved registering a slew of common surnames into the .com or .org domain on the theory that one could sell them to individuals who wanted domains named after their own surnames. Some of them went into it with honest intentions: they wanted to offer companies with no web presence web-hosting services, and went ahead and registered potential customers' marks as domain names as a initial step in their business plan. Others decided to use the domains they registered for porn sites, on the theory that someone would come along looking for the White House and type whitehouse.com, where they'd find all sorts of pornography that might entice them to stick around.

Whatever motives they had, though, during the couple of years between the time that Network Solutions started registering .com domain names on a first-come first-served basis and the moment that all the businesses in the Western World figured out that they wanted a domain name based on their trademarks, a fair number of domain names that someone else might also want got snapped up.

Of course, many more people turned out to want .com domain names much more quickly than anyone had anticipated, so, after the initial craziness, Network Solutions persuaded the National Science Foundation to let it charge a couple of hundred dollars to register each domain name in .com, both to keep folks from stockpiling a bunch of names and to help it to pay for some more employees and computer resources and so forth to keep up with the demand.

You can see that the whole situation was a collision waiting to happen: Out here in meat space, we can have a whole bunch of different owners of ACME as a trademark—the last time I counted there were more than 100 different trademark registrations, in addition to all the local unregistered ACME marks you can find by just looking in the telephone book. On the Internet, only one person can own acme.com. Jef Poskanzer, the Wile E Coyote fan I mentioned earlier, happens to be the lucky guy. He doesn't own *any* Acme trademarks, but he got there first.

That offends some people, who think that when Jef Poskanzer came knocking on Network Solutions' door, it should have done a quick trademark search, and when it discovered that Jef didn't own an ACME trademark and someone else did, it should have refused to give him acme.com, and instead hung onto it for the trademark owner.

Once it became clear that the Internet was important, even essential to business, a bunch of companies had decided to get themselves an Internet domain, and found that the ones they wanted had already been registered by someone else, under Network Solutions's first-come-first-served registration policy. They were outraged. They sued. Some won; some lost.

Hasbro toys was interested in offering an online version of its CLUE game at clue.com, but, it discovered that Clue Computing had gotten there first. Hasbro also considered putting together an online version of its CANDYLAND game, but then it found out that Candyland.com belonged to a company named the Internet Entertainment Group, which was using it for a pornographic website. The Amazon Bookstore, the oldest feminist bookstore in the United States, wanted to register amazon.com, but Amazon.com had gotten there first. Panavision, the movie camera company, went to Network Solutions to register panavision.com, and discovered it already belonged to a guy named Dennis Toeppen, and that Mr. Toeppen was willing to convey the domain name to Panavision, *if* Panavision forked over $13,000.

. . . .

Hasbro sued Clue Computing. It lost.[22] It sued Internet Entertainment Group, and it won.[23] Panavision sued Mr. Toeppen, and it actually won a dilution claim, although the court had to do a fair amount of maneuvering to find commercial use in commerce—it decided that Toeppen's practice of selling domain names to the companies who owned the relevant trademarks was itself commercial use in commerce.[24]

There were a bunch of lawsuits, and the courts seemed to be working it out. Mr. Toeppen and other domain name speculators struck courts as profoundly offensive, so they called them cybersquatters and ruled against

---

22. Hasbro, Inc. v. Clue Computing, 66 F.Supp.2d 117 (D.Mass.1999), URL: <http://www.clue.com/legal/hasbro/d2.html>.

23. Hasbro, Inc. v. Internet Entertainment Group, 40 U.S.P.Q.2d 1479 (W.D.Wash. 1996).

24. Panavision International v. Toeppen, 141 F.3d 1316 (9th Cir.1998).

them. People who capitalized on famous trademarks to divert consumers to their sites, especially pornographic sites, also lost. Companies that had legitimate claim to their domain names, like Clue Computing, often didn't lose, but they spent millions of dollars in attorneys fees and court costs. The millions-of-dollars thing meant that some trademark owners offered to buy out domain name registrants rather than litigate. It also meant that when a number of different domain name registrants got bigfoot letters from trademark owners' lawyers, they decided to fold.

We had a system in which a trademark owner who wanted a domain name that had been registered by someone else might be able to get it by litigating but might not. For lots of trademark owners, that wasn't good enough. They felt *entitled* to occupy the domain names incorporating their trademarks, and if the system didn't give it to them, they needed to change the system.

Some of them sued *Network Solutions* for trademark infringement and dilution. That didn't work, and it shouldn't. If Dennis Toeppen isn't breaking the law when he registers panavision.com, Network Solutions surely isn't breaking the law when it lets him. Nonetheless, Network Solutions hated being dragged into court, and it lost it. I don't know who represented Network Solutions, but whoever it was must have frightened the company silly, because it set out to try to ensure that nobody could ever sue it for anything ever again. It adopted a new set of rules designed to placate trademark owners. The new rules first required all domain name registrants past and future to indemnify it for anything, and then insisted that if some trademark owner showed up with a certificate of registration complaining about a domain name, it could give the domain name registrant thirty days to prove that it's rights were superior to the trademark owner's, and, if it didn't, Network Solutions would suspend the domain name.

That didn't prevent Network Solutions from being sued; it just meant that domain name registrants had to go to court to stop Network Solutions from inactivating their domains.

The Roadrunner Computer Systems registered roadrunner.com, and then one day, Warner Brothers Studios (home of Wile E. Coyote) decided that *it* wanted roadrunner.com. Warner Brothers has been using a road runner character in its cartoons since the 1930s, but didn't actually register the trademark until 1991; a bunch of other people own registrations for ROAD RUNNER for tires, a restaurant, construction services, tractors, treadmills, although Roadrunner computer systems isn't one of them. As the holder of a trademark registration, is Warner Brothers entitled to oust Roadrunner Computers? If so, what happens if the owner of Roadrunner Tires wants to oust Warner Brothers—its trademark registration was, after all, first?

Warner Brothers' came in with its registration for Roadrunner, and Network Solutions sent a 30 day letter to Roadrunner computer systems. Roadrunner is an Internet Service Provider. If its domain name gets cut off, all of its customers lose their Internet addresses for some indefinite period, and it as good as gets run out of business entirely. Roadrunner Computer did the only thing it could think of: it filed suit against Network Solutions to stop the cut-off. That worked. So, as other domain name owners got 30 day letters, they went and found trademark lawyers and sued to enjoin the cut-off.

Network Solutions tried to impose a revised, revised policy. That didn't stop the lawsuits either. It also sent out more and more thirty-day letters as more and more trademark owners threatened to sue it. That got the community of Internet domain owners really mad, and they decided that Network Solutions had to be stopped.

By now, this little company wasn't so little anymore, and it was pulling in millions and millions of dollars registering all these domain names. If other entities got into the registration business, folks figured, they could both offer a better alternative to NSI and make lots and lots of money doing so. An ad hoc International group of Internet organizations and trademark owners decided to replace the entire edifice with a new one, in which, incidentally, they would take over the registration business themselves, and introduce a bunch of new generic top level domains.

The crux of the proposal, for our purposes, is that it would have given companies who didn't get in in time to get a domain name based on their trademarks a new opportunity. Expanding the number of generic top level domains would give multiple claimants access to domains containing the same alphanumeric strings. Jef Poskanzer could keep acme.com, and Warner Brothers could take acme.biz, while the Acme glass company could have acme.glass and so forth. That proposal made the trademark bar unhappy. They argued that increasing the number of generic top level domains would just multiply the potential for confusion.[33]

As a prediction, that one is flawed. Consumers know that there are lots of different businesses named Acme, and don't expect any given Acme to be the particular Acme they have in mind. If consumers learned that there were lots of acme-based domain names on the web, they wouldn't expect any particular one to belong to either Poskanzer or Warner Brothers. They wouldn't be confused. Yes, that might prevent Warner Brothers from grabbing a valuable marketing tool, but Warner Brothers doesn't have the acme.com domain as it is, so it isn't any worse off. Increasingly, however, the rhetoric about consumer confusion camouflaged efforts to leverage trademark rights into stronger property interests in the use of desirable alphanumeric strings on the Internet, even in the absence of any plausible likelihood of consumer confusion. In fact, the consumer confusion issues are not hard to solve, but some trademark interests perceived the domain name conundrum as an opportunity to expand their rights beyond the limits imposed by traditional trademark law. That trademark owners

33. *See* International Trademark Association, *INTA Response to the U.S. Government Paper on the Improvement of Technical Management of Internet Names and Address-* es (March 18, 1998), URL: <http://www.ntia. doc.gov/ntiahome/domainname/130dftmail/ scanned/INTA.htm>.

should pursue such a course is easy to understand, but there is no policy reason why we should design the architecture of the system to assist them.

The proposal to add new generic top level domains had additional potential advantages only tangentially related to trademark law. Because of successful advertising, a large segment of the public had come to view .com as the only "real" domain. The combined registration activities of businesses trying to do business on the World Wide Web and domain name speculators had led to the registration of essentially every word in a typical English-language dictionary as a second level domain in .com. New entrants into the world of e-commerce were necessarily settling for increasingly unwieldy domain names. The fact that there were few easy-to-remember alphanumeric strings left unregistered served as an entry barrier to new firms seeking to do business on the web, and gave their earlier competitors a marketing advantage that was difficult to overcome. In addition, it inflated the value of the resale market in .com domain names, encouraging the activities of domain name speculators. If the speculators were a significant part of the problem, parsimonious limits on the expansion of domain name space would only make the problem worse.

Most representatives of trademark owners were undoubtedly sincere in their efforts to protect trademarks from infringement and dilution, although their single-minded pursuit of that goal caused them to elevate trademark concerns over all others. (People who own trademarks appear to be doomed to perceive their marks as stronger and more valuable than their customers and competitors do.) Other trademark lobbyists may have gotten greedy, hoping to enshrine in domain name space the trademark rules that they felt should be the rules in meat space, but weren't.

The trademark bar started claiming that the only legitimate domain name use of a word that was also a trademark was a trademark use by the trademark owner, and demanded a system that allowed trademark owners to oust non-trademark owners of domain names incorporating their marks, and that permitted trademark owners to prevent any subsequent registration of any domain name incorporating their marks in any top level domain.

That's in a lot of ways an outrageous demand. This is not a particularly new problem. We have seen it in the United States with 1–800 telephone numbers, which are given out on a first-come first served basis, it's not that hard to solve. Trademark laws give businesses some powerful tools to prevent confusion and dilution, but they don't confer on anyone a right to own the phone number 1–800–trademark or the domain name trademark.com, much less trademark.net, trademark.org, or trademark.uk.

Moreover, a rule that a trademark owner had the right to any and all domain names of the form trademark.domain wouldn't make any sense and would be impossible to administer. For one thing, how are we supposed to pick which trademark owner? Dell Books has been around since 1943. Dell computers has been around since 1988. Both of them own trademark registrations for Dell. Which one is entitled to the domain name "dell.com"? And how do you decide? It gets worse if the dell you choose will presumptively have a claim on dell.org, dell.net, dell.us, dell.uk, dell.biz, and so forth. The BUDWEISER beer mark belongs to Anheuser–Busch in the United States and to the Budvar brewery in the Czech Republic. Anheuser–Busch's Budweiser beer is the more famous; Budvar's Budweiser was first. Only one of them, however, can own the domain name budweiser.com, and that domain will be accessible from computers in the United States, in the Czech Republic, and in any other country connected to the Internet. How should a domain name allocation system choose between them? The Apple Computer Company and Apple Records have shared the APPLE trademark without incident for more than 20 years, selling computers and recorded music, respectively, throughout the world. Only one of them can operate the apple.com domain. The British record company adopted the name first; the California computer company's business, however, is more intimately connected to the Internet. Does one of them have the superior claim, and, if so, which one?

. . . .

Congress enacted the *Anticybersquatting Consumer Protection Act* [in 1999]. The new law establishes a new cause of action for registration, trafficking or use of a domain name confusingly similar to or dilutive of a trademark or personal name. It contains provisions for capturing domain names from registrants who are not subject to a federal court's *in personam* jurisdiction. It allows trademark owners to recover substantial statutory damages as well as an order for the transfer of a domain name when the domain name is registered or used "with a bad faith intent to profit" from its similarity to a trademark. The Second Circuit availed itself of an early opportunity to apply the new law to a case tried before its enactment, and adopted a liberal interpretation of the phrase "bad faith intent to profit."[64] The district court had found that defendant's operation of the sportys.com website was unlikely to cause confusion, but diluted plaintiff's registered mark. The court held, however, that defendant's dilution was not willful. Without disturbing the trial court's findings of no likelihood of confusion and no willful intent to dilute, the Second Circuit ordered recovery under the *Anticybersquatting Consumer Protection Act*, holding that defendant's actions showed a "bad faith intent to profit" as defined in the new law.

B. ANTICYBERSQUATTING CONSUMER PROTECTION ACT

15 U.S.C. § 1125(d)(1) (LANHAM ACT § 43(d)(1)):

(1)(A) A person shall be liable in a civil action by the owner of a mark, including a personal name which is protected as a mark under this section, if, without regard to the goods or services of the parties, that person—

---

64. *See* Sporty's Farm LLC v. Sportsman's Market, Inc., 202 F.3d 489 (2d Cir. 2000).

(i) has a bad faith intent to profit from that mark, including a personal name which is protected as a mark under this section; and

(ii) registers, traffics in, or uses a domain name that—

    (I)   in the case of a mark that is distinctive at the time of registration of the domain name, is identical or confusingly similar to that mark;

    (II) in the case of a famous mark that is famous at the time of registration of the domain name, is identical or confusingly similar to or dilutive of that mark; or

    (III) is a trademark, word, or name protected by reason of section 706 of title 18, United States Code, or section 220506 of title 36, United States Code.

(B)(i) In determining whether a person has a bad faith intent described under subparagraph (A), a court may consider factors such as, but not limited to—

    (I)   the trademark or other intellectual property rights of the person, if any, in the domain name;

    (II)   the extent to which the domain name consists of the legal name of the person or a name that is otherwise commonly used to identify that person;

    (III)   the person's prior use, if any, of the domain name in connection with the bona fide offering of any goods or services;

    (IV)   the person's bona fide noncommercial or fair use of the mark in a site accessible under the domain name;

    (V)   the person's intent to divert consumers from the mark owner's online location to a site accessible under the domain name that could harm the goodwill represented by the mark, either for commercial gain or with the intent to tarnish or disparage the mark, by creating a likelihood of confusion as to the source, sponsorship, affiliation, or endorsement of the site;

    (VI)   the person's offer to transfer, sell, or otherwise assign the domain name to the mark owner or any third party for financial gain without having used, or having an intent to use, the domain name in the bona fide offering of any goods or services, or the person's prior conduct indicating a pattern of such conduct;

    (VII) the person's provision of material and misleading false contact information when applying for the registration of the domain name, the person's intentional failure to maintain accurate contact information, or the person's prior conduct indicating a pattern of such conduct;

    (VIII) the person's registration or acquisition of multiple domain names which the person knows are identical or confusingly similar to marks of others that are distinctive at the time of registration of such domain names, or dilutive of famous marks of others that are famous at the time of registration of such domain names, without regard to the goods or services of the parties; and

(IX)   the extent to which the mark incorporated in the person's domain name registration is or is not distinctive and famous within the meaning of subsection (c)(1) of section 43.

(ii) Bad faith intent described under subparagraph (A) shall not be found in any case in which the court determines that the person believed and had reasonable grounds to believe that the use of the domain name was a fair use or otherwise lawful.

(C) In any civil action involving the registration, trafficking, or use of a domain name under this paragraph, a court may order the forfeiture or cancellation of the domain name or the transfer of the domain name to the owner of the mark.

Sporty's Farm L.L.C. v. Sportsman's Market, Inc.

202 F.3d 489 (2d Cir.2000).

■ CALABRESI, CIRCUIT JUDGE:

This case originally involved the application of the Federal Trademark Dilution Act ("FTDA") to the Internet. While the case was pending on appeal, however, the Anticybersquatting Consumer Protection Act ("ACPA"), Pub. L. No. 106–113 (1999), was passed and signed into law. That new law applies to this case.

Plaintiff–Counter–Defendant–Appellant–Cross–Appellee Sporty's Farm L.L.C. ("Sporty's Farm") appeals from a judgment, following a bench trial, of the United States District Court for the District of Connecticut (Alfred V. Covello, Chief Judge) dated March 13, 1998. Defendant–Third–Party–Plaintiff–Counter–Claimant–Appellee–Cross–Appellant Sportsman's Market, Inc. ("Sportsman's") cross-appeals from the same judgment.

The district court held: (1) that the Sportsman's trademark ("*sporty's*") was a famous mark entitled to protection under the FTDA; (2) that Sporty's Farm and its parent company, Third–Party–Defendant–Appellee Omega Engineering, Inc. ("Omega"), diluted the *sporty's* mark by using the Internet domain name "sportys.com" to sell Christmas trees and by preventing Sportsman's from using its trademark as a domain name; (3) that applying the FTDA to Sporty's Farm through an injunction requiring it to relinquish sportys.com was both equitable and not a retroactive application of the statute; (4) that Sportsman's was limited to injunctive relief since the conduct of Sporty's Farm and Omega did not constitute a willful intent to dilute under the FTDA; and (5) that Sporty's Farm and Omega did not violate the Connecticut Unfair Trade Practices Act ("CUTPA"), Conn. Gen. Stat. Ann. § § 42–110a to 42–110q (West 1992 & Supp. 1999). We apply the new anticybersquatting law and affirm the judgment in all respects, but, given the new law, on different grounds from those relied upon by the district court.

BACKGROUND

. . . .

II

Sportsman's is a mail order catalog company that is quite well-known among pilots and aviation enthusiasts for selling products tailored to their needs. In recent years, Sportsman's has expanded its catalog business well beyond the aviation market into that for tools and home accessories. The company annually distributes approximately 18 million catalogs nation-wide, and has yearly revenues of about $50 million. Aviation sales account for about 60% of Sportsman's revenue, while non-aviation sales comprise the remaining 40%.

In the 1960s, Sportsman's began using the logo "*sporty*" to identify its catalogs and products. In 1985, Sportsman's registered the trademark *sporty's* with the United States Patent and Trademark Office. Since then, Sportsman's has complied with all statutory requirements to preserve its interest in the *sporty's* mark. *Sporty's* appears on the cover of all Sports-man's catalogs; Sportsman's international toll free number is 1–800–4sportys; and one of Sportsman's domestic toll free phone numbers is 1–800–Sportys. Sportsman's spends about $10 million per year advertising its *sporty's* logo.

Omega is a mail order catalog company that sells mainly scientific process measurement and control instruments. In late 1994 or early 1995, the owners of Omega, Arthur and Betty Hollander, decided to enter the aviation catalog business and, for that purpose, formed a wholly-owned subsidiary called Pilot's Depot, LLC ("Pilot's Depot"). Shortly thereafter, Omega registered the domain name sportys.com with NSI. Arthur Holland-er was a pilot who received Sportsman's catalogs and thus was aware of the *sporty's* trademark.

In January 1996, nine months after registering sportys.com, Omega formed another wholly-owned subsidiary called Sporty's Farm and sold it the rights to sportys.com for $16,200. Sporty's Farm grows and sells Christmas trees, and soon began advertising its Christmas trees on a sportys.com web page. When asked how the name Sporty's Farm was selected for Omega's Christmas tree subsidiary, Ralph S. Michael, the CEO of Omega and manager of Sporty's Farm, explained, as summarized by the district court, that in his own mind and among his family, he always thought of and referred to the Pennsylvania land where Sporty's Farm now operates as *Spotty's farm*. The origin of the name ... derived from a childhood memory he had of his uncle's farm in upstate New York. As a youngster, Michael owned a dog named Spotty. Because the dog strayed, his uncle took him to his upstate farm. Michael thereafter referred to the farm as Spotty's farm. The name Sporty's Farm was ... a subsequent derivation.

There is, however, no evidence in the record that Hollander was considering starting a Christmas tree business when he registered sportys. com or that Hollander was ever acquainted with Michael's dog Spotty.

In March 1996, Sportsman's discovered that Omega had registered sportys.com as a domain name. Thereafter, and before Sportsman's could take any action, Sporty's Farm brought this declaratory action seeking the right to continue its use of sportys.com. Sportsman's counterclaimed and also sued Omega as a third-party defendant for, *inter alia*, (1) trademark infringement, (2) trademark dilution pursuant to the FTDA, and (3) unfair competition under state law. Both sides sought injunctive relief to force the other to relinquish its claims to sportys.com. While this litigation was ongoing, Sportsman's used "sportys-catalogs.com" as its primary domain name.

After a bench trial, the court rejected Sportsman's trademark infringement claim and all related claims that are based on a "likelihood of [consumer] confusion" since "the parties operate wholly unrelated businesses [and t]herefore, confusion in the marketplace is not likely to develop." But on Sportsman's trademark dilution action, where a likelihood of confusion was not necessary, the district court found for Sportsman's. The court concluded (1) that *sporty's* was a *famous* mark entitled to protection under the FTDA since "the '*Sporty's*' mark enjoys general name recognition in the consuming public," and (2) that Sporty's Farm and Omega had diluted *sporty's* because "registration of the 'sportys.com' domain name effectively compromises Sportsman's Market's ability to identify and distinguish its goods on the Internet.... [by] precluding Sportsman's Market from using its 'unique identifier,'" *id.* at 289. The court also held, however, that Sportsman's could only get injunctive relief and was not entitled to "punitive damages ... profits, and attorney's fees and costs" pursuant to the FTDA since Sporty Farm and Omega's conduct did not constitute willful dilution under the FTDA.

. . . .

The district court then issued an injunction forcing Sporty's Farm to relinquish all rights to sportys.com. And Sportsman's subsequently acquired the domain name. Both Sporty's Farm and Sportsman's appeal....

III

As we noted above, while this appeal was pending, Congress passed the ACPA. That law was passed "to protect consumers and American businesses, to promote the growth of online commerce, and to provide clarity in the law for trademark owners by prohibiting the bad-faith and abusive registration of distinctive marks as Internet domain names with the intent to profit from the goodwill associated with such marks—a practice commonly referred to as 'cybersquatting'." S. REP. NO. 106–140, at 4. In particular, Congress viewed the legal remedies available for victims of cybersquatting before the passage of the ACPA as "expensive and uncertain." H.R. REP. NO. 106–412, at 6. The Senate made clear its view on this point:

> While the [FTDA] has been useful in pursuing cybersquatters, cybersquatters have become increasingly sophisticated as the case law has developed and now take the necessary precautions to insulate themselves from liability. For example, many cybersquat-

ters are now careful to no longer offer the domain name for sale in any manner that could implicate liability under existing trademark dilution case law. And, in cases of warehousing and trafficking in domain names, courts have sometimes declined to provide assistance to trademark holders, leaving them without adequate and effective judicial remedies. This uncertainty as to the trademark law's application to the Internet has produced inconsistent judicial decisions and created extensive monitoring obligations, unnecessary legal costs, and uncertainty for consumers and trademark owners alike.

S. REP. NO. 106–140, at 7. In short, the ACPA was passed to remedy the perceived shortcomings of applying the FTDA in cybersquatting cases such as this one.

The new act accordingly amends the Trademark Act of 1946, creating a specific federal remedy for cybersquatting. New 15 U.S.C. § 1125(d)(1)(A) reads:

> A person shall be liable in a civil action by the owner of a mark, including a personal name which is protected as a mark under this section, if, without regard to the goods or services of the parties, that person—
>
> (i) has a bad faith intent to profit from that mark, including a personal name which is protected as a mark under this section; and
>
> (ii) registers, traffics in, or uses a domain name that—
>
> > (I) in the case of a mark that is distinctive at the time of registration of the domain name, is identical or confusingly similar to that mark;
> >
> > (II) in the case of a famous mark that is famous at the time of registration of the domain name, is identical or confusingly similar to or dilutive of that mark;
>
> . . . .

The Act further provides that "a court may order the forfeiture or cancellation of the domain name or the transfer of the domain name to the owner of the mark," 15 U.S.C. § 1125(d)(1)(C), if the domain name was "registered before, on, or after the date of the enactment of this Act," Pub. L. No. 106–113, § 3010. It also provides that damages can be awarded for violations of the Act,[9] but that they are not "available with respect to the registration, trafficking, or use of a domain name that occurs before the date of the enactment of this Act." *Id.*

---

9. The new Act permits a plaintiff to "elect, at any time before final judgment is rendered by the trial court, to recover, instead of actual damages and profits, an award of statutory damages in the amount of not less than $1,000 and not more than $100,000 per domain name, as the court considers just." Pub. L. No. 106–113, § 3003. If the plaintiff does not so elect, the court may award damages under 15 U.S.C. § 1117(a) and (b), based on damages, profits, and the cost of the action. *See id.*

DISCUSSION

This case has three distinct features that are worth noting before we proceed further. First, our opinion appears to be the first interpretation of the ACPA at the appellate level. Second, we are asked to undertake the interpretation of this new statute even though the district court made its ruling based on the FTDA. Third, the case before us presents a factual situation that, as far as we can tell, is rare if not unique: A Competitor X of Company Y has registered Y's trademark as a domain name and then transferred that name to Subsidiary Z, which operates a business wholly unrelated to Y. These unusual features counsel that we decide no more than is absolutely necessary to resolve the case before us.

A. *Application of the ACPA to this Case*

The first issue before us is whether the ACPA governs this case. The district court based its holding on the FTDA since the ACPA had not been passed when it made its decision. Because the ACPA became law while this case was pending before us, we must decide how its passage affects this case. As a general rule, we apply the law that exists at the time of the appeal. [Citations]

But even if a new law controls, the question remains whether in such circumstances it is more appropriate for the appellate court to apply it directly or, instead, to remand to the district court to enable that court to consider the effect of the new law. We therefore asked for additional briefing from the parties regarding the applicability of the ACPA to the case before us. After receiving those briefs and fully considering the arguments there made, we think it is clear that the new law was adopted specifically to provide courts with a preferable alternative to stretching federal dilution law when dealing with cybersquatting cases. Indeed, the new law constitutes a particularly good fit with this case. Moreover, the findings of the district court, together with the rest of the record, enable us to apply the new law to the case before us without difficulty. Accordingly, we will do so and forego a remand.

B. *"Distinctive" or "Famous"*

Under the new Act, we must first determine whether *sporty's* is a distinctive or famous mark and thus entitled to the ACPA's protection. See 15 U.S.C. § 1125(d)(1)(A)(ii)(I), (II). The district court concluded that *sporty's* is both distinctive and famous. We agree that *sporty's* is a "distinctive" mark. As a result, and without casting any doubt on the district court's holding in this respect, we need not, and hence do not, decide whether *sporty's* is also a "famous" mark.

. . . .

C. *"Identical and Confusingly Similar"*

The next question is whether domain name sportys.com is "identical or confusingly similar to" the *sporty's* mark. 15 U.S.C. § 1125 (d)(1)(A)(ii)(I). As we noted above, apostrophes cannot be used in domain names. . . . As a result, the secondary domain name in this case (sportys) is indistinguishable from the Sportsman's trademark (*sporty's*). We therefore conclude that, although the domain name sportys.com is not precisely identical to the *sporty's* mark, it is certainly "confusingly similar" to the protected mark under § 1125(d)(1)(A)(ii)(I).

D.   *"Bad Faith Intent to Profit"*

We next turn to the issue of whether Sporty's Farm acted with a "bad faith intent to profit" from the mark *sporty's* when it registered the domain name sportys.com. 15 U.S.C. § 1125(d)(1)(A)(i). The statute lists nine factors to assist courts in determining when a defendant has acted with a bad faith intent to profit from the use of a mark. But we are not limited to considering just the listed factors when making our determination of whether the statutory criterion has been met. The factors are, instead, expressly described as indicia that "may" be considered along with other facts. *Id.* § 1125(d)(1)(B)(i).

We hold that there is more than enough evidence in the record below of "bad faith intent to profit" on the part of Sporty's Farm (as that term is defined in the statute), so that "no reasonable factfinder could return a verdict against" Sportsman's. First, it is clear that neither Sporty's Farm nor Omega had any intellectual property rights in sportys.com at the time Omega registered the domain name. See id. § 1125(d)(1)(B)(i)(I). Sporty's Farm was not formed until nine months after the domain name was registered, and it did not begin operations or obtain the domain name from Omega until after this lawsuit was filed. Second, the domain name does not consist of the legal name of the party that registered it, Omega. See id. § 1125(d)(1)(B)(i)(II). Moreover, although the domain name does include part of the name of Sporty's Farm, that entity did not exist at the time the domain name was registered.

The third factor, the prior use of the domain name in connection with the bona fide offering of any goods or services, also cuts against Sporty's Farm since it did not use the site until after this litigation began, undermining its claim that the offering of Christmas trees on the site was in good faith. See id. § 1125(d)(1)(B)(i)(III). Further weighing in favor of a conclusion that Sporty's Farm had the requisite statutory bad faith intent, as a matter of law, are the following: (1) Sporty's Farm does not claim that its use of the domain name was "noncommercial" or a "fair use of the mark," *see id.* § 1125(d)(1)(B)(i)(IV), (2) Omega sold the mark to Sporty's Farm under suspicious circumstances, *see Sporty's Farm v. Sportsman's Market*, No. 96CV0756 (D. Conn. Mar. 13, 1998), (describing the circumstances of the transfer of sportys.com); 15 U.S.C. § 1125(d)(1)(B)(i)(VI), and, (3) as we discussed above, the *sporty's* mark is undoubtedly distinctive, *see id.* § 1125(d)(1)(B)(i)(IX).

The most important grounds for our holding that Sporty's Farm acted with a bad faith intent, however, are the unique circumstances of this case, which do not fit neatly into the specific factors enumerated by Congress but may nevertheless be considered under the statute. We know from the record and from the district court's findings that Omega planned to enter into direct competition with Sportsman's in the pilot and aviation consumer market. As recipients of Sportsman's catalogs, Omega's owners, the Hollanders, were fully aware that *sporty's* was a very strong mark for consumers of those products. It cannot be doubted, as the court found below, that Omega registered sportys.com for the primary purpose of keeping Sportsman's from using that domain name. Several months later, and after this lawsuit was filed, Omega created another company in an unrelated business that received the name Sporty's Farm so that it could (1) use the sportys.com domain name in some commercial fashion, (2) keep the name away from Sportsman's, and (3) protect itself in the event that Sportsman's brought an infringement claim alleging that a "likelihood of confusion" had been created by Omega's version of cybersquatting. Finally, the explanation given for Sporty's Farm's desire to use the domain name, based on the existence of the dog Spotty, is more amusing than credible. Given these facts and the district court's grant of an equitable injunction under the FTDA, there is ample and overwhelming evidence that, as a matter of law, Sporty's Farm's acted with a "bad faith intent to profit" from the domain name sportys.com as those terms are used in the ACPA.

E.   Remedy

Based on the foregoing, we hold that under § 1125(d)(1)(A), Sporty's Farm violated Sportsman's statutory rights by its use of the sportys.com domain name. The question that remains is what remedy is Sportsman's entitled to. The Act permits a court to "order the forfeiture or cancellation of the domain name or the transfer of the domain name to the owner of the mark," § 1125(d)(1)(C) for any "domain name[] registered before, on, or after the date of the enactment of [the] Act," Pub. L. No. 106–113, § 3010. That is precisely what the district court did here, albeit under the pre-existing law, when it directed a) Omega and Sporty's Farm to release their interest in sportys.com and to transfer the name to Sportsman's, and b) permanently enjoined those entities from taking any action to prevent and/or hinder Sportsman's from obtaining the domain name. That relief remains appropriate under the ACPA. We therefore affirm the district court's grant of injunctive relief.

We must also determine, however, if Sportsman's is entitled to damages either under the ACPA or pre-existing law. Under the ACPA, damages are unavailable to Sportsman's since sportys.com was registered and used by Sporty's Farm prior to the passage of the new law. *See id.* (stating that damages can be awarded for violations of the Act but that they are not "available with respect to the registration, trafficking, or use of a domain name that occurs before the date of the enactment of this Act.").

But Sportsman's might, nonetheless, be eligible for damages under the FTDA since there is nothing in the ACPA that precludes, in cybersquatting cases, the award of damages under any pre-existing law. *See* 15 U.S.C § 1125(d)(3) (providing that any remedies created by the new act are "in addition to any other civil action or remedy otherwise applicable"). Under the FTDA, "the owner of the famous mark shall be entitled only to injunctive relief unless the person against whom the injunction is sought willfully intended to trade on the owner's reputation or to cause dilution of the famous mark." Id. § 1125(c)(2) (emphasis added). Accordingly, where willful intent to dilute is demonstrated, the owner of the famous mark is— subject to the principles of equity—entitled to recover (1) damages (2) the dilutor's profits, and (3) costs. *See id.; see also id.* § 1117(a) (specifying remedies).

We conclude, however, that damages are not available to Sportsman's under the FTDA. The district court found that Sporty's Farm did not act willfully. We review such findings of "willfulness" by a district court for clear error. Thus, even assuming the *sporty's* mark to be famous, we cannot say that the district court clearly erred when it found that Sporty's Farm's actions were not willful. To be sure, that question is a very close one, for the facts make clear that, as a Sportsman's customer, Arthur Hollander (Omega's owner) was aware of the significance of the *sporty's* logo. And the idea of creating a Christmas tree business named Sporty's Farm, allegedly in honor of Spotty the dog, and of giving that business the sportys.com domain name seems to have occurred to Omega only several months after it had registered the name. Nevertheless, given the uncertain state of the law at the time that Sporty's Farm and Omega acted, we cannot say that the district court clearly erred in finding that their behavior did not amount to willful dilution. It follows that Sportsman's is not entitled to damages under the FTDA.

. . . .

QUESTION

The court affirms the trial court's determination, under the FTDA, that Sporty's Farm did not act willfully, but also holds that "there is ample and overwhelming evidence that, as a matter of law, Sporty's Farm's acted with a 'bad faith intent to profit' from the domain name sportys.com. . . ." Are those two holdings consistent?

Lucas Nursery and Landscaping, Inc. v. Grosse

359 F.3d 806 (6th Cir.2004).

■ R. GUY COLE, JR., CIRCUIT JUDGE.

. . .

I. BACKGROUND

This case arises from a dispute related to landscaping work that was performed by Lucas Nursery at the residence of Michelle Grosse. In March 2000, Grosse hired Lucas Nursery to correct a dip in the soil (known as a swale) that ran horizontally through the center of her front yard. Lucas Nursery's representative, Bob Lucas, Jr., stated that the swale could be corrected by using five large loads of topsoil. Lucas Nursery performed the work on May 16, 2000.

Grosse contends that the work was performed inadequately. After allegedly contacting Lucas Nursery on numerous occasions to express her displeasure with the work and to seek some repair, Grosse filed a complaint with the Better Business Bureau ("the BBB"). After the BBB ended its investigation without making a recommendation, Grosse remained dissatisfied by what she felt had been poor service by Lucas Nursery, and decided to inform others about her experience with the company.

On August 12, 2000, Grosse registered the domain name "lucasnursery.com." She then posted a web page for the sole purpose of relaying her story to the public. The web page was titled, "My Lucas Landscaping Experience." The web page included complaints regarding the poor preparation of the soil prior to Lucas Nursery's laying of the sod, the hasty nature of Lucas Nursery's work, the ineffectiveness of the BBB in addressing her complaint, and the fact that she had to pay an additional $5,400 to a second contractor to repair the work originally performed by Lucas Nursery.

On September 27, 2000, Grosse received a letter from Lucas Nursery's attorney demanding that she cease operating the web site. On October 2, 2000, Grosse removed the web site's content. However, after removing the web site's content, Grosse contacted the Michigan Bureau of Commercial Services Licensing Division and the U.S. Patent & Trademark Office to determine whether there was a registered trademark for Lucas Nursery. After learning that no trademark registration existed, Grosse concluded that Lucas Nursery could not prevent her from retaining the web site. On April 13, 2001, Grosse posted a new narrative on the web site, again describing her experience with Lucas Nursery.

Lucas Nursery filed suit against Grosse on August 17, 2001. Thereafter, each party moved for summary judgment. On April 23, 2002, the district court denied Lucas Nursery's motion for summary judgment and granted Grosse's motion for summary judgment.

II.   ANALYSIS

. . .

In order for liability to attach under the ACPA a court must conclude that the defendant's actions constitute "bad faith." ACPA § 3002 (codified at 15 U.S.C. § 1125(d)(1)(A)–(B)). An analysis of whether a defendant's actions constitute bad faith within the meaning of the ACPA usually begins with consideration of several factors, nine of which are listed in the ACPA. *See Sporty's Farm v. Sportsman's Market, Inc.*, 202 F.3d 489, 498 (2d Cir. 2000). The first four factors are those that militate against a finding of bad faith by providing some reasonable basis for why a defendant might have registered the domain name of another mark holder. These factors focus on: whether the defendant has trademark or other rights in the domain name; the extent to which the domain name consists of the defendant's legal name or other common name; any prior use of the domain name for the offering of goods and services; and the bona fide noncommercial use of the site.

Each of the first three factors cuts against Grosse. She does not hold a trademark or other intellectual property rights to the domain name or names included in the registered domain name. The domain name neither consists of her legal name or any name used to refer to her. Grosse has also not used the domain name in connection with any offering of goods or services. The fourth factor cuts in Grosse's favor because the site was used for noncommercial purposes.

Factors five through eight are indicative of the presence of bad faith on the part of the defendant. These factors focus on: whether the defendant seeks to divert consumers from the mark holder's online location either in a way that could harm good will or tarnish or disparage the mark by creating a confusion regarding the sponsorship of the site; whether there has been an offer to transfer or sell the site for financial gain; whether the defendant provided misleading contact information when registering the domain name; and whether the defendant has acquired multiple domain names which may be duplicative of the marks of others.

. . .

None of these factors militates against Grosse. There is no dispute that Lucas Nursery did not have an online location, and hence Grosse's creation of a web site to complain about Lucas Nursery's services could not have been intended "to divert consumers from the mark owners's online location." Nor is there any evidence that Grosse ever sought to mislead consumers with regard to the site's sponsorship. The web site explicitly stated that the site was established by Grosse for the purposes of relaying her experience with Lucas Nursery. Moreover, Grosse never offered to sell the site to Lucas Nursery. She also did not provide misleading contact information when she registered the domain name. Finally, she has not acquired any additional domain names, which would be indicative of either an intent to sell such names to those entities whose trademarks were identical or similar, or exploit them for other uses.

. . .

Lucas Nursery seeks to buttress its argument with *Toronto–Dominion Bank v. Karpachev*, 188 F.Supp.2d 110 (D. Mass. 2002). There, the district court granted Toronto–Dominion's motion for summary judgment against the defendant, concluding that there was sufficient evidence to show that the defendant had acted in bad faith under the ACPA. The defendant, a disgruntled customer, registered sixteen domain names composed of various misspellings of the name tdwaterhouse.com. *Id.* at 111. On the web sites associated with these names, the defendant attacked Toronto–Dominion for "webfacism" and involvement with white collar crime, among other things. *Id.* at 112. The court concluded that the defendant had acted in bad faith, citing four factors: (1) his intention to divert customers from the "tdwaterhouse" web site by creating confusion as to its source or sponsorship; (2) the fact that he had registered sixteen domain names; (3) the fact that he offered no goods or services on the site; and (4) the fact that he had no intellectual property rights in the site. *See id.* at 114.

Although Grosse's actions would arguably satisfy three of the four aforementioned factors, she does not fall within the factor that we consider central to a finding of bad faith. She did not register multiple web sites; she only registered one. Further, it is not clear to this Court that the presence of simply one factor that indicates a bad faith intent to profit, without more, can satisfy an imposition of liability within the meaning of the ACPA. The role of the reviewing court is not simply to add factors and place them in particular categories, without making some sense of what motivates the conduct at issue. The factors are given to courts as a guide, not as a substitute for careful thinking about whether the conduct at issue is motivated by a bad faith intent to profit. Perhaps most important to our conclusion are, Grosse's actions, which seem to have been undertaken in the spirit of informing fellow consumers about the practices of a landscaping company that she believed had performed inferior work on her yard. One of the ACPA's main objectives is the protection of consumers from slick internet peddlers who trade on the names and reputations of established brands. The practice of informing fellow consumers of one's experience with a particular service provider is surely not inconsistent with this ideal.

CONCLUSION

For the foregoing reasons, we AFFIRM the district court's grant of summary judgment in favor of Grosse.

SECTION 43(D) AND "GRIPE" SITES

Recent cases have found the reasoning of *Lucas Nursery* persuasive. In *TMI v. Maxwell*, 368 F.3d 433 (5th Cir.2004), the Court of Appeals for the 5th Circuit followed *Lucas Nursery* in dismissing both dilution and ACPA claims against a cyber-griper. After an unsatisfactory experience seeking to purchase a home from TrendMarker Homes, Defendant Maxwell had posted a site at <www.trendmakerhome.com> complaining about his experience. TrendMaker sued Maxwell for cybersquatting and dilution. The Fifth Circuit held that "Maxwell's conduct is not the kind of harm the ACPA is designed to prevent." In *Mayflower Transit, LLC v. Prince*, 314 F.Supp.2d 362 (D.N.J.2004), the court applied the reasoning of *Lucas Nursery* to a cyber-griping case involving the registration of multiple domain names. Brett Prince engaged Lincoln Storage, an intrastate moving company affiliated with Mayflower Van Lines, to move his worldly goods from West Orange, New Jersey to Freehold, New Jersey. Enroute, thieves broke in to the parked moving truck and stole much of Prince's property. Prince sued both the Lincoln and Mayflower, and registered the domain name <mayflowervanlinebeware.com>. He posted a website describing his moving experience under the headline "Beware of Lincoln Storage Warehouse. Beware of Mayflower Van Lines." The website urged consumers contemplating a move to avoid both companies. Prince subsequently registered the domain names <mayflowevanline.com>, <lincolnstorageware-house.com>, <newjerseymovingcompany.com>, and posted similar materi-al to those sites. Mayflower sued Prince under the ACPA. The court, relying on *Lucas Nursery*, held that Mayflower had failed to show that Prince had a "bad faith intent to profit," concluding that "genuine cyber-gripers . . . are not covered by the ACPA." Prince's registration and use of multiple domain names did not persuade the court that he acted in bad faith.

In *Coca–Cola Company v. Purdy*, 382 F.3d 774 (8th Cir. 2004), howev-er, the Court of Appeals for the Eighth Circuit distinguished *Lucas Nursery* and upheld a finding of bad faith intent to profit. The case involved the registration and use of domain names for a gripe site that was unrelated to the products or services sold by the owners of trademarks used in the contested domain names. William Purdy set up an anti-abortion web page at <www.abortionismurder.com>, where he posted antiabortion commen-tary and graphic photos of aborted fetuses. Purdy also posted links to a website offering to sell hats, neckties, and tee shirts adorned with antiabor-tion messages. Purdy registered the domains <drinkcoke.com>, <mycoca-cola.com>, <my-washingtonpost.com>, <mypepsi.org>, and others, and used those domain names to redirect browsers to <abortionismurder.com>. The trademark owners brought suit under the ACPA. In distinguishing *Lucas Nursery*, the Eighth Circuit emphasized that "[t]he content available at abortionismurder.com contained no references to plaintiffs, their prod-ucts, or their alleged positions on abortion."

Finally, in *Bosley Medical Institute, Inc. v. Kremer*, 403 F.3d 672 (9th Cir.2005), the Court of Appeals for the 9th Circuit dismissed a trademark infringement and dilution claim over a gripe site, but declined to dismiss the ACPA claim. Plaintiff Bosley Medical sued its former hair-transplant patient when he posted a site at <www.BosleyMedical.com> criticizing plaintiff's hair transplant services. The Ninth Circuit concluded that defen-dant's site did not violate the Lanham Act, because Kremer's actions were not "commercial use in commerce:"

> The dangers that the Lanham Act was designed to address are simply not at issue in this case. The Lanham Act, expressly enacted to be applied in commercial contexts, does not prohibit all unauthorized uses of a trademark. Kremer's use of the Bosley Medical mark simply cannot mislead consumers into buying a competing product—no cus-tomer will mistakenly purchase a hair replacement service from Krem-er under the belief that the service is being offered by Bosley. Neither is Kremer capitalizing on the good will Bosley has created in its mark. Any harm to Bosley arises not from a competitor's sale of a similar product under Bosley's mark, but from Kremer's criticism of their services. Bosley cannot use the Lanham Act either as a shield from Kremer's criticism, or as a sword to shut Kremer up.

The court remanded the ACPA claim for trial, however, noting that section 43(d) of the Lanham Act does not expressly require commercial use and that other circuits had interpreted it to make non-commercial as well as commercial cybersquatting actionable.

QUESTION

1. The ACPA limits liability to those domain name registrants who register, use or traffic in a domain name with "a bad faith intent *to profit.*" 15 U.S.C. § 1125(d)(1)(A). How does that differ from simple "bad faith intent?" In what sense was Purdy's activity calculated to yield a "profit?" How does intent to profit differ from commercial use?

2. America Online (AOL) is the world's largest online service provider, with more than 20 million subscribers. AOL encourages subscribers to connect to its service using proprietary (free) software that is advertised as being easy to use. Since 1989, AOL has been using the phrases "You have mail!" and "You've got mail!" to signal to its subscribers that they have unread electronic messages. The current version of the AOL software greets subscribers with a welcome screen that tells them "you have mail", while a pleasant male voice says *"Welcome. You've got mail!"*

Madelene Sabol is a first-time author who lives in Denver, Colorado. Her self-published Internet dating book is a how-to manual for women seeking romance with men they find on the Internet. Sabol named the book "You've Got Male." The book offers tips on picking up men online along with advice on things to avoid. Sabol has said that she wrote the book after a particularly bad Internet dating experience.

Sabol registered the domain name youve- got-male.com, and uses it for a website promoting the book. Sabol's site, at www.youve- got-male.com includes a picture of Sabol holding her book, promotional blurbs about the book, and a link to Amazon.com to facilitate immediate purchase of a copy of the book. AOL has demanded that Sabol rename her book because of the title's confusing similarity to its famous trademark "You've got mail!" and that she immediately convey ownership of the youve- got-male.com domain to AOL. Can AOL secure cancellation or transfer of the domain name under section 43(d)? Is it likely to recover under section 43(a) or 43(c)?

LIABILITY OF DOMAIN NAME BROKERS AND DOMAIN NAME AUCTIONEERS

Ford v. Greatdomains.com, 177 F.Supp.2d 635 (E.D.Mich.2001). Ford Motor Company brought an ACPA claim against Greatdomains.com, a domain name auction site that lists domain names for sale in return for a commission. Greatdomains.com had allegedly hosted auctions of multiple domain names that were confusingly similar to Ford's trademarks. Ford also sued the individual sellers of the disputed domain names. The court dismissed the claim against Greatdomains.com:

> The issue with regard to Great Domains is whether Ford has sufficiently alleged the first necessary element of a cybersquatting claim, *i.e.*, whether Great Domains either (1) "registers," (2) "traffics in," or (3) "uses" the domain names at issue in this case.

15 U.S.C. § 1125(d)(1)(A)(ii). It is undisputed that Great Domains has not "registered" any of the challenged domain names. Moreover, § 1125(d) expressly provides that a person may not be held liable for "using" a domain name under the statute unless that person "is the domain name registrant or that registrant's authorized licensee." § 1125(d)(1)(D). Thus, the court's inquiry must focus on whether Ford can demonstrate that Great Domains has "trafficked in" a domain name. 15 U.S.C. § 1125(d)(1)(A)(ii).

The phrase "traffics in" is defined in the ACPA as "referring to transactions that include, but are not limited to, sales, purchases, loans, pledges, licenses, exchanges of currency, and any other transfer for consideration or receipt in exchange for consideration." 15 U.S.C. § 1125(d)(1)(E). The specific terms listed in this definition are susceptible to broad interpretation and, moreover, are merely illustrative. Nonetheless, the concluding catch-all phrase "any other transfer . . . or receipt in exchange for consideration" provides the context in which they must be understood. Specifically, the language "any other transfer . . . or receipt" clarifies that the defining terms are all ways in which a domain name may be transferred or received. The key words—"transfer" and "receipt"—both denote some level of ownership or control passing between the person transferring and the person receiving. Thus relying upon the plain meaning of the statute, the court concludes that the phrase "traffics in" contemplates a direct transfer or receipt of ownership interest in a domain name to or from the defendant.

Great Domains's commercial activity does not fit within this definition. As an auctioneer, Great Domains does not transfer or receive for consideration the domain names that are sold over its website. Although it does provide a forum at which such transfers and receipts may take place, the property interests associated with each domain name remain with the person "transferring" and pass directly to the person "receiving," thus bypassing Great Domains entirely. Accordingly, the court concludes that the ACPA does not cover Great Domain's provision of ancillary services, which merely facilitate the statutorily targeted transfers and receipts. *Accord Bird v. Parsons*, 127 F. Supp. 2d 885 (S.D. Ohio 2000) ("Registration of a domain name does not constitute use within the trademark laws. The same logic applies to providing a site at which domain names can be sold." (internal citation omitted)); *cf. Lockheed Martin Corp. v. Network Solutions, Inc.*, 141 F. Supp. 2d 648, 655 (N.D. Tex. 2001) (finding "no summary judgment evidence that [a domain name registrar] had engaged in transactions of any of those kinds" listed to define the phrase "traffics in").

In addition to the plain language of the statute, the ACPA's "bad faith intent" requirement lends further support to the conclusion that only persons directly transferring or receiving a property interest in the domain name can be liable as cybersquatters. First, as discussed previously, the bad faith factors set forth in the ACPA focus on the relationship between the domain name and the defendant, directing attention to the legitimacy of the defendants' use. Such an analysis is not purposeful when applied to a person or entity that did not register the domain name, has no ownership interest in the domain name, and does not otherwise use the domain name. *Cf. Lockheed*, 141 F. Supp. 2d at 655 ("Although the list is not exclusive, none of the conditions and conduct listed would be applicable to a person functioning solely as a registrar or registry of domain names."). The court believes that if Congress had intended to extend the anticybersquatting law to auction, banking, or other similar auxiliary service providers, it would have set forth factors that meaningfully could be applied in determining whether such entities had acted in bad faith.

Second, subjecting ancillary service providers such as Great Domains to liability under the statute would significantly hinder the case-by-case analysis intended in "balancing the property interests of trademark owners with the legitimate interests of Internet users and others who seek to make lawful uses of others' marks." S. Rep. No. 106–140, at 13; H.R. Rep. No. 106–412, at 10. Great Domains has little ability to ascertain whether a domain name seller wishes to sell based on a "bad faith intent to profit" or because some previous legitimate use has proven unsuccessful or undesirable. This is particularly true where, as here, a domain name incorporates another's trademark, but is not identical to that trademark. In such circumstances, a defendant easily can set forth a facially legitimate reason for having registered the disputed domain. The [individual] Defendants' explanations for having registered domains such as "volvoguy.com" ("volvoguy" is registrant's nickname arising from his work as a Volvo repair specialist), "jaguarcenter.com" (site for publication of issues surrounding preservation of jaguar cats), "vintagevolvos.com" (site for vintage Volvo enthusiasts to connect with each other and share resources), and so forth, amply illustrate this point. For a court to determine whether such proffered uses are, in fact, legitimate requires legal analysis of whether the disputed domain is "confusingly similar to or dilutive of" a mark and the weighing of evidence, particularly each individual defendant's credibility. Imposing liability under the ACPA upon Great Domains would require it to engage in a similarly complex process, essentially forcing Great Domains to discontinue any trafficking in domain names that contain protected trademarks. Such a result would be contrary to Congress's intent not to hinder the legitimate buying and selling of domain names over the Internet. For these reasons, the court concludes that, in addition to the plain meaning of "traffics in," the bad faith element further mandates that the ACPA be limited in its application to persons directly transferring or receiving a property interest in the domain name at issue.

3. *Contributory liability*

Ford argues that even if it cannot directly state a cybersquatting claim against Great Domains, the law supports a claim of contributory liability. This argument is premised on Ford's allegations that Great Domains (1) auctions domain names "to the highest bidder" through the "greatdomains.com" website; (2) "collects a commission on the sale of domain names purchased through its web site" and thus "shares its customers' interest in selling their domain names at the highest possible price"; and (3) encourages cybersquatting by explaining in the "valuation model" found on its website that "the value of a domain name is driven by its ability to deliver traffic and revenue," which ability, Ford adds, is greatly enhanced if the domain name incorporates a trademark. These claims are insufficient to support contributory liability in the cybersquatting context.

. . . .

§ 43(d)(2) AND *IN REM* JURISDICTION

The ACPA also includes a section 43(d)(2), which permits an *in rem* civil action to obtain forfeiture or cancellation of an infringing domain name:

43(d)(2)(A). The owner of a mark may file an in rem civil action against a domain name in the judicial district in which the domain name registrar, domain name registry, or other domain name authority that registered or assigned the domain name is located if—

(i)   the domain name violates any right of the owner of a mark registered in the Patent and Trademark Office, or protected under subsection (a) or (c); and

(ii)   the court finds that the owner—
  (I)   is not able to obtain in personam jurisdiction over a person who would have been a defendant in a civil action under paragraph (1); or
  (II) through due diligence was not able to find a person who would have been a defendant in a civil action under paragraph (1). . . .

(D)(i) The remedies in an in rem action under this paragraph shall be limited to a court order for the forfeiture or cancellation of the domain name or the transfer of the domain name to the owner of the mark. . . .

(4) The in rem jurisdiction established under paragraph (2) shall be in addition to any other jurisdiction that otherwise exists, whether in rem or in personam.

In *Caesars World v. Caesars–Palace.Com*, 112 F.Supp.2d 502 (E.D.Va. 2000), the District Court for the Eastern District of Virginia upheld the constitutionality of § 43(d)(2)'s *in rem* provision against a due process challenge. In *Lucent Technologies v. Lucentsucks.com*, 95 F.Supp.2d 528 (E.D.Va.2000), however, the court held that a plaintiff could invoke the *in rem* action only after a reasonable, good faith effort to locate and obtain personal jurisdiction over the registrant of a disputed domain name. The court dismissed Lucent's *in rem* action against the lucentsucks.com domain name, noting that plaintiff had failed to wait a reasonable time for the registrant to respond to its notice before filing an *in rem* action, and had continued to proceed with its *in rem* suit after it became aware of the registrant's current address. Where the identity and address of the registrant is known and *in personam* jurisdiction is possible, the court held, a § 43(d)(2) *in rem* cause of action is not available.

Harrods Limited v. Sixty Internet Domain Names

302 F.3d 214 (4th Cir. 2002).

■ MICHAEL, CIRCUIT JUDGE:

This case involves a dispute over Internet domain names between two companies named "Harrods," both with legitimate rights to the "Harrods" name in different parts of the world. The plaintiff, Harrods Limited ("Harrods UK"), is the owner of the well-known Harrods of London department store. The defendants are 60 Internet domain names ("Domain Names" or "Names") registered in Herndon, Virginia, by Harrods (Buenos Aires) Limited ("Harrods BA"). Harrods BA, once affiliated with Harrods UK, is now a completely separate corporate entity that until recently operated a "Harrods" department store in Buenos Aires, Argentina. Harrods UK sued the 60 Domain Names under 15 U.S.C. § 1125(d)(2), the in rem provision of the recently enacted Anticybersquatting Consumer Protection Act (ACPA), Pub. L. No. 106–113, 113 Stat. 1501A–545 (codified in scattered sections of 15 U.S.C.) (1999). Harrods UK alleged that the Domain Names infringed and diluted its American "Harrods" trademark and that Harrods BA registered the Names in bad faith as prohibited by 15 U.S.C. § 1125(d)(1). ...

I.

Harrods UK and its predecessors have operated a department store named "Harrods" in the Knightsbridge section of London, England, since 1849. In 1912 Harrods UK created a wholly owned subsidiary, Harrods South America Limited, to carry on business in South America. Harrods South America Limited created Harrods BA as an independent company, and in 1914 Harrods BA opened a department store under the name "Harrods" in a new building in downtown Buenos Aires designed to look like Harrods UK's historic London building. Over the following decades Harrods BA registered "Harrods" as a trademark in Argentina, Brazil, Paraguay, Venezuela, and a number of other South American countries. Harrods UK and Harrods BA quickly drifted apart: by the 1920s Harrods BA was operating largely independently of Harrods UK, and the last remaining legal ties between the two companies were severed in 1963.

In the early 1990s Harrods UK and Harrods BA entered into negotiations for Harrods UK to buy Harrods BA's South American trademark rights in the name "Harrods." At one point Harrods UK offered $10 million for the rights, but the parties never reached agreement.... Here, we have not been asked to conclusively determine the legitimacy and scope of Harrods BA's rights in the name "Harrods" throughout South America. It appears, however, that Harrods BA has the right to use the name "Harrods" in Argentina and much of South America, and for the limited purposes of this litigation Harrods UK does not attempt to prove otherwise.

Harrods UK, for its part, has exclusive trademark rights in the name "Harrods" in much of the rest of the world, including the United States, where retail catalog and Internet sales generate millions of dollars in revenue each year. Harrods UK's retail business has thrived in recent years, but Harrods BA's business has been in decline since the early 1960s. Over the years, Harrods BA occupied less and less of its large Buenos Aires department store building and leased more and more of the space to other vendors. Some time around 1998 Harrods BA ended its department store operation entirely, and the building now sits vacant. Harrods BA's only current revenue is about $300,000 annually from the continued operation of the building's parking garage.

In February of 1999 Harrods UK launched a website at the domain name harrods.com, and the website became a functioning online retail store in November of 1999. Harrods BA executives testified that sometime in 1999 they also began planning to launch a Harrods store on the Internet. Toward that end, Harrods BA hired a consultant, a Mr. Capuro, to prepare a proposal for an online business. In the fall of 1999, around the same time that Harrods UK was launching its Internet business (and announcing this in the press), Harrods BA began registering the first of what eventually became around 300 Harrods-related domain names. The 60 Domain Names that are defendants in this case were registered with Network Solutions, Inc. (NSI), a domain name registry located in Herndon, Virginia. At that time NSI served as the exclusive worldwide registry for domain names using .com, .net, and .org.

. . .

Harrods BA registered each of its Harrods-related domain names under the .com, .net., and .org top-level domains. For example, Harrods BA registered the second-level domain harrodsbuenosaires as harrodsbuenosaires.com, harrodsbuenosaires.net, and harrodsbuenosaires.org. This case involves 20 distinct second-level domain names, each registered under the three top-level domains .com, .net, and .org, for a total of 60 defendant Domain Names.[5] All told, Harrods BA registered about 300 Harrods-related domain names in the United States. The 20 second-level domain names at

---

5. For simplicity's sake we will refer to the names by the second-level domains, such as harrodsbuenosaires, with the understanding that this reference encompasses the three permutations of that second-level domain created by combining it with the three top-level domains, .com, .net, and .org.

issue in this case are harrodsbuenosaires, harrodsargentina, harrodssudamerica, harrodssouthamerica, harrodsbrasil, harrodsbrazil, harrodsamerica, tiendaharrods, cyberharrods, ciberharrods, harrodsbank, harrodsbanking, harrodsfinancial, harrodsservices, harrodsvirtual, harrodsstore, shoppingharrods, harrodsshopping, harrodsbashopping, and harrodsshoppingba.

. . .

On February 16, 2000, Harrods UK sued 60 of the Harrods-related domain names in the United States District Court for the Eastern District of Virginia. Harrods UK sued under 15 U.S.C. § 1125(d)(2), which permits the owner of a protected mark to bring an in rem action against domain names that violate "any right of the owner of a mark," subject to certain limitations. For example, the in rem action is available only when the plaintiff cannot find or cannot obtain personal jurisdiction over the domain name registrant. Harrods UK claimed that the Domain Names violated 15 U.S.C. § 1125(d)(1), which prohibits bad faith registration of domain names with intent to profit, and 15 U.S.C. §§ 1114, 1125(a) & (c), which together prohibit trademark infringement and dilution. Harrods BA was easily identified as the registrant of the defendant Domain Names, but the mere act of registering the Domain Names in Virginia was deemed insufficient to provide personal jurisdiction over Harrods BA. *See, e.g., Heathmount A.E. Corp. v. Technodome.com*, 106 F.Supp.2d 860, 866–69 (E.D. Va. 2000). Because Harrods UK could not obtain personal jurisdiction over Harrods BA, the suit was filed in rem against the 60 Domain Names themselves.

. . .

II

. . .

On appeal the Domain Names claim that the district court's exercise of in rem jurisdiction over them violates the Due Process Clause because they lack sufficient minimum contacts with the forum. The Due Process clause of the Fifth Amendment permits a federal court to exercise personal jurisdiction over a defendant only if that defendant has "certain minimum contacts with [the forum] such that the maintenance of the suit does not offend 'traditional notions of fair play and substantial justice.' " *Int'l Shoe Co. v. Washington*, 326 U.S. 310, 316, 90 L. Ed. 95, 66 S. Ct. 154 (1945) (*quoting Milliken v. Meyer*, 311 U.S. 457, 463, 85 L. Ed. 278, 61 S. Ct. 339 (1940))....

In the case of disputes involving property, the presence of the property in the jurisdiction does not always justify the exercise of in rem jurisdiction, but "when claims to the property itself are the source of the underlying controversy between the plaintiff and the defendant, it would be unusual for the State where the property is located not to have jurisdiction." *Shaffer* [*v. Heitner*, 433 U.S. 186 (1977)], 433 U.S. at 207 (internal footnote omitted). ...Specifically, the Supreme Court said in *Shaffer* that in rem jurisdiction is appropriate in "suits for injury suffered on the land of an absentee owner, where the defendant's ownership of the property is conceded but the cause of action is otherwise related to rights and duties growing out of that ownership." *Shaffer*, 433 U.S. at 208. The dispute in this case is roughly analogous to such a suit. Harrods UK has allegedly suffered injury by way of property, the Domain Names, owned by Harrods BA, an absentee owner. Harrods BA's initial ownership of the Names is conceded, but the cause of action is related to Harrods BA's rights and duties arising out of that ownership.

Likewise, Virginia's "interests in assuring the marketability of property within its borders and in providing a procedure for peaceful resolution of disputes about the possession of that property" also support the exercise of in rem jurisdiction in this case. *Id.* (internal footnote omitted). Moreover, Virginia's interest in not permitting foreign companies to use rights emanating from, and facilities located in, its territory to infringe U.S. trademarks also supports the exercise of in rem jurisdiction. By registering these Domain Names in Virginia, Harrods BA exposed those Names to the jurisdiction of the courts in Virginia (state or federal) at least for the limited purpose of determining who properly owns the Domain Names themselves. This is not a case where "the only role played by the property is to provide the basis for bringing the defendant into court." *Id.* at 209. Rather, because "claims to the property itself are the source of the underlying controversy," *id.* at 207, and because Virginia has important interests in exercising jurisdiction over that property (the Names), we conclude that courts in Virginia, the state where the Domain Names are registered, may constitutionally exercise in rem jurisdiction over them. Thus, the district court's exercise of in rem jurisdiction over the Domain Names was constitutional.

. . .

Harrods UK argues that § 1125(d)(2) provides for in rem jurisdiction against domain names for traditional infringement and dilution claims under §§ 1114, 1125(a) & (c) as well as for claims of bad faith registration with the intent to profit under § 1125(d)(1). The Domain Names argue that the district court correctly limited the scope of the in rem provision to claims under § 1125(d)(1) for bad faith registration of a domain name with the intent to profit. This argument has not yet been settled by any federal circuit court. . . . While we consider this to be a close question of statutory interpretation, we ultimately conclude that § 1125(d)(2) is not limited to violations of § 1125(d)(1); it also authorizes in rem actions for certain federal infringement and dilution claims.

We begin our analysis with the text of the statute. Section 1125(d)(2)(A) provides that the "owner of a mark" may file an in rem action against a domain name if:

> (i) the domain name violates any right of the owner of a mark registered in the Patent and Trademark Office, or protected under subsection (a) [infringement] or (c) [dilution]; and

> (ii) ... the owner—
>> (I) is not able to obtain in personam jurisdiction over a person who would have been a defendant in a civil action under paragraph (1) [§ 1125(d)(1)]; or
>> (II) through due diligence was not able to find a person who would have been a defendant in a civil action under paragraph (1)....

15 U.S.C. § 1125(d)(2)(A). We start with the first clause, subsection (d)(2)(A)(i), which provides that an in rem action is available if "(i) the domain name violates *any right* of the owner of a mark registered in the Patent and Trademark Office, or protected under subsection (a) or (c)." 15 U.S.C. § 1125(d)(2)(A)(i) (emphasis added). The broad language "any right of the owner of a mark" does not look like it is limited to the rights guaranteed by subsection (d)(1), but appears to include any right a trademark owner has with respect to the mark. The language, by itself, would include rights under § 1125(d)(1), and it would also include, for example, rights under § 1125(a) against trademark infringement and rights under § 1125(c) against trademark dilution. If Congress had intended for subsection (d)(2) to provide in rem jurisdiction only for subsection (d)(1) claims, it could easily have said so directly. For example, Congress could have said that an in rem action is available if "the domain name violates subsection (d)(1)." Again, if the first key phrase Congress gave us—"any right of the owner of a mark"—is considered in isolation, it would authorize the in rem pursuit of any of the actions that could be brought in personam under U.S. trademark law, including infringement (subsection (a)), dilution (subsection (c)), and cybersquatting (subsection (d)(1)). ...

Of course, subsection (d)(2)(A)(i) does not create a claim for the owner of any mark, but rather for the owner of "a mark registered in the Patent and Trademark Office [PTO], or protected under subsection (a) or (c)." Thus, to understand the scope of subsection (d)(2)(A)(i), we must also consider the implications of this additional language. Generally speaking, trademark protection is a common law right that arises from the use of a mark to identify the source of certain goods or services. *Brittingham v. Jenkins*, 914 F.2d 447, 452 (4th Cir. 1990); 3 McCarthy § 19:3. By its terms, subsection (d)(2)(A)(i) does not provide an in rem action for the owner of any type of mark protected under trademark law, but only for the owner of a mark that is either (1) registered in the PTO or (2) protected under §§ 1125(a) or (c).

First, we consider the protection offered a mark registered in the PTO. The owner of a mark may register that mark with the PTO. 15 U.S.C. § 1051. While it is the use of a mark, not its registration, that confers trademark protection, *Brittingham*, 914 F.2d at 452, registration does confer certain benefits on the owner; for example, it serves as prima facie evidence of the mark's validity. Id.; 15 U.S.C. § 1057(b). Subsection (d)(2)(A)(i) provides an additional benefit for registration of a mark: registration now entitles the owner of the mark to proceed on an in rem basis under § 1125(d)(2). The rights of an owner whose mark is registered in the PTO are not limited to rights under § 1125(d)(1), however. They also include, for example, rights against infringement of a registered mark under § 1114.

Second, subsection (d)(2)(A)(i) ends with the provision that even if a mark is not registered, the mark's owner may proceed on an in rem basis under § 1125(d)(2) if the mark is "protected under subsection (a) or (c)." Subsections (a) and (c) are the infringement and dilution provisions of § 1125. Because subsection (d)(2) provides for an in rem action for the violation of "any right . . . of a mark . . . protected under subsection (a) or (c)," it seems to provide in rem jurisdiction over a domain name that infringes a mark under § 1125(a) or dilutes a famous mark under § 1125(c). . . . If in rem jurisdiction is only available for subsection (d)(1) bad faith claims, we cannot understand why Congress described the types of marks covered under subsection (d)(2) as those "registered in the [PTO], or protected under subsection (a) or (c)." Subsection (d)(2)(A)(i)'s reference to a mark "registered in the [PTO], or protected under subsection (a) or (c)" reinforces our sense that the phrase "any right" includes more than just subsection (d)(1) rights.

According to the Domain Names, the problem with interpreting subsection (d)(2) as covering more than just bad faith claims under subsection (d)(1) is that subsection (d)(2)(A)(ii) conditions the availability of in rem jurisdiction on proof that the plaintiff is unable to find or obtain personal jurisdiction over the "person who would have been a defendant in a civil action [for bad faith registration] under paragraph (1)," that is, § 1125(d)(1). As the district court explained, "because Congress chose to include in the in rem action the definition of potential defendants used in paragraph (1), we must therefore conclude that Congress intended for the 'bad faith intent to profit' element to be part of any in rem action." *Harrods Ltd. v. Sixty Internet Domain Names*, 110 F.Supp.2d 420, 426 (E.D. Va. 2000). We realize that it is possible to get the impression from reading subsection (d)(2)(A)(ii) that the in rem action is available only for subsection (d)(1) violations. But it is important to distinguish between the language discussing the subject matter covered by the in rem provision and the language discussing the proper defendant in a cybersquatting case. Subsection (d)(2)(A)(i) deals with the former, and subsection (d)(2)(A)(ii) deals with the latter. Subsection (d)(2)(A)(i) identifies the substantive rights actionable under the in rem provision, stating in broad terms that the in rem provision protects "any right of the owner of a mark" that is registered in the PTO or "protected under subsection (a) or (c)." Subsection (d)(2)(A)(ii) deals with the proper defendant to a cybersquatting claim, stating that in rem jurisdiction is available only when personal jurisdiction over the registrant is lacking. It would be odd for Congress to have placed a significant limitation on the scope of the substantive rights identified in subsection (d)(2)(A)(i), which deals with the subject matter of in rem actions, by indirectly tacking something on to subsection (d)(2)(A)(ii), which deals with the proper defendant in cybersquatting actions.

If the only way to understand the phrase "a person who would have been a defendant in a civil action under paragraph (1)" was as a reference to subsection (d)(1)'s bad faith requirement, we would be forced to confront the tension between this language and subsection (d)(2)(A)(i)'s broad language of "any right of the owner of a mark." However, the phrase "a person who would have been a defendant in a civil action under paragraph (1)" can fairly be understood as a shorthand reference to the current registrant of the domain name. . . .

Nonetheless, it is possible to disagree about the meaning of the phrase "a person who would have been a defendant in a civil action under paragraph (1)." As noted above, the district court understood this language not as a shorthand reference to the current domain name registrant, but as limiting in rem jurisdiction to subsection (d)(1) bad faith claims. *Harrods Ltd.*, 110 F.Supp.2d at 426. Because the meaning of this phrase in conjunction with the phrase "any right of the owner of a mark" is not altogether clear, it is appropriate to "look to the legislative history for guidance in interpreting the statute." *United States v. Childress*, 104 F.3d 47, 53 (4th Cir. 1996). The legislative history confirms that the phrase "a person who would have been a defendant in a civil action under paragraph (1)" should be read as a shorthand reference to the domain name registrant, not as requiring a bad faith element in all in rem actions. The House Report says that "in rem jurisdiction is . . . appropriate in instances where personal jurisdiction cannot be established over the domain name registrant." H.R. Rep. No. 106–412, at 14 (1999). The registrant is the person who would be the defendant both in a subsection (d)(1) bad faith registration action and in a traditional infringement or dilution action involving the improper use of a domain name.

. . .

On balance, we are left with the following. On its face, subsection (d)(2)(A)(i) provides an in rem action for the violation of "any right" of a trademark owner, not just rights provided by subsection (d)(1). Moreover, subsection (d)(2)(A)(i) authorizes in rem jurisdiction for marks "protected under subsection (a) or (c)," the very subsections underlying two of the claims that were dismissed by the district court as outside the scope of subsection (d)(2). While subsection (d)(2)(A)(ii) provides that the in rem action is available only if the plaintiff is unable to find or obtain personal jurisdiction over the "person who would have been a defendant in a civil action under paragraph (1)," we believe this language is best understood as a shorthand reference to the current registrant of the domain name, who would be the defendant in any trademark action involving a domain name. Finally, the legislative history of the ACPA specifically discussing the in rem provision speaks in terms of domain names that violate "substantive Federal trademark law" or that are "infringing or diluting under the Trademark Act." Sen. Rep. No. 106–140, at 10–11. This reinforces the language of subsection (d)(2)(A)(i), which suggests that the in rem provision is not limited to bad faith claims under subsection (d)(1). Thus, we conclude that the best interpretation of § 1125(d)(2) is that the in rem provision not only covers bad faith claims under § 1125(d)(1), but also covers infringement claims under § 1114 and § 1125(a) and dilution claims under § 1125(c).

QUESTIONS

1. Judge Michael dismisses the Domain Names' due process challenge to § 43(d)(2)'s in rem provisions because of the presence of the disputed property in the state of Virginia. In what sense are the domain names located in Virginia? Is the analogy to "suits for injury suffered on the land of an absentee owner" persuasive?

2. The court concludes that the in rem jurisdiction in section 43(d) allows suits for substantive trademark violations as well as claims for bad faith registration. Do you agree? What are the best arguments supporting a contrary interpretation? What remedies are available in an in rem action for trademark infringement or dilution?

3. The court finds it significant that section 43(d)(2) "does not create a claim for the owner of *any* mark," but only for owners of marks that are registered in the PTO or protected under section 43(a) or 43(c). What trademarks does that exclude?

Cable News Network LP v. CNNews.com, 56 Fed. Appx. 599, 66 U.S.P.Q.2d (BNA) 1057 (4th Cir. 2003). The Cable News Network brought an in rem action against the domain name cnnews.com, registered and operated by a Chinese Internet service provider, Shanghai Maya. Shanghai Maya used the website to provide Chinese-language news and information, and argued that the domain name stood for "China Network News." The Court of Appeals rejected Shanghai Maya's argument that district court for the Eastern District of Virginia lacked jurisdiction to order the transfer of the domain name because Shanghai Maya lacked minimum contacts with the forum. It also was unsympathetic to Shanghai Maya's objection that application of the ACPA to a Chinese language website operated in China for a Chinese audience would impermissibly extend the reach of United States trademark law to regulate extraterritorial activity. Relying on its analysis in *Harrods*, the court upheld the exercise of in rem jurisdiction. Although the trial court had analyzed whether Shanghai Maya had registered and used the domain name in bad faith, the Fourth Circuit interpreted its opinion in *Harrods* to establish that no showing of bad faith was required to prevail in an in rem action under the ACPA. It therefore vacated the trial court's bad faith analysis and summarily affirmed the order transferring the CNNews.com domain name to the Cable News Network.

IN REM ACTIONS REGARDING U.S. REGISTRATIONS OF FOREIGN–HELD DOMAIN NAMES CORRESPONDING TO FOREIGN TRADEMARKS

Just as a domain name registrant need not be a U.S. business or resident, so the plaintiffs in these proceedings may be foreign enterprises. Sometimes neither the plaintiff nor the registrant are U.S. businesses or residents. Because the *in rem* proceeding concerns a *res* (the registration) localized in the U.S., the nationality or residence of the parties should not matter. Nonetheless, the role of U.S. law in providing a special procedural mechanism and a substantive norm may seem problematic when the parties not only are from countries other than the U.S., but also are both from the same foreign country. In **Heathmount A.E. Corp. v. Techno-dome.com**, 106 F.Supp.2d 860 (E.D.Va.2000), the defendant, a Canadian corporation, urged the court to decline jurisdiction when the plaintiff was also a Canadian corporation, and the witnesses and documents were likely to be located in Canada. The court nonetheless retained jurisdiction:

> [P]ublic factors bearing on the question lean toward retaining the matter in this District. A Canadian court would be less familiar with the provisions of the ACPA than is this Court. Even if it prevailed, Plaintiff might face difficulties enforcing the Canadian court's judgment in the United States, which would arguably undercut its U.S. trademark rights in its "technodome" mark. A trademark holder seeking to enforce its U.S.-registered marks against infringing domain name registrants should not be penalized in the exercise of those rights merely because the parties involved are not United States citizens.
>
> On a more basic level, Plaintiff may not be able to assert the same rights in Canada, which lacks a body of law equivalent to the ACPA and whose enforcement of its trademark laws cannot extend into the United States. Defendants suggest that Canadian intellectual property law, drawing upon recent English case law, might view the registration of a trademark-infringing domain name as an actionable trademark violation. This outcome is particularly likely, Defendants argue, in a case like the one at bar, involving both registration and use of the mark. However, Defendants' prediction of what the Canadian courts will do when presented with this issue is necessarily speculative and provides little support for the argument that Canada is a satisfactory alternative forum for this lawsuit.

QUESTIONS

1. The plaintiff was clearly "forum shopping" for the E.D. Va., whose *in rem* jurisdiction permits it to adjudicate cybersquatting claims against a domain name registrant not subject to U.S. courts' *in personam* jurisdiction. But, if a Canadian court has jurisdiction over the parties, and can apply the ACPA, why should plaintiff's forum choice be respected? How persuasive are the reasons the E.D. Va. offers for rejecting the registrant's arguments that the matter should be heard by a Canadian court? Are there more persuasive reasons?

2. Would the availability of an international administrative dispute resolution proceeding that allowed trademark owners to challenge registration of domain names that resembled their marks change the calculus? Why or why not?

C.   ICANN and the Uniform Trademark Domain Name Dispute Resolution Policy

By the mid–1990s, the explosive growth of the Internet had persuaded everyone that the extant method of administering the domain name system needed to change. Stakeholders began discussing alternative regimes, focusing heavily on proposals to add more generic top level domains and to introduce competition into the business of registering them. Meanwhile, intellectual property owners complained loudly that the domain name system needed to be more responsive to their concerns.

In 1997, the United States Government put together an interagency working group to formulate official U.S. policy on privatizing the Domain Name System. In June 1998, the Commerce Department released a proposal to turn over U.S. government involvement in the DNS system to a new non-profit corporation. The new corporation would decide whether to open new generic Top Level Domains [gTLDs], and how to do so. It would open up the business of registering gTLDs to multiple registrars, which could compete with Network Solutions, but it would make whatever changes it made gradually, with the first priority being stability of the Internet. The U.S. plan resorted to vague language on most of the controversial topics: resolving most disputes by delegating them to the yet-to-be-devised new corporation. Internet stakeholders had tentatively coalesced around a different plan to turn over oversight of the DNS to an international organization based in Europe, but most of the interested organizations agreed that they could accept the proposed U.S. framework, and began to try to exert their influence on the details. In response to intellectual property owner complaints, the U.S. government proposal had called upon the World Intellectual Property Organization (WIPO) to conduct a study of the intellectual property issues posed by the current domain name system, and to make recommendations for reform.

The idea of a new private non-profit corporation to administer the domain name system evolved into ICANN (the name is an acronym for Internet Corporation for Assigned Names and Numbers). The United States Department of Commerce signed an agreement with ICANN in the fall of 1998, which envisioned a gradual transition from U.S. government control of the DNS to autonomous ICANN control over a period of several years. The newly appointed ICANN interim Board met, elected officers, and began to try to figure out what it was the new organization was supposed to do, where it was going to get its funding, and how it was supposed to behave.

Nine years later, Network Solutions has been absorbed by Verisign and continues to control the .com and .net registries, but ICANN has accredited other registrars to compete with it in registering domain names. After a byzantine consideration process, ICANN introduced 11 new gTLDs: .biz, .info, .name, .museum, .coop, .aero, .pro, .cat, .jobs, .mobi, and .travel. Following a brief flirtation with allowing individual Internet users to become members of ICANN and elect the members of its Board of Directors, ICANN reorganized itself to eliminate Board elections. The Department of Commerce has subjected ICANN to only minimal oversight, and has repeatedly extended its memorandum of understanding authorizing ICANN to continue to perform the functions it performs, without completely giving up its supervisory role. Meanwhile, the United Nations Working Group on Internet Governance has been urging a greater role for the United Nations in overseeing the DNS.

ICANN's most notable achievement so far is probably its imposition of a mandatory trademark dispute resolution policy on all domain name registrants. In April of 1999, the World Intellectual Property Association issued its report recommending changes to the domain name system to reduce conflicts between the domain name system and trademark rights. It suggested that domain name registrars collect and make publicly available reliable contact information for domain name registrants. It also suggested that ICANN adopt a mandatory administrative dispute resolution process to handle cases of alleged "cybersquatting" expeditiously without litigation. It recommended that ICANN introduce a procedure that allowed the owners of famous marks to prevent the registration of their marks in some or all top level domains by anyone other than the mark owner. Finally, it suggested caution in the introduction of new generic top level domains.

ICANN acted quickly to adopt a mandatory administrative dispute resolution procedure in the autumn of 1999.

Uniform Domain Name Dispute Resolution Policy

(As Approved by ICANN on October 24, 1999).
URL: <http://www.icann.org/udrp/udrp-policy–24oct99.htm >

1. *Purpose.* This Uniform Domain Name Dispute Resolution Policy (the "Policy") has been adopted by the Internet Corporation for Assigned Names and Numbers ("ICANN"), is incorporated by reference into your Registration Agreement, and sets forth the terms and conditions in connection with a dispute between you and any party other than us (the registrar) over the registration and use of an Internet domain name registered by you. Proceedings under Paragraph 4 of this Policy will be conducted according to the Rules for Uniform Domain Name Dispute Resolution Policy (the "Rules of Procedure"), which are available at <http://www. icann.org/udrp-rules–24oct99.htm>, and the selected administrative-dispute-resolution service provider's supplemental rules.

2. *Your Representations.* By applying to register a domain name, or by asking us to maintain or renew a domain name registration, you hereby represent and warrant to us that (a) the statements that you made in your Registration Agreement are complete and accurate; (b) to your knowledge, the registration of the domain name will not infringe upon or otherwise violate the rights of any third party; (c) you are not registering the domain name for an unlawful purpose; and (d) you will not knowingly use the

domain name in violation of any applicable laws or regulations. It is your responsibility to determine whether your domain name registration infringes or violates someone else's rights.

3. *Cancellations, Transfers, and Changes.* We will cancel, transfer or otherwise make changes to domain name registrations under the following circumstances:

a. subject to the provisions of Paragraph 8, our receipt of written or appropriate electronic instructions from you or your authorized agent to take such action;

b. our receipt of an order from a court or arbitral tribunal, in each case of competent jurisdiction, requiring such action; and/or

c. our receipt of a decision of an Administrative Panel requiring such action in any administrative proceeding to which you were a party and which was conducted under this Policy or a later version of this Policy adopted by ICANN. (See Paragraph 4(i) and (k), below.)

We may also cancel, transfer or otherwise make changes to a domain name registration in accordance with the terms of your Registration Agreement or other legal requirements.

4. *Mandatory Administrative Proceeding.* This Paragraph sets forth the type of disputes for which you are required to submit to a mandatory administrative proceeding. These proceedings will be conducted before one of the administrative-dispute-resolution service providers listed at www. icann.org/udrp/approved-providers.htm (each, a "Provider").

a. *Applicable Disputes.* You are required to submit to a mandatory administrative proceeding in the event that a third party (a "complainant") asserts to the applicable Provider, in compliance with the Rules of Procedure, that

(i) your domain name is identical or confusingly similar to a trademark or service mark in which the complainant has rights; and

(ii) you have no rights or legitimate interests in respect of the domain name; and

(iii) your domain name has been registered and is being used in bad faith.

In the administrative proceeding, the complainant must prove that each of these three elements are present.

b. *Evidence of Registration and Use in Bad Faith.* For the purposes of Paragraph 4(a)(iii), the following circumstances, in particular but without limitation, if found by the Panel to be present, shall be evidence of the registration and use of a domain name in bad faith:

(i) circumstances indicating that you have registered or you have acquired the domain name primarily for the purpose of selling, renting, or otherwise transferring the domain name registration to the complainant who is the owner of the trademark or service mark or to a competitor of that complainant, for valuable consideration in excess of your documented out-of-pocket costs directly related to the domain name; or

(ii) you have registered the domain name in order to prevent the owner of the trademark or service mark from reflecting the mark in a corresponding domain name, provided that you have engaged in a pattern of such conduct; or

(iii) you have registered the domain name primarily for the purpose of disrupting the business of a competitor; or

(iv) by using the domain name, you have intentionally attempted to attract, for commercial gain, Internet users to your web site or other on-line location, by creating a likelihood of confusion with the complainant's mark as to the source, sponsorship, affiliation, or endorsement of your web site or location or of a product or service on your web site or location.

c. *How to Demonstrate Your Rights to and Legitimate Interests in the Domain Name in Responding to a Complaint.* When you receive a complaint, you should refer to Paragraph 5 of the Rules of Procedure in determining how your response should be prepared. Any of the following circumstances, in particular but without limitation, if found by the Panel to be proved based on its evaluation of all evidence presented, shall demonstrate your rights or legitimate interests to the domain name for purposes of Paragraph 4(a)(ii):

(i) before any notice to you of the dispute, your use of, or demonstrable preparations to use, the domain name or a name corresponding to the domain name in connection with a bona fide offering of goods or services; or

(ii) you (as an individual, business, or other organization) have been commonly known by the domain name, even if you have acquired no trademark or service mark rights; or

(iii) you are making a legitimate noncommercial or fair use of the domain name, without intent for commercial gain to misleadingly divert consumers or to tarnish the trademark or service mark at issue.

d. *Selection of Provider.* The complainant shall select the Provider from among those approved by ICANN by submitting the complaint to that Provider. The selected Provider will administer the proceeding, except in cases of consolidation as described in Paragraph 4(f).

e. *Initiation of Proceeding and Process and Appointment of Administrative Panel.* The Rules of Procedure state the process for initiating and conducting a proceeding and for appointing the panel that will decide the dispute (the "Administrative Panel").

f. *Consolidation.* In the event of multiple disputes between you and a complainant, either you or the complainant may petition to consolidate the disputes before a single Administrative Panel. This petition shall be made to the first Administrative Panel appointed to hear a pending dispute between the parties. This Administrative Panel may consolidate before it any or all such disputes in its sole discretion, provided that the disputes being consolidated are governed by this Policy or a later version of this Policy adopted by ICANN.

g. *Fees.* All fees charged by a Provider in connection with any dispute before an Administrative Panel pursuant to this Policy shall be paid by the complainant, except in cases where you elect to expand the Administrative Panel from one to three panelists as provided in Paragraph 5(b)(iv) of the Rules of Procedure, in which case all fees will be split evenly by you and the complainant.

h. *Our Involvement in Administrative Proceedings.* We do not, and will not, participate in the administration or conduct of any proceeding before an Administrative Panel. In addition, we will not be liable as a result of any decisions rendered by the Administrative Panel.

i. *Remedies.* The remedies available to a complainant pursuant to any proceeding before an Administrative Panel shall be limited to requiring the cancellation of your domain name or the transfer of your domain name registration to the complainant.

j. *Notification and Publication.* The Provider shall notify us of any decision made by an Administrative Panel with respect to a domain name you have registered with us. All decisions under this Policy will be published in full over the Internet, except when an Administrative Panel determines in an exceptional case to redact portions of its decision.

k. *Availability of Court Proceedings.* The mandatory administrative proceeding requirements set forth in Paragraph 4 shall not prevent either you or the complainant from submitting the dispute to a court of competent jurisdiction for independent resolution before such mandatory administrative proceeding is commenced or after such proceeding is concluded. If an Administrative Panel decides that your domain name registration should be canceled or transferred, we will wait ten (10) business days (as observed in the location of our principal office) after we are informed by the applicable Provider of the Administrative Panel's decision before implementing that decision. We will then implement the decision unless we have received from you during that ten (10) business day period official documentation (such as a copy of a complaint, file-stamped by the clerk of the court) that you have commenced a lawsuit against the complainant in a jurisdiction to which the complainant has submitted under Paragraph 3(b)(xiii) of the Rules of Procedure. (In general, that jurisdiction is either the location of our principal office or of your address as shown in our Whois database. See Paragraphs 1 and 3(b)(xiii) of the Rules of Procedure for details.) If we receive such documentation within the ten (10) business day period, we will not implement the Administrative Panel's decision, and we will take no further action, until we receive (i) evidence satisfactory to us of a resolution between the parties; (ii) evidence satisfactory to us that your lawsuit has been dismissed or withdrawn; or (iii) a copy of an order from such court dismissing your lawsuit or ordering that you do not have the right to continue to use your domain name.

5. *All Other Disputes and Litigation.* All other disputes between you and any party other than us regarding your domain name registration that are not brought pursuant to the mandatory administrative proceeding provisions of Paragraph 4 shall be resolved between you and such other party through any court, arbitration or other proceeding that may be available.

. . . .

QUESTIONS

1. How different is the UDRP from section 43(d) as a substantive matter? For example, § 43(d)(1)(A)(ii) appears to apply to anyone who registers, traffics in, *or* uses a domain name with bad faith intent to profit, while section 4(a)(iii) of the UDRP seems to require both bad faith registration *and* bad faith use. Is that difference likely to be determinative of the results in actual cases? What other provisions seem to be the principal substantive differences? In what sorts of cases is a court adjudicating a dispute under section 43(d) likely to reach a different result from an arbitrator adjudicating the same dispute under the UDRP?

2. In *Referee Enterprises v. Planet Ref*, National Arbitration Forum No. FA0004000094707 (June 26, 2000), a UDRP panel dismissed a complaint filed by the owner of the registered mark REFEREE for magazines against the registrant of ereferee.com, noting that "Referee is generic for an official who serves as an umpire officiating at sports events and is a weak mark," and "Respondent has a legitimate interest in the Domain name in view of the sports background of the principal of Respondent and there is no bad faith use." Complainant then filed a Lanham Act suit in federal district court. Judge Clevert concluded that "the plaintiff is likely to establish that it is threatened with dilution, trademark infringement, unfair competition and false designation of origin," and enjoined the registrant from:

using the mark REFEREE or any other mark confusingly similar to Referee Enterprise's REFEREE trademark, either alone or in combination with other words, specifically including, but not limited to: eReferee, ereferee.com, ereferee.net, ereferee.org, refereecamp.com, refereecamps.com, refereeclinics.com, refereeforum.com, refereeinsurance.com, refreemail.com and refereeresume.com; as a mark, domain name or highlighted term or in any way other than in common textual reference, any other mark or second-level domain name including the term "referee" in any form. . . .

Referee Enterprises v. Planet Ref, No. 00–C–1391 (E.D. Wi. 2001) What arguments should the defendant make on appeal? How should REFEREE magazine respond?

ICANN's Uniform Dispute Resolution Policy took effect on January 1, 2000. By the following year, ICANN had approved four different administrative dispute resolution providers. Between January 1 and April 19, 2001, trademark owners filed 3499 proceedings under the UDRP, involving 6203 different domain names. By April 19, 2001, arbitrators had already resolved 2639 of those disputes. Arbitrators had ordered the transfer or cancellation of 3734 domain names in 2101 disputes. In 519 decisions, involving 658 domain names, arbitrators decided that the domain name registrants were entitled to retain their domain names under the policy. ICANN's most recent tabulation of UDRP statistics, dated May 2004, notes 7700 UDRP decisions involving 13311 domain names. 1468 of those decisions upheld the domain name registrant's right to retain its domain name, while 6215 ordered the domain name transferred to the complainant and 15 ordered the cancellation of domain name. As of February, 2007, trademark owners have filed more than 12,000 proceedings. Administrative dispute panel decisions are posted on the Internet at the websites of the different approved dispute resolution providers and accessible via ICANN's site at URL: <http://www.icann.org/udrp/udrp.htm>. The most notable advantage of the UDRP is that it provides a resolution that is both cheap and quick in comparison with litigation. The UDRP has come under attack based on studies that tend to show that its procedures, as actually implemented, favor trademark-owner complainants over domain name registrant respondents. *See* Michael Geist, *Fair.com? An Examination of the Allegations of Systemic Unfairness in the ICANN UDRP*, 27 Brooklyn Journal of International Law 903–38 (2002).

Dial–A–Mattress Operating Corp. v. Moakely

WIPO Arbitration and Mediation Center Case No. D2005–0471 (July 1, 2005).

■ Towns, Panelist

1. The Parties

The Complainant is Dial–A–Mattress Operating Corp., Long Island City, New York, United States of America, represented by Sarah E.

Greenless, Esq., Dial–A–Mattress Operating Corp., United States of America.

The Respondent is Christopher E. Moakely, Coplay, Pennsylvania, United States of America.

2. *The Domain Name and Registrar*

The disputed domain name <1–800mattress.com> is registered with Melbourne IT trading as Internet Name Worldwide.

3. *Procedural History*

The Complaint was filed with the WIPO Arbitration and Mediation Center (the "Center") on April 28, 2005. On April 29, 2005, the Center transmitted by email to Melbourne IT trading as Internet Name Worldwide a request for registrar verification in connection with the domain name at issue. On May 12, 2005, Melbourne IT trading as Internet Name Worldwide transmitted by email to the Center its verification response confirming that the Respondent is listed as the registrant and providing the contact details for the administrative, billing, and technical contact. In response to a notification by the Center that the Complaint was administratively deficient, the Complainant filed an amendment to the Complaint on May 25, 2005. The Center verified that the Complaint together with the amendment to the Complaint satisfied the formal requirements of the Uniform Domain Name Dispute Resolution Policy (the "Policy"), the Rules for Uniform Domain Name Dispute Resolution Policy (the "Rules"), and the WIPO Supplemental Rules for Uniform Domain Name Dispute Resolution Policy (the "Supplemental Rules").

In accordance with the Rules, Paragraphs 2(a) and 4(a), the Center formally notified the Respondent of the Complaint, and the proceedings commenced on May 26, 2005. In accordance with the Rules, Paragraph 5(a), the due date for Response was June 15, 2005. The Respondent did not submit any response. Accordingly, the Center notified the Respondent's default on June 17, 2005.

The Center appointed William R. Towns as the sole panelist in this matter on June 20, 2005. The Panel finds that it was properly constituted. The Panel has submitted the Statement of Acceptance and Declaration of Impartiality and Independence, as required by the Center to ensure compliance with the Rules, Paragraph 7.

4. *Factual Background*

The Complainant is a retailer in the field of mattresses and bedding products. Best known since 1988, as a telemarketer selling mattresses using the toll free number 1–800–MATTRESS, the Complainant also operates retail stores and sells mattresses and bedding products over the internet at "www.mattress.com". The Complainant has used the trade name "1–800–MATTRESS" since 1994, in connection with these activities.

The Complainant is the owner of the service marks 1–800–MATTRES, AND LEAVE OFF THE LAST S THAT'S THE S FOR SAVINGS, and 1–800–MATTRESS. The first mark was registered with the United States Patent and Trademark Office (PTO) on December 22, 1990, and the second mark obtained PTO registration on January 4, 2005. The PTO registration for 1–800–MATTRESS reflects that the mark was first used in commerce on December 31, 1995.

The Respondent, a former employee of the Complainant, registered the disputed domain name <1–800mattress.com> on February 7, 2000. The disputed domain name currently resolves to temporary website apparently maintained not by the Respondent but by the web host, and there is no indication in the record that the Respondent has ever made any commercial or noncommercial use of the domain name. On or about March 17, 2005, the Complainant contacted the Respondent, requesting that the Respondent cease and desist using the disputed domain name and transfer the domain name to the Complainant. The Respondent chose not to honor this request.

5. Parties' Contentions

A. Complainant

The Complainant contends that the disputed domain name <1–800mattress.com> is confusingly similar to its federally registered service marks, 1–800–MATTRES, AND LEAVE OFF THE LAST S THAT'S THE S FOR SAVINGS, and 1–800–MATTRESS. The Complainant also maintains that the Respondent has no rights or legitimate interests with respect to the disputed domain name, because (1) the Complainant has not authorized the Respondent to use the domain name, (2) the Respondent has never been commonly known by the domain name, and (3) there is no evidence that the Respondent has used or made demonstrable preparations to use the domain name in connection with a *bona fide* offering of goods or services or for any legitimate noncommercial purpose. Further, the Complainant avers that the Respondent, a former employee of the Complainant, registered and is using the disputed domain name in bad faith. Accordingly, the Complainant seeks the transfer of the disputed domain name.

B. Respondent

The Respondent did not reply to the Complainant's contentions.

6. Discussion and Findings

A. Scope of the Policy

The Policy is addressed to resolving disputes concerning allegations of abusive domain name registration and use. *Milwaukee Electric Tool Corporation v. Bay Verte Machinery, Inc. d/b/a The Power Tool Store*, WIPO Case No. 2002–0774. Accordingly, the jurisdiction of this Panel is limited to providing a remedy in cases of "the abusive registration of domain names", also known as "cybersquatting". *Weber-Stephen Products Co. v. Armitage Hardware*, WIPO Case No. D2000–0187. See Report of the WIPO Internet Domain Name Process, Paragraphs 169 & 170. Paragraph 15(a) of the Rules provides that the Panel shall decide a complaint on the basis of statements and documents submitted and in accordance with the Policy, the Rules and any other rules or principles of law that the Panel deems applicable.

Paragraph 4(a) of the Policy requires that the Complainant prove each of the following three elements to obtain a decision that a domain name should be either cancelled or transferred:

> (i) The domain name registered by the Respondent is identical or confusingly similar to a trademark or service mark in which the Complainant has rights; and

> (ii) The Respondent has no rights or legitimate interests with respect to the domain name; and

> (iii) The domain name has been registered and is being used in bad faith.

Cancellation or transfer of the domain name are the sole remedies provided to the Complainant under the Policy, as set forth in Paragraph 4(i).

Paragraph 4(b) sets forth four situations under which the registration and use of a domain name is deemed to be in bad faith, but does not limit a finding of bad faith to only these situations.

Paragraph 4(c) in turn identifies three means through which a respondent may establish rights or legitimate interests in the domain name. Although the complainant bears the ultimate burden of establishing all three elements of Paragraph 4(a), a number of panels have concluded that Paragraph 4(c) shifts the burden to the respondent to come forward with evidence of a right or legitimate interest in the domain name, once the complainant has made a prima facie showing. See, e.g., *Document Technologies, Inc. v. International Electronic Communications Inc.*, WIPO Case No. D2000–0270.

B.   Identical or Confusingly Similar

The Panel finds that the disputed domain name <1–800mattress.com> is confusingly similar to the Complainant's registered service marks 1–800–MATTRES, AND LEAVE OFF THE LAST S THAT'S THE S FOR SAVINGS, and 1–800–MATTRESS. For purposes of Paragraph 4(a)(i), a domain name incorporating a complainant's mark generally will be considered confusingly similar unless accompanied by other terms that effectively disclaim any association. *See Lockheed Martin Corporation. v. Dan Parisi*, WIPO Case No. D2000–1015; The *Salvation Army v. Info–Bahn, Inc.*, WIPO Case No. D2001–0463. The disputed domain name contains no additional terms that would distinguish it from the Complainant's service marks, and for this reason the Panel concludes that persons viewing the disputed domain name likely would think that the domain name is in some way connected to the Complainant. This is known as "initial interest confusion", which occurs when a member of the public sees the disputed domain name and thinks that it may lead to a website associated with the Complainant. See *Covance, Inc. and Covance Laboratories Ltd. v. The Covance Campaign*, WIPO Case No. D2004–0206.

The Complainant has established rights in the two service marks through registration and use. The Panel notes that the Complainant did not obtain registration of the 1–800–MATTRESS mark was until January 4, 2005, some five years after the Respondent registered the disputed domain name, but the federal registration indicates that the mark had been used in commerce since December 1995. Even had there been no use of this mark prior to the registration of the disputed domain name, a majority of Panels have held for purposes of Paragraph 4(a)(i) that a complainant can have rights in a trademark or service mark corresponding to the domain name even where those rights first arise after the registration of the domain name. See, e.g., *Digital Vision, Ltd. v. Advanced Chemill Systems*, WIPO Case No. D2001–0827; *Kangwon Land, Inc. v. Bong Woo Chun (K.W.L. Inc.)*, WIPO Case No. D2003–0320; *AB Svenska Spel v. Andrey Zacharov*, WIPO Case No. D2003–0527; *Iogen Corporation v. Iogen*, WIPO Case No. D2003–0544; *Madrid 2012, S.A. v. Scott Martin–MadridMan Websites*, WIPO Case No. D2003–0598. See *PC Mall, Inc. v. Pygmy Computer Systems, Inc.*, WIPO Case No. D2004–0437.

C. Rights or Legitimate Interests

The Complainant has not authorized the Respondent to use its service marks or to register domain names reflecting these marks. There is no evidence that the Respondent has never been commonly known by the domain name. The record is not indicative of the Respondent's use of, or demonstrable preparations to use, the disputed domain name in connection with any offering of goods or services. Nor is there any indication that the Respondent is making any noncommercial use of the domain name.

Given the foregoing, the Panel finds that the Complainant has made a *prima facie* showing under Paragraph 4(a)(ii). The circumstances set forth in the Complaint are sufficiently evocative of cybersquatting to require the Respondent to come forward with evidence under Paragraph 4(c) of the Policy demonstrating rights to or legitimate interests in the disputed domain name. See, *e.g., Document Technologies, Inc. v. International Electronic Communications Inc.*, WIPO Case No. D2000–0270; *Compagnie de Saint Gobain v. Com–Union Corp.*, WIPO Case No. D2000–0020.

Pursuant to Paragraph 4(c) of the Policy, the Respondent may establish rights to or legitimate interests in the disputed domain name by demonstrating any of the following:

(i) before any notice to it of the dispute, the respondent's use of, or demonstrable preparations to use, the domain name or a name corresponding to the domain name in connection with a *bona fide* offering of goods or services; or

(ii) the respondent has been commonly known by the domain name, even if it has acquired no trademark or service mark rights; or

(iii) the respondent is making a legitimate noncommercial or fair use of the domain name, without intent for commercial gain, to misleadingly divert consumers or to tarnish the trademark or service mark at issue.

The Respondent has not submitted a formal response to the Complaint, and in the absence of any such submission this Panel may accept all reasonable inferences and allegations included in the Complaint as true. See, *Talk City, Inc. v. Robertson*, WIPO Case No. D2000–0009. Nevertheless, the ultimate burden of proof on the legitimacy issue remains with the Complainant. *Document Technologies, Inc. v. International Electronic Communications Inc.*, WIPO Case No. D2000–0270. Accordingly, the Panel considers it appropriate to examine the record in its entirety to determine whether any evidence exists to support a claim by Respondent of rights or legitimate interests in the disputed domain name.

The record as a whole discloses nothing even remotely suggesting that the Respondent has been commonly known by the disputed domain name, nor any indication of any legitimate noncommercial or fair use of the domain name. The domain name currently resolves to a "temporary" website, apparently maintained by the website host to advertise its services, but there is no indication that the Respondent is using or has made demonstrable preparations to use the disputed domain name in connection with any offering of goods or services. In fact, the record reveals no plausible basis upon which the Respondent could claim any rights or legitimate interests in the disputed domain name. Accordingly, the Panel finds that the Complainant has met its burden under Paragraph 4(a)(ii).

D.   Registered and Used in Bad Faith

Paragraph 4(b) of the Policy states that any of the following circumstances, in particular but without limitation, shall be considered evidence of the registration or use of a domain name in bad faith:

(i) circumstances indicating that the Respondent registered or acquired the domain name primarily for the purpose of selling, renting, or otherwise transferring the domain name registration to the Complainant (the owner of the trademark or service mark) or to a competitor of that Complainant, for valuable consideration in excess of documented out-of-pocket costs directly related to the domain name;

(ii) circumstances indicating that the Respondent registered the domain name in order to prevent the owner of the trademark or service mark from reflecting the mark in a corresponding domain name, provided that the Respondent has engaged in a pattern of such conduct;

(iii) circumstances indicating that the Respondent registered the domain name primarily for the purpose of disrupting the business of a competitor; or

(iv) circumstances indicating that the Respondent intentionally is using the domain name in an attempt to attract, for commercial gain, internet users to its website or other on-line location, by creating a likelihood of confusion with the Complainant's mark as to the source, sponsorship, affiliation, or endorsement of the Respondent's website or location or of a product or service on its website or location.

The overriding objective of the Policy is to prevent abusive domain name registration and use for the benefit of legitimate trademark owners, and the Panel notes that the examples of bad faith registration and use set forth in Paragraph 4(b) are not meant to be exhaustive of all circumstances from which such bad faith may be found. See, *Telstra Corporation Limited v. Nuclear Marshmallows*, WIPO Case No. D2000–0003. Under *Telstra*, passive holding of a domain name can be considered as bad faith where it is not possible to conceive of any plausible actual or contemplated active use of the disputed domain name that would not be illegitimate. See, also *Salomon Smith Barney, Inc. v. Salomon Internet Services*, WIPO Case No. D2000–0668.

The *Telstra* requirements are met where "the Complainant proves that the registration was undertaken in bad faith *and* that the circumstances of the case are such that Respondent is continuing to act in bad faith." *Telstra Corporation Limited v. Nuclear Marshmallows*, WIPO Case No. D2000–0003 (emphasis in original). A finding that the domain name "has been registered in bad faith" can be reached under *Telstra* where the totality of the circumstances persuades the panel that the primary motive for the respondent's acquisition of the disputed domain name was cybersquatting.

This Panel is persuaded from the circumstances of this case that the Respondent's primary motive in registering the disputed domain name was cybersquatting. The Respondent was employed by the Complainant during 1994 and 1995, and his wife also worked for the Complainant until her job position was eliminated in 2003. Clearly, the Respondent would have been aware of the Complainant's service marks at the time he registered the disputed domain name in February 2000. Moreover, the Respondent has failed to make any active use of the domain name, and the Panel cannot conceive of any plausible actual or contemplated active use for which the Respondent could have registered the domain name that "would not be illegitimate, such as by being a passing off, an infringement of consumer protection legislation, or an infringement of the Complainant's rights under trademark law." *Telstra Corporation Limited v. Nuclear Marshmallows*, WIPO Case No. D2000–0003. The Panel therefore concludes that the Respondent's registration of the disputed domain name "was undertaken in bad faith *and* that the circumstances of the case are such that Respondent is continuing to act in bad faith." *Id.* (emphasis in original). Accordingly, the Panel finds that the Complainant has met its burden under Paragraph 4(a)(iii).

7. Decision

For all the foregoing reasons, in accordance with Paragraphs 4(i) of the Policy and 15 of the Rules, the Panel orders that the domain name <1–800mattress.com> be transferred to the Complainant.

———

In **Dial–A–Mattress Franchise Corp. v. Page**, 880 F.2d 675 (2d Cir.1989), Dial–A–Mattress, which had for years sold mattresses over the telephone in New York City using the local phone number 628–8737 (MATTRES)sought an injunction preventing a competitor from advertising its telephone number 1–800–628–8737 as 1–800–MATTRESS in the New York City metropolitan area. Defendant argued that mattress was a generic word that plaintiff was not entitled to monopolize. The court was not persuaded:

> Plaintiff does not lose the right to protection against defendant's use of a confusingly similar number and a confusingly similar set of letters that correlate with that number on the telephone dial just because the letters spell a generic term. The principles limiting protection for the use of generic terms serve to prevent a marketer from appropriating for its exclusive use words that must remain available to competitors to inform their customers as to the nature of the competitor's business or product. These principles do not require that a competitor remain free to confuse the public with a telephone number or the letters identifying that number that are deceptively similar to those of a first user.

In *Holiday Inns v. 800 Reservation, Inc.*, 86 F.3d 619 (6th Cir.1996), however, Holiday Inn, which had the vanity telephone number 1–800–HOLIDAY [465–4329], was unsuccessful in its suit against a competitor that had acquired the telephone number 1–800–405–4329. Holiday Inns argued that because consumers frequently misdial zero instead of the letter "o", defendant's phone number would cause confusion in violation of section 43(a). The Sixth Circuit disagreed. 800 Reservations, it held, "did not create the consumers' confusion, but ... merely took advantage of confusion already in existence." Moreover, since 800 Reservations didn't publicize the number, it did not use it in commerce. In *DaimlerChrysler AG v. Bloom*, 315 F.3d 932 (8th Cir.2003), similarly, defendant obtained the telephone number 1–800–637–2333 (1–800–MERCEDE) and used it to launch a commercial service for the benefit of Mercedes dealerships, but did not advertise the number to consumers. The court concluded that defendant had not used the Mercedes mark in commerce. One prevalent source of domain name disputes is the practice known as "typosquatting"—registering a common misspelling of a famous mark as a domain name. Assuming that the typosquatter engages in no advertising or promotion of its domain name, should the telephone number cases control the resulting domain name disputes? Why or why not?

Estate of Frank Gorshin v. Martin

WIPO Arbitration and Mediation Center Case No. D2005–0803 (Oct. 31, 2005).

■ ZADRA–SYMES, PANELIST.

.   .   .   .

3.   *Factual Background*

Complainant is the estate of the actor Frank Gorshin whose numerous television roles have included the role of "The Riddler" on the *Batman* program and, just prior to his death on May 17, 2005, playing himself on *CSI Crime Scene Investigation* on CBS–TV. Complainant contends that Mr. Gorshin was a well-known and internationally recognizable actor and impressionist whose high profile and worldwide presence has been seen and heard in television and film for close to the last 50 years.

Upon the death of her late husband in May 2005, Christina Gorshin, the estate's executrix, determined to register his name as a domain name in order to market and advertise his profile to his fans and other interested persons. At such time, Complainant learned that Respondent had previously registered the Domain Name on or about December 27, 1998.

5.   *Parties' Contentions*

A.   *Complainant*

Complainant contends that Respondent does not have the right to use the name "Frank Gorshin" in respect of Respondent's web site and, in doing so, is in violation of Complainant's rights.

Complainant contends that Respondent is an autograph hound who attends various tradeshows, notably "Star Trek," "Babylon 5" and other science fiction conventions, where he prevails on celebrities to sign autographs and, in some cases, to pose for photographs with him.

Complainant alleges that in order to market such items relating to Frank Gorshin Respondent created a so-called "official Web-site," and in doing so, is and has been cyber-squatting upon the decedent's name, in violation of Complainant's trademark and right of publicity. Complainant contends that the Web site promotes Respondent as the decedent's "Web master" and the items sought to be sold in a false light, without authority.

Complainant alleges that during the decedent's lifetime, the decedent made repeated effort to put an end to the online business which Respondent touts as "The Official Frank Gorshin Web Site." As evidence of such effort, Complainant originally submitted only one email, dated April 17, 2005, from John Stacks, allegedly the builder of the decedent's own Web site when living ("www.therealfrankgorshin.com"). In that email, Mr. Stacks wrote to Respondent Terry Martin asking him to transfer the

Domain Name to the decedent. According to Complainant, this request was ignored.

Complainant contends that Respondent also purports to operate "The Official Web Site[s]" of several other professional actors and that such conduct evidences a pattern of willful infringement of the rights of others.

Complainant has entered into agreements authorizing certain other websites, notably "www.therealfrankgorshin.com", to market products bearing the name and likeness of Frank Gorshin. Complainant contends that this is the only "official" Frank Gorshin Web site.

. . . .

B.   Respondent

Respondent contends that he entered into an agreement with Frank Gorshin over seven years ago to create the "www.frankgorshin.com" site at the decedent's request and at Respondent's initial and continued expense. Respondent contends that he paid the decedent to sign Respondent's photos that Respondent then merchandised on the "www.frankgorshin.com" site. Respondent contends that all the photos were sent to the decedent with full payment for each signature, and that Respondent was "in contact with this arrangement with Frank until the month he died." Respondent further contends that during the seven year duration of Respondent's contract with the decedent, the decedent signed a contract for additional items, including trading cards, and continually received photos and checks for his autographs. Respondent further contends that, even though a friend of the decedent had created an additional site to sell his figures and drawings, the decedent told Respondent not to transfer the name to anyone, and that the arrangement between the decedent and Respondent was by far the decedent's best producing site.

Respondent also claims that no one from the estate of Frank Gorshin had contacted Respondent until Respondent received a copy of the filed Complaint.

Finally, Respondent claims that he has never sold a domain name.

6.   Discussion and Findings

According to Paragraph 4(a) of the Policy, Complainant must prove that:

(i) the Domain Name is identical or confusingly similar to a trademark or service mark in which Complainant has rights; and

(ii) Respondent has no rights or legitimate interests in respect of the Domain Name; and

(iii) the Domain Name has been registered and is being used in bad faith.

A.   Identical or Confusingly Similar

Frank Gorshin is the actual birth name of the actor, Frank Gorshin, and was used by him professionally in motion picture and television since the mid 1950's. Complainant contends that the actor developed common law trademark rights in his name and that the Domain Name bears a confusing similarity to that name.

Complainant contends that persons seeking to reach out to Frank Gorshin have been misled and confused by the similarity of Complainant's and the decedent's trademark and the contested Domain Name. Complainant contends that the Domain Name adopted by Respondent infringes upon the name and trademark of Complainant and clearly causes a likelihood of confusion.

The Panel finds that the actor Frank Gorshin developed common law trademark rights in his name and that the Domain Name is identical or confusingly similar to that name.

B. Rights or Legitimate Interests

Complainant must show that Respondent has no rights or legitimate interests in respect of the Domain Name. Respondent may establish a right or legitimate interest in a disputed Domain Name... in accordance with Paragraph 4(a)(ii) of the Policy....

Complainant contends that Respondent has received no license or other grant of authority from the decedent or Complainant to use the mark embodied in the Domain Name.

In his uncertified Response, Respondent contends that he had an agreement with the decedent, Frank Gorshin, to pay for the actor's signatures on photographs and trading cards that were subsequently offered for sale on Respondent's web site. However, despite the Panel's request that Respondent submit evidence of such agreement, Respondent has not submitted any such evidence.

Complainant contends that "decedent made repeated effort to put an end to the [Respondent's] online business" and submitted an email sent to Respondent in April 2005 from John Stacks, "the builder of the decedent's own Web site when living ('www.therealfrankgorshin.com')." In that email, Mr. Stacks states:

"Terry I ask again that you consider the transferring the domain www.frankgorshin.com to Frank. Terry I am sure you are aware of Cyber Squatting and the WIPO Arbitration and Mediation Center http://www.wipo.int/amc/en/center/faq/domains.html. Terry if this can not be resolve with you surrendering the domain, then Frank will file a complaint. Please try to work with him on this, you will find if you have a problem with Frank it could cause more problems with your other clients. Please respond ASAP ... John Stacks"

In response to the Panel's request for further evidence of Complainant's or Frank Gorshin's repeated demands that Respondent transfer the disputed domain name, Complainant submitted additional emails sent to Respondent in May and December 2004, in which Mr. Stacks stated that he was working with Frank Gorshin's family "in trying to get all his things in order" and invited Respondent to contact Frank Gorshin if Respondent had any doubt that Frank Gorshin wanted the domain name to be transferred.

In the event there was a consent from the actor, by filing its Complaint in this dispute, the Estate of Frank Gorshin has revoked such prior consent to use the decedent's name in the Domain Name. The Panel concludes that Respondent has no rights or legitimate interests in respect of the Domain Name.

C.   Registered and Used in Bad Faith

. . . .

The record lacks any evidence to support Respondent's assertions of an agreement with Frank Gorshin allowing Respondent to register and maintain the disputed domain name. The record indicates that Respondent's use of the disputed domain name is causing a likelihood of confusion with Complainant's mark as to the source, sponsorship, affiliation or endorsement of Respondent's web site or location or of products on Respondent's web site or location.

Based on the case file, the Panel finds that Respondent's registration and use of the disputed Domain Name is in bad faith.

7.   Decision

For the foregoing reasons, the Panel directs that the disputed domain name be transferred to Complainant.

The Orange Bowl Committee, Inc. v. Front and Center Tickets, Inc./Front and Center Entertainment

WIPO Arbitration and Mediation Center Case No. D2004–0947 (January 20, 2005).

■ PARTRIDGE, PRESIDING PANELIST.

1.   The Parties

The Complainant is The Orange Bowl Committee, Inc., Miami, Florida, of United States of America, represented by Hunton & Williams, United States of America.

The Respondent is Front and Center Tickets, Inc./Front and Center Entertainment, Fort Lauderdale, Florida, of United States of America, represented by Mark Halpern.

2.   The Domain Names and Registrar

The disputed domain names <orangebowl.net> and <orangebowltickets.net> ("Domain Names") are registered with Dotster, Inc.

. . . .

4. Factual Background

Complainant has used the ORANGE BOWL mark since 1935, for one of the nation's best-known college football tournaments. It has also expanded use of the mark to a variety of other goods and services, including a tennis tournament, a basketball championship, a golf tournament and various types of merchandise.

The ORANGE BOWL tournament has been the subject of extensive advertising and media attention and is watched annually by millions of spectators. The television rights alone to broadcast the ORANGE BOWL game involve fees in excess of $100,000,000.00.

Complainant sells millions of tickets and hundreds of thousands of goods under the ORANGE BOWL mark, some of which are sold via Complainant's websites at "www.orangebowl.com" and "www.orangebowl.org".

Complainant obtained a federal trademark registration for the mark ORANGE BOWL on December 12, 1995, but inadvertently allowed that registration to lapse on September 14, 2002, due an administrative error. Complainant is the co-owner federal trademark registrations for FEDEX ORANGE BOWL (Reg. No. 2,129,760; 2,037,172) and reapplied for federal registration of the mark ORANGE BOWL on December 10, 2002. Respondent admits that ORANGE BOWL is a famous name.

Respondent is engaged in the online resale of tickets for sporting and entertainment events. The domain name <orangebowltickets.net> was registered on April 14, 1999. The domain name <orangebowl.net> was registered on June 24, 1999.

At the time the Complainant in this action was filed, Respondent used the respective Domain Names for a site that offered tickets to various events, including college bowl game tickets and National Football League tickets, as well as "all concert tickets—all sporting event tickets—all theater tickets." The site included a disclaimer stating: "The National Collegiate Athletic Association (NCAA) has neither licensed or endorsed Front and Center Entertainment Group to sell goods and services in conjunction with NCAA and regular season or championship games." There was no disclaimer relating to Complainant.

The domain name <orangebowl.net> is no longer active, and Respondent has agreed to transfer it to Complainant.

The domain name <orangebowltickets.net> now leads to a modified site that prominently bears the heading "Orange Bowl National Championship Tickets." There is also a new disclaimer stating:

> "Orangebowltickets.net is a private ticket broker and the FedEx Orange Bowl has neither licensed nor endorsed Front and Center Entertainment Group to sell goods and services in conjunction with The FedEx Orange Bowl and regular season or championship games."

The page continues to offer tickets for other events, including other college bowl games, NFL games and the Superbowl, with several links from the site leading to Respondent's "frontrow.com" website where it offers tickets to other events, including tickets to Las Vegas Shows, Broadway Shows, NASCAR races, and concerts by performers such as Celine Dion, Elton John and Cher.

. . . .

6. Discussion and Findings

The Respondent states that it has no argument regarding the domain name <orangebowl.net> and agrees to transfer the name to Complainant. Therefore, the entirety of the Panel finds in favor of Complainant on that domain name.

With respect to the domain name <orangebowltickets.net>, Paragraph 4(a) of the Policy requires the Complainant to establish each of the following elements:

(i) that the domain name registered by the Respondent is identical or confusingly similar to a trademark or service mark in which the Complainant has rights;

(ii) that the Respondent has no rights or legitimate interest in respect of the domain name; and

(iii) that the domain name has been registered and is being used in bad faith.

The majority of the Panel finds as follows on these elements.

A. Identical or Confusingly Similar

Respondent does not dispute that Complainant owns trademark rights in the mark ORANGE BOWL. Respondent further concedes that the ORANGE BOWL name is famous.

The issue is whether the addition of "tickets" is sufficient to avoid a finding of confusingly similarity. In reaching a conclusion under this element of the Policy, prior decisions primarily base the test on a comparison of the mark and the domain name on their own, without regard to the content of the site. See *AT&T Corp. v. Amjad Kausar*, WIPO Case No. D2003–0327.

It is generally well-established the addition of merely descriptive or non-distinctive matter to another's mark is not sufficient to avoid confusion. See *NCAA v. Randy Pitkin*, WIPO Case No. D2000–0903. Thus, the addition of ".com" is held to be insufficient to avoid confusion. *Id.*

Similarly, in the other Panel decisions considering the issue, including decisions involving this Respondent, the addition of "tickets" to the name of an event has uniformly been held to be insufficient to avoid confusion. See *National Collegiate Athletic Association and March Madness Athletic Association, LLC v. Mark Helpern and Front & Center Entertainment*, WIPO Case No. D2000–0700 (transferring domain names including <final-

fourtickets.net> to the complainant); *HBP, Inc. v. Front and Center Tickets, Inc.,* WIPO Case No. D2002–0802 (transferring the domain name <daytona500tickets.net> to the complainant); *ISL Worldwide and The Federal Internationale de Football Association v. Western States Ticket Service,* WIPO Case No. D2001–0070 (transferring <fifatickets.com>); *The Professional Golfers' Association of America v. 24/7 Ticket Service,* WIPO Case No. D2002–0258 (transferring <pgachampiontickets.com>); *NCAA v. Randy Pitkin,* WIPO Case No. D2000–0903 (finding in favor of complainant on this issue, but ruling in favor of respondent on other grounds); *Southwest Airlines Co. v. Patrick Orly,* WIPO Case No. D2003–0761 (transferring <southwestairlinestickets.com>).

Similarly, the Panel finds that Respondent's addition of "tickets" is not sufficient to avoid confusion since it is a generic or merely descriptive term for the goods offered by Complainant under the ORANGE BOWL mark. Accordingly, we conclude that the remaining domain name at issue is confusingly similar to a mark in which Complainant has rights under Paragraph 4(a)(i) of the Policy.

B. *Rights or Legitimate Interests*

Complainant contends that Respondent has no rights or legitimate interest in the Domain Name. The record shows that Respondent has no relationship with or authorization from Complainant for the use of the ORANGE BOWL mark. Further, it appears that Respondent is known as Front & Center Entertainment, not the name ORANGEBOWLTICKETS.NET.

Respondent contends that it is using the domain name for a bona fide offering of ORANGE BOWL tickets. Indeed, the record shows that Respondent sells ORANGE BOWL tickets, along with tickets for a wide range of other events. However, whether or not this use is a bona fide use depends on whether or not Respondent's use of the ORANGE BOWL is legitimate, non-infringing use. Otherwise, a respondent could rely on an intentional infringement to demonstrate a legitimate interest. See *Madonna Ciccone, p/k/a Madonna v. Dan Parisi and "Madonna.com",* WIPO Case No. D2000–0847 (holding that infringing use of <madonna.com> to sell services did not create legitimate interest).

Respondent acknowledges that it is using Complainant's trademark in a domain name to promote its commercial ticket brokering services. Thus, our inquiry focuses on whether that use is permitted or not.

. . . .

We conclude that the Respondent's use of Complainant's mark in Respondent's domain name fails to meet the test for fair use because the ORANGE BOWL mark is used in Respondent's domain name not merely to describe, but also as an attention-getting device to attract Internet users to Respondent's site to sell other products, and because the domain name is used to sell products that it does not describe (e.g., Broadway show tickets, Las Vegas tickets, NFL tickets and tickets for competing college bowl events). By using the mark in the domain name, Respondent is using Complainant's mark more prominently than is necessary merely to describe its services. Moreover, the Complainant's mark is used in a way that triggers initial interest confusion regarding the relationship with Complainant in a way that is not adequately dispelled, for reasons more fully discussed below.

. . . .

Accordingly, for the reasons discussed above, we conclude that Respondent's use of Complainant's ORANGE BOWL mark in a domain name used in connection with the resale of tickets not only to the ORANGE BOWL game but also for tickets to a variety of unrelated and competing events is not fair use under the Policy. We further conclude, therefore, that Respondent lacks any right or legitimate interest in the use of ORANGE BOWL in its domain name and find in Complainant's favor on Paragraph 4(a)(ii) of the Policy.

C. *Registered and Used in Bad Faith*

The Policy lists several nonexclusive criteria to show bad faith registration and use of a domain name. Paragraph 4(b)(iv) indicates that bad faith use and registration may be found when the Respondent is intentionally attempting to attract, for commercial gain, Internet users to its website, by creating a likelihood of confusion with the complainant's mark.

Respondent concedes that it intentionally registered and is using Complainant's mark to attract Internet users to its website. It does this for commercial gain. We believe Respondent does so by creating a likelihood of confusion with and by trading on Complainant's mark. Persons initially encountering Respondent's domain name are likely to be confused as to the source, sponsorship, affiliation or endorsement of the domain name due to the use of the famous ORANGE BOWL mark. They may thus be drawn into the site trusting that they may obtain tickets from an authorized source.

Respondent is using Complainant's well known mark as a principal means (i.e., via the domain name) to advertise and sell products of third parties. A disclaimer may or may not be sufficient to dispel confusion as to the source of products at the "point of sale" (i.e. on Respondent's website). However, at this point Respondent has already misused Complainant's mark to bring consumers into its shop. Once in the shop, consumers are offered competitors' products. In the words of the Seventh Circuit, this is "plain misdescription, in fact false advertising" (*Ty Inc. v. Perryman*, No. 02–1771, (7th Cir.), decided October 4, 2002). The panel majority does not consider that Respondent's disclaimer is adequate to cure this exercise of bad faith use of Complainant's famous and distinctive mark.

Even assuming that a disclaimer might be effective to remedy initial interest confusion in a way that would remedy the initial problematic use, Respondent's disclaimer does not dispel the initial interest confusion caused by the domain name itself and is inadequate to avoid likelihood of confusion at the site. Prior to this action, Respondent's website featured a disclaimer of affiliation with the NCAA that did not mention Complainant or the ORANGE BOWL mark. This was obviously inadequate to dispel confusion about the relationship of Respondent and its site with Complainant. Subsequent to the filing of this action, Respondent has modified its site and disclaimer.

The new disclaimer is also problematic. It states that "the FedEx Orange Bowl has neither licensed or endorsed Front and Center Entertainment Group to sell goods and services in conjunction with the FedEx Orange Bowl." The disclaimer is confusing in that it is limited the sale of "goods and services" in conjunction with the event and fails to address Respondent's relationship to Complainant with respect to the sale of "tickets." A person reading and understanding the disclaimer is not clearly informed whether or not Respondent as "a private ticket broker" is authorized by Complainant to resell ORANGE BOWL tickets.

We acknowledge that Respondent in part uses the domain name to resell ORANGE BOWL tickets, and in that limited sense persons are accurately informed about some of Respondent's products. However, they are not adequately informed about the relationship of Complainant to Respondent's site and tickets, and may incorrectly conclude Respondent's conduct, including pricing and sale of tickets to other events, is endorsed by Complainant, when in fact that is not the case.

In sum, as a result of Respondent's use of the famous and distinctive ORANGE BOWL mark in its domain name, consumers are likely to be brought to Respondent's website mistakenly believing it is authorized, "official" or endorsed by Complainant. Respondent is thereupon offering to sell tickets to events which compete with that of Complainant. This is a bad faith use of Complainant's mark. Once at the website, consumers are likely to continue to believe mistakenly that Complainant has authorized or endorsed Respondent's use of the ORANGE BOWL mark in connection with the resale of tickets to the ORANGE BOWL game and for other events.

Therefore, we conclude that Complainant has established bad faith registration and use under Paragraph 4(b)(iv) of the Policy.

7. *Decision*

For all the foregoing reasons, in accordance with Paragraphs 4(i) of the Policy and 15 of the Rules, we order that the domain name <orangebowl.net> and <orangebowltickets.net> be transferred to the Complainant.

■ SMITH, PANELIST, DISSENTING.

I believe that the Panel should rule for the Respondent for the reasons enunciated in the prior decision of the WIPO panel in *NCAA v. Randy Pitkin* WIPO Case No. D2000–0903.

In this case the portion of the domain name that is at issue is also the name of an event, which cannot otherwise easily be otherwise described, coupled with the word "tickets," where the website is being used for the purpose of advertising the sale of tickets to the event. It is my belief that the use of such a domain name including, as it does, the word "tickets" is not cybersquatting under the rules governing the Uniform Dispute Resolution Policy.

While the Internet domain name using only the trademark name of the event might be cybersquatting, and thus I agree with the award of the Internet domain name <orangebowl.net> to Complainant, a concession which apparently Respondent makes in its Reply Brief, without admission, I do not believe that this applies to the use of the name of the actual event coupled with the generic word "ticket."

When the trademark is also the name of an event, such as the Orange Bowl, use of the name of the event is not always a trademark use, but may be a nominative fair use, where the words "Orange Bowl" although they be a trademark, are being used for the name of the event. It is difficult to identify the event, particularly this one, since it is one of several "bowl" games, and cannot be identified by its date, which varies from year to year, and this year, for some reason, is on a Tuesday!

I submit that the Orange Bowl event is even harder to identify, without using the words which also are a trademark, then even the Super Bowl, since various words preceding the word Bowl are used to distinguish this game from others on nearby dates, which mark also apparently indicates a major product of the Florida location in which this particular bowl game is played. It cannot be distinguished by the identification of the teams, since USC, which often commands a seat at the Rose Bowl, this year is in the Orange Bowl.

To the extent that the Orange Bowl is the name of a venue, *i.e.*, the particular coliseum or stadium where the Orange Bowl game is played, then it is also the name of venue for which the ticket will provide a seat license for the holder to sit in, and likewise the identification of this venue, together with the generic word "tickets" where the sale of tickets for this event in this location is being held, is also not, in my view, an unfair use.

It is my belief therefore that it is not bad faith to register the domain name which is also the "name of the game," together with the generic word "tickets" in this circumstance. Respondent has also placed a prominent disclaimer of sponsorship or association with the Orange Bowl on the face of its website, and understands the need to avoid a likelihood of confusion or mistake, if such exists. It may well be that selling a plethora of tickets to the named event at much higher prices then are normally garnered for this game, will also help avoid any likelihood of confusion or mistake in the use of the Internet domain name <orangebowltickets.com>.

Finally, I take note of the decision of the United States Supreme Court in *KP Permanent Make Up v. Lasting Impressions*, ___ U.S. ___, No. 03–409 decided December 8, 2004 S.C. (December 2004), where the United States Supreme Court, in the jurisdiction where both respondent and complainant reside, and the jurisdiction where the tickets and event were sold and is held, determined that where a trademark is being used by a defendant fairly to describe, in this case, the event and/or the event tickets, then the possible existence of even actual confusion does not provide a basis for the finding of trademark infringement and unfair competition under United States law. The United States Supreme Court, specifically rejected the view of the United States Court of Appeals for the Ninth Circuit which had held that the existence of confusion might trump infringement, and/or that there would be a burden on one party or another to prove the existence of, or absence of, confusion, when a mark is being used fairly and descriptively.

The panel majority attempts to distinguish this case as one where the famous mark is being used by another "to attract Internet users to a website offering products in competition with the trademark holder's product." I do not believe this to be the case, since the tickets being offered are the trademark holder's product, and are to attend the trademark holder's product, its Orange Bowl games.

Finally, I note that the new phenomenon of corporate sponsorship has made even the trademark use of the Orange Bowl trademark, less likely to cause confusion, since it is now the, presumably "FedEx" or "Federal Express" "brand" Orange Bowl game, stadium, venue, and/or ticket therefor.

QUESTIONS

1. You represent Fiber Shield Ltd., a Canadian company that has not registered its corporate name as a trademark. When your client tried to register fibershield.com as a domain name, it discovered that fibershield.com was unavailable, and had been registered by Fiber–Shield Industries of New York. Your client therefore registered the domain name fibershield.net. Last week, it received a letter from Fiber–Shield industries attaching a copy of a U.S. Trademark registration for the mark "FIBER–SHIELD", and demanding that it surrender the domain name fibershield.net immediately. The letter insists that because your client knew of the prior registration of fibershield.com before it registered fibershield.net, it registered fibershield.net in bad faith. What result under the UDRP? Under section 43(d)? *See Fiber–Shield Industries v. Fiber Shield (Toronto) Ltd.*, National Arbitration Forum Case No. FA0001000092054 (Feb. 29, 2000).

2. CTA Computers has operated a computer resale business on the Internet at www.buypc.com for the past four years, and uses "BuyPC.com" as a common law service mark. Last year, CTA failed to pay the fees due for renewing the domain name, and its domain name registration lapsed. Recently, a domain name speculator registered buypc.com and offered it for sale at its website. CTA wishes to regain the buypc.com domain name without paying the domain name speculator's price. Is it likely to succeed in a dispute under the UDRP? Under § 43(d)? *See Cedar Trade Associates, Inc. v. Ricks*, Nat'l Arbitration Forum Case No. FA0002000093633 (Feb. 25, 2000).

3. Seth Sanders, a long time *Star Wars* fan, has registered the domain name obiwankenobi.com and operates an unauthorized *Star Wars* fan website at www.obiwankenobi.com, with special attention to the Obi–Wan Kenobi character from the original and most recent *Star Wars* movies. Lucasfilm, the producer of the *Star Wars* movies and the owner of seven registered trademarks for OBI–WAN KENOBI sent Mr. Sanders a cease-and-desist letter. Enraged that Lucasfilm would so mistreat a longstanding fan, Sanders redirected his obiwankenobi.com site to a randomly selected pornographic web business. Lucasfilm has now filed a UDRP complaint. What result should the panel reach? *Cf. Telaxis Communications Corp. v. Minkle*, WIPO Arbitration and Mediation Center Case No. D2000–0005 (March 5, 2000). Should a court deciding the dispute under § 43(d) reach a different result? Why or why not?

Direct Line Group Ltd v. Purge I.T.

WIPO Arbitration and Mediation Center Case No. D 2000–0583 (Aug. 13, 2000).

■ CORNISH, PANELIST:

. . . . .

3. Factual Background

(1) The Complainants are a group of United Kingdom companies of which the first-named is the parent. Between them they do considerable business in that country in insurance, mortgages and other loans, life assurance, savings accounts and other financial services, the sixth Complainant providing various service and contracting functions to the others. The Complaint has furnished detailed evidence of the considerable amounts of business undertaken by the second to the fifth Complainants, all of which employ the mark, "Direct Line", for their services and products.

On behalf of the Direct Line group, the second Complainant is proprietor of 20 registrations of trade marks in the United Kingdom, consisting of or incorporating as a major feature the words, "Direct Line". The registrations are held for various insurance and other financial services and also for considerable categories of goods and all date from before registration of the Domain Name in dispute.

(2) The Complainants also hold 52 TLDs which incorporate "direct-line" or "directlines". Many of these add a further word without any break, as in "directlineinsurance.com", "directlineclub.com".

(3) The Complaint forms one of a series against the Respondents or the corporate Respondent alone. The Response to these cases has been by a single document, which indicates that the Domain Name Registrations in issue were made in pursuit of the same business objective. The Complainants have demonstrated by WhoIs database searches that the Respondents have registered with Network Solutions the names or abbreviations of eighteen well-known British enterprises with the addition of "sucks". All were obtained on May 11, 1999. Five have resulted in the parallel complaints which have been referred conjointly to the present Panel. The other four are D2000–0584 (dixonssucks.com), D2000–0585 (freeservesucks.com),

D2000–0636 (natwestsucks.com) and D2000–0681(standardchartered-sucks.com).

. . . .

5. Discussion and Findings

In accordance with the Dispute Resolution Policy, Paragraph 4(a), the Complainants bear the burden of demonstrating three elements.

Element 1: *That the Complainants have rights in a trade or service mark, with which the Respondents' Domain Name is identical or confusingly similar.*

As they have clearly demonstrated in their Complaint, the Complainants have a well-known trade mark for banking and associated services in the United Kingdom. This reputation is protected by the registration of the trade marks already referred to in Paragraph 3(1) and further enhanced by the use which they make of their Domain Names also there referred to. The Respondents' explanation of the conduct which they have pursued in relation to the names of various major enterprises is as follows:

> The company was set up in response to an article in The Times newspaper referring to disgruntled consumers registering domain names such as walmartsucks.com to host complaints sites against companies.

The Respondents' registration, consisting of the Complainants' name with the suffix, "sucks" (plus ".com"), is not identical to the Complainants' marks and the question arises whether the registration is confusingly similar to those marks.

Given the apparent mushrooming of complaints sites identified by reference to the target's name, can it be said that the registration would be recognised as an address plainly dissociated from the Complainants? In the Panel's opinion, this is by no means necessarily so. The first and immediately striking element in the Domain Name is the Complainants' name and adoption of it in the Domain Name is inherently likely to lead some people to believe that the Complainants are connected with it. Some will treat the additional "sucks" as a pejorative exclamation and therefore dissociate it after all from the Complainants; but equally others may be unable to give it any very definite meaning and will be confused about the potential association with the Complainants. The Complainants have accordingly made out the first element in its Complaint (see the rather similar conclusion on this element in Case D 2000–0477 (walmartcanadasucks.com)).

Element 2: *The Respondents must be shown to have no rights or legitimate interests in the Domain Name.*

The Complainants' reputation was well established before the Respondents began their activity, as is evident from their own statement of purpose, which is said to be, to help protect enterprises against being bothered by customer sites at which grievances are aired. Complaints sites are only likely to be set up against businesses with considerable reputations. Those who have genuine grievances against others or wish [to] express criticisms of them—whether the objections are against commercial or financial institutions, against governments, against charitable, sporting or cultural institutions, or whatever—must be at liberty, within the confines set by the laws of relevant jurisdictions, to express their views. If today they use a website or an email address for the purpose, they are entitled to select a Domain Name which leads others easily to them, if the name is still available.

The Respondents, contrarily, make it plain that their purpose is to have none of such free expression. They want, so they say, to protect against such engines of free speech. They claim as their own legitimate interest that they are in the business of obtaining Domain Names which might embarrass well-known enterprises if the names were allowed to fall into the hands of critics. The Respondents do not, however, act in a wholly altruistic spirit, since, as will be discussed further under Element 3, they seek substantial sums beyond their own costs before they will transfer over the offending registration. This latter aspect has to be brought into account in considering whether the Respondents therefore have any "right or legitimate interest" in the Domain Name, with which they otherwise have no association whatsoever and which they admit to have selected by reference to the Complainants' reputation in their own marks. The Panel finds that there is no justification for the role of officious interferer which the Respondents have taken upon themselves to provide in the manner in which they have chosen to do so. The Complainants have accordingly made out the second. . . .

Element 3: *That the Respondents registered and are using the Domain name in bad faith, in one of the senses of that term set out in Paragraph 4b of the Dispute Settlement Policy.*

The first Complainant received a letter of February 9 2000 from the Respondents offering to transfer the domain name for a "five figure sum" to be paid directly to a charity chosen by the Respondents. This must be read as a reference to a sum of at least GBP 10,000. Subsequently, according to attendance notes whose content has not been challenged by the Respondents, the Complainants' solicitor had two conversations with Mr Joseph Rice of Purge (on March 6 and 29, 2000). The upshot of these was an indication that a payment of somewhere in the region of GBP 5,000, paid directly to Purge, would, subject to checking, be needed to compensate for the time and expense involved. Taken together with Mr Rice's assurance that the whole purpose of registering the name was to enable its transfer to the Complainants, the Panel finds that these facts constitute plain evidence of circumstances indicating that the Respondents registered the name primarily for the purpose of selling, renting or otherwise transferring the domain name registration to the Complainants who are the owners of the relevant marks for valuable consideration in excess of documented out-of-pocket costs directly related to the domain name. Paragraph 4(b)(i) of the Dispute Resolution Policy states that such conduct is of itself to count as registration and use of the Domain Name in bad faith. Accordingly the third and final Element of the Complaint is made out.

6. Decision

The Panel decides, in accordance with the Uniform Domain Name Dispute Resolution Policy, Paragraph 4a and 4b,

—that the Domain Name in dispute is confusingly similar to the registered trade and service marks of the Complainants;

—that the Respondents have no rights or legitimate interests in respect of the Domain Name; and

—that the Domain Name has been registered and is being used in bad faith.

The Panel accordingly requires that the Domain Name DIRECTLINE-SUCKS.COM be transferred forthwith to the Second Complainant as specified in the Complaint.

QUESTIONS

1. Do you agree with the panel that directlinesucks.com is confusingly similar to complainant Direct Line's family of marks because some people "will be confused about the potential association with complainants?" Could Direct Line recover on these facts under § 43(a)? Section 43(c)? 43(d)?

2. Wal–Mart is a well-known chain of discount stores. Harvey registers walmartsucks.com, and offers to sell it to Wal–Mart for 5 million dollars. Wal–Mart declines. Harvey then uses the domain name to operate a website, which solicits and posts criticism of Wal–Mart from disgruntled employees and dissatisfied customers. Wal–Mart files a complaint under the UDRP. What result? *See Wal–Mart Stores Inc. v. walmartcanadasucks.com*, WIPO Arbitration & Mediation Center Case No. D2000–1104 (Nov. 23, 2000); *Wal–Mart Stores, Inc. v. Walsucks*, WIPO Arbitration & Mediation Center Case No. D2000–0477 (July 20, 2000).

———

In the seven years since ICANN's UDRP took effect, the dispute resolution service provided by the World Intellectual Property Organization, WIPO, has come to dominate UDRP dispute resolution. In 2005, the WIPO Arbitration and Mediation Center posted an informal overview of the weight of WIPO panel authority on UDRP legal issues. The overview is available online at http://arbiter.wipo.int/domains/search/overview/index. html?lang=eng. The overview summarizes WIPO panels' determinations on a number of recurrent legal questions. For example, in connection with questions of confusing similarity under the UDRP, the overview presents this précis:

1.3 Is a domain name consisting of a trademark and a negative term confusingly similar to the complainant's trademark? ("sucks cases")

Majority view: A domain name consisting of a trademark and a negative term is confusingly similar to the complainant's mark. Confusing similarity has been found because the domain name contains a trademark and a dictionary word; or because the disputed domain name is highly similar to the trademark; or because the domain name may not be recognized as negative; or because the domain name may be viewed by non-fluent English language speakers, who may not recognize the negative connotations of the word that is attached to the trademark.

Relevant decisions:

- Wal–Mart Stores, Inc. v. Richard MacLeod d/b/a For Sale D2000–0662 <walmartsucks.com>, Transfer

- A & F Trademark, Inc. and Abercrombie & Fitch Stores, Inc. v. Justin Jorgensen D2001–0900 <abercrombieandfilth.com>, Transfer

- Berlitz Investment Corp. v. Stefan Tinculescu D2003–0465 <berlitzsucks.com>, Transfer

- Wachovia Corporation v. Alton Flanders D2003–0596 <wachovia-sucks.com> among others, Transfer

Minority view: A domain name consisting of a trademark and a negative term is not confusingly similar because Internet users are not likely to associate the trademark holder with a domain name consisting of the trademark and a negative term.

Relevant decisions:

- Lockheed Martin Corporation v. Dan Parisi D2000–1015 <lockheedmartinsucks.com>, Denied

- McLane Company, Inc. v. Fred Craig D2000–1455 <mclanenortheastsucks.com>, Denied

- America Online, Inc. v. Johuathan Investments, Inc., and Aollnews.com D2001–0918 <aollnews.com>, <fucknetscape.com> Transfer, Denied in Part

Deutsche Welle v. Diamondware Limited, WIPO Arbitration & Mediation Center Case No. D 2000–1202 (2001). Deutsche Welle, a German television broadcaster that used the registered mark "DW" brought a complaint over the domain name "dw.com." The domain had been registered by a U.S. software firm, which had done business under the "DW" acronym since 1994. Diamondware had registered the domain name in December of 1994 and operated an active business website at <www.dw.com>. In July, 2000, Deutsche Welle wrote to Diamondware and demanded the transfer of the domain name. Diamondware responded "Thank you for your interest in our domain name, dw.com. We are not currently offering this property for sale on the open market, however it has recently been attracting enquiries. Therefore, we would consider an offer above $3,750,000 (three million, seven hundred fifty thousand US Dollars) from an accredited buyer...." Deutsche Welle filed a UDRP complaint.

The three-member panel concluded that the dw.com domain name was identical to Deutsche Welle's registered trademark. It found, however, that Diamondware had provided ample evidence of its legitimate interest in the domain name. It also declined to find Diamondware's offer to consider selling the domain name for $3,750,000 to be evidence of bad faith:

> The Panel does not interpret the Policy to mean that a mere offer for sale of a domain name for a large sum of money is, of itself, proof of cybersquatting. It may, in certain circumstances, provide some evidence, but it is not conclusive evidence. Indeed, some of the largest sums of money paid for domain names have been for generic names and it is clear to anyone who follows reports of domain name sales that two-letter .com registrations are extremely prized. In any event, in this case the Respondent, with a substantial underlying business interest in the Domain Name, had every reason to demand a substantial sum of money for transfer of the Domain Name.

> The Panel finds that the Complainant has not met the burden of proving bad faith.

Finally, a majority of the panel upheld Diamondware's claim that Deutsche Welle's complaint amounted to "reverse domain name hijacking" under the UDRP:

> The Policy is only designed to deal with a very narrow category of case, namely cybersquatting. It was never intended to be a substitute for trade mark infringement litigation. Manifestly, ... this was never a case of cybersquatting. The Policy is clear. To succeed in the Complaint, the Complainant has to prove, at the very least, that the Domain Name was registered in bad faith. When the Complainant conducted its Whois search and found that the Domain Name registration dated back nearly 6 years, it was alerted to the fact that registration of the Domain Name was most unlikely to have been undertaken "primarily" for any bad faith purpose directed at the Complainant. The Complainant has not produced one shred of evidence to suggest why the Respondent, a company in the United States, should have been aware of the existence of the Complainant, a German broadcasting service, back in 1994 when it registered the Domain Name. When the Complainant visited the Respondent's website (its letter of July 13, 2000 makes it clear that it was aware of the website) any doubts it may have had were removed. The Domain Name connects to an active website through which the Respondent conducts a bona fide business and in relation to which the acronym "DW" is apt. In such circumstances, the price the Respondent put on the Domain Name in the year 2000 was completely irrelevant to its motives when registering the Domain Name in 1994. None of this is addressed in the Complainant's response. In the view of [the majority], the Complainant's behaviour, which has wrongfully resulted in the

Respondent having to incur what must be substantial legal fees, should be condemned as an abuse of the administrative procedure.

D.   THE UDRP IN THE U.S. COURTS

Sallen v. Corinthians Licenciamentos LTDA, 273 F.3d 14 (1st Cir.2001). The owner of the Brazilian soccer team Corinthiao brought a successful UDRP proceeding against Jay Sallen, the registrant of the domain name <corinthians.com>. Sallen then filed suit under section 43(d)(2)(v) seeking the return of his domain name and a declaration that his registration and use of <corinthians.com> was not unlawful:

> Sallen asserts that (1) this provision of the ACPA creates an explicit cause of action for a declaration that a registrant who has lost a domain name under the UDRP has lawfully registered and used that domain name; (2) this declaration overrides the WIPO panel's decision to the contrary; and (3) federal courts may order the domain name reactivated or transferred back to the aggrieved registrant. Sallen's position is that, despite the terms of his domain name registration agreement, and despite the WIPO panel's interpretation of those terms, he is entitled to retain registration and use of corinthians.com if his registration and use of the domain name is consistent with the ACPA.

> This case raises an issue of first impression, requiring us to determine whether a domain name registrant, who has lost in a WIPO-adjudicated UDRP proceeding, may bring an action in federal court under § 1114(2)(D)(v) seeking to override the result of the earlier WIPO proceeding by having his status as a nonviolator of the ACPA declared and by getting an injunction forcing a transfer of the disputed domain name back to him. The answer to this question turns on the relationship between the ACPA, in particular § 1114(2)(D)(v), and decisions of administrative dispute resolution panels contractually empowered to adjudicate domain name disputes under the UDRP.

> The district court dismissed Sallen's complaint on the grounds that no actual controversy existed between the parties since CL never claimed that Sallen violated the ACPA. We hold that, although CL represented that it had "no intent to sue [Sallen] under the ACPA for his past activities in connection with corinthians.com," an actual controversy did exist between the parties concerning rights to corinthians.com, and that the district court incorrectly dismissed Sallen's complaint. Section 1114(2)(D)(v) grants domain name registrants who have lost domain names under administrative panel decisions applying the UDRP an affirmative cause of action in federal court for a declaration of nonviolation of the ACPA and for the return of the wrongfully transferred domain names. Accordingly, we reverse and remand to the district court.

Dluhos v. Strasberg, 321 F.3d 365 (3d Cir.2003). The estate of Lee Strasberg, a famous acting teacher who died in 1982, filed a UDRP proceeding against Dluhos, the registrant of <leestrasberg.com>. Rather than contesting the UDRP proceeding, Dluhos filed an action in federal court challenging the constitutionality of the UDRP. After the UDRP panel ruled that the <leestrasberg.com> should be transferred to the Strasberg estate, Dluhos amended his complaint to add a count seeking the reinstatement of his domain. The district court dismissed Dluhos's constitutional challenge. In reviewing the UDRP decision, the court applied the deferential standard imposed by the Federal Arbitration Act, and upheld the award. On appeal, the Third Circuit held that UDRP decisions are not subject to review under the Federal Arbitration Act, but may be challenged under the ACPA:

> At issue before us then is whether the nonbinding domain name resolution policy (UDRP) proceeding that shifted Appellant's registered domain name to the Strasberg defendants constitutes arbitration under the FAA. If this proceeding qualifies as arbitration under the FAA, then the dispute resolution is subject to extremely limited review. If it does not fall under the FAA umbrella, then the district court lacked jurisdiction to examine—and thus to affirm—the result under the lax FAA review standards.

> IV.

> We begin our analysis of the FAA's applicability by examining the specific arbitration agreement at issue, a contract-based arrangement for handling disputes between domain name registrants and third parties who challenge the registration and use of their trademarks. In our view, the UDRP's unique contractual arrangement renders the FAA's provisions for judicial review inapplicable.

> A.

> First, the UDRP obviously contemplates the possibility of judicial intervention, as no provision of the policy prevents a party from filing suit before, after or during the administrative proceedings. See UDRP § 4(k) (stating that domain-name resolution proceedings shall not stop either party from "submitting the dispute to a court of competent jurisdiction for independent resolution"); *Sallen v. Corinthians Licenciamentos Ltda.*, 273 F.3d 14, 26 (1st Cir. 2001) (discussing the likelihood that the "judicial outcome will override the UDRP one"). In that sense, this mechanism would not fall under the FAA because "the dispute will [not necessarily] be settled by this arbitration." *Harrison [v. Nissan Motor Corp.*, 111 F.3d 343, 350 (3d Cir. 1997)], at 349.

> The UDRP was intended to ensure that the parties could seek independent judicial resolution of domain name disputes, regardless of whether its proceeding reached a conclusion. *See World Intellectual Property Organization, The Management of Internet Names and Addresses: Intellectual Property Issues: Final Reporter of the WIPO Internet Domain Name Process* 139, 150(iv), at http://wipo2.wipo.int/process

1/report/finalreport.html (Apr. 30, 1999) (remarking that the parties should be permitted to seek "de novo review" of a UDRP-based dispute resolution); *see also Sallen*, 273 F.3d at 26 (affording independent complete review of a UDRP proceeding rather than addressing it under the FAA); *Weber-Stephen Prods. Co. v. Armitage Hardware & Bldg. Supply, Inc.*, 2000 U.S. Dist LEXIS 6335 (N.D. Ill. May 3, 2000) (concluding that the UDRP takes account of the possibility of parallel litigation in federal court, and that federal courts are "not bound by the outcome of the administrative proceedings").

Indeed, unlike methods of dispute resolution covered by the FAA, UDRP proceedings were never intended to replace formal litigation. *See Parisi* [*v. Netlearning, Inc.*, 139 F.Supp.2d 745 (E.D. Va. 2001)], at 752 (citing the FAA's requirement that parties to arbitration "agree[ ] that a judgment of the court shall be entered upon the award made pursuant to the arbitration," 9 U.S.C.S. 9, and noting the absence of such an agreement in the UDRP); David E. Sorkin, *Judicial Review of ICANN Domain Name Dispute Decisions*, 18 SANTA CLARA COMPUTER & HIGHTECH L.J. 35, 51–52 (2001) ("Unlike conventional arbitration, the UDRP is not meant to replace litigation, but merely to provide an additional forum for dispute resolution, with an explicit right of appeal to the courts."). Rather, the UDRP contemplates truncated proceedings. It "is fashioned as an 'online' procedure administered via the Internet," *Parisi*, 139 F.Supp.2d at 747, which does not permit discovery, the presentation of live testimony (absent exceptional circumstances), or any remedy other than the transfer or cancellation of the domain name in question. [Citations]

To shove Dluhos' square-peg UDRP proceeding into the round hole of the FAA would be to frustrate this aim, as judicial review of FAA-styled arbitration proceedings could be generously described only as extremely deferential.

B.

Second, because the trademark holder or the trademark holder's representative is not required to avail itself of the dispute resolution policy before moving ahead in the district court, these proceedings do not qualify as the type that would entail a court's compelling party participation prior to independent judicial review—thus removing the proceeding from the warmth of the FAA blanket. Under § 4 of the FAA, a district court may "stay the trial of the action until such arbitration has been had in accordance with the terms of the agreement." 9 U.S.C. § 4. Although "[s]ome courts, relying in part on their inherent equitable powers, have stayed litigation and compelled participation in non-binding procedures so long as there are 'reasonable commercial expectations' that the procedures would 'settle' disputed issues," *Parisi*, 139 F.Supp.2d at 750 n.10 (*quoting AMF*, 621 F.Supp. at 460–461), a UDRP proceeding settles a domain-name dispute only to the extent that a season-finale cliffhanger resolves a sitcom's storyline—that is, it doesn't. It is true that the language of the resolution policy describes the dispute-resolution process as "mandatory," but "the process is not 'mandatory' in the sense that either disputant's legal claims accrue only after a panel's decision." *Parisi*, 139 F.Supp.2d at 751 (*quoting Bankers Ins. Co.*, 245 F.3d at 319). Only the domain-name registrant is contractually obligated to participate in the proceeding if a complaint is filed. Even then, the panel may "decide the dispute based on the complaint" if the registrant declines to participate. UDRP § 5(e). That Dluhos could do precisely that by eschewing the NAF proceeding and filing suit in district court only demonstrates the dispute resolution policy's outcome's relative hollowness. Indeed, it is not the district court litigation that could be stayed pending dispute resolution, but rather the dispute-resolution mechanism itself. *See* UDRP § 18 (giving arbitration panel "the discretion to decide whether to suspend or terminate the administrative proceeding, or to proceed to a decision" while a lawsuit is pending). And that is exactly what the NAF panel did.

C.

The bottom line is that a registrant who loses a domain name to a trademark holder "can effectively suspend [a] panel's decision by filing a lawsuit in the specified jurisdiction and notifying the registrar in accordance with [UDRP § 4(k)]." *Parisi*, 139 F.Supp.2d at 752. From that provision, it is evident that the UDRP provides "'parity of appeal,' affording a 'clear mechanism' for 'seeking judicial review of a decision of an administrative panel canceling or transferring the domain name.'" *Id.* (*quoting* ICANN, *Staff Report on Implementation Documents for the Uniform Dispute Resolution Policy* (Sept. 29, 1999)).

Accordingly, we hold that UDRP proceedings do not fall under the Federal Arbitration Act.More specifically, judicial review of those decisions is not restricted to a motion to vacate arbitration award under § 10 of the FAA, which applies only to binding proceedings likely to "realistically settle the dispute." The district court erred in reviewing the domain name proceeding under limitations of FAA standards.

V.

Because the UDRP—a private covenant—cannot confer federal jurisdiction where none independently exists, the remaining question is whether the Congress has provided a cause of action to challenge its decisions. In the Anticybersquatting Consumer Protection Act, we hold that it has.

The ACPA, 15 U.S.C. § 1114(2)(D)(v), "provide[s] registrants ... with an affirmative cause of action to recover domain names lost in UDRP proceedings." *Sallen*, 273 F.3d at 27. Under this modern amendment to the Lanham Act, a registrant whose domain name has been "suspended, disabled, or transferred" may sue for a declaration that the registrant is not in violation of the Act, as well as for an injunction returning the domain name. 15 U.S.C. § 1114(2)(D)(v). Congress' authorization of the federal courts to "grant injunctive relief to the domain name registrant, including the reactivation of the domain name or transfer of the domain name to the domain name registrant" gives the registrant an explicit cause of action through which to redress the loss of a domain name under the UDRP. *Id.*

Accordingly, as to the CMG and Strasberg defendants, we will reverse and remand the case for further proceedings consistent with this opinion. This decision in no way reflects an intimation that the NAP panel erred in its judgment, but merely that UDRP resolutions do not fall under the limited judicial review of arbitrators of the FAA.

Barcelona.com, Inc. v. Excelentisimo Ayuntamiento De Barcelona

330 F.3d 617 (4th Cir.2003).

■ NIEMEYER, CIRCUIT JUDGE:

Barcelona.com, Inc. ("Bcom, Inc."), a Delaware corporation, commenced this action under the Anticybersquatting Consumer Protection Act against Excelentisimo Ayuntamiento de Barcelona (the City Council of Barcelona, Spain) for a declaratory judgment that Bcom, Inc.'s registration and use of the domain name <barcelona.com> is not unlawful under the Lanham Act (Chapter 22 of Title 15 of the United States Code). The district court concluded that Bcom, Inc.'s use of <barcelona.com> was confusingly similar to Spanish trademarks owned by the City Council that include the word "Barcelona." Also finding bad faith on the basis that Bcom, Inc. had attempted to sell the <barcelona.com> domain name to the City Council for a profit, the court ordered the transfer of the domain name to the City Council.

Because the district court applied Spanish law rather than United States law and based its transfer order, in part, on a counterclaim that the City Council never filed, we reverse the judgment of the district court denying Bcom, Inc. relief under the Anticybersquatting Consumer Protection Act, vacate its memorandum opinion and its order to transfer the domain name <barcelona.com> to the City Council, and remand for further proceedings consistent with this opinion.

I

In 1996, Mr. Joan Nogueras Cobo ("Nogueras"), a Spanish citizen, registered the domain name <barcelona.com> in the name of his wife, also a Spanish citizen, with the domain registrar, Network Solutions, Inc., in Herndon, Virginia. In the application for registration of the domain name, Nogueras listed himself as the administrative contact. When Nogueras met Mr. Shahab Hanif, a British citizen, in June 1999, they developed a business plan to turn <barcelona.com> into a tourist portal for the Barcelona, Spain, region. A few months later they formed Bcom, Inc. under Delaware law to own <barcelona.com> and to run the website, and Nogueras, his wife, and Hanif became Bcom, Inc.'s officers. Bcom, Inc. was formed as an American company in part because Nogueras believed that doing so would facilitate obtaining financing for the development of the website. Although Bcom, Inc. maintains a New York mailing address, it has no employees in the United States, does not own or lease office space in the United States, and does not have a telephone listing in the United States. Its computer server is in Spain.

Shortly after Nogueras registered the domain name <barcelona.com> in 1996, he placed some Barcelona-related information on the site. The site offered commercial services such as domain registry and web hosting, but did not offer much due to the lack of financing. Before developing the business plan with Hanif, Nogueras used a web-form on the City Council's official website to e-mail the mayor of Barcelona, Spain, proposing to "negotiate" with the City Council for its acquisition of the domain name <barcelona.com>, but Nogueras received no response. And even after the development of a business plan and after speaking with potential investors, Nogueras was unable to secure financing to develop the website.

In March 2000, about a year after Nogueras had e-mailed the Mayor, the City Council contacted Nogueras to learn more about Bcom, Inc. and its plans for the domain name <barcelona.com>. Nogueras and his marketing director met with City Council representatives, and after the meeting, sent them the business plan that was developed for Bcom, Inc.

On May 3, 2000, a lawyer for the City Council sent a letter to Nogueras demanding that Nogueras transfer the domain name <barcelona.com> to the City Council. The City Council owned about 150 trademarks issued in Spain, the majority of which included the word Barcelona, such as "Teatre Barcelona," "Barcelona Informacio I Grafic," and "Barcelona Informacio 010 El Tlefon Que Ho Contesta Tot." . . .

. . .

Upon Bcom, Inc.'s refusal to transfer <barcelona.com> to the City Council, the City Council invoked the Uniform Domain Name Dispute Resolution Policy ("UDRP") promulgated by the Internet Corporation for Assigned Names and Numbers ("ICANN") to resolve the dispute.

The administrative complaint was resolved by a single WIPO panelist who issued a ruling in favor of the City Council on August 4, 2000. The WIPO panelist concluded that <barcelona.com> was confusingly similar to the City Council's Spanish trademarks, that Bcom, Inc. had no legitimate interest in <barcelona.com>, and that Bcom, Inc.'s registration and use of <barcelona.com> was in bad faith. To support his conclusion that Bcom, Inc. acted in bad faith, the WIPO panelist observed that the only purpose of the business plan was "to commercially exploit information about the City of Barcelona . . . particularly . . . the information prepared and provided by [the City Council] as part of its public service." The WIPO panelist ordered that Bcom, Inc. transfer the domain name <barcelona.com> to the City Council.

In accordance with the UDRP's provision that required a party aggrieved by the dispute resolution process to file any court challenge within ten business days, Bcom, Inc. commenced this action on August 18, 2000 under the provision of the Anticybersquatting Consumer Protection Act (the "ACPA") that authorizes a domain name owner to seek recovery or restoration of its domain name when a trademark owner has overstepped its authority in causing the domain name to be suspended, disabled, or transferred. *See* 15 U.S.C. § 1114(2)(D)(v). Bcom, Inc.'s complaint sought a declaratory judgment that its use of the name <barcelona.com> "does not infringe upon any trademark of defendant or cause confusion as to the origin, sponsorship, or approval of the website <barcelona.com>; . . . [and] that [the City Council] is barred from instituting any action against [Bcom, Inc.] for trademark infringement."

Following a bench trial, the district court entered a memorandum opinion and an order dated February 22, 2002, denying Bcom, Inc.'s request for declaratory judgment and directing Bcom, Inc. to "transfer the domain name <barcelona.com> to the [City Council] forthwith." 189 F.Supp.2d 367, 377 (E.D. Va. 2002). Although the district court concluded that the WIPO panel ruling "should be given no weight and this case must be decided based on the evidence presented before the Court," the court proceeded in essence to apply the WIPO panelist opinion as well as Spanish law. *Id.* at 371. The court explained that even though the City Council did not own a trademark in the name "Barcelona" alone, it owned numerous Spanish trademarks that included the word Barcelona, which could, under Spanish law as understood by the district court, be enforced against an infringing use such as <barcelona.com>. *Id.* Adopting the WIPO panelist's decision, the court stated that "the WIPO decision was correct in its determination that [Bcom, Inc.] took 'advantage of the normal confusion' of an Internet user by using the 'Barcelona route' because an Internet user would 'normally expect to reach some official body . . . for . . . the information.' " *Id.* at 372. Referring to the facts that Bcom, Inc. engaged in little activity and attempted to sell the domain name to the City Council, the court concluded that "these factors clearly demonstrate a bad faith intent on the part of the Plaintiff and its sole shareholders to improperly profit from their registration of the domain name <barcelona.com>." At bottom, the court concluded that Bcom, Inc. failed to demonstrate, as required by 15 U.S.C. § 1114(2)(D)(v), that its use of <barcelona.com> was "not unlawful." *Id.* at 373.

. . .

From the district court's order of February 22, 2002, Bcom, Inc. filed this appeal.

II

. . .

[D]omain names are issued pursuant to contractual arrangements under which the registrant agrees to a dispute resolution process, the UDRP, which is designed to resolve a large number of disputes involving domain names, but this process is not intended to interfere with or modify any "independent resolution" by a court of competent jurisdiction. Moreover, the UDRP makes no effort at unifying the law of trademarks among the nations served by the Internet. Rather, it forms part of a contractual policy developed by ICANN for use by registrars in administering the issuance and transfer of domain names. Indeed, it explicitly anticipates that judicial proceedings will continue under various nations' laws applicable to the parties.

. . .

Moreover, any decision made by a panel under the UDRP is no more than an agreed-upon administration that is *not* given any deference under the ACPA. To the contrary, because a UDRP decision is susceptible of being grounded on principles foreign or hostile to American law, the ACPA authorizes reversing a panel decision if such a result is called for by application of the Lanham Act.

In sum, we conclude that we have jurisdiction over this dispute brought under the ACPA and the Lanham Act. Moreover, we give the decision of the WIPO panelist no deference in deciding this action under § 1114(2)(D)(v). [Citations] Thus, for our purposes, the WIPO panelist's decision is relevant only to serve as the reason for Bcom, Inc.'s bringing an action under § 1114(2)(D)(v) to reverse the WIPO panelist's decision.

III

Now we turn to the principal issue raised in this appeal. Bcom, Inc. contends that in deciding its claim under § 1114(2)(D)(v), the district court erred in applying the law of Spain rather than the law of the United States. Because the ACPA explicitly requires application of the Lanham Act, not foreign law, we agree.

Section 1114(2)(D)(v), the reverse domain name hijacking provision, states:

> A domain name registrant whose domain name has been suspended, disabled, or transferred under a policy described under clause (ii)(II) may, upon notice to the mark owner, file a civil action to establish that the registration or use of the domain name by such registrant is not unlawful under this chapter. The court may grant injunctive relief to the domain name registrant, including the reactivation of the domain name or transfer of the domain name to the domain name registrant.

15 U.S.C. § 1114(2)(D)(v). Thus, to establish a right to relief against an "overreaching trademark owner" under this reverse hijacking provision, a plaintiff must establish (1) that it is a domain name registrant; (2) that its domain name was suspended, disabled, or transferred under a policy implemented by a registrar as described in 15 U.S.C. § 1114(2)(D)(ii)(II); (3) that the owner of the mark that prompted the domain name to be suspended, disabled, or transferred has notice of the action by service or otherwise; and (4) that the plaintiff's registration or use of the domain name is not unlawful under the Lanham Act, as amended.

. . .

It is the last element that raises the principal issue on appeal. Bcom, Inc. argues that the district court erred in deciding whether Bcom, Inc. satisfied this element by applying Spanish law and then by concluding that Bcom, Inc.'s use of the domain name violated Spanish law.

It appears from the district court's memorandum opinion that it indeed did resolve the last element by applying Spanish law. Although the district court recognized that the City Council did not have a registered trademark in the name "Barcelona" alone, either in Spain or in the United States, it observed that "under Spanish law, when trademarks consisting of two or more words contain one word that stands out in a predominant manner, that dominant word must be given decisive relevance." *Barcelona.com, Inc.*, 189 F.Supp.2d at 371–72. The court noted that "the term 'Barcelona' has been included in many trademarks consisting of two or more words owned by the City Council of Barcelona. In most of these marks, the word 'Barcelona' is clearly the dominant word which characterizes the mark." 189 F.Supp.2d at 372. These observations regarding the substance and effect of Spanish law led the court to conclude that the City Council of Barcelona "owns a legally valid Spanish trademark for the dominant word 'Barcelona.' " *Id.* The district court then proceeded to determine whether Bcom's "use of the Barcelona trademark is not unlawful." *Id.* In this portion of its analysis, the district court determined that there was a "confusing similarity between the <barcelona.com> domain name and the marks held by the Council," *id.*, and that "the circumstances surrounding the incorporation of [Bcom, Inc.] and the actions taken by Nogueras in attempting to sell the domain name evidenced a bad faith intent to profit from the registration of a domain name containing the Council's mark," *id.* Applying Spanish trademark law in this manner, the court resolved that Bcom, Inc.'s registration and use of <barcelona.com> were unlawful.

It requires little discussion to demonstrate that this use of Spanish law by the district court was erroneous under the plain terms of the statute. The text of the ACPA explicitly requires application of the Lanham Act, not foreign law, to resolve an action brought under 15 U.S.C. § 1114(2)(D)(v). Specifically, it authorizes an aggrieved domain name registrant to "file a civil action to establish that the registration or use of the domain name by such registrant is *not unlawful under this chapter*." 15 U.S.C. § 1114(2)(D)(v) (emphasis added). It is thus readily apparent that the cause of action created by Congress in this portion of the ACPA requires the court adjudicating such an action to determine whether the registration or use of the domain name violates the Lanham Act. Because the statutory language has a plain and unambiguous meaning that is consistent with the statutory context and application of this language in accordance with its plain meaning provides a component of a coherent statutory scheme, our statutory analysis need proceed no further. [Citation]

By requiring application of United States trademark law to this action brought in a United States court by a United States corporation involving a domain name administered by a United States registrar, 15 U.S.C.

§ 1114(2)(D)(v) is consistent with the fundamental doctrine of territoriality upon which our trademark law is presently based. . . .

When we apply the Lanham Act, not Spanish law, in determining whether Bcom, Inc.'s registration and use of <barcelona.com> is unlawful, the ineluctable conclusion follows that Bcom, Inc.'s registration and use of the name "Barcelona" is not unlawful. Under the Lanham Act, and apparently even under Spanish law, the City Council could not obtain a trademark interest in a purely descriptive geographical designation that refers only to the City of Barcelona. *See* 15 U.S.C. § 1052(e)(2); *see also* Spanish Trademark Law of 1988, Art. 11(1)(c) (forbidding registration of marks consisting exclusively of "geographical origin"). Under United States trademark law, a geographic designation can obtain trademark protection if that designation acquires secondary meaning. *See, e.g., Resorts of Pinehurst, Inc. v. Pinehurst Nat'l Corp.*, 148 F.3d 417, 421 (4th Cir. 1998). On the record in this case, however, there was no evidence that the public—in the United States or elsewhere—associates "Barcelona" with anything other than the City itself. Indeed, the Chief Director of the City Council submitted an affidavit stating that "the City does not own and is not using any trademarks in the United States, to identify any goods or services." Therefore, under United States trademark law, "Barcelona" should have been treated as a purely descriptive geographical term entitled to no trademark protection. *See* 15 U.S.C. § 1052(e)(2). It follows then that there was nothing unlawful about Nogueras' registration of <barcelona.com>, nor is there anything unlawful under United States trademark law about Bcom, Inc.'s continued use of that domain name.

For these reasons, we conclude that Bcom, Inc. established entitlement to relief under 15 U.S.C. § 1114(2)(D)(v) with respect to the domain name <barcelona.com>, and accordingly we reverse the district court's ruling in this regard.

QUESTION

Assume the district court was correct in concluding that Bcom's registration and use of <barcelona.com> violated the trademark law of Spain. Indeed, assume that the Barcelona City Council has obtained a Spanish court judgment to that effect. Should Bcom nonetheless be entitled to prevail in an action to recover the domain name on the ground that its registration and use of the domain name does not violate United States law?

CHAPTER 12

Trademarks as Speech

Robert C. Denicola, Trademarks as Speech: Constitutional Implications of the Emerging Rationales for the Protection of Trade Symbols, 1982 Wis. L. Rev. 158, 158–59 (footnotes omitted)

For a time, the concept of freedom of speech did not reach the mundane communications at issue in the typical trademark infringement action. The information conveyed through the use of a trademark generally relates not to the momentous philosophical or political issues of the day, but rather to the details of prospective commercial transactions—the source or quality of specific goods or services. Restrictions on such "commercial speech" were long thought exempt from constitutional scrutiny. Although speech relating solely to commercial exchange is only tangentially relevant to many of the interests that inspire the commitment to freedom of expression, its complete excision from the first amendment was nevertheless difficult to justify. Recent years have seen this arbitrary division replaced by a more flexible model in which even purely commercial speech merits constitutional protection, although not necessarily equivalent to that afforded communications more intimately associated with fundamental first amendment values. The ability to restrict, untruthful or deceptive commercial speech, however, has remained unquestioned. Traditional trademark and unfair competition theory, with its historic emphasis on consumer deception and confusion, thus rests comfortably within contemporary constitutional principles. But this confusion rationale has come under quiet attack. The notion of trademark misappropriation even in the absence of any likelihood of confusion is evident in much of the current case law, and the long dormant concept of trademark dilution appears poised to further expand the scope of trademark rights. To say that the law appears increasingly willing to accord trademarks the status of property may not be a particularly helpful characterization of modern trademark law, but it does emphasize that today's doctrine somehow differs from yesterday's. Emboldened by hints of a more expansive monopoly, trademark owners are pressing claims in areas beyond the reach of traditional theory. The struggle to extend the scope of trademark protection is interesting in its own right, and has also raised for the first time the possibility of genuine conflict between trademark law and the first amendment.

San Francisco Arts & Athletics, Inc. v. United States Olympic Committee

483 U.S. 522, 107 S.Ct. 2971, 97 L.Ed.2d 427 (1987).

■ JUSTICE POWELL delivered the opinion of the Court:

In this case, we consider the scope and constitutionality of a provision of the Amateur Sports Act of 1978, 36 U.S.C. §§ 371–396, that authorizes the United States Olympic Committee to prohibit certain commercial and promotional uses of the word "Olympic."

I

Petitioner San Francisco Arts & Athletics, Inc. (SFAA), is a nonprofit California corporation. The SFAA originally sought to incorporate under the name "Golden Gate Olympic Association," but was told by the California Department of Corporations that the word "Olympic" could not appear in a corporate title. App. 95. After its incorporation in 1981, the SFAA nevertheless began to promote the "Gay Olympic Games," using those words on its letterheads and mailings and in local newspapers. *Ibid.* The games were to be a 9–day event to begin in August 1982, in San Francisco, California. The SFAA expected athletes from hundreds of cities in this country and from cities all over the world. *Id.*, at 402. The Games were to open with a ceremony "which will rival the traditional Olympic Games." *Id.*, at 354. See *id.*, at 402, 406, 425. A relay of over 2,000 runners would carry a torch from New York City across the country to Kezar Stadium in San Francisco. *Id.*, at 98, 355, 357, 432. The final runner would enter the stadium with the "Gay Olympic Torch" and light the "Gay Olympic Flame." *Id.*, at 357. The ceremony would continue with the athletes marching in uniform into the stadium behind their respective city flags. *Id.*, at 354, 357, 402, 404, 414. Competition was to occur in 18 different contests, with the winners receiving gold, silver, and bronze medals. *Id.*, at 354–355, 359, 407, 410. To cover the cost of the planned Games, the SFAA sold T-shirts, buttons, bumper stickers, and other merchandise bearing the title "Gay Olympic Games." *Id.*, at 67, 94, 107, 113–114, 167, 360, 362, 427–428.

Section 110 of the Amateur Sports Act (Act), 92 Stat. 3048, 36 U.S.C. § 380, grants respondent United States Olympic Committee (USOC) the right to prohibit certain commercial and promotional uses of the word "Olympic" and various Olympic symbols.[4] In late December 1981, the executive director of the USOC wrote to the SFAA, informing it of the

---

4. Section 110 of the Act, as set forth in *36 U.S.C. § 380,* provides:

"Without the consent of the [USOC], any person who uses for the purpose of trade, to induce the sale of any goods or services, or to promote any theatrical exhibition, athletic performance, or competition—

"(1) the symbol of the International Olympic Committee, consisting of 5 interlocking rings;

"(2) the emblem of the [USOC], consisting of an escutcheon having a blue chief and vertically extending red and white bars on the base with 5 interlocking rings displayed on the chief;

existence of the Amateur Sports Act, and requesting that the SFAA immediately terminate use of the word "Olympic" in its description of the planned Games. The SFAA at first agreed to substitute the word "Athletic" for the word "Olympic," but, one month later, resumed use of the term. The USOC became aware that the SFAA was still advertising its Games as "Olympic" through a newspaper article in May 1982. In August, the USOC brought suit in the Federal District Court for the Northern District of California to enjoin the SFAA's use of the word "Olympic." The District Court granted a temporary restraining order and then a preliminary injunction. The Court of Appeals for the Ninth Circuit affirmed. After further proceedings, the District Court granted the USOC summary judgment and a permanent injunction.

The Court of Appeals affirmed the judgment of the District Court. 781 F.2d 733 (1986). It found that the Act granted the USOC exclusive use of the word "Olympic" without requiring the USOC to prove that the unauthorized use was confusing and without regard to the defenses available to an entity sued for a trademark violation under the Lanham Act, 60 Stat. 427, as amended, 15 U.S.C. § 1051 *et seq.* . . . Three judges dissented, finding that the panel's interpretation of the Act raised serious First Amendment issues. 789 F.2d 1319, 1326 (1986).

We granted certiorari, 479 U.S. 913 (1986), to review the issues of statutory and constitutional interpretation decided by the Court of Appeals. We now affirm.

. . . .

"(3) any trademark, trade name, sign, symbol, or insignia falsely representing association with, or authorization by, the International Olympic Committee or the [USOC]; or

"(4) the words 'Olympic', 'Olympiad', 'Citius Altius Fortius', or any combination or simulation thereof tending to cause confusion, to cause mistake, to deceive, or to falsely suggest a connection with the [USOC] or any Olympic activity;

"shall be subject to suit in a civil action by the [USOC] for the remedies provided in the Act of July 5, 1946 (60 Stat. 427; popularly known as the Trademark Act of 1946 [Lanham Act]) [*15 U.S.C. § 1051 et seq.*]. However, any person who actually used the emblem in subsection (a)(2) of this section, or the words, or any combination thereof, in subsection (a)(4) of this section for any lawful purpose prior to September 21, 1950, shall not be prohibited by this section from continuing such lawful use for the same purpose and for the same goods or services. In addition, any person who actually used, or whose assignor actually used, any other trademark, trade name, sign, symbol, or insignia described in subsections (a)(3) and (4) of this section for any lawful purpose prior to September 21, 1950 shall not be prohibited by this section from continuing such lawful use for the same purpose and for the same goods or services.

"(b) The [USOC] may authorize contributors and suppliers of goods or services to use the trade name of the [USOC] as well as any trademark, symbol, insignia, or emblem of the International Olympic Committee or of the [USOC] in advertising that the contributions, goods, or services were donated, supplied, or furnished to or for the use of, approved, selected, or used by the [USOC] or United States Olympic or Pan-American team or team members.

"(c) The [USOC] shall have exclusive right to use the name 'United States Olympic Committee'; the symbol described in subsection (a)(1) of this section; the emblem described in subsection (a)(2) of this section; and the words 'Olympic', 'Olympiad', 'Citius Altius Fortius' or any combination thereof subject to the preexisting rights described in subsection (a) of this section."

III

This Court has recognized that "national protection of trademarks is desirable ... because trademarks foster competition and the maintenance of quality by securing to the producer the benefits of good reputation." *Park 'N Fly, Inc.* v. *Dollar Park and Fly, Inc.*, 469 U.S. 189, 198 (1985). In the Lanham Act, 15 U.S.C. § 1051 *et seq.*, Congress established a system for protecting such trademarks. Section 45 of the Lanham Act defines a trademark as "any word, name, symbol, or device or any combination thereof adopted and used by a manufacturer or merchant to identify and distinguish his goods, including a unique product, from those manufactured or sold by others." 15 U.S.C. § 1127 (1982 ed., Supp. III). Under § 32 of the Lanham Act, the owner of a trademark is protected from unauthorized uses that are "likely to cause confusion, or to cause mistake, or to deceive." § 1114(1)(a). Section 33 of the Lanham Act grants several statutory defenses to an alleged trademark infringer. § 1115.

The protection granted to the USOC's use of the Olympic words and symbols differs from the normal trademark protection in two respects: the USOC need not prove that a contested use is likely to cause confusion, and an unauthorized user of the word does not have available the normal statutory defenses. The SFAA argues, in effect, that the differences between the Lanham Act and § 110 are of constitutional dimension. First, the SFAA contends that the word "Olympic" is a generic word that could not gain trademark protection under the Lanham Act. The SFAA argues that this prohibition is constitutionally required and thus that the First Amendment prohibits Congress from granting a trademark in the word "Olympic." Second, the SFAA argues that the First Amendment prohibits Congress from granting exclusive use of a word absent a requirement that the authorized user prove that an unauthorized use is likely to cause confusion. We address these contentions in turn.

A

. . . .

The history of the origins and associations of the word "Olympic" demonstrates the meritlessness of the SFAA's contention that Congress simply plucked a generic word out of the English vocabulary and granted its exclusive use to the USOC. Congress reasonably could find that since 1896, the word "Olympic" has acquired what in trademark law is known as a secondary meaning—it "has become distinctive of [the USOC's] goods in commerce." Lanham Act, § 2(f), 15 U.S.C. § 1052(f). See *Park 'N Fly, Inc.* v. *Dollar Park and Fly, Inc.*, 469 U.S., at 194. The right to adopt and use such a word "to distinguish the goods or property [of] the person whose mark it is, to the exclusion of use by all other persons, has been long recognized." *Trade–Mark Cases, supra,* at 92. Because Congress reasonably could conclude that the USOC has distinguished the word "Olympic" through its own efforts, Congress' decision to grant the USOC a limited property right in the word "Olympic" falls within the scope of trademark law protections, and thus certainly within constitutional bounds.

B

Congress also acted reasonably when it concluded that the USOC should not be required to prove that an unauthorized use of the word "Olympic" is likely to confuse the public. To the extent that § 110 applies to uses "for the purpose of trade [or] to induce the sale of any goods or services," *36 U. S. C. § 380*(a), its application is to commercial speech. Commercial speech "receives a limited form of First Amendment protection." *Posadas de Puerto Rico Assoc.* v. *Tourism Company of Puerto Rico,* 478 U.S. 328, 340 (1986); *Central Hudson Gas & Electric Corp.* v. *Public Service Comm'n of New York,* 447 U.S. 557, 562–563 (1980). Section 110 also allows the USOC to prohibit the use of "Olympic" for promotion of theatrical and athletic events. Although many of these promotional uses will be commercial speech, some uses may go beyond the "strictly business" context. See *Friedman v. Rogers,* 440 U.S. 1, 11 (1979). In this case, the SFAA claims that its use of the word "Olympic" was intended to convey a political statement about the status of homosexuals in society. Thus, the SFAA claims that in this case § 110 suppresses political speech.

By prohibiting the use of one word for particular purposes, neither Congress nor the USOC has prohibited the SFAA from conveying its message. The SFAA held its athletic event in its planned format under the names "Gay Games I" and "Gay Games II" in 1982 and 1986, respectively. See n. 2, *supra.* Nor is it clear that § 110 restricts purely expressive uses of the word "Olympic." Section 110 restricts only the manner in which the SFAA may convey its message. The restrictions on expressive speech properly are characterized as incidental to the primary congressional purpose of encouraging and rewarding the USOC's activities. The appropriate inquiry is thus whether the incidental restrictions on First Amendment freedoms are greater than necessary to further a substantial governmental interest. *United States v. O'Brien,* 391 U.S. 367, 377 (1968).

One reason for Congress to grant the USOC exclusive control of the word "Olympic," as with other trademarks, is to ensure that the USOC receives the benefit of its own efforts so that the USOC will have an incentive to continue to produce a "quality product," that, in turn, benefits the public. See 1 J. McCarthy, Trademarks and Unfair Competition § 2:1, pp. 44–47 (1984). But in the special circumstance of the USOC, Congress has a broader public interest in promoting, through the activities of the USOC, the participation of amateur athletes from the United States in "the great four-yearly sport festival, the Olympic Games." Olympic Charter, Rule 1 (1985). The USOC's goal under the Olympic Charter, Rule 24(B), is to further the Olympic movement, that has as its aims: "to promote the development of those physical and moral qualities which are the basis of sport"; "to educate young people through sport in a spirit of better understanding between each other and of friendship, thereby helping to build a better and more peaceful world"; and "to spread the Olympic principles throughout the world, thereby creating international goodwill." *Id.,* Rule 1. See also *id.,* Rule 11 (aims of the IOC). Congress' interests in promoting the USOC's activities include these purposes as well as those specifically enumerated in the USOC's charter. Section 110 directly advances these governmental interests by supplying the USOC with the means to raise money to support the Olympics and encourages the USOC's activities by ensuring that it will receive the benefits of its efforts.

The restrictions of § 110 are not broader than Congress reasonably could have determined to be necessary to further these interests. Section 110 primarily applies to all uses of the word "Olympic" to induce the sale of goods or services. Although the Lanham Act protects only against confusing uses, Congress' judgment respecting a certain word is not so limited. Congress reasonably could conclude that most commercial uses of the Olympic words and symbols are likely to be confusing. It also could determine that unauthorized uses, even if not confusing, nevertheless may harm the USOC by lessening the distinctiveness and thus the commercial value of the marks. See Schechter, *The Rational Basis of Trademark Protection*, 40 Harv. L. Rev. 813, 825 (1927) (one injury to a trademark owner may be "the gradual whittling away or dispersion of the identity and hold upon the public mind of the mark or name" by nonconfusing uses).

In this case, the SFAA sought to sell T-shirts, buttons, bumper stickers, and other items, all emblazoned with the title "Gay Olympic Games." The possibility for confusion as to sponsorship is obvious. Moreover, it is clear that the SFAA sought to exploit the "commercial magnetism," see *Mishawaka Rubber & Woolen Mfg. Co. v. S. S. Kresge Co.*, 316 U.S. 203, 205 (1942), of the word given value by the USOC. There is no question that this unauthorized use could undercut the USOC's efforts to use, and sell the right to use, the word in the future, since much of the word's value comes from its limited use. Such an adverse effect on the USOC's activities is directly contrary to Congress' interest. Even though this protection may exceed the traditional rights of a trademark owner in certain circumstances, the application of the Act to this commercial speech is not broader than necessary to protect the legitimate congressional interest and therefore does not violate the First Amendment.

Section 110 also extends to promotional uses of the word "Olympic," even if the promotion is not to induce the sale of goods. Under § 110, the USOC may prohibit purely promotional uses of the word only when the promotion relates to an athletic or theatrical event. The USOC created the value of the word by using it in connection with an athletic event. Congress reasonably could find that use of the word by other entities to promote an athletic event would directly impinge on the USOC's legitimate right of exclusive use. The SFAA's proposed use of the word is an excellent example. The "Gay Olympic Games" were to take place over a 9–day period and were to be held in different locations around the world. They were to include a torch relay, a parade with uniformed athletes of both sexes divided by city, an "Olympic anthem" and "Olympic Committee," and the award of gold, silver, and bronze medals, and were advertised under a logo of three overlapping rings. All of these features directly parallel the modern-day Olympics, not the Olympic Games that occurred in ancient Greece. The image the SFAA sought to invoke was exactly the image carefully cultivated by the USOC. The SFAA's expressive use of the word cannot be divorced from the value the USOC's efforts have given to it. The mere fact that the SFAA claims an expressive, as opposed to a purely commercial, purpose does not give it a First Amendment right to "appropriat[e] to itself the harvest of those who have sown." *International News Service v. Associated* Press, 248 U.S., at 239–240. The USOC's right to prohibit use of the word "Olympic" in the promotion of athletic events is at the core of its legitimate property right.

. . . .

V

Accordingly, we affirm the judgment of the Court of Appeals for the Ninth Circuit. *It is so ordered.*

■ JUSTICE BRENNAN, with whom JUSTICE MARSHALL joins, *dissenting:*

The Court wholly fails to appreciate both the congressionally created interdependence between the United States Olympic Committee (USOC) and the United States, and the significant extent to which § 110 of the Amateur Sports Act of 1978, 36 U.S.C. § 380, infringes on noncommercial speech. I would find that the action of the USOC challenged here is Government action, and that § 110 is both substantially overbroad and discriminates on the basis of content. I therefore dissent.

. . . .

Section 110(a)(4) prohibits "any person" from using the word "Olympic" "without the consent of the [USOC] for the purpose of trade, to induce the sale of any goods or services, or to promote any theatrical exhibition, athletic performance, or competition." The Court construes this section to give the USOC authority over use of the word "Olympic" which far surpasses that provided by a standard trademark. The Court ignores the serious First Amendment problems created by its interpretation. It holds that § 110(a)(4) regulates primarily commercial speech, and that this section imposes only those incidental restrictions on expressive speech necessary to further a substantial governmental interest. *Ante,* at 535–541.

I disagree. The statute is overbroad on its face because it is susceptible of application to a substantial amount of non-commercial speech, and vests the USOC with unguided discretion to approve and disapprove others' noncommercial use of "Olympic." Moreover, by eliminating even noncommercial uses of a particular word, it unconstitutionally infringes on the SFAA's right to freedom of expression. The Act also restricts speech in a way that is not content neutral. The Court's justifications of these infringements on First Amendment rights are flimsy. The statute cannot be characterized as a mere regulation of the "manner" of speech, and does not serve any Government purpose that would not effectively be protected by giving the USOC a standard commercial trademark. Therefore, as construed by the Court, § 110(a)(4) cannot withstand the First Amendment challenge presented by petitioners.

ROCHELLE COOPER DREYFUSS, EXPRESSIVE GENERICITY: TRADE-MARKS AS LANGUAGE IN THE PEPSI GENERATION, 65 Notre Dame L. Rev. 397–98, 412–17 (footnotes omitted) (1990)

Trademarks have come a long way. Originating in the stratified econo-my of the middle ages as a marketing tool of the merchant class, these symbols have passed into popular culture. During the journey, ideograms that once functioned solely as signals denoting the source, origin, and quality of goods, have become products in their own right, valued as indicators of the status, preferences, and aspirations of those who use them. Some trademarks have worked their way into the English language; others provide bases for vibrant, evocative metaphors. In a sense, trade-marks are the emerging lingua franca: with a sufficient command of these terms, one can make oneself understood the world over, and in the process, enjoy the comforts of home.

Trademark law has not kept pace with trademark practice. Concerned initially with maintaining the lines of communication between the mercan-tile class and its customers, the law encouraged entrepreneurs to invest in quality-producing activities by protecting the goodwill that inhered in their source-identifying marks. Thus, in both state unfair competition cases and federal trademark actions, claims focused on the impact of the mark on purchasing decisions. By the same token, defenses centered on the commer-cial requirements of the competitive marketplace. The terms that delimited the reach of trademark law—consumer confusion, gap bridging, fair use, genericity, abandonment—were understood strictly by reference to these commercial interests.

But as trademark owners have begun to capitalize on the salience of these symbols in the culture, the justifications that formerly delineated the scope of the law have lost significance. The Mets' right to prevent others from selling banners, caps, and tee shirts marked with its logo could not initially be explained on quality-promotion grounds so long as it was clear that fans are not confused, and that they did not regard the franchise as insuring the quality of anything but a baseball team. Nor does traditional trademark law offer an account for, or limits to, McDonald's claim to control non-food uses of the prefix "Mc," or George Lucas's attempt to exclude public interest groups from utilizing the title of his movie, "Star Wars."

. . . .

The Gay Olympics case is a good context in which to consider the connection between the vehicles of speech and the efficacy of communica-tion because in claiming that the word "Olympic" was generic and avail-able to all, SFAA essentially made the argument that the loss of the ability to use "Olympic" was effectively suppression of its speech. Although somewhat opaque on this point, the Court managed to duck the constitu-tional issue. Instead, it held that since "Gay Games" informed potential customers that tickets would entitle them to view athletic competitions, that term was an adequate substitute for the challenged mark, "Gay Olympic Games."

In fact, this substitution is highly inadequate. SFAA was not an impresario of sporting events, similar in function and purpose to the NBA, NFL, or PGA. Rather, a nonprofit corporation organized under California law, its mission was to educate the public about homosexuality, to portray it positively, to provide recreation for homosexuals, and to create a climate of friendship and cooperation among people of all sexual preferences. To further that goal by demonstrating that gay people are as athletic as anyone else, SFAA created a series of competitive sporting events. To recall the tenets of the ancient Greeks and to evoke their spirit of cooperation, mutual acceptance, and international friendship, it called the tournament the "Gay Olympic Games." While the events could easily be called "Gay Games," that title conveys none of this history and elicits none of these associations. Thus, no matter how successful "Gay Games" were in the marketplace of athletic events, it is doubtful that a society accustomed to receiving information in easily swallowed "sound bites" fully appreciated the message that SFAA was trying to interject into the marketplace of ideas.

It is not only ironic that in a case about communication, the Court managed to misinterpret the message that SFAA was attempting to convey. In translating "Olympic" as "game" and missing the rich set of connotations that surround the former expression, the Court illustrated just how much words and their paraphrases differ. There is an open texture to certain words that makes them much more than "a short cut from mind to mind." This openness comes, in part, from the fact that some words have core denotations (definitions that can be found in a dictionary), and a set of connotations that depend upon their history, derivation, and identification with users. These peripheral meanings are often highly individualized to the speaker, the listener, and possibly to the method by which they interact or perceive one another. When such words are used, they become infused with the listener's own associations, and their message is incorporated into the listener's own frame of reference. The result is that the expression as perceived can have much greater impact on the recipient's thinking than the words that were actually transmitted.

Studies of cognition reveal that words can be open-textured in a stronger sense as well. Because words sometimes have several core meanings, particular usages can require listeners to consider several denotations, their respective connotations, and the connections between them. This effort can lead to a new level of understanding, which might not have been achieved by words lacking the same associational set. Nor would these insights be produced by an expanded statement of meaning because a paraphrase of a word, like a paraphrase of any other metaphor, closes the set of associations and constrains the field of connections that are necessary to the expansion of perception.

Paradoxically, words can advance understanding not only by splintering and juxtaposing associations, but also by crystallizing the relationship between diverse experiences. For example, the early stage of scientific inquiry can be understood as a process of proposing nominal definitions, which are expressions naming concepts and defining the criteria for deciding when the concepts apply. The defined terms are then utilized in higher level manipulation, such as ordering, empirical testing, and, ultimately, the formulation of theoretical constructs. Although it is the empirical import of these constructs—their explanatory and predictive capacity—that is the essence of scientific advance, it is the definitional and classification procedure that enables scientists to find the correlations between observables that makes theorizing possible.

Linguists understand the role that specific words play in structuring thought and organizing experience. They observe the phenomenon described above as reflected in the correlation between language patterns and theoretical constructs, and also the rapidity with which cultures devise words to fit new conceptualizations. Were the relationship between a word and its paraphrase merely a short cut, language groups could afford to take time developing words to suit new needs. Instead, even the French, who zealously guard linguistic integrity, are quick to fill empty vocabulary slots, even if that requires borrowing phrases from other languages.

Similarly, physicians who treat aphasia, the loss of language, find that it is a more profound disorder than muteness, the loss of speech. The inability of aphasics to comprehend particular words interferes with the operations that they need to think. A grasp of literal meaning is not helpful, as cognition is often mediated by the metaphorical character of words, which provoke comparisons between phenomena, or by their metonymic significance, which induce understanding of the whole of a phenomenon from consideration of a part of it. Thus, it is not only that technology has shortened attention span to the point where only messages packaged into "sound bites" are heard, though that phenomenon is certainly important to consider when contemplating claims to individual words. It may well be the case that the human intellect is constructed such that it is the density with which information is packed that is critical. If densely packed units—words infused with sets of denotations and associated connotations—are processed more readily than longer, less concentrated linguistic segments, loss of words can, in a very real sense, be equated with loss of the ability to communicate.

Of course, even if the connection between words and thought is conceded, it could be argued that no particular word is essential to communication, as the process of nominal definition could be utilized to induce a shift in concept identifiers. So, for example, If SFAA felt that not enough meaning were packed into "Gay Games," it could redefine the idea of cooperation, acceptance, international friendship, and competition by announcing, "let 'Grekko' stand for 'Olympic.'" Calling the sporting events "Gay Grekko Games" would then have as much impact as the title that utilized "Olympic." Since this process demands some use of the trademark, accepting it would require recognition of a limited form of fair use (a sort of definitional use), but trademark owners like the USOC would be fully protected without sacrificing expressive concerns.

The difficulty with such a procedure is that words do not become part of the effective language as easily as this process would require. At any given time, speakers experiment with a wide variety of sound groups (phonemes), but only a small number of these potential words actually enter the vocabulary. Although linguists have not developed a complete theory for predicting which sounds become words, the innovations that are successful tend to share certain traits. They are made up of sound clusters that are euphonious, readily pronounced, easily inflected, and accommodate well to grammatical rules. Either because there are a large number of initial users or because the phonemes contain internal cues, the meaning of successful words are quickly grasped. They are introduced by prestigious speakers whom others wish to emulate, or by speakers who are mobile enough to spread the new word efficiently. Not every group of phonemes meets the first set of requirements; finding ones that do can be expensive, especially if the word is to enter more than one language. Added to this is the cost of educating the right seed group so that the new word and its meaning spread to others.

Since the process of producing a word is expensive, the real question in requiring substitution through nominal definition is, who should pay the cost. As between members of the public (such as SFAA) who wish to use trademarks expressively and trademark owners (such as the USOC), the latter appears to be the superior choice. First, the cost of developing perfect synonyms for marks could be considered part of the quid pro quo for acquiring control over them. It is, in contrast, difficult to see how a single expressive user could capture enough of the benefits of a new word to compensate for the cost of developing it. Although this user could ask for contributions from the public, which would also benefit from the naming of new conceptualizations, the transaction costs involved in such an enterprise are likely to be prohibitive. Second, trademark owners are already in the business of developing words and advertising their meaning. The marginal cost of developing two words for the same concept is surely lower than the cost that a member of the public would incur in creating only one word. Moreover, words are most readily adopted into language when they fill conceptual voids; indeed, most trademarks that have passed into the language have done so precisely because there was no other word to describe the product they signified. Since trademark owners control timing, they are in the best position to exploit the window of opportunity provided by the existence of empty language slots.

In fact, the notion of imposing this duty on trademark owners is not new, for the doctrine of genericity works exactly this way. It protects the efficacy of communication by recognizing the public's need for a trademark that becomes the common signifier for the set to which the product on which it appears belongs. Such marks are considered generic, and a successful demonstration of genericity is a defense to infringement actions. Not only does the doctrine protect public access to important words, it has a significant side effect. An owner that does not wish to lose its mark will often introduce a second word, which it educates the public to use for the category. The trademark itself can then retain its role as a signal. Thus,

General Foods has successfully promoted the term "decaffeinated coffee" to protect "Sanka" from genericization and Xerox is currently working on public acceptance for "photocopy." As a result of these efforts, the public obtains more than just a few new words: it acquires the vehicles necessary to formulate questions about whether Sanka is the best decaffeinated coffee, or Xerox the best photocopier. Indeed, SFAA had suggested precisely this approach in Gay Olympics. Had it been successful, the Court's declaration that the 2000–year old Greek word was generic would have forced Congress to release "Olympic" to the public and to emulate General Foods and Xerox by developing a second series of terms for the USOC to sell.

But SFAA's failure to convince the Court of the genericity of "Olympic" may hold the key to resolving the problem of public access to marks in a legal regime intent on expanding proprietary rights. Thus, the explanation for the Court's willingness to accept "games" as a substitute for "Olympic" may lie in the fact that it compartmentalized the vocabulary into expressive and competitive components. Since it took the genericity defense solely in its traditional form, as a claim about the competitive vocabulary, it evaluated the word in only the competitive context, as a word denoting athletic tournaments, and came to the conclusion that ample synonyms were readily available. Had it instead focused on the expressive significance of "Olympic," and looked for replacements that would evoke the tenets of the ancient Greeks, it might have reached a different result on the genericity issue.

QUESTION

When the International Olympic Committee adopted the OLYMPIC service mark, the word already had a long history and possessed multiple connotations. Like many initially descriptive marks, it went on to build up substantial secondary meaning, but some portion of its goodwill reflected the meanings the term had acquired before its adoption as a mark. In that circumstance, the public's interest in using the term seem especially compelling. Do the same considerations apply in cases in which an arbitrary or fanciful trademark enters the language as a metaphor? Mickey Mouse,® Twinkies,® Star Wars,® and Spam® have all acquired non-trademark significance in part because of their popularity. The Marlboro® Man is an instantly recognizable symbol, which embodies both the goodwill of a distinct brand of cigarette and a medley of associations related to smoking and tobacco. Should the trademark owners' interests in protecting their marks from infringement and dilution yield whenever the public appropriates a trademark and gives it new connotations?

A.   REFERENTIAL USE

New Kids on the Block v. News America Publishing

971 F.2d 302 (9th Cir.1992).

[The opinion is *supra* chapter 6.C.2.c, page 462]

Dow Jones & Company, Inc. v. International Securities, 451 F.3d 295 (2d Cir.2006). Dow Jones and McGraw–Hill sued an options trading exchange, which had announced its intention to institute options trading pegged to plaintiffs' stock indices. Plaintiffs argued that defendants' use of the underlying indices misappropriated their intellectual property interests in the indices and infringed and diluted their trademarks. The trial court dismissed both plaintiffs' complaints. The Court of Appeals for the Second Circuit affirmed. Assuming without deciding that plaintiffs did own intellectual property rights in their stock indices, the court held that none of defendant's behavior misappropriated those rights:

> Plaintiffs intentionally disseminate their index values to inform the public. They cannot complain when the defendants do nothing more than draw information from that publication of the index values. The complaints do not specify any use of the indexes likely to be made by the defendants that would constitute misappropriation.

Plaintiff's infringement and dilution claims focused on defendant's use of the trademarks for plaintiffs' indices in promoting its options. The court found that those claims failed as a matter of law:

> While a trademark conveys an exclusive right to the use of a mark in commerce in the area reserved, that right generally does not prevent one who trades a branded product from accurately describing it by its brand name, so long as the trader does not create confusion by implying an affiliation with the owner of the product.

Kassbaum v. Steppenwolf Productions, Inc.

236 F.3d 487 (9th Cir.2000).

■ GOULD, CIRCUIT JUDGE:

In 1967, John Kay, Jerry Edmonton, Michael Monarch and Goldie McJohn formed a musical band called "Steppenwolf." In 1968, Nicholas Kassbaum, who is professionally known as "Nick St. Nicholas," joined Steppenwolf as a bass player. That year, the band members entered into a partnership agreement whereby the members became co-equal partners and owners in Steppenwolf, and agreed to share equally the band's expenses and income. Also in 1968, the band members signed a recording agreement with Dunhill Records both as partners and as Steppenwolf band members.

From late 1968 until late April 1970, Steppenwolf, with Kassbaum as its bass player, toured the world in concerts and recorded Steppenwolf's well-received music. Kassbaum appeared prominently on Steppenwolf record album covers and authored Steppenwolf compositions. In 1971, John Kay, who had asserted control over Steppenwolf, excluded Kassbaum from the band.

. . . .

[In 1980, Kassbaum signed an agreement acknowledging that Steppenwolf Productions, Inc. owned the "Steppenwolf" service mark.]

From 1980, when the contract was executed, until 1996, Kassbaum performed as "Lone Wolf." During that time, without objection from the parties to the 1980 contract, Kassbaum referred to his historical association with Steppenwolf, describing himself as a "former member of" or "previous member of" "Steppenwolf."

From 1996 until the present, Kassbaum has performed in a group called World Classic Rockers. The group is comprised of former members of various musical groups well known to rock music fans including: Randy Meiser, a former member of "Wings;" Spencer Davis, a former member of the "Spencer Davis Group;" Bruce Gary, a former member of "Knack;" and Michael Monarch and Kassbaum, former members of Steppenwolf. While performing as the World Classic Rockers, Kassbaum and the other band members often identified themselves by referring to their former musical associations. For example, one advertisement identifies Kassbaum as "NICK ST. NICHOLAS former member of Steppenwolf." Kassbaum also promoted himself as being a "Former Original Member of Steppenwolf," "Original Founding Member of Steppenwolf," and "Formerly of Steppenwolf."

In response to these promotional claims, SPI and SI sent Kassbaum cease and desist letters asserting that Kassbaum's historical references to Steppenwolf violated federal trademark law and the 1980 contract. Kassbaum then filed a complaint in federal district court seeking a declaration that he is entitled to refer to himself as "Formerly of Steppenwolf," an "Original Member of Steppenwolf," and an "Original Founding Member of Steppenwolf." SPI answered and filed a counterclaim alleging trademark infringement, unfair competition and breach of contract. Thereafter, SPI and SI moved for summary judgment on Kassbaum's complaint for declaratory relief and SPI's counterclaim for breach of contract. SPI and SI also sought permanently to enjoin Kassbaum and his agents from using the name Steppenwolf.

The district court granted SPI and SI's motion for summary judgment on Kassbaum's complaint for declaratory relief, granted SPI's counterclaim for breach of contract, dismissed Kassbaum's complaint for declaratory relief, and granted SPI and SI's request for a permanent injunction forbidding Kassbaum from using the designations "Formerly of Steppenwolf," "Original Member of Steppenwolf" and "Original Founding Member of Steppenwolf," in promotional materials.

Kassbaum appeals, contending that the district court erred. We agree, and we reverse and remand.

DISCUSSION

. . . .

B. Lanham Act

Kassbaum's complaint requests, inter alia, a declaratory judgment that section 32(1)(a) of the Lanham Act, 15 U.S.C § 1114(1)(a), does not bar him from stating, particularly in promotional materials, that he was

"Formerly of Steppenwolf," an "Original Member of Steppenwolf," or an "Original Founding Member of Steppenwolf." The district court dismissed Kassbaum's complaint and granted SPI and SI's motion for summary judgment. We reverse.

. . . .

The purpose of a trademark is to allow customers to identify the manufacturer or sponsor of a good or the provider of a service. *New Kids on the Block v. News. Am. Pub., Inc.*, 971 F.2d 302, 305 (9th Cir.1992). Actual consumer confusion is not required for profit recovery; it is sufficient to show a likelihood of confusion combined with willful infringement. *Gracie v. Gracie*, 217 F.3d 1060, 1068 (9th Cir.2000). For the reasons that follow, we believe that Kassbaum's references to himself in promotional materials as "Formerly of Steppenwolf," an "Original Member of Steppenwolf," and an "Original Founding Member of Steppenwolf," do not cause a likelihood of confusion.

First, we believe the phrases "Formerly of," "Original Member of" and "Original Founding Member of," immediately preceding the name "Steppenwolf" in the promotional materials for World Classic Rockers greatly reduce the likelihood of confusion about the source of the band's music.

Additionally, the context of the historical references to Kassbaum's affiliation with Steppenwolf in World Classic Rockers' promotional materials further reduces any likelihood of confusion between these two bands. In all promotional materials presented to the district court, references to World Classic Rockers are more prominent than are references to Steppenwolf. The materials display the title "World Classic Rockers" on the top or at the center of the page, while references to the band members' former groups, including Steppenwolf, are displayed on the bottom or around the edges of the page. Also, the title "World Classic Rockers" appears in large and bold lettering, while smaller and plainer lettering is used for the titles of the former groups, including Steppenwolf. Finally, while the materials mention multiple former groups, the materials promote only World Classic Rockers, not Steppenwolf, or any other former band.

Our holding is supported by cases in similar contexts. For example, in *Kingsmen v. K–Tel International Ltd.*, 557 F. Supp. 178 (S.D.N.Y.1983), the district court distinguished the likelihood of confusion that exists when a former member of a band re-records a song under the name of the original band from the likelihood of confusion that exists when the former member re-records a song under his own name with the designation "formerly of" the original band displayed on the recording. . . .

. . . .

Finally, we wholeheartedly agree with Justice Holmes's statement about the limits of trademark protection in *Prestonettes, Inc. v. Coty*, 264 U.S. 359, 368, 68 L. Ed. 731, 44 S. Ct. 350 (1924): "When the mark is used in a way that does not deceive the public we see no such sanctity in the word as to prevent its being used to tell the truth. It is not taboo." We reverse the district court's order granting summary judgment to SPI and SI and dismissing Kassbaum's complaint for declaratory judgment as to the Lanham Act issue.

. . . .

REVERSED and REMANDED.

Playboy Enterprises, Inc. v. Welles

279 F.3d 796 (9th Cir.2002).

Playboy Metatag Case [handwritten]

■ T.G. NELSON, CIRCUIT JUDGE:

Playboy Enterprises, Inc. (PEI), appeals the district court's grant of summary judgment as to its claims of trademark infringement, unfair competition, and breach of contract against Terri Welles; Terri Welles, Inc.; Pippi, Inc.; and Welles' current and former "webmasters," Steven Huntington and Michael Mihalko. We have jurisdiction pursuant to 28 U.S.C. § 1291, and we affirm in part and reverse in part.

. . .

I.

Background

Terri Welles was on the cover of Playboy in 1981 and was chosen to be the Playboy Playmate of the Year for 1981. Her use of the title "Playboy Playmate of the Year 1981," and her use of other trademarked terms on her website are at issue in this suit. During the relevant time period, Welles' website offered information about and free photos of Welles, advertised photos for sale, advertised memberships in her photo club, and promoted her services as a spokesperson. A biographical section described Welles' selection as Playmate of the Year in 1981 and her years modeling for PEI. After the lawsuit began, Welles included discussions of the suit and criticism of PEI on her website and included a note disclaiming any association with PEI.[1]

PEI complains of four different uses of its trademarked terms on Welles' website: (1) the terms "Playboy" and "Playmate" in the metatags of the website;[2] (2) the phrase "Playmate of the Year 1981" on the masthead of the website; (3) the phrases "Playboy Playmate of the Year 1981" and "Playmate of the Year 1981" on various banner ads, which may be transferred to other websites; and (4) the repeated use of the abbreviation "PMOY '81" as the watermark on the pages of the website.[3] PEI

---

1. The disclaimer reads as follows: "This site is neither endorsed, nor sponsored, nor affiliated with Playboy Enterprises, Inc. PLAYBOY® PLAYMATE OF THE YEAR® AND PLAYMATE OF THE MONTH® are registered trademarks of Playboy Enterprises, Inc."

2. Metatags are hidden code used by some search engines to determine the content of websites in order to direct searchers to relevant sites.

3. PEI claims that "PMOY" is an unregistered trademark of PEI, standing for "Playmate of the Year."

claimed that these uses of its marks constituted trademark infringement, dilution, false designation of origin, and unfair competition. The district court granted defendants' motion for summary judgment. PEI appeals the grant of summary judgment on its infringement and dilution claims. We affirm in part and reverse in part.

. . .

III.

Discussion

A. Trademark Infringement

Except for the use of PEI's protected terms in the wallpaper of Welles' website, we conclude that Welles' uses of PEI's trademarks are permissible, nominative uses. They imply no current sponsorship or endorsement by PEI. Instead, they serve to identify Welles as a past PEI "Playmate of the Year."[7]

We articulated the test for a permissible, nominative use in *New Kids On The Block v. New America Publishing, Inc.* The band, New Kids On The Block, claimed trademark infringement arising from the use of their trademarked name by several newspapers. The newspapers had conducted polls asking which member of the band New Kids On The Block was the best and most popular. The papers' use of the trademarked term did not fall within the traditional fair use doctrine. Unlike a traditional fair use scenario, the defendant newspaper was using the trademarked term to describe not its own product, but the plaintiff's. Thus, the factors used to evaluate fair use were inapplicable. The use was nonetheless permissible, we concluded, based on its nominative nature.

We adopted the following test for nominative use:

> First, the product or service in question must be one not readily identifiable without use of the trademark; second, only so much of the mark or marks may be used as is reasonably necessary to identify the product or service; and third, the user must do nothing that would, in conjunction with the mark, suggest sponsorship or endorsement by the trademark holder.[12]

We noted in *New Kids* that a nominative use may also be a commercial one.

In cases in which the defendant raises a nominative use defense, the above three-factor test should be applied instead of the test for likelihood of confusion set forth in [*AMF v.*] *Sleekcraft*.[14] The three-factor test better

---

7. *See New Kids on the Block v. News America Publ'g, Inc.,* 971 F.2d 302, 306 (9th Cir.1992) (describing a nominative use as one that "does not imply sponsorship or endorsement of the product because the mark is used only to describ e thing, rather than to identify its sou .

12. *New Kids,* 971 F.2d at 308 (footnote omitted).

14. 599 F.2d at 348–49. [Editors' note: The *Sleekcraft* factors are the 9th Circuit's eight-factor test for likelihood of confusion.]

evaluates the likelihood of confusion in nominative use cases. When a defendant uses a trademark nominally, the trademark will be identical to the plaintiff's mark, at least in terms of the words in question. Thus, application of the *Sleekcraft* test, which focuses on the similarity of the mark used by the plaintiff and the defendant, would lead to the incorrect conclusion that virtually all nominative uses are confusing. The three-factor test—with its requirements that the defendant use marks only when no descriptive substitute exists, use no more of the mark than necessary, and do nothing to suggest sponsorship or endorsement by the mark holder—better addresses concerns regarding the likelihood of confusion in nominative use cases.

We group the uses of PEI's trademarked terms into three for the purpose of applying the test for nominative use. First, we analyze Welles' use of the terms in headlines and banner advertisements. We conclude that those uses are clearly nominative. Second, we analyze the use of the terms in the metatags for Welles' website, which we conclude are nominative as well. Finally, we analyze the terms as used in the wallpaper of the website. We conclude that this use is not nominative and remand for a determination of whether it infringes on a PEI trademark.

1. *Headlines and banner advertisements.*

To satisfy the first part of the test for nominative use, "the product or service in question must be one not readily identifiable without use of the trademark[.]" This situation arises "when a trademark also describes a person, a place or an attribute of a product" and there is no descriptive substitute for the trademark. In such a circumstance, allowing the trademark holder exclusive rights would allow the language to "be depleted in much the same way as if generic words were protectable." In *New Kids*, we gave the example of the trademarked term, "Chicago Bulls." We explained that "one might refer to the 'two-time world champions' or 'the professional basketball team from Chicago,' but it's far simpler (and more likely to be understood) to refer to the Chicago Bulls." Moreover, such a use of the trademark would "not imply sponsorship or endorsement of the product because the mark is used only to describe the thing, rather than to identify its source." Thus, we concluded, such uses must be excepted from trademark infringement law.

The district court properly identified Welles' situation as one which must also be excepted. No descriptive substitute exists for PEI's trademarks in this context. The court explained:

> There is no other way that Ms. Welles can identify or describe herself and her services without venturing into absurd descriptive phrases. To describe herself as the "nude model selected by Mr. Hefner's magazine as its number-one prototypical woman for the year 1981" would be impractical as well as ineffectual in identifying Terri Welles to the public.

We agree. Just as the newspapers in *New Kids* could only identify the band clearly by using its trademarked name, so can Welles only identify herself clearly by using PEI's trademarked title.

The second part of the nominative use test requires that "only so much of the mark or marks may be used as is reasonably necessary to identify the product or service[.]" *New Kids* provided the following examples to explain this element: "[A] soft drink competitor would be entitled to compare its product to Coca–Cola or Coke, but would not be entitled to use Coca–Cola's distinctive lettering." Similarly, in a past case, an auto shop was allowed to use the trademarked term "Volkswagen" on a sign describing the cars it repaired, in part because the shop "did not use Volkswagen's distinctive lettering style or color scheme, nor did he display the encircled 'VW' emblem." Welles' banner advertisements and headlines satisfy this element because they use only the trademarked words, not the font or symbols associated with the trademarks.

The third element requires that the user do "nothing that would, in conjunction with the mark, suggest sponsorship or endorsement by the trademark holder." As to this element, we conclude that aside from the wallpaper, which we address separately, Welles does nothing in conjunction with her use of the marks to suggest sponsorship or endorsement by PEI. The marks are clearly used to describe the title she received from PEI in 1981, a title that helps describe who she is. It would be unreasonable to assume that the Chicago Bulls sponsored a website of Michael Jordan's simply because his name appeared with the appellation "former Chicago Bull." Similarly, in this case, it would be unreasonable to assume that PEI currently sponsors or endorses someone who describes herself as a "Playboy Playmate of the Year in 1981." The designation of the year, in our case, serves the same function as the "former" in our example. It shows that any sponsorship or endorsement occurred in the past.[25]

In addition to doing nothing in conjunction with her use of the marks to suggest sponsorship or endorsement by PEI, Welles affirmatively disavows any sponsorship or endorsement. Her site contains a clear statement disclaiming any connection to PEI. Moreover, the text of the site describes her ongoing legal battles with the company.[26]

For the foregoing reasons, we conclude that Welles' use of PEI's marks in her headlines and banner advertisements is a nominative use excepted from the law of trademark infringement.

Welles includes the terms "playboy" and "playmate" in her metatags. Metatags describe the contents of a website using keywords. Some search engines search metatags to identify websites relevant to a search. Thus, when an internet searcher enters "playboy" or "playmate" into a search

25. We express no opinion regarding whether an individual's use of a current title would suggest sponsorship or endorsement.

26. By noting Welles' affirmative actions, we do not mean to imply that affirmative actions of this type are necessary to establish nominative use. *New Kids* sets forth no such requirement, and we do not impose one here.

engine that uses metatags, the results will include Welles' site.[28] Because Welles' metatags do not repeat the terms extensively, her site will not be at the top of the list of search results. Applying the three-factor test for nominative use, we conclude that the use of the trademarked terms in Welles' metatags is nominative.

As we discussed above with regard to the headlines and banner advertisements, Welles has no practical way of describing herself without using trademarked terms. In the context of metatags, we conclude that she has no practical way of identifying the content of her website without referring to PEI's trademarks.

A large portion of Welles' website discusses her association with Playboy over the years. Thus, the trademarked terms accurately describe the contents of Welles' website, in addition to describing Welles. Forcing Welles and others to use absurd turns of phrase in their metatags, such as those necessary to identify Welles, would be particularly damaging in the internet search context. Searchers would have a much more difficult time locating relevant websites if they could do so only by correctly guessing the long phrases necessary to substitute for trademarks. We can hardly expect someone searching for Welles' site to imagine the same phrase proposed by the district court to describe Welles without referring to Playboy—"the nude model selected by Mr. Hefner's organization...." Yet if someone could not remember her name, that is what they would have to do. Similarly, someone searching for critiques of Playboy on the internet would have a difficult time if internet sites could not list the object of their critique in their metatags.

There is simply no descriptive substitute for the trademarks used in Welles' metatags. Precluding their use would have the unwanted effect of hindering the free flow of information on the internet, something which is certainly not a goal of trademark law.[29] Accordingly, the use of trademarked terms in the metatags meets the first part of the test for nominative use.

We conclude that the metatags satisfy the second and third elements of the test as well. The metatags use only so much of the marks as reasonably necessary and nothing is done in conjunction with them to suggest sponsorship or endorsement by the trademark holder. We note that our decision might differ if the metatags listed the trademarked term so repeatedly that Welles' site would regularly appear above PEI's in searches for one of the trademarked terms.

---

28. We note that search engines that use their own summaries of websites, or that search the entire text of sites, are also likely to identify Welles' site as relevant to a search for "playboy" or "playmate," given the content of the site.

29. Admittedly, this hindrance would only occur as to search engines that use metatags to direct their searches.

3.   *Wallpaper/watermark.*

The background, or wallpaper, of Welles' site consists of the repeated abbreviation "PMOY '81," which stands for "Playmate of the Year 1981."[32] Welles' name or likeness does not appear before or after "PMOY '81." The pattern created by the repeated abbreviation appears as the background of the various pages of the website. Accepting, for the purposes of this appeal, that the abbreviation "PMOY" is indeed entitled to protection, we conclude that the repeated, stylized use of this abbreviation fails the nominative use test.

The repeated depiction of "PMOY '81" is not necessary to describe Welles. "Playboy Playmate of the Year 1981" is quite adequate. Moreover, the term does not even appear to describe Welles—her name or likeness do not appear before or after each "PMOY '81." Because the use of the abbreviation fails the first prong of the nominative use test, we need not apply the next two prongs of the test.

Because the defense of nominative use fails here, and we have already determined that the doctrine of fair use does not apply, we remand to the district court. The court must determine whether trademark law protects the abbreviation "PMOY," as used in the wallpaper.

B.   *Trademark Dilution*

The district court granted summary judgment to Welles as to PEI's claim of trademark dilution. We affirm on the ground that all of Welles' uses of PEI's marks, with the exception of the use in the wallpaper which we address separately, are proper, nominative uses. We hold that nominative uses, by definition, do not dilute the trademarks.

. . . .

When Welles refers to her title, she is in effect referring to a product of PEI's. She does not dilute the title by truthfully identifying herself as its one-time recipient any more than Michael Jordan would dilute the name "Chicago Bulls" by referring to himself as a former member of that team, or the two-time winner of an Academy Award would dilute the award by referring to him or herself as a "two-time Academy Award winner." Awards are not diminished or diluted by the fact that they have been awarded in the past.

Similarly, they are not diminished or diluted when past recipients truthfully identify themselves as such. It is in the nature of honors and awards to be identified with the people who receive them. Of course, the conferrer of such honors and awards is free to limit the honoree's use of the title or references to the award by contract. So long as a use is nominative, however, trademark law is unavailing.

The one exception to the above analysis in this case is Welles' use of the abbreviation "PMOY" on her wallpaper. Because we determined that

---

32.   "PMOY" is not itself registered as a trademark. PEI argued before the district court that it is nonetheless protected because it is a well-known abbreviation for the trade-marked term "Playmate of the Year." In this court PEI cites one affidavit that supports this argument.

this use is not nominative, it is not excepted from the anti-dilution provisions. Thus, we reverse as to this issue and remand for further proceedings. We note that if the district court determines that "PMOY" is not entitled to trademark protection, PEI's claim for dilution must fail. The trademarked term, "Playmate of the Year" is not identical or nearly identical to the term "PMOY." Therefore, use of the term "PMOY" cannot, as a matter of law, dilute the trademark "Playmate of the Year."

IV.

Conclusion

For the foregoing reasons, we affirm the district court's grant of summary judgment as to PEI's claims for trademark infringement and trademark dilution, with the sole exception of the use of the abbreviation "PMOY." We reverse as to the abbreviation and remand for consideration of whether it merits protection under either an infringement or a dilution theory.

. . .

QUESTIONS

1. Would the 2006 amendment to section 43(c) change the result of the court's dilution analysis?

2. Apple Computer Company introduced the iPod MP3 player in October of 2001. It is currently the leading portable MP3 player. Apple filed a trademark application on October 18, 2001 to register "IPOD" as a trademark for portable and handheld electronic devices and associated computer software. Registration issued on April 27, 2004. At the time of Apple's registration, there were several prior registrations for the word "IPOD" for different products, including IPOD Office Furniture, IPOD pulse oximeters, and IPOD financial services. Apple subsequently introduced the iPod Mini, a smaller MP3 player in fruit sherbet colors, and the iPod Photo, a player designed to store and display photos as well as storing and playing music. Apple has not sought registration for "IPOD MINI" or "IPOD PHOTO."

Playboy operates a website at www.playboy.com. Recently, Playboy introduced a new "iBod" feature, which it made available to the public at www.playboy.com/features/features/ibod. Playboy's iBod site invited members of the public to download 25–image slideshows with pictures of naked women. The site is labeled "**Playboy.com Features iBod—Portable photo technology puts Playboy's sexiest models at your fingertips.**"

The website explained:

> Portable MP3 players and other handheld media toys are this year's must-have geek gadgets. The latest thing is Apple's new-generation iPod—the iPod Photo—which does for pictures what the original iPod did for music. Now you can view individual images or entire slide shows in the palm of your hand at the tap of

a button to beautify your dull commute or just to pass the time in the lecture hall.

Playboy has harnessed this latest digital innovation so some of our sexiest girls next door can be added right to your portable player. Simply download this free image gallery to your desktop from Playboy.com and upload it to your iPod Photo handheld device. If iPod Photo is "a feast for the eyes" on its own, it's a veritable ocular orgy now that Playboy.com has dialed up the heat a few notches.

Two slideshows are available at no cost. To download additional slideshows, it is necessary to join the Playboy Cyber Club for $19.95 per month. Is Playboy's "iBod" site actionable under the Lanham Act?

B. PARODY

Mutual of Omaha Insurance Co. v. Novak

836 F.2d 397 (8th Cir.1987), *cert. denied*, 488 U.S. 933, 109 S.Ct. 326, 102 L.Ed.2d 344 (1988).

■ BOWMAN, J.:

Mutual of Omaha Insurance Company (Mutual) brought suit against Franklyn Novak (Novak) alleging trademark infringement and trademark disparagement. The District Court found for Mutual on the infringement issue and granted a permanent injunction, but rejected the disparagement claim. Novak appeals the decision concerning infringement and Mutual appeals the disparagement decision. We affirm the District Court's infringement decision and do not reach the disparagement issue.

Beginning in 1952, Mutual acquired trademark registrations for marks used in connection with its insurance services and a television program it sponsors. These marks include the familiar "Indian head" logo and the designations "Mutual of Omaha" and "Mutual of Omaha's Wild Kingdom."

In 1983 Novak produced a design reminiscent of the Mutual marks. It uses the words "Mutant of Omaha" and depicts a side view of a feather-bonneted, emaciated human head. Novak initially put the design on T-shirts along with the words "Nuclear Holocaust Insurance." Novak marketed approximately 4000 of these shirts before Mutual obtained a preliminary injunction. He also had the design placed on sweatshirts, caps, buttons, and coffee mugs, which he has offered for sale at retail shops, exhibitions, and fairs. Novak also has advertised such merchandise on television and in newspapers and magazines.

After a trial on the merits of Mutual's claims, the District Court ruled that Novak had infringed Mutual's trademarks. The District Court found that Novak's use of the design created a likelihood of confusion as to

[handwritten margin note: Parody of Image for commercial gain]

Mutual of Omaha's

 Wild Kingdom

Mutual's sponsorship of or affiliation with Novak's merchandise, and therefore held such use to be in violation of both federal and state law. Accordingly, the District Court permanently enjoined Novak from advertising or marketing T-shirts, coffee mugs, and other products featuring the designations "Mutant of Omaha," "Mutant Kingdom," and "Mutant of Omaha's Mutant Kingdom," or confusingly similar designations, and also permanently enjoined Novak from using as a logo a design confusingly similar to Mutual's "Indian head" logo.

Like most trademark cases, this case revolves around the "likelihood of confusion" issue. Specifically, the ultimate issue here is whether Novak's design so resembles Mutual's marks that it is likely to cause confusion among consumers as to whether Mutual has sponsored, endorsed, or is otherwise affiliated with the design. . . .

In resolving the likelihood of confusion issue, the District Court considered the factors that this Court enumerated in *SquirtCo*, 628 F.2d at 1091: 1) the strength of the trademark; 2) the similarity between the trademark and the defendant's mark; 3) the competitive proximity of the products on which the respective marks are placed; 4) the intent of the alleged infringer to pass off his goods as those of the trademark holder; 5) the incidents of actual confusion; and 6) the degree of care likely to be exercised by potential customers of the trademark holder. [The court evaluated the district court's weighing of each factor. It gave the most weight to the fifth factor.]

. . . .

As to incidents of actual confusion, Mutual produced evidence of actual confusion in the form of a survey conducted by Sorenson Marketing and Management Corporation of New York. We consider this appropriate, for surveys are often used to demonstrate actual consumer confusion. Sorenson interviewed at random four hundred people over the age of twenty-one in New York, Denver, Chicago, and San Francisco. While viewing Novak's design on a T-shirt, approximately forty-two percent of those surveyed said that Mutual of Omaha came to mind. Of that group, twenty-five percent said that they believe Mutual "goes along" with the T-shirts "in order to help make people aware of the nuclear war problem." Thus, approximately ten percent of all the persons surveyed thought that Mutual "goes along" with Novak's product. Because manifestations of actual confusion serve as strong evidence of a likelihood of confusion, and may, in fact, be the best such evidence, this survey should be given substantial weight unless seriously flawed.

The District Court acknowledged that there may be some ambiguity in the "goes along" question used in the survey, but found the survey as a whole "credible evidence of a likelihood of confusion as to source or sponsorship." Novak presents no persuasive reason for overriding the District Court's evaluation of the reliability of the survey. Hence, we cannot say that the District Court erred in giving the survey significant weight. Courts frequently give substantial weight to properly conducted surveys.

. . . .

The cases Novak relies upon to support his view that there is no likelihood of confusion here, but merely obvious parody, lack persuasiveness in relation to the situation before us. Those cases either did not involve surveys demonstrating confusion or involved surveys of doubtful validity. For example, in *Carson v. Here's Johnny Portable Toilets, Inc.*, 698 F.2d 831 (6th Cir.1983), the plaintiffs presented no surveys demonstrating confusion, and in *Tetley, Inc. v. Topps Chewing Gum, Inc.*, 556 F. Supp. 785, 793 (E.D.N.Y.1983), the court noted that the plaintiff presented no evidence at all of either the likelihood of or actual confusion. . . .

Novak argues that his use of the design in question is an exercise of his right of free speech and is protected by the First Amendment. We believe, however, that the protection afforded by the First Amendment does not give Novak license to infringe the rights of Mutual. Mutual's trademarks are a form of property, and Mutual's rights therein need not "yield to the exercise of First Amendment rights under circumstances where adequate alternative avenues of communication exist." Given the circumstances of this case, Mutual's property rights should not yield. The injunction our decision upholds prohibits Novak's conduct only insofar as Novak uses Mutual's marks as logos or "to market, advertise, or identify [his] services or products." Other avenues for Novak to express his views exist and are unrestricted by the injunction; for example, it in no way infringes upon the constitutional protection the First Amendment would provide were Novak to present an editorial parody in a book, magazine, or film. Because the injunction leaves open many such avenues of expression, it deprives neither Novak nor the public of the benefits of his ideas. We therefore conclude that in the circumstances of this case failure to protect Mutual's trademark rights would amount to an "unwarranted infringement of property rights," for it would "diminish [those] rights without significantly enhancing the asserted right of free speech." It follows that the District Court did not violate Novak's First Amendment rights by issuing the injunction. . . .

We conclude that the District Court's finding of a likelihood of confusion between Mutual's valid trademarks and Novak's design is not clearly erroneous. That finding warrants the District Court's issuance of a permanent injunction restricting Novak's further use of his infringing design.

The judgment of the District Court is AFFIMED.

■ HEANEY, J., *dissenting*:

I respectfully dissent. In my view, the trial court's finding that there exists a likelihood of confusion is clearly erroneous. Moreover, the majority's holding sanctions a violation of Novak's first amendment rights. The T-shirts simply expressed a political message which irritated the officers of Mutual, who decided to swat this pesky fly buzzing around in their backyard with a sledge hammer (a federal court injunction). We should not be a party to this effort.

. . . .

The only *SquirtCo* factor really in dispute in this case is whether consumers could be "actually confused" as to who sponsored or produced the T-shirts.

The evidence on this issue consisted solely of a survey by a nationally recognized firm. Four hundred persons over the age of twenty-one were interviewed at shopping malls in New York, Denver, Chicago and San Francisco. Neither T-shirts nor insurance were featured at the shopping malls where the interviews were conducted. No one was asked whether he or she was interested in buying a T-shirt or insurance.

The interviewees were shown the T-shirts described in the majority opinion and asked: "Does anything come to your mind when you look at this tee shirt?" Ninety-two percent said yes. Those answering yes, were then asked: "What comes to your mind when you see this tee shirt?" Twenty-one percent answered Mutual of Omaha, or the TV program Wild Kingdom sponsored by Mutual. Interviewees were then asked, "anything else?" and an additional eight percent then mentioned Mutual of Omaha.

As recognized by the majority, the only possible evidence of actual confusion is contained in the following question: "Would you say that Mutual of Omaha goes along with or does not go along with these tee shirts in order to make people aware of the nuclear war problem?" Twelve percent of those who mentioned Mutual of Omaha in the earlier questions gave an affirmative answer to this question.

This survey question, however, is fundamentally flawed and should be given little evidentiary weight. The question is blatantly suggestive. It plants the idea of nuclear war in the mind of the interviewee. Thus, an interviewee who only casually glances at the T-shirt or who doesn't understand the message in the T-shirt is tipped off by the question that the T-shirt has something to do with nuclear war. But, if the interviewer had not tipped these people off about the message on the T-shirts, many would never have even come to the misconception that Mutual sponsored the message on the T-shirt.

The only class of interviewees that really matter in this case are those who, *on their own,* recognized the T-shirt contained a message about nuclear war and also believed that Mutual sponsored it. This survey gives us no firm data on how many of these interviewees there were, except that the percentage is somewhere from zero to twelve percent. That is not compelling evidence. It is at most an inference of the possibility of confusion, and such a showing is not sufficient to prove infringement.

. . . .

The majority justifies its assault on Novak's first amendment rights by stating that "protection afforded by the first amendment does not give Novak license to violate the [property] rights of Mutual where adequate alternative avenues of communication exist." Unfortunately, neither the district court nor the majority identifies how Mutual's property rights were harmed by the message on the T-shirts—its feelings, yes, but its reputation, highly unlikely.

. . . .

In sum, the evidence in this case shows at most a possibility of trademark confusion, no real evidence of actual harm to property, and, most importantly, a significant intrusion upon the defendant's first amendment rights. For these reasons, I dissent.

Cliffs Notes, Inc. v. Bantam Doubleday Dell Publishing Group, Inc.

886 F.2d 490 (2d Cir.1989).

■ FEINBERG, J.:

Defendant Bantam Doubleday Dell Publishing Group, Inc. appeals from an order, dated August 2, 1989, of the United States District Court for the Southern District of New York, Shirley Wohl Kram, J., enjoining defendant-appellant from distributing Spy Notes, a parody of the Cliffs Notes series of paperback books published by plaintiff-appellee Cliffs Notes, Inc. This appeal raises basic questions over application of trademark law to an allegedly infringing literary parody. For reasons given below, we vacate the injunction.

Background

The appeal involves three principals, although only two of them are parties. The first is plaintiff-appellee, which publishes a series of study guides, known as Cliffs Notes. As many college students are aware, Cliffs Notes are condensed versions, with brief analyses, of various short stories, plays and books. The cover of a typical Cliffs Notes book lists the name of the work that is to be condensed and discussed in the pages that follow. Although appellee asserts that a variety of readers, and not just students, purchase Cliffs Notes, students apparently form the primary audience for the books. This is reflected in the roster of available Cliffs Notes, which contains most of the titles that one would expect to encounter in college literature and English classes.

The second principal is defendant-appellant, a well-known publishing company, which publishes Spy Notes. The third principal is Spy magazine, which appellant does not publish. Spy magazine contains a mixture of journalism, humor and satire. Its purpose is to provide political and social commentary in an entertaining manner, and its style of humor is quite sharp. Even though the magazine was founded only three years ago, it has a substantial circulation and has received considerable acclaim. Spy editors have been featured or interviewed in the press and on television. Recently, Spy magazine received the accolade of being itself the subject of a full-blown parody called "Sty," published by Random House.

Although Spy magazine is not a party to this lawsuit, it played a key role as one of the two creators, along with defendant-appellant, of Spy Notes. The idea behind Spy Notes was to create a double parody. First, Spy Notes would poke fun at certain novels—Tama Janowitz's *Slaves of New York*, Brett Ellis's *Less Than Zero* and Jay McInerney's *Bright Lights, Big City*—which a Spy editor described in the district court as defining "a genre

CLIFFS NOTES on $3.75

SALINGER'S   **CATCHER IN THE RYE**

Cliffs®
NOTES INC.
YOUR KEY TO THE CLASSICS

of savvy, urban novels depicting the drug abuse, promiscuity and post-adolescent angst of the 1980s." The editor further noted that "[b]ecause of their literary shortcomings and their familiarity to Spy readers, these novels were a natural target for Spy's satirical commentary." In addition,

Spy Notes would satirize Cliffs Notes. Spy magazine editors thought that a study guide would provide an ideal vehicle for a parody of these works, because "[t]he flat, straightforward, academic style" of Cliffs Notes "would appear incongruous with the cool, ironic, sophisticated, urbane novels and thus greatly enhance the humor of the satire.'' Furthermore, ''because most college graduates and students have seen or heard of'' Cliffs Notes, the readers of Spy and the audience targeted for Spy Notes would be ''familiar with the format and style'' of Cliffs Notes.

Appellant and the Spy editors produced Spy Notes, a onetime parody of Cliffs Notes. Appellant readily admitted that it copied the prominent features of Cliffs Notes in order to make Spy Notes an effective parody. Thus, just as a Cliffs Notes book does, Spy Notes lists on the cover the works it condenses, *i.e.*, the three novels referred to above. In addition, the cover of Spy Notes replicates the distinctive, yellow color, black diagonal stripes and black lettering of Cliffs Notes, a design that is the subject of appellee's registered trademark.

At the same time, there are some important differences between the two books. (We will focus on the covers, as the district court did, because appellee's trademark protects the cover of Cliffs Notes; however, the humorous content of Spy Notes is also quite different from the serious condensation and analysis of Cliffs Notes.) For example, the cover of Spy Notes, unlike that of Cliffs Notes, prominently states ''A Satire'' five times in bright red lettering (and the back similarly states it four times), bears the notation ''A Spy Book'' with the logo of Spy magazine against a bright red background, uses the word ''Spy'' four times, and shows a clay sculpture of New York City rather than the clay sculpture of a mountain that typically appears on Cliffs Notes. Also, the cover of Spy Notes contains red, blue and white—colors that are not used on the cover of Cliffs Notes—and bears wry notations not found on a Cliffs Notes cover, such as ''All Those Other Hip Urban Novels Of The 1980s,'' and ''Even Funnier Than The Originals.'' In addition, the Spy Notes cover price ($7.95) is substantially higher than that of Cliffs Notes ($3.50). Further, the cover of Spy Notes states prominently in red that it ''Includes The Spy Novel–O–Matic Fiction–Writing Device!'' This tool, which a prospective purchaser can inspect simply by opening Spy Notes, allows the ''young, world-weary urban author'' to create ''16,765,056 different plot possibilities'' by manipulating a card. A Cliffs Notes book contains no such obviously absurd shortcut to success. Finally, appellant plans to market Spy Notes in distinctive prepacks of 10 copies in a manner that prominently features the Spy name.

Early in July 1989, after the Spy Notes books had been bound but before the copies had been shipped to bookstores, appellee sued appellant. Appellee alleged that the cover of Spy Notes violated the Lanham Trademark Act, because it would give consumers the false impression that Spy Notes was actually appellee's product. Appellee also asserted that the cover violated the New York common law of unfair competition, as well as section 368–d of the New York General Business Law. Appellee sought preliminary and final injunctions against the distribution of Spy Notes, and other relief.

On August 2, 1989, the district court granted a preliminary injunction, reaching only appellee's claims under section 43(a) of the Lanham Act. The court rejected what it characterized as appellant's ''general theory that the

First Amendment gives the parodist unbridled freedom to use a registered trademark as part of a parody or satire," and went on to analyze appellee's trademark claims under the eight-factor balancing test of *Polaroid Corp. v. Polarad Elec. Corp.*, 287 F.2d 492, 495 (2d Cir.), *cert. denied*, 368 U.S. 820 (1961). Finding "a profound likelihood of confusion" between the cover of Spy Notes and that of Cliffs Notes, the district court held that appellee had demonstrated irreparable injury and a likelihood of success on the merits. The judge therefore preliminarily enjoined appellant from distributing the parody with its current cover design and ordered appellant to so advise the retail trade.

. . . .

Discussion

. . . .

We start with the proposition that parody is a form of artistic expression, protected by the First Amendment. For example, the Supreme Court has held that the First Amendment bars recovery "for the tort of intentional infliction of emotional distress by reason of" publication of satire "without showing in addition that the publication contains a false statement of fact which was made with 'actual malice.' " *Hustler Magazine v. Falwell*, 108 S. Ct. 876, 882 (1988). Similarly, our decisions have recognized "the broad scope permitted parody in First Amendment law." *Groucho Marx Prod., Inc. v. Day and Night Co.*, 689 F.2d 317, 319 n. 2 (2d Cir.1982); *see Elsmere Music, Inc. v. National Broadcasting Co.*, 623 F.2d 252, 253 (2d Cir.1980) (per curiam) ("in today's world of often unrelieved solemnity, copyright law should be hospitable to the humor of parody . . ."). We have stated the "general proposition" that "parody and satire *are* deserving of substantial freedom—both as entertainment and as a form of social and literary criticism." *Berlin v. E.C. Publications, Inc.*, 329 F.2d 541, 545 (2d Cir.) (emphasis in original), *cert. denied*, 379 U.S. 822 (1964).

At the same time, "[t]rademark protection is not lost simply because the allegedly infringing use is in connection with a work of artistic expression." *Silverman v. CBS Inc.*, 870 F.2d 40, 49 (2d Cir.), *cert. denied*, 109 S. Ct. 3219 (1989). Books are "sold in the commercial marketplace like other more utilitarian products, making the danger of consumer deception a legitimate concern that warrants some government regulation." *Rogers v. Grimaldi*, 875 F.2d 994, 997 (2d Cir.1989).

Conflict between these two policies is inevitable in the context of parody, because the keystone of parody is imitation. It is hard to imagine, for example, a successful parody of Time magazine that did not reproduce Time's trademarked red border. A parody must convey two simultaneous—and contradictory—messages: that it is the original, but also that it is not the original and is instead a parody. To the extent that it does only the former but not the latter, it is not only a poor parody but also vulnerable under trademark law, since the customer will be confused.

Thus, the principal issue before the district court was how to strike the balance between the two competing considerations of allowing artistic expression and preventing consumer confusion. We believe that the correct approach in this case was foreshadowed by our decision in *Rogers v. Grimaldi,* upon which appellant relies heavily . . . .

It is true that *Rogers,* though a Lanham Act case, was concerned with a very different problem from the one we have here. As indicated, the claim there was that a title was false or at least misleading because it could be (mis)understood to mean that Ginger Rogers was the subject of the work or that she had endorsed it. This case is not about whether a title is false advertising but whether the appearance of a work's cover is confusingly similar to the trademark elements of an earlier cover. Furthermore, the present case contains the added element of parody.

Appellee argues that the *Rogers* approach is not relevant to this case and that we should simply apply the *Polaroid* factors, as the district judge did. Appellee points out that the *Rogers* rule—that the Lanham Act's false advertising prohibition does not apply to titles with some artistic relevance to the underlying work unless they are explicitly misleading—does not protect "misleading titles that are confusingly similar to other titles." Since appellee claims that the cover of Spy Notes is highly misleading, and points out that the judge so found, appellee seizes upon the quoted language in *Rogers* as support for its position that the case has no application here. However, that language says only that where a title is complained about because it is confusingly similar to another title, the *Rogers* rule that titles are subject to the Lanham Act's false advertising prohibition only if explicitly misleading is inapplicable. But that does not mean, as appellee appears to claim, that nothing in the *Rogers* opinion is relevant to this case.

We believe that the overall balancing approach of *Rogers* and its emphasis on construing the Lanham Act "narrowly" when First Amendment values are involved are both relevant in this case. That is to say, in deciding the reach of the Lanham Act in any case where an expressive work is alleged to infringe a trademark, it is appropriate to weigh the public interest in free expression against the public interest in avoiding consumer confusion. *Id.* at 998–99. *See also Silverman,* 870 F.2d at 48 ("In the area of artistic speech . . . enforcement of trademark rights carries a risk of inhibiting free expression. . . ."). And just as in *Rogers,* where we said that the expressive element of titles requires more protection than the labeling of ordinary commercial products, so here the expressive element of parodies requires more protection than the labeling of ordinary commercial products. Indeed, we have said, in the context of alleged copyright infringement, that a parody is entitled "at least" to conjure up the original and can do more. *Elsmere Music, Inc.,* 623 F.2d at 253 n. 1.

Thus, we hold that the *Rogers* balancing approach is generally applicable to Lanham Act claims against works of artistic expression, a category that includes parody. This approach takes into account the ultimate test in trademark law, namely, the likelihood of confusion " 'as to the source of the goods in question.' " [Citations omitted]. At the same time, a balancing approach allows greater latitude for works such as parodies, in which expression, and not commercial exploitation of another's trademark, is the primary intent, and in which there is a need to evoke the original work being parodied. *Cf. Dallas Cowboys Cheerleaders, Inc. v. Pussycat Cinema, Ltd.*, 604 F.2d 200, 206–07 (2d Cir.1979) (upholding an injunction, despite First Amendment claims, in a case concerning a pornographic movie with blatantly false and explicitly misleading advertisements).

To apply the *Rogers* approach in this case, we begin by noting the strong public interest in avoiding consumer confusion over Spy Notes. As we put it in *Rogers*, the purchaser of a book, "like the purchaser of a can of peas, has a right not to be misled as to the source of the product." *Rogers*, 875 F.2d at 997–98. But, taking into account that somewhat more risk of confusion is to be tolerated when a trademark holder seeks to enjoin artistic expression such as a parody, the degree of risk of confusion between Spy Notes and Cliffs Notes does not outweigh the well-established public interest in parody. In other words, we do not believe that there is a likelihood that an ordinarily prudent purchaser would think that Spy Notes is actually a study guide produced by appellee, as opposed to a parody of Cliffs Notes. And although the district court found a strong likelihood of confusion between the cover of Spy Notes and that of Cliffs Notes, based on its review of the eight *Polaroid* factors,[3] that determination is a legal conclusion which is reviewable by this court as a matter of law. [Citations omitted].

As indicated, we believe that the district court erred. This conclusion is based upon a number of factors. First, the district court apparently thought that the parody here had to make an obvious joke out of the cover of the original in order to be regarded as a parody. We do not see why this is so. It is true that some of the covers of the parodies brought to our attention, unlike that of Spy Notes, contain obvious visual gags. [Citations omitted]. But parody may be sophisticated as well as slapstick; a literary work is a parody if, taken as a whole, it pokes fun at its subject. Spy Notes surely does that, and there are sufficient reasons to conclude that most consumers will realize it is a parody. For example, a substantial portion of the potential audience for Spy Notes—*i.e.,* college students or college-educated adults—overlaps with that for Cliffs Notes. Spy magazine, like Cliffs Notes, is widely read on some college campuses, although presumably for different reasons. As a result, the name "Spy" in the title, the notation "A Spy Book" emblazoned on the cover of Spy Notes and the use of a prepack marketing device prominently displaying the "Spy" name should alert the buyer that Spy Notes is a parody of some sort, or, at least, that it is not the same product as Cliffs Notes.

---

3. As indicated, appellee argues that the *Polaroid* factors supply the relevant standard and that the district court correctly applied them. The *Polaroid* test has its origin in cases of purely commercial exploitation, which do not raise First Amendment concerns. Thus, the *Polaroid* test is at best awk-ward in the context of parody, which must evoke the original and constitutes artistic expression. In such a situation, the *Polaroid* factors should be applied with proper weight given to First Amendment considerations, something the district court did not do here.

Furthermore, while the cover of Spy Notes certainly conjures up the cover of Cliffs Notes, the two differ in many respects. In addition to the differences listed in the following paragraphs, which indicate that Spy Notes is a parody of Cliffs Notes, the cover of Spy Notes contains red, blue and white, colors that do not appear on the cover of Cliffs Notes. Also, the Spy Notes cover shows a clay sculpture of New York City rather than a clay sculpture of a bare cliff. In addition, the price quoted on the cover of Spy Notes is about twice the price at which Cliffs Notes is sold, and appellant plans to market Spy Notes in large part through prepacks of 10 copies, which prominently present the Spy name.

In addition, a Cliffs Notes book is not likely to be bought as an impulse purchase. A prospective reader of Cliffs Notes probably has a specific book in mind when going to the bookstore for a study guide. And, even if a consumer did go to a store looking for a Cliffs Notes summary of any of the three books condensed in Spy Notes, that purchaser would not find one. Appellee does not produce Cliffs Notes for these novels, and has no plans to do so. There may be a few purchasers who have been assigned to read the novels who would buy the parody thinking it is a serious work and is produced by Cliffs Notes. In view of the public interest in free expression, that slight risk should be taken in order to allow the parody to be sold. Similarly, it is conceivable, though hardly likely, that some purchaser may mistakenly think that Cliffs Notes itself produced the parody, but that small chance does not justify the injunction here. There is no requirement that the cover of a parody carry a disclaimer that it is not produced by the subject of the parody, and we ought not to find such a requirement in the Lanham Act.

The label "A Satire" is also prominently used five times on the cover (and four on the back) of Spy Notes. Appellee conceded at oral argument that "satire," for this purpose, is the same as "parody." In addition, the prepack, a major promotional tool in which the books will appear in most, although not all, bookstores, bears the legend "The Outrageous Parody from the Creators of Separated at Birth" (the latter was a very popular book authored by Spy magazine editors). These measures should alert most consumers that Spy Notes is, in fact, a parody. Moreover, even for those few readers who might be slightly confused by the cover, the most likely reaction would be to open the book. Both the title page and the copyright notice page indicate that the book is written by the editors of Spy magazine and published by appellant. The copyright notice page states, "Spy Notes is a parody of Cliffs Notes." Furthermore, the reader would encounter the Spy Novel–O–Matic Fiction–Writing Device, which is an immediate tip-off that something non-serious is afoot.[5]

Finally, with few exceptions, most Cliffs Notes are summaries of the traditional "great books," rather than contemporary works or those some-

---

5. By mentioning the items inside the book that would contribute to dispelling whatever risk of confusion might arise, we do not mean to suggest that a parody could copy the trademark aspects of the cover of a book without adequate indication on its own cover that it was a parody.

what outside the mainstream. As indicated above, the Spy editors certainly thought that the three novels were obviously not in the former category and that the purchaser would be aware of the humor of having Cliffs Notes summarize them. Moreover, the books that Spy Notes summarizes are characterized by their spare, stripped-down prose, and uncomplicated plots. The idea of condensing them at all is something of a parody. Thus, the consumer would likely be put on notice from the first that Spy Notes was not Cliffs Notes.

Conclusion

We conclude that the parody cover of Spy Notes, although it surely conjures up the original and goes to great lengths to use some of the identical colors and aspects of the cover design of Cliffs Notes, raises only a slight risk of consumer confusion that is outweighed by the public interest in free expression, especially in a form of expression that must to some extent resemble the original. The district court's ruling unjustifiably impos-es the drastic remedy of a pre-publication injunction upon the cover of a literary parody. Accordingly, for the reasons set forth above, we vacate the injunction against appellant.

QUESTIONS

1. One possible resolution of the tension between trademark and First Amendment protections would limit injunctive relief to those instances in which the trademark owner demonstrated likely (or perhaps only actual) confusion. Does the court's disposition of the likelihood of confusion issue in *Mutual of Omaha* suggest that this resolution works well in practice?

2. The *Cliffs Notes* court appears to acknowledge that the effectiveness of a parody lies in its ability to engender initial confusion between the parody and the parodied subject. So long as the initial misimpression is dispelled, then there is no actionable confusion. In *Cliffs Notes* the parodist adopted a variety of disclaimers, which the court found sufficient to alleviate confu-sion. Do all trademark parodies lend themselves to the kinds of elaborate disclaimers "Spy Notes" employed?

3. What are "alternative avenues of communication" for trademark paro-dies? Are you persuaded by those suggested in *Mutual of Omaha*? Are there others?

4. Section 43(c) of the Lanham Act (as amended in 2006) now expressly excludes dilution liability for parodies:

> "The following shall not be actionable as dilution by blurring or dilution by tarnishment under this subsection:
>
> "(A) Any fair use, including a nominative or descriptive fair use, or facilitation of such fair use, of a famous mark by another person other than as a designation of source for the person's own goods or services, including use in connection with—
>
> . . . .

(ii) identifying and parodying, criticizing, or commenting upon the famous mark owner or the goods or services of the famous mark owner."

Does this language limit the parody exception to parodies whose target is the trademark owner or its products?

5. Can the language of section 43(c), quoted above, be read to exempt parodies from infringement and false designation of origin claims as well as dilution claims? Should it be?

Anheuser–Busch, Inc. v. Balducci Publications, 28 F.3d 769 (8th Cir.1994), *cert. denied*, 513 U.S. 1112 (1995). When *Snicker* magazine ran a parody of a "Michelob Dry" ad on the back cover of its April, 1989, issue, the Court of Appeals for the Eighth Circuit had an opportunity to revisit the analysis it applied in *Mutual of Omaha Insurance Co. v. Novak* in the light of recent cases from other circuits. Defendants' parody was a mock advertisement for a product named "Michelob Oily," with the slogan "One Taste and You'll Drink it Oily" (a take-off on plaintiff's federally registered phrase "ONE TASTE AND YOU'LL DRINK IT DRY"®.) According to the court of appeals:

> The accompanying graphics include a partially-obscured can of Michelob Dry pouring oil onto a fish, an oil-soaked rendition of the A & Eagle design (with the eagle exclaiming "Yuck!") below a Shell Oil symbol, and various "Michelob Oily" products bearing a striking resemblance to appellants' Michelob family. This resemblance was quite intentional, as evidenced by the admitted use of actual Anheuser–Busch "clip-art" in replicating several of the protected trademarks. In smaller text the ad opines, "At the rate it's being dumped into our oceans, lakes and rivers, you'll drink it oily sooner or later, anyway." Finally, the following disclaimer is found in extremely small text running vertically along the right side of the page: "Snicker Magazine Editorial by Rich Balducci. Art by Eugene Ruble. Thank goodness someone still cares about quality (of life)."

Anheuser–Busch sued for trademark infringement, unfair competition, and dilution. The trial court ruled for defendants, finding that, notwithstanding the intentional use of plaintiff's registered marks, there was no likelihood of confusion and no cognizable threat of dilution. *Anheuser–Busch, Inc. v. Balducci Publications*, 814 F.Supp. 791 (E.D.Mo.1993). Judge Hamilton noted that the *Mutual of Omaha* court had stated that its injunction did not restrict Novak's first amendment activity in part because "it in no way infringes upon the constitutional protection the first amendment would provide were Novak to present an editorial parody in a book, magazine, or film." 814 F.Supp. at 794 (*quoting Mutual of Omaha*, 836 F.2d at 402). The trial court then reviewed Cliffs Notes Inc. v. Bantam Doubleday Dell; L.L. Bean, Inc. v. Drake Publishers; *and* Rogers v. Grimaldi, and concluded that the traditional, multifactored test for likelihood of confusion should be applied "with special sensitivity to the purposes of

trademark law and the First Amendment Rights of the Defendants.'' 814
F.Supp. at 795–96.

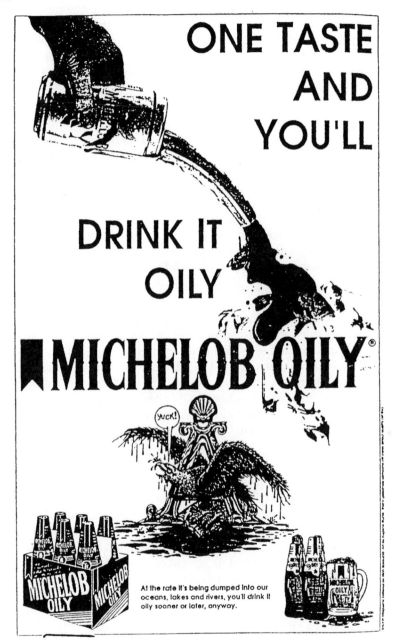

The court of appeals reversed:

Rather than first considering whether Balducci's ad parody
was likely to confuse the public and then considering the scope of

First Amendment protection, the district court conflated the two. The court essentially skewed its likelihood of confusion analysis in an attempt to give "special sensitivity" to the First Amendment, holding Anheuser Busch to a higher standard than required in a "classic trademark infringement case." Since we cannot separate the court's factual finding of confusion from its legal conclusions, we conduct a de novo review of the well-developed record before us.

Many courts have applied, we believe correctly, an expansive interpretation of likelihood of confusion, extending "protection against use of [plaintiff's] mark on any product or service which would reasonably be thought by the buying public to come from the same source, or thought to be affiliated with, connected with, or sponsored by, the trademark owner." McCarthy, Trademarks and Unfair Competition § 24.03, at 24–13 (3d ed. 1992); *Novak*, 836 F.2d at 398. This approach seems consistent with congressional intent, as evidenced by the express inclusion during the 1989 revision of the Lanham Act of protection against confusion as to "origin, sponsorship, or approval." 15 U.S.C. § 1125(a).

Anheuser–Busch possessed several very strong trademarks that Balducci displayed virtually unaltered in the ad parody. Thus, the first two *SquirtCo* factors weigh heavily in favor of Anheuser–Busch. The third factor, competitive proximity, is less one-sided. Balducci does not directly compete with Anheuser–Busch. Confusion, however, may exist in the absence of direct competition. Moreover, Balducci published the parody on the back cover of a magazine—a location frequently devoted to real ads, even in Snicker. This location threatens to confuse consumers accustomed to seeing advertisements on the back cover of magazines.

Our analysis of Balducci's intent relies, of necessity, on circumstantial evidence. According to Richard Balducci, he sought to comment on certain social conditions through parody. Other factors, however, suggest Balducci had, if not an intent to confuse, at least an indifference to the possibility that some consumers might be misled by the parody. For example, no significant steps were taken to remind readers that they were viewing a parody and not an advertisement sponsored or approved by Anheuser–Busch. Balducci carefully designed the fictitious ad to appear as authentic as possible. Several of Anheuser–Busch's marks were used with little or no alteration. The disclaimer is virtually undetectable. Balducci even included a (R) symbol after the words Michelob Oily.

The survey evidence, whether considered as direct or indirect evidence of actual confusion, tilts the analysis in favor of Anheuser–Busch. Over half of those surveyed thought Balducci needed Anheuser–Busch's approval to publish the ad. Many of these presumably felt that such approval had in fact been obtained. Six percent thought that the parody was an actual Anheuser–Busch advertisement. Other courts have accepted similar survey findings. In *Novak,* for example, "approximately ten percent of all the persons surveyed thought that Mutual 'goes along' with Novak's product." 836 F.2d at 400. The court found this persuasive despite the existence of "some ambiguity" in the survey question. *Id.* Thus, we are left with evidence, obtained by means of a valid consumer survey, that strongly indicates actual consumer confusion.

[W]e are convinced that the First Amendment places no bar to the application of the Lanham Act in this case. As we have discussed, Balducci's ad parody was likely to confuse consumers as to its origin, sponsorship or approval. This confusion might have to be tolerated if even plausibly necessary to achieve the desired commentary—a question we need not decide. In this case, the confusion is wholly unnecessary to Balducci's stated purpose. By using an obvious disclaimer, positioning the parody in a less-confusing location, altering the protected marks in a meaningful way, or doing some collection of the above, Balducci could have conveyed its message with substantially less risk of consumer confusion. Other courts have upheld the use of obvious variations of protected marks. *See, e.g., Cliffs Notes,* 886 F.2d at 496 ("Spy Notes" held not to infringe "Cliffs Notes" mark). The First Amendment does not excuse Balducci's failure to do so. As the Second Circuit observed:

> A parody must convey two simultaneous—and contradictory—messages: that it is the original, but also that it is not the original and is instead a parody. To the extent that it does only the former but not the latter, it is not only a poor parody but also vulnerable under trademark law, since the customer will be confused.

Cliffs Notes, 886 F.2d at 494. Balducci's ad, developed through the nearly unaltered appropriation of Anheuser–Busch's marks, conveys that it is the original, but the ad founders on its failure to convey that it is not the original. Thus, it is vulnerable under trademark law since the customer is likely to be confused, as the record before the district court demonstrated.

QUESTIONS

1. What about the ad does the court find is likely to confuse consumers? Is the problem that consumers may believe that the law requires parodists to secure the permission of the owners of any trademarks parodied? If this likelihood of confusion about the law is actionable, won't the law necessarily respond by requiring trademark owner permission in more and more circumstances, even though confusion about the source of any advertised product is highly unlikely?

2. Is the *Polaroid* factors test problematic in contexts in which defendants' use may be controversial, or is the flexibility of the factors a strength in cases where free speech interests may be at stake?

In **Yankee Publishing v. News America Publishing**, 809 F.Supp. 267 (S.D.N.Y.1992), the publisher of the *Farmer's Almanac* sued *New York* magazine for the cover of its December 3, 1990 issue, which copied the

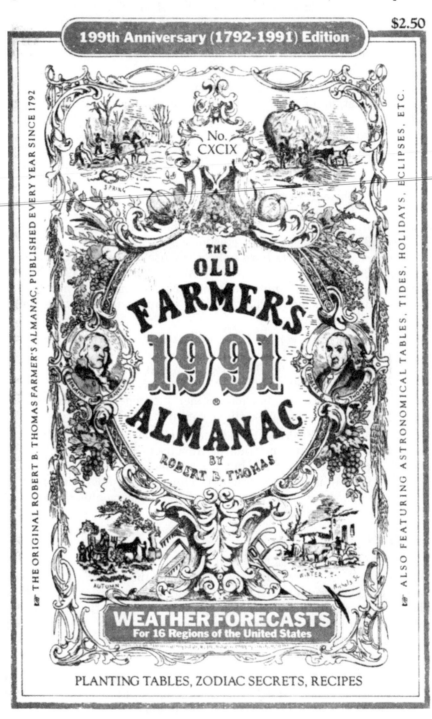

Almanac's trade dress and which purported to include the *New York* "1990 CHRISTMAS GIFTS ALMANAC by Corky Pollan." Characterizing the copying as a "referential joke," rather than a parody, District Court Judge

Pierre Leval applied the *Polaroid* factors, and found no likelihood of confusion. Judge Leval described the plaintiff's mark as strong, but held that its strength in the case of a referential joke made confusion less likely rather than more. Although both uses involved magazine covers, Judge Leval concluded that the two uses were "quite different," because plaintiff used its mark as a source identifier, while defendant used it as "part of a jest." He characterized the products as far apart because the two publications appealed to different customers. Plaintiff, moreover, was unlikely to bridge the gap. There was no evidence of actual confusion, a lack the Judge characterized as "significant." The court found that New York magazine had copied the trade dress in good faith, "as part of a joking commentary on the economic times, and not as an attempt to misuse or abuse Yankee's trademark rights." The defendant's magazine was of high quality and the judge characterized magazine purchasers as sophisticated. All eight of the *Polaroid* factors, thus, cut in defendant's favor.

In **MGM–Pathe Communication Co. v. Pink Panther Patrol**, 774 F.Supp. 869 (S.D.N.Y.1991), decided months earlier by the same judge, the motion picture studio that produced the *Pink Panther* movies sued a New York City gay rights organization for calling itself "The Pink Panther Patrol." Defendant's organization patrolled the Greenwich Village area with cameras to deter street violence against homosexuals. It had chosen its name after an editorial in *Outweek* magazine had suggested it because of its allusion to other activist panther organizations like the Black Panthers and the Grey Panthers and because pink was a color associated with gay activism. To evaluate the likelihood that consumers be confused by the patrol's name, Judge Leval applied the *Polaroid* factors. The Pink Panther mark, he found, was strong and distinctive, which "increases the likelihood of confusion and entitles the mark to a broad cloak of protection." Although plaintiff and defendant used the pink panther mark in different contexts, the court found a "high degree of similarity between plaintiff's The Pink Panther and defendants' Pink Panther Patrol." Although the court acknowledges a substantial difference between MGM's movies and the service offered by the patrol, "it does not negate the likelihood of confusion." This was so because "the Patrol seeks public recognition for its name and mission in the news media, which is not so distant from plaintiff's field of entertainment." Similarly, the size of the gap between filmmaking and protecting homosexuals from attack was less important in a case, such as this one, which both plaintiff and defendant were "promoting their marks in the same marketplace–the general public for television entertainment and news." There was no proof of actual confusion, but Judge Leval remarked that "[a] court may use common sense inference from established facts to determine whether confusion is likely, even if proof of such existing confusion has not been offered." With respect to Defendant's good or bad faith, the court held "[a]lthough I do not suggest that defendants had any desire to create confusion between themselves and the promoters of the comic entertainment figure, there is nonetheless an element of piggybacking in the adoption of a name which the commercial efforts of another have made famous." MGM conceded that the quality of the patrol's services weren't relevant to the likelihood of confusion in this case, but the judge remarked that MGM "concedes too much." The difference between the mental images of lighthearted entertainment associated with plaintiff's mark and the associations of "political activism, violence, defiance, homosexuality and angry confrontation" attaching to the patrol's use of the mark threatened harm to plaintiff's trademark. Finally, the court characterized the public as unsophisticated. With seven of the eight factors pointing in plaintiff's favor, Judge Leval found confusion likely and enjoined defendant's use of the Pink Panther Patrol name.

Does the multi-factored *Polaroid factor* test give judges too much discretion to find confusion likely when they don't approve of defendants' use and unlikely when they do?

Mattel, Inc. v. Universal Music International

296 F.3d 894 (9th Cir. 2002), *cert. denied*, 537 U.S. 1171, 123 S.Ct. 993 (2003).

Barbie Girl Case

■ KOZINSKI, CIRCUIT JUDGE:

If this were a sci-fi melodrama, it might be called Speech–Zilla meets Trademark Kong.

I

Barbie was born in Germany in the 1950s as an adult collector's item. Over the years, Mattel transformed her from a doll that resembled a "German street walker," as she originally appeared, into a glamorous, long-legged blonde. Barbie has been labeled both the ideal American woman and a bimbo. She has survived attacks both psychic (from feminists critical of her fictitious figure) and physical (more than 500 professional makeovers). She remains a symbol of American girlhood, a public figure who graces the aisles of toy stores throughout the country and beyond. With Barbie, Mattel created not just a toy but a cultural icon.

With fame often comes unwanted attention. Aqua is a Danish band that has, as yet, only dreamed of attaining Barbie-like status. In 1997, Aqua produced the song Barbie Girl on the album Aquarium. In the song, one bandmember impersonates Barbie, singing in a high-pitched, doll-like voice; another bandmember, calling himself Ken, entices Barbie to "go party." ... Barbie Girl singles sold well and, to Mattel's dismay, the song made it onto Top 40 music charts.

Mattel brought this lawsuit against the music companies who produced, marketed and sold Barbie Girl ... (collectively, "MCA"). MCA in turn ... brought a defamation claim against Mattel for statements Mattel made about MCA while this lawsuit was pending. The district court concluded it had jurisdiction over the foreign defendants and under the Lanham Act, and granted MCA's motion for summary judgment on Mattel's federal and state-law claims for trademark infringement and dilution. The district court also granted Mattel's motion for summary judgment on MCA's defamation claim.

Mattel appeals the district court's ruling that Barbie Girl is a parody of Barbie and a nominative fair use; that MCA's use of the term Barbie is not likely to confuse consumers as to Mattel's affiliation with Barbie Girl or dilute the Barbie mark; and that Mattel cannot assert an unfair competition claim under the Paris Convention for the Protection of Industrial Property. MCA cross-appeals the grant of summary judgment on its defamation claim as well as the district court's jurisdictional holdings.

. . .

III

A.   A trademark is a word, phrase or symbol that is used to identify a manufacturer or sponsor of a good or the provider of a service. *See New Kids on the Block v. News Am. Publ'g, Inc.*, 971 F.2d 302, 305 (9th Cir. 1992). It's the owner's way of preventing others from duping consumers into buying a product they mistakenly believe is sponsored by the trademark owner. A trademark "informs people that trademarked products come from the same source." *Id.* at 305 n.2. Limited to this core purpose—avoiding confusion in the marketplace—a trademark owner's property rights play well with the First Amendment. "Whatever first amendment rights you may have in calling the brew you make in your bathtub 'Pepsi' are easily outweighed by the buyer's interest in not being fooled into buying it." *Trademarks Unplugged*, 68 N.Y.U.L. Rev. 960, 973 (1993).

The problem arises when trademarks transcend their identifying purpose. Some trademarks enter our public discourse and become an integral part of our vocabulary. How else do you say that something's "the Rolls Royce of its class?" What else is a quick fix, but a Band–Aid? Does the average consumer know to ask for aspirin as "acetyl salicylic acid?" *See Bayer Co. v. United Drug Co.*, 272 F. 505, 510 (S.D.N.Y. 1921). Trademarks often fill in gaps in our vocabulary and add a contemporary flavor to our expressions. Once imbued with such expressive value, the trademark becomes a word in our language and assumes a role outside the bounds of trademark law.

Our likelihood-of-confusion test, *see AMF Inc. v. Sleekcraft Boats*, 599 F.2d 341, 348–49 (9th Cir. 1979), generally strikes a comfortable balance between the trademark owner's property rights and the public's expressive interests. But when a trademark owner asserts a right to control how we express ourselves—when we'd find it difficult to describe the product any other way (as in the case of aspirin), or when the mark (like Rolls Royce) has taken on an expressive meaning apart from its source-identifying function—applying the traditional test fails to account for the full weight of the public's interest in free expression.

The First Amendment may offer little protection for a competitor who labels its commercial good with a confusingly similar mark, but "trademark rights do not entitle the owner to quash an unauthorized use of the mark by another who is communicating ideas or expressing points of view." *L.L. Bean, Inc. v. Drake Publishers, Inc.*, 811 F.2d 26, 29 (1st Cir. 1987). Were we to ignore the expressive value that some marks assume, trademark rights would grow to encroach upon the zone protected by the First Amendment. *See Yankee Publ'g, Inc. v. News Am. Publ'g, Inc.*, 809 F. Supp. 267, 276 (S.D.N.Y. 1992) ("When unauthorized use of another's mark is part of a communicative message and not a source identifier, the First Amendment is implicated in opposition to the trademark right."). Simply put, the trademark owner does not have the right to control public discourse whenever the public imbues his mark with a meaning beyond its source-identifying function. *See Anti–Monopoly, Inc. v. Gen. Mills Fun Group*, 611 F.2d 296, 301 (9th Cir. 1979) ("It is the source-denoting function which trademark laws protect, and nothing more.").

B.   There is no doubt that MCA uses Mattel's mark: Barbie is one half of Barbie Girl. But Barbie Girl is the title of a song about Barbie and Ken, a reference that—at least today—can only be to Mattel's famous couple. We expect a title to describe the underlying work, not to identify the producer, and Barbie Girl does just that.

The Barbie Girl title presages a song about Barbie, or at least a girl like Barbie. The title conveys a message to consumers about what they can expect to discover in the song itself; it's a quick glimpse of Aqua's take on their own song. The lyrics confirm this: The female singer, who calls herself Barbie, is "a Barbie girl, in [her] Barbie world." She tells her male counterpart (named Ken), "Life in plastic, it's fantastic. You can brush my hair, undress me everywhere/Imagination, life is your creation." And off they go to "party." The song pokes fun at Barbie and the values that Aqua contends she represents. *See Cliffs Notes, Inc. v. Bantam Doubleday Dell Publ'g Group*, 886 F.2d 490, 495–96 (2d Cir. 1989). The female singer explains, "I'm a blond bimbo girl, in a fantasy world/Dress me up, make it tight, I'm your dolly."

The song does not rely on the Barbie mark to poke fun at another subject but targets Barbie herself. *See Campbell v. Acuff–Rose Music, Inc.*, 510 U.S. 569, 580, 127 L. Ed. 2d 500, 114 S. Ct. 1164 (1994); *see also Dr. Seuss Ents., L.P. v. Penguin Books USA, Inc.*, 109 F.3d 1394, 1400 (9th Cir. 1997). This case is therefore distinguishable from *Dr. Seuss*, where we held that the book *The Cat NOT in the Hat!* borrowed Dr. Seuss's trademarks and lyrics to get attention rather than to mock *The Cat in the Hat!* The defendant's use of the Dr. Seuss trademarks and copyrighted works had "no critical bearing on the substance or style of" *The Cat in the Hat!*, and therefore could not claim First Amendment protection. *Id.* at 1401. *Dr. Seuss* recognized that, where an artistic work targets the original and does not merely borrow another's property to get attention, First Amendment interests weigh more heavily in the balance. *See id.* at 1400–02; *see also Harley–Davidson, Inc. v. Grottanelli*, 164 F.3d 806, 812–13 (2d Cir. 1999) (a parodist whose expressive work aims its parodic commentary at a trademark is given considerable leeway, but a claimed parodic use that makes no comment on the mark is not a permitted trademark parody use).

The Second Circuit has held that "in general the [Lanham] Act should be construed to apply to artistic works only where the public interest in avoiding consumer confusion outweighs the public interest in free expression." *Rogers v. Grimaldi*, 875 F.2d 994, 999 (2d Cir. 1989); *see also Cliffs Notes*, 886 F.2d at 494 (quoting *Rogers*, 875 F.2d at 999). *Rogers* considered a challenge by the actress Ginger Rogers to the film *Ginger and Fred*. The movie told the story of two Italian cabaret performers who made a living by imitating Ginger Rogers and Fred Astaire. Rogers argued that the film's title created the false impression that she was associated with it.

At first glance, Rogers certainly had a point. Ginger was her name, and Fred was her dancing partner. If a pair of dancing shoes had been labeled Ginger and Fred, a dancer might have suspected that Rogers was associated with the shoes (or at least one of them), just as Michael Jordan has endorsed Nike sneakers that claim to make you fly through the air. But Ginger and Fred was not a brand of shoe; it was the title of a movie and, for the reasons explained by the Second Circuit, deserved to be treated differently.

A title is designed to catch the eye and to promote the value of the underlying work. Consumers expect a title to communicate a message about the book or movie, but they do not expect it to identify the publisher or producer. *See Application of Cooper*, 45 C.C.P.A. 923, 254 F.2d 611, 615–16 (C.C.P.A. 1958) (A "title . . . identifies a specific literary work, . . . and is not associated in the public mind with the . . . manufacturer." (internal quotation marks omitted)). If we see a painting titled "Campbell's Chicken Noodle Soup," we're unlikely to believe that Campbell's has branched into the art business. Nor, upon hearing Janis Joplin croon "Oh Lord, won't you buy me a Mercedes–Benz?," would we suspect that she and the carmaker had entered into a joint venture. A title tells us something about the underlying work but seldom speaks to its origin?.

Rogers concluded that literary titles do not violate the Lanham Act "unless the title has no artistic relevance to the underlying work whatsoever, or, if it has some artistic relevance, unless the title explicitly misleads as to the source or the content of the work." *Id.* at 999 (footnote omitted). We agree with the Second Circuit's analysis and adopt the *Rogers* standard as our own.

Applying *Rogers* to our case, we conclude that MCA's use of Barbie is not an infringement of Mattel's trademark. Under the first prong of *Rogers*, the use of Barbie in the song title clearly is relevant to the underlying work, namely, the song itself. As noted, the song is about Barbie and the values Aqua claims she represents. The song title does not explicitly mislead as to the source of the work; it does not, explicitly or otherwise, suggest that it was produced by Mattel. The *only* indication that Mattel might be associated with the song is the use of Barbie in the title; if this were enough to satisfy this prong of the *Rogers* test, it would render *Rogers* a nullity. We therefore agree with the district court that MCA was entitled to summary judgment on this ground. We need not consider whether the district court was correct in holding that MCA was also entitled to summary judgment because its use of Barbie was a nominative fair use.[1]

IV

Mattel separately argues that, under the Federal Trademark Dilution Act ("FTDA"), MCA's song dilutes the Barbie mark in two ways: It diminishes the mark's capacity to identify and distinguish Mattel products, and tarnishes the mark because the song is inappropriate for young girls. *See* 15 U.S.C. § 1125(c); *see also Panavision Int'l, L.P. v. Toeppen*, 141 F.3d 1316, 1324 (9th Cir. 1998).

"Dilution" refers to the "whittling away of the value of a trademark" when it's used to identify different products. 4 J. Thomas McCarthy, *McCarthy on Trademarks and Unfair Competition* § 24.67 at 24–120; § 24.70 at 24–122 (2001). For example, Tylenol snowboards, Netscape sex shops and Harry Potter dry cleaners would all weaken the "commercial magnetism" of these marks and diminish their ability to evoke their original associations. Ralph S. Brown, Jr., *Advertising and the Public Interest: Legal Protection of Trade Symbols*, 57 Yale L.J. 1165, 1187 (1948), *reprinted* in 108 Yale L.J. 1619 (1999). These uses dilute the selling power of these trademarks by blurring their "uniqueness and singularity," Frank I. Schechter, *The Rational Basis of Trademark Protection*, 40 Harv. L. Rev. 813, 831 (1927), and/or by tarnishing them with negative associations.

By contrast to trademark infringement, the injury from dilution usually occurs when consumers aren't confused about the source of a product: Even if no one suspects that the maker of analgesics has entered into the snowboard business, the Tylenol mark will now bring to mind two products, not one. Whereas trademark law targets "interference with the source signaling function" of trademarks, dilution protects owners "from an appropriation of or free riding on" the substantial investment that they have made in their marks. *I.P. Lund Trading ApS v. Kohler Co.*, 163 F.3d 27, 50 (1st Cir. 1998).

Originally a creature of state law, dilution received nationwide recognition in 1996 when Congress amended the Lanham Act by enacting the FTDA.[2] The statute protects "the owner of a famous mark ... against another person's commercial use in commerce of a mark or trade name, if such use begins after the mark has become famous and causes dilution of the distinctive quality of the mark." 15 U.S.C. § 1125(c). Dilutive uses are prohibited unless they fall within one of the three statutory exemptions discussed below. *See* pp. 10495–96 *infra*. For a lucid and scholarly discus-

---

1. The likelihood-of-confusion test also governs Mattel's state law claims of unfair competition. *Cleary v. News Corporation*, 30 F.3d 1255, 1262–63 (9th Cir.1994) (citing *Academy of Motion Picture Arts & Sciences v. Creative House Promotions, Inc.*, 944 F.2d 1446, 1457 (9th Cir.1991)). Therefore, the district court properly granted summary judgment on these claims as well.

2. Even at the state level, dilution is of relatively recent vintage. The first anti-dilution statute was enacted in Massachusetts in 1947, *see* Mass. Gen. Laws Ann. Ch. 110B, § 12 (West 1992). By the time the FTDA was enacted in 1996, only twenty-six states had anti-dilution statutes on the books. *See* 4 *McCarthy* § 24:80, at 24–136.2 n. 2; H.R.Rep. No. 104–374, at 3–4 (1995), *reprinted in* 1995 U.S.C.C.A.N. 1029, 1030–31.

sion of the statutory terms, as well as the purposes of the federal dilution statute, we refer the reader to Judge Leval's opinion in *Nabisco, Inc. v. PF Brands, Inc.*, 191 F.3d 208, 214–17 (2d Cir. 1999). Barbie easily qualifies under the FTDA as a famous and distinctive mark, and reached this status long before MCA began to market the Barbie Girl song. The commercial success of Barbie Girl establishes beyond dispute that the Barbie mark satisfies each of these elements.

We are also satisfied that the song amounts to a "commercial use in commerce." Although this statutory language is ungainly, its meaning seems clear: It refers to a use of a famous and distinctive mark to sell goods other than those produced or authorized by the mark's owner. *Panavision*, 141 F.3d at 1324–25. That is precisely what MCA did with the Barbie mark: It created and sold to consumers in the marketplace commercial products (the Barbie Girl single and the Aquarium album) that bear the Barbie mark.

MCA's use of the mark is dilutive. MCA does not dispute that, while a reference to Barbie would previously have brought to mind only Mattel's doll, after the song's popular success, some consumers hearing Barbie's name will think of both the doll and the song, or perhaps of the song only. This is a classic blurring injury and is in no way diminished by the fact that the song itself refers back to Barbie the doll. To be dilutive, use of the mark need not bring to mind the junior user alone. The distinctiveness of the mark is diminished if the mark no longer brings to mind the senior user alone.

We consider next the applicability of the FTDA's three statutory exemptions. These are uses that, though potentially dilutive, are nevertheless permitted: comparative advertising; news reporting and commentary; and noncommercial use. 15 U.S.C. § 1125(c)(4)(B). The first two exemptions clearly do not apply; only the exemption for noncommercial use need detain us.

A "noncommercial use" exemption, on its face, presents a bit of a conundrum because it seems at odds with the earlier requirement that the junior use be a "commercial use in commerce." If a use has to be commercial in order to be dilutive, how then can it also be noncommercial so as to satisfy the exception of section 1125(c)(4)(B)? If the term "commercial use" had the same meaning in both provisions, this would eliminate one of the three statutory exemptions defined by this subsection, because any use found to be dilutive would, of necessity, not be noncommercial.

Such a reading of the statute would also create a constitutional problem, because it would leave the FTDA with no First Amendment protection for dilutive speech other than comparative advertising and news reporting. This would be a serious problem because the primary (usually exclusive) remedy for dilution is an injunction.[5] As noted above, tension with the First Amendment also exists in the trademark context, especially

---

5. The FTDA provides for both injunctive relief and damages, but the latter is only available if plaintiff can prove a willful intent to dilute. 15 U.S.C. § 1125(c)(2).

where the mark has assumed an expressive function beyond mere identification of a product or service. *See* pp. 10487–89 *supra*; *New Kids on the Block v. News Am. Publ'g, Inc.*, 971 F.2d 302, 306–08 (9th Cir. 1992). These concerns apply with greater force in the dilution context because dilution lacks two very significant limitations that reduce the tension between trademark law and the First Amendment.

First, depending on the strength and distinctiveness of the mark, trademark law grants relief only against uses that are likely to confuse. *See* 5 *McCarthy* § 30:3 at 30–8 to 30–11; *Restatement* § 35 cmt. c at 370. A trademark injunction is usually limited to uses within one industry or several related industries. Dilution law is the antithesis of trademark law in this respect, because it seeks to protect the mark from association in the public's mind with wholly unrelated goods and services. The more remote the good or service associated with the junior use, the more likely it is to cause dilution rather than trademark infringement. A dilution injunction, by contrast to a trademark injunction, will generally sweep across broad vistas of the economy.

Second, a trademark injunction, even a very broad one, is premised on the need to prevent consumer confusion. This consumer protection rationale—averting what is essentially a fraud on the consuming public—is wholly consistent with the theory of the First Amendment, which does not protect commercial fraud. *Cent. Hudson Gas & Elec. v. Pub. Serv. Comm'n*, 447 U.S. 557, 566, 65 L. Ed. 2d 341, 100 S. Ct. 2343 (1980); *see Thompson v. W. States Med. Ctr.*, 152 L. Ed. 2d 563, 122 S. Ct. 1497 (2002) (applying *Central Hudson*). Moreover, avoiding harm to consumers is an important interest that is independent of the senior user's interest in protecting its business.

Dilution, by contrast, does not require a showing of consumer confusion, 15 U.S.C. § 1127, and dilution injunctions therefore lack the built-in First Amendment compass of trademark injunctions. In addition, dilution law protects only the distinctiveness of the mark, which is inherently less weighty than the dual interest of protecting trademark owners and avoiding harm to consumers that is at the heart of every trademark claim.

Fortunately, the legislative history of the FTDA suggests an interpretation of the "noncommercial use" exemption that both solves our interpretive dilemma and diminishes some First Amendment concerns: "Noncommercial use" refers to a use that consists entirely of noncommercial, or fully constitutionally protected, speech. *See* 2 Jerome Gilson *et al.*, *Trademark Protection and Practice* § 5.12[1][c][vi] at 5–240 (this exemption "is intended to prevent the courts from enjoining speech that has been recognized to be [fully] constitutionally protected," "such as parodies"). Where, as here, a statute's plain meaning "produces an absurd, and perhaps unconstitutional, result[, it is] entirely appropriate to consult all public materials, including the background of [the statute] and the legislative history of its adoption." *Green v. Bock Laundry Mach. Co.*, 490 U.S. 504, 527, 104 L. Ed. 2d 557, 109 S. Ct. 1981 (1989) (Scalia, J., concurring).

The legislative history bearing on this issue is particularly persuasive. First, the FTDA's sponsors in both the House and the Senate were aware of the potential collision with the First Amendment if the statute authorized injunctions against protected speech. Upon introducing the counterpart bills, sponsors in each house explained that the proposed law "will not prohibit or threaten noncommercial expression, such as parody, satire, editorial and other forms of expression that are not a part of a commercial transaction." 141 Cong. Rec. S19306–10, S19310 (daily ed. Dec. 29, 1995) (statement of Sen. Hatch); 141 Cong. Rec. H14317–01, H14318 (daily ed. Dec. 12, 1995) (statement of Rep. Moorhead). The House Judiciary Committee agreed in its report on the FTDA. H.R. Rep. No. 104–374, at 4 (1995), *reprinted* in 1995 U.S.C.C.A.N. 1029, 1031 ("The bill will not prohibit or threaten 'noncommercial' expression, as that term has been defined by the courts.").[6]

The FTDA's section-by-section analysis presented in the House and Senate suggests that the bill's sponsors relied on the "noncommercial use" exemption to allay First Amendment concerns. H.R. Rep. No. 104–374, at 8, *reprinted* in 1995 U.S.C.C.A.N. 1029, 1035 (the exemption "expressly incorporates the concept of 'commercial' speech from the 'commercial speech' doctrine, and proscribes dilution actions that seek to enjoin use of famous marks in 'non-commercial' uses (such as consumer product reviews)"); 141 Cong. Rec. S19306–10, S19311 (daily ed. Dec. 29, 1995) (the exemption "is consistent with existing case law[, which] recognizes that the use of marks in certain forms of artistic and expressive speech is protected by the First Amendment"). At the request of one of the bill's sponsors, the section-by-section analysis was printed in the Congressional Record. 141 Cong. Rec. S19306–10, S19311 (daily ed. Dec. 29, 1995). Thus, we know that this interpretation of the exemption was before the Senate when the FTDA was passed, and that no senator rose to dispute it.

To determine whether Barbie Girl falls within this exemption, we look to our definition of commercial speech under our First Amendment caselaw. See H.R. Rep. No. 104–374, at 8, *reprinted* in 1995 U.S.C.C.A.N. 1029, 1035 (the exemption "expressly incorporates the concept of 'commercial' speech from the 'commercial speech' doctrine"); 141 Cong. Rec. S19306–10, S19311 (daily ed. Dec. 29, 1995) (the exemption "is consistent with existing [First Amendment] case law"). "Although the boundary between commercial and noncommercial speech has yet to be clearly delineated, the 'core notion of commercial speech' is that it 'does no more than propose a commercial transaction.'" *Hoffman v. Capital Cities/ABC, Inc.*, 255 F.3d 1180, 1184 (9th Cir. 2001) (quoting *Bolger v. Youngs Drug Prods Corp.*, 463 U.S. 60, 66, 77 L. Ed. 2d 469, 103 S. Ct. 2875 (1983)). If speech is not

---

6. Our interpretation of the noncommercial use exemption does not eliminate all tension between the FTDA and the First Amendment because the exemption does not apply to commercial speech, which enjoys "qualified but nonetheless substantial protection." *Bolger v. Youngs Drug Prod's Corp.*, 463 U.S. 60, 68, 103 S.Ct. 2875 (1983) (applying *Central Hudson Gas & Electric Corp. v.* *Pub. Serv. Comm'n,* 447 U.S. 557, 100 S.Ct. 2343, 65 L.Ed.2d 341 (1980)). *See also Thompson,* 535 U.S. at ___, 122 S.Ct. at 1503–04 (same). It is entirely possible that a dilution injunction against purely commercial speech would run afoul of the First Amendment. Because that question is not presented here, we do not address it.

"purely commercial"—that is, if it does more than propose a commercial transaction—then it is entitled to full First Amendment protection. *Id.* at 1185–86 (internal quotation marks omitted).

In *Hoffman*, a magazine published an article featuring digitally altered images from famous films. Computer artists modified shots of Dustin Hoffman, Cary Grant, Marilyn Monroe and others to put the actors in famous designers' spring fashions; a still of Hoffman from the movie "Tootsie" was altered so that he appeared to be wearing a Richard Tyler evening gown and Ralph Lauren heels. Hoffman, who had not given permission, sued under the Lanham Act and for violation of his right to publicity. *Id.* at 1183.

The article featuring the altered image clearly served a commercial purpose: "to draw attention to the for-profit magazine in which it appeared" and to sell more copies. *Id.* at 1186. Nevertheless, we held that the article was fully protected under the First Amendment because it included protected expression: "humor" and "visual and verbal editorial comment on classic films and famous actors." *Id.* at 1185 (internal quotation marks omitted). Because its commercial purpose was "inextricably entwined with [these] expressive elements," the article and accompanying photographs enjoyed full First Amendment protection. *Id.*

Hoffman controls: Barbie Girl is not purely commercial speech, and is therefore fully protected. To be sure, MCA used Barbie's name to sell copies of the song. However, as we've already observed, *see* pp. 10489–90 *supra*, the song also lampoons the Barbie image and comments humorously on the cultural values Aqua claims she represents. Use of the Barbie mark in the song Barbie Girl therefore falls within the noncommercial use exemption to the FTDA. For precisely the same reasons, use of the mark in the song's title is also exempted.

. . .

VI

After Mattel filed suit, Mattel and MCA employees traded barbs in the press. When an MCA spokeswoman noted that each album included a disclaimer saying that Barbie Girl was a "social commentary [that was] not created or approved by the makers of the doll," a Mattel representative responded by saying, "That's unacceptable. . . . It's akin to a bank robber handing a note of apology to a teller during a heist. [It] neither diminishes the severity of the crime, nor does it make it legal." He later characterized the song as a "theft" of "another company's property."

MCA filed a counterclaim for defamation based on the Mattel representative's use of the words "bank robber," "heist," "crime" and "theft." But all of these are variants of the invective most often hurled at accused infringers, namely "piracy." No one hearing this accusation understands intellectual property owners to be saying that infringers are nautical cutthroats with eyepatches and peg legs who board galleons to plunder cargo. In context, all these terms are nonactionable "rhetorical hyperbole," *Gilbrook v. City of Westminster*, 177 F.3d 839, 863 (9th Cir. 1999). The parties are advised to chill.

AFFIRMED.

QUESTIONS

1. Ignoring for the moment any first amendment interest in recording a parody aimed at Barbie dolls, how likely is it that members of the public would be confused about the source or sponsorship of the Aqua song?

2. The version of section 43(c) in force when the *Barbie Girl* case came before the Ninth Circuit provided in subsection 43(c)(4)(B): "The following shall not be actionable under this section: . . . Noncommercial use of a mark." Examine the current language of section 43(c)(3). Does Judge Kozinksi's analysis still hold?

Mattel Inc. v. Walking Mountain Productions, 353 F.3d 792 (9th Cir.2003).

Thomas Forsythe, aka "Walking Mountain Productions," is a self-taught photographer who resides in Kanab, Utah. He produces photographs with social and political overtones. In 1997, Forsythe developed a series of 78 photographs entitled "Food Chain Barbie," in which he depicted Barbie in various absurd and often sexualized positions. Forsythe uses the word "Barbie" in some of the titles of his works. While his works vary, Forsythe generally depicts one or more nude Barbie dolls juxtaposed with vintage kitchen appliances. For example, "Malted Barbie" features a nude Barbie placed on a vintage Hamilton Beach malt machine. "Fondue a la Barbie" depicts Barbie heads in a fondue pot. "Barbie Enchiladas" depicts four Barbie dolls wrapped in tortillas and covered with salsa in a casserole dish in a lit oven.

"Barbie Enchiladas"

"Malted Barbie"

. . .

Forsythe's market success was limited. He displayed his works at two art festivals—the Park City Art Festival in Park City, Utah, and the Plaza Art Fair in Kansas City, Missouri.[2] He promoted his works through a postcard, a business card, and a website. Forsythe printed 2000 promotional postcards depicting his work, "Barbie Enchiladas," only 500 of which were ever circulated. Of those that were circulated, some were distributed throughout his hometown of Kanab and some to a feminist scholar who used slides of Forsythe's works in her academic presentations. He also sold 180 of his postcards to a friend who owned a book store in Kanab so she could resell them in her bookstore and

2. Additionally, Forsythe's works were chosen for display in various exhibitions, including the Dishman Competition at Lamar University in Texas, and the Through the Looking Glass Art Show in Los Alamos, New Mexico. Some of his "Food Chain Barbie" photographs were also selected for exhibition by the Deputy Director and Chief Curator of the Guggenheim Museum of Modern Art in New York.

sold an additional 22 postcards to two other friends. Prior to this lawsuit, Forsythe received only four or five unsolicited calls inquiring about his work. The "Food Chain Barbie" series earned Forsythe total gross income of $3,659.[3]

. . .

On August 23, 1999, Mattel filed this action in the United States District Court for the Central District of California (the "Los Angeles federal district court") against Forsythe, alleging that Forsythe's "Food Chain Barbie" series infringed Mattel's copyrights, trademarks, and trade dress.

. . .

The limited purpose of trademark protections set forth in the Lanham Trade-Mark Act, 15 U.S.C. § 1051 *et. seq.*, is to "avoid confusion in the marketplace" by allowing a trademark owner to "prevent[ ] others from duping consumers into buying a product they mistakenly believe is sponsored by the trademark owner." [*Mattel, Inc. v.*] *MCA* [*Records*, 296 F.3d 894 (9th Cir. 2002)] at 900. Trademark law aims to protect trademark owners from a false perception that they are associated with or endorse a product. . . .

As we recently recognized in *MCA*, however, when marks "transcend their identifying purpose" and "enter public discourse and become an integral part of our vocabulary," they "assume[ ] a role outside the bounds of trademark law." 296 F.3d at 900. Where a mark assumes such cultural significance, First Amendment protections come into play. *Id.* In these situations, "the trademark owner does not have the right to control public discourse whenever the public imbues his mark with a meaning beyond its source-identifying function." *Id.* See also *New Kids on the Block v. News Am. Publ'g Inc.*, 971 F.2d 302, 307 (9th Cir. 1992).

As we determined in *MCA*, Mattel's "Barbie" mark has taken on such a role in our culture. 296 F.3d at 898–99. In *MCA*, Mattel brought an identical claim against MCA Records, producers of a song entitled "Barbie Girl" that contained lyrics that parodied and mocked Barbie. *296 F.3d* at 894. Recognizing that First Amendment concerns in free expression are particularly present in the realm of artistic works, we rejected Mattel's claim. In doing so, we adopted the Second Circuit's First Amendment balancing test for applying the Lanham Act to titles

---

3. Purchases by Mattel investigators comprised at least half of Forsythe's total sales.

of artistic works as set forth in *Rogers v. Grimaldi*, 875 F.2d 994, 999 (2d Cir. 1989). *MCA*, 296 F.3d at 902.

. . .

Application of the *Rogers* test here leads to the same result as it did in *MCA*. Forsythe's use of the Barbie mark is clearly relevant to his work. . . .The Barbie mark in the titles of Forsythe's works and on his website accurately describe the subject of the photographs, which in turn, depict Barbie and target the doll with Forsythe's parodic message. . . .The photograph titles do not explicitly mislead as to Mattel's sponsorship of the works. . . .

Accordingly, the public interest in free and artistic expression greatly outweighs its interest in potential consumer confusion about Mattel's sponsorship of Forsythe's works.

B. *Trade dress*

Mattel also claims that Forsythe misappropriated its trade dress in Barbie's appearance, in violation of the Lanham Act, 15 U.S.C. § 1125. Mattel claims that it possesses a trade dress in the Superstar Barbie head and the doll's overall appearance. The district court concluded that there was no likelihood that the public would be misled into believing that Mattel endorsed Forsythe's photographs despite Forsythe's use of the Barbie figure.

Arguably, the Barbie trade dress also plays a role in our culture similar to the role played by the Barbie trademark—namely, symbolization of an unattainable ideal of femininity for some women. Forsythe's use of the Barbie trade dress, therefore, presumably would present First Amendment concerns similar to those that made us reluctant to apply the Lanham Act as a bar to the artistic uses of Mattel's Barbie trademark in both *MCA* and this case. But we need not decide how the *MCA/Rogers* First Amendment balancing might apply to Forsythe's use of the Barbie trade dress because we find, on a narrower ground, that it qualifies as nominative fair use.

. . .

In the trademark context, we recently held that a defendant's use is *classic* fair use where "a defendant has used the plaintiff's mark *only* to describe his own product, *and not at all to describe the plaintiff's product.*" *Cairns*[*v. Franklin Mint*], 292 F.3d at 1151 (emphasis in original). In contrast, a defendant's use of a plaintiff's mark is *nominative* where he or she "used the plaintiff's mark to describe the plaintiff's product, *even if the defendant's ultimate goal is to describe his own product.*" *Id.* (emphasis in original). The goal of a nominative use is generally for the "purposes of comparison, criticism [or] point of reference." *New Kids on the Block*, 971 F.2d at 306. These two mutually exclusive forms of fair use are equally applicable here in the trade dress context.

Applying these fair use standards to the trade dress context, we hold that a defendant's use is *classic* fair use where the defendant has used the plaintiff's dress to describe or identify the defendant's own product and not at all to describe or identify the plaintiff's product. Likewise, a defendant's use is *nominative* where he or she used the plaintiff's dress to describe or identify the plaintiff's product, even if the defendant's ultimate goal is to describe or identify his or her own product.

Forsythe's use of the Barbie trade dress is nominative. Forsythe used Mattel's Barbie figure and head in his works to conjure up associations of Mattel, while at the same time to identify his own work, which is a criticism and parody of Barbie. *See Cairns*, 292 F.3d at 1151. Where use of the trade dress or mark is grounded in the defendant's desire to refer to the plaintiff's product as a point of reference for defendant's own work, a use is nominative.

Fair use may be either nominative or classic. *Id.* at 1150. We recognize a fair use defense in claims brought under § 1125 where the use of the trademark "does not imply sponsorship or endorsement of the product because the mark is used only to describe the thing, rather than to identify its source." *New Kids on the Block*, 971 F.2d at 306. Thus, we recently reiterated that, in the trademark context, nominative use becomes nominative *fair use* when a defendant proves three elements:

> First, the plaintiff's product or service in question must be one not readily identifiable without use of the trademark; second, only so much of the mark or marks may be used as is reasonably necessary to identify the plaintiff's product or service; and third, the user must do nothing that would, in conjunction with the mark, suggest sponsorship or endorsement by the trademark holder.

Cairns, 292 F.3d at 1151 (quoting *New Kids on the Block*, 971 F.2d at 308).

. . .

We hold that Forsythe's use of Mattel's Barbie qualifies as nominative fair use. All three elements weigh in favor of Forsythe. Barbie would not be readily identifiable in a photographic work without use of the Barbie likeness and figure. Forsythe used only so much as was necessary to make his parodic use of Barbie readily identifiable, and it is highly unlikely that any reasonable consumer would have believed that Mattel sponsored or was affiliated with his work. The district court's grant of summary judgment to Forsythe on Mattel's trade dress infringement claim was, therefore, proper.

C. *Dilution*

Mattel also appeals the district court's grant of summary judgment on its trademark and dress dilution claims. The district court found that Forsythe was entitled to summary judgment because his use of the Barbie mark and trade dress was parody and thus "his expression is a non-commercial use."

Dilution may occur where use of a trademark "whittles away . . . the value of a trademark" by "blurring their uniqueness and singularity" or by "tarnishing them with negative associations." *MCA*, 296 F.3d at 903 (internal citations omitted). However, "tarnishment caused merely by an editorial or artistic parody ·which satirizes plaintiff's product or its image is not actionable under an anti-dilution statute because of the free speech protections of the First Amendment. . . ." 4 McCarthy, *supra*, § 24:105, at 24–225. A dilution action only applies to purely commercial speech. *MCA*, 296 F.3d at 904. Parody is a form of noncommercial expression if it does more than propose a commercial transaction. *See id.* at 906. Under *MCA*, Forsythe's artistic and parodic work is considered noncommercial speech and, therefore, not subject to a trademark dilution claim.

We reject Mattel's Lanham Act claims and affirm the district court's grant of summary judgment in favor of Forsythe. Mattel cannot use "trademark laws to . . . censor all parodies or satires which use [its] name" or dress. *New Kids on the Block*, 971 F.2d at 309.

C. TRADEMARKS AS SPEECH

ROBERT C. DENICOLA, TRADEMARKS AS SPEECH: CONSTITUTIONAL IMPLICATIONS OF THE EMERGING RATIONALES FOR THE PROTECTION OF TRADE SYMBOLS, 1982 Wis. L. Rev. 158, 206–07 (excerpt).

Judicial antipathy toward the enrichment that flows to the copyist has carried trademark owners to a series of triumphs over competing contentions. At some point, however, extensions of the trademark monopoly must be tempered by the realization that unlimited control over the use of trade symbols will at times interfere with the exercise of basic first amendment rights.

Trademark law, even if more by chance than design, has generally avoided such constitutional confrontations. Traditional theory, with its reliance on the confusion rationale, poses no threat to freedom of speech. Even the misappropriation and dilution rationales, whatever their substantive merits, do not endanger free speech interests when directed at the decorative or trademark use of another's mark. When the trademark is utilized as a vehicle for the communication of ideas, however, constitutional interests can no longer be ignored.

That the protection of trademarks does not on the whole exceed permissible bounds is no consolation to one whose constitutional rights are jeopardized. Nor is judicial intuition alone, however well educated, a sufficiently secure barrier against the infringement of free speech interests. When substantive standards offer the convenient malleability that characterizes the law of trademarks, nothing short of a candid examination of the constitutional implications of asserted rights can satisfactorily defend constitutional preserves.

———

Rogers v. Grimaldi

875 F.2d 994 (2d Cir.1989).

[text of opinion *supra* chapter 10B page 699]

Parks v. LaFace Records

329 F.3d 437 (6th Cir.2003).

■ HOLSCHUH, DISTRICT JUDGE.

This is a dispute over the name of a song. Rosa Parks is a civil rights icon who first gained prominence during the Montgomery, Alabama bus boycott in 1955. She brings suit against LaFace Records, a record producer, and OutKast, a "rap" (or "hip-hop") music duo, as well as several other named affiliates, for using her name as the title of their song, *Rosa Parks*. Parks contends that Defendants' use of her name constitutes false advertising under § 43(a) of the Lanham Act, 15 U.S.C. § 1125(a), and intrudes on her common law right of publicity under Michigan state law. Defendants argue that they are entitled to summary judgment because Parks has failed to show any violation of the Lanham Act or her right of publicity. Defendants further argue that, even if she has shown such a violation, their First Amendment freedom of artistic expression should be a defense as a matter of law to each of these claims. . . .

For the reasons hereafter set forth, we believe that, with respect to Rosa Parks' claims under the Lanham Act and under the common law right of publicity, "the evidence is such that a reasonable jury could return a verdict for the nonmoving party." We therefore conclude that the district court erred in granting Defendants' motion for summary judgment on those claims. . . .

I.   BACKGROUND

A.   Facts

Rosa Parks is an historical figure who first gained prominence as a symbol of the civil rights movement in the United States during the 1950s and 1960s. In 1955, while riding in the front of a segregated bus in Montgomery, Alabama, she refused to yield her seat to a white passenger and move to the back of the bus as blacks were required to do by the then-existing laws requiring segregation of the races. A 381–day bus boycott in Montgomery flowed from that one event, which eventually became a catalyst for organized boycotts, sit-ins, and demonstrations all across the South. Her single act of defiance has garnered her numerous public accolades and awards, and she has used that celebrity status to promote various civil and human rights causes as well as television programs and books inspired by her life story. She has also approved a collection of gospel recordings by various artists entitled *Verity Records Presents: A Tribute to Mrs. Rosa Parks* (the *"Tribute"* album), released in 1995.

Defendants are OutKast, comprised of recording artists Andre "Dre" Benjamin and Antwan "Big Boi" Patton; their record producers, LaFace, founded by and named after Antonio "L.A." Reid and Kenny "Babyface" Edmonds; and LaFace's record distributors, Arista Records and BMG Entertainment (collectively "Defendants"). In September 1998, Defendants released the album *Aquemini*. The album's first single release was a song titled *Rosa Parks*, described as a "hit single" by a sticker on the album. The same sticker that contained the name *Rosa Parks* also contained a Parental Advisory warning of "explicit content." Because, as later discussed, the critical issue in this case is a determination of the artistic relevance of the title, *Rosa Parks*, to the content of the song, the lyrics obviously must be considered in their entirety. They are as follows:

(Hook)

Ah ha, hush that fuss
Everybody move to the back of the bus
Do you wanna bump and slump with us
We the type of people make the club get crunk

Verse 1: (Big Boi)

Many a day has passed, the night has gone by
But still I find the time to put that bump off in your eye
Total chaos, for these playas, thought we was absent
We takin another route to represent the Dungeon Family
Like Great Day, me and my nigga decide to take the back way

We stabbing every city then we headed to that bat cave
A–T–L, Georgia, what we do for ya
Bull doggin hoes like them Georgetown Hoyas
Boy you sounding silly, thank my Brougham aint sittin pretty
Doing doughnuts round you suckas like then circles around titties
Damn we the committee gone burn it down
But us gone bust you in the mouth with the chorus now

(Hook)

Verse 2: (Andre)

I met a gypsy and she hipped me to some life game
To stimulate then activate the left and right brain
Said baby boy you only funky as your last cut
You focus on the past your ass'll be a has what
Thats one to live by or either that one to die to
I try to just throw it at you determine your own adventure
Andre, got to her station here's my destination
She got off the bus, the conversation lingered in my head for hours
Took a shower kinda sour cause my favorite group ain't comin with it

But I'm witcha you cause you probably goin through it anyway
But anyhow when in doubt went on out and bought it
Cause I thought it would be jammin but examine all the flawsky-wawsky
Awfully, it's sad and it's costly, but that's all she wrote
And I hope I never have to float in that boat
Up shit creek it's weak is the last quote
That I want to hear when I'm goin down when all's said and done
And we got a new joe in town
When the record player get to skippin and slowin down
All yawl can say is them niggas earned that crown but until then
. . .

(Hook)

(Harmonica Solo)

(Hook till fade)

B. Procedural History

Parks sued Defendants in the Wayne County Circuit Court of Michigan alleging, *inter alia*, that Defendants' unauthorized use of her name infringes on her right to publicity, defames her character, and interferes with an ongoing business relationship. Defendants removed this case to the District Court for the Eastern District of Michigan. Parks thereafter filed an amended complaint that reiterated her state law claims and added a false advertising claim under § 43(a) of the Lanham Act.

The parties entered into a stipulation of the facts ("Stipulated Facts") and filed cross-motions for summary judgment. Applying *Rogers v. Grimaldi*, 875 F.2d 994 (2d Cir. 1989), the district court concluded that the First Amendment, as a matter of law, was a defense to Parks' Lanham Act and right of publicity claims. *See Parks v. LaFace Records*, 76 F.Supp.2d 775, 780–84 (E.D. Mich. 1999). Specifically, the court found that (1) an "obvious relationship" between the content of the song and its title *Rosa Parks* renders the right of publicity inapplicable as a matter of law, *id.* at 780; (2) with respect to the Lanham Act, there was no explicit representation that the work was endorsed by Parks, *id.* at 783; (3) the prominent appearance of OutKast's name on their album cured any likelihood of consumer confusion between Plaintiff's and Defendants' albums as a matter of law, *id.* at 784; and (4) even if there were some likelihood of consumer confusion, such risk was outweighed by the First Amendment interests of the Defendants, 76 F. Supp. 2d at 783. . . .

II. DISCUSSION

* * *

[T]he scope of § 43(a) extends beyond disputes between producers of commercial products and their competitors. It also permits celebrities to vindicate property rights in their identities against allegedly misleading commercial use by others. *See Waits v. Frito–Lay, Inc.*, 978 F.2d 1093, 1110

(9th Cir. 1992) (celebrity suit against snack manufacturer for unauthorized use of his distinctive voice in a commercial); *Allen v. Nat'l Video, Inc.*, 610 F. Supp. 612, 624–25 (S.D.N.Y. 1985) (celebrity suit against a video retailer for use of a celebrity look-alike in its advertisements); *Landham v. Lewis Galoob Toys, Inc.*, 227 F.3d 619, 626 (6th Cir. 2000) (actor sued toy company for creating an action figure named after one of his movie characters); *Abdul–Jabbar v. Gen. Motors Corp.*, 85 F.3d 407, 410 (9th Cir. 1996) (professional basketball player sued car manufacturer for using his birth name to sell cars). Celebrities have standing to sue under § 43(a) because they possess an economic interest in their identities akin to that of a traditional trademark holder. *See Waits*, 978 F.2d at 1110. *See also* 4 J. Thomas McCarthy, *McCarthy on Trademarks and Unfair Competition* § 28:15 (4th ed. 2002)(discussing cases).

In order to prevail on a false advertising claim under § 43(a), a celebrity must show that use of his or her name is likely to cause confusion among consumers as to the "affiliation, connection, or association" between the celebrity and the defendant's goods or services or as to the celebrity's participation in the "origin, sponsorship, or approval" of the defendant's goods or services. *See* 15 U.S.C. § 1125(a)(1)(A); *Landham*, 227 F.3d at 626; *Wendt v. Host Int'l, Inc.*, 125 F.3d 806, 812 (9th Cir. 1997); *Cardtoons, L.C. v. Major League Baseball Players Ass'n*, 95 F.3d 959, 966 (10th Cir. 1996); *White v. Samsung Elecs. Am., Inc.*, 971 F.2d 1395, 1399 (9th Cir. 1992). Consumer confusion occurs when "consumers ... believe that the products or services offered by the parties are affiliated in some way," *Homeowners Group, Inc. v. Home Mktg. Specialists, Inc.*, 931 F.2d 1100, 1107 (6th Cir. 1991), or "when consumers make an incorrect mental association between the involved commercial products or their producers," *Cardtoons*, 95 F.3d at 966 (*quoting San Francisco Arts & Athletics, Inc. v. United States Olympic Comm.*, 483 U.S. 522, 564, 97 L. Ed. 2d 427, 107 S. Ct. 2971 (1987) (Brennan, J., dissenting)). A "likelihood" means a "probability" rather than a "possibility" of confusion....

Parks contends that Defendants have violated the Lanham Act because the *Rosa Parks* title misleads consumers into believing that the song is about her or that she is affiliated with the Defendants, or has sponsored or approved the *Rosa Parks* song and the *Aquemini* album. She argues that the risk of confusion is enhanced by the fact that her authorized *Tribute* album is in the marketplace alongside Defendants' album featuring the *Rosa Parks* single. As additional evidence for her claim, Parks points to Defendants' concession that they have used the *Rosa Parks* title to advertise and promote both the song and the *Aquemini* album. She also supplies twenty-one affidavits from consumers affirming that they either believed Defendants' song was about Parks or was connected to the *Tribute* album authorized by her.

Defendants respond that Parks' Lanham Act claim must fail for two reasons. First, they claim that Parks does not possess a trademark right in her name and Defendants have not made a trademark use of her name, as allegedly required for a cause of action under the Lanham Act. Second, they contend that even if use of the title posed some risk of consumer confusion, the risk is outweighed by Defendants' First Amendment right to free expression.

1. Trademark Right In and Trademark Use of Parks' Name

Citing *Rock & Roll Hall of Fame & Museum, Inc. v. Gentile Productions*, 134 F.3d 749, 756 (6th Cir. 1998), Defendants contend that Parks' § 43(a) claim must fail because they have made no trademark use of her name. However, Defendants misconceive the legal basis of a Lanham Act claim. It is not necessary for them to make a "trademark" use of Rosa Parks' name in order for her to have a cause of action for false advertising under § 43(a) of the Lanham Act.

Rosa Parks clearly has a property interest in her name akin to that of a person holding a trademark. It is beyond question that Parks is a celebrity. The parties have stipulated to her international fame and to her prior authorization of television programs and books. We have already established, *supra*, that courts routinely recognize a property right in celebrity identity akin to that of a trademark holder under § 43(a). *See, e.g., Landham*, 227 F.3d at 626; *Waits*, 978 F.2d at 1110; *Allen*, 610 F. Supp. at 624–25. We find Parks' prior commercial activities and international recognition as a symbol of the civil rights movement endow her with a trademark interest in her name the same as if she were a famous actor or musician.

Therefore, even though Rosa Parks' name might not be eligible for registration as a trademark, and even though Defendants were not selling Rosa Parks-brand CD's, a viable cause of action also exists under § 43(a) if consumers falsely believed that Rosa Parks had sponsored or approved the song, or was somehow affiliated with the song or the album. We turn then to Defendants' second argument, that even if Parks could establish some likelihood of confusion, the First Amendment protects Defendants' choice of title.

* * *

The application of *Rogers* ... in cases decided in other circuits, persuades us that *Rogers* is the best test for balancing Defendants' and the public's interest in free expression under the First Amendment against Parks' and the public's interest in enforcement of the Lanham Act. We thus apply the *Rogers* test to the facts before us.

3. Application of the Rogers Test

a. Artistic Relevance Prong

The first prong of *Rogers* requires a determination of whether there is any artistic relationship between the title and the underlying work. *Rogers*, 875 F.2d at 999. Parks contends that a cursory review of the *Rosa Parks* title and the lyrics demonstrates that there is no artistic connection between them. Parks also submits two articles in which members of OutKast are purported to have admitted that the song was not about her. As further evidence, she offers a "translation" of the lyrics of the song

Rosa Parks, derived from various electronic "dictionaries" of the "rap" vernacular to demonstrate that the song truly has nothing to do with Parks herself. The "translation" of the chorus reads as follows:

> "Be quiet and stop the commotion. OutKast is coming back out [with new music] so all other MCs [mic checkers, rappers, Master of Ceremonies] step aside. Do you want to ride and hang out with us? OutKast is the type of group to make the clubs get hyped-up/excited."

Pl. Br. at 5.

Defendants respond that their use of Parks' name is "metaphorical" or "symbolic." They argue that the historical association between Rosa Parks and the phrase "move to the back of the bus" is beyond dispute and that Parks' argument that the song is not "about" her in a biographical sense is simply irrelevant.

The district court was of the opinion that the artistic relationship between the title and the song was "so obvious that the matter is not open to reasonable debate." *Parks*, 76 F.Supp.2d at 782. The court said:

> Rosa Parks is universally known for and commonly associated with her refusal ... to ... "move to the back of the bus." The song at issue makes unmistakable reference to that symbolic act a total of ten times. Admittedly, the song is not about plaintiff in a strictly biographical sense, but it need not be. Rather, defendants' use of plaintiff's name, along with the phrase "move to the back of the bus," is metaphorical and symbolic.

Id. at 780.

Contrary to the opinion of the district court, we believe that the artistic relationship between the title and the content of the song is certainly not obvious and, indeed, is "open to reasonable debate" for the following reasons.

It is true that the phrase "move to the back of the bus" is repeatedly used in the "hook" or chorus of the song. When the phrase is considered *in the context of the lyrics*, however, the phrase has absolutely nothing to do with Rosa Parks. There could be no stronger, no more compelling, evidence of this fact than the admission of "Dre" (Andre "Dre" Benjamin) that, "We (OutKast) never intended for the song to be about Rosa Parks or the civil rights movement. It was just symbolic, meaning that we comin' back out, so all you other MCs move to the back of the bus." J.A. at 333. The composers did *not* intend it to be about Rosa Parks, and the lyrics are *not* about Rosa Parks. The lyrics' sole message is that OutKast's competitors are of lesser quality and, therefore, must "move to the back of the bus," or in other words, "take a back seat." We believe that reasonable persons could conclude that there is no relationship of any kind between Rosa Parks' name and the content of the song—a song that is nothing more and nothing less than a paean announcing the triumph of superior people in the entertainment business over inferior people in that business. *Back of the Bus*, for example, would be a title that is obviously relevant to the content of the song, but it also would not have the marketing power of an icon of the civil rights movement.[6] Choosing Rosa Parks' name as the title to the song unquestionably enhanced the song's potential sale to the consuming public.

The *Rogers* court made an important point which clearly applies in this case. The court said, "poetic license is not without limits. The purchaser of a book, like the purchaser of a can of peas, has a right not to be misled as to the source of the product." *Rogers*, 875 F.2d at 997. The same is also true regarding the content of a song. The purchaser of a song titled *Rosa Parks* has a right not to be misled regarding the content of that song. While the expressive element of titles admittedly requires more protection than the labeling of ordinary commercial products, "[a] misleading title with no artistic relevance cannot be sufficiently justified by a free expression interest," *id.* at 999, and the use of such a title, as in the present case, could be found to constitute a violation of the Lanham Act. Including the phrase "move to the back of the bus" in the lyrics of this song, in our opinion, does not justify, as a matter of law, the appropriation of Rosa Parks' name for the title to the song, and the fact that the phrase is repeated ten times or fifty times does not affect the question of the relevancy of the title to the lyrics. . . .

While Defendants' lyrics contain profanity and a great deal of "explicit" language (together with a parental warning), they contain absolutely nothing that could conceivably, by any stretch of the imagination, be considered, explicitly or implicitly, a reference to courage, to sacrifice, to the civil rights movement or to any other quality with which Rosa Parks is identified. If the requirement of "relevance" is to have any meaning at all, it would not be unreasonable to conclude that the title *Rosa Parks* is *not* relevant to the content of the song in question. The use of this woman's name unquestionably was a good marketing tool—*Rosa Parks* was likely to sell far more recordings than *Back of the Bus*—but its use could be found by a reasonable finder of fact to be a flagrant deception on the public regarding the actual content of this song and the creation of an impression that Rosa Parks, who had approved the use of her name in connection with the *Tribute* album, had also approved or sponsored the use of her name on Defendants' composition.

It is certainly not dispositive that, in response to an interview following the filing of this lawsuit, one of the OutKast members said that using Rosa Parks' name was "symbolic." Where an artist proclaims that a celebrity's name is used merely as a "symbol" for the lyrics of a song, and such use is highly questionable when the lyrics are examined, a legitimate question is presented as to whether the artist's claim is sincere or merely a guise to escape liability. Our task, it seems to us, is not to accept without question whatever purpose Defendants may now claim they had in using Rosa Parks' name. It is, instead, to make a determination as to whether,

---

6. Suggesting that "Back of the Bus" would have been an appropriate title is not meant to be an application of the "alternative avenues" test discussed *supra*. It simply shows that such a title would clearly be artistically relevant under the first prong of *Rogers*.

applying the law of *Rogers*, there is a genuine issue of material fact regarding the question of whether the title is artistically relevant to the content of the song. As noted above, crying "artist" does not confer *carte blanche* authority to appropriate a celebrity's name. Furthermore, crying "symbol" does not change that proposition and confer authority to use a celebrity's name when none, in fact, may exist.

It appears that the district court's rendition of summary judgment for OutKast was based on the court's conclusion that Defendants' use of Plaintiff's name as the song's title was "metaphorical and symbolic." *Id.* at 780. The obvious question, however, is *symbolic of what*? There is no doubt that Rosa Parks is a symbol. As the parties agree, she is "an international symbol of freedom, humanity, dignity and strength." There is not even a hint, however, of any of these qualities in the song to which Defendants attached her name. In lyrics that are laced with profanity and in a "hook" or chorus that is pure egomania, many reasonable people could find that this is a song that is clearly *antithetical* to the qualities identified with Rosa Parks. Furthermore, the use of Rosa Parks' name in a metaphorical sense is highly questionable. A metaphor is "a figure of speech in which a word or phrase denoting one kind of object or action is used in place of another to suggest a likeness or analogy between them." *Webster's Third New International Dictionary* 1420 (Phillip Babcock Gove, ed. 1976). The use of the phrase "go to the back of the bus" may be metaphorical to the extent that it refers to OutKast's competitors being pushed aside by OutKast's return and being forced to "take a back seat." The song, however, is not titled *Back of the Bus*. It is titled *Rosa Parks*, and it is difficult to equate OutKast's feeling of superiority, metaphorically or in any other manner, to the qualities for which Rosa Parks is known around the world. We believe that reasonable people could find that the use of Rosa Parks' name as the title to this song was not justified as being metaphorical or symbolic of anything for which Rosa Parks is famous. To the contrary, reasonable people could find that the name was appropriated solely because of the vastly increased marketing power of a product bearing the name of a national heroine of the civil rights movement.

We do not mean to imply that Rosa Parks must always be displayed in a flattering manner, or that she should have the ability to prevent any other characterization of her. She is a celebrity and, as such, she cannot prevent being portrayed in a manner that may not be pleasing to her.... The present case, however, does not involve any claim of caricature, parody or satire. It involves, instead, the use of a celebrity's name as the title to a song when it reasonably could be found that the celebrity's name has no artistic relevance to the content of the song. It involves, in short, a reasonable dispute whether the use of Rosa Parks' name was a misrepresentation and false advertising or whether it was a legitimate use of a celebrity's name in some recognized form of artistic expression protected by the First Amendment.

In *Rogers*, the court, in discussing the title to the movie *Ginger and Fred*, observed that "there is no doubt a risk that some people looking at the title 'Ginger and Fred' might think the film was about Rogers and Astaire in a direct, biographical sense. For those gaining that impression, the title is misleading." 875 F.2d at 1001. Likewise, in the present case, some people looking at the title *Rosa Parks* might think the song is about Rosa Parks and for those gaining that impression (as twenty-one consumer affidavits filed in this case indicate happened, J.A. at 342–62), the title is misleading. This, standing alone, may not be sufficient to show a violation of the Lanham Act *if* the title is nevertheless artistically relevant to the content of the underlying work.

There is a clear distinction, however, between the facts in *Rogers* and the facts in the present case. In *Rogers*, the court had no difficulty in finding that the title chosen for the movie *Ginger and Fred* had artistic relevance to the content of the movie. "The central characters in the film are nicknamed 'Ginger' and 'Fred,' and these names are not arbitrarily chosen just to exploit the publicity value of their real life counterparts but instead have genuine relevance to the film's story." 875 F.2d at 1001. The *Rogers* court further pointed out that the title *Ginger and Fred* is "entirely truthful as to its content in referring to the film's fictional protagonists who are known to their Italian audience as 'Ginger and Fred.'" *Id.* In other words, the title in *Rogers* was obviously relevant and truthful as to the film's content, because the film was about the main characters known in the film as Ginger and Fred. In contrast, it cannot be said that the title in the present case, *Rosa Parks*, is clearly truthful as to the content of the song which, as OutKast admits, is not about Rosa Parks at all and was never intended to be about Rosa Parks, and which does not refer to Rosa Parks or to the qualities for which she is known.

* * *

There is a genuine issue of material fact whether the use of Rosa Parks' name as a title to the song and on the cover of the album is artistically related to the content of the song or whether the use of the name Rosa Parks is nothing more than a misleading advertisement for the sale of the song.

b.   *Misleading Prong*

In *Rogers*, the court held that if the title of the work is artistically relevant to its content, there is no violation of the Lanham Act *unless* the "title explicitly misleads as to the source or the content of the work." 875 F.2d at 999.

* * *

We considered all the facts presented to us and concluded that, with reference to the first prong of the *Rogers* analysis, the issue of artistic relevance of the title *Rosa Parks* to the lyrics of the song is highly questionable and cannot be resolved as a matter of law. However, if, on remand, a trier of fact, after a full evidentiary hearing, concludes that the title *is* used in some symbolic or metaphorical sense, application of the *Rogers* analysis, under the particular facts of this case, would appear to be complete. In the present case, the title *Rosa Parks* "makes no explicit statement that the work is about that person in any direct sense." In other words, Defendants did not name the song, for example, *The True Life Story of Rosa Parks* or *Rosa Parks' Favorite Rap.*

In short, whether the title *Rosa Parks* has any artistic relevance to the content of the song is an issue that must be resolved by a finder of fact following an evidentiary hearing and not by a judge as a matter of law upon the limited record submitted in support of a motion for summary judgment. If, on remand, the finder of fact determines that OutKast placed the title *Rosa Parks* on a song to which it had no artistic relevance at all, then this would constitute a violation of the Lanham Act and judgment should be entered in favor of Plaintiff. However, if the finder of fact determines that the title is artistically relevant to the song's content, then the inquiry is at an end because the title "is not explicitly misleading as to the content of the work." In that event, judgment should be entered in favor of Defendants.

C.   *Right of Publicity*

* * *

a.   *Cognizability of a First Amendment Defense*

Because a plaintiff bears a reduced burden of persuasion to succeed in a right of publicity action, courts and commentators have recognized that publicity rights carry a greater danger of impinging on First Amendment rights than do rights associated with false advertising claims. *See Rogers,* 875 F.2d at 1004; *see also Cardtoons,* 95 F.3d at 967 (noting that publicity rights offer "substantially broader protection" than laws preventing false endorsement); [citation omitted]

We have recognized the importance of a First Amendment defense to right of publicity actions in a recent case. In *Ruffin–Steinback v. dePasse,* friends and family members of the Motown group, the "Temptations," sued the makers of a televised mini-series for the manner in which they and the former group members were portrayed in the film. 82 F.Supp.2d 723, 726–27 (E.D. Mich. 2000), *aff'd,* 267 F.3d 457 (6th Cir. 2001). The plaintiffs alleged that their likenesses were appropriated to endorse a product, the film, without their permission. The court found in that case that the plaintiffs could not overcome the defendant's First Amendment defense, even where the portrayal of the plaintiffs was partly fictionalized, and even where the likenesses of the plaintiffs were used to promote a videocassette version of the mini-series. *Id.* at 730–31; *see also Seale,* 949 F. Supp. at 337 (holding that the film *Panther,* which used the name and likeness of Black Panther founder Bobby Seale, was protected by the First Amendment).

As with the Lanham Act, then, we must conduct another balancing of interests—Parks' property right in her own name versus the freedom of artistic expression. . . .

b.   *Application of a First Amendment Defense*

In *Rogers*, the Second Circuit held that movie titles are protected from right of publicity actions unless the title is "wholly unrelated" to the content of the work or was "simply a disguised commercial advertisement for the sale of goods or services." 875 F.2d at 1004. This test is supported in the context of other expressive works by comment c of § 47 of the *Restatement (Third) of Unfair Competition*. It states that "use of another's identity in a novel, play, or motion picture is ... not ordinarily an infringement [of the right of publicity, unless] the name or likeness is used solely to attract attention to a work that is not related to the identified person." The *Rogers* formulation is also supported by the decision in *dePasse*. In *dePasse*, the court cited *Seale*, 949 F. Supp. at 337, for the proposition that the relationship between a plaintiff's identity and the content of the work is an element of a defense to a right of publicity action....

For the same reasons we have stated earlier and need not repeat, we believe that Parks' right of publicity claim presents a genuine issue of material fact regarding the question of whether the title to the song is or is not "wholly unrelated" to the content of the song. A reasonable finder of fact, in our opinion, upon consideration of all the evidence, could find the title to be a "disguised commercial advertisement" or adopted "solely to attract attention" to the work. *See Rogers*, 875 F.2d at 1004–05.

* * *

III.   CONCLUSION

We are not called upon in this case to judge the quality of Defendants' song, and whether we personally regard it as repulsive trash or a work of genius is immaterial to a determination of the legal issues presented to us....

In this case, for the reasons set forth above, the fact that Defendants cry "artist" and "symbol" as reasons for appropriating Rosa Parks' name for a song title does not absolve them from potential liability for, in the words of Shakespeare, filching Rosa Parks' good name.[12] The question of that liability, however, should be determined by the trier of fact after a full evidentiary hearing and not as a matter of law on a motion for summary judgment.

[*Editors' Note*: The case settled without going to trial. *See* D. Shepardson and J. Menard, "Parks Settles Outkast Suit," *Detroit News* (April 15, 2005).]

QUESTIONS

1. What is the basis of Ms. Parks' Lanham Act claim? If OutKast were to move for reconsideration in light of *Dastar*, how should the court rule?

---

12. Who steals my purse steals trash; 'tis something, nothing;
  'Twas mine, 'tis his, and has been slave to thousands;
  But he that filches from me my good name
Robs me of that which not enriches him
And makes me poor indeed.

William Shakespeare, *Othello*, act 3, sc. 3.

2.   The district court found that Rosa Parks' name had "obvious relevance" to OutKast's song. The court of appeals found it obviously irrelevant. The district court found the song's reference to Ms. Parks to be symbolic and protected by the first amendment. The court of appeals agreed Ms. Parks was a symbol, but not of anything to do with the song. Does *Rogers v. Grimaldi* oblige courts to engage in literary analysis of the references to named celebrities? Does *Parks v. LaFace* suggest courts are particularly competent to do it?

MasterCard International Inc. v. Nader 2000 Primary Committee, Inc.

70 U.S.P.Q.2d (BNA) 1046 (S.D.N.Y.2004).

■ George B. Daniels, District Judge:

. . .

MasterCard, a Delaware corporation with its principal place of business in New York, is a large financial institution that engages in the interchange of funds by credit and debit payment cards through over 23,000 banks and other foreign and domestic member financial institutions. Since Fall of 1997, MasterCard has commissioned the authorship of a series of advertisements that have come to be known as the "Priceless Advertisements." These advertisements feature the names and images of several goods and services purchased by individuals which, with voice overs and visual displays, convey to the viewer the price of each of these items. At the end of each of the Priceless Advertisements a phrase identifying some priceless intangible that cannot be purchased (such as "a day where all you have to do is breathe") is followed by the words or voice over: "Priceless. There are some things money can't buy, for everything else there's MasterCard."

In August 2000, MasterCard became aware that Ralph Nader and his presidential committee were broadcasting an allegedly similar advertisement on television that promoted the presidential candidacy of Ralph Nader in the 2000 presidential election. That political ad included a sequential display of a series of items showing the price of each ("grilled tenderloin for fund-raiser; $1,000 a plate;" "campaign ads filled with half-truths: $10 million;" "promises to special interest groups: over $100 billion"). The advertisement ends with a phrase identifying a priceless intangible that cannot be purchased ("finding out the truth: priceless. There are some things that money can't buy"). The resulting ad (the "Nader ad") was shown on television during a two week period from August 6–17, during the 2000 presidential campaign, and also appeared on the defendants' web site throughout that campaign. Plaintiff sent defendants a letter explaining its concern over the similarity of the commercials, and suggested that defendants broadcast a more "original" advertisement. When plaintiff contacted representatives of defendants a few days later, plaintiff MasterCard advised defendants to cease broadcasting their political advertisement due to its similarity with MasterCard's own commercial advertisement and resulting infringement liability.

When the parties could not come to an agreement, on August 16, 2000, MasterCard filed a complaint alleging the following counts against Ralph Nader and his presidential committee; trademark infringement and false designation of origin in violation of Section 43(a) of the Lanham Act; infringement of a registered trademark in violation of Section 32(1) of the Lanham Act; dilution in violation of Section 43(c) of the Lanham Act; copyright infringement in violation of the Copyright Act; unfair competition; misappropriation; infringement of New York Common Law Trademark Rights; dilution under New York law; and deceptive trade practices. Plaintiff sought a preliminary injunction during the 2000 presidential campaign which was denied by this Court. Thereafter, defendants moved for summary judgment on all nine of plaintiff's counts.

DISCUSSION

. . .

1. Trademark Infringement

MasterCard's first count is based on Section 43(a) of the Trademark Act, 15 U.S.C. Section 1125(a). Plaintiff claims that defendants have used two of MasterCard's service marks—"THERE ARE SOME THINGS MONEY CAN'T BUY. FOR EVERYTHING ELSE THERE'S MASTERCARD," and "PRICELESS" to misrepresent that the 2000 presidential candidacy of Ralph Nader for the office of President of the United States was endorsed by MasterCard. . . .

In trademark infringement cases, the Court must apply the undisputed facts to the balancing test outlined in *Polaroid Corp. v. Polarad Elecs., Corp.*, 287 F.2d 492, 495 (2d Cir. 1961), and may grant summary judgment where it finds, as a matter of law, that there is no likelihood of confusion to the public. . . .

[The court analyzed the *Polaroid* factors. Nader conceded that Mastercard's marks were strong, and that the Nader commercials used "there are some things money can't buy" and "priceless" in a way that created the same look, sound, and impression. The court concluded that there was little similarity between Mastercard's credit card business and Nader's political campaign, and little likelihood of Mastercard's bridging the gap. There was no evidence of actual confusion. The court found no evidence that Ralph Nader intended to pass himself off as associated with Mastercard:]

There is no basis to argue that the Ralph Nader political ad which has the clear intent to criticize other political candidates who accept money from wealthy contributors, at the same time, attempts or intends to imply that he is a political candidate endorsed by MasterCard. There is uncontradicted testimony that neither Ralph Nader, nor his committees, had any such intent

The seventh factor, the quality of defendants' products or services, is of insignificant weight in this case. There is no reasonable comparison to be made between the quality of the products and services provided by MasterCard and the value of defendants' politics. . . .

The eighth and final factor to be weighed is the level of consumer sophistication in either of the relevant markets for credit card services or for political candidates. Unless otherwise demonstrated, it is reasonable to conclude that the general American public is sophisticated enough to distinguish a Political Ad from a commercial advertisement. Rarely, if ever, is there a realistic opportunity to confuse the two. . . .

. . . Thus, after balancing the Polaroid factors, this Court finds that there is no genuine issue of material fact with regard to any likelihood of confusion between MasterCard's Priceless Advertisements and Ralph Nader's Political Ad which could constitute a violation of the Trademark Act.

    . . .

3.   Dilution

Counts Three and Eight of plaintiff's complaint allege against defendants federal and state dilution of plaintiff's trademarks. The Federal Trademark Dilution Act, 15 U.S.C. § 1125(c) and the New York anti-dilution law, New York Gen. Bus. Law § 360–1, protect against the unauthorized use of marks that impairs the goodwill and value of plaintiff's mark. . . . Under both federal and New York law, dilution can involve either blurring or tarnishment. [Citations]

    . . .

The Federal Trademark Dilution Act specifically exempts noncommercial uses of a mark from its coverage. Section 1125(c)(4) provides that "the following shall not be actionable under this section: . . . (B) Noncommercial use of a mark." Therefore, prior to even addressing whether defendants have actually diluted plaintiff's marks under the federal law, the Court must first determine whether defendants' use of the marks is "commercial," and thereby, whether that use is even covered by the statute.

Plaintiff argues that Ralph Nader's Political Ad is commercial in nature even though it neither sells products or services, is not designed to entice consumers to buy products or services, and does not propose any kind of commercial transaction. MasterCard asserts that contributions to the Nader 2000 General Committee "increased from $5125 before the Ad ran to $818,000 in August 2000, after the Ad ran through the 'DONATE ON–LINE' icon or otherwise." . . . Although the Nader Ad ran before a large sum of contributions were made to his campaign, plaintiff offers no evidence of a causal connection between the Ad and the contributions. There is nothing in the record other than the inference to be drawn from the proximity in time that advances the notion that the contributions Ralph Nader and his political committee received were a direct result of the Ad.

Even assuming the Nader Ad caused greater contributions to be made to his political campaign, this would not be enough to deem Ralph Nader's Ad "commercial." If so, then presumably, as suggested by defendants, all political campaign speech would also be "commercial speech" since all political candidates collect contributions. Ralph Nader's Political Ad attempts to communicate that other presidential candidates can be bought, but that the "truth," represented by himself, cannot. The Nader Ad is a strong political message which expresses his personal opinion on presidential campaigning. The legislative history of the Lanham Act clearly indicates that Congress did not intend for the Act to chill political speech. In speaking about the amendments to Section 43(a) that expanded what was actionable as deceptive advertisements, one of the new law's sponsors, United States Representative Robert Kastenmeier, pointed out that political advertising and promotion are not meant to be covered by the term "commercial." He stated that the statute

> uses the word "commercial" to describe advertising or promotion for business purposes, whether conducted by for-profit or non-profit organizations or individuals. *Political advertising and promotion is political speech, and therefore not encompassed by the term "commercial."* This is true whether what is being promoted is an individual candidacy for public office, or a particular political issue or point of view ...

134 Cong. Rec. H. 1297 (daily ed. April 13, 1989) (statement of Wisconsin Rep. Kastenmeier) (emphasis added).

Plaintiff MasterCard urges the Court to rely on *United We Stand America, Inc. v. United We Stand, America New York, Inc.*, 128 F.3d 86 (2d Cir. 1997) to conclude that Ralph Nader's activities are "commercial" in nature. That case is not instructive in determining whether or not MasterCard has a basis to bring a claim against defendants under the Federal Trademark Dilution Act. In *United We Stand*, the Court was determining whether a certain political activity fell under the scope and the meaning of the word "services" and "use in commerce" of the Lanham Trademark Act, § 32(1)(a), 15 U.S.C.A. § 1114(1)(a). That particular section of the Lanham Act does not have a commercial activity requirement, nor does it exempt from liability noncommercial use of a mark. *See Planned Parenthood Federation of America Inc. v. U.S. District Court Southern District of New York*, 42 U.S.P.Q.2d 1430, 1434 (S.D.N.Y. 1997). However, the Federal Trademark Dilution Act, 15 U.S.C.A. § 1125 (c), specifically exempts from the scope of all provisions of Section 1125 the "noncommercial use of a mark." See Id., at 1433.

Though not binding, this Court finds the analysis in *American Family Life Insurance Company v. Hagan, et al.*, 266 F. Supp.2d 682 (N.D.Ohio 2002), to be relevant and persuasive. In that case, similar to the case at hand, the plaintiff, American Family Life Insurance Company, or AFLAC, ran well-known "AFLAC Duck" commercials which featured a white duck quacking the company's name "AFLAC." *Id.*, at 684. One of the defendants was a candidate for Governor of the State of Ohio running against the incumbent Governor Robert Taft. The candidate and his Campaign, developed internet commercials that " 'borrow[ed]' from AFLAC's commercials. Specifically, the internet commercials included a crudely animated character made up of the incumbent Governor's head sitting on the body of a white cartoon duck; the duck quacks 'TaftQuack' several times during each commercial," which defendants ran on their website, www.taftquack.com.

Id. Defendants' website also contained a link which visitors could use to make campaign contributions. Id. at 686–87. Among other claims, plaintiff sued defendants for federal trademark dilution and moved for a preliminary injunction.

In denying the plaintiff's motion for a preliminary injunction, and finding that the plaintiff was not likely to prevail on its dilution claim, the court also found that defendants' speech was political, rather than commercial. Specifically, the court stated that the candidate was "using a quacking cartoon character, which admittedly brings to mind AFLAC's marks, *as part of his communicative message,* in the context of expressing political speech." *Id.*, at 700 (emphasis in original). The court added that though "the consuming public may associate the AFLAC Duck and the TaftQuack character-a proposition the Court accepts-[this] is an insufficient predicate to support injunctive relief of political speech." *Id.*, at 701. The court further noted that though defendants included in their website a mechanism for visitors to make campaign contributions, "it is arguable whether [the candidate's] speech proposes a commercial transaction at all." *Id.*, at 697. The court stated that defendants' solicitation of contributions, and the resulting making of contributions, "is much more than merely a commercial transaction. Indeed, this exchange is properly classified not as a commercial transaction at all, but completely noncommercial, political speech." *Id.*

This Court finds that Ralph Nader's use of plaintiff's trademarks is not commercial, but instead political in nature and that therefore, it is exempted from coverage by the Federal Trademark Dilution Act. However, even if Ralph Nader's use of plaintiff's trademarks could be deemed commercial in nature, such use did not dilute plaintiff's marks. Defendants do not dispute that plaintiff's marks are famous, distinctive, or that they used plaintiff's marks after such marks became famous. However, there is no evidence in the record that defendants' use of plaintiff's marks actually caused dilution of the distinctiveness of plaintiff's marks. Plaintiff does not offer evidence that defendants' limited use of the Priceless marks lessened its value or the capacity of these marks to identify and distinguish plaintiff's goods or services. Further, plaintiff does not claim, nor is there any evidence in the record, that due to defendant's use of plaintiff's marks, plaintiff altered or lessened its use of the marks to identify MasterCard's products or services.

Count Three of plaintiff's complaint alleging dilution of plaintiff's trademarks is dismissed on defendants' motion for summary judgment. Ralph Nader's use of plaintiff's trademarks is political in nature, not within a commercial context, and is therefore exempted from coverage by the Federal Trademark Dilution Act. Furthermore, there is no evidence on the record that Ralph Nader's use of plaintiff's trademarks diluted plaintiff's trademarks.

Planned Parenthood Federation of America, Inc. v. Bucci, 42 U.S.P.Q.2d (BNA) 1430 (S.D.N.Y.1997), *aff'd mem.*, 152 F.3d 920 (2d Cir.1998). Plaintiff owned service mark registrations for PLANNED PAR-

ENTHOOD and operated an informational World Wide Web site at URL: <http://www.ppfa.org>. Defendant, an anti-abortion activist, set up a "Planned Parenthood" website and home page at URL: <http://www.plannedparenthood.com> containing anti-abortion texts. Planned Parenthood filed suit under sections 32, 43(a)(1)(A), 43(a)(1)(B) and 43(c). The court applied the *Polaroid* factors and found confusion under sections 32 and 43(a)(1). Defendant raised a first amendment defense:

> Defendant also argues that his use of the "planned parenthood" mark is protected by the First Amendment. As defendant argues, trademark infringement law does not curtail or prohibit the exercise of the First Amendment right to free speech. I note that plaintiff has not sought, in any way, to restrain defendant from speech that criticizes Planned Parenthood or its mission, or that discusses defendant's beliefs regarding reproduction, family, and religion. The sole purpose of the Court's inquiry has been to determine whether the use of the "planned parenthood" mark as defendant's domain name and home page address constitutes an infringement of plaintiff's trademark.

> Defendant's use of another entity's mark is entitled to First Amendment protection when his use of that mark is part of a communicative message, not when it is used to identify the source of a product. *Yankee Publishing, Inc. v. News America Publishing, Inc.*, 809 F.Supp. 267, 275 (S.D.N.Y.1992). By using the mark as a domain name and home page address and by welcoming Internet users to the home page with the message "Welcome to the Planned Parenthood Home Page!" defendant identifies the web site and home page as being the product, or forum, of plaintiff. I therefore determine that, because defendant's use of the term "planned parenthood" is not part of a communicative message, his infringement on plaintiff's mark is not protected by the First Amendment.

> Defendant argues that his use of the "Planned Parenthood" name for his web site is entitled to First Amendment protection, relying primarily on the holding of *Yankee Publishing*, 809 F. Supp. at 275. In that case, Judge Leval noted that the First Amendment can protect unauthorized use of a trademark when such use is part of an expression of a communicative message: "the Second Circuit has construed the Lanham Act narrowly when the unauthorized use of the trademark is for the purpose of a communicative message, rather than identification of product origin." *Id.* Defendant argues that his use of the "Planned Parenthood" name for his web site is a communicative message.

> However, *Yankee Publishing* carefully draws a distinction between communicative messages and product labels or identifications:

> > When another's trademark ... is used without permission for the purpose of source identification, the trademark

> law generally prevails over the First Amendment. Free
> speech rights do not extend to labeling or advertising
> products in a manner that conflicts with the trademark
> rights of others.

Id. at 276. Defendant offers no argument in his papers as to why
the Court should determine that defendant's use of "plannedpar-
enthood.com" is a communicative message rather than a source
identifier. His use of "plannedparenthood.com" as a domain name
to identify his web site is on its face more analogous to source
identification than to a communicative message; in essence, the
name identifies the web site, which contains defendant's home
page. The statement that greets Internet users who access defendant's web site, "Welcome to the Planned Parenthood Home
Page," is also more analogous to an identifier than to a communication. For those reasons, defendant's use of the trademarked
term "planned parenthood" is not part of a communicative message, but rather, serves to identify a product or item, defendant's
web site and home page, as originating from Planned Parenthood.

Defendant's use of plaintiff's mark is not protected as a title
under *Rogers v. Grimaldi*, 875 F.2d 994, 998 (2d Cir.1989). There,
the Court of Appeals determined that the title of the film "Ginger
and Fred" was not a misleading infringement, despite the fact that
the film was not about Ginger Rogers and Fred Astaire, because of
the artistic implications of a title. The Court of Appeals noted that
"filmmakers and authors frequently rely on word-play, ambiguity,
irony, and allusion in titling their works." *Id.* The Court of
Appeals found that the use of a title such as the one at issue in
Rogers was acceptable "unless the title has no artistic relevance to
the underlying work"; even when the title has artistic relevance, it
may not be used to "explicitly mislead[] [the consumer] as to the
source or content of the work." *Id.* Here, even treating defendant's
domain name and home page address as titles, rather than as
source identifiers, I find that the title "plannedparenthood.com"
has no artistic implications, and that the title is being used to
attract some consumers by misleading them as to the web site's
source or content. Given defendant's testimony indicating that he
knew, and intended, that his use of the domain name "planned-
parenthood.com" would cause some "pro-abortion" Internet users
to access his web site, he cannot demonstrate that his use of
"planned parenthood" is entitled to First Amendment protection.

Because defendant's use of plaintiff's mark is subject to the
Lanham Act, because the *Polaroid* factors demonstrate that there
is a likelihood of confusion arising from defendant's use of plaintiff's mark, and because defendant has not raised a defense that
protects his use of the mark, plaintiff has met its burden of
demonstrating that a preliminary injunction against defendant's
use of plaintiff's mark is warranted.

Jews for Jesus v. Brodsky, 993 F.Supp. 282 (D.N.J.1998), *aff'd mem.*, 159 F.3d 1351 (3d Cir.1998). This controversy, like *Planned Parenthood*, involved registration of a domain name and posting of a website by an antagonist of the named organization. The registrant and website operator in this case sought to attract websurfers seeking the Jews for Jesus organization, in order to protest that organization's activities, and to lead potential strays back into the fold of traditional Jewish organizations. In addition to criticizing the Jews for Jesus organization, the website included a hyperlink to the "Outreach Judaism" organization. Brodsky's site also included a disclaimer: "The website is an independent project which reflects the personal opinion of its owner, and is in no way affiliated with the Jewish organization Outreach Judaism, or the Christian organization, Jews for Jesus." After holding that defendant's disclaimer did not remove the likelihood that the Internet-using public would be confused as to the source of defendant's jewsforjesus.org and jews-for-jesus.com sites, the court turned to the dilution claim:

In this case, the Defendant is using the Mark and the Name of the Plaintiff Organization to lure individuals to his Internet site where he makes disparaging statements about the Plaintiff Organization. His site then refers these individuals, via a hyperlink, to the Internet site maintained by the Outreach Judaism Organization which also contains information critical of and contrary to the teachings of the Plaintiff Organization. Such conduct amounts to "blurring" and "tarnishment" of the Mark and the Name of the Plaintiff Organization. *See Panavision [v. Toepper*, 945 F.Supp. 1296] at 1304....

In this case, the use by the Defendant in his domain name of the Mark and the Name of the Plaintiff Organization has resulted in not only the loss of control over the Mark and the Name of the Plaintiff Organization, but also in the reality that views directly contrary to those of the Plaintiff Organization will be disseminated through the unauthorized use of the Mark and the Name of the Plaintiff Organization. As such, irreparable harm has resulted....

c. The Use by Defendant of the Mark and the Name of the Plaintiff Organization Constitutes Commercial Speech

The Defendant contends his conduct is exempted from the dilution law because it is "non-commercial speech." Specifically, the Defendant claims his speech is non-commercial because "it is meant to call attention to issues of public importance."

"The non-commercial use of a domain name that impedes a trademark owner's use of that domain name does not constitute dilution" because such use is excluded from Section 1125(c). *Lockheed Martin Corp. v. Network Solutions, Inc.*, 985 F.Supp. 949 (C.D.Cal.1997) ... As such, the mere registration of a domain name, without more, is not a "commercial use" of a trademark. [Citations omitted.] "The exception for non-commercial use of a famous mark is intended to prevent courts from enjoining constitutionally protected speech. That is, the exclusion encompasses conduct such as parodies and consumer product reviews." *Panavision . . . .*

In this case, the Defendant has done more than merely register a domain name. He has created, in his words, a "bogus 'Jews for Jesus' "site intended to intercept, through the use of deceit and trickery, the audience sought by the Plaintiff Organization. Moreover, the Defendant Internet site uses the Mark and the Name of the Plaintiff Organization as its address, conveying the impression to Internet users that the Plaintiff Organization is the sponsor of the Defendant Internet site. Although the Defendant Internet site does not solicit funds directly like the defendant's site did in Planned Parenthood, the Outreach Judaism Organization Internet site (available through the hyperlink) does do so through the sale of certain merchandise. The Defendant does not argue that the Outreach Judaism Organization site is not commercial in nature. Considering the limited nature of the Defendant Internet site and its hyperlink to the Outreach Judaism Organization Internet site, it is apparent the Defendant Internet site is a conduit to the Outreach Judaism Organization Internet site, notwithstanding the statement in the Disclaimer that "this website . . . is in no way affiliated with the Jewish organization Outreach Judaism . . . ."

The conduct of the Defendant also constitutes a commercial use of the Mark and the Name of the Plaintiff Organization because it is designed to harm the Plaintiff Organization commercially by disparaging it and preventing the Plaintiff Organization from exploiting the Mark and the Name of the Plaintiff Organization. *See Panavision*, 945 F. Supp. at 1303. In addition, the Defendant Internet site has and will continue to inhibit the efforts of Internet users to locate the Plaintiff Organization Internet site. *See id.*

The Plaintiff Organization has demonstrated a likelihood of success on its claim of dilution under Section 1125(c).

In response to defendant's contention that its domain name and website were not an actionable use "in connection with any goods or services" under § 43(a), the court rejoined:

The Defendant contends, without any explanation or analysis, that the Plaintiff has not demonstrated that his activities are done "in connection with any goods or services." This contention is without merit.

The requirement that the activities of an infringer be done "in connection with any goods or services," does not require the infringer to actually cause goods or services to be placed into the stream of commerce. *See Juno*, 979 F. Supp. at 691 (finding mere acquisition of domain name constituted "in connection with goods and services"). Rather, all that is needed is that the trademark violation be "in connection" with any goods or services.

The activities of the Defendant are "in connection" with goods and services for several reasons. First, the hyperlink in the Defendant Internet site to the Outreach Judaism Organization Internet site is designed to promote the viewpoint of the Outreach Judaism Organization and to encourage the purchase of the products and services offered by that organization. Second, as explained in *Planned Parenthood,*

> the defendant's use of plaintiff's mark is "in connection with the distribution of services" because it is likely to prevent some Internet users from reaching plaintiff's own Internet web site. Prospective users of plaintiff's services who mistakenly access defendant's web site may fail to continue to search for plaintiff's own home page, due to anger, frustration, or the belief that plaintiff's home page does not exist. . . . Therefore, defendant's action in appropriating plaintiff's mark has a connection to plaintiff's distribution of its services.

Planned Parenthood, 1997 U.S. Dist. LEXIS 3338, *14 (discussing "in connection with goods or services" requirement in context of Section 1114 claim). In this case, because of the similarity of the domain name used by the Defendant with the Mark and Name of the Plaintiff Organization, the conduct of the Defendant is not only designed to, but is likely to, prevent some Internet users from reaching the Internet site of the Plaintiff Organization; as well it diverts visitors to the Outreach Judaism Organization site which is commercial in nature. As such, the conduct of the Defendant is "in connection with goods and services" as that term is used in Section 1125(a).

WHS Entertainment Ventures v. United Paperworkers International Union, 997 F.Supp. 946 (M.D.Tenn.1998). Union organizers distributed leaflets publicizing health code violations at plaintiff's "Whitehorse Saloon" bar and restaurant. The leaflets also bore a disparaging version of the restaurant's logo: instead of a robust long-maned horse enclosed by two rings of triangles, the leaflet showed a sweaty and emaciated horse similarly enclosed. The restaurant's proprietors alleged that the leaflets' distribution violated Lanham Act protections against confusion and dilution under §§ 43(a) and (c). The court determined that both claims failed, for lack of "use in commerce." The court reviewed the § 45 definition of "use in commerce," and concluded:

> [I]t is clear that the Union's conduct does not fit within the reach of the term "use in commerce." If the flyers being distributed by the Union are themselves considered "goods," these "goods" are not "sold or transported in commerce," as required by the Act. The flyers are not being sold, as the Union is distributing these

flyers for the purposes of publicizing the Wildhorse Saloon's health violations, at no cost to the recipient. *Cf. Tax Cap Committee v. Save Our Everglades, Inc.*, 933 F.Supp. 1077, 1081 (S.D.Fla.1996). [Other citations omitted.] Furthermore, the flyers are not being "transported in commerce" because the Plaintiffs have alleged that they have only been distributed "on the premises at the Restaurant and immediately outside the Restaurant." This limited geographical area in which the flyers are being distributed cannot by any stretch of the term be considered a "transportation" of the flyers in commerce.

Furthermore, the Union's use of the trademark was not related to the "sale or advertising of a service." The parody of the Wildhorse Saloon logo exhibited on the flyers distributed by the Union were not used to sell the Union's services, or for that matter, to promote the Union entity itself. The Union was not using the Wildhorse Saloon logo in flyers that were intended, for example, to attract new members, or to solicit donations. It is true that the flyers were used to further the Union's position in a labor dispute, and the act of negotiating on behalf of union members is, in turn, a service that is provided by the Union. However, this action is too far removed from the "sale or advertising" of the Union's services to be considered as such under the Lanham Act. [Citations omitted.]

Although the Court's research has not uncovered any federal opinions in the Sixth Circuit which discuss whether the distribution of flyers during a labor dispute can be considered a "use in commerce," at least one other judge has agreed with the Court's reasoning in the present case. In *IAM v. Winship Green Nursing Center*, 103 F.3d 196 (1st Cir.1996), Judge Saris, a district judge sitting by designation, addressed in her concurrence the issue of whether two pieces of campaign literature were "used in commerce" under facts analogous to the ones at bar. The case involved the attempt by the International Association of Machinists and Aerospace Workers Union ("IAM") to organize the non-professional employees at Winship Green Nursing Center. In response to this campaign, the company circulated two sets of flyers, consisting of several pages each. Each set included a page which was written on what appeared to be IAM letterhead, which itself bore the IAM service mark. One of the flyers purported to be a letter from the union requesting that Winship terminate an employee due to his or her failure to pay union dues. The second was a simulated invoice from the union, listing a series of dues payable to it, as well as some other commentary. *Id.* Two of the judges from the panel determined that Winship's actions did not violate the Lanham Act, because they were not "likely to confuse." Though she agreed with much of the majority's holding, Judge Saris also concluded that Winship's "use" of the IAM service mark was not prohibited by the Lanham Act. She first noted that "trial courts have rejected efforts to extend the Lanham Act to cases where the defendant is not using or displaying the trademark in the sale, distribution or advertising of its goods or services." [Citations omitted.] Judge Saris then determined that the use of mark in labor dispute was not a use in "commercial sale or advertising" because it was not directed at advertising or promoting the union itself.

As Judge Saris noted in *IAM*, there may be some instances in which a union's use of a company trademark may constitute "commercial sale or advertising" for purposes of the Act. *Id.* at 210. One of the cases cited by Judge Saris to illustrate an instance where liability may incur was *Brach Van Houten Holding, Inc. v. Save Brach's Coalition for Chicago*, 856 F.Supp. 472, 475–76 (N.D.Ill.1994), a case also extensively cited by the Plaintiffs. In *Brach*, a non-profit organization (Save Brach's) whose purpose was to prevent the Brach company from closing a certain candy factory in Chicago adopted the Brach company logo as its own. The Save Brach's coalition included a labor union, presumably the union organized for the candy factory workers. The Court concluded that Save Brach's provided a "service" for purposes of the Lanham Act because it was "engaged in soliciting donations, preparing press releases, holding public meetings and press conferences, propounding proposals for the reorganization of Brach's ownership and/or management, and other activities designed to bring about change in the Brach's organization and enhance the stability of workers' jobs." Consequently, although this argument was not explicitly made by the Save Brach's court, Judge Saris noted that the organization's act of adopting the logo as its own was also a "use in commerce," because the logo was used in buttons and bumper stickers which were in turn used to publicize Save Brach's.

In contrast, in the present case the Union's purpose in distributing the flyers bearing the Wildhorse Saloon restaurant was not to advertise itself or its services, but to pressure an employer in a labor dispute. Thus, the Union did not "use in commerce" the Wildhorse Saloon logo and could not be held liable under either § 43(a) or (c) of the Lanham Act.

People for the Ethical Treatment of Animals v. Doughney

263 F.3d 359 (4th Cir.2001).

■ GREGORY, CIRCUIT JUDGE:

People for the Ethical Treatment of Animals ("PETA") sued Michael Doughney ("Doughney") after he registered the domain name peta.org and created a website called "People Eating Tasty Animals." PETA alleged claims of service mark infringement under 15 U.S.C. § 1114 and Virginia common law, unfair competition under 15 U.S.C. § 1125(a) and Virginia common law, and service mark dilution and cybersquatting under 15 U.S.C.

§ 1123(c). Doughney appeals the district court's decision granting PETA's motion for summary judgment. . . . Finding no error, we affirm.

I.

PETA is an animal rights organization with more than 600,000 members worldwide. PETA "is dedicated to promoting and heightening public awareness of animal protection issues and it opposes the exploitation of animals for food, clothing, entertainment and vivisection."

Doughney is a former internet executive who has registered many domain names since 1995. For example, Doughney registered domain names such as dubyadot.com, dubyadot.net, deathbush.com, RandallTerry.org (Not Randall Terry for Congress), bwtel.com (BaltimoreWashington Telephone Company), pmrc.org ("People's Manic Repressive Church"), and ex-cult.org (Ex–Cult Archive). At the time the district court issued its summary judgment ruling, Doughney owned 50–60 domain names.

Doughney registered the domain name peta.org in 1995 with Network Solutions, Inc. ("NSI"). When registering the domain name, Doughney represented to NSI that the registration did "not interfere with or infringe upon the rights of any third party," and that a "nonprofit educational organization" called "People Eating Tasty Animals" was registering the domain name. Doughney made these representations to NSI despite knowing that no corporation, partnership, organization or entity of any kind existed or traded under that name. Moreover, Doughney was familiar with PETA and its beliefs and had been for at least 15 years before registering the domain name.

After registering the peta.org domain name, Doughney used it to create a website purportedly on behalf of "People Eating Tasty Animals." Doughney claims he created the website as a parody of PETA. A viewer accessing the website would see the title "People Eating Tasty Animals" in large, bold type. Under the title, the viewer would see a statement that the website was a "resource for those who enjoy eating meat, wearing fur and leather, hunting, and the fruits of scientific research." The website contained links to various meat, fur, leather, hunting, animal research, and other organizations, all of which held views generally antithetical to PETA's views. Another statement on the website asked the viewer whether he/she was "Feeling lost? Offended? Perhaps you should, like, exit immediately." The phrase "exit immediately" contained a hyperlink to PETA's official website.

Doughney's website appeared at "www.peta.org" for only six months in 1995–96. In 1996, PETA asked Doughney to voluntarily transfer the peta.org domain name to PETA because PETA owned the "PETA" mark ("the Mark"), which it registered in 1992. See U.S. Trademark Registration No. 1705,510. When Doughney refused to transfer the domain name to PETA, PETA complained to NSI, whose rules then required it to place the domain name on "hold" pending resolution of Doughney's dispute with

PETA.[1] Consequently, Doughney moved the website to www.mtd.com/tasty and added a disclaimer stating that "People Eating Tasty Animals is in no way connected with, or endorsed by, People for the Ethical Treatment of Animals."

In response to Doughney's domain name dispute with PETA, The Chronicle of Philanthropy quoted Doughney as stating that, "if they [PETA] want one of my domains, they should make me an offer." Non–Profit Groups Upset by Unauthorized Use of Their Names on the Internet, THE CHRONICLE OF PHILANTHROPY, Nov. 14, 1996. Doughney does not dispute making this statement. Additionally, Doughney posted the following message on his website on May 12, 1996:

> "PeTa" has no legal grounds whatsoever to make even the slightest demands of me regarding this domain name registration. If they disagree, they can sue me. And if they don't, well, perhaps they can behave like the polite ladies and gentlemen that they evidently aren't and negotiate a settlement with me.... Otherwise, "PeTa" can wait until the significance and value of a domain name drops to nearly nothing, which is inevitable as each new web search engine comes on-line, because that's how long it's going to take for this dispute to play out.

PETA sued Doughney in 1999, asserting claims for service mark infringement, unfair competition, dilution and cybersquatting. PETA did not seek damages, but sought only to enjoin Doughney's use of the "PETA" Mark and an order requiring Doughney to transfer the peta.org domain name to PETA.

Doughney responded to the suit by arguing that the website was a constitutionally-protected parody of PETA. Nonetheless, the district court granted PETA's motion for summary judgment on June 12, 2000. *People for the Ethical Treatment of Animals, Inc. v. Doughney, 113 F.Supp.2d 915 (E.D. Va. 2000)*. The district court rejected Doughney's parody defense, explaining that

> [o]nly after arriving at the "PETA.ORG" web site could the web site browser determine that this was not a web site owned, controlled or sponsored by PETA. Therefore, the two images: (1) the famous PETA name and (2) the "People Eating Tasty Animals" website was not a parody because [they were not] simultaneous.

Id. at 921.

. . .

II.

. . .

---

1. When Doughney registered *peta.org,* he agreed to abide by NSI's Dispute Resolution Policy, which specified that a domain name using a third party's registered trademark was subject to placement on "hold" status.

A. Trademark Infringement/Unfair Competition

. . .

There is no dispute here that PETA owns the "PETA" Mark, that Doughney used it, and that Doughney used the Mark "in commerce." Doughney disputes the district court's findings that he used the Mark in connection with goods or services and that he used it in a manner engendering a likelihood of confusion.

1.

To use PETA's Mark "in connection with" goods or services, Doughney need not have actually sold or advertised goods or services on the www. peta.org website. Rather, Doughney need only have prevented users from obtaining or using PETA's goods or services, or need only have connected the website to other's goods or services.

While sparse, existing caselaw on infringement and unfair competition in the Internet context clearly weighs in favor of this conclusion. For example, in *OBH, Inc. v. Spotlight Magazine, Inc.*, the plaintiffs owned the *"The Buffalo News"* registered trademark used by the newspaper of the same name. 86 F.Supp.2d 176 (W.D.N.Y. 2000). The defendants registered the domain name thebuffalonews.com and created a website parodying *The Buffalo News* and providing a public forum for criticism of the newspaper. *Id.* at 182. The site contained hyperlinks to other local news sources and a site owned by the defendants that advertised Buffalo-area apartments for rent. *Id.* at 183.

The court held that the defendants used the mark "in connection with" goods or services because the defendants' website was "likely to prevent or hinder Internet users from accessing plaintiffs' services on plaintiffs' own web site." *Id.*

> Prospective users of plaintiffs' services who mistakenly access defendants' web site may fail to continue to search for plaintiffs' web site due to confusion or frustration. Such users, who are presumably looking for the news services provided by the plaintiffs on their web site, may instead opt to select one of the several other news-related hyperlinks contained in defendants' web site. These news-related hyperlinks will directly link the user to other news-related web sites that are in direct competition with plaintiffs in providing news-related services over the Internet. Thus, defendants' action in appropriating plaintiff's mark has a connection to plaintiffs' distribution of its services.

Id. Moreover, the court explained that defendants' use of the plaintiffs' mark was in connection with goods or services because it contained a link to the defendants' apartment-guide website. *Id.*

Similarly, in *Planned Parenthood Federation of America, Inc. v. Bucci*, the plaintiff owned the "Planned Parenthood" mark, but the defendant registered the domain name plannedparenthood.com. 1997 U.S. Dist. LEX-

IS 3338, 42 U.S.P.Q.2D (BNA) 1430 (S.D.N.Y. 1997). Using the domain name, the defendant created a website containing information antithetical to the plaintiff's views. 42 U.S.P.Q.2D (BNA) at 1435. The court ruled that the defendant used the plaintiff's mark "in connection with" the distribution of services.

> because it is likely to prevent some Internet users from reaching plaintiff's own Internet web site. Prospective users of plaintiff's services who mistakenly access defendant's web site may fail to continue to search for plaintiff's own home page, due to anger, frustration, or the belief that plain tiff's home page does not exist.

Id.

> The same reasoning applies here. As the district court explained, Doughney's use of PETA's Mark in the domain name of his website is likely to prevent Internet users from reaching[PETA's] own Internet web site. The prospective users of[PETA's] services who mistakenly access Defendant's web site may fail to continue to search for [PETA's] own home page, due to anger, frustration, or the belief that [PETA's] home page does not exist.

Doughney, 113 F.Supp.2d at 919 (quoting *Bucci,* 1997 U.S. Dist. LEXIS 3338, 42 U.S.P.Q.2D (BNA) at 1435). Moreover, Doughney's web site provides links to more than 30 commercial operations offering goods and services. By providing links to these commercial operations, Doughney's use of PETA's Mark is "in connection with" the sale of goods or services.

2.

The unauthorized use of a trademark infringes the trademark holder's rights if it is likely to confuse an "ordinary consumer" as to the source or sponsorship of the goods. *Anheuser–Busch, Inc. v. L & L Wings, Inc.,* 962 F.2d 316, 318 (4th Cir. 1992) (citing 2 J. McCarthy, *Trademarks and Unfair Competition* § 23:28 (2d ed. 1984)). To determine whether a likelihood of confusion exists, a court should not consider "how closely a fragment of a given use duplicates the trademark," but must instead consider "whether the use in its entirety creates a likelihood of confusion." *Id.* at 319.

Doughney does not dispute that the peta.org domain name engenders a likelihood of confusion between his web site and PETA. Doughney claims, though, that the inquiry should not end with his domain name. Rather, he urges the Court to consider his website in conjunction with the domain name because, together, they purportedly parody PETA and, thus, do not cause a likelihood of confusion.

A "parody" is defined as a "simple form of entertainment conveyed by juxtaposing the irreverent representation of the trademark with the idealized image created by the mark's owner." *L.L. Bean, Inc. v. Drake Publishers, Inc.,* 811 F.2d 26, 34 (1st Cir. 1987). A parody must "convey two simultaneous—and contradictory—messages: that it is the original, but also that it is not the original and is instead a parody." *Cliffs Notes, Inc. v.*

Bantam Doubleday Dell Publ. Group, Inc., 886 F.2d 490, 494 (2d Cir. 1989) (emphasis in original). To the extent that an alleged parody conveys only the first message, "it is not only a poor parody but also vulnerable under trademark law, since the customer will be confused." *Id.* While a parody necessarily must engender some initial confusion, an effective parody will diminish the risk of consumer confusion "by conveying [only] just enough of the original design to allow the consumer to appreciate the point of parody." *Jordache Enterprises, Inc. v. Hogg Wyld, Ltd.*, 828 F.2d 1482, 1486 (10th Cir. 1987).

Looking at Doughney's domain name alone, there is no suggestion of a parody. The domain name peta.org simply copies PETA's Mark, conveying the message that it is related to PETA. The domain name does not convey the second, contradictory message needed to establish a parody—a message that the domain name is not related to PETA, but that it is a parody of PETA.

Doughney claims that this second message can be found in the content of his website. Indeed, the website's content makes it clear that it is not related to PETA. However, this second message is not conveyed simultaneously with the first message, as required to be considered a parody. The domain name conveys the first message; the second message is conveyed only when the viewer reads the content of the website. As the district court explained, "an internet user would not realize that they were not on an official PETA web site until after they had used PETA's Mark to access the web page 'www.peta.org.'" *Doughney*, 113 F.Supp.2d at 921. Thus, the messages are not conveyed simultaneously and do not constitute a parody. *See also Morrison & Foerster LLP v. Wick*, 94 F.Supp.2d 1125 (D. Co. 2000) (defendant's use of plaintiffs' mark in domain name "does not convey two simultaneous and contradictory messages" because "only by reading through the content of the sites could the user discover that the domain names are an attempt at parody"); *Bucci*, 1997 U.S. Dist. LEXIS 3338, 42 U.S.P.Q.2D (BNA) at 1435 (rejecting parody defense because "seeing or typing the 'planned parenthood' mark and accessing the web site are two separate and nonsimultaneous activities"). The district court properly rejected Doughney's parody defense and found that Doughney's use of the peta.org domain name engenders a likelihood of confusion. Accordingly, Doughney failed to raise a genuine issue of material fact regarding PETA's infringement and unfair competition claims.

B. *Anticybersquatting Consumer Protection Act*

The district court found Doughney liable under the Anticybersquatting Consumer Protection Act ("ACPA"), 15 U.S.C. § 1125(d)(1)(A). To establish an ACPA violation, PETA was required to (1) prove that Doughney had a bad faith intent to profit from using the peta.org domain name, and (2) that the peta.org domain name is identical or confusingly similar to, or dilutive of, the distinctive and famous PETA Mark. 15 U.S.C. § 1125(d)(1)(A).

Doughney makes several arguments relating to the district court's ACPA holding: (1) that PETA did not plead an ACPA claim, but raised it for the first time in its motion for summary judgment; (2) that the ACPA, which became effective in 1999, cannot be applied retroactively to events that occurred in 1995 and 1996; (3) that Doughney did not seek to financially profit from his use of PETA's Mark; and (4) that Doughney acted in good faith.

None of Doughney's arguments are availing.

. . .

Doughney's third argument—that he did not seek to financially profit from registering a domain name using PETA's Mark—also offers him no relief. It is undisputed that Doughney made statements to the press and on his website recommending that PETA attempt to "settle" with him and "make him an offer." The undisputed evidence belies Doughney's argument.

Doughney's fourth argument—that he did not act in bad faith—also is unavailing. Under 15 U.S.C. § 1125(d)(1)(B)(i), a court may consider several factors to determine whether a defendant acted in bad faith,.... In addition to listing ... nine factors, the ACPA contains a safe harbor provision stating that bad faith intent "shall not be found in any case in which the court determines that the person believed and had reasonable grounds to believe that the use of the domain name was fair use or otherwise lawful." 15 U.S.C. § 1225(d)(1)(B)(ii).

The district court reviewed the factors listed in the statute and properly concluded that Doughney (I) had no intellectual property right in peta.org; (II) peta.org is not Doughney's name or a name otherwise used to identify Doughney; (III) Doughney had no prior use of peta.org in connection with the bona fide offering of any goods or services; (IV) Doughney used the PETA Mark in a commercial manner; (V) Doughney "clearly intended to confuse, mislead and divert internet users into accessing his web site which contained information antithetical and therefore harmful to the goodwill represented by the PETA Mark"; (VI) Doughney made statements on his web site and in the press recommending that PETA attempt to "settle" with him and "make him an offer"; (VII) Doughney made false statements when registering the domain name; and (VIII) Doughney registered other domain names that are identical or similar to the marks or names of other famous people and organizations. *People for the Ethical Treatment of Animals*, 113 F.Supp.2d at 920.

Doughney claims that the district court's later ruling denying PETA's motion for attorney fees triggers application of the ACPA's safe harbor provision. In that ruling, the district court stated that

> Doughney registered the domain name because he thought that he had a legitimate First Amendment right to express himself this way. The Court must consider Doughney's state of mind at the time he took the actions in question. Doughney thought he was within his First Amendment rights to create a parody of the plaintiff's organization.

People for the Ethical Treatment of Animals, Inc. v. Doughney, 2000 U.S. Dist. LEXIS 13421, *5, Civil Action No. 99–1336–A, Order at 4 (E.D. Va. Aug. 31, 2000). With its attorney's fee ruling, the district court did not find that Doughney "had reasonable grounds to believe" that his use of PETA's Mark was lawful. It held only that Doughney thought it to be lawful.

Moreover, a defendant "who acts even partially in bad faith in registering a domain name is not, as a matter of law, entitled to benefit from [the ACPA's] safe harbor provision." *Virtual Works, Inc.,* 238 F.3d at 270. Doughney knowingly provided false information to NSI upon registering the domain name, knew he was registering a domain name identical to PETA's Mark, and clearly intended to confuse Internet users into accessing his website, instead of PETA's official website. Considering the evidence of Doughney's bad faith, the safe harbor provision can provide him no relief. . . .

QUESTIONS

1. Can this case be reconciled with *Cliffs Notes v. Bantam Doubleday Dell*? Is there a variant domain name Mr. Doughney might adopt that would signal that his web site criticizes or pokes fun at PETA, without running afoul of the Lanham Act?

2. Since 1955, the Phillip Morris Company has featured cowboys in its Marlboro® cigarette ads, and the cowboy figure has become widely known as the "Marlboro Man." In 1997 the California State Health Department introduced a series of anti-smoking billboards, including the one below:

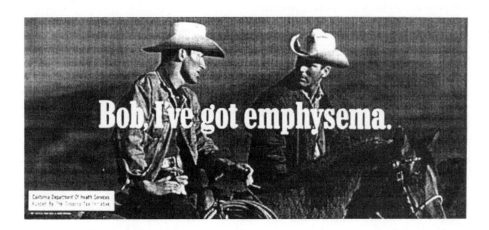

The billboard appeared on freeways throughout the state. It was reproduced in a variety of different news publications. A 1999 wall calendar featuring ad parodies used it for the month of October. The advertising agency that created the billboard features it on its website as an example of its work. Has Phillip Morris any recourse under the Lanham Act?

3. SNITCH, the Northfield environmental group responsible for the CHUGGING CHAINSAW protest, has now published a newspaper advertisement deploring recent U.S. Forest Service policies. The advertisement depicts the well-known Forest Service symbol, Smokey the Bear, with a chainsaw partially hidden behind his back, and the legend "Say it ain't so, Smokey." The remainder of the advertisement consists of text criticizing the Forest Service's management of public lands. The Forest Service has initiated a trademark infringement suit. How would you analyze the environmental group's likelihood of success? *Cf. LightHawk, The Environmental Air Force v. Robertson*, 812 F.Supp. 1095 (W.D.Wash.1993) .

Lamparello v. Falwell

420 F.3d 309 (4th Cir.2005).

■ DIANA GRIBBON MOTZ, CIRCUIT JUDGE:

Christopher Lamparello appeals the district court's order enjoining him from maintaining a gripe website critical of Reverend Jerry Falwell. For the reasons stated below, we reverse.

I.

Reverend Falwell is "a nationally known minister who has been active as a commentator on politics and public affairs." *Hustler Magazine, Inc. v. Falwell*, 485 U.S. 46, 47, 99 L. Ed. 2d 41, 108 S. Ct. 876 (1988). He holds the common law trademarks "Jerry Falwell" and "Falwell," and the registered trademark "Listen America with Jerry Falwell." Jerry Falwell Ministries can be found online at "www.falwell.com," a website which receives 9,000 hits (or visits) per day.

Lamparello registered the domain name "www.fallwell.com" on February 11, 1999, after hearing Reverend Falwell give an interview "in which he expressed opinions about gay people and homosexuality that [Lamparello] considered ... offensive." Lamparello created a website at that domain name to respond to what he believed were "untruths about gay people." Lamparello's website included headlines such as "Bible verses that Dr. Falwell chooses to ignore" and "Jerry Falwell has been bearing false witness (Exodus 20:16) against his gay and lesbian neighbors for a long time." The site also contained in-depth criticism of Reverend Falwell's views. For example, the website stated:

> Dr. Falwell says that he is on the side of truth. He says that he will preach that homosexuality is a sin until the day he dies. But we believe that if the reverend were to take another thoughtful look at the scriptures, he would discover that they have been twisted around to support an anti-gay political agenda ... at the expense of the gospel.

Although the interior pages of Lamparello's website did not contain a disclaimer, the homepage prominently stated, "This website is NOT affiliated with Jerry Falwell or his ministry"; advised, "If you would like to visit

Rev. Falwell's website, you may click here''; and provided a hyperlink to Reverend Falwell's website.

At one point, Lamparello's website included a link to the Amazon.com webpage for a book that offered interpretations of the Bible that Lamparello favored, but the parties agree that Lamparello has never sold goods or services on his website. The parties also agree that "Lamparello's domain name and web site at www.fallwell.com," which received only 200 hits per day, "had no measurable impact on the quantity of visits to [Reverend Falwell's] web site at www.falwell.com."

Nonetheless, Reverend Falwell sent Lamparello letters in October 2001 and June 2003 demanding that he cease and desist from using www. fallwell.com or any variation of Reverend Falwell's name as a domain name. Ultimately, Lamparello filed this action against Reverend Falwell and his ministries (collectively referred to hereinafter as "Reverend Falwell"), seeking a declaratory judgment of noninfringement. Reverend Falwell counter-claimed, alleging trademark infringement under 15 U.S.C. § 1114 (2000), false designation of origin under 15 U.S.C. § 1125(a), unfair competition under 15 U.S.C. § 1126 and the common law of Virginia, and cybersquatting under 15 U.S.C. § 1125(d).

The parties stipulated to all relevant facts and filed cross-motions for summary judgment. The district court granted summary judgment to Reverend Falwell, enjoined Lamparello from using Reverend Falwell's mark at www.fallwell.com, and required Lamparello to transfer the domain name to Reverend Falwell. However, the court denied Reverend Falwell's request for statutory damages or attorney fees, reasoning that the "primary motive" of Lamparello's website was "to put forth opinions on issues that were contrary to those of [Reverend Falwell]" and "not to take away monies or to profit.".

Lamparello appeals the district court's order; Reverend Falwell cross-appeals the denial of statutory damages and attorney fees. We review de novo a district court's ruling on cross-motions for summary judgment. *See People for the Ethical Treatment of Animals v. Doughney*, 263 F.3d 359, 364 (4th Cir. 2001) [hereinafter "PETA"].

II.

We first consider Reverend Falwell's claims of trademark infringement and false designation of origin.

A.

.   .   .

Trademark law serves the important functions of protecting product identification, providing consumer information, and encouraging the production of quality goods and services. *See Qualitex Co. v. Jacobson Prods. Co.*, 514 U.S. 159, 164, 131 L. Ed. 2d 248, 115 S. Ct. 1300 (1995). But protections " 'against unfair competition' ''cannot be transformed into " 'rights to control language.' " *CPC Int'l, Inc. v. Skippy Inc.*, 214 F.3d 456, 462 (4th Cir. 2000) (*quoting* Mark A. Lemley, The Modern Lanham Act and the Death of Common Sense, 108 Yale L.J. 1687, 1710–11 (1999)). "Such a transformation" would raise serious First Amendment concerns because it would limit the

> ability to discuss the products or criticize the conduct of companies that may be of widespread public concern and importance. Much useful social and commercial discourse would be all but impossible if speakers were under threat of an infringement lawsuit every time they made reference to a person, company or product by using its trademark.

Id. (internal quotation marks and citations omitted).

Lamparello and his amici argue at length that application of the Lanham Act must be restricted to "commercial speech" to assure that trademark law does not become a tool for unconstitutional censorship. The Sixth Circuit has endorsed this view, *see Taubman Co. v. Webfeats*, 319 F.3d 770, 774 (6th Cir. 2003), and the Ninth Circuit recently has done so as well, *see Bosley Med. Inst., Inc. v. Kremer*, 403 F.3d 672, 674 (9th Cir. 2005).

In its two most significant recent amendments to the Lanham Act, the Federal Trademark Dilution Act of 1995 ("FTDA") and the Anti-cybersquatting Consumer Protection Act of 1999 ("ACPA"), Congress left little doubt that it did not intend for trademark laws to impinge the First Amendment rights of critics and commentators. The dilution statute applies to only a "commercial use in commerce of a mark," 15 U.S.C. § 1125(c)(1), and explicitly states that the "noncommercial use of a mark" is not actionable. Id. § 1125(c)(4). Congress explained that this language was added to "adequately address[] legitimate First Amendment concerns," H.R. Rep. No. 104–374, at 4 (1995), *reprinted in* 1995 U.S.C.C.A.N. 1029, 1031, and "incorporated the concept of 'commercial' speech from the 'commercial speech' doctrine." *Id.* at 8, *reprinted in* 1995 U.S.C.C.A.N. at 1035. . . . Similarly, Congress directed that in determining whether an individual has engaged in cybersquatting, the courts may consider whether the person's use of the mark is a "bona fide noncommercial or fair use." 15 U.S.C. § 1125(d)(1)(B)(i)(IV). The legislature believed this provision necessary to "protect[] the rights of Internet users and the interests of all Americans in free speech and protected uses of trademarked names for such things as parody, comment, criticism, comparative advertising, news reporting, etc." S. Rep. No. 106–140 (1999), 1999 WL 594571, at *8.

In contrast, the trademark infringement and false designation of origin provisions of the Lanham Act (Sections 32 and 43(a), respectively) do not employ the term "noncommercial." They do state, however, that they pertain only to the use of a mark "in connection with the sale, offering for sale, distribution, or advertising of any goods or services," 15 U.S.C. § 1114(1)(a), or "in connection with any goods or services," *Id.* § 1125(a)(1). But courts have been reluctant to define those terms narrowly. Rather, as the Second Circuit has explained, "the term 'services' has been interpreted broadly" and so "the Lanham Act has . . . been applied to defendants furnishing a wide variety of non-commercial public and civic benefits." *United We Stand Am., Inc. v. United We Stand, Am. N.Y., Inc.*, 128 F.3d 86, 89–90 (2d Cir. 1997). Similarly, in *PETA* we noted that a website need not actually sell goods or services for the use of a mark in that site's domain name to constitute a use " 'in connection with' goods or services." *PETA*, 263 F.3d at 365; *see also Taubman Co.*, 319 F.3d at 775 (concluding that website with two links to websites of for-profit entities violated the Lanham Act).

Thus, even if we accepted Lamparello's contention that Sections 32 and 43(a) of the Lanham Act apply only to commercial speech, we would still face the difficult question of what constitutes such speech under those provisions. In the case at hand, we need not resolve that question or determine whether Sections 32 and 43(a) apply exclusively to commercial speech because Reverend Falwell's claims of trademark infringement and false designation fail for a more obvious reason. The hallmark of such claims is a likelihood of confusion—and there is no likelihood of confusion here.

B.

1.

"The use of a competitor's mark that does not cause confusion as to source is permissible." *Dorr–Oliver, Inc. v. Fluid–Quip, Inc.*, 94 F.3d 376, 380 (7th Cir. 1996). Accordingly, Lamparello can only be liable for infringement and false designation if his use of Reverend Falwell's mark would be likely to cause confusion as to the source of the website found at www.fallwell.com. This likelihood-of-confusion test "generally strikes a comfortable balance" between the First Amendment and the rights of markholders. *Mattel, Inc. v. MCA Records, Inc.*, 296 F.3d 894, 900 (9th Cir. 2002).

We have identified seven factors helpful in determining whether a likelihood of confusion exists as to the source of a work, but "not all these factors are always relevant or equally emphasized in each case." *Pizzeria Uno Corp. v. Temple*, 747 F.2d 1522, 1527 (4th Cir. 1984)....

Reverend Falwell's mark is distinctive, and the domain name of Lamparello's website, www.fallwell.com, closely resembles it. But, although Lamparello and Reverend Falwell employ similar marks online, Lamparello's website looks nothing like Reverend Falwell's; indeed, Lamparello has made no attempt to imitate Reverend Falwell's website. Moreover, Reverend Falwell does not even argue that Lamparello's website constitutes advertising or a facility for business, let alone a facility or advertising similar to that of Reverend Falwell. Furthermore, Lamparello clearly created his website intending only to provide a forum to criticize ideas, not to steal customers.

Most importantly, Reverend Falwell and Lamparello do not offer similar goods or services. Rather they offer opposing ideas and commentary. Reverend Falwell's mark identifies his spiritual and political views; the website at www.fallwell.com criticizes those very views. After even a quick glance at the content of the website at www.fallwell.com, no one seeking Reverend Falwell's guidance would be misled by the domain name—www.fallwell.com—into believing Reverend Falwell authorized the content of that website. No one would believe that Reverend Falwell sponsored a site criticizing himself, his positions, and his interpretations of the Bible. *See New Kids on the Block v. News Am. Publ'g, Inc.*, 971 F.2d 302, 308–09 (9th Cir. 1992) (stating that use of a mark to solicit criticism of the markholder implies the markholder is not the sponsor of the use).

Finally, the fact that people contacted Reverend Falwell's ministry to report that they found the content at www.fallwell.com antithetical to Reverend Falwell's views does not illustrate, as Reverend Falwell claims, that the website engendered actual confusion. To the contrary, the anecdotal evidence Reverend Falwell submitted shows that those searching for Reverend Falwell's site and arriving instead at Lamparello's site quickly realized that Reverend Falwell was not the source of the content therein.

For all of these reasons, it is clear that the undisputed record evidences no likelihood of confusion. In fact, Reverend Falwell even conceded at oral argument that those viewing the content of Lamparello's website probably were unlikely to confuse Reverend Falwell with the source of that material.

2.

Nevertheless, Reverend Falwell argues that he is entitled to prevail under the "initial interest confusion" doctrine. This relatively new and sporadically applied doctrine holds that "the Lanham Act forbids a competitor from luring potential customers away from a producer by initially passing off its goods as those of the producer's, even if confusion as to the source of the goods is dispelled by the time any sales are consummated." *Dorr–Oliver*, 94 F.3d at 382. According to Reverend Falwell, this doctrine requires us to compare his mark with Lamparello's website domain name, www.fallwell.com, without considering the content of Lamparello's website. Reverend Falwell argues that some people who misspell his name may go to www.fallwell.com assuming it is his site, thus giving Lamparello an unearned audience—albeit one that quickly disappears when it realizes it has not reached Reverend Falwell's site. This argument fails for two reasons.

First, we have never adopted the initial interest confusion theory; rather, we have followed a very different mode of analysis, requiring courts to determine whether a likelihood of confusion exists by "examining the allegedly infringing use *in the context in which it is seen by the ordinary consumer.*" *Anheuser–Busch, Inc. v. L & L Wings, Inc.*, 962 F.2d 316, 319 (4th Cir. 1992) (emphasis added) (citing cases); *see also What–A–Burger of Va., Inc. v. WHATABURGER, Inc.*, 357 F.3d 441, 450 (4th Cir. 2004).

Contrary to Reverend Falwell's arguments, we did not abandon this approach in *PETA*. Our inquiry in *PETA* was limited to whether Doughney's use of the domain name "www.peta.org" constituted a successful enough parody of People for the Ethical Treatment of Animals that no one was likely to believe www.peta.org was sponsored or endorsed by that organization. For a parody to be successful, it "must convey two simultaneous—and contradictory—messages: that it is the original, but also that it is not the original and is instead a parody." *PETA*, 263 F.3d at 366 (internal quotation marks and citation omitted). Doughney argued that his domain name conveyed the first message (that it was PETA's website) and that the content of his website conveyed the requisite second message (that it was not PETA's site). Id. Although "the website's content made it clear that it was not related to PETA," *id.*, we concluded that the website's content could not convey the requisite second message because the site's content "was not conveyed *simultaneously* with the first message, [i.e., the domain name itself,] as required to be considered a parody." *Id.* at 366. Accordingly, we found the "district court properly rejected Doughney's parody defense." *Id.* at 367.

PETA simply outlines the parameters of the parody defense; it does not adopt the initial interest confusion theory or otherwise diminish the necessity of examining context when determining whether a likelihood of confusion exists. Indeed, in *PETA* itself, rather than embracing a new approach, we reiterated that "to determine whether a likelihood of confusion exists, a court should not consider how closely a *fragment* of a given use duplicates the trademark, but must instead consider *whether the use in its entirety creates a likelihood of confusion.*" *Id.* at 366 (internal quotation marks and citation omitted) (emphasis added). When dealing with domain names, this means a court must evaluate an allegedly infringing domain name in conjunction with the content of the website identified by the domain name.[4]

Moreover, even if we did endorse the initial interest confusion theory, that theory would not assist Reverend Falwell here because it provides no basis for liability in circumstances such as these. The few appellate courts that have followed the Ninth Circuit and imposed liability under this theory for using marks on the Internet have done so only in cases involving a factor utterly absent here—one business's use of another's mark for its own financial gain. [Citations]

Profiting financially from initial interest confusion is thus a key element for imposition of liability under this theory.[5] When an alleged

---

4. Contrary to Reverend Falwell's suggestions, this rule does not change depending on how similar the domain name or title is to the mark. Hence, Reverend Falwell's assertion that he objects only to Lamparello using the domain name www.fallwell.com and has no objection to Lamparello posting his criticisms at "www.falwelliswrong.com," or a similar domain name, does not entitle him to a different evaluation rule. Rather it has long been established that even when alleged infringers use the *very marks at issue* in titles, courts look to the underlying *content* to determine whether the titles create a likelihood of confusion as to source. *See, e.g., Parks v. LaFace Records,* 329 F.3d 437, 452–54 (6th Cir.2003); *Mattel,* 296 F.3d at 901–02; *Westchester Media v. PRL USA Holdings, Inc.,* 214 F.3d 658, 667–68 (5th Cir.2000); *Rogers v. Grimaldi,* 875 F.2d 994, 1000–01 (2d Cir. 1989).

5. Offline uses of marks found to cause actionable initial interest confusion also have involved financial gain. *See Elvis Presley Enters., Inc. v. Capece,* 141 F.3d 188, 204 (5th Cir.1998); *Mobil Oil Corp. v. Pegasus Petroleum Corp.,* 818 F.2d 254, 260 (2d Cir.1987). And even those courts recognizing the initial interest confusion theory of liability but finding no actionable initial confusion involved one business's use of another's mark for profit. *See, e.g., Savin Corp. v. The Savin Group,* 391 F.3d 439, 462 n. 13 (2d Cir.2004); *AM Gen. Corp. v. DaimlerChrysler Corp.,* 311 F.3d 796, 827–28 (7th Cir.2002); *Checkpoint Sys., Inc. v. Check Point Software Techs., Inc.,* 269 F.3d 270, 298 (3d Cir.2001); *Hasbro, Inc. v. Clue Computing, Inc.,* 232 F.3d 1, 2

infringer does not compete with the markholder for sales, "some initial confusion will not likely facilitate free riding on the goodwill of another mark, or otherwise harm the user claiming infringement. Where confusion has little or no meaningful effect in the marketplace, it is of little or no consequence in our analysis." *Checkpoint Sys. v. Check Point Software Techs., Inc.*, 269 F.3d 270, 296–97 (3d. Cir. 2001). For this reason, even the Ninth Circuit has stated that a firm is not liable for using another's mark in its domain name if it "could not financially capitalize on [a] misdirected consumer [looking for the markholder's site] even if it so desired." *Interstellar Starship Servs., Ltd. v. Epix, Inc.*, 304 F.3d 936, 946 (9th Cir. 2002).

This critical element—use of another firm's mark to capture the markholder's customers and profits—simply does not exist when the alleged infringer establishes a gripe site that criticizes the markholder. See Hannibal Travis, The Battle For Mindshare: The Emerging Consensus that the First Amendment Protects Corporate Criticism and Parody on the Internet, 10 Va. J.L. & Tech. 3, 85 (Winter 2005)....[6] Applying the initial interest confusion theory to gripe sites like Lamparello's would enable the markholder to insulate himself from criticism—or at least to minimize access to it. We have already condemned such uses of the Lanham Act, stating that a markholder cannot " 'shield itself from criticism by forbidding the use of its name in commentaries critical of its conduct.' " *CPC Int'l*, 214 F.3d at 462 (*quoting L.L. Bean, Inc. v. Drake Publishers, Inc.*, 811 F.2d 26, 33 (1st Cir. 1987)). "Just because speech is critical of a corporation and its business practices is not a sufficient reason to enjoin the speech." *Id.*

In sum, even if we were to accept the initial interest confusion theory, that theory would not apply in the case at hand. Rather, to determine whether a likelihood of confusion exists as to the source of a gripe site like that at issue in this case, a court must look not only to the allegedly infringing domain name, but also to the underlying content of the website. When we do so here, it is clear, as explained above, that no likelihood of

(1st Cir.2000); *Syndicate Sales, Inc. v. Hampshire Paper Corp.*, 192 F.3d 633, 638 (7th Cir.1999); *Rust Env't & Infrastructure, Inc. v. Teunissen*, 131 F.3d 1210, 1217 (7th Cir. 1997); *Dorr–Oliver*, 94 F.3d at 383.

6. Although the appellate courts that have adopted the initial interest confusion theory have only applied it to profit-seeking uses of another's mark, the district courts have not so limited the application of the theory. Without expressly referring to this theory, two frequently-discussed district court cases have held that using another's domain name to post content antithetical to the markholder constitutes infringement. *See Planned Parenthood Fed'n of Am., Inc. v. Bucci*, No. 97 Civ. 0629, 1997 WL 133313 (S.D.N.Y. March 24, 1997), *aff'd*, 152 F.3d 920 (2d Cir.1998) (table) (finding use of domain name "www.plannedparenthood.com" to provide links to passages of anti-abortion book constituted infringement); *Jews for Jesus v. Brodsky*, 993 F.Supp. 282 (D.N.J.1998), *aff'd*, 159 F.3d 1351 (3d Cir.1998) (table) (finding use of "www.jewsforjesus.org" to criticize religious group constituted infringement). We think both cases were wrongly decided to the extent that in determining whether the domain names were confusing, the courts did not consider whether the websites' content would dispel any confusion. In expanding the initial interest confusion theory of liability, these cases cut it off from its moorings to the detriment of the First Amendment.

confusion exists. Therefore, the district court erred in granting Reverend Falwell summary judgment on his infringement, false designation, and unfair competition claims.

. . .

IV.

For the foregoing reasons, Lamparello, rather than Reverend Falwell, is entitled to summary judgment on all counts. Accordingly, the judgment of the district court is reversed and the case is remanded for entry of judgment for Lamparello.

QUESTION

Is the court's basis for distinguishing its decision in *PETA* persuasive?

CHAPTER 13

REMEDIES

Editors' Note: The student should consult 15 U.S.C. §§ 1116–21 (Lanham Act §§ 34–39), in the Statutory Supplement.

A. INJUNCTIVE RELIEF

1. INJUNCTIONS

Nova Wines, Inc. v. Adler Fels Winery LLC

467 F.Supp.2d 965 (N.D.Cal.2006).

■ MARILYN HALL PATEL, DISTRICT JUDGE.

On September 29, 2006, plaintiff Nova Wines, Inc. ("Nova" or "plaintiff") brought this action against defendants Adler Fels Winery LLC ("Adler Fels"), Saal Brown, Inc. dba Pacific Licensing ("Pacific Licensing"), Gary Saal ("Saal"), and Tom Kelly Studios, Inc. ("TKS") (collectively "defendants") asserting claims for trademark infringement, trade dress infringement, unfair competition and passing off. Now before the court is plaintiff's motion for a preliminary injunction. . . .

BACKGROUND

Plaintiff Nova Wines, a St. Helena, California winery, does business as Marilyn Wines and sells wines bearing photographs of Marilyn Monroe. Plaintiff has produced wine under the Marilyn Merlot brand name since 1987, the Marilyn Cabernet brand name since 1993, the Norma Jeane brand name since 1998 and the Velvet Collection brand name since 2004. . . . Since 1989, plaintiff has held an exclusive license to use, on wine, the registered trademark "Marilyn Monroe," as well as common law trademarks for Monroe's name, image and likeness from the Monroe estate. Plaintiff has been the sole winery using photographs of Marilyn Monroe on wine for nearly twenty years.

Defendant TKS holds copyrights for a series of nude photographs taken of Marilyn Monroe by Tom Kelley, Sr., in 1949. While Marilyn Monroe was still alive, she signed a model release consenting to use of her "name, portraits, and pictures and reproductions thereof" of the photographs taken by Kelley. Defendant Saal Brown, Inc., doing business as Pacific Licensing, is the licensing agent for TKS. In 1999 or 2000, TKS began using the term "Red Velvet Collection" as a trademark for the collection of Kelley photographs. . . .

In 1999 Pacific first contacted plaintiff to propose licensing the Red Velvet Collection images to plaintiff. Pacific and Nova did not enter a license agreement at that time, in part because the Monroe estate and the Tobacco Tax and Trade Bureau ("TTB") would likely not approve of nude photos of Monroe on wine labels. In 2003, Pacific worked with the TTB and other consultants to develop a "modesty overlay" to cover Monroe's breasts and buttocks in the Red Velvet Collection photographs, and ultimately did acquire approval for a wine label from the TTB.

In 2004 TKS and plaintiff entered a license agreement for use of Red Velvet Collection photos. In May and June of 2005, relations between the parties began to deteriorate, and TKS notified plaintiff that it would "establish[] a new licensee. . . ."

In June or July 2006, plaintiff learned that defendant Adler Fels was marketing a wine bearing a photograph from the Velvet Collection . . . On July 5, 2006 counsel for plaintiff Wines informed Adler Fels that "no one else" besides plaintiff had "the right to produce wines [bearing Marilyn Monroe's] likeness," and that plaintiff would "aggressively protect" its rights. Counsel representing Adler Fels, TKS and Pacific Licensing responded on July 7, 2006 that his clients "decline to succumb to your threats." Defendants subsequently informed plaintiff that they would not release a 1.5–liter bottle in the fall of 2006. However, defendants' counsel also advised plaintiff that defendants might release a 750–milliliter bottle using Red Velvet Collection labels in Fall 2006. This was the last communication between parties before plaintiff filed its complaint on September 29, 2006.

In late August 2006 Adler Fels began marketing 750–milliliter bottles of its "Red Velvet Collection . . . ultra-fine wines." Adler Fels invested more than one hundred work hours, and has spent $140,000 in development and production of its initial run of 2,500 cases of the Red Velvet Collection line. Pre-orders for Adler Fels' Red Velvet Collection line number 2,000 cases. Defendants forecast that the Red Velvet Collection will sell 15,000 cases in its first year of release, and estimate revenues totaling four million dollars from these sales. Adler Fels originally scheduled October 23, 2006 as its bottling date for the Red Velvet Collection wine, with a ship date of early November 2006.

In September 2006 plaintiff received an announcement regarding Adler Fels' Red Velvet Collection wine, urging consumers to place orders by September 15. The announcement attached a "mock-up" of the wine bottle for Adler's Red Velvet Collection line. The mock-up showed a photograph from TKS's Red Velvet Collection series on a bottle of red wine, though not a photo that plaintiff had used on any of its wines.

Plaintiff filed its complaint for trademark infringement, trade dress infringement, unfair competition and passing off on September 29, 2006. Plaintiff served its complaint on defendants on October 5, 2006. That same day, plaintiff filed its ex parte application for a temporary restraining order and motion for preliminary injunction. This court granted a temporary restraining order on October 10, 2006, pending briefing and determination of plaintiff's request for preliminary injunction. On October 26, the court heard arguments regarding plaintiff's request for preliminary injunction.

LEGAL STANDARD

"A preliminary injunction is a provisional remedy, the purpose of which is to preserve status quo and to prevent irreparable loss of rights prior to final disposition of the litigation." *Napa Valley Publ'g Co. v. City of Calistoga*, 225 F. Supp.2d 1176, 1180 (N.D. Cal. 2002). In light of these considerations, a plaintiff seeking preliminary injunctive relief must demonstrate either: "(1) a likelihood of success on the merits and the possibility of irreparable injury; or (2) that serious questions going to the merits [have been] raised and the balance of hardships tips sharply in [the plaintiff's] favor." *Southwest Voter Registration Educ. Project v. Shelley*, 344 F.3d 914, 917 (9th Cir. 2003) (en banc) (per curiam); (citation omitted). The components of these two tests, together with the added consideration of the public interest, operate on a sliding scale or "continuum." *Southwest Voter Registration Educ. Project*, 344 F.3d at 918. Consequently, "the less certain the district court is of the likelihood of success on the merits, the more plaintiffs must convince the district court that the public interest and balance of hardships tip in their favor." *Id.* (citation omitted).

As in any other civil proceeding, the likelihood of success on the merits and the balance of hardships are the critical considerations in determining whether a preliminary injunction should issue in a trademark infringement action. (citation omitted) To prevail on the merits of a trademark infringement claim, a plaintiff must establish "that the defendant's use of its mark gives rise to a 'likelihood of confusion' in the consuming public." *Metro Publ'g, Ltd. v. San Jose Mercury News*, 987 F.2d 637, 640 (9th Cir. 1993) (quoting *E. & J. Gallo Winery v. Gallo Cattle Co.*, 967 F.2d 1280, 1290 (9th Cir. 1992)). "Once the plaintiff has demonstrated a likelihood of confusion, it is ordinarily presumed that the plaintiff will suffer irreparable harm if injunctive relief is not granted." *Brookfield Commc'ns, Inc. v. West Coast Entm't Corp.*, 174 F.3d 1036, 1066 (9th Cir. 1999) (quoting *Metro Publ'g*, 987 F.2d at 640). Such an injunction may issue even if the plaintiff's mark has not been registered with the PTO. (Citation omitted).

DISCUSSION

Plaintiff seeks protection for ... the common law trademarks consisting of the images and likenesses of Marilyn Monroe, ... and the trade dress comprised of "high quality, distinctive photographs of Marilyn Monroe in various poses taken at different times during her career that show her, [sic] beauty, glamour and sex appeal" ("the Marilyn Wines trade dress"). With the exception of "Velvet Collection" and the Marilyn Wines trade dress, plaintiff asserts that these marks are each owned by the Marilyn Monroe estate, which has granted plaintiff an exclusive license to use the marks in connection with wine. Significantly, plaintiff seeks protection for these marks and dresses *only* as they are used on wine bottles.

. . . .

D. Likelihood of Confusion

. . . .

. . . [T]he court finds the following *Sleekcraft* factors weigh in favor of plaintiff: the similarity of the trade dresses, the strength of the Marilyn Wines trade dress, the relatedness of the parties' goods, and the degree of care likely to be exercised by purchasers of the parties' products. Although the intent in choosing the trade dress weighs in favor of defendant, lack of intent is of little probative value in assessing likelihood of confusion. The remaining factors are of little importance under the circumstances and do not favor either party. Because all of the probative factors, including the all-important similarity factor, weigh in favor of plaintiff, the court finds that plaintiff has established by a preponderance of the evidence that it will able to prove a likelihood of consumer confusion at trial.

. . . Because plaintiff has asserted a valid trade dress inference and shown a likelihood of confusion, the court finds that plaintiff has demonstrated a likelihood of success on the merits. "Once the plaintiff has demonstrated a likelihood of confusion, it is ordinarily presumed that the plaintiff will suffer irreparable harm if injunctive relief is not granted." *Brookfield Commc'ns., 174 F.3d at 1066.* Plaintiff is therefore entitled to injunctive relief.

II. Balance of Hardships

While plaintiff's demonstration of likelihood of confusion is sufficient to warrant injunctive relief, the court further finds that injunctive relief is warranted under the Ninth Circuit's alternative test: serious questions going to the merits of the case combined with the balance of hardships tipping sharply in favor of the plaintiff. (Citation omitted). As the sole purveyor of Marilyn Monroe wines for the past twenty years, plaintiff may suffer immeasurable and irreparable damage to its reputation and goodwill if other wineries are able to sell wines with nearly identical packaging outside the control of plaintiff.

In contrast, defendants have made very little showing of hardship should an injunction issue. Defendants claim that they will suffer irreparable harm through loss of "market time," injury to reputation by being unable to follow through with its planned introduction of its Marilyn Monroe wines, and a negative perception in the marketplace as an infringer without proof that plaintiff has any rights or that defendants have violated those rights. Defendants assert that they will suffer financial losses in excess of $4 million should an injunction issue, based on their inability to fill orders and exploit "initial publicity and buzz" in time to make holiday season sales. Defendants offer no data to support this figure.

Defendants cite cases in which parties suffered harm by being forced to withdraw their products or were effectively shut down by the injunction.(Citations omitted). Defendants seem to ignore the crucial fact that Adler Fels' product has not yet been released into the market place. There are thus no products to withdraw, and it is unlikely that defendants will be "shut down" by being temporarily prevented from releasing a particular product. Notably, defendants have offered no explanation as to why they cannot simply use a different, clearly non-infringing label for the particular wine they have chosen as their Red Velvet Collection wine. As there can be no possible relationship between the image of Marilyn Monroe and the flavor of the wine, that which we call Marilyn Monroe wine, by any other name, would taste as sweet. *See* William Shakespeare, Romeo and Juliet, act 2, sc. 2. In addition, Adler Fels has been in the business of selling wine under a wide variety of names and labels. Given the large number of unclaimed names and images that Adler Fels could select for its wines, it is difficult to see how Adler Fels' business will be adversely affected by being barred from using the name or image of one particular individual.

Finally, defendants claim that plaintiff's delay in filing its TRO application and motion for preliminary injunction militate against granting a preliminary injunction. The court does not find undue delay here. Although the initial controversy erupted in June or July 2006, plaintiff did not learn that Adler Fels was actually marketing its upcoming Red Velvet Collection wine until September, and the earlier communications between the parties did not indicate that Adler Fels would be selling such a wine. Plaintiff served its complaint, TRO application, and motion for a preliminary injunction, the following month. This time frame was reasonable and therefore does not bar injunctive relief.

Accordingly, the court finds that the balance of hardships tips sharply in plaintiff's favor.

CONCLUSION

For the reasons stated above, the court GRANTS plaintiff's motion for a preliminary injunction.

. . . .

QUESTIONS

1. What if instead of moving for a preliminary injunction soon after learning that Adler Fels was going to market wine with Marilyn Monroe images, Nova Wines had waited for a year? Should the delay affect the grant of a preliminary injunction? Why or why not? *See, e.g., Citibank N.A. v. Citytrust*, 756 F.2d 273 (2d Cir.1985). Are there any other factors that might undercut a finding of irreparable harm?

2. Should a presumption of irreparable harm be applied in a case in which likelihood of success on the merits has been shown with respect to a dilution claim but not with respect to an infringement claim? *Cf. Federal Express Corp. v. Federal Expresso, Inc.*, 201 F.3d 168 (2d Cir.2000). In such a case, should it matter how local the dilution is likely to be? Compare

Federal Express (involving local coffee shops) with *Nabisco Inc. v. PF Brands, Inc.*, 191 F.3d 208 (2d Cir.1999) (involving a national rollout of competing cracker products).

3. Can injunctive relief under the Lanham Act be obtained against infringements by state and/or federal government entities? *See* definition of "person" in section 45 of the Lanham Act, 15 U.S.C. § 1127, and *Preferred Risk Mutual Insurance Co. v. United States*, 86 F.3d 789 (8th Cir.1996), *cert. denied*, 520 U.S. 1116 (1997). Do the Supreme Court's decisions in *College Savings Bank v. Florida Prepaid Postsecondary Education Expense Board* and in *Florida Prepaid Secondary Education Expense Board v. College Savings Bank* (Chapter 6.D, *supra*) change the analysis? Why or why not?

4. Once an injunction is granted, are there any circumstances that would justify a modification of this relief? Consider the situation in which a registrant for a mark for Mexican cheese products was enjoined in 1988 in 4 states on the basis of the other party's prior common law rights in those states to a similar mark for Mexican cheese products. Do the facts that the Latino population has become more dispersed in the United States and that Spanish networks offering national advertising have emerged since the injunction issued justify a modification to the injunction allowing the defendant to advertise nationally in Spanish media? *See V&V Food Products, Inc. v. Cacique Cheese Co.*, 66 U.S.P.Q.2d 1179 (N.D.Ill.2003).

CENTRALITY OF INJUNCTIVE RELIEF AND USE OF ALTERNATE DISPUTE RESOLUTION

Injunctive relief has been termed "the remedy of choice for trademark and unfair competition cases." *Century 21 Real Estate Corp. v. Sandlin*, 846 F.2d 1175, 1180 (9th Cir.1988). Injunctive relief is critical to trademark owners to halt infringing uses for which it has been held that "there is no adequate remedy at law for the injury caused." *Id.* A likelihood of confusion or dilution risks non-quantifiable damage to the trademark owner's reputation or to the goodwill or distinctiveness associated with its mark. As a result, trademark owners frequently seek preliminary injunctive relief as in *Nova Wines, supra,* as well as permanent injunctive relief. Moreover, an injunction is often the only remedy trademark owners realistically can obtain in non-counterfeiting cases. Actual damages are difficult to prove, and an award of defendant's profits is not routine. Attorney's fees are awarded only in "exceptional cases." 15 U.S.C. § 1117(a).

Litigation can provide no certain answers in advance to many trademark, trade dress and related disputes. The "answer" may not be known until after there has been a motion for a temporary restraining order, followed by a motion for a preliminary injunction, an appeal to the Court of Appeals, then a trial, and a further appeal. Such litigation is not only enormously expensive but the uncertainty that lingers until a final decision issues can also destroy a business plan. Perhaps partly because there is no perceived likelihood of monetary compensation coupled with the uncertainty and expense of litigation, litigants sometimes resort to alternate methods of dispute resolution, including mediation and arbitration. These methods can reduce uncertainty by ensuring a rapid final decision, and can lower the cost of resolving disputes. They also avoid the gambling aspect of having such matters tried before a jury or a judge who is unfamiliar with trademarks.

In mediation, the disputing parties voluntarily meet with a neutral facilitator who tries to facilitate resolution. If the parties cannot agree on how to deal with their problem, either party can choose to litigate the issue in court, or to arbitrate. A number of the leading companies in the cereal industry, for example, have agreed that any trade dress dispute among them will be subject to mediation for a period of 90 days. If the matter is not resolved within that time, either party is free to fight it out in the courts.

The International Trademark Association (INTA) in a joint venture with the Center for Public Resources (CPR) Institute for Dispute Resolution established a national panel of mediators/arbitrators, all of whom are veteran trial lawyers in the trademark, trade dress, false advertising and unfair competition areas. The panelists are trained by CPR and are available either to mediate or to arbitrate disputes in these areas. An example of how the CPR/INTA panel works is instructive. Two major consumer goods competitors were engaged in a dispute involving a 30 second commercial that had just appeared on national television. Among other things, the commercial referred to the competitor's principal trademark in a way that gave offense to the owner of the mark. The parties agreed to arbitrate before a single arbitrator from the CPR/INTA panel. The arbitration agreement provided that the hearing before the arbitrator would take place within 20 days and that the arbitrator would render the decision within 10 days. It was further agreed that pending the arbitrator's decision, the commercial would not be televised. Within 2 weeks of the signing of the arbitration agreement, a hearing was held, and 10 fact witnesses testified along with four experts. The arbitrator rendered a decision within 4 days after closing arguments. Thus, the parties, by this method, received a prompt and confidential resolution by a knowledgeable arbitrator. In addition, the cost of resolving the dispute was significantly reduced.

Recently, domain name disputes have become fertile ground for arbitration proceedings since the institution of ICANN's Dispute Resolution Policy. *See* Chapter 11, *supra*. Rather than undergoing the time and expense of bringing court actions for trademark infringement, dilution and/or cyberpiracy, many trademark owners are utilizing the relatively speedy and cost-effective arbitration procedure specified in ICANN's policy.

2. DISCLAIMERS

Home Box Office v. Showtime

832 F.2d 1311 (2d Cir.1987).

■ LUMBARD, J.:

. . . .

I.

HBO and Showtime are competitors in the subscription television field. Both programming services offer a variety of movies, concerts, sporting events and other programs. Both sell their television services primarily to cable operators who then sell them to consumer subscribers.

HBO identifies its service through its federally registered servicemark and trademark "HBO" which appears at the beginning of each program. HBO frequently promotes its companion "Cinemax" television service in tandem with its "HBO" service with slogans such as "HBO & CINEMAX." Showtime also frequently promotes its companion service, "The Movie Channel," along with its "Showtime" service with slogans such as "SHOW-TIME/THE MOVIE CHANNEL."

At the National Cable Television Association Convention held in Las Vegas on May 17–20, 1987 (an industry trade show), Showtime launched a new advertising and promotional campaign using a new slogan as its theme. The primary slogan used was "SHOWTIME & HBO. It's Not Either/Or Anymore." (the "slogan"); the related slogans were: "THE MOVIE CHANNEL & HBO. Together is Better.", "Why SHOWTIME & HBO make such a perfect pair.", and "Play the Showtime PERFECT (HBO, Showtime) PAIR Instant Winner Game." The slogan was featured on a number of materials displayed or distributed at or near the Convention site. The materials included an outdoor highway billboard and a hot air balloon located outside the Convention Center; a rolling billboard that was driven around the Convention area; promotional videotapes played in public at the Las Vegas airport and in Convention hotel rooms; signs located in Showtime's Convention booth; promotional pens, tote bags, sunglasses, buttons and cookies distributed at Showtime's booth and/or to the hotel rooms of Convention attendees; advertisements that were distributed at the Convention and which appeared in trade publications at or about the time of the Convention; packages of promotional material distributed to Showtime's cable affiliates at or about the time of the Convention; game cards; and a brochure emphasizing the value of subscribing to both HBO and Showtime. Some, but not all, of these materials contained disclaimers stating that HBO and Showtime were unrelated services.

. . . .

HBO maintains that the slogan is confusing because it suggests that HBO and Showtime have merged or are engaged in a cooperative promotional campaign. To prove this, HBO produced evidence in the district court which tended to show that the slogan was the source of confusion because some observers perceived it to be part of a joint promotional campaign. The evidence presented by HBO included the promotional materials or representations of the materials used by Showtime at the Convention, a *Boston Globe* article that described the confusion caused by the slogan at the Convention among members of the cable television trade and a consumer reaction study in four cities that tested reactions to the videotaped commercial and the billboard that Showtime used at the Convention.

Showtime maintains that it adopted the slogan and undertook the related promotional campaign to educate consumers that Showtime has exclusive movies that are not available from HBO. Showtime asserts that its goal in using the slogan was to differentiate the two services and to convince consumers to subscribe to its service as well as to HBO. Showtime thus emphasizes that it sought to inform the public that Showtime and HBO are different, not to suggest any link between the services. It points to the disclaimers of any link between HBO and Showtime, and especially to the new promotional materials presented to the district court at the preliminary injunction hearing that featured disclaimers more prominently than did the materials that Showtime displayed and distributed at the Convention.

. . . . .

Although finding that the slogan was not "patently false," Judge Daranco credited the results of HBO's study and found that, if used alone without "adequate disclaiming information appropriate to the selected medium," it was ambiguous and likely to confuse and mislead consumers. Based on its findings, the district court enjoined Showtime from using the slogan and the related slogans "unless a prominent disclaimer, appropriate to the selected medium accompanies their use." The court thus enjoined the materials used at the Convention and any other materials not featuring an adequate disclaimer but it specifically exempted the materials presented at the hearing from the terms of the order. This court granted HBO's motion to hear this appeal on an expedited basis.

II.

Although we agree with the district court's application of the likelihood of confusion standard to Showtime's promotional materials, our view of the proper role of disclaimers in trademark infringement cases is somewhat different. . . . In many circumstances a disclaimer can avoid the problem of objectionable infringement by significantly reducing or eliminating consumer confusion by making clear the source of a product. *See Soltex Polymer Corporation v. Fortex Industries, Inc.*, No. 87–7245, slip op. (2d Cir. November 3, 1987) (minimal to moderate amount of consumer confusion found by district court could be cured effectively through the use of a disclaimer). We believe, however, that the record before us is not sufficient to support a finding that the disclaimers proposed by Showtime will be effective in substantially reducing consumer confusion. In fact, our examination of some of the promotional materials first submitted to the district court by Showtime as exhibits at the preliminary injunction hearing indicates to us that some of the potentially confusing statements are not effectively disclaimed because the disclaiming information does not appear in sufficiently close proximity to the infringing statements. As an example, we find Showtime's use of disclaimers to be especially problematic in the case of one of the multiple panel brochures submitted to the district court which had an infringing use on its back panel and a disclaimer only appearing on an inside panel. . . .

Requiring infringing users such as Showtime to demonstrate the effectiveness of proposed disclaimers is supported by cases from other circuits in which the use of a disclaimer by an infringing user has been found not to be sufficient to avoid consumer confusion in the marketplace. *See, e.g., United States Jaycees v. Philadelphia Jaycees,* 639 F.2d 134, 142 (3d Cir.1981); *Miss Universe, Inc. v. Flesher,* 605 F.2d 1130, 1134–35 (9th Cir.1979). In addition, we note that there is a body of academic literature that questions the effectiveness of disclaimers in preventing consumer confusion as to the source of a product. *See* Jacoby & Raskoff, *Disclaimers as a Remedy for Trademark Infringement Litigation: More Trouble Than They Are Worth?,* 76 Trademark Rept. 35 (1986); Radin, *Disclaimers as a Remedy for Trademark Infringement: Inadequacies and Alternatives,* 76 Trademark Rept. 59 (1986).

These authors have concluded that disclaimers are frequently not effective. One discussion concluded that disclaimers, especially those (like the disclaimers in question in this case) which employ brief negator words such as "no" or "not," are generally ineffective. *See Jacoby & Raskopf, supra* at 54. This conclusion was based on a study of the effect of disclaimers on football jerseys, an example of the effect of corrective advertising, and a generalized framework involving behavioral science research. The authors recommended that courts should consider the effectiveness of a proposed disclaimer more carefully and "[w]henever disclaimers are considered, empirical studies should be used to evaluate their likely impact. At the very least, no disclaimer should issue without a full hearing regarding its likely effectiveness." *Id.* at 57–58 (citations omitted), *see also* Radin, *supra* at 72. Radin also advocates the use of other methods either to make a disclaimer more effective or wholly unnecessary; the primary method he advocates is altering the context in which the infringing use occurs to make consumer confusion less likely. *Id.* at 71.

Although it is conceivable that a disclaimer could alleviate the likelihood of confusion that the district court found in this case, the court did not have before it sufficient evidence regarding the revised promotional materials to decide that their disclaimers rendered them significantly less likely to confuse consumers so that they might be exempted from the injunction. This is especially so as HBO had no opportunity to consider the proposed disclaimers and produce evidence as it had with respect to the slogans and disclaimers that Showtime used at the Convention.

In further proceedings before the district court, Showtime should be free to apply for relief from the injunction, on the basis of its use of disclaimers or otherwise, after it gives adequate notice to HBO.

Upon such an application, there would be a heavy burden on Showtime to come forward with evidence sufficient to demonstrate that any proposed materials would significantly reduce the likelihood of consumer confusion. We do not believe that Showtime, at any point in this litigation, has met this burden and until it satisfies the district court on the basis of proper showing, it may not use HBO's trademark in its slogan or the related slogans.

We appreciate that this assignment of the burden of proof unlike the method utilized by the district court might make it significantly more difficult for Showtime ever to use these slogans. Nevertheless, we believe that it is an appropriate allocation of burdens between these parties for several reasons. First, it acknowledges that by granting the preliminary injunction, the district court found that HBO had adequately proved that the slogan as Showtime first employed it was likely to cause consumer confusion. Second, it recognizes that by using the slogans as they were presented at the Convention, Showtime is infringing on HBO's trademark and, therefore, that Showtime has no right to use the mark unless and until it can demonstrate that, because of some change in the slogan or the context in which it is presented, its use will no longer constitute an infringement. Third, it alleviates the necessary hardship that could be imposed on HBO if it repeatedly had to catch up with Showtime's use of its trademark by adequately demonstrating that each new permutation of the slogan and its context was likely to mislead consumers. Fourth, and finally, it is the allocation of the burden of proof which best accords with our interpretation of the Lanham Act as a means of protecting trademark holders and the public from confusion as to the source and promotion of products.

We affirm the district court's issuance of a preliminary injunction but vacate that portion of the order which allowed Showtime to continue using the slogan if it utilizes an appropriate disclaimer and that portion which exempted the revised promotional materials presented to the district court at the hearing conducted before the district court on July 15, 1987. We deny Showtime's cross appeal. This case is remanded for further proceedings consistent with this opinion.

Soltex Polymer Corp. v. Fortex Industries, Inc.

832 F.2d 1325 (2d Cir.1987).

■ ALTIMARI, J.:

This appeal presents the interesting question of whether a finding of any likelihood of consumer confusion between two products bearing the same mark necessarily mandates the use of an absolute injunction in favor of the owner of that trademark. The instant appeal arises from an order of the United States District Court for the Eastern District of New York, McLaughlin, J., following a bench trial in which the court refused to issue an injunction in favor of plaintiff-appellant Soltex Polymer Corporation ("Soltex") against defendants-appellees Fortex Industries, Inc. ("Fortex") and Fortiflex, Inc. ("Fortiflex") barring the use of plaintiff's mark FORTI-FLEX on plastic containers. The district court instead directed defendants to use a disclaimer on a certain product line of containers after the court concluded, with respect to that product line, that the defendants had infringed upon plaintiff's mark. Because the district court did not abuse its discretion in fashioning an appropriate remedy given the limited nature of defendants' infringement as evidenced by the court's factual findings, we affirm.

I. *Background*

Soltex is a manufacturer of polyprophylene and other raw plastic materials ... The company was formed ... to acquire a high-density polyethylene ("HDPE") business from Celanese Corporation ("Celanese"). Soltex also acquired the ownership rights to the registered trademark FORTIFLEX from its predecessor in interest, Celanese.

Soltex sells its raw plastic materials to other manufacturers who fabricate them into various finished plastic products such as containers for industrial uses and gallon milk jugs. Soltex's HDPE resin is in the form of a granular white powder and is sold under the trademark FORTIFLEX, primarily in either 50 pound bags, 1,000 pound boxes or 180,000 pound railway hopper cars. The FORTIFLEX as well as the SOLTEX trademarks appear on all bags and boxes containing the resin and on all bills of lading accompanying rail car shipments. Both marks currently are displayed prominently in the company's advertising.

. . . .

Fortex is a Puerto Rico corporation owned primarily by members of the Ballester family and is a manufacturer of finished rubber products, including various types of containers. During the late 1960s, ... Fortex wanted to start a new company which could manufacture containers made from a composite of rubber and plastic. With regard to this new product line, Fortex had to decide whether the products would carry the company's existing FORTEX trademark or whether a new mark should be selected. The Ballesters ultimately decided to adopt a mark that, while similar to Fortex, would clearly establish a new identity and would emphasize their rubber/plastic products' qualities of strength and flexibility. Fortex also recognized the advantage of disassociating its new product line from existing FORTEX products in the event that the new product line prove unsuccessful. Consequently, the Ballesters chose "FORTIFLEX," a name which, like their FORTEX mark, uses the Latin root, "fort," for strength, yet suggests the product's flexible qualities.

Much to his chagrin, Jose Ballester later discovered that FORTIFLEX already was being used by Celanese for HDPE resin and by another company not connected with this litigation for rolling pins. He apparently satisfied himself that the uses of the mark by those two companies were on non-competing goods. In addition, he asked an attorney for a legal opinion as to whether Fortex could register the FORTIFLEX mark. The attorney quickly discovered the trademarks held by the other two companies but agreed with Ballester that Fortex could adopt and use the mark since the prior registrations related to products that were substantially different from those contemplated by Fortex.

Fortiflex then was incorporated in 1975 and commenced operation in Puerto Rico. Over the past ten years, the company has sold finished plastic products, including industrial containers such as buckets and pails as well as commercial animal feeders, under the mark FORTIFLEX. Fortiflex's bucket and container line of products has been sold principally in Puerto Rico because these "straight-walled" products cannot be telescoped one inside the other and thus are expensive to ship. Since 1977, however, the company's "animal-feeder" line of products has been marketed successfully in the United States, and its sales in this country are approximately $1,000,000 annually. As with Soltex's products, Fortiflex's products and related advertisements prominently display the FORTIFLEX mark as well as the company's name.

The district court heard testimony indicating that, as early as the fall of 1975, Soltex was aware of defendant's attempts to register the mark FORTIFLEX in Puerto Rico. Nothing was done, however, to prevent such registration. Soltex's management evidently concluded, at least initially, that Soltex's relatively low volume of business in Puerto Rico did not warrant an extensive effort to protect against the use of the mark by a small company. Several months thereafter during a routine marketing visit to the Fortiflex plant, an official of Soltex observed some plastic containers bearing the name FORTIFLEX and several bags of Soltex's FORTIFLEX HDPE resin. Soltex apparently confronted Ballester with its objection to defendants' use of the FORTIFLEX mark but also indicated that a solution could be "worked out."

Although, as the district court found, this conciliatory atmosphere continued over the next few years, the parties' discussions eventually were discontinued. . . .

Following its analysis of the various *Polaroid* factors, the district court concluded:

> [A]s to defendant's use of the FORTIFLEX mark on its animal feeder and agricultural products line, there is little, if any, likelihood of consumer confusion. As to defendant's container line, however, the Court finds that the *Polaroid* factors cut minimally or moderately in favor of a holding that an appreciable number of ordinarily prudent purchasers may be confused as to the source of defendant's goods or defendant's association with the plaintiff.

After balancing the equities to determine the propriety of injunctive relief, the court denied Soltex injunctive relief with respect to defendants' animal-feeder and industrial container lines, but required defendants to use the following disclaimer in conjunction with the FORTIFLEX mark and logo on its industrial container line: "Not connected with Soltex Polymer Corporation of Houston, Texas."

II. Discussion

. . . .

B. *Appropriateness of the relief granted*

Soltex's principal argument on appeal is that the district court abused its discretion in refusing to issue an injunction against the use of appellant's mark on defendants' industrial container line of products upon finding a minimal or moderate likelihood of consumer confusion. As the district court recognized, the crucial issue in a trademark infringement action is whether there is substantial likelihood of consumer confusion with respect to the goods in question. Soltex argues that once the district court determined that there was any likelihood of confusion, it was entitled to injunctive relief as a matter of law in view of the Lanham Act's principal purpose to provide effective relief against infringement and thereby protect trademarks and the goodwill associated with them. *See* S. Rep. No. 1333, 79th Cong., 2d Sess., *reprinted in* 1946 U.S. Code Cong. Serv. 1274.

A basic principle of the law of equitable remedies, however, is that the relief granted should be no broader than necessary to cure the effects of the harm caused. Defendants maintain that this principle supports their contention that the district court did not abuse its discretion in ordering a disclaimer in lieu of an injunction.

A district court has a "wide range of discretion in framing an injunction in terms it deems reasonable to prevent wrongful conduct." *Springs Mills, Inc. v. Ultracashmere House, Ltd.*, 724 F.2d 352, 355 (2d Cir.1983) (citation omitted). We have emphasized before the "flexible approach" characteristic of our *Polaroid* decisions. *See Vitarroz Corp. v. Borden, Inc.*, 644 F.2d 960, 966 (2d Cir.1981) (citations omitted). Indeed, we have rejected expressly an "all-or-nothing" or per se rule mandating the use of an absolute injunction whenever likelihood of confusion is found. *Id.* at 967–68; *see Springs Mills*, 724 F.2d at 355 ("district court did not err in devising an appropriate limited injunction"). This flexible approach also is in accord with the function of a court of equity.

The court's determination of whether to grant relief in the form of an absolute injunction or through the use of a disclaimer will not be disturbed on appeal, therefore, unless there has been an abuse of discretion. Although disclaimers may not always provide an effective remedy against an infringing use, a careful review of the record in this case satisfies us that the district court did not abuse its discretion. Several factors convinced the district court that an absolute prohibition against defendants' use of the FORTIFLEX mark was inappropriate. These included the court's factual findings that defendants adopted the FORTIFLEX mark in good faith, took substantial steps to present the mark only in conjunction with defendants' own stylized logo, and have a legitimate interest in preserving their rights in the "FORT" family of marks used by the Ballesters for many years. All of these findings are supported by the record.

In addition, given the undisputed fact that the market for defendants' industrial containers consists of relatively sophisticated buyers, the district court reasonably concluded that the minimal or moderate amount of potential confusion found could be cured effectively by use of a disclaimer. We find no abuse of discretion here, particularly in view of the district court's careful balancing of the equities to reach an *appropriate* result protective of the interests of both parties. Whether or not, as a matter of first impression, we would have reached the same result as the district court in refusing to enjoin defendants from using the FORTIFLEX mark on the industrial container line is beside the point. We simply cannot say that the district court abused its discretion in ordering a disclaimer instead of an absolute injunction. While we are aware that two other opinions filed today by panels of this court cast doubt on the effectiveness of disclaimers in trademark infringement cases involving a substantial likelihood of consumer confusion, *Home Box Office,* 832 F.2d at 1315, *Charles of the Ritz Group,* 832 F.2d at 1324, where, as here, the likelihood of consumer confusion is far less than substantial, we believe that it is within the district court's discretion to grant disclaimer relief. . . .

QUESTIONS

1. Can the reasoning in the *Home Box Office* and *Soltex* decisions be reconciled? Can the difference in result be explained by the effectiveness (or lack thereof) of the disclaimers at issue? Or by a balancing of the equities involved?

2. What kind of empirical evidence would be useful to a defendant trying to establish the effectiveness of a disclaimer in eliminating or substantially reducing a likelihood of confusion?

3. Should a disclaimer be more readily considered as an acceptable remedy if the mark at issue implicates First Amendment interests, such as a magazine title? *Cf. Westchester Media v. PRL USA Holdings, Inc.,* 214 F.3d 658 (5th Cir.2000).

4. If a defendant uses a disclaimer, may an adverse inference be drawn from such use?

5. Consider the facts in *Pebble Beach Co. v. Tour 18 I Ltd.,* 155 F.3d 526 (5th Cir.1998). Tour 18 copied golf holes from well known golf courses, a fact which it promoted on the course and in advertising and promotional materials. Tour 18 employed disclaimers on the course and in some advertising materials. The appellate court permitted Tour 18 to make referential use of plaintiff's marks, subject to use of conspicuous disclaimers, even though plaintiffs' survey of golfers who had played on defendant's Tour 18 course, still evidenced some confusion. Should an absolute injunction have been granted? Is it necessary to tolerate some level of confusion in order to permit nominative fair use? *Cf. Toho Co. v. Wm. Morrow & Co.,* 33 F.Supp.2d 1206 (C.D.Cal.1998) (disclaimer on back cover of book prominently entitled GODZILLA! in stylized lettering similar to that used by plaintiff inadequate to render use a nominative fair use).

6. Where a domain name is found to be confusingly similar to a trademark, would a disclaimer of association with the trademark owner on the defendant's website be an adequate remedy? Why or why not? *See, e.g., OBH Inc. v. Spotlight Magazine Inc.,* 86 F.Supp.2d 176 (W.D.N.Y.2000); *Planned Parenthood Federation of America, Inc. v. Bucci,* 42 U.S.P.Q.2d 1430 (S.D.N.Y.1997), *aff'd mem.,* 152 F.3d 920 (2d Cir.), *cert. denied,* 525 U.S. 834 (1998).

3. Recalls and Destruction

Perfect Fit Indus. v. Acme Quilting Co.

646 F.2d 800 (2d Cir.1981).

■ Kearse, J.:

[The district court held that defendant's J-board trade dress for mattress pads violated plaintiff's common law unfair competition rights under N.Y. law and ordered defendant to deliver the infringing product inventory to plaintiff for destruction and to write to customers of the last 6 months requesting the return of the package inserts. Defendant appealed the order.]

. . . .

We turn ... to the propriety of the recall provision of the district court's May 19 order. The recall provision is an unusual, and perhaps unprecedented, remedy for a violation of New York's law of unfair competition. Nonetheless, we conclude that the imposition of a recall requirement is well within the district court's broad powers as a court of equity, and that the district court properly exercised these powers in the present case.

It is well settled that the district court's equity jurisdiction empowers it "to mould each decree to the necessities of the particular case." ... State law does not govern the scope of the equity powers of the federal court; and this is so even when state law supplies the rule of decision.

... [T]here is federal precedent for use of the recall remedy in cases such as this. *See Kiki Undies Corp. v. Promenade Hosiery Mills, Inc.,* 308 F. Supp. 489 (S.D.N.Y.1969) (on remand from 411 F.2d 1097 (2d Cir.1969), *cert. dismissed,* 396 U.S. 1054 (1970)). The circumstances in *Kiki Undies* were remarkably similar to those of the present case, except that the plaintiff's claim was decided under federal trademark laws rather than under state laws of unfair competition. The injunctive order fashioned by the district court required the defendant, *inter alia,* to use its best efforts, on a continuing basis, to withdraw the offending materials from all customers, retailers and other persons. The district court here had no less power to order Acme to make a single request to its distributees to return the offending J-boards.

We conclude that this was an appropriate case for the exercise of the court's power to require a recall. The district court found that Acme had intentionally copied Perfect Fit's trade dress, and on appeal we held that, as a matter of law, Acme's trade dress was likely to cause confusion among customers, *see* 618 F.2d at 954–55. Acme's infringing trade dress was therefore likely to divert customers from Perfect Fit's product to Acme's. Particularly because the first appeal had prolonged the litigation and therefore increased the probable injury to Perfect Fit, the district court was entirely justified in fashioning swift and complete relief for Perfect Fit. The recall procedure would naturally hasten the removal of the offending materials from public view and therefore seek to end quickly the injury to Perfect Fit.

Acme's argument that the recall provision is unduly burdensome is unpersuasive. Of course, a district court should carefully consider the likely burden and expense of a recall before it imposes the remedy. In some circumstances the imposition of a recall may be unduly onerous, as where the defendant's products are widely distributed and particularly expensive to ship. Or the probable benefit to the plaintiff from a recall may not outweigh the burden to the defendant in some cases even if that burden is relatively light. These are matters to be weighed in the first instance by the district court, and we see no abuse here of the district court's discretion. Nothing in the record developed below suggests that appropriate consideration was not given to these questions or indicates that Acme would suffer unduly under the May 19 order. The order did not require Acme to take extensive action to retrieve the J-boards. The company need only have written its customers requesting a return of the boards and paid the cost of the return for those customers who complied. *Compare Kiki Undies, supra.* Acme's evidence concerning the cost of this program was wholly speculative and was founded on the unwarranted assumption that every person contacted would return not only the J-boards, as requested, but the mattress covers as well. Given the flimsiness of Acme's showing of burden, we can hardly say that the district judge abused her discretion in granting the remedy.

. . . .

Nikon, Inc. v. Ikon Corp., 987 F.2d 91 (2d Cir.1993). After affirming that defendant's IKON mark for cameras infringed plaintiff's NIKON mark for cameras, the Second Circuit also affirmed the district court's recall order, reasoning as follows:

> [Defendant] claims that the recall order was unduly harsh under the circumstances, asserting that Nikon delayed the trial, causing it to last three years. IPC says that Nikon was in no hurry to get IPC products off the market and that a recall is not justified.
>
> We hold that the recall order was appropriate. The district court has broad discretion as to recall orders which are part of permanent injunctions. *Perfect Fit Industries v. Acme Quilting Co.*, 646 F.2d 800, 805 (2d Cir.1981), *cert. denied*, 459 U.S. 832 (1982). As Nikon asserts, IPC was warned by its counsel that the trademarks were similar and that IPC should add to its mark to avoid confusion. IPC also withheld from its counsel its intention to enter the 35 mm market. This is evidence of bad faith on the part of IPC. Moreover, while affixing stickers on the cameras warning customers about Ikon's infringement might be said to be less harsh than a recall, there is no guarantee that retailers would affix the stickers. Further, IPC still could remove the trademark from the cameras and sell them to stores like Job Lot. Although IPC asserts it is a harsh remedy, there is no evidence in the record

before us to show that the court abused its discretion in ordering the immediate recall.

Gucci America, Inc. v. Daffy's, Inc.

354 F.3d 228 (3d Cir.2003).

■ McKEE, CIRCUIT JUDGE.

[The district court found defendant Daffy's, Inc., a discount retailer, liable for selling high quality counterfeit GUCCI handbags that defendant had acquired from its supplier without all the usual indicia of authenticity. Daffy's had taken a bag to a Gucci outlet store where the store clerk indicated that the bag was authentic. Daffy's also sent one bag to Gucci for repair, and it was repaired without comment. When Gucci sent a cease and desist letter, Daffy's withdrew the few remaining bags from sale and also instituted a policy of not selling Gucci merchandise. Despite finding liability, the district court denied *inter alia* a recall order and a permanent injunction. Gucci appealed].

. . . .

A. Recall Order

We review the district court's denial of Gucci's request for recall of the counterfeit handbags for an abuse of discretion. (Citations omitted)

Both Daffy's and Gucci agree that the propriety of the court's recall decision is governed by:

1. the willful or intentional infringement by the defendant;

2. whether the risk of confusion to the public and injury to the trademark owner is greater than the burden of the recall to the defendant; and

3. substantial risk of danger to the public due to the defendant's infringing activity.

See Theodore C. Max *Total Recall: A Primer on a Drastic Form of Equitable Relief*, 84 Trademark Rep. 325, 327 (1994) (listing these factors); *see also Perfect Fit Industries v. Acme Quilting Co,* 646 F.2d 800, 807 (2d Cir 1981) (weighing the first two factors in decision to order recall).

. . . .

Gucci does not argue that Daffy's conduct created a substantial risk of danger to the public, nor does Gucci contest the district court's conclusion that Daffy's was "an innocent infringer," . . . Therefore, we may focus our discussion on the court's resolution of the balancing of harms required under the second factor set forth above. . . .

. . . . [W]e agree with the district court's determination that the public benefit of a recall does not outweigh the equities counseling against it. A recall would have a financial impact upon Daffy's. It would also likely injure the company's goodwill as consumers may well assume that Daffy's was guilty of intentional wrongdoing no matter how carefully Daffy's explained the circumstances leading to any recall. Since the counterfeit bags were virtually indistinguishable from Gucci manufactured bags, the district court quite reasonably concluded that "a recall would harm Daffy's with little real benefit to Gucci" or the public.

Gucci invokes a post-sale confusion theory, which presumes that "the senior user's potential purchasers or ongoing customers might mistakenly associate the inferior quality work of the junior user with the senior user and, therefore, refuse to deal with the senior user in the future." *Acxiom Corp. v. Axiom, Inc.*, 27 F. Supp. 2d 478, 497 (D. Del. 1998); (citation omitted). Yet, Gucci does not challenge the district court's conclusion that, given the quality of the counterfeit bags, third party observers would not perceive anything inferior about them. Accordingly, consumers would not attribute substandard merchandise to Gucci. Gucci does, however, claim that the district court gave short shrift to its concerns over ongoing confusion of Daffy's consumers who unknowingly possess a counterfeit "Gucci."

Although this position has some initial surface appeal, it does not withstand scrutiny. As we noted above, the district court considered the dangers of customer confusion. It gave "serious consideration to the fact that denying a recall will leave Daffy's customers under the continued misapprehension that they own a real Gucci product." However, the court was convinced that this did not justify a recall because the quality of the counterfeit bags and the relatively high price Daffy's customers were willing to pay for them undermined claims of a tarnished Gucci trademark. Finally, in the absence of sufficient evidence regarding the comparative durability of Daffy's bags and Gucci's bags, Gucci's conclusion that counterfeit bags would require greater maintenance rests upon pure speculation. Accordingly, the district court stated the following in explaining why the equities precluded ordering a recall:

> The potential for damage to Daffy's goodwill with its customers is too obvious to be belabored. Daffy's marketing niche, distress sales of designer goods at significant discounts, would mean nothing if the consumer lacked confidence that the goods were what they purport to be. Daffy's also points out that a recall would require credit card records available only from the issuing banks.

. . . . The court's factual conclusions are not clearly erroneous. Given the careful application of the correct equitable standard to the evidence before it, it is clear to us that the district court did not abuse its discretion in refusing to order a recall.

B. Summary Judgment–Injunctive Relief . . .

We review the district court's decision to grant or deny an injunction for an abuse of discretion . . .

1. Injunctive Relief

In deciding whether to grant a permanent injunction, the district court must consider whether: (1) the moving party has shown actual success on the merits; (2) the moving party will be irreparably injured by the denial of injunctive relief; (3) the granting of the permanent injunction will result in even greater harm to the defendant; and (4) the injunction would be in the public interest.

Shields v. Zuccarini, 254 F.3d 476, 482 (3d Cir. 2001). Although we have said that "trademark infringement amounts to irreparable injury as a matter of law," dissent at 27 (quoting *S & R Corp. v. Jiffy Lube Int'l, Inc.,* 968 F.2d 371, 378, 1992 U.S. App. LEXIS 14267 (1992)), the irreparable injury we referred to was not intended to swallow the remaining prongs of the permanent injunction inquiry.

In *S & R Corp.,* we stated:

Grounds for irreparable injury include loss of control of reputation, loss of trade, and loss of goodwill. Lack of control amounts to irreparable injury regardless of allegations that the infringer is putting the mark to better use. Irreparable injury can also be based on the possibility of confusion. Finally, and most importantly for this case, trademark infringement amounts to irreparable injury as a matter of law.

968 F.2d at 378 (citations omitted). We cited *Opticians Assoc. of America v. Indept. Opticians of America* in support of our pronouncement that trademark infringement constitutes irreparable injury as a matter of law. A closer look at *Opticians* will therefore further inform our analysis of the district court's denial of injunctive relief here.

In *Opticians,* we concluded that infringement constitutes a *per se* injury "even if the infringer's products are of high quality, . . ." *Opticians Ass'n of America v. Independent Opticians of America,* 920 F.2d 187, 196, 1990 U.S. App. LEXIS 20690 (1990). This is because infringement inhibits the owner's "ability to control its own Guild marks, which in turn creates the *potential* for damage to its reputation. Potential damage to reputation constitutes irreparable injury for the purpose of granting a preliminary injunction in a trademark case." *Id.* However, ... Gucci argued injury from loss of control for the first time on appeal, and that aspect of irreparable injury has therefore been waived. Accordingly, the district court correctly focused on the *actual* injury to Gucci's reputation and goodwill in finding that Gucci had not established irreparable harm for purposes of injunctive relief.

. . . We believe that conclusion was reasonable, and that the district court did not abuse its discretion in denying Gucci the injunction given this record and the inquiry properly undertaken under *Shields.*

. . . . .

IV. Conclusion

For all of the above reasons, we will affirm the orders of the district court denying Gucci's request for a recall. We will also affirm the district court's order denying Gucci's request for summary judgment which precluded both injunctive relief . . .

■ ROSENN, CIRCUIT JUDGE, DISSENTING:

. . . .

The District Court ignored the purpose of the trade-mark statute to protect the public from deceit and secure to the business community the advantages of its good name and reputation. It left the purchasers of 588 highly expensive counterfeit bags without any relief or even notice that the bags they were carrying were not genuine. . . . [T]he court denies the innocent trademark owner an injunction against future infringement and a recall of the spurious goods sold under the producer's trade-mark and good name. Because the majority affirms that decision, I respectfully dissent.

. . . .

The District Court found that Daffy's unintentionally sold counterfeit bags. However, as between a sophisticated chain of discount stores in the high risk business of selling products acquired outside the customary chain of retail distribution and without the usual authenticating documentation and an innocent infringed, the District Court . . . has favored and enriched the infringer and left the innocent and innovative creator of a famous product and trademark owner without any remedy whatsoever. Moreover, the court has denied protection against future infringement. . . .

II.

Gucci is . . . entitled to an injunction to protect it from future unintentional infringement by Daffy's. Although the District Court found that Daffy's infringement was unintentional, there is still a danger that Daffy's will harm Gucci in the future through an incident of unintentional infringement. . . .

Although the majority acknowledges, as it must, that "trademark infringement amounts to irreparable injury as a matter of law," it jumps to an inexplicable conclusion that Gucci's failure to argue in the District Court that the "loss of control" over its trademarked goods by the infringement also amounts to a waiver of irreparable harm "for purposes of injunctive relief." This holding incredibly transforms the "control of quality" argument asserted by Gucci in its contention that the District Court committed legal error in failing to order a recall of the counterfeit goods into a general waiver of irreparable harm "for purposes of injunctive relief." Irreparable harm was and is a basic element of plaintiff's case from its inception. Implying a *sub silentio* waiver, as the majority does, of the fundamental legal principal that "trademark infringement amounts to irreparable injury" is highly unwarranted and imprudent.

. . . .

By proving infringement, Gucci proved irreparable injury as a matter of law. Upon proving irreparable injury, the burden shifted to Daffy's to prove that the injury will not recur in the future. "It is well established that the voluntary discontinuance of challenged activities by a defendant does not necessarily moot a lawsuit." *Lyons P'ship, L.P. v. Morris Cos-*

tumes, Inc., 243 F.3d 789, 800 (4th Cir. 2001) (internal quotation marks omitted). "That rule is subject to the caveat that an injunction is unnecessary when there is *no* reasonable expectation that the wrong will be repeated." *Id.* (citing *United States v. W.T. Grant Co.*, 345 U.S. 629, 633, 97 L. Ed. 1303, 73 S. Ct. 894 (1953)) (emphasis in original) (internal quotation marks omitted). Daffy's cannot show that its putative policy against selling infringed goods moots Gucci's motion for an injunction. To show that an injunction is unnecessary and further proceedings are mooted by Daffy's plans not to sell any more Gucci products, Daffy's must meet its "heavy burden" of showing that future infringement is "practically speaking, nearly impossible." *Lyons P'ship*, 243 F.3d at 800.

Daffy's argues that it now has a policy of not buying any Gucci goods. It points out that if it does not buy any Gucci branded goods, it cannot even unintentionally infringe Gucci's trademark. That is true as long as the policy lasts, but that is of little comfort to Gucci because Daffy's has the ability to change the policy at any time. Moreover, Gucci argues that Daffy's does not point to any evidence in the record in support of its statement that it has adopted a policy never to sell Gucci goods in the future. Even now, Daffy's has no policies or procedures to authenticate merchandise. In response to our question at oral argument, Daffy's attorney would not stipulate that Daffy's will never sell Gucci's products. It merely claimed that its present policy is not to do so. No legal obligation prevents Daffy's from changing its mind tomorrow and immediately resuming sales of purported Gucci products.

Daffy's unwillingness to stipulate forbodes the possibility of future infringements, and once an infringement is shown, the trademark owner is not required to prove that the infringer is likely to infringe again. *Hard Rock Cafe Licensing Corp. v. Concession Services, Inc.*, 955 F.2d 1143, 1151 (7th Cir. 1992); *Basic Fun, Inc. v. X–Concepts, LLC.*, 157 F. Supp. 2d at 457 ("If the infringers sincerely intended not to infringe, the injunction harms them little; if they do, it gives [the trademark owner] substantial protection of its trademark."). Once infringement has been proven, a "heavy burden" falls on the infringer to demonstrate that there is no possibility of further recurrence of the infringement. *Lyons P'ship*, 243 F.3d at 800. The unwillingness of Daffy's to stipulate that in the future it would not sell Gucci bags obviously inspires no confidence in its present policy.

... Gucci sought to enjoin Daffy's only from future infringement "through sales of unauthorized goods and false advertising." It was erroneous as a matter of law for the court to place the burden on Gucci to prove that trademark infringement would continue in the future. *Shields v. Zuccarini*, 254 F.3d 476, 482 (3d Cir. 2001), merely identifies the four factors to be considered by the court in granting an injunction. Once an act of infringement is proven, federal courts do not require the plaintiff to show that the defendant is likely to infringe again in the future. *Levi Strauss & Co. v. Shilon*, 121 F.3d 1309, 1314 (9th Cir. 1997)(any doubt regarding extent of injunctive relief "must be resolved in [the plaintiff's] favor as the innocent producer and against the [defendant]"); (citation omitted). Once an infringement is demonstrated, a "heavy burden" shifts to the defendant to prove that there is no possibility of future recurrence of the infringement. *Lyons P'ship,* 243 F.3d at 800. Daffy's made no effort, beyond its non-binding policy, to prove that in the future it will not infringe upon Gucci's trademarks through sales of counterfeits.

For the reasons set forth above, the denial of the injunction constituted reversible error. . . .

———

Section 36 of the Lanham Act, 15 U.S.C. § 1118, also authorizes the destruction of articles that infringe a registered mark, section § 43(a) or section 43(c) (if willful).

QUESTIONS

1. As the *Perfect Fit* and *Nikon* cases illustrate, recall can be an extremely powerful remedy for trademark owners, and a corresponding calamity for infringers. While many considerations can support a recall order, one rationale is that recall acts as a deterrent to the defendant and to others against engaging in infringing conduct. Is this a proper consideration? What other reasons might support a recall order? In opposition to a recall, would it be wise for a defendant to stress the harm that such an order would cause to it as the defendant in *Gucci* did?

2. Is a recall order appropriate only when the infringement is willful? Is that why the *Gucci* court denied a recall remedy?

3. Was the majority or dissenting opinion in *Gucci* correct about the recall order? About the permanent injunction?

4. Entry of a destruction order is within the court's discretion, but only after plaintiff has established a violation of its rights after full trial, or after entry of summary judgment in its favor. If the infringing mark can be removed without destroying the product, should the court nonetheless order the destruction of the goods? What arguments would support an application for destruction in these circumstances?

———

B. MONETARY RELIEF

1. ASSESSING PROFITS AND/OR DAMAGES

Taco Cabana Int'l, Inc. v. Two Pesos, Inc.

932 F.2d 1113 (5th Cir.1991), *aff'd,* 505 U.S. 763, 112 S.Ct. 2753, 120 L.Ed.2d 615 (1992).

■ REAVLEY, J.:

[*See* the Supreme Court's decision, *supra* Chapter 7.B, for a discussion of the facts in the case.]

. . . .

III. *Remedies*

The jury awarded $306,000 for lost profits, $628,300 for lost income, and nothing for loss of good will.... Finding intentional and deliberate infringement, the district court doubled the damages to $1,868,600 for the trade dress infringement, and awarded attorneys' fees of $937,550. The court further ordered Two Pesos to make several changes in the design of its Texas restaurants, and to dispel customer confusion by displaying a prominent sign for a year acknowledging that Two Pesos had unfairly copied Taco Cabana's restaurant concept.

Taco Cabana claims injury, under the so-called "headstart" theory, from Two Pesos' preemption of the Houston market and other areas. According to Two Pesos, the jury based damages on an initial franchise fee of $10,000 per store and continuing royalty of 1% (which is substantially below what Taco Cabana or Two Pesos requires of actual franchisees). The lost profits calculation apparently assumes a foreclosure of five restaurants in the Houston area at a 6% profit margin on sales of $1.7 million per store with an incremental fixed over-head of $204,000. The jury heard abundant evidence on the foregoing remedies, including detailed damage models yielding totals substantially exceeding the jury's award.

A. *Trade–Dress Infringement Remedies*

> ... Section 35 provides that a prevailing plaintiff may, subject to the principles of equity ... recover (1) defendant's profits, (2) any damages sustained by the plaintiff, and (3) the costs of the action.... In assessing damages the court may enter judgment, according to the circumstances of the case, for any sum above the amount found as actual damages, not exceeding three times such amount. Such sum ... shall constitute compensation and not a penalty. The court in exceptional cases may award reasonable attorney fees to the prevailing party.

15 U.S.C.A. § 1117(a) (West Supp. 1991)....

. . . .

C. *Profits and Damages*

Two Pesos argues that a monetary award requires evidence of actual confusion, and that only diverted sales provide a proper measure of damages. We disagree, as we did in *Boston Professional Hockey*, 507 F.2d at 75–76 (plaintiff's failure to quantify any damages from diverted sales did not preclude recovery for deprivation of economic benefits that would have accrued from licensing); *see also Shen Mfg. Co. v. Suncrest Mills, Inc.*, 673 F. Supp. 1199, 1206 (S.D.N.Y.1987) (defendant's intentional copying entitles plaintiff to profits based on unjust enrichment theory despite failure to prove any instance of actual confusion). Because we embrace the "head-start" theory as the apt framework for monetary recovery, we need not pursue the issue of actual diverted sales.

Especially given the volatility of the restaurant industry, and the significant value of securing the image of "market leader," we believe the "headstart" theory provides an apt framework for Taco Cabana's monetary recovery. Two Pesos' infringement foreclosed the Houston market, which Gabriel Gelb characterized as "one of the most affluent Mexican food markets in the country." Based on the Houston market alone, Gelb estimated lost profits of $4.4 million. Other damage models produced even higher figures. The jury award easily qualifies as reasonable compensation to Taco Cabana.

D.   *Enhanced Damages*

Finding that Two Pesos' conduct was willful and deliberate, the district court doubled the jury award for infringement. Judge Singleton asserted that "[u]nder the facts of this case and listening to the witnesses and judging the credibility myself, I can come to no other conclusion than to find that Two Pesos' actions were willful in the sense that it was deliberate.... The evidence was overwhelming." Intentional imitation alone—as opposed to intentional infringement—would not suffice for the requisite bad faith, but as his Order recites, Judge Singleton found "that Two Pesos intentionally and deliberately infringed Taco Cabana's trade dress."

We must respect the fact that section 35 endows the district court with considerable discretion in fashioning an appropriate remedy for infringement. An enhancement of damages may be based on a finding of willful infringement, but cannot be punitive. *Playboy Enterprises, Inc. v. P.K. Sorren Export Co.*, 546 F. Supp. 987, 998 (S.D.Fla.1982); *see* 15 U.S.C.A. § 1117(a) (West Supp. 1991) (any sum in excess of actual damages must "constitute compensation and not a penalty").

It is anomalous to say that an enhancement of damages, which implies an award exceeding the amount found "compensatory," must be "compensatory" and not "punitive." Responding to that anomaly, we have suggested that enhancement could, consistent with the "principles of equity" promoted in section 35, provide proper redress to an otherwise undercompensated plaintiff where imprecise damage calculations fail to do justice, particularly where the imprecision results from defendant's conduct. *Boston Professional Hockey*, 597 F.2d at 77 (increased damages justified when defendant withholds or misrepresents available sales records or otherwise obstructs ascertainment of damages); *accord P.K. Sorren*, 546 F. Supp. at 998–99 (award of excess damages appropriate where "record strongly indicates that plaintiff's damages and defendant's profits were both greater than the amounts conclusively proven"). We find no evidence of information obstruction by Two Pesos, but we acknowledge the trial court's superior capacity to discern the elements of equitable compensation. Given the substantial evidence of willful infringement, the jury finding of trade secret misappropriation, and the evidence of substantial damages not reflected in the jury award, we cannot say that Judge Singleton abused his discretion.

.   .   .   .

Banjo Buddies, Inc. v. Renosky

399 F.3d 168 (3d Cir.2005).

■ ROTH, CIRCUIT JUDGE:

This appeal requires us to decide whether a showing of willful infringement is a prerequisite to an accounting of a trademark infringer's profits for a violation of section 43(a) of the Lanham Act. We hold that wilfulness is an important equitable factor but not a prerequisite to such an award, noting that our contrary position in *SecuraComm Consulting Inc. v. Securacom Inc.*, 166 F.3d 182, 190 (3d Cir. 1999), has been superseded by a 1999 amendment to the Lanham Act. We further affirm the District Court's resolution of several other damages issues, with a single exception explained below.

I.   *Factual Background and Procedural History*

Joseph Renosky was a member of the board of directors of Banjo Buddies, Inc., ("Banjo Buddies" or "BBI") from February 1996 until May 1999. Banjo Buddies' principal product during that time was an extremely successful fishing lure called the Banjo Minnow, which Renosky helped develop.

The Banjo Minnow was principally advertised via "infomercial" broadcast, and was also sold in sporting goods catalogs and sporting goods stores. Tristar Products, Inc., obtained exclusive rights to advertise and sell the Banjo Minnow through all forms of "direct response marketing, . . . print media, and retail distribution." BBI received 48% of Tristar's net profits in return. Renosky agreed to provide the manufactured Banjo Minnow lure kit through his corporation, Renosky Lures, Inc., to both Tristar and BBI at $5.20 per kit. Renosky received additional shares of BBI stock in exchange for producing the Banjo Minnow kits at a "fair price." . . .

During the Banjo Minnow's early success in 1996, Renosky presented an idea to the BBI board for a "new and improved" Banjo Minnow called the Bionic Minnow. The board took no formal action on the proposal, and a month later Renosky advised one of BBI's directors that he would develop the new lure independently. At least two board members urged Renosky against this course of action, but Renosky could not be swayed. He immediately began developing the Bionic Minnow through Renosky Lures and ultimately marketed the new lure via infomercial and other means beginning in February 1999.

After Renosky failed to comply with a "cease and desist" letter, BBI brought suit . . . that Renosky violated section 43(a) of the Lanham Act, 15 U.S.C. § 1125(a), by developing and marketing the Bionic Minnow in such a way that customers would believe the Bionic Minnow was a Banjo Buddies product . . .

The District Court ... found that Renosky was liable for "false designation of origin" under § 43(a) of the Lanham Act ... [and] concluded that Renosky should be forced to disgorge the net profits of the Bionic Minnow project under section 35(a) of the Lanham Act, 15 U.S.C. § 1117(a), which provides for such accountings as an equitable remedy for Lanham Act violations....

Accordingly, the District Court ordered Renosky to pay to Banjo Buddies the net profits earned by the Bionic Minnow project, and to produce "verified financial records" attesting to this amount. Renosky never produced these records, despite numerous delays and court orders. Renosky did ultimately retain an independent financial analysis (the "Alpern Report"), which the District Court accepted for purposes of establishing the total sales of the Bionic Minnow through November 2002. However, the court rejected that report's conclusion that the Bionic Minnow project suffered a net loss. Accordingly, the court calculated Renosky's profits by multiplying the total sales figure by 16%, based on testimony from Renosky's business manager that Renosky Lures products typically earn a "bottom line" of between 15–17%. The court also determined that Renosky should be forced to disgorge all of the distributions (based on gross sales) made to him as a shareholder in the Bionic Minnow project. The court entered judgment in March 2003 against Renosky in the amount of $1,589,155.

. . . .

III. Discussion

A. Willfulness Is a Factor, Not a Prerequisite.

Renosky argues that the District Court erred by awarding profits from the Bionic Minnow project to Banjo Buddies under section 35(a) of the Lanham Act because Renosky's violation of section 43(a) of that statute was not willful or intentional. Renosky relies on *SecuraComm Consulting, Inc. v. Securacom, Inc.*, 166 F.3d 182 (3d Cir. 1999), in which this court held that "a plaintiff must prove that an infringer acted willfully before the infringer's profits are recoverable" under § 35(a) of the Lanham Act. *Id. at 190* (citing *George Basch Co. v. Blue Coral, Inc.*, 968 F.2d 1532, 1537 (2d Cir. 1992)). The District Court's findings related to the issue of Renosky's intent are ambiguous and possibly contradictory.[5] However, we need not decide whether the District Court found or should have found that Renosky acted willfully, because we conclude that *SecuraComm*'s bright-line willfulness requirement has been superseded by statute and that, based on all the

---

5. On the one hand, that District Court found that Renosky exhibited "a considerable lack of good faith and fair dealing" by producing a nearly identical product in identical packaging, using the same primary marketing tool (the infomercial) with similar content, and by presenting himself as the developer of the Banjo Minnow in marketing materials for the Bionic Minnow. On the other hand, the court found that even though Renosky copied the successful format of the Banjo Minnow product and infomercial, "there is no evidence that [Renosky] deliberately intended by that copying to confuse consumers into believing that the Bionic Minnow was a Banjo Buddies project."

relevant equitable factors, the District Court did not abuse its discretion by ordering an accounting of Renosky's profits.

SecuraComm's bright-line rule was the dominant view when *Secura-Comm* was issued in January 1999. *See, e.g., Quick Technologies, Inc. v. Sage Group PLC,* 313 F.3d 338, 347–48 (5th Cir. 2002) (collecting cases, including *SecuraComm*); *George Basch Co.,* 968 F.2d at 1537; *Restatement (Third) of Unfair Competition § 37 (1995); J.* Thomas McCarthy, 5 *McCarthy on Trademarks and Unfair Competition* § 30:62 (4th ed. 1996). In August 1999, however, Congress amended § 35. Prior to the amendment, that section provided as follows:

> When a violation of any right of the registrant of a mark registered in the Patent and Trademark Office, or a violation under section 43(a) [15 U.S.C. § 1125(a)], shall have been established . . . the plaintiff shall be entitled . . ., subject to the principles of equity, to recover (1) defendant's profits, (2) any damages sustained by the plaintiff, and (3) the costs of the action.

See SecuraComm, 166 F.3d at 186 (quoting former 15 U.S.C. § 1117(a)). The 1999 amendment replaced "or a violation under *section 43(a)*" with "a violation under *section 43(a),* or a *willful* violation under *section 43(c),*" *see* Pub. L. No. 106–43, § 3(b), 113 Stat. 219 (Aug. 5, 1999) (emphasis added). The plain language of the amendment indicates that Congress intended to condition monetary awards for *§ 43(c)* violations, but not *§ 43(a)* violations, on a showing of willfulness.[6]

We presume Congress was aware that most courts had consistently required a showing of willfulness prior to disgorgement of an infringer's profits in Lanham Act cases, despite the absence of the word "willful" in the statutory text prior to 1999. (Citation omitted). By adding this word to the statute in 1999, but limiting it to § 43(c) [dilution] violations, Congress effectively superseded the willfulness requirement as applied to § 43(a).

This conclusion is supported by *Quick Technologies,* 313 F.3d at 349, the only other appellate decision to reach the issue. The Fifth Circuit in *Quick Technologies* considered the effect of the 1999 amendment and held that, based on earlier decisions of that court as well as "the plain language of *[§ 43(a)]*," willful infringement was not a prerequisite to an accounting of the infringer's profits. *Id.* The court noted the wealth of contrary authority, including *SecuraComm,* but pointed out that all of those cases

---

6. The statute has been twice amended since August 1999, *see* Pub. L. No. 106–113, Div. B, § 1000(a)(9), 113 Stat. 1536, 1501A–54 (Nov. 29, 1999), *and* Pub. L. No. 107–273, Div. C, Tit. III, § 13207(a), 116 Stat. 1906 (Nov. 2, 2002), and now reads as follows:

> When a violation of any right of the registrant of a mark registered in the Patent and Trademark Office, a violation under section 1125(a) or (d) of this title, or a willful violation under section 1125(c) of this title, shall have been established in any civil action arising under this chapter, the plaintiff shall be entitled, subject to the provisions of sections 1111 and 1114 of this title, and subject to the principles of equity, to recover (1) defendant's profits, (2) any damages sustained by the plaintiff, and (3) the costs of the action.

15 U.S.C. § 1117(a).

preceded the statutory change. *Id. at 347–48.* The *Quick Technologies* court reaffirmed the factor-based approach elaborated in prior Fifth Circuit cases, including *Pebble Beach Co. v. Tour 18 I,* 155 F.3d 526, 554 (5th Cir. 1998), explaining that the infringer's intent was an important—but not indispensable—factor in evaluating whether equity supports disgorging the infringer's profits. *Quick Techs.,* 313 F.3d at 349. These factors "include, but are not limited to (1) whether the defendant had the intent to confuse or deceive, (2) whether sales have been diverted, (3) the adequacy of other remedies, (4) any unreasonable delay by the plaintiff in asserting his rights, (5) the public interest in making the misconduct unprofitable, and (6) whether it is a case of palming off." *Id.* (internal citations omitted).

.... For the reasons explained above, we now hold that *SecuraComm* has been superceded by the 1999 amendment. Relying on the *Quick Technologies* factor-based approach ... [W]e further conclude that the District Court did not abuse its discretion by ordering an accounting of Renosky's profits.... Because the District Court's findings concerning Renosky's intent are difficult to reconcile, *see supra* note 5, we will assume that factor is neutral. Nonetheless, all of the other *Quick Technologies* factors support an award of profits here.

It is likely that Renosky's conduct diverted sales from Banjo Buddies. *See Quick Techs.,* 313 F.3d at 349 (factor two). The District Court found that Renosky's marketing for the Bionic Minnow was confusingly similar to that of the Banjo Minnow, noting numerous material similarities in the infomercials used to market each product. The court also found that the two lure kits were "nearly identical" and were packaged identically. The court further found that the markets for the two products were "either the same or substantially overlapping." The District Court's observations concerning the close similarities of the products as well as their packaging and marketing schemes also strongly support the conclusion that Renosky was "palming off" the Bionic Minnow as a Banjo Buddies product. *See id.* (factor six). The public has an interest in discouraging this type of behavior, as it interferes with the consumer's ability to make informed purchasing decisions. *See id.* (factor five).

Next, there are no other adequate remedies. *See id.* (factor three). The District Court rejected Banjo Buddies' estimation of its damages (for both the Lanham Act claims and the state law claims) as too speculative. If Renosky's profits are not assessed, Banjo Buddies will be wholly uncompensated for Renosky's infringing actions. Finally, Banjo Buddies did not delay in bringing suit to stop Renosky's infringing actions. *See id.* (factor four). Accordingly, we conclude that the District Court did not abuse its discretion in deciding to order an accounting of Renosky's profits.

B.   *The District Court's Estimation of Profits.*

.   .   .   .

Section 35(a) provides that "in assessing profits the plaintiff shall be required to prove defendant's sales only; defendant must prove all elements of cost or deduction claimed." 15 U.S.C. § 1117(a); (citation omitted). The

District Court accepted the Alpern report's figure for total sales of the Bionic Minnow through November 22, 2002. Thus, Banjo Buddies' burden of proof was satisfied by Renosky's accountant's financial report.

However, the District Court held that Renosky failed to satisfy his burden of proof regarding costs and deductions ... [and] rejected the Alpern report's conclusion that Renosky suffered a loss of $492,699.00 for several reasons. ...First, the court observed that the Alpern report's summary of direct expenses associated with the Bionic Minnow project— totaling almost five million dollars—was sorely lacking in detail, lumping costs into six broad categories with no explanation of what specific expenses those categories represented....

Renosky fails to address the District Court's remaining reasons for rejecting the Alpern report's analysis of costs associated with the Bionic Minnow project. Most important, Renosky makes no attempt to explain why he twice failed to produce verified financial records supporting his claimed costs and deductions as ordered by the court. The court also observed several unexplained discrepancies between the Alpern report's summary of direct expenses and other evidence in the record. Next, the court rejected the Alpern report's conclusion that "shared expenses" associated with the Bionic Minnow project were $1,416,050. The court explained that the Alpern report did not show how "each item of general expense contributed to the production of the infringing items in issue and offer a fair and acceptable formula for allocating a given portion of overhead to the particular infringing items at issue." (citing *Design v. K-Mart Apparel Corp.*, 13 F.3d 559, 565–66 (2d Cir. 1994)). Finally, the court found that the Alpern report's "bottom line" lacked credibility. The court doubted that Renosky would allow the Bionic Minnow to lose nearly half a million dollars, and noted that Renosky's claimed loss was inconsistent with his attempt to secure clarification that profits accrued after November 22, 2002, would belong to him and not Banjo Buddies. Considering the collective strength of these arguments together with Renosky's failure to address most of them, we conclude that the District Court's rejection of the Alpern report's cost analysis was not clearly erroneous.

Because Renosky failed to meet his burden of proving costs and deductions, the District Court was forced to use an alternative method to estimate Renosky's profits. The court decided to rely on the trial testimony of Renosky's business manager, Denice Altemus, who stated that Renosky Lures products "always [make] a bottom line of between 15 and 17%." Renosky argues that there is no direct evidence that the Bionic Minnow earned a profit in this range. While this is true, the onus of producing such evidence is clearly placed by § 35(a) on Renosky, not Banjo Buddies. 15 U.S.C. § 1117(a). The District Court has broad discretion in shaping remedies under § 35(a), *see Burger King Corp. v. Weaver*, 169 F.3d 1310, 1321 (11th Cir. 1999), and did not abuse that discretion by estimating ... a profit of 16%.

Renosky further argues that Banjo Buddies is only entitled to 48% of whatever profits were earned by the Bionic Minnow project. That is, if

Banjo Buddies had produced the Bionic Minnow, it would have received only 48% of the profits earned from the sale of the lure under its contract with TriStar. We first note that this contention is impossible to evaluate on appeal as a factual matter. Presumably Tri–Star provided some services in exchange for its profit-sharing agreement with Banjo Buddies, and presumably Renosky procured those same services through services contracts rather than a profit-sharing agreement. There is no way for this court to determine which party struck the better deal.

Further, this argument also fails as a matter of law, because there is no requirement that the defendant's profits approximate the plaintiff's damages. Section 35(a) permits a plaintiff to recover, "subject to the principles of equity . . ., (1) defendant's profits, (2) any damages sustained by the plaintiff, and (3) the costs of the action." 15 U.S.C. § 1117(a). As the Second Circuit observed in *George Basch*, 968 F.2d at 1537, an accounting of the infringer's profits is available if the defendant is unjustly enriched, if the plaintiff sustained damages, or if an accounting is necessary to deter infringement. These rationales are stated disjunctively; any one will do. *See id.* Allowing Renosky to keep half the estimated profits of his infringing activities would not serve the Congressional purpose of making infringement unprofitable—Renosky would be unjustly enriched and other would-be infringers would be insufficiently deterred.(Citations omitted). Even if Banjo Buddies receives a windfall in this case—which, as discussed in the previous paragraph, is impossible for this court to determine—it is preferable that Banjo Buddies rather than Renosky receive the benefits of Renosky's infringement. (Citation omitted).

Finally, we agree with Renosky that the District Court clearly erred by adding distributions made to Renosky as a shareholder in the Bionic Minnow project to the profits award because these distributions were already accounted for in the court's estimation of profits . . .

. . . .

IV.   Conclusion

For the reasons given above, we will affirm the District Court's award of Renosky's estimated profits on the Bionic Minnow project but reverse the District Court's decision to add Renosky's shareholder distributions to that amount. We will affirm the District Court's judgment in all other respects.

QUESTIONS

1.   Is there still room for a court to conclude that a willfulness finding is required to award a defendant's profits after the amendment of section 1117(a) or is the reasoning in *Banjo Buddies* dispositive?

2.   Is there any way a victim of trademark infringement can gain an award of punitive damages? *See, e.g., Transgo, Inc. v. Ajac Transmission Parts Corp.*, 768 F.2d 1001 (9th Cir.1985), (upholding award of punitive damages under California law), *cert. denied*, 474 U.S. 1059 (1986); *Big O Tire*

Dealers, Inc. v. Goodyear Tire & Rubber Co., infra (upholding award of punitive damages under Colorado law).

3. If the Lanham Act forbids punitive damage awards in a non-counterfeiting case, why should such relief continue to be available under state law?

4. Section 1117(a) provides that actual damages may be enhanced up to three times the amount and that profits may be adjusted up or down if the court finds that recovery is inadequate or excessive. Can a court add profits and damages together and apply a multiplier up to three times? *See Thompson v. Haynes*, 305 F.3d 1369 (Fed.Cir.2002).

2. Corrective Advertising

Big O Tire Dealers, Inc. v. Goodyear Tire & Rubber Co.
561 F.2d 1365 (10th Cir.1977).

■ Lewis, J.:

[Big O, a $200,00 a year company, sued Goodyear Tire for a false designation under section 43(a) and for common law trademark infringement based on Goodyear's national campaign using the term "Bigfoot" to advertise one of its tires. Although Goodyear's search did not reveal Big O's prior common law use of BIGFOOT in connection with tires, the use came to Goodyear's attention shortly before the advertising launch. Despite Big O's insistence that it did not want money but only wanted Goodyear to halt the campaign as soon as possible, Goodyear refused.]

... Big O filed suit on November 27, 1974. The district court denied Big O's request for a temporary restraining order and a preliminary injunction. After judgment was entered on the jury's verdict for Big O, Goodyear appealed to this court. Goodyear's allegations of error are discussed below.

.   .   .   .

[The court affirmed the lower court's rulings on the merits and on jury instructions.]

VII.

... Goodyear challenges the jury's verdict awarding Big O $2.8 million in compensatory damages.... Goodyear contends Big O failed to prove either the fact or the amount of damages. Big O asserts the evidence supporting the fact of damages falls into two categories: (1) Goodyear's enormous effort to adopt, use, and absorb Big O's trademark virtually destroyed Big O's ability to make any effective use of its "Big Foot" trademark and (2) Goodyear's false statements that "Bigfoot" was available only from Goodyear created the appearance of dishonesty and wrongful conduct by Big O thereby harming its reputation within the trade and with the public. We agree with the district court that there is sufficient evidence to support the jury's finding of the fact of damages.

Big O also asserts the evidence provided the jury with a reasonable basis for determining the amount of damages. Big O claims the only way it can be restored to the position it was in before Goodyear infringed its trademark is to conduct a corrective advertising campaign. Big O insists it should be compensated for the advertising expenses necessary to dispel the public confusion caused by Goodyear's infringement. Goodyear spent approximately $10 million on its "Bigfoot" advertising campaign. Thus, Big O advances two rationales in support of the $2.8 million award: (1) there were Big O Tire Dealers in 28 percent of the states (14 of 50) and 28 percent of $10 million equals the amount of the award; and (2) the Federal Trade Commission generally orders businesses who engage in misleading advertising to spend approximately 25 percent of their advertising budget on corrective advertising and this award is roughly 25 percent of the amount Goodyear spent infringing on Big O's trademark. The district court used the first rationale in denying Goodyear's motion to set the verdict aside. The second rationale was presented by Big O at oral argument.

The purpose of general compensatory damages is to make the plaintiff whole. Big O concedes it was unable to prove with precision the amount necessary to make itself whole. However, the district court concluded "[the] damages awarded by the jury would enable Big O to do an equivalent volume of advertising in the states in which there are Big O dealers to inform their customers, potential customers, and the public as a whole about the true facts in this dispute or anything else necessary to eliminate the confusion." 408 F. Supp. 1232. Moreover, the Supreme Court has pointed out that a plaintiff's ability to prove with precision the amount necessary to make itself whole does not preclude recovery since [the] most elementary conceptions of justice and public policy require that the wrongdoer shall bear the risk of the uncertainty which his own wrong has created.

Bigelow v. RKO Radio Pictures, Inc., 327 U.S. 251, 265.

There is precedent for the recovery of corrective advertising expenses incurred by a plaintiff to counteract the public confusion resulting from a defendant's wrongful conduct. [Here, however,] Big O did not spend any money prior to trial in advertising to counteract the confusion from the Goodyear advertising. It is clear from the record Big O did not have the economic resources to conduct an advertising campaign sufficient to counteract Goodyear's $9,690,029 saturation advertising campaign. We are thus confronted with the question whether the law should apply differently to those who have the economic power to help themselves concurrently with the wrong than to those who must seek redress through the courts. Under the facts of this case we are convinced the answer must be no. Goodyear contends the recovery of advertising expenses should be limited to those actually incurred prior to trial. In this case the effect of such a rule would be to recognize that Big O has a right to the exclusive use of its trademark but has no remedy to be put in the position it was in prior to September 16,

1974, before Goodyear effectively usurped Big O's trademark. The impact of Goodyear's "Bigfoot" campaign was devastating. The infringing mark was seen repeatedly by millions of consumers. It is clear from the record that Goodyear deeply penetrated the public consciousness. Thus, Big O is entitled to recover a reasonable amount equivalent to that of a concurrent corrective advertising campaign.

As the district court pointed out, the jury's verdict of $2.8 million corresponds to 28 percent of the approximately $10 million Goodyear spent infringing Big O's mark. Big O has dealers in 14 states which equals 28 percent of the 50 states. Big O also points out the jury's award is close to 25 percent of the amount Goodyear spent infringing on Big O's mark. Big O emphasizes that the Federal Trade Commission often requires businesses who engage in misleading advertising to spend 25 percent of their advertising budget on corrective advertising.

Taking cognizance of these two alternative rationales for the jury's award for compensatory damages we are convinced the award is not capable of support as to any amount in excess of $678,302. As the district court implied in attempting to explain the jury's verdict, Big O is not entitled to the total amount Goodyear spent on its nationwide campaign since Big O only has dealers in 14 states, thus making it unnecessary for Big O to run a nationwide advertising campaign. Furthermore, implicit in the FTC's 25 percent rule in corrective advertising cases is the fact that dispelling confusion and deception in the consuming public's mind does not require a dollar-for-dollar expenditure. In keeping with " '[the] constant tendency of the courts . . . to find some way in which damages can be awarded where a wrong has been done,' "we hold that the maximum amount which a jury could reasonably find necessary to place Big O in the position it was in before September 16, 1974, vis-a-vis its "Big Foot" trademark, is $678,302. We arrive at this amount by taking 28 percent of the $9,690,029 it was stipulated Goodyear spent on its "Bigfoot" campaign, and then reducing that figure by 75 percent in accordance with the FTC rule, since we agree with that agency's determination that a dollar-for-dollar expenditure for corrective advertising is unnecessary to dispel the effects of confusing and misleading advertising.

. . . .

U–Haul International, Inc. v. Jartran, Inc.

793 F.2d 1034 (9th Cir.1986).

■ SNEED, CIRCUIT JUDGE:

U–Haul International, Inc. (U–Haul) sued Jartran, Inc. (Jartran) for false comparative advertising under section 43(a) of the Lanham Act, 15 U.S.C. § 1125(a), and under the common law. The district court awarded U–Haul $40 million and attorney fees, as well as a permanent injunction against certain Jartran advertisements. *U–Haul International, Inc. v. Jartran, Inc.,* 601 F. Supp. 1140 (D. Ariz. 1984). Jartran appeals on several grounds.

I.

FACTS

The U–Haul System has dominated the self-move consumer rental industry for many years. In mid–1979, Jartran entered that market on a national basis. It engaged in a nationwide newspaper advertising campaign comparing itself to U–Haul. The campaign lasted from the summer of 1979 to December of 1980 and included advertisements in forty-one states and the District of Columbia. While Jartran's revenues increased from $7 million in 1979 to $80 million in 1980, revenues of the U–Haul System declined for the first time in its history, from $395 to $378 million. The tremendous success of the advertisements is demonstrated not only by the financial growth of Jartran, but also by Jartran's receipt of the prestigious "Gold Effie" award, which the American Marketing Association awards annually in recognition of effective advertising campaigns.

. . . .

The district judge calculated damages with respect to each claim under two distinct methods. . . . The second theory relied on the cost of the advertising campaign to Jartran, $6 million, and the cost of corrective advertising by the U–Haul System, $13.6 million. This . . . produced an award of $20 million. On the Lanham Act count, the district court doubled the $20 million under section 35 of the Lanham Act . . . Because we affirm the calculation of the award based on advertising expenditures and the doubling of the award under section 35 of the Lanham Act, we need not address Jartran's challenges to the [alternative method]. . . .

Jartran raises three challenges to the district judge's conclusion that Jartran is liable to U–Haul. First, it argues that the injury suffered by U–Haul was insufficiently direct to support a recovery under the Lanham Act. Second, it argues that the actual deception and reliance of consumers can be proved only by surveys of actual consumers. Finally, it argues that it is inappropriate to presume actual deception and reliance from proof of Jartran's intent to deceive. Because we reject the first and third challenges, we affirm the district court's findings of deception and reliance. Addressing the second challenge thus becomes unnecessary.

. . . .

B. *Presumption of Consumer Deception and Reliance*

. . . . [T]he district court held that "publication of deliberately false comparative claims gives rise to a presumption of actual deception and reliance. . . ."

To support the district court's conclusion, U–Haul cites a false advertising case granting injunctive relief, *McNeilab, Inc. v. American Home Products Corp.,* 501 F. Supp. 517 (S.D.N.Y. 1980), and two of our "palming off" cases granting damages, *National Van Lines v. Dean,* 237 F.2d 688, 692 (9th Cir. 1956); *National Lead Co. v. Wolfe,* 223 F.2d 195, 202, 205 (9th Cir.), *cert. denied,* 350 U.S. 883, 76 S. Ct. 135, 100 L. Ed. 778, 107 U.S.P.Q.

(BNA) 362 (1955). Jartran responds by pointing out that *McNeilab* was an injunction case, in which the burden of proof is substantially lower, and that the two "palming off" cases are not comparative advertising cases as is this one.

Jartran's distinctions do not undermine the force of U–Haul's argument. It is not easy to establish actual consumer deception through direct evidence. The expenditure by a competitor of substantial funds in an effort to deceive consumers and influence their purchasing decisions justifies the existence of a presumption that consumers are, in fact, being deceived. He who has attempted to deceive should not complain when required to bear the burden of rebutting a presumption that he succeeded.

The district judge's application of this presumption was fair and in keeping with our early "palming off" precedents. We hold that it was correct to apply it in this context.

CALCULATION OF THE AWARD

A. *Calculation of Damages*

Jartran does not dispute the propriety of basing a damage award on corrective advertising expenditures. *See, e.g., Otis Clapp & Son, Inc., v. Filmore Vitamin Co.,* 754 F.2d 738, 745 (7th Cir. 1985). Jartran does argue, however, that the district court did not have discretion to award damages for corrective advertising expenditures more than twice the size of the original advertising expenditures. Jartran relies on *Big O Tire Dealers, Inc. v. Goodyear Tire & Rubber Co.,* 561 F.2d 1365, 1375 (10th Cir. 1977), *cert. dismissed under* Sup. Ct. R. 60, 434 U.S. 1052, 98 S. Ct. 905, 54 L. Ed. 2d 805 (1978). There the court reversed a jury verdict and held that the plaintiff's recovery for corrective advertising was limited to 25% of the defendant's wrongful expenditures. *Big O*, however, is plainly inapplicable. It explicitly distinguishes itself from the plentiful earlier precedent allowing recovery of *actual* corrective advertising expenditures. In *Big O* the plaintiff had not made any corrective advertising expenditures. *See id.; see also Cuisinarts, Inc. v. Robot–Coupe International Corp.,* 580 F. Supp. 634, 641 (S.D.N.Y. 1984) (limiting *Big O* in the same manner). It provides no basis for overturning the district court's award in this case of actual corrective advertising expenditures.

Jartran's complaints as to the propriety of U–Haul's corrective advertising campaign should have been addressed to the district court. That court did consider arguments that the advertising was not necessary to correct harm to the U–Haul trademark; but it rejected them. We agree with the district court's conclusion.

. . . .

AFFIRMED IN PART; MODIFIED IN PART; REVERSED IN PART; and REMANDED FOR FURTHER PROCEEDINGS.

QUESTIONS

1. Do you agree with the *Big O* court's determination of the sum to award for corrective advertising? What other measures might you apply?

2. Once plaintiff has been awarded compensatory damages for corrective advertising, must it in fact devote that money to corrective advertising?

3. The jury in *Big O* also awarded plaintiff $16,800,000 in punitive damages under the state law claim. Under Colorado law, exemplary damages must bear some relation to the compensatory award. The jury award thus bore a 6:1 ratio to the jury's compensatory award. Is this "reasonable"? Should the appellate court apply a 6:1 ratio to the reduced compensatory award in determining exemplary damages?

4. Was the court in *U–Haul* correct in allowing plaintiff all of its expenses for corrective advertising even though the amount exceeded that incurred by the defendant for its advertising?

———

3.   ATTORNEY'S FEES

Securacomm Consulting, Inc. v. Securacom Inc.

224 F.3d 273 (3d Cir.2000).

■ SLOVITER, J.:

This appeal marks the second time the remedial portion of this trademark case has come before us. In the first appeal, defendants Securacom Incorporated, KuwAm Corporation, and Wirt D. Walker, III (collectively "Securacom New Jersey") sought reversal of the District Court's award of profits, treble damages, and attorney's fees after the court found that Securacom New Jersey had willfully infringed the trademark of SecuraComm Consulting, Inc. We . . . remanded as to the award of attorney's fees. *See SecuraComm Consulting Inc. v. Securacom Inc.*, 166 F.3d 182 (3d Cir.1999) (*"SecuraComm Consulting I"*).

On remand, the District Court again awarded attorney's fees . . . Securacom New Jersey appeals. It argues primarily that the District Court erred in awarding fees under § 35(a) of the Lanham Act, 15 U.S.C. § 1117(a), which authorizes an award of fees to the prevailing party only in "exceptional cases."

I.

The underlying trademark dispute involved the adoption by two security systems consulting firms of similar marks, the mark "SecuraComm" by plaintiff SecuraComm Consulting (who with its principal Ronald Libengood will be referred to as "SecuraComm Pennsylvania") and the mark "Securacom" by defendant Securacom New Jersey. . . . SecuraComm Pennsylvania remained a relatively small company, with average annual revenues between 1992 and 1996 of slightly more than $250,000 per year.

In 1993, Libengood applied for registration of "Securacomm" as a service mark for security communication consulting and systems engineering; the mark was registered on the principal register on May 20, 1997. Plaintiff is licensed by Libengood to use the mark.

Defendant Securacom New Jersey, the other firm in the dispute, is the successor of a firm formed by Sebastian Cassetta in 1987. The firm affiliated with the engineering firm Burns & Roe, and operated under the name Burns & Roe Securacom. Burns & Roe Securacom's business was confined primarily to the nuclear security field.

Libengood first became aware of Burns & Roe Securacom in 1987 at a trade conference where he saw Cassetta throw a business card bearing the name "Burns & Roe Securacom" into a fish bowl. Libengood promptly approached Cassetta about the use of the name. Cassetta told him that he knew about Libengood's firm but that his attorneys had informed him that the similarity in the companies' names would not cause problems. Cassetta noted that the "Securacom" in his company name was preceded by "Burns & Roe" and that the two companies, SecuraComm Consulting and Burns & Roe Securacom, served different clienteles. As a result of the conversation, Libengood took no action.

In 1992, Burns & Roe Securacom hired Ronald Thomas as its chief executive officer, and terminated Cassetta's employment within two days. The company soon became independent of Burns & Roe after it received a substantial investment from KuwAm Corporation, a venture capital firm of which Wirt D. Walker, III is a shareholder and officer. The new, independent company expanded its activities into the full range of security services and changed its name to Securacom Incorporated.

In January 1993, Libengood learned that Burns & Roe Securacom had changed its name to Securacom Incorporated and had expanded its range of security services. Shortly thereafter, he mailed a cease-and-desist letter to Securacom New Jersey. For the next two and a half years, Libengood and Thomas attempted to settle the dispute. Libengood met with Thomas on two occasions and exchanged correspondence in which Libengood maintained his ownership of the mark, but stated that although he was not interested in selling his business, he would be willing to change his name if Securacom New Jersey were willing to pay for it. In fact, Libengood hired an appraiser in November 1994 who valued the SecuraComm Pennsylvania mark, together with the cost of changing its name, at $275,000.00. Libengood provided the appraisal to Thomas in May 1995.

In June 1995, Libengood informed Thomas that, as he had received no response concerning his offer to sell the SecuraComm Pennsylvania mark, he would institute legal proceedings after 30 days. Some time later, Thomas informed Libengood that he would have to deal with Walker, the chairman of the board of Securacom New Jersey. When Libengood spoke with Walker, Walker became abusive and told Libengood that if he filed suit,

Walker would bury him financially and take everything he had. On October 19, 1995, Libengood filed suit against Securacom New Jersey (later amended to add as defendants KuwAm Corporation and Walker) alleging, inter alia, service mark infringement and false designation of origin in violation of the Lanham Act, 15 U.S.C. §§ 1114 and 1125(a)....

On November 13, 1995, Securacom New Jersey filed an answer, defenses and counterclaims, including the same four claims that Secura-Comm Pennsylvania had asserted, plus a fifth claim for libel, and also filed a third-party complaint against Libengood. Thereafter, ... the attorneys for Securacom New Jersey filed a separate suit against Libengood and his attorney in Superior Court of New Jersey charging them with attempted extortion, business interference and interruption, malicious prosecution, scheming and artifice to defraud and to obtain money by means of false and fraudulent pretenses and misrepresentations, and RICO violations.... The state suit was ultimately removed to federal court, consolidated with the existing Lanham Act action, and dismissed as meritless. Securacom New Jersey subsequently filed a petition to cancel Libengood's trademark with the Patent and Trademark Office, seeking the same relief that it sought in its counterclaims in this case. Further, in June 1997 Securacom New Jersey filed another action in the District of Columbia Superior Court, alleging service mark infringement. The action was removed to the District Court of the District of Columbia. The District Court in this case enjoined Securacom New Jersey from proceeding with that action pending this trial.

The case was tried before the District Court in a bench trial in October 1997.... [T]he court found that the facts "conclusively establish Libengood's ownership" of the name "Securacomm" *SecuraComm Consulting, Inc. v. Securacom Inc.*, 984 F. Supp. 286, 298 (D.N.J.1997). It also found that confusion was likely and concluded that Securacom New Jersey had infringed the valid trademark of SecuraComm Pennsylvania. The court enjoined Securacom New Jersey's use of the word "Securacom" throughout the United States and Puerto Rico. Further, although it did not enter an amount of compensatory damages on the ground the damages could not "be measured with reasonable precision," *id.* at 303, the court awarded SecuraComm Pennsylvania ten percent of Securacom New Jersey's profits. It trebled that amount based on the "egregious circumstances" of the case and awarded attorney's fees to SecuraComm Pennsylvania in the amount of $233,600.26. *Id.* at 302–04.

Securacom New Jersey appealed ...

We reversed the award of damages on the ground that the record did not support a finding of willful infringement.... We remanded as to the attorney's fees, stating: Since the District Court's finding of willful infringement appears to be a substantial basis for the award of attorneys' fees, we are required to reverse and remand on the issue of whether exceptional circumstances, other than willful infringement, exist warranting an attorneys' fees award.

[T]he court awarded SecuraComm Pennsylvania attorney's fees in the amount of $233,600.26 pursuant to § 35 of the Lanham Act, 15 U.S.C.

§ 1117(a). The court determined that this was an "exceptional case" warranting fees under § 35 based on its finding that Securacom New Jersey "sought to secure use of the trademark Securacom not simply through fair and vigorous use of the legal process ... [but] by first engaging in bad faith negotiations and then seeking to destroy a financially weaker adversary through oppressive litigation tactics." *SecuraComm Consulting, Inc. v. Securacom Inc.*, No. 95–5393, slip op. at 5 (D.N.J. Apr. 12, 1999) (hereafter "slip op.").

. . . .

B.   *The Fee Award*

Section 35(a) of the Lanham Act, ... provides in pertinent part that "the court in exceptional cases may award reasonable attorney fees to the prevailing party." 15 U.S.C. § 1117(a)....

. . . .

Congress added the attorney's fee provision of § 35(a) to the Lanham Act in 1975 in response to the Supreme Court's decision in *Fleischmann Distilling Corp. v. Maier Brewing Co.*, 386 U.S. 714, 18 L. Ed. 2d 475, 87 S. Ct. 1404 (1967), holding that attorney's fees were not available in trademark cases under the Lanham Act absent express statutory authority. *See* S. Rep. No. 93–1400, at 2 (1974), *reprinted in* 1974 U.S.C.C.A.N. 7132, 7133. Although the statute now expressly provides for an award of attorney's fees at the discretion of the court in "exceptional cases," 15 U.S.C. § 1117(a), it does not define an "exceptional case."

In *Ferrero*, we held that an exceptional case under § 35(a) must involve culpable conduct on the part of the losing party. *See* 952 F.2d at 47. We were persuaded by the cases in other circuits holding that "a district court must make a finding of culpable conduct on the part of the losing party, such as bad faith, fraud, malice, or knowing infringement, before a case qualifies as 'exceptional.'" *Id.* ... One of the factors we emphasized was that it was a case in which defendant had imported gray market goods which legitimately bore the trademark of plaintiff's foreign affiliate. We found that at the time the importation began, the legality of importation of gray goods was unsettled. *Id.* at 49. We concluded that the district court had relied on an erroneous legal standard in finding exceptionality, and we reversed the award of fees.

We did not hold in *Ferrero*, as Securacom New Jersey asserts, that willful infringement is the only culpable conduct by a defendant that renders a case exceptional. On the contrary, by explicitly referring to "bad faith," "fraud," or "malice" as other examples of culpable conduct that might warrant a finding of exceptionality, *id.* 952 F.2d at 47, we recognized that culpable conduct comes in a variety of forms and may vary depending on the circumstances of a particular case....

Securacom New Jersey next argues that in this case the District Court's finding of the defendant's culpable conduct was not centered on the infringing use but on its litigation conduct. Although culpability is often based on the infringing acts, we have not suggested that that was the only conduct that would qualify as exceptional enough to warrant a fee award. In cases in which the defendant is the prevailing party in a trademark infringement case and seeks fees from the plaintiff, the plaintiff's culpable conduct will necessarily center on the act of filing the lawsuit rather than on the infringement. Yet the language of § 35(a) authorizing attorney's fees to the prevailing party in the discretion of the court is the same for defendants as well as plaintiffs. It does not preclude using litigating conduct as a basis for the fee.

Nor does the legislative history of the Lanham Act fee provision support the restrictive view that Securacom New Jersey takes of its scope. Although the Senate Report states that "[Attorney's fees] should be available in exceptional cases, i.e., in infringement cases where the acts of infringement can be characterized as 'malicious,' 'fraudulent,' 'deliberate,' or 'willful,' "S. Rep. No. 93–1400, at 2 (1974), *reprinted in* 1974 U.S.C.C.A.N. 7132, 7133, the report further explains:

> [The attorney's fee provision] provides that attorney fees may be awarded to the prevailing party in actions under the federal trademark laws, when equitable considerations justify such awards. It would make a trademark owner's remedy complete in enforcing his mark against willful infringers, and would give defendants a remedy against unfounded suits.

S. Rep. No. 93–1400, at 6 (1974), *reprinted in* 1974 U.S.C.C.A.N. 7132, 7137 (*emphasis added*).

Securacom New Jersey relies on the Report's reference to "willful infringers" to argue that a defendant's vexatious litigation conduct is not included in the definition of an exceptional case. As the first sentence of the same passage reaffirms, whether a case qualifies as exceptional ultimately turns on consideration of the equities in full. In fact, the Senate Report states the purpose of the fee provision as "authorizing award of attorney fees to the prevailing party in trademark litigation where justified by equitable considerations." S. Rep. No. 93–1400, at 1 (1974), reprinted in 1974 U.S.C.C.A.N. 7132, 7132 (*emphasis added*).

By using the term "equitable considerations," we think it clear that Congress intended to invoke the tradition of equity, a hallmark of which is the ability to assess the totality of the circumstances in each case. Accordingly, although culpable conduct of a defendant in the act of infringement is a relevant factor to consider, it is not exclusive of other equitable considerations.

. . . .

Applying the Lanham Act fee provision to the case at hand, we see no abuse of discretion in the District Court's finding that this case was exceptional. The case involved a deliberate effort by Securacom New Jersey to "bury" Libengood financially and "take everything he had" by filing multiple suits and complaints against him and his attorneys in a variety of legal fora. As the District Court found, based on documents and testimony presented at trial, Securacom New Jersey "did not confine itself to litigating the case fairly on the merits. Rather, it tried to prevail by crushing Libengood and his corporation." The facts of this case support the District Court's conclusion that this is an exceptional case involving culpable conduct on the part of Securacom New Jersey.

National Assn. of Professional Baseball Leagues, Inc. v. Very Minor Leagues, Inc.

223 F.3d 1143 (10th Cir.2000).

■ EBEL, J.:

The National Association of Professional Baseball Leagues, Inc. ("Professional Baseball Leagues") owns the trademark "Professional Baseball The Minor Leagues" and its accompanying logo. Very Minor Leagues, Inc. ("Very Minor Leagues") is an Oklahoma corporation that manufactures, markets, and sells baseball caps and t-shirts featuring the names and logos of fictitious baseball teams.

Very Minor Leagues applied to the United States Patent and Trademark Office ("PTO") for registration of the mark "Very Minor Leagues" on June 30, 1994. Very Minor Leagues' application was published for opposition on April 18, 1995. Professional Baseball Leagues filed a Notice of Opposition to Very Minor Leagues's application on August 21, 1995 ... In its Notice of Opposition, Professional Baseball Leagues contended it owned common law trademarks in "The Minor Leagues" and "Minor League Baseball," and that registration of the trademark requested by Very Minor Leagues would create confusion among consumers, tarnish Professional Baseball Leagues' marks, and dilute Professional Baseball Leagues' trademark and trademark rights.

. . . .

In late spring or early summer of 1996, The Hearst Corporation, King Features Syndicates Division ("King Features") contacted Very Minor Leagues regarding the possibility of a licensing agreement between Very Minor Leagues and King. During the course of negotiations, Very Minor Leagues revealed the pending trademark dispute with Professional Baseball Leagues. Counsel for Very Minor Leagues informed Professional Baseball Leagues counsel on June 27, 1996, that the trademark opposition proceedings were inhibiting culmination of an agreement between Very Minor Leagues and an international company. On June 28, 1996, Very Minor Leagues filed a motion for summary judgment with the Trademark Trial and Appeal Board. . . .

While Very Minor Leagues' motion for summary judgment in the opposition proceeding remained pending, Professional Baseball Leagues initiated this litigation in the United States District Court for the Middle District of Florida. In its complaint, Professional Baseball Leagues alleged trademark infringement, false designation of origin, trademark dilution, and unfair competition under federal statutes and common law. On April 1,

1997, the TTAB granted a request by Professional Baseball Leagues to suspend the opposition proceedings pending the outcome of the judicial proceedings. The litigation was then transferred to the Western District of Oklahoma in July 1997.

King Features withdrew its offer to enter into any licensing agreement with Very Minor Leagues. Very Minor Leagues alleges this was because of the dispute with Professional Baseball Leagues ... The jury returned a verdict in favor of Very Minor Leagues on Professional Baseball Leagues' trademark infringement, false designation of origin, unfair competition, and trademark dilution claims. Very Minor Leagues filed a motion for attorney fees as the prevailing party, which the district court denied. According to the district court, recovery of attorney fees under 15 U.S.C. § 1117(a) required, for both prevailing plaintiffs and prevailing defendants, a showing that the other party had acted in bad faith, and Very Minor Leagues had failed to make such a showing.

Very Minor Leagues appeals the district court's order denying it attorney fees....

. . . .

In assessing Very Minor Leagues' claim that the district court should have awarded it attorney fees, we are governed by the relevant provision of the Lanham Act. That provision provides that "the court in exceptional cases may award reasonable attorney fees to the prevailing party." *See* 15 U.S.C. § 1117(a) (emphasis added). Thus, being the prevailing party is not, by itself, enough to justify an award of attorney fees. Moreover, even in exceptional cases, the award of attorney fees is vested in the discretion of the district court. The statute itself does not define "exceptional cases," but the legislative history to the statute suggests two considerations for prevailing defendants who seek attorney fees. One, an objective consideration, is whether the suit was "unfounded." *See* S. Rep. No. 93–1400, at 2 (1974), *reprinted in* 1974 U.S.C.C.A.N. 7132, 7133. The other, a subjective consideration, is whether the suit was brought by the trademark owner "for harassment and the like." *Id.* The legislative history further advises that an award of attorney fees to a prevailing party is authorized where "justified by equitable considerations." *Id.* at 1, *reprinted in* 1974 U.S.C.C.A.N. 7132.

No one factor is determinative, and an infringement suit could be "exceptional" for a prevailing defendant because of (1) its lack of any foundation, (2) the plaintiff's bad faith in bringing the suit, (3) the unusually vexatious and oppressive manner in which it is prosecuted, or (4) perhaps for other reasons as well. The Lanham Act largely vests in the district court the discretion to determine when a losing plaintiff's claims or conduct in the litigation are so "exceptional" as to warrant the assessment of attorney fees. The focus of the analysis is not only on whether the defendant prevailed, or concomitantly, whether the plaintiff lost. Not every losing suit is without foundation, and not every strategic decision by a plaintiff in bringing suit and in prosecuting it in a manner to enhance the prospects of success is done for the purpose of harassment or another improper purpose.

. . . .

[W]hile we do not specifically adopt the approach of any of the other circuits, we note that many of the standards used by other circuits in analyzing the attorney fee issue for prevailing defendants are essentially consistent with our approach. The Eighth and Ninth Circuits, for example, use a standard of whether a plaintiff's claim is "groundless, unreasonable, vexatious, or pursued in bad faith." *See Stephen W. Boney, Inc. v. Boney Services, Inc.,* 127 F.3d 821, 827 (9th Cir.1997); *Hartman v. Hallmark Cards, Inc.,* 833 F.2d 117, 123 (8th Cir.1987). That standard focuses on the same objective and subjective factors we derive from the legislative history. The terms "groundless" and "unreasonable" reflect the objective merits of the case, and emphasize that it is not enough that the plaintiff does not prevail. Rather, to be an "exceptional" case within the meaning of the statute, the plaintiff's suit must lack any reasonable foundation. The terms "vexatious" and "bad faith" look to the subjective motivation and manner in which the case is prosecuted.

Similarly, the Fourth and D.C. Circuits have looked to factors such as "economic coercion," "groundless arguments," and "failure to cite controlling law." *See Ale House Management, Inc. v. Raleigh Ale House, Inc.,* 205 F.3d 137, 144 (4th Cir.2000) (*citing Noxell Corp. v. Firehouse No. 1 Bar–B–Que Restaurant,* 248 U.S.App.D.C. 329, 771 F.2d 521, 526 (D.C.Cir.1985)). Once again, those factors seem to track the objective and subjective elements in the legislative history. Some circuits point out, we think correctly, that the test should not focus solely on bad faith, but rather should incorporate a broader range of factors. *See Door Systems, Inc. v. Pro–Line Door Systems, Inc.,* 126 F.3d 1028, 1031 (7th Cir.1997) (stating that "bad faith is not the correct standard for determining whether to award attorneys' fees to the defendant in a Lanham Act case"); *Noxell,* 771 F.2d at 526 (stating, in the context of a claim for attorney fees by a prevailing defendant, that "something less than 'bad faith,' we believe, suffices to mark a case as 'exceptional.'"). *But see Conopco, Inc. v. Campbell Soup Co.,* 95 F.3d 187, 194 (2d Cir.1996) (applying bad faith standard for prevailing defendant).

Here, Professional Baseball Leagues argues that the strict "bad faith" standard should apply, and thus Very Minor Leagues, the prevailing defendant, should only be eligible for attorney fees if Professional Baseball Leagues acted in bad faith in bringing its suit. Professional Baseball Leagues' argument is as follows: (1) when the plaintiff is the prevailing party, he or she can only get attorney fees when it is proven that the defendant has engaged in acts of infringement in bad faith, *see Takecare Corp. v. Takecare of Oklahoma, Inc.,* 889 F.2d 955, 957 (10th Cir.1989) (stating, in the context of a prevailing plaintiff's claim for attorney fees, that "running through the case law, which has developed around a § 1117(a) award of attorney fees, is the implicit recognition that some degree of bad faith fuels the infringement at issue"); (2) the standard for awarding attorney fees should be the same for a prevailing defendant, *see Fogerty v. Fantasy, Inc.*, 510 U.S. 517, 534, 114 S. Ct. 1023, 1033, 127 L. Ed. 2d 455 (1994) (holding that prevailing plaintiffs and prevailing defendants seeking attorney fees are to be "treated alike").

We agree with Professional Baseball Leagues' first proposition that plaintiffs only get attorney fees when defendant's acts of infringement are in bad faith; however, we disagree that there should be, or even could be, perfect harmony between the standard for awarding attorney fees to a prevailing plaintiff and a prevailing defendant. The underlying conduct under scrutiny is different. When attorney fees are awarded against a defendant, the court looks to whether the defendant's acts of infringement were pursued in bad faith. When attorney fees are awarded against a plaintiff, the court looks to the plaintiff's conduct in bringing the lawsuit and the manner in which it is prosecuted.[4]

We recognize that in *Fogerty*, the Supreme Court, considering the issue of attorney fees under the Copyright Act, held that prevailing plaintiffs and prevailing defendants should be treated alike. *Fogerty*, however, was a Copyright Act case, not a Lanham Act case, and the Copyright Act gives discretion to the district court to award attorney fees to the "prevailing party" without the further significant limitation found in the Lanham Act that the award be limited to "exceptional cases." *Compare* 17 U.S.C. § 505, with 15 U.S.C. § 1117(a). In any event, in *Fogerty*, the Court was concerned with, and disapproved of, a great dichotomy between the standards being used for prevailing defendants and prevailing plaintiffs.... In rejecting the "dual" standard, *Fogerty* did not specify that the standard for prevailing plaintiffs and prevailing defendants had to be identical; rather it stated that the parties should be "treated alike." The standards to which we subscribe for prevailing plaintiffs and prevailing defendants under the Lanham Act are not identical because we are looking to different kinds of conduct for each party; however, we believe our approach is even-handed and treats plaintiffs and defendants essentially alike for the respective conduct that is at issue. In both cases, the party seeking attorney fees will have to show that the other party acted in an "exceptional" manner, rather than merely in a wrong manner, before attorney fees can be awarded.

The district court here specifically found that Professional Baseball Leagues' claims were not unfounded and we agree. In support of its claims, Professional Baseball Leagues provided some evidence of similarity between its mark and Very Minor Leagues' mark, as well as some evidence of consumer confusion from independent experts, including one expert who

---

4. Of necessity, there is not complete transportability between the standard used for prevailing plaintiffs and the standard used for prevailing defendants under the Lanham Act. Courts, guided by the legislative history, have looked to whether the defendant's acts of infringement were "malicious, fraudulent, deliberate or willful" in determining the propriety of attorney fees for pre- vailing plaintiffs. *See* S. Rep. No. 93–1400, at 2 (1974), *reprinted in* 1974 U.S.C.C.A.N. 7132, 7133. Every lawsuit is both "deliberate" and "willful"; therefore, if the same standard were applied for prevailing defendants, attorney fees could be awarded automatically. *See Door Systems, Inc.*, 126 F.3d at 1032 (discussing this point).

testified that he believed it was deceptive to use the words "minor league" in connection with fictional baseball teams. Another expert testified that Very Minor Leagues' use of "minor leagues" inferred an association or affiliation with Professional Baseball Leagues, and that he was confused about whether Very Minor Leagues' products were licensed by Professional Baseball Leagues. That evidence indicates that Professional Baseball Leagues' suit was not unfounded.

Admittedly, a suit may have some underlying merit and yet be pursued in such a meritless and improper manner that it becomes unfounded, or that subjective considerations of "harassment and the like" may justify an award of attorney fees. That is what Very Minor Leagues argues occurred here. However, Professional Baseball Leagues' filing of the federal lawsuit while the TTAB proceeding was nearing completion does not demonstrate that the judicial suit was unfounded or, as Very Minor Leagues argues, that it was brought only to avoid an unfavorable ruling at the TTAB. There was nothing inappropriate about Professional Baseball Leagues seeking a judicial, rather than administrative, determination of its rights. Similarly, the fact that Professional Baseball Leagues originally filed the suit in the Middle District of Florida does not indicate that the suit was brought in an unreasonable manner or to harass Very Minor Leagues. Professional Baseball Leagues' allegation of jurisdiction in Florida was based on the fact that Very Minor Leagues marketed its products in Florida and took and filled orders for its products from customers in Florida. Although the case was ultimately transferred to the Western District of Oklahoma, we cannot say that the initiation of the action in the Middle District of Florida was without jurisdictional basis.

We find that Professional Baseball Leagues' suit was not "unfounded" or brought for "harassment and the like," and therefore we hold that the district court did not abuse its discretion in denying attorney fees to Very Minor Leagues.

QUESTIONS

1. Should a court consider the fact that a judgment is entered by default in determining whether circumstances are "exceptional" for purposes of awarding attorney's fees? *Cf. Reed Pub. B.V. v. Execulink, Inc.*, 1998 WL 812246 (D.N.J.1998).

2. Did the *Securacomm* and *Very Minor Leagues* opinions agree that a prevailing plaintiff can only recover attorney's fees when the defendant's infringement is in bad faith? If not, which decision articulated the better view?

3. The Lanham Act provides that attorney's fees should be awarded only in "exceptional circumstances" in non-counterfeiting cases. Are there ever any circumstances where attorney's fees can be awarded as part of damages? What if a plaintiff files an opposition in the TTAB as well as a lawsuit, can its opposition expenses be considered part of damages? *See Attrezzi, LLC v. Maytag Corp.*, 436 F.3d 32 (1st Cir. 2006).

4. Where both federal and state infringement claims are brought and state law provides for the award of attorney's fees to a prevailing plaintiff without any showing of the "exceptional circumstances" required by the Lanham Act, is the state statute preempted? *See Attrezzi LLC v. Maytag Corp., supra.*

C. TRADEMARK COUNTERFEITING

The Problem of Counterfeiting

Counterfeiting remedies present a marked contrast to those available for federal trademark infringement, dilution, unfair competition or cybersquatting and include criminal penalties, ex parte civil seizure orders, and statutory damages as well as mandatory attorney's fees and treble damages absent "extenuating circumstances" where there has been an "intentional" use of a counterfeit mark. The enhanced remedies exist to combat not only the normal harms trademark owners can suffer, such as diverted sales, reputation loss and potential injury to mark distinctiveness and goodwill, and that potential purchasers can suffer, such as obtaining the wrong goods or increased search costs, but also to redress other potential injuries to the public.

The International Chamber of Commerce estimates that counterfeit goods are worth $350 billion, representing about 7% of world trade. "Facts on Fakes," International Anticounterfeiting Coalition <http://www.iacc.com>. If accurate, this figure translates into a very substantial effect on the global economy, including lost jobs and tax revenues. For example, one estimate suggests that auto part counterfeiting costs the auto industry $12 billion in lost sales and could account for 200,000 lost jobs. *Id.*

Moreover, the Justice Department has noted the dangers that counterfeits can pose to public safety and health:

> Counterfeit marks ... can mask serious health or safety risks to consumers as in the case of counterfeit food products, batteries, prescription drugs, or auto parts.... Airline passengers are victims of counterfeit airplane parts, coronary patients are victims of counterfeit heart pumps, and children are victims of counterfeit infant formula ...

"Computer Crimes & Intellectual Property Section," U.S. Dept. Of Justice, <http://www.cybercrime.gov/ipmanual/03ipma.html>. The FAA, for example, estimates that 2% of airplane parts are counterfeit, and the World Health Organization estimates that about 10% of pharmaceuticals are counterfeit. "Facts On Fakes," *supra.* Resulting illness, death and crashes have been documented. *Id.*

Further, links have been reported between counterfeit operations and both organized crime and terrorist organizations, which have allegedly used counterfeiting as a money laundering or funding device. *Id.*

In reviewing the materials in this section, ask yourself whether the special remedies for counterfeiting are efficacious or necessary to protect against these harms.

1. PROCEDURAL ISSUES

15 U.S.C. § 1116(d) [LANHAM ACT § 34(d)], as amended by the Trademark Counterfeiting Act of 1984 and subsequent amendments

(d) *Civil actions arising out of use of counterfeit marks.*

(1)(A) In the case of a civil action arising under section 32(1)(a) of this Act (15 U.S.C. 1114) or section 220506 of Title 36 with respect to a violation that consists of using a counterfeit mark in connection with the sale, offering for sale, or distribution of goods or services, the court may, upon ex parte application, grant an order under subsection (a) of this section pursuant to this subsection providing for the seizure of goods and counterfeit marks involved in such violation and the means of making such marks, and records documenting the manufacture, sale, or receipt of things involved in such violation.

(B) As used in this subsection the term ''counterfeit mark'' means—

> (i) a counterfeit of a mark that is registered on the principal register in the United States Patent and Trademark Office for such goods or services sold, offered for sale, or distributed and that is in use, whether or not the person against whom relief is sought knew such mark was so registered; or

> (ii) a spurious designation that is identical with, or substantially indistinguishable from, a designation as to which the remedies of this Act are made available by reason of section 220506 of Title 36; but such term does not include any mark or designation used on or in connection with goods or services of which the manufacturer or producer was, at the time of the manufacture or production in question authorized to use the mark or designation for the type of goods or services so manufactured or produced, by the holder of the right to use such mark or designation.

(2) The court shall not receive an application under this subsection unless the applicant has given such notice of the application as is reasonable under the circumstances to the United States attorney for the judicial district in which such order is sought. Such attorney may participate in the proceedings arising under such application if such proceedings may affect evidence of an offense against the United States. The court may deny such application if the court determines that the public interest in a potential prosecution so requires.

(3) The application for an order under this subsection shall—

(A) be based on an affidavit or the verified complaint establishing facts sufficient to support the findings of fact and conclusions of law required for such order; and

(B) contain the additional information required by paragraph (5) of this subsection to be set forth in such order.

(4) The court shall not grant such an application unless—

(A) the person obtaining an order under this subsection provides the security determined adequate by the court for the payment of such damages as any person may be entitled to recover as a result of a wrongful seizure or wrongful attempted seizure under this subsection; and

(B) the court finds that it clearly appears from specific facts that—

(i) an order other than ex parte seizure order is not adequate to achieve the purposes of section 1114 of this title;

(ii) the applicant has not publicized the requested seizure;

(iii) the applicant is likely to succeed in showing that the person against whom seizure would be ordered used a counterfeit mark in connection with the sale, offering for sale, or distribution of goods or services;

(iv) an immediate and irreparable injury will occur if such seizure is not ordered;

(v) the matter to be seized will be located at the place identified in the application;

(vi) the harm to the applicant of denying the application outweighs the harm to the legitimate interests of the person against whom seizure would be ordered of granting the application; and

(vii) the person against whom seizure would be ordered, or persons acting in concert with such person, would destroy, move, hide, or otherwise make such matter inaccessible to the court, if the applicant were to proceed on notice to such person.

(5) An order under this subsection shall set forth—

(A) the findings of fact and conclusions of law required for the order;

(B) a particular description of the matter to be seized, and a description of each place at which such matter is to be seized;

(C) the time period, which shall end not later than seven days after the date on which such order is issued, during which the seizure is to be made;

(D) the amount of security required to be provided under this subsection; and

(E) a date for the hearing required under paragraph (10) of this subsection.

(6) The court shall take appropriate action to protect the person against whom an order under this subsection is directed from publicity, by or at the behest of the plaintiff, about such order and any seizure under such order.

(7) Any materials seized under this subsection shall be taken into the custody of the court. The court shall enter an appropriate protective order with respect to discovery by the applicant of any records that have been seized. The protective order shall provide for appropriate procedures to assure that confidential information contained in such records is not improperly disclosed to the applicant.

(8) An order under this subsection, together with the supporting documents, shall be sealed until the person against whom the order is directed has an opportunity to contest such order, except that any person against whom such order is issued shall have access to such order and supporting documents after the seizure has been carried out.

(9) The court shall order that service of a copy of the order under this subsection shall be made by a Federal law enforcement officer (such as a United States marshall or an officer or agent of the United States Customs Service, Secret Service, Federal Bureau of Investigation, or Post Office) or may be made by a state or local law enforcement officer, who, upon making service, shall carry out the seizure under the order. The court shall issue orders, when appropriate, to protect the defendant from undue damage from the disclosure of trade secrets or other confidential information during the course of the seizure, including, when appropriate, orders restricting the access of the applicant (or any agent or employee of the applicant) to such secrets or information.

(10)(A) The court shall hold a hearing, unless waived by all the parties, on the date set by the court in the order of seizure. That date shall be not sooner than ten days after the order is issued and not later than fifteen days after the order is issued, unless the applicant for the order shows good cause for another date or unless the party against whom such order is directed consents to another date for such hearing. At such hearing the party obtaining the order shall have the burden to prove that the facts supporting findings of fact and conclusions of law necessary to support such order are still in effect. If that party fails to meet that burden, the seizure order shall be dissolved or modified appropriately.

(B) In connection with a hearing under this paragraph, the court may make such orders modifying the time limits for discovery under the Rules of Civil Procedure as may be necessary to prevent the frustration of the purposes of such hearing.

(11) A person who suffers damage by reason of a wrongful seizure under this subsection has a cause of action against the applicant for the order under which such seizure was made, and shall be entitled to recover such relief as may be appropriate, including damages for lost profits, cost of materials, loss of good-will, and punitive damages in instances where the seizure was sought in bad faith, and, unless the court finds extenuating circumstances, to recover a reasonable attorney's fee. The court in its discretion may award prejudgment interest on relief recovered under this paragraph, at an annual interest rate established under section 6621 of Title 26, commencing on the date of service of the claimant's pleading setting forth the claim under this paragraph and ending on the date such recovery is granted, or for such shorter time as the court deems appropriate.

QUESTIONS

1. Do you believe that an ex parte seizure order would be available against an enterprise such as Wal–Mart were it selling counterfeit NIKE sneakers? Why or why not?

2. Suppose the Los Angeles Lakers team owns a federal registration for LAKERS for t-shirts, hats and sweatshirts. Would an ex parte seizure order be available against a factory making counterfeit LAKERS scarves that are being sold outside the Lakers' arena?

3. How successfully does the Trademark Counterfeiting Act respond to interests in both due process and effective protection of trademarks? Suppose you are a producer of designer luggage, or shirts, or watches, etc. You observe street vendors selling probable counterfeits on a major pedestrian thoroughfare. Does the Trademark Counterfeiting Act give you the means to pursue and seize the goods from the vendors? If you are a vendor whose goods have been wrongfully seized, do the provisions provide an adequate remedy? Consider *Waco Int'l, Inc. v. KHK Scaffolding Houston Inc.* and *Skierkewiecz v. Gonzalez, infra,* in answering this question.

Waco International, Inc. v. KHK Scaffolding Houston Inc.

278 F.3d 523 (5th Cir.2002).

■ JANE A. RESTANI, CIRCUIT JUDGE:

The primary issues before the court are (1) whether the district court applied the proper standard for a Lanham Act wrongful seizure claim . . . and (4) whether a cross-appellant is entitled to additional attorney fees. We affirm the district in all respects.

FACTUAL AND PROCEDURAL HISTORY

Plaintiff–Appellant Waco International Inc. ("Waco") . . . manufactures scaffolding and shoring products. Waco owns the federally registered trademarks "WACO" and "HI–LOAD." Waco's scaffolding and shoring products are marked with a decal bearing the Waco mark. . . .

KHK Scaffolding Houston, Inc. ("KHK") . . . sells scaffolding manufactured by its parent company in Dubai, United Arab Emirates . . . KHK sells scaffolding that is compatible with products manufactured and sold by Waco and other companies. In its sales brochure, KHK indicates the compatibility of its scaffolding by abbreviated designations . . . The scaffolds themselves do not bear the Waco mark or a KHK mark. The scaffolds are stamped "made in the U.A.E." . . .

In early 1998, KHK mailed brochures and solicitation letters to prospective customers. Some of those materials stated that KHK was offering "Waco" products. On April 2, 1998, Waco sent a cease and desist letter to KHK. On April 20, 1998, Waco's investigator purchased scaffold frames from KHK. The investigator was given an original "sales report" that identified the frames as "WACO" frames. On April 20, 1998, KHK sent a letter to Waco's counsel stating that one of KHK's salespersons mistakenly quoted "Waco Red" and "Waco Blue" to six potential customers in the midst of his sales presentation, and that KHK would take measures to prevent such representations.

On April 30, 1998, Waco sued KHK . . . and sought and obtained an *ex parte* seizure order under 15 U.S.C. § 1116(d)(1)(A). The seizure order permitted Waco to enter KHK's place of business and seize KHK's red and blue scaffolding and certain business records.

A post-seizure hearing was held on May 15, 1998, and a preliminary injunction hearing was held on June 8–10, 1998. The magistrate judge found that injunctive relief was not appropriate with respect to KHK's use of Waco Red and/or Waco Blue in describing the *style* or *compatibility* of its KHK products[2]. She found, however, that "invoices purporting to sell 'Waco Red' or 'Waco Blue' scaffolding . . . demonstrate a likelihood of confusion, warranting injunctive relief." The magistrate judge recommended an injunction "enjoining KHK from quoting, describing, or purporting to sell, its products as 'Waco' products, 'Waco Red,' or 'Waco Blue' " [and] also recommended that the seizure order be dissolved pursuant to section 1116(d)(10)(A), reasoning that the products seized did not carry a "counterfeit mark." On July 20, 1998, the district court adopted the magistrate judge's recommendation in full.

KHK filed a counterclaim for compensatory and punitive damages for wrongful seizure under 15 U.S.C. § 1116(d)(11). . . . On August 16, 1999, the magistrate judge recommended . . . that the court grant KHK's motion in part, reasoning that the seizure was wrongful as a matter of law because the KHK frames were "legitimate non-infringing merchandise." The judge recommended denial of summary judgment on KHK's claim for damages, noting that "evidence shows that the measure of damages allegedly sus-

---

2. The magistrate judge found that "in most cases, KHK is using the [Waco] mark in a descriptive sense, advertising its product as 'Waco Red style' or 'Waco Red compatible,' or 'interchangeable with Waco.' "

tained by KHK from the wrongful seizure is disputed." On September 16, 1999, the district court adopted the magistrate judge's memorandum and recommendation in full.

. . . .

The jury made the following findings, *inter alia*: (1) KHK had infringed Waco's trademarks, but that KHK's use constituted "fair use;" (2) KHK did not use a counterfeit mark in connection with the sale, offering for sale, or distribution of goods or services; . . . (3) Waco had seized goods that were predominantly non-infringing and had acted in bad faith in seeking the seizure order. The jury also awarded KHK $730,687 in attorney fees, $185,196 in costs, and $250,000 in punitive damages. The jury found, however, that KHK suffered $0 in lost profits and $0 in lost goodwill from the seizure. . . .

. . . .

A. Wrongful Seizure Liability

. . . .

. . . Congress intentionally left the definition of "wrongful seizure" to "case-by-case interpretation." *See* Joint Statement on Trademark Counterfeiting Legislation, 130 Cong. Rec. H12076, at 12083 (Oct. 10, 1984). Congress did identify, however, several guidelines for determining whether a seizure was wrongful. Congress indicated that a seizure may be wrongful: (1) where an applicant acted in "bad faith" in seeking the order; *or* (2) if the goods seized are predominately legitimate merchandise, even if the plaintiff acted in good faith. *See* Senate Comm. on the Judiciary, S. Rep. No. 98–526, at 8 (1984), *reprinted in* 1984 U.S.C.C.A.N. 3627, 3634. . . .

. . . It is apparent that the district court referred to sections 1116(d)(1) and (d)(4) to indicate the authority under which the court granted the order. In fact, the district court specifically identified section 1116(d)(11) as the statutory provision under which it deemed the seizure wrongful:

> In seeking an *ex parte* seizure order, [Waco] assumed the risk imposed by section 1116(d)(11) that it would be liable for damages for a wrongful seizure if its position was not ultimately sustained upon completion of the adversarial process [i.e., the post-seizure hearings].

Waco claims error on the ground that the seizure was of "counterfeit goods" because the Waco mark was used on sales invoices issued "in connection with" the sale of KHK's scaffolding. Waco argues that the Lanham Act imposes liability for trademark counterfeiting on any person who shall, without the consent of the registrant, "use in commerce . . . any counterfeit . . . of a registered mark *in connection with* the sale, offering for sale, distribution, or advertising of any goods or services on or in connection with which such use is likely to cause confusion, or to cause mistake, or to deceive. . . ." 15 U.S.C. § 1114(1)(a) (emphasis added). Waco's argument lacks merit.

First, that KHK may be *liable* under the Lanham Act for its representations in connection with the sale of its goods does not necessarily mean that the *seizure* was warranted. The *ex parte* seizure remedy must be narrowly construed, and is *not* coextensive with liability for any Lanham Act claim. *Martin's Herend Imports v. Diamond & Gem Trading,* 112 F.3d 1296, 1306 (5th Cir. 1997) (*"Martin's I"*) (importation of gray market goods, although held to constitute infringement, was not an act of counterfeiting and thus *ex parte* seizure applicant could be liable under section 1116(d)(11) for wrongful seizure). Thus, even if Waco ultimately had prevailed at trial on its trademark infringement claim, its application for *ex parte* seizure still could be found wrongful.

Second, the primary focus of an *ex parte* seizure order is on the goods themselves, rather than any business practice or representation that may give rise to liability for trademark infringement or unfair competition. In light of this purpose, Congress has stated that "a seizure must be considered wrongful when the *material* to be seized is legitimate, non-infringing merchandise." 130 Cong. Rec. H–12076 (October 10, 1984) (emphasis added). Waco admits that the seized goods did not bear the Waco trademark. *See* Waco Brief at 7–8. Waco also admits that the KHK scaffolding bore both an imprint of its country of origin (U.A.E.) and a safety label with KHK's name and telephone number. *See id.* There is no support for the proposition that any unauthorized use of a mark not on the goods themselves precludes a finding that a seizure was sought wrongfully.

Even if use of the Waco mark "in connection with" the sale of unmarked goods could support a seizure order, the jury found that, as a factual matter, KHK did not "use a counterfeit of any of the listed Waco registered marks in connection with the sale, offering for sale, or distribution of goods or services." *See* Jury Question 4, RE1–3–5. We decline Waco's invitation to second-guess the jury's factual finding.

. . . .

E. *Whether KHK is "a person who suffers damage"*

Waco contends that because the jury found that KHK had not suffered "lost profit" or "loss of good will," KHK suffered no actual damages and therefore it is not "a person who suffers damage" as required by section 1116(d)(11) ("A person who suffers damage by reason of a wrongful seizure under this subsection has a cause of action against the applicant ...."). Waco mischaracterizes a finding of lost profits and/or loss of good will as a statutory prerequisite for a wrongful seizure claim. McCarthy on Trademarks, at § 30:44 specifies that a claimant must prove as an element of a wrongful seizure claim that "Claimant was in fact damaged by reason of the seizure." McCarthy further explains that attorney fees are to be considered part of actual damage:

> One who proves damage from a wrongful seizure can recover all appropriate damages, including compensation for lost goods or materials, damage to good will and business reputation, and *all*

other elements of actual damage, including a reasonable attorney fee.

Id.

Even if actual damages are, as Waco suggests, limited to lost profits and/or loss of good will, the statute does not, as Waco insists, apply only to claimants who have suffered "actual damages" but to those who have suffered "damage," which can include costs and fees incurred in bringing the wrongful seizure counterclaim. According to the legislative history, "the sponsors recognize that *ex parte* seizure orders are an extraordinary remedy, and that a person who is subject to a wrongful *ex parte* seizure should be *fully compensated* by the party who obtained the seizure order." 130 Cong. Rec., at H12082–83 (emphasis added). Thus, Congress apparently intended that wrongful seizure claimants be compensated for the attorney fees and costs expended in bringing the counterclaim, assuming the claimant prevails in establishing "bad faith" or that the goods were predominately legitimate. Failure to show lost profit or loss of good will does not necessarily preclude recovery of attorney's fees under the wrongful seizure statute.

F. Attorney Fees

Under section 1116(d)(11), "unless the court finds extenuating circumstances, [a claimant is entitled] to recover a reasonable attorney's fee...." Waco claims that such circumstances exist and that attorney fees must be denied. For example, Waco points to evidence that KHK was not awarded damages for lost profit or good will, that it produced "bogus" invoices in discovery, and that it altered business records. Waco Brief at 40. Even if such evidence could support a finding of "extenuating circumstances," there is no support for the proposition that the district court was under an affirmative obligation to make such a finding. The district court did not abuse its discretion in allowing KHK to recover attorney fees.

. . . .

CONCLUSION

Accordingly, we AFFIRM the final judgment, the award of attorney's fees, the order denying prejudgment interest, and the order denying a permanent injunction.

Skierkewiecz v. Gonzalez

711 F.Supp. 931 (N.D.Ill.1989).

■ CHARLES P. KOCORAS, UNITED STATES DISTRICT JUDGE.

This case comes before the Court on defendants John J. Brown's, David C. Hilliard's, Pattishall, McAuliffe, Newberry, Hilliard & Geraldson's, (hereinafter "Defendant Attorneys"), Charles Baley's, Mark Hinchy's, and Baley, Hinchy, Downes & Associates, Inc.'s, (hereinafter "Defendant Investigators"), Motion to Dismiss pursuant to Rule 12(b) of the Federal Rules of Civil Procedure. Defendants contend that Counts I through IV of the Complaint must be dismissed for failure to state a claim against these defendants and that the remaining counts must be dismissed because they name only defendants previously dismissed by plaintiffs. For the following reasons, the defendants' motion is granted in part and denied in part.

FACTS

. . . .

On April 29, 1988, Defendant Attorneys appeared in chambers . . . and presented their Motion for *Ex Parte* Seizure Order and affidavits in support. Judge Parsons entered the *Ex Parte* Temporary Restraining Order and Order for Seizure.

On May 4, 1988, two United States Marshals executed the Court's April 29, 1988, Order for Seizure at the . . . Defendants' office and warehouse in Chicago. Subsequently, the . . . Defendants brought a motion to vacate the seizure order to obtain the return of their goods.

On May 27, 1988, Judge Parsons addressed the defendants' motion to vacate and issued his Memorandum Opinion and Order in which he was highly critical of Defendant Attorneys. Judge Parsons detailed the numerous misrepresentations which had been made to him by the Defendant Attorneys at the *Ex Parte* hearing and made it clear that he would not have ordered the seizure in the absence of the false portrayal of the plaintiffs as counterfeiters. Nevertheless, Judge Parsons found it necessary to issue a preliminary injunction, enjoining the . . . Defendants from selling tennis rackets marked with the word "Panther" or hang tags used as advertising pieces depicting a panther in any position.

On August 19, 1988, the plaintiffs filed the Complaint which is the subject of the Defendants' Motion to Dismiss. In Count I of plaintiffs' Complaint, plaintiffs seek damages against Defendant Attorneys for wrongful seizure pursuant to 15 U.S.C. § 1116(d)(11). In Count II, plaintiffs attempt to state a claim for abuse of process. Finally, Counts III and IV allege that Defendant Attorneys and Defendant Investigators committed trespass to chattel and trespass to land, respectively, during the execution of the April 29, 1988, Order for Seizure.

DISCUSSION

. . . .

The defendants first contend that plaintiffs' claim for wrongful seizure (Count I) against the Defendant Attorneys must be dismissed. The defendants argue that the plaintiffs are merely seeking recovery for representations made by the Defendant Attorneys in the course of representing their client's legitimate trademark interest in obtaining the Order of Seizure and that these representations are protected under Illinois law. (Citation omitted). The defendants maintain that an attorney has a conditional privilege in advising and acting on behalf of his client which cannot be attacked absent a showing of malice, or the attorney's desire to harm which is separate and apart from the attorney's desire to protect his client. (Citation omitted).

The plaintiffs argue, however, that defendants have ignored the fact that plaintiffs' claim for wrongful seizure is brought pursuant to the federal cause of action created by 15 U.S.C. § 1116(d)(11) and have wrongfully read into this statute a conditional privilege for an attorney accused of obtaining a wrongful seizure. We agree.

When Congress passed 15 U.S.C. § 1116(d), it created an extraordinary remedy, an *ex parte* order authorizing seizure of alleged counterfeit marks . . . However, . . . Congress recognized that the remedy should only be used in extreme circumstances, and Congress expressly required the courts to use extreme caution before issuing a seizure order without first providing the targeted defendant with any measure of due process. The purpose behind such extraordinary action was to provide the plaintiff and the court with an effective weapon against those "fly-by-night" counterfeiters who will, if given notice of court proceedings, dispose of their goods to someone else in the counterfeit network or destroy them to escape legal liability. *See Slazengers Ltd. v. Stoller*, 1988 U.S. Dist. LEXIS 5194, No. 88 C 3722, at 4 (May 27, 1988) *citing* House Report to Trademark Counterfeiting Act of 1984, Rept. 98–997 p. 15, 98th Congress 2d Session, Sept. 7, 1984.

By enacting 15 U.S.C. § 1116(d)(11), Congress provided a means of preventing potential abuse by persons wishing to obtain *ex parte* seizure orders. The section allows recovery by the person who suffered damages by reason of a wrongful seizure where the seizure order was sought in bad faith. Section 1116(d)(11) does not explicitly or implicitly require the plaintiff to show the applicant acted with malice in obtaining the order, even where the applicant was an attorney allegedly acting on his client's behalf. Moreover, this Court believes that to read a malice requirement into the section would thwart its purpose of deterring applicants from requesting the seizure order except where absolutely necessary. Accordingly, no such conditional privilege recognized by the Illinois courts is applicable to a federal cause of action against an attorney who acted as an applicant for a seizure order in violation of 15 U.S.C. § 1116(d)(11).

In Count I, plaintiffs allege that Defendant Attorneys improperly sought and obtained the *Ex Parte* Seizure Order through the use of misleading statements presented to the Court. The Complaint further states that the *Ex Parte* Seizure Order was sought in bad faith in violation of 15 U.S.C. 1116(d)(11). The Court finds that these allegations are sufficient to state a claim against Defendant Attorneys, and consequently, defendants' motion to dismiss Count I is denied.

. . . . .

The defendants next contend that Counts III and IV of plaintiffs' Complaint, which allege trespass to land and trespass to chattle, must be dismissed because the Defendant Attorneys and Defendant Investigators were authorized by the Seizure Order to enter upon plaintiffs' premises and seize certain goods and records. The defendants maintain that such an entry upon land pursuant to court order cannot constitute a trespass.

It is true that a party cannot be liable for trespass if acting pursuant to and within the scope of a valid court order. (Citation omitted). However, a party cannot stand behind a court order which was obtained through the party's own wrongful conduct. Thus, this Court believes that Count III must be dismissed as to the Defendant Investigators because they played no role in obtaining the Order of Seizure from Judge Parsons and they acted pursuant to and within the scope of a facially valid Order of Seizure in seizing certain goods and records. This Court will not, however, dismiss Count III as stated against the Defendant Attorneys. The facts, when taken as true, allege that the Defendant Attorneys wrongfully obtained and executed the Order of Seizure. These allegations are sufficient to state a claim for trespass to chattel against Defendant Attorneys.

With respect to plaintiffs' claim for trespass to land in Count IV, the Court believes the count should stand against both the Defendant Attorneys and Defendant Investigators. First, for the reason stated in the preceding paragraph, the Court rejects defendants' argument that the Seizure Order immunizes the Defendant Attorneys from liability for trespass to land. In addition, both the Defendant Attorneys and the Defendant Investigators allegedly acted beyond the scope of the Order of Seizure when they remained on the premises without the U.S. Marshals. The *Ex Parte* Order of Seizure provides in pertinent part as follows:

> FURTHER ORDERED, that plaintiff's attorneys and representatives be allowed to accompany the Marshal, or other authorized persons, for the purpose of identifying goods and records subject to this Order;

Thus, the plaintiffs properly state a claim for trespass to land when they allege in Count IV that after the Marshal left the premises, Russell Stoller demanded that the Defendant Attorneys and Defendant Investigators leave the premises and they refused. Accordingly, defendants' motion to dismiss Count IV is denied.

Based on the foregoing discussion, the defendants' Motion to Dismiss is granted in part and denied in part. . . .

2.   SUBSTANTIVE ISSUES

18 U.S.C. § 2320 (TRADEMARK COUNTERFEITING ACT OF 1984, as amended)

§ 2320.   Trafficking in counterfeit goods or services

(a) Whoever intentionally traffics or attempts to traffic in goods or services and knowingly uses a counterfeit mark on or in connection with such goods or services, or intentionally traffics or attempts to traffic in labels, patches, stickers, wrappers, badges, emblems, medallions, charms, boxes, containers, cans, cases, hangtags, documentation, or packaging of any type or nature, knowing that a counterfeit mark has been applied thereto, the use of which is likely to cause confusion, to cause mistake, or to deceive, shall, if an individual, be fined not more than $2,000,000 or imprisoned not more than 10 years, or both, and, if a person other than an individual, be fined not more than $5,000,000. In the case of an offense by a person under this section that occurs after that person is convicted of another offense under this section, the person convicted, if an individual, shall be fined not more than $5,000,000 or imprisoned not more than 20 years, or both, and if other than an individual, shall be fined not more than $15,000,000.

(b)(1) The following property shall be subject to forfeiture to the United States and no property right shall exist in such property:

(A) Any article bearing or consisting of a counterfeit mark used in committing a violation of subsection (a).

(B) Any property used, in any manner or part, to commit or to facilitate the commission of a violation of subsection (a).

. . . .

(c) All defenses, affirmative defenses, and limitations on remedies that would be applicable in an action under the Lanham Act shall be applicable in a prosecution under this section. In a prosecution under this section, the defendant shall have the burden of proof, by a preponderance of the evidence, of any such affirmative defense.

. . . .

(e) For the purposes of this section—

(1) the term "counterfeit mark" means—

(A) a spurious mark—

(i) that is used in connection with trafficking in any goods, services, labels, patches, stickers, wrappers, badges, emblems, medallions, charms, boxes, containers, cans, cases, hangtags, documentation, or packaging of any type or nature;

(ii) that is identical with, or substantially indistinguishable from, a mark registered on the principal register in the United States Patent and Trademark Office and in use, whether or not the defendant knew such mark was so registered;

(iii) that is applied to or used in connection with the goods or services for which the mark is registered with the United States Patent and Trademark Office, or is applied to or consists of a label, patch, sticker, wrapper, badge, emblem, medallion, charm, box, container, can, case, hangtag, documentation, or packaging of any type or nature that is designed, marketed, or otherwise intended to be used on or in connection with the goods or services for which the mark is registered in the United States Patent and Trademark Office; and

> (iv) the use of which is likely to cause confusion, to cause mistake, or to deceive; or

(B) a spurious designation that is identical with, or substantially indistinguishable from, a designation as to which the remedies of the Lanham Act are made available by reason of section 220506 of title 36; but such term does not include any mark or designation used in connection with goods or services, or a mark or designation applied to labels, patches, stickers, wrappers, badges, emblems, medallions, charms, boxes, containers, cans, cases, hangtags, documentation, or packaging of any type or nature used in connection with such goods or services, of which the manufacturer or producer was, at the time of the manufacture or production in question, authorized to use the mark or designation for the type of goods or services so manufactured or produced, by the holder of the right to use such mark or designation.

(2) the term "traffic" means to transport, transfer, or otherwise dispose of, to another, for purposes of commercial advantage or private financial gain, or to make, import, export, obtain control of, or possess, with intent to so transport, transfer, or otherwise dispose of;

(3) the term "financial gain" includes the receipt, or expected receipt, of anything of value; and

(4) the term "Lanham Act" means the Act entitled "An Act to provide for the registration and protection of trademarks used in commerce, to carry out the provisions of certain international conventions, and for other purposes", approved July 5, 1946 (*15 U.S.C. 1051* et seq.).

(f) Nothing in this section shall entitle the United States to bring a criminal cause of action under this section for the repackaging of genuine goods or services not intended to deceive or confuse.

United States v. Torkington

812 F.2d 1347 (11th Cir.1987).

■ KRAVITCH, J.:

The definition of the term "counterfeit mark" under section 2320(d)(1)(A) of the Trademark Counterfeiting Act of 1984 (the Act), 15 U.S.C. §§ 1116–1118, 18 U.S.C. § 2320, is at issue in this case of first impression. The district court held that a mark is not "counterfeit" under section 2320(d)(1)(A) unless the use of the mark in connection with the goods in question would be likely to cause direct purchasers to be confused, mistaken or deceived. The court found that, given the enormous price differential between the allegedly counterfeit goods and the authentic goods, it was unlikely, as a matter of law, that direct purchasers would be confused, mistaken or deceived. The court therefore dismissed the indictment.

We find that the district court's ruling that section 2320(d)(1)(A) requires a showing that direct purchasers would be likely to be confused, mistaken or deceived is not supported by either the language or the legislative history of the section. Accordingly, we hold that section 2320(d)(1)(A) does not require a showing that direct purchasers would be confused, mistaken or deceived; rather, the section is satisfied where it is shown that members of the purchasing public would be likely to be confused, mistaken or deceived. Moreover, we find that this likely confusion test includes the likelihood of confusion in a post-sale context.

I.   *Background*

On June 2, 1985, Edward Little, a private investigator with Rolex Watch U.S.A., Inc., visited a booth operated by appellee John Torkington at the Thunderbird Swap Shop Indoor Flea Market in Fort Lauderdale, Florida. Little noticed a salesman at the booth showing customers two watches bearing both the name "Rolex" and the Rolex crown trademark emblem. The watches were virtually indistinguishable from authentic Rolex watches. These allegedly counterfeit Rolex watches had been kept under the counter; there were no such watches on display.

Little asked to see those watches as well as other models of replica Rolex watches. The salesman showed him several. The salesman said that the watches were $27 each. Little asked the salesman whether the watches were guaranteed. The salesman responded that they were not guaranteed but said that Little could return any watch that broke to the booth and the salesman would fix it. Little purchased a watch. The salesman handed it to him in a pouch bearing the Rolex crown mark. It is undisputed that Little knew that he had purchased a replica Rolex watch and not an authentic one.

On June 23, 1985, a deputy marshal executed a search and seizure order on Torkington's booth at the Thunderbird Flea Market. He seized 742 replica Rolex watches bearing both the Rolex name and crown trademarks.

On October 3, 1985, a federal grand jury in the Southern District of Florida charged Torkington with two counts of trafficking and attempting to traffic in counterfeit Rolex watches, in violation of 18 U.S.C. § 2320(a). Count I of the indictment is based on the June 2, 1985 sale of the watch to Little. Count II is based on the 742 replica Rolex watches that were seized from Torkington's booth on June 23, 1985.

. . . Following hearings on the matter, the court issued an order on February 10, 1986 dismissing both counts of the indictment on the ground that the replica Rolex watches were not "counterfeit" under section 2320(d)(1)(A). The United States appealed.

II. *Definition of "Counterfeit Mark"*

The district court concluded that the replica Rolex watches in question were not "counterfeit" under section 2320(d)(1)(A)(iii) because it determined that the section is not satisfied unless the use of the mark would be likely to cause direct purchasers of the allegedly counterfeit goods to be confused, mistaken or deceived. The court concluded that the government could not prove a section 2320 violation in the instant case because "it [is] unlikely ... that the purchaser of a replica or fake Rolex watch that sold for $27.00 would be confused, mistaken or deceived into thinking that he was purchasing a genuine Rolex watch, which may sell for approximately $1,000 to $8,000." The court also ruled that the likely confusion of members of the public who encounter the allegedly counterfeit watches in a post-sale context is irrelevant to the section 2320(d)(1)(A)(iii) inquiry. We disagree with both of these conclusions.

Section 2320 of the Trademark Counterfeiting Act was enacted in order to increase the sanctions for the counterfeiting of certain registered trademarks above the purely civil remedies available under the Trademark Act of 1946, 15 U.S.C. § 1051 *et seq.* [hereinafter the Lanham Act].

Section 2320 is narrower in scope than is the Lanham Act, however. In particular, its sanctions are available only where the defendant "knowingly uses a counterfeit mark on or in connection with" the goods or services in question. 18 U.S.C. § 2320(a).

The section defines "counterfeit mark" as:

(A) a spurious mark—

(i) that is used in connection with trafficking in goods or services;

(ii) that is identical with, or substantially indistinguishable from, a mark registered for those goods or services on the principal register in the United States Patent and Trademark Office and in use, whether or not the defendant knew such mark was so registered; and

(iii) the use of which is likely to cause confusion, to cause mistake, or to deceive;

18 U.S.C. § 2320(d)(1)(A) (emphasis added).

A. *Confusion of the Purchasing Public*

The "likely to cause confusion, to cause mistake, or to deceive" test of section 2320(d)(1)(A)(iii) is broadly worded. Nothing in the plain meaning of the section restricts its scope to the use of marks that would be likely to cause direct purchasers of the goods to be confused, mistaken or deceived.

The legislative history indicates that Congress intentionally omitted such limiting language. Congress easily could have inserted language restricting the scope of section 2320(d)(1)(A)(iii) to cases where it is likely that direct purchasers would be confused, mistaken or deceived. Congress in fact had used such limiting language in a similar context in the original version of section 1114(1) of the Lanham Act. Congress therefore had before it language it could have used to restrict section 2320(d)(1)(A)(iii) to situations where direct purchasers would be likely to be confused, mistaken, or deceived. Congress chose not to use either this or similar limiting language and we will not construe section 2320(d)(1)(A)(iii) in a way that adds a restriction that Congress chose not to include.

Moreover, not only did Congress omit the limiting language of the original version of section 1114(1) from section 2320(d)(1)(A)(iii), but it explicitly employed the language of the current version of section 1114(1) of the Lanham Act. In our view, Congress thereby manifested its intent that section 2320(d)(1)(A)(iii) be given the same interpretation as is given the identical language in section 1114(1) of the Lanham Act.

The current version of section 1114(1) of the Lanham Act differs from the original version in that it does not contain the likely to confuse direct purchasers requirement of the original section. Courts interpreting the current version of section 1114(1) have held that the section does not require a showing that direct purchasers would be likely to be confused, mistaken or deceived. Instead, they construe section 1114(1) to require simply the likely confusion of the purchasing public—a term that includes individuals who are potential purchasers of the trademark holders goods as well as those who are potential direct purchasers of the allegedly counterfeit goods.

Given our conclusion that section 2320(d)(1)(A)(iii) should be interpreted similarly to the identical language in section 1114(1), we hold that section 2320(d)(1)(A)(iii) also is satisfied when the use of the mark in connection with the goods or services in question would be likely to confuse the purchasing public.

B. *Post–Sale Context*

In its order the district court also concluded that the likelihood of post-sale confusion is irrelevant to the section 2320(d)(1)(A)(iii) inquiry. We disagree.

Under section 1114(1) of the Lanham Act, the likely to confuse test is satisfied when potential purchasers of the trademark holder's products would be likely to be confused should they encounter the allegedly counterfeit goods in a post-sale context—for example, in a direct purchaser's possession. Consequently we conclude that the likely to confuse test of section 2320(d)(1)(A)(iii) also is satisfied by a showing that it is likely that members of the public would be confused, mistaken or deceived should they encounter the allegedly counterfeit goods in a post-sale context.

This conclusion is supported by the policy goals of the Trademark Counterfeiting Act. Like the Lanham Act, the Trademark Counterfeiting Act is not simply an anti-consumer fraud statute. Rather, a central policy goal of the Act is to protect trademark holders' ability to use their marks to identify themselves to their customers and to link that identify to their reputations for quality goods and services.[6]

---

6. It also is important to recognize that the enforcement of trademark laws benefits consumers even in cases where there is no possibility that consumers will be defrauded.

It is essential to the Act's ability to serve this goal that the likely to confuse standard be interpreted to include post-sale confusion. A trademark holder's ability to use its mark to symbolize its reputation is harmed when potential purchasers of its goods see unauthentic goods and identify these goods with the trademark holder. This harm to trademark holders is no less serious when potential purchasers encounter these counterfeit goods in a post-sale context. Moreover, verbal disclaimers by sellers of counterfeit goods do not prevent this harm.

III. *Whether Dismissal is Appropriate*

. . . .

We therefore hold that the district court erred in dismissing the indictment because it was incorrect in concluding that the marks are not counterfeit as a matter of law. Accordingly, we reverse the dismissal of the indictment and remand.

REVERSED and REMANDED.

QUESTIONS

1. In footnote 6 of the *Torkington* decision, the court notes the consumer's interest in protecting even against post-sale confusion. How persuasive is this reasoning?

2. How does the consumer's interest in protecting against counterfeit ROLEX watches compare with the interest against counterfeit pharmaceuticals? Does the law recognize this difference?

3. Could a consumer who knowingly purchases a ROLEX watch for himself be prosecuted for criminal counterfeiting? Review the definition of "traffic" in section 2320(e)(2).

Rolex Watch, U.S.A., Inc. v. Michel Co.

179 F.3d 704 (9th Cir.1999).

■ TASHIMA, J.:

Micha Mottale, doing business as Michel Co. ("Mottale"), reconditions used Rolex watches with parts that are not provided or authorized by Rolex Watch, U.S.A., Inc. ("Rolex"), and sells the altered watches, as well as generic replacement parts fitting Rolex watches, to jewelry dealers and selected retail jewelers. In addition, Mottale provides the service of specially

---

For, to the extent that trademarks provide a means for the public to distinguish between manufacturers, they also provide incentives for manufacturers to provide quality goods. Traffickers of these counterfeit goods, however, attract some customers who would otherwise purchase the authentic goods. Trademark holders' returns to their investments in quality are thereby reduced. This reduction in profits may cause trademark holders to decrease their investments in quality below what they would spend were there no counterfeit goods. This in turn harms those consumers who wish to purchase higher quality goods.

reconditioning used Rolex watches. The district court held that Mottale's retention of the original Rolex trademarks on the altered "Rolex" watches that he sells constituted trademark counterfeiting under section 32(1)(a) of the Trademark Act of 1946 ("Lanham Act"), 15 U.S.C. § 1114(1)(a), as interpreted by our decision in *Westinghouse Electric Corp. v. General Circuit Breaker & Electric Supply Inc.*, 106 F.3d 894, 899–900 (9th Cir.), *cert. denied*, 522 U.S. 857, 118 S. Ct. 155, 139 L. Ed. 2d 101 (1997). On that basis, the district court permanently enjoined Mottale from selling such altered watches without (1) adding permanent independent marks on the non-Rolex parts, and (2) including a written disclosure concerning the generic replacement parts on tags, invoices, promotions, and advertising.

Rolex appeals, principally arguing that the relief ordered by the district court is inadequate because the changes that Mottale makes to used Rolex watches are so basic that they result in a different product. We agree, and accordingly direct the district court to enjoin Mottale from retaining Rolex's trademarks on the altered watches he sells. In addition, we reverse the district court's denial of Rolex's request for its attorney's fees on this claim and remand that request for consideration under section 35(b) of the Lanham Act, 15 U.S.C. § 1117(b).

I. FACTUAL AND PROCEDURAL BACKGROUND

. . . .

Rolex sells new Rolex watches exclusively through official Rolex jewelers. Rolex and official Rolex jewelers service Rolex watches. Rolex watches have a one-year warranty from Rolex; the addition of parts that are not provided or authorized by Rolex voids the watch's warranty. Rolex also will not service watches that have been modified with non-Rolex parts.

Mottale sells jewelry and used luxury watches at wholesale, primarily to jewelry dealers at jewelry trade shows. In addition, Mottale reconditions used luxury watches in response to orders from retail jewelers, typically on behalf of a retail customer. Mottale's gross receipts were over $2.5 million for 1995.

Mottale sells the following products related to Rolex watches: (1) used Rolex watches; (2) used Rolex watches that have been "reconditioned" or "customized" with non-Rolex parts, which we call "altered 'Rolex' watches;" (3) used Rolex watch replacement parts; and (4) generic replacement parts fitting Rolex watches. Mottale customizes used Rolex watches by replacing their bezels (the ring that surrounds the crystal and affixes it to the watch casing), dials, and bracelets, and/or by inserting diamonds into their dials. These replacement parts are not authorized or provided by Rolex. The altered "Rolex" watches retain their original Rolex trademarks on their dials and bracelets, except when Mottale replaces the bracelet. Some examples of the replacement bracelets used by Mottale bear an imitation of the Crown Device logo. The other replacement parts added by Mottale bear no independent mark.

. . . .

The district court held that Mottale's sale of altered "Rolex" watches constituted counterfeit trademark use under section 32(1)(a) as construed in *Westinghouse*, 106 F.3d 894. In *Westinghouse*, we held that retaining the original Westinghouse trademarks on used, reconditioned circuit breakers sold by circuit breaker vendors constituted trademark counterfeiting under section 32(1)(a). *See id.* at 899–900. We rejected the vendors' suggestion that duplication of a trademark is necessary for trademark counterfeiting:

> [A] copy of a mark is no more likely to confuse the public than is the original; in fact, the public is more likely to be deceived by an original mark because it serves as a perfect imitation. In short, the distinction between using a duplication versus using an original has no relevance to the purposes of trademark law. When an original mark is attached to a product in such a way as to deceive the public, the product itself becomes a "counterfeit" just as it would if an imitation of the mark were attached.

Id. at 900.

Here the district court found that retention of the original Rolex marks on altered "Rolex" watches, in the absence of adequate disclosures that the altered watches contain non-Rolex parts, was deceptive and misleading as to the origin of the non-Rolex parts, and likely to cause confusion to subsequent or downstream purchasers, as well as to persons observing the product. Accordingly, under *Westinghouse*, the district court concluded that this confusing use of Rolex's trademarks in connection with the sale of altered "Rolex" watches constituted a counterfeit use of the trademarks. Based on this finding of liability, the district court issued a permanent injunction. The district court found that the changes Mottale made to the used Rolex watches were not so extensive that Mottale should be completely enjoined from retaining Rolex's trademarks on the used Rolex watches he sells. Rather, the district court required Mottale to place an independent, permanent mark on the non-Rolex replacement parts that he adds to Rolex watches, such as "Michel Co.," and to include a written disclosure in tags, promotions, and advertising of his altered "Rolex" watches.[3] The district court denied Rolex's request for attorneys' fees attributable to the prosecution of this claim, and for treble profits from Mottale's sales of altered "Rolex" watches.[4]

---

3. The district court required the following disclosure:

This watch contains non-Rolex parts which are not supplied by an official Rolex jeweler. The addition of non-Rolex parts voids the Rolex warranty. Rolex Watch, U.S.A., Inc. may no longer service a watch containing non-Rolex parts.

4. The district court also found that Mottale sold two watches bearing Rolex trademarks that have no official Rolex parts, and one watch band bearing Rolex trademarks that is not a Rolex band at trade shows. It concluded that Mottale's sale of these completely counterfeit watches and bracelet violated section 32(1)(a) of the Lanham Act, and issued a permanent injunction, granted Rolex treble profits from these watches, and its attorneys' fees under 15 U.S.C. § 1117(b). Mottale did not appeal this ruling.

II. DISCUSSION

A. *Adequacy of Injunctive Relief*

.   .   .   .

Our analysis of Rolex's plea for greater injunctive relief begins with *Champion Spark Plug Co. v. Sanders,* 331 U.S. 125, 91 L. Ed. 1386, 67 S. Ct. 1136 (1947). In *Champion*, the manufacturer of Champion brand spark plugs brought a trademark infringement action against a business that repaired and reconditioned used Champion spark plugs and resold them. *See id*. at 126. The reconditioned spark plugs retained their original Champion trademark and were sold in boxes stamped with the word "Champion." *See id*. The Supreme Court upheld an injunction that permitted the business to continue to sell the reconditioned spark plugs bearing their original Champion trademark so long as the words "Used" or "Repaired" were also stamped on the plugs and the cartons included a more complete disclosure that the plugs were used and reconditioned. *See id*. 127–28, 130. The Court reasoned that it is permissible for a secondhand dealer to get some advantage from the trademark "so long as the manufacturer is not identified with the inferior qualities of the product resulting from wear and tear or the reconditioning by the dealer." *Id*. at 130 (citing *Prestonettes, Inc. v. Coty*, 264 U.S. 359, 68 L. Ed. 731, 44 S. Ct. 350 (1924)). In reaching the conclusion that stamping "Used" or "Repaired" on the plugs gave the manufacturer all the trademark protection to which it was entitled, the Court acknowledged that "cases may be imagined where the reconditioning or repair would be so extensive or so basic that it would be a misnomer to call the article by its original name, even though the words 'used' or 'repaired' were added." 331 U.S. at 129. *Champion* did not pose such as case because "the repair or reconditioning of the plugs does not give them a new design," but rather was no more than "a restoration, so far as possible, of their original condition." *Id*.

Rolex argues that this is a case where the alterations Mottale makes to Rolex's products are so basic that it is a misnomer to permit Mottale to retain Rolex's marks on the altered watches he sells. Mottale refurbishes the Rolex dial, sometimes adding diamonds to it, changes the watch bracelet, and/or replaces the Rolex watch bezel. Rolex asserts that the watch bezel as well as the workmanship involved in inserting diamonds into the face of the watch go to the basic performance and durability of the watch: The quality of the bezel and how it is attached affect the waterproofing of the watch; the insertion of diamonds on the face of the watch can affect the functioning of the watch hands. Rolex also contends that the durability of the watch bracelet and clasp affect the usefulness and longevity of the watch.

.   .   .   .

We ... conclude that the alterations that Mottale makes to the used Rolex watches he sells, ... result in a new product, although one containing a Rolex movement and casing. In this light, the district court's requirement that Mottale put an independent mark, such as "Michel Co.," on the non-Rolex parts is [not] adequate to prevent consumer confusion . . . Neither conveys basic changes that have been made to the watch. Nor would the face of the watch support a more adequate legend. Hence, under *Champion*, the retention of Rolex's trademarks on Mottale's altered watches is a misnomer—and a trademark infringement. We accordingly hold that the district court abused its discretion in not completely enjoining the use of Rolex's trademarks on the altered watches that Mottale sells.[8]

B. *Attorney's Fees*

Rolex argues that the district court erred in declining to award attorney's fees for its claim that Mottale's altered "Rolex" watches constituted trademark counterfeiting . . .

There are two potential provisions under which the district court could have awarded Rolex attorney's fees for the prosecution of this claim. First, under 15 U.S.C. § 1117(a), "the court in exceptional cases may award reasonable attorney fees to the prevailing party." A trademark infringement is viewed as "exceptional" under § 1117(a) "when the infringement is malicious, fraudulent, deliberate or willful." [Citations omitted]. Second, under 15 U.S.C. § 1117(b), in cases in which the violation of section 32(1)(a), 15 U.S.C. § 1114(1)(a), consists of "intentionally using a mark or designation, knowing such mark or designation is a counterfeit mark," the court shall grant the prevailing party a reasonable attorney's fee, unless it finds "extenuating circumstances." We have said that "in counterfeiting cases, 'unless the court finds extenuating circumstances,' treble damages and reasonable attorney's fees are available." [Citations omitted] Under both sections 1117(a) and 1117(b), awards are "never automatic and may be limited by equitable considerations." [Citation omitted]

The district court found that, except for Mottale's sale of three completely counterfeit items, Mottale's trademark violations were not exceptional under section 1117(a). The district court did not, however, make a determination of whether Rolex is entitled to attorney's fees under section 1117(b) for the prosecution of its claims that Mottale's altered "Rolex" watches violate trademark counterfeiting prohibitions. Where, as here, the district court finds trademark counterfeiting in violation of section 1114(1)(a), the district court must, when requested, address whether the prevailing party is entitled to the remedies provided by section 1117(b) for those violations. *See* 15 U.S.C. § 1117(b) (providing treble profits or damages and a reasonable attorney's fee for certain trademark counterfeit violations of 15 U.S.C. § 1114(1)(a)).

Both parties urge us to resolve whether Rolex is entitled to these fees under section 1117(b) on the current record. We decline to do so.

---

8. Rolex noted at oral argument that it did not seek, and had not sought in the district court, an injunction preventing individual owners of Rolex watches from altering their watches with non-Rolex parts. Neither the district court's injunction, nor the injunction we direct it to enter, enjoins Mottale from altering Rolex watches at the specific request of an individual watch owner.

... Accordingly, we reverse the district court's denial of Rolex's request for attorney's fees attributable to its claim that Mottale's altered "Rolex" watches involved counterfeit use of Rolex's trademarks and remand for a determination of whether Rolex is entitled to those fees under section 1117(b).

. . . .

III. CONCLUSION

Because the changes that Mottale makes to used Rolex watches are so basic that they result in a different product, we reverse the permanent injunction entered by the district court to the extent that it permitted Mottale to retain Rolex's trademarks on the altered "Rolex" watches he sells, and remand with directions to enter a permanent injunction consistent with this opinion. We also reverse the district court's denial of Rolex's request for attorney's fees under its claim that Mottale's sale of altered "Rolex" watches violated its trademark rights, and remand this claim for consideration under 15 U.S.C. § 1117(b).

Hunting World, Inc. v. Reboans, 24 U.S.P.Q.2d 1844 (N.D.Cal. 1992). Defendant, who had been denied a license to sell Hunting World articles in the San Francisco area, went directly to the Italian manufacturer of Hunting World leather goods, and there acquired merchandise which it sold in San Francisco without plaintiff's permission. In response to plaintiff's action under the Anti-counterfeiting Act, defendant asserted that, as a seller of genuine goods, it could not be engaged in counterfeiting under the Act. The court held for plaintiff:

Regardless of whether [defendants'] story is true and the allegedly counterfeit bags were obtained from the [plaintiff's] factory, there is a fundamental problem with defendants' position. Defendants cite cases holding that the unauthorized sale of trademarked goods alone does not give rise to a claim for trademark infringement. However, none of the authorities cited by defendants support the proposition that goods subverted from the factory are not counterfeit and do not infringe plaintiff's trademark rights. As noted in *H.L. Hayden Co. v. Siemens Medical Systems, Inc.*, 879 F.2d 1005, one of the cases cited by defendants, although "the unauthorized sale of a genuine trademarked product does not in itself constitute trademark infringement ... identical goods sold in an unauthorized manner are not 'genuine' for purposes of the Lanham Act." *Id.* at 1023 (citations omitted).

In *El Greco Leather Products Co. v. Shoe World, Inc.*, 806 F.2d 392, 395 (2d Cir.1986), the court held that even if the goods were originally ordered by the trademark owner, if the goods are not inspected by the trademark owner to insure quality, they are not genuine. In so holding, the court noted that "One of the most valuable and important protections afforded by the Lanham Act is the right to control the quality of the goods manufactured and sold under the holder's trademark." *Id.* (citations omitted). Similarly, in *Shell Oil Co. v. Commercial Petroleum, Inc.*, 928 F.2d 104 (4th Cir.1991), the court held the use of Shell's trademark by a bulk oil wholesaler violated the Lanham Act because "a product in not truly 'genuine' unless it is manufactured and distributed under quality control established under the manufacturer." *Id.* at 107.

The court finds the reasoning in *El Greco* and *Shell* to be persuasive. Defendants claim to have purchased the merchandise at issue from the same factory that manufactures the goods for Hunting World. However, there has been no showing that Hunting World inspected or approved the goods at issue. Indeed, defendants' own experts admitted that the seized bags had certain defects. According to the testimony of Mr. Antognoli [plaintiff's factory production manager], defective or slightly imperfect bags are not sold, but are either destroyed or "cannibalized," i.e., the acceptable parts are used to make new bags. If the bags were not subjected to Hunting World's quality control procedures, they are not "genuine" for purposes of the Lanham Act.

In addition, the Ninth Circuit has held under similar facts that there is a likelihood of confusion. *Model Rectifier Corp. v. Takachiho Int'l, Inc.*, 709 F.2d 1517 (9th Cir.1983). The use of the Hunting World marks implies that the goods are subject to the Hunting World quality control guidelines. Plaintiffs have presented evidence that the goods sold by defendants did not meet Hunting World's strict quality control standards. Thus, defendants' use of Hunting World's marks is likely to confuse consumers who rely on the trademarks as an indication of quality. Accordingly, the court finds that plaintiff has demonstrated a strong likelihood of success on the merits.

QUESTIONS

1. Could the defendant in *Hunting World* have been prosecuted for criminal counterfeiting? Why or why not?

2. How, if at all, do the Trademark Counterfeiting Act and its judicial interpretation affect concepts of trademarks as "property?"

———

3. MANDATORY TREBLE DAMAGES AND ATTORNEY'S FEES

Section 35(b) requires imposition of treble damages and an award of attorney's fees where there has been an intentional use of a counterfeit mark or designation unless the court finds "extenuating circumstances." Consider the following decision's analysis of "intentional."

Chanel, Inc. v. Italian Activewear of Florida, Inc.

931 F.2d 1472 (11th Cir.1991).

■ EDMONSON, J.:

. . . .

I.

Plaintiff-appellee Chanel, Inc. sells luxury items using registered well-known trademarks. Defendant-appellant Italian Activewear was a Florida corporation selling imported goods under various labels, including Chanel. Defendant-appellant Mervyn Brody was president and chief operating officer of Italian Activewear. Defendant-appellant Myron Greenberg is a friend and business associate of Brody. Although not an employee, Greenberg sometime sold merchandise on behalf of Italian Activewear or Brody and would "keep an eye on things" at the store when Brody was out of town.

Italian Activewear, through Brody, imported and began marketing a shipment of handbags and belt buckles bearing Chanel trademarks. Brody purchased these goods from Sola, a European broker from whom Brody had earlier purchased other shipments of luxury items under various labels. Part of the shipment of Chanel-labeled goods was immediately resold to some California businessmen. . . .

The Chanel-labeled goods purchased from Sola were counterfeit. In addition to minor differences in physical construction, these handbags lacked several indicia of authenticity possessed by genuine Chanel bags: each authentic Chanel bag has a uniquely numbered sticker affixed to an inconspicuous location inside the bag and comes with a separate "certificate of authenticity" bearing the same number; and each bag is packaged inside a felt bag and then inside a "shiny black box," both of which also bear Chanel trademarks. Authentic Chanel belt buckles, moreover, are not sold without Chanel belts, as these were.

In his deposition testimony, Brody stated that he did not know where Sola got the bags and buckles and that he did not ask. He also said he was aware the bags should have had certificates of authenticity but that these bags did not. He said he had made efforts to ensure the goods were genuine (by comparing them with products he knew to be genuine). Brody's verification efforts were further attested to by one of his employees at the preliminary injunction hearing.

Chanel first acted in California, seizing the counterfeit goods held by the Californians who received part of the Sola shipment. The Californians informed Greenberg—who was "minding the store" at Italian Activewear while Brody was away—of the seizure. Greenberg sent Brody the following facsimile:

Att Merv. [Brody]

Big trouble. Marshell (sic) & Chanel closed down Calif. Took bags and there will be lawsuit. They want to stop new shipments— and they are right. They know about this store and probably will be in here shortly. Trying to get your lawyer but I know he won't be able to do anything.

Call back right away.

Mike [Myron Greenberg]

He gathered up all the Chanel-labeled goods and removed them from the store, putting them in the trunk of a car which was then parked several blocks away.

Chanel sued Italian Activewear and Brody for trademark infringement in violation of 15 U.S.C.A. § 1114(1)(a). Greenberg was added as a defendant by later amendment. The district court granted plaintiff Chanel's motion for summary judgment in full, concluding as a matter of law not only that the trademark had been infringed, but also that the infringement had been intentional. It thus awarded the treble damages ($208,433.25) and attorneys' fees ($71,859.61) statutorily mandated in cases of intentional violation of 15 U.S.C.A. § 1114(1)(a). *See* 15 U.S.C.A. § 1117(b). . . .

II.

The Lanham Act prohibits, among other things, the use in commerce of a counterfeit trademark in a manner likely to cause confusion; and the Act further provides that anyone using a counterfeit trademark in such manner shall be liable in a civil action to the registrant of the trademark. *See* 15 U.S.C.A. § 1114(1)(a). The remedies available to the registrant are set forth in 15 U.S.C.A. § 1117. In addition to injunctive relief, a registrant whose rights are violated may generally recover the defendant's profits from the infringing activity (or its own damages or both) together with costs of the action. Based on equitable considerations, the trial court may, in its discretion, reduce or enhance the resulting award up to three times the original amount, and may, in exceptional cases, award attorneys' fees. 15 U.S.C.A. § 1117(a). If the infringement is *intentional*, however, § 1117(b) governs: unless the court finds extenuating circumstances, treble damages and attorneys' fees are mandated. 15 U.S.C.A. § 1117(b).

The interplay of these provisions demonstrates that a showing of intent or bad faith is unnecessary to establish a violation of § 1114(1)(a), or to seek remedies pursuant to § 1117(a). But where, as here, a registrant seeks the mandatory treble damages and attorneys' fees provided for in § 1117(b), the plaintiff must prove the defendants' intent to infringe.

III.

. . . .

The district court's grant of summary judgment on this issue rested chiefly on two undisputed facts: (1) the counterfeit goods lacked all indicia of authenticity, and Brody knew that indicia of authenticity generally accompanied genuine Chanel products; and (2) Brody knew Sola was not an authorized distributor of Chanel products, yet failed to ask Sola the origin of his Chanel-labeled products. Based on these facts, the court concluded Brody had been willfully blind, and "[w]illful blindness is knowledge enough." *See Louis Vuitton S.A. v. Lee*, 875 F.2d 584, 590 (7th Cir.1989).

We accept this dicta from the Seventh Circuit: willful blindness could provide the requisite intent or bad faith. But whether a defendant has been willfully blind will depend on the circumstances[5] and, like intent itself, will generally be a question of fact for the factfinder after trial. The undisputed facts relied on by the district court could certainly support an inference of knowledge or willful blindness. But they do not so clearly compel that conclusion as to warrant finding intent as a matter of law.

Chanel calls our attention to several other occurrences it feels bolster its position. First, it points out Brody has been involved in trademark infringement litigation twice in the past (in the mid–1980's). Second, it points to Greenberg's actions after hearing of the seizure of Chanel-labeled goods in California: he sent a warning fax to Brody; and then removed all Chanel-labeled merchandise from the premises, putting it in the trunk of a car. But these additional facts are, at best, simply further circumstantial evidence strengthening the inference of knowledge or intent. That these facts do even this is uncertain; for they could cut both ways. Looking at the facts in the light most favorable to Brody and Greenberg as non-moving parties, Brody's past experiences with trademark infringement laws might in fact make his evidence of attempted verification of authenticity more believable. Greenberg's pointed-to actions all occurred *after* the infringing activities; and all are consistent with the possibility that he first heard about the infringement from the Californians after the raid and was simply taking actions to stop the infringing activities and minimize the damage.

Chanel further suggests summary judgment was proper because, in response to its lengthy and well-documented motion, appellants filed only three pages of argument and one affidavit from Brody. Once a moving party has sufficiently supported its motion for summary judgment, the non-moving party must come forward with significant, probative evidence demonstrating the existence of a triable issue of fact. *See Ferguson v. National Broadcasting Co., Inc.*, 584 F.2d 111, 114 (5th Cir.1978). But— particularly where, as here, the moving party is also the party with the burden of proof on the issue—it is important to remember the non-moving party must produce its significant, probative evidence only after the movant has satisfied its burden of demonstrating there is no genuine dispute on any material fact. And, as previously noted, there is no genuine dispute only if a reasonable jury could not return a verdict for the non-moving party. Chanel's evidence does not demonstrate lack of a genuine dispute on intent; so appellants did not have to present the significant, probative evidence *Ferguson* requires.[7]

AFFIRMED in part, VACATED in part, and REMANDED for further proceedings.

---

5. In *Lee*, for example, the defendants had purchased obviously poorly crafted goods from an itinerant peddler at bargain-basement prices. 875 F.2d at 590.

7. Our conclusion that appellants' intent was not a proper subject for summary judgement is further confirmed by a brief look at other trademark infringement cases in which intent has been found. In *Louis Vuitton S.A. v. Lee*, for example, the "willful blindness" case discussed briefly above, the defendant had actually conceded knowledge in a pretrial stipulation. 875 F.2d 584 (7th

QUESTIONS

1. Do you agree with the district court or appellate court in *Chanel* concerning the plausible interpretations of Greenberg's actions after the raid?

2. Section 35(b) does not require mandatory treble damages and attorney's fees where "extenuating circumstances" are found. What might constitute such extenuating circumstances? *See Gucci America, Inc. v. Daffy's, Inc., supra* this chapter, page 929.

D. Border Control Measures

15 U.S.C. § 1124 [LANHAM ACT § 42]

Importation of goods bearing infringing marks or names forbidden

Except as provided in subsection (d) of section 1526 of Title 19, no article of imported merchandise which shall copy or simulate the name of any domestic manufacture, or manufacturer, or trader, or of any manufacturer or trader located in any foreign country which, by treaty, convention, or law affords similar privileges to citizens of the United States, or which shall copy or simulate a trademark registered in accordance with the provisions of this Act or shall bear a name or mark calculated to induce the public to believe that the article is manufactured in the United States, or that it is manufactured in any foreign country or locality other than the country or locality in which it is in fact manufactured, shall be admitted to entry at any customhouse of the United States.

1. Goods Subject to Seizure and Forfeiture

The Statutory Scheme

In *Ross Cosmetics Distribution Ctrs. v. United States*, 34 U.S.P.Q.2d 1758 (Ct. Int'l Trade 1994), reported *infra*, the court set forth the statutory

Cir.1989). And in *Louis Vuitton S. A. v. Spencer Handbags Corp.*, plaintiffs had a videotape of defendants bragging to a potential associate about their trademark infringement activities. 765 F.2d 966 (2d Cir.1985). Intent was based on more circumstantial evidence (like that present in this case) in *Polo Fashions, Inc. v. Rabanne*, 661 F. Supp. 89 (S.D.Fla.1986), and *Vuitton et Fils, S. A. v. Crown Handbags*, 492 F. Supp. 1071 (S.D.N.Y.1979), *aff'd without opinion*, 622 F.2d 577 (2d Cir. 1980); but the findings of intent in these cases were made only after full bench trials, *see Rabanne*, 661 F. Supp. at 99; *Crown Handbags*, 492 F. Supp. at 1072. *See also Finity Sportswear v. Airnit, Inc.*, 631 F. Supp. 769 (S.D.N.Y.1985) (knowledge or intent to infringe not appropriate subject of summary judgment). *But see Fendi S.A.S. Di Paola Fendi E. Sorelle v. Cosmetic World, Ltd.*, 642 F. Supp. 1143 (S.D.N.Y.1986) (summary judgment on willfulness granted where defendant admitted in deposition that he told retail merchants to whom he sold products that the products were "imitations," but that retail merchants' customers would likely think they were buying genuine Fendi products).

bases and criteria for preventing entry into the U.S. of goods bearing counterfeit or infringing trademarks:

The applicable statutes are the Trademark Act of 1946 (the Lanham Act), 15 U.S.C. §§ 1051–1127, and sections under title 19 of the United States Code concerning the protection of trademark rights by the Customs Service. In general, goods that infringe the rights of United States trademark owners are not permitted importation; infringing goods are subject to seizure and forfeiture by the Customs Service. *See* 15 U.S.C. §§ 1124, 1125 (1988); 19 U.S.C. §§ 1526(e), 1595a(c).

a. Applicable Statutory Violations

Section 42 of the Lanham Act, 15 U.S.C. § 1124, forbids importation of any goods that "copy or simulate" a trademark registered with the PTO. "A 'copying or simulating' mark" is either "an actual counterfeit of the recorded mark or name[,] or is one which so resembles it as to be likely to cause the public to associate the copying or simulating mark with the recorded mark or name." 19 C.F.R. § 133.21(a) (1993).

Section 43(b) of the Lanham Act, 15 U.S.C. § 1125(b), forbids importation of any goods "marked or labeled in contravention of" section 43(a).... By virtue of th[e] broad coverage of section 43, Customs' protection of trademark rights extends to all trademarks and trade dresses, regardless of whether they are registered with the PTO or recorded with Customs.

b. Penalties

Under 19 U.S.C. § 1526(e), any merchandise "bearing a counterfeit mark" imported into the United States in violation of 15 U.S.C. § 1124 "shall be seized and, in the absence of the written consent of the trademark owner, forfeited for violations of the customs laws." A "counterfeit" is defined as "a spurious mark which is identical with, or substantially indistinguishable from, a registered mark." 15 U.S.C. § 1127 (1988).

Under 19 U.S.C. § 1595(c), any merchandise imported into the United States "may be seized and forfeited" if the merchandise or its packaging violates section 1124, 1125, or 1127 of title 15 of the United States Code, or section 2320 of title 18 of the United States Code, which imposes criminal liability on any person who intentionally traffics in counterfeit goods. 19 U.S.C. § 1595a(c)(2)(C).

c. Counterfeit v. Confusingly Similar

In order to facilitate the enforcement of trademark protection at the border, Customs currently divides trademark infringement cases into two categories: those which bear a "counterfeit" mark, and those which bear a "confusingly similar" mark. A "counterfeit" mark is defined in accordance with 15 U.S.C. § 1127. A "confusingly similar" mark is defined by Customs as one "that is likely to cause confusion, or to cause mistake, or to deceive the consumer as to the origin, affiliation, or sponsorship of the goods in question." This definition appears to track the language contained in section 43(a) of the Lanham Act. In addition, Customs draws a distinction between trademarks that are registered and recorded with Customs, and trademarks that are registered but not recorded with Customs.

Thus, imported articles bearing "counterfeit" versions of marks recorded with Customs are subject to seizure and forfeiture under 19 U.S.C. § 1526(e). Imported articles bearing "counterfeit" versions of marks not recorded with Customs are subject to seizure and forfeiture under 19 U.S.C. § 1595a(c) for violation of 18 U.S.C. § 2320.

Imported articles bearing "confusingly similar" versions of marks recorded with Customs are ultimately subject to seizure and forfeiture under 19 U.S.C. § 1595a(c) for violation of 15 U.S.C. § 1124. Imported articles bearing "confusingly similar" versions of marks not recorded with Customs are currently not prohibited for importation.

3. Counterfeit v. Mere Infringement

Under Customs laws and regulations, goods that infringe upon rights of trademark owners are classified into two categories. The first category consists of counterfeit merchandise which bears "a spurious mark which is identical with, or substantially indistinguishable from, a registered mark." 15 U.S.C. § 1127. Usually, "counterfeit merchandise is made so as to imitate a well-known product in all details of construction and appearance so as to deceive customers into thinking that they are getting genuine merchandise." 3 J. Thomas McCarthy, McCarthy on Trademarks and Unfair Competition § 25.01[5][a] (3d ed. 1992).

The second category consists of "merely infringing" goods which are not counterfeits but bear marks likely to cause public confusion. This category includes merchandise which bears a mark that "copies or simulates" a registered mark so as to be likely to cause the public to associate the copying or simulating mark with the registered mark. See 15 U.S.C. § 1124; 19 C.F.R. § 133.21; see also *Montres Rolex, S.A. v. Snyder*, 718 F.2d 524, 527–28 (2d Cir.1983) *cert. denied*, 465 U.S. 1100 (1984) (distinguishing copying or simulating mark that is counterfeit mark from copying or simulating mark that is a merely infringing mark). Also included in this category is merchandise which uses any word, name, symbol, or any combination thereof, in such a manner that is likely to cause public confusion as to the origin, sponsorship, or approval of the merchandise by another person. See 15 U.S.C. § 1125(a)(2).

The significance of the distinction between counterfeits and merely infringing goods lies in the consequences attached to the two categories. Counterfeits must be seized, and in the absence of the written consent of the trademark owner, forfeited. See 19 U.S.C. § 1526(e); 19 C.F.R. § 133.23a(b) (1993). Merely infringing goods, on the other hand, may be seized and forfeited for violating 15 U.S.C. §§ 1124 or 1125. 19 U.S.C. § 1595a (c)(2)(C). Under Customs regulations, merely infringing goods may be imported if the "objectionable mark is removed or obliterated prior to importation in such a manner as to be illegible and incapable of being reconstituted." 19 C.F.R. § 133.21(a), (c)(4).

Ross Cosmetics Distribution Ctrs. v. United States

34 U.S.P.Q.2d 1758 (Ct. Int'l Trade 1994).

■ DICARLO, CHIEF JUDGE:

... Plaintiff, an importer of cosmetics, toiletries, and related products, requested Customs to issue a pre-importation ruling pursuant to 19 C.F.R. § 177.2 (1993), regarding whether its packaging for certain bath oils and fragrance oils proposed for importation conformed with Customs-administered laws and regulations relating to trademarks, trade names, and similar intellectual property rights. Specifically, plaintiff's packages for its bath oil product[] GORGEOUS ... bear language inviting customers to compare these products to the well-known products of GIORGIO ... Plaintiff's products are sold at a fraction of the price of the well-known products.

Customs issued its initial ruling on June 27, 1991, Rul. Ltr. 451142. The Agency held that, because "GIORGIO" [is a] trademark[] registered with the United States Patent and Trademark Office (PTO) and recorded with Customs for protection against infringing importation, plaintiff's use of these marks on its packaging constituted a counterfeit use of these marks. Accordingly, plaintiff's products, if imported, would be subject to seizure and forfeiture for violation of 19 U.S.C. § 1526 (1988).... Plaintiff filed this action challenging Customs' initial ruling and seeking a judgment upon the agency record. The court issued a decision on August 10, 1993, holding that the Ruling was arbitrary, capricious, an abuse of discretion, or otherwise not in accordance with law. The court held that before Customs could conclude plaintiff's products were counterfeits, Customs must first make a finding that plaintiff's packages were "identical with or substantially indistinguishable from" the registered marks, and that Customs had failed to do so. The court also held that the Ruling was arbitrary, because in finding that plaintiff's packages were likely to cause customer confusion, Customs simply compared plaintiff's packages to the facsimile copies of the recorded marks, rather than to the actual packages of the products, or a reasonable reproduction representing the design and color of the trademarks. The court remanded the Ruling to Customs for redetermination.

On November 10, 1993, Customs issued its remand determination. The remand determination ruled: ... plaintiff's products using the trademark[] "GIORGIO" are considered to infringe the rights of the respective trademark owners, and constitute a counterfeit use of these trademarks. Because "GIORGIO" [is] recorded with Customs ..., products using the trademark[] "GIORGIO" ..., if imported, would be subject to seizure and forfeiture under 19 U.S.C. § 1526(e) ...

Plaintiff now contests Customs' remand determination concerning plaintiff's use of the trademark[] "GIORGIO" ...

Discussion

This court's review will be limited to that part of the remand determination challenged by plaintiff; that is, Customs' decision concerning plaintiff's use of the trademark "GIORGIO" on the proposed packaging of its product GORGEOUS.

1.   The Products

   a.   "GIORGIO" v. "GORGEOUS"

The trademark "GIORGIO" is owned by Giorgio Beverly Hills, Inc., which has three valid trademark registrations with both the PTO and Customs for GIORGIO perfume and toiletry products: (1) the word mark "GIORGIO;" (2) a GIORGIO crest design; and (3) a design of alternating yellow and white vertical stripes. The GIORGIO packages use the stripe design as background, and bears the GIORGIO crest and the word mark "GIORGIO" in various styles and sizes.

The proposed package of plaintiff's product GORGEOUS invites the consumer to compare GORGEOUS to GIORGIO. The package of GORGEOUS uses diagonal yellow and white stripes as the background. A crest design appears above the name "GORGEOUS." At the top of the front panel is the language "COMPARE TO GIORGIO YOU WILL SWITCH TO ... ," in which the word mark "GIORGIO" is followed by the registered trademark symbol and appears in a bold and larger size print than the rest of the words. At the bottom of the front panel is a disclaimer: "OUR PRODUCTS IS IN NO MANNER ASSOCIATED WITH, OR LICENSED BY, THE MAKERS OF GIORGIO." The word mark "GIORGIO" is again followed by the registered trademark symbol. All words in the disclaimer appear to be in the same size print.

. . . .

4.   Whether Plaintiff's Use of Registered Trademarks Constitutes Counterfeit Use

Customs determined that plaintiff's use of the word mark "GIORGIO" on the packaging of its own products constituted a counterfeit use of these marks, because plaintiff applied marks "identical to the registered trademarks" to its goods without the authorization of the trademark owners. The court disagrees.

It is clear that plaintiff's products are not counterfeits. Plaintiff's product GORGEOUS do[es] not imitate the well-known product GIORGIO in all details of construction and appearance. Rather, plaintiff uses the mark "GIORGIO" to market its product GORGEOUS.

The use of another person's trademark in the context of marketing one's own product is not prohibited by law unless it creates a reasonable likelihood of confusion as to the source, identity, or sponsorship of the product. [citations omitted] Customs' practice shows its acceptance of this principle. See e.g., C.S.D. 89–172, 3 Cust. B. & Dec. 547, 549 (1988) (holding that reference to trademarks NINTENDO and NINTENDO EN-TERTAINMENT SYSTEM on packages for video game joystick to indicate its compatibility with NINTENDO system is permissible); C.S.D. 79–318, 13 Cust. B. & Dec. 1476, 1477 (1978) (holding that packaging of doll clothes referring to trademarked doll name would not infringe upon rights of trademark owner of doll name).

Thus, at issue is not whether plaintiff may use the mark "GIORGIO" on the packaging of its own product, but whether such use is likely to cause consumer confusion. If a likelihood of confusion exists, plaintiff's use of the marks would constitute trademark infringement, but not a counterfeit use of the marks.

In reaching the conclusion that plaintiff's use of the marks constitutes a counterfeit use, Customs misapplied 15 U.S.C. § 1127, which defines a counterfeit as a spurious mark "identical with, or substantially indistin-guishable from, a registered mark." According to Customs, any reference to another person's mark in the context of marketing one's own goods (whether a parallel use or comparative advertising) would constitute coun-terfeit use if a likelihood of confusion is found. This is because, under Customs' reasoning, the mark used in such a context would be necessarily "identical" to the registered mark. Customs' application of the statutory definition of counterfeit ignores the distinction between counterfeit and mere infringement, and therefore is not in accordance with law.

5.   Whether Plaintiff's Use of Registered Trademarks Constitutes Infringe-ment

Having held that plaintiff's use of the mark "GIORGIO" does not constitute a counterfeit use, the court must now address whether such use nevertheless infringes the rights of the trademark owner . . . .

In this case, Customs applied commonly accepted factors, and deter-mined that the use of the mark "GIORGIO" on the packaging of GOR-GEOUS is likely to cause confusion, and that the disclaimers on the packaging are insufficient to dispel the likelihood of confusion. Plaintiff agrees that the factors Customs used to determine the likelihood of confusion are appropriate. Plaintiff asserts, however, that Customs incor-rectly applied these factors to the two packages, and that Customs was arbitrary in finding the disclaimers ineffective . . . .

Applying the list of factors relevant to the determination of likelihood of confusion, Customs found the following:

(a) The word mark "GIORGIO," as used on fragrance and toiletry products, is inherently distinctive, and is therefore a strong mark entitled to a broad scope of protection.

(b) "GORGEOUS" and "GIORGIO" are used on identical products—perfumes and toiletries are listed in the same class (International Class—3) for the purposes of the Trademark Office. This factor enhances the likelihood of confusion.

(c) There is a high degree of similarity between the two packages. GIORGIO is covered by a pattern of alternating vertical white and yellow stripes; GORGEOUS by a pattern of alternating diagonal white and yellow stripes, of the same width as the GIORGIO stripes. GIORGIO has the red, black, and gold GIORGIO crest; GORGEOUS a red and gold crest. On the GIORGIO packaging, the word "GIORGIO" appears slightly above the center of the front panel and in close proximity to the GIORGIO crest; on the GORGEOUS packaging, the word "GORGEOUS" also appears slightly above the center of the front panel and in close proximity to its crest. In addition, the words "GORGEOUS" and "GIORGIO" share consonants, vowels, and sounds in their pronunciation.

(d) The fact that plaintiff selected and combined the three design elements utilized on GIORGIO boxes for use on its packaging (the word mark "GIORGIO," the image of a crest, and the yellow and white stripes), and the fact that the word mark "GIORGIO" appears in a prominent location on the front panel and in a darker and bigger print than the surrounding language inviting comparison, strongly suggest that plaintiff intentionally designed its packaging to be similar to GIORGIO, and thus did not develop its design in good faith.

(e) Since the quality of GORGEOUS is not comparable to that of GIORGIO, GORGEOUS would be sold in discount and low-end retail stores, whereas GIORGIO is normally sold in boutiques and fine department stores. However, there is a possibility GIORGIO would be sold in the same store as GORGEOUS. Customs' survey revealed that both GIORGIO and plaintiff's products were sold by a Wal–Mart store, and that a major retail drug store chain sold both GIORGIO products and various brands of "smell-alike" products. The possibility that the two products could be sold in the same stores enhances the likelihood of confusion.

(f) While a typical buyer of GIORGIO products may be expected to exercise care before purchasing because of the higher prices involved, a typical buyer of GORGEOUS would be less likely to make more than a cursory inspection of the product because low-priced items are often the subject of impulse purchasing. The nature of plaintiff's product as a target of impulse purchasing enhances the likelihood of confusion.

On balance, Customs found the factors that enhance the likelihood of confusion outweigh the factors that diminish the likelihood of confusion. Therefore, "there is a substantial likelihood that consumers could be confused as to the source of the Ross product."

Customs then examined whether the disclaimer used is sufficient to eliminate the confusion. Customs found that the disclaimer on the package of GORGEOUS is located at the bottom of the front panel, far from the word mark "GIORGIO" which appears in a prominent position at the top of the panel, and that the disclaimer is written in a smaller type size than any other words on the box. Customs concluded that the disclaimer could be easily overlooked by consumers and therefore is insufficient to dispel the likelihood of confusion.

The court holds that Customs properly applied the relevant factors in determining a likelihood of confusion, and that Customs' examination of the adequacy of the disclaimer was consistent with the applicable law. Although the court may not necessarily come to the same conclusion if reviewing the case de novo, it finds there is a rational connection between the facts found and the determination made by Customs.

The court sustains Customs' finding of a likelihood of confusion with respect to plaintiff's packaging for GORGEOUS. Accordingly, packages identical to that of GORGEOUS shall be denied entry and, if imported, are subject to seizure and forfeiture under 19 U.S.C. § 1595a(c).

2.   THE GRAY MARKET/PARALLEL IMPORTS

K Mart Corp. v. Cartier, Inc.

486 U.S. 281, 108 S.Ct. 1811, 100 L.Ed.2d 313 (1988).

■ JUSTICE KENNEDY announced the judgment of the Court, and delivered the opinion of the Court with respect to Parts I and II–A which REHNQUIST, C. J., and WHITE, BLACKMUN, O'CONNOR, and SCALIA, JJ., joined, an opinion with respect to Part II–B which WHITE, J., joined, and an opinion for the Court with respect to Part II–C which REHNQUIST, C.J., and BLACKMUN, O'CONNOR, and SCALIA, JJ., joined:

A gray-market good is a foreign-manufactured good, bearing a valid United States trademark, that is imported without the consent of the U.S. trademark holder. These cases present the issue whether the Secretary of the Treasury's regulation permitting the importation of certain gray-market goods, 19 C.F.R. § 133.21 (1987), is a reasonable agency interpretation of § 526 of the Tariff Act of 1930 (1930 Tariff Act), 46 Stat. 741, as amended, 19 U.S.C. § 1526.

I

A

The gray market arises in any of three general contexts. The prototypical gray-market victim (case 1) is a domestic firm that purchases from an

independent foreign firm the rights to register and use the latter's trademark as a U.S. trademark and to sell its foreign-manufactured products
here. Especially where the foreign firm has already registered the trademark in the United States or where the product has already earned a
reputation for quality, the right to use that trademark can be very
valuable. If the foreign manufacturer could import the trademarked goods
and distribute them here, despite having sold the trademark to a domestic
firm, the domestic firm would be forced into sharp intrabrand competition
involving the very trademark it purchased. Similar intrabrand competition
could arise if the foreign manufacturer markets its wares outside the
United States, as is often the case, and a third party who purchases them
abroad could legally import them. In either event, the parallel importation,
if permitted to proceed, would create a gray market that could jeopardize
the trademark holder's investment.

The second context (case 2) is a situation in which a domestic firm
registers the U.S. trademark for goods that are manufactured abroad by an
affiliated manufacturer. In its most common variation (case 2a), a foreign
firm wishes to control distribution of its wares in this country by incorporating a subsidiary here. The subsidiary then registers under its own name
(or the manufacturer assigns to the subsidiary's name) a U.S. trademark
that is identical to its parent's foreign trademark. The parallel importation
by a third party who buys the goods abroad (or conceivably even by the
affiliated foreign manufacturer itself) creates a gray market. Two other
variations on this theme occur when an American-based firm establishes
abroad a manufacturing subsidiary corporation (case 2b) or its own unin-
corporated manufacturing division (case 2c) to produce its U.S. trademarked goods, and then imports them for domestic distribution. If the
trademark holder or its foreign subsidiary sells the trademarked goods
abroad, the parallel importation of the goods competes on the gray market
with the holder's domestic sales.

In the third context (case 3), the domestic holder of a U.S. trademark
authorizes an independent foreign manufacturer to use it. Usually the
holder sells to the foreign manufacturer an exclusive right to use the
trademark in a particular foreign location, but conditions the right on the
foreign manufacturer's promise not to import its trademarked goods into
the United States. Once again, if the foreign manufacturer or a third party
imports into the United States, the foreign-manufactured goods will compete on the gray market with the holder's domestic goods.

B

Until 1922, the Federal Government did not regulate the importation
of gray-market goods, not even to protect the investment of an independent
purchaser of a foreign trademark, and not even in the extreme case where
the independent foreign manufacturer breached its agreement to refrain
from direct competition with the purchaser. That year, however, Congress
was spurred to action by a Court of Appeals decision declining to enjoin the
parallel importation of goods bearing a trademark that (as in case 1) a

domestic company had purchased from an independent foreign manufacturer at a premium. *See A. Bourjois & Co. v. Katzel*, 275 F. 539 (C.A.2 1921), *rev'd*, 260 U.S. 689 (1923).

In an immediate response to *Katzel*, Congress enacted § 526 of the Tariff Act of 1922, 42 Stat. 975. That provision [was] later reenacted in identical form as § 526 of the 1930 Tariff Act, 19 U.S.C. § 1526....

The regulations implementing § 526 for the past 50 years have not applied the prohibition to all gray-market goods. The Customs Service regulation now in force provides generally that "[f]oreign-made articles bearing a trademark identical with one owned and recorded by a citizen of the United States or a corporation or association created or organized within the United States are subject to seizure and forfeiture as prohibited importations." 19 CFR § 133.21(b) (1987). But the regulation furnishes a "common-control" exception from the ban, permitting the entry of gray-market goods manufactured abroad by the trademark owner or its affiliate:

> (c) *Restrictions not applicable.* The restrictions ... do not apply to imported articles when:
>
> > (1) Both the foreign and the U.S. trademark or trade name are owned by the same person or business entity; [or]
>
> > (2) The foreign and domestic trademark or trade name owners are parent and subsidiary companies or are otherwise subject to common ownership or control....

The Customs Service regulation further provides an "authorized-use" exception, which permits importation of gray-market goods where

> > (3) [t]he articles of foreign manufacture bear a recorded trademark or trade name applied under authorization of the U.S. owner ... 19 CFR § 133.21(c) (1987).

Respondents, an association of U.S. trademark holders and two of its members, brought suit in Federal District Court in February 1984, seeking both a declaration that the Customs Service regulation, 19 CFR § 133.21(c)(1)–(3) (1987), is invalid and an injunction against its enforcement. *Coalition to Preserve the Integrity of American Trademarks v. United States*, 598 F. Supp. 844 (D.D.C.1984). They asserted that the common-control and authorized-use exceptions are inconsistent with § 526 of the 1930 Tariff Act. Petitioners K Mart and 47th Street Photo intervened as defendants.

The District Court upheld the Customs Service regulation, 598 F. Supp., at 853, but the Court of Appeals reversed, *Coalition to Preserve the Integrity of American Trademarks v. United States*, 252 U.S. App. D.C. 342, 790 F.2d 903 (1986), holding that the Customs Service regulation was an unreasonable administrative interpretation of § 526. We granted certiorari to resolve a conflict among the Courts of Appeals....

A majority of this Court now holds that the common-control exception of the Customs Service Regulation, 19 CFR § 133.21(c)(1)–(2) (1987), is consistent with § 526. A different majority, however, holds that the author-ized-use exception, 19 CFR § 133.21(c)(3) (1987), is inconsistent with § 526. We therefore affirm the Court of Appeals in part and reverse in part.

II

A

In determining whether a challenged regulation is valid, a reviewing court must first determine if the regulation is consistent with the language of the statute. "If the statute is clear and unambiguous 'that is the end of the matter, for the court, as well as the agency, must give effect to the unambiguously expressed intent of Congress.' . . . The traditional deference courts pay to agency interpretation is not to be applied to alter the clearly expressed intent of Congress." In ascertaining the plain meaning of the statute, the court must look to the particular statutory language at issue, as well as the language and design of the statute as a whole. If the statute is silent or ambiguous with respect to the specific issue addressed by the regulation, the question becomes whether the agency regulation is a permissible construction of the statute. If the agency regulation is not in conflict with the plain language of the statute, a reviewing court must give deference to the agency's interpretation of the statute.

B

Following this analysis, I conclude that subsections (c)(1) and (c)(2) of the Customs Service regulation, 19 CFR § 133.21(c)(1) and (c)(2) (1987), are permissible constructions designed to resolve statutory ambiguities. All Members of the Court are in agreement that the agency may interpret the statute to bar importation of gray-market goods in what we have denoted case 1 and to permit the imports under case 2a. As these writings state, "owned by" is sufficiently ambiguous, in the context of the statute, that it applies to situations involving a foreign parent, which is case 2a. This ambiguity arises from the inability to discern, from the statutory language, which of the two entities involved in case 2a can be said to "own" the U.S. trademark if, as in some instances, the domestic subsidiary is wholly owned by its foreign parent.

A further statutory ambiguity contained in the phrase "merchandise of foreign manufacture," suffices to sustain the regulations as they apply to cases 2b and 2c. This ambiguity parallels that of "owned by," which sustained case 2a, because it is possible to interpret "merchandise of foreign manufacture" to mean (1) goods manufactured in a foreign country, (2) goods manufactured by a foreign company, or (3) goods manufactured in a foreign country by a foreign company. Given the imprecision in the statute, the agency is entitled to choose any reasonable definition and to interpret the statute to say that goods manufactured by a foreign subsid-iary or division of a domestic company are not goods "of foreign manufac-ture."

C

(1)

Subsection (c)(3), 19 CFR § 133.21(c)(3) (1987), of the regulation, however, cannot stand. The ambiguous statutory phrases that we have already discussed, "owned by" and "merchandise of foreign manufacture," are irrelevant to the proscription contained in subsection (3) of the regulation. This subsection of the regulation denies a domestic trademark holder the power to prohibit the importation of goods made by an independent foreign manufacturer where the domestic trademark holder has authorized the foreign manufacturer to use the trademark. Under no reasonable construction of the statutory language can goods made in a foreign country by an independent foreign manufacturer be removed from the purview of the statute.

(2)

The design of the regulation is such that the subsection of the regulation dealing with case 3, § 133.21(c)(3), is severable. The severance and invalidation of this subsection will not impair the function of the statute as a whole, and there is no indication that the regulation would not have been passed but for its inclusion. Accordingly, subsection (c)(3) of section 133.21 must be invalidated for its conflict with the unequivocal language of the statute.

III

We hold that the Customs Service regulation is consistent with § 526 insofar as it exempts from the importation ban goods that are manufactured abroad by the "same person" who holds the U.S. trademark, 19 CFR § 133.21(c)(1) (1987), or by a person who is "subject to common ... control" with the U.S. trademark holder, § 133.21(c)(2). Because the authorized-use exception of the regulation, § 133.21(c)(3), is in conflict with the plain language of the statute, that provision cannot stand. The judgment of the Court of Appeals is, therefore, reversed insofar as it invalidated §§ 133.21(c)(1) and (c)(2), but affirmed with respect to § 133.21(c)(3).

It is so ordered.

QUESTION

Are you persuaded that the customs regulations at issue in *K–Mart* reasonably construed an "ambiguity" in the statute?

Bourdeau Bros. v. ITC

444 F.3d 1317 (Fed.Cir.2006).

■ Clevenger, Senior Circuit Judge.

Appellants Bourdeau Bros., Inc. (Bourdeau), Sunova Implement Co. (Sunova), and OK Enterprises (OK), (collectively, appellants) appeal the decision of the United States International Trade Commission (ITC) affirm-

ing the Initial Determination and Recommended Remedy Determination
(Initial Determination) of Administrative Law Judge Luckern (ALJ) that
the importation of certain Deere European version forage harvesters infringed one or more of Deere's federally registered trademarks, Certain
Agric. Vehicles & Components Thereof, Inv. No. 337–TA–487 (Jan. 13,
2004) (Initial Determination), and granting a general exclusion order
covering those forage harvesters as well as cease and desist orders against
Bourdeau, OK, and other respondents, Certain Agric. Vehicles & Components Thereof, Inv. No. 337–TA–487 (Int'l Trade Comm'n Sept. 24, 2004)
(ITC Remedy Determination). We vacate and remand.

I

On January 8, 2003, Intervenor Deere & Co. (Deere) filed a complaint
with the ITC alleging violations of 19 U.S.C. § 1337 (section 1337) by the
importation into the United States, and sale in the United States, of certain
used agricultural vehicles that infringed United States Registered Trademark Nos. 1,503,576, 1,502,103, 1,254,339, and 91,860 (the Deere trademarks). In particular, Deere alleged that Deere forage harvesters that had
been manufactured solely for sale in Europe (the European version forage
harvesters) were being imported into the United States. Deere argued that
the European version forage harvesters were materially different from the
forage harvesters manufactured and authorized for sale in the United
States (the North American version forage harvesters). Thus, Deere
claimed that the European version forage harvesters constituted "gray
market goods" such that they infringed Deere's trademarks. The ITC
commenced an investigation on February 7, 2003. On January 13, 2004, the
ALJ issued his Initial Determination in which he found that appellants'
importation of used Deere European version forage harvesters violated
section 1337. The ALJ recommended that the ITC issue a general exclusion
order covering the infringing Deere forage harvesters and cease and desist
orders against Bourdeau, OK, and other non-appellant respondents. Appellants filed a Petition for Review on January 23, 2004, and on March 30,
2004, the ITC issued a notice indicating that it had decided not to review
the Initial Determination. On May 14, 2004, after analyzing the proposed
remedy and the effect of any remedial orders on the public interest, the
ITC followed the ALJ's recommendation and issued both the general
exclusion order and the cease and desist orders. Appellants timely filed a
notice of appeal. We have jurisdiction pursuant to 28 U.S.C. § 1295(a)(6).

* * *

III

Section 1337(a)(1)(c) forbids "[t]he importation into the United States,
the sale for importation, or the sale within the United States after importation by the owner, importer, or consignee, of articles that infringe a valid
and enforceable United States trademark registered under the Trademark
Act of 1946." Thus, section 1337 grants the ITC the power to prevent the
importation of goods that, if sold in the United States, would violate one of
the provisions of the federal trademark statute, the Lanham Act.

Many of the goods that are forbidden from importation under section 1337 are what are referred to as "gray market goods": products that were "produced by the owner of the United States trademark or with its consent, but not authorized for sale in the United States." *Gamut Trading Co. v. Int'l Trade Comm'n*, 200 F.3d 775, 777 (Fed. Cir. 1999). The rationale behind preventing importation of these goods is that the public associates a trademark with goods having certain characteristics. *Id.* at 778–79. To the extent that foreign goods bearing a trademark have different characteristics than those trademarked goods authorized for sale in the United States, the public is likely to become confused or deceived as to which characteristics are properly associated with the trademark, thereby possibly eroding the goodwill of the trademark holder in the United States. *Id.* at 779.

Thus, gray market theory recognizes both the territorial boundaries of trademarks and a trademark owner's right to control the qualities or characteristics associated with a trademark in a certain territorial region. As such, the basic question in gray market cases "is not whether the mark was validly affixed" to the goods, "but whether there are differences between the foreign and domestic product and if so whether the differences are material." *Id.* We have applied "a low threshold of materiality, requiring no more than showing that consumers would be likely to consider the differences between the foreign and domestic products to be significant when purchasing the product." *Id.*

However, even though the threshold of materiality is low, "a plaintiff in a gray market trademark infringement case must establish that all or substantially all of its sales are accompanied by the asserted material difference in order to show that its goods are materially different." *SKF*, 423 F.3d at 1315 (emphasis added). As we noted in *SKF*, the sale by a trademark owner of the very same goods that he claims are gray market goods is inconsistent with a claim that consumers will be confused by those alleged gray market goods. *Id.* "To permit recovery by a trademark owner when less than 'substantially all' of its goods bear the material difference . . . would allow the owner itself to contribute to the confusion by consumers that it accuses gray market importers of creating." *Id.* That is, a trademark owner has the right to determine the set of characteristics that are associated with his trademark in the United States; however, a trademark owner cannot authorize the sale of trademarked goods with a set of characteristics and at the same time claim that the set of characteristics should not be associated with the trademark.

This case involves the importation and sale of used forage harvesters manufactured by Deere. Deere sells 5000 and 6000 series forage harvesters in both the United States and Europe through a network of authorized dealers and distributors. The 5000 series is manufactured exclusively in the United States, regardless of the market for which it is destined, while the 6000 series is manufactured exclusively in Germany. Both the 5000 and 6000 series forage harvesters fit generally into two categories: the North American version forage harvesters, which are manufactured for sale in the

United States and North America, and the European version forage harvesters, which are manufactured for sale in Europe. Although the North American and European version forage harvesters are sold under the same series numbers, they have certain differences, including labeling differences and differences in certain safety features, discussed at greater length below.

Appellants are involved in the importation into the United States and the resale of used European version forage harvesters of both the 5000 and 6000 series. The ITC determined that the European versions of these forage harvesters are materially different from their North American counterparts and that the importation and sale of these forage harvesters violates section 1337.

IV

As a threshold matter, appellants argue that, because the 5000 series forage harvesters are manufactured in the United States, they are not "gray market goods" and thus that importation and sale of these forage harvesters cannot violate section 1337. Appellants point to the Supreme Court's decision *K Mart Corp. v. Cartier, Inc.*, 486 U.S. 281, 108 S.Ct. 1811, 100 L.Ed.2d 313 (1987), in which the Court, while addressing whether certain Customs regulations were consistent with 19 U.S.C. § 1526, discussed the meaning of the term "gray market goods." The Court noted that a gray market good is "a foreign-manufactured good, bearing a valid United States trademark, that is imported without the consent of the United States trademark holder." *K Mart*, 486 U.S. at 285.... Appellants argue that the Court did not include ... a case in which a domestic firm manufactures a product in the United States for sale abroad and that good is re-imported to the United States for later sale without the trademark owner's permission. Thus, appellants argue that a good manufactured domestically for export cannot be a "gray market good" and hence cannot violate section 1337.

However, *K Mart* did not address violations of either section 1337 or of the Lanham Act. Rather, the case discussed gray market theory as the background to an analysis of whether certain Customs regulations were consistent with section 526 of the Tariff Act of 1930, 19 U.S.C. § 1526, which attempted to regulate, for the first time, the importation of "gray market goods." See *K Mart*, 486 U.S. at 285–87. Both the regulation at issue, 19 C.F.R. § 133.21, and 19 U.S.C. § 1526 specifically refer to "[f]oreign-made articles" or "merchandise of foreign manufacture." Id. at 287–88 (quoting 19 C.F.R. § 133.21 (1987) and 19 U.S.C. § 1526). Thus, it is not surprising that the Court's description of gray market theory focused on goods of foreign manufacture. Further, the Court noted that "[t]he regulations implementing § 526 ... have not applied the prohibition to all gray-market goods." *Id.* at 288. Thus, *K Mart* should not be read to limit gray market theory, as it is applied in the context of section 1337, to goods of foreign manufacture.

In addition, the ITC has already determined that trademarked goods manufactured in the United States exclusively for sale in foreign countries may violate section 1337 if they are imported into the United States without the trademark owner's permission and if they are materially different from the trademarked goods authorized for sale in the United States. See Certain Cigarettes & Packaging, Thereof, Inv. No. 337–TA–424, USITC Pub. 3366, Commission Opinion at 2, n. 2 (Int'l Trade Comm'n, Oct. 16, 2000) (Cigarettes) (finding that cigarettes manufactured in the United States but intended for sale exclusively abroad violated section 1337). Although the ITC expressly declined to refer to the goods in Cigarettes as "gray market goods," using instead the terms "for-export" or "re-imported," the ITC analyzed whether the goods violated section 1337 using the "material difference" standard we applied in *Gamut*.

Indeed, section 1337(a)(1)(c) makes no reference to the term "gray market." In addition, unlike the statute at issue in *K Mart*, it does not distinguish between goods of domestic manufacture and goods of foreign manufacture. Rather, the statute simply declares unlawful "[t]he importation into the United States, the sale for importation, or the sale within the United States after importation by the owner, importer, or consignee, of articles that infringe a valid and enforceable United States trademark registered under the Trademark Act of 1946." 19 U.S.C. § 1337(a)(1)(c).

Finally, although this court noted in *Gamut* that "[t]he term 'gray market goods' refers to genuine goods that in this case are of foreign manufacture," we did not expressly limit the term "gray market goods"-nor yet the reach of section 1337–to foreign-manufactured goods. 200 F.3d at 778 (emphasis added). Rather, we noted that "[t]he principle of gray market law is that the importation of a product that was produced by the owner of the United States trademark or with its consent, but not authorized for sale in the United States, may, in appropriate cases infringe the United States trademark." *Id.* at 777. Thus, gray market law is not concerned with where the good was manufactured, nor is it concerned with whether the trademark owner controlled the manufacture of the product or authorized the use of the trademark on that product in another country. Instead, gray market law is concerned with whether the trademark owner has authorized use of the trademark on that particular product in the United States and thus whether the trademark owner has control over the specific characteristics associated with the trademark in the United States.

As such, we agree with the ITC, and we hold that the importation and sale of a trademarked good of domestic manufacture, produced solely for sale abroad and not authorized by the owner of the trademark for sale in the United States, may violate section 1337 if the imported good is materially different from all or substantially all of those goods bearing the same trademark that are authorized for sale in the United States.

V

In order to find a violation of section 1337, the imported goods must be materially different from all or substantially all of those trademarked goods authorized for sale in the United States. The materiality threshold is low, "requiring no more than showing that consumers would be likely to consider the differences between the foreign and domestic products to be significant when purchasing the product, for such differences would suffice to erode the goodwill of the domestic source." *Gamut*, 200 F.3d at 779. Indeed, there need only be one material difference between a domestic and a foreign product in order to determine that the latter is a gray market good eligible for exclusion. *See, e.g., id.* at 780–82 (affirming ITC finding of material difference based solely on the absence of English-language warning and instructional labels on foreign goods). However, the "plaintiff . . . must establish that all or substantially all of its sales are accompanied by the asserted material difference in order to show that its goods are materially different." *SKF*, 423 F.3d at 1315.

In this case, the ALJ found that there were numerous differences between the European and North American versions of both the 5000 and 6000 series forage harvesters that a customer in the United States would be likely to consider significant when purchasing the product. Initial Determination, slip op. at 19. While, for the most part, the appellants do not contest the existence of differences between the North American and European version forage harvesters, they argue that substantial evidence does not support the ALJ's findings that these differences are material.

However, substantial evidence supports the ALJ's determination that there are several differences between the North American and European version forage harvesters of both the 5000 and 6000 series that a customer would be likely to consider significant when purchasing the product. Both the 5000 and 6000 series harvesters contain differences in safety features that a customer would be likely to consider significant when purchasing the product. First of all, there are material differences between the lighting configuration and lighting functions of the North American and European forage harvesters, including the type of lights used during transport, the manner in which hazard lights and turn signals function, and whether safety warning lamps exist. There are also material differences between the warning labels and safety decals on the North American forage harvesters, which carry pictures and English writing, and European forage harvesters, which carry only pictures. *See In Re Certain Agric. Tractors Under 50 Power Takeoff Horsepower Investigation*, 44 U.S.P.Q.2d 1385, 1402 (Int'l Trade Comm'n 1997) ("*Tractors*") (finding that the absence of English-language warning and instructional labels on foreign goods constituted a material difference), *aff'd, Gamut*, 200 F.3d 775.

There are several other material differences between the North American and European versions of both the 5000 and 6000 series forage harvesters. There is a material difference in the hitch mechanism of the North American and European forage harvesters, as the mechanism in the European forage harvesters is not compatible with wagons used in North America. In addition, the operator's manuals of the European version forage harvesters are in the language of the target country, while the American forage harvesters' manuals are in English. Although appellants claim that North American manuals are often provided to purchasers of European version forage harvesters, this only serves to heighten confusion, as the North American and European manuals contain different information due to other differences in the products.

Finally, there are differences in the services provided along with the machines, including the Deere Product Improvement Programs (PIPs) and Service Information System (SIS). Although all three types of Deere's PIPs—mechanical, fix-it fail, and safety—are free to customers who have purchased American forage harvesters, the owners of European forage harvesters only qualify for safety PIPs. Further, the SIS, which records details about past PIPs, differs depending on the PIPs for which a machine is available, such that more information is available for North American forage harvesters than European forage harvesters. [The court vacated and remanded the case, however, for a determination whether Deere had itself sold the European forage harvesters in the U.S.]

* * *

QUESTION

Can genuine goods become spurious? Suppose that a licensee has been manufacturing and selling trademarked goods. When the license terminates or is otherwise revoked, may the licensee continue selling its inventory of trademarked goods, or will doing so violate the Lanham Act? Compare *Glovaroma, Inc. v. Maljack Productions, Inc.*, 71 F.Supp.2d 846 (N.D.Ill. 1999) with *Rogers v. HSN Direct Joint Venture*, 1999 WL 728651 (S.D.N.Y. 1999). *See also Abercrombie & Fitch v. Fashion Shops of Ky.*, 363 F.Supp.2d 952 (S.D. Ohio 2005) (licensed Abercrombie & Fitch clothing that failed U.S. quality standards, but whose sale abroad was permitted, was resold by unlicensed third party in the U.S.); *American Circuit Breaker Corp. v. Oregon Breakers Inc.*, 406 F.3d 577 (9th Cir.2005) (resale in U.S. of circuit breakers made under license for the Canadian market; only difference between U.S.-destined and Canada-destined goods is the nonfunctional color of the plastic housing).

INDEX

References are to pages.

†